EARLY CHRISTIANITY AND ITS SACRED LITERATURE

EARLY CHRISTIANITY AND ITS SACRED LITERATURE

Lee Martin McDonald
Stanley E. Porter

HENDRICKSON PUBLISHERS

© 2000 by Hendrickson Publishers, Inc.
P. O. Box 3473
Peabody, Massachusetts 01961–3473
All rights reserved
Printed in the United States of America

First Printing — November 2000

Library of Congress Cataloging-in-Publication Data

McDonald, Lee Martin, 1942–
     Early Christianity and its sacred literature   /   Lee Martin McDonald and Stanley E. Porter.
     Includes bibliographical references and indexes.
     ISBN 1-56563-266-4 (cloth)
     1. Bible. N.T.—Introductions.   I. Porter, Stanley E., 1956–   II. Title.
BS2330.2 M34 2000
225.6′1—dc21   00-039529

Photo Credits

ROHR PRODUCTIONS

Page number: 48[a], 51, 52[b], 53[a], 53[b], 55[b], 57[a], 58[b], 59, 65[a], 65[b], 81, 87, 123, 135[a], 135[b], 137, 138[a], 138[b], 139, 141, 143[a], 143[b], 145, 146[a], 146[b], 146[c], 146[d], 146[e], 146[f], 148[b], 149, 150, 151[a], 151[b], 154[a], 154[b], 156, 157, 159, 161, 162, 163, 165, 179, 225, 226, 231[b], 233, 235, 236, 237, 244, 246, 247, 249[a], 249[b], 261, 327[a], 327[b], 327[c], 327[d], 330[a], 330[b], 335[a], 335[b], 338, 343, 346, 351, 354, 378, 387, 423[a], 423[b], 426[a], 426[b], 431, 434, 439, 442[a], 442[b], 447, 450, 519[a], 519[b], 522[a], 522[b], 527[a], 527[b], 530[a], 530[b], 530[c], 530[d], 530[e], 530[f], 535[a], 535[b], 538[a], 538[b], 543, 546[a], 546[b], 579

LEE MARTIN MCDONALD

Page number: 48[b], 49, 50[a], 50[b], 52[a], 54, 55[a], 56[a], 56[b], 57[b], 58[a], 60, 74, 75, 77, 83[a], 83[b], 85, 120, 129, 131, 132, 133[a], 133[b], 134, 136, 140, 142, 144[a], 144[b], 148[a], 153, 155, 230, 231[a], 245, 255, 256, 259, 293, 334, 336, 341, 345, 366[a], 366[b], 372[a], 372[b], 373[a], 373[b], 374[a], 374[b], 375[a], 375[b], 377[a], 377[b], 380, 381, 382, 384, 385, 416, 429, 430[a], 430[b], 435[a], 435[b], 436[a], 436[b], 437, 462, 463, 467, 472, 475, 476, 548, 555, 556, 557[a], 557[b]

Dedicated to

Craig A. Evans

a good scholar and a special friend,
but most of all,
a fellow servant of Jesus Christ

TABLE OF CONTENTS

PREFACE

There are several reasons for the existence of this volume, reasons that should make it serviceable especially for students, but also for scholars in many, if not most, regards. Few introductions focus on the historical context in which early Christianity and its sacred literature emerged. Some recent introductions still perpetuate that practice, often with just a few pages given to explanation of the Jewish context of early Christianity and even less to the Greco-Roman background of many of the events described in the New Testament. But the situation is changing. Many are seeing the importance of presenting a greater focus on the historical context out of which the New Testament writings emerged. But we also know more about that context than we did a generation ago thanks to the work of many fine scholars, Jewish, Christian, and otherwise. Many previous assumptions about that context are now being discarded. There is also a growing awareness among New Testament scholars that the historical setting of early Christianity includes the Greco-Roman world and its literature, but also a Jewish context different from that previously assumed.

Today we are aware that the writers of the early Christian literature that eventually became our canon of Scriptures were also informed by ancient writings other than the books that currently make up our Old Testament canon. Some of the peculiarities of New Testament writers' interpretation of the Old Testament have parallels in the rabbinic writings of the second century and later. The context of the New Testament and early Christianity has been broadened significantly by the work of a generation of scholars who have tried to share more clearly what earlier scholars already knew—that the church and its Scriptures did not emerge out of a historical vacuum or from the narrow, limited context of Judaism as it was previously understood, but in a much richer, diverse social setting. There is always a need to shed more light on the current state of research in the scholarly world. We hope that *Early Christianity and Its Sacred Literature* will be especially helpful for those making their first journey through the fascinating and rewarding collection of Christian writings called the New Testament and will also aid them in their understanding of the primary issues and concerns addressed by the early church. For students we offer an introduction to the major issues in the study of the writings of the New Testament. For scholars we offer a critical analysis of a variety of scholarly interpretations of these issues, along with our resulting synthesis.

Throughout this study it is assumed that something happened in the lives of Jesus' earliest followers that not only gave them hope and confidence to face the complexities and frustrations of their day but dispelled their sense of despair that Jesus had been arrested, publicly mocked, and crucified. What happened also generated in them a sense of mission to all humanity. That "something," with which the New Testament writings are particularly concerned, is prior to what the disciples experienced and has to do with what God accomplished in the life, death, resurrection, ministry, and teaching of Jesus of Nazareth. It is a further assumption that the work of God through Jesus' life is fundamentally important for all humanity and thus for every generation. The story of Jesus as told in the New Testament and other early Christian literature has changed people's lives, giving them hope in hopeless circumstances. Early Christianity had a message that not only brought transformation to the lives of a band of disciples in Palestine two thousand years ago but still transforms people today. No apologies are made for these prior understandings or assumptions about the Christian story. Indeed, we think that they are essential if we are to glean the full meaning of the subject matter we are about to explore.

Understanding the faith of early Christianity necessarily involves examining the writings of the New Testament. Some of the Christian literature that makes up our current New Testament was recognized by a few church fathers as Scripture on a par with their Old Testament Scriptures beginning around the middle of the second century A.D. By the end of the fourth century A.D. most, if not all, of the rest of that collection of writings had also similarly been recognized, and many had been cherished in churches almost from the beginning of the Christian community. In the most general sense, the Christian literature that makes up our New Testament, especially the Gospels, tells us the story of Jesus and his teachings and of the mission of the community of faith that followed him. By the middle of the second century, some Christians were beginning to call some of this literature "scripture," and by the last quarter of that century, some were also speaking of a few of these writings as a "new testament"—bearing witness to a different relationship between God and God's people, both Jews and Gentiles.

Eventually that New Testament[1] came to include for most Christians the twenty-seven books of the New Testament that are familiar to us today. The writings of the New Testament include "Gospels," which are something like ancient biographies; an interpretive history of the church in the book of Acts; and letters, from Paul and others prominent in the early church, which were written mostly to Christian communities called "churches" or "assemblies of God" but also to individuals (as in

the Pastoral Epistles [1 and 2 Timothy and Titus] and Philemon). The book of Hebrews, possibly an extended sermon based on Psalm 110, and the book of Revelation, an interesting collection of visionary messages from a late-first-century follower of Jesus, round out the literature that makes up the New Testament. This literature is the primary witness of the origins of early Christianity, but as will be seen later, it is not the only ancient Christian witness to the church's birth and early growth or even to the story of Jesus and his significance.

Understanding the writings of the New Testament and other ancient literature is not easy, even though it may be fascinating and exciting. We consider that the time spent in careful examination of the origins of Christianity and its sacred literature will be more than worth the effort involved. At almost every turn there are teachings that are hard to understand, passages that are not easily reconciled with others, writers who appear at first glance not to agree with other New Testament writers on their teachings about Jesus, and writings that appear to differ on how to respond to his message. These difficulties, instead of being obstacles to understanding Jesus and the origins of early Christianity, can actually open up a fresh way of seeing that community of faith and how it allowed for more diversity than have many subsequent generations of the church. For the patient and diligent student or scholar these apparently contradictory voices in the early church can become vehicles for understanding not only the rapid expansion of early Christianity but also the nature of the Christian faith and the vitality of the life in Christ the New Testament proclaims. We do not offer a simplistic harmonization of divergent views in early Christian literature but allow those views to stand in bold relief, thereby showing how differences can enable one to see the beauty and necessity of the diverse composition of the church today. When the New Testament and other writings were first penned, it was not clear what view would finally emerge as the essence of Christian faith or what the appropriate theological understanding of Jesus' life and ministry might be. In some cases, the church struggled for generations to arrive at a meaningful understanding of who Jesus was and what was involved in his mission. The creeds of the church bear witness to this process.

Many who study the New Testament and the origins of early Christianity have preconceived ideas about what will be found in the investigation. Since many have some experience in a Christian church, it is only natural to come to the biblical text with assumptions handed on by others. When those assumptions appear to be questioned or challenged, the reader should look for an opportunity to grow in his or her understanding and be patient with those who have previously guided them in their theological pilgrimage, those who are attempting to take them further, and those they may be attempting to guide and instruct. Generally, it is precisely when earlier assumptions and prejudices about the Bible are challenged that we are able to learn the most about our faith and grow in our understanding of the Bible and the nature of Christian faith itself. Users of this book may not choose to change their earlier assumptions, but when they examine the Bible, they should learn to articulate their own presuppositions about the biblical text with more clarity than before and identify more effectively the strengths and weaknesses of their earlier understanding. Those who call assumptions and prejudices into question can challenge others to formulate a more defensible theology, one that they can support and proclaim with conviction. Near the turn of the second century A.D. a wise Christian teacher said to his students, "If our faith is such that it is destroyed by force of argument, then let it be destroyed; for it will have been proved that we do not possess the truth" (Clement of Alexandria, *Strom.* 6.10.80 [*ANF*]). His words are still valid for those of us today who engage in a serious study of the Bible.

When we examine the great teachings of the Scriptures and ask what our response to them ought to be, we soon see that our task, though greatly rewarding, is just beginning. In the complexity of some of the issues to be explored there is an opportunity for unimagined growth in understanding. The simplest Christian can sometimes grasp the essence of the gospel in certain ways that some scholars cannot, namely, that there is a call in the Scriptures to obedience to God and to a regular communion with God.

Scholars should be able to profit from reading sections of this book that discuss topics in more detail, even though they will already be familiar with many of the more general discussions. Some sections of this book may be of less value to the beginner than to the more advanced student, and perhaps a word of caution should go to those teaching from this book to make assignments user-friendly. We have tried to be sensitive to a wider readership and trust that we have shed more light, rather than cast darkness, on some of the most important issues. Those who seek a deeper understanding of biblical faith must be willing to pay the price of time, energy, persistence, and often frustration to achieve their goal. Precision in their understanding of the early church, the New Testament, and the faith it proclaims will be their reward.

Finally, there are always critical issues to rethink and reassess. Students and scholars alike must raise questions that require attention and further inquiry. Because of the nature of early Christian literature and the faith it proclaims, dealing with many questions of ultimate significance, we should always expect to be personally challenged in studying early Christianity and its sacred literature in their historical and faith dimensions. That is the goal of this inquiry.

This volume has truly been a collaborative effort. Although those who know our work will be able to detect which portions were written by each author, we have read each other's material several times and have felt free to offer extended comments and corrections. On many, if not most, issues we agree with each other, but in a few significant areas we simply disagree. On the complex issues related to the nature and limits of historical inquiry, the authorship of various books, pseudonymity, and canon, we have not resolved all our differences. Scholars have debated these issues at length without resolution for years, and we find that the same thing is true with us. This is not a weakness unless one believes that perfect agreement must exist before persons can work together. We have been able to learn much from each other's work and the questions we have raised about each other's contributions, and we agree far more often than we disagree. We hope that these differences have made us more sensitive to representing as fairly as possible the wide range of positions on most topics in the study of early Christianity and the New Testament so that readers will more easily make up their minds for themselves. If we have succeeded, this book will prove a valuable resource.

In the course of producing such a volume, we have incurred a number of debts. Lee McDonald would like to thank the members and friends of the First Baptist Church of Alhambra, California, for their generosity in allowing him time to pursue and complete this project in the midst of busy pastoral responsibilities. He also expresses his gratitude to his former professors Hugh A. Anderson and Helmut Koester for their significant help and many kindnesses in guiding him in his earlier study of the New Testament; surely they will not share all of the conclusions expressed in this volume, but their impact on his critical development has been considerable and very much appreciated. He also is grateful for the love and generous support of his wife, Mary, who patiently has also tolerated his carrying a computer and books on more vacations than was reasonable or fair under any conditions! Stanley Porter would like to thank his wife, Wendy, not only for reading the manuscript several times but for being a better friend and companion than any man has a right to expect or hope for. This was especially true during a period of many impending publishing deadlines. He would also like to thank several former and current research students—Craig Allert, Kent D. Clarke, and Youngchul Whang—for reading the manuscript as potential teachers of it; Jeffrey T. Reed for his usual critical acumen on Paul; his colleague Brook W. R. Pearson for his timely and detailed comment on the entire manuscript; and the University of Surrey Roehampton, London, for the opportunity of serving as professor in a group of outstanding fellow scholars. Finally, both of us wish to express our deep appreciation and respect for our dear friend and colleague of many years, Craig A. Evans. He first encouraged us to work together on this project. He will be especially surprised to find out that we both decided long ago to dedicate this volume to him!

---

[1]The word "testament" is used for a special genre of literature that, as H. Koester notes (*Introduction to the New Testament* [2 vols.; FFNT; Philadelphia: Fortress, 1982; 2d ed. of vol. 1, 1995], 1:416), is a "modification of the covenant formula in which the historical introduction is replaced by the biographical description of an individual (patriarch or apostle). This individual, who may already be dead at the time of writing, then gives instructions and pronounces curses and blessings." The use of the term "testament" for the collections of both the OT and the NT literature occurs for the first time at the end of the second century A.D. in the writings of Irenaeus and Tertullian.

ABBREVIATIONS

BIBLE VERSIONS

NA[27]	*Novum Testamentum Graece,* Nestle–Aland, 27th ed.
NEB	New English Bible
NIV	New International Version
NRSV	New Revised Standard Version
RSV	Revised Standard Version
UBS [2,3,4]	*The Greek New Testament,* United Bible Societies, 2d, 3d, 4th ed.

OLD TESTAMENT PSEUDEPIGRAPHA

1 En.	*1 Enoch (Ethiopic Apocalypse)*
2 Bar.	*2 Baruch (Syriac Apocalypse)*
Apoc. Mos.	*Apocalypse of Moses*
Ascen. Isa.	*Ascension of Isaiah*
Assum. Mos.	*Assumption of Moses*
Jub.	*Jubilees*
Let. Aris.	*Letter of Aristeas*
Pss. Sol.	*Psalms of Solomon*
Sib. Or.	*Sibylline Oracles*
T. Ab.	*Testament of Abraham*
T. Benj.	*Testament of Benjamin*
T. Jos.	*Testament of Joseph*
T. Jud.	*Testament of Judah*
T. Levi	*Testament of Levi*
T. Sim.	*Testament of Simeon*

DEAD SEA SCROLLS AND RELATED TEXTS

1Q, 2Q, etc.	Qumran caves numbered
CD	*Damascus Document* (from Cairo Genizah)
1QapGen	*Genesis Apocryphon*
1QpHab	*Pesher on Habakkuk*
1QS	*Manual of Discipline* (*Rule of the Community, Serek hayyaḥad*)
3Q15	*Copper Scroll* (3QTreasure)
3QHym	*Hymn Scroll*
4QFlor	*Florilegium (Eschatological Midrashim)*
4QMMT	*Miqsat Maaseh ha-Torah*
4Q521	4QMessianic Apocalypse
11QMelch	*Melchizedek*

PHILO

Abraham	*On the Life of Abraham*
Contempl. Life	*On the Contemplative Life*
Dreams 1, 2	*On Dreams* 1, 2
Embassy	*On the Embassy to Gaius*
Flaccus	*Against Flaccus*
Good Person	*That Every Good Person Is Free*
Moses 1, 2	*On the Life of Moses* 1, 2
Providence 1, 2	*On Providence* 1, 2
Quest. Exodus 1, 2	*Questions and Answers on Exodus* 1, 2
Spec. Laws	*On the Special Laws*
Unchangeable	*That God Is Unchangeable*

JOSEPHUS

Ag. Ap.	*Against Apion*
Ant.	*Jewish Antiquities*
War	*Jewish War*

MISHNAH, TALMUD, AND RELATED LITERATURE

b.	Babylonian Talmud (*Bavli, Babli*)
m.	Mishnah
t.	Tosephta
y.	Jerusalem Talmud (*Yerushalmi*, sometimes also abbreviated *j*)
B. Bat.	*Baba Bathra*
Ber.	*Berakot*
Giṭṭ.	*Giṭṭin*
Ḥul.	*Ḥullin*

Naz.	*Nazir*
Ned.	*Nedarim*
Qidd.	*Qiddušin*
Roš Haš.	*Roš Haššana*
Šabb.	*Šabbat*
Sanh.	*Sanhedrin*
Yad.	*Yadayim*

OTHER RABBINIC TERMS AND WORKS

bar.	*Baraita*
Ber. Rab.	*Berešit Rabbah*
Koh. Rab.	*Koheleth Rabbah*
Sop.	*Soperim*

APOSTOLIC FATHERS

Barn.	*Barnabas*
1, 2 Clem.	*1, 2 Clement*
Did.	*Didache*
Diogn.	*Diognetus*
Herm. *Mand.*	Shepherd of Hermas, *Mandate*
Herm. *Sim.*	Shepherd of Hermas, *Similitude*
Herm. *Vis.*	Shepherd of Hermas, *Vision*
Ign. *Eph.*	Ignatius, *To the Ephesians*
Ign. *Magn.*	Ignatius, *To the Magnesians*
Ign. *Phld.*	Ignatius, *To the Philadelphians*
Ign. *Pol.*	Ignatius, *To Polycarp*
Ign. *Rom.*	Ignatius, *To the Romans*
Ign. *Smyrn.*	Ignatius, *To the Smyrnaeans*
Ign. *Trall.*	Ignatius, *To the Trallians*
Mart. Pol.	*Martyrdom of Polycarp*
Pol. *Phil.*	Polycarp, *To the Philippians*

NAG HAMMADI CODICES

Ap. Jas.	I,*2 Apocryphon of James*
Ap. John	III,*1 Apocryphon of John*
1 Apoc. Jas.	V,*3 (First) Apocalypse of James*
Gos. Truth	XII,*2 Gospel of Truth*

NEW TESTAMENT APOCRYPHA AND PSEUDEPIGRAPHA

Acts Paul	*Acts of Paul*
Acts Pet.	*Acts of Peter*

Acts Pil.	*Acts of Pilate*
Apoc. Pet.	*Apocalypse of Peter*
Apos. Con.	*Apostolic Constitutions and Canons*
Gos. Eb.	*Gospel of the Ebionites*
Gos. Eg.	*Gospel of the Egyptians*
Gos. Heb.	*Gospel of the Hebrews*
Gos. Naass.	*Gospel of the Naassenes*
Gos. Pet.	*Gospel of Peter*
Gos. Thom.	*Gospel of Thomas*
Inf. Gos.	*Infancy Gospels*
Prot. Jas.	*Protevangelium of James*
Ps.-Clem.	*Pseudo-Clementines*

ANCIENT CHRISTIAN WRITERS

	Did. apost.	*Didascalia apostolorum*
	Pass. Perp.	*Passion of Perpetua and Felicitas*
Ambrose	*Ep.*	*Epistulae*
Athenagoras	*Leg.*	*Legatio pro Christianis*
Augustine	*City*	*The City of God*
	Harm.	*Harmony of the Gospels*
Clement of	*Extracts*	*Extracts from the Prophets*
Alexandria	*Misc.*	*Miscellanies*
	Salvation	*Salvation of the Rich*
	Tutor	*Tutor*
Ephraem the	*Hymni*	*Hymni contra haereses*
Syrian		
Epiphanius	*Mens. et pond.*	*De mensuris et ponderibus*
	Pan.	*Panarion (Adversus haereses)*
Eusebius	*Const.*	*Life of Constantine*
	Hist. eccl.	*Ecclesiastical History*
Hippolytus	*Comm. Dan.*	*Commentarium in Danielem*
	Comm. Gen.	*Commentarium in Genesim*
	Haer.	*Refutatio omnium haeresium*
Irenaeus	*Haer.*	*Adversus haereses*
Jerome	*Comm. Matt.*	*Commentariorum in Matthaeum libri IV*
	Ep.	*Epistulae*
	Vir. ill.	*De viris illustribus*
Justin	*1 Apol.*	*Apologia 1*
	2 Apol.	*Apologia 2*
	Dial.	*Dialogus cum Tryphone*
Minucius Felix	*Oct.*	*Octavian*
Origen	*Cels.*	*Contra Celsum*
	Comm. Jo.	*Commentarii in evangelium Joannis*
	Comm. Matt.	*Commentarium in evangelium Matthaei*
	Comm. Rom.	*Commentarii in Romanos*

	Did.	Didascalia
	Hom. Gen.	Homiliae in Genesim
	Hom. Jerem.	Homiliae in Jeremiam
	Hom. Judic.	Homiliae in Judices
	Or.	De oratione
	Philoc.	Philocalia
	Princ.	De principiis
Paulus Orosius	Hist. pag.	Historiae adversus paganos
Rufinus	Symb.	Commentarius in symbolum apostolorum
Socrates Scholasticus	Hist. eccl.	Historia ecclesiastica
Sozomen	Hist. eccl.	Historia ecclesiastica
Tertullian	Ag. Jews	Against the Jews
	Ag. Marc.	Against Marcion
	Ag. Prax.	Against Praxeas
	Ag. Val.	Against the Valentinians
	Apparel	The Apparel of Women
	Bapt.	Baptism
	Modesty	Modesty
	Prescr.	Prescription against Heretics
	Res.	The Resurrection of the Flesh
	Scorp.	Antidote for the Scorpion's Sting
Theophilus	Autol.	Ad Autolycum
Victorinus	Apoc.	Apocalypsis Joannis

ANCIENT NON-CHRISTIAN WRITERS

Aratus	Phaen.	Phaenomena
Athenaeus	Deipn.	Deipnosophistae (Deipnosophists)
Cicero	Att.	Epistulae ad Atticum
	Flac.	Pro Flacco
Dio Cassius	Rom.	Roman History
Dionysius of Halicarnassus	Ant. rom.	Antiquitates romanae
Epictetus	Diatr.	Diatribae (Dissertationes)
Euripides	Bacch.	Bacchae
Flavius Arrian	Anab.	Anabasis
Herodotus	Hist.	History
Homer	Od.	Odyssey
Lucian	Hist. conscr.	Quomodo historia conscribenda sit
	Merc. cond.	De mercede conductis
	Peregr.	De morte Peregrini
Macrobius	Sat.	Saturnalia
Marcus Aurelius	Med.	Meditations
Maximus of Tyre	Or.	Orationes

Philostratus	*Apollo.*	*Vita Apollonii*
Plato	*Rep.*	*Republic*
Pliny the Elder	*Nat.*	*Natural History*
Pliny the Younger	*Ep.*	*Epistulae*
Plutarch	*Alex. fort.*	*De Alexandri magni fortuna aut virtute*
	Def. orac.	*De defectu oraculorum*
Polybius	*Hist.*	*History*
Seneca	*Ep.*	*Epistulae morales*
Strabo	*Geog.*	*Geographica*
Suetonius	*Aug.*	*Divus Augustus*
	Claud.	*Divus Claudius*
	Dom.	*Domitianus*
Tacitus	*Ann.*	*Annales*
	Hist.	*Historiae*
Xenophon	*Anab.*	*Anabasis*

PAPYRI

P.Cairo	Papyrus Cairo
P.Cair.Zen	Papyrus Cairo Zenon
P.Egerton	Papyrus Egerton
P.Eleph.	Papyrus Elephantine
P.Köln	Papyrus Köln
P.Lond.	Papyrus London
P.Magd.	Papyrus Magdalen
P.Oxy.	Papyrus Oxyrhynchus
P.Paris	Papyrus Paris
P.Ryl.	Papyrus Rylands
P.Tebt.	Papyrus Tebtunis
P.Vindob.	Papyrus Vindobonensis

ABBREVIATIONS OF JOURNALS AND SERIES

AB	Anchor Bible
ABD	*Anchor Bible Dictionary.* Ed. D. N. Freedman. 6 vols. New York, 1992
ABRL	Anchor Bible Reference Library
AGJU	Arbeiten zur Geschichte des antiken Judentums und des Urchristentums
ALGHJ	Arbeiten zur Literatur und Geschichte des hellenistischen Judentums
AnBib	Analecta biblica
ANF	*Ante-Nicene Fathers*
ANRW	*Aufstieg und Niedergang der römischen Welt: Geschichte und Kultur Roms im Spiegel der neueren Forschung.* Ed. H. Temporini, W. Haase. Berlin, 1972–
APOT	*Apocrypha and Pseudepigrapha of the Old Testament.* Ed. R. H. Charles. 2 vols. Oxford, 1913
ASNU	Acta seminarii neotestamentici upsaliensis

BAR	*Biblical Archeology Review*
BASPSup	Bulletin of the American Society of Papyrologists: Supplement
BBR	*Bulletin for Biblical Research*
BETL	Bibliotheca ephemeridum theologicarum lovaniensium
BGU	*Aegyptische Urkunden aus den Königlichen* (later *Staatlichen*) *Museen zu Berlin, Griechische Urkunden. Berlin.* III: 1903.
Bib	*Biblica*
BibSem	The Biblical Seminar
BIS	Biblical Interpretation Series
BJRL	*Bulletin of the John Rylands Library*
BJS	Brown Judaic Studies
BNTC	Black's New Testament Commentaries
BR	*Biblical Research*
BRev	*Bible Review*
BTB	*Biblical Theology Bulletin*
BZNW	Beiheft zur Zeitschrift für die neutestamentliche Wissenschaft
CBQ	*Catholic Biblical Quarterly*
CGTC	Cambridge Greek Testament Commentary
CGTSC	Cambridge Greek Testament for Schools and Colleges
CHB	*The Cambridge History of the Bible*
CRBR	*Critical Review of Books in Religion*
CSEL	Corpus scriptorum ecclesiasticorum latinorum
CSR	*Christian Scholar's Review*
CTM	*Concordia Theological Monthly*
CurTM	*Currents in Theology and Mission*
DJD	Discoveries in the Judaean Desert
DJG	*Dictionary of Jesus and the Gospels.* Ed. J. B. Green and S. McKnight. Downers Grove, Ill., 1992
DPL	*Dictionary of Paul and His Letters.* Ed. G. F. Hawthorne and R. P. Martin. Downers Grove, Ill., 1993
ECF	*Early Christian Fathers*
EEC	*Encyclopedia of Early Christianity.* Ed. E. Ferguson. 2 vols. 2d ed. New York, 1997
EncJud	*Encyclopaedia Judaica.* 16 vols. Jerusalem, 1972
EvQ	*Evangelical Quarterly*
ExpT	*Expository Times*
FCI	Foundations for Contemporary Interpretation
FFNT	Foundations and Facets: New Testament
FN	*Filología neotestamentaria*
GBS	Guides to Biblical Scholarship
GCS	Die griechische christliche Schriftsteller der ersten drei Jahrhunderte
GR	*Greece and Rome*
HBD	*Harper's Bible Dictionary.* Ed. P. Achtemeier. San Francisco, 1985
	HarperCollins Bible Dictionary. Ed. P. J. Achtemeier et al. 2d ed. San Francisco, 1996
HBT	*Horizons in Biblical Theology*

HDB	*Hastings Dictionary of the Bible.* E. J. Hastings. 5 vols. Edinburgh, 1898–1904.
HeyJ	*Heythrop Journal*
HNT	Handbuch zum Neuen Testament
HNTC	Harper's New Testament Commentaries
HTR	*Harvard Theological Review*
HTS	Harvard Theological Studies
HUCA	*Hebrew Union College Annual*
HUT	Hermeneutische Untersuchungen zur Theologie
IB	*Interpreter's Bible.* Ed. G. A. Buttrick et al. 12 vols. New York, 1951–1957
IBR	Institute for Biblical Research
ICC	International Critical Commentary
IDB	*The Interpreter's Dictionary of the Bible.* Ed. G. Buttrick. 4 vols. Nashville, 1962
IDBSup	*Interpreter's Dictionary of the Bible: Supplementary Volume.* Ed. K. Crim. Nashville, 1976
IG	*Inscriptiones graecae.* Editio minor. Berlin, 1924–
IGR	Inscriptiones graecae ad res romanas pertinentes
Int	*Interpretation*
ISBE	*International Standard Bible Encyclopedia.* Ed. G. W. Bromiley. 4 vols. Grand Rapids, 1979–1988
JBC	*Jerome Biblical Commentary.* Ed. R. E. Brown et al. Englewood Cliffs, 1968.
JBL	*Journal of Biblical Literature*
JBR	*Journal of Bible and Religion*
JETS	*Journal of the Evangelical Theological Society*
JSNT	*Journal for the Study of the New Testament*
JSNTSup	Journal for the Study of the New Testament: Supplement Series
JSOT	*Journal for the Study of the Old Testament*
JSOTSup	Journal for the Study of the Old Testament: Supplement Series
JSP	*Journal for the Study of the Pseudepigrapha*
JSPSup	Journal for the Study of the Pseudepigrapha: Supplement Series
LCL	Loeb Classical Library
LEC	Library of Early Christianity
McCQ	*McCormick Quarterly*
MNTC	Moffatt New Testament Commentary
NCB	New Century Bible
NewDocs	*New Documents Illustrating Early Christianity.* Ed. G. H. R. Horsley and S. Llewelyn. 8 vols. to date. North Ryde, N.S.W., 1981–
NHL	*Nag Hammadi Library in English.* Ed. J. M. Robinson. 4th rev. ed. Leiden, 1996
NHS	Nag Hammadi Studies
NIB	*New Interpreter's Bible*
NIBC	New International Bible Commentary
NICNT	New International Commentary on the New Testament
NIGTC	New International Greek Testament Commentary
NovT	*Novum Testamentum*

NovTSup	Novum Testamentum Supplement Series
NPNF1, 2	*Nicene and Post-Nicene Fathers,* Series 1, 2
NTL	New Testament Library
NTS	*New Testament Studies*
NTTS	New Testament Tools and Studies
OAA	*Oxford Annotated Apocrypha, RSV Edition*
OBS	Oxford Bible Series
OCT	Oxford Classical Texts
OGIS	*Orientis graeci inscriptiones selectae.* Ed. W. Dittenberger.
OS	Oudtestamentische studiën
OTM	Oxford Theological Monographs
OTP	*Old Testament Pseudepigrapha.* Ed. J. H. Charlesworth. 2 vols. Garden City, N.Y., 1983
OTS	Old Testament Studies
PB	Jewish Prayer Book
PG	Patrologia graeca. Ed. J.-P. Migne. 162 vols. Paris, 1857–1886
PL	Patrologia latina. Ed. J.-P. Migne. 217 vols. Paris, 1844–1864
PNTC	Pelican New Testament Commentaries
QR	*Quarterly Review*
RelS	*Religious Studies*
RGG	*Religion in Geschichte und Gegenwart.* Ed. K. Galling. 7 vols. 3d ed. Tübingen, 1957–1965
RILP	Roehampton Institute London Papers
SB	Sammelbuch griechischer Urkunden aus Ägypten
SBG	Studies in Biblical Greek
SBLDS	Society of Biblical Literature Dissertation Series
SBLMS	Society of Biblical Literature Monograph Series
SBLRBS	Society of Biblical Literature Resources for Biblical Study
SBLSBS	Society of Biblical Literature Sources for Biblical Study
SBLSP	*Society of Biblical Literature Seminar Papers*
SBT	Studies in Biblical Theology
Scrip	*Scriptura*
SD	Studies and Documents
SE	Studia evangelica I, II, III, etc. (= Texte und Untersuchungen 73 [1959], 87 [1964], 88 [1964]), etc.
SecCent	*Second Century* (see *Journal of Early Christian Studies*)
SECT	Sources of Early Christian Thought
SJLA	Studies in Judaism in Late Antiquity
SJT	*Scottish Journal of Theology*
SNTSMS	Society for New Testament Studies: Monograph Series
SP	Sacra Pagina
SPAW.PH	Sitzungsberichte der preussischen Akademie der Wissenschaften, Philosophisch-historische Klasse
SR	*Sciences religieuses*
SBLSS	Society of Biblical Literature Symposium Series
StNT	Studien zum Neuen Testament

StPatr	Studia patristica
StTh	*Studia theologica*
SUNT	Studien zur Umwelt des Neuen Testaments
TDNT	*Theological Dictionary of the New Testament.* Ed. G. Kittel and G. Friedrich. Trans. G. W. Bromiley. 10 vols. Grand Rapids, 1964–1976
Theol	*Theology*
ThStKr	*Theologische Studien und Kritiken*
ThTo	*Theology Today*
TNTC	Tyndale New Testament Commentaries
TS	*Theological Studies*
TU	Texte und Untersuchungen
TynB	*Tyndale Bulletin*
TZ	*Theologische Zeitschrift*
USQR	*Union Seminary Quarterly Review*
VC	*Vigiliae christianae*
VT	*Vetus Testamentum*
VTSup	Supplements to Vetus Testamentum
WBC	Word Biblical Commentary
WDB	Westminster Dictionary of the Bible
WTJ	*Westminster Theological Journal*
WUNT	Wissenschaftliche Untersuchungen zum Neuen Testament
ZNW	*Zeitschrift für die neutestamentliche Wissenschaft und die Kunde der älteren Kirche*

OTHER ABBREVIATIONS

ca.	around, approximately
A.D.	anno Domini (Lat. "in the year of our Lord"), same as C.E. ("Christian/Common Era")
Aram.	Aramaic
B.C.	before Christ, same as B.C.E. ("before the Christian/Common Era")
bk.	book
cent.	century
cf.	confer, compare
ch(s).	chapter(s)
d.	died
ed(s).	editor(s), edited by, edition(s)
esp.	especially
f(f).	and following
fig.	figure
fl.	*floruit* (flourished)
frg.	fragment
FS	Festschrift
Ger.	German
Gk.	Greek

Heb.	Hebrew
Lat.	Latin
lit.	literally
LXX	Septuagint (the Greek OT)
MS(S)	manuscript(s)
MT	Masoretic Text
n.	note
n.d.	no date
n.p.	no place; no publisher
no.	number
NT	New Testament
OL	Old Latin
OT	Old Testament
per.	person
pl.	plural
R.	Rabbi
rev.	revised, revised by
sec.	section
trans.	translator, translated by
v(v).	verse(s)
vs	versus
vol(s).	volume(s)
Vulg.	Vulgate

HISTORY AND FAITH:
Critical Assumptions for the Study of the New Testament

1. THE PROBLEM OF HISTORY

Christianity makes its boldest claim when it speaks about a God who acts in time and space through events in history such as the exodus of the Jews from Egypt or the resurrection of Jesus from the dead. This claim has always been part of the Christian message, but since the time of the Enlightenment and the development of the historical-critical method, it has become the focal point of numerous debates among Christian theologians. Does God in fact work in ways that can be observed, detected, or experienced through the sensory perceptions of human beings? Is it conceivable that God would intervene in history by raising someone from the dead or by suspending or contravening the laws of nature in other ways?

The purpose of this chapter is, first, to identify some of the problems that the modern approach to history continues to pose for Christian faith and, second, to set forth an appropriate, meaningful means of understanding the biblical message.[1] This approach does not skirt major issues of our day, nor does it pressure one to retreat into untenable conclusions about the biblical text (some of which issues are discussed in more detail in ch. 6, where the focus is on the resurrection of Jesus).

Since the time of the Enlightenment (17th and 18th cents.), the notion of God's activity in human affairs has been seriously called into question. In the Age of Reason, which questioned the authority, activity, and even existence of an independent divine being, the miracles often referred to by earlier historians were also called into question. Is there a God as traditionally understood? Does God act in history? Do miracles occur? Did Jesus rise from the dead? Was there a miraculous rescue of the Israelites from the Egyptians in the waters of the Red Sea? With the Enlightenment came the rise of biblical criticism, a new methodology for understanding the Bible. The problem was that the new criteria employed in examining the past were also an indictment against the biblical worldview, which confessed faith in a God who acts in history in phenomenal ways.

Whether in principle or in practice, the tide began to turn against the traditional confessions of the church, especially in terms of its focus on miracles. This new approach to history was clearly troublesome to many Christians. Some from within the Christian community tried to apply the new and developing historical criteria to biblical traditions, with devastating results for conservative

Christian beliefs. Many debates ensued within the church. Some teachers within the church responded by claiming that the results of a historical inquiry that in principle or in practice ignores the activity of God in human affairs cannot be a valid tool of biblical inquiry nor can its results be trusted by those within the church.

Many scholars of the Christian tradition, such as F. C. Baur, Ernst Renan, Friedrich Schleiermacher, and David Strauss,[2] wanted to find a means of wedding Christian thought to contemporary critical thinking, but the results of their inquiry were mixed and uneasiness over their work grew within the church. Some scholars began to argue that the biblical picture of God's activity in history was clearly mythological, stemming from an earlier and more primitive worldview (Ger. *Weltanschauung*) that simply was no longer tenable in the modern age of the Enlightenment. They tried to ground the basis for Christian faith in a historical person, Jesus of Nazareth, who was not a miracle worker but a great teacher of ethics and wisdom. This picture drew some converts within the church, but most Christians continued to reject it. There appeared to be no acceptable way to account for the transformation of the disciples and the birth of the church by using the newly established historical methodology; it was dominated by assumptions that from the outset denied in principle God's miraculous activity in Jesus and especially Jesus' resurrection from the dead.

In the last century, no NT theologian has challenged the traditional understanding of Christianity more than the German scholar Rudolf Bultmann. His often radical application of the historical-critical method to the biblical writings, with the resulting denigration of miracles or supernatural events recorded in Scripture, has nevertheless been helpful in clarifying some of the major problems the church faces in secular society today. More than anyone, he raised the question of the relevance, for modern society, of talk of the supernatural and attempted to translate the message of the NT into meaningful twentieth-century language. His goal, however well he did or did not achieve it, was noble in that he was trying to identify the true "stumbling block" (1 Cor 1:23) of the Christian message and to present it with clarity to his generation. He believed, however, that the stumbling block of Christian faith was not simply its focus on miracles and the supernatural elements of the traditional Christian message but, rather, the message that God calls one to abandon all worldly securities and, in radical obedience, to surrender to Christ in order to discover authentic Christian living.

Bultmann was a historian par excellence as well as a philosophical theologian and NT scholar. It is precisely at the point where Christian faith and history intersect that Bultmann brought all three of his interests together to engage modern thinkers in a careful understanding of the Christian message. Whether he adequately understood the church's Easter message or handled the NT traditions that confess the resurrection of Jesus will be explored later. As a historian, however, Bultmann challenged the church to rethink the viability of its confession of God's activity in history and the kind of history in which God acts. Does God act openly in history through miracles or supernatural interventions, as described in the Bible, for example, in the exodus of the Jews from Egypt and in the resurrection of Jesus? Is God's activity open for all to see and therefore objectifiable in history? Or does God always act in more hidden ways, as in the case of one's personal encounter with God, which comes through hearing the preached word of God, or in the various circumstances of life, when God speaks in ways indiscernible to the objective and unprejudiced historian? Although a Christian need not opt for one or the other of these positions, Bultmann chose the latter position—that God acts in hidden ways in human history—and as a historian he asked the church to speak honestly when it speaks historically about God's activity. He did not deny the activity of God in history but maintained that such activity is not verifiable through the historian's method of inquiry and does not involve a violation of the natural order of events, such as he saw proclaimed on the pages of the NT, especially in the case of the resurrection of Jesus from the dead. All such talk, he said, is mythological and grows out of a pre-enlightened view of the world. Bultmann, rather than rejecting or discarding the "myth" of the NT, chose to reinterpret it in terms of human self-understanding. In other words, the ancient belief in the supernatural interventions of God in history was the church's way of concretizing the "otherworldly" activity of God in terms of "this-worldly" experiences.

Bultmann believed that all historical events, or events of history, should be open to the historian and that, if there is no empirical historical evidence to support a historical statement such as that Jesus rose from the dead, then there is no way for the church to confess its faith in such an event. He taught that the results of historical inquiry are the same for the Christian as for the non-Christian. Bultmann maintained, however, that Christian faith can never be tied to the ever-changing results of the historian's inquiry; therefore, the Christ according to the flesh, or the Jesus of historical inquiry, is largely irrelevant for Christian faith.

In terms of the radical implications for Christian faith that stem from the application of historical-critical methodology to the study of the life of Jesus, he said that what the historian could do with that tradition was of no consequence to him and that he "let it [the traditional picture of Jesus in the Gospels] burn peacefully, for I see that that which burns is all fantasy-pictures of the life-of-Jesus theology, that is, the Christ according to the flesh. But the Christ according to the flesh is irrelevant for us; I do not know and do not care to know the inner secrets of the heart of Jesus."[3] For Bultmann, the manner in which the Easter faith arose in the disciples "has been obscured in the tradition by legend and is not of basic importance."[4] In a now famous essay, he stated unequivocally that "an historical fact that involves a resurrection from the dead is utterly inconceivable!"[5] In that same essay, he made another declaration that brought an equally strong reaction from more conservative Christian theologians around the world: Bultmann concluded that the ancient worldview that made room for angels, demons, miracles, and resurrections is outdated and no longer tenable for Christians in the twentieth century. He argued that "it is impossible to use electric light and the wireless [radio] and to avail ourselves of modern medical and surgical discoveries and at the same time to believe in the New Testament world of spirits and miracles."[6] Referring to the conclusions of existentialist philosopher Karl Jaspers, Bultmann argued emphatically that "he is as convinced as I am that a corpse cannot come back to life or rise from the grave."[7] For Bultmann, Christian faith in the resurrection meant that "death was not swallowed up into Nothing, but that the same God, who is always coming to us, also comes to us in our death. In this sense,

faith in the resurrection is the criterion for whether someone is a Christian or a non-Christian."[8]

Although many twentieth-century theologians disagreed with Bultmann's conclusions, no one can question that he raised the pivotal questions about understanding history, questions to be answered prior to one's investigation of the NT. More than any other biblical scholar of the twentieth century, he showed that one's worldview plays a significant role in the conclusions drawn from an investigation of the NT. Others after Bultmann have applied these radical criteria to the Bible with equally radical consequences. For these reasons, we will focus briefly on the meaning and methodological assumptions of modern historiography and how their application to the message of the NT can have important, but also often highly negative, results. Is modern historical methodology adequate for evaluating or appropriating the fact and significance of God's work in history, especially that view of the activity of God which speaks of divine intervention in history through the suspension or contravention of the laws of nature? Before we can answer this question, we must first decide what history is and seek to understand the philosophy of history most common today as well as the methodology it uses in its field of inquiry.[9] Following this, we will apply commonly accepted principles and assumptions of the historical methodology to Jesus' resurrection, the primary NT example of God's intervention in history and the basis of Christian preaching. In the final two sections of this discussion, we will set forth an alternate approach to the unique activity of God in history, one that both appreciates its relation to history and shows the possibility of confessing more clearly faith in a God who acts in history.

2. HISTORY AND THE HISTORICAL METHOD

A. The Meaning and Subject of History

Although the word "history" is derived from the Greek ἱστορία and ἱστορέω (*historia, historeō*; from ἵστωρ [*histōr*], meaning "learned" or "skilled"), referring to an inquiry or a visit with the purpose of coming to know someone, and later came to mean an account of knowledge about someone or something, the term is seldom used in this wide sense today.[10] Often the term "history" is used to distinguish reality from myth or legend.[11] In this sense history refers to that which really happened, and it can be used to designate not only human events but also natural phenomena, such as volcanic eruptions, hurricanes, etc., whether or not experienced by humans.

More recently the terms "history" and "historical" have been used in a more limited way in reference to humankind and those events that have affected human beings in their social environment. The terms have now become inseparable from describing the past actions of human beings. In most universities today, the history department is found either in the social-sciences faculty or in the humanities faculty. History therefore is not to be confused with nature, which is not of primary interest to historians. Fuller correctly sees that nature can be a part of history, but still contends that the primary concern of the historian is human behavior. He maintains that although nature—that is, storms, pestilences, hereditary characteristics, etc.—does affect the course of human history, it is not the primary focus of the historian. Rather, he observes that "human behavior in reaction to its environment is the mainspring of history. Hence most historical explanations become attempts to account for human behavior."[12]

Collingwood claims that history is a kind of research or inquiry that attempts to find out things done in the past by human beings.[13] He summarizes current understanding of the meaning and subject of history, together with the task of the historian, in his definition of history as "(a) a science, or an answering of questions; (b) concerned with human actions in the past; (c) pursued by interpretation of evidence; and (d) for the sake of human self-knowledge."[14]

Walsh limits the historian's field even further by saying that the historian is concerned only with the past actions of humankind that are no longer open or available to direct inspection.[15] Anderson holds, however, that a survey of the present and the future is also a part of the historian's field of inquiry. He explains that "man's insatiable curiosity to know what happened or what happens is the sanction of scientific historical research as it has always been the inspiration of the natural sciences."[16] Anderson is certainly correct when he

claims that the historian is interested in "what happened"; not a few historians, however, would disagree on his second point that the historian is interested in "what happens." It is true that the natural scientist is interested in "what happens," but as we will soon argue, this is one of the distinguishing marks between the natural scientist's subject and that of the historian. The historian is not primarily interested in "what happens" or in establishing rules that govern the present and the future.

Historians use certain philosophical rules and assumptions that enable them to understand the past. It is the philosopher or "prophet" of history who enjoys the vantage point of surveying the entire historical process and who not only points out characteristics of past events unnoticed by the practicing historian but, in addition, tells us what the future will be like before it actually occurs.[17] History, therefore, is essentially limited to a study of the reality of the human past; and since the future is not yet reality and not yet the past, it does not properly lie within the historian's prescribed field of inquiry.[18] Jaspers, agreeing with this, claims that historical science is confined to the past. He denies that the historian's work involves a study of any laws that govern either the present or the future. He maintains that all recognizable necessities, whether evident connections of meaning or causal inevitabilities, are outside the scope of the historian's field of inquiry and that "the course of history as a whole knows no necessity. 'It had to come' is not a scientific sentence."[19] Jaspers, further limiting the role of the historian, claims that as a scientist the historian "has to make no valid present forecasts either."[20] Daniels agrees with Jaspers but adds that history is the past experience of humankind, more precisely "the memory of the past experience as it has been preserved largely in written records." He goes on to say that since history treats human affairs, it is most logically studied in its chronological dimension.[21] Within this chronological development of history, one can further subdivide history into geographical locations as well as into political, cultural, and other areas of human interest.

The nineteenth-century historical positivists[22] held that history was nothing more than ascertaining facts, sifting through them, and then framing general laws from them. Although in their labors

the positivists never fully carried out their definition beyond the ascertaining of facts, this notion of
history was a strong influence upon their work and
has continued in a slightly varied form in the works
of many, if not most, historians today. The positivists
defined historical knowledge as the reality of the
past, and this reality is found in facts whose essence is historical or obtained through the historical process.[23]

The historian is constantly looking at the past
in order to understand humanity's development
and present condition, and is also looking for that
which will enable modern individuals to understand themselves in their social environment. Historians are therefore interested in those past events
that relate most directly to humankind. This is essentially what Gogarten says when he explains the
particular interest of historians: "Man has discovered his power to transform the earth and has understood himself as the substance of history, which
constantly refers back to itself."[24] The substance
and the subject of history, therefore, is humankind.

Another limitation on the subject of history,
which is more difficult to locate in any one author
but seems to be everywhere assumed, is that it is
only concerned with those events that happen within
the space-time continuum. Events in the spiritual
realm, whether real or imagined, are not proper
subjects for the historian. Explaining why, Wand
contends that "history has no tools by which it can
deal with such events. In so far as it is scientific,
history is a form of measurement. It can estimate
the amount of evidence for or against a given event
and can sometimes measure the credibility of the
evidence. But the evidence is documentary, whether
of stone, parchment or paper, including evidence of
an archaeological nature; and none of these belongs to the intangible sphere of spirit."[25]

Although there is no final agreement on the
exact meaning of history, there is general agreement on its subject. Perhaps the least one can say
about history is that it is a critical investigation or
inquiry into the past actions of human beings or
into those events in the past that directly relate to
human beings, for example, an earthquake or tidal
wave as it may have had an impact upon the social
condition of a person, city, or nation. Whether it is
the historian's duty to frame laws about the nature
of humanity in light of the facts that have been dis-

covered (so argued the positivists) is a question
that will be taken up presently.

B. The Task of the Historian

Today historians would not deny that a major
part of their historical task is centered around the
discovery of facts. Most historians would also see as
their task the interpretation of those facts. Facts
seldom, if ever, speak for themselves, and this is
where conceptual and logical thinking is required
of the historian. As Gardiner has remarked, historical writing is "not merely an uninterrupted ag-
glomeration of symbols without reference to experience."[26] For him, every historian has the obligation of acting as an interpreter of history. The
practicing historian attempts through historical
methodology to describe past events, considering
each event unique. Gardiner holds that historians
must not only describe past events but also assess
them in light of present understanding about the
laws of nature, such as the uniformity of nature.[27]
Walsh also agrees with this and stresses that history is not only a descriptive science but one that
requires assessment. Therefore, a historian must
answer questions about the meaning and purpose
of the events of history as well as offer a description
of them.[28]

Historians generally agree that even apart from
their own conscious judgments about facts or
events they are describing, written history continually reflects current thought and interpretation
about past events. It was Benedetto Croce who, in a
somewhat pessimistic view of the scientific nature
of history, coined the phrase that "all history is
contemporary philosophy."[29] Certainly not all historians would be as pessimistic as this. Walsh, for
instance, argues that a historian's value judgments
only "slant" history; they do not determine its details.[30]

It is this philosophizing aspect of the historian's
task that Stephen Neill has understood as the cause
of some of the major debates among theologians on
the subject of history, especially NT history. He
urges the historian to keep the task limited to
simply obtaining the facts and not to interpret
them.[31] What Neill is opposed to is the use of certain philosophical assumptions or rules that the
historian uses as criteria for interpreting past events.
Although Neill is somewhat naive in thinking that

the historian can be separated from assessing evidence, he is correct in realizing that this is the very place where differences and difficulties especially arise in the investigation and interpretation of the biblical narratives. Indeed, a traditional Christian historian would no doubt interpret the resurrection narratives differently than would a historian who denies in practice the presence and activity of God in human affairs. The evidence that both historians examine is the same, but their interpretation and assessment of that evidence undoubtedly differ in many respects because of the former's openness to God's unique activity in history and the latter's refusal of such a possibility. The source of their disagreement is their assumptions about what is possible in history.[32]

When scholars study history, they have before them certain documents or relics of the past. Their business is to discover what the past was that has left these relics behind. In this sense, the historian's task cannot be viewed apart from the sources, whether they be pottery, papyrus, or other written or printed documents. According to Fuller, the historian investigates the "tracks which men leave behind," which fall into two categories: intentional and unintentional.[33] Following *The Historian's Craft* by Bloch, Fuller explains that "intentional tracks" are left behind when a person deliberately records the events that occurred in a certain span of history. "Unintentional tracks," on the other hand, are those things that "range all the way from the artifacts left by a cave dweller to correspondence that men have exchanged. They include anything that indicates how men lived in the past."[34]

Historians must first sift through the various sources available to them and choose the best, or most reliable, on the subject they are exploring. Second, they must investigate and evaluate these sources for understanding, plausibility, and consistency.[35] This is done in part by a study of words or terms that may be particularly significant in NT studies, such as "Abba," "Son of Man," "messiah," and "atonement." Determining the historical circumstances in which these terms were found is important. This is accomplished by comparing these pieces of information with one another and any other external evidence available on the same topic. In doing this, Daniels claims, "the historian is made aware of the inherent defects in most of his sources—not only deliberate bias or deception, but also the errors of memory that cause eye witnesses to disagree, as well as the incompleteness caused by the loss of sources or the failure to make certain records in the first place."[36] Third, there must be a synthesis of the historical data obtained. This is most properly called the interpretive step, in which the historian puts in narrative form a reconstruction of how the examined event is believed to have occurred. Collingwood informs us that the historian must at this point rethink the thought of the author of the sources being examined. He makes the point that historical inquiry involves not only an event but also the thoughts behind the original author's/historian's composition. For Collingwood, history cannot be separated from the historian's attempt to know the thoughts and activities of someone else's thinking about the past.[37]

Often the evidence available to the historian is not sufficient to make dogmatic conclusions or assertions about past events that gave rise to the sources; it is at this point that the historian must make a careful conjecture. In such places explanations and judgments may be called for that will involve the historian's own personality, moral values, and assumptions. Because it is incumbent upon the historian to make arguments and statements that can be rationally assessed, caution must be exercised in the use of such conjectures. A careful historian will also clarify the framework or assumptions from which the conclusions are drawn or assertions made.

C. The Framework of the Historian

Although many biblical scholars have exercised great care and skill in sifting through and evaluating the biblical narratives, very few of their discoveries or conclusions have gained unanimous acceptance among theologians. How is it that competent biblical scholars can examine the same set of sources and yet interpret them differently? To be sure, a part of the answer lies in the complex nature of the sources they evaluate, but other factors often determine the results of their research. More than one person has described the resurrection of Jesus as the best-attested fact in history. We may properly ask, however, why not all historians have accepted the resurrection as an attested historical fact if it truly is such. Indeed, it may be very difficult to find any modern historians who would make any such claim about this biblical event. Why is it that what one well-educated and highly skilled person considers to be an incontestable fact of history can be judged to be nonsensical or mythical by another qualified inquirer? The answer to this question sheds a great deal of light on the problem of historically understanding the resurrection of Jesus and other remarkable stories in the Bible.

The problem of Jesus' resurrection is somewhat different today than it was in the time of Jesus. The question then, especially among the Pharisees, was not whether the dead could rise but whether in fact Jesus of Nazareth had been raised from the dead. The question today is not so much whether Jesus was raised from the dead but whether anyone has ever been raised from the dead. On what basis can an informed person of today decide the answer to this question? Willi Marxsen, along with Bultmann, contends that a person today who thinks historically, and therefore critically, cannot accept the ancient belief held by the first Christians that the resurrection of Jesus, or any similarly reported event, actually took place.[38] He contends that a modern person must reject the miraculous element in the NT in accordance with the current understanding of historical inquiry that developed at the time of the Enlightenment. He claims that "we simply must (in spite of the unequivocal belief of those narrators and early readers [of the Bible]) raise the question of historicity and then answer this question in accordance with *our own* historical judgment and knowledge."[39] In accordance with his own historical judgment, Marxsen rejects the resurrection of Jesus as a historical event. He argues that one must decide in advance about the resurrection of Jesus quite apart from any support that the Bible might set forth in its defense. The big question for him is not whether Jesus was raised from the dead but whether any person can be raised from the dead. Harvey agrees that one must make a decision about the historical nature of the resurrection of Jesus apart from, and in advance of, any arguments that the NT might bring forth in its support. He rejects the conclusion that since so much evidence stood in favor of the emptiness of the tomb of Jesus and so little definite and convincing evidence against it, the resurrection is probably historical:

When dealing with an event so initially improbable as the resurrection of a dead man, the two-thousand-year-old narratives of which are limited to the community dedicated to propagating the belief and admittedly full of "legendary features, contradictions, absurdities, and discrepancies," how could a critical historian argue that since much can be said for it and no convincing evidence against it, it is probably historical?[40]

Prior to an investigation of the resurrection of Jesus in the NT, must there be a commitment to a particular interpretation of that event before investigating it? Léon-Dufour believes that one must answer the major question about the possibility of such an event before the evidence in favor of it can be assessed. Concerning the resurrection, he says that "the problem facing the historian is here at its most acute, since it is impossible for him to assess any evidence for the resurrection without first making a personal option about the possibility of a person rising to life from the grave."[41] He also finds it impossible for a person objectively to approach historical evidence for an event if that person has already rejected in advance the possibility of the occurrence of that event.[42] Obviously the view one takes with respect to the possibility of the resurrection of the dead will greatly influence one's evaluation of the evidence for the resurrection of Jesus. This kind of "prior understanding" (Ger. *Vorverständnis*) is what Gardiner has in mind when he speaks about the temptation of the historian to ask the big questions first and, having answered them, then to "deal with the subject along a course set by those answers."[43]

On what basis, however, shall we determine whether one can rise from the dead? What evidence can be brought forth that will enable us to decide either way in advance? Why will some persons accept the resurrection as a possibility and others reject it? Are there any commonly accepted criteria that will enable us to make this kind of a decision? These questions are perplexing to modern historians as well as to critical biblical scholars. The reason for differing responses to the idea of the unique or supernatural intervention of God in history, as in the case of the resurrection of Jesus, is, in large measure, the fact that historians have failed to develop a set of generally accepted canons of interpretation that all who call themselves historians accept.[44] Historians do not generally agree on the criteria or rules for judging one event historical and another unhistorical. This is especially true in the case of Christian historians. The reasons historians disagree among themselves in the interpretation and assessment of past events are also the reasons for the current debates in modern theology about the resurrection of Jesus.

It is the historian's framework for specific types of events that determines how the historian will decide the question. Walsh believes that the work of a historian must be thought of in terms of an artist expressing his or her own personality. What historians bring with them to their work obviously will significantly affect their conclusions.[45] Coming back to the resurrection of the dead, the reason one historian will accept this alleged event as true and another who examines the same evidence or sources rejects it is that both historians bring something to their sources not found in the evidence itself. That something is found in their own peculiar interests and personalities as well as in their philosophies about the universe in which they live. Walsh argues quite convincingly that the way historians tell a story depends not merely on what they have to say but also on their own interests and preconceptions. He holds that there is a subjective element in every historical inquiry that determines what the historian will accept or reject. It is this subjective element that Walsh describes as the limiting factor in any truly scientific or historical investigation of the past:[46] history "is always written from a particular point of view, a phrase which includes the acceptance of a certain moral outlook."[47] This moral outlook slants the way one assesses the evidence for an alleged event.

Walsh's "moral outlook" is what Paul Tillich calls the historian's "historic consciousness," which is "one cause of the endless differences in historical presentations of the same factual material."[48] Tillich maintains that it is impossible to sever this historical consciousness from the historian, and stresses that there is no history without factual occurrences and the reception and interpretation of them by historical consciousness.[49] He also recognizes that historical documents, whether legend, chronicle, or scholarly report, are all interpreted through one's own philosophical framework. Tillich claims that this interpretation also has many levels:

> It includes the selection of facts according to the criterion of importance, the valuation of causal

dependences, the image of personal and communal structures, a theory of motivation in individuals, groups, and masses, a social and political philosophy, and underlying all of this, whether admitted or not, an understanding of the history [that is] in unity with the meaning of existence in general.[50]

Walsh, however, cautions that there is no scientific way to justify the moral outlook of one investigator over another, that at least none has yet been found to determine whether one's moral judgment is more correct than another's.[51] Even though the sources that historians handle cannot be altered by their assumptions or moral outlook, their conclusions about these sources cannot always be independently verified by a thorough examination of them. If historians refuse to accept the moral outlook or worldview of others, it may be claimed that they are unreasonable, irresponsible, or ignorant, but it cannot be argued that they are necessarily standing in opposition to the facts. Worldviews are exceedingly difficult, if not impossible, to substantiate or support.

D. History and Science

Whether history can rightly be called a science is an age-old question that still garners no consensus among historians and scientists. In a very broad sense, history may be called a science because, like scientific inquiry, it seeks to discover or find out things. When the term "science" is applied to knowledge, however, certain factors must exist, according to Walsh. This knowledge (1) is methodically arrived at and systematically related; (2) consists of, or at least includes, a body of general truths; (3) enables one to make successful predictions and so to control the future course of events, in some measure at least; and (4) is objective, in the sense that it is such as all unprejudiced observers ought to accept if the evidence were put before them, whatever their personal predilections or private circumstances.[52] Obviously, some of these criteria are not true of history. For example, it would be difficult to find a British historian who would agree with an American historian on the causes, effects, and even particular battles of the American Revolutionary War. The same could be said about the French Revolution if it were interpreted by German and French historians.

If the above assumptions regarding science are valid, however, as Gardiner believes they are, then history as such is not a science.[53] There are no experimental and inductive processes in history by which its conclusions can be tested. History cannot be demonstrated by controlled observation. Gardiner points to four primary arguments used by some historians to show that there is a distinction between the practice of history and the general understanding of scientific inquiry: (1) historical events are past events and hence cannot be known in the manner in which present events are known; (2) historical events are unique and unclassifiable; (3) history describes the actions, statements, and thoughts of human beings, not the behavior of matter, with which science is concerned; and (4) historical events have an irreducible richness and complexity.[54]

These distinctions between history and science have long been debated among historians, but they do bring out the essential features of historical writing. A natural scientist observes phenomena in order to discover certain detectable laws about the behavior of all such phenomena in the same given circumstances. Historians, though not able to divorce themselves from thinking about certain events within the framework of basic laws that govern the universe, are primarily concerned with describing past events and telling not only what, how, and why they happened but also their relevance for human self-understanding. Although they are not free to disregard general laws when reconstructing the past, historians do not set out to establish these or any other laws through their work.[55] Historians are interested primarily in what happened in the past and its relevance for today, not what generally happens, even though they cannot dissociate their conclusions from perceptions about what happens. Natural scientists, on the other hand, are primarily concerned with what happens and continually happens under repeated observations of controlled experiments. A person who uses past events to illustrate certain laws or patterns by which future events or actions of human behavior can be predicted or determined is not properly a historian but something more difficult to describe.[56] The historian's interest is more appropriately directed to particular events than to universal laws.

Whether history is a science and whether it can be called scientific is a debate that cannot be settled here, but certain characteristics of history must be noted. In the natural sciences laws are demonstrable through controlled observation, but in history, laws are assumed that are not easily illustrated by the results of the historical inquiry. The preconceptions that the historian brings to the text often determine the interpretation that emerges. Objectivity is always the aim of conscientious historians, but honesty must also compel them to make known their presuppositions and assumptions about history when these assumptions affect a reconstruction of the past in any way. If historians are to distinguish their work from mere propaganda, they must strive for objectivity and impartiality in their work. They must be honest enough to indicate when their own preconceptions and interests have not only guided some of their pursuits but swayed them in their conclusions. Jaspers observes that this relationship between the historian's objectivity and moral outlook, or framework, in the scientific study of history is one of the limiting factors in modern historical research:

> The presentation of historic realities—events, conditions, periods, personalities—is always a work of art on a scientific basis. If successful, it is scientifically based in all its parts; but on the whole, in the choice of the theme and in the selection and arrangement of facts, it will arise only from motives which transcend science, though they must accept its limitations.[57]

Consequently, if historical inquiry is limited to this framework, we are not able to examine adequately some of the prominent assumptions employed by most contemporary historians in their craft.

3. PRINCIPLES AND ASSUMPTIONS OF MODERN HISTORIOGRAPHY

In his classic book *Jesus and His Story*, Ethelbert Stauffer sought to minimize the subjective element in historical research and determined to let the facts speak for themselves concerning the biblical testimony about Jesus. In his attempt to argue for the resurrection of Jesus, he systematically set out to prove the emptiness of the tomb in which Jesus was buried. But as Anderson has observed, "Even if Stauffer had proven the empty tomb beyond reasonable doubt, the Erlangen [Germany, Stauffer's home] historian would then have given us only an empty tomb and not a risen Lord."[58] What Stauffer failed to see was that facts do not speak for themselves; they must be interpreted. If the facts are to be meaningful, the historian must interpret them, and how historical facts are interpreted will, in large measure, be determined by the methodology and assumptions the historian adopts. In the preceding discussion, we showed that there are certain philosophical preconceptions and assumptions that guide historians in their work and that this framework helps us to explain some of the differences among historians. We will now identify some of these assumptions or principles and show how they create difficulties for biblical interpretation today.

A. The Principle of Autonomy

The revolution of thought brought about by the Enlightenment primarily concerned authority and autonomy. Immanuel Kant saw the Enlightenment as essentially an autonomy from authority. Humanity's release from all authority would give the freedom to think without direction from another.[59] Reason reigned supreme after the overthrow of the old authority. Prior to the Enlightenment, mediation between past and present events was accomplished chiefly by means of testimony, the historian knowing the past simply by accepting or rejecting an authority who was a witness to past events. Collingwood labels this form of knowledge a "scissors and paste" history.[60] He argues that insofar as one accepts the testimony of an authority and treats it as historical truth, that person "obviously forfeits the name of historian; but we have no other name by which to call him."[61] Before the Enlightenment, the essential function of the historian was to compile and synthesize testimonies of so-called authorities or eyewitnesses. The historian was primarily (though not exclusively) an editor and harmonizer of the sources. Examples of this can be seen in Eusebius's *Ecclesiastical History*, from the fourth century, and Sozomen's *Ecclesiastical History*, from the fifth century. Collingwood concludes that these kinds of works, though useful, are not actually history because they contain little criticism or interpretation and there is little reliving or re-creating the experience of the past in one's own mind.[62] Harvey explains that one of the primary tasks of a modern

historian is not to be so loyal to the texts under investigation that the historian cannot see where the author failed to do justice to the subject matter. Harvey also believes that using the principle of autonomy is a major part of the critical theologian's task in relation to exegesis:

> One must, to be sure, listen to and wrestle with Paul, but that also means to see where Paul himself sometimes failed to communicate properly his vision. One must, in other words, determine the degree to which the subject matter really has achieved adequate expression in the words and statements of the author. One cannot assume that even Paul spoke only in the spirit of Christ, for other spirits also come to expression through him.[63]

Although historians cannot function apart from their sources, the sources never dictate the conclusions. In this sense, autonomy is an accepted principle used by most modern historians.

B. A Closed Causal Nexus

Although not always acknowledged by historians, one of the primary presuppositions of historical inquiry is that history must be viewed as occurring within a closed continuum of cause-and-effect events. This prevailing view of history among its modern practitioners, whether assumed consciously or unconsciously, had its roots in the Enlightenment and was both designed and refined by nineteenth-century positivists. Braaten observes that history, according to the current positivistic assumptions, is a constant state of immanent interconnections of cause and effect.[64] Each event emerges out of, and must be understood in relation to, the historical context in which it appears. This closed causal nexus is what Macquarrie, following Ernst Troeltsch, refers to as the principle of correlation: "Although there may be distinctive events, and even highly distinctive events, all events are of the same order, and all are explicable in terms of what is immanent in history itself. Thus there can be no divine irruptions or interventions in history."[65] Macquarrie adds that the effect of this principle of correlation upon the activity of God in history is that God reveals himself but "his activity is immanent and continuous. It is not the special or sporadic intervention of a transcendent deity."[66] Although an event may qualify and transform the future course of history in significant ways, it never appears within the historical process as an inexplicable bolt from the blue. Kaufman notes that the task of the modern historian is "to explain and interpret the movement of man's history entirely by reference to the interaction of human wills, the development of human institutions and traditions, and the effects of natural events and processes, i.e., exclusively in intramundane terms."[67]

Clearly, this view of history had significant consequences for traditional and more conservative notions about the activity of God in history. Because of the naturalistic mold in which the historian has chosen to work, Kaufman concludes that the inevitable result is a denial of the existence of God and, hence, "God is dead."[68] The consequence of this understanding of history, in methodology at least, is that it excludes acknowledgment of God's activity in history as it has normally been defined in the exodus event and the resurrection of Jesus or other supernatural interventions in history. The modern historian presupposes the interrelation and interconnection of all events in an unbroken line of immanent causes and, according to Gogarten, "seeks the driving force of a historical process in mankind itself." Gogarten argues that this assumption was based on the premise that human beings are responsible for the world and what takes place in it, completely denying to God responsibility. This exclusion, he is careful to explain, is not in principle but because of "purely methodological reasons."[69] In his own work, however, it is difficult to distinguish what is "in principle" and what is "methodological" in matters related to God's activity in history.

The assumption of a closed universe concludes that all historical events are therefore natural events and have natural (intramundane) explanations. They are an uninterrupted series of events that are continuous with one another and cannot be explained apart from one another. Something within the historical circumstances surrounding an event naturally gives rise to the resulting event. This assumption may be illustrated by a historian's argument that a particular war was won because the general on the winning side had better-trained soldiers, the best military equipment available, a larger supply of munitions, or even weather and terrain in his favor, as when Wellington faced Napoleon. The historian as a historian does not conclude that Wellington won the battle because God was on his side.

Again, since all events are of the same order, no particular event can be called final, and therefore it is neither absolute nor unique. The net result of the application of this principle to Christianity, as Macquarrie concludes, is that Christianity becomes a relative religion. "Christianity belongs within the sphere of religious and human history as a whole, and no absolute claim can be made for it. The life and work of Jesus Christ himself may be a very distinctive event, but it cannot be absolute or final or of a different order from other historical events."[70] The historian is therefore primarily concerned with describing past events and indicating why and how they took place, but the historian may not treat them as unique in the sense that they occur suddenly from nowhere. All historical events, according to the notion of a closed causal nexus, occur inside the course of history and are always connected to other events of the same order. A revolution does not simply occur; it must be seen as the result of many historical causes that gave rise to it. All historical explanation is based on the idea of continuity: the circumstances surrounding an event in some way bring it about, and all historical events are interconnected in the sense that one event somehow causes another naturally, not through something that comes from above.

C. The Principle of Analogy

Besides adopting in principle the notion of a closed causal nexus, modern historiography investigates its subject on the basis of analogy. Analogy essentially means that historical knowledge relies upon what is known in order to find out what is unknown. It assumes that history is repetitive and constant and that what is absolutely unique either does not occur in history or is unknowable. Braaten explains that events of the past are knowable only because historians can find some connection between them and modern-day events with which they are familiar.[71] Macquarrie observes that in historical analogy we assume that all events of the past are analogous to events that we ourselves experience in the present. It follows, then, that events analogous to our experience are more likely to be reckoned true than those events for which we can find no analogy.[72]

It may be assumed that the Battle of Waterloo was a single occurrence in history and, in that sense, unique. But there have been other major battles in history in which well-known generals have fought and lost. In this sense, Napoleon's defeat at Waterloo has analogy. There was only one Napoleon who ruled France and brought the rest of Europe to its knees through his military conquests, but there have been other rulers in history who have conquered vast segments of territory. Napoleon, therefore, is not without analogy.

In favor of this principle, it may be argued that historians have no other means of interpreting history than through their knowledge and sensory perceptions of the world. What historians know about the repetition of nature, its constancy, and the general laws within which nature operates helps in understanding the scope of history. Therefore, since events tend to repeat themselves and since knowledge can only proceed from the known to the unknown, an event cannot be considered historical if it is without analogy to other events in history.

Gardiner, objecting to this line of thinking, says that the historian's primary interest is in establishing past events in their unique setting. He maintains that "history is about what happened on particular occasions. It is not about what usually happens or what always happens under certain circumstances; for this we go to science."[73] He nevertheless argues that the historian cannot be divorced from certain laws that govern the field of inquiry. Although he holds that the historian is only concerned with describing past events and indicating how and why they occurred when they did, he also admits that the historian, for all of the attention given to the individual and the unique, is still not free to disregard general laws in the work of reconstruction.[74] By this he means that a historian cannot ignore natural laws, such as the assumption of a closed causal nexus but especially the principle of analogy.

Braaten questions the viability of this principle because, if rigidly adhered to, history cannot reflect anything new—it can only discover what it already knows, and consequently it has little to say.[75] Although there is much to be said for Braaten's position, that is, that history is open to the unique activity of God, he has not answered the age-old criticism that what is absolutely unique is absolutely unknowable. One might support Braaten by invoking Christian theology, that the absolutely unique is knowable if it has been revealed by God. A Christian might thus argue that God has uniquely revealed himself through his Son, Jesus Christ. Revelation appears to be the best answer Christians can muster in defense of the uniqueness of Jesus and of God's activity in raising him from the dead. But the historian as a historian cannot treat uniqueness in the same manner as the Christian theologian. Such a step by a historian would violate the procedures used to describe and interpret past events.

D. The Principle of Probability

It is difficult to find the principle of probability discussed in detail, but it appears to be universally assumed by historians. Gardiner calls this principle a commonsense explanation.[76] When historians use common sense, they fall back upon their own experience and do not employ high degrees of precision. When we encounter the phrase "The cow jumped over the moon," for example, we do not ask about the kind of cow involved or the circumstances related to the action; we simply call the notion absurd or a myth because we have neither seen nor heard of such a thing. We may have seen a cow jump a few feet, but based on our experience with such animals, we safely conclude that such a phenomenon is impossible and therefore did not happen. The story is thus regarded as a myth or fairy tale, and no credence is given to the facticity of the story. There are many such things that, according to our own experience and knowledge, are highly improbable. For instance, it is highly improbable, within our current knowledge, that any person could run a three-minute mile, that a person could make an axe head float on the water, or that dead people whom we have buried would rise from the grave in a few days. On the other hand, to use the battle analogy of Napoleon, it is probable that at least one great general will lose a battle sometime; our experience in other events of history informs us that greatness does not ensure success. The primary criterion of the principle of probability is the sensory experience, perception, and reflection of the historian investigating the past. Our current understanding of life strongly suggests not only that a person is unable to run a three-minute mile but also that a virgin cannot conceive and bear a son and that dead people do not come back to life. The implications of these principles of modern historical inquiry for Christian faith are obvious for traditional beliefs about a God who intervenes precisely in these ways to accomplish his purposes in the world.

Some scholars are now addressing the issue of miracles in the Bible using certain criteria for authenticity. Few doubt that Jesus was a miracle worker in the sense that he was able to perform various kinds of healings for individuals in need, but this has analogy in the history of human experience and is not therefore unique. Such healing miracles have parallels in numerous stories of individuals being healed from various infirmities through the abilities of certain persons. This can be accounted for, however, on the basis of psychosomatic abilities that are not completely clear and that are not attributed to the intervention of God in human affairs.

4. HISTORICAL ASSUMPTIONS AND GOD'S ACTIVITY IN HISTORY

When the above assumptions and principles are applied to the Bible, their application, if they are valid, will have a major effect on interpreting the biblical narratives that tell of God's special interventions in history, whether creation itself, miracles of healing, the calming of storms, the parting of the waters of the Red Sea, or resurrections from the dead. When the assumptions are applied to the primary traditions of the Christian faith, Christianity is deprived of its miraculous and supernatural assertions. All of its proclamations about unique, absolute, or supernatural events must be discarded or, according to Rudolf Bultmann, redefined in terms of what they say about human existence. If the assumptions are correct, it appears that Christianity can no longer be considered absolute or final but only sufficient for some people. Bultmann, however, never drew this conclusion. He argued that only through the unique Christ experience, that is, submission to the Christ who calls us as heard in the preaching of the gospel, can one find authentic human existence.

If the assumptions are true, however, it would appear that Christianity has been reduced simply to a historical religious phenomenon, to be understood naturally within the religious development of humankind. When they are applied as an appropriate guide for interpreting the resurrection of Jesus, the conclusions are rather dismal for traditional Christian faith. Such conclusions need not be so negative, however, when a larger perspective is taken.

First, the subject of the resurrection of Jesus is God, not humanity. It was God, according to the NT, who raised up Jesus from the dead.[77] If historians are only interested in human beings and their past actions in their social environment, then, in a technical sense, they have ruled out the resurrection of Jesus as a historical event. On the basis of current notions of the subject of history, Moltmann is right when he concludes:

> If, as has frequently been pointed out, it is true that the experiences of history on the basis of which the concepts of the historical have been constructed have nowadays an anthropocentric character, that "history" is here man's history and man is the real subject of history . . . then it is plain that on this presupposition the assertion of the raising of Jesus by God is a "historically" impossible and therefore a "historically" meaningless statement.[78]

Second, since the NT writers view God as the author of this supernatural, or at least out-of-the-ordinary, event, then their perspective on history does not view events as occurring only within a closed continuum of cause and effect. The resurrection of Jesus, according to the NT, was accomplished by one who is outside and beyond the boundaries and limitations of natural causation. To the NT writers, history is an open continuum wherein God, though separate from nature, is free and powerful enough to perform redemptive deeds within it and to make his will known to humankind in ways that are not our ways.

Third, there are no analogies to the resurrection of Jesus that will enable the historian to interpret properly such an event. The historian proceeds from the known to the unknown in an inductive style of investigation. Therefore, what is absolutely unique must in turn be absolutely unknowable. This is true unless one accepts, as do the NT writers, the biblical understanding of revelation, that is, that God has revealed his uniqueness in the person of his Son. The biblical writers accept another form of knowledge, not experienced through historical methodology but only through the special revelation of God—whether through redemptive deeds, as in the resurrection of Jesus or the exodus, or through direct verbal communication, as in the giving of the law at Sinai. But the historian has no objective criteria with which to examine such revelations. They are without analogy and beyond the historian's own experience.

Fourth, there are no natural causes in the circumstances surrounding the resurrection of Jesus that could give rise to that event. Jesus was arrested, beaten, crucified, and buried. His disciples abandoned him, fled, and were filled with despair and gloom. In these circumstances there is nothing in the experience of the historian or in known natural laws that leads one to conclude that a resurrection must be forthcoming. On the contrary, what the historian knows through experience and demonstrable natural laws forces the conclusion that the earthly and human life of Jesus ended finally and completely at the cross.

Fifth, under the principle of probability, Jesus must remain in the tomb. It is simply not probable, under known circumstances, that a dead person should rise from the grave. Traditional Christianity argues that Jesus was not simply just another man but in fact the Son of God, unique in every way, and that it is therefore improbable that death should contain such a person. Against this line of reasoning is the complete inability of the historian to establish Jesus' uniqueness through historical methodology, any more than his resurrection from the grave. There are no known categories of thought available that enable the historian to get behind the faith statements of the early NT writers and demonstrate that Jesus was in fact "Lord," "Christ," "Son of Man," or "Son of God." It should be noted that, unlike some contemporary Christian apologists, NT writers work from the event of Jesus' resurrection to establish or recognize the uniqueness of the person of Jesus and not the other way around (cf. Acts 2:32–36; Rom 1:3–4; Phil 2:5–11).

It should be clear that the above described historical method presents serious difficulties for the biblical view of the resurrection of Jesus. If history is a closed continuum, then history is also closed to the kind of divine deeds found frequently in the Bible, whether the floating of an axe head, walking on water, or the past or future resurrection of a dead person. Moltmann again draws the proper conclusions from a rigid application of this historical methodology when he maintains that "in face of the positivistic and mechanistic definition of the nature of history as a self-contained system of cause and effect, the assertion of a raising of Jesus by God appears as a myth concerning a supernatural incursion which is contradicted by all our experience of the world."[79] When viewed through the modern historical method, supernatural or miraculous events appear absurd.

The problem now for theologians is to decide whether historical methodology has reached its objective limits or whether it has built-in limitations that prevent it from properly assessing the resurrection of Jesus and other supernatural events in the biblical narratives. Are there real events of the past that are not discernible through the modern historical methods of investigation?

From this discussion, it is clear that any modern theologian who wishes to confess Jesus as the risen Lord must grapple with the problems of the relationship between history and faith. Whether it is possible or even desirable for a modern Christian to have a faith like Paul or the twelve apostles in the risen Lord Jesus will depend, to a great extent, on the view of history adopted and its relation to faith.

The Gospel writers did not intend to write historical or biographical documents in the modern technical senses of those terms but, rather, sought to write confessions of faith, in the form of abbreviated biographies, that were meant to call persons to faith in their risen Lord. They were indeed interested in the biography of their Lord and other historical information available to them, but only as these things aided them in their evangelistic calling of persons to faith in Jesus as the Christ. They were certain that the resurrection of Jesus and the other events they described had actually happened. They also confessed that the earthly Jesus could not be understood apart from the Easter faith they proclaimed. Ernst Käsemann, who also recognizes the implications of modern historiography for Christian faith, states, "Primitive Christianity is obviously of the opinion that the earthly Jesus cannot be understood otherwise than from the far side of Easter, that is, in his majesty as Lord of the community and that, conversely, the event of Easter cannot be adequately comprehended if it is looked at apart from the earthly Jesus."[80]

Whatever historical statements may be made about the Gospel narratives, one must conclude that the writers of these narratives believed that Jesus of Nazareth was raised from the dead and was seen by human beings. Marxsen correctly observes that the resurrection of Jesus is the presupposition for the fact that Jesus later became the object of preaching.[81]

From here the question naturally arises whether the modern historian who accepts the historical assumptions discussed in this chapter can agree with the declaration of Easter faith, namely, that Jesus is risen from the dead. Ladd does not believe this is possible:

> The critical historian, as historian, cannot talk about God and his acts in the Incarnation, the Resurrection, and the Parousia; for although such events occur within the history of our world, they have to do not merely with the history of men, but with God in history; and for the historian as historian, the subject matter of history . . . is man. Therefore the historical-critical method has self-imposed limitations which render it incompetent to interpret redemptive history.[82]

It seems fair to say that if Christians wish to affirm faith in the resurrection of Jesus today, they must either do so in opposition to the conclusions of modern historical science or find some other way to confess their faith in the risen Lord, one that will speak responsibly both historically and kerygmatically. If the currently accepted historical methodology is not valid for establishing all of the past, then its weaknesses or limitations must be demonstrated. The theologian may wish to classify the resurrection as an unhistorical event, since it does not fit in with the popular notion of what is historical, but as Moltmann argues, "He must look around for other ways for modern, historically determined man to approach and appropriate the reality of the resurrection."[83] The NT focuses on faith as the appropriate medium for grasping the significance of the resurrected Jesus and the experience of God's salvation.

5. HISTORICAL AND "THEOLOGICAL" EXPLANATION

Is there a reality of the past that is beyond the scope of the historian's inquiry? Christian faith, in-

cluding that of Bultmann, answers a resounding "yes!" Whether that activity is limited to a new self-understanding (so Bultmann)[84] or to the intervention of God into the events of time and space, many Christians agree that God is not limited to the scope of the historian's inquiry. The primary question for the Christian community is whether God has intervened in the course of human affairs by suspending the laws of nature in order to accomplish his will. Can one reasonably account for the origins of Christianity apart from a belief in God's supernatural intervention in the course of history? The historian, as historian, cannot answer reasonably about the origins of Christian faith, but what of Christians? Is it possible to arrive at some other approach that accounts for Christian origins and is, at the same time, historically responsible? This new approach would recognize that there are self-imposed limitations on the current historical method. Although it rightly enables the historian to assess much of human history, the current method does not have the ability to accommodate or account for the activity of God. This new method would contend that the historical method is incapable of examining all factual events of history because of its significant self-imposed limitations.

Is it possible that an event of history can be discovered or encountered apart from historical-critical inquiry? Can a so-called historical-theological approach better account for the origins of the Christian faith? Is there something in the nature of a theological method that can recover unique or supernatural events of the past? Christian faith has traditionally confessed the unique activity of God in history, yet it must be conceded that there are no scientific or strictly objective historical ways of proving that such unique activity ever occurred. But if this is so, why should such events have anything to do with the Christian proclamation? For Bultmann the activity of God took place in history in the death of Jesus on the cross, but only through the eyes of faith was the meaning of this revealed to the disciples. For the historian the cross could only be seen as a tragic end of a good individual, but through faith alone its full meaning was disclosed to Jesus' followers. The Christian proclamation is so completely wrapped up, however, with an assurance of God's unique activity in Jesus, which culminates in his resurrection from the dead and his consequent exaltation, that the church cannot easily reject its roots in a unique and supernatural event in history as Bultmann has done. Indeed, one's credulity is stretched beyond all limits to suppose that Christian faith is based solely upon a new understanding of an historically unverifiable resurrection, or even a new self-understanding disclosed in the resurrection. Bultmann is right to say that the cross posed a question to the followers of Jesus; but that the cross could in itself "disclose to them its meaning"[85] stretches one's faith as much as, or more than, believing, as the disciples did, that God raised Jesus from the dead. The testimony of the NT writings is that it was the resurrection of Jesus that gave a new understanding of the cross to the disciples, not the cross itself, which only promoted doubt, discouragement, and despair. An examination of the earliest Christian preaching in Acts 2–5 shows that the early church's Christology and understanding of salvation were based not upon the cross but upon its belief in the resurrection of Jesus.[86]

Christian faith does not depend on the historian's ability to examine the past or upon any ambiguous event of the past, including the empty tomb, but on the certainty that God has acted uniquely and decisively in Jesus of Nazareth, not only in his death but also in his resurrection from the dead. This confession is not empirically perceived or mediated through any historical methods but, rather, through the certainty of Christian faith, which comes through the proclamation of the gospel. In the proclamation, the hearer is called upon to submit to, or confess as Lord, the Christ who reveals himself in preaching (see Rom 10:9–10; 1 Cor 15:3–9).

If the historian could prove the unique actions of God in history, there would indeed be no need for faith at all (2 Cor 5:7). Yet even though one cannot prove it historically, to deny the resurrection of Jesus is to deny the very heart of the Christian proclamation (1 Cor 15:17). In other words, though it is not possible to prove the activity of God in Christ through any wisdom of this world (Paul suggests as much in 1 Cor 1:18–29), the denial of this unique activity, it would seem, denies the validity of the Christian faith altogether. The Christian message is neither transmitted nor received through logic, reason, or even historical research, but is believed on the basis of a revelation from God through the proclaimed gospel (1 Cor 15:11) and is an obedient submission to the call of God.[87] Christian faith believes that God speaks through the proclamation of the Christ (Rom 10:14–17). Although faith is not primarily an assent to a series of facts, Christian faith cannot deny the truthfulness of the kerygma to which it submits. The aliveness of the risen Christ is demonstrated by the Holy Spirit in the life of the believer who submits to the call of God. The Christian can therefore proclaim that Christ is alive not only because the early disciples said so but because the Christian has encountered him in the Christian message. The truthfulness of the Christian message, then, is known through a submission to the call of God that comes through the proclamation of that message and is verified by his Spirit to the person of faith (see, e.g., Acts 5:32). The Christian's confession of God is a confession of trust and confidence in one who "gives life to the dead and calls into existence the things that do not exist" (Rom 4:17b). We suggest here that the one who has encountered God in history does not close history to the activity of God. In large measure, Bultmann would agree with this last statement, but we contend here that his view of what God can do in history has been more determined by the historian than by the act of God. In this we must take exception with him.

The historical method has never been capable of discovering God's activity in history (and Bultmann surely agrees). The accuracy of this statement can be seen in the impotent life-of-Jesus research of the great nineteenth-century liberal "quest." Jesus was never called Lord because of his ethical teachings, and it is almost universally admitted that the inchoate band of disciples after Jesus' crucifixion had no basis in their prior contact with him to continue together in his name. What initiated (or reinitiated) their faith in him after his death has never been on public display for the critical historian because what happened was unique and revelatory and therefore beyond the scope of the historian's inquiry. The unique, supernatural, and revelatory activity of God is beyond objective inquiry because the historian is limited to examining only the natural and usual kinds of events in history. Historians can only be involved with what they already know through their own sensory experience and what has analogy to other known events of the past. In regard to the unique activity of God, they have no means of objective inquiry.

Geering argues that the resurrection of Jesus should be removed from the class of events that are properly called historical and open to historical investigation.[88] It is not the kind of event that can be subjected to historical scrutiny. The creeds of the church may be open to the unique activity of God in history, but the creeds of the historian preclude such a confession. Those who contend that the resurrection of Jesus is a historical event for historical inquiry[89] appear to be unaware of the background and development of the historian's craft. The resurrection of Jesus is best left out of the realm of the historical, in the most technical sense of the term, and allowed to be confessed as a unique and revelatory event brought about by the activity of God. The reality of the resurrection of Jesus is only known through an encounter with the living Christ.

There is indeed a subjective element found in the study of the past, not just on the part of the historian but also on the part of the Christian. Christian faith maintains that God is known only through an obedience of faith to the call of God (Rom 1:5; 10:9–17). Only through submission to the Christ who comes to us through the message of the word of God can the truthfulness of the message concerning him be finally demonstrated with assurance. The aliveness of Christ is seen today in the participation in, and submission to, the message about him. In one of the earliest confessions of the church, it can be seen that the resurrection of Jesus from the dead and his lordship were first confessed and believed in the heart, not demonstrated through reason or science (Rom 10:8–10). The subjective element is trust in God, not in the human resources of wisdom (1 Cor 1:18–21). It is God's Spirit who testifies to the Christian about the validity of the proclamation (Acts 5:32) and assures the Christian of a place in God's kingdom (Rom 8:14–16).

This discussion may appear to be an unwillingness to submit the resurrection of Jesus, or the uniqueness of God's activity in Jesus of Nazareth, to historical analysis; the contention, however, is simply that the final judgment about the supernatural intervention of God in history, including his raising of Jesus from the dead, is reserved for faith, not for historical-critical inquiry. To the extent possible, we will make a critical investigation of the church's belief in the resurrection of Jesus by carefully scrutinizing the traditions passed on to us (ch. 6), but even then we will bring to the attention of the reader the limits of each inquiry. No apology is made for this statement, for truly there appear to be no strictly rational, scientific, or historical reasons for confessing the lordship of Jesus Christ. Indeed, from a historian's perspective, how can it possibly be that one who has suffered a humiliating death on a cross is also the exalted Lord of the church? Only after God's disclosure of his unique work in raising Jesus from the dead did Christian faith become a possibility in the first place.

Christian faith cannot defend itself against the claim that it is a subjective religion except by saying that faith is a response to a genuine call from God. It is objective, however, in the sense that this faith is not produced from one's own longings but is initiated by the risen Christ himself, who comes to the obedient hearer through the Christian message. This is not history in the narrow sense defined above, however, but theology, and there is a theological way of knowing that is not available to historical-critical inquiry. The Christian realizes that his or her new life is a gift from God and is not due to any self-motivated psychological feelings, even though there are no objective ways to prove otherwise. God's speaking to the believer cannot be detected through a historical-critical investigation but only through the obedience of faith to the call of God that comes to us in the message of the risen Christ. In this sense, it has always been possible to prove God's existence, but only by a proof known through the eye of faith. It is proof known by means of theological encounter, not historical inquiry.

In closing, the nature of the resurrection appearances themselves is not such as would allow a historian to evaluate them. Jesus' resurrection was not like the resuscitation of Lazarus but, rather, a resurrection to a new mode of life (see 1 Cor 15). Even the Gospels and the book of Acts suggest that the appearances of Jesus were of another kind than a mere resuscitation. Paul saw Jesus on the Damascus road while those with him only heard something (Acts 9:7) or saw some flash of light (Acts 22:9). Also, though the disciples saw the risen Jesus firsthand, some of the disciples still doubted after they had seen him (Matt 28:17). Again, Jesus suddenly appeared and disappeared following his resurrection (Matt 24:12ff.), and Mary, as well as the disciples on the road to Emmaus, had difficulty recognizing him (John 20:14; Luke 24:16). (We return again to these and other related issues in ch. 6.) Whatever else may be said of the objective nature of the resurrection, it is not clear that an impartial observer could have witnessed the appearances of the risen Jesus. Apart from the Apostle Paul and perhaps James the brother of Jesus, none of the witnesses of the appearances could have claimed empirically based objectivity, since they had been followers of Jesus before his death. The disciples had hoped in him before his death, but not James and Paul. The resurrection of Jesus, as a resurrection to a new mode of existence, may not have been objectively identifiable. From the Easter traditions in the NT, it is clear that the resurrection of Jesus was *revealed* to the disciples through the Easter appearances and was not based on logical deduction about an empty tomb, even less about the cross itself.

BIBLIOGRAPHY

BAGNALL, R. S. *Reading Papyri, Writing Ancient History.* London: Routledge, 1995.

BARTSCH, H.-W., ed. *Kerygma and Myth.* Trans. R. H. Fuller. 2 vols. New York: Harper & Row, 1961.

BRAATEN, C. E. *History and Hermeneutics.* Philadelphia: Westminster, 1966.

BULTMANN, R. *Essays: Philosophical and Theological.* Trans. J. C. G. Greig. London: SCM, 1966.

———. *Theology of the New Testament.* Trans. K. Grobel. 2 vols. London: SCM, 1951–1955.

COLLINGWOOD, R. G. *The Idea of History.* Oxford: Oxford University Press, 1946.

FINLEY, M. I. *Ancient History: Evidence and Models.* London: Chatto & Windus, 1985.

FULLER, D. P. *Easter Faith and History.* London: Tyndale, 1968.

GARDINER, P. *The Nature of Historical Explanation.* London: Oxford University Press, 1968.

GOGARTEN, F. *Christ the Crisis.* London: SCM, 1970.

HARVEY, V. A. *The Historian and the Believer: The Morality of Historical Knowledge and Christian Belief.* Urbana: University of Illinois Press, 1966; 2d ed., 1996.

JOHNSON, L. T. *The Real Jesus: The Misguided Quest for the Historical Jesus and the Truth of the Traditional Gospels.* San Francisco: HarperCollins, 1996.

LÉON-DUFOUR, X. *The Gospels and the Jesus of History.* Ed. and trans. J. McHugh. London: Collins, 1968.

MACQUARRIE, J. *Twentieth-Century Religious Thought.* London: SCM, 1970.

MCINTIRE, C. T., and R. A. Wells, eds. *History and Historical Understanding.* Grand Rapids: Eerdmans, 1984.

MARXSEN, W. *The Resurrection of Jesus of Nazareth.* Trans. M. Kohl. London: SCM, 1970.

MOLTMANN, J. *Theology of Hope.* Trans. J. W. Leitch. London: SCM, 1969.

NEILL, S., and N. T. Wright. *The Interpretation of the New Testament, 1861–1986.* Rev. ed. Oxford: Oxford University Press, 1988.

WALSH, W. H. *An Introduction to Philosophy of History.* London: Hutchinson, 1967.

NOTES TO CHAPTER 1
HISTORY AND FAITH

pages 1–4

1. Essays that attempt a similar task at more length are found in C. T. McIntire and R. A. Wells, eds., *History and Historical Understanding* (Grand Rapids: Eerdmans, 1984).
2. See W. G. Kümmel, *The New Testament: The History of the Investigation of Its Problems* (trans. S. McL. Gilmour and H. C. Kee; Nashville: Abingdon, 1972), passim.
3. R. Bultmann, *Essays: Philosophical and Theological* (trans. J. C. G. Greig; London: SCM, 1966), 101.
4. R. Bultmann, *Theology of the New Testament* (trans. K. Grobel; 2 vols.; London: SCM, 1951–1955), 1:44.
5. R. Bultmann, "The New Testament and Mythology," in *Kerygma and Myth* (ed. H.-W. Bartsch; trans. R. H. Fuller; 2 vols.; New York: Harper & Row, 1961), 1:39.
6. Ibid., 1:5; see also 1:13–15.
7. R. Bultmann, "The Case for Demythologizing," in *Kerygma and Myth*, 2:184; see also 1:8.
8. R. Bultmann, "Is Jesus Risen as Goethe?" in *Der Spiegel on the New Testament* (ed. W. Harenberg; trans. J. H. Burtness; London: Macmillan, 1970), 236.
9. This is not to suggest that the following comments are accepted by all contemporary historians. Indeed, most of what will be said in this discussion is still under examination by many modern historians. The point is that the approach we have to history needs careful scrutiny, since our understanding of it has a significant impact on the conclusions we draw from the surviving ancient documents of early Christianity. What the historian brings to the biblical text determines in large measure what conclusions are drawn from the text.
10. The reliance upon the history of a word, or its etymology, can often be quite misleading. For example, the English word "nice" comes from a Latin word meaning "ignorant," but normal usage does not include the latter sense today. See S. E. Porter, "Studying Ancient Languages from a Modern Linguistic Perspective: Essential Terms and Terminology," *FN* 2 (1989): 161–62.
11. J. Peter, *Finding the Historical Jesus* (London: Collins, 1965), 77.
12. D. P. Fuller, *Easter Faith and History* (London: Tyndale, 1968), 24.
13. R. G. Collingwood, *The Idea of History* (Oxford: Oxford University Press, 1946), 9.
14. Ibid., 10–11.
15. W. H. Walsh, *An Introduction to Philosophy of History* (London: Hutchinson, 1967), 19.
16. H. Anderson, *Jesus and Christian Origins* (New York: Oxford University Press, 1964), 59.
17. P. Gardiner, *The Nature of Historical Explanation* (London: Oxford University Press, 1968), ix, tries to make this point.
18. It is here that A. Toynbee has received his strongest criticism. He begins *A Study of History* (12 vols.; London: Oxford University Press, 1948–1961) endeavoring to be a historian of preceding civilizations, but he gradually lapses into the role of a prophet of what will take place in all subsequent civilizations. Cf. criticisms of Toynbee in Walsh, *Introduction*, 160–64.
19. K. Jaspers, *Philosophical Faith and Revelation* (trans. E. B. Ashton; London: Darton, Longman & Todd, 1967), 186.
20. Ibid., 187.
21. R. V. Daniels, "History: (1) Methodology," in *Encyclopedia Americana* (22 vols.; New York: Americana Corporation, 1971), 14:226–27; quotation, p. 226.

pages 4–7

22. Collingwood (*Idea of History*, 127–29) has defined "historical positivism" as a philosophy, acting in the service of natural science, whose duties include the ascertaining of facts obtained by sense perception. Laws are then framed by the inductive method, and from this a positivistic historiography arises. The rules used to ascertain these facts are basically twofold: first, there is an analysis of the sources in question to determine earlier and later elements in the material, thereby enabling the historian to discriminate between more and less trustworthy portions; second, internal criticism is applied to determine how the author's point of view might affect his statement of the facts, thereby enabling the historian to make allowances for the distortions thus produced. Ibid., 126–30.
23. See ibid., 30ff., for a more complete discussion of this topic.
24. F. Gogarten, *Christ the Crisis* (London: SCM, 1970), 158.
25. W. Wand, *Christianity: A Historical Religion?* (London: Hodder & Stoughton, 1971), 23.
26. Gardiner, *Nature*, 42.
27. Ibid., 70–112.
28. Walsh, *Introduction*, 184.
29. Cited by Wand, *Christianity*, 27.
30. Walsh, *Introduction*, 180.
31. S. Neill and N. T. Wright, *The Interpretation of the New Testament, 1861–1986* (rev. ed.; Oxford: Oxford University Press, 1988), 301–2.
32. That this kind of dispute is not confined to NT scholars is well illustrated in the recent work of R. S. Bagnall on the use of papyri in historical understanding. See his *Reading Papyri, Writing Ancient History* (London: Routledge, 1995).
33. Fuller, *Easter Faith*, 21.
34. Ibid., 21.
35. See Daniels, "History," 229.
36. Ibid., 229.
37. Collingwood, *Idea of History*, 282–301. Harvey is not in agreement with Collingwood at this point. He does not believe that it is important to know all or any of the thought processes of an original author and questions strongly whether such a task is even possible. Cf. V. A. Harvey, *The Historian and the Believer: The Morality of Historical Knowledge and Christian Belief* (2d ed.; Urbana: University of Illinois Press, 1996), 89–99. Harvey has good objections to the heavy reliance upon knowing the thoughts of the authors of documents from the past, but the validity of trying to achieve this goal cannot be easily pushed aside. Quite often the meaning and interpretation of an event can be enhanced by striving to know the thoughts of the original authors of those documents. To be sure, caution is required in this area, and the results, if any, are not always accurate. Gardiner's criticism of Collingwood on this question is quite clear. He argues that not all of history is thought out but that it is often routine, unskilled, or impulsive. He adds that Collingwood's view omits the thoughts of groups who have performed actions in the past. See Gardiner, *Nature*, 49.
38. W. Marxsen, "The Resurrection of Jesus as a Historical and Theological Problem," in *The Significance of the Message of the Resurrection for Faith in Jesus Christ* (ed. C. F. D. Moule; trans. D. M. Barton and R. A. Wilson; London: SCM, 1968), 16.
39. Ibid., 16–17.
40. Harvey, *Historian*, 109.
41. X. Léon-Dufour, *The Gospels and the Jesus of History* (ed. and trans. J. McHugh; London: Collins, 1968), 254.

42. Ibid., 254.
43. Gardiner, *Nature*, xi.
44. So argues Walsh, *Introduction*, 21.
45. Ibid., 22.
46. Ibid., 169–87.
47. Ibid., 182.
48. P. Tillich, *Systematic Theology* (3 vols.; Digswell Place, England: James Nisbet, 1968), 3:321.
49. Ibid., 3:322.
50. Ibid., 3:372.
51. Walsh, *Introduction*, 182–85.
52. Ibid., 37.
53. Gardiner, *Nature*, 28–29.
54. Ibid., 34.
55. Ibid., 43.
56. It is here that Gardiner, in addition to Walsh, chooses to label Spengler and Toynbee as "prophets" of the future rather than as historians of the past. Ibid., 44.
57. Jaspers, *Philosophical Faith*, 187.
58. Anderson, *Jesus and Christian Origins*, 60.
59. See Harvey, *Historian*, 39, for a more detailed explanation of this principle.
60. Collingwood, *Idea of History*, 282.
61. Ibid., 256.
62. Ibid., 204.
63. Harvey, *Historian*, 40.
64. C. E. Braaten, *History and Hermeneutics* (Philadelphia: Westminster, 1966), 81.
65. J. Macquarrie, *Twentieth-Century Religious Thought* (London: SCM, 1970), 143.
66. Ibid., 143.
67. G. D. Kaufman, "On the Meaning of 'Act of God,' " *HTR* 61 (1968): 187.
68. Ibid., 187.
69. Gogarten, *Christ the Crisis*, 158–59.
70. Macquarrie, *Religious Thought*, 143. It should be noted that Macquarrie is giving the consequences of Troeltsch's historical method as it is applied to Christianity, but Macquarrie's conclusions on this issue are not much different from those of Troeltsch.
71. Braaten, *History*, 44.
72. Macquarrie, *Religious Thought*, 142.
73. Gardiner, *Nature*, 40.
74. Ibid., 45.
75. Braaten, *History*, 44–46.
76. Gardiner, *Nature*, 5–23.
77. Although most references to the resurrection of Jesus in the NT refer to God as the author of Jesus' resurrection, there are a few passages that allow for Jesus' self-resurrection. Cf. Mark 16:6; Matt 28:6–7; Luke 24:6, 34; but esp. John 10:17–18. The earliest references to the resurrection of Jesus, however, have Jesus as the subject of a passive sentence, with God as the agent who raises him up. See 1 Cor 15:4, but also Acts 2:23–24; 4:10; 5:30–31.
78. J. Moltmann, *Theology of Hope* (trans. J. W. Leitch; London: SCM, 1969), 174.
79. Ibid., 177.
80. E. Käsemann, *Essays on New Testament Themes* (trans. W. J. Montague; London: SCM, 1968), 25.

pages 7–14

81. W. Marxsen, *Anfangsprobleme der Christologie* (Kassel: Gutersloher, 1960), 51.
82. G. E. Ladd, "The Problem of History in Contemporary New Testament Interpretation," in *SE V* (ed. F. L. Cross; Berlin: Akademie, 1968), 99.
83. Moltmann, *Theology of Hope*, 177.
84. For further reading on Bultmann's understanding of the activity of God in history, besides the works mentioned above, see his *Jesus Christ and Mythology* (London: SCM, 1966); *History and Eschatology* (Gifford Lectures; Edinburgh: Edinburgh University Press, 1957); "History and Eschatology," *NTS* 1 (1954–1955): 5–16; and "On the Problem of Demythologizing," in *New Testament Issues* (ed. R. Batey; London: SCM, 1970), 35–44.
85. Bultmann, "New Testament and Mythology," 1:38.
86. Whether one dates the book of Acts early (ca. A.D. 60–70) or late (ca. A.D. 100), the sources used by its author are certainly a reflection of the earliest strands of Jewish Christianity in Jerusalem, even if they are a bit oversimplified and idealistic.

pages 15–17

87. No one has explained this better than Bultmann, "πιστεύω, πίστις," *TDNT* 6:174–228.
88. L. Geering, *Resurrection: A Symbol of Hope* (London: Hodder & Stoughton, 1971), 216.
89. See M. C. Tenney, *The Reality of the Resurrection* (Chicago: Moody, 1972); and "The Historicity of the Resurrection," in *Jesus of Nazareth: Savior and Lord* (ed. C. F. H. Henry; London: Tyndale, 1966), 133–44.

EXAMINING THE BIBLE CRITICALLY

1. INTRODUCTION

When historical methods of inquiry were developing in the eighteenth and nineteenth centuries, it did not take long for biblical scholars to begin applying to the Bible these new approaches developed for ancient literary documents. Some, no doubt, hoped to uncover the original meaning of the Bible by this application of critical inquiry to the biblical text. But as Phyllis Bird observes, other biblical scholars used the new criticism as a tool for "unmasking religion and rejecting its supernatural claims by exposing the Bible's human character, its crudeness, and fallibility."[1] She notes that both groups challenged the traditional understanding of the Bible, especially in regard to inspiration, authorship, and authority, but it was the second group that became better known, for some occasionally expressed wild and destructive claims that caused many within the church to retreat from applying the critical methodology of historians to the Bible. Attempts to defend the traditional understanding of the Bible, most frequently through the use of dogmatic and philosophical argumentation, have only served to obscure further the original meaning of the biblical literature. Rejection of the critical methodology altogether, however, prevents the church from coming to grips with real issues that the biblical writers raised, issues that also have significant application for this age. Although

some scholars may have differing motives in radically applying the assumptions of the developing critical methodologies, the insights of this critical approach have helped the church immensely in trying to recover the original meaning of the literature that comprises the Bible and the faith that was first proclaimed in the church. The meaning that critical biblical interpretation has uncovered has often been a prophetic word of God to the church, summoning it to a more radical obedience to the call of God than was understood earlier, when the Bible's message was controlled by dogma.

This chapter discusses the methodology for attempting to recover the original meaning of the biblical text—an exegetical methodology. Exegesis is the process of analyzing, explaining, and finally interpreting the Bible within its own historical and cultural context. The word comes from the Greek noun ἐξήγησις *(exēgēsis)*, which means "interpretation," "explanation." The verb form of the word is ἐξηγέομαι *(exēgeomai)*, which means "explain," "describe," "interpret." When speaking of an exegetical method in the study of the Bible, we are referring to the whole process of determining the meaning of the Bible: the historical inquiry into the context, the study of literary features, the analysis of language within its historical and social context, including observation of the various nuances of the grammar of the text, and, ultimately, the attempt to understand the Bible within our own context. In order for the Bible to have meaning, it has to be translated into our framework of human experience. As Guelich has ably observed, exegesis of the Bible involves

> analysis, explanation and interpretation of a text that makes use of the critical historical tools to gain perspective from the historical context of the authorial process, the "sender"; that makes use of the lexico-grammatical tools for decoding the foreign language of the "text"; and that makes use of the literary critical tools to enhance the "receiver's" reading of the parts of the text in terms of the whole.[2]

The value of this process is that it enables the interpreter of Scripture to understand better a text that comes as the word of God, worthy of our best efforts to interpret it correctly (2 Tim 2:15). A valuable reward awaits us at the end of our journey of careful critical biblical inquiry. As we handle that word responsibly and interpret it carefully, it will inevitably have a significant effect upon our lives and the lives of those who hear the results of our inquiry. The following sections of this chapter discuss some of the more important concepts involved in this process of interpretation.

2. THE IMPORTANCE OF CRITICAL BIBLICAL INQUIRY

Because there is a historical, cultural, and linguistic gap between the earliest Christian communities and Christians of today, there is a need for careful analysis of those documents, produced by the church, we call the NT. The same can be said for the OT Scriptures, which are commonly called the Hebrew Bible. This careful analysis is what we mean when we speak of biblical criticism. The term "biblical criticism," for a layperson, may suggest that those engaged in its practice are criticizing the Bible in some pejorative manner. This view may suggest itself not only because of the current use of the term "critical" in social discourse but perhaps also because many scholars who have practiced biblical criticism in its various disciplines have been rather negative in their conclusions about the Bible, especially on questions of historical reliability, miracles, and the viability of the church's proclamation. Nevertheless, whenever one asks

questions about the historical context of the Bible (date, authorship, provenance, etc.), the identity of certain groups of individuals named within it, or the definition of certain technical terms, for instance, "Son of Man," "Son of God," "Lord," or even "eternal," "kingdom," "grace," and "peace," we are asking critical questions. The more one reads the Bible, the more such questions arise. The raising of such questions and probing for answers regarding the Bible is what is called biblical criticism.

Throughout church history many gifted biblical scholars have endeavored to expose the meaning of the Bible to the Christian community in as careful and clear a way as possible for their time. Those teachers have also tended to teach the Bible as the very word of God, not simply as an ancient artifact of the church's past. They have labored under the assumption that the Bible has something important to say about and for the Christian faith. The early church assumed that, generally, what we call the OT (although usually in its Greek form, called today the Septuagint, abbreviated LXX) had an unquestioned authority within the community of faith, and they employed these Scriptures to teach and proclaim their faith in Jesus as the Christ. This was true even when the complete scope of which writings were canonical in their OT or NT Scriptures was unclear to them. They also used their Scriptures both to admonish and to offer models and guidelines for behavior. By the early second century, several Christian writers were using the NT writings not only to proclaim Jesus as Lord and Christ but to clarify what it meant to be a man or woman of God (see 1 Clement, the Didache, and the writings of Ignatius). Like most of our ancient predecessors, we too study the biblical literature in order to understand who we are as a community of God's people and to find direction from God for living. What a Christian is and how a Christian is to live are answered within the pages of the church's Scriptures in a variety of ways but also with continuity. In a very real sense, the church's true identity is found most clearly in the writings of the NT and, to some degree, also in the OT. Without any fear of exaggeration, then, we can affirm that if the church ever loses sight of its Scriptures, it will also lose sight of its own identity and reason for being.

For those who believe that they already know what the Bible teaches and consequently do not need to wrestle with its interpretation, their job is a relatively simple one, however uninformed. Unfortunately, such individuals rarely learn anything new from the Bible, and for them it often ceases to function as a prophetic and inspired book. When we allow the Bible to call into question our behavior and beliefs, then it functions as a prophetic voice to the church. This happens to the extent that we take the time and energy to study its message rather than use it to support our own prejudices. In the latter case, the Bible merely becomes a collection of proof texts to support an already well-defined system of beliefs. The Bible must be studied afresh in every generation, which will ask of it the pertinent and tough questions of the age in which Christians find themselves. When we critically study the Bible, we must appreciate previous interpretation, but we cannot be shackled to the creeds and covenants of a previous era, which often do not allow us to be challenged and criticized by the Bible itself. When we allow for open-minded inquiry of the Bible—that is, biblical criticism—it can be of tremendous value to the church.

All of the Gospel writers wrote their narratives a number of years after Jesus' death and resurrection and from the perspective of Christian faith. This critical observation of the biblical text has enormous implications for the study of the Gospels. Christian faith and the significance of Jesus for faith were expressed for the church in the Gospels. The writers were not trying to write as if the importance of the events they were describing were either unknown to them or of little consequence. Biblical criticism is not primarily interested in what the Bible means for this generation but, rather, with what it meant to those who received the text when it was first written. In this sense, biblical criticism is interested primarily in the compositional stage of development. It seeks to discover the perspectives of the writers and of the communities to whom the writers wrote. It also assumes that there should be some direct relationship between what a text of Scripture meant and what it means for the church today.

A critical study of the Bible is not optional if we are to be relevant in preaching to our own generation. When the church simply repeats its cherished creeds without serious study of its sacred traditions and Scriptures, it defeats itself and becomes irrelevant to its own generation. It further loses sight of the fact that as an inspired book, the Bible, when

properly interpreted, has a continuing and living voice for every generation (see ch. 13, below). A critical investigation of the Bible must be accompanied, however, by the honesty and integrity of the interpreter. If a question presents itself that cannot be answered, we should be willing to say so and not try to cover up the question by simplistically appealing to traditions, creedal formulations, or even piety. Those who approach the Bible critically and are willing to listen intently to its message will soon see that the Bible often criticizes our simplistic answers. Doing this kind of inquiry is never easy, but it has significant value in that it allows the prophetic nature of the Scriptures to be unleashed in our midst. In serious biblical criticism, difficult questions are not shoved under the carpet or given facile answers but are dealt with honestly, with the critical ability and faith that initiated the study in the first place.

A historical-critical study of the Bible does not necessarily deny the unique or divine origins of the Scriptures as some Christians suppose. It merely recognizes that the Bible, though uniquely inspired of God, nevertheless was written by human beings in particular historical contexts and that their work is subject to historical assessment and analysis. We can, for instance, study the vocabulary, grammar, and even the theological priorities of the various authors of the biblical literature. In many cases, we can also determine fairly accurately the occasion and context the author was addressing in his text, and thereby clarify the meaning of the author's words. The information gleaned from such studies can in no way be considered irrelevant for the study of the Bible if we acknowledge that the Bible was written by human beings whose personalities, abilities, and even shortcomings[3] affected the writings they produced. There are significant differences in the ways in which the Gospel writers describe particular events in the life of Jesus, especially in the death and resurrection narratives but also elsewhere. How do we account for these differences? Historically, many Christians, perhaps out of embarrassment or out of a sense of need to protect a particular view of biblical inspiration, have tried to harmonize these differences and, as a result, have often missed the point that each writer was trying to make. Finally, even though the Bible was written in a historical context and its message cannot be fully gleaned if we ignore this historical context and other historical questions implied in the text (e.g., date, authorship, consistency, etc.), historical criticism alone cannot account for the faith of the earliest Christian community. Historical research can never be a substitute for Christian faith, and Christian faith can never be arrived at through scientific research alone. In order to get into the mind-set or perspective of the NT writers, people must be open to the call of God that comes through the message of Scripture, and they must also be willing to submit to this call of God to obedience and surrender. Only then can the faith of which the NT speaks be initiated and experienced. Properly understood, biblical criticism is a servant of faith and can never be its master or its substitute.

3. TYPES OF BIBLICAL CRITICISM

The following types of biblical criticism are the most important fields of inquiry that skilled interpreters of the Bible use to determine the meaning of the NT.[4] Some of these critical methods have been utilized in biblical studies for some time and consequently have been refined over the years. Others are relatively new and are still in the process of establishing their place as a legitimate model of interpretation. We can do no more than briefly introduce them here and refer to works that offer further discussion. The student may think that we are suggesting that one must become proficient in all of the disciplines listed below in order to understand the Bible; this is not the case. Very few, if any, biblical scholars have competence in all of these areas. Nevertheless, we think that this brief exposure to these disciplines will show how many avenues of inquiry are available for biblical study. Those already familiar with these methods will understand the seriousness with which those who do critical investigation of the Bible take their responsibilities.

A. Textual Criticism

The first area of responsibility for any interpreter of the Bible is to determine precisely what the author of a passage or text wrote.[5] The primary goal of textual criticism is to establish the original wording of a text as far as that is possible. Sometimes textual criticism is also called "lower" criti-

cism because it is the foundational work on which all other studies are based. Unless there is some relative agreement on the original wording of a biblical passage, it is difficult, if not impossible, to have any meaningful interpretations of the Scriptures. This is not to suggest, however careful the work done here, that it will yield exact information for every passage of the Bible. Many texts of Scripture are still unclear to biblical scholars today, but the process of evaluating these texts goes on and the most recent conclusions are incorporated into critical translations of the Bible, as in the case of the *New Revised Standard Version*, the *Revised English Bible*, the *New International Version*, and the *New Jerusalem Bible*.

One of the peculiarities of the early Christian community was its preference, by around A.D. 100, for use of the codex—the ancient predecessor of the modern book—over the scroll. C. H. Roberts has evaluated the many possible reasons for this (economy, compactness, comprehensiveness, convenience of use, and ease of reference, among others) and concludes that none of the most obvious explanations answer the question why the Christians, more than anyone else, preferred the codex. He suggests that the practice began in Jerusalem with the Christians opting for another means of transmitting their sacred literature than the scrolls used by the Jews.[6] The early church did not have the opportunity, because of the slower development of the codex, to combine all of the books of the NT or OT into one volume. Early in the second century, the most that could be circulated together in one codex was the four Gospels, some 220 pages or 110 leaves. By the fourth century, however, the process for making a codex, especially with parchment, made possible the combining of all the biblical books into one volume. Those writings that circulated in the same codex become very significant in canonical discussions. Along with these codices (many of which are still in existence), numerous copies of lectionaries (biblical excerpts used for reading in services) survive that may preserve an early form of the biblical text. Some of the oldest translations of the Bible, the Coptic or the Old Syriac for example, were based on earlier texts of the NT; consequently, these translations are quite valuable for recovering the original work of the biblical writers.

After the books of the NT were first written, preserved, and circulated in the churches, they were all hand-copied for centuries by well-intentioned and dedicated individuals. There are thousands of Greek manuscripts and fragments of manuscripts of the NT; about 8 percent of them cover most of the NT, but the vast majority contain only portions of the NT or exist in fragmentary form. Although, for the most part, the copyists were very meticulous in their transmission of the biblical text, they still made mistakes by adding or omitting letters, words, or lines. Some copyists, however, made deliberate changes that they thought would clarify the text or make it more relevant to their own communities. In many of these cases the changes in the text were passed on for centuries in subsequent copies. In time some of the copyists saw that certain older manuscripts differed from the ones they were familiar with, and they made what they thought were corrective changes in order to get back to what they believed was the original text of Scripture. Not all such "errors" were caught, however, and questions about the authentic or most original text persist among scholars.

There are no original manuscripts, known as autographs, remaining from either the OT (either the Hebrew Bible or the LXX) or the Greek NT. In modern times, and with the discovery of many more manuscripts of various textual types, scholars have, by detailed comparison, been able to make better-informed decisions about what the original biblical texts must have looked like. In a number of cases, however, we still cannot be certain of the original reading. Variants in the Greek NT, along with the best available estimate of the original text, are found in critical editions (see ch. 12, below).

B. Historical Criticism

Historical criticism, often called documentary criticism or higher criticism, deals with introductory matters in the study of the NT: the dating of a book, its authorship, the location where the book was produced, its destination, the historical context or setting of the book, and the occasion for its writing. These are basic historical questions, essential for any serious study of a passage of Scripture. An understanding of geography and archaeology is also an important aspect of historical criticism, which enables the historian to re-create more carefully the context of the story about Jesus and the community of faith, called the church, that emerged after his death and resurrection. Ultimately, the historical critic will have done his or her job best when the distance between the biblical writings and the modern reader can be bridged or at least considerably narrowed. The goal of historical criticism is to put the modern reader in the time frame and mood of the community that first heard and responded to the message of the Bible. We can say that we are doing historical-critical research when we try to determine the meaning the writer of a given piece of literature had in mind when he wrote that document to the original readers. Knowing the context of both the writer and the readers, as well as the occasion for the writing and any vocabulary and grammatical relationships within the document, is of immense value in finding out what the writer meant by the words he employed in the writing. Insofar as it is possible, historical criticism also seeks to discover a chronology for the biblical writings. Concerning the NT, the historical critic tries, for example, to discover the historical sequence of the activities of Jesus and the early church. To a large extent, much of this present volume is an exercise in historical criticism.

C. Source Criticism

Many of the writers of the Bible used sources when they produced their literature. NT research most often focuses on this area of investigation when discussing the literary relationships among the Gospels, but it is also applicable to the rest of the NT. As we will see later, among the canonical Gospels there are close literary relationships that suggest a literary dependency. Not only did Matthew and Luke apparently make use of Mark; they also seem to have used other sources, written or oral—those sometimes called the "Synoptic Sayings Source" or "Q" as well as the traditions found only in Matthew and only in Luke—that were circulating among the churches in the last half of the first century. Source criticism focuses, in part, on these relationships and seeks to identify sources in the Gospels themselves and in the other literature of the NT. Source criticism was applied first to the Hebrew Scriptures, primarily to the Pentateuch, and subsequently to the NT

Gospels (see the discussion of the Gospels and their reliability in ch. 8, below).

D. Form Criticism

Sometimes known as the stepchild of source criticism and historical criticism, form criticism made the valuable discovery that particular texts of Scripture may have had a separate history of their own before their inclusion in the biblical narratives. The two parables in Mark 2:18–22, for example, are widely acknowledged to have circulated in churches before Mark included them in his Gospel. The same is true of portions of the parable of the Sower and the Seeds in Mark 4:3–9 and its interpretation in 4:13–20. In the canonical Gospels a number of parallels are found in the appearance stories following Jesus' resurrection. They include the common description of the situation (the disciples being bereft), the appearance of Jesus, the greeting, the recognition by the disciples, and the word of command by Jesus. The similarities of form here suggest that these stories circulated widely in the early Christian communities before being written down and were probably used for instructional or catechetical purposes. It is also often (although not universally) thought that some of the creedal formulations in Paul's letters (e.g., Rom 10:9–10; 1 Cor 15:3–9; Phil 2:6–11) were early Christian affirmations of faith incorporated by him into his letters and that many of the hymns employed by the NT writers (e.g., in Luke 1:46–55, 69–79; and possibly John 1:1–14; 1 Pet 1:18–21; 1 Tim 3:16; Col 1:15–20) reflect early Christian hymns.

The forms of these texts, it is sometimes argued, may have originated in oral discourse or teaching and have subsequently gone through several oral or written stages of development before they appeared in the biblical text. Reconstructing the history of the biblical text is called tradition criticism. Those who investigate the history of the text of the NT generally contend that these different forms often reveal more about the use of tradition in the communities of faith and the life setting (Ger. *Sitz im Leben*) of the churches from which these forms of tradition emerged than they do about the events they purport to describe.

There is no agreement among scholars today on the exact forms to be found in the Gospels, though the categories employed by Rudolf Bultmann in his well-known *History of the Synoptic Tradition* have been largely accepted by many scholars.[7] These include apophthegms (short pithy sayings or maxims, also called aphorisms), sayings, miracle stories, historical stories, and legends. Some other scholars have added to these the distinction between "Jesus stories" and "Christ stories."[8] The forms in the Gospels, however, are basically two-fold: narrative material and sayings sources, or, as some scholars prefer, narratives and discourses, with considerable overlap. The primary goal of form criticism is to discover the life setting of the text. The more radical NT form critics (such as Dibelius and Bultmann) argued that the forms or traditions of the NT Gospels tell us more about the life setting of the early church than about the actual "historical Jesus." Although many scholars have seen the value of studying the various forms of the NT literature and even its value for telling us about the communities from which those traditions emerged, most have not shared the skepticism of Bultmann and others on the ability of those texts to shed light on Jesus himself. Several scholars have thus rejected the notion that the synoptic tradition was only created or formed in the later Christian community and that it does not represent a reliable reflection of Jesus. Nevertheless, the application of form criticism to the NT has caused many of its practitioners to focus more on the community from which the various units of tradition arose and less on the overall message of the writers and the final form of the writing. This deficiency led to the development of the next critical discipline, which focuses on those who compiled, edited, or wrote the biblical narratives and on their perspective when they presented their material in the way they did.

E. Redaction Criticism

One of the values of form criticism is that it raises appropriate questions about the setting of the biblical narratives and emphasizes the importance of the historical context in which they developed. Redaction criticism took that a significant step further, arguing that the writers themselves wrote from a particular perspective that gave shape to the material they passed on. The redaction critic focuses on the way in which the editor/compiler of the biblical text put together his sources and on the particular emphases he had in composing his text.

Redaction criticism continues the work begun by source criticism in that it presumes that there were other written sources employed by the final editor or redactor of the Gospels. It advances the inquiry by acknowledging that the editor had a particular view or perspective in mind when compiling and redacting his text, and it seeks to discover the specific purpose each writer had in producing his Gospel.

The term itself comes from the German *Redaktionsgeschichte* ("redaction history") and sometimes is described as "composition criticism." By evaluating the manner in which the editor produced his Gospel, the investigator may examine both the historical context and the theological perspective of the redactor himself and perhaps his community. Redaction criticism had its beginnings in the work of Günther Bornkamm on Matthew, but the most significant use of the new methodology came with Hans Conzelmann's work on Luke and with Willi Marxsen's work on Mark, in which he also set forth principles for its use in Gospel research.[9] He argued that while the form critic seeks the *Sitz im Leben* (social context and circumstance) of Jesus and the early church, the redaction critic also seeks the *Sitz im Leben* of the evangelists themselves. Redaction critics are primarily interested in how authors used their sources and the special theological emphases that each author brought to his material. Since the sources are clearest in the Gospels, most of the redaction-critical work has been focused here, although scholars have also discovered sources that were employed in the production of Acts, the epistles of Paul, and elsewhere.

It is taken for granted that theological motives are not behind every difference in the Gospels, but they are behind some, and the redaction critic seeks out the perspectives and nuances that distinguish each writer. The redaction critic therefore focuses on the way in which the editor/compiler of the biblical text put together his sources and on the particular emphases he had in composing his text. For example, by comparing how Luke and Matthew added to, changed, and omitted elements from their source Mark, it is possible to see some of the theological motifs and perspectives of each evangelist. Rather than viewing the Gospel writers as merely "scissors and paste" compilers of traditions about Jesus, we are made more aware through the work of redaction critics that each evangelist had a theological perspective in mind. Where they are discernible, the redaction

critic examines how each evangelist made changes in his sources and how he combined traditions/sources to produce the final product. Because Mark was used as a source, it is more difficult to do redaction-critical work on Mark; the Gospel of John also poses difficulties. Nevertheless, we can see, as Stein observes, that Luke, unlike Mark and Matthew, emphasizes the role of the Spirit both during and after Jesus' temptation when he began his ministry in Galilee.[10] Likewise, Matthew's frequent insertion of the words "this was to fulfill what was spoken by the prophet" (1:22; 2:15, 17, 23; 4:14; 8:1; 13:35; etc.) and Mark's and Luke's lack of this expression demonstrate that scriptural fulfillment was a major motif of Matthew's work.

Most scholars today recognize the value of redaction criticism, particularly because it serves as a corrective to form-critical analysis, which tended to get lost in the detail of recovering the life settings of the early Christian communities and often missed the point the evangelists were trying to make. We should not overlook, however, the limitations of this discipline. It is easy to confuse the theological emphases of an evangelist with the entire theology of that evangelist, focusing on the diversity of the writers rather than on those matters on which they agree. Although there is considerable diversity in the canonical Gospels, they hold even more in common in their story of Jesus.

F. Literary Criticism

Although source criticism has also been called literary criticism, and redaction criticism has many similarities to it, what most interpreters of the NT now call literary criticism is a discipline in its own right.[11] Having its basis in the study of nonsacred literature, such as novels, literary criticism of the NT applies the criteria of the discipline of literary study to the various forms of NT writing, especially the Gospels. Even though literary criticism of the NT is a fairly recent arrival on the scene, it has already developed in several different ways.

Since literary criticism of the NT began as an apparent reaction to the kinds of source- and form-critical readings often offered by NT scholars, many literary critics of the Bible argue that the final form of the biblical text is the one that should be analyzed. Although some of this NT literary criticism is by literary scholars, most of it is by biblical scholars. They were trained in the traditional critical methods but have made conscious efforts to move away from looking *behind* the text to concentrate on what is *in* the text. Especially in Gospels research, there have been a number of important studies. For example, an early work by Rhoads and Michie concentrates on Mark's Gospel as a "unified narrative."[12] With this assumption about the narrative, they are able to find and analyze the author's consistent perspective and coherent plot and characters. What distinguishes this approach, according to the authors, is that any historical information not germane is not introduced into their study. Rhoads and Michie's treatment has inspired the work of many others, usually having in common the emphasis upon the story within the text rather than upon the world surrounding the text.

Although many continue to offer the kinds of reading that Rhoads and Michie offer, a number of readers of the NT have moved away from the text as an item in and of itself to examine the responses generated by the text. Drawing upon what has been called reader-response criticism in literary studies, this kind of criticism is often focused not upon the contemporary reader but upon the first-century reader. A better term for this kind of interpretation may be reader-oriented criticism. The most convincing and useful forms of reader-oriented criticism for NT study pay attention to various details in the text that help to control and guide the reader, or allow the reader to participate in creating the meaning of the text. This method, which opposes the idea that the text is a repository of fixed meanings waiting to be uncovered by interpreters, allows the interpreter to have a creative role in interpretation. With a focus upon the original reader, much of this criticism takes on a historical-critical sense, although most reader-oriented critics wish to focus upon the dynamic relationship between text and reader.[13]

In a further development called deconstruction or postmodernist criticism, the text is subjected to critical suspicion.[14] By placing even more emphasis upon the determinative role of the interpreter, so much so that the interpreter takes a position of preeminence over the text, deconstruction questions the assumption that the text is a literary unity. Indeed, the assumption seems to be that a text is not inherently unified and that any perceived unity can be quickly dispelled by examination of the text. As a result, a deconstructive critic such as Seeley

can find insurmountable difficulties in Paul's Letter to the Romans, such as the problem that in Rom 2 one can be righteous through the doing of the law while in Rom 3 one can only be justified through faith apart from works.[15] Deconstruction has passed out of favor in literary criticism, and it apparently is doing so in biblical interpretation as well. Besides a number of philosophical problems with such an approach, it fails to account for the strength and durability of texts, and the resultant readings have not proved convincing.

Whereas most literary criticism has been applied to narrative texts, such as the Gospels and Acts, there have been a few attempts to appreciate the literary dimension of the letters of Paul. In a highly challenging treatment that also draws on social-scientific criticism, Petersen examines the letter of Paul to Philemon.[16] Petersen defines narrative in terms of plotting events and then applies this to Philemon, reconstructing the narrative of the letter from the events mentioned or alluded to by the author. From this he is able to extrapolate a number of social relations that seem to be at play in the letter. Besides Petersen's and a few other efforts, there has been relatively little significant literary analysis of the Epistles, with much potential for more important work.

The strengths of NT literary criticism include its attention to details often overlooked, its recognition of the value of story and textual integrity, an interest in the process of writing and reading, an appreciation of how texts work, and the resultant interesting readings that emerge. However, there are also limitations to the method. Some of these are a failure to pay attention to the history of interpretation and to learn from past scholarly opinion, the lack of explicit criteria for what constitutes evidence in an analysis, readings that are sometimes not as insightful as those arrived at through more traditional methods, and the neglect of evident theology. Despite these limitations—all of which have been addressed and can be overcome—literary analysis of the NT continues to be a fruitful area of interpretation.[17]

G. Rhetorical Criticism

Rhetorical criticism is one of the most popular forms of criticism of the NT today. The way it is practiced by many interpreters allows for a combination of literary and historically based criticism. The literary dimension is the attention paid to the unfolding argument of the text. As a result, most rhetorical critics either assume or find unity in the text. The historical dimension is the grounding of rhetorical theory in the practice of ancient rhetoricians or public speech makers, such as Demosthenes, Lysias, and Isocrates.[18] As a result, rhetorical criticism takes two major forms. There are those who treat the NT writings as if they were ancient speeches either read or delivered, which allows them to be analyzed according to the standards that were used in the writing of ancient speeches. In other words, the same categories that are found in the rhetorical handbooks (handbooks on how to write speeches, by such people as Quintilian, the ancient teacher of rhetoric) are used to analyze the NT writings. There are others who believe that the ancient rhetorical handbooks and ancient rhetorical practice, as well as medieval and modern rhetoric, follow certain universal principles for how best to construct an argument and attempt to persuade an audience. The NT, for these rhetorical critics, can be analyzed like any piece of language to discover its rhetorical elements. Thus, for example, a letter of Paul may be analyzed in terms of whether it is related to the courtroom (judicial), praise and blame (epideictic), or a considered course of action (deliberative), in the same way that an ancient speech may have addressed these issues.

The history of NT rhetorical criticism can be discussed in terms of the work of three rhetorical critics. The first is George Kennedy, whose work on rhetoric has been instrumental in reviving interest in what was a neglected area even in classical studies. In an important study, Kennedy maintained that the writings of the NT, from portions of the Gospels to various letters and even parts of letters, could be analyzed rhetorically.[19] Although Kennedy seems to believe that there is something pervasive about rhetoric, in the sense that the popular use of rhetoric was simply a part of what it meant to live in the ancient Greco-Roman world, the categories that he uses are the formal ones of the ancient writers. As a result, Galatians may be analyzed in terms of a proem, or introduction (1:6–10); a *probatio*, or proof (1:11–5:1)—in which there are various elements, including a *narratio*, or discussion of background (1:13–2:14), an argument (2:15–21), various topics of discussion, and a personal appeal

(4:12–20)—a moral exhortation (5:2–6:10); and an epilogue (6:11–18).[20] The Sermon on the Mount is characterized as deliberative rhetoric, since it endorses a course of action.

The second major rhetorical critic is Hans Dieter Betz, who wrote a commentary on Galatians in which he outlined the book according to a rhetorical model,[21] as if it were a speech. Much more based on the handbooks than Kennedy, Betz seems to believe that this letter is simply a speech with epistolary opening and closing attached. Whereas a major weakness of Kennedy's approach is his assumption that to be a member of the ancient world virtually guaranteed competence in rhetoric, the weakness in Betz's work is that, in order to make his outline fit, he must either utilize categories in ways that they are not used in the ancient world or practically invent new categories. Both Kennedy and Betz have had numerous followers of their methods. One question not often raised, however, is whether such analysis, since it purports to come out of the ancient world, would have been recognizable by the ancients themselves. In other words, did the ancients analyze, for example, the Gospels or the Letters using the categories of rhetoric? There does not appear to be substantive evidence that this is the case.

As a consequence, the work of Wilhelm Wuellner has been very important. Rather than confine himself to the categories of ancient rhetoric, Wuellner follows the so-called New Rhetoric, especially that developed in the study of law.[22] He believes that these universal categories of persuasion allow analysis of any writing for its rhetorical elements. One can thus examine a Pauline Letter, a Gospel, or portions of each without being confined by the terminology and categories of the ancients. Whereas some have wanted to ground their rhetorical criticism in the ancient categories, Wuellner's method does not allow for the same certainty; consequently, his work has not been as widely accepted as that of Kennedy and Betz.

Although there is great advantage in appreciating the persuasive elements of the biblical texts—and thus rhetorical analysis, in that sense, should have a place in critical biblical study—several questions have been posed.[23] The first is whether rhetorical criticism is a method or an interpretive perspective. In other words, is rhetorical criticism simply a set of tools that can be used in conjunction with other methods, such as various forms of historical criticism, or is it a perspective in its own right, with various claims and viewpoints on larger issues, such as the nature of human communication. A second question is how to reconcile the various perspectives noted above. At present, most rhetorical critics use similar language, sometimes without realizing the differing assumptions they make regarding its use. Rhetorical criticism is still a very new type of criticism, but one that can be expected to continue to be used in NT study.

H. Social-Scientific Criticism

Although social-scientific criticism can be considered one of the more recent methods of NT interpretation and criticism, in another sense it has been in use for most of the last century. It is in the twentieth century that the social sciences have developed, including not only sociology but psychology and anthropology as well. As awareness has grown that a human being is not a creature who lives in isolation but one who lives in groups, scholars have attempted to describe these relationships. Social-scientific criticism of the NT reflects these interests.

In its earliest shape, concern for the social element of the NT took the form of social description. Various scholars, such as Adolf Deissmann and F. C. Grant,[24] attempted to describe the various groups that existed in the ancient world, including those of the early church. Their categories of thought were very much dependent upon the extent of knowledge of the classical world mediated through classical studies, so their descriptions reflected an emphasis upon what some would contend was a skewed perspective of the ancient world, with perhaps too much polarity created between the haves and the have-nots. They also reflected the change in social perspective of the nineteenth century and, with it, the rise of such emphases as the social-gospel movement. As a result, in some circles Christianity was often described as a peasant religion, with an itinerant peasant as leader, without any formal or institutional ties to those with money and power. This kind of description was part of the set of presuppositions of the form-critical agenda in the twentieth century as well and has influenced how various literary types in the NT have been viewed in terms of their creation and transmission.

In a more technical sense and as a distinct critical approach, social-scientific criticism of the NT is only about twenty-five years old. Current social-scientific description can be divided into two categories. The first includes those who are still concerned to do social description. This is not to say that these scholars continue to perpetuate the analyses of the previous group; their orientation is to allow their sets of classifications to grow out of the data gleaned from the ancient texts. Judge and Malherbe,[25] and a number who have followed them, have utilized this approach. A recent example is Clarke's analysis of 1 Cor 1–6, in which he examines the language of the letter to classify the social relations at Corinth.[26] He also draws upon extrabiblical evidence, such as inscriptions. He concludes that the Corinthian church had a mix of people from various social strata, which were parts of a system of benefaction. The concept of the benefactor, an important one in the ancient world, was responsible for organizing lines of dependency and benefit up and down the social scale.

The second group of social-scientific critics consists of those who are doing social analysis or sociology proper; that is, they are utilizing models from contemporary social-scientific criticism to examine social structures in the ancient world. Various scholars have proposed different models for analysis of the data of the NT. For example, Meeks has examined the Pauline churches from the standpoint of their presence in the urban world of the first century. John Elliott focuses upon key vocabulary in 1 Peter related to the house and household to formulate theories regarding Christianity as a social minority in the alien Greco-Roman world. Holmberg uses a model from the sociologist Max Weber, including analysis of Paul in terms of authority and his charismatic leadership.[27]

There are several apparent problems that social-scientific criticism must confront. One is an unfortunate tendency, when it is applied to the NT, to impose categories from the modern world upon the ancient people and their texts. Another is to draw contrasts that are too sharp between various parts of the ancient world, such as the Hellenistic versus the Jewish elements, and then to side with one against the other on almost every point. A final problem is a tendency to stereotype not only the modern world but also the ancient world, neglecting a wealth of data that are sometimes intractable.[28] Nevertheless, through this method important insights have been gained into the social structure of the NT world.

I. Canonical Criticism

Canonical criticism of the Bible seeks to understand a writing not so much within its own historical context and development as within its place and arrangement in the biblical canon. Canonical criticism also focuses, in part, on the question of how the biblical text came to be recognized as authoritative Scripture within the community of faith. It is interested not so much in the original meaning of a text, as argued by the historical-critical scholar, but in the final form of the biblical text in conjunction with the other parts of the Bible, which spoke to a community of faith. The primary focus of canonical criticism is on the Bible seen as a whole and on how each part of that whole functioned as authoritative in the life of the church. Canonical critics acknowledge that the original meaning of a book, or even its original text, may have been changed by a later community of Christians and that the message originally intended by the author is secondary to its canonical significance. The basis for canonical authority in antiquity, however, was directly related to such questions as authorship and the writing's proximity to the time of the apostles. The apostolic witness, the earliest witness of the Christian community to the Christ event, was what the canonical communities of the fourth and fifth centuries believed they had incorporated into their biblical canon. The goal of those Christian communities, therefore, was to identify their sacred Scriptures, employing the criteria of apostolicity, orthodoxy, and antiquity (see ch. 13, below), and thus forming a composite work that now functions as the basis for present-day canonical criticism.

The explicit theological agenda of canonical criticism developed in direct response to the growing lack of confidence in the Bible and to the consequent minimal use of it in ministry. One of its major exponents, Brevard Childs, stepping forward to respond to this "crisis," gave his attention to unlocking the Bible from its historical-critical past, which he believed had undermined its authoritative role in the church.[29] James Sanders, reflecting some of the same concerns, believed that there was need for a reevaluation of the formation and function of the biblical canon.[30] Childs and Sanders agreed that the Bible had become, for the specialist, a catalogue of isolated texts that led to its fragmentation and to what Childs called the "atomization" of the biblical text. Childs stressed that historical criticism's practice of dividing the biblical passages into their various historical stages and developments (a "diachronic approach") often destroyed the "synchronic" dimension of the text.[31] He rejected the fragmentation of the biblical text and instead called for a synchronic approach that viewed the Bible as a whole, in its final form, rather than in its various literary stages of development or as a collection of isolated texts. For him, the Bible comes to us not just from individuals but primarily from ancient communities of faith. He and Sanders both agree that "the Bible, the sum as well as all of its parts, comes to us out of the liturgical and instructional life of early believing communities."[32] For Childs, however, the canon of the Bible, or its continuing authority in the church, includes the contributions of the later editors of its texts, the superscriptions that were later added by the communities of faith, and "all the redactional seams." The shift here is from what scholars call their quest for an *Urtext*, that is, the earliest form of a text, to its final form, which was frozen by the church and passed on in its communities of faith. Childs specifically rejects the use of the term "canonical criticism" as a description of his work, while Sanders embraces it. Sanders defines it differently than does Childs, calling it a subdiscipline of biblical criticism that is a means of "unlocking the Bible from the past into which criticism has tended to seal it."[33] Because of the often negative value biblical criticism has had for believing communities, Childs rejects the use of the term "criticism" altogether.[34] He contends that the focus on how a document functioned as canon in the religious community is an essential feature of theological inquiry—about this he and Sanders are in agreement.

This relatively new approach to the biblical literature has been launched chiefly through the writings of Sanders and Childs,[35] but it is also carried on by several other capable scholars who agree with their goal of a canonical understanding of the Bible.[36] Their canonical focus asks, in part, which form of the biblical text is authoritative for the church today. Sanders views the biblical text from a number of contexts in which it is ever renewing itself as canon within the communities of faith. Childs shows interest only in the latest stage of this development though he is not uninformed about its earlier stages.

Childs is undoubtedly correct that the Bible's message is not fully grasped through the descriptive work of biblical exegesis alone but, rather, in an encounter with the living God. This encounter with God, however, need not be separated from a careful interpretation of the biblical text, employing the various critical disciplines available for the theologian to explicate its meaning.[37] But this is nothing new. Last century, both Karl Barth and Rudolf Bultmann agreed that biblical faith could not be understood apart from the obligation of faith to surrender to the call of God that comes in the preaching of the Christian message.

Childs's major limitation is his focus on the biblical text at the *end* of the canonical process—including both the scribal and the editorial material added to the writer's original message and possibly at variance with the very perspective of the canonical community he is anxious to preserve. Why should the second-to-fourth-century additions to the biblical text be combined with the canon of the church or be given weight equal to those of the apostolic community? Why should a later Christian generation's text, which admittedly has been corrupted by mistakes, glosses, and deliberate changes, be given priority over the earliest recoverable text? Childs does not answer these questions satisfactorily. His work, in practice, denies the value of textual criticism as well as the work of the historical critics who have made great strides in recovering the historical context, date, authorship, and provenance of many of the biblical writings.

The Christian communities of the second to the fourth centuries did not see themselves as the canonical community but instead sought to build their faith upon what they believed were the traditions and writings from the earliest Christian community.[38] Since this appeal to the earliest witnesses was made by the very community that handed to us our "received text," why should the church not be as interested in their quest today, especially if we can come closer to it than the churches of the fourth and fifth centuries did? The apostolic witness, that is, the earliest witness of the earliest Christian community to the Christ event, was precisely what the canonical community of the fourth and fifth centuries believed it had incorporated into its biblical canon. The recovery of the earliest text or the compositional form of the text was one of the important goals of exegesis and proclamation from the perspective of the early Christian communities.

J. Linguistic Criticism

The form of criticism that is perhaps the most underutilized and in its most rudimentary form of development for NT studies is linguistic criticism.[39] Linguistic criticism includes several different subtypes, including semantics (especially found in lexicography) and pragmatics, sociolinguistics, and discourse analysis. All of these areas of investigation work from the assumption that the principles of modern linguistics must take precedence over the categories of traditional philology. Traditional philology used categories from the study of Latin, emphasized historical issues such as the origin and development of a word or word-form (i.e. etymology), and gave undue attention to the literature (rather than the documents of everyday life, such as the papyri) of the ancient Greeks and Romans. Modern linguistics analyzes language according to a different set of criteria. These criteria include the emphasis of synchrony over diachrony, that is, contemporary usage over the history of usage, a view of language as system rather than as a series of separate, discrete elements, and an estimation of common usage as more important than literary artifacts.[40]

As a result, in the study of semantics (meaning) and pragmatics (meaning in context), linguistic criticism analyzes contemporary usage of words and word-forms. This can usefully be discussed in terms of two axes, the paradigmatic and the syntagmatic. The paradigmatic axis discusses the other possible linguistic choices in a given context. For example, when selecting a given word, such as a noun, a writer may have had any number of other nouns to choose from in constructing the sentence. The syntagmatic axis is concerned with how strings of elements are combined together into such things as phrases, clauses, and sentences. Thus the semantics of a language is based upon choice at two levels, from among similar items (selection) and in relation to how these elements are combined (combination). Pragmatics is concerned with the context in which these elements are used. Various linguistic means are employed by speakers and writers to ground a particular set of words in a meaningful context. These include what are often called deictic indicators. Deictic indicators contain a reference to person, time, place, and even discourse factors. Pragmatics is also concerned with the various presuppositions and implications of the use of language, realizing that the meaning of a stretch of language is not arrived at simply by adding up the meanings of the individual units. Thus, a lexicon based upon semantic domains—the meaningful spaces occupied by conceptually related words—such as the Louw and Nida lexicon,[41] is a necessary tool for linguistic criticism. Similarly, discussions of such elements of Greek structure as the verb (e.g., why the present tense rather than the aorist is used in a given passage) or the case of a noun in terms of the choices available to the language user would also be necessary.[42]

Sociolinguistics is concerned with the important social dimension of language usage. In other words, sociolinguistics recognizes that all language is used in human contexts of varying types, and these must be appreciated in order to understand the language. Thus, most users of languages have several different types of language at their disposal, often referred to as registers. Registers are the various ways in which language is utilized in given contexts, such as formal or informal, business or pleasure, etc. Registers are different from dialects. "Dialect" may be defined in different ways. Although dialect is often associated with accent, it is perhaps better understood in terms of regional variations in usage that would include not only accent but other differences as well. The language of the Greek of the NT has often been discussed in terms of how much influence Semitic languages may have had on it and whether it constitutes its own form of language or not,[43] but the kind of linguistic criticism meant here is concerned with varieties of usage according to whether one is writing a Gospel or an epistle, a homily or an apocalypse.

Discourse analysis (sometimes called text-linguistics) is one of the latest areas of important development.[44] Much linguistic work in the last century has concentrated on the sentence as the largest unit of meaning, but discourse analysis posits that units for meaningful analysis must be understood in terms of an entire discourse. The entire discourse, which may be as small as a single utterance or as large as an entire multivolume work, must be taken into account. In a number of ways, discourse analysis includes not only all that we have been discussing about a linguistic analysis of the NT (i.e., semantics and pragmatics) but also more besides. Discourse analysis, in its concern for the entire complexity of human communication, considers the role of the speaker or writer, the hearer or reader, the medium of communication, and the context, both social and otherwise. Discourse-analytical models vary according to the interpreter, but usually include a balance between attention to the individual elements of usage (such as connecting words, or patterns in vocabulary) and formulation of larger patterns. It is through attention to these details that one is able to discover the various linguistic means by which an author may unify the discourse or choose to bring to prominence and emphasize various other features.

4. BIBLICAL THEOLOGY: WHAT COMES AFTER BIBLICAL CRITICISM?

Thus far we have been primarily concerned with what has commonly been called the historical-critical method and several of the newer forms of criticism that have been offering challenges to it. Several of these methods have proved valuable in recent criticism of the NT. As the survey indicates, various questions are addressed by the various methods, and different—even competing—answers are given. Apart from the interests of canonical criticism, however, very little has been said about the theological dimensions of the NT texts. These concerns are also of importance in NT study.

Biblical criticism is the presupposition and foundation for all biblical theology. When we speak about biblical theology, we are recognizing that the Bible has the peculiarity of being a theological book. Clearly it is not only a historical account of a few ancient events that affected the lives of some Jews and Gentiles in antiquity. Although it includes this, it is significantly more; it is history and theology combined. By "theology" we are referring to the belief of the early Christians that the writings of the NT were inspired by God, that they told the overwhelming story of Jesus of Nazareth, who was both Lord and Christ of the church. These are theological statements, based on the experience of some men and women of antiquity who saw more in Jesus than those who can only see him as the poor unfortunate wisdom teacher who was rejected by the majority of his people but later was embraced in faith by the Gentiles. The Bible was written from a theological perspective, and the study of Scripture is not complete when we have simply focused on the so-called historical issues. The perspectives advocated and advanced in the Bible are the theology of the biblical text. Robert Grant cautions his readers not to forget, in their study of the NT, that its authors "had a purpose for writing and that unless this purpose is kept in view the analysis of their writings will be fragmentary and will produce nothing but a collection of fragments."[45]

The essential goal of a biblical theology of the NT is to reconstruct the message or kerygma of the NT writings. If these writings define what it means to be a Christian or a follower of Jesus, or express the faith that caused its writers to write them and subsequent Christians to preserve them, then it is important to determine what is advocated or demanded in the biblical text. In this sense, a biblical theology is, in the first place, a descriptive enterprise that engages the NT interpreter in discovering the teachings of the NT, *from its own perspective*, about God, humanity (especially humanity in relation to God), the plan of redemption or salvation, ethical behavior that is informed by the perspective of the Bible, and the eternal destiny of humanity. After this, the interpreter seeks to understand the individual writings or groups of writings, noting their similarities and differences. To the extent that the activity of God described in the NT sets out theological statements about God, it is important to understand the NT's perspective on that activity. How does God act in history or in human affairs? What is the NT's perspective on these matters? How do the different writers of the Bible respond to these questions?

The biblical theologian first must try to clarify what theological statements in the NT mean. It is not sufficient simply to do a descriptive study and state what the NT says. One must also see how the text says the reader must respond. Therefore, "description" and "prescription" are both important parts of biblical theology, even though scholars differ on how these elements are combined. The theologian assumes that the biblical text has something to say that is significant for the present; in other words, there is an understanding of reality and human existence in the NT that has relevance for today. George Ladd captures this idea when he concludes that "biblical theology is far more than an intellectual discipline; it has a spiritual goal, namely, personal knowledge of God."[46]

Because the Bible features prominently in the Christian tradition and because the church has historically sought to ground its faith in the message of the Bible, those who would study the Bible's content and meaning must inevitably go beyond the initial task of description, even though it is possible to describe the theology of the NT and leave the matter there. On the other hand, as Bruce Chilton notes, "[New Testament] theology demands that the study of documents be related to an account of God," and he concludes that "the study of the New Testament is irrevocably a part of theological discussion."[47] The theology of the NT emerged from the deep-seated conviction of the writers, and anyone who wants to understand the NT must try to understand the source and nature of this conviction.

How does one do biblical theology of the NT? In the descriptive side of the task, the student of the NT should first examine each writer, not assuming automatically that they all say the same thing, and identify main expositional passages in the letter or book (look for the longest or most repeated themes), then analyze them in terms of key issues or controlling concepts—keeping in mind the more polemical passages as well. For example, in Gal 2, Paul is at variance with Peter, James, and the Jerusalem leaders. What accounts for this? Second, it is important to trace cognate themes and concepts elsewhere in the same book or letter, asking how similar themes function in the main expositional passages. For example, how does God's interest in poor, lowly, or insignificant persons and sinners play a role in Luke's Gospel? How does the way Luke deals with the birth, genealogy, and temptations of Jesus factor into that picture or perspective? Why is it that Luke has lowly shepherds come to the Christ child in a barn (cave?) or manger scene while Matthew has wise men (magi) from the east come to a house to visit the Christ child and present expensive gifts? What accounts for this different perspective in the text? How does Luke's emphasis here fit with his parables of the lost sheep, coin, and son or, later, with his story that one of the thieves on the cross next to Jesus cried out to be remembered by Jesus and Jesus assured him that he would be with him in paradise that day? In other words, what was Luke trying to say through these various but overlapping stories? This is the focus of biblical theology. Third, the NT theologian should also consider the material that appears to have a special place in the writer's argument, for example, the kerygmatic affirmations or proclamations. A clear example of this is in Luke 19:10, where the author seems to step away from the immediate situation to explain why all of these events occurred, namely, because it is the goal of the Son of Man to seek to save those who are lost. In Acts several summary passages show the author's concern to emphasize the ongoing growth and development of the Christian community (e.g., Acts 2:41–42, 43–47; 4:32–34; 5:11–12a; 5:42). Finally, one should also organize the findings of these first three steps, seeking to determine how these various conceptions are related and whether the overall argument of the writing is driven or shaped by a particular theological perspective.[48]

5. CONCLUSION

This brief overview of the field of critical analysis of the NT has included a description of the types of biblical criticism and the ways of viewing and assessing the writings of the NT from a theological perspective. What has been said often has an equally valid application to the study of the OT, or the Hebrew Scriptures. Indeed, many of these criticisms were first employed in the study of the OT. The mastering of the discipline of a critical study of the Bible will not automatically enable the student of the text to understand the perspective of the writers of the Bible and their message. The biblical writers wrote not as unbiased and unprejudiced scholars but as proclaimers. Although the above methodologies, if carefully applied, will allow for important historical and theological insights into the message of the Bible, there is still a significant gulf between this scholarly approach and the experience of what caused the writers to write in the first place. The interpreter must go beyond the surface facts to explore the particular understanding of existence and reality expressed in the text. It is here that scholars and laypeople alike must humble themselves before the text and enter into a more complete understanding of the Scriptures by faith. Ultimately, questions about the preached Christ of the NT cannot be settled through historical research alone, but when critical inquiry is combined with faith in the One who comes through the biblical proclamation, there is a greater likelihood of discovering the rich meaning of the text and experiencing the reality it was trying to express in its ancient context. It should be stressed again, however, that there are great benefits to be gained from a critical study of the NT. Without it, Christian faith inevitably becomes irretrievably locked into the interpretations of the past without any way of getting beyond them to a clearer picture of the Christ of the NT and his demands upon those who acknowledge him as Lord.

BIBLIOGRAPHY

This bibliography is generally divided up according to the sections discussed above. Only a small number of the most important works can be cited. Cross-reference is also made to other places in this volume, where more detailed bibliographies are provided. A work that provides annotations on a number of the most important sources for critical study of the NT is: Porter, S. E., and L. M. McDonald. *New Testament Introduction.* IBR Bibliographies 12. Grand Rapids: Baker, 1995.

1. BASIC TOOLS FOR CRITICAL STUDY

A. Bible Dictionaries and Encyclopedias

Anchor Bible Dictionary. Ed. D. N. FREEDMAN. 6 vols. New York: Doubleday, 1992.

Interpreter's Dictionary of the Bible. Ed. G. BUTTRICK and K. CRIM. 4 vols. and supplement. Nashville: Abingdon, 1962.

International Standard Bible Encyclopedia. Ed. G. BROMILEY. 4 vols. Grand Rapids: Eerdmans, 1979–88.

The Illustrated Bible Dictionary. Ed. J. D. DOUGLAS. 3 vols. Wheaton, Ill.: Tyndale, 1980.

Harper's Bible Dictionary. Ed. P. ACHTEMEIER. New York: Harper & Row, 1985.

B. New Testament Introductions

BROWN, R. E. *An Introduction to the New Testament.* ABRL. New York: Doubleday, 1997.

CHILTON, B. *Beginning New Testament Study.* Grand Rapids: Eerdmans, 1986.

COLLINS, R. F. *Introduction to the New Testament.* Garden City, N.Y.: Doubleday, 1983.

EPP, E., and G. W. MACRAE, eds. *The New Testament and Its Modern Interpreters.* Atlanta, Ga.: Scholars Press, 1989.

GUNDRY, R. H. *A Survey of the New Testament.* 3d ed. Grand Rapids: Zondervan, 1994.

GUTHRIE, D. *New Testament Introduction.* 4th ed. Downers Grove: InterVarsity, 1990.

JOHNSON, L. T. *The Writings of the New Testament: An Interpretation.* Philadelphia: Fortress, 1986.

KEE, H. C. *Understanding the New Testament.* 5th ed. Edgewood Cliffs, N.J.: Prentice-Hall, 1993.

KOESTER, H. *Introduction to the New Testament.* 2 vols. FFNT. Philadelphia: Fortress, 1982; 2d ed. of vol. 1, 1995; vol 2, 2000.

KÜMMEL, W. G. *Introduction to the New Testament.* Trans. H. C. Kee. Nashville: Abingdon, 1975.

MARTIN, R. P. *New Testament Foundations: A Guide for Christian Students.* 2d ed.; 2 vols. Grand Rapids: Eerdmans, 1986.

MOULE, C. F. D. *The Birth of the New Testament.* 3d ed. San Francisco: Harper & Row, 1982.

PERKINS, P. *Reading the New Testament: An Introduction.* Rev. ed. Mahwah, N.J.: Paulist, 1988.

PUSKAS, C. B. *An Introduction to the New Testament.* Peabody, Mass.: Hendrickson, 1989.

ZAHN, T. B. *Introduction to the New Testament.* Trans. J. M. TROUT et al. 3 vols. New York: Scribners, 1909.

2. TYPES OF BIBLICAL CRITICISM

A. Textual Criticism

The reader should consult ch. 12, below, for more information.

ALAND, K., and B. ALAND. *The Text of the New Testament: An Introduction to the Critical Editions and to the Theory and Practice of Modern Textual Criticism.* Trans. E. F. RHODES. 2d ed. Grand Rapids: Eerdmans, 1989.

GREENLEE, J. H. *Introduction to New Testament Textual Criticism.* Rev. ed. Peabody, Mass.: Hendrickson, 1995.

METZGER, B. M. *The Text of the New Testament: Its Transmission, Corruption, and Restoration.* 3d ed. Oxford: Clarendon, 1992.

METZGER, B. M. *A Textual Commentary on the Greek New Testament.* Rev. ed. New York: United Bible Societies, 1995.

B. Historical Criticism and Exegesis

Many of the following works of collected essays have individual chapters on the various forms of criticism discussed in this chapter.

BLACK, D. A., and D. S. Dockery. *New Testament Criticism and Interpretation.* Grand Rapids: Zondervan, 1991.

BROWN, R. E. *The Critical Meaning of the Bible.* New York: Paulist, 1981.

CONZELMANN, H., and A. LINDEMANN. *Interpreting the New Testament: An Introduction to the Principles and Methods of New Testament Exegesis.* Trans. S. S. SCHATZMANN. Peabody, Mass.: Hendrickson, 1988.

FEE, G. D. *New Testament Exegesis: A Handbook for Students and Pastors.* 2d ed. Louisville: Westminster John Knox, 1993.

HAYES, J. H., and C. R. HOLLADAY. *Biblical Exegesis: A Beginner's Handbook.* 2d ed. Atlanta: John Knox, 1987.

KAISER, O., and W. G. KÜMMEL. *Exegetical Method: A Student's Handbook.* Trans. E. V. N. Goetchius and M. J. O'CONNELL. 2d ed. New York: Seabury, 1981.

McKenzie, S. L., and S. R. Haynes, eds. *To Each Its Own Meaning: An Introduction to Biblical Criticisms and their Application.* Louisville: Westminster John Knox, 1993.

Marshall, I. H., ed. *New Testament Interpretation: Essays on Principles and Methods.* Grand Rapids: Eerdmans, 1977.

Porter, S. E., ed. *Handbook to Exegesis of the New Testament.* NTTS 25. Leiden: Brill, 1997.

Porter, S. E., and D. Tombs, eds. *Approaches to New Testament Study.* JSNTSup 120. Sheffield: Sheffield Academic Press, 1995.

Porter, S. E., and C. A. Evans, eds. *New Testament Interpretation and Methods: A Sheffield Reader.* BibSem 45. Sheffield: Sheffield Academic Press, 1997.

Stenger, W. *Introduction to New Testament Exegesis.* Grand Rapids: Eerdmans, 1993.

Tuckett, C. *Reading the New Testament: Methods of Interpretation.* London: SPCK, 1987.

C. Form Criticism

Bultmann, R. *The History of the Synoptic Tradition.* Trans. J. Marsh. Rev. ed. 1963; repr., Peabody, Mass.: Hendrickson, 1993.

Dibelius, M. *From Tradition to Gospel.* Trans. B. L. Woolf. London: Ivor Nicholson and Watson, 1934.

Jeremias, J. *The Parables of Jesus.* Trans. S. H. Hooke. 2d ed. New York: Scribners, 1972.

Kelber, W. *The Oral and the Written Gospel.* Philadelphia: Fortress, 1983.

McKnight, E. V. *What Is Form Criticism?* GBS. Philadelphia: Fortress, 1969.

Sanders, E. P. *The Tendencies of the Synoptic Tradition.* SNTSMS 9. Cambridge: Cambridge University Press, 1969.

Stanton, G. "Form Criticism Revisited." Pages 13–27 in *What about the New Testament? Essays in Honour of Christopher Evans.* Ed. M. Hooker and C. Hickling. London: SCM, 1975.

Stein, R. H. *The Method and Message of Jesus' Teachings.* Rev. ed. Louisville: Westminster John Knox, 1994.

Taylor, V. *The Formation of the Gospel Tradition.* London: Macmillan, 1945.

D. Source Criticism

Corley, B., ed. *Colloquy on New Testament Studies: A Time for Reappraisal and Fresh Approaches.* Macon: Mercer University Press, 1983.

Farmer, W. R. *The Synoptic Problem: A Critical Analysis.* New York: Macmillan, 1964.

Kloppenborg, J. *The Formation of Q.* Philadelphia: Fortress, 1987.

Longstaff, T. R. W. *Evidence of Conflation in Mark? A Study in the Synoptic Problem.* SBLDS 87. Missoula, Mont.: Scholars Press, 1977.

Rist, J. M. *On the Independence of Matthew and Mark.* SNTSMS 32. Cambridge: Cambridge University Press, 1978.

Sanday, W., ed. *Oxford Studies in the Synoptic Problem.* Oxford: Clarendon, 1911.

Stein, R. H. *The Synoptic Problem: An Introduction.* Grand Rapids: Baker, 1987.

Streeter, B. H. *The Four Gospels: A Study of Origins.* London: Macmillan, 1924.

Tuckett, C. M. *The Revival of the Griesbach Hypothesis: An Analysis and Appraisal.* SNTSMS 44. Cambridge: Cambridge University Press, 1983.

_____, ed. *Synoptic Studies: The Ampleforth Conferences of 1982 and 1983.* JSNTSup 7. Sheffield: JSOT Press, 1984.

Westcott, B. F. *An Introduction to the Study of the Gospels.* 6th ed. Cambridge: Macmillan, 1881.

E. Redaction Criticism

Black, C. C., II. *The Disciples according to Mark: Markan Redaction in Current Debate.* JSNTSup 27. Sheffield: JSOT Press, 1989.

Bornkamm, G., G. Barth, and H.-J. Held. *Tradition and Interpretation in Matthew.* Trans. P. Scott. NTL. Philadelphia: Westminster, 1963.

Conzelmann, H. *The Theology of St. Luke.* Trans. G. Buswell. New York: Harper & Row, 1960.

Marshall, I. H. *Luke: Historian and Theologian.* Grand Rapids: Zondervan, 1970.

Martin, R. P. *Mark: Evangelist and Theologian.* Grand Rapids: Zondervan, 1972.

Marxsen, W. *Mark the Evangelist: Studies on the Redaction History of the Gospel.* Trans. J. Boyce et al. Nashville: Abingdon, 1969.

Neirynck, F. *Duality in Mark: Contributions to the Study of the Markan Redaction.* Leuven: Leuven University Press/Peeters, 1988.

Perrin, N. *What Is Redaction Criticism?* GBS. Philadelphia: Fortress, 1970.

Smalley, S. S. *John: Evangelist and Interpreter.* Grand Rapids: Zondervan, 1978.

STANTON, G. N. *Jesus of Nazareth in New Testament Preaching.* SNTSMS 27. Cambridge: Cambridge University Press, 1974.

STEIN, R. H. "What Is *Redaktionsgeschichte?" JBL* 88 (1969): 45–56.

F. Literary Criticism

AUNE, D. E. *The New Testament in Its Literary Environment.* LEC. Philadelphia: Westminster, 1987.

BAILEY, J. L., and L. D. Vander Broek. *Literary Forms in the New Testament.* Louisville: Westminster John Knox, 1992.

CULPEPPER, R. A. *Anatomy of the Fourth Gospel: A Study in Literary Design.* FFNT. Philadelphia: Fortress, 1983.

LONGMAN, T., III. *Literary Approaches to Biblical Interpretation.* FCI 3. Grand Rapids: Zondervan, 1987.

McKNIGHT, E. V. *The Bible and the Reader: An Introduction to Literary Criticism.* Philadelphia: Fortress, 1985.

McKNIGHT, E. V., and E. S. MALBON, eds. *The New Literary Criticism and the New Testament.* JSNTSup 109. Sheffield: JSOT Press, 1994.

MOORE, S. D. *Literary Criticism and the Gospels: The Theoretical Challenge.* New Haven: Yale University Press, 1989.

PETERSEN, N. R. *Literary Criticism for New Testament Critics.* GBS. Philadelphia: Fortress, 1978.

RHOADS, D., and D. MICHIE. *Mark as Story: An Introduction to the Narrative of a Gospel.* Philadelphia: Fortress, 1982.

G. Rhetorical Criticism

ANDERSON, R. D., Jr. *Ancient Rhetorical Theory and Paul.* Kampen: Kok Pharos, 1996.

KENNEDY, G. A. *New Testament Interpretation through Rhetorical Criticism.* Chapel Hill: University of North Carolina Press, 1984.

MACK, B. L. *Rhetoric and the New Testament.* GBS. Minneapolis: Fortress, 1990.

PORTER, S. E., ed. *Handbook of Classical Rhetoric in the Hellenistic Period, 330 B.C.–A.D. 400.* Leiden: Brill, 1997.

PORTER, S. E., and T. H. Olbricht, eds. *Rhetoric and the New Testament: Essays from the 1992 Heidelberg Conference.* JSNTSup 90. Sheffield: JSOT Press, 1993.

_____, eds. *The Rhetorical Analysis of Scripture: Essays from the 1995 London Conference.* JSNTSup 146. Sheffield: Sheffield Academic Press, 1997.

WATSON, D. F., ed. *Persuasive Artistry: Studies in New Testament Rhetoric in Honor of G. A. Kennedy.* JSNTSup 50. Sheffield: JSOT Press, 1991.

WATSON, D. F., and A. J. HAUSER. *Rhetorical Criticism of the Bible: A Comprehensive Bibliography with Notes on History and Method.* BIS 4. Leiden: Brill, 1994.

H. Social-Scientific Criticism

ELLIOTT, J. H. *What Is Social-Scientific Criticism?* GBS. Minneapolis: Fortress, 1993.

HOLMBERG, B. *Sociology and the New Testament: An Appraisal.* Minneapolis: Fortress, 1990.

KEE, H. C. *Christian Origins in Sociological Perspective.* Philadelphia: Westminster, 1980.

JUDGE, E. A. *The Social Pattern of Christian Groups in the First Century.* London: Tyndale, 1960.

MALHERBE, A. J. *Social Aspects of Early Christianity.* 2d ed. Philadelphia: Fortress, 1983.

MALINA, B. J. *The New Testament World: Insights from Cultural Anthropology.* Atlanta: John Knox, 1981.

MEEKS, W. A. *The Moral World of the First Christians.* LEC. Philadelphia: Westminster, 1986.

OSIEK, C. *What Are They Saying about the Social Setting of the New Testament?* Rev. ed. New York: Paulist, 1992.

STAMBAUGH, J., and D. BALCH. *The New Testament in Its Social Environment.* LEC. Philadelphia: Westminster, 1986.

TIDBALL, D. *The Social Context of the New Testament: A Sociological Analysis.* Grand Rapids: Zondervan, 1984.

I. Canonical Criticism

The reader should consult ch. 13, below, for more information.

CHILDS, B. S. *Biblical Theology of the Old and New Testaments: Theological Reflection on the Christian Bible.* Philadelphia: Fortress, 1993.

_____. *The New Testament as Canon: An Introduction.* Philadelphia: Fortress, 1985.

PATZIA, A. G. *The Making of the New Testament: Origin, Collection, Text, and Canon.* Downers Grove, Ill.: InterVarsity, 1995.

SANDERS, J. A. *Canon and Community: A Guide to Canonical Criticism.* GBS. Philadelphia: Fortress, 1984.

_____. *From Sacred Story to Sacred Text: Canon as Paradigm.* Philadelphia: Fortress, 1987.

WALL, R. W., and E. E. Lemcio. *The New Testament as Canon: A Reader in Canonical Criticism.* JSNTSup 76. Sheffield: JSOT Press, 1992.

J. Linguistic Criticism

BLACK, D. A., with K. BARNWELL and S. Levinsohn, eds., *Linguistics and New Testament Interpretation: Essays on Discourse Analysis.* Nashville: Broadman, 1992.

COTTERELL, P., and M. TURNER. *Linguistics and Biblical Interpretation.* London: SPCK, 1989.

PORTER, S. E. *Idioms of the Greek New Testament.* 2d ed. Biblical Languages: Greek 2. Sheffield: JSOT Press, 1994.

_____. "Studying Ancient Languages from a Modern Linguistic Perspective: Essential Terms and Terminology." *FN* 2 (1989): 147–72.

PORTER, S. E., and D. A. CARSON, eds. *Biblical Greek Language and Linguistics: Open Questions in Current Research.* JSNTSup 80. Sheffield: JSOT Press, 1993.

_____, eds. *Discourse Analysis and Other Topics in Biblical Greek.* JSNTSup 113. Sheffield: JSOT Press, 1995.

PORTER, S. E., and J. T. REED. "Greek Grammar since BDF: A Retrospective and Prospective Analysis." *FN* 4 (1991): 143–64.

REED, J. T. "Modern Linguistics and the New Testament: A Basic Guide to Theory, Terminology, and Literature." Pages 222–65 in *Approaches to New Testament Study.* Ed. S. E. PORTER and D. TOMBS. JSNTSup 120. Sheffield: Sheffield Academic Press, 1995.

_____. *A Discourse Analysis of Philippians: Method and Rhetoric in the Debate over Literary Integrity.* JSNTSup 136. Sheffield: Sheffield Academic Press, 1997.

SILVA, M. *Biblical Words and Their Meaning: An Introduction to Lexical Semantics.* Rev. ed. Grand Rapids: Zondervan, 1994.

3. NEW TESTAMENT THEOLOGY

BULTMANN, R. *Theology of the New Testament.* Trans. K. Grobel. 2 vols. London: SCM, 1951–1955.

CAIRD, G. B. *New Testament Theology.* Ed. L. D. HURST. Oxford: Clarendon, 1994.

CONZELMANN, H. *An Outline of the Theology of the New Testament.* New York: Harper & Row, 1968.

DUNN, J. D. G. *Unity and Diversity in the New Testament: An Inquiry into the Character of Earliest Christianity.* Philadelphia: Westminster, 1977.

DUNN, J. D. G., and J. P. MACKEY. *New Testament Theology in Dialogue.* Philadelphia: Westminster, 1987.

FULLER, R. H. *The Foundations of New Testament Christology.* New York: Collins-Fontana Library, 1969.

GOPPELT, L. *Theology of the New Testament.* Trans. J. Alsup. 2 vols. Grand Rapids: Eerdmans, 1981–1982.

JEREMIAS, J. *New Testament Theology.* Trans. J. BOWDEN. London: SCM, 1971.

KRAFTCHICK, S. J., C. D. MYERS Jr., and B. C. OLLENBURGER, eds. *Biblical Theology: Problems and Perspectives.* Nashville: Abingdon, 1995.

KÜMMEL, W. G. *The Theology of the New Testament.* Trans. D. STEELEY. Nashville: Abingdon, 1973.

LADD, G. E. *A Theology of the New Testament.* Ed. D. A. HAGNER. Rev. ed. Grand Rapids: Eerdmans, 1993.

LONGENECKER, R. N. *The Christology of Early Jewish Christianity.* London: SCM, 1970.

MARSHALL, I. H. *The Origins of New Testament Christology.* Downers Grove, Ill.: InterVarsity, 1976.

MORGAN, R. *The Nature of New Testament Theology.* London: SCM, 1973.

MORRIS, L. *The Apostolic Preaching of the Cross.* 3d ed. Grand Rapids: Eerdmans, 1965.

_____. *New Testament Theology.* Grand Rapids: Zondervan, 1986.

MOULE, C. F. D. *The Origin of Christology.* Cambridge: Cambridge University Press, 1977.

NEILL, S. *Jesus through Many Eyes.* Philadelphia: Fortress, 1976.

PERRIN, N. *A Modern Pilgrimage in New Testament Christology.* Philadelphia: Fortress, 1974.

REUMANN, J. *Variety and Unity in New Testament Thought.* Oxford Bible Series. Oxford: Oxford University Press, 1991.

RICHARDSON, A. *An Introduction to the Theology of the New Testament.* New York: Harper & Row, 1958.

pages 23–28

1. P. A. Bird, *The Bible as the Church's Book* (Philadelphia: Westminster, 1982), 54. Bird discusses the negative impact such critical methodology has had upon the church and the resulting opposition to it (pp. 53–66). She shows how the church retreated behind its traditional dogma rather than come to grips with this new methodology and see it as a means of reforming itself by bringing itself more into line with the real intent of the biblical message.

2. R. A. Guelich, "On Becoming a Minister of the Word," *Theology, News, and Notes* (June 1993): 8.

3. E.g., most scholars agree that the Greek of Mark's Gospel is of a different and more straightforward style than that of Luke and Matthew and perhaps, as we shall see later, even more bluntly direct. Both Matthew and Luke saw the need to change the language of Mark, even softening it on occasion.

4. For a detailed analysis of interpreting the biblical text from a historical-critical perspective, see H. Conzelmann and A. Lindemann, *Interpreting the New Testament: An Introduction to the Principles and Methods of New Testament Exegesis* (trans. S. S. Schatzmann; Peabody, Mass.: Hendrickson, 1988). This work is useful in describing the many facets of biblical criticism, including the meaning and practice of textual, literary, form, and redaction criticism. It provides guidance into NT exegesis (interpretation) as well as introductory materials for understanding NT literature. For a less critical introduction, but one that is highly readable and presents well-informed guidelines for the beginning student, see G. D. Fee and D. Stuart, *How to Read the Bible for all Its Worth: A Guide to Understanding the Bible* (2d ed.; Grand Rapids: Zondervan, 1993). The latter work focuses on how to interpret the various kinds of literature, or literary genres, found in the Bible.

5. See L. D. Reynolds and N. G. Wilson, *Scribes and Scholars: A Guide to the Transmission of Greek and Latin Literature* (2d ed.; Oxford: Clarendon, 1974), 186.

6. C. H. Roberts and T. C. Skeat, *The Birth of the Codex* (London: Oxford University Press, 1983), 45–61. This explanation is combined with another Christian phenomenon, the use of *nomina sacra*, shortened forms of special divine or holy names—Lord, Father, Jesus, Son, etc.—with a short line over the top of the abbreviated word (see ch. 12, sec. 4, below). Skeat shows that this activity in the Christian church developed at the same time as the outburst of activity among Jewish scholars in the land of Israel that led to the standardization of the Hebrew Bible. The use of both *nomina sacra* and the codex helped distinguish Christian writing from Jewish and pagan writing. See ibid., 7–61.

7. R. Bultmann, *The History of the Synoptic Tradition* (trans. J. Marsh; 2d ed.; 1963; repr., Peabody, Mass.: Hendrickson, 1993). Other important studies include M. Dibelius, *From Tradition to Gospel* (trans. B. L. Woolf; London: Ivor Nicholson & Watson, 1934; repr., Cambridge: J. Clarke, 1971); V. Taylor, *The Formation of the Gospel Tradition* (London: Macmillan, 1945). More recent summaries are in S. H. Travis, "Form Criticism," in *New Testament Interpretation: Essays on Principles and Methods* (ed. I. H. Marshall; Grand Rapids: Eerdmans, 1977), 153–64, and D. R. Catchpole, "Source, Form, and Redaction Criticism," in *Handbook to Exegesis of the New Testament* (ed. S. E. Porter; NTTS 25; Leiden: Brill, 1997), 167–88.

8. See E. V. McKnight, "Form and Redaction Criticism," in *The New Testament and Its Modern Interpreters* (ed. E. J. Epp and G. W. MacRae; Atlanta: Scholars Press, 1989), 150–51.

pages 29–32

9. See G. Bornkamm, G. Barth, and H. J. Held, *Tradition and Interpretation in Matthew* (trans. P. Scott; NTL; Philadelphia: Westminster, 1963); H. Conzelmann, *The Theology of St. Luke* (trans. G. Buswell; New York: Harper & Row, 1960); W. Marxsen, *Mark the Evangelist: Studies on the Redaction History of the Gospel* (trans. J. Boyce et al.; New York: Abingdon, 1969). A general introduction is N. Perrin, *What Is Redaction Criticism?* (GBS; Philadelphia: Fortress, 1970).

10. R. H. Stein, "Redaction Criticism (NT)," *ABD* 5:648.

11. See S. D. Moore, *Literary Criticism and the Gospels: The Theoretical Challenge* (New Haven: Yale University Press, 1989).

12. D. Rhoads and D. Michie, *Mark as Story: An Introduction to the Narrative of a Gospel* (Philadelphia: Fortress, 1982), 2. See also J. A. Darr, *On Character Building: The Reader and the Rhetoric of Characterization in Luke–Acts* (Literary Currents in Biblical Interpretation; Louisville: Westminster John Knox, 1992).

13. See R. Fowler, *Let the Reader Understand: Reader-Response Criticism and the Gospel of Mark* (Minneapolis: Fortress, 1991). Many others call themselves reader-response critics, although not all are convincing. See S. E. Porter, "Why Hasn't Reader-Response Criticism Caught on in New Testament Studies?" *Literature and Theology* 4 (1990): 278–92.

14. See S. Moore, *Mark and Luke in Poststructuralist Perspectives: Jesus Begins to Write* (New Haven: Yale University Press, 1992); *Poststructuralism and the New Testament: Derrida and Foucault at the Foot of the Cross* (Minneapolis: Fortress, 1994).

15. D. Seeley, *Deconstructing the New Testament* (BIS 5; Leiden: Brill, 1994).

16. N. R. Petersen, *Rediscovering Paul: Philemon and the Sociology of Paul's Narrative World* (Philadelphia: Fortress, 1985). See also S. E. Porter, "A Newer Perspective on Paul: Romans 1–8 through the Eyes of Literary Analysis," in *The Bible in Human Society: Essays in Honour of John Rogerson* (ed. M. D. Carroll R., D. J. A. Clines, and P. R. Davies; JSOTSup 200; Sheffield: Sheffield Academic Press, 1995), 366–92.

17. For a development of these comments, see S. E. Porter, "Literary Approaches to the New Testament: From Formalism to Deconstruction and Back," in *Approaches to New Testament Study* (ed. S. E. Porter and D. Tombs; JSNTSup 120; Sheffield: Sheffield Academic Press, 1995), 77–128; cf. B. W. R. Pearson, "New Testament Literary Criticism," in *Handbook to Exegesis of the New Testament* (ed. Porter), 241–66.

18. See G. A. Kennedy, *The Art of Persuasion in Greece* (Princeton: Princeton University Press, 1963).

19. G. A. Kennedy, *New Testament Interpretation through Rhetorical Criticism* (Chapel Hill: University of North Carolina Press, 1984).

20. See ibid., 146–51, although his arrangement of the parts is not entirely clear.

21. H. D. Betz, *Galatians* (Hermeneia; Philadelphia: Fortress, 1979).

22. See W. Wuellner, "Hermeneutics and Rhetorics," *Scrip S* 3 (1989). He follows the work of C. Perelman and L. Olbrechts-Tyteca, *The New Rhetoric: A Treatise on Argumentation* (trans. J. Wilkinson and P. Weaver; Notre Dame: Notre Dame University Press, 1969).

23. See D. L. Stamps, "Rhetorical Criticism of the New Testament: Ancient and Modern Evaluations of Argumentation," in *Approaches to New Testament Study* (ed. Porter and Tombs), 129–69.

24. See, e.g., A. Deissmann, *Paul: A Study in Social and Religious History* (2d ed.; trans. W. E. Wilson; 1927; repr. New York: Harper, 1957); F. C. Grant, *Roman Hellenism and the New Testament* (Edinburgh: Oliver & Boyd, 1962).

25. E. A. Judge, *The Social Pattern of Christian Groups in the First Century* (London: Tyndale, 1960); A. J. Malherbe, *Social Aspects of Early Christianity* (2d ed.; Philadelphia: Fortress, 1983).

26. A. D. Clarke, *Secular and Christian Leadership in Corinth: A Socio-Historical and Exegetical Study of 1 Corinthians 1–6* (AGJU 28; Leiden: Brill, 1993).

27. W. A. Meeks, *The First Urban Christians: The Social World of the Apostle Paul* (New Haven: Yale University Press, 1983); J. H. Elliott, *A Home for the Homeless: Social-Scientific Criticism of 1 Peter, Its Situation and Strategy* (2d ed.; Minneapolis: Fortress, 1990); B. Holmberg, *Paul and Power: The Structure of Authority in the Primitive Church as Reflected in the Pauline Epistles* (Philadelphia: Fortress, 1978).

28. A volume that falls victim to some of these criticisms is J. J. Pilch and B. J. Malina, eds., *Biblical Social Values and Their Meaning: A Handbook* (Peabody, Mass.: Hendrickson, 1993).

29. B. S. Childs, "Interpretation in Faith: The Theological Responsibility of an Old Testament Commentary," *Int* 18 (1964): 432–49; see esp. *The New Testament as Canon: An Introduction* (Philadelphia: Fortress, 1985).

30. See the essays in J. A. Sanders, *From Sacred Story to Sacred Text: Canon as Paradigm* (Philadelphia: Fortress, 1987); cf. *Canon and Community: A Guide to Canonical Criticism* (GBS; Philadelphia: Fortress, 1984).

31. This criticism of the biblical-theology movement appears in B. S. Childs, *Biblical Theology in Crisis* (Philadelphia: Westminster, 1970).

32. J. A. Sanders, "Canonical Context and Canonical Criticism," *HBT* 2 (1980): 182.

33. Ibid., 187.

34. B. S. Childs, *Introduction to the Old Testament as Scripture* (Philadelphia: Fortress, 1979), 82.

35. For a summary of their work, see K. D. Clarke, "Canonical Criticism: An Integrated Reading of Biblical Texts for the Community of Faith," in *Approaches to New Testament Study* (ed. Porter and Tombs), 170–221.

36. See, e.g., R. W. Wall and E. E. Lemcio, *The New Testament as Canon: A Reader in Canonical Criticism* (JSNTSup 76; Sheffield: JSOT Press, 1992).

37. See S. E. Porter and K. D. Clarke, "Canonical-Critical Perspective and the Relationship of Colossians and Ephesians," *Bib* 78 (1997): 57–86.

38. This is discussed in more detail in L. M. McDonald, *The Formation of the Christian Biblical Canon* (rev. ed.; Peabody, Mass.: Hendrickson, 1995).

39. See J. T. Reed, "Modern Linguistics and the New Testament: A Basic Guide to Theory, Terminology, and Literature," in *Approaches to New Testament Study* (ed. Porter and Tombs), 222–65.

40. See S. E. Porter, "Studying Ancient Languages from a Modern Linguistic Perspective: Essential Terms and Terminology," *FN* 2 (1989): 159–68; S. E. Porter and J. T. Reed, "Greek Grammar since BDF: A Retrospective and Prospective Analysis," *FN* 4 (1991): 143–64.

41. J. P. Louw and E. A. Nida, eds., *Greek–English Lexicon of the New Testament Based on Semantic Domains* (2 vols.; New York: United Bible Societies, 1988).

42. See S. E. Porter, *Idioms of the Greek New Testament* (2d ed.; Biblical Languages: Greek 2; Sheffield: JSOT Press, 1994).

43. See S. E. Porter, ed., *The Language of the New Testament: Classic Essays* (JSNTSup 60; Sheffield: JSOT Press, 1991), for a selection of representative essays.

pages 32–35

44. See S. E. Porter, "Discourse Analysis and New Testament Studies: An Introductory Survey," in *Discourse Analysis and Other Topics in Biblical Greek* (ed. S. E. Porter and D. A. Carson; JSNTSup 113; Sheffield: Sheffield Academic Press, 1995), 14–35, along with the essays by George Guthrie, Stephen Levinsohn, and Jeffrey Reed.

45. R. M. Grant, *A Historical Introduction to the New Testament* (New York: Simon & Schuster, 1972), 92.

46. G. E. Ladd, "Biblical Theology," *ISBE* 1.508.

47. B. Chilton, *Beginning New Testament Study* (Grand Rapids: Eerdmans, 1986), 174–75.

48. These steps have been adapted from V. P. Furnish, "Theology in 1 Corinthians," in *1 and 2 Corinthians*, vol. 2 of *Pauline Theology* (ed. D. M. Hay; Minneapolis: Fortress, 1993), 59–89.

pages 35–37

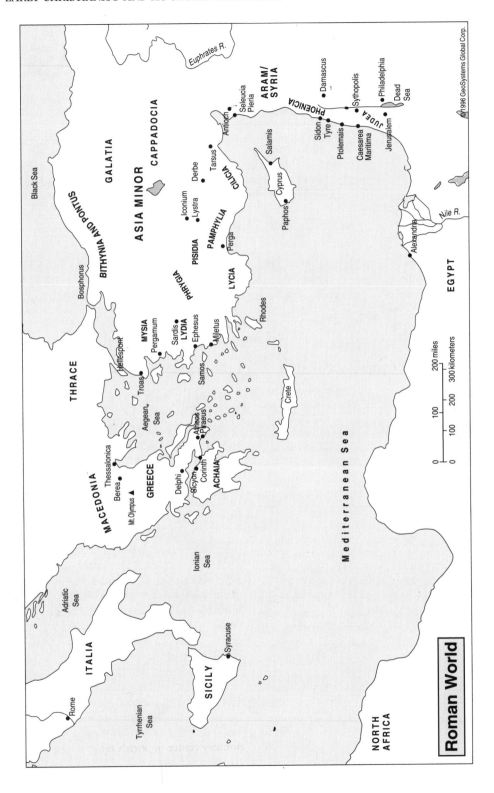

Roman World

THE HISTORICAL CONTEXT OF EARLY CHRISTIANITY

1. FROM CYRUS TO AUGUSTUS

A. Persian Domination of Palestine

After the disastrous events surrounding the destruction of Jerusalem in 587/586 B.C. with its consequent deportation of thousands of Jews to Babylon, several social and religious changes came to the Jews. Their written and oral language was no longer predominantly Hebrew but instead was replaced by Aramaic along with the more square letters of the Aramaic script. Also, after the decree of Cyrus (ca. 538–532 B.C.) that allowed the Jews to return to their homeland (see Ezra 1:2–4; 6:2–5), most of them did *not* return home, preferring instead to remain in the peaceful environment of Persia, where many were prospering. Some of them migrated to Greece, Asia Minor, Rome, Egypt, and elsewhere (see Acts 2:8–11). Since Palestine was largely in ruins, there was little to encourage the Jews to come back to their land, even though thousands did return.[1] The Jews who remained in Persia or moved to other places outside Palestine came to be known as the Dispersion or the Diaspora Jews (James writes to the Christian Jews, or "the twelve tribes in the Dispersion" [διασπορά, *diaspora*], in Jas 1:1). By NT times the number of Jews in the Dispersion was around five to six million, with an additional one to two million living in Palestine.

More important, those Jews who returned to the land, beginning with Ezra the scribe, believed that they had been deported as a result of their failure to keep the law of Moses. From that time on, Ezra and the rest of the Jews devoted themselves to rebuilding the temple and its walls but especially to understanding their religious heritage, which resulted in a new emphasis on interpreting the Law. Neither the Prophets nor the Writings (see sec. 2.B, below) were viewed as sacred Scripture yet, nor did they play a discernibly major role in the religious life of Israel. While in Babylon, the Jews were unable to offer their animal sacrifices, which were the dominant form of their cultic religious expression in pre-exilic times. Although some believe that the synagogue emerged during the captivity in Babylon to meet the religious needs of the people, its precise origins are obscure; other scholars claim that its origins are in the early second century B.C. in Palestine, but more likely the synagogue emerged later in the second century B.C. during Hasmonean times (after 140 B.C.) In any case, the synagogue, which was apparently common both inside and outside Palestine in the first century A.D. and later (although the archaeological evidence is scarce), became the primary center of Jewish religious life after the destruction of the temple in A.D. 70. Rather than a priest-led liturgy, which focused on temple worship with its sacrifices, the synagogue was primarily a lay-oriented community that stressed reading of the Scriptures, exposition of the Sriptures (when persons were present who could do it), singing of hymns, and offering of prayers. After the temple was destroyed, the form of worship used in the synagogue became the only surviving worship expression of Judaism. The earliest Christian community in Jerusalem also organized and practiced worship after the manner of the synagogue.

The traditional Mount Sinai with one of several small chapels surrounding it. Photo © Rohr Productions. Used with permission.

It is probable that the widespread recognition of the divine origins and authority of the law of Moses took place during the time of the Jewish exile in Babylon, when the Jews were without a temple. This does not negate the impact of the reforms inspired by the law on the Jews in the days of Josiah in the sixth century B.C. (2 Kgs 22–23), but they were in effect only for a brief period before the destruction of the nation and its religious cult. The call for restoring the temple (see Haggai and Zech 1–8) was also important during the period of Persian domination (which extended from ca. 530 to 330 B.C.), but from the Babylonian exile forward, the law and the reforms it brought to the people of Israel were among the highest priorities of the nation. There were conflict and instability in the land, and they continued well into the time of the Latter Prophets. For example, Zech 9–14 foretold the major cleansings within Israel (see esp. chs. 12–14) and even within the royal family. The emphasis was on a future transformed time when Yahweh would be the king of a renewed people.

After the devastation of the nation that began in 596/595 B.C. and concluded with the subsequent destruction of the temple and deportation of the people in 587/586 B.C., what remained for the Jews who returned to Palestine after the exile was a story about their heritage, including an experience with Yahweh.[2] As mentioned, they had concluded that the destruction of their homeland and temple was due to their own failure to keep their covenant with Yahweh. The school of interpretation that began with Ezra added a new focus on the law and its practical implications in the lives of the Jewish people. In the renewal of their covenant with God (see Ezra 10:1–5; Neh 7:73–9:38), they also rebuilt the temple under Zerubbabel by around 515 B.C., as noted above, and then rebuilt the walls around the city (no later than ca. 445–443 B.C.). During the rebuilding of the walls, the Jews met with opposition from Sanballat, the governor of Samaria (Neh 4:2). This is the first time the Samaritans are mentioned by name.

Ancient steps carved in the hillside leading to the temple of Samaria. Photo Lee M. McDonald.

Later, by the time of the NT, the Samaritans are generally looked upon with disdain by the Jews (see John 4:4–12, 19); nevertheless, in the parable of the Good Samaritan in Luke 10:25–37, Jesus made the point that even a natural enemy of the Jews, a Samaritan, can be a good neighbor. The Samaritans built their own temple ca. 330 B.C., but ca. 128–125 B.C., John Hyrcanus, king of the Hasmoneans, destroyed the rival Samaritan temple, although not the Samaritans' devotion to Mount Gerizim, where the temple had been built. (For further discussion of this topic, see sec. 2.I.5, below.) The remainder of

*Petra in Jordan, home of Aretas, who defeated Herod the Great in battle
(Josephus,* Ant. *17.287; 18.109–115). Photo Lee M. McDonald.*

the period of Persian domination of Palestine (ca. 530–330 B.C.) was often turbulent, but in comparison with the time of the Seleucid domination (198–142 B.C.), it was relatively peaceful. Evidence for upheaval during the Persian period may be recorded in the second portion of Zechariah (chs. 9–14). Many scholars place these chapters between 330 and 150 B.C., since in 9:14 the rise of the Greeks had already occurred; if that is the case, then the period of relative calm that has been frequently attributed to this period did not prevail.

B. Greek Domination of Palestine

With the conquests of Alexander "the Great" (334–323 B.C.), Palestine fell under Greek control and the influence of Alexander's ambitious goals of revolutionizing the cultural, linguistic, religious, and political structures of the communities he captured.[3] The opening sentences of 1 Maccabees (ca. 104–100 B.C.) describe the enormous impact that Alexander made on the ancient world:

After Alexander son of Philip, the Macedonian, who came from the land of Kittim, had defeated King Darius of the Persians and the Medes, he succeeded him as king. (He had previously become king of Greece.) He fought many battles, conquered strongholds, and put to death the kings of the earth. He advanced to the ends of the earth, and plundered many nations. When the earth became quiet before him, he was exalted, and his heart was lifted up. He gathered a very strong army and ruled over countries, nations, and princes, and they became tributary to him. (1 Macc 1:1–4)

The Greek language came to be spoken almost everywhere during this time, and Greek culture was disseminated through, among other avenues, the Greek gymnasiums, which were the major places of both learning and physical training. During the Greek domination there was a move toward syncretism of both the architectural and the religious heritages of the Greek and Oriental peoples. Many Jews were opposed to these syncretistic moves, though many Jews, especially the educated class, were quite favorable to Hellenistic influences in Palestine.

Steps of the ancient Pnyx in Athens, the meeting place of the popular assembly after 507 B.C. and the birthplace of democracy. Photo Lee M. McDonald.

Part of the success for Alexander's program, apart from his military prowess, was due to his vision for the peoples he conquered. Alexander reportedly gave a famous speech at Opis, a town on the Tigris River near Babylon, in 324 B.C. The speech was undoubtedly embellished by Eratosthenes (the third director of the library of Alexandria in the second century B.C.) and by Ptolemy (one of Alexander's famous generals), who reportedly heard the speech, but enough of it has been reported in various contexts to be able to determine the substance of Alexander's words. Supposedly delivered to some nine thousand "dignitaries and notables of all races," the speech emphasized brotherhood and the reconciliation of all persons. The shortest report of this speech comes from the Roman historian Flavius Arrian (ca. 130 A.D.): "And Alexander prayed for all sorts of blessings, and especially for harmony (ὁμόνοιαν, *homonoian*) and fellowship (κοινωνίαν, *koinōnian*) in the empire between Macedonians and Persians."[4]

After Alexander's death there was confusion in his empire until it was divided among his generals, called the Diadochi (διάδοχοι, *diadochoi*)—Antipater and his son Cassander, Lysimachus, Ptolemy I, Antigonus I, and Seleucus. Their vision for the empire was not as great as Alexander's, and divisions were inevitable. By 280 B.C. there remained three major Greek dynasties tracing their descent from Alexander. Palestine at first fell under the control of the Ptolemaic dynasty, which had established its headquarters in Alexandria, Egypt. The Seleucid dynasty, which controlled Asia Minor to Syria and Persia to the Euphrates River, was headquartered in Damascus, with major units of its army and gov-

Egyptian architecture at Petra in Jordan. It dates from the period of the Alexandrian conquests. Photo Lee M. McDonald.

ernment at Antioch of Syria. Finally, there were the Antigonids, who controlled Greece and Thrace. Under the Ptolemies, the Jews experienced a relatively peaceful time of religious toleration and prosperity, since they were basically self-governing. During this time a major project of translating the Hebrew Scriptures into Greek was begun in Alexandria, perhaps at the instigation of the ruler of the Ptolemies, Ptolemy II Philadelphus (if the testimony of the second-century B.C. *Letter of Aristeas* is to be trusted),[5] though more likely it was instigated by the Jews themselves sometime around 250–225 B.C. This new translation came to be referred to as the Septuagint (LXX), a probable reference to the seventy or seventy-two elders of Judah reported to have been translators in the project. The LXX, which was not completed until around 100 B.C., became the most commonly used translation of the Bible among Diaspora Jews and many Palestinian

*Caesarea Philippi (Baniyas/Banias/Paneas, Syria) before recent excavations with details of
a spring and a cave. Photo © Rohr Productions. Used with permission.*

Jews until the second century A.D. It was used and preserved in the church by the Christian community almost from its beginnings.

The Ptolemic regime ruled Palestine until the Seleucid king Antiochus III ("the Great") defeated the Egyptian forces (ca. 200–198 B.C.) led by Ptolemy V at Panion (Paneas, or Caesarea Philippi in the NT), which lies at the southern end of Mount Hermon. From this time, the Jews were under the Seleucids, who controlled by far the largest part of Alexander's kingdom. When Antiochus III's grandson, Antiochus IV Epiphanes ("Manifestation"), became ruler of the Seleucid dynasty in 175 B.C., new pressures were brought on the Jews to conform to the religion and culture of the Greeks. One of Antiochus Epiphanes' early moves was to depose the high priest in Jerusalem, Onias III, and appoint Jason, a Jew sympathetic to the Hellenism of the Seleucids. Jason was chosen mostly because of his large gift of money to Antiochus. After three years, Menelaus offered Antiochus an even larger gift for the office of high priest, which was then awarded to him. This move greatly angered the Jews and

caused rebellion among them. Subsequently, when the Jews believed that Antiochus had been killed in battle with the Egyptians, Jason, the previous high priest, forced Menelaus out of office. Antiochus, on the brink of reestablishing Seleucid reign in Egypt, had been thwarted by the intervention of the Romans. When Antiochus returned from Egypt to Palestine, humiliated by his defeat, and found out what Jason had done, he was enraged and reinstated Menelaus, plundered the temple and its treasury, and took some of its furniture to Antioch of Syria. He then tore down the walls of the temple and in 167 B.C. made an offering to Zeus on the altar in the sacred Jewish temple in Jerusalem. It is probably this act that is described in detail in Dan 11:21–45, calling it the "abomination of desolation" (11:31). The impact of this event on Israel was so devastating and infuriating to the Jews that when Jesus later described the ultimate catastrophe of the great tribulation of the end times, he spoke of it in terms of this event (Matt 24:15).

Many of the more educated Jews willingly accepted the hellenization being imposed on them,

*A section of a frieze among the ruins at Hierapolis
(Pamukkale ["Cotton Castle"], Turkey).
Photo Lee M. McDonald.*

some even committing religious apostasy by undergoing "epispasm"—a surgical procedure to remove the marks of circumcision—and embracing Greek religion. Antiochus went further, trying to force all the Jews to sacrifice to Zeus and even to violate their religious dietary laws by eating pork. Such acts of sacrilege resulted in a rebellion among the Jews led by Mattathias, a Jewish priest from Modein and a member of the influential Hasmonean family. After he refused to obey a command from a Seleucid officer to make a sacrifice to Zeus on a Jewish alter in Modein and another Jew stepped forward to do so, Mattathias and his sons killed both the Jew and the officer and then fled to the hills to organize guerrilla warfare against the Seleucids. Mattathias was soon killed, and his son Judas "the Maccabee" (probably meaning "hammer") led the Jews into battles against the Seleucids with many successes. He and his brothers were joined by the Hasideans (*hasadim*, "the pious")—a devoutly religious group who were probably the forerunners of the Essenes and the Pharisees (see sec. 2.I, below)—to rid the Seleucids from their land.[6] These successes became a major source of pride and inspiration for all subsequent generations

*A portion of the western wall of the Old City of Jerusalem near the ruins of the Hasmonean wall.
Photo © Rohr Productions. Used with permission.*

of Jews. In 164 B.C. the Jews were able to take over the temple in Jerusalem, even cleansing it and re-dedicating it for use in sacrifices.

C. Jewish Independence and the Hasmoneans

The Jews were aided in their battles against the Seleucids when Antiochus IV Epiphanes had to withdraw many of his forces from Palestine and send them to fight the Parthians in the east, leaving his forces divided and Lysias, his general, in charge of half of his troops. While Antiochus IV was in Persia, Judas recaptured the temple in Jerusalem in 164, later commemorated in the Jewish festival Hanukkah, (e.g., John 10:22). After Antiochus IV died in Persia in 163 B.C., his successors were never able to mount a sustained offensive against the Jews. Judas, killed in battle in 160 B.C., was succeeded by his brother Jonathan. He led the Jewish forces in the attempt to oust from Palestine the remaining Seleucid armies from 160 to 154 B.C., and he became the high priest in 152 B.C.

Simon (142–135 B.C.), a younger brother, who began his rule after Jonathan's death, became not only high priest like Jonathan but also king, beginning the Hasmonean dynasty in Palestine. By 142 B.C. Simon had forced the Seleucids from their last garrison in Palestine and freed the Jews from their heavy taxation. He later even minted his own coins for currency. By 142–140 B.C., all Seleucids were out of the land, and the Jews extended their borders under Simon, and later John Hyrcanus I

A bronze coin of Alexander Jannaeus (103–76 B.C.). Greek inscription: "Of Alexander the King"; the Hebrew: "Jonathan the King." Photo © Rohr Productions. Used with permission.

(135–104 B.C.), to include an even larger territory than that ruled earlier by Solomon. John Hyrcanus also invaded Idumea and forced the inhabitants of that territory to follow Judaism.[7] His successor, Aristobulus, who only reigned one year (103 B.C.), followed John Hyrcanus's lead and ruthlessly imposed circumcision on the Idumeans. From 102 to 76 B.C., Alexander Jannaeus reigned over the Hasmonean dynasty and significantly increased the territorial boundaries. He was succeeded by his wife, Salome Alexandra, who ruled as queen (76–67 B.C.) and named her son Hyrcanus II high priest. She made a tentative peace with the Pharisees, who

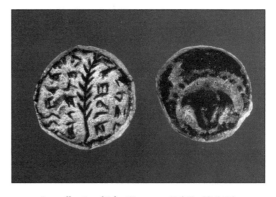

A small coin of John Hyrcanus II (63–40 B.C.), which reads, "Yohanan the High Priest and the Assembly of the Jews." Photo © Rohr Productions. Used with permission.

still apparently exerted significant influence, and ruled a warrior nation. After her death, she was succeeded by her son Aristobulus II, who was locked into a major battle with Hyrcanus II, his brother, to succeed his mother. Although Aristobulus reigned for a time (67–63 B.C.), he was then imprisoned in Rome by Pompey, who had invaded Palestine and Syria in 63 B.C.; soon afterwards Hyrcanus II came to power and ruled as high priest, though not as king.

D. Roman Domination of Palestine and Herodian Rule

During the waning years of the Hasmonean dynasty, its power was divided because the Hasideans rejected the Hasmoneans' control of the priesthood. Some Hasideans (probably some of those who later became known as the Essenes) withdrew

A swimming pool located at the winter palace of Herod the Great in NT Jericho. It is the probable drowning site of Aristobulus, the high priest and last of the heirs to the Hasmonean dynasty (Josephus, Ant. 15.50–56). Photo Lee M. McDonald.

to the desert and other places, often in isolation from public life; others (probably the Pharisees) worked within society to help reform it. The Pharisees, like the Essenes, rejected the combination of kingship and priesthood in the same family, and the Hasmonean priesthood altogether.[8] What made the transition in power even more complex was the entry into Palestine of the Parthians from the east who supported the rule and high priesthood of Antigonus (40–37 B.C.).

From 63 to 37 B.C. the Hasmoneans ruled Palestine with the support of Pompey. Antigonus, the last of the Hasmonean kings, ruled in Israel from 40 to 37 B.C., a time of conflict, until a political realignment allowed Antipater and his famous son, Herod the Great, to gain power with the aid of the Romans.

Antipater, who came from Idumea, was called upon to serve in the Hasmonean dynasty and was promoted to a high place of influence. Later (55–43 B.C.), he was appointed by the Romans as procurator of Judea. His son, Herod the Great, aligned himself with Rome. During the struggles for power when the arch-enemy of Rome, the Parthians from the east, supported the rule and high priesthood of Antigonus, Herod gained control of Judea. Through several politically astute moves, Herod was able to win the favor of Rome and came to power as king in 37 B.C. with the help of a decree from Rome.[9] He took control of the territory, solidifying his kingdom in Palestine often in a most ruthless manner. The story reported about him in Matt 2:16 is certainly in keeping with other reports about his behavior. According to Josephus (see esp. *Ant.* 15.14–17, 199; *War* 1.435–669), he murdered his favorite wife, Mariamne (who was a Hasmonean), and allowed two of his sons by her, Alexander and Aristobulus, to be tried by the Romans and put to death.[10]

During his reign from 37 to 4 B.C. Herod built an impressive harbor in Caesarea Maritima that enabled him to bring spices (a very important

The excavation of a bathhouse at Herod's winter palace in Jericho (1st cent. B.C.), where Herod died (Ant. 17.173–199). Photo Lee M. McDonald.

commodity in the ancient world) through his country and ship them out to the rest of the Roman world. Through this venture, and because he also controlled the trade routes overland and imposed heavy taxation on the people, Herod became very rich, using his monies to build magnificent palaces, fortresses, aqueducts, and especially the temple in Jerusalem, begun in 20–19 B.C. Although still under construction, this temple was the pride of the Jews in the time of Jesus and was the structure destroyed in A.D. 70 by Titus, the Roman general who later became emperor after his father Vespasian. Herod the Great, by far the most famous builder of the first century B.C., was able to build his harbor at Caesarea by using a method—likely borrowed from the Romans—of drying cement under water.

He initiated major building enterprises in some twenty cities in Palestine as well as in several other cities in the Greco-Roman world. Josephus claims that Athens and other cities were recipients of Herod's building projects (*War* 1.422–425). Two inscriptions found on the Athenian Acropolis, between the Propylaea and the Erechtheum, thank Herod for his generosity. The first reads, "The people [erect this monument to] King Herod, Lover of Romans, because of the benefaction and good will [shown] by him"; the second reads, "The people [erect this monument to] King Herod, Devout and a Lover of Caesar, because of his virtue and benefaction."[11] Because of his consummate love of Roman architecture, Herod designed most of his buildings after their typical structural style, as in

the temple he built for the burial of the Abrahamic family in Hebron, not far from ancient Machpelah.

After Herod's death, his kingdom was divided among his sons: Archelaus, a son by Malthace, ruled Judea from 4 B.C. to A.D. 6; Herod Antipas, another son by Malthace, ruled Galilee and Perea from 4 B.C. to A.D. 39; and Philip the Tetrarch, a son by Cleopatra, ruled Iturea and Trachonitis from 4 B.C. to A.D. 34.

Herod Archelaus (see Matt 2:22) was deposed because of his many cruelties and the consequent rebellion by the Jews in A.D. 6. The Roman procurators then ruled Judea until Palestine was again briefly unified under the rulership of Herod Agrippa I, grandson of Herod the Great, from A.D. 41 to 44. Agrippa had succeeded Philip and ruled his territory from A.D. 37 to 41. Acts 12:20–23 and Josephus (*Ant.* 19.346–350) record his sudden and tragic death. From A.D. 50 to around A.D. 100 Herod Agrippa II ruled over the same territory as his father, Agrippa I.[12]

2. THE JEWISH CONTEXT OF EARLY CHRISTIANITY

A. *Jewish Identity and Religious Beliefs*

Although Judaism of the first century, when Jesus lived, is sometimes confused with a single set of beliefs and often referred to as "normative Judaism," the fact is that there were many competing

A bronze coin of Herod the Great (37 B.C.). Greek inscription: "Of Herod the King, Year Three." Photo © Rohr Productions. Used with permission.

orthodoxies or beliefs at that time. Among the most commonly known theological views of first-century Judaism are those of the Pharisees, the Sadducees, the Essenes, the Samaritans, the Zealots, and also the Christians. The Christians were at first a Jewish

A low-level aqueduct, dating from the fourth or fifth century A.D., that brought water to Caesarea from three miles north of the city. Photo Lee M. McDonald.

The remains of the pier built by Herod the Great at Caesarea Maritima ("by the sea"). Photo Lee M. McDonald.

sect, that is, a religious group, like the Pharisees, within the broad Jewish religious tradition and claiming heir to the Scriptures and traditions of the Jewish people. A common characteristic among these various Judaisms—with perhaps the exception of the Sadducees and the Samaritans—that distinguished them from later rabbinic Judaism (2d cent. A.D.) was a widespread apocalyptic belief that from God would come a messiah who would establish the kingdom of God and bring to an end the repressiveness of evil rulers and the occupiers of the land of Israel—the Romans. This belief led to two revolts against Rome (A.D. 66–70 and 132–135), but because of their tragic failure, it all but disappeared among the Jews in the second century. Still, in the first century, Judaism was more characerized by its practices than by its specific catalog of beliefs. It was not so much doctrinally oriented as life-oriented: what one did was more important than what one thought. There was a reasonable amount of theological toleration in the nation of Israel as long as Jews did what Jews were supposed to do, namely, respect the Sabbath, keep the religious holy days and purification rites, and do the things that demonstrated their loyalty to the covenant of God. Although the study of the law, temple worship, and deeds of charity were generally recognized as the pivotal features of Judaism (see *m.*

ʾ*Abot* 1.2, which may reflect first-century practice), they were known primarily for their observance of male circumcision, Sabbath rest, and the holy days.

First-century Jews were also known for their strong monotheism, or faith in one God (the God of Israel), their belief that Israel was specially chosen, and their recognition of the special status of the Torah (the law given by God to the Jewish people), which was read regularly in their assemblies.[13] They had little optimism, however, as there had been before the deportation of the Jews in 587/586 B.C., that history was redeemable. Many had become pessimistic about the salvation of Israel as a whole, thinking that only a remnant would see that salvation, and only through future traumatic events when the next world of the new age would be introduced. As mentioned, this apocalyptic fervor is the chief feature distinguishing the Pharisaic tradition of the first century from the rabbinic Judaism of the second century A.D. The other Judaisms of the first century (Sadducees, Essenes, Zealots) were almost totally rejected by the surviving Judaism of the rabbinic sages, who codified the oral traditions teaching how to keep faithfully the law of God in its two dimensions, oral and written. This rabbinic Judaism prevailed among most Jews in the last two-thirds of the second century A.D. The apocalyptically influenced Judaisms that had torn apart the nation and contributed to its two major revolts against Rome were no longer as attractive to those who survived the catastrophe. The Roman imperial system, which victimized the Jews, had perhaps led to this apocalyptic fervor and the

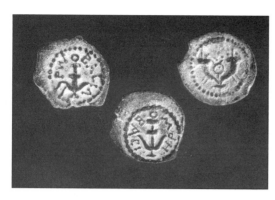

Bronze coins of Herod the Great (37–4 B.C.), depicting anchors and double cornucopias. Greek inscription: "Of Herod the King." Photo © Rohr Productions. Used with permission.

traumatic events that followed.[14] While we have pointed out some characteristics that were common among the various first-century Jewish religious groups, very few things could be said to

characterize all of the various Judaisms of that time. One must resist the unhelpful tendency to impose the more uniform thinking of later rabbinic Judaism back on the first century.

B. The Hebrew Scriptures

Although there was no final fixed canon of the OT, whether in Greek or Hebrew, in the time of Jesus, it is likely that the books now recognized as the OT were generally thought of then as authoritative by most Jews in Palestine. Only the Sadducees held to a more conservative biblical canon, accepting only the five books of Moses. Many other books that did not later become a part of the Hebrew Bible (or the later Protestant biblical canon of OT Scriptures) were also acknowledged as authoritative literature both among Jews of the first century and among Christians (e.g., the Wisdom of Solomon and Sirach). Some of them became part of what has become known as the Apocrypha

The Herodium with a Roman pool in the foreground. Herod the Great reportedly was buried in this cone-shaped fortress (Josephus, Ant. 17.196–199). It was one of three fortresses that Herod the Great built in Judea (Masada, Machaerus, Herodium). Photo Lee M. McDonald.

(among Catholics, the deuterocanonical literature). In addition, many Jews before and during the time of Jesus read an even larger body of literature now commonly called the Pseudepigrapha. A likely reference to the inspired status of this literature is found in 2 Esd 14:44–48:

> So during the forty days, ninety-four books were written. And when the forty days were ended, the Most High spoke to me, saying, "Make public the twenty-four books that you wrote first, and let the worthy and the unworthy read them; but keep the seventy that were written last, in order to give them to the wise among your people. For in them is the spring of understanding, the fountain of wisdom, and the river of knowledge." And I did so.

The extent to which the Pseudepigrapha also informed the theology of the earliest Christian community will be discussed in chs. 13 and 14, below. Pious Jews of the first century A.D. read closely from the three major categories of Scriptures—the Law, the Prophets, and the Writings—though it is less clear whether these categories contained all the books they now possess and whether they read only these books as sacred Scripture. The three sections of the current Hebrew Bible are often identified by the acronym "Tanak," which stands for Torah (the first five books of the Bible, the Law), Neviim (the Prophets, including both the Former Prophets and the Latter Prophets), and Ketuvim (the Writings, the remaining OT books, which were not fixed in Judaism until late in the second century A.D., or possibly even later). Although the term "Tanak" does not come from the first century but from later Judaism, it is a convenient designation for what eventually became the Hebrew Scriptures of Judaism.

Early Christianity shared with Judaism its recognition of the divinely inspired status of the Writings, but attached itself more to the Prophets, many Christians going so far as to use the term "Prophets" for all the Scriptures by the second century (see Justin, 1 Apol. 67). The Jews, on the other hand, often used the term "law" for all of their Scriptures (see John 10:34).[15]

The three constant reminders of the law to Jews of a Pharisaic bent were the zizith (fringes or tassels worn on the ends of garments—see Num 15:37–41; Deut 22:19), the mezuzah (a small container for selected Scriptures, hung on the doorpost—see Deut 6:9; 11:20), and the tefillin, or phylacteries (prayer straps containing passages of

The temple in Hebron built by Herod the Great and believed to be the burial place of Abraham. The temple walls resemble walls in the Jerusalem temple except for the top few feet, which were added when the site came under Moslem control. Photo Lee M. McDonald.

Scriptures, worn on one's arm and head—see Exod 13:9, 16; also Matt 23:5). These were designed to recall to the Jews their loyalty to God and the law of God.

Since many Jews thought that the destruction of the holy city Jerusalem and their deportation to Babylon in 587/586 B.C. were due to their failure to keep the law of Moses, they dedicated themselves to the preservation and study of the law (see 2 Bar. 85:3) after the end of their captivity. They also instituted a special class of interpreters of the law called the *soferim*, or scribes. They taught that the law consisted of instructions or teachings and that the primary meaning of the Torah had to be fol-

A bronze coin of Sepphoris (Diocaesarea), struck under Trajan (A.D. 98–117) and depicting a palm tree. Greek inscription: "Of People of Sepphoris." Photo © Rohr Productions. Used with permission.

lowed at all costs. At first this absolute scriptural observance applied only to the five books of Moses, but eventually for most Jews, including the Pharisees and those of the later rabbinic tradition, it was expanded to include the Prophets and the Writings. During the influence of the Pharisaic schools of the first century A.D., which preceded the rabbinic tradition, there emerged also oral traditions that focused on the religious prescriptions and proscriptions believed essential to the religious observances of the Jews (see Jesus' reference to this in Mark 7:5–13). These oral traditions came to be codified in the Mishnah under the leadership of Rabbi Judah ha-Nasi ("the Prince") (fl. c. A.D. 200–215). Later these traditions also became a part of the Jewish sacred tradition, along with the literature that interpreted it—the Tosefta, the two Talmudim, and the Jewish interpretations of the Scriptures called midrashim (e.g., *Genesis Rabbah* and *Leviticus Rabbah*). In the Hebrew Scriptures themselves the scribes found some 613 commandments (365 negative and 248 positive) (see *Mekilta* 67a). It was believed that the law applied to all of life and that if one had any difficulty making an appropriate application, then one needed to "turn it and turn it again for everything is in it" (*m. ʾAbot* 5:22).

C. The Rabbinic Tradition and Literature of Ancient Judaism

The primary schools of biblical interpretation flourishing in the time of Jesus were those of Hillel and Shammai (ca. 30 B.C.–A.D. 10). The latter was more popular in Israel in the years before the destruction of Jerusalem in A.D. 70, but Hillel's interpretation later prevailed and became foundational for the surviving Judaism of the late first and second centuries. Many of the teachings of Hillel were passed on to his best known pupil in the first century A.D., Rabbi Gamaliel, the teacher of the Apostle Paul (Acts 22:3). It was said, in a Jewish form of hyperbole intended to praise a prominent teacher of the law, that when Gamaliel died, "the glory of the law ceased and purity and abstinence died in Israel" (*m. Soṭa* 9:15). After the destruction of Jerusalem and the temple, Rabbi Johanan ben Zakkai reorganized Judaism. He had to deal with the problem of how Judaism, which had been so directly tied to the temple cultus with its many sacrifices, could survive without its very important sacrificial system. He was instrumental in the

reorganization of Israel's religious life through the rabbinic academy that is reported to have met at Jamnia (Jabneh) ca. A.D. 90. After him Rabbis Eliezer and Gamaliel II became prominent, but the latter had a less tolerant attitude toward the Christian community than his grandfather had (Acts 5:34–42). Gamaliel II reportedly introduced the twelfth of the Eighteen Benedictions *(Shemoneh-Esreh)*, which were repeated by pious Jews three times daily, in the morning, at noon, and in the evening, and were an essential part of the daily synagogue service. The twelfth benediction was a curse on heretics, which undoubtedly included Christians: "For apostates let there be no hope, and the dominion of arrogance [Rome] do Thou speedily root out in our days; and let the Nazarenes [Christians] and the heretics perish as in a moment, let them be blotted out of the book of the living and let them not be written with the righteous. Blessed art Thou, O Lord, who humblest the arrogant!"[16] This is also called a *Birkath ha-Minim*, a malediction for the heretics.

Rabbi Akiba, the leading rabbinic figure from A.D. 120 to 140, recognized and supported the claims of Simeon bar Koziba (also known as Simeon bar Kokhba) to be the King Messiah. Bar Koziba led an uprising against Rome in A.D. 132–135, seeking to make the Jewish state independent from Roman rule. The Jews had initial success against Rome and for a while minted their own coins, but their attempts were ultimately futile, ending in an overwhelming defeat of the Jews and the death of Bar Koziba. After their defeat the Roman emperor Hadrian (A.D. 135) excluded the Jews from Jerusalem

The reading of the Talmud, the wisdom teaching of rabbinic Judaism that many believe put a wall of safety around the Jews. Photo © Rohr Productions. Used with permission.

and renamed the city Aeolia Capitolina. Because of this massive defeat and punishment, the Jews called Bar Koziba a liar who had committed sins worthy of death. He was then called Bar *Kozeba* ("lie"), a play on words that referred to his deceit and the deception of the people (see *Mishneh Torah, Melakhim* 11.3).

After the death of Rabbi Akiba, Rabbi Meir (ca. A.D. 140) began the process of codifying the oral traditions, which served as a "hedge" around the law and guarded its proper implementation in the lives of the Jews in Palestine. The codification, which was completed under the direction of Rabbi Judah ha-Nasi the Patriarch ("the Prince") in the early third century, was called the Mishnah. It was essentially a codification of the halakah (from the Heb. *halak,* "walk")—legal traditions that focused on how to conduct oneself, or walk, according to the law. The Mishnah emphasized the legal aspects of keeping the law, and eventually it became the second canon of the Jews. Almost from the time of its codification, it was believed to be so important that whole traditions of interpreting it began to develop. When a rabbi commented on the meaning of the Mishnah, his commentary was called Gemara (from the Heb. *gemar,* "complete"). The Mishnah and its Gemara were combined to form the Talmud. There were two basic Talmuds produced by the Jews, each including portions in both Aramaic and Hebrew: the Jerusalem (*Yerushalmi;* also called the Palestinian) Talmud and the Babylonian (*Bavli* or *Babli*) Talmud.[17] The Jerusalem Talmud is our primary source about Palestinian Judaism in late antiquity. The Babylonian Talmud, covering almost 6,000 folio pages, is much more extensive and conservative than the Jerusalem. About one-third of it contains halakah (legal prescriptions for obeying the law); two-thirds of it is haggadah (short stories and anecdotes). Although the Babylonian Talmud comments on only thirty-six and a half of the tractates in the Mishnah and the Jerusalem on thirty-nine, the former is almost four times as long as the latter. To these documents was added the Tosefta ("Supplement")—a collection of interpretations contemporary with the Mishnah but excluded from it. Together the Mishnah and the Tosefta formed the core of the second sacred canon of later Judaism. Other traditions, dating from the second century A.D. (the earliest period of rab-

binic Judaism is known as the Tannaitic period—roughly the first and second centuries A.D.) and possibly earlier but not included in the Mishnah, are sometimes called *baraita* ("external," "outside"; pl. *baraitoth*). The *baraitoth* did not have sufficient status among the people to be included in the Mishnah, and it is questionable whether they obtained that authoritative status later during the period of the Amoraim (rabbinic sages from the third to sixth centuries A.D.), but a *baraita* does come from an early period and may have represented the beliefs of some Jews of this early period.

We may wonder why this literature, which was largely produced well after the time of Jesus and the origins of early Christianity, has any significance for understanding early Christianity and its sacred Scriptures. The answer is that the Mishnah is the codification of the oral traditions that *in some cases* may have been contemporary with Jesus or even have originated from a time before his ministry. The Mishnah provides, in several instances, background material for understanding Jesus' teachings. For example, the tractate *Shabbath* in the second division focuses on the observance of the Sabbath, and *Nedarim* ("Vows") in the third division and *Shebuoth* ("Oaths") in the fourth division offer a context for understanding Jesus' teaching on oaths (Matt 5:33–37). There are other parallels that provide background to Jesus' teaching on marriage and divorce (Mark 10:2–11; Matt 19:3–12) and on the two greatest commandments, on which all of the law hangs (Mark 12:28–34; Matt 22:34–40). To be sure, one needs to be cautious in

A sign at Sepphoris with words from the Babylonian Talmud telling of the journey of the Sanhedrin after the destruction of Jerusalem in A.D. 70. Photo Lee M. McDonald.

the use of the Mishnah. Some of it probably dates back to or before the time of Jesus, but much does not. It is a temptation among scholars of early Christianity to project second- and third-century rabbinic traditions back on the first century, but such traditions may well have emerged for the first time after the traumatic events surrounding the destruction of Jerusalem and its temple cultus (A.D. 66–70) or after the Bar Kokhba rebellion in A.D. 132–135.

Just as the Christians needed another testament to complete the sense of their OT, so the adherents of Judaism in the second century believed that they needed the Mishnah and its interpretations to complete the understanding of the Hebrew Scriptures for them and explain its relevance for everyday life.

The Mishnah was written in Hebrew and has six divisions *(sedarim)*, which are made up of sixty-three tractates.[18] It is concerned with holy life lived in the context of Palestine, not with life in the Diaspora. The divisions are as follows:

FIRST DIVISION, *ZERAIM* ("SEEDS")
Berakoth ("Benedictions")
Peah ("Gleanings")
Demai ("Produce not certainly tithed")
Kilaim ("Diverse Kinds")
Shebiith ("The Seventh Year")
Terumoth ("Heave-Offerings")
Maaseroth ("Tithes")
Maaser Sheni ("Second Tithe")
Hallah ("Dough-offering")
Orlah ("Fruit of Young Trees")
Bikkurim ("First-fruits")

SECOND DIVISION, *MOED* ("SET FEASTS")
Shabbath ("The Sabbath")
Erubin ("The Fusion of Sabbath Limits")
Pesahim ("Feast of Passover")
Shekalim ("The Shekel Dues")
Yoma ("The Day of Atonement")
Sukkah ("The Feast of Tabernacles")
Yom Tob or Betzah ("Festival-days")
Rosh ha-Shanah ("Feast of the New Year")
Taanith ("Days of Fasting")
Megillah ("The Scroll of Esther")
Moed Katan ("Mid-Festival Days")
Hagigah ("The Festal Offering")

THIRD DIVISION, *NASHIM* ("WOMEN")
Yebamoth ("Sisters-in-law")
Ketuboth ("Marriage Deeds")
Nedarim ("Vows")
Nazir ("The Nazarite Vow")
Sotah ("The Suspected Adulteress")
Gittin ("Bills of Divorce")
Kiddushin ("Betrothels")

FOURTH DIVISION, *NEZIKIN* ("DAMAGES")
Baba Kamma ("The First Gate")
Baba Metzia ("The Middle Gate")
Baba Bathra ("The Last Gate")
Sanhedrin ("The Sanhedrin")
Makkoth ("Stripes")
Shebuoth ("Oaths")
Eduyoth ("Testimonies")
Abodah Zarah ("Idolatry")
Aboth ("The Fathers")
Horayoth ("Instructions")

FIFTH DIVISION, *KODASHIM* ("HALLOWED THINGS")
Zebahim ("Animal-offerings")
Menahoth ("Meal-offerings")
Hullin ("Animals killed for food")
Bekhoroth ("Firstlings")
Arakhin ("Vows of Valuation")
Temurah ("The Substituted Offering")
Kerithoth ("Extirpation")
Meilah ("Sacrilege")
Tamid ("Daily Whole-offering")
Middoth ("Measurements")
Kinnim ("The Bird-offerings")

SIXTH DIVISION, *TOHOROTH* ("CLEANLINESS")
Kelim ("Vessels")
Oholoth ("Tents")
Negaim ("Leprosy-signs")
Parah ("Red Heifer")
Tohoroth ("Cleanliness")
Mikwaoth ("Immersion-pools")
Niddah ("The Menstruant")
Makshirin ("The Predisposers")
Zabim ("They that suffer a flux")
Tebul Yom ("He that immersed himself that day")
Yadaim ("Hands")
Uktzin ("Stalks")

D. The Home

The importance of the home was recognized by the Jews and their Greco-Roman neighbors, although for different reasons. The Greco-Roman household was considered a very important social and economic institution. Although the economic dimension of the Jewish household was also important, this was not considered its major function. Owing to the command in Deut 6:7–10, the Jews recognized the home as a major place for religious instruction. This passage, popularly known among the Jews as the *Shema* (the term is taken from the first Hebrew word of the passage, "*Hear*, O Israel . . ."), was cited often among the Jews as a call to remember who they were and what God required of them: to keep his commands not only in social contacts and at work but also in the home. In conjunction with important religious instruction, the home was also the place for fulfillment of certain religious rituals, such as circumcision and the observance of the Passover meal, in which the Jews celebrated their freedom from bondage in Egypt. In a real sense, the faith of Israel was tied to what happened at home. Their religious faith was observed not only in the temple but also in the home.

E. The Temple

The temple that was visited by Jesus was begun by Herod the Great (20–19 B.C.) but was not yet completed during the time of Jesus' ministry (John 2:20). It was the pride of Israel and, as Stephen saw in Acts 7, the Jews did not tolerate criticism of it. Many Jews living in Palestine in the time of Jesus believed strongly in the need for the sacrificial system, in which the blood of animals was taken into the temple as an offering to God for the forgiveness of sins as well as for thanksgiving. This practice was believed to be in keeping with the admonitions of Deut 12:5–14. The temple was clergy-oriented in that the priests alone could offer to God the sacrifices of the people in the temple. All Jews living within twenty miles of the temple were expected to come there at least three times a year. Many of the more affluent Jews visited it from great distances (see, e.g., Acts 2:5–11; 8:27–28).

The temple and the chief priests constituted not only the religious center of Palestinian Judaism but also its political and symbolic center. The three events that all Jewish males in Palestine were expected to attend at the temple in Jerusalem were the celebration of Passover, the Festival of Weeks, and the Festival of Booths. Public prayers and services in the temple required the functioning of both priests and Levites—a lower class of priest involved in temple worship. The sacrifices performed in the temple demonstrated the faith of the participants, affirmation of their covenant with God, and their thanksgiving to God.

The temple also had a military significance. The temple that Herod built, like those of Solomon and Zerubbabel, was also a strong military fortification—indeed the strongest military fortification in Jerusalem. The Romans had troops stationed next to it in the Antonia Fortress (which Herod the Great built to honor Mark Antony) in order to keep order and to neutralize the temple's military potential. Within the temple area, the administrative, legislative, economic, and judicial authorities of Judea also met and decided matters related to the total life of the people. It was not only the place for the collection of tithes but also the center for tax collection of all Judea and for teaching related to the law and traditions of Judaism. The temple was the center for the administration of justice in the land. Jerusalem and the temple "bore the burden and potential of Israel's history and tradition. . . . The symbolic center and apocalyptic hopes, the stability of the social order and revolutionary potential of the people freed from Egypt long ago all rested on Jerusalem and in the Temple."[19]

F. The Synagogue

The origins of the synagogue are obscure. Although it is believed by many scholars to have developed in Babylon during the time of the Jewish captivity (ca. 586–532 B.C.), its origins (as noted above) were probably during the time of the Hasmoneans in the second century B.C.[20] The synagogue (Gk. συναγωγή, *synagōgē*, "assembly") was a lay-oriented movement comprising at least ten Jewish men (women and children were welcome to attend, but were not allowed to sit in the same location as the men). Some scholars believe that one of the earlier designations for the synagogue was προσευχή (*proseuchē*, ["house of] prayer"), a term also employed by Jews in Egypt.[21] Other scholars, however, make a distinction between the function of the "house of prayer" and the synagogue (cf. Acts 16:13, where it is unclear whether the "place of prayer" is a synagogue; in Mark 11:17 Jesus said that the temple was a "house of prayer"). The service carried on in the synagogue included primarily the offering of prayers, the reading of Scriptures, the exposition of the Scriptures if someone present was capable of teaching them (see Luke 4:16–22), and the singing of hymns. The synagogue was also the place of organized charity and hospitality, as well as a place of instruction, in which one would receive education in the Scriptures and in their applicability to life. In the time of Jesus there were synagogues all over the Roman Empire including the east. This institution was especially meaningful to the many hundreds of thousands of Jews who were unable to get to Jerusalem to visit the temple. The synagogue was also quite popular in Palestine itself. On the basis of documentary evidence (archaeological evidence is very scarce), it is thought that Jerusalem alone had more than sixty synagogues in the first century A.D., though it is not clear how many of these had buildings specifically set aside only for that purpose. So far, less than a handful of synagogues dating to the first century A.D. have been found by archaeologists in Israel. Two of these are quite small (at the Herodium and at Masada), able to seat comfortably only about fifty at most. This may be typical of the others. A greater number of synagogues, such as the large one at Capernaum and the one at Sardis, date to the second and third centuries A.D.[22] Although there were many synagogues in the Diaspora, most of those in Palestine in the first century apparently were in public buildings that functioned as the center of civic life; in some cases, they were the homes of the wealthiest persons in the area.

After the destruction of Jerusalem in A.D. 70 the synagogue became the primary place of Jewish worship even in Palestine. In the book of Acts it is apparent that the early Christian church in Jerusalem was organized after the typical pattern of the synagogue, with a body of elders and overseers. Early Christian worship also followed the basic pattern of worship in the synagogue, and some Christians may have used the term "synagogue" for their gathering. James 2:2 uses συναγωγή (*synagōgē*) for

a Christian gathering, and Lucian (*Peregr.* 11) calls the Christian assembly a synagogue when he uses the term ξυναγωγεύς (*xynagōgeus*).

G. Conversion to Judaism

Judaism apparently was appealing to many in the Greco-Roman world, especially because of its strong focus on monotheism, its high ethical standards, its nonsacrificial worship (apart from the temple), its possession of an ancient and inspired written revelation of the will of God, and the social cohesiveness of the Jewish community. That it had such appeal is somewhat surprising, since first-century Judaism, while welcoming proselytes, apparently did not have what might be considered an aggressive "missionary" effort in the Greco-Roman world.[23] It is fair to say that there were probably more people attracted to Judaism than actually converted. To convert to Judaism was to join the Jewish community. More specifically, it meant circumcision for the males, baptism with several witnesses, acceptance of the Jewish law, and, before A.D. 70, the making of an offering in the temple. Because of the general disgust among first-century Gentiles with the practice of circumcision (it was considered bodily mutilation), most converts to Judaism were women and children. Those who accepted the basic tenets of Judaism but rejected the practice of circumcision were apparently known as "Godfearers"[24] and were generally treated well by the Jews. Many Jews, however, were not in favor of Gentile converts and rejected them as part of the social life of the Jewish community. Priests could not marry a Gentile convert and, of the two major schools of interpretation, Shammai and Hillel, only Hillel had a positive attitude toward Gentile converts. Those Gentiles who practiced the seven "Noachic commandments"[25] were believed by the Jews to have a share in the life to come. Conversions to Judaism among Gentiles is well attested not only in Jewish literature but also in the NT (see Matt 23:15) and in non-Jewish and Christian literature (see the discussion on the attractiveness of Judaism in ch. 7, below).

H. Apocalypses and Messiahs

From the mid-second century B.C., many social-reform movements arose in Palestine in response to persecutions, and later to the Roman occupation (43 B.C.) and heavy taxation. Beginning with Seleucid rule of Palestine in the second century B.C. and continuing throughout Roman domination, especially after the destruction of Jerusalem and the outbreaks of persecution of the Christians, there were many movements offering hope to those people who were faithful to God. One kind of literature coming out of this period was the apocalypse (lit., "revelation"). Some Greco-Roman literature had apocalyptic elements, but the genre was essentially an intertestamental Jewish literary form. Usually the author reported a vision from God, interpreted to a famous figure of the past by an angel, which told of God's overcoming the evil within the land and of political and social reform in which the righteous would prevail over their wicked oppressors (e.g., *1 Enoch; 2 Baruch*). These apocalypses encouraged the faithful in their obedience to God and God's covenant. The language is often heavily symbolic—perhaps to help the writer avoid persecution—and designed to encourage the faithful to have confidence in God's power and justice.

Some scholars today deny that this stream of religious piety also influenced Jesus and was incorporated by him in his message to the people of his day (see Mark 13). It was certainly a factor, however, in the eschatological beliefs of many of Jesus' followers (see 1 Thess 4:13–5:11; 2 Tim 3:1–9; 2 Peter 2–3)[26] and also the belief of John the Baptist before him (all four canonical Gospels indicate that John was preparing his hearers for the imminent coming of the kingdom of God). Jesus' ministry began in the context of John's ministry, and John had a significant influence on Jesus' preaching (Mark 1:9, 14–15). The book of Revelation, which makes use of the imagery of Daniel among other works, has many examples of apocalyptic visionary language. All of the Gospels also place some of this language on the lips of Jesus (Mark 13; Matt 24; Luke 21; John 5:25–28). Through the mid–second century, this literature played a significant role in other segments of Judaism in Palestine. The apocalyptic writings were normally anonymous revelations of hidden knowledge concerning the end of history. In the OT, examples appear in Daniel, Zech 1–8, Ezekiel, and Isa 24–27. Ferguson observes that although there was no "manual of style" for apocalypses, most followed one of three basic forms: a farewell

discourse, a predictive discourse, or an account of a vision.[27] Often the message is pessimistic about history and sees that the only hope for the faithful is an intervention of God in human affairs at the end of the age. All history is moving toward a climax expected to be imminent, and hope for the righteous is only in God and in the beyond, that is, after God has intervened in history.

Just as apocalyptic literature developed, so did the understanding of "messiah" (Heb. *meshiach*, lit., "anointed," "one who is anointed").[28] In the OT, kings and high priests were anointed as they began office (e.g., David in 1 Sam 16:12–13). When the Davidic kingdom had ceased, the term took on new meaning and increasingly began to refer to the one who would restore the kingdom to Israel (2 Sam 7:10–17). Even Cyrus the Persian king, who was instrumental in the return of the Jews to Palestine, is called a "messiah" (Isa 45:1). Although the members of the Qumran community used the term in reference to the one who would restore the Davidic kingdom, they also spoke of a priestly "messiah of Aaron."[29] In the first century A.D., for the Christians and most of Pharisaic Judaism, the Messiah was a Davidic messiah who would restore the kingdom to Israel.

In the period from around the birth of Jesus to the early second century A.D., messianic claimants included (1) Judas, son of the bandit leader Hezekiah in Galilee (4 B.C.); (2) Simon, a Herodian slave living in Perea (4 B.C.); (3) Athronges, a shepherd living in Judea (4 B.C.); (4) Menahem, an inhabitant of Galilee and grandson of Judas the Galilean (A.D. 66); (5) Simon, son of Gioras (A.D. 68–70); and (6) Simeon bar Kokhba, also known as Simeon bar Koziba, who (as noted above) led a revolt against the Roman occupation of Palestine in A.D. 132–135.[30] Like others before him, Jesus was recognized by some as a messiah when he began his ministry in the region of Galilee (see ch. 5, sec. 2, below). This was a region that had been conquered by the Romans and was sternly ruled by a Jewish aristocracy answerable to Rome, a region that suffered heavy taxation with no avenue of appeal for the people and with no possibility of control over their land or destiny. Jesus' call for renewal of society and the reversal of social order made him very popular, especially in this region, but, at the same time, a very real threat to those who tried to keep the residents of Galilee in their hopeless condition. Since 90 percent of the population was involved with farming and since taxes on the farm ranged from 30 to 70 percent of the produce, it is easy to understand the process by which many farmers lost their farms and became tenant farmers or daily workers going to the marketplace in the hope of finding work for the day (Matt 20:1–16). Apocalyptic and messianic views were understandably popular in the first century, especially in those areas of Palestine most oppressed.[31]

I. Primary Jewish Religious Sects

Apart from a general belief in Yahweh as the one true God who would send a messiah to establish his kingdom, as well as the recognition of the authority of the law of Moses for all Jews, there was little else upon which all the Jews of the first century A.D. agreed. Along with the priesthood, which was responsible for the oversight of the temple and the sacrificial system, there were several religious sects in Israel claiming to have a true understanding of the law of God and to be the proper interpreters of the way and the will of God. These included especially the Sadducees, the Pharisees, the Scribes, and the Essenes.[32] The same could be said of the Zealots, but they were more a group of political insurrectionists, motivated by religious beliefs, whose primary aim was to free the Jews from their bondage to the Romans under the yoke of heavy taxation. Our primary source for this taxonomy is Josephus (*Ant.* 18.11–25; *War* 2.119–166), but his work must always be used with care (see ch. 13, sec. 3, below).

1. The Sadducees

Essentially a wealthy priestly group, the Sadducees were made up mostly of aristocratic families. They were especially responsible for public order and cooperated with the Romans in order to insure that the Jewish sacrifices would not be interrupted. They have a poor reputation in the NT as well as in much other ancient Jewish literature, especially that of rabbinic Judaism. After the destruction of Jerusalem and its temple in A.D. 66–70, the Sadducees did not survive long in the religious life of Israel. The little that remains about them suggests the following.

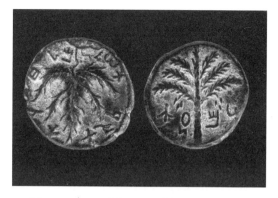

A bronze coin struck by Bar Kokhba in A.D. 134–135 and depicting a vine leaf and a tree. Hebrew inscriptions: "To the Freedom of Jerusalem" and, on the opposite side around the palm tree, "Simon." Photo © Rohr Productions. Used with permission.

a. Their Name. Although "Sadducee" is known in the Greek σαδδουκαῖος (*saddoukaios*), Hebrew *seduqi*, and Aramaic (through the Syriac *zadduqaya*), the origins of those who were called Sadducees in the NT are unknown. This is partly because at present there is no surviving literature from them—with the possible exception of Ecclesiastes, according to some recent scholarly opinion. Three explanations are proffered for their origin. First, it is possible, but unlikely, that their name is a derivative of the OT person Zadok (from the line of Aaron), whose sons were recognized to be the legitimate priests of Israel (Ezek 40:46). Both Ezra (Ezra 7:2) and the high priests of the postexilic and

A silver tetradrachm struck by Bar Kokhba in Judea in A.D. 135 and depicting the façade of the Jerusalem temple with four kinds of tabernacles. Inscriptions: "Simon" around tabernacles and, on the opposite side, "To the freedom of Jerusalem." Photo © Rohr Productions. Used with permission.

pre-Maccabean period (1 Chron 24:3; Hag 1:1; Sir 51:12) founded their reigns as priests after the order of Zadok. There is nothing in the sources to support this derivation, however, and there is sufficient reason to reject it because the Sadducees themselves reportedly supported the non-Zadokite priesthood of Annas (Acts 4:1; 5:17). Only the Essenes claimed to be the spiritual sons of Zadok (1QS V, 2; CD IV, 4ff.). Second, it is possible that the Sadducees' name is derived from the Hebrew term *saddiq* ("righteous"), but since many religious groups used that designation of themselves, it is difficult to substantiate this explanation. Third, and most likely, the name Sadducee came from the term *sadduqim*, which is a Hebraization of the Greek word σύνδικοι *(syndikoi)*, meaning "members of the council." This is more in keeping with the role assigned to the Sadducees in the NT. Still, no strong case can be made for any of these options.

b. Their Beliefs and Scriptures. Religiously, the Sadducees were both conservative and traditional. They cooperated with the Romans for pragmatic reasons because by doing so they were allowed to keep the sacrificial system going in Israel; but they, like most other Jews, despised the Romans for occupying their homeland. Not much is known about their religious beliefs, but the traditional view is that they only recognized the law of Moses as authoritative Scripture, that is, the Pentateuch or the Torah. Since a belief in the resurrection from the dead is not clearly supported in the Torah, the Sadducees rejected this popular belief, as well as the messianic beliefs of many Jews in the first century A.D. The debate between the Pharisees and the Sadducees when Paul was arrested in the temple area (Acts 23:6–10) is understandable in this light.

Was the biblical canon of the Sadducees really different from that of other forms of Judaism? A number of scholars have recently argued that there was no essential difference between the Sadducees and the Pharisees and even the Essenes in this regard. F. F. Bruce, for example, disagrees with the traditional view, claiming that the notion of a more limited Sadducee biblical canon comes from a common misunderstanding of Josephus's references to the Sadducees, in which he claims that they "admit no observance at all apart from the laws" (*Ant.* 18.16). This has usually been taken to mean that only the law of Moses was sacred to the Sadducees

and that they excluded all other authoritative writings accepted by the Pharisees. Bruce claims instead that the passage in Josephus was in fact only a reference to their rejection of the oral traditions of the Jews, not the Prophets and the Writings.[33] The full text in Josephus reads:

> The Sadducees hold that the soul perishes along with the body. They own no observance of any sort apart from the laws; in fact, they reckon it a virtue to dispute with the teachers of the path of wisdom that they pursue. There are but few men to whom this doctrine has been made known, but these are practically nothing, however. For whenever they assume some office, though they submit unwillingly and perforce, yet submit they do to the formulas of the Pharisees, since otherwise the masses would not tolerate them. (Josephus, *Ant.* 18.16–17 [Feldman, LCL])

Bruce also cites another passage that, he claims, makes clear that Josephus intended in the above text only the oral traditions of the Pharisees and not the Prophets and the Writings:

> For the present I wish merely to explain that the Pharisees had passed on to the people certain regulations handed down by former generations and not recorded in the Laws of Moses, for which reasons they are rejected by the Sadducaean group, who hold that only those regulations should be considered valid which were written down (in Scripture) and that those which had been handed down by former generations need not be observed. (Josephus, *Ant.* 13.297 [Marcus, LCL])

Based on this text alone, however, the Sadducees could have rejected the Prophets, the Writings, *and* the oral traditions of the Jews. This seems to be a more reasonable conclusion, especially in light of the fact that their rejection of belief in the resurrection is well established and it would be difficult to maintain that such books as Isaiah, Ezekiel, and Daniel are a part of the Sadducees' canon when they speak against the notion of resurrection from the dead. (See, e.g., Isa 26:19, Ezek 37:4–14, and Dan 12:2.)[34]

What is more important in deciding the matter is Jesus' argument against the Sadducees' denial of the resurrection in Matt 22:23–33 (see also Mark 12:18–27). It is not based on those books (Isaiah, Ezekiel, and Daniel) that have been thought clearest on the subject, as would be expected if the Sadducees accepted them as Scripture. He appeals instead to the law of Moses (Exod 3:6). This also fits best with the obvious implications of the passage in

Acts 23:6–10, that the Sadducees rejected the notion of the resurrection from the dead:

> When Paul noticed that some were Sadducees and others were Pharisees, he called out in the council, "Brothers, I am a Pharisee, a son of Pharisees. I am on trial concerning the hope of the resurrection of the dead." When he said this, a dissension began between the Pharisees and the Sadducees, and the assembly was divided. (The Sadducees say that there is no resurrection, or angel, or spirit; but the Pharisees acknowledge all three.) Then a great clamor arose, and certain scribes of the Pharisees' group stood up and contended, "We find nothing wrong with this man. What if a spirit or an angel has spoken to him?" When the dissension became violent, the tribune, fearing that they would tear Paul to pieces, ordered the soldiers to go down, take him by force, and bring him into the barracks.

For some time scholars argued that Ecclesiastes was a Sadducee book, and that may well be, but there is no other surviving material from them to suggest what their view of the biblical canon was. Josephus, the comments from Jesus in Matt 22:23–33, and the passage in Acts 23:6–10 are still the most important sources for deciding the issue. Supporting this conclusion are Origen (*Cels.* 1.49) and Jerome (*Comm. Matt.* 22:31ff.), both of whom agree that the Sadducees accepted only the law of Moses as Scripture. They may have depended on Josephus for their information, as Bruce claims,[35] though this is not certain. But both writers also had independent access to informed Jews in their own communities.[36]

c. Their Position in Israel. From A.D. 6, when Judea became a Roman province, until A.D. 66, when the Zealots seized power in Jerusalem, the high priests were regularly selected from among wealthy Saducean families. These families dominated the Sanhedrin ("body of elders"), which was the city council, or *gerousia*, of Jerusalem in the time of Jesus. (See Matt 21:45; John 7:32; Mark 14:53; Luke 22:2; Acts 4:5, 23; 22:30 for references to their activities.)

d. Christianity and the Sadducees. There is no evidence that the Christian message ever had much effect upon the Sadducees. They were very active in opposing the Christian message and in persecuting the Christians, as the above references show. The intensity of their persecution may also have stemmed from the fact that if Christianity had been adopted, there would have begun a significant new social reform that would have called into question their prestige and power, no doubt creating social unrest. An examination of the Beatitudes in Matt 5:3–12, with its transposition of social values, indicates this. Also, Christianity could not be separated from its strong belief in the resurrection from the dead (1 Cor 15:12–22), which was soundly rejected by the Sadducees.

2. The Pharisees

In the NT the Pharisees, like the Sadducees, are typically represented unfavorably. Seeing them depicted as the wicked antagonists of Jesus and as strongly legalistic in their orientation, most Christians have had very little good to say about them. In Matthew, for instance, they are seen as arrogant, treacherous, and fundamentally hypocritical. For example, John the Baptist makes scathing comments about the Pharisees in Matt 3:7 ("you brood of vipers"), and Jesus describes them in Matt 23:27 as "whitewashed tombs." Paul does not condemn them as such and even claims to have been a Pharisee (Phil 3:5), but the Gospels generally present a negative picture of them.

A cautionary note should be added here that the Pharisees contemporary with Matthew, who may have written his Gospel as late as ca. A.D. 80–85, may not have been the same as those who lived during Jesus' lifetime. Matthew's Gospel was probably written primarily for a Jewish-Christian community, possibly somewhere in the area of Syria (Antioch?), which seems to have been locked in a struggle with other Jews over the question of which group was more faithful to the law. In other words, was the more faithful Jew who best fulfilled the righteousness promised by the law the one who accepted Jesus as Messiah, or was it the one who rejected him as God's Messiah? Matthew claims that Jesus did not reject the law but offered a "fuller righteousness" than was offered in the law alone. This is seen, for example, in the Sermon on the Mount in Matt 5–7, especially in the sayings of Jesus that begin with "You have heard that it was said. . . . But I say to you" (5:21, 27, 31, 33, 38, 43). This theme is also combined with a derogatory comment about the Pharisees when Jesus says, "unless your righteousness exceeds that of the . . . Pharisees" (5:20). This perspective on righteousness is also the reason for Jesus' baptism in Matt

3:13–15. Matthew apparently was convinced that those who followed Jesus were more faithful Jews than those who rejected him, especially the Pharisees (see ch. 8, below, on the Gospels and Acts).

Much of the NT's picture of the Jews, and the Pharisees in particular, may have been shaped by circumstances shortly before the persecution of the Christians in Palestine in A.D. 62–64, which led many Christians to move northeast from Jerusalem to Pella. Events just before the destruction of Jerusalem in A.D. 70 had considerable impact on the view that Matthew presents of the Pharisees. As a Jewish Christian, he was also competing with the Jewish traditions near the end of the first century, when the Jews themselves who survived the events of A.D. 70 were seeking to reestablish their identity in light of the devastating loss of Jerusalem, the temple, and its sacrifices (see ch. 8, below). Paul himself never speaks ill of the Pharisees in particular but of the Jews in general who rejected Jesus as their Messiah and persecuted the Christians (1 Thess 2:14–16). Most of the criticisms against the Pharisees, especially in the Gospels of Matthew and Luke, were probably written after the experiences of the 60s, when persecution of the Christians was growing in various pockets of the Roman Empire (Rev 2:9), but especially in Palestine. The term "Jew" is probably not the equivalent of "Pharisee" in John's and Paul's writings, even though it may be so in Matthew's Gospel.

a. Characteristics. The Pharisees were apparently the most influential religious-renewal sect in Palestine in the time of Jesus, attracting both Jews and Gentiles from inside and outside Palestine with their religious teachings. Their influence, however, declined among non-Jews after the destruction of Jerusalem and almost completely after the Bar Kokhba rebellion in A.D. 135.

Unlike the Sadducees, the Pharisees were neither doctrinal nor biblical fundamentalists, nor were they priestly aristocrats anxious to maintain the status quo. They were open to the development of law and doctrine, and they argued that temple purity was not to be reserved for priests alone but that such religious purity before God was for all Jews in everyday life. They believed that holiness was practical and that it applied to all spheres of life, for instance, at work, at rest, and in all human relations. They did not deny the validity and importance of temple worship, however. Indeed, it is probable that the movement was begun by priests in the second century B.C. who rejected the Hasmonean dynasty's combination of priesthood with kingly power and were dissatisfied with what they believed was the Hasmonean dynasty's compromising of the will of God.

In the NT era the Pharisaic movement was made up primarily of laypeople. The Pharisees were especially popular among members of the emerging class of artisans and merchants of Palestine, but also among the Diaspora (Jews living outside Palestine) who benefited from the Pax Romana (Roman peace) begun in the reign of Caesar Augustus. The Apostle Paul, for instance, was a Pharisee before his conversion and an artisan (tentmaker) who was born in the Diaspora—his home was in Tarsus, a hellenized city and Roman colony, which gave to him the very highly prized Roman citizenship (see ch. 9, below, for more detailed discussion).

The message of the Pharisees was especially appealing to urban dwellers, who no longer depended on the agrarian (farming) lifestyle that was so much emphasized in the festivals of the temple cult. Passover, Pentecost, and the Feast of Tabernacles were based largely on the lifestyles of those who tended flocks or farmed. Because the Pharisees were more flexible in their understanding of the significance of the law and the temple, they were sometimes branded as a liberal movement. Their collection of sacred and authoritative Scriptures was apparently considerably larger than that of their more conservative counterparts, the Sadducees. The Pharisaic Scriptures in common use before the separation of Christians from the practice of Judaism, at least as it existed in Palestine in A.D. 62, were probably very similar to the recognized collection of Scriptures for the first Christians. It included most of what we now call the OT and probably some, if not most, of what we identify as the apocryphal and pseudepigraphal literature. As will be discussed later, the collection at that time was ill defined for Judaism—and therefore also for early Christianity, since Christianity drew heavily upon the common views of the Judaisms in Palestine before its complete separation from Judaism in the late first or early second century A.D.

The Pharisees were unenthusiastic about the Romans, but they were willing to tolerate them so long as their own religious practices were not affected. There is no clear evidence that they supported the insurrectionist activities of the Zealots, nor did they advise their people to withdraw from society, as some of the Essenes did. They were not a monastic movement. The Pharisees tried to preserve their Jewish religious identity but, at the same time, attempted to respond to the cultural challenge posed by Hellenism, especially as it affected the middle class. The Pharisees exerted their influence primarily in the synagogues of the towns and villages, though for a brief time during the reign of Queen Salome Alexandra (76–67 B.C.), they had also held considerable political power and exerted it often with the same intensity with which many of their opponents earlier had employed it against them. They wanted to apply the laws that originally applied only to the priests to everyone, thereby making the whole nation obedient to their version of the law.

b. Schools of Interpretation. The Pharisees emphasized careful interpretation of the law. They believed that the law had essentially two forms: (1) that which was written down and (2) that which was handed down by word of mouth (oral tradition). Jesus was severely critical of the Pharisees in regard to their oral traditions, some of which he believed were contrary to the law of God (Mark 7:1–23). The Pharisees, like the Essenes and Sadducees, also believed that they alone rightly interpreted the Scriptures. There were two major schools of interpretation in the time of Jesus, centering around the work of two famous teachers whose careers extended from around 30 B.C. to A.D. 10. The first of these teachers of the law was Shammai, who was conservative in his outlook and tended to be somewhat rigid. His teaching on divorce is similar to the one Jesus adopted and taught in Matt 19:3–12. Shammai's teachings, which were Palestinian in orientation and focused on Jewish obedience to the law in terms of the temple and its sacrificial system, were dominant in Palestine until after the destruction of the temple in A.D. 70. The other famous teacher of the law was Hillel, who was more liberal in his understanding of the law and much less rigid. It is probable that he was raised in Babylon, or at least had early roots there, and so was less interested in the temple orientation of Shammai and more focused on the practical implications of the law. He taught that all of the requirements of the law were fulfilled in loving God

with all of one's heart and also loving one's neighbor. According to Matt 22:34–40, Jesus shared the same perspective on the law. As we would expect, when observance of the sacrificial system was no longer possible after the destruction of the temple, Hillel's teachings were more influential than those of Shammai, except for a brief period between A.D. 115–35. The more open teachings of Hillel became the primary theological perspective adopted by Jews after the destruction of Jerusalem, when they were seeking to discover how Judaism might continue without the temple and a sacrificial system.[37]

c. Christianity and the Pharisees. Christianity shared much with the Pharisees, including a call for social reform and beliefs in a coming messiah who would bring about the kingdom of God, in the resurrection of the dead, in rewards and punishments at the end of the ages, and in the existence of angels and demons. Jesus, however, seems to have understood that the crisis of Jewish identity in the first century could not be resolved through a renewal movement such as that proposed by the Pharisees. They had simply heightened or intensified the norms for fuller observance of the law, thereby hoping to satisfy the call of God to righteousness, but Jesus taught that only by a new relationship to God could a person finally satisfy the claims of God upon his or her life. The old forms of religion were not adequate to handle what God had prepared for his followers (Mark 2:21–22). Jesus also taught that everyone was a sinner and needed humbly to receive the grace and forgiveness of God; in turn, those who received these from God must also offer them to others (Matt 6:12–14; 18:21–35; Luke 18:9–14; John 3:3–18). He contrasted this with the self-righteousness of the Pharisees, who saw no need of repentance or forgiveness of sins and had little sympathy for those who did (Luke 18:9–14). Jesus also called for freedom from all laws or traditions that restrict the proper caring for human need (Mark 2:23–3:6) and called upon his hearers to love God with all their heart, to love their neighbors (Matt 22:34–40), even to love their enemies (Matt 5:43–48), and to abandon worldly securities (Mark 8:34–37). Pharisaic Judaism had a profound influence upon the early Christian community, but evidently a fair number of the Pharisees themselves later became Christians (Acts 15:5), the most famous being the Apostle Paul.[38]

3. The Scribes

a. Origins of the Term. The term "scribe" comes from the Hebrew *sofer,* which refers to a person who is able to "cipher" or write. From this notion came the idea of a secretary and eventually a scribe. In Jer 36:26, a scribe was an official who had charge of legal documents (see also Jer 32:12–15) and who had a special place in the royal palace. According to 2 Kgs 22:3–7, Shaphan the scribe appears to have been a minister of finance, and in Isa 36:3 (cf. 22:15), Shebna the scribe functioned like a secretary of state. In preexilic times (before 587 B.C.) the scribal office was generally a secular position without any special religious significance. Although there were no religious scribes as such before the time of the exile, still there were those scribes who were specialists in understanding and transcribing the law.

b. Scribes as "Doctors" of the law. The scribal function as a doctor or teacher of the law had its origins probably in the period of the exile and shortly thereafter, when the law became the center of all Jewish life. The scribes were seen as the wise men or men of understanding (see Dan 11:33–35; 12:3) by no later than 160–150 B.C. It was probably the scribes who were responsible for fixing the canon of Jewish Scriptures to be included in the Law around 500 B.C. and the Prophets sometime after 200 B.C. The third category of the Hebrew Scriptures, the Writings, was more precisely defined in the rabbinic tradition in the second to the fifth centuries A.D. During the intertestamental period, the scribes were the ones who gathered together Israel's sacred literature, interpreted it, and copied it. It was probably Ezra the scribe who gave the impetus for the scribes to become a distinctive and influential class of teachers and interpreters of the law (Ezra 7:6; Neh 8:1, 4, 9, 13; 12:26, 36).

c. Scribes in the New Testament. In the NT, scribes (γραμματεῖς, *grammateis*) are the same as the teachers of the law (διδάσκαλοι τοῦ νόμου, *didaskaloi tou nomou*) and the lawyers (νομικοί, *nomikoi*) (cf. Luke 2:46; 5:17; 7:30). They are most often listed in conjunction with the Pharisees in the Gospels, although it appears that they came from the families of the priests and Levites (cf. 1 Chron 2:55). It is not surprising that scribes are most often associated with Pharisees, since Pharisees were devoted to the keeping of the law and the scribes were its primary interpreters. In the time of the Seleucid hellenizing of Israel, the scribes, called a "synagogue of the scribes," were the religious backbone of the resistance movement (see 1 Macc 7:11–17; cf. 2:42, where there is a possible link with the Hasideans). In Matt 23:34, Jesus mentions the scribes, along with the prophets and wise men, as holy men sent to Israel by God but rejected by the people. This indicates their prominent religious standing in the time of Jesus. According to Matt 7:28–29, however, the scribes, even though they were teachers of the law, apparently had little or no authority.

Mark 2:16, Luke 5:30, and Acts 23:9 speak of the "scribes of the Pharisees" (but cf. Mark 7:5; Matt 15:1), which suggests that there may have been several schools of scribes, some related to the Pharisees.[39] It is interesting that Matthew indicates that it was the high priest, Caiaphas, the chief priests, and the elders who gathered together to condemn Jesus (Matt 26:3–4), but the earlier writer Mark says that the scribes were also present at the trial (Mark 15:1). Luke adds that it was the chief priests, the assembly of the elders, and the scribes who consulted at Jesus' trial (22:66). Luke later says that it was the chief priests and the scribes who accused Jesus (23:10), but in 23:13–17 concludes that it was the chief priests and the "rulers" who brought Jesus before Pilate and called for his crucifixion. It is possible that some scribes served in the party of the Pharisees in Jerusalem and that some also served as part of the ruling class in the Sanhedrin of Jerusalem. According to Acts 5:27–34, for example, Gamaliel, who was a teacher of the law (a scribe) and a Pharisee, was also a member of the council. In this same vein, Josephus (ca. A.D. 85–90) speaks of "priestly scribes" (Ἱερογραμματεῖς, *hierogrammateis*) (*War* 6.291).

The main business of the scribes in the NT era was that of teaching, interpreting, and copying the law. They were the primary preservers of Judaism in the Greco-Roman period. Their authority was recognized everywhere in Palestine, but according to Jesus, they were not known for consistency in their behavior (cf. Matt 23:1–3). There are very few references to the scribes in rabbinic literature, and much about them remains obscure.[40]

4. The Zealots

Until recently, not much was known about the Zealots or whether they were an organized religious or political group during the time of Jesus. With the publication of Martin Hengel's foundational work, *The Zealots*,[41] however, more light has come to bear on this rather obscure group, which is mentioned only marginally in the NT. The name itself is probably derived from the story of Phinehas in Num 25:1–13, who took radical measures to purify the nation of Israel in its devotion to God and to prevent the anger of the Lord from falling upon the nation. He was praised by the Lord and given his "covenant of peace" because he was "zealous for his God and made atonement for the Israelites." According to 1 Macc 2:22–54, the story of Phinehas was a major part of the inspiration of Mattathias Hasmoneus, the priest of Modein who initiated the Maccabean conflict. The term may therefore represent those in Palestine during the time of Jesus who were zealous to purify the nation from its corruption brought on by Roman occupation, but it also reflects an eschatological perspective, the expectation of the violent overthrow of the Roman armies. Such individuals may have taken radical and even revolutionary measures against Rome, as in the case of Judas the Galilean in A.D. 6 (cf. Acts 5:37; Josephus, *Ant.* 18.4–10).[42] Mattathias Hasmoneus served as an example for the Zealotic movement, which became more organized in the early A.D. 60s, just before the siege of Jerusalem and the destruction of the temple (see Josephus, *War* 2.647–651; 4.158–161). Following the Roman occupation of Palestine in 63 B.C., the Zealots were those who opposed the Roman occupation and on many occasions took steps, including violence, to rid Palestine of the Roman presence. According to Josephus (*Ant.* 18.23), before the revolt against Rome in A.D. 66–70, an organized nationalistic party called the Zealots (a fourth religious party or "philosophy," with similarities to the Pharisees) emerged to challenge Rome's authority over Palestine, but it is not certain that Josephus's account is reliable. The uncertainty centers on his identification of Judas the Galilean as head of a movement (*Ant.* 18.9) and his blaming the war with Rome on a small revolutionary faction instead of acknowledging the Zealots as but one of many such factions in the war.

In Acts 21:20–21, there were some Jews who had become Christians and were "zealous for the law." The extent to which one demonstrated zealousness for the law could vary greatly. The most frightening of those zealous for the law were the *sicarii*, "assassins," who made vows to destroy anyone who they believed opposed the law. The group drew its name from the knives its members were known to conceal in their clothing. At public festivals they would kill community figures or celebrities who were under suspicion or who had violated the law. Their theology was probably Pharisaic, but this is not certain. They were zealous enough for the law, however, to be willing to lay down their lives for its preservation.

Whether Luke's reference to one of Jesus' disciples as "Simon the Zealot" (Luke 6:15; Acts 1:13) suggests a member of the later and more actively organized Zealotic movement is doubtful. If Simon had been a member of such a fanatical party, he apparently left it when he followed Jesus. The fact that he could serve alongside a tax collector, Levi (Mark 2:14), indicates that he underwent a radical change in his behavior as a result of his association with Jesus. His relation to such a party, however, is currently impossible to prove. The term "Zealot" may be an anachronism on Luke's part, but possibly also a reference to a loosely organized opposition to Rome even in Jesus' day. Far more difficult to substantiate is the view, based on a supposed parallel between Judas the Galilean (Acts 5:37) and Jesus, that Jesus was a member of such a party. Mark 12:17 suggests that Jesus was unwilling to so align himself. Further, there is nothing in the Gospels to indicate that Jesus ever advocated the overthrow of the Roman government, saw his kingdom as one in conflict with Rome, or raised an army to further his aims. Jesus' rejection of the use of power and his rebuke of his own disciples who may have considered such tactics (Mark 8:33; 10:39–40; Luke 24:21; Acts 1:6) also speak against this supposition. The strongest argument for the position that Jesus sympathized with the Zealots, which for some interpreters suggests that he was part of that movement, is the superscription placed over Jesus' head on the cross accusing him of being king of the Jews (Mark 15:26). The understanding here, of course, is that Jesus was an insurrectionist and was crucified for such activity. If the Romans had taken that accusation seriously, however, they would no doubt have rounded up Jesus' disciples after his death and tried to stop the activities of the church; such was not the case. On the other hand, Hengel has made a strong case that, despite some points of contact, the early church "represented the overcoming of the Zealots' attempt to bring about God's rule on earth by violence."[43] And as Rhoads observes, "No early Christian writing advocated armed revolution as a way of expressing devotion to God."[44]

The term "robbers" (λῃσταί, lēstai) was used to identify those who were crucified with Jesus (Matt 27:44; Mark 15:27). Josephus often uses the same Greek term for "revolutionaries" (Ant. 20.97–98; cf. 18.3–10; War 2.118), and Barabbas, whose place Jesus evidently took, was known as an insurrectionist (Mark 15:6–7). All of this may indicate that a group of organized revolutionaries was known in the time of Jesus; still, it is difficult to date an organized revolutionary party known as the Zealots that early, and even more difficult (if not impossible) to establish Jesus' participation in such a group. The one who invited his followers to turn the other cheek to those who did violence against them and to go an extra mile, giving what was asked of them (Matt 5:39–41), cannot reasonably have belonged to this kind of movement. It is also inaccurate to say that all who participated against Rome in the Jewish uprising in A.D. 66–70 were identified with such a party, since many Jews throughout Palestine participated in the ill-fated rebellion.

5. The Samaritans

a. Origins. Although the Samaritans are part of the wide range of diverse and well-known sects of Judaism in the first century, their earliest history is unclear. There are many negative comments about them in Jewish literature, especially in Josephus's writings but also in the Hebrew Scriptures (2 Kgs 17:24–41) and the rabbinic tradition of the second and following centuries A.D. The most common view used to be that they were the descendants of the tribes of northern Israel that had intermarried with the pagan population of Samaria after the Assyrian colonization of northern Palestine in the late eighth century B.C. From this perspective, which was a view perpetuated by Josephus, the Samaritans had their origins in the corrupt and syncretistic community of northern Palestine that became known as Samaria (Josephus, Ant. 9.277–291). The rabbinic traditions, which are less polemical than

Josephus, mention the Samaritans in the Talmud (Qidd. 76a; Ber. 47b; Giṭṭ. 10a; Ḥul. 4a, 6a; Ned. 31a; Soṭa 33b; Sanh. 90b). But today very few scholars give significant weight to Josephus's account of Samaritan origins; instead, most distinguish between "Samaritans" as a religious party and "Samarians" who were residents of Samaria.

The religious sect of the Samaritans probably originated in postexilic times during a schism with the Jewish priests in Jerusalem. Josephus speaks of disenfranchised Jewish priests going over to the Samaritans who established a rival sanctuary on Mount Gerizim during the days of Alexander the Great (330–325 B.C.). He also claims that Alexander the Great granted permission to Sanballat II to build the temple there (Josephus, Ant. 11.297–347). Most scholars, with some reservations, agree today that the beginnings of the Samaritan sect we read about in the NT came from this time. The rift over the place of worship is highlighted in John 4:19–26 in the story of the woman at the well (see also Luke 17:16; John 8:48). The extent to which the Samaritans developed their religious ideas independently of the Jews in the south is not clear; what is certain in the NT is that they were looked upon as foreigners and with distaste among the Jews. The point of Jesus' parable about the "good" Samaritan (Luke 10:25–37) may have been to shame the priests and Levites with the fact that even the most despised individuals can befriend those in need and fulfill God's will toward their neighbors, whereas those with religious positions who ignore human need violate God's law to love one's neighbor.

The Samaritans probably emerged as a distinct religious group at the same time other religious sects were beginning to distinguish themselves from the primary religious leadership and traditions in Jerusalem. This occurred during the middle of the second century B.C., although the Samaritans' origins are certainly prior to that. The earliest references to this religious group come from the second century B.C. in the writings of Ben Sira (Sir 50:25–26) (ca. 180 B.C.) and later in 2 Macc 5–6 (as well as in the T. Levi 5–7 and Jub. 30).

The Samaritans revered the law and Moses but chose instead to worship on Mount Gerizim on the basis of their version of Deut 27:4, which may have been more accurate than the Masoretic Text of today's Hebrew Bible. The Samaritans believed that Ezra corrupted the Pentateuch and changed Gerizim to Ebal in Deut 27:4. For them, Gerizim was where Abel built his altar and where Abraham was willing to sacrifice Isaac. They also taught that Mount Gerizim was the "navel" of the universe.[45]

In the second century B.C. (ca. 129/128), John Hyrcanus of the Hasmonean dynasty in Jerusalem destroyed the Samaritan temple on Mount Gerizim, but this did not affect the Samaritans' reverence for the mountain as their true place of worship. The Samaritans had built an altar to Yahweh at Shechem near Mount Ebal and their temple on nearby Mount Gerizim. Their reverence for worship there seems to have been one of the most distinguishing characteristics of their religious faith. Many of these individuals apparently embraced the Christian faith as a result of the early Christian mission (Acts 8:4–25).

b. Their Identity. The Samaritans, who today comprise a small group of only around five hundred individuals, were a strict Law-observing community who referred to themselves as the rightful heirs of the Israelite traditions. They had their own Samaritan Pentateuch, which they believed was more accurate than that of the Jews. One name they gave themselves was *samerim*, "keepers" (of the Law), which distinguished them from the other inhabitants of Samaria. Mostly, however, they preferred to call themselves Hebrews or Israelites, believing that they were the true descendants of Manasseh and Ephraim of the northern Israelite tribes. Along with the Sadducees, the Samaritans held to a much smaller biblical canon than did the Pharisees and most groups in Judaism, accepting only the law of Moses, and like the Sadducees, they rejected notions of resurrection from the dead. Like other Jewish sects in the first century, including the Christian community, they also shared a messianic-type theology that believed in the coming of the Taheb ("one who restores") as a fulfillment of Deut 18:18. The Restorer, they believed, would herald the day of God's judgment and reward, restore the temple on Mount Gerizim, and reinstate sacrifices. Finally, they believed that the heathen would be converted and at the Last Judgment the faithful would enter the Garden of Eden and the sinful would be delivered to the flames of judgment.

Like the Qumran covenanters (the Essenes), they rejected the Jerusalem priesthood and its temple and spoke of themselves as the true "sons of light." Also like them, they emphasized the divine

relationship to "word." There are obvious parallels here also with early Christianity, especially with the Gospel of John (1:1, 14), Stephen's speech in Acts 7, and possibly the audience of the book of Hebrews. The long list of heroes of the faith in Heb 11:1–31 comes from the Pentateuch and in 11:32–38 only summarily from other OT works. The Pentateuch was recognized as sacred by the Samaritans, and the list in Heb 11 is similar to the heroes found in the Samaritan documents. Their history shows that they were open to other religious influences, including Christianity and later even Islam. For example, they refer to God not only as Yahweh but also as Ela (similar to Heb. *Elohim* and Islamic *Allah*). Although they reverence the name of God, they, unlike the Jews, do not hesitate to speak the name of God, Yahweh.

6. The Essenes

Although the Essenes are not mentioned by name in the NT, their presence was certainly known in Palestine in the time of Jesus. They were known in Asia Minor between Colossae and Ephesus during Paul's and John's ministry and in Egypt during the early life of Jesus (Philo, *Contempl. Life* 3.25–28). There are similarities between what is known of the Essene community at Qumran and 2 Cor 6:14–7:1; some scholars call this passage a "post-Pauline interpolation," but others consider it the actual "first" letter of Paul to the Corinthians that is referred to in 1 Cor 5:9 (see ch. 10, below). There are also purported parallels in Essene literature with Paul's focus on "mystery," "flesh and spirit," "perfect," "truth," and "justification," as well as numerous parallels with the Gospel of John. For instance, John's focus on "sons of light" and "the spirit of truth" has parallels in the Qumran literature. It may also be possible that the heresy mentioned in Paul's letter to the Christians at Colossae was an Essene-type theology, but this is not certain (see ch. 10, below). These similarities may simply be a part of the shared characteristics of first-century Judaism.

a. Historical Background. It is possible that the Essenes' historical roots go back to the time when the Jews were in Babylon. An attractive theory is that the Essenes were an offshoot of the Hasidim ("pious ones," also called Hasideans) who helped the Maccabees overthrow the Seleucid dynasty's control of Palestine between 164 and 140 B.C. Like the Pharisees, they rejected the political priesthood of the Hasmonean dynasty, which took over the rule of Israel after several defeats of the Seleucids in Palestine. When the Hasidim saw that the Zadokite priesthood of the OT era had been forsaken by the Hasmoneans, they evidently were divided over what to do about it. The Pharisees (probably also a party of the Hasidim) decided to remain in the social life of Israel seeking to reform it, but some of the Essenes rejected that option and removed themselves to the desert to "prepare the way for the coming of the Lord," although we know from Josephus that some did remain involved in public life (*War* 2.120–161). The group that went to Qumran was but one sect of the larger body of Essenes, but unfortunately it is the only one of which we have firsthand awareness.

Their founder was apparently referred to as the Teacher of Righteousness, but his exact identity has been lost. This teacher, called a saint, was betrayed by a scoffer and persecuted by the Wicked Priest (CD I; 1QpHab I). The reference to a wicked priest may well have been an allusion to the Maccabean hero Jonathan, the son of Mattathias, who was very prominent in the revolution against the Seleucids. The founder of the Essene community may well have been a Zadokite who acted as priest in 152 B.C. but refused to serve under Jonathan (CD I, 4–12).

Ironically, the Qumran community suffered the same fate as befell Jerusalem with its despised temple and priesthood. In A.D. 68 or perhaps as late as A.D. 70, the Essenes at Qumran abandoned their settlement, which was destroyed by the Romans after already being partly destroyed by an earthquake in 31 B.C. It is possible that some or all of those at Qumran went south to Masada and joined with the Zealots who had taken control of that mountaintop fortress. The basis for this conjecture is that some of the writings found at Masada have only been found at one other location, Qumran.

b. Characteristics and Beliefs. Much could be said about this religious sect, but included here are some of the central themes in their writings. They saw themselves as the holy remnant of God whose purity of life outshone that of the "sons of darkness," the priesthood in Jerusalem that regulated temple worship. Their literature is rife with the language of apocalypticism, seen in the dualism found in the con-

A view of Cave 4 at Qumran and the site of the first discovery of scrolls near the ancient Essene community. Photo Lee M. McDonald.

trasts of the Teacher of Righteousness with the Wicked Priest, the sons of light with the sons of darkness, and the holy congregation with the company of Satan. The community awaited the dramatic intervention of God in history to end their suffering and to avenge their enemies. They expected an eschatological war or climactic battle in which their beliefs would be vindicated, their enemies crushed, and a new age ushered in. Finally, they tried to create an alternative temple community characterized by utter purity in desert camps that were far removed from the defiled presence of Jerusalem. Qumran is an example of this kind of community, but not the only one, as was noted above.

c. Parallels to Early Christianity. A number of parallels between the Christian community and the one at Qumran have led to wild speculation about Christianity's dependence on the group or its emergence from it, but all the parallels may be nothing more than what was commonly shared by the many Judaisms of the first century, of which the Essenes and the Christians were but two. The parallels are, nevertheless, worth mentioning, but this listing will be followed by some significant differences in section (d) below. (1) The Essenes had a strong focus on the "last days," an apocalyptic focus on end times and a dualistic emphasis on good versus evil (similar to the book of Revelation, Matt 24, Mark 13, Luke 21, and 2 Peter). (2) They believed in a coming messiah who would establish God's kingdom (Matt 6:10; Acts 1:6–7). (3) The Teacher of Righteousness and his followers represented the faithful remnant who went out into the wilderness to prepare the way of the Lord, as in Isaiah's prophecy (Isa 40:3). This is the very text referred to in the Synoptic Gospels when John the Baptist's ministry was looked upon as preparing the way for and introducing Jesus the Christ (Matt 3:3; Mark 1:1–4; Luke 3:2–6).[46] (4) Baptisms were very common in the Qumran community as ritual cleansings, but the act of baptism was significant only if it was the outward sign of a purified and humble soul within (1QS III, 1–12). This was true of both John the Baptist's practice of baptism (Matt 3:1–6) and that followed by the Christians in Acts (2:37–38). (5) The Essenes emphasized a common meal at which the priestly head of the theocracy and the Messiah of Israel would be present (1QS VI, 1–8). Some scholars have argued that the meal may have been viewed as quasi-sacrificial, in other words, a holy meal. The meal had an eschatological focus similar to the kingdom banquet mentioned by Jesus in Matt 8:11–12. (6) The Essenes believed that martyrdom was something to be desired. In Mark 8:34–35, Jesus emphasized the giving up of one's life for the sake of the gospel in order to be his disciple, and this view had an important impact on the developing church at the beginning of the early second century A.D., when Ignatius of Antioch desired martyrdom as a means of "getting to God." His example is not unlike the Qumran emphasis on martyrdom as something to be desired because it would bring justification to the martyr (1QS V, 6; IX, 3–5). (7) The Essenes gave up all property to the community and added a penalty for deceit in turning over the property. Although this is a voluntary act in the NT (Acts 4:32–37; 5:4) the practice was similar. The penalties at Qumran for holding some of the money back, however, were not as severe as one finds in the early church (Acts 5:5–6). (8) The Essenes often determined the will of God by casting lots. This reminds us of Acts 1:26, where lots were cast to determine the replacement of Judas Iscariot. (9) They were organized in a hierarchy, not unlike the churches in the late first century and afterwards, especially in Antioch of Syria and Asia Minor under the leadership of Ignatius, the bishop of Antioch. (10) Many of the writings that the residents of Qumran deemed sacred were also among the writings that most of early Christianity considered sacred. Besides the OT writings (all of the OT writings except Esther have been discovered at Qumran), other books have been found that played a role in the developing churches, such as *1 Enoch*

The descent through the Wadi Qumran. The Dead Sea is in the upper left. Photo Lee M. McDonald.

(see Jude 14, 15), *Assumption of Moses*, and a sizable collection of apocalyptic literature also alluded to in the NT and other early Christian literature. (11) The Essenes saw themselves as "holy ones" or "saints" who were separated unto God. In the NT these are common terms for Christians (Rom 1:7; 1 Cor 1:2; Phil 1:1; etc.), and Paul calls upon his hearers to come out from among the evil ones and be separate (2 Cor 6:17–18). (12) They spoke of "two ways" in their *Manual of Discipline*, which was built upon Deut 30:15. This same kind of exposition is found in the first six chapters of the early Christian document called the *Didache* (ca. A.D. 70–90) and in the second-century Christian document called the *Epistle of Barnabas* (ca. A.D. 130). It is also reminiscent of Jesus' speaking of two ways, one that leads to life and the other to destruction (Matt 7:13). In Acts 9:2; 19:9, 23; 22:4; 24:14, 22, the earliest name used for the followers of Jesus was "the Way." In the Qumran literature the believer chooses the right way of the two ways. In Acts 16:17; 18:25–26 there is also mention of the "way of salvation," "the Way of the Lord," and "the Way of God."

d. Differences between Early Christianity and the Essenes. Despite the many parallels between the two groups, there are also several significant differences between the Essenes at Qumran and the early Christians. (1) The early Christians believed that the "age to come" had already arrived in the events of the life, death, and resurrection of Jesus. The Essenes believed that this age was still to come. (2) Although the Christians believed that they would rule and reign with Christ in his kingdom, their response to this, unlike at Qumran, involved no organization for war or preparation for battle. The early church had no Masada. Unlike the Essenes, early Christians preached love for neighbor and enemy alike (Matt 5:43–48). (3) The Essenes were sectarian, believing that only their few chosen ones would make it into the kingdom of God, but Christians believed that their message was universal in scope and not limited to a select group of Jews. (4) The Essenes believed that the Scriptures had their primary fulfillment in their own community, whereas the Christians believed that they had their fulfillment in the life, death, and resurrection of Jesus. (5) Finally, Christianity was not a monastic religion (at least not at first!), nor a priestly religion, except in the broadest sense when it claimed the priesthood of all believers (1 Pet 2:5, 9). Nor did the earliest church regularly practice celibacy (1 Cor 9:5). Both of these aspects, however, were common in the Essene community.

e. The Qumran Literature. Among the various renewal movements in Palestine in the time of Jesus, only the community at Qumran produced a literature that sheds direct light on Judaism as it existed in the earliest decades of the first century. The Dead Sea Scrolls from the Qumran community on the northwestern side of the Dead Sea were mostly found in the late 1940s and 1950s and are thought to be products of an Essene religious sect at Qumran dating from approximately 200–150 B.C. to A.D. 70 (or A.D. 68, when they were threatened by the Romans). The manuscripts or scrolls, with fragments of about 600 works, were found in eleven caves near the Qumran community. Many of the manuscripts were wrapped in linen and placed in jars. It has been assumed that the scrolls were stored in the caves by the residents as the Romans

were advancing on their positions around A.D. 70, but this is not certain. Kahle has suggested that the documents were intentionally stored and hidden over a period of time in inaccessible places. According to him, the motive may have been that the community was on the verge of dying and so hid the documents to preserve them as long as possible. The caves have been numbered 1 through 11 and the various manuscripts are identified in part by their cave number. (Thus 1QS is a document designated S found in cave 1.) Although there most certainly were other Essene communities in existence in Palestine in the first century and probably in Alexandria and elsewhere, the Essene literature that has survived is that from the Qumran community (a copy of the *Damascus Document* [CD] was found in Cairo; see below). A large number of the documents discovered at Qumran have only recently been published, and their significance for the study of early Christianity and Judaism of the first century continues to emerge. The range of literature includes the following texts.[47]

(1) Canonical Old Testament Texts. With the unlikely exception of a small fragment of a manuscript that some have claimed is from the Gospel of Mark, no NT texts have been found at Qumran.[48] All of the OT books except Esther have been found at or near Qumran, some in a number of different versions. Copies and fragments of Isaiah amount to about twenty different manuscripts, and there are seventeen manuscripts of the Psalms.

(2) Sectarian Literature. What is most generally recognized as peculiarly Essene literature consists of nine different documents and various other fragments. See Table 3–1.

(3) Biblical Commentaries. The commentaries found at Qumran consist of passages from the OT texts accompanied by *pesharim*, literalistic and eschatological interpretations of the scriptural books in the light of the life and history of the community at Qumran. These constituted the true meaning of the OT texts in the eyes of the residents of Qumran.

(4) Late Jewish Apocryphal and Pseudepigraphical Works. Several apocryphal and pseudepigraphical writings have been found at Qumran. They include the Hebrew version of Sirach (ca. 180 B.C.), Tobit (190–170 B.C.), an Aramaic version of Tobit, a Greek version of the Epistle of Jeremiah (ca. 50 B.C.), *Jubilees* (150 B.C.), an Aramaic version of *Enoch* (ca. A.D. 1–10 but no date available for the original

form of *Enoch*), and the *Testaments of the Twelve Patriarchs* (pre–A.D. 70), all of which are of special interest because they indicate the theological outlook and "nonorthodox" tendencies in Palestine during early Christianity.

(5) The Significance of These Finds for Understanding the Development of the Old Testament Canon. All of the writings of the current OT canon except Esther were found at Qumran. The implication that many scholars draw from this is that the Qumran community had the same biblical canon as those in the rabbinic tradition of the second century A.D. Bruce, for instance, concludes that "it is probable, indeed, that by the beginning of the Christian era the Essenes (including the Qumran community) were in substantial agreement with the Pharisees and Sadducees about the limits of the Hebrew scripture."[49] Beckwith also argues that the presence of the OT canonical books at Qumran, save Esther, points to the acceptance of the same biblical canon as the one found in Pharisaic Judaism.[50] Parallels with Pharisaic Judaism in some of the books found at Qumran, however, do not support the conclusion that they utilized the same biblical canon. The Qumran texts include more than the OT canonical books, which suggests that their collection of sacred texts was considerably broader than the current OT biblical canon.

Yigael Yadin, for example, has argued convincingly that the *Temple Scroll* was venerated as the Essene Torah and held to be equal in importance to the traditional Torah.[51] He points out that the Tetragrammaton, the four letters YHWH that form the unpronounced name of God in the Hebrew Scriptures, is replaced in the Pentateuch with the personal pronouns "I" or "me." He cites an example from Num 30:3 in which the *Temple Scroll* states, "When a woman vows a vow *to me*," replacing the traditional Torah, which says instead, "when a woman vows a vow *to the Lord*."[52] His point is that the author wished to present the law as if it came directly from God himself rather than

A view from Cave 5 at Qumran with the Dead Sea in the background and the site of Cave 4 in the center. Photo Lee M. McDonald.

through Moses. Yadin also observes that a square Aramaic script is used in the *Temple Scroll* to write the name of God just as in the other biblical books, a further indication to him that this scroll was viewed canonically, or as sacred literature, by the people at Qumran. More important, however, is Yadin's observation that the scroll, though thirty feet long, was copied several times at Qumran, more times than the scroll of Isaiah. This leads him, among other reasons, to conclude that "the Temple Scroll was, for the Essenes, a holy canonical book on par, for them, with the other books of the Bible."[53]

There also existed at Qumran a common practice of altering and changing the biblical texts. This did not seem to them to violate any understanding of the sacredness of the texts they were examining. In the OT and the NT, as well as in the rabbinic tradition, there is a command against changing or altering the sacred text. For instance, Deut 4:2 commands: "You must neither add anything to what I command you nor take away anything from it, but keep the commandments of the LORD your God with which I am charging you." The command is repeated in Deut 12:32: "You must diligently observe everything that I command you; do not add to it or take anything from it." Finally, in Rev 22:18–19, the author employs the Deuteronomy tradition to establish the sacredness of his own work and commands his readers:

> I warn everyone who hears the words of the prophecy of this book: if anyone adds to them, God will add to that person the plagues described in this book; if anyone takes away from the words of the book of this prophecy, God will take away that person's share in the tree of life and in the holy city, which are described in this book.

The Essene community, however, changed and altered the sacred texts regularly. Silver has brought to our attention how the scribes at Qumran not only felt free to alter the order and wording of the Psalms, even to the point of adding the refrain "Praised be the Lord and praised be His name forever and ever" after each verse of Ps 145, but also changed the script, spelling, grammar, and content of the two scrolls of Isaiah found in cave 1. He underscores that at the time of the writing of the scrolls at Qumran there were no agreed-upon formal methods for the presentation of the sacred writings. Even the Torah, Prophets, and Writings

had sentences deleted or added, and such matters as word division, syntax, and spelling do not appear to have been of primary concern to the scribes at Qumran. He concludes from this that although in prerabbinic times the Law, Prophets, and Psalms carried a large degree of authority in the Qumran community, they had not as yet attained the status given to Scripture by later rabbinic schools that copied every letter and word as accurately as possible.[54] This supports the idea that the concept of Scripture as inviolable was not uniformly understood or followed by at least the Essenes in the first century A.D. Did the Essenes have a different view of the Scriptures than other sects of Judaism?

Neusner accepts that the Essene community held to a much wider collection of sacred and authoritative literature than the other Jews in the land of Israel.

> The Essene's library at Qumran encompassed a diverse group of writings, surely received as authoritative and holy, that other Jews did not know within their canon. . . . We have no evidence that the relation to the canon of Scripture of the Manual of Discipline, the Hymns, the War Scroll, or the Damascus Covenant perplexed the teacher of righteousness and the other holy priests of the Essene community. To the contrary, these documents at Qumran appear side by side with the ones we now know as canonical Scripture.[55]

This evidence argues for notions of Scripture and canon in the Judaisms of the first century A.D. different from those in later rabbinic and Christian traditions.

f. The Influence and Significance of the Essenes. Several observations should be made about Qumran and the Essenes before concluding this discussion. (1) There were Essene centers besides that at Qumran. As noted, some of their literature (though in a much later form) has been found in a *genizah* of an old synagogue in Cairo. Philo, a Jewish writer approximately contemporary with Jesus, lived in Egypt and was apparently aware of the Essenes (*Good Person* 12–13.75). (2) John the Baptist, who was born into a priestly family (Luke 1:5–10), evidently rejected his rightful claim to be a priest and came "out of the wilderness" (Mark 1:4–5) preaching the message of Isa 40:3, a very popular text among the Essenes. He was wearing clothing common among them and eating food typical of their diet (Mark 1:6). His message focused on the coming kingdom of God and called for a baptism of repentance for the forgiveness of sins (Mark 1:4–5). These teachings, too, were characteristic of the Qumran community; John's particular kind of baptism, however, was different from that at Qumran. (3) Not all of the Essenes stayed at camps such as the one at Qumran; some of them sold their goods in the market. Although most of them appear to have practiced celibacy, some of them also allowed marriage. It is possible that their influence and sympathetic hearing in Egypt influenced Christians at the end of the second century A.D. especially in their views of marriage and monasticism. These views are expressed quite clearly and approvingly by Clement of Alexandria ca. A.D. 170–180. (4) The OT manuscripts found at Qumran are in Hebrew and are fully a thousand years earlier than all previously found copies of the Hebrew Scriptures.

g. Final Questions. Did early Christianity borrow any of its views or ideas from the Essenes? It is difficult to answer that question with any precision, even though there are numerous parallels between the two groups and, as noted above, they may have influenced a later generation of Christians. If some Essenes did respond to the Christian message, it is not unlikely that many of the Essene ideas and practices were brought with them into the Christian faith. There certainly were precedents for this. On the other hand, since the Christian writings of Paul and quite possibly Mark were likely written before A.D. 70 and the only other Jewish literature from this period is the writings

TABLE 3-1

QUMRAN SECTARIAN DOCUMENTS

Damascus Document (CD)	Zadokite fragment found in Cairo, 1895. The Qumran manuscripts are versions of CD, which appears to be a later version of the *Rule of the Community* in IQS.
Manual of Discipline (Rule of the Community, Serek hayyaḥad) (1QS)	Rules of life for the community, including (a) aims and ideals, (b) annual-census instructions covering moral outlook (humility), (c) a treatise on the spirits of good and evil, (d) regulations regarding obedience, (e) an oath of allegiance, and (f) a hymn about calendar details and secrecy of doctrine.
Appendix A *(Rule of the Congregation)* to 1QS (1QSa)	Supplementary provisions for instruction that describe the treatment of the aged and mentally ill and offer more council rules.
Appendix B *(Blessings)* to 1QS (1QSb)	A handbook of benedictions for members and officials.
War Scroll (1QM) *(Milḥamah)*	A nineteen-column document containing instructions on the preparations for the great eschatological battle, when the universal dominion of God's holy race will be established (cf. Ezek 38–39; Daniel).
Hodayot (Thanksgiving Hymns) (1QH)	Scroll containing thirty hymns, many of which are thanksgivings for salvation and knowledge. Somewhat parallel to the canonical Psalms, they are more individualistic.
Fragments	Liturgical and astrological
Florilegia (or testimony books)	Three fragments from cave 4 with assembled selections from OT passages.
Genesis Apocryphon (Lamech Scroll) (1QapGen)	Similar to *Jubilees* and contains a rewritten and "modernized" version of parts of Genesis in Aramaic.
Temple Scroll (11QTemple)	Over 30 feet long, highly influential in the Qumran community. This document is discussed above.

found at Qumran, the similarities could reflect more an example of what was typical of the various expressions of Judaism in the first century than some dependence or influence by one group on the other. After the destruction of Jerusalem in A.D. 70 and the fall of Masada in A.D. 73, some of the Essenes joined with the Ebionite Christians. These were conservative Jewish Christians who kept the law and believed that Jesus was a human being, an angel, or a spirit but not a divine being. These Christians lived in Palestine and Syria and continued to keep the Mosaic law and confess faith in Jesus as their Messiah.

3. THE GRECO-ROMAN CONTEXT OF EARLY CHRISTIANITY

A. The Social World

1. The Sources

There are many primary resources available for dealing with the social context of the Greco-Roman world at the time when Christian faith was born. The sources include numerous ancient histories; biographies; biblical commentaries; theological and philosophical treatises; the writings of Pliny, Josephus, Tacitus, Suetonius, Philo, Cicero, and Clement of Rome; many second-century Christian texts that reflect the social context of the Roman Empire and early Christianity, including those of Polycarp and Ignatius; and the writings of the fourth-century church historian Eusebius. Indeed, it is accurate to say that the Greco-Roman world is the best-documented society of the ancient world.[56]

2. The Broader Context

With the civil wars and murder of Julius Caesar in 44 B.C., the Roman republic came to an end. The successor to the republic was Octavian (Caesar Augustus, 27 B.C.–A.D. 14), who became the architect for the emergence of the Roman Empire and the establishment of what is known as the Pax Romana, a period of almost two hundred years of relative tranquility in the Mediterranean world.[57] The change from republic to empire made little difference to those already subject to Rome, but with the reign of Octavian, many of the inner turmoils and

conflicts in the empire came to an end. Several changes in this period dramatically affected the way things were done, including the development of a better means for collecting taxes. Instead of private companies—which frequently extorted the citizens with heavy taxations—now civil servants were employed. The situation did improve for the people under this system, even though there were still isolated pockets of the empire where extortion continued. Roman control over local affairs remained much the same, in that many of the provinces in the empire were administered by Roman governors, or by procurators who were agents of the state and looked after its affairs in the absence of the governors. Normally the procurators were freedmen or members of the equestrian class (see sec. 3, below), and in the imperial provinces the procurator was under a legate (or envoy of the emperor) who looked after the interests of the emperor. Procurators were most often dependent upon the governors of larger provinces, and so it seems that Pilate was subject to Quirinius of Syria (Luke 2:1–2). The authority of the governors and the procurators was supported by legionary or ancillary military troops. There were, for example, twenty-four to twenty-eight legions stationed in various trouble spots on the frontiers of the empire. A legion consisted of approximately 5,400 to 6,000 men. Two such legions were located in Egypt in the first century. An Italian cohort was normally stationed where loyalty was especially important and where it was suspected that trouble would likely emerge; one such was apparently at Caesarea (Acts 10:1).

3. The Social Structure[58]

The social structure of the Roman Empire consisted essentially of five classes of people: (1) members of the Roman senatorial families, who had such positions because of great wealth; (2) members of the equestrian class, who arrived at their positions because of wealth or because of significant contributions to the service of the state; (3) freemen and freewomen, who were born as free Roman citizens and who may or may not have been wealthy; (4) freed men and women, who had bought their freedom or had it purchased for them; (5) slaves, whose indenture ran the gamut from immensely dangerous work, such as in mines, to trusted positions in a household. Some slaves were allowed to buy their freedom and citizenship, but their wages were often quite low, making it extremely difficult to do this.[59] The rights of citizens included the right of appeal, even to the emperor or

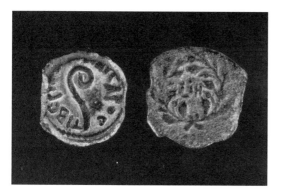

A bronze coin of the Roman procurator Pontius Pilate, struck in A.D. 31. Greek inscriptions: "Of Tiberius Caesar" and, around the wreath, "Year 18." Photo © Rohr Productions. Used with permission.

to his highest court if need be, the right of trial, and exemption from some of the local taxes and certain forms of punishment. Citizenship was clearly a highly prized possession, and in Acts we can see that Paul's Roman citizenship and consequent rights helped him out of several difficulties and even saved his life (Acts 16:37–39; 22:25–29; 25:9–12).[60]

4. Trade

Trade, quite active in the first century A.D., was the primary purpose for the development of an elaborate network of well-built roads and safe shipping routes. Food, especially grain, was regularly brought to Rome from the Nile Valley in Egypt, as seen in Acts 27:6, where, for his journey to Rome, Paul was placed on a commercial ship delivering food from Egypt. Rhodes supplied wine to cities all over the Mediterranean world, and spices were brought to the west from the east through Caesarea Maritima on the coast of Palestine. This port was built by Herod the Great, who played a major role in the shipping of spices to other parts of the empire, spices being essential for preserving foods without refrigeration in the ancient world.

As a result of the advanced roads and shipping lines, it was possible to transport troops throughout the empire. Correspondence was sent to most of the empire's cities with little or no difficulty, although there was no official system of transportation for private mail. As a result of the low wages for slaves, wages for freemen and freewomen were low throughout the empire, but this also meant that prices were low. The rich, who usually had their riches from land ownership and tended to become richer and richer, enjoyed many privileges from the state but could also be the objects of very real threat from the emperors, risking the loss of everything they had acquired by the wrong political choices and their support or lack of support for political candidates.

5. Education

Considerable emphasis was placed on education in the first century, and there was relatively high literacy in many parts of the Roman Empire. It is estimated that, at the very most, 20–30 percent of males in the Hellenistic world were literate—that is, able to read and write their own language.[61] It was expected that those higher up on the social and economic scale would be literate, while those lower down were less likely to be. The educational system was divided into three stages, with elementary, intermediate, and advanced training. Although girls could participate in the lowest level, the higher levels were reserved mostly for boys and men, including the highest level, the gymnasium. Whereas basic reading and writing were learned at the lowest level, at the highest level the student learned how to be a good citizen and received formal training in rhetoric.[62] Rhetorical training was a complex process that included taking various theses and defending or opposing them. Rhetoric was designed to enable the student to undertake the necessary advocacy of ideas that a citizen might be called upon to render. There is considerable discussion about how applicable ancient rhetoric is to interpreting the NT (see ch. 2, above). Examples of rhetoric can be found in several places in the NT, such as in Acts 17:22–31, where Paul addresses the philosophers in Athens.[63] Only skeptics argued for the relativity of all human opinions, especially in regard to religion. Most others had opinions that were strongly defended.

Throughout the empire, there was a common acceptance of belief in the gods and in the importance of strong moral teaching, regardless of widespread moral decadence. Doctrines about the gods were generally given less value than those emphasizing virtue. The Stoics were largely responsible for this, focusing on four main virtues: justice, courage, sobriety (see Eph 5:18), and understanding.[64] They often compiled lists of virtues and vices (see parallels in Gal 5:22–23; 5:19–21a). They published summaries of the duties of fathers to children and vice versa, as well as the household duties of husbands and wives, masters and slaves (see similar lists in Eph 5:21–6:9; Col 3:18–22). The Stoics also exhorted individuals to accept social responsibility, the primary way to find inner freedom. In their exhortations, they developed the "diatribe," which was a lively moral address delivered in a semiconversational style. Examples of this can be found throughout Romans, especially chs. 2–3, 6–7. Paul appears to have been well versed in Stoic and other Hellenistic patterns of communication.[65]

6. The Cosmos

Beliefs about the earth as the center of the universe were widespread in the Greco-Roman world. Pliny the Elder in his *Natural History* also taught that the earth was spherical, not flat. We see a similar idea in Isa 40:22, where the circle or sphere of the earth is mentioned. Although many people followed the examples of the Roman emperors and believed that the stars governed people's lives, Christian writers insisted upon freedom from astral determination. The statements in Col 1:20 that Christ reconciles all things, whether things upon the earth or things in the heavens, and in Col 2:15 that all "rulers and authorities" are overcome might well be direct responses to Hellenistic cosmology[66] (cf. also Rom 8:39, where there may be a reference to astral notions).

As the gospel was going out into the Greco-Roman world, the Christian message had to be adapted to the intellectual, social, and theological situation of its audience. Paul's teachings on the future and the wrath of God, for example, made no sense to his hearers until he spoke of moral responsibility and consequently of God's judgment (Rom 1:18–3:20). The author of 2 Peter reflects Stoic views of the cosmos when he states that the earth was made out of water and through water (2 Pet 3:5) and that a fiery catastrophe awaits the end of the age (3:7, 10, 12).[67]

B. Religion

1. The Gods

Most religions in the Roman Empire were civic; that is, the gods were recognized by the state and by local cities. Priesthoods, including those in Palestine, were reserved in most instances for prominent citizens. Before the first century, similarities in the Greek and Roman deities were widely recognized, and in several instances they were acknowledged to be identical. Jupiter and Zeus, for example, were seen as the same god.

Religion in the Greco-Roman world was varied and complex. In essence, it was polytheistic and closely related to astrology and magic. In Rome, religion was more public and less private than in other parts of the empire and was supported and regulated by the state. Many new cults emerged during the Roman era, and most were respected by the state; at times they were even embraced by the Romans, who often built temples in honor of foreign deities.

During the first century B.C., Julius Caesar, Lepidus, and Augustus (Octavian) took upon themselves the title *pontifex maximus* (chief priest) of the state. The title became essentially political, but when Augustus came to power, he rebuilt and restored some eighty-two temples, taking the title very seriously. The term was also used by the bishop of Rome from the fifth century onward. The deeply religious Romans were basically followers of a peasant farmer's religion. Sacrifices and sacred processions were employed to bless the fields. The peasantry believed themselves to be surrounded, protected—or threatened—by gods or powers. A strict formalism, therefore, was involved in the observance of religion, whether in sacramental acts or in prayer.

Among the Roman gods Jupiter was by far the most powerful deity, lord of heaven's vault of thunderbolts. He became the Roman state deity. Other gods in the pantheon included Juno (Hera, in Greek mythology), the protectress of women, queen of heaven, and wife of Jupiter, and Minerva (Athena), the goddess of craftsmen. Besides this powerful

The temple of Apollo at Delphi, north of the Corinthian Gulf. The Delphic inscription that identifies Gallio in Corinth (see Acts 18:12) and provides one of the few sure dates of the NT era was found here. Photo Lee M. McDonald.

Roman triad, Mars (Ares) was the god of war and of hard labor in the fields, Saturn (Cronus) the god of agriculture, and Vesta (Hestia) the guardian of the fire entrusted to the care of the vestal virgins.

Also important in the Roman pantheon were Ceres (Demeter), the goddess of fertility; Mercury (Hermes), the protector of shopkeepers; and Vulcan (Hephaestus), the god of fire and smiths. Neptune (Poseidon) was recognized as the deity of all waters and seas, Diana (Artemis) as the patron goddess of women and slaves, and Fortuna as the mistress of good luck; later Venus (Aphrodite) became the goddess of love. To these more prominent gods many others were added. Foreign deities were readily accepted by the Romans, who wanted to appease the foreign sources of supernatural power.[68]

The importance of the gods to the Romans is seen in Livy's *History:* "You will find that those who followed the gods had every success, while those who disregarded them were visited with misfortune" (5.51.5). The Romans did not directly communicate with their deities or pray to them in the way that Christians think of prayer. The importance of addressing the proper gods by their proper names and in the proper ways meant that prayer often took place with the aid of someone else, such

The Polygonal Wall at Delphi dates to the sixth century B.C. and contains numerous inscriptions. Photo Lee M. McDonald.

as state priests *(pontifices)*.[69] The *pontifices* were often men of great power, and the majority of them reached official political positions at the consulate and praetorship levels.

By and large, the Romans were tolerant of foreign cults, but this tolerance was matched by intolerance and hostility toward any threat to the morality taught by the state, to the traditions of the Romans, and to public order. Often persecutions of Christians came when these interests of the Romans were perceived to be threatened. When Christians were accused, for example, of incest, atheism, and cannibalism,[70] the state believed that it should intervene. When Christians questioned or refused to worship or sacrifice to the state-recognized gods, then Christianity was deemed a threat to the empire and in need of strict monitoring, if not extermination.

As a part of the hellenization of the Roman Empire, there was a tendency to amalgamate cults and gods and mix various sets of religious and philosophical beliefs.[71] This syncretism, for example, is seen in the worship of the Egyptian goddess Isis in Rome during the first century A.D. A special temple, sometimes called the Red Hall and later the Red Court—eventually converted into a Christian church—still partly stands in Pergamum, built in the second century by the Romans in honor of the Egyptian god Serapis. Gods and goddesses of subject peoples throughout the empire found wide acceptance in Rome. Worship of the gods was led and conducted primarily by priests who wore vestments and perpetuated rituals often of an exotic nature—using incense, for example. Purification and/or initiatory rites were required in most state-recognized religions, and such rites were believed to lead to a better moral character.

2. Emperor Worship

After the death of Julius Caesar, the Roman senate often voted to deify emperors who had died—for example, Claudius, Vespasian, and Titus, according to Suetonius.[72] Often a prominent person in the empire testified to seeing the soul of the befallen emperor wing heavenward when the body was cremated (cf. Acts 1:8–11). In the first century three emperors claimed that they were divine (Caligula, Nero, and Domitian), but when they died, the Roman senate did not vote them so. It appears that those who made such a decision for themselves were rejected by the Roman senate.

Precedent for the divinization of rulers went back at least as far as Alexander the Great, and it was encouraged by various Hellenistic kings, especially in the east. The practice of emperor worship was never universal, and its regulated practice seems to have originated in Asia Minor, the center of the ancient imperial cult (Rev 13:15). After Julius Caesar's death, Augustus had him deified. Although Augustus was careful not to be seen as promoting his own deification in Rome, he allowed himself to be heralded as "son of God" and "savior" in some eastern cities. Augustus allowed himself to be venerated as a god, but he would only allow a temple to be erected in his honor if the goddess Roma was also included. Suetonius writes of Augustus: "Although it was already known to him that even proconsuls often had temples erected in their honor, he never allowed this to be done in his own case unless the name of the goddess Roma was added to his" (*Aug.* 52). The first temples erected for Roma and Augustus were at Pergamum and Nicomedia in 29 B.C. More interesting for the study of early Christianity are some of the titles attributed to Augustus and other Caesars. Perhaps three of the most famous records for these are the Priene inscription of 9 B.C. that heralds Augustus's birthday as the "good news" of the birthday of the god (*OGIS* 458), an inscription on a column from Pergamum that calls Augustus "god" and "son of God" (IGR 4.309), and an inscription from Greece proclaiming Julius Caesar as "savior" (*IG* 12.5.557). What Augustus started became increasingly formalized in the first century. The first example of compulsory veneration or worship of an emperor is recorded in the writings of the Roman governor Pliny the Younger (ca. A.D. 112) during an investigation of Christians (*Ep.* 10). It was clearly present at Pergamum, where Hadrian had an imperial sanctuary, the Trajaneum, built where both his adoptive father, Trajan, and Zeus were honored and worshiped. Later Hadrian himself was also honored there.[73]

3. The Mystery Religions[74]

The growing inclusion of foreign deities brought confusion to the Roman people, and there was a blurring of the ancient religious distinctions common

A wall with inscriptions of sacred oracles at Delphi. Photo Lee M. McDonald.

to Rome. The result was more interest in the monotheistic religions of the east, Judaism and Christianity. Of particular interest to Christian origins is the study of the mystery religions of the east, originating with the Great Mother, Kybele. Our knowledge of some of the mystery religions is limited. One major source, the Hermetic Corpus,[75] is a compilation of various documents, largely written several hundred years after the religions had flourished. These religions focused primarily on weak, suffering, and insecure persons and promised cleansing and purification as well as salvation and eternal bliss. Interestingly, the Roman army was especially interested in Mithraism. Mystery religions offered to every individual direct encounters with the divine and communion with the deity whose death and resurrection were again and again experienced. They also had an initiatory rite of baptism. The parallels with early Christianity are in some instances remarkable and have been the source of numerous scholarly discussions and debates. The mysteries of the Persian god Mithras were introduced among the Romans by men captured from Cilicia during Roman military campaigns and brought back to Rome by Pompey. The greatest period of influence among the Romans was during the second and third centuries A.D., when officers of the Roman legions openly espoused this religious practice. In the second century, even Aurelian and other emperors recognized Mithras as the supreme deity of the empire.[76] The parallels with Christianity have been overdrawn, however, since most forms of mystery religions did not flourish in the areas where Christianity did until after Christianity was well established. Paul, on the other hand, may be addressing a form of mystery cult when he instructs the Christians of Ephesus (Eph 5:18) not to be drunk with wine but to be filled with the spirit (see Euripides, *Bacch.* 278–301), but it is clear that he rejects their influence.

4. Sibylline and Delphic Oracles

Sibylla, the name of a legendary prophetess in ancient Greece, was given to a group of women who made prophetic utterances, often in an apocalyptic and charismatic style. Romans and Greeks applied the term "sibyl" to aged and inspired women who, in a state of ecstasy, prophesied coming events and gave to their listeners the decisions of the gods, especially Apollo, on important matters facing the state or individuals. Augustus considered some of the oracles subversive and had two thousand volumes of sibylline oracles destroyed. Some Jews used the oracle as a means of disseminating propaganda, claiming that the daughter-in-law of Noah was cast into this role and made prophecies (*Sib. Or.* 3:823–827). Some of the Christians also adopted this sibylline style of prophesying from the Jews. Many of them even embraced some of the Latin sibylline oracles without critical discernment.

In the sixth century A.D., both Jewish and Christian oracles were gathered together into fifteen books, the *Sibylline Oracles,* of which twelve now survive. Books 9, 10, and 15 are missing. Books 6–8 and 13 are Christian; in them the Christians' hatred for the Romans is intense. Books 3–5 are mostly Jewish; in them the unity and sovereignty of God are emphasized, as is opposition to the practice of idolatry and the moral corruptions of paganism. There is also considerable discussion of God's judgments of various groups of people. Book 3 also contains elements from both Egyptian and Roman traditions dating from 170 to 116 B.C. and from 43 to 30 B.C. Book 4 sheds light on events in Palestine from A.D. 68 to 69. Book 5 is concerned with Jerusalem shortly after the destruction of Jerusalem in A.D. 70 and the eruption of Mount Vesuvius. Probably composed in Egypt, it speaks about the Roman emperors Hadrian, Antoninus Pius, Marcus Aurelius, and Lucius Verus.[77]

Of special interest here is the impact that the inspirational Delphic oracles had on people throughout the Roman Empire in the first century A.D. The oracles had possessed their greatest significance several centuries before the Christian era, but they still had considerable influence in the world of the first Christian missionaries. The Greek god Apollo, the son of Zeus, had a stronger influence on Greek culture than any other god of the Greek pantheon. It was believed that he was the god who punished humans and whose arrows brought destruction and death to people. He is most often pictured with a bow and arrows. He was also believed to be the helper of people and the father of medicine.

There were numerous oracles offered in the name of Apollo at Delphi, a small city located at the foot of Mount Parnassus in Phocis, and people came from all over the Greco-Roman world to consult with Apollo through the women who were the media for receiving and transmitting the oracles. The temple there was constructed over a cavern from which vapors arose. Some believed that the vapors were the breath of Apollo influencing the oracles to speak. As the priestesses sat upon a tripod over the cavern and inhaled the vapors, they reportedly would go into a trance and mutter words that were then written down and interpreted by the attending priest, called a προφήτης (*prophētēs;* "prophet," "seer"). Some scholars have argued that the vapors from the cavern were gaseous fumes that produced the trances, but this is not certain. Some of the words from the trances were probably not unlike the sounds of tongues that are mentioned in 1 Cor 12–14 and in Acts 2:4; 19:6. The prophets would give the translation of these words to the pilgrims who ventured to Delphi for answers to both personal issues and major issues, such as whether to go out in battle against a certain enemy or whether to raise or decrease taxes.

Delphi was the city from which the proconsul of Achaia, Gallio, came to visit Corinth in A.D. 51/52 (Acts 18:12–16). Gallio was the brother of the philosopher Seneca, who was then proconsul of Asia. Gallio's presence in Corinth is evidence that there was important contact between the two cities. In the NT, the only place where there seems to have been a problem with an overemphasis on "tongues" was Corinth, which is but a brief journey by boat almost straight south from Delphi, and just a little longer by land. Since divinations were an important part of Delphi, it is easy to see how this gift would be prized among the Christians at Corinth. In the ancient world, there were two very important goods that every Greek desired from the gods: prophetic advice and healing. Prophetic advice was found especially at Delphi from Apollo's oracular shrine, and healing came from the various Asclepion sanctuaries spread throughout Greece and Asia Minor, chiefly at Epidaurus, Corinth, Athens, and Pergamum but also elsewhere, including two reportedly found in Jerusalem.[78]

One of the most certain dates for establishing the time of Paul's epistles comes from a comment in Acts 18:12–17, in which Paul stands before

Gallio. A Latin inscription bearing Gallio's name has been found at Delphi. His full name was Lucius Junius Annaeus Gallio, and he held several important civil posts in the Roman Empire. The inscription bearing his name indicates that Gallio was proconsul at Achaia at the time of the twenty-sixth accolade given to Emperor Claudius, which can be dated between A.D. 51/52 and A.D. 52/53. From this and Paul's testimony in 1 Cor 3:5–15, it appears that Paul was in Corinth in A.D. 51/52, and appeared before Gallio somewhere between July and October of A.D. 51/52, shortly after Gallio came to office. From this, the dates of the journeys of Paul can be calculated according to the sequence of events in Acts. The inscription reads in English as follows, with probable restorations in brackets:

Tiberius [Claudius] Caesar Augustus Germanicus . . . [in his tribunician] power [year 12, acclaimed emperor] the 26th time, father of the country . . . [Lucius] Junius Gallio my friend and [pro]consul [of Achaia wrote] . . .[79]

The city of Delphi and its oracles were referred to in various ways in the ancient world; see, for example, Homer, *Od.* 8.80, 11.580. The city, which the Greeks believed to be the center of the earth, was earlier called Pytho. Later the name Pythian Apollo was given to the shrine at Delphi. The spirit that inspired the priestess was known as the Python. Annual Pythian games held at the stadium at Delphi drew large crowds of forty to fifty thousand. The woman who was exorcised by Paul in Acts 16:16 at Philippi is said to have had a "spirit of divination"; the Greek word here for "divination" is πύθωνα *(pythōna)*! The young woman was probably an oracle of Apollo, possibly even from Delphi; at least she functioned like one.

C. Christianity and Hellenism

Christianity, although based in its earliest stages within Judaism, was from the outset a part of Greco-Roman thought and culture. Indeed, both

In the left center is a second-temple mausoleum. To the right is the family tomb of Herod the Great, with the modern King David Hotel in back. See references to this tomb in Josephus, War 1.581; 5.108; and possibly 1.228. Photo © Rohr Productions. Used with permission.

Christianity and Judaism were part of the larger world of Hellenistic culture and thought and show significant signs of developing within this milieu.[80]

One of the primary accomplishments of Alexander the Great was to spread Greek culture wherever he went. On the other hand, Hellenism also accommodated, and even assimilated, many other religions and cultures. Hellenism was characterized by this syncretism—an amalgamation of the arts, philosophies, and faiths of all peoples. In the process of dissemination, Hellenism itself experienced a modification and transformation no less profound.

At the birth of Christianity, although Rome had become the dominant power in terms of military strength, economics, and governmental structures, the Greek language remained dominant for several centuries even in Rome itself. Because of the size of the Hellenistic world surrounding the Mediterranean Sea, and the sense many had of being part of a large and increasingly impersonal world, there was an emphasis upon the individual and his or her place in such a world. Many had also become concerned with their eternal destinies. Roman conquests had flooded the slave markets with people whose value to society was considered little; consequently, many slaves were being exploited. In this atmosphere, many philosophers began to focus on the value of the human soul. As a result, Paul could preach effectively on the "redemption" of the individual, and Christianity found fertile soil for its message of a Redeemer who frees people from bondage and prepares them to meet God. Idolatry was also prevalent in the Roman Empire (Acts 17:6), and in the first century the practice had many critics. Strabo (*Geog.* 9.1.12, 16), for instance, wrote, "Attica is a possession of the gods who seized it as a sanctuary for themselves"—a reference to the pagan shrines in and around Athens. Many people seemed ready for a change, and the religions that offered the only real alternatives to polytheism were Judaism and Christianity.

As Christians moved forward into the Greco-Roman world with their gospel, the availability of a single language and culture, which allowed for easy communication, the well-constructed Roman roads, and the Pax Romana greatly facilitated their ability to evangelize. These factors, along with an openness and readiness in many sectors of the empire, brought remarkable successes in the early church's mission.

BIBLIOGRAPHY

1. GENERAL RESOURCES

BARRETT, C. K. *The New Testament Background: Selected Documents.* Rev. ed. San Francisco: Harper & Row, 1987.

BOARDMAN, J., J. GRIFFIN, and O. MURRAY, eds. *The Oxford History of the Classical World.* New York: Oxford University Press, 1986.

BURY, J. B., et al., ed. *Cambridge Ancient History.* 11 vols. Cambridge: Cambridge University Press, 1924–1936. Especially relevant are vol. 7, on Hellenistic monarchies, and vols. 8–10, on various dimensions of Roman civilization.

DEISSMANN, A. *Light from the Ancient East.* Trans. L. R. N. STRACHAN. 4th ed. 1927. Repr., Peabody, Mass.: Hendrickson, 1995.

EVANS, C. A. *Noncanonical Writings and New Testament Interpretation.* Peabody, Mass.: Hendrickson, 1992.

EVANS, C. A., and S. E. PORTER, eds. *New Testament Backgrounds: A Sheffield Reader.* Sheffield: Sheffield Academic Press, 1997.

FERGUSON, E. *Backgrounds of Early Christianity.* 2d ed. Grand Rapids: Eerdmans, 1993.

2. JUDAISM

A. General Studies

ALEXANDER, P. S., ed. and trans. *Textual Sources for the Study of Judaism.* Manchester: Manchester University Press, 1984.

BILDE, P. *Flavius Josephus between Jerusalem and Rome: His Life, His Works, and Their Importance.* JSPSup 2. Sheffield: JSOT Press, 1988.

BORGEN, P., and S. GIVERSEN, eds. *The New Testament and Hellenistic Judaism.* Peabody, Mass.: Hendrickson, 1997.

BOWKER, J. *The Targums and Rabbinic Literature: An Introduction to Jewish Interpretations of Scripture.* Cambridge: Cambridge University Press, 1969.

CHARLESWORTH, J. H. *The Pseudepigrapha and Modern Research.* Rev. ed. Missoula, Mont.: Scholars Press, 1981.

_____, ed. *The Old Testament Pseudepigrapha.* 2 vols. Garden City, N.Y.: Doubleday, 1983–1985.

CHILTON, B., and J. NEUSNER. *Judaism in the New Testament: Practices and Beliefs.* New York: Routledge, 1995.

COHEN, S. J. D. *From the Maccabees to the Mishnah.* LEC. Philadelphia: Westminster, 1987.

DANBY, H. *The Mishnah.* Oxford: Oxford University Press, 1933.

DAVIES, W. D., and L. FINKELSTEIN, eds. *The Hellenistic Age.* Vol. 2 of *The Cambridge History of Judaism.* Cambridge: Cambridge University Press, 1989.

EPSTEIN, I., ed. *The Babylonian Talmud.* 35 vols. London: Soncino, 1935–1948. Repr. in 18 vols., 1961.

FELDMAN, L. H., and G. HATA, eds. *Josephus, Judaism, and Christianity.* Detroit: Wayne State University Press, 1987.

FITZMYER, J. A. *A Wandering Aramean: Collected Aramaic Essays.* SBLMS 25. Chico, Calif.: Scholars Press, 1979.

GOODENOUGH, E. W. *Jewish Symbols in the Greco-Roman World.* Ed. J. Neusner. Princeton: Princeton University Press, 1988.

GRABBE, L. L. *Judaism from Cyrus to Hadrian.* 2 vols. Minneapolis: Fortress, 1991.

HENGEL, M. *Judaism and Hellenism: Studies in Their Encounter in Palestine during the Early Hellenistic Period.* Trans. J. BOWDEN. 2 vols. Philadelphia: Fortress, 1974.

HORSLEY, R. A. *Bandits, Prophets, and Messiahs: Popular Movements at the Time of Jesus.* San Francisco: Harper, 1985.

JEREMIAS, J. *Jerusalem in the Time of Jesus: An Investigation into Economic and Social Conditions during the New Testament Period.* Trans. F. H. CAVE and C. H. CAVE. Philadelphia: Fortress, 1969.

KRAFT, R.A., and G. W. E. NICKELSBURG, eds. *Early Judaism and Its Modern Interpreters.* Atlanta: Scholars Press, 1986.

MCLAREN, J. S. *Power and Politics in Palestine: The Jews and the Governing of Their Land, 100 B.C.–A.D. 70.* JSNTSup 63. Sheffield: JSOT Press, 1991.

MCNAMARA, M. *Palestinian Judaism and the New Testament.* Good News Studies 4. Wilmington, Del.: Glazier, 1983.

_____. *Targum and Testament: Aramaic Paraphrases of the Hebrew Bible—a Light on the New Testament.* Grand Rapids: Eerdmans, 1972.

MASON, S. *Josephus and the New Testament.* Peabody, Mass.: Hendrickson, 1992.

MONTEFIORE, C. G., and H. LOEWE, eds. *A Rabbinic Anthology.* London: Macmillan, 1938.

MOORE, G. F. *Judaism in the First Centuries of the Christian Era: The Age of the Tannaim.* 1927–1930. Repr., 3 vols. in 2, Peabody, Mass.: Hendrickson, 1997.

MURPHY, F. J. *The Religious World of Jesus: An Introduction to Second Temple Palestinian Judaism.* Nashville: Abingdon, 1996.

NEUSNER, J. *Introduction to Rabbinic Literature.* ABRL. Garden City, N.Y.: Doubleday, 1994.

_____. *Judaism in the Beginning of Christianity.* Philadelphia: Fortress, 1984.

NICKELSBURG, G. W. E. *Jewish Literature between the Bible and the Mishnah: A Historical and Literary Introduction.* Philadelphia: Fortress, 1981.

PATTE, D. *Early Jewish Hermeneutic in Palestine.* SBLDS 22. Missoula, Mont.: Scholars Press, 1975.

RAJAK, T. *Josephus: The Historian and His Society.* Philadelphia: Fortress, 1984.

SALDARINI, A. J. *Pharisees, Scribes, and Sadducees in Palestinian Society: A Sociological Approach.* Wilmington, Del.: Glazier, 1988.

SANDERS, E. P. *Judaism: Practice and Belief, 63 B.C.E.–66 C.E.* Philadelphia: Trinity Press International, 1992.

_____. *Paul and Palestinian Judaism: A Comparison of Patterns of Religion.* Philadelphia: Fortress, 1977.

SCHÄFER, P. *The History of the Jews in Antiquity: The Jews of Palestine from Alexander the Great to the Arab Conquest.* Trans. D. CHOWCAT. Luxembourg: Harwood, 1995.

SCHÜRER, E. *The History of the Jewish People in the Age of Jesus Christ (175 B.C.–A.D. 135).* Trans., rev., and ed. G. VERMES, F. MILLAR, M. GOODMAN, and M. BLACK. 3 vols. Edinburgh: T. & T. Clark, 1973–1987.

SHANKS, H., ed. *Christianity and Rabbinic Judaism: A Parallel History of Their Origins and Early Development.* Washington, D.C.: Biblical Archaeology Society, 1992.

STRACK, H. L., and G. STEMBERGER. *Introduction to the Talmud and Midrash.* Trans. M. BOCKMUEL. Minneapolis: Fortress, 1992.

TALMON, S., ed. *Jewish Civilization in the Hellenistic Roman Period.* Philadelphia: Trinity Press International, 1991.

B. Dead Sea Scrolls and Qumran

CHARLESWORTH, J. H., ed. *Jesus and the Dead Sea Scrolls.* ABRL. New York: Doubleday, 1992.

_____. *John and the Dead Sea Scrolls.* New York: Crossroad, 1990.

CROSS, F. M., Jr. *The Ancient Library of Qumran and Modern Biblical Studies.* Garden City, N.Y.: Doubleday, 1958. Repr., Sheffield: Sheffield Academic Press, 1994.

FITZMYER, J. A. *The Dead Sea Scrolls: Major Publications and Tools for Study.* 2d ed. SBLRBS 20. Atlanta: Scholars Press, 1990.

KAMPEN, J., and M. J. BERNSTEIN, eds. *Reading 4QMT: New Perspectives on Qumran Law and History.* SS 2. Atlanta: Scholars Press, 1996.

GARCÍA MARTÍNEZ, F. *The Dead Sea Scrolls Translated: The Qumran Texts in English.* 2d ed. Leiden: Brill, 1996.

MURPHY-O'CONNOR, J., ed. *Paul and the Dead Sea Scrolls.* Rev. ed. New York: Crossroad, 1990.

SCHIFFMANN, L. H. *Reclaiming the Dead Sea Scrolls: Their True Meaning for Judaism and Christianity.* ABRL. New York: Doubleday, 1994.

VANDERKAM, J. C. *The Dead Sea Scrolls Today.* Grand Rapids: Eerdmans, 1994.

VERMES, G. *The Dead Sea Scrolls in English.* 4th ed. London: Penguin, 1995.

3. THE GRECO-ROMAN WORLD

A. Historical Surveys and General Introductions

BAGNALL, R. S., and P. DEROW. *Greek Historical Documents: The Hellenistic Period.* Chico, Calif.: Scholars Press, 1981.

CARY, M. *A History of Rome down to the Reign of Constantine.* 2d ed. London: Macmillan, 1954.

_____. *The Legacy of Alexander: A History of the Greek World from 323 to 146 B.C.* New York: Dial, 1932.

FREND, W. H. C. *The Rise of Christianity.* Philadelphia: Fortress, 1984.

GLOVER, T. R. *The Conflict of Religions in the Early Roman Empire.* 2d ed. London: Methuen, 1909.

GRANT, M. *The Hellenistic Greeks from Alexander to Cleopatra.* London: Weidenfeld & Nicolson, 1982.

_____. *The Twelve Caesars.* London: Weidenfeld & Nicolson, 1996.

GRANT, R. M. *Augustus to Constantine: The Rise and Triumph of Christianity in the Roman World.* Rev. ed. New York: Harper & Row, 1990.

GREEN, P. *Alexander to Actium: The Historical Evolution of the Hellenistic Age.* Berkeley: University of California Press, 1990.

KOESTER, H. *Introduction to the New Testament.* 2 vols. FFNT. Minneapolis: Fortress, 1982; 2d ed. of vol. 1, 1995; vol. 2, 2000.

LEWIS, N. *Life in Egypt under Roman Rule.* Oxford: Clarendon, 1983.

MILLAR, F. *The Roman Near East, 31 B.C.–A.D. 337.* Cambridge: Harvard University Press, 1993.

NEWSOME, J. D. *Greeks, Romans, Jews: Currents of Culture and Belief in the New Testament World.* Philadelphia: Trinity Press International, 1992.

SALMON, E. T. *A History of the Roman World, 30 B.C. to A.D. 138.* 6th ed. London: Routledge, 1968.

STARR, C. G. *A History of the Ancient World.* 4th ed. New York: Oxford University Press, 1991.

TARN, W., and G. T. Griffith. *Hellenistic Civilisation.* 3d ed. London: Edward Arnold, 1952.

B. Greek and Hellenistic Background to the New Testament

ANDREWES, A. *Greek Society.* Harmondsworth, England: Penguin, 1967.

BEVAN, E. *Hellenism and Christianity.* London: Allen & Unwin, 1921.

BICKERMAN, E. J. *The Jews in the Greek Age.* Cambridge: Harvard University Press, 1988.

BORGEN, P. *Early Christianity and Hellenistic Judaism.* Edinburgh: T. & T. Clark, 1996.

CONZELMANN, H. *Gentiles–Jews–Christians: Polemics and Apologetics in the Greco-Roman Era.* Trans. M. E. BORING. Minneapolis: Fortress, 1992.

DEISSMANN, A. *Light from the Ancient East.* Trans. L. R. N. Strachan. 4th ed. 1927. Repr., Peabody, Mass.: Hendrickson, 1995.

FINLEY, M. I., ed. *The Legacy of Greece: A New Appraisal.* Oxford: Oxford University Press, 1984.

HENGEL, M. *The "Hellenization" of Judaea in the First Century after Christ.* London: SCM, 1989.

_____. *Jews, Greeks, and Barbarians: Aspects of the Hellenization of Judaism in the Pre-Christian Period.* Trans. J. BOWDEN. London: SCM, 1980.

_____. *Judaism and Hellenism: Studies in Their Encounter during the Early Hellenistic Period.* Trans. J. BOWDEN. 2 vols. Philadelphia: Fortress, 1974.

HILL, C. C. *Hebrews and Hellenists: Reappraising Division within the Earliest Church.* Minneapolis: Fortress, 1992.

HOEHNER, H. *Herod Antipas.* SNTSMS 17. Cambridge: Cambridge University Press, 1972.

JAEGER, W. *Early Christianity and Greek Paideia.* Cambridge: Harvard University Press, 1960.

LONG, A. A. *Hellenistic Philosophy: Stoics, Epicureans, Sceptics.* 2d ed. London: Duckworth, 1986.

SANDERS, E. P., ed. *Jewish and Christian Self-Definition.* Vol. 1. *The Shaping of Christianity in the Second and Third Centuries.* Vol. 2. Edited with A. I. BAUMGARTEN and A. MENDELSON. *Aspects of Judaism in the Graeco-Roman Period.* Vol. 3. Edited with B. F. MEYER. *Self-Definition in the Graeco-Roman World.* Philadelphia: Fortress, 1980–1982.

STAMBAUGH, J. E., and D. L. BALCH. *The New Testament in Its Social Environment.* LEC. Philadelphia: Westminster, 1986.

TAYLOR, D. *Roman Society.* London: Macmillan, 1980.

WALBANK, F. W. *The Hellenistic World.* Rev. ed. Glasgow: Collins Fontana, 1992.

WRIGHT, N. T. *The New Testament and the People of God.* Minneapolis: Fortress, 1992.

C. Roman Background to the New Testament

ALEXANDER, L., ed. *Images of Empire.* JSOTSup 122. Sheffield: JSOT Press, 1991.

ARNOLD, W. T. *The Roman System of Provincial Administration to the Accession of Constantine the Great.* Rev. ed. Oxford: Blackwell, 1906.

BARTCHY, S. S. *First-Century Slavery and 1 Corinthians 7:21.* SBLDS 11. Atlanta: Scholars Press, 1973.

BENKO, S. *Pagan Rome and the Early Christians.* Bloomington: Indiana University Press, 1984.

CHRIST, K. *The Romans: An Introduction to Their History and Civilization.* Trans. C. HOLME. Berkeley: University of California Press, 1984.

GRANT, F. C. *Roman Hellenism and the New Testament.* New York: Scribners, 1962.

HARRILL, J. A. *The Manumission of Slaves in Early Christianity.* HUT 32. Tübingen: Mohr–Siebeck, 1995.

LUTTWAK, E. L. *The Grand Strategy of the Roman Empire: From the First Century A.D. to the Third.* 2d ed. Baltimore: Johns Hopkins University Press, 1979.

MARTIN, D. B. *Slavery as Salvation: The Metaphor of Slavery in Pauline Christianity.* New Haven: Yale University Press, 1990.

MOMMSEN, T. *The Provinces of the Roman Empire from Caesar to Diocletian.* Trans. W. P. DICKSON. 2 vols. London: Macmillan, 1909.

SHERWIN-WHITE, A. N. *Roman Society and Roman Law in the New Testament.* Oxford: Clarendon, 1963.

SMALLWOOD, E. M. *The Jews under Roman Rule: From Pompey to Diocletian.* SJLA 20. Leiden: Brill, 1976.

STARR, C. G. *The Ancient Romans.* New York: Oxford University Press, 1971.

WATSON, A. *The Law of the Ancient Romans.* Dallas: Southern Methodist University Press, 1970.

WELLS, C. *The Roman Empire.* Stanford, Calif.: Stanford University Press, 1984.

D. Greco-Roman Religion and the New Testament

AUNE, D. E. *Prophecy in Early Christianity and the Ancient Mediterranean World.* Grand Rapids: Eerdmans, 1983.

BURKERT, W. *Greek Religion.* Trans. J. Raffan. Cambridge: Harvard University Press, 1985.

DODDS, E. R. *The Greeks and the Irrational.* Berkeley: University of California Press, 1951.

FERGUSON, J. *The Religions of the Roman Empire.* Ithaca, N.Y.: Cornell University Press, 1970.

FINEGAN, J. *Myth and Mystery: An Introduction to the Pagan Religions of the Biblical World.* Grand Rapids: Baker, 1989.

GRANT, R. M. *Gods and the One God.* LEC. Philadelphia: Westminster, 1986.

GUTHRIE, W. K. C. *The Greeks and Their Gods.* Boston: Beacon, 1950.

KIRK, G. S. *The Nature of Greek Myths.* Harmondsworth, England: Penguin, 1974.

LANE FOX, R. *Pagans and Christians.* New York: Harper & Row, 1987.

LIEBESCHUETZ, J. H. W. G. *Continuity and Change in Roman Religion.* Oxford: Clarendon, 1979.

MACMULLEN, R. *Paganism in the Roman Empire.* New Haven: Yale University Press, 1981.

MACMULLEN, R., and E. N. LANE, eds. *Paganism and Christianity, 100–425 C.E.: A Sourcebook.* Minneapolis: Fortress, 1992.

MARTIN, L. H. *Hellenistic Religions: An Introduction.* New York: Oxford University Press, 1987.

MURRAY, G. *Five Stages of Greek Religion.* London: Watts, 1935.

NOCK, A. D. *Conversion: The Old and the New in Religion from Alexander the Great to Augustine of Hippo.* Oxford: Oxford University Press, 1933.

OGILVIE, R. M. *The Romans and Their Gods in the Age of Augustus.* London: Chatto & Windus, 1969.

RICE, D. G., and J. E. Stambaugh. *Sources for the Study of Greek Religion.* Atlanta: Scholars Press, 1979.

ROSE, H. J. *Religion in Greece and Rome.* New York: Harper & Brothers, 1959.

**NOTES TO CHAPTER 3
THE HISTORICAL
CONTEXT OF EARLY
CHRISTIANITY**

pages 47–52

1. "Palestine" is from the ancient Greek derivation of the OT word "Philistine." It was first used by Herodotus (*History* 7.89) to designate the "sea people" invaders of the coastland regions of Canaan in the twelfth century B.C., when the Hebrew peoples also entered the land east of there (Jordan). The Philistines occupied the land later known as Philistia, which extended from approximately twenty miles north of Joppa to some twenty miles south of Gaza and eastward to the Judean mountain range of Canaan. Although "Palestine" originally referred to the narrow southern coastal strip of land these invaders occupied in the twelfth century B.C., it came to be used to designate the whole region including western Jordan and the land of Israel. After being ignored for centuries, the term was revived by the British after World War I as a designation for the region. The designation "Palestine" is used in an excellent summary of the Jewish history of the period: P. Schäfer, *The History of the Jews in Antiquity: The Jews of Palestine from Alexander the Great to the Arab Conquest* (Luxembourg: Harwood, 1995).

2. J. A. Sanders, *From Sacred Story to Sacred Text* (Philadelphia: Fortress, 1987), 127–47, 175–90, explains that it was not a cultus, a monarchy, or anything other than a story of Israel's life and heritage, wrapped up in the call of Yahweh, that gave Israel its identity and the incentive to continue its existence in the face of overwhelming odds.

3. An excellent treatment of this period is M. Cary, *The Legacy of Alexander: A History of the Greek World from 323 to 146 B.C.* (New York: Dial, 1932), esp. 1–112, 167–230. For the time leading up to it, see J. B. Bury and R. Meiggs, *A History of Greece to the Death of Alexander the Great* (4th ed.; New York: St. Martin, 1975), esp. 414–500. On Alexander the Great, see R. Lane Fox, *Alexander the Great* (London: Allen Lane, 1973).

4. Flavius Arrian, *Anab.* 7.11.9 (LCL). The Strabo (64 B.C.–ca. A.D. 23) version of the story (*Geography* 1.4.9) claims that Alexander, transcending the old distinctions between Greek and Barbarian, said that the real distinction between people was not a matter of race but whether they were good or bad. The speech has taken many forms (see also Plutarch, *Alex. fort.* 1.6), but the themes of brotherhood and reconciliation are in all of them. For a careful discussion of this story, see esp. W. W. Tarn, *Alexander the Great* (2 vols.; Cambridge: Cambridge University Press, 1948), 2:434–49; also N. G. L. Hammond, *A History of Greece to 323 B.C.* (Oxford: Clarendon, 1959), 641–42; and Bury and Meiggs, *A History of Greece,* 547.

5. The Greek text of the letter, with an introduction, can be found in H. St. J. Thackeray, "Appendix: The Letter of Aristeas," in H. B. Swete, *An Introduction to the Old Testament in Greek* (Cambridge: Cambridge University Press, 1902), 501–74. A translation is available by R. J. H. Shutt in *OTP* 2:7–34. For discussion of the LXX's date and related issues, see S. Jellicoe, *The Septuagint and Modern Study* (Oxford: Clarendon, 1968), 29–58.

6. This story, together with the Jewish successes in battle against the Seleucids, is recorded in 1 and 2 Maccabees. An excellent history of the time is still W. O. E. Oesterley and T. H. Robinson, *From the Fall of Jerusalem, 586 B.C., to the Bar-Kokhba Revolt, A.D. 135,* vol. 2 of *A History of Israel* (2 vols.; Oxford: Clarendon, 1932). On the revolt itself, as well as the sources and some of their difficulties, see D. J. Harrington, *The Maccabean Revolt: Anatomy of a Biblical Revolution* (OTS; Wilmington, Del.: Glazier, 1988).

7. See J. Sievers, *The Hasmoneans and Their Supporters: From Mattathias to the Death of John Hyrcanus* (South Florida Studies in the History of Judaism; Atlanta: Scholars Press, 1990).

8. The Essenes were not, strictly speaking, a wilderness movement. A recent archaeological find has shown the likelihood that an Essene community lived in the time of Jesus in the Hinnom Valley just outside the Essene Gate, cut into the southern wall of Jerusalem's Old City. Evidence for the gate was found near ritual baths and latrines just outside the wall. See B. Pixner, "Jerusalem's Essene Gateway—Where the Community Lived in Jesus' Time," *BAR* 23 (3, 1997): 23–31.

9. See M. Grant, *Herod the Great* (London: Weidenfeld & Nicolson, 1971), for a survey of the life and accomplishments of this man. For the Roman domination of Palestine, see M. Cary, *A History of Rome down to the Reign of Constantine* (2d ed.; London: Macmillan, 1954), esp. 346–519.

10. It is reported that, because Herod had several of his sons killed and because he observed Jewish dietary laws, Augustus said (Macrobius, *Sat.* 2.f.2) that he would rather be a pig than a son of Herod. There is a play upon the Greek words for pig, ὗς (*hys*), and son, υἱός (*huios*).

11. Trans. J. McRay, *Archaeology and the New Testament* (Grand Rapids: Baker, 1991), 92, who also gives the Greek, citing Pittafes, *Archaiologike Ephemeris*, nos. 3442 (p. 1798), 3768 (p. 1935).

12. A summary of Herodian rule is found in Oesterley and Robinson, *History of Israel*, 2:373–75. See also J. S. McLaren, *Power and Politics in Palestine: The Jews and the Governing of their Land, 100 B.C.–A.D. 70* (JSNTSup 63; Sheffield: JSOT Press, 1991).

13. For a discussion of Jewish beliefs in the first century A.D., see E. Ferguson, *Backgrounds of Early Christianity* (rev. ed.; Grand Rapids: Eerdmans, 1993), 480–527.

14. E. Rivkin, "What Crucified Jesus?" in *Jesus' Jewishness: Exploring the Place of Jesus within Early Judaism* (ed. J. H. Charlesworth; New York: Crossroad, 1991), 226–57, here 250–57.

15. See Ferguson, *Backgrounds*, 508. In the first century there was a lack of precision, in both Judaism and early Christianity, about which Scriptures made up the Hebrew Bible. See ch. 13, sec. 3, below.

16. Trans. C. W. Dugmore, *The Influence of the Synagogue upon the Divine Office* (Oxford: Oxford University Press, 1944), 114–25, reproduced in Ferguson, *Backgrounds*, 543–44. Ferguson observes in n. 314 that the phrase "and let the Nazarenes" is often contested as an original part of the Benedictions, but it is not out of keeping with the kinds of comments said about early Christians and others by the Jews on other occasions. See L. T. Johnson, "The New Testament's Anti-Jewish Slander and the Conventions of Ancient Polemic," *JBL* 108 (1989): 434–41. Johnson has shown that Jewish polemic against the pagans was quite common in ancient times and that some of the language later used by Christians against the Jews was also used earlier by the Jews in reference to their pagan enemies. For example, in his *On the Embassy to Gaius* Philo describes his Alexandrian neighbors as "promiscuous and unstable rabble" (18.120 [LCL]) and says that the Egyptians were a "seed bed of evil in whose souls both the venom and temper of the native crocodiles and wasps are reproduced" (26.166). Similar examples are found in Philo's *On the Contemplative Life*, as well as in the earlier Wisdom of Solomon (ca. 1st cent. B.C. in Alexandria). Johnson lists numerous references in Josephus to Jewish violence and hostilities, including Josephus's own frequent use of

malicious terms to describe his opponents and the enemies of the Jews in his *Against Apion.* The point is that we should probably not take too literally the strongly hostile language commonplace in the ancient world and should also not be too surprised when we find it in the Eighteen Benedictions.

17. Tractates from the Talmud are generally identified by a *j* or a *y* (for Jerusalem or *Yerushalmi*) or by a *b* (for Babylonian or *Bavli*).

18. The following list and its translation are found in H. Danby, *The Mishnah: Translated from the Hebrew with Introduction and Brief Explanatory Notes* (Oxford: Oxford University Press, 1933), ix–x. For a table of abbreviations to this collection and other Jewish and rabbinic writings, see *The SBL Handbook of Style* (Peabody, Mass.: Hendrickson, 1999).

19. A. J. Saldarini, "Within Context: The Judaism Contemporary with Jesus," in *Within Context: Essays on Jews and Judaism in the New Testament* (ed. D. P. Efroymson, E. J. Fisher, and L. Klenicki; Collegeville, Minn.: Liturgical, 1993), 33–34.

20. J. Gutmann, "Synagogue Origins: Theories and Facts," in *Ancient Synagogues: The State of Research* (ed. J. Gutmann; BJS 22; Chico, Calif.: Scholars Press, 1981), 1–6. The entire volume provides important information on the synagogue.

pages 60–64

21. There are a number of Jewish inscriptions in Egypt that use the term προσευχή. See W. Horbury and D. Noy, eds., *Jewish Inscriptions of Graeco-Roman Egypt* (Cambridge: Cambridge University Press, 1992).

22. The same could be said of Christian meeting places in the first two centuries. They were quite small and mostly in homes. On occasion, Christians would also meet in a community building or hall designed for special meetings (Acts 19:9).

23. See S. McKnight, *A Light among the Gentiles: Jewish Missionary Activity in the Second Temple Period* (Minneapolis: Fortress, 1991), esp. 48; cf. J. C. Paget, "Jewish Proselytism at the Time of Christian Origins: Chimera or Reality?" *JSNT* 62 (1996): 65–103; P. Borgen, *Early Christianity and Hellenistic Judaism* (Edinburgh: T. & T. Clark, 1996), 45–69.

24. Scholars such as A. T. Kraabel ("The Disappearance of the 'God-Fearers,' " *Numen* 28 [1981]: 113–26) have rejected the depiction of the Godfearers in Acts, claiming that there was no extrabiblical evidence for such a category of followers. But with the publication of the third-century A.D. Aphrodisias inscription and other possible texts (J. Reynolds and R. Tannenbaum, *Jews and God-Fearers at Aphrodisias: Greek Inscriptions with Commentary* [Cambridge, England: Cambridge Philological Society, 1987]), scholars are now much more willing to recognize that the depiction in Acts regarding Godfearers reflects the first-century situation. See M. C. De Boer, "God-Fearers in Luke–Acts," in *Luke's Literary Achievement* (ed. C. M. Tuckett; JSNTSup 116; Sheffield: Sheffield Academic Press, 1995), 50–71; I. Levinskaya, *The Book of Acts in Its Diaspora Setting* (vol. 5 of *The Book of Acts in Its First Century Setting*; ed. B. W. Winter; Grand Rapids: Eerdmans, 1996), 51–126.

25. The seven Noachic commandments, stated by Rabbi Johanan, comprised seven laws binding on the descendants of Noah; the laws, for instance, established courts and forbade blasphemy, worship of other gods, murder, incest and adultery, theft and robbery, and eating the flesh of an animal before it died. See *b. Sanh.* 56a.

26. In 1960, E. Käsemann ("The Beginnings of Christian Theology," in *New Testament Questions of Today* [trans. W. J. Montague; Philadelphia: Fortress, 1969], 102) pronounced that apocalyptic was the

pages 64–69

"mother of all Christian theology." This has been disputed by, among others, W. G. Rollins, "The New Testament and Apocalyptic," *NTS* 17 (1971): 454–76.

27. Ferguson, *Backgrounds,* 446–49.

28. See R. S. Hess, "The Messiah in the Old Testament," in *Images of Christ: Ancient and Modern* (ed. S. E. Porter, M. A. Hayes, and D. Tombs; RILP 2; Sheffield: Sheffield Academic Press, 1997), 22–33.

29. J. J. Collins, "A Pre-Christian 'Son of God' among the Dead Sea Scrolls," *BR* 19 (3, 1993): 36.

30. These and other messianic claimants are discussed in C. A. Evans, *Jesus and His Contemporaries: Comparative Studies* (AGJU 25; Leiden: Brill, 1995), 61–73, with reference to the important ancient sources.

31. See Saldarini, "Within Context," 22–25, 35–38, for a summary of this period.

32. The extent to which all of these groups may be called religious sects is highly debated today. S. J. D. Cohen (*From the Maccabees to the Mishnah* [LEC; Philadelphia: Westminster, 1987], 125–27, 166–67) defines a sect as a "small, organized group that separates itself from a larger religious body and asserts that it alone embodies the ideals of the larger group because it alone understands God's will" (p. 125). In this sense he also defines Christianity as a Jewish sect until it no longer kept the law and traditions of Judaism. Religious sects generally see themselves as the only ones fulfilling the purpose and tradition of the larger religious body and separate themselves from it. With the possible exception of the Samaritans, all of these groups, plus early Christianity, can probably be called religious sects, but there is no evidence that these groups separated themselves from Israel. For a discussion of the sources, esp. for the Pharisees and Sadducees, see T. R. Hatina, "Jewish Religious Backgrounds of the New Testament: Pharisees and Sadducees as Case Studies," in *Approaches to New Testament Study* (ed. S. E. Porter and D. Tombs; JSNTSup 120; Sheffield: Sheffield Academic Press, 1995), 46–76.

33. F. F. Bruce, *The Canon of Scripture* (Glasgow: Chapter House, 1988), 40–41.

34. Beckwith recognizes the force of this argument but rejects it, claiming that the Sadducees also rejected a belief in angels, which is taught even in the Torah. He claims that this line of reasoning would then imply that the Sadducees also rejected the law of Moses, since angels are clearly found in Gen 19:1, 15; 28:12; 32:1 and elsewhere. R. Beckwith, *The Old Testament Canon of the New Testament Church and Its Background in Early Judaism* (Grand Rapids: Eerdmans, 1985), 87–88. See his earlier discussion of the Sadducees, pp. 30–39.

35. Bruce, *Canon,* 40–41. See also his n. 41.

36. The difference in the biblical canons of the Pharisees and the Sadducees is unclear in the NT, but it is obvious that there was a lack of belief in the resurrection by the Sadducees. The differences between the Sadducees and the Pharisees in the Mishnah (see *Yad.* 4:6) are primarily over matters of purity, and this distinction is carried on later in the Tosefta (*t. Para* 3.7). For additional references to the Sadducees in the Mishnah, Tosefta, and Talmudim, see G. G. Porton, "Sadducees," *ABD* 5:892–93.

37. Hillel's teachings also form the roots of modern-day Judaism, especially among Conservative and Orthodox Jews.

38. For a discussion of the Pharisees, see A. J. Saldarini, *Pharisees, Scribes, and Sadducees: A Sociological Approach* (Wilmington, Del.: Glazier, 1988); and "Pharisees," *ABD* 5:289–303. Also helpful is R. A.

Horsley and J. S. Hanson, *Bandits, Prophets, and Messiahs: Popular Movements in the Time of Jesus* (San Francisco: Harper, 1985).

39. There are scholars who have called into question the accuracy of Mark's portrayal of the role of the scribe, adding that since Matthew and Luke used Mark, their reports also are unreliable.

40. See G. G. Porton, "Diversity in Post-biblical Judaism," in *Early Judaism and Its Modern Interpreters* (ed. R. A. Kraft and G. W. E. Nickelsburg; Atlanta: Scholars Press, 1986), 60; and M. Black, "Scribe," *IDB* 4:246–48.

41. M. Hengel, *The Zealots: Investigations into the Jewish Freedom Movement in the Period from Herod I until 70 A.D.* (trans. D. Smith; Edinburgh: T. & T. Clark, 1989).

42. See Evans, *Jesus and His Contemporaries*, 63–64.

43. Hengel, *Zealots*, 379.

44. D. Rhoads, "Zealots," *ABD* 6:1043–54; here 1052.

45. For further study, see Ferguson, *Backgrounds*, 499–502; R. T. Anderson, "Samaritans," *ISBE* 4:303–8; and for an update on the current state of Samaritan studies and an extensive bibliography, J. D. Purvis, "The Samaritans and Judaism," in *Early Judaism and Its Modern Interpreters* (ed. Kraft and Nickelsburg), 81–98; and, more recently, R. T. Anderson, "Samaritans," *ÁBD* 5:941–47.

pages 70–80

46. On John and Qumran, see J. H. Charlesworth, ed., *John and the Dead Sea Scrolls* (New York: Crossroad, 1990).

47. The following is a list of the main documents found there and is based in part on J. T. Milik, *Ten Years of Discovery in the Wilderness of Judaea* (trans. J. Strugnell; SBT 26; London: SCM, 1959), ch. 2. For a discussion of some of the most recently released documents, see F. García Martínez, *The Dead Sea Scrolls Translated: The Qumran Texts in English* (Leiden: Brill, 1994).

48. For a discussion of whether 7Q5 is a fragment of Mark 6:52–53, see G. Stanton, *Gospel Truth? New Light on Jesus and the Gospels* (London: HarperCollins, 1995), 20–32. He concludes that it is not.

49. Bruce, *Canon*, 40.

50. Beckwith, *Canon*, 19.

51. Y. Yadin, "The Temple Scroll—the Longest and Most Recently Discovered Dead Sea Scroll," *BAR* 10 (September/October 1984), 33–49; repr. in *Archaeology and the Bible: The Best of BAR, Archaeology in the World of Herod, Jesus, and Paul* (ed. H. Shanks and D. P. Cole; 2 vols.; Washington, D.C.: Biblical Archaeology Society, 1990), 2:161–77. See also his impressive work on the scrolls, *The Temple Scroll* (3 vols.; Jerusalem: Israel Exploration Society, 1983).

52. Yadin, "Temple Scroll," 168.

53. Ibid., 172.

54. D. J. Silver, *The Story of Scripture: From Oral Tradition to the Written Word* (New York: Basic Books, 1990), 136–41.

55. J. Neusner, *The Talmud, A Close Encounter* (Minneapolis: Fortress, 1991), 174.

56. For introductions to the literature of the Greco-Roman world, see C. R. Beye, *Ancient Greek Literature and Society* (2d ed.; Ithaca: Cornell University Press, 1987); and as applicable to the NT, D. E. Aune, *The New Testament in Its Literary Environment* (LEC; Philadelphia: Westminster, 1987).

57. See K. Wengst, *Pax Romana and the Peace of Jesus Christ* (trans. J. Bowden; London: SCM, 1987), for a realistic assessment of this time. Cf. also L. Alexander, ed., *Images of Empire* (JSOTSup 122; Sheffield: JSOT Press, 1991); P. Garnsey and R. Saller, *The Early Principate:*

Augustus to Trajan (Oxford: Clarendon, 1982); J. B. Campbell, *The Emperor and the Roman Army* (Oxford: Clarendon, 1984), 17ff. On Augustus, see A. H. M. Jones, *Augustus* (Ancient Culture and Society; London: Chatto & Windus, 1980).

58. A recent discussion, with bibliography, of Roman social structure and its application to the NT, is found in J. N. Kraybill, *Imperial Cult and Commerce in John's Apocalypse* (JSNTSup 132; Sheffield: Sheffield Academic Press, 1996), 57–82. See also A. R. Burn, *The Government of the Roman Empire from Augustus to the Antonines* (London: George Philip, 1952); J. E. Stambaugh and D. L. Balch, *The New Testament in Its Social Environment* (LEC; Philadelphia: Westminster, 1986), esp. 138–67.

59. On slavery in the Roman Empire, see K. R. Bradley, *Slaves and Masters in the Roman Empire: A Study in Social Control* (New York: Oxford University Press, 1987); J. A. Harrill, *The Manumission of Slaves in Early Christianity* (HUT 32; Tübingen: Mohr–Siebeck, 1995).

60. See B. Rapske, *The Book of Acts and Paul in Roman Custody* (vol. 3 of *The Book of Acts in Its First Century Setting*; ed. B. W. Winter; Grand Rapids: Eerdmans, 1994), 71–112.

61. W. V. Harris, *Ancient Literacy* (Cambridge: Harvard University Press, 1989), 145, and 233–48 on schooling.

62. See S. F. Bonner, *Education in Ancient Rome: From the Elder Cato to the Younger Pliny* (London: Methuen, 1977); cf. D. L. Clark, *Rhetoric in Greco-Roman Education* (New York: Columbia University Press, 1957); G. A. Kennedy, *The Art of Rhetoric in the Roman World, 300 B.C.–A.D. 300* (Princeton: Princeton University Press, 1972).

63. See M. L. Soards, *The Speeches in Acts: Their Content, Context, and Concerns* (Louisville: Westminster John Knox, 1994), esp. 95–100.

64. See F. H. Sandbach, *The Stoics* (London: Chatto & Windus, 1975), esp. 28–68; A. A. Long, ed., *Problems in Stoicism* (London: Athlone, 1971), with essays on various topics in Stoicism.

65. See D. E. Aune, ed., *Greco-Roman Literature and the New Testament* (SBLSBS 21; Atlanta: Scholars Press, 1988), with chapters by D. L. Balch, "Household Codes," 25–50, and S. K. Stowers, "The Diatribe," 71–83, among others.

66. See G. H. C. Macgregor and A. C. Purdy, *Jew and Greek: Tutors unto Christ—the Jewish and Hellenistic Background of the New Testament* (London: Ivor Nicholson & Watson, 1936), 335.

67. Ibid., 334.

68. For a discussion of the Roman deities, see K. Christ, *The Romans* (trans. C. Holme; Berkeley, Calif.: University of California Press, 1984), 157–68; and the classic treatment by H. J. Rose, *Religion in Greece and Rome* (New York: Harper & Brothers, 1959). A listing of both Greek and Roman gods, as well as their functions and attributes, is found in McRay, *Archaeology and the New Testament*, 411.

69. See R. M. Ogilvie, *The Romans and Their Gods* (London: Chatto & Windus, 1969), 24–40.

70. In Roman terms, the accusation of incest would have arisen from the familial language Christians used to refer to each other; that of atheism, from their worship of non-Roman deities; and that of cannibalism, from the Lord's Supper, since they spoke of eating the body and drinking the blood of Jesus. See S. Benko, *Pagan Rome and the Early Christians* (Bloomington: Indiana University Press, 1984), 54–78.

71. See F. C. Grant, *Roman Hellenism and the New Testament* (Edinburgh: Oliver & Boyd, 1962), 54–80; concerning change in Roman religion, esp. under the influence of Stoicism, see J. H. W. G. Liebeschuetz,

pages 80–84

Continuity and Change in Roman Religion (Oxford: Clarendon, 1979), esp. 55–200.

72. For an excellent recent survey, see L. J. Kreitzer, "The Apotheosis of the Roman Emperor," in *Striking New Images: Roman Imperial Coinage and the New Testament World* (JSNTSup 134; Sheffield: Sheffield Academic Press, 1996), 69–98, with bibliography on 69–70 (p. 70 for the reference to Suetonius). Very valuable collections of primary texts are found in L. R. Taylor, *The Divinity of the Roman Emperor* (Middletown, Conn.: American Philological Association, 1931); and V. Ehrenberg and A. H. M. Jones, *Documents Illustrating the Reigns of Augustus and Tiberius* (2d ed.; Oxford: Clarendon, 1955), 81–97, which requires, however, Greek and Latin.

73. For a discussion of these and other temples at Pergamum, see E. M. Yamauchi, *New Testament Cities in Western Asia Minor: Light from Archaeology on Cities of Paul and the Seven Churches of Revelation* (Grand Rapids: Baker, 1980), 41–45.

74. For collections of primary sources, with commentary, see M. W. Meyer, ed., *The Ancient Mysteries: A Sourcebook* (San Francisco: Harper & Row, 1967); A. S. Geden, *Select Passages Illustrating Mithraism* (London: SPCK, 1925).

75. See B. P. Copenhaver, *Hermetica: The Greek Corpus Hermeticum and the Latin Asclepius in a New English Translation, with Notes and Introduction* (Cambridge: Cambridge University Press, 1992). For a collection of pertinent texts in translation, see Geden, *Select Passages Illustrating Mithraism*.

76. R. M. Grant, *Augustus to Constantine: The Rise and Triumph of Christianity in the Roman World* (San Francisco: Harper & Row, 1970), 19–20.

77. See J. J. Collins, "The Sibylline Oracles," *OTP* 1:317–472.

78. R. Parker, "Greek Religion," in *The Oxford History of the Classical World* (ed. J. Boardman, J. Griffin, and O. Murray; New York: Oxford University Press, 1986), 260, 267.

79. Trans. Ferguson, *Backgrounds*, 549. The text is conveniently found and discussed in A. Deissmann, *Paul: A Study in Social and Religious History* (2d ed.; trans. W. E. Wilson; 1927; repr., New York: Harper, 1957), 261–86.

80. For a series of chapters illustrating the Hellenistic elements of the Judaism into which Christianity was born, see M. E. Stone and D. Satran, eds., *Emerging Judaism: Studies on the Fourth and Third Centuries B.C.E.* (Minneapolis: Fortress, 1989), including selections by such reputable scholars of Judaism as Elias Bickerman, Michael Stone, Victor Tcherikover, Morton Smith, Arnaldo Momigliano, and Martin Hengel. See also H. Koester, *Introduction to the New Testament* (2 vols.; FFNT; Minneapolis: Fortress, 1982; 2d ed. of vol. 1, 1995), vol. 1.

THE QUEST FOR THE HISTORICAL JESUS:
Recent Life-of-Jesus Research

1. INTRODUCTION TO LIFE-OF-JESUS RESEARCH

Before focusing on the primary events in the life of Jesus, it is important to understand something of the history and background of research in this area of study. Although many laypersons in the church are unaware of this field, it plays a significant role in most academic centers for theological study and ministry preparation today. Indeed, life-of-Jesus research (Ger., *Leben Jesu Forschung*), sometimes known as "historical Jesus" research, where Jesus' life and ministry are examined from a historical perspective, is often at variance with the so-called Christ of faith of the church's confessions and ministry. We will examine the major events of Jesus' life and teaching in the next two chapters (chs. 5 and 6) from both historical and faith perspectives. In other words, while we are examining the story of Jesus, we will try to be faithful to the historian's craft without diminishing the value of the Christ who is experienced through faith. To justify this approach, however, we must make a brief detour to clarify what has been going on in life-of-Jesus research. As noted in the chapter on historical methodology, Jesus' life demands a different set of historical assumptions from those normally used in simple historical reconstructions of

past events or personalities. Some aspects of Jesus' life are not historically verifiable, since they do not match the experience of the critical historian and are loaded with theological implications. These events are, however, recorded in the canonical Gospels and form part of the image of the "real Jesus" for the church.

2. THE QUEST FOR THE HISTORICAL JESUS

Speaking of the historical Jesus brings to mind the possibility of an "unhistorical Jesus." What are scholars talking about when they talk and write about the historical Jesus? Some scholars believe that the Jesus of the church's confession is "unreal"—a product of legend and mythology. The "real Jesus" for them is a human being who lived in antiquity without all of the ecclesiological accretions that have been added to him over the years as the object of the church's confessions. The real Jesus, according to some scholars, did not walk on water, did not believe that he was the Messiah, and was not resurrected. Whom, then, are scholars talking about when they talk and write about the historical Jesus? We will answer this question in part by surveying the four phases of the quest to discover the identity of the Jesus of history.

A. The First Quest for the Historical Jesus

The term "historical Jesus" became common parlance among biblical scholars when Albert Schweitzer wrote his *Quest for the Historical Jesus*,[1] a book that described the results of the various historical attempts, from the mid–eighteenth century to the early part of the twentieth century, to discover who Jesus was, what he said, and what he did from a historical-critical perspective. These so-called empirical approaches, which were later labeled a "quest," employed a positivistic approach to history and tended to be more autobiographical than historical; that is, they reflected the biases of the scholars who wrote rather than clarified who Jesus was. They also tended to reflect the understanding of history that had developed out of the Enlightenment. Shortly after the turn of this century, Schweitzer described these attempts to recover Jesus as he "actually was" as a dead-end street that did not capture the essence of Jesus. Schweitzer effectively ended the first historical search when he observed that those who wrote lives of Jesus were, in effect, writing their own stories rather than the story of Jesus.

Hermann Samuel Reimarus (1695–1768) was identified as the founder of this first quest, even though it was actually begun earlier by the English deists, who denied the possibility of divine intervention in human and worldly affairs after creation was complete. Reimarus, however, was one of the most notable of the early contributors to the quest for the historical Jesus. He feared the publication of his conclusions, which denied the supernatural origins of Christian faith and relativized the Christ of the church's confessions. His findings were, however, published after his death by his student and friend, the German philosopher Gottlob Lessing (1729–1781).[2] Reimarus's emphasis on a historical portrayal of Jesus influenced by a methodology that denied, in principle at least, the supernatural intervention of God in history strongly affected the work of David Friedrich Strauss, who advanced the positions earlier held by Reimarus. Strauss called for an unprejudiced investigation of the life of Jesus, assuming that the Gospels were filled with

myth and could no longer be accepted as accurate reflections of what Jesus said and who he was.[3] Another voice in early historical Jesus research was that of Joseph Ernst Renan (1823–1892), whose *Life of Jesus*, like that of Strauss, created no small stir over its similar conclusions.[4] Besides these highly influential scholars, other well-known scholars also pursued the ever elusive historical Jesus, especially F. C. Baur (1792–1860), Heinrich Julius Holtzmann (1832–1910), Johannes Weiss (1863–1914), William Wrede (1859–1906), Martin Kähler (1835–1912), Adolf Harnack (1851–1930), and finally Schweitzer himself (1875–1965).[5] It has been estimated that a hundred thousand lives of Jesus were written during the eighteenth, nineteenth, and early twentieth centuries, sixty thousand of which were published in the nineteenth century alone.[6]

Most of these "lives" were written from a historical perspective that was opposed to the church's belief in the uniqueness of Jesus and was closed to the notion of the intervention of God into human affairs. Such activity described in the Bible was seen as myth and consequently rejected and dismissed from consideration. These scholars found ways to explain away or deny the miracles of the Bible, especially the activity of God in creation, the exodus, and the resurrection of Jesus from the dead. The underlying assumption was that the Jesus of history was a more reliable foundation for the church's faith than the traditional Christ of faith in the church's confessions. In these studies, the alternative to the historical Jesus became the "Christ of faith," as Martin Kähler called him, that is, the one whom the early disciples believed had performed miracles, had a unique relationship with God, was crucified for the sins of the world and raised from the dead, and will come again to usher in the kingdom of God.

Kähler wrote a compelling work that influenced all subsequent historical Jesus studies by effectively calling into question the limitations of historical-critical methodology and its assumptions when applied to the study of the life of Jesus.[7] He denied the distinction between the historical Jesus and the Christ of faith, arguing that the former, or the real Jesus, was known only through the proclaimed Christ who comes in the church's proclamation. For Kähler, the primary sources for this Jesus were the canonical Gospels. He rejected the notion that Christian faith was dependent upon the ever-changing results of historical inquiry.

These eighteenth- and nineteenth-century scholars seeking the historical Jesus, like those of today, brought to their inquiry their own historical presuppositions and philosophical assumptions about history and reality. The influence of these scholars was enormous, significantly affecting the emergence of what was later called liberal theology, especially that of Friedrich Schleiermacher (1768–1834), who argued that faith could not be based on the church's dogma or on a tenuous historical foundation but should be located, rather, in the realm of feeling and experience.[8] Scholars today are much more aware of the assumptions of historical inquiry than were those of the eighteenth and nineteenth centuries. Many then believed that they were writing purely objective history without philosophical assumptions. The primary assumption was that if one could somehow reconstruct the historical Jesus apart from all of the actions attributed to him by the church (miracles, resurrection from the dead, and other "mythological" elements added by the early church), then it would be possible to recover the essence of Jesus, and that would somehow have significance for the church. These scholars recognized that church dogma throughout history has tended to obscure the Jesus of antiquity and has presented mostly the Christ of the church's faith. They tried to understand Jesus apart from the miracle stories in the Gospels and the accounts of his resurrection from the dead, looking instead for explanations how he came to be confessed as Lord by the church. He was essentially viewed as a religious sage who gave new ethical teaching to his followers (e.g., in the Sermon on the Mount).

The problem with this enterprise, however, was how to account for the large following of Jesus and for why anyone would want to crucify him. In order to explain this, Schweitzer suggested that central to the life and teachings of Jesus was a radical, apocalyptic eschatology: Jesus fully expected the imminent advent of the kingdom of God. Schweitzer stated that Jesus was simply wrong on this point. He concluded that the kingdom did not come as Jesus had hoped and proclaimed but that it was impossible to understand Jesus apart from this perspective. Subsequent studies of Jesus sought to minimize this role of apocalyptic eschatology in Jesus' thinking and claimed that for Jesus the king-

dom of God had manifested itself in his ministry ("realized eschatology"). Even today, some scholars deny the importance of the apocalyptic eschatological perspective for understanding Jesus.[9]

Although Jesus certainly taught that in some sense the kingdom of God had been realized in his ministry (Matt 12:28; Luke 4:18–29), still, according to the canonical Gospels, the fullness of that kingdom for Jesus was future (Matt 6:10; Mark 9:1; 14:25). Many scholars today recognize that in Jesus' ministry there was a tension between the "already" and the "not yet" of the kingdom and that the notion of a coming kingdom of God bringing judgment and blessing was also a part of his basic teaching. John the Baptist was clearly an apocalyptic thinker who focused on preparation for the imminently coming kingdom of God, and most scholars also recognize that Jesus' ministry was begun in conjunction with John's ministry and with a similar focus on preparation for the coming kingdom of God (see Mark 1:14–15). If the most influential person in Jesus' formative ministry, John, was an apocalyptic thinker and Jesus' earliest followers were also (and no one seems to deny this), it is at least plausible that Jesus, too, was interested in that same perspective rather than solely in the politicized and realized kingdom some have suggested. It is less plausible that Jesus' followers misunderstood him than that he was a Jew highly influenced by the apocalyptic thought of his day.

B. The "No Quest" for the Historical Jesus

As a result of the work of Schweitzer, the importance of the quest for the historical Jesus was significantly minimized and essentially abandoned by leading scholars in the early decades of this century. The most important scholars who championed this "no quest" position included Karl Ludwig Schmidt, Martin Dibelius, Rudolf Bultmann, and Friedrich Gogarten—scholars who flourished between the 1920s and the 1950s and who developed the use of form criticism for the analysis of the Gospels. They concluded that the pursuit for the historical Jesus would not be profitable for the church, since the object of the church's faith was never the Jesus of history but, rather, the Christ of faith. Bultmann, for example, contended that the *fact* of Jesus (his "thatness") was the presupposition for

Christian faith, but he disregarded the importance of the historical details of Jesus' ministry and life.[10] Shelter from the radical conclusions of the earlier historians was found in the Christ of the church's proclamation. For Bultmann, God was always a subject, and never an object, of study. Consequently, any information gleaned by historical-critical inquiry was largely irrelevant for Christian faith. Bultmann was strongly influenced by Kähler, and agreed with him that Christian faith cannot depend upon the ever-changing uncertainties of historical research. He went further than Kähler, however, when he argued that any historical information about Jesus other than his "thatness" was irrelevant for Christian faith. Although the Jesus of the church's faith was not called the "unhistorical Jesus" by Bultmann and others, he in essence became such when he was identified as the mythical Jesus of the early church's faith and hopes, not the actual Jesus as he really was. Bultmann rightly rejected the idea that the Jesus of history (the historian's Jesus) was the object of the church's hope, but he did not conclude that the real Jesus was the Jesus of the church's proclamation. For him, this Jesus (Christ) was a mythological figure who needed to be "demythologized," that is, reinterpreted in the appropriate modern existential categories that could be grasped by the current generation. For Bultmann, the activity of God comes in the preaching of the cross and the risen Christ—Easter faith was the disciples' interpretation of the significance of the cross that was disclosed to them by God. The identity of Jesus in Bultmann's work is vague, and his Christ appears to be little more than a cipher or symbol to initiate faith.

C. The "New Quest," or Second Quest, for the Historical Jesus

Not all of Bultmann's students followed his skeptical assessment of the value of historical inquiry about Jesus for Christian faith. Ernst Käsemann,[11] along with Günther Bornkamm, Ernst Fuchs and James Robinson, held that if historical information about Jesus was obtainable, then it could not be irrelevant for Christian faith. Most scholars agreed that Christianity made historical claims about events that reportedly took place in history and that are inextricably connected with a person who lived and died in Palestine in the first century. Unlike Bultmann, several of his students believed that much could be known about Jesus and that such information was important for Christian faith. With their efforts came the so-called new quest for the historical Jesus. The attempt to transfer interest from history to theology, which had been characteristic of Bultmann's approach—and indeed the interest in distinguishing early Christianity from Jesus himself—had been one of the results, if not the aim, of the form criticism that had abandoned the original quest for the historical Jesus. With the new quest of the 1950s to the late 1970s, the interest in the theology of the evangelists and the early church did not subside, and the emphasis on the differences between the historical Jesus and how he was confessed in the emerging church continued. Scholars recognized, however, that although the material of the Gospels did not readily or clearly disclose the life situation (*Sitz im Leben*) of those who transmitted the Gospels, it did show that the material used had been selected and modified to fit the interests of Jesus' later followers. How could it have been otherwise? The story of Jesus was relevant to the needs of the community that first received it, and the evangelists (now called redactors or editors) geared their message to those varying needs, as seen in the differences in the Gospels themselves. The new quest seemed more interested in the connection between kerygma, or Christian proclamation, and history, since biblical faith at least was in Jesus of Nazareth, a historical figure. Whether this quest produced significant results is contested within the scholarly community.

D. The "Third Quest" for the Historical Jesus

In the 1980s, a significant number of scholars began to look again at the sources (both canonical and noncanonical) that could offer a picture of who Jesus was and to try to establish the facts about him that a person could reasonably accept. Although many have wanted to see this as a new phase in research into the historical Jesus, labeling it the "third quest,"[12] others see it as simply a continuation of the second quest, but with many more participants from a wider diversity of backgrounds. Some scholars in this "third quest" tend to draw generally negative conclusions about the most significant events advanced in the Gospels, but others, at times in something of an apologetic tone, find perhaps more than is knowable through the historical methodologies they employ. To some extent, both groups of scholars have shown a tendency to ignore what others are saying about Jesus. Significant volumes have been written on the life of Jesus over the past few years, and several are receiving considerable and, in some cases, well-deserved attention, even in the popular media.[13] Scholars who are generally more negative toward the traditional understanding of Jesus portrayed in the canonical literature include Morton Smith, Robert Funk, John Dominic Crossan, Burton Mack, and Marcus Borg, who writes more popular works. Several of these scholars have been associated with the well-known Jesus Seminar organized by Robert Funk. Borg, for example, prefers to make the distinction between the pre-Easter Jesus (the historical Jesus) and the post-Easter Jesus (the Christ of the church's faith). He does not deny the reality of the latter, but he rejects the uniqueness of Jesus and interprets his ministry and teaching as he does other religious persons throughout history. He challenges the authenticity of many of the traditional affirmations about Jesus' person and activity, and about 80 percent of the sayings attributed to him in the canonical Gospels.[14]

Two interesting and quite valuable studies that interpret Jesus' life and ministry from within the context of Judaism include the work of Geza Vermes and E. P. Sanders. If there is one significant difference between current life-of-Jesus studies and those of previous generations, it is the emphasis on interpreting Jesus within the context of Judaism.[15] In earlier studies, the Judaism often considered to be the context of early Christianity was in fact more reflective of the Judaism of second-century rabbinic Judaism than that of the first century A.D. These studies tended to examine history anachronistically, that is, posit that everything true of Judaism of the second century (after the destruction of the temple in A.D. 70 and the later Bar Kokhba rebellion in 132–135 A.D.) was also true of Judaism before those events. More recently, scholars have focused on the Judaisms of the first century that were contemporary with Jesus, namely, those of the Qumran community that produced the Dead Sea Scrolls, of Philo of Alexandria, and, to some extent, of the Jewish historian Josephus, as well as that of the Gospels.

Discussions of Jesus that have a historical-critical perspective but also respect the faith dimensions of NT literature include the work of John Meier, Ben Witherington III, and William R. Farmer, along with the older work of Ben F. Meyer and A. E. Harvey.[16] These scholars do not ignore historical investigation but generally agree that the basis for the church's faith cannot be established by it. Luke Johnson, in an important evaluation of the conclusions about Jesus drawn by those in the Jesus Seminar, argues similarly.[17] He exposes some of the Seminar's commonly held perspectives: (1) favoring many of the noncanonical texts over the canonical Gospels as sources for knowing who Jesus was; (2) ignoring the rest of the canonical writings (esp. Acts and Paul) as sources for establishing who Jesus was; (3) emphasizing the social aspects of Jesus' ministry rather than his religious interests; (4) rejecting the most important "theological" confessions of the traditional church; and (5) viewing, implicitly or explicitly, historical knowledge as normative for faith and theology. Johnson points to these scholars' lack of self-criticism in establishing their reconstruction of Jesus. Meier similarly rejects what he believes are the negative and unwarranted conclusions of the Jesus Seminar and contends, with Johnson, that there is much that is historical (or true) about Jesus in the Gospels and in the rest of early Christian literature, and that this material is not irrelevant for Christian faith.[18] Both insist, however, that faith in the Christ of the church's proclamation does not depend upon what one can or cannot establish about Jesus through modern historical research.

The most important issues that emerge in this "third quest" concern Jesus' relationship with the Judaism of his day, his self-conscious identity and sense of mission, the factors that led to his death, and the factors that gave rise to the emergence of the early church.[19] Noting the controversy and lack of agreement among scholars on these items, Crossan has raised the question of the propriety of much that has been termed historical investigation of the life of Jesus. He even calls the whole quest "something of a scholarly bad joke" because of the many and conflicting so-called scholarly attempts to describe Jesus, concluding that this "stunning diversity is an academic embarrassment" and that "it is impossible to avoid the suspicion that historical

Jesus research is a very safe place to do theology and call it history, to do autobiography and call it biography."[20] Crossan concludes that Jesus was essentially a Jewish peasant Cynic philosopher. He himself, however, has contributed to the strange state of affairs in Jesus research by insisting on the priority of noncanonical sources over those in the NT canon to establish his image of Jesus. He gives priority to material that most of the academic world has considered secondary at best and, in all probability, spurious. He disregards the reliability of most of the NT writings, and most of all he ignores the contributions of Paul and Acts as sources for the study of the historical Jesus. He proposes instead that behind the second-century apocryphal *Gospel of Peter* lies a Cross Gospel written sometime in the middle of the first century and that this Cross Gospel is the source of the passion narrative in all four canonical Gospels. Meier cogently argues that the *Gospel of Peter* and even Crossan's Cross Gospel clearly depend upon the canonical Gospels, rather than the other way around. Crossan generally values the apocryphal *Gospel of Thomas*, the Egerton Papyrus (P.Egerton 2), the *Gospel of Peter*, and Morton Smith's allegedly discovered Secret Gospel of Mark over the canonical Gospels, but all of these noncanonical sources have dubious support and most likely depend on the canonical Gospels. According to Meier, there is nothing in these materials that can serve as a legitimate source in the quest for the historical Jesus.[21]

Neusner seems puzzled that so many scholars in the Christian community prefer a historical approach to their Christian faith and, on purely historical grounds, make claims not only about who Jesus was but also about who he was not:

Why [do some Jesus scholars] insist that there is a kind of knowledge about Jesus that not only conforms to the kind of knowledge we have about George Washington but also distinguishes between the epiphenomena of piety and the hard facts of faith? "Who he really was" also means "who he really was not." I cannot point to another religion besides Christianity that has entertained in the intellectual centers of the faith a systematic exercise in learning commencing with unfaith; certainly not Islam, as Salman Rushdie's awful fate has shown, and certainly not Judaism, where the issues of theological learning—Talmud study and scripture study, for example—do not confuse secular history with the pattern of religious truth or ask Moses to submit to the mordant wit of Voltaire.[22]

As we begin our journey into the story of Jesus in the following chapter, we are under no illusion that what can be determined from the historian's perspective is *essential* for Christian faith, but we agree that it has value, even if it is not yet clear what the full value of the historical investigations of the origins of Christian faith might be. Nevertheless, there is a growing tendency among historical-Jesus scholars to say quite freely that they believe they can know a good deal about the historical Jesus. Sanders, for instance, concludes that "the dominant view today seems to be that we can know pretty well what Jesus was out to accomplish, that we can know a lot about what he said, and that those two things make sense within the world of first-century Judaism."[23] In this book, we are unashamedly starting with the premise that God has acted in Jesus in a manner unparalleled in human history and that in him something remarkable has been accomplished for all humanity. Our discussion of the life of Jesus in the following chapter is not an unprejudiced accounting of the story of Jesus, though we hope to present a perspective that is both fair and faithful to the biblical narratives and other available evidence. We are concerned, however, to present a reliable biblical account of these events.

3. THE USE OF Q IN RECOVERING THE HISTORICAL JESUS

One of the most intriguing issues in the quest for the historical Jesus concerns use of the so-called Gospel of Q, which, as noted in ch. 2, above, is essentially composed of those portions of Matthew and Luke that are common to each other but not found in Mark.[24] Crossan and others assume that they have discovered the exact parameters of this source (preserved especially in Luke[25] but also in Matthew) and that nothing else (oral traditions or other writings) with a passion or Easter tradition influenced or informed those for whom this source was produced.

For some time now, certain scholars have argued that Q (Ger. *Quelle*, "source") was a document separate from other canonical sources and reflects an earlier and separate stage of the community of Jesus (when they did not call themselves "Christians").[26] There is no way to demonstrate that the producer of Q was uninformed or unconcerned about other traditions of the death and resurrection of Jesus, but this is crucial to the conclusions of some scholars of the Jesus Seminar. This community of followers of Jesus (the Q community), so the argument goes, did not have a passion or resurrection tradition in their Gospel but essentially only the sayings of Jesus. In other words, the very events and perspectives that are at the heart of the canonical Gospels are missing from this so-called earlier source now called Q. The opinion that all such events and teachings of the death and resurrection of Jesus are late in the development of the church and that the earliest group of followers of Jesus did not have such views is a remarkable perspective clearly out of step with historic Christianity. Scholars who hold to this view have yet to produce any documents from the first century that support this claim.

What bolsters the view for many of the historical-Jesus scholars that there existed a Q community of followers of Jesus without knowledge or acceptance of a passion and resurrection tradition is that there is another writing—indeed, it was historically the first document to claim that it is a "Gospel"—that has no passion or resurrection narratives. This is the *Gospel of Thomas*, a gnostic document in Coptic that was not known in modern times until the 1945 discovery of the gnostic library at Nag Hammadi in Egypt.[27] There is some scholarly debate about the dating of this document, whether it originated in the first century or in the second and whether it depends on the canonical Gospels or preceded them and was independent of them. If the *Gospel of Thomas* dates from before the canonical Gospels (so the argument goes), then there is support for the Q hypothesis that there were writings about Jesus in the early church that did not have a passion or resurrection narrative, thereby representing a form of Christianity that is distinct from the orthodox model that has survived in the church. When we consider that the gnostics denied both the incarnation and the bodily resurrection, however, it is understandable how such a group could emerge near the end of the first century, when notions such as theirs were becoming commonplace. In 1 John 4:2, the writer focuses on the problem of Docetism, emerging in the churches of Asia Minor in the last decade of the first century, which denied the humanity of Jesus. There is no evidence, however, that such a brand of Christianity existed before the end of the first century. It is not clear, therefore, that the *Gospel of Thomas* is a reasonable parallel with the supposed Q source. Even if the *Gospel of Thomas* may, as has been argued, contain several authentic sayings of Jesus (some scholars claim that as many as twenty-two of these sayings are authentic), they are packaged in a document that has, to say the least, bizarre conclusions about women and those who are fit for the kingdom of God, among other strange teachings.[28]

A number of other serious difficulties beset this thesis, not the least of which is that neither Paul nor the rest of the NT mentions or acknowledges a form of Christianity such as that assumed to have existed in the Q community. The hypothesis (commonly associated with Burton Mack) that there was such a form of Christianity assumes that the canonical literature was, at best, wrong about Jesus and, at worst, fraudulent in its depiction of who Jesus was.[29] If Paul was alone in his understanding of the death and resurrection of Jesus, however, it is nowhere apparent, as the rest of the canonical literature amply demonstrates by affirming both the death and the resurrection of Jesus (esp. Acts, Hebrews, 1 Peter, Revelation, and even James). The difficulty in postulating, as Mack does, that a community that denied the traditional understanding of passion and resurrection of Jesus existed before the emergence of the gospel presented by Paul is twofold: first, there are no existing documents that can demonstrate the existence of such a community (Q notwithstanding, since Q is found only in two sources, Matthew and Luke, both of which include a passion and resurrection); and second, there was simply not sufficient time for such a tradition to emerge before the conversion of Paul, nor is there any evidence of one like it holding sway in the church before his time. Few would deny that Peter and the Twelve were part of the inner circle of Jesus and were closest to him. In 1 Cor 15:3–8, after stating "that Christ died for our sins" and "that he was raised on the third day," Paul indicates that the risen Lord appeared first to Peter, then to the Twelve, then to some five hundred followers of Jesus, then to James and the rest of the apostles, and last of all to himself. Paul concludes that the tradition of 1 Cor 15:3–8, which in its current form shows many signs of having been circulated orally before Paul received it,[30] was believed by the earliest followers of Jesus by pointing out that this is what Paul, Peter, the Twelve, James, and the rest of the apostles preached and what the Corinthians believed (1 Cor 15:11). Paul clearly aligns himself and his understanding of the Christian proclamation with those he concluded were the earliest followers of Jesus. They, he claims, centered their faith on the resurrection of Jesus from the dead. Had the case been otherwise, it would doubtless be reflected somewhere in the NT writings themselves, but this is nowhere to be found. Nor is such a community ever mentioned in the Apostolic Fathers or the church fathers of the patristic era, who never hesitated to deal with what they considered a "heresy" or anything that they felt was an affront to the Christian faith.[31] If something like a Q community existed, it was marginal at best, had no significant leadership, and played no important part in the formation of early Christianity. The conversion of Paul took place sometime around A.D. 33 or 34 at the latest (Gal 1:11–17), and he claims that his gospel was acknowledged by the leadership ("pillars") of the church in Jerusalem (Peter, James, and John) and that he and his gospel were accepted by them in Jerusalem (Gal 2:2–10). Paul's gospel is compatible with the passion and resurrection stories of the canonical Gospels. These were written thirty-five to seventy years, at the most, after the death of Jesus, and they clearly depend on earlier traditions. There was simply not enough time for the church's traditions to change so radically—as the existence of a Q community presupposes—in such a brief period of time.

It cannot be demonstrated that Paul's view of the death and resurrection of Jesus influenced the other writers of the NT or that he was the source of a tradition that was in some way contrary to the views held by earliest Christianity. On the contrary, Paul and the other biblical and early church writers express their awareness of the death and resurrection of Jesus because it was central to the earliest strands of their faith.

Although a Q document has never been found, nor even been mentioned in any literature of antiquity, advocates continue to make more of its existence than is warranted by the evidence. There probably was an additional source (or sources) to which Matthew and Luke appealed, though much of the material that they have in common may well have been oral traditions that circulated in the churches in the last half of the first century (hence the variations in portions of the material they hold in common) rather than written sources. If Q was a written document that represented another community of Jesus' followers without an Easter tradition, its positions and views were never acknowledged by anyone in antiquity. To postulate a kind of Christianity that restricted itself to an appreciation of the sayings of Jesus, even the subversive or alternative wisdom sayings (as Borg puts it),[32] is completely unwarranted.[33]

There are several other assumptions about Q that are not as yet supportable but are regularly made by scholars who advocate some kind of a Q community without an awareness of, or devotion to, an Easter tradition. Johnson has listed the most important of these: (1) the material common to Matthew and Luke comes from the same single source; (2) what is contained in the source as we now have it is all that it ever contained; (3) the original form of Q can be determined by omitting the alterations of it that appear primarily in Matthew but also in Luke; (4) the source as it presently exists constituted the entire literature of a specific community of followers of Jesus; (5) it is possible to detect stages in the development of Q; (6) each of these stages is thematically unified; (7) stages of development or redaction correspond exactly to the community's social development; and (8) the group that read this document was an early form of a Jesus movement unaffected by the Jerusalem church and the Pauline "Christ cult." Johnson contends not only that there is not one shred of evidence for any of these assumptions but that, if they were true, they would leave the question of Christian origins unanswerable, since this would leave the Christian church without an impressive founder or any "founding experience."[34] At best, Q appears to be a convenient descriptive title for material that is common to Matthew and Luke but not found in Mark. Nothing more or less is required from the evidence available. It is possible that parts of it came from a written source, but the evidence that all of it was written is lacking. Evidence that all of it came from the same source or that we have all of that source (two of the weightiest assumptions of the advocates of the Q community) is lacking. We are therefore unconvinced of the validity of an important assumption made by some current scholars in Jesus research.

4. CRITERIA FOR AUTHENTICITY

Most NT scholars today agree that the testimony of each early witness to the story of Jesus must be individually weighed to determine its connection with the historical Jesus, but what are the ways of determining the historical reliability or probability of the words and activities of Jesus that are reported in the Gospels? A first step is to recognize that the writers of the Gospels, although they were not unprejudiced scholars of history, were vitally interested in the historical truthfulness of what they were reporting or proclaiming. The events of Jesus' life and ministry were obviously important to the early Christians who followed him, and those events became the earliest canon or authoritative base for Christian preaching, teaching, and behavior in the first church of the first century as well as in the church of the second century. For example, Paul cites the words of Jesus to support his comments about relationships between husbands and wives (1 Cor 7:10) and distinguishes his own words from those of Jesus in a manner that shows that Jesus' words were clearly more authoritative (1 Cor 7:12; 11:23; Phil 4:15). In Acts, Paul cites the words of Jesus to support his comments to the Ephesian elders (Acts 20:35). Not only was what Jesus said important to early Christians; it was also significant to them that Jesus could raise the dead, heal a leper or a blind man, and deal with the critical and everyday circumstances of life. When the church was facing difficulties at a later time, this information was especially encouraging to Christian faith.

Determining the authenticity of a reported or proclaimed event or teaching in the Gospels is a difficult process. There is no general agreement on this topic among scholars, and no commonality in their application of historical criticism to the NT and other literature. C. F. Evans, questioning Pannenberg's view of the resurrection of Jesus and his uncritical acceptance of biblical traditions, remarks that Pannenberg's position "rests upon a predominantly receptive attitude towards traditions and their continuity, whereas the historical-critical method has frequently felt itself able to advance only by a suspicious attitude towards tradition and by uncovering discontinuities."[35] Wherein should the burden of proof lie when we try to determine the authenticity of a report? McArthur argues that when three or four Gospel writers agree on an item or tradition, the burden of proof is with those who deny the authenticity of the tradition, though he admits that this does not necessarily establish or negate a passage.[36] This is essentially what is called the criterion of multiple attestation. Other criteria are also used to establish the authentic historical-Jesus tradition, but the three most important are the following: (1) The criterion of dissimilarity (or discontinuity) claims that traditions that are neither an expression of Jewish piety or beliefs nor an expression of Christian piety or beliefs are more likely to be authentic. (2) The criterion of coherence states that a tradition is more likely to be authentic if it coheres with the hard core of facts already established as authentic through the first principle of dissimilarity. (3) The criterion of multiple attestation argues that a tradition found in several strands of the Synoptic Gospels is more likely to be authentic (more recently some scholars include noncanonical sources such as the *Gospel of Thomas*, the Egerton Papyrus, and other sources).[37] None of these criteria can finally determine authenticity but, rather, only where the burden of proof should rest. In other words, if an event or item in the Gospel traditions is attested by several strands of tradition, the burden of proof is with those who would deny its historicity. A strong attestation, for example, would be a combination of Mark, Q (see sec. 3, above), and John; here there are essentially three primary traditions, Mark, Q, and John since Matthew and Luke primarily depend upon Mark and Q in the production of their Gospels.

The first of these principles, the principle of dissimilarity or discontinuity, is highly suspect, since it wrongly assumes that there was little connection between Jesus and his historical surroundings. Essentially, the principle of discontinuity gives us a picture of a Jesus who was not a Jew, and a Christian community that was uninterested in Jesus! This unique Jesus, isolated from his Jewish context and unremembered in the Christian community, cannot have had much value for the church and clearly cannot be the Jesus who lived in Palestine and presumably learned from that environment. Those who emphasize the principle of dissimilarity are seeking an absolute minimum that can be said about Jesus. The problem with this procedure, however, is that this minimum soon becomes the maximum, and the picture of Jesus drawn from such an examination is distorted. Since Jesus was a first-century Jew, it should be expected that some of his teachings indicate his Jewish heritage, as indeed is the case. The Lord's Prayer (Matt 6:9–13), for example, is a typical Jewish prayer. Characteristically Jewish also is the view that all the law hangs on loving God with all one's heart and soul and mind and one's neighbor as oneself (Matt 22:37–40). In addition, Jesus was the founder of the church; that is, he expected his followers to be a part of a renewed Israel and to carry on his ministry (see ch. 6, below). Without him there simply would be no church. It is logical, therefore, to expect that his teachings and the story of his career would be meaningful, not to say useful, to the church and would provide an authoritative base for Christian preaching and teaching. It is only reasonable to assume that the church would have preserved its traditions about Jesus, which is precisely our suggestion here.

Other criteria are employed with some regularity in this quest, but we will examine only one more in some detail—the criterion of embarrassment. This criterion posits that it is unlikely that the early church would have included material that was embarrassing to it unless it was based on firm tradition. It is not likely that a religious movement would have invented the stories of the disciples' fear and flight at the arrest of Jesus (Mark 14:50 and parallels), or of its leaders fleeing and even denying him during the time of their Lord's greatest trial (Mark 14:66–72 and parallels). The same could be said about Jesus' cry on the cross (Mark 15:34; Matt 27:46), which is not found in Luke or John, and even the rejection of Jesus by the Roman and Jewish authorities that resulted in his death. There is nothing that would make it advantageous for the church to circulate these stories unless they accurately reflected what had happened. The unflattering story of Jesus' disciples (James and John) coming to him in an almost childish manner asking to have places of preeminence in his kingdom (Mark 10:35–45) cannot be the invention of a later religious community seeking to advance its image in the Jewish or non-Jewish community. Jesus' family or those around him trying to restrain him because of the accusation by some that he was deranged is another example of an unflattering story (Mark 3:21, 31–34) that the church would not invent; as it could be of no advantage to the church, it bears the marks of authenticity.

Besides these criteria, Meier lists what he calls secondary or dubious criteria of authenticity. These cannot be relied upon to establish authenticity, although many scholars have used them. These include emphasizing (1) traces of Aramaic (a tradition found with traces of Aramaic grammar, style, and vocabulary as opposed to Greek), (2) the Palestinian environment (sayings and deeds of Jesus that reflect the Palestinian environment), (3) vividness of narration (events and sayings that supply concrete details not germane to the event or saying itself), (4) tendencies of the developing synoptic tradition in Matthew and Luke, and (5) a historical presumption (according to which the burden of proof is with those who claim that the leaders of the church would mislead the early Christians by reporting things that did not happen in the life of Jesus).[38]

What conclusions emerge from the application of these and other criteria? Charlesworth, summarizing the range of conclusions of many recent Jesus scholars, finds that twenty facts are generally held to be true about Jesus: (1) Jesus was a Jew; (2) his earliest followers did have a historical interest in him; (3) we possess considerable knowledge about Jesus that allows us to conclude something of Jesus' mission and teachings within the context of Judaism; (4) Jesus must be studied not only in light of the early church but also in light of the Judaism of his day; (5) Jesus led some kind of renewal movement; (6) Jesus' attack against the moneychangers was a major factor leading to his arrest and crucifixion; (7) Jesus' disciples, with the possible exception of Judas, came from Galilee, and Jesus' mission must be interpreted in light of the views of the Messiah that were current there; (8) Jesus was a devout Jew who was concerned with keeping the law; (9) Jesus was aware of noncanonical writings, as were Jews at Qumran and elsewhere in Palestine; (10) Jesus' awareness of these books did not lead him to quote from them but only from *some* of the canonical books of the Hebrew Scriptures; (11) Jesus was influenced by apocalyptic thought, and his message was eschatological; (12) Jesus' parables are thoroughly Jewish, with parallels in some cases in the later rabbinic writings; (13) Jesus, as the recent archaeology of Palestine shows, interpreted purification in keeping with the traditions found in later rabbinic writings and in the *Temple Scroll* at Qumran but not like the wealthy aristocrats in Jerusalem; (14) sociology, anthropology, and some branches of psychology have a valid role in interpreting Jesus; (15) Jesus was recognized as unusual because of the power and authority he claimed; (16) Jesus thought of himself in terms of current messianic and eschatological understanding; (17) many of the healing miracles of Jesus are authentic; (18) Jesus began his ministry with John the Baptist and couched his message in similar eschatological terms; (19) Jesus did not belong to any of the popular groups in Palestine but had clashes or differences with all of them (Pharisees, Sadducees, Zealots, Essenes); and (20) Jesus could be remarkably offensive in his dealings with, and responses to, individuals.[39] These twenty widely accepted facts about Jesus provide a useful starting point for further discussion of the historical Jesus. Johnson further summarizes seventeen reliable statements about Jesus attested by the rest of the NT outside the canonical Gospels; several of them are also attested in non-Christian writings. Much of the picture of Jesus offered in the Gospels is also supported in other sources often ignored by several historical Jesus scholars (esp. Paul and Acts, but other sources as well; see ch. 5, below). In terms of the multiple attestation of independent sources, the burden of proof, Johnson argues, now lies with those who reject the picture of Jesus presented in the canonical Gospels.[40]

5. PROBLEMS FOR CHRISTIAN FAITH

Is the historical Jesus of historical-critical scholarship opposed to the Christ of the church's faith? To some extent, yes. This is true especially if one is hoping to objectify the activity of God in history so that the unbiased observer can fully understand the Christian faith. A dimension besides that of scientific inquiry is needed. Nevertheless, such investigation of the Gospels and other literature of antiquity has often had positive results that enable the believer to understand more clearly dimensions

of the faith that was preached and handed on in the church. There is still much about the context of early Christianity that is unclear even when viewed through the eyes of faith, and those who labor in their research of ancient literature to elucidate the historical context of early Christianity do the church a great favor. Critical scholars who investigate Christian origins do not necessarily have a negative bias against the church and its traditions. Many seek only a greater clarity in understanding the message proclaimed in the Bible than was previously available.

The distinction between the Jesus of history and the Christ of faith, of which we spoke earlier, is still an important issue for Christian faith today. Is the Jesus of historical-critical research the object of the church's faith? Is the Christ of the church's confession a mythological figure? Are there any historical data to support the church's confession about the uniqueness of Jesus as an object of faith and the bringer of God's salvation to humanity? Such issues are not irrelevant and indeed still play a role in NT historical and theological inquiry. Jesus is remembered not only as a teacher of the past but also as the living Lord of the present. Paul and the other non-Gospel writers of the NT showed little interest in simply preserving the life of Jesus. In fact, as James Dunn has noted, all that Paul and the other epistle writers of the NT said about the historical Jesus, if combined, could be put on the back of a postcard (though perhaps a relatively large card).[41] The tradition preserved in the Gospels often reflects the life setting of the early church more than that of Jesus, which is what one might expect from a later community seeking to continue the sayings of Jesus relevant for itself. The various traditions often reflect the needs of the church for evangelism, worship, teaching, and apologetics. The Gospels do not reflect a desire on the part of the evangelists simply to remember Jesus as he was and what he said while on earth. The traditions of the Gospels—emphasizing the continuing relevance of Jesus—are also an expression of the faith of early Christianity.

There is every probability that the first Christians were anxious to preserve and pass on memories of Jesus' ministry, but apart from the Gospels and some apocryphal stories that did not gain much credibility in the church, there was little interest in the early church to pass on large amounts of detailed information about Jesus' earthly career. This is a far cry, however, from saying that the church invented whatever stories it needed for the sake of its own development and was not interested in Jesus as he actually was. Dunn observes that "it would have been unusual indeed if the followers of such a leader had not been concerned to preserve memories of the exploits and utterances which first drew them to him and sustained their loyalty to him."[42] Converts to the Christian faith would surely have asked at least basic questions about who Jesus was and what he did. Dunn goes a step further and argues that "we must accept the probability that the earliest Christian teachers were charged with the task of preserving and retelling the distinctive features of Jesus' ministry which first drew disciples to him."[43]

Faith in Jesus as the Christ is, in at least a limited sense, a historical phenomenon. Christian faith is centered in God's activity in a historical person who lived and died in Palestine in the first century. Because of this, Christians cannot avoid having a serious concern for historical questions. This concern with history is a strength of Christianity, but its faith in a God who acts in history exposes it also to the risks of critical research. Christian faith is directly related to historical events (the death and resurrection of Jesus), but also to a person who lived and ministered in historical circumstances, many of which are clear to the historian as well as to the believer. Historical inquiry can sharpen the church's focus on the life and witness of Jesus of Nazareth, which are relevant for Christian faith, but the limitations of such an approach and the critical assumptions employed in such research are often at odds with the claims and beliefs of Christians. When this conflict arises, the person of faith must not necessarily be dissuaded from confidence in the God who acts in history and has acted in the life of Jesus, but must realize that personal appropriation of that activity cannot be found in the historical-critical dimension but only through faith.

BIBLIOGRAPHY

ANDERSON, H. A. *Jesus.* Englewood Cliffs, N.J.: Prentice-Hall, 1967.

BORG, M. J. *Jesus, a New Vision: Spirit, Culture, and the Life of Discipleship.* San Francisco: HarperCollins, 1991.

_____. *Jesus in Contemporary Scholarship.* Valley Forge, Penn.: Trinity Press International, 1994.

_____. *Meeting Jesus Again for the First Time: The Historical Jesus and the Heart of Contemporary Faith.* San Francisco: HarperCollins, 1994.

_____, ed. *Jesus at 2000.* Boulder, Colo.: Westview/HarperCollins, 1997.

BOWDEN, J. *Jesus: The Unanswered Questions.* London: SCM, 1988.

CHARLESWORTH, J. H., ed. *Jesus' Jewishness: Exploring the Place of Jesus in Early Judaism.* New York: Crossroad, 1991.

CHARLESWORTH, J. H., and W. P. WEAVER, eds. *Images of Jesus Today.* Faith and Scholarship Colloquies. Valley Forge, Penn.: Trinity Press International, 1994.

CHILTON, B. *Pure Kingdom: Jesus' Vision of God.* Studying the Historical Jesus. Grand Rapids: Eerdmans; London: SPCK, 1996.

CHILTON, B., and C. A. Evans, eds. *Studying the Historical Jesus: Evaluations of the State of Current Research.* NTTS 19. Leiden: Brill, 1994.

CROSSAN, J. D. *The Historical Jesus: The Life of a Mediterranean Jewish Peasant.* San Francisco: Harper, 1991.

_____. *Who Killed Jesus? Exposing the Roots of Anti-Semitism in the Gospel Story of the Death of Jesus.* San Francisco: HarperSanFrancisco, 1995.

DUNN, J. D. G. *The Living Word.* Philadelphia: Fortress, 1987.

ELLIOTT, J. K. *The Apocryphal Jesus: Legends of the Early Church.* Oxford: Oxford University Press, 1996.

EVANS, C. A. *Jesus and His Contemporaries: Comparative Studies.* AGJU 25. Leiden: Brill, 1995.

EVANS, C. A., and S. E. PORTER, eds. *The Historical Jesus: A Sheffield Reader.* BibSem 33. Sheffield: Sheffield Academic Press, 1995.

FARMER, W. R. *The Gospel of Jesus: The Pastoral Relevance of the Synoptic Tradition.* Louisville: Westminster John Knox, 1994.

_____. *Jesus and the Gospel: Tradition, Scripture, and Canon.* Philadelphia: Fortress, 1982.

FUNK, R. W. *Honest to Jesus: Jesus for a New Millennium.* New York: HarperCollins, 1996.

GRANT, M. *Jesus: An Historian's View of the Gospels.* New York: Macmillan, 1977.

HARVEY, A. E. *Jesus and the Constraints of History.* Philadelphia: Westminster, 1982.

JOHNSON, L. T. *The Real Jesus: The Misguided Quest for the Historical Jesus and the Truth of the Traditional Gospels.* San Francisco: HarperCollins, 1996.

KECK, L. E. *A Future for the Historical Jesus: The Place of Jesus in Preaching and Theology.* Philadelphia: Fortress, 1981.

LINNEMANN, E. *Is There a Synoptic Problem? Rethinking the Literary Dependence of the First Three Gospels.* Trans. R. W. Yarbrough. Grand Rapids: Baker, 1992.

MACK, B. L. *The Lost Gospel of Q: The Book of Q and Christian Origins.* San Francisco: Harper, 1993.

_____. *A Myth of Innocence: Mark and Christian Origins.* Philadelphia: Fortress, 1988.

MEIER, J. P. *A Marginal Jew: Rethinking the Historical Jesus.* Vol. 1. *The Roots of the Problem and the Person.* Vol. 2. *Mentor, Message, and Miracles.* 3 vols. ABRL. Garden City, N.Y.: Doubleday, 1991–1994.

MEYER, B. F. *The Aims of Jesus.* London: SCM, 1979.

NEUSNER, J. *Rabbinic Literature and the New Testament: What We Cannot Show, We Do Not Know.* Valley Forge, Penn.: Trinity Press International, 1994.

SANDERS, E. P. *The Historical Figure of Jesus.* London: Allen Lane/Penguin, 1993.

_____. *Jesus and Judaism.* Philadelphia: Fortress, 1985.

SMITH, M. *The Secret Gospel: The Discovery and Interpretation of the Secret Gospel according to Mark.* New York: Harper & Row, 1973.

THEISSEN, G. *The Shadow of the Galilean: The Quest of the Historical Jesus in Narrative Form.* Philadelphia: Fortress, 1987.

VERMES, G. *Jesus the Jew: A Historian's Readings of the Gospels.* Philadelphia: Fortress, 1973.

WITHERINGTON, B., III. *The Christology of Jesus.* Minneapolis: Fortress, 1990.

_____. *The Jesus Quest: The Third Search for the Jew of Nazareth.* Downers Grove, Ill.: InterVarsity, 1995.

_____. *Jesus the Sage: The Pilgrimage of Wisdom.* Minneapolis: Fortress, 1993.

WRIGHT, N. T. *Following Jesus: Biblical Reflections on Discipleship.* Grand Rapids: Eerdmans, 1994.

_____. *Jesus and the Victory of God.* Minneapolis: Fortress, 1996.

_____. *Who Was Jesus?* Grand Rapids: Eerdmans, 1992.

pages 101–104

1. The full English title of the translated 1906 German edition was *The Quest for the Historical Jesus: A Critical Study of Its Progress from Reimarus to Wrede* (New York: Macmillan, 1910). The German title was *Von Reimarus zu Wrede: Eine Geschichte des Leben-Jesu-Forschung* (Tübingen: Mohr, 1906).
2. H. S. Reimarus, *Reimarus: Fragments* (trans. R. S. Fraser; Philadelphia: Fortress, 1970). This work originally appeared as *Von dem Zwecke Jesu und seiner Jünger: Noch ein Fragment des Wolfenbüttelschen Ungenannten—Fragment 7* (ed. G. E. Lessing; Braunschweig: n.p., 1778).
3. D. F. Strauss, *The Life of Jesus Critically Examined* (trans. G. Eliot; 3 vols.; 1835; repr., Philadelphia: Fortress, 1972). The German title was *Das Leben Jesu kritisch bearbeitet* (2 vols.; Tübingen: Osiander, 1835–1836).
4. E. Renan, *The Life of Jesus* (trans. C. E. Wilbour; London: Trübner, 1864). The original title was *La vie de Jésus* (Paris: Michel Lévy Frères, 1863).
5. For a bibliography of Jesus research, see C. A. Evans, *Life of Jesus Research: An Annotated Bibliography* (2d ed.; NTTS 13; Leiden: Brill, 1996).
6. H. Anderson, *Jesus* (Englewood Cliffs, N.J.: Prentice-Hall, 1967), 16.
7. M. Kähler, *The So-Called Historical Jesus and the Historic, Biblical Christ* (trans. C. E. Braaten; Philadelphia: Fortress, 1964). The original title was *Der sogenannte historische Jesus und der geschichtliche, biblische Christus* (Leipzig: Deichert, 1892).
8. A. C. Thiselton, *New Horizons in Hermeneutics* (Grand Rapids: Zondervan, 1992), 204–36.
9. This view held that the end of the ages was soon to come with a violent overthrow of this world's kingdoms by God and his messiah. The righteous would then be blessed and the wicked would be judged by God.
10. The classic statement is the opening line of R. Bultmann, *Theology of the New Testament* (trans. K. Grobel; 2 vols.; New York: Scribners, 1951–1955), 1:3: "*The message of Jesus* is a presupposition for the theology of the New Testament rather than a part of that theology itself."
11. In 1953 E. Käsemann delivered a lecture contradicting his teacher Bultmann. The essay is published in English as "The Problem of the Historical Jesus," in *Essays on New Testament Themes* (trans. W. J. Montague; SBT 41; Naperville, Ill.: Allenson, 1964), 15–47.
12. See S. Neill and T. Wright, *The Interpretation of the New Testament, 1861–1986* (rev. ed.; Oxford: Oxford University Press, 1988), 379.
13. See, e.g., D. van Biema, "The Gospel Truth?" *Time*, 8 April 1996, 52–59; K. L. Woodward, "Rethinking the Resurrection," *Newsweek*, 8 April 1996, 60–70; J. L. Sheler, M. Tharp, and J. J. Seider, "In Search of Jesus," *U.S. News and World Report*, 8 April 1996, 46–53.
14. M. Borg, *Meeting Jesus Again for the First Time: The Historical Jesus and the Heart of Contemporary Faith* (San Francisco: HarperCollins, 1994), 15–16, 20–24; *Jesus in Contemporary Scholarship* (Valley Forge, Penn.: Trinity Press International, 1994), 160–79.
15. See, for instance, J. H. Charlesworth, ed., *Jesus' Jewishness: Exploring the Place of Jesus in Early Judaism* (American Interfaith Institute; New York: Crossroad, 1991), for a collection of interfaith essays that explore this question.
16. From a different viewpoint, the prominent rabbinic scholar Jacob Neusner evaluates Smith's, Crossan's and Meier's work on the historical

Jesus with important conclusions about the whole enterprise of trying to understand the biblical Jesus from a historian's perspective. See J. Neusner, "Who Needs 'the Historical Jesus'?" in *Rabbinic Literature and the New Testament: What We Cannot Show, We Do Not Know* (Valley Forge, Penn.: Trinity Press International, 1994), 169–84.

17. L. T. Johnson, *The Real Jesus: The Misguided Quest for the Historical Jesus and the Truth of the Traditional Gospels* (San Francisco: HarperCollins, 1996), esp. 20–27, 54–56.

18. See J. P. Meier, "Reflections on Jesus-of-History Research Today," in *Jesus' Jewishness* (ed. Charlesworth), 84–107.

19. N. T. Wright, *Who Was Jesus?* (Grand Rapids: Eerdmans, 1992), 17–18, has an excellent discussion of these issues. See also his "Quest for the Historical Jesus," *ABD* 3:796–802.

20. J. D. Crossan, *The Historical Jesus: The Life of a Mediterranean Jewish Peasant* (San Francisco: Harper, 1991), xxvii, xxviii.

21. J. P. Meier, *A Marginal Jew: Rethinking the Historical Jesus* (3 vols.; ABRL; Garden City, N.Y.: Doubleday, 1991–), 1:114–39 (2 vols. have appeared so far). He offers a careful analysis of these apocryphal texts and concludes that those who use these sources to reconstruct the historical Jesus, namely, Crossan, Koester, and Robinson, "are simply on the wrong track" (p. 123).

pages 104–107

22. See J. Neusner, *Rabbinic Literature and the New Testament* (Valley Forge, Penn.: Trinity Press International, 1994), 171; but see his much longer argument, pp. 171–78.

23. See E. P. Sanders, *Jesus and Judaism* (Philadelphia: Fortress, 1985), 2.

24. For a more detailed discussion of Q, see ch. 8, sec. 2.C, below.

25. References to Q usually follow the versification in Luke.

26. See, e.g., H. Koester, *Ancient Christian Gospels: Their History and Development* (Philadelphia: Trinity Press International, 1990), 86.

27. Three Greek papyrus fragments (P.Oxy. 1, 654, 655) were found at the end of the last century and the beginning of this, but they were not known to come from this document until the entire document was found in 1945.

28. See, e.g., *Gos. Thom.* 114, which says, "Simon Peter said to them [the disciples and Jesus] 'Let Mary leave us, for women are not worthy of life.' Jesus said, 'I myself shall lead her in order to make her a male, so that she too may become a living spirit resembling you males. For every woman who will make herself a male will enter the Kingdom of Heaven' " (transl. W. Barnstone, ed., *The Other Bible* [San Francisco: HarperSanFrancisco, 1984], 307).

29. B. Mack, *The Lost Gospel: The Book of Q and Christian Origins* (San Francisco: Harper, 1993), esp. 42–49, 245–50. For a careful response, see E. Linnemann, *Is There a Synoptic Problem? Rethinking the Literary Dependence of the First Three Gospels* (trans. R. W. Yarbrough; Grand Rapids: Baker, 1992), 177–85, who argues the time factor cogently. Linnemann and Farmer are well known for their arguments against the existence of the Q document and also against Mark and Q as the primary sources for Matthew and Luke.

30. Symmetry is seen in the four statements that are introduced by the Greek word ὅτι, *hoti* ("that") in each of the clauses of vv. 3–5, the balance in the uses of εἶτα (*eita*) or ἔπειτα (*epeita*) ("then"/"then") in vv. 5–8, and the balances of emphases in vv. 3–5 and in vv. 5–8. This is evidence of a tradition arranged for easy memory and transmission in oral form.

31. E. Linnemann, "Is There a Gospel of Q?" *BRev* 11 (August 1995): 20.

32. Borg, *Meeting Jesus Again*, 70.

33. For further arguments against this use of Q to postulate a supposed strange and different community of followers of Jesus that existed before Paul, see W. R. Farmer, *The Gospel of Jesus: The Pastoral Relevance of the Synoptic Problem* (Louisville: Westminster John Knox, 1994); and Linnemann, *Is There a Synoptic Problem?* and, more recently, "Is There a Gospel of Q?" 18–23, 42–43.

34. Johnson, *The Real Jesus*, 52–53.

35. C. F. Evans, *Resurrection and the New Testament* (London: SCM, 1970), 179, responding to W. Pannenberg, *Jesus, God and Man* (trans. L. L. Wilkins and D. A. Priebe; Philadelphia: Westminster, 1968).

36. H. K. McArthur, "The Burden of Proof in Historical Jesus Research," *ExpT* 82 (1971): 119. See also his "Basic Issues: A Survey of Recent Gospel Research," in *In Search of the Historical Jesus* (ed. H. K. McArthur; New York: Scribners, 1969), 139–44; and his introduction, 3–20. For a more recent discussion of these and other criteria, see C. A. Evans, "Authenticity Criteria in the Life of Jesus Research," *CSR* 19 (1989): 6–31. These and other criteria are discussed in detail in Meier, *Marginal Jew*, 1:167–95.

37. On the nature and use of these noncanonical sources, see J. H. Charlesworth and C. A. Evans, "Jesus in the Agrapha and Apocryphal Gospels," in *Studying the Historical Jesus: Evaluations of the State of Current Research* (ed. B. Chilton and C. A. Evans; Leiden: Brill, 1994), 479–533.

38. Meier, *Marginal Jew*, 1:177–83. Both Evans and Meier have applied many of these primary and secondary criteria to the miracle stories of Jesus, and both conclude that the miracle tradition, however it was to be accounted for, was an actual part of the ministry of Jesus. See C. A. Evans, "Life-of-Jesus Research and the Eclipse of Mythology," *TS* 54 (1993): 3–36; and Meier, *Marginal Jew*, 2:617–31.

39. J. H. Charlesworth, "Jesus Research Expands with Chaotic Creativity," in *Images of Jesus Today* (ed. J. H. Charlesworth and W. P. Weaver; Valley Forge, Penn.: Trinity Press International, 1994), 5–15.

40. See Johnson, *Real Jesus*, 121–22.

41. J. D. G. Dunn, *The Living Word* (Philadelphia: Fortress, 1988), 25–26. Cf. D. Wenham, *Paul: Follower of Jesus or Founder of Christianity?* (Grand Rapids: Eerdmans, 1995).

42. Dunn, *Living Word*, 27.

43. Ibid., 29

pages 107–111

THE STORY OF JESUS, PART A:
From Birth to Burial

1. INTRODUCTION

This study of the life of Jesus examines the events and focus of his life and ministry from the perspective of the Gospel writers, but it also uses the historical-critical method described earlier. Some of these events are not historically quantifiable (see ch. 1, above), since they are reported as divine activity and are surrounded with theological implications. Nevertheless, they are recorded in the Gospels as events in the life of Jesus, and so they will be examined from both critical and theological perspectives. In other words, we will ask what happened and what the evangelists were trying to say that these events meant by the way they recorded them.

Although some events in the life of Jesus are recorded in all four canonical Gospels, there are only a few events about which the four evangelists, or Gospel writers, agree in terms of sequence. Scholars generally agree on the sequence of the following events or stories in the life of Jesus. Items marked with an asterisk are in all four Gospels and in roughly the same order.

(1) Birth. This is found only in Matt 1:18–25 and Luke 1:26–38; 2:1–20, and these accounts are clearly independent of each other. The other evangelists, Mark and John, start their story with the ministry of John the Baptist and the beginning of Jesus' ministry.

(2) Childhood. Only Luke (2:21–52) records anything about the so-called hidden years of Jesus, namely, from his birth to his baptism. Even then he speaks only about Jesus' dedication in the temple and Jesus' journey to Jerusalem to celebrate the Passover at age twelve. Although Luke portrays Jesus as a remarkable child, he is nonetheless described as a child who grew in a natural manner (2:52).

*(3) Baptism. All three synoptic evangelists agree that Jesus was baptized by John the Baptist in the Jordan River before beginning his ministry. John announces Jesus while he is baptizing others (John 1:28), but the author of the Fourth Gospel does not actually say that Jesus was baptized by John (1:29–34) even though he reports that John saw the Spirit descend upon Jesus (1:32).

(4) Temptation. This event is mentioned only in the Synoptic Gospels (Matt 4:1–11; Mark 1:12–13; Luke 4:1–13) and is described in detail only in Matthew and Luke.

*(5) Early Galilean Ministry. All four evangelists agree that Jesus' earlier ministry was in the region of Galilee (Matt 4:12; Mark 1:14; Luke 4:14;

John 1:43), although they do not agree on which villages were visited or the order in which they were visited. For John, Jesus' ministry began in Galilee shortly after the scene at the Jordan and Jesus' calling of his disciples (John 1:43–2:12).

(6) Transfiguration. The story of the transfiguration of Jesus is found in roughly the same place in the Synoptic Gospels (Matt 17:1–8; Mark 9:2–8; Luke 9:28–36), just before Jesus' journey south to Jerusalem, where he was arrested and crucified. The event was evidently intended to give assurances to the disciples about the coming of Jesus into his kingdom in the relatively near future. It is not mentioned in John's Gospel, but there is an apparent reference to it in 2 Pet 1:16–18. Similarities between the appearance of Jesus in the transfiguration and his resurrection appearances have prompted some form critics to hypothesize that the story is a resurrection story put back into the earthly life of Jesus, that is, a transposed resurrection narrative.

*(7) Triumphal Entry into Jerusalem. All the Gospel writers agree that when Jesus came to Jerusalem, he was well received by the common people and rejected by the religious leaders (Matt 21:1–19; Mark 11:1–10; Luke 19:28–38; John 12:12–19). The OT references in each of the Gospels (see discussion below) indicate that Jesus was being hailed as the coming Messiah in Jerusalem by the crowds of people just days before he was arrested and crucified.

*(8) The Last Supper. Each of the evangelists records that just before the arrest of Jesus, he shared a final meal, the Passover, with his disciples (Matt 26:26–29; Mark 14:22–25; Luke 22:14–23). It is not clear in John (13:1–17:25) that this was the Passover meal, but see John 6:41–59, where Jesus shares a similar meal with his disciples in the region of Galilee.

*(9) Arrest and Trial. All the evangelists essentially agree on the time of the arrest and trial or hearing before the Sanhedrin—sometime after the last supper, while Jesus was praying in the garden at Gethsemane. There are, however, some differences in the details of the various accounts (Matt 26:36–56; Mark 14:32–50; Luke 22:39–54; John 18:1–11).

*(10) Crucifixion and Resurrection. The four Gospels all have these events at the conclusion of Jesus' arrest and trial. The details, however, vary in accordance with the theological motifs of each evangelist.

(11) Ascension. Only Luke and John have an ascension story, but the time of this event differs in their narratives. John has an ascension between the first and second appearance of Jesus (John 20:17), but Luke has it at the end of all of Jesus' appearances to the disciples (Luke 24:50–51; Acts 1:1–11). Both writers, however, give the same significance to this event and have it in a similar sequence—resurrection, ascension (and thereby glorification of Jesus), and giving of the Spirit.

2. THE LIFE OF JESUS: FROM BIRTH TO BURIAL

The following discussion is a brief outline of the life of Jesus (the reader should consult the more exhaustive works listed in the footnotes and bibliographies provided below). The discussion is not restricted to what a historical-critical approach can deduce, although it will present aspects of that approach throughout the section and will also focus on some of the theological motives of the evangelists as they tell the story of Jesus.

A. The Birth of Jesus

Matthew and Luke use the story of Jesus' birth to communicate their understanding of the good news about him.[1] The earliest and latest of the four Gospels, Mark and John, do not have such a story. There is no other reference in the NT to this event, and no theology outside Matthew and Luke built upon it. Its significance has therefore been problematic for many NT scholars and laypersons alike.

1. Location

Since only Matthew and Luke discuss the birth of Jesus and their quite different stories agree that the birth of Jesus took place in Bethlehem, it is reasonable to conclude that this was the location, even though Jesus grew up in Nazareth. The information found in the rest of the NT says that he came from Nazareth. Bethlehem was in keeping with Jewish tradition about the place where the coming Messiah was to be born (Mic 5:2–5). The shepherd king who would come to rescue Israel was, like David (1 Sam 17:12), not to be from the capital city, Jerusalem, but instead from the city of promise, Bethlehem. Both Matthew and Luke see

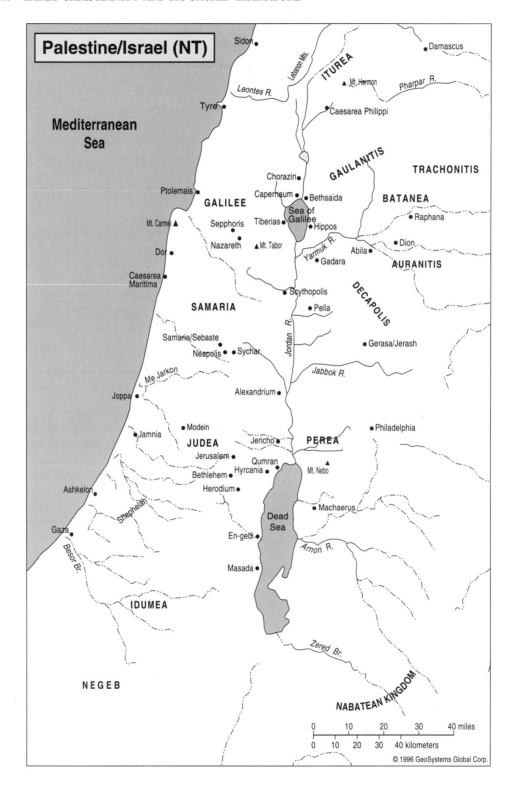

Palestine/Israel (NT)

the birth of Jesus as fulfilling this promise. Some scholars reject the view that Jesus was born in Bethlehem and focus instead on Nazareth even though both Matthew and Luke (though for different reasons) depict Joseph and Mary in Bethlehem and departing to Nazareth (cf. Matt 2:1–23 with Luke 2:1–20, 39–40). Does the point common in both narratives, namely, that the future Messiah king would come out of Bethlehem, have additional attestation in John 7:42? This is not a clear reference to Jesus coming from Bethlehem but may be a use of irony in referring to the people's debate over Jesus' messiahship and their affirmation that the Messiah must come from Bethlehem. Whether this is so, John elsewhere only mentions that Jesus is from Nazareth (18:5, 7). If we did not have the infancy narratives of Matthew and Luke, we might well conclude from the Gospels that Jesus was born in Nazareth. As in the genealogies, which we will examine below, and the nature of the birth itself, the question is whether to assume that the reference to Bethlehem is a theological statement rather than a historical one.

Another matter related to location is Matthew's flight into Egypt, which is apparently incompatible with the account given by Luke, who simply has Joseph and Mary return to Nazareth after they complete all that is appropriate following the birth of their child. Possibly the account of Joseph and Mary's flight to Egypt has another motive, namely, the recognition of Jesus as the Son of God. Matthew 2:15 suggests this when Hos 11:1 is cited from the Hebrew (MT), which says, "out of Egypt I called my son," rather than from the Greek (LXX) version, which says, "out of Egypt I called his children." It may also be, as Brown suggests, that the quotation of the Hosea passage in Matthew has an exodus motif; that is, the reference to the exodus precedes the exile.[2] He reasons that Matthew's story of the flight to Egypt and the wailing over the loss of children (citing texts that refer to the exodus [Hos 11:1] and the children of Israel in exile [Jer 31:15]) ties the story of Jesus into the two most significant moments in the life of the people Jesus came to save.

2. Date of the Birth of Jesus

The traditional dating of the birth of Jesus was due to a miscalculation of some four to five years by Dionysius Exiguus, a Roman abbot (ca. A.D. 525) whose calculations were accepted by the archbishop and biblical scholar James Ussher (1581–1656). In his two-volume work, *Annales Veteris et Novi Testamenti* (1650–1654), which was used for centuries in various editions of the King James Bible, including the well-known *Scofield Reference Bible* notes, Ussher argued for a date of 4004 B.C. for the creation of the world. He used the birth of Jesus as the center of history and dated all events as happening before the birth of Christ or after (B.C./A.D.).[3] Recent support for an earlier dating of Jesus' birth is all but universally accepted. The primary arguments for changing the traditional date to around 6–4 B.C. are based on the following factors.

a. Evidence from Matthew. According to Matt 2:1–16, Jesus was born in the days of Herod the Great. Our best available evidence on the death of Herod comes from Josephus, who says that Herod's death occurred after he had reigned for thirty-four years and that his reign began three years after he had been made king by the Romans (*Ant.* 17.191; *War* 1.665). In other words, his death was probably around March or April of 4 B.C., although it may have been as early as December of 5 B.C.

If Matthew's reference to Jesus' birth during the reign of Herod is reliable, then the time of Jesus' birth has to be pushed back to somewhere around 6–4 B.C., but no later than 4 B.C. Also, since Herod reportedly put to death a large number of boys under the age of two, the oldest that he thought the child might be (Matt 2:16, 20), this would also support the 6–4 B.C. dating. Matthew implies that Herod was hoping to insure that he had destroyed the child who was described by the Magi and who he thought might threaten his rule (2:16–20).

b. Evidence from Luke. Since John the Baptist was born during Herod's rule (Luke 1:5) and Jesus was born about six months later (see Luke 1:24–57), it is reasonable to suggest that Jesus also was born in the days of Herod, as we see in Matt 2:1–4. For the date of Jesus' birth, the following should be noted: (1) Luke dates the baptism of Jesus and the beginning of his ministry during the time of John the Baptist's ministry, which he places in the fifteenth year of the reign of Tiberius Caesar (Luke 3:1), whose reign as emperor began in A.D. 14 after the death of Augustus (Octavian). The first two years of his reign may have been a coregency in conjunction with the reign of Augustus, but none of the ancients date Tiberius's reign before the death of his stepfather, Augustus. If we add fifteen years to that time, then Jesus' baptism and the beginning of his ministry began sometime around A.D. 29. (2) Luke claims that Jesus was about thirty years old when John baptized him (3:23), which means that Jesus was born around 1 B.C. or sooner. Luke, however, was not being precise in 3:23, and the "about thirty" could be more or less than thirty by a couple of years. Since Luke places the birth of John the Baptist, and by inference that of Jesus, in the reign of Herod the Great (1:5), then a birth around 6–4 B.C. is still most plausible.

c. The Problem of Quirinius. Luke 2:1–2 says that Quirinius was governor of Syria when Jesus was born, but Tacitus (*Ann.* 6.41) states that Quirinius began as governor only after Archelaus was expelled from office in A.D. 6. Josephus (*Ant.* 18; *War* 2.117; 7.253) claims that Quirinius ordered a census for tax purposes in A.D. 6–7 that caused a rebellion. If Tacitus and Josephus are correct, then by Luke's accounting, the birth of Jesus comes too late and Luke is out of step with other historians of the time. Geldenhuys, however, argued that Quirinius had a dual reign and also a dual enrollment or registration as Luke 2:2 indicates, the first being in the first decade B.C. and the second in the first decade A.D., which is probably also referred to in Acts 5:37 and in Josephus, *Ant.* 20.97–105.[4] Josephus, however, does not mention that Quirinius served as magistrate in Syria on more than one occasion, and this has some importance since he refers to Quirinius's rule in *Ant.* 17.353 and 18.1–4. A marble slab from Tivoli (Tibur), dated sometime after A.D. 14 and currently in the Vatican Museum, mentions an unnamed official who served as legate of Syria on two occasions, but there is nothing in the inscription that specifically ties it to Quirinius. A second inscription, found in Pisidian Antioch in 1912, is dedicated to G. Caristanius Fronto, a colonist of Antioch who served as a prefect for two magistrates. It reads, "prefect of P. Sulpicius Quirinius, chief magistrate *(duumvir)*, prefect of M. Servilius." A third inscription, though similar, specifies that Fronto is now the prefect of a third magistrate as well.[5] From these inscriptions, however, it is impossible to prove conclusively a dual reign of Quirinius. Publius

The burial site for the family of Herod the Great in Jerusalem in the Hinnom Valley (Josephus, War 1.581; see also 5.108, 507). Photo Lee M. McDonald.

Sulpicius Quirinius could have become consul in Syria in 12 B.C. and died in A.D. 21 (see Tacitus, *Ann.* 3.48; Strabo, *Geog.* 12.6.5), but there is much conjecture in this.

More difficult to explain is the reason for calling a census for the taxation of the people by Augustus when Herod the Great was king and he himself had his own taxes and tax collectors. The client king paid tributes to Rome but was free to collect his own taxes. In examples where Rome levied taxes directly upon the people, significant changes had occurred. For instance, after Herod the Great died and his ruthless son Archelaus was deposed by the emperor in A.D. 6, Judea was no longer a Herodian tetrarchy but a Roman province under the direction of Syria and directly taxed. As a result, there was widespread rebellion in the land, and Judas the Galilean led a revolt against Rome (Josephus, *Ant.* 18.1–6). Does Luke confuse this time with the time of the birth of Jesus? He certainly uses the taking of a census to indicate why Joseph and Mary arrived in the town of Bethlehem, the city of the promise of a shepherd king. A papyrus of A.D. 104 indicates that, for Egyptian censuses, those making declarations were to go to their areas of origin.[6] Luke has the same word (ἀπογραφή, *apographē*) for census as that widely used in the abundant Egyptian papyri, in which almost continuous records indicate that censuses were taken at regular intervals from 11/10 B.C. to A.D. 257/58. These censuses took place every fourteen years from A.D. 33/34 on but were probably at seven-year intervals before that. If censuses were held at the same times outside Egypt, and this is far from certain, the census Luke refers to could be the one held in 4/3 B.C. There is apparently no simple answer available to this difficult issue of correlating Luke's story of the birth of Jesus with available historical data, and questions remain about Luke's understanding of the historical context of the birth of Jesus.[7]

d. The Argument from John. In John's Gospel, during the cleansing of the temple, placed near the beginning of Jesus' ministry in Jerusalem, earlier than in the Synoptic Gospels, Jesus responds to his antagonists, who ask for evidence that he has authority to do what he has done, by saying, "Destroy this temple, and in three days I will raise it up" (John 2:19). His critics answer that the temple had been in the making for forty-six years (2:20) and that they doubt that Jesus would raise it up in three days. According to Josephus (*Ant.* 15.380), the temple was begun by Herod in the eighteenth year of his reign. This refers either to 20/19 B.C., eighteen years after he was made king by the Romans in 37 B.C., or to 23/22 B.C., eighteen years after he in fact began to rule in 40 B.C. This ambiguity could account for Josephus's reference in *War* 1.401 to the building of the temple in the fifteenth year of Herod's reign. Most scholars argue from the date of the conferral of Herod's kingship by the Romans in 37 B.C. and follow *Ant.* 15.380 in the matter. The historical significance of this is that if the temple was begun in 20/19 B.C., then forty-six years later would put the beginning of Jesus' ministry around A.D. 26. That the temple was unfinished during the time of Jesus is supported by the fact that building was still going on both in and around the temple in the early A.D. 60s during the time of the high priesthood of Albinus (see Josephus, *Ant.* 20.219). The difficulty with using this passage to date the origins of Jesus' ministry or to correlate the date of his birth is that this incident, the cleansing of the temple, is reported in the Synoptic Gospels at the Passover just before Jesus' death but in John at the beginning of Jesus' ministry two or three years before his death. There is considerable difficulty in saying anything more precise than that Jesus' ministry began somewhere around A.D. 27 at the earliest and no later than A.D. 30. A round figure of thirty years of age (Luke 3:23) still allows his birth to be sometime before the death of Herod in 4 B.C. Again, the dates are at best approximate.

That Jesus may have been older than thirty, and perhaps in his forties, has been suggested by the debate between Jesus and the "Jews" in John

8:52–59. After Jesus responds to the question whether he is greater than Abraham, the Jews ask, "You are not yet fifty years old, and have you seen Abraham?" (8:57). This reference is too imprecise for arguing his exact age, however. All that can be said from this polemical passage is that Jesus appeared to the Jews on that occasion to be younger than fifty, perhaps in his forties or less. This text is thus in keeping with the view that Jesus was ministering in his thirties and possibly late thirties or early forties. If he had been born two or more years before the death of Herod (4 B.C.) and if he had been active in his ministry for some time according to John 8, then this passage overlaps somewhat with the dating presented in Matthew and Luke; we cannot, however, be sure from the available data.

John's Gospel is also helpful regarding the length of Jesus' ministry and the time of his death. According to all the Gospels, the time of Jesus' death is fixed with the Jewish Passover after either one year of ministry (as Matthew, Mark, and Luke suggest) or two and a half to three years (which John requires on the basis of the number of Passover meals that Jesus celebrated in Jerusalem). If the latter is so, the beginning of Jesus' ministry would be around A.D. 26/27 and his death around 29/30. If he began his ministry around 30 years of age, we still have a probable date for Jesus' birth that precedes the traditional dating offered by Ussher's chronology. Those who would prefer more precision should consider Meier's conclusion that, for a marginal person of Greco-Roman history, "these figures are remarkably good, and perhaps they are the best we can hope for."[8]

3. Questions about Jesus' Birth

What is the point of the birth stories in Matthew and Luke? Why do only Luke and Matthew have stories of Jesus' phenomenal birth, and why are their stories so different? Why is there no theology in the rest of the NT built on the so-called virgin birth (better referred to as the virginal conception)? Why are there no explicit or even implicit references to Jesus' phenomenal birth elsewhere in the NT, not even in Gal 4:4–5, Mark 6:3 ("son of Mary"), John 1:13, and John 7:41–42? Do Matthew and Luke say more with the virgin birth story than Mark, John, and Paul do without it? How should Isa 7:14 be understood in Matt 1:23 and in Isaiah itself? Do the virgin birth stories presume too much about Mary's and Joseph's understandings of Jesus, as suggested by subsequent reports of Mary's concern for Jesus' behavior and her lack of understanding about his mission (Mark 3:21, 31)? Is it possible that Mary did not grasp the significance of Jesus after all that had happened to her? How credible, then, is this story in Matthew and Luke? The ancients were familiar with remarkable births, both in the Old and New Testaments (Samuel, John the Baptist) and in pagan lore (the pharaohs, Alexander the Great, Augustus [Octavian], and even Apollonius of Tyana),[9] although these stories have few clear parallels to the virgin birth stories of Matthew and Luke.

What is the origin of the notion of a virginal conception in Matthew and Luke? Although Matthew appeals to Isa 7:14, clearly this is not the origin of his understanding of the birth of Jesus; rather, he has adapted the Greek text of that OT passage (which spoke of only a "young" girl) to suit his own purposes. Luke does not mention that passage, however, but continues the tradition of Jesus' remarkable birth. Where does the story originate? It may have been a logical inference drawn from the early church's affirmation of Jesus as the Son of God or perhaps, as Brown has suggested, from a theology of the sinlessness of Jesus. As Brown insists, however, the surviving evidence from that period does not allow one to make assertions about the matter.[10] Both evangelists in their own peculiar way say that Jesus was born without the agency of a human father. Whatever one concludes about the historical basis of the virgin birth, it is clear that, at the least, the authors were making a christological statement about the person of Jesus, namely, that he is the Christ, or Messiah of God, who is in a peculiar relationship with God reserved for no other and, in the case of Matthew, is the rightful heir to the throne of David.

When we compare the birth stories in Matthew and Luke, we see that Matthew focuses on royalty (birth in a house, not a stable; the special gifts of the Magi from the east), while Luke focuses on the lowliness of the birth (the poor shepherds coming to the manger scene to witness the new birth; no room for Jesus in the inn). According to Matthew, evidently Joseph and Mary lived in Bethlehem after Jesus' birth, and only after the threat to the life of the newborn child did they consider leaving Bethlehem, going first of all to Egypt and then to Naza-

reth. Luke tells nothing of the threat to Jesus' life and indicates that Joseph and Mary originally came from Nazareth and returned there only after all that was necessary regarding purification and dedication of the child in the temple had taken place. Why does Matthew have Jesus taken down to Egypt while Luke simply says that Joseph and Mary returned to Nazareth with their child? In Matt 2:22, Joseph was warned in a dream to go to Nazareth to avoid dealing with Herod Archelaus. Nothing of this kind of threat is found in Luke. Luke says nothing of the massacre of children in Matt 2. Why are these birth and infancy narratives so different? These questions are not easily answered, but it is probable that the construction of each of these accounts was based on a different theological agenda. Meier says that the point of these widely differing stories is that the church, not Mary or Jesus, wished to make the major theological point that "what Jesus Christ was fully revealed to be at the resurrection (Son of David, Son of God by the Power of the Holy Spirit) he really was from his conception onward."[11]

Because of the considerable differences in these narratives and because they appear to serve early church apologetics, many, if not most, critical scholars do not see much historical evidence for the life of Jesus in the birth stories of Matthew and Luke. But if the criterion of multiple attestation is taken seriously, in light of the fact that the birth stories of Matthew and Luke appear to represent independent traditions, much more credibility should be given to various dimensions of the account. There are basic facts, such as the agreement that Jesus was born in Bethlehem and that Jesus' birth took place during the reign of Herod the Great (Matt 2:1; Luke 1:50), who died ca. 5/4 B.C. There are also more significant factors—angelic visitations, the special circumstances of conception, and visitors attesting to the special qualities of this child—that should not be neglected. These point to the significance of Jesus for both Matthew and Luke.

B. The Genealogy of Jesus

The Gospel narratives state that Jesus descended from the line of David (Matt 1:1, 6, 17; Luke 2:4). This is supported elsewhere in the NT in Rom 1:3–4, the creedal formulation of 2 Tim 2:8, and throughout the Gospels and Acts (Mark 10:47; 12:35–37;

Matt 9:27; 12:23; 15:22; 20:30; 21:9, 15; 22:42–45; Luke 3:31; 18:38–39; 20:41–44; Acts 2:25–31; 13:22–23). Although Jesus' line of descent functions in a theological context in the Gospels, nevertheless, because of its multiple attestation in the Gospels and elsewhere in the NT, it is not likely that the descent was invented and inserted into the traditions of the church. Nor is it likely that the superscription "King of the Jews" over the head of Jesus on the cross is the source for such a designation, since the title of king of the Jews was given to many non-Davidic persons from the time of the Hasmoneans, including the Idumeans, from whom Herod descended.[12] Still, as one examines the two significantly different genealogies of Jesus listed in Matt 1:2–17 and Luke 3:23–38, there are apparent points of conflict. Scholars have discussed possibilities ranging from Matthew offering the genealogy of Joseph and Luke the genealogy of Mary to both lists having a strictly theological function. Some have argued that both Matthew and Luke took over existing lists and modified them to suit their own purposes. Most current scholars, however, have seen in the genealogies an attempt by both evangelists to make a statement about Jesus and his mission. Luke's genealogy is considerably longer than Matthew's, containing some fifty-five names in the same time frame from Abraham to Jesus in which Matthew has forty-one names (forty-two names were intended; cf. 1:17). Matthew starts his genealogy with Abraham and descends to Jesus, while Luke starts with Jesus and goes back by way of Adam to God.

Before analyzing these genealogies and their importance for each evangelist, it should be noted that in the ancient world biblical genealogies often had several different forms and characteristics that were employed for a variety of reasons. Sometimes they ran from parent to child (1 Chron 9:39–44), but they could also begin with the child and go back to the parent (1 Chron 9:14–16). They were generally characterized by fluidity: some names could be deliberately deleted because certain family members had fallen into disgrace or were considered unimportant, or the differences may have reflected changes in social relationships. On occasion, simple error may have caused changes in a genealogy (see possibly 1 Chron 4:39), but differing social structures may also have been at the root of the changes (Gen 36:9–14, 15–19; 1 Chron 1:35–36). Some changes in genealogies may reflect political

and geographical realignments (see, e.g., Gen 46:9, 12, 17; 1 Chron 7:23). Linear genealogies were also used to legitimize one's rightful authority to rule as king of a people.[13] This is apparently Matthew's intention, as is demonstrated by the repeated focus on David; this view is supported by the visit of the Magi to see Jesus and to present royal gifts to him.

A bronze coin of Herod Archelaus (4 B.C.–A.D. 6), struck in Jerusalem. Greek inscriptions: "Herod" and, around the galley, "Ethnarch" ("Governor"). Photo © Rohr Productions. Used with permission.

One should thus not be surprised if the genealogies of Jesus are different from each other and serve different theological functions. The fact that Matthew has three evenly divided sections in his genealogy of Jesus, each consisting of fourteen generations, should prompt us to ask whether Matthew ever intended it to be taken literally or whether he meant it to be taken figuratively to tell his particular message about Jesus. On the other hand, is there a reason why Luke has the reverse order in his genealogy and provides so many names (77–78 compared to the 41 in Matthew)? Why does Luke's genealogy come at the end of ch. 3 rather than at the beginning of his Gospel, as in Matthew? What is Luke's purpose for introducing this genealogy? Looking at these and other questions below, we will maintain that each evangelist has a peculiar story to tell with his genealogy and that theological issues are involved.

1. Matthew's Genealogy

Matthew's genealogy (1:2–17) seems to serve several important functions in his Gospel. These functions are seen most clearly at the beginning of his Gospel in his attempt to show that Jesus is the legitimate heir to the Davidic messiahship and kingship that was anticipated by many of the Jews of that day. David is mentioned once in v. 1, twice in v. 6, and twice in v. 17. The three major divisions of fourteen generations identify the premonarchical period, the monarchical period, and the time from the exile to Jesus.

Matthew was apparently a relatively sophisticated Jewish sage, if not a highly trained Pharisee, steeped in the Judaism of his day and aware of the interpretive skills of his fellow Jews.[14] He was also familiar with the Hellenistic mentality and language of his age and could appeal to both the Hebrew Scriptures and the LXX. This helps us to understand his use of symbolic language to convey his message about Jesus, to understand the meaning of what may be a symbolic or artificial, rather than literal, genealogy. Many scholars have looked for explanations for the highly rigid structure of this genealogy, but most likely Matthew is using the genealogy to focus on the identity of Jesus as the rightful heir to the throne of David. Notice, for example, that in the gematria[15] of the passage there is a focus on fourteen. The number may well represent the numerical equivalent of David's name. In the Hebrew numerical system, the three consonants of David's name, ד ו ד $(d + v + d)$, is $4 + 6 + 4$, totaling 14. The strong emphasis on David's name (5 times in 1:1–17) and the fact that his name can account for the presence of the three (consonants in his name) and the fourteen (numerical equivalent of his name) suggest that the solution to the meaning of Matthew's genealogy is to be found here. It is probably also important that David's name is the fourteenth name listed. There is precedent elsewhere for the use of gematria in genealogies. For instance, the genealogy in Gen 46:8–27 has a strong focus on the number seven. Gad is the seventh in the list of sons, and his name has the numerical equivalent of seven. He also had seven sons. In the same passage, Rachel bore fourteen sons and Bilhah seven sons to Jacob, and the number of Jacob's family who went with him to Egypt was seventy. Although there are other numbers in this list, the number seven and numbers divided by seven stand out. That numbers are important to Matthew can be seen in Table 5–1 below, which

gives examples of his preference for reporting activities or teachings in categories of three.

Also in Matthew, Jesus' ancestry is traced through the line of kings, though three kings (Ahaziah, Joash, and Amaziah) are omitted after Joram in v. 8 and the actual number of names in vv. 12–16 is not fourteen but thirteen, in spite of the statement in v. 17. This may be due simply to an oversight in Matthew's calculations. Matthew mentions four women in Jesus' genealogy (Tamar, Rahab, Ruth, and Bathsheba)—perhaps as a means of selecting women who could in some sense be identified with Mary. Brown suggests that these four women were chosen because there was something irregular, if not scandalous, about their union with their husbands and because each of the women played an important part in the plan of God. Consequently, each could be identified as one through whom the Holy Spirit worked, just as Matthew suggests happened with Mary.[16] Matthew's genealogy focuses upon Jesus as the Messiah, that is, the Anointed One or the Christ, and his right to be the heir of David's throne. We should finally note that all of the names after Zerubbabel from Abiud to Jacob are unknown. According to Matthew, Joseph's father was Jacob, not Heli as Luke claims (Luke 3:23).

2. Luke's Genealogy

Luke's genealogy (3:23–38) follows the beginning of Jesus' ministry, *after* Jesus has been anointed by the Spirit and identified as God's servant/son. There is a possible allusion here to Moses, whose genealogy is not given when he is first introduced in relation to his parents in Exod 2:1–2 but only later, after he had received his call from God in the wilderness (Exod 6:14–27). In Exod 2:1, 2, not even Moses' parents' names are given. Whether this identification with Moses was Luke's intention or not, there are definite parallels. Several features of Luke's genealogy merit further attention. For instance, Luke begins his genealogy with Jesus and proceeds backwards to Adam and ultimately to God (Luke 3:38), a possible means of introducing Jesus as the Son of God and the Son of Man. In Hebrew, *ʾadam* is the word for "human." The genealogy in Luke's Gospel may serve his universalistic understanding of the gospel by showing that Jesus is related to the whole of the human race. Perhaps

T A B L E   5 - 1

MATTHEW'S USE OF THE NUMBER THREE

Description	Matthean Reference
a. Three incidents in Jesus' childhood	ch. 2
b. Three incidents before Jesus' ministry	chs. 3–4
c. Three temptations of Jesus	4:1–11
d. Threefold interpretation of "Do not commit murder"	5:22
e. Three illustrations of righteousness	6:1–18
f. Three prohibitions	6:19–7:6
g. Three injunctions	7:7–27
h. Three miracles of power	(8:23–9:8)
i. Three complaints of Jesus' adversaries	(9:1–17)
j. Three responses to the question of fasting	(9:14–17)
k. Three examples of hostility from the Pharisees	(ch. 12)
l. Three parables of sowing	(13:1–22)
m. Three sayings about "little ones"	(ch. 18)
n. Three parables of prophecy	(21:38–22:14)
o. Three parables of warning	(24:32–25:30)[17]

also Luke is emphasizing Jesus' role as Son of Man, a representative suffering servant in the tradition of Isa 53:10–12. It is likely that through his genealogy Luke identifies Jesus with the whole human race and even with God.

Luke includes seventy-seven names where Matthew only has forty-one. The period from Abraham to Jesus has fifty-six names in Luke, and even here, only half of the names are the same as those in Matthew's list, except for those after the time of the captivity. Many of the names after the exile in both Luke's and Matthew's lists are not found anywhere else. There may be a pattern of eleven sevens in Luke's list, but a pattern of sevens is not as evident with Luke as with Matthew.

Both Matthew and Luke offer the genealogy of Joseph, not Mary. The widely held view that Luke offers the genealogy of Mary and Matthew presents the genealogy of Joseph was first proposed in 1490 by Annius, the bishop of Viterbo in central Italy. That view, though obviously intended to account for the clear differences between Matthew and Luke, fails to deal adequately with the fact that both genealogies mention Joseph, but not Mary.

C. The Early Childhood of Jesus

Not much is known about the childhood of Jesus, apart from the one passage in Luke 2:39–52, which tells of Jesus' childhood visit to Jerusalem and the temple. The following information, however, may be gleaned and inferred from the Gospels.

It can be inferred from Luke 2:24 that Joseph and Mary's offering in the temple was that of a poor family and that Jesus was probably brought up in relatively poor surroundings. Although the vast majority of the population would have been considered poor, the fact that Jesus had the trade of carpenter or stonemason probably put him into a higher socioeconomic level. Being a carpenter meant that Jesus would have been a member of the artisan class or a tradesman. From what we know of the growth of cities in the Decapolis region, especially Sepphoris (although this city is not mentioned in the NT), people with various skills and subtrades such as Jesus' were in high demand. He was likely to have been strong in stature, since in antiquity a carpenter normally cut his own timber and hauled it to his workshop. It should be noted that the term "carpenter" or "wood-craftsman" (τέκτων, tektōn) was also used of stonemasons, who often carried huge rocks. Jesus' ability to chase the moneychangers out of the temple, whether it was a few or all of them, as the four Gospel writers report, is not out of step with a man of considerable strength such as we might expect from a carpenter in the prime of life.

From Mark 6:3, where Jesus is described as the son of Mary (a not uncommon way of describing a son whose father had died), we might also infer that he had important responsibilities in his family early on, since he was the oldest male child in his home. It may also be that the early death of Joseph resulted in poverty for the family as Jesus was growing up, but this is merely supposition. Joseph is not mentioned after the birth stories in Matthew and Luke except for Jesus' visit to Jerusalem in Luke 2:39–52, his baptism in Luke 3:23, and the start of his ministry in Luke 4:22. On the other hand, Joseph is mentioned as the father of Jesus in John 6:42, with the possible implication that Joseph and Mary were both still living at the time of Jesus' ministry. In John 1:45 Jesus is identified as the son of Joseph, and in Luke 4:22 the same occurs with no indication of Joseph's death. Mary's name, however, seldom occurs outside the infancy narratives

(see Mark 6:3; Matt 13:55; Acts 1:14). Mary was the mother of Jesus and Joseph was the reputed father, but it is not certain that Joseph was still living as Jesus approached adulthood. What seems clear is his rejection of family ties and social contacts (Mark 3:21, 31–35; 6:1–6; and esp. Luke 14:25–26; John 7:3–9). Jesus was from a fairly large family that included four brothers and at least two sisters (Mark 6:3). From Mark, it appears that Jesus' family did not follow him or believe in him during the days of his ministry (esp. 3:21, 31–35).

Jesus' references to common things reveal his familiarity with an agrarian community. He uses these illustrations: sewing patches on a garment (Mark 2:21), the growth of a farmer's crop (Mark 4:26–29), the growth of the lilies of the field and the grass of the field (Matt 6:28–30), the farmer with two barns (Luke 12:16–21), the sower who sowed seed (Mark 4:1–9), the price of small birds (Matt 10:29–31; Luke 12:6–7), and the amount of a common worker's daily wages (Matt 20:1–2).

A typical Jewish boy in Palestine in the first century would have been educated in the synagogue, taken annually to the temple in Jerusalem (if the family had the means), and given religious training in the home. Jesus' attendance at the synagogue and his visits to the temple, as well as his references to the law and its practice, all suggest that he had such a training. This training, however, was not the same as that received by clergy. Jesus was a layperson in his theological education. Meier is probably right to understand the well-known parable of the Good Samaritan (Luke 10:30–37), with its reference to the priest and the Levite, as an "anticlerical joke" shared with Galileans who were distrustful of the clergy of their day.[18] It certainly was not a story from one who shared their ranks.

The region where Jesus grew up had a large Gentile population, and he likely learned enough Greek to do business with the Gentiles of Galilee, possibly even teaching in Greek occasionally. Even so, his usual language was probably Aramaic, and because of his synagogue training, he probably also had some knowledge of Hebrew. His contacts with Gentiles and his ability to communicate with them are well attested in the Gospels. For instance, Jesus almost certainly spoke Greek with the Syrophoenician woman in Mark 7:24–30 and with Pilate in Mark 15:2. Indeed, it is probable that we have the actual words of Jesus in Mark 15:2 (parallels in Matt 27:11; Luke 23:3; cf. John 18:18–37) in his dialogue with Pilate, when he affirms that he is the king of the Jews. It may even be that Jesus' conversation with his disciples in Matt 16:13–20 in the region of Caesarea Philippi, a Greek-speaking area, record his actual words.[19]

D. John the Baptist and the Baptism of Jesus

All four of the Gospels indicate that Jesus began his ministry during the time of John the Baptist's preaching. For them, the story of Jesus begins in conjunction with the ministry of John. Jesus' message was closely tied to that of John, and like John, Jesus called for true repentance as the preparation for the coming kingdom of God (see Mark 1:4, 15), and for baptism as the sign or seal of the reception of his preaching (see Mark 1:4; John 3:22–27). The popularity of John is attested not only in all four canonical Gospels and Acts, where John's disciples were preaching as far away as Ephesus (Acts 19:1–7), but also in Josephus, whose comments about John merit attention:

> But to some of the Jews the destruction of Herod's army seemed to be divine vengeance, and certainly a just vengeance, for his treatment of John, surnamed the Baptist. For Herod had put him to death, though he was a good man and had exhorted the Jews to lead righteous lives, to practice justice towards their fellows and piety towards God, and so doing to join in baptism. In his view this was a necessary preliminary if baptism was to be acceptable to God. They must not employ it to gain pardon for whatever sins they committed, but as a consecration of the body implying that the soul was already thoroughly cleansed by right behaviour. When others too joined the crowds about him, because they were aroused to the highest degree by his sermons, Herod became alarmed. Eloquence that had so great an effect on mankind might lead to some form of sedition, for it looked as if they would be guided by John in everything that they did. Herod decided therefore that it would be much better to strike first and be rid of him before his work led to an uprising, than to wait for an upheaval, get involved in a difficult situation and see his mistake. Though John, because of Herod's suspicions, was brought in chains to Machaerus, the stronghold that we have previously mentioned, and there put to death, yet the verdict of the Jews was that the destruction visited upon Herod's army was a vindication of John, since God saw fit to inflict such a blow on Herod. (*Ant.* 18.116–119; Feldman, LCL)

Much has been made of the dress and diet of John the Baptist (Mark 1:6), his practice of baptism in the Jordan, and the origin of his ministry in the Judean wilderness. Could there be a connection between John and the Essene community at Qumran or a similar community in that area? This is improbable, but it is interesting that John evidently rejected his priestly heritage (he was the son of Zechariah the priest, according to Luke 1:5). It is even possible that John, born to parents who were already getting old (Luke 1:7), was orphaned as a child and grew up in a community, like Qumran, known for taking in orphans. A connection with such a community, however, is not mentioned either in the NT or in Josephus, and there are clear distinctions between the kind of baptism of repentance John practiced and the daily ablutions at Qumran.

John was the first prophet in Israel in more than three hundred years, and his influence upon his nation was considerable. His impact on Galilee is obvious, for Jesus himself came from Nazareth in Galilee to be baptized by him (Mark 1:9). Later, Jesus' disciples practiced baptism as the sign and seal of the reception of their message, just as John had done.

Scholars generally agree that Jesus identified himself with the preaching of John the Baptist and was soon thereafter baptized by John in the Jordan, shortly before he began his own ministry around A.D. 28. There is little doubt that Jesus was baptized by John, as the Synoptics clearly state (Mark 1:9–11; Matt 3:13–17; Luke 3:21–22; cf. Acts 10:37–38). John, who recounts the same story of the Spirit descending upon Jesus (1:29–34), does not mention baptism as the agency of that descending Spirit, or the occasion for the divine approval ("This is my Son, the Beloved"); he does not mention Jesus' baptism at all. John apparently made a conscious decision to deal in this way with an obvious embarrassment for the church, namely, that Jesus the Christ received a baptism of repentance. There appears to be no reason why the church would invent such a story or pass it along in its traditions if there was not some basis in reality for it.

If the tradition is authentic, why was Jesus baptized? If Jesus was sinless, as many early Christians proclaimed (2 Cor 5:21), why would he have submitted to John's baptism, a baptism of repentance

(Mark 1:4; Matt 3:2–6, 11; Luke 3:3, 7–8, 10–14)? Meier suggests that it was because Jesus identified with John's message of the "imminent disaster that was threatening Israel in the last days of its history, a disaster to be avoided only by national repentance."[20] Jesus continued several themes of John's preaching throughout his ministry, including that of God's care for those who are dispossessed and unfortunate (Matt 25:31–46; cf. Luke 3:7–14; Matt 3:7–10). To be sure, Jesus had a more "realized eschatology" than did John and less of a focus on the observance of holy days (Mark 2:18–22; Luke 5:33–39), but both emphasized the imminent kingdom, concern for the physically impaired (Luke 14:1–6) and the poor (Luke 14:12–14, 21–24), a changed life (repentance) as a prerequisite for entering into that kingdom, and baptism as the sign and seal under which that kingdom is accepted.

Perhaps we should differentiate between what the baptism by John meant to Jesus and what it meant to the evangelists. They clearly connected it with the identity of Jesus as the Son of God ("This is my Son, the Beloved")—the fulfillment of Ps 2:7—and as the servant of the Lord in Isa 42:1, cited in the declaration at his baptism (see Mark 1:11; Matt 3:17; Luke 3:21–22) or at the time that John was baptizing (John 1:34). For the evangelists, the initiation of Jesus' public ministry at his baptism indicates that the fulfillment of prophecy is at hand and that "the Son of God, the royal Davidic messiah, is anointed with God's spirit to be the final prophet and servant of the Lord sent to a sinful people."[21]

Meier argues that Jesus' and John's acceptance of the practice of baptism shows that they were centering their lives around a new ritual or rite that lacked the sanction of tradition and the temple authorities. They thereby were calling into question the sufficiency of the temple and synagogue worship as it was practiced by the Jews at that time.[22]

But did the reception of John's baptism mean more for Jesus than just this? Did Jesus consider himself a sinner before God? The mere raising of that question takes us well beyond the available data in our sources and beyond the scope of the historian to respond. The church has clearly answered with a resounding no, speaking beyond historically quantifiable data and in theological terms. Meier concludes that the texts do "not yield sufficient data to form a judgment in the matter"[23] and reminds us that the acknowledgment of sin in antiquity was not like the experience we often think of today, in which one confesses a list of personal sins. It included, rather, an awareness that one was part of the history of sin because one was part of a sinful people. He finds examples of this in the prayers of confession of Ezra, who identified with his people and confessed their sin as a people to God (Ezra 9:6–7, 10–11, 15; but see also 1QS I, 18–II, 2). Meier concludes that we cannot know with any certainty what was going on in Jesus' mind at his baptism but that we can at least assume the following: Jesus acknowledged John as an eschatological prophet of God;[24] he agreed with John on the imminent judgment of God on a sinful Israel; and he submitted to John's baptism "as a seal of his own resolve to change his life and as a pledge of salvation as part of a purified Israel."[25] Borg understands the meaning of Jesus as eschatological prophet in the following way: "To say that Jesus was the eschatological prophet is to say that he saw himself as the prophet of the end who proclaimed the end of the world in his own time and the urgency of repentance before it was too late. That was the core of his message and mission."[26] Although Borg, with others, does not believe that this picture was true of the historical Jesus—that is, that Jesus understood himself as an eschatological prophet—it is difficult to argue historically that Jesus was not drawn to the message of John the Baptist, who himself announced the coming of the end times. Jesus identified his ministry with that of John the Baptist, who proclaimed the near arrival of the end times and called upon the Israelites to prepare themselves for it (Matt 3:2; Mark 1:2–4; Luke 3:2–9; John 1:19–23, as the quotation from Mal 4:5 indicates).

The synoptic evangelists themselves viewed Jesus' baptism as an announcement that he was the Son of God, but there were other messages as well. For Mark, the first witness to this event, it was God showing his approval of Jesus' mission (compare Mark 1:11 with Ps 2:7 and Isa 42:1). For Matthew, it was understood as necessary for Jesus' consecration to ministry (Matt 3:14, 15) to fulfill the demands of righteousness. According to Acts 10:37–38, the baptism was evidently viewed as God's anointing of Jesus with the Spirit as he began his ministry. In Luke's Gospel, the baptism may have been a

Machaerus (Mukāwir, Jordan), the site of Herod the Great's easternmost fortress and the place where John the Baptist was beheaded (Mark 6:14–29; Josephus, Ant. 18.116-119). A Roman siege ramp is in the foreground.
Photo Lee M. McDonald.

part of the Lukan motif of identifying Jesus with those he came to save; hence, after Jesus was born, he was dedicated in the temple, was baptized along with the others coming to John, was identified with the human race in his genealogy (Luke 3:23–38), and, like all humanity, was tempted but did not sin (Luke 4:1–13).

Finally, there was a time when John sent his own disciples to Jesus to ask whether he was the Messiah of God or whether he should continue seeking another (Luke 7:18–19). Luke 7:21, with its parallel in Matt 11:2–6, states that "Jesus had just then cured many people of diseases, plagues, and evil spirits, and had given sight to many who were blind." Jesus then tells them of the activity of the expected Messiah, saying "Go and tell John what you have seen and heard: the blind receive their sight, the lame walk, the lepers are cleansed, the deaf hear, the dead are raised, the poor have good news brought to them. And blessed is anyone who takes no offense at me" (Luke 7:22–23; cf. Isa 29:18–19; 35:5–6; 61:1). In a recently published text

from Qumran, 4QMessianic Apocalypse (4Q521), there is a similar interpretation of the Isaiah passages by another form of Judaism of the first century, the Essenes. This text suggests that several Jewish groups of the early first century had similar understandings of what phenomena would accompany the coming of the Messiah:

[for the heav]ens and the earth will listen *to his Messiah,* [and all] that is in them will not turn away from the holy precepts. Be encouraged, you who are seeking the Lord in his service! . . . Will you not, perhaps, encounter the lord in it, all those who hope in their heart? For the Lord will observe the devout, and call the just by name, and upon the poor he will place his spirit, and the faithful he will renew with his strength. For he will honour the devout upon the throne of eternal royalty, freeing prisoners, *giving sight to the blind,* straightening out the twisted. Ever shall I cling to those who hope. In his mercy he will jud[ge] for *he will heal the badly wounded and will make the dead live, he will proclaim good news to the meek* [and] *give lavishly* [to the need]y, *lead the exiled and enrich the hungry.* [. . .] and all [. . .]. (4Q521 2 II)[27]

The exchange between Jesus and John's disciples in Luke 7 is very important because it is an early reference to Jesus' understanding of his messianic role. This so-called Q passage, quite similar to the wording in both Matthew and Luke, suggests that it was a very early tradition in the church. Members of the Jesus Seminar have voted against the authenticity of this passage,[28] but apparently without sufficient cause, just a prior assumption that Jesus could not have said about himself anything related to an apocalyptic figure who would establish an apocalyptic kingdom of God. But this passage is well attested, and there is every reason to believe that it essentially came from Jesus himself. Other voices of first-century Judaism also believed that the coming messiah would be accompanied by remarkable phenomena.

E. The Temptation of Jesus

Matthew and Luke, following Mark and Q, indicate that Jesus was tempted in the wilderness after his baptism, before the beginning of his ministry. The story is not mentioned in John. The only other references to this temptation in the NT are found in Heb 2:18 and 4:15, where the author claims that Jesus was tempted so that he could identify with humanity and understand what humanity faces in its temptations. The purpose of the temptations is not clearly stated in the Synoptics, but it may be that, in the view of the evangelists, there were several motives. In Luke, these appear to be related to the theme of Jesus' identity with humanity: his birth in lowly circumstances, his baptism with the people of Israel, his genealogy connecting him to all of humanity (through Adam) as well as God, and his temptations such as others face. When combined, these stories present a vivid picture of Jesus' interest in, and identification with, humanity in all of its frailty and vulnerability. It may also be that Luke (4:1–13) and Matthew (4:1–11) viewed the manner in which Jesus faced his temptations as a model for the church to follow. It is instructive that Luke has the Spirit descend upon Jesus at his baptism (3:22) and empower him during his temptations (4:1) and at the beginning of his ministry (4:14). In his opening ministry at the synagogue in Nazareth, Jesus is invited to read from Isa 61:1–2 (cf. 58:6), which begins, "The Spirit of the Lord is upon me" (Luke 4:16–21). Luke may have tried to point out to the church how to overcome temptation, even as Jesus overcame it, by showing that the ability to overcome is available to those who rely upon the power of the Spirit when they face trials, and to those who depend upon the sacred Scriptures. This was undoubtedly an important message for the early church, indeed for the church of any age.

Finally, it is difficult not to see the parallels and contrasts between the temptation of Jesus and the temptations of Israel in the wilderness. The number forty is prominent in both Jesus' and Israel's temptations, and both temptations, or trials, take place in the wilderness. Physical hunger was a part of both (Luke 4:3; cf. Num 11:1–15). The contrasts are also clear. Jesus was obedient to God; the Israelites were not, save Joshua and Caleb (Num 13:26–33). For the forty days of spying there were forty years of wandering in the wilderness. Jesus' temptations were for forty days, during which he was obedient to God and dependent upon God (the Holy Spirit) for strength.

F. The Early Galilean Ministry

Jesus grew up in Galilee, which, as we have mentioned, had a large Gentile population and seems to have been a place where the Jews were strongly nationalistic. The region, the most fertile and agriculturally productive land in the nation, yielded many kinds of fruit, and the Sea of Galilee, also called Gennesaret, was well known for its plentiful fish. One of the oldest descriptions of the area, near the time of Jesus, comes from Josephus:

> Skirting the lake of Gennesar [Galilee], and also bearing that name, lies a region whose natural properties and beauty are very remarkable. There is not a plant which its fertile soil refuses to produce, and its cultivators in fact grow every species; the air is so well-tempered that it suits the most opposite varieties. The walnut, a tree which delights in the most wintry climate, here grows luxuriantly, beside palm-trees, which thrive on heat, and figs and olives, which require a milder atmosphere. One might say that nature had taken pride in thus assembling, by a *tour de force*, the most discordant species in a single spot, and that, by a happy rivalry, each of the seasons wished to claim this region for her own. For not only has the country this surprising merit of producing such diverse fruits, but it also preserves them: for ten months without intermission it supplies those kings of fruits, the grape and the fig; the rest mature on the

trees the whole year round. Besides being favoured by its genial air, the country is watered by a highly fertilizing spring, called by the inhabitants Capharnaum; some have imagined this to be a branch of the Nile, from its producing a fish resembling *coracin* found in the lake of Alexandria. This region extends along the border of the lake which bears its name for a length of thirty furlongs and inland to a depth of twenty. Such is the nature of this district. (*War* 3.516–521; Thackeray, LCL)

This is the region where Jesus began his ministry. The Sea of Galilee is thirteen miles long and eight miles at its widest point. On its north shore in the first century was the little village of Capernaum, which had a population of 1,000 to 1,500. It was here that Jesus established the headquarters for his ministry in Galilee. On the east and west sides of Galilee and on the eastern and western sides of the Jordan River to the south were ten Gentile cities called the Decapolis, a league of cities; Sepphoris, the capital of Galilee and one of the Decapolis cities, was located only three to four miles northwest of Nazareth. Jesus made two brief visits to this area during his ministry (Mark 5:1–20; 7:31–37).

Clay jars modeled after those in which the scrolls from the Dead Sea were preserved.

From there he also went north and west to the region of Tyre and Sidon on the Phoenician seacoast (Mark 7:24–30). The Gospels do not record that he went into the cities in either area. One might wonder whether Jesus went into the larger cities, such as Sepphoris, Tiberias, or Scythopolis, and if he did not, why not. For whatever reasons, he apparently went instead to the small towns, villages, and countryside in Galilee for most of his ministry.

The inhabitants of Galilee included low- to moderate-income farmers or fishermen (Mark 1:16–17) as well as many rootless peasants and itinerant craftsmen (Matt 20:1–16). The Jewish aristocracy of the region lived mostly in Sepphoris, Tiberias, and Scythopolis. Most of the lesser officials in the region—judges, civil administrators, tax collectors, stewards for absentee landlords— came from Jerusalem and were resented by the residents of Galilee. For example, Jesus' parable of the absentee landlord sending his servants to collect payment from wicked tenants for the use of his land (Mark 12:1–12) is stinging in its indictment, since Jesus told it to members of the Sanhedrin—chief priests, scribes, and elders (see the context in Mark 11:27).[29] It appears that most of the citizens of Galilee were deprived, not well schooled, uncultured, and even ridiculed by other Jews. Notice, for instance, the view that Jesus' disciples were uneducated (Acts 4:5–13, when Peter and John stood before the Sanhedrin) and the question in John 1:46 whether anything good could come out of Nazareth.[30] Not all who came from the region were uneducated, but it appears that this was more the case than a few exceptions might suggest. Sepphoris, the location of Herod Antipas's "ornament of all Galilee" (Josephus, *Ant.* 18.27) and home of the local Jewish aristocracy, was resented by the majority of the Jews in the region, especially during the rebellion of A.D. 66–70, when the citizens of that community remained loyal to Rome. In A.D. 25 Herod Antipas built Tiberias as a new capital city of the region, but Sepphoris continued to serve as a home for the wealthy and educated. Sepphoris was well within the view of the residents of Nazareth, since both towns were on opposite sides of a valley. The discovery of a Greek inscription from a Roman-period synagogue at Sepphoris may indicate that there was a Jewish-Christian synagogue

A modern replica of ancient boats (so-called Jesus boats) on the Sea of Galilee. Photo Lee M. McDonald.

there in the late first or second century, since the inscription has the typical Christian Chi-Rho monogram at the end.[31] By the fifth century, there was clearly a strong Christian presence in the city, evidenced by the presence of a bishop from Sepphoris at the Council of Chalcedon in A.D. 451. There are also second-century reports of a Jewish Christian named Jacob who talked about Jesus at Sepphoris and gained permission to start a church.[32]

In Galilee Jesus proclaimed a new order of reality coming in the near future. He argued that the kingdom of God would reverse the social order and bring equality, liberation, and justice. This was Jesus' message in the synagogue in Nazareth (Luke 4:16–19), and he commented on at least three occasions that "the last will be first, and the first will be last" (Matt 20:16; Mark 10:31; Luke 13:30). It is clear from the Gospels that Jesus led a movement of disciples whom he had personally called to a radical change of lifestyle. He called them to renounce their home (Mark 1:16; 10:28–31; Matt 8:20) or families (Luke 14:26–27), to give up their possessions (Matt 10:1–10; Mark 10:25), to reject self-protection (Matt 5:38–39), and to live a life of self-denial (Mark 8:34–37).

All four Gospels portray Jesus as an itinerant preacher who was homeless and without a source of income. His disciples accompanied him on his journeys in Galilee, and it appears that on occasion women also accompanied him, especially on his journey to Jerusalem. Jesus said to a would-be disciple in Matt 8:20, "Foxes have holes, and birds of the air have nests; but the Son of Man has nowhere to lay his head." All the evangelists agree on this picture, and we find that Jesus frequently eats at the homes of others and is cared for by his followers (Mark 2:15–17; Luke 7:36–50; 11:37–44; 19:1–10), especially by the women (Luke 8:1–3). Indeed, it appears that the main source of care came from women who became followers of Jesus (see also Matt 27:55–56; Mark 15:40–41).

Jesus' earliest followers became wandering vagabonds who could be asked to endure such hardships of deprivation and trials because the kingdom of God was imminent and the call to men and women was urgent (Matt 9:35–38). He asked for a

Ruins at the hot-spring baths, from Roman times, at Tiberias beside the Sea of Galilee. Photo Lee M. McDonald.

radical decision from all who would follow him (Matt 8:18–22; Luke 9:57–62). He seemed to reject wealth on the part of his followers, and he is recorded to have said that it would be easier for a camel to go through the eye of a needle than for a rich man to enter the kingdom of God (Mark 10:25).

Those persons who were most likely to hear Jesus' message and to be especially drawn to such a movement were the disenfranchised, who had everything to gain and nothing to lose from such a significant change in the social order. Jesus' call for justice, love of the poor, and the giving of mercy to the least in society (Luke 4:16–21; Matt 5:3ff.; 25:31–46) would especially have appealed to those who were deprived of justice, love, and mercy. Galilee was an area by and large filled with the dispossessed and oppressed (Matt 9:35–38). Paul's comments about the makeup of the church in Corinth shows that the Gospel appealed to a similar kind of people outside Palestine as well (cf. 1 Cor 1:26–27).

Not all of Jesus' followers in Galilee, however, were "down-and-outers." For example, Zebedee had hired laborers (Mark 1:20); those who were

An olive press from Roman times found at Capernaum. Photo Lee M. McDonald

able to hire laborers had a certain status in village communities. Also, one of Jesus' disciples was a tax collector (Matthew or Levi), and further south in Jericho Zacchaeus, a wealthy "chief" tax collector, became a follower of Jesus (Luke 19:1–10). One of Jesus' followers was a Zealot (Simon), one was a rich member of the town council (Joseph; cf. Matt

A unique column discovered at Chorazin; it has a companion in the Israeli Archaeological Museum in Jerusalem. Photo Lee M. McDonald.

27:57; Luke 23:50–51); even a Roman military officer came to Jesus (Luke 7:2–10). Jesus apparently could move freely among all groups of people, but those most likely to listen to him and most open to a radical change were those who were the most vulnerable in society and had nothing to lose in following him—the poor. The large numbers of poor and uneducated members of the church even in the second century prompted Celsus to write: "Let no one educated, no one wise, no one sensible draw near [to the Christians]. For those abilities are thought by us to be evils. But as for anyone ignorant, anyone stupid, anyone uneducated, anyone who is a child, let him come boldly" (Origen, *Cels.* 3.44 [LCL]).

That some, but not many, educated and prosperous persons joined the Christian community in the early development of the church is no doubt behind Paul's comments in 1 Cor 1:26–29:

Consider your own call, brothers and sisters: not many of you were wise by human standards, not many were powerful, not many were of noble birth. But God chose what is foolish in the world to shame the wise; God chose what is weak in the world to shame the strong; God chose what is low and despised in the world, things that are not, to reduce to nothing things that are, so that no one might boast in the presence of God.

Well into the second century, Christians were laughed at and mocked because of the large number of uneducated and uncultured adherents. Only after the mid–second century A.D. did the church begin to have a respectable number of philosophers and scholars advocating the Christian faith, such as Justin Martyr, Irenaeus, Clement of Alexandria, and Origen. One of them, Aristo, came from the unlikely community of Pella in the region of Galilee.

Considerable discussion has been raised about whether Jesus intended to found a religious community, the new Israel. Although there is nothing in the Gospels to indicate how Jesus wanted that community organized, it is obvious from the very selection of the Twelve[33] that he had decided to establish some kind of community faithful to the Lord. His disciples, convinced that they would have authority in that community, were even debating among themselves over who would be greatest in that kingdom (Mark 8:33–37). It is not likely that the early church would have invented the notion of the Twelve, later inserting it into the story of Jesus, especially since one of the Twelve, Judas Iscariot, is identified as the one who betrayed him. Meier is no doubt correct when he concludes that this could hardly be an invention of church propaganda. He observes the lesson from Qumran that some scholars have ignored, that Jesus' view on the imminent judgment of God and the coming of the eschatological kingdom did not mean that he was uninterested in organization. Qumran, an eschatological community with similar views about the coming kingdom of God, was also a very organized community.[34]

Thanks to John's Gospel, we learn that Jesus ministered frequently in Jerusalem, which helps us to understand why a strong church developed there after his death, but also from John we get a different idea of the length of Jesus' ministry (see sec. A, above). The Synoptic Gospels mention only one Passover and appear to reduce the ministry of Jesus to a period of less than one year. The Passover meal was the occasion for the Last Supper of

The northeastern Sea of Galilee with Hippos, one of the Decapolis cities, to the left of center.
© Rohr Productions. Used with permission.

The Jezreel Valley with a view to Mount Tabor. © Rohr Productions. Used with permission.

A view of the plains of Megiddo (Harmagedon), where some believe the last great battle of humanity will take place (Rev 16:12–16). Photo Lee M. McDonald.

Jesus with his disciples (Mark 14:12–16; Matt 26:17–19; Luke 22:7–13), and this is supported by Paul's reference to Jesus as "our pascal lamb" (1 Cor 5:7). John, on the other hand, mentions three or possibly four such occasions during the career of Jesus (John 2:13; possibly 5:1; 6:4; 11:55; 12:1); this may well be more accurate than the synoptic tradition that follows Mark. In these matters, John probably preserves a more accurate account of the duration of Jesus' ministry.

G. Healings, Teachings, and the Nature of Jesus' Appeal

Among the chief characteristics of Jesus' ministry are reports about his remarkable activity of healing persons from illnesses and physical ailments such as blindness and engaging in such phenomena as calming a storm. From the time of the Enlightenment, when miracles were called into question by David Hume and his contemporaries, many theologians have tried to ground their Christian faith in a Jesus of history, that is, in a Jesus without the so-called mythological reports about miracles that were attributed to him. All such stories about remarkable healings, walking on the water, and the like were summarily dismissed without distinction and removed from the Gospels as inauthentic material. Even Bultmann, who acknowledged that Jesus was a miracle worker—that he was known to have performed a number of healings—accepted this aspect of Jesus but attributed it not to the miracle-working power of God but, rather, to often dimly understood religious and psychological phenomena. These so-called miracles were not viewed as extramundane phenomena but were explained on the basis of common religious and/or psychosomatic experiences. More recently, scholars have generally accepted as a part of the historical Jesus his ability to do remarkable healings among people. In a survey of NT scholarship on the matter, Craig Evans has applied the traditional criteria for authenticity to the miracles of Jesus and concluded that the older notion of myth can no longer be ap-

Ruins caused by an earthquake in the mid–eighth century on top of Hippos on the eastern side of Galilee. Perhaps this city is referred to in Jesus' saying "a city set on a hill cannot be hid" (Matt 5:14). Photo © Rohr Productions. Used with permission.

plied to the Gospel stories. Evans claims that the notion "that miracles played a role in Jesus' ministry is no longer seriously contested," concluding that "we are in what I think should be understood as a post-mythological era in life-of-Jesus research."[35] This does not mean that historical-critical scholars now affirm that the source of Jesus' ability to do miracles came from "a bolt from the blue" (or God) but only that such phenomena did occur and are to be explained in intramundane closed-causal-nexus categories. Rather than get bogged down in philosophical discussion on the possibility of miracles, Meier argues that it is appropriate simply to recognize that faith healers and miracle workers are common phenomena not only in the ancient world but in the present age as well.[36]

Although parallels to Jesus' miracles are sometimes sought in the examples of Honi the Circle Drawer, who lived in Palestine in the first century B.C., and Rabbi Hanina ben Dosa, who lived perhaps before A.D. 70, these parallels are not impressive and are not at all similar to the stories about

the miracles of Jesus in the Gospels.[37] Others have tried to show parallels with the first-century itinerant philosopher Apollonius of Tyana, but significant contrasts outweigh the parallels.

Jesus' preaching and teaching brought a message of hope for the hopeless and a warning to those who were comfortable with their securities in this world (Luke 12:16–21). He called for the abandonment of worldly securities and obedience to the call of God (Mark 8:34–37) and spoke of alertness and preparation for the coming kingdom of God and day of judgment that would test every person's preparation and vigilance (Mark 13:32–37; Matt 24:36–51). He warned that every person would be judged on how they treated the hungry, thirsty, poor, naked, sick, and imprisoned (Matt 25:31–46). In his response to John the Baptist's question issued through his disciples, "Are you the one who is to come, or are we to wait for another?" (Luke 7:18), Jesus replied that the blind see and the lame walk—in other words, the answer was in his miracles. Brown concludes that Jesus believed that in

Tiberias, built by Herod Antipas, with the Jordan Valley in the upper center. The ancient ruins and mineral baths are located just south of the modern city of the same name. © Rohr Productions. Used with permission.

An earlier view of the largely unexcavated Beth Shean, the location of the Hellenistic city Scythopolis that was inhabited in the New Testament era by Gentiles and wealthy Jewish landowners. The Roman theater is in the lower right. More recently all of this area has been excavated in significant detail. © Rohr Productions. Used with permission.

Capernaum, the location of Jesus' headquarters during his Galilean ministry.
Photo © Rohr Productions. Used with permission.

his mission of preaching, exorcisms, and healing the kingdom of God was not only at hand but also present to some extent (see Matt 12:28; Luke 17:21).[38] In a way, in the ministry of Jesus the "not yet" of the kingdom of God was already present, although not completely. Although many scholars choose either the imminent apocalyptic understanding of the kingdom of God (it is near but not yet here) in the teaching of Jesus or the so-called realized eschatology, in which the kingdom is fulfilled in his ministry, it is more probable that both are in view. The future has broken into the present in Jesus, but its fullness is yet future.

Jesus was not as strict in observance of the law as were those at Qumran or those in the strict Pharisaic tradition. He did not allow human need to take second place to the keeping of the ritual of the law and its traditions. He associated freely with those the righteous considered unclean and of low esteem (Mark 2:15–17), was not concerned with keeping the traditional fasting days (Mark 2:18–22), and even felt free to violate traditions about work-

ing or healing on the Sabbath (Mark 2:23–27; 3:1–6). It was regarding the Sabbath that such offense was taken by the Pharisees that they began to look for ways to destroy him (Mark 3:6). On the other hand, Jesus' motivation to keep what the Scriptures said about the purity of the temple caused him to overturn the moneychangers' tables there, a story found in all four Gospels (Mark 11:15–18; Matt 21:12–13; Luke 19:45–48; John 2:13–17). Jesus appears to announce a new morality, a new standard by which people were to be evaluated and judged by God. This is seen in his "You have heard it said" messages in Matthew's Sermon on the Mount (see esp. 5:21–48), in which he intensifies the meaning and application of the law to levels not heard of before. Although there is considerable opposition to the idea that Jesus actually said these words, in part because they fit with Matthew's apologetic in showing Jesus to be more faithful in keeping the law than were the Pharisees, they fit the picture of Jesus that is portrayed in the Gospels. He did not abandon the law even though he placed greater

Perhaps a third-century synagogue at Capernaum. It is built on top of an earlier synagogue structure, dating from the time of Jesus. Photo Lee M. McDonald.

value on the law's call to care for human need than on its many rituals. This is clear in his teaching of the greatest commandments, loving God and one's neighbor, which have parallels to teachings of Hillel before him (Mark 12:28–34; Luke 10:25–28; Matt 22:37–40). Luke supplies a further parable that illustrates this very point, and isolates Jesus' understanding of the meaning of the Law from that of the religious people of his day. In the parable of the Good Samaritan (Luke 10:29–31), Jesus stated that the end of the law was to love God and one's neighbor. Challenged by a scribe or lawyer to explain who his neighbor was, Jesus told him not only who his neighbor was—anybody in need—but also how to be a neighbor, to care for human need. In the parable he contrasted the actions of a traditional enemy, the Samaritan, with those of the traditional religious people, the priest and the Levite.

The long-standing Jewish view of the temple was that it was a house of prayer and worship. It was also a place where the Gentiles could go and worship in the larger courtyard, which in the time of Jesus was noisy with animals and moneychang-ers. When Jesus saw the moneychangers in the outer courtyard of the temple and heard the noise such an activity would cause, he was apparently so incensed that he upset the tables of the money-changers and drove them out of the temple (Mark 11:15–19; Matt 21:12–16; Luke 19:45–48; John 2:13–22). The multiple attestation to the cleansing of the temple strongly witnesses to the authenticity of this event, even though we are not certain how many were involved in the incident. Jesus' verbal response includes references or allusions to Isaiah, who said that the temple was to be a place of prayer (Isa 56:1–7) and focused on the place of the Gentiles in such worship (56:7–8). Also mentioned in this story are passages in Jer 7:2–14 (v. 11 in particular) and 26:8 that focus on holiness in God's house and persecution of the prophets (cf. also Exod 30:13; Lev 1:14). John, who places this event at the beginning of Jesus' ministry (John 2:13–22), appeals to Ps 69:9 for justification of Jesus' actions. Standing behind this passage may be an understanding of Zech 14:21, which focuses on holiness and the absence of a trader in the house of the Lord

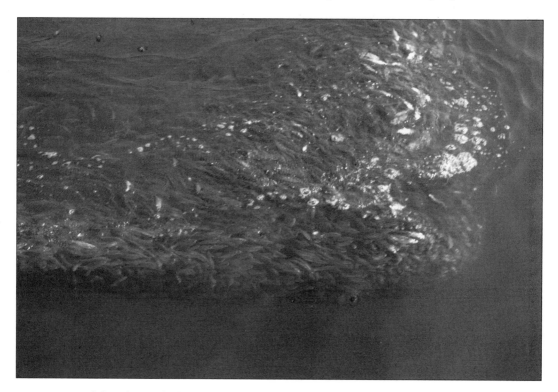

Fish from the Sea of Galilee. It was not unusual to catch many fish at one time with a large net (see Luke 5:1–9; John 21:4–11). Photo © Rohr Productions. Used with permission.

(which Jesus may have taken to be the same as moneychangers). The significance of this event in the Synoptics is their depiction of it as one of the primary activities of Jesus, during his last week of ministry in Jerusalem, that led to his arrest (Mark 11:18–19; Luke 19:45–48).[39] It also shows Jesus' concern for true worship and possibly even a concern for the Gentiles, who had no other place to go.

At the heart of Jesus' teaching and preaching was the message of the kingdom of God and how one should prepare for its coming. Jesus, in some sense, saw the kingdom of God and God himself present in his ministry and person. This was also a factor that led to his arrest and crucifixion.

H. The Transfiguration of Jesus

The transfiguration is one of the events that is found only in the Synoptic Gospels (Mark 9:2–8; Matt 17:1–8; Luke 9:28–36) (see table 5–2). It is, however, referred to one other time in 2 Pet 1:16–19. Since the transfiguration is beyond normal human experience and appears to have a theological function in the Gospels, most scholars have either written this event off as a transposed resurrection narrative (e.g. Bultmann) or dismissed it altogether. It is not discussed in most historical-Jesus studies. Like the virginal conception stories, the transfiguration simply does not fit into natural human experience. But is there more that can be said about this story? What is its purpose in the Gospel narratives? How does it function to further the story that each evangelist tells?

The story is laden with several important theological motifs and seems to function, after the confession of Peter in the previous section, as a foreshadowing of the coming kingdom and as an encouragement to that inner circle of disciples who witnessed it. It is also wrapped up with Mark's "messianic secret" motif.[40] In the transfiguration, the evangelists describe Jesus in his heavenly glory as the Messiah, the Son of God. Matthew calls this a vision (ὅραμα, *horama*, 17:9), but the exact nature of the experience appears to go beyond other

The ancient city of Gerasa (Jerash, Jordan), one of the cities of the Decapolis and also a major route to Damascus during the time of the apostle Paul. It is doubtful that Jesus performed the miracle of exorcizing the pigs in this community (see Matt 8:28; Luke 8:26; Mark 5:1), since it is thirty-seven miles southeast of Galilee.
Photo Lee M. McDonald.

visionary experiences mentioned in the OT and NT. As in other passages, such as Paul's encounter with the risen Christ on the Damascus road (Acts 9:3), brilliance is associated with visionary experiences, but in the transfiguration accounts the parallel of Moses' experience with God on Mount Sinai (Exod 34:29–35) is more likely because of their description of Moses. Exodus 24:12–18 states that Moses was on Mount Sinai for forty days while he encountered God and was given assurances that God was with him as he continued his journey taking the children of Israel through the wilderness (Exod 33:7–23; 34:29–35). His appearance was changed as a result of this encounter.

A few other parallels are worth noting as well. For example, Mark refers to "six days" (Mark 9:2; cf. Exod 24:16), three companions were taken on the journey (Mark 9:2; cf. Exod 24:1), the experience took place on a mountain (Mark 9:2; Matt 17:1; Luke 9:28; cf. Exod 24:12), a cloud covered the mountain (Mark 9:7; cf. Exod 24:16), God's voice came from the cloud (Mark 9:7; cf. Exod 24:16), an appearance was transformed (Mark 9:3; cf. Exod 34:30), and there was a fearful reaction (Mark 9:6; cf. Exod 34:30). In Exod 24:13 Moses takes Joshua up with him. In Hebrew the name Jesus is Joshua. Whether this is veiled typology is not certain, but it appears to be.

Luke likewise makes a clear connection with Moses in his telling of this story and makes a few additions to it. He reverses Mark's order in the names (Luke 9:30) and emphasizes the discussion about Jesus' exodus, or departure (v. 31). Also, Luke tells of the disciples seeing Jesus' glory (v. 32), a familiar parallel with Exod 24:16, where the glory of the Lord was on the mountain, and with Exod 33:18–23, where Moses asked to see God's glory. Luke also says that Jesus' face or countenance was changed (Luke 9:29; cf. Exod 34:30, 35). Only Luke mentions the "eight days

The Sea of Galilee during a windstorm (see John 6:16–21). © Rohr Productions. Used with permission.

A view of Chorazin with Galilee in the background. © Rohr Productions. Used with permission.

The pool of Siloam in Jerusalem (John 9:7–11), the site also of an Asclepion, a Greco-Roman place of healing. Photo Lee M. McDonald.

Baptist, and since then the good news of the kingdom has been preached. The implication is that in Jesus a new day has dawned. In Luke 24:27, Jesus says that Moses and the prophets spoke of him. In his appearance to the disciples, he shows references to himself in Moses (the law), the prophets, and the Psalms (Luke 24:44–45).

After he had appeared to his disciples for forty days after his resurrection, Jesus was taken up in a cloud (Acts 1:3, 9). It is difficult not to draw a parallel with Moses, who also entered the cloud and was with God on the mountain for forty days in Exod 24:15–18. Did Luke anticipate Jesus' ascension into heaven with the transfiguration story? Does this passage focus on Jesus' glory, which was to be found later at his resurrection? Was the transfiguration intended by the evangelists as a foreshadow-

after," instead of the six days in Mark and Matthew. There is a parallel with Lev 23:33–44: seven days of offerings for the feast of Tabernacles or Booths, and on the eighth day a holy convocation, during which time the people were to dwell in booths or tents to remind them of the exodus (Lev 23:42–43). A "holy convocation" in Luke includes Moses the law-giver, Elijah the first of the prophets, and Jesus God's Son. To the heavenly voice announcing Jesus as God's Son, Luke 9:35 adds the words "my Chosen," a possible reference to Isa 42:1. "Listen to him" is probably a reference to Deut 18:15, where Moses commanded the people to listen to the prophet whom God would raise up some day. These parallels are quite extensive, and are too obvious to be coincidental. There appears to be a Moses motif running throughout this passage. Later, in Luke 16:16, Jesus says that the day of the law and the prophets concluded with the ministry of John the

Water from the springs flowing from under the grotto at Caesarea Philippi (Mark 8:27–30). Photo Lee M. McDonald.

A sacred niche in a mountain wall honoring the god Pan at Caesarea Philippi. Photo © Rohr Productions. Used with permission.

ing of the resurrection Jesus had predicted in Mark 8:31, 9:1, Luke 9:22, 27, and Matt 16:21, 28?

The climax of the transfiguration story is the divine identification of Jesus: "This is my Son, the Beloved" (Mark 9:7; Matt 17:5; Luke 9:35 has "my Chosen" instead of "my Beloved"). What are the implications of this in the Gospels? The announcement by God of his special relationship with Jesus is made either to the disciples or to Moses and Elijah ("This is," not "You are").

How did this event contribute to the message of the evangelists? Was it understood as a fulfillment of Mark 8:38–9:1 (see Matt 16:28; Luke 9:27), that is, as a foretaste of when "the Son of Man . . . comes in the glory of his Father," which would be shared with all of the disciples? Was Mark 9:1 a reference to the resurrection of Jesus? If so, why does Jesus say only "some" will witness it whereas all but Judas witnessed his resurrection appearances and no one actually witnessed the resurrection? Does it refer to the coming of the apocalyptic kingdom of God that Jesus proclaimed, as a number of scholars have suggested, adding that Jesus was wrong in his understanding? Again, this would seem a strange meaning of the text, since all of Jesus' disciples, and not only some, would have witnessed such an event if it were imminent. It is also unlikely that he was referring to the destruction of Jerusalem, which took place in A.D. 70, even though Jesus may well have believed that the nation stood under the condemnation of God and would be destroyed for its faithlessness (Luke 13:34–35; Matt 23:37–39). To make Mark 9:1 and its parallels in Matthew and Luke refer to this destruction is not necessitated by the text. Some scholars have argued that this was a reference to the coming of the Holy Spirit as seen in

T A B L E   5 - 2

THE TRANSFIGURATION OF JESUS: Parallel Accounts

Mark 9:2–13	Luke 9:28–36	Matthew 17:1–8
1. After six days . . .	About eight days after . . .	After six days . . .
2. Peter, James, and John accompanied Jesus.	same	same
3. Jesus went to a high mountain with the three.	Jesus went to a mountain to pray.	Jesus led the disciples to a high mountain.
4. Jesus was transfigured before them.	As he was praying, his countenance was altered.	Jesus was transfigured before them.
5. His garments became intensely white.	same	His garments became white as light.
6. Elijah and Moses appeared talking to Jesus.	Moses and Elijah appeared to speak of Jesus' departure (exodus).	Moses and Elijah appeared talking to Jesus.

The ancient synagogue in Tiberias. It may be the site of the tomb of Rabbi Meir Ba'al Ha-nes, a name associated with various rabbis of antiquity but most popularly with the tanna Meir who was a pupil of Rabbi Akiba ben Joseph in the second century A.D. © Rohr Productions. Used with permission.

Tiberias by the Sea of Galilee, the general site where the Talmud of the Land of Israel (the Yerushalmi) was produced. © Rohr Productions. Used with permission.

The ruins of Chorazin, made of basalt, with the slopes of the Mount of Beatitudes, north of the Sea of Galilee, in the upper background. © Rohr Productions. Used with permission.

The traditional site of the Sermon on the Mount on the northern shore of the Sea of Galilee. Such contours in the mountainside are conducive to speaking to large audiences. © Rohr Productions. Used with permission.

The Mosque of Abraham in Hebron. It was built by Herod the Great around the Cave of Machpelah. © Rohr Productions. Used with permission.

Caesarea Maritima (upper left) with the remains of Herod's harbor (upper left of center) and the remains of the hippodrome (center). © Rohr Productions. Used with permission.

Acts 1:8 and evidenced in Acts 2:1–42. Again, the word "some" does not fit this reference, since all but Judas Iscariot experienced the coming of the Holy Spirit. It is more likely that the evangelists had the transfiguration in mind, as that took place only for a few and is the most immediate context of the prediction. This interpretation is supported by 2 Pet 1:16–19, the only other passage in the NT to mention the transfiguration as a time when the glory of Jesus was revealed to his disciples. It appears, then, that the evangelists were drawing parallels with Moses in the transformation of Jesus at his transfiguration. The glory of Jesus was revealed in each of the accounts of the transfiguration story, perhaps with the purpose of assuring and encouraging the three disciples as they began their journey toward Jerusalem. Nevertheless, it was not sufficient to carry the disciples through the pain of seeing their Messiah arrested and crucified.

I. The Triumphal Entry

The story of the triumphal entry into Jerusalem is told in all four Gospels (Mark 11:1–10; Matt 21:1–9; Luke 19:28–38; John 12:12–15),[41] along with the story of the cleansing of the temple. In these stories, which do not appear to be creations of the evangelists, Jesus' relationship to God and his awareness of his mission as king of a renewed Israel are emphasized. The same texts of Scripture are cited in each of these stories (Zech 9:9 in all four, along with Ps 118:26 in the Synoptics and Isa 62:11 in Matthew). The objections by the Pharisees in Luke 19:39 show that what was done and said at Jesus' entry into Jerusalem was considered blasphemous, and John 12:19 likewise records a response of exasperation by the Pharisees. Coupled with his cleansing of the temple (Mark 11:15–17; Matt 21:12–13; Luke 19:45–48; John 2:13–17) and the response to it (Mark 11:18), as well as his prophecy concerning the destruction of the temple, Jesus' opponents believed they had grounds to destroy him (see sec. 3.A, below). These references fit in with the record of Jesus' trial, where the charge of blasphemy is raised against him (Mark 14:61–64).[42]

J. The Passion Predictions of Jesus

Several times during his ministry, the evangelists note that Jesus predicted his own death (Mark 8:31; 9:10–12, 32; Luke 9:45; John 2:21; 12:32–33). It is not difficult to understand that Jesus might have understood the natural consequences of his teaching, especially his challenging of the religious structures of his day, but one of the problems with the predictions is that the disciples seem ill prepared to understand or accept the arrest and crucifixion of Jesus in Jerusalem when it actually happens. If Jesus predicted his death, why was there an apparent lapse of faith by his disciples—and by Jesus himself, according to many scholars on the basis of his cry on the cross, "My God, my God, why have you forsaken me?" (Mark 15:34)—when he died?

As a result, some scholars have suggested that Jesus did not predict his death, that his predictions were later attributed to him by the early church to help it deal with the scandal of the cross and the embarrassment it caused (see sec. K, below). Others have argued that Jesus' predictions were more abbreviated than they appear in the Gospels and were not as clear as they were made out to be in the postresurrection church. In other words, the Gospel writers had the advantage of hindsight, and we should not expect them to make obscure in their passages what they understood more clearly even if only at a later time. One could also say that the disciples heard Jesus' predictions but were simply not attuned to understand them because of their excitement about going to Jerusalem, the city of fulfillment, and their anticipation of their roles in the coming kingdom of God. They expected a ruling king who would establish a political kingdom, not a crucified Messiah.

Whatever the solution to the problem, it is clear that nothing Jesus had said to his disciples influenced their behavior at the time of his arrest or changed their minds about what was taking place until after his resurrection. This might be the key for understanding the earliest preaching in Acts, where the cross does not play a significant role but is simply in the plan of God that death cannot destroy (Acts 2:23). The resurrection of Jesus was at the heart of their preaching, not the cross, until the latter became central to Paul's preaching a short time later (1 Cor 1:17–18, 23–24).[43]

K. The Arrest and Trial of Jesus

The setting for the arrest of Jesus has five important factors. (1) Jesus made personal claims to

A burial chamber in a garden at Bethphage (see
Matt 21:1; Mark 11:1; Luke 19:29).
Photo Lee M. McDonald.

have a special relationship with God, claims that
included his acceptance of the acclaim of the
people in the triumphal entry (see Luke 19:39).
(2) Jesus cleansed the temple. (3) Jesus rejected
the traditional application of the law to daily
practice, as shown in his healings on the Sabbath
(Mark 3:1–6), in allowing his disciples to collect
grain on the Sabbath (Mark 2:23–28), and in rejecting the traditional days of fasting (typically
Mondays and Thursdays, since it was believed
that Moses ascended and descended Mount Sinai
on those days [Mark 2:18–22]). (4) The charge
of insurrection against Rome was brought against
Jesus; that is, it was alleged that Jesus had become a political threat to Rome by substituting
himself as king in place of Caesar (Mark 15:1–3;
Luke 23:1–5; Matt 27:11–14; John 19:33–37). That
one of Jesus' disciples was called a Zealot has led
many to conclude that he was influenced by this
revolutionary party, which sought the overthrow
of Roman domination of Palestine (see sec. 3,
below). That one of Jesus' disciples was carrying a
sword when Jesus was arrested in the garden
(Mark 15:47) has also led to speculation that his
followers were not so passive as tradition has led
us to believe but could be quite reactionary.
These were characteristics of the revolutionaries that eventually led to the confrontation
with Rome in A.D. 66 and the destruction of the
temple and the city of Jerusalem in A.D. 70. (5) Je-

The Old City of Jerusalem with a view of the temple platform (left to center) and the site of the ancient Antonia
Fortress. The Via Dolorosa (Way of Sorrow) is in the center. Photo © Rohr Productions. Used with permission.

sus' popularity among the people was a growing concern to the leaders in Jerusalem. It was for this reason that they had to use caution, choosing to arrest him and bring charges against him late in the evening (Mark 14:2; Matt 26:5). According to John 6:15, the people even wanted to force him to be their king, perhaps seeing him as a liberator from oppression, a person who would care for the hungry and homeless and correct the abusive system that kept so many in poverty.

Scholars debate the merits of each of these factors, but there is little question that Jesus' neglect of the oral traditions that focused on how to keep the law (e.g., how far one could walk on the Sabbath, healing on the Sabbath, various kinds of ritual cleansings, and the focus on keeping the letter of the law) eventually led the religious leaders in Jerusalem to see Jesus as a threat; therefore, they sought to destroy him (e.g., Mark 3:1–6). All the evangelists agree on this point. Whether Jesus made remarkable claims about himself and his relationship to God, however, is debated among historical-Jesus scholars. Did Jesus make such claims? What passages suggest this, and to what extent might they be considered later church additions to the story of Jesus? There is no question that the Gospels report that Jesus made such claims (see also John 20:26–29, where Jesus accepts such recognition from Thomas), but are these accurate reports? Jesus' special relationship with God is announced in the earliest Christian proclamation (Rom 1:3–4; 10:9–10; Phil 2:11; 1 Cor 16:22), but how soon was this recognized by the followers of Jesus? We suggest that these acclamations stem from the ministry and teaching of Jesus himself.

For one known to have performed exorcisms, healings, and nature miracles (calming a storm, breaking five loaves and two fish to feed a multitude of thousands, etc.) and to have proclaimed the coming kingdom of God, the question must have ultimately arisen, "Who is this man?" His actions provoked questions from those who witnessed

The Western Wall of the Temple Mount in Jerusalem. This wall dates back to the time of Herod the Great, and recent discoveries at the base of the wall can be dated to the time of Solomon. Photo © Rohr Productions. Used with permission.

Olive trees from a garden on the Mount of Olives in Jerusalem. Jesus was arrested in the Garden of Gethsemane in this vicinity (Mark 14:26–50). Photo © Rohr Productions. Used with permission.

them (Mark 4:41; Luke 8:25; Matt 8:27). Along with the spectacular elements of his ministry, Jesus was known as a teacher and proclaimer as well as one who received the outcasts of society. Who was he? According to the synoptic tradition, Jesus himself raised the question with his disciples (Mark 8:27–30; Matt 16:13–20; Luke 9:20). He appears to have accepted acclaim from his disciples (ibid.; see also John 20:28–29), and the early church itself acknowledged him as "Lord," as in the early Christian confession of Rom 10:9–10, and the earlier form of this confession, which told of the early church's hope for the return of the risen Christ who is the Lord, in 1 Cor 16:22.[44] Even if it is maintained that these acclamations did not originate until after the Easter event (Rom 1:3–4), where did such ideas come from? Are they a reasonable inference of what Jesus himself taught or an accurate deduction from his words to his followers? The titles attributed to Jesus by others and those he used for himself may be helpful here. Table 5-3 lists the most frequent designations of Jesus, along with their use in the OT and noncanonical Jewish literature.

What do these titles imply about the early church's understanding of Jesus? Does Jesus' reference to himself as the Son of Man infer anything more than that he was a part of the human race, such as we see in the some eighty uses of the term in Ezekiel (2:1, 3, 6, 8; 3:1, 3, 17; etc.)? Does this title refer instead to a *divine* man who comes as the representative of God at the end of the age to bring the salvation of God, an eschatological figure, as we can infer from Dan 7:13–14? Some of the references in the NT could have both meanings, but it is the idea of a divine man with which we are most concerned. If Jesus had this understanding in mind, then his self-awareness of being in a special, if not unique, relation to God is certain. See, for example, Mark 2:10, 28; 8:38; 9:9; 13:26; 14:62; Matt 13:41; 16:27; 24:27, 30, 37; 25:31; Luke 12:40; 17:24; 21:27; John 3:13; 12:23; 13:31. In each of these instances, as well as the others in the Gospels, it is Jesus who is speaking. The early church almost never used

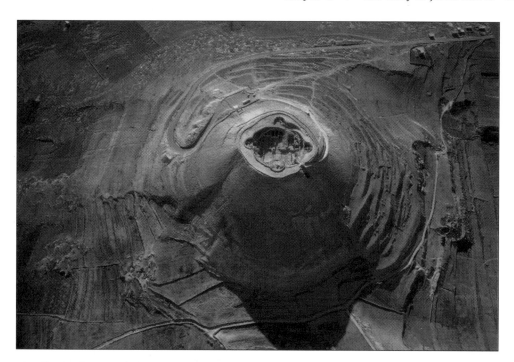

The Herodium, Herod the Great's fortification east of Jerusalem and his burial site according to Josephus, Ant. 17.199 and War 2.673. © Rohr Productions. Used with permission.

Mount Tabor, the traditional site of the transfiguration (Mark 9:2–9), from the Jezreel Valley. © Rohr Productions. Used with permission.

this term as a reference to Jesus, and outside the Gospels the term is found only in Acts 7:56 and Rev 1:13; 14:14. It is hardly possible that the term was an invention by the church, since the church does not seem to have referred to Jesus this way and there is widespread attestation that Jesus used it in reference to himself. Did he have in mind the eschatological figure that is found not only in Dan 7:13–14 and in most of the examples cited above but also in noncanonical literature (*1 En.* 37–71, esp. the vision of 46:1–8; 2 Esdras 13:3–4, 25–32, 51–52) referring to a messianic and eschatological figure? In many of the Gospel passages where Jesus speaks of himself as the Son of Man, it does appear that he has this apocalyptic and messianic figure in mind. Was part of the reason for the rejection of Jesus precisely that he appeared to the religious leaders of his day to be a blasphemer, that is,

T A B L E   5 - 3

TITLES FOR JESUS

Christ, Anointed One	2 Sam 22:51; Ps 2:2; 18:50; Dan 9:25, 26; *1 En.* 52:4; John 1:41; Mark 8:29; Luke 4:18
King	Matt 21:5 (see Zech 9:9); Luke 19:38; Matt 2:2; Mark 15:32; John 18:33; etc.
Son of David	Prov 1:1; Qoh 1:1; *Pss. Sol.* 17:21; Matt 1:1; Mark 10:47–48
Son	Ps 2:7; Isa 7:14; 9:6; Mark 1:1, 11; 3:11; 5:7; 9:7; 13:32; etc.
Son of Man	80 references in Ezekiel; Ps 8:4; esp. Dan 7:13–14. Cf. *1 En.* 48:2; 62:7; 71:17. Most common self-designation of Jesus in the Gospels, e.g., Matt 12:8, 32; 13:37; Mark 2:10, 28; 8:38; 9:12; 13:26; 14:62; Luke 12:8, 10, 40
Servant	Isa 42:1–4; 49:1–13; 50:1–11; 52:13–53:12; Matt 12:18 (Isa 42:1); Acts 4:27, 30; Mark 10:45
Branch	Isa 11:1; Jer 23:5; 33:15; Zech 3:8; 6:12. In the NT this may be an equivalent to Jesus being a Nazarene (Matt 2:23)
Prophet	Deut 18:15–18; Matt 11:9; 21:11, 46; 23:31, 37; Mark 6:4, 15; 8:28; Luke 7:16; 24:19; John 6:14; 7:40; Acts 3:22–23; 7:37
Priest	Gen 14:18; Ps 110:4; *T. Sim.* 7:2; *T. Jud.* 21:2; *T. Jos.* 19:6. Jesus as priest is found explicitly only in Heb 5:5–10 and 7:1–10:18 but also implicitly in the ministry of Jesus. See his forgiveness of sin (Mark 2:5; Luke 7:47–48), shedding of his blood for a new covenant (Mark 14:24), promise of a "new temple" (John 2:19; Mark 12:1–11; 14:58), and role as mediator (1 Tim 2:5–6)
Holy One	2 Kgs 19:22; Isa 5:24; 43:3, 15; 45:11; Jer 50:29; Mark 1:24; Luke 4:34; John 6:69
Chosen/Elect One	Isa 53:11; Jer 23:5; Zech 9:9; *1 En.* 53:6. See the "righteous one" in 1 John 2:1; 3:7; Luke 23:47; Acts 3:14
Lord Messiah	*Pss. Sol.* 17:32; 18:7; Mark 2:28. Note: Though not a messianic title, Jesus is called "Lord" in Mark 2:28; Matt 14:30; 15:22; John 20:28; and passim
Rabbi, Teacher	John 1:38; 3:2, 26 (cf. Matt 23:7–8; "the Word," John 1:1, 14; *1 En.* 61:7)
Son of God	Matt 3:17; 4:3, 6; Mark 1:1; 3:11; 9:7; 14:61; 15:39; and passim

speaking of a special relationship with God, his Father? That he should on occasion say to others that the kingdom of God was present in his activity of healing and preaching suggests this very thing.

After Jesus' entry into Jerusalem, in which some Pharisees were troubled by the acclaim he had received and evidently accepted (Luke 19:39), he entered into the temple and overturned the tables of the moneychangers in the outer courtyard (Mark 11:15–17). When the chief priest and scribes heard of this, they began to look for ways to kill him (11:18). After leaving the temple with his disciples, Jesus also predicted its destruction (Mark 13:1–2). Did others hear him make this pronouncement? Later, just before the outbreak of the war against Rome in A.D. 66, there was a man by the name of Jesus, son of Ananus, who pronounced woes against Jerusalem and against the temple (the "holy house"), for which he was beaten several times and eventually killed with a stone (Josephus, *War* 6.300–309). To say something against the temple or the city of Jerusalem, or even the religious people of Jerusalem, was a serious matter (see also Jesus' woes pronounced against the religious leaders of Jerusalem in Matt 23:13–36). Jesus was on a collision course with the religious leaders of his day, but the evangelists all say that he was aware of the consequences of this behavior (Mark 8:31; Matt 16:22; see also Luke 9:21–22 and similar predictions in Mark 9:30–32, 10:33–34, and parallels; and in Mark 10:21–28; John 12:27–36). In Mark 10:44–45, Jesus made reference to giving his life as "a ransom for many." And at the Last Supper, he referred to the cup as his "blood of the covenant, which is poured out for many," then, in an apparent farewell statement, said that he would not drink of the fruit of the vine again until he did so in the kingdom of God (Mark 14:24–25; see also Matt 26:26–28; Luke 22:15–20). The independent tradition in John 6:51–58 is considerably different. Even stripped of its theological meaning, which speaks to the concerns of the church of a later generation, the Johannine tradition still attests to Jesus' sharing a meal with his followers and speaking of his own sacrifice. In the final Passover meal with the disciples in John 13:1–38, before the time of the arrest in the garden, Jesus appears to have been aware that he had been betrayed by Judas (13:21–30). Supporting this is the tradition in Paul, who speaks about the supper of the Lord in which Jesus himself spoke of the elements of bread and wine as representing his body and blood (1 Cor 11:23–27). These various strands of tradition, when combined, strongly suggest that Jesus knew he would be in conflict in Jerusalem and would soon die (see also Matt 23:37–39; Luke 13:31–34). After he predicted his death in Mark 10:32–34, the disciples obviously did not grasp what Jesus had said, and two of them, James and John, approached him to ask for places of prominence in his kingdom. He asked them if they were able to drink from the cup that he drinks from and be baptized with the baptism that he is baptized with, speaking about his death. According to the Gospel tradition, Jesus was

The Dome of the Rock in Jerusalem, a Moslem shrine that was begun in A.D. 688 and completed in 691. Islam's first major sanctuary, it has survived largely intact. Built to honor the Islamic tradition that Muhammad ascended to heaven from this place, it was intended to compete with the grandeur of the Christian temples, especially the church of the Holy Sepulcher in Jerusalem. Photo Lee M. McDonald.

The northern Jordan River, running south into the Sea of Galilee. © Rohr Productions. Used with permission.

The Horns of Hattin in the foreground, where the Crusaders were defeated by Saladin on July 4, 1187. In the upper-right corner is the descent by way of Mount Arbel, overlooking the Sea of Galilee. © Rohr Productions. Used with permission.

not taken unawares when he was arrested and put to death.

If this is so, why does Jesus apparently suffer a lapse on the cross, as some scholars have argued, with his words "My God, my God, why have you forsaken me?" (Mark 15:34; Matt 27:46)? Although this cry is only found in two of the four evangelists, it is unlikely that the early church invented it, since, on the surface, it makes Jesus appear to be facing death believing that God has forsaken him and that something tragic has happened to his plans. Jesus' cry of despair, however, may in fact be more of an affirmation of hope at his death, since what he says are the opening words of Psalm 22. Years ago Martin Dibelius argued that an ancient manner of citing Scripture was to give the opening of the first verse with the rest of the passage understood to be in mind. Since Psalm 22 concludes with great confidence in the faithfulness of God (vv. 25–31), Dibelius concluded that "no pious Jew dying with these words on his lips could have thought himself abandoned by God."[45]

Whether Jesus was an insurrectionist needs little comment. There simply are no elements in Jesus' behavior or teachings to suggest that he was a revolutionary anxious to overthrow the Roman government. He only asked that his followers should give to the emperor the things that belong to the emperor (taxes) and to God what belongs to God (Mark 12:17). This teaching was carried on in the earliest Christian churches (Rom 13:7). If Jesus was a revolutionary, he obviously had no following, and no army was ever called for, or established, by the early church.

The arrest and trial of Jesus, therefore, were caused by several factors. Chief among them were his claims to be in a special relationship with God, his cleansing of the temple, his rejection of the religious traditions of his day (especially when they interfered with human need), and his growing popularity with the people. He was perceived as a threat, arrested, tried, and crucified. According to Mark 14:10–11, he was betrayed by one of his own followers, Judas Iscariot, who gave information to the chief priests on Jesus' whereabouts.[46] Judas knew where to find Jesus (John 18:2; Luke 22:39) and brought the temple guards to him. The religious leaders of the Jews wanted to kill Jesus, but because of his popularity with the people, this was not an easy job. Their formal grievances against

him were not sufficient matters of legality to have him killed, and convicting Jesus on a minor charge would not have stopped him.

It is fairly certain that it was Judas Iscariot who betrayed Jesus and turned him over to the Jewish religious authorities (the Sanhedrin and the temple guard). The tradition is too widespread in the Gospel narratives and is not the kind of story that the church would fabricate, that one of Jesus' trusted followers betrayed him for a sum of money. The question is, however, why did Judas betray Jesus? Was it because of the rebuke Jesus gave to Judas earlier for his rebuke of Mary (Mark 14:6–8; Matt 26:8–10; see also John 12:4)? Did he simply want to force Jesus' hand to take a more prominent role in Israel, as he had come to expect? The evangelists have little good to say about him, focusing on the money he received as an incentive. But Judas's remorse is recorded in Matt 27:3–10, although there is no reference to his guilt in the different account in Acts 1:18. Both accounts connect his death with a cemetery for foreigners.

It is probably safest to say that no formal trial as such took place but, rather, it took some time to bring accusations against Jesus. According to Mark 14:43–53, after Jesus was arrested, he was taken before the Sanhedrin by night, evidently to allow them to deal with the matter as quickly as possible and to avoid conflict with his followers and admirers. Because of difficulty finding adequate reasons to condemn Jesus, they tried to get him to incriminate himself (Mark 14:55–59). Earlier at least a portion of the Sanhedrin, made up of chief priests, scribes, and elders, had met with Jesus to have him

A miqveh (ritualistic cleansing pool or bath) next to the southern steps of the Herodian temple, dating from the first century A.D. Photo Lee M. McDonald.

Sunrise over Jerusalem, looking eastward toward the Mount of Olives with the Dome of the Rock in the center.
Photo © Rohr Productions. Used with permission.

condemn himself or give them grounds to arrest him, but without success (Mark 11:27–33). This time they were more determined to convict him, and the whole Sanhedrin met (Mark 14:54). Although the time of the meeting was unusual, the concern they had over Jesus' arrest was great, and they wanted to deal with him quickly and privately. This meeting went on until past dawn (Mark 15:1). The solicited testimonies against Jesus did not agree (Mark 14:55–59), and according to Num 35:30, at least two witnesses were needed to condemn a person to death (cf. Deut 19:15–21). The lack of agreement at Jesus' hearing before the Sanhedrin left them with no alternative but to try to get Jesus to convict himself. At this point, according to Mark, the high priest, Caiaphas, asked Jesus if he was the Messiah, the son of the Blessed, that is, God (Mark 14:61). Jesus answered that he was, and began to quote Dan 7:13, the messianic text that refers to the apocalyptic Son of Man, with Ps 110:1 and possibly 110:5 in view. Although Jesus answered Caiaphas, we see in Mark 14:62 that he also included the

whole Sanhedrin in his response, as the change to a plural verb indicates (ὄψεσθε, *opsesthe*, 2d per. pl., lit. "you [plural] can expect to see").

Much has been made of the irregularity of this trial and of Jesus' response. The point is apparently that if the trial did not take place as Mark claims— and the trial there appears to have violated the general laws governing its procedures—then Jesus' affirmation that he was indeed the Messiah and Son of God must also be fabricated. A shift in opinion seems to be taking place among NT scholars, however, and more credibility has been given to this trial or hearing before the Sanhedrin. Gundry, for instance, admits that the procedures that took place at the trial according to Mark are unusual, but argues that they are not without precedence given the circumstances. To the extent that the Mishnaic legal regulations that were codified in the late second century and early third century A.D. were also in effect in the time of Jesus, as Gundry concludes is likely, then Jesus' trial appears as unjust and, in Mark's account, also tendentious,

The Orthodox monastery of St. Onofrius on the traditional site of the "Field of Blood" (Akeldama)
(Matt 27:7, 8; Acts 1:19) with tombs enclosed. The open area has tombs from the Herodian period.
Photo © Rohr Productions. Used with permission.

according to Gundry. He argues that ancient texts such as Susanna (vv. 44–59) and 11QTemple LXI, 9 show the concern for justice at the time of Jesus and provide early enough background to understand some of the concerns about his trial. Gundry acknowledges the irregularities in the passage; for example, the meeting place is the high priest's house rather than the "Chamber of Hewn Stone," as called for in *m. Sanh.* 11:2, and the trial takes place on Passover eve, which is forbidden in *m. Sanh.* 4:1. Nevertheless, according to *b. Sanh.* 46a, allowances were made for emergencies when the protection of the Torah was in view.[47] Since the circumstances were unusual and they believed that the religious traditions were placed in danger by the actions of Jesus, who both violated their traditions about the Sabbath and interrupted the temple, it is understandable why they took such unusual measures.

The charge against Jesus was blasphemy (Mark 14:63–64), which meant that he was believed to have encroached upon an area reserved for God alone when he claimed to have a special relationship with God. As Evans has pointed out, however, it was not Jesus' claim to be the Messiah that warranted his condemnation. Others had claimed such a status and had not been put to death. It was that Jesus, in citing Dan 7:13 with Ps 110:1, positioned himself on the chariot throne of God, seated next to him when God comes in judgment against the Jewish people.[48] This was blasphemy. The penalty for this act was death, but because the Sanhedrin did not have the power to put persons to death in the current political climate, they took Jesus before Pontius Pilate, the Roman prefect. They charged him with insurrection, that is, claiming to be a king (Mark 15:1–5; Luke 23:1–5), and with opposition to paying taxes to Rome (Luke 23:2). These charges are supported by the *titulus*, or sign, on the cross—mentioned in each of the four Gospels—that Pilate placed over his head indicating the accusation (Mark 15:26, 32; Matt 27:37, 39–42; Luke 23:36–37, 38; John 19:1–3, 15–16, 19). What adds more credibility to this report is that the title was contested by the "Jews" (Sanhedrin?), who asked that it be changed. It is likely that the charge against Jesus of claiming to be both king and Messiah is authentic. Supporting this is Pilate's question to Jesus asking whether he was the king of the Jews (Luke 23:3; Matt 27:11–12; Mark 15:2–3; John 18:29–33). It is not likely that the reference to Jesus as Messiah came after the cross but, rather, that he was acknowledged as such by his disciples during his ministry (Mark 8:29; Matt 16:16; Luke 9:20; cf. John 1:41–42). Some scholars have rejected the authenticity of this confession and Jesus' acceptance of it. But when it is placed in the context of the disciples leaving their businesses and following Jesus to Jerusalem, even debating among themselves who would be greatest in his kingdom, it surely reflects their view that he had a special relationship with God and their anticipation that he would establish the apocalyptic kingdom he had proclaimed (Mark 10:35–40; Matt 20:20; Luke 22:24–27). There can be little question that Jesus' disciples believed that he was the expected Messiah who was going to establish God's kingdom. The fact that he chose twelve disciples, even if we are uncertain of their names, indicates that he believed he was going to establish a renewed people of Israel for the new day of the coming kingdom of God.

Although Jesus accepted the messianic title in private from his followers, he did not use the title of Messiah for himself in his ministry but only in his appearance before Caiaphas and the Sanhedrin. He thus made this claim in public only once (Mark 14:60–62).

Pilate was evidently unconvinced that Jesus had done anything worthy of death (Luke 23:1–5; John 18:33–38), and he wanted the Jews to handle the matter themselves (John 18:30–31). Perhaps seeking to find an easy way to deal with the matter, he tried to pass the problem over to Herod Antipas (Luke 23:6–12). Antipas likewise found no fault in Jesus that was worthy of death (Luke 23:13–16) and sent him back to Pilate. Pilate therefore gave the Jews a choice of releasing either Jesus or Barabbas, and the "Jews" (the Sanhedrin, but possibly also the crowds that they had incited by this time) chose to have Barabbas released (Mark 15:6–15; Luke 23:25). Pilate then had Jesus handed over to his guards for crucifixion as an insurrectionist, as the title on his cross shows. Jesus was beaten and humiliated by soldiers (Mark 15:16–20), then prepared for crucifixion.

L. The Death and Burial of Jesus

1. Crucifixion

Crucifixion was used by the Romans and others, including Jews, as a form of capital punishment from the sixth century B.C. to the fourth century A.D. Josephus reports that the practice was viewed as one of the most horrible manners of death among the Jews, and tells us that the Hasmonean king Alexander Janneaus (reigned 103–76 B.C.) used this form of punishment for his Jewish (Pharisaic) enemies:

> The most powerful among them, however, he shut up and besieged in the city of Bethoma, and after taking the city and getting them into his power, he brought them back to Jerusalem; and there he did a thing that was as cruel as could be: while he feasted with his concubines in a conspicuous place, he ordered some eight hundred of the Jews to be crucified, and slaughtered their children and wives before their eyes of the still living wretches. This was the revenge he took for the injuries he had suffered; but the penalty he exacted was inhuman for all that. (*Ant.* 13.380–381; Marcus, LCL)

Later the Pharisees under the protection of Queen Salome Alexandra, the successor of Alexander Janneaus, convinced the queen to crucify those who had persuaded Alexander to crucify these eight hundred men (Josephus, *Ant.* 13.410).

Crucifixion was not generally used on Roman citizens except in cases of very serious crimes such as high treason.[49] Normally this practice was reserved only for slaves and subject peoples (see fig. 1). Its practice was banned in A.D. 337 by Constantine out of respect for Jesus. Although it was practiced in the Hellenistic-Hasmonean period (165–63 B.C.), it was not used against the Jews by Herod the Great. The Romans, however, did not hesitate to use crucifixion to pacify the Jews after the invasion of Pompey in 63 B.C. *Assumption of Moses* 6:8–9 reports the practice of crucifixion, possibly by Pompey: "there will come into their land a powerful king of the West who will subdue them; and he will take captives, and a part of their temple he will burn with fire. He will crucify some of them around the city."[50] This was a hated form of death among the Jews, and the reference in Deut 21:23 (see also Gal 3:13) helps explain why a crucified Messiah was a stumbling block to them (1 Cor 1:23).

Crucifixion was normally preceded by scourging, after which the criminal would sometimes

A view of northern Galilee with Mount Arbel on the right, where the Syrians slaughtered partisans in 161 B.C. and where Herod the Great fought against the supporters of his rival Antigonus in 38 B.C. (Josephus, Ant. 14.423–426). © Rohr Productions. Used with permission.

carry his own cross or the crossbar from the place of judgment to the place of execution. More notorious criminals were often hung higher than others. It is also possible that Jesus took the place of Barabbas, a convicted robber.

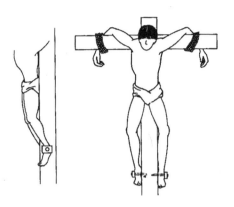

Other forms of crucifixion existed, including crucifixion on a single post in which the hands were clasped together over the head and the feet were affixed below.

Nails were normally driven through the wrists, and the feet were fastened on a peg by either a nail or cords, but this was not uniformly done. Normally, the person who was crucified died of exposure to heat and the elements, lack of nourishment, and asphyxiation when the legs gave out. This usually took a day or two. Jesus did not spend much time on the cross—perhaps a few hours, three to six hours at the most—before he died, which may indicate the severity of his beating. Even Pilate was surprised that it took so little time for Jesus to die (Mark 15:44–45).

Each of the evangelists tells the story of Jesus' crucifixion to make an important theological point. Matthew, for example, includes the story of the earthquake (27:51), the temple curtain torn in two (27:51), and the bodies rising out of the graves and going through the streets of Jerusalem (27:52–53, a signal of the resurrection at the end of the age). These events show that in the death of Jesus the end of the age had come (see Matt 24:7–8) and, through the death of Jesus, access to God was then open. Matthew also indicates that, in Jesus' death, he was seen to be the Son of God (27:54). Table 5-4 shows how each evangelist listed accompanying

phenomena at the death of Jesus. Each of these phenomena is laden with theological significance.

2. Burial Narratives

Although there are a number of differences in the Gospel stories of the burial of Jesus, the many consistencies indicate a common origin for the accounts. We will briefly look at the similarities before looking at the differences. In all four Gospel narratives, for instance, it is Joseph of Arimathea who requested and received from Pilate the body of Jesus for burial purposes, and it is Joseph who prepared the body with a linen shroud and placed it in the tomb (John 19:39–40 says that Nicodemus helped in both chores). All four Gospels agree that the day of the burial was the Day of Preparation (Friday) just before the beginning of the Sabbath.

Beyond these common agreements, Mark and Matthew both say that Joseph rolled the stone against the door of the tomb after the body was placed inside (Mark 14:46; Matt 27:59–60). Luke and John make no mention of Joseph rolling the stone against the tomb, but the possibility that someone had sealed up the tomb could be inferred from the surprise of the women in the next chapter (Luke 24:2–4), or from Mary's surprise in John 20:1 at the stone being rolled away. It is somewhat surprising that the stone's being rolled away is mentioned in Luke and John, since neither records that the tomb was sealed. This could be an indication of Luke's and John's dependence upon a common source. Mark says Jesus' body was placed in a tomb (15:46), while Matthew calls it "his own new tomb, which he [evidently Joseph] had hewn in the rock" (27:60). Luke and John are once again in agreement when they describe the tomb as one in which "no one had ever been laid" (Luke 23:53; John 19:41). Luke and John differ here only in that Luke calls the tomb "rock-hewn" and John calls it "new," although these two descriptions are far from incompatible.

Furthermore, in John 19:38 Joseph asks for the body in secret, but Mark 15:43 says Joseph "went boldly to Pilate" to request the body. The secret nature of the request in John is evidently unknown to Matthew, who shows that the whereabouts of Joseph's tomb in which Jesus' body was placed was known to the Roman guard and Jewish leaders.

And according to John 20:1, Mary, who was a Galilean, also knew where to go to find the body of Jesus. Further, the Synoptics make no mention of Joseph adding spices or ointments to the body during the preparation for burial. John alone introduces this element, along with the only mention of Nicodemus's helping Joseph prepare the body (John 19:39–42). John is also alone in not mentioning the presence of the women at the burial of Jesus. Since none of the Gospel writers indicates that the women saw the preparation for Jesus' burial, it may be that the women were unaware of the specific preparations, but this is not explicitly stated in the Gospel tradition. Mark says that Mary Magdalene and Mary, the mother of Joses, watched the burial. Matthew simply says it was Mary Magdalene and the "other Mary" who watched, while Luke says that it was the women who came with Jesus from Galilee who watched.

Besides the above minor differences in the burial stories, a few other problems should be mentioned. First, it is not clear who supplied the anointing spices and ointments. Mark and Luke say that it was the women who came to the tomb on the first day of the week to bring spices, but John says that the spices and ointments were brought by Nicodemus before Jesus was placed in the tomb. Second, we must ask whether the careful burial preparation (John 19:40; Mark 15:46) is consistent with the claim that haste had to be made because of the rapidly approaching Sabbath (John 19:42; Luke 23:54). Third, Bultmann argues that the coming of the women to the tomb to embalm the body of Jesus after two nights and a day would be impossible given the climate of the Middle East.[51] Fourth, Bultmann further contends that the burial of Jesus was complete and the women were obviously witnesses to this fact (Mark 15:47); but if so, why did the women come to the tomb at all on the first day of the week?[52] Finally, there is the question of who buried Jesus. Was it Joseph of Arimathea (as in all four evangelists), whom Matthew calls a disciple of Jesus (Matt 27:57), or was Jesus buried by his enemies as Acts 13:28–29 may imply?

The Church of the Holy Sepulcher, the traditional site of the crucifixion and burial of Jesus in Jerusalem, begun in the fourth century by the mother of Constantine. Photo © Rohr Productions. Used with permission.

Machaerus, Herod the Great's easternmost fortress, on the Jordanian side of the Dead Sea. It is the place of execution of John the Baptist (Josephus, Ant. 18:116–119). © Rohr Productions. Used with permission.

The so-called Tomb of Zechariah in the Kidron Valley, dating from the early Roman conquest of Judea, ca. the second half of the second century B.C. (see 2 Chron 24:20ff.). On the tomb to the left, the priestly family name of Bene Hezir (1 Chron 24:15) was found above the two Doric columns. Photo © Rohr Productions. Used with permission.

The problems of the burial stories are not nearly so great as those of the empty-tomb and appearances stories (see ch. 6, below). In the burial stories, Luke and John tend to have many agreements, and the same is true between Matthew and Mark. There is no mention in Mark or Matthew of a new tomb "where no one had ever been laid" and no reference to the linen clothes in the empty tomb, which clothes are mentioned in both Luke and John. These similarities may provide further evidence for a common source behind Luke and John. Further similarities between these two include the following: two angels are present at the tomb in both Luke and John, but only one individual (angel? angel of the Lord?) is mentioned in Mark and Matthew; the location of the Easter appearances of Jesus is Jerusalem in both Luke and John but Galilee in both Matthew and Mark; and the ascension of Jesus is mentioned in both Luke–Acts and John but not in Mark and Matthew. Each similarity, in and of itself, conveys very little, but together the several parallels tend to suggest a common source used by both Luke and John in their death and resurrection narratives, which narratives may or may not be as early as the Markan tradition. Since Luke was almost certainly written earlier than John and since John shows little dependence upon Luke or similarity to him in his depiction of the appearances of Jesus, it seems likely that they both had a common source. Apart from the material form of the appearances and their location, John and Luke are quite different; for example, Luke's empty tomb story, the disciples on the road to Emmaus, the appearance to the disciples, and Luke's understanding of the ascension of Jesus are quite foreign to John. Unlike John, Luke has no major emphasis on the Holy Spirit in his Gospel except in the temptation story in 4:1, 14 and in the promise of the Spirit in 24:49. The kind of ascension that John portrays, which comes in the midst of the resurrection appearances, rather than at their conclusion as in the case of Luke, suggests a lack of dependence of either Gospel on the other. It seems, therefore, that the similarities in Luke and

T A B L E   5 - 4

THE DEATH OF JESUS IN THE GOSPELS

Event	Matthew 27:32–54	Mark 15:21–39	Luke 23:39–49	John 19:12–37
Thieves	Both thieves revile Jesus	Both thieves revile Jesus	One thief reviles Jesus and one asks to be remembered. Request granted	Thieves mentioned, but no reviling
Time	From the 6th hour to the 9th hour	From the 6th hour to the 9th hour	From the 6th hour to the 9th hour	About 6th hour (vv. 13, 14) Jesus stands before Pilate
Jesus' cry	"Eli, Eli, lema sabachthani?" (Heb.)	"Eloi, Eloi, lema sabachthani?" (Aram.)	"Father, into your hands I commend my spirit."	Jesus' reference to his mother; "I am thirsty"; "It is finished."
Jesus offered a drink	Sponge with vinegar	Sponge with vinegar	Vinegar, but offered at a different time	Sponge full of vinegar on a hyssop
Accompanying phenomena	*Darkness	*Darkness	*Darkness	*Scripture fulfilled: 19:24, 28, 36, 37
	*Temple curtain torn in two from top to bottom	*Temple curtain torn in two from top to bottom	*Temple curtain torn in two	
	*Earthquake			
	*Tombs of the dead opened and the dead rise to life			
	*Centurion: "Truly this man was God's Son."	*Centurion: "Truly this man was God's Son!"	*Centurion: "Certainly this man was innocent."	
Sign over Jesus	"This is Jesus, the King of the Jews"	"The King of the Jews"	"This is the King of the Jews"	"Jesus of Nazareth, the King of the Jews"

John are due to dependence upon a common tradition. There appears, then, to be a Markan tradition (Matthew showing dependence upon Mark) and a separate Easter tradition common to both Luke and John. These traditions dominate the resurrection narratives, though each evangelist takes the liberty to add what contributes to his own purposes. Matthew, for example, adds the apologetic story of the guard at the tomb, while Luke includes the story of the disciples on the road to Emmaus; John,

showing concern for a later generation of Christians, adds the story of the special appearance of Jesus to Thomas (see ch. 6, below).

The following discussion includes three of the more obvious discrepancies in the burial stories and some suggested solutions to the other problems mentioned above.

a. Who provided the spices? Is there a discrepancy between John on the one hand, who says the

The so-called Tomb of Absalom in the Kidron Valley (based on 2 Sam 18:18) actually dates from the first century B.C. Photo © Rohr Productions. Used with permission.

spices were provided by Nicodemus, and Mark and Luke on the other, who say that the women brought the spices? The answer may lie in the ignorance of the women on how the body was prepared for burial. Having seen only the burial itself and not the preparation of the body, they might well have considered coming back to prepare the body appropriately for burial. Is much to be made of the silence of John and Matthew about the women (or of John about Mary) and the spices? Should it be assumed that in all four Gospels the women (or woman, in John) came to the tomb on the first day of the week to anoint the body with spices? To make that conjecture is an argument from silence, though not impossible as some have claimed. Bultmann's view that Mark 15:46 indicates that the burial of Jesus was complete and needed nothing further[53] does not take into consideration the possible ignorance of the women regarding what had already occurred. Also, his view does not allow that this act, according to the evangelists, was simply an act of devotion on the part of the women.

Because of the lateness of the day when Jesus was buried, the women may well have not had time to pay their final respects of devotion and honor to their fallen Master. On the Day of Preparation (παρασχευή, *parascheuē*), there was only enough time to perform the most necessary of obligations; any further acts of devotion would have to be postponed until after the Sabbath.

b. Elaborate burial procedures. All of the evangelists indicate that a rather elaborate preparation, or wrapping, of Jesus' body in a shroud took place and that the Sabbath was fast approaching, forcing those who prepared the body to do so somewhat hastily (see Matt 27:57; Mark 15:42; Luke 23:54; John 19:42). Long ago Lilly noted that the Talmud, in the treatise dealing with the Sabbath rest, permits all necessary steps to be taken for a decent burial on the Sabbath and that "the duty of burying the dead was thus regarded as taking precedence over other laws whenever there should be a conflict."[54] It may well be, as Lilly argues, that what had obtained in Judaism in a later generation was also true in the time of Jesus. Since Deut 21:23 expressly states that the body of a condemned man could not hang upon a tree all night but had to be buried "that same day," there seems to be no contradiction in the elaborate nature of Jesus' burial, which took place on a late Friday afternoon as the Sabbath was approaching. Also, this elaborate burial (Mark 15:46; John 19:39–41) is not necessarily in conflict with the lateness of the Day of Preparation as the Sabbath was approaching or with the fact that Jesus died a criminal's death, since "they may make ready (on the Sabbath or on a feast day) all that is needful for the dead, and anoint it and wash it, provided that they do not move any member of it" (*m. Šabb.* 23:5).[55] Therefore, everything necessary for a decent burial, including the washing and anointing of a body, as the evangelists mention, was possible within the proper keeping of the law by the Jews. For this reason, Lilly says that the evangelists, who were familiar with Palestinian conditions and customs, could not have attributed to the women the intention of coming to embalm the body of Jesus three days after burial. The intention of the women, Lilly claims, was in keeping with an ancient Palestinian custom of visiting graves for three days after burial. This custom stemmed from the belief that the soul of the deceased remained in or near the body during this time. The Palestinian custom of bringing spices and ointments for anointing was similar to the modern custom of bringing flowers or wreaths to the graveside of loved ones. Lilly cites as proof an example from Josephus (*Ant.* 17.196–199), in which five hundred pounds of perfumes were brought for the burial of Herod the Great in addition to those used to embalm the body.[56] Although we may agree with Bultmann that according to Mark 15:46 the burial of Jesus was complete, we should ask whether Mark 16:1 and Luke 24:1 suggest otherwise. If Lilly is correct, it is possible that Nicodemus supplied all the necessary spices for the burial and that the women only intended to offer their spices and ointments out of love and devotion.

This is speculation, of course, and we may be reading into the text something not explicitly there, but it does offer a possible solution to the problem posed above. But the question of why the women visited the tomb should not be one of great importance here. Whether it was to anoint the body of Jesus, as in Mark and Luke, or just to visit the tomb, as in Matthew and John, does not detract significantly from the message of the evangelists. Several motivations for the women coming to the tomb are plausible, but the important fact is that, as Bode puts it, "the women came and that is enough."[57]

c. Who buried Jesus? One of the most significant problems in the burial stories is the question of who buried Jesus. All four Gospels state quite clearly that it was Joseph of Arimathea, but Acts 13:29 strangely attributes this act to the enemies of Jesus, the Jews.

Grass holds that the Acts passage is pre-Lukan and represents an accurate portrayal of the burial of Jesus. He believes that the Joseph of Arimathea burial story is late in the traditions about Jesus and that Jesus was laid in a common grave without special burial preparation, contrary to what the Gospels indicate, because this was the normal procedure for executed criminals in that day.[58] Following Grass, Fuller concludes that Mark 16:1–8 is more naturally an earlier part of the Gospel tradition (contra Bultmann) and that the burial stories of the Gospels can be explained as a subsequent addition to the original tradition with the purpose of preventing Jesus from suffering the final shame of an improper burial.[59] He claims that the story of the women coming to the tomb to complete the burial rites was in order since, before then, the body of Jesus had simply been handled by those who buried him (his enemies, Acts 13:29). The elaborate burial story in the Gospels, according to Fuller, was an expansion begun by Mark in order to make the final act of hostility toward Jesus into one of charity. Mark's statement that Joseph of Arimathea was a respected member of the council and was looking for the kingdom of God (15:43) was, according to Fuller, later developed in the Gospel tradition to the point where Joseph eventually was even called a "disciple" (Matt 27:57). Fuller then concludes that it was the Markan burial story on which all of the evangelists drew, not the empty-tomb story, which was at variance with the rest of the resurrection narratives. He believes that the difference in the names of the women in the burial and empty-tomb stories can be attributed to later attempts to square the empty-tomb tradition with the names in the burial story. He claims that originally there was only Mary Magdalene at the tomb (John 20:1), and agrees with Wilckens's thesis that when the disciples returned from Galilee after receiving their visions, they heard the report from Mary Magdalene about the empty tomb and were pleased with the story because it was in accord with their experience.[60] Accordingly, Mary's report was later attached to the passion narrative as a vehicle for proclaiming the resurrection of Jesus.

O'Collins, on the other hand, contends that Luke used an unreliable source in the Acts 13 speech, which was reportedly given by Paul, because in the witnesses to the resurrection in v. 31 there is no mention of Paul (see 1 Cor 15:8). This passage, according to O'Collins, represents Paul "not as appealing to his own encounter with the risen Christ but as relying exclusively on other witnesses to the resurrection! As Luke fails in this speech to portray accurately the historical Paul, we can hardly insist on the strict reliability of a vague remark about Jesus' burial."[61] Conzelmann accepts the inconsistency, but says that this "pre-Lukan" passage (Acts 13:29) was simply not adopted in Luke's Gospel narrative of the burial story. He says that Luke was not aware of the original meaning of this passage.[62]

Rather than opt for one tradition over another, Bruce says that it is possible to work out a harmony of the two stories by allowing the enemies of Jesus to remove the body from the cross, as seems possible from John 19:31, and at the same time having Joseph (and Nicodemus) take care of the burial itself. This, however, does not seem to solve all of the problems, especially because Acts 13:29 has the enemies of Jesus not only taking him down from the cross but also placing him in the tomb. Munck calls the final clause of Acts 13:29 a passive construction: "A passive construction is used instead of the active 'they took him down' for the agent might be Romans, the Jews, or the disciples."[63] This, he believes, would allow for the disciples taking care of the burial rather than Jesus' enemies. In the clause in question, however, the participle καθελόντες (*kathelontes*, "taking down") and the verb ἔθηκαν (*ethēkan*, "placed") are both in the active voice. It would be difficult to argue for a passive construction when there is no passive verb in the whole clause. Perhaps the correct way to view this problem is to say with Bruce that both verbs are "generalizing" plurals, that is, that Luke does not specifically wish to say that the

enemies of Jesus actually buried him.[64] Hanson, apparently concurring, says that Luke's representation of the Jews as burying Jesus is a result of his "condensed style" and not his deliberate intention.[65] The author of Luke–Acts probably would not have had Joseph of Arimathea perform the burial rites in one part of his work (Luke) and then be inconsistent with this in the second part of his work (Acts).

There are clearly a number of alternative ways of explaining a discrepancy between the Gospels and Acts. Whatever the explanation, we find it difficult to call the very strong testimony of four evangelists into question, since they are more agreed on the burial of Jesus than on any other area of the resurrection narratives.

Regarding Joseph, Bode argues that, since Joseph did not hold any place of remembrance or honor in the organization of the earliest community of Christians, he is to be regarded as something of an outsider and consequently not the kind of person who would likely have been drawn into an invented story.[66] Geering, on the other hand, holds that because Arimathea is not known as a place from any other source, it is an imagined site like the later Emmaus. The name Joseph, he says, may have been used to personalize the unknown Jew who was presumed by Mark to have been responsible for the burial of Jesus. He suggests that "Joseph" was used "because of the biblical tradition which told of the care with which Joseph, the patriarch, transported the body of his father all the way back to Machpelah for burial." He concludes that the form and content of Mark's burial story is no guarantee of its genuineness and that this "Joseph story" was a later addition to his narrative.[67]

The location of Arimathea is not as unknown as Geering would have us believe, however, and certainly not as problematic as the whereabouts of Emmaus. Although it cannot be conclusively demonstrated, many scholars are willing to equate Ἀριμαθαία (*Arimathaia*) with Ramathaim-zophim (= "The Two Heights" or "Twin Ramahs"), the city of Elkanah and Samuel (1 Sam 1:1), near Diospolis in the district of Timnah. The LXX form of Ramathaim is Ἀρμαθαίμ (*Armathaim*).[68] Also, the virtual lack of any similarity between Joseph of Arimathea and the Joseph in Gen 50:1–14 makes Geering's view far from convincing. The basic problem in identifying Joseph of Arimathea concerns whether he was indeed a follower of Jesus ("a disciple," Matt 27:57). Mark 15:43 only claims that he was a respected member of the council (presumably the town council of Jerusalem, though this is not stated) and that he "was also himself waiting expectantly for the kingdom of God." Matthew takes this to mean that he was a disciple, and Luke 23:50–51 understands that Joseph "was a good and righteous man" and "was waiting expectantly for the kingdom of God." If this understanding is correct, one must still wonder why the women did not participate in the burial that is mentioned in all four Gospels, since they would presumably have had nothing to fear by doing so. In the Synoptic Gospels they are observers, but one gathers that it was from a distance. If, on the other hand, Joseph was in fact not a follower of Jesus but simply a respected member of "the council" who was anxious to do what was right and proper on the Sabbath day, then Acts 13:29 may be right when it says that the burial of Jesus was performed by his enemies. The problem here is to explain why, if Joseph were not a follower of Jesus, he would have provided such an expensive burial place for him. John also calls Joseph a "disciple" of Jesus and includes another disciple (by inference Nicodemus?) in the burial story. Joseph of Arimathea, therefore, was probably both a disciple of Jesus and responsible for his burial. The fourfold testimony of this in the Gospels should outweigh the problematic assertion of Acts 13:29 that the enemies of Jesus buried him.

In spite of the variations in the accounts of the burial story, at least one basic message is found in all, including the Acts 13 speech—that it was Jesus of Nazareth who died on a cross and who was buried in a tomb. The evangelists also agree that this same Jesus who was placed in a tomb was also raised from that tomb to life.

3. WHAT FACTORS AND PEOPLE WERE INVOLVED IN THE DEATH OF JESUS? FURTHER COMMENT

Significant attention has recently been given to the question of who crucified Jesus. Some scholars have tried to eliminate Jewish complicity altogether, placing blame solely on the "Roman imperial system,"[69] while some Christians have unwittingly and unjustly blamed the Jewish race for the death of Jesus. Neither position has credible support. The question, however, has been so emotionally packed for such a long time that clarity on the matter has not been easy.

In the time of Jesus it was the primary responsibility of the Roman prefect to keep order in the region of Judea. More specifically, during this time it was the official responsibility of Pontius Pilate, the Roman prefect from 26 to 36 A.D. The actual, indirect authority for keeping peace in Judea and making sure that the Jews were obedient to Roman authority and its various laws was the high priest in Jerusalem. For almost five hundred years before the Roman conquest of Palestine in 63 B.C., the Jews were used to being governed by a high priest. During the Hasmonean Dynasty, the final eighty years of that time (ca. 140–63 B.C.), the Jews were ruled by a king who was also the high priest over the nation. After Rome intervened in Judean affairs, Herod the Great became the client king who was responsible to Rome for governance of the region. After his death, Herod's territory was divided among his sons, and one son, Herod Archelaus, did so poorly as a ruler that he was replaced by Roman prefects who governed Judea from 6 A.D. on, with the brief exception of the years 41–44 A.D., when Agrippa I ruled until his untimely death (Acts 12:20–23; cf. Josephus, *Ant.* 19.343–350).

Pontius Pilate ruled from the coastal city of Caesarea and was known for his ruthless dealing with rebellion and maintaining a strong posture toward the inhabitants of his region. In the day-to-day control of the region, the high priest had the right to make recommendations to the prefect, including capital punishment, which he himself did not have the authority to carry out. Caiaphas evidently did a good job as high priest, at least in the eyes of the Romans, since he served eighteen years in that role, longer than any other high priest of the first century.

A. Circumstances Surrounding Jesus' Death

As discussed above, the immediate factors that led to the arrest and death of Jesus probably included the following: his triumphal entry, when the Pharisees told Jesus to stop his disciples from their confession of him as king (Mark 11:1–11; cf. Luke 19:38–40); the cleansing of the temple (Mark 11:15–19); and his prediction of the demise of the temple (Mark 13:1–2). As Jesus came out of the temple, he said to his disciples that there would not be one stone on another that would not be torn down (Mark 13:1–2).[70] Sanders notes that many in antiquity claimed that the temple would be replaced or destroyed, such as the author of *1 Enoch* and the author of the Qumran *Temple Scroll* (11QTemple XXIX, 8–10). But Jesus' actions and words, combined with the fact that he had a following, caused alarm among the religious and political leaders. Sanders argues that Caiphas had Jesus arrested because he mistakenly thought that Jesus had personally threatened the temple.[71] Did Jesus threaten to destroy the temple? Probably not (but cf. Mark 15:29–30 and the criticisms against him from the passersby). The importance of such allegations must be understood in light of the significance of the temple in Judaism in the time of Jesus. Its centrality in the political, social, and religious life of first-century Judaism cannot be overestimated.[72]

Jesus' actions and teachings were considered a threat to the stability of the region by the religious authorities and, as a result, also by Pilate. So Jesus was arrested by Caiphas, who apparently believed that the death of one person was far better than the destruction of the whole land (John 11:50). Upon his recommendation, Pilate had Jesus beaten and crucified. Sanders argues that the NT references to Pilate's hesitation to have Jesus put to death (see Matt 27:24–25; Luke 23:42–47; but also Mark 15:6–15; John 18:38) was the word of a later generation of Christians who were trying to reduce conflict between Rome and the early Christian movement.[73] Although it is reasonable that later Christians went to considerable lengths to show that the church was not in conflict with Rome and thereby reduce sources of harm for their community, the reliability of the Gospel reports still has considerable support, especially since they are found to some extent in all four Gospels.

Carroll and Green observe that while the Gospels may be correct in Pilate's findings that the charges against Jesus were baseless and that he posed no serious threat to Rome, Pilate's reputation in noncanonical sources (Philo, *Embassy* 302) and in the NT (Luke 13:1–5) shows that he needed little or no persuasion to move against Jesus.[74] Philo, for instance, spoke of Pilate's "corruption, and his acts of insolence, and his rapine, and his habit of insulting people, and his cruelty, and his continual murders of people untried and uncondemned, and his never ending, and gratuitious, and most grievous inhumanity" (*Embassy* 302).[75] Josephus observes that Pilate was removed from office by the Syrian governor Vitellius and returned to Rome "because of the matters with which he was charged" (*Ant.* 18.89), and he added that in conjunction with this action he also removed Caiaphas from office and appointed Jonathan in his place (*Ant.* 18.95). Crossan notes that Pilate's and Caiaphas's tenures in Judea overlapped by ten years and that the close cooperation between them probably offended Jewish sensibilities and made it necessary to remove them both.[76]

The key factors that led to the death of Jesus probably also included his earlier conflicts with Jewish teachers, especially the Pharisees, during his public career in Galilee (Mark 3:1–6). Jesus was a charismatic figure who challenged the religious and social norms of his day and, as a result, had a following.[77] Along with this, if Jesus was a messianic claimant (see discussion above), we have further reasons for his downfall. He did not normally refer to himself as a Messiah or king in public, but in his questioning by Caiaphas in Mark 14:61–62, Jesus acknowledged that he was the Messiah, "the Son of the Blessed One." This fits with a number of clues in the Gospels. According to Matt 11:4–6 (cf. Luke 7:22–23), in which Jesus is questioned by the disciples of John about his identity, he answers with a reference to Isa 29:18–19 and 35:5, 6 (cf. Luke 7:18–35). Jesus' response in the so-called Q passage (Luke 7:22–23; cf. Matt 11:4–6) appears to make a messianic claim. If 4QMessianic Apocalypse (cited in sec. 2.D, above) reflects a first-century Jewish understanding of the role of the Messiah, as appears likely, then it may be that Jesus made such a claim to John's disciples.[78] Jesus' reference to the nature of his ministry in Luke 4:18–19, when he cites Isa 61:1, 2 (see also 58:6), also suggests that he at least saw himself as an eschatological prophet, if not a messianic figure. Stanton, citing *Melchizedek* (11QMelch) in conjunction with 4QMessianic Apocalypse, contends that Jesus' reference to Isa 61:1–2 shows that he was making an indirect messianic claim.[79]

There were no ancient models of a crucified Messiah, and it is debatable how the title Messiah was applied to Jesus after his death. It does not automatically refer to a king, and had Jesus openly claimed to be a king early in his ministry, this could have been fatal.[80] The early church did not call Jesus their king, and even a nonkingly messianic reference is difficult to find on the lips of Jesus in the Gospels. He seldom appealed to the title Messiah, and even when Peter confessed that Jesus was the Christ (Messiah), Jesus did not affirm the acclamation but instead predicted his rejection and death (Mark 8:29–31). Suffering and rejection were not parts of messianic expectations in the first century. This makes the despair of the disciples after Jesus' death more understandable. When Jesus was crucified as king of the Jews by Pilate, however, we have some indication at least that his actions had been interpreted by his followers as well as by his enemies to mean that he was a Messiah figure or claimant.[81] The title or accusation against Jesus that was placed on his cross suggests that he was passed off to Pilate as a messianic king and was thus condemned. Sanders argues that Jesus' three symbolic acts just before his death (his triumphal entry into Jerusalem, cleansing of the temple, and transformation of the Passover meal into a religious ceremony with a different significance) all point to Jesus' belief in the coming of a new kingdom and his leadership role within it.[82]

Although the temple cleansing and the predictions against the temple were the immediate causes for Jesus' arrest, he also had opposition from both the Pharisees and the Scribes dating back to the early days of his ministry in Galilee, when they took exception to him for not agreeing with them on their views of keeping the Sabbath, the various purification laws, and fasting laws (Mark 2:18–3:6; 7:1–23). The Pharisees generally disappear as opponents of Jesus after his ministry in Galilee, but after the chief priests and scribes and elders had confronted Jesus on his authority (Mark 11:27), they sent some Pharisees and Herodians to try to trap him in what he said in the temple precincts (Mark 12:13–17). Their opposition evidently followed him from the early days of his ministry (Mark 3:6). Jesus was also accused of being a magician who cast out demons by the power of the devil, or Beelzebub (Matt 9:34; 10:25; 12:24, 27; see Jesus' response, 12:25–32), and of being a false prophet who led the

people astray (Luke 23:2, 5, 14). Early opposition to Jesus is not negligible among the factors that brought Jesus to the cross. It is likely that news of the growing opposition to his ministry, even in Galilee, contributed to his rejection in Jerusalem, even if the decisive events that led to his arrest were the temple cleansing and his predictions about its destruction. The temple cleansing itself was probably more of a prophetic act intended to make a statement about Jesus' mission rather than simply a cleaning up of the temple. Stanton contends that it would have taken an army to halt the buying and selling in the temple and that therefore Jesus' actions are better understood as "a prophetic gesture against the Temple itself" than as a protest against the moneychangers in the temple area.[83]

Whatever his motives, the incident in the temple and Jesus' words about its destruction (Mark 13:1–2) were the most likely immediate causes for his arrest and crucifixion.[84] The religious leaders in Jerusalem perceived a threat from these actions and feared that Jesus could present major problems to the stability and tenuous peace with Rome, problems that might lead to Roman intervention. Adding to this, Jesus had a following, even though there is nothing to suggest that he ever enlisted an army to accomplish his ends or was a member of the Zealots or even sympathetic to such a group (if such a group ever existed; see ch. 3, sec. 2, above).[85] The size of his following at the time of his death is uncertain, but it was noticeable (Mark 11:18; Luke 19:39). Both the Jewish religious leaders and Pilate therefore decided that they could not allow him to continue.

Jesus evidently had the opportunity to defend himself both to Caiaphas and to Pilate, who could essentially have dismissed the charges against him, but Jesus chose not to do so (Mark 14:60–61; 15:1–5; Luke 22:66–70; 23:3–4, 8–9; Matt 26:62–64; 27:11–14; John 18:19–24, 28–38). Sanders affirms the historicity of these reports, saying that Jesus conceivably "could have talked his way out of execution had he promised to take his disciples, return to Galilee and keep his mouth shut. He seems not to have tried."[86]

B. Responsibility for Jesus' Death

Because Crossan does not believe that the NT writings present much historically accurate information about the life and ministry of Jesus, it is not surprising that he also dismisses the historical accuracy of the passion narratives and their implication that there was some Jewish participation in Jesus' condemnation and death.[87] He does not find much historical information in the Gospels but, rather, what he calls "prophecy historicized rather than history recalled."[88] Crossan rightly rejects Jewish responsibility (i.e., of the whole nation) and Roman innocence, but he fails to satisfy the question why there was such strong reaction against the Jewish people in early Christian writings. Without question, not all of the Jews of Palestine could be held accountable for the death of Jesus, not even a sizable percentage. No doubt there were some Jews who did not accept Jesus as a messianic figure and perceived that he was some kind of a charlatan. Some wanted to dismiss him, some even wanted to execute him, and some believed in him. In no case were all the Jewish people guilty of, or responsible for, his death.

There is no good reason to deny, however, that certain religious leaders in Jerusalem believed that the death of one person who threatened the religious and social structure of the region could keep the nation safe from Roman interference in their affairs (John 11:50). Since the Jewish authorities did not have the authority to execute, the local Roman prefect, Pilate, and the soldiers under his command were responsible for the actual death itself. The execution probably did come as a recommendation from the high priest, but Pilate was under no mandate to carry out the high priest's wishes. Pilate made the final decision, evidently quickly, since none of the Gospels indicate that he tarried long in his deliberation. The execution itself took place on the same day within a few hours after Jesus was brought to him.

The number of those responsible for Jesus' death was eventually and unfortunately expanded by the church to include the whole Jewish nation and even all Jews of all times. Some references in the NT probably contributed to this conclusion, for example, John 8:34–59 and 1 Thess 2:13–16. This unreasonable understanding of Jewish texts by Gentiles of a later era has led to many tragedies for the Jewish people throughout history. It is an overstatement to say that no Jews in authoritative places were responsible for the death of Jesus, but it is likewise unreasonable to say that all of Israel should be held accountable.

What may have led to the expansion of Jewish responsibility for the death of Jesus is the fact that the Jews did not convert to Christianity and that many early Christians still found Judaism attractive well into the fifth century A.D. There also appears to have been some Jewish involvement in the persecution of the Christians, such as turning Christians over to Roman authorities when the Christian faith had been outlawed in certain sectors of the empire. In some cases, Jews were no doubt responsible for turning in Christians to Roman authorities, who punished Christians for their faith, as in the case of the death of Polycarp (*Mart. Pol.* 12.2; 13.1; 17.2; 18.1).[89]

From a biblical perspective, however, early Christian writers began to argue that the death of Jesus was in the plan of God (Acts 2:23) and that his death was for "our sins," that is, he died in the place of sinners (Rom 5:8; 2 Cor 5:19–21). Stein is certainly correct when he concludes that "Christians know that *they* are the cause for Jesus' death. Ultimately it is the believer, for whom Christ died, who is responsible for his death"; those who need a scapegoat "need only look in the mirror."[90] The time for blaming the whole Jewish nation for the crimes against Jesus is long since over, and Christians should consider Stein's able advice.

BIBLIOGRAPHY

ANDERSON, H. A. *Jesus.* Englewood Cliffs, N.J.: Prentice-Hall, 1967.

BORG, M. J. *Jesus, a New Vision: Spirit, Culture, and the Life of Discipleship.* San Francisco: HarperCollins, 1991.

BORNKAMM, G. *Jesus of Nazareth.* Trans. I. and F. McLuskey with J. M. Robinson. New York: HarperCollins, 1960.

BROWN, R. E. *The Birth of the Messiah: A Commentary on the Infancy Narratives in the Gospels of*

Matthew and Luke. Rev. ed. ABRL. Garden City, N.Y., 1993.

_____. *The Death of the Messiah: A Commentary on the Passion Narratives*. 2 vols. ABRL. New York: Doubleday, 1994.

BOWDEN, J. *Jesus: The Unanswered Questions*. London: SCM, 1988.

CHARLESWORTH, J. H., ed. *Jesus' Jewishness: Exploring the Place of Jesus in Early Judaism*. New York: Crossroad, 1991.

CHARLESWORTH, J. H., and W. P. WEAVER, eds. *Images of Jesus Today*. Faith and Scholarship Colloquies. Valley Forge, Penn.: Trinity Press International, 1994.

CROSSAN, J. D. *The Historical Jesus: The Life of a Mediterranean Jewish Peasant*. San Francisco: Harper, 1991.

_____. *Who Killed Jesus? Exposing the Roots of Anti-Semitism in the Gospel Story of the Death of Jesus*. San Francisco: HarperSanFrancisco, 1995.

EVANS, C. A. *Jesus and His Contemporaries: Comparative Studies*. AGJU 25. Leiden: Brill, 1995.

_____. *Life of Jesus Research: An Annotated Bibliography*. Rev. ed. NTTS 13. Leiden: Brill, 1996.

FARMER, W. R. *The Gospel of Jesus: The Pastoral Relevance of the Synoptic Problem*. Philadelphia: Westminster, 1993.

HENGEL, M. *Crucifixion in the Ancient World and the Folly of the Message of the Cross*. Philadelphia: Fortress, 1977.

MEIER, J. P. *A Marginal Jew: Rethinking the Historical Jesus*. Vol. 1. *The Roots of the Problem and the Person*. Vol. 2. *Mentor, Message, and Miracles*. 3 vols. ABRL. Garden City, N.Y.: Doubleday, 1991–.

NEUSNER, J. *Rabbinic Literature and the New Testament: What We Cannot Show, We Do Not Know*. Valley Forge, Penn.: Trinity Press International, 1994.

SANDERS, E. P. *The Historical Figure of Jesus*. London: Allen Lane/Penguin, 1993.

_____. *Jesus and Judaism*. London: SCM, 1985.

STANTON, G. *Gospel Truth? New Light on Jesus and the Gospels*. Valley Forge, Penn.: Trinity Press International, 1995.

STAUFFER, E. *Jesus and His Story*. London: SCM, 1960.

THEISSEN, G. *Miracle Stories of the Early Christian Tradition*. Edinburgh: T. & T. Clark, 1984.

WITHERINGTON, B., III. *Jesus the Sage: The Pilgrimage of Wisdom*. Minneapolis: Fortress, 1993.

pages 117–126

1. The name Jesus is from the Greek form of the Hebrew *Yeshua,* or Joshua. It was a common name in the first century A.D. and has numerous parallels in the century before and after the time of Jesus. Because of the rise of Christianity, the Jews then reverted back to using the earlier form, Joshua. Josephus mentions some ten persons by the name of Jesus. See, e.g., in his *Ant.* 20.223 a reference to Jesus, the son of Gamaliel.

2. R. E. Brown, *The Birth of the Messiah: A Commentary on the Infancy Narratives in Matthew and Luke* (rev. ed.; ABRL; Garden City, N.Y.: Doubleday, 1993), 216–21.

3. The more recent method of dating history (B.C.E. = before the Christian/Common Era, and C.E. = in the Christian/Common Era) continues to date historical events on the basis of Ussher's dating method, even though the best available evidence for dating shows that the traditional time of Jesus' birth was a few years later than the actual date.

4. N. Geldenhuys, *The Gospel of Luke* (NICNT; Grand Rapids: Eerdmans, 1951), 100.

5. The first inscription can be read in W. M. Ramsay, *Was Christ Born in Bethlehem?* (New York: Putnam, 1898), 273; the second and third, in *The Bearing of Recent Discovery on the Trustworthiness of the New Testament* (London: Hodder & Stoughton, 1915), 285, 291.

6. P.Lond. III 904 (LCL; *Select Papyri* 2:220.18–27). A. S. Hunt and C. C. Edgar, *Select Papyri* (2 vols.; LCL; Cambridge: Harvard University Press, 1932–1934).

7. For a more detailed analysis of this problem, see Brown, *Birth of the Messiah,* 551–55. On the Egyptian census, see R. S. Bagnall and B. W. Frier, *The Demography of Roman Egypt* (Cambridge: Cambridge University Press, 1994), esp. 1–5; cf. 14–16.

8. J. P. Meier, *A Marginal Jew: Rethinking the Historical Jesus* (3 vols.; ABRL; Garden City, N.Y.: Doubleday, 1991–), 1:382.

9. See Philostratus, *Apoll.* 1.4–6, in which the origins of the first-century itinerant philosopher Apollonius are considered divine: the child bears the image of the divine Proteus, the mother has a remarkable birth, and the child is called a "son of Zeus."

10. Brown, *Birth of the Messiah,* 527–28.

11. Meier, *Marginal Jew,* 1:213.

12. Ibid., 1:219, 241–42.

13. R. R. Wilson, "Genealogy, Genealogies," *ABD* 2:929–32.

14. See D. E. Orton, *The Understanding Scribe: Matthew and the Apocalyptic Ideal* (JSNTSup 25; Sheffield: JSOT Press, 1989).

15. Gematria is a method of interpreting the Scriptures by calculating the numerical value of words. It focuses on discovering a hidden meaning within a passage by adding up or studying the numerical value of words and numbers in the text. See, e.g., the highly charged number 666 in Rev. 13:18 and the number 7, used elsewhere in that book.

16. Brown, *Birth of the Messiah,* 71–74.

17. A more complete listing of this feature in Matthew is in W. D. Davies and D. C. Allison, *A Critical and Exegetical Commentary on the Gospel according to Matthew* (3 vols.; ICC; Edinburgh: T. & T. Clark, 1988–1997), 1:85–87.

18. J. P. Meier, "Reflections on Jesus-of-History Research Today," in *Jesus' Jewishness: Exploring the Place of Jesus in Early Judaism* (ed. J. H. Charlesworth; New York: Crossroad, 1991), 89.

19. See S. E. Porter, "Did Jesus Ever Teach in Greek?" *TynB* 44 (2, 1993): 199–235.

20. Meier, "Reflections," 89.

21. J. P. Meier, *Marginal Jew*, 2:106.

22. Ibid., 2:110.

23. Ibid., 2:113.

24. Eschatology, from the Greek ἔσχατος, *eschatos* ("last"), is the study of the end times of history and the divine judgment of God. An eschatological prophet is one who announces that the end of time or history and God's intervention into human affairs has come or is about to happen.

25. Meier, *Marginal Jew*, 2:116.

26. M. Borg, *Jesus, A New Vision: Spirit, Culture, and the Life of Discipleship* (San Francisco: Harper, 1987), 11; cf. 14–16, 20 n. 25.

27. Trans. Florentino García Martínez, *Dead Sea Scrolls Translated: The Qumran Texts in English* (Leiden: Brill, 1994), 394. Square brackets [ ] represent gaps in the manuscript where the translator has supplied the words within. The italics are ours.

28. See R. W. Funk et al., *The Five Gospels: The Search for the Authentic Words of Jesus* (New York: Macmillan, 1993), 301–2.

29. Although some members of the Jesus Seminar do not believe this parable comes from Jesus (R. Funk, B. B. Scott, and J. R. Butts, *The Parables of Jesus, Red Letter Edition: A Report of the Jesus Seminar* [Sonoma, Calif.: Polebridge, 1988], 50–51), we believe it is authentic and find nothing in it unfamiliar to a resident of Galilee of the first century, such as someone who was raised in Nazareth.

30. It is interesting, as Crossan has observed, that Josephus, who gives the names of forty-five towns in Galilee, and the Talmud, which refers to sixty-three towns from the region, never mention Nazareth. See J. D. Crossan, *The Historical Jesus: The Life of a Mediterranean Jewish Peasant* (San Francisco: Harper, 1991), 15, citing J. Finegan's research. Nazareth was obviously not significant in the first few centuries A.D.

31. For a reconstruction of the inscription, see E. Meyers, E. Netzer, and C. Meyers, *Sepphoris* (Winona Lake, Ind: Eisenbrauns, 1992), 15.

32. Ibid., 16–17. They also recall the strong tradition, supported in patristic literature and still upheld in the Roman Catholic Church, that Joakim and Anna, the parents of Mary the mother of Jesus, were residents of Sepphoris.

33. The exact identity of the Twelve is not clear from the accounts in the Gospels. All four Gospels mention Peter (called Simon and, in Paul's writings, Cephas), Andrew his brother, James and John (called the Sons of Thunder or sons of Zebedee), Philip, Thomas, and Judas Iscariot. Matthew, Mark, Luke, and Acts also mention Bartholomew, Matthew, James the son of Alphaeus, and Simon the Zealot or the Cananaean. Matthew and Mark add Thaddaeus. Luke, Acts, and John add Judas the son of James (or in the case of John, "Judas (not Iscariot)"), and John adds Nathanael. This totals fourteen names. Clearly the number twelve was intended, but there is confusion about who makes up the Twelve, including uncertainty that Matthew and Levi, both called tax collectors, are the same. See E. P. Sanders, *The Historical Figure of Jesus* (London: Allen Lane/Penguin, 1993), 291.

34. Meier, "Reflections," 90–91.

35. C. A. Evans, "Life-of-Jesus Research and the Eclipse of Mythology," *TS* 54 (1993): 3–36; here 34, 36.

pages 127–137

36. Meier, "Reflections," 93.

37. For a discussion of these individuals and of miracles in the story of Jesus, see Meier, *Marginal Jew*, 2:581–88; also on the miracles of Jesus and on his understanding of miracles in general, see 2:509–1038. Cf. G. Theissen, *Miracle Stories of the Early Christian Tradition* (trans. F. McDonagh; Edinburgh: T. & T. Clark, 1983), who offers a valuable historical and sociological context for interpreting the significance of the miracle stories.

38. S. Brown, *The Origins of Christianity: A Historical Introduction to the New Testament* (OBS; Oxford: Oxford University Press, 1984), 57.

39. Besides the temple cleansing, Jesus' willingness to violate Sabbath laws, his triumphal entry, which demonstrated his awareness of his role as Messiah, and his negative comments about the temple were all factors that led to Jesus' crucifixion. See sec. 3, below.

40. This motif, associated with the scholar W. Wrede (*The Messianic Secret* [trans. J. C. C. Greig; Cambridge, England: J. Clarke, 1971; originally published in 1901]), recognizes that Jesus at several places in Mark's Gospel instructs the disciples and others not to tell anyone about what they have seen him do. Explanations of the origins and meaning of this motif vary considerably.

41. Matthew has Jesus' disciples secure two animals for this occasion (Matt 21:2–7) whereas the other evangelists mention only one animal. It appears that Matthew took the Hebrew letter *waw* in Zech 9:9 to be a connective ("and") rather than an explicative ("even"). Even in the Greek text the problem would be the same with the word καί (*kai*, which can be translated "and," "even," or "also").

42. A number of scholars have rejected the authenticity of the trial of Jesus before Caiaphas, especially the response of Jesus. We believe, however, that they fit the rest of the pattern of Jesus' career and message and should thus be accepted as a part of the authentic tradition about him.

43. Although Acts was written years after the epistles of Paul, we believe that a summary of the preaching of the early church is well preserved in the early chapters of Acts. The fact that Acts presents a simple and idealistic view of the early church in summary form does not detract from this conclusion about its preservation of the essence of early Christian preaching.

44. The words "Our Lord, come!" originally were written in Aramaic and transliterated into Greek as μαρανα θα (or possibly μαραν αθα, "Our Lord has come"). The fact that Paul shares these words in Aramaic with Greeks from Corinth strongly indicates that they had an earlier history in Palestine and did not originate on Hellenistic soil as some scholars have earlier argued.

45. M. Dibelius, *From Tradition to Gospel* (London: Nicholson & Watson, 1934), 193–94. See also his *Jesus* (trans. C. B. Hedrick and F. C. Grant; Philadelphia: Westminster, 1949).

46. An excellent work on this topic is R. E. Brown, *The Death of the Messiah* (2 vols.; New York: Doubleday, 1994). See also P. Benoit, *The Passion and Resurrection of Jesus Christ* (New York: Herder & Herder, 1969).

47. R. H. Gundry, *Mark: A Commentary on His Apology for the Cross* (Grand Rapids: Eerdmans, 1993), 893.

48. See C. A. Evans, *Jesus and His Contemporaries: Comparative Studies* (AGJU 25; Leiden: Brill, 1995), 407–34, where he also defends the authenticity of the trial scene.

pages 137–157

49. See M. Hengel, *Crucifixion in the Ancient World and the Folly of the Message of the Cross* (Philadelphia: Fortress, 1977), 39–45, who cites several examples of Romans who were crucified. He summarizes the practice of crucifixion on pp. 86–90.

50. Trans. J. H. Charlesworth, *OTP* 1:930.

51. R. Bultmann, *The History of the Synoptic Tradition* (trans. J. Marsh; rev. ed.; Oxford: Blackwell, 1972), 285. W. Marxsen (*The Resurrection of Jesus of Nazareth* [trans. M. Kohl; London: SCM, 1970], 45) believes Matthew deliberately altered Mark's text at this point because on reflection he knew it was impossible to undertake the anointing of a body on the third day, "for the process of mortification would have already begun. Consequently Matthew strikes out this feature of his copy [of Mark]." It is more probable, however, that Matthew omitted the story about the spices because he already had stated that the tomb was sealed and a guard posted (27:66). For Matthew, the women probably came to the tomb out of simple devotion and not necessarily with the purpose of anointing the body of Jesus, although this is not certain.

52. Bultmann (*Synoptic Tradition*, 285 n. 1) believes that this inconsistency in Mark points to the secondary nature of the empty-tomb tradition in Mark and that 16:1–8 was not constructed with the chronology that controls Mark in mind.

53. Ibid., 274.

54. J. L. Lilly, "Alleged Discrepancies in the Gospel Accounts of the Resurrection," *CBQ* 2 (1940): 103–104.

55. Trans. H. Danby, *The Mishnah* (Oxford: Oxford University Press, 1980), 120.

56. Ibid., 104–105.

57. E. L. Bode, *The First Easter Morning: The Gospel Accounts of the Women's Visit to the Tomb of Jesus* (Rome: Biblical Institute Press, 1970), 173.

58. H. Grass, *Ostergeschehen und Osterberichte* (Göttingen: Vandenhoeck & Ruprecht, 1962), 179–80.

59. R. H. Fuller, *Formation of the Resurrection Narratives* (London: SCM, 1972), 54–56. Bultmann (*Synoptic Tradition*, 284–85) argued that the story of the women coming to the tomb on Easter morning was secondary because it did not fit with the previous section in Mark. After giving the names in 15:40, 47, it would not be necessary to do so again as in 16:1; also, their intention to embalm the body does not agree with 15:46, where there is no indication that the burial was incomplete.

60. Fuller, *Formation*, 54–55.

61. G. O'Collins, *The Easter Jesus* (London: Darton, Longman, & Todd, 1973), 39.

62. H. Conzelmann, *The Theology of St. Luke* (trans. G. Buswell; London: Faber & Faber, 1960), 88, 202.

63. J. Munck, *The Acts of the Apostles* (AB 31; Garden City, N.Y.: Doubleday, 1967), 123.

64. F. F. Bruce, *The Acts of the Apostles* (3d ed.; Grand Rapids: Eerdmans, 1990), 308.

65. R. P. C. Hanson, *The Acts* (Oxford: Clarendon, 1967), 143.

66. Bode, *Easter Morning*, 173.

67. L. Geering, *Resurrection: A Symbol of Hope* (London: Hodder & Stoughton, 1971), 47.

68. For other possibilities, see K. W. Clark, "Arimathea," *IDB* 1:219; and J. A. Pattengale, "Arimathea," *ABD* 1:378.

69. See E. Rivkin, *What Crucified Jesus? The Political Execution of a Charismatic* (Nashville: Abingdon, 1984); and H. Cohn, *The Trial and Death of Jesus* (New York: Harper & Row, 1971).

70. Sanders, *Historical Figure*, 257, says that the fact that this did not literally happen shows that the prediction predates the destruction of the temple and may well go back to Jesus himself.

71. Ibid., 262, 271.

72. For a brief discussion of the function and importance of the Jewish temple in the time of Jesus, see E. Ferguson, *Backgrounds of Early Christianity* (2d ed.; Grand Rapids: Eerdmans, 1993), 527–32; also M. O. Wise, "Temple," *DJG* 811–17; and the instructive discussion of the significance of the cleansing incident in W. R. Herzog II, "Temple Cleansing," *DJG* 817–21; and esp. in Sanders, *Historical Figure*, 35–43, 254–62, 270–73.

73. Sanders, *Historical Figure*, 274.

74. J. T. Carroll and J. B Green, *The Death of Jesus in Early Christianity* (Peabody, Mass.: Hendrickson, 1995), 202–3.

75. Trans. C. D. Yonge, *The Works of Philo: Complete and Unabridged* (rev. ed.; Peabody, Mass.: Hendrickson, 1993), 784.

76. J. D. Crossan, *Who Killed Jesus? Exposing the Roots of Anti-Semitism in the Gospel Story of the Death of Jesus* (San Francisco: Harper, 1996), 148.

77. Carroll and Green, *Death of Jesus*, 201–2; and G. Stanton, *Gospel Truth? New Light on Jesus and the Gospels* (Edinburgh: T. & T. Clark, 1995), 183–87.

78. Stanton (*Gospel Truth?* 185–87) makes this claim.

79. Ibid., 187.

80. Ibid., 179.

81. Ibid.

82. Sanders, *Historical Figure*, 253–64.

83. Stanton, *Gospel Truth?* 182–83.

84. Sanders, *Historical Figure*, 265.

85. Contra S. G. F. Brandon, *Jesus and the Zealots* (Manchester: Manchester University Press, 1967), who portrayed Jesus as sympathetic to the Zealots, which led to Jesus' death.

86. Sanders, *Historical Figure*, 267.

87. Crossan, *Who Killed Jesus?* 147–59.

88. Ibid., 159.

89. For a more detailed discussion, see ch. 7, below, and L. M. McDonald, "Anti-Judaism in the Early Church Fathers," in *Anti-Semitism and Early Christianity* (ed. C. A. Evans and D. A. Hagner; Minneapolis: Fortress, 1993), 215–52, esp. 236–49.

90. R. Stein, *Jesus the Messiah: A Survey of the Life of Christ* (Downers Grove, Ill.: InterVarsity Press, 1996), 239.

THE STORY OF JESUS, PART B:

Easter Faith and the Resurrection Narratives

1. INTRODUCTION

The most important event of the NT, which is also foundational for the establishment of the church, is the resurrection of Jesus from the dead. The earliest NT Christologies (see Rom 1:3–4), eschatologies (1 Cor 15:20–28; Phil 3:21; Rom 8:9–11, 22–24), and other doctrines, including the salvation of humanity (1 Cor 15:12–20), are based on this event. Without the resurrection of Jesus, according to Paul, there is no basis for Christian proclamation and an inadequate explanation of how the proclaimer, Jesus, became the proclaimed in the Christian tradition. It was in his resurrection that Jesus' message was authenticated and faith was born in his disciples (Acts 2:22–36); it was in the proclamation of the resurrection that forgiveness of sins and hope beyond the grave were extended to the earliest communities of believers in Jesus. There are, however, a number of obscurities in the Easter narratives about precisely what happened in the resurrection of Jesus. Although Paul precedes the Gospel writers, he does not describe the appearances of Jesus or the empty-tomb tradition that is found in all the canonical Gospels. This silence has been used as a basis for calling into question the authenticity of the Gospel narratives. A brief comparison of the Gospels and the Pauline testimony in 1 Cor

15 shows the difficulties with which scholars have struggled for centuries. The united testimony from the early church, however, is that God raised up Jesus from the dead, even though there are many unsettled questions about the event. The basic message of the Gospels remains: Jesus of Nazareth was crucified, buried, and raised from the dead and then was seen (or will be seen; cf. Mark 16:7) by witnesses. This message is also at the heart of the entire NT witness to the glorification of Jesus and Christian hope (1 Cor 15:3–8; 1 Pet 1:3–5; Rev 1:5; etc.). Because an understanding of the Easter story and its proclamation is critical for understanding the origins of Christian faith and the birth of the church, this examination of the primary NT texts about the resurrection will be fairly detailed.

2. ORIGINS OF THE NOTION OF RESURRECTION

There was no single understanding of life after death adopted by all Jews in the time of Jesus, even though the view that prevailed was that of the Pharisees, who believed in the resurrection of the

The gatehouse of the Golden Gate, also called Solomon's Throne, on the Eastern Wall of the Temple Mount in Jerusalem. Photo © Rohr Productions. Used with permission.

body at the end of the ages. In his summary of the primary texts on resurrection, Nickelsburg has shown that belief in meaningful life after death was, in fact, a rather late development in the history of Israelite religion.[1] This notion appears to begin with Jewish speculation that there was life beyond this one in spite of physical death (e.g., Psalms 16, 49, 73; Isa 24–27, esp. 25:6–8, 26:14–19). Scholars debate the dating of all these texts, but most put them late in OT history. The context of persecution against the people of God and belief in God's vindication after death may be the source of such early notions of life after death. This is the case, for example, in *1 En.* 22–27, especially ch. 22. In these chapters, the blessing of God comes to the righteous after death, as does the eternal judgment of God upon the sinner. The nature of existence in the afterlife is not fully described here, but what description is offered is given in nonphysical terms (e.g. 22:3–14) except in 22:13, where the souls of the righteous are assumed to rise on the day of judgment but not the souls of the unrighteous. In 25:6, however, the "fragrance" of the holy place

"shall (penetrate) their [the righteous] bones," and "long life will they live on earth such as your fathers lived in their days."[2] If it is like that of the fathers before them, their mode of life is likely perceived here to be a physical one. These, and other similar passages, may be directly dependent on Isa 65–66 (perhaps ca. late or early fifth century B.C.), which speaks of the blessings of the faithful and the judgment of sinners.

The notion of the blessing and judgment of God is also present in *Jub.* 23:11–31 and 2 Macc 7:9–14. In 4 Maccabees (perhaps late first century B.C. or early first century A.D.), the writer mentions the blessing that God promises to those who are faithful and live by the law (4 Macc 2:23). Later, in 17:11–12, after the faithful martyrdoms of an aged priest, a mother, and her seven sons, it is reported that the prize for victory is "immortality in endless life." Finally, in 18:23, with their "victorious mother" they "are gathered together into the chorus of the fathers, and have received pure and immortal souls from God."[3] In the Wisdom of Solomon (probably late first century B.C.), chs. 1–5 (1:15; 2:22–23; 3:1,

8; 5:15), the blessing of God after death comes in the form of immortality of the soul. *Fourth Ezra* 7 (2 Esdras; late first century A.D.) speaks of immortality of the soul for the righteous (v. 13), who escape what is corruptible in order "to receive and enjoy [spacious liberty in] immortality" (vv. 96–99), while the wicked face the judgment of God (vv. 76–87). Qumran and related Jewish literature also refers to rewards for godly living and punishment for the unjust in the life to come (e.g., 3QHymn III, 19–23; XI, 3–14; CD III, 13–IV, 26; *cf. T. Ab.* 11–12).[4]

McDonald observes that there is very little language about the notion of resurrection from the dead in the OT, and what there is of it is both late in the history of Israel and in a context of suffering. Like Nickelsburg, he claims that the idea of resurrection emerges in the context of "theodicy," or the "attempt to affirm the goodness and omnipotence of God in the face of evil in the world."[5] When so much of the promise of God to Israel was voiced in terms of possession of the land of Palestine, how could it be that the people of God, even if a remnant, would die in captivity in Babylon after the destruction of their homeland and temple? At this time, there was an attempt to come to terms with God's goodness in the face of evil. Ezekiel was one of the first to speak of God reconstituting the nation in terms of a resurrection of "dry bones" (Ezek 37:1–14). In symbolic language, the nation is reconstituted. Similarly, Isa 26:19 (see all of Isa 24–27) makes this same point using resurrection imagery. These may be the earliest texts to discuss the notion of the resurrection and reward of the righteous (Isaiah scholars dispute the dating of chs. 24–27, many contending that they are postexilic in origin).

The notion of the resurrection of the righteous is more clearly presented in the intertestamental literature, where we begin to see several references to the resurrection from the grave. For example, in Dan 12:2, a text that was written in its final form in the mid–second century B.C., we find reference to a resurrection for the faithful and the unfaithful to blessing and condemnation respectively. The context of the book is persecution of the righteous, and resurrection is the means by which God corrects injustice (chs. 9–10). Daniel 12:2 can be compared with *Assum. Mos.* 10 and *Jub.* 23:27–31, where there are similar interests in resurrection as a means of both reward and punishment. *Testament of Judah* 25

is also a close parallel. In 2 Macc 7:7–23, we see a description of the physical tortures of the Jews by Antiochus (167–165 B.C.) and an affirmation that God will "raise us up to an everlasting renewal of life, because we have died for his laws" (v. 9). Other similar passages include *Pss. Sol.* 3:11 and *1 En.* 22, which focus on the rewards and punishments of both the righteous and sinners. *First Enoch* 25:6 anticipates the rising of the righteous to new life in the new Jerusalem, but it is not clear whether the unrighteous will rise for punishment. These passages, and others, bear witness that belief in a resurrection from the grave was not uniform in the intertestamental literature. Wisdom of Solomon 2:23–24; 3:1, for instance, does not speak of resurrection but, rather, the immortality of the soul (see also *Jub.* 23:32; *1 En.* 103; cf. Ps 73:24–26). On the other hand, *1 En.* 102:4–104:8 (ca. early second century B.C.) argues that the day of judgment will come to those who oppress the poor and that the souls of the righteous who grieve in Sheol will come back to life and receive the reward that their fleshly bodies missed. On the basis of these passages, McDonald concludes that resurrection language is essentially eschatological and is related to an apocalyptic worldview.[6]

That there was no single Jewish teaching about life after death is illustrated by Josephus when he claims that the Pharisees believed in the resurrection of the body, the Sadducees did not hold to any view of life after death, whether for rewards or punishments, and the Essenes held to the immortality of the soul (*War* 2.154–166; *Ant.* 18.12–20; see also 13.171–173).[7] The NT agrees that this was one of the points of contention between the Sadducees and the Pharisees (Mark 12:18–23; cf. Matt 22:23–33; Luke 20:27–39; Acts 23:6–8). The NT writers, however, generally agree with the Pharisees that for those who have faith in God life after death will be by resurrection of the body (1 Thess 4:13–17; Rev 20:4; 1 Cor 15:3–5, 35–58). A possible exception to this is in Hebrews, where the author, though he does not use the typical resurrection language in reference to Jesus' exaltation, does affirm the notion of resurrection from the dead (Heb 6:2; 13:20). The nature of the resurrection is described differently in Luke 24:36–43 and Paul (1 Cor 15:38–45, 50), but both focus on a bodily resurrection from the grave, even if Paul emphasizes a transformed bodily resurrection (1 Cor 15:51–54) and contends that "flesh and blood cannot inherit the kingdom of God" (15:50). Although according to second-century rabbinic Judaism "all Israelites have a share in the world to come" except those who say "that there is no resurrection of the dead prescribed in the law" (*m. Sanh.* 10:1),[8] this does not mean that these were the uniform views of Judaism between 100 B.C. and 100 A.D.[9]

3. THE RESURRECTION OF JESUS IN HISTORY AND IN THE EASTER TRADITIONS

There is little doubt that the kingdom of God and its coming played a significant role in the thinking of Jesus' disciples and, indeed, in the thinking of Jesus himself. The disciples anticipated an early establishment of the kingdom of God and even quarreled over who would be greatest in this kingdom (Matt 18:1). They appear to have believed that Jesus was the one who would initiate the coming of the kingdom among them. So, when Jesus died, his disciples were shattered, along with their hopes for the early establishment of the kingdom.

After Jesus was arrested, his disciples abandoned him and fled (Mark 14:50); they were filled with deep discouragement (Luke 24:17). The death of Jesus must certainly have spelled the end of the disciples' hopes and led them to question who Jesus really was. As Bultmann argues, the cross presented the disciples with a question that had to be answered.[10] According to Paul, it was the major stumbling block the Jews had to overcome (1 Cor 1:23). How could confidence be restored in Jesus in such a short space of time after his ignoble death? The writers of the NT contend that it was because Jesus was raised from the dead and exalted by God that faith became a possibility and the church was born.

Several generally accepted historical facts surround the resurrection of Jesus: (1) Jesus died on a cross in Jerusalem; (2) his disciples lost their faith and confidence in him as the one who would establish the kingdom of God; (3) within a relatively short period of time the disciples regained faith and confidence in Jesus as the bringer of God's salvation; and (4) the Christian community grew as a result of the disciples' preaching about the resurrection of Jesus. A fifth and more disputed historical fact to be discussed later is the report, recorded

in the canonical Gospels, of the empty tomb. All of these facts are congruent with the earliest Christian proclamation that God raised Jesus from the dead. The sheer improbability of such an event taking place, however, along with the confusing narratives that tell this story, have caused many interpreters of Christian origins to be cautious and even skeptical in their conclusions about the Easter story. The first issue, therefore, is the problem of knowing what precisely happened in the resurrection of Jesus.

Because there is a tendency among those critical scholars who reject the resurrection of Jesus as an event of history to emphasize the discrepancies within the resurrection narratives, we will focus on some of these problems, not so much with harmonization in mind as with the aim of trying to discover what actually happened in Jesus' resurrection according to the NT. Even though several serious discrepancies[11] can be found in the resurrection narratives, including problems of consistency within a single narrative (John 20:1–18), the essential message of each evangelist is quite clear—that Jesus of Nazareth who was crucified was also raised from the dead. Besides a brief outline of a few lesser issues, the following discussion will address three basic issues: the empty-tomb tradition, the appearance stories, and the nature of the resurrection of Jesus.

The Gospel writers never describe the resurrection itself; they only proclaim that Jesus was raised from the dead and describe various appearances of Jesus to the disciples. There were no eyewitnesses to the resurrection, and so we cannot know exactly what happened in the resurrection itself. The NT writings, unlike the apocryphal *Gospel of Peter*,[12] do not describe or narrate the Easter event, what actually happened to Jesus during his resurrection. There is no doubt in the minds of the NT writers, however, that Jesus was again alive and that the best way to proclaim this fact was through the story of his resurrection from the dead. The evangelists narrate the discovery of an empty tomb and the appearances of Jesus to the disciples, but the resurrection itself was an inference drawn from the appearances, as was its nature from the empty-tomb stories.[13] Even though he himself does not accept that the tomb of Jesus had been vacated by a miracle from God, Lüdemann agrees that this was a part of the beliefs of the earliest Christian community.[14] Some of the earliest Easter proclamations only mention the fact of the resurrection and call for a confession of it without having narrated the event at all (see Rom 10:9). Paul, for example, mentions the resurrection of Jesus as a means of introducing his letters to Christians (see Gal 1:1; Rom 1:3–4). In some of the early Christian proclamation there existed the belief that, by the resurrection, God did not allow Jesus' flesh to see corruption (Acts 2:24–31) but, rather, raised him up and exalted him (Acts 2:32–33).

From the perspective of Paul as well as the evangelists, the basis for proclaiming Easter faith was the postresurrection appearances of Jesus. Indeed, without them, it is difficult to account for the birth of Christianity. The earliest Christian message is that God raised up Jesus from the dead and exalted him and that, as a result, there was hope for the forgiveness of sins and participation in the coming kingdom of God (Acts 2:38; 3:19; 5:30–31; 13:39; and passim).[15] That Jesus was seen alive after his death is attested in Matt 28, Luke 24, and John 20 and 21, may be presumed in Mark 16:7, and is affirmed by Paul (1 Cor 9:1–2; 15:3–8); all offer assurances that Jesus was alive after his death. The later Easter traditions in the Gospels employed the empty-tomb story as a means of proclaiming the resurrection of Jesus. For example, this is the message of the angel(s) at the empty tomb in the Synoptic Gospels (Mark 16:6; Luke 24:4–7; Matt 28:1–7) and, in a different way, in John 20:1–18, though it should not be concluded that an empty tomb in and of itself was the basis for belief in the resurrection. The appearances of Jesus and the empty-tomb tradition were the two vehicles for proclaiming the resurrection of Jesus; because of the appearances of Jesus Easter faith was initiated, while the empty tomb added credibility to the nature of these appearances, namely, that they were bodily or corporeal. Easter faith proclaims, then, that God raised Jesus from the dead, but how God raised him up remains, to some extent, a mystery.

Another difficulty in ascertaining what happened in the resurrection of Jesus stems from the fact that the only sources about the event were not written until some thirty or more years later, even though they are unquestionably based on earlier oral traditions that circulated in churches (e.g., 1 Cor 15:11). As the message of Easter was carried on largely by word of mouth, it is likely that the traditions were passed on with some alterations or mod-

ifications. Indeed, the expansion of the Easter traditions can be seen in the addition of the empty-tomb stories themselves to the proclamation of Easter. The earliest Easter traditions in the NT (1 Cor 15:3–8; Rom 10:9–10) do not employ the empty-tomb story. This does not mean that the empty-tomb tradition is a late invention of the early church, only that its inclusion in the mainstream of the Easter tradition was not in the earliest preaching of the resurrection of Jesus. Neither does this mean that the story was unknown or unimportant to the earliest Christians. The addition of the story to the Easter tradition was perhaps prompted by a later need to show that Jesus' resurrection was not simply a spiritual event but a bodily event. This is speculation, of course, but is offered only as a possible explanation for the church's need to add this story.[16] Matthew 28:11–15 records a Jewish polemic that the disciples stole Jesus' body. This polemic assumes that the tomb was empty and tries to account for how it became that way, lending further credence to the earliness of the empty-tomb tradition.

In any event, it is difficult to believe that the Easter traditions used in early Christian preaching and teaching (during the rather lengthy oral stage of their development) could have remained static. Although certain changes are discernible in the Easter traditions, it does not follow that what initiated the faith of the earliest followers of Jesus and the birth of the church has been lost or completely obscured in the traditions, as some scholars contend. The message is still clear that God raised up Jesus from the dead, and that belief is what stands behind the birth of the church (Rom 10:9).

Despite this affirmation, a number of difficulties still remain in the narratives. Among these are the number of angels at the empty tomb, their message, their location, the number and names of the women coming to the tomb, the time of their arrival, the nature and location of the resurrection appearances, and the message that the risen Lord proclaims in the appearances. Along with these difficulties, we also mention the various accompanying phenomena included by the four evangelists at the death and resurrection of Jesus in all of the Gospels; they may well be part of the Gospels' various theological interpretations of the events they describe. Those who believe that Jesus did rise from the grave often tend to minimize historical objections to the Easter story and to discount the growth and development of the traditions, while those who reject it tend to emphasize the differences in the traditions, saying that what happened is so obscured in the Gospels that it is not possible to decide what it was that initiated Christian faith.[17] How significant are the differences in the Gospels and those between Paul and the Gospels? It is wrong, on the one hand, to deemphasize the problems and unfair, on the other hand, to spend so much time on them that the common elements in the stories are lost. There is a common message in each of the surviving traditions that should not be over-looked. Still, there are problems of considerable importance, for example, the nature of the resurrection appearances and their location. Nevertheless, the basic assertion in the Easter traditions is the aliveness of Jesus after his crucifixion, the significance of which is considerable for all who place their trust in him. To what extent, however, is the credibility of the resurrection of Jesus in doubt if some of the details of this event cannot be harmonized? Is there a way to explain the difficulties in the sources that makes more credible the message they proclaim? Is it possible to know what actually happened in the resurrection of Jesus? The following is an attempt to deal fairly with the narratives without forcing them into a brittle and unrealistic harmony.

4. THE EMPTY-TOMB TRADITION

It is quite common among scholars to point to the various problems in the empty-tomb tradition as evidence that the story is a later addition to the resurrection narratives in the development of the Gospel tradition. To some extent they are correct, but it does not follow that the tradition is a complete fabrication, as some argue. In this section we will discuss some of the more serious discrepancies in the narratives, and simply list some of the others. Then we will focus on some of the consistencies in the empty-tomb narratives (see table 6-1).

A. The Time of the Discovery

Although all four Gospels indicate that the day of the women's (or Mary's) discovery was early on the first day of the week, the specific time seems to vary in the accounts. In Mark 16:2 the discovery

came "when the sun had risen"; in John 20:1 "while it was still dark"; in Matt 28:1 "as the first day of the week was dawning"; and in Luke 24:1 "at early dawn." There is an obvious difference between Mark and John ("the sun had risen" vs. "while it was still dark"), but Matthew and Luke are quite similar. It also appears that Matthew and Luke are here closer to John than to Mark, though Matthew and Luke could be made to agree with either John or Mark.

Lilly offers two explanations for the difference between Mark and John.[18] First, he says it is possible that while the women were on their way to the tomb, they needed to purchase the spices. Mary Magdalene left this task to the other women and went to the tomb by herself, and the others came later, "when the sun had risen," to join her. His second explanation is derived from a possible translation of ἔρχεται πρωὶ σκοτίας ἔτι οὔσης *(erchetai prōi skotias eti ousēs)* in John 20:1. If Mary "is on her way before daylight," then, according to Lilly, the emphasis is on the *beginning* of the journey to the tomb, while it was still dark. Lilly's first explanation, however, is foreign to Mark, who writes that the women went (3d per. pl. ἔρχονται, *erchontai*, here "they went") to the tomb when the sun had risen. Mark makes no room for a separation or parting of the women. Lilly's second explanation, which emphasizes the present tense of ἔρχονται (John 20:1), fails to consider that such a literalistic translation, even if possible in this context, would demand that he translate the ἔρχονται in Mark 16:2 with the same present force.[19] If this were done, the women in Mark would begin their trip "when the sun had risen" and Mary in John would begin her journey "while it was still dark." Such explanations are not convincing; they do not seem to make a coherent explanation of the differences or allow them to stand in the text.

Jeremias has argued that in Mark, when two references to time are given and one of the references appears to be unnecessary, there seems to be a tendency for the latter to explain the former. Thus, in Mark 16:2, "very early" (λίαν πρωΐ, *lian prōi*) could be before the sun had risen or even afterwards, but here "when the sun had risen" is intended, according to Jeremias, to clarify the "very early."[20] If this is correct, Hebert's theological explanation that "very early" refers to the time but "when the sun had risen" refers to Jesus himself is even less plausible than it is fanciful.[21] Brown suggests that the "darkness" is appropriate for John's theological emphasis because the empty tomb meant to Mary that someone had stolen the body of Jesus.[22] Although John frequently uses signs or themes in his Gospel to point to the significance of the work of Christ, it has not been argued convincingly that John had anything in mind other than the time element, namely, that the women came to the tomb "while it was still dark." John's frequent use of the terms "light" (φῶς, phōs) in reference to Christ (e.g., 8:12; 9:5; 12:35) and "darkness" (σκοτία, skotia) in contrast to the "light" (e.g., 1:5; 3:19; 12:35, where "darkness" is a reference to unrighteousness or evil) bears no parallel to his use of the terms in 20:1.

There appears to be no way to reconcile the time of the discovery of the empty tomb in John and Mark. All of the evangelists are agreed, however, that it took place early in the morning on the

T A B L E   6 - 1

THE EMPTY-TOMB STORY

	Matthew 28	Mark 16	Luke 24	John 20
Time of the visit	First day of the week at growing light	Very early on the first day of the week when the sun has risen	First day of the week at first dawn	Early on the first day of the week while still dark
Those who come to the tomb	Mary Magdalene and the other Mary	Mary Magdalene, Mary the mother of James, and Salome	Mary Magdalene, Mary the mother of James, Joanna, and others	Mary Magdalene comes but goes away confused (but note the "we" in v. 2)
			Then Peter comes but does not understand what took place (v. 12).	Then Peter and the other disciple come. The other disciple sees and believes, but not Peter
Purpose in coming	Women come to see the tomb	They bring aromatic oils to anoint the body	They have aromatic oils from Friday and bring them along	No word on the purpose of the visit
Visual phenomena	Earthquake; an angel of the Lord descends, rolls back stone, and sits on the stone *outside*	Stone is already rolled back; a youth sits *inside* on the right	Stone is already rolled back; *two* men stand *inside*	Stone is already rolled away; *two* angels are sitting *inside*
Conversation at the tomb	Angel: Do not fear. Jesus is not here. He is raised. Tell disciples that he is going to Galilee. There you will see him	Youth: Not to fear. Jesus is not here. He is raised. Tell disciples that he is going to Galilee. There you will see him	Men: Why do you seek living among the dead? Jesus is not here. He is raised. As he told you while still in Galilee	Angels to Mary (later): Why do you weep? Mary: They took my Lord away. Jesus, not the angels, then gives Mary a message for the disciples: I am ascending to my Father

first day of the week, that is, Sunday. Both Mark and John use the term πρωΐ (*prōi*), which means "early," though it is not definite how early. Luke's ὄρθρου βαθέως (*orthrou batheōs*) in 24:1 means simply "at early dawn," and Matthew's ὀψὲ . . . σαββάτων (*opse . . . sabbatōn*, "after the sabbath") in 28:1 is a difficult expression because of the repetition of σαββάτων in v. 1. The second σαββάτων refers to the "first day of the week," literally "first (day) of the sabbath," but it is unlikely that the words τῇ ἐπιφωσκούσῃ εἰς μίαν σαββάτων ἦλθεν (*tē epiphōskousē eis mian sabbatōn ēlthen*, "at the dawn of the first day of the sabbath she came") means "late on the sabbath," especially because of ἐπιφωσκούσῃ (the "break of dawn," "nearing of dawn"). It is more likely that Matthew, like the other evangelists, is simply saying that the discovery took place early on the first day of the week near dawn.

B. The Number and Names of the Women

A simple reading of the four Gospels shows that the evangelists disagree on who came to the empty tomb on the first Easter morning. Mark 16:1 says that the three women who made the journey to the tomb were Mary Magdalene, Mary the mother of James, and Salome. Matthew 28:1, however, mentions only Mary Magdalene and "the other Mary," while Luke 24:10 says that it was Mary Magdalene, Joanna, Mary the mother of James, and "the other women with them." Perhaps Luke wanted to include the women who came with Jesus from Galilee and who are mentioned earlier in the passion account at 23:55. John 20:1 mentions Mary Magdalene; while there is no direct mention of any other women present, Lilly has used the first person plural "we" of the verb οἴδαμεν (*oidamen*, "we know") in v. 2 to try to bring John into line with the other evangelists.[23] Jeremias, on the other hand, claims that the first person plural of v. 2 is simply the influence of Galilean Aramaic, in which the substitution of "we know" for "I know" (οἶδα [*oida*]) would be idiomatic. He points to the return to the singular οἶδα in v. 13 as support for this view. He also claims that the presence of οἴδαμεν could be the result of a synoptic influence on John.[24] Bultmann calls John 20:2 an "editorial connec-

tive" for the purpose of joining vv. 1, 11ff. with vv. 3–10 and agrees with Jeremias that the "we" of v. 2 is a Semitic way of speaking and not a genuine plural.[25] Brown disagrees with both Bultmann and Jeremias here because, according to him, they do not explain adequately the switch back to οἶδα in v. 13. If "we" was used for the first person singular, he asks, why go back to the singular? Brown believes it is probable that the "we" of John 20:2 is a reference to the other women who were present with Mary at the tomb.[26] Eduard Schweizer says that the church's tendency to expand its traditions leads him to the conclusion that John's empty-tomb story is the earliest such tradition, because Mary Magdalene alone is common to all of the evangelists and she alone, according to John, was at the tomb first. He adds, however, that if this story were a late fabrication included to prove the reality of the resurrection of the body, as many have suggested, then it would probably have included more witnesses who could "testify" to that fact. He also thinks it unlikely that Jesus' resurrection could have been preached in Jerusalem if anyone knew of a tomb containing the body of Jesus.[27]

At any rate, John clearly wished to highlight only Mary Magdalene in his empty-tomb story. If there were other women present, John only pays a passing reference to them (οἴδαμεν). It is uncertain why Matthew, who drew upon Mark, omitted Salome from his list of women. It is also puzzling that all three of the synoptic accounts mention two Marys, Mary Magdalene and Mary the mother of James (or the "other Mary," Matt 28:1), while only Mark mentions "Salome" (16:1) and only Luke mentions "Joanna" (24:10). The "other women with them" in Luke may be parallel to John's "we" (20:2), but this is uncertain. If Schweizer's view on the early church's tendency for expansion is correct and the original story in John, with only Mary being present at the tomb, was expanded by Mark's addition of Mary the mother of James and Salome, then we must ask why Matthew, who had Mark's Gospel available to him, reduced the number of women coming to the tomb to Mary Magdalene and "the other Mary" (28:1).

There appear to be only two solutions. Either we admit with Schweizer and others that only Mary Magdalene was present at the tomb on the first Easter and the Synoptic Gospels expanded this tradition to fit their own apologetic needs, that is, to have more witnesses to the event of the resurrection. Or we admit that several other women besides Mary Magdalene were present and each evangelist took the freedom to mention the name or names he wanted, either out of loyalty to a particular tradition or from personal preference. But in either case, it is doubtful that the women would have been called upon for apologetic purposes, since in ancient times the supporting testimony of women would certainly have been suspect in such an important matter.[28] It is possible that the synoptic tradition, which includes several women coming to the tomb, is the correct one but that Mary Magdalene was the leading figure among them and was therefore given priority in the Synoptics and sole recognition in John.

Whatever the solution, it is clear in the Gospel tradition that the tomb in which Jesus was buried was discovered empty on the first day, not by the Twelve but by the women who accompanied Jesus from Galilee. The women, or Mary Magdalene, were the first to report that the tomb was empty, and this was then confirmed by the disciples (Peter in Luke 24:12; Peter and the "beloved disciple" in John 20:2–10).

Bultmann has argued that the discrepancies in the empty-tomb stories, especially in the Gospel of Mark, on which the other evangelists depend, point to the lateness of the tradition. He cites as further evidence the cumbersome repetition of the women's names in Mark 16:1 from 15:40, 47.[29] This repetition, however, does not necessarily indicate the introduction of a new or secondary tradition into Mark's Gospel. In 15:40 the women accompanying Mary Magdalene are Mary, the mother of James the younger and of Joses, and Salome. In 15:47 only Mary Magdalene and Mary, the mother of Joses, see the burial. In 16:1, however, all three of the women (see 15:40) go to anoint Jesus' body, rather than just the two women who saw Jesus buried the Friday before. That Mary the mother of James and Joses is mentioned as only the mother of Joses in 15:47 but only of James in 16:1 probably should not be a cause for concern, since it is clear from 15:40 that the same Mary is in mind in both places. Perhaps the names are reintroduced in 16:1 because Salome, who did not see the burial (15:47), joined the two Marys for the subsequent anointing and Mark simply wanted to express her devotion

along with that of the other two women. This admittedly rather rigid following of the text may open up possibilities for understanding the duplication of names.

C. The Problem of Opening the Tomb

Bultmann argues that the secondary nature of the empty-tomb tradition in Mark 16:1–8, on which the other evangelists rely, can be seen in the failure of the women to consider ahead of time how they would open the tomb (16:3).[30] It is only in Mark 16:3 that the women worry about opening the tomb to anoint the body of Jesus. Matthew, for example, says only that the women went to see the sepulcher where Jesus was placed; there is no mention of spices (28:1). Luke states simply that the women brought spices to the tomb, and they found the stone rolled away from before it (24:2). John, like Matthew and Luke, has no mention of the difficulty of moving the stone. C. F. Evans, noting this, claims that according to Matthew the women knew of the sealing of the tomb and therefore only came to visit the tomb, not to anoint the body.[31]

This problem does not appear so great, since both Mark 15:46 and Matt 27:60 indicate that Joseph of Arimathea himself closed the tomb by rolling the stone against it. To this should be added the fact that since one man closed the tomb, it would be possible for one man to have opened it, and probably also two or more women. When Jesus appears to Mary in John 20:15, she supposes him to be a gardener. Is it possible that there would have been someone in the vicinity of the tomb upon whom the women could have prevailed to open the tomb? It may well be that the anxious hope of the women was strong enough that they began their journey to the tomb thinking they would find someone to open it for them. Also, these women were from Galilee (Luke 23:55), not from Jerusalem. They therefore probably had few friends in Jerusalem upon whom they could call for help, other than the disciples who had fled, abandoning Jesus in his hour of trial. In such circumstances, probably the only chance of receiving help would have been from someone in the neighborhood of the tomb itself, from either a gardener or someone else in that area. Mark 16:3 seems to allow for this possibility.

D. The Opening of the Tomb

Mark 16:4 says that the tombstone was already rolled back when the women arrived. This is followed by Luke, who says that the women "found the stone rolled away from the tomb" (24:2), and John, who claims that Mary "saw that the stone had been removed from the tomb" (20:1). Unlike these three reports, which claim that the tomb was already opened when the women arrived, Matthew says that the women and the guards (28:4) saw an "angel of the Lord" descend from heaven and roll back the stone (28:2). He adds that "a great earthquake" (28:2) preceded the event. How can such differences between Matthew and the other evangelists be reconciled? Perhaps Matthew's description of the opening of the tomb was his attempt to support the testimony to the resurrection of Jesus by including the guards as witnesses, thereby strengthening the women's testimony. Undoubtedly Matthew also points to the significance of Jesus' resurrection through the story of the earthquake and the angel of the Lord descending. Apologetical and theological motives seem to influence Matthew's account, especially when he dispels the Jewish polemic against the resurrection of Jesus (28:4, 11–15). Perhaps the key to understanding Matthew's intentions is found in his reference to the "great earthquake." In the OT, an earthquake was a mark of Yahweh's presence for revelation (Exod 19:18), but it could also be one of destructive judgment (Isa 29:6). Elsewhere in Matthew earthquakes are among the catastrophic phenomena of the last days (Matt 24:7). It is therefore possible that the earthquake in the tomb story was intended by Matthew to emphasize the revelatory and apocalyptic nature of this event. The description of the angel of the Lord (28:2–3) and the results of his activity (v. 4) are, aside from the earthquake, almost direct parallels to Dan 10:5–7, as we see in the "appearance like lightning" (v. 3; cf. Dan 10:6), the fear of those present (v. 4; cf. Dan 10:7), and the admonition not to fear (v. 5; cf. Dan 10:12). Daniel 10:2–21 is clearly an apocalyptic passage speaking about the approaching activity of Yahweh. At the death of Jesus all of the synoptic evangelists record accompanying physical, miraculous phenomena. All three mention the tearing of the temple curtain (Mark 15:38; Matt 27:51; Luke 23:45), but along with this Matthew adds an earthquake (27:51, 54) and an unusual story of the res-urrection of the bodies of many saints, who went walking through the streets of Jerusalem (vv. 52–53). Matthew probably intended these phenomena to indicate that an eschatological event was taking place in which one was viewing the dawn of a new age. Notice that Matt 24:7, Mark 13:8, and Luke 21:11 all mention earthquakes in the last days before God's coming judgment and kingdom. Jeremias points out that the passage in Matt 28:18–20 is not unlike Dan 7:13–15, which also speaks of the kingdom and dominion of the Son of Man. He concludes from Matt 28:18 that Matthew means that the view "that the Son of man would one day be enthroned as ruler of the world was fulfilled in the resurrection."[32]

Matthew does not appear to set forth supernatural phenomena primarily for apologetic purposes; rather, he is trying to point to the significance of the events he is describing: in the death and resurrection of Jesus a new age has begun. This understanding of the dawning of a new age dominates both Matthew's empty-tomb story and his appearance stories.

E. The Women Entering the Tomb

All of the Synoptic Gospels suggest that the women entered the tomb when they saw that it was open (Mark 16:4; Luke 24:3; by implication Matt 28:6, in which the women are invited to "Come, see where he lay"). John, however, states that Mary Magdalene saw that the stone had been rolled away and then ran to tell Peter and the "other disciple" (presumably John) that the body was missing (20:2). She only sees the stone rolled away yet tells the disciples that the body had been taken. Not until v. 11 does Mary stoop to look into the tomb, after Peter and the "other disciple" have entered (vv. 3–10). Bultmann believes that John 20:2 is simply a connective joining two different stories. According to him, the story of Mary goes from v. 1 to v. 11, with another story about Peter and the "other disciple" sandwiched in the middle.[33]

The difference between John and the Synoptics here may well lie in John's concern to preserve the priority of Peter in his narrative. He thus prevents Mary from entering the tomb until after Peter had done so. This is supported by the unusual waiting of the "beloved disciple" until after Peter had entered the tomb (John 20:5, 8). On the other hand, John, without expressly stating so, could have assumed that Mary entered the tomb at her first visit; otherwise Mary's comment about the missing body (v. 2) is difficult to follow. How would she know without entering? But, it may be asked, if she went in or had even stopped to look in at her first visit to the tomb (v. 1), why did she not see the grave clothes (vv. 6–7)? There may be several motives for the form of this story in John, for example, to affirm the priority of Peter, to sew together two rather distinct traditions, and to stress the special nature of the resurrection itself (see vv. 24–27).

Again, why did Mary not see the grave clothes, which had earlier impressed the "other disciple" (vv. 6–8), when she looked into the tomb in v. 11? She saw only the angels, who failed to communicate anything significant to her. It may be correct to see two different empty-tomb stories in John 20:1–18. It may also be possible to clarify the many difficulties in this passage by recognizing the rough, composite nature of this section of John's resurrection narrative. Brown lists the elements in John's account that point to its awkwardness: (1) Mary comes to the tomb alone in v. 1 but speaks as "we" in v. 2; (2) she states that the body was stolen (v. 2) but fails to look into the tomb until v. 11; (3) frequent duplication occurs in the story about Peter and the beloved disciple—for example, two "to" phrases in v. 2 and a repetition in what was seen in v. 5 and v. 6; (4) the belief of the beloved disciple has no effect on Mary or anyone else (v. 19); (5) it is not clear how or when Mary returns to the tomb in v. 11; (6) it is not clear why Mary sees angels but not the grave clothes in v. 12; (7) in v. 13 the message of the angels reveals nothing about the fate of Jesus (or anything else, for that matter); (8) Mary is said to have turned to Jesus two times (vv. 14, 16).[34]

F. The Angels in the Empty-Tomb Stories

There are several differences among the four evangelists about the angels attending the empty tomb. First, how many angels were there? Mark mentions only one individual, a young man in a white robe.[35] Matthew 28:2 here agrees with Mark, but Luke 24:4 indicates that two men "in dazzling apparel" appeared to the women. John 20:12 is again in agreement with Luke at this point. Why is there a difference between Mark and Matthew, on the one hand, and Luke and John, on the other, about the number of attending angels? The identical words, literally "Behold two men," are found in Luke's stories of the transfiguration (Luke 9:30) and the empty tomb (but not in Mark 9:4), and two angels are also found in the ascension story of Acts 1:10. Could it be that Luke is trying to connect Moses and Elijah (9:30) with these three events, the transfiguration, the resurrection, and the ascension, as van Daalen suggests?[36] Or is this use of the number two an indication of a common tradition behind Luke and John (see John 20:12)? As we have seen before, such parallels between Luke and John are not necessarily insignificant. Another interesting parallel is that in each of these references in Luke the two men stood by: in Luke 9:32 they "stood with" Jesus (perfect participle of συνίστημι, sunistēmi), in Luke 24:4 they "stood beside" the women (aorist of ἐφίστημι, ephistēmi), and in Acts 1:10 they "stood by" the apostles (pluperfect of παρίστημι, paristēmi). Such similarities may not be easily dismissed as unintentional or insignificant trivia.

Another explanation for the differences in the number of angels at the tomb is that Luke usually has two witnesses to confirm major events—for example, Simeon and Anna praising God for the birth of Jesus (2:25–38), Herod and Pilate attesting to the innocence of Jesus (23:1–25), two men observing the transfiguration (9:30–34), the disciples sent out two by two (10:1), two men attending the empty tomb (24:4), two men walking on the road to Emmaus (24:13–32), etc. Elsewhere Luke uses numbers to make a significant point beyond the number itself. For example, he uses the number forty in Luke 4:2 and Acts 1:3; these easily parallel the same number in several other OT texts where Yahweh is active (Noah's flood, the giving of the law, Moses at Sinai, the wilderness wanderings, Elijah at Mt. Horeb). The number two is one of the most commonly used numbers in the Gospels and, along with seven, one of the most popular in the NT. Luke–Acts employs it more than any other books in the NT, although it is common in the other Gospels. It is difficult to find a consistent use for the number, but we frequently find it in Jesus' parables or in stories where Jesus makes pronouncements.

Lillie may be correct when he suggests that originally only one angel was mentioned and that Luke and John, perhaps following a tradition also found in the later Christian document *Ascension of Isaiah*, where two angels (Michael and "the angel of the Holy Spirit") are identified at the tomb of Jesus, may have introduced the second angel because the Jews were accustomed to the idea of angels participating in a resurrection.[37]

Whether special significance is to be attached to the number two in the empty-tomb narratives, and what that significance might be, are not clear, but the above possibilities show the direction in which one might pursue the question. The frequency of the number two in Luke may be an indication of intended theological significance that is not part of Mark's and Matthew's orientation. Both Luke and John mention two angels, Luke attributing to them an interpretive role, while John mentions them but does not give them an essential role in the empty-tomb story other than that they may indicate the significance of the resurrection by their presence.

A second difference in the empty-tomb stories is Mary's lack of amazement or fear when she encounters the angels in John 20:12–13. In Matt 28:5, fear and joy are mentioned; in Mark 16:6, 8, amazement and fear; and in Luke 24:5, fear. Evidently John is willing to subdue the role of the angels in his story, but their presence in his source or sources was probably too pronounced for him to dismiss them altogether. For John, they simply occasion Mary's encounter with the risen Lord. At any rate, Luke and John may both depend upon a common tradition for their information on the number of angels present at the tomb, as they also may have for other elements of their passion and resurrection narratives, especially in the location of the appearances (see below).

Third, there is the difference in the location of the angels. Mark's angel was *inside*, evidently sitting on "the right side" of where Jesus' body was placed (16:5). Matthew's angel descended from heaven, rolled back the stone from before the tomb, and *sat down outside*, on the stone (28:2). Luke's angels were *inside and standing* (24:4), but John's angels were *inside sitting* "where the body of Jesus had been lying, one at the head and the other at the feet" (20:12).

Fourth, the initial comments of the angels have interesting parallels. In Mark 16:6 the angel tells the women, "Do not be alarmed; you are looking for Jesus of Nazareth, who was crucified." Matthew 28:5 is similar: "Do not be afraid; I know that you are looking for Jesus who was crucified." The angels in Luke 24:5, on the other hand, say nothing to dispel the fear of the women but ask, "Why do you look for the living among the dead?" The angels in John 20:13 simply ask Mary, who believed the body was stolen, "Woman, why are you weeping?"—the question about seeking Jesus, unlike in the Synoptic Gospels, being left for Jesus himself to ask. In John 20:15, Jesus combines the angels' question with one similar to the angelic statement in the Synoptics and asks, "Woman, why are you weeping? Whom are you looking for?" Only in John does the initial revelation about the emptiness of the tomb come from Jesus himself; in the Synoptics the angel or angels give the message that Jesus is risen: "He has been raised; he is not here" (Mark 16:6); "He is not here; for he has been raised, as he said" (Matt 28:6); "He is not here, but has risen" (Luke 24:5).

Fifth, the additional message of the angels shows several interesting discrepancies. In Mark 16:6, the angel invites the women to look at the location where Jesus was placed. In Matt 28:6, the angel invites the women, "Come, see the place where he lay," indicating that they had not yet entered the tomb. Mark's angel then tells the women to tell the disciples and Peter that "he is going ahead of you to Galilee; there you will see him, just as he told you" (16:7). Matthew's version of the angelic command is somewhat more expanded than Mark's. His angel tells the women to tell the disciples, "He has been raised from the dead, and indeed he is going ahead of you to Galilee; there you will see him. This is my message for you" (28:7). Matthew has strangely omitted Peter from the angelic command, added the statement that Jesus had been raised from the dead, and changed Mark's "as he has told you" to "This is my message for you." Luke's angels do not give a command to go to Galilee or even to tell the disciples, but call instead upon the women to remember Jesus' words "while he was still in Galilee" (24:6) concerning his crucifixion and subsequent resurrection "on the third day" (24:7; cf. 1 Cor 15:4). The differences here may be due in part to the theological motivation of Luke to make Jerusalem the center of the new Christian missionary endeavors of the church. This will be discussed later when we look at the problem of the location of the appearances. John likewise does not tell of any command to go to Galilee but, rather, reports that Jesus, after telling Mary about his ascension, commands her to report his ascension to the disciples (20:17).

The problems concerning the angels at the tomb seem trivial but, when taken together, suggest possible confusion in the traditions employed by the evangelists or even a lack of attention to details. Perhaps there are theological emphases that are not altogether clear to modern interpreters. What, then, can be made of such discrepancies? What in fact did the angels say? What was each writer trying to convey when he introduced the angel or angels? Matthew evidently wanted to point to the eschatological nature of the events he was trying to describe, namely, that the future had just broken into the present through the death and resurrection of Jesus. Mark and Luke employ the angel or angels to interpret the significance of the empty tomb to the women. John, however, may be the key to understanding all of the passages. He evidently uses the angels to show the importance of the resurrection of Jesus, though strangely Mary does not understand this until Jesus speaks to her. In John the angels do not advance the message of the risen Lord as they do in the other Gospels. It is likely that the angels in his empty-tomb tradition are intended to point to the significance of the resurrection itself. Perhaps no angels were present in the earliest form of the empty-tomb traditions but were later employed by the evangelists to heighten the significance of the resurrection of Jesus, or at least the empty tomb. The presence of the angels in all four Gospels does have multiple and varied attestation in the tradition, but the differences in the narratives suggest that they are a late addition, employed for apologetic or theological purposes.

G. The Response of the Women to the Angelic Message

In the Synoptic Gospels, the response to the angelic presence is varied. In Mark 16:8 the women flee from the tomb and say "nothing to anyone, for they were afraid."[38] Matthew, however, says that the women departed from the tomb "with fear and great joy, and ran to tell his disciples" (28:8). Luke says nothing about the joy of the women but states

almost blandly that after the women were told of the meaning of the empty tomb, they "remembered his [Jesus'] words, and returning from the tomb, they told all this to the eleven and to all the rest" (24:8–9). Luke 24:10 almost seems like a second thought by Luke to remember all of the women who were at the tomb. It is difficult to know whether this was Luke's attempt to make his Gospel correspond to the other evangelists, especially since he adds "the other women with them" to show that others were present at the tomb. Luke obviously feels free to depart from the Markan tradition, if in fact he was even acquainted with this part of it, and adds some of the names of the women from Galilee (23:55). Perhaps it is also significant that Luke introduces the title "apostle" here in his Easter story (24:10), a term that has special importance in the second half of Luke–Acts.

H. The Response of the Disciples to the Message of the Women

Mark says nothing of the disciples' response to the message of the women, since his Gospel ends so abruptly, but Matthew tells us that the women went to tell the disciples (28:11) and that the disciples responded to their message by going to Galilee (28:16). Matthew intends for his readers to understand that the disciples believed the women and went back to Galilee. Luke, however, says that the apostles did not accept the women's report because "these words seemed to them an idle tale, and they did not believe them" (24:11). Even Peter in 24:12 visits the tomb and leaves with questions in his mind, not faith. Matthew does not show any lack of belief in the women's report, even though some doubted after they had seen Jesus (28:17), but Luke reserves faith for a subsequent time when Jesus appears to the disciples and breaks bread with them (24:30–34). John says nothing about the disciples' response to Mary's report of Jesus' appearance to her (20:18). He only mentions the response of the two disciples to the report about the empty tomb when they went to investigate for themselves (20:2–10).

I. The Grave Clothes

In John 20:3–10, upon receiving news from Mary Magdalene that "they have taken the Lord out of the tomb" (v. 2), Peter and the beloved disciple ran to the tomb to check her report. Verses 4 and 5 state that both disciples ran toward the tomb but that the "other disciple" reached the tomb first and, looking inside without entering, saw the grave clothes ("linen wrappings"). Peter came and, entering the tomb, saw the clothes lying in their (evidently) peculiar place. The "other disciple" then entered the tomb and responded with faith to what he saw. Note the conceptual parallel between "he saw" and "[he] believed" (cf. 20:29). The faith of the beloved disciple here does not fit with the statement in v. 9, "for as yet they did not understand the Scripture, that he must rise from the dead."

If faith was reached at the tomb by the other disciple, why is it that this faith was not shared with Mary, who is left standing at the entrance of the tomb weeping (v. 11), or, for that matter, with the rest of the disciples (vv. 19–23)? It is important here to refer to the similar passage in Luke 24:12. Bultmann argues that the faith expressed in John 20:8 refers to both disciples. He reasons that if the writer intended only one of the disciples to come to faith, then the two disciples would have been set over against one another and it would have been expressly stated that Peter had not believed.[39] But was this distinction not precisely what the writer was trying to make?

Luke does not mention the other disciple accompanying Peter to the tomb, but he does say that Peter saw the grave clothes lying by themselves, "then he went home, amazed at what had happened" (24:12). Since Luke's account says that there was only Peter and that only confusion or wondering resulted from this visit, John's story is at odds with Luke's only in his mentioning of the other disciple and in that disciple's coming to faith. If Luke's version of the story is correct and if the story of the beloved disciple was intended by John to show what the ideal disciple of Jesus ought to be like, then the conflict in John's story between believing (John 20:8) and not mentioning it to Mary (v. 11) or the other disciples (vv. 19ff.) is understandable. Indeed, if the act of believing by the other disciple is not original to the tradition in John about the grave clothes (common to both Luke and John), then "for as yet they did not understand" (οὐδέπω γὰρ ἤδεισαν, *oudepō gar ēdeisan*) (v. 9) becomes more intelligible (and also more in harmony with Luke). If this is so, then the reason the beloved

disciple did not share his faith with the other disciples (vv. 19ff.) becomes obvious: in the original story no one believed when they saw the grave clothes. The failure of the two disciples to understand at this point (οὐδέπω, "not yet") the Scripture about the resurrection of Jesus would, then, be somewhat parallel to the conclusion of Luke's version of the same story ("amazed at what had happened," πρὸς ἑαυτὸν θαυμάζων τὸ γεγονός, *pros heauton thaumazōn to gegonos*, Luke 24:12).[40] If this suggestion is correct, then John's narrative would be more consistent with itself as well as with the Lukan tradition.

If the above suggestion is correct, it raises the question why John would insert the story of the ideal or beloved disciple into his narrative. It appears as though he was trying to shape a well-known tradition—the story of the grave clothes—into a vehicle for expressing what the other Gospels express through the angels, namely, the interpretation of the empty tomb. But if this is so, there is still the puzzle why Peter and Mary did not come to the same conclusion as did the beloved disciple. Brown argues that John tried to introduce here not only the significance of the empty tomb but also a loving relation to Jesus that Peter did not have. He believes that John was not necessarily trying to detract from Peter but was, rather, trying to build up the image of the beloved disciple. He also discredits the view that John was trying to point to the blessedness of the beloved disciple because he believed without seeing (contrast John 20:29). He agrees with Cullmann that, because the beloved disciple "saw and believed" (v. 8), he could not have been one of those in v. 29 who had not seen and yet believed. Brown contends that John was making a special hero of the beloved disciple, who was closely connected to Jesus. He concludes that the writer of John used the story of the race to the tomb to show that the other disciple was bound closest to Jesus in love and was the "quickest to look for him and the first to believe in him."[41] John's interpretation of the empty tomb and his pointing to the faith of the beloved disciple are probably later additions to the tradition, seen more clearly in Luke 24:12, about the grave clothes.

Luke 24:24's reference to "some of those who were with us" going to the tomb stands in opposition to the implication from 24:12 that only Peter went to the tomb. This may be resolved if Luke's point in the text was to emphasize the priority of Peter (cf. 24:34) and his intention was not necessarily to rule out the possibility of others being present at the tomb. It is also quite possible that, in Luke 24:12, another disciple may have been with Peter on his visit to the tomb and perhaps even more than two, as Luke 24:24 suggests. Reiser claims that Luke 24:12 and 24 depend on an earlier form of the Johannine tradition of the disciples at the tomb and says that it is possible Luke knew of Peter's visit to the tomb and also of the accompanying beloved disciple but "would not have considered him worth mentioning for it would not have suited his purpose."[42]

The double witness to the grave clothes suggests that a common early tradition about this story was available both to Luke and to John. John introduces a new element into the story, the faith of the beloved disciple, in order to express both the meaning of the empty tomb and the exalted status of the beloved disciple. If the beloved disciple's act of believing is deleted from the passage, there will be fewer problems in understanding the continuing sorrow of Mary (v. 11) and the failure of the beloved disciple to tell the other disciples of his discovery.

J. The Guard at the Tomb

The story of the guard at the tomb in Matt 27:62–66 and 28:11–15 has been widely acknowledged as a later apologetic legend in the Gospel tradition. This is because of the clearly apologetic nature of the story, the apocalyptic coloring throughout the passage (e.g., the earthquake and the angel of the Lord) and the fact that no other Gospel mentions the presence of soldiers at the tomb. The story does, however, help to substantiate the authenticity of the empty tomb itself. Fuller, agreeing with Bultmann that the story is an "apologetic legend," nevertheless contends that it helps to establish that the Jewish understanding at that time was of resurrection from the dead as bodily. He argues that "the use of the Jewish polemic is of considerable importance, for it shows that 'resurrection' to the Jewish mind naturally suggested resurrection from the grave. It was to the Christian kerygma that Christ 'had been raised from the dead' that they [the Jews] replied by the allegation that the empty tomb was a fraud."[43] Fuller also believes that this story supports the earliest belief of the church concerning the time of the resurrection of Jesus, that it was on the "third day" (1 Cor 15:4) or "after three days" (Matt 27:63–64). Although the reference to the Jewish authorities' awareness of Jesus' prediction about his resurrection led Evans to endorse further the legendary nature of the passage, he says that the reference to Jesus having claimed, "After three days I shall rise" (Matt 27:63), cannot be related to any public statement of Jesus but, rather, "reflects again the later Christian preaching of the resurrection."[44]

Marxsen argues that this story contradicts itself in at least three places. First, when the guards experience the opening of the tomb (Matt 28:2–4), they return to tell the chief priest. Why would they report to the Jewish authorities if they were Romans? Second, he raises the problem of the inner conflict in the story of the chief priests telling the guards to pass a story on to the people (28:13). Third, Marxsen then raises his major question against the story: "How can anyone say what happened while he was asleep?"[45] Such inner contradictions in the story, he concludes, force one to say that the story of the guard at the tomb has no basis in fact or at least could not have occurred as it is written. On the other hand, the objection about the report of the guards to the high priests does not pose a problem, since in Matt 27:62–66 Pilate offered the guard to the chief priests and Pharisees. Why would they not report to the Jewish authorities if Pilate had assigned this guard to them?

The story of the guard at the tomb—regardless of its authenticity—appears to set forth two important elements of the early Easter tradition. First, both the enemies of the church and the church itself recognized that the tomb of Jesus was empty. The only disagreement was on how it got that way. Second, the tradition points to the nature of the resurrection of Jesus as it was first preached and believed in the early Christian communities—that it was bodily from the grave.

Before looking at other consistencies in the empty-tomb stories, we note further that the basic reliability of the empty-tomb tradition is attested by the church's lack of tampering with the several variations in the details of these stories.[46] Surely these cannot have escaped the attention of the ancient church that received them.

K. Consistencies in the Empty-Tomb Tradition and Their Importance

Often omitted in discussions about the empty-tomb tradition are the important consistencies in the traditions and their significance for our understanding of what happened in the Easter event proclaimed in the NT.

First, all of the evangelists are clear that the tomb in which Jesus' body was placed was empty early on the first day of the week and that this was testified to by several witnesses. This was witnessed first of all by women (this is probably also true of John, as can be seen in "we do not know" [οὐκ οἴδαμεν], 20:2), in Luke 24:12, 24 and in John 20:3–9. The empty tomb was also witnessed by two of Jesus' disciples. If Matthew and Mark do not claim that the disciples examined the tomb, neither do they deny it. If the disciples were in Jerusalem when they received the women's report, it would not be extraordinary for them to check the tomb if they knew of its whereabouts, especially in view of the disturbing report given to them by the women. This is speculation, of course, but not unreasonable to consider.

Second, in each of the Gospels there is an angelic presence at the site of the tomb on Easter morning. In all three Synoptic Gospels, the angels (or angel) interpret the significance of the tomb by saying that Jesus is risen, even though the angels in John only ask a question, leaving the explanation of the significance of the empty tomb to the risen Lord himself (John 20:11–18; cf. also Matt 28:8–10). The message of the angels varies according to each evangelist, but their very presence indicates that the empty tomb and events surrounding it were perceived to have far-reaching, if not eschatological, implications. Angels (or men in white robes) are also present at the ascension of Jesus in Acts 1:10–11, interpreting what has taken place as referring to the return of the risen Lord in triumph. The evangelists evidently wanted their readers to understand the eschatological significance of the events that occurred at the tomb. Perhaps because the empty tomb by itself could only lead to wonder or doubt, each writer saw the need to interpret the significance of the tomb by angelic reports (Mark and Luke), the grave clothes (Luke and John), the appearance of Jesus (John), or the angelic reports and the appearances of Jesus (Matthew).

Other scholars have argued differently, however. Bode, who does not wish to deal with the question of the existence of angels, omits all angelic appearances from the historical nucleus of the empty-tomb tradition. He concludes that the women neither experienced the appearance of an angel nor received a heavenly message at the tomb, primarily because he finds too many kerygmatic and redactional elements in the angelic message. He asks, "How could the angel have spoken in the kerygmatic language of the primitive church according to Mark, with the authority of God as his messenger to announce the predicted resurrection according to Matthew, with the themes of Lukan theology according to the third gospel and without any message according to John?"[47] He reasons that the angelic appearance and message can be dismissed from the historical nucleus of the empty-tomb tradition because the angels constitute a biblically acceptable literary motif for presenting a divinely authoritative message. Also, he believes that the exclusion of the angels from the empty-tomb tradition gives better insight into the tradition and its development. The women, he claims, came to the tomb early on the first day of the week and found the tomb empty. For them, indeed for everyone, the significance of the tomb remained ambiguous until it was later interpreted by the proclamation of the resurrection and by references to the appearance of Jesus to his disciples. Bode rejects the authenticity of the account of the disciples going to the tomb (Luke 24:12, 24; John 20:3–9) and argues instead that the women kept silent about the tomb until the resurrection proclamation began to be preached. Bode further claims that the virtual silence about the empty tomb in all of the appearance stories (except in the Emmaus account) argues for an independent origin of both traditions.[48]

Wilckens agrees with Bode, adding that early on the Diaspora Jews in Jerusalem came to believe in Jesus through contact with the primitive Christian community. For these Jews the resurrection of Jesus was central, but they were unacquainted with the developing tradition, the empty-tomb story, which Bode claims originated in Jerusalem at a later time. This group of Christians was influenced by Hellenism and set forth a "cosmic christology" that "included in its assertions scarcely a word about the ministry and teaching of the historical Jesus himself."[49] It was this growing tradition in the church, he argues, that had a powerful influence and prepared the way for varieties of Gnosticism in early Christianity. Consequently, the reverse tendency appeared in the later resurrection stories, in which the preresurrection identity of Jesus is seen in his corporeal appearances, such as in Luke 24:36ff. Lüdemann concludes that the reports of the corporeality of the resurrection of Jesus are all late and legendary. They had the purpose of answering the objection that Jesus was not raised from the dead but the disciples only experienced a phantom or a spirit.[50] He contends that the revival of a corpse is *"not a historical fact, but a verdict of faith,"* that Jesus' tomb *"was not empty, but full, and his body did not disappear, but rotted away,"* and that "with the scientific view of the world, the statements about the resurrection of Jesus have irrevocably lost their literal meaning."[51] These conclusions, however, are based almost completely on an argument from silence and include a false assumption about what is generally accepted as a worldview by modern humanity.

Furthermore, merely because the empty-tomb tradition is found not in the epistles but only in the Gospels does not prove that the tradition of the bodily resurrection of Jesus was unknown to the writers of the epistles. Wilckens's view, with Lüdemann's, presupposes that during Paul's visits to Jerusalem (Gal 1:18; 2:1–10) he did not come into contact with any presynoptic traditions concerning Jesus or, if he did, they did not interest him.[52] This view also assumes that the empty-tomb tradition emerged in the middle to late 60s at the earliest, and was well entrenched in the church by the early 70s, the latest date presumed for the writing of Mark's Gospel. This argument, however, cannot be sustained historically.[53] Although Lüdemann believes that Paul was unaware of the empty-tomb tradition and that historically Jesus' tomb was not empty, he posits that Paul nevertheless "imagines the resurrection of Jesus in bodily form, which seems to require the emergence of the body of Jesus from the empty tomb." Disregarding the clear implications of 1 Cor 15:50, Lüdemann states, "The fate of the physical body of Jesus cannot have been unimportant to Paul."[54]

The empty-tomb tradition is referred to in only one of the appearance stories, the Emmaus account in Luke 24, and is absent from the oldest tradition about the resurrection in the NT (1 Cor 15:3–8), but the independence of this tradition from the appearance stories would still only be short-lived if Bode is correct. We can find no reasonable argument against the visit of the disciples to the tomb (Luke and John), and indeed, since all four Gospels agree that the tomb was discovered early on the first day of the week, the disciples were probably still in Jerusalem at the time; otherwise they would have had to leave Jerusalem on the Sabbath, an unlikely scenario. Also, the disciples would probably have heard about the empty tomb from the women. Not only do Luke 24:12, 24 and John 20:2ff. give this impression; in all of the Gospel reports the angels (or Jesus, in John) command the women to tell the disciples, who are still in Jerusalem at the time, about the tomb. The message that "he [Jesus] is not here" must refer to the tomb (Mark 16:6; Matt 28:6; also John 20:13; Luke 24:3). In every Gospel account the women (or just Mary) tell the disciples about their experience at the tomb.[55] Consequently, the empty-tomb story could not have been separated long, if at all, from the proclamation of the resurrection of Jesus; the disciples therefore probably already knew of the tomb when Jesus appeared to them.

The argument for the separation of the empty-tomb stories from the appearance stories is not as convincing as it might first appear, since neither the evangelists nor the rest of the NT traditions about Christian belief make the tomb an object of faith. The early church did not venerate the tomb because it was empty; it never was an object of worship, unlike the tombs of many of the early martyrs of the church.[56] Why should the tomb be recalled in the appearance stories? The purpose of the appearances was evidently to assure the disciples of the reality of Jesus' aliveness after his death and to give to them their missionary task. In their proclamation of the resurrection of Jesus, Paul and the other NT writers had no need to provide a narration about the tomb, since this was not the basis of Easter faith. In the Gospels, however, there was a keen interest on the part of the evangelists to tell the story of Jesus. It could well be that the apologetic needs of the Christian community at the time of the writing of the Gospels called for assurance of the corporeality of the resurrection appearances or even for further support of the event itself. At what place could the evangelists more appropriately include an explanation for the empty tomb, which was by that time common knowledge, than in a narrative concerning the life, death, resurrection, and significance of Jesus? Since all four evangelists include this story, the argument for its early existence is certainly more enhanced, especially in light of the obviously free handling of traditions by the evangelists. When they felt free to draw upon or omit numerous items in the Easter tradition, why would all of them include the story of the tomb unless it occupied a dominant place in the traditions long before them?

A brief survey of several recent interpreters of the empty-tomb tradition highlights the major issues. McDonald realizes that the empty tomb is disorientating in the Easter narratives, producing shock, fear, weeping, and the like, and is not celebrated by joy. While McDonald admits that one can cite Jewish beliefs about the physical nature of the resurrection, he contends that not all Jews of Jesus' time held to this. He believes that the examples of the translation of highly esteemed persons—Enoch, Elijah, and Moses, for example, who left no human remains on earth—are more to the point. Instead, the empty tomb is a basic presupposition of early Christian preaching that is "not in itself explained, though it is verified."[57] He cites an interview he had with J. C. O'Neill, who said, "My massive argument is that the preaching of the resurrection could not have arisen on any basis other than the empty tomb. There is positive evidence that the tomb was empty. . . . Negatively, nobody produced the body, although it would have been required for any refutation of the resurrection claims that a body be produced."[58]

Davis similarly concludes that the empty-tomb stories not only are compatible with Christian preaching about the resurrection but are required by it. In spite of the competing theories of life after death in the first century, the NT writers had bodily resurrection in mind:[59] "Resurrection from the grave is what Jews of Jesus' day *would naturally have meant* by the term 'raised from the dead' (even though they could have *understood* alternative theories). And in the absence of compelling evidence for the claim that they had some other theory in mind, . . . the proper conclusion is that the NT writers had bodily resurrection in mind."[60] He contends that all NT accounts of Jesus' resurrection present it as a bodily transformation rather than a resuscitation or spiritual resurrection, even in 1 Cor 15. He asks why, if the empty tomb stories are a

late tradition, early Jewish tradition did not dispute the claim. The fact that it did not strongly suggests "that the empty tomb was a fact agreed upon by all parties early in the game."[61]

Some scholars still insist, nevertheless, that the many differences in the empty-tomb stories constitute a major reason for disputing their credibility. Lorenzen, for instance, questions whether we should readily accept the empty-tomb tradition, because of the problems in dating the sources and accounting for their many differences as well as in what they seem to imply. He observes that Paul, who wrote earlier than the evangelists, spoke of the resurrection of Jesus without a reference to the empty tomb. Since Paul was writing an apology for the resurrection in 1 Cor 15:3–11, it would have strengthened his case considerably to have included the story had he known about it. Lorenzen also points to the lack of a uniform view of the nature of the resurrection body in the first century and contends that resurrection faith could have been proclaimed without an empty-tomb story. He argues that this possibility allows for the early church creating the tradition of the empty tomb in order to assist in its proclamation of Jesus' resurrection from the dead. If this was the case, it is probable that the early church employed the empty-tomb tradition to guard the Christian message against the docetic and spiritualizing distortions of its faith. He concludes that Paul's ignorance of this tradition speaks for its lateness and that it could easily have evolved as a deduction of the confession that God raised Jesus from the dead. For Lorenzen, the body of Jesus that was raised from the tomb was not his physical body but, rather, and strangely, Jesus himself in his identity, mission, and effect on the world. This was the "body" that was raised, not the one that was placed in a tomb. While Lorenzen agrees that there may have been some historical kernel of truth to the emptiness of the tomb, he concludes that it was relatively unimportant and not a part of the apologetic for the resurrection of the earliest Christians. Faith was proclaimed as a result of the appearances of the risen Christ to his followers. It was only when the reality of the resurrection was later questioned, along with the emergence of questions about the fate of Jesus' body, that the matter of the empty tomb was raised.[62]

In spite of the several differences in the message of the angels at the tomb and the variations in the stories, we still observe that all of the Gospel traditions agree that Jesus' body was no longer in the tomb. This could not be considered inconsequential. In the story of Mary at the tomb, the angels become the occasion for Mary's announcement that the body is gone (John 20:12–13), and then the meaning of the absence of his body is given by Jesus himself (John 20:14–17). Matthew confirms the message of the angel with an appearance of the risen Jesus to the women at the tomb (28:9–10), but in all of these stories the message is still the same: Jesus' body is not in the tomb, he has risen from the dead, and his aliveness is affirmed.

The angelic message to the women at the tomb is a heavenly revelation that the women convey to the disciples and that was later put into the church's proclamation. Dodd, trying to account for the presence of the angels in the Easter proclamations, suggests that when angels are introduced in biblical narratives, it is frequently a sign that a truth is being conveyed that is beyond the reach of the senses, a "revelation." Concerning the angelic visit to the empty tomb, he explains that "what the women saw [the empty tomb] brought only perplexity; then by a leap beyond the evidence of the senses, they knew what it meant. But it still awaited verification from later experience."[63] The variation in the angels' message in the Synoptics is evidence for an early dating of that tradition if we agree that traditions tend to expand with time as they are passed along. On the other hand, John's rather different role for the angels is difficult to understand. Perhaps John held onto the story of the presence of the angels at the tomb because it was part of the tradition he received, although he focused instead on the fact that the first appearance of Jesus was to the women (or Mary), rather than to Peter. Matthew (see 28:9–10), the only Gospel that does not mention Peter, is also apparently trying to establish this point. The reason why John has no angelic message as such is not clear, but since his angels add little or nothing to the story of the resurrection of Jesus, it is a wonder John chose to include them at all, unless the tradition he received was so strong that he felt it necessary to include them, or he believed that they pointed to the "revelatory" nature of the tomb.

The empty-tomb tradition in its present form in the Gospel traditions allows for Easter faith without receiving an appearance from the risen Lord. This is apparent especially in Matt 28:8, Luke 24:8–11, and John 20:8. Mark also allows for this possibility (16:6–7), but in his account the women do not believe, at least not up to the point where his Gospel breaks off in v. 8. In Matthew the disciples evidently believe the women's report and set off for Galilee (28:16). In the rest of the NT, apart from the Gospels, Easter faith for the disciples is a result of meeting the risen Lord, not because of events at the empty tomb. The significance of the empty tomb was at first probably ambiguous, causing only confusion (Mark 16:8; Luke 24:12, 24; John 20:1–2), but after the appearances, it became a signpost indicating to the early Christians that the great anticipated eschatological act of God had taken place in history in the risen Christ. It may also have pointed them to the bodily nature of the resurrection. The empty-tomb story itself eventually became a vehicle for proclaiming the resurrection of Jesus.[64]

Finally, Dunn, after surveying the conflicting stories about the empty tomb, maintains that the empty-tomb tradition is both early and accurate: the body of Jesus was not in the tomb in which he had been buried. In light of the arguments for the authenticity of the tradition, Dunn concludes that "as a matter of historical reconstruction, the weight of evidence points firmly to the conclusion that Jesus' tomb was found empty and that its emptiness was a factor in the first Christians' belief in the resurrection of Jesus."[65] The claim of the Christians that the tomb of Jesus was empty was not challenged even by the enemies of the followers of Jesus. Johnson thus correctly concludes that what empowered the community of faith was not the absence of a body but a new form of presence that needed explanation: "Whatever the character of the ministry of Jesus for the 'Jesus movement' before his death, it is the experience of the transformed Jesus as Lord that begins the 'Christian movement.'"[66]

From this brief survey of scholarship and of the biblical texts, we see that the emptiness of the tomb, although ambiguous by itself, was well established quite early in both Christian and non-Christian communities and elicited numerous interpretations. For example, the Jews said the disciples had taken the body, while Mary thought that someone else had taken it. It is possible that because of this the emphasis in the narratives shifted from the ambiguity of the tomb to the appearances of Jesus as confirmation of the fact of the resurrection. The vacant tomb could never stand on its own as evidence of the resurrection of Jesus, but it could help corroborate the conclusions drawn from the appearances and point to the bodily nature of the event.

5. THE APPEARANCE STORIES

When it comes to the resurrection appearances, the only cohesion in the Gospels seems to be their order—all of the appearances reported in the Gospels follow the discovery of the empty tomb. Beyond that, there is not much that is common. Dodd has noted that there is a basic pattern in the appearance stories: the situation (generally, the disciples' state of gloom, despair, and unbelief), the appearance of Jesus, his greeting, the disciples' recognition of Jesus, and a word of command.[67] But even though a pattern can be found, there are striking differences in the persons involved in the appearances, the circumstances surrounding the appearances, and their various locations. The presence of these discrepancies suggests that the early church did not go to great lengths to harmonize the Gospels. When Tatian in his second-century *Diatessaron* made such an attempt, his efforts were rejected by the church at large. Perhaps the early church could see more clearly what some of the differences meant to the evangelists than we are able to discern today, assuming that several Gospels were known in various early Christian communities. Why else would so many differences have remained after such a long history of changes to the text during its transmission? We do not deny, however, the seriousness of the matter or the still significant problems in the narratives. Indeed, denying that such problems exist is not honest, and harmonizing them does not appear possible. This should not lead to a neglect of the inconsistencies in resurrection narratives but, rather, to attempts to clarify their meaning because of their fundamental significance for the Christian community. Sometimes the differences can be accounted for by the theological stance of the writer and the message he was trying to convey, as shown in our dis-

cussion of the empty-tomb traditions in the Gospels. After examining the narratives, we will attempt to discover some cohesion in the appearance traditions. Table 6-2 lists the reported postresurrection appearances of Jesus.

A. The Location of the Appearances

One of the major difficulties in reconstructing the events of the first Easter is the problem of locating the resurrection appearances of Jesus. Mark 14:28 and 16:7 indicate that the forthcoming appearances will take place in Galilee. Bultmann believes that both of these passages are footnotes put by Mark into the narrative, which he took from an older tradition that told of the disciples' flight to Galilee. According to Bultmann, since Mark had dispensed with the story of the disciples' flight, he found it "necessary to have the disciples artificially dispatched to Galilee in order to achieve congruity with the old Easter tradition."[68] Matthew, evidently following Mark's lead, places the appearance of Jesus to the disciples in Galilee (28:16–20), though he has an appearance to the women ("Mary Magdalene and the other Mary") in Jerusalem (28:8–10). The close parallels between Mark 14:28, 16:7 and Matt 28:7 argue convincingly for Matthew's dependence upon Mark or his awareness of a similar tradition here. On the other hand, neither Luke nor John mentions any appearances of Jesus in Galilee. For them, the appearances all took place in and around Jerusalem. Luke includes the appearance on the road to Emmaus, as well as appearances in Jerusalem and Bethany (Luke 24:13ff., 33ff., 50ff.). John mentions only Jerusalem. The Galilean appearances of Jesus in John 21 are not included here. As Mark 16:9–20 is generally recognized by biblical scholars as a late addition to Mark, so John 21 is also considered by many scholars to be an epilogue added by the church or later editor(s) sometime after the original work (chs. 1–20) had been composed (see 21:24). No doubt these additions were an attempt to harmonize existing traditions and possibly to answer questions that were later raised against the early church.

How can these two strongly differing traditions about the location of the appearances be brought together? In current scholarly opinion, there appear to be three possibilities: (1) the appearances of Jesus took place both in Galilee and in Jerusalem;

T A B L E   6 - 2

POSTRESURRECTION APPEARANCES OF JESUS

There are at least eleven distinguishable appearance stories in the Gospel narratives (incl. Mark 16:9–20; John 21) in which the risen Lord appears to his followers.

Matt 28:9–10: to the women at the tomb

Matt 28:16–20: to the eleven disciples in Galilee

Luke 24:13–35: to the two disciples on the road to Emmaus (the appearance to Peter in Luke 24:34 is only stated and not narrated)

Luke 24:36–53: to the disciples in Jerusalem (vv. 50–53 are treated as part of the same appearance)

John 20:11–18: to Mary Magdalene at the tomb

John 20:19–23: to the disciples in Jerusalem

John 20:24–29: to Thomas in Jerusalem

*John 21:1–22: to the eleven disciples at the Sea of Tiberias (the dialogue with Peter, vv. 15–22, is evidently in the presence of the others)

*Mark 16:9–11: to Mary Magdalene

*Mark 16:12–13: to the two disciples walking in the country (Emmaus?)

*Mark 16:14–20: to the eleven disciples in Jerusalem (?) (this concludes with his ascension)

To these we add Paul's list (1 Cor 15:5–8), which includes not only appearances to Cephas and "the twelve" but also appearances to "five hundred" followers of Jesus, James the brother of Jesus, "all the apostles," and Paul himself.

*Probably not an original part of the Gospel in which it appears, at least as originally planned.

---

(2) the appearances took place solely in Galilee; or (3) the appearances took place solely in and around Jerusalem. Most scholars have attempted to reconcile the geographical differences, but others have emphasized that the appearances occurred in only one of the two locations. This raises the question why there were two locations mentioned in the Easter traditions and what theological significance might be connected with either place, if any. Could it also be that the differences in location may answer the question of the nature of the appearances, that they were visionary experiences of the disciples?

Lohmeyer, raising the question of the theological significance of the two locations, suggests that the reason for the variation in the tradition is that Galilee represented the place of preaching and the "son of man christology" as well as the land of fulfillment but Jerusalem represented the place of the "messiah christology."[69] Many scholars today give support to Lohmeyer's contention that there are theological reasons for the references to Galilee and Jerusalem in the appearance stories, but few agree on precisely what those reasons are. O'Collins observes that since the 1930s, when Lohmeyer first published his work, scholars have not always understood Mark's references to Galilee in a geographical sense. Some have argued instead that Galilee denotes not only the place of preaching but also the land of the Gentiles, which would point instead to the worldwide mission of the church.[70] If Mark does not intend Galilee to be taken in a geographical sense, then it would probably be best to accept Jerusalem as the actual place of all the appearances. On the other hand, if Bultmann is correct that Mark deleted the oral tradition of the disciples' flight to Galilee and only included the appearance stories (in the original unmutilated ending of his Gospel), then the report on the location of the appearances probably originated in Galilee.[71]

O'Collins concludes, however, that even though Mark may use the term "Galilee" with some theological value in mind, it is probably best to follow Mark rather than Luke and place all of the appearances in Galilee; he thinks it is more likely that Luke altered Mark's text for theological reasons than the other way around.[72] Marxsen, on the other hand, takes Mark 16:7 and 14:28 as references not to a resurrection appearance but to the Parousia, or coming, of Christ, which Mark expected to occur soon in Galilee. He argues that, while the Gospels and Paul (1 Cor 15) use the term ὤφθη (*ōphthē*, "he was seen," "he appeared") for the resurrection appearances, Mark uses instead ὄψεσθε (*opsesthe*, "you will see"), thus referring to the Parousia. Mark, therefore, was pointing to the Parousia by referring to Galilee, where the disciples would see Jesus in his coming, not simply his resurrection appearance.[73] Fuller observes, however, that both Paul and John use ὄψομαι ("will see") for a resurrection appearance (1 Cor 9:1; John 20:18, 25, 29) and that Matthew undoubtedly understood Mark 16:7 as a resurrection appearance (Matt 28:7, 10, 16–20). The decisive argument against Marxsen's interpretation, however, as Fuller is quick to note, is the fact that Mark names Peter and the other disciples—a clear indication of the two appearances listed by Paul in 1 Cor 15:5: "If Mark 16:7 were pointing forward to the parousia it is hard to see why Peter should be singled out for special mention. But if it points to resurrection appearances, the reason for the mention of Peter is obvious."[74]

So where did the appearances of the risen Christ take place? Was it in Galilee, in Jerusalem, or in both places? There have been several major attempts to resolve this difficulty. Moule has proposed a solution that brings the two different traditions together. He asks whether it is possible to hold that the appearances took place first in Jerusalem and then in Galilee. He suggests that the location of the resurrection appearances might be understood in terms of the festival pilgrimages. The disciples of Jesus were all Galileans and consequently were in Judea only as pilgrims for the Passover festival, just as Jesus had been. Within the week after the end of Passover they naturally returned to Galilee. During that week some of the disciples could have seen Jesus in Jerusalem and then later in Galilee. Accepting that the appearances were spread over a longer period of time, that is, forty or fifty days, Moule believes that it is possible the disciples returned to Jerusalem for the next pilgrim feast, Pentecost, and there Jesus appeared to them again in Jerusalem.[75] Moule admits this is a rather rigid interpretation of the narratives, but believes that it makes sense of Mark 16:7 and Luke's recorded admonition from the risen Christ to the disciples to remain in Jerusalem (Luke 24:49; Acts 1:4). As he says, "Such literalism may seem absurd; but it seems to make sense of the Marcan 'he goes before you into Galilee' (16:7)—it would mean, when you return home you will find him already there—and of the injunction in Luke–Acts not to leave Jerusalem after Pentecost (Luke 24:48, Acts 1:4)—it would mean, this time, do not return to Galilee, as you did after Passover."[76] Moule's proposal has been criticized by several scholars not only because it is a rather wooden interpretation of difficult passages but also because it is not supported by the resurrection narratives themselves and raises the difficult problem of separating Luke 24:36–53 (presumably between vv. 43 and 44) in order to allow for a Galilean appearance before the command of 24:48 to remain in Jerusalem. It is therefore questionable whether Moule's interpretation comes to grips with the fact that Mark and Matthew have opted so strongly for Galilee but Luke and John for Jerusalem.

The same could be said for Lilly's somewhat traditional solution to the problem, which is based on the refusal of the disciples to believe the women's report of the empty tomb and on the command from the angel to go to Galilee. Lilly suggests that at first Jesus intended for the disciples to leave the hostile atmosphere of Jerusalem for the more tranquil territory of Galilee, where he would reveal himself to them and give his final commission. However,

> the holy women delayed to report the direction to the Apostles, and when finally the message did reach them, they remained incredulous, labeled the report contemptuously "idle tales." The only way, at least the most effective way, to overcome this incredulity was for Jesus to appear to the Apostles directly, establish faith in their minds as to the reality of His resurrection and prepare them for the final and more important appearances in Galilee.[77]

Lilly's attempt at a reconciliation does not account for John's rather clear preference for Jerusalem as the location for appearances, or for Luke 24:49, where the author may have been aware of the Markan tradition but simply rejected it (see 24:6).

Another attempt at harmonizing the location of the appearances comes from C. F. Evans, whose translation of προάγειν (proagein, "precede," "go before") in Mark 14:28 and 16:7 is based on Mark's earlier use of this term in 10:32. The normal meaning given for this term in these locations is "precede." Evans believes that it can mean "lead" (the verb comes from a root meaning "lead"). If he is right, would Jesus have had to lead his disciples from Jerusalem to Galilee, thereby appearing in both Jerusalem and then all the way up in Galilee?[78] But this translation, however well suited it may be for Mark 10:32 or 14:28, is ill suited for 16:7, since there the angel clearly says "there (ἐκεῖ, ekei) you will see him," referring to Galilee.

Marxsen takes the differences in the location of the appearances to be an indication that each evangelist aimed only at showing one important truth: "the cause of Jesus goes on beyond Good Friday—in a miraculous way," and "the fact that it goes on is always due to a new emergence and intervention of Jesus, to a new commission."[79] For him, the evangelists' selection and arrangement of the material for their Gospels depended on their own perspective and circumstance. That selection was determined chiefly by the period during which they wrote, the readers for whom they wrote, and the varying theological problems with which each had to deal separately. The details of the Easter tradition were basically unimportant, and the mode of the resurrection of Jesus was neither an article of faith nor a part of a universal Christian conviction. This interpretation, however, does not square with the fact that in every tradition or resurrection nar-

rative the resurrection of Jesus always means Jesus who was raised from the dead and was seen (or appeared). In Mark's Gospel this can be concluded from the angelic comment, "He has been raised; he is not here" (16:6), especially since it is said in the setting of the empty tomb. The reference to the place where the disciples will see Jesus (16:7) is also in line with all other resurrection traditions, including Paul's in 1 Cor 15. Indeed, Paul's emphasis on the resurrection body, with all of its difficulties, still means that the old body (of flesh) is incorporated into the new (see vv. 42–46). It is possible that the knowledge of an empty tomb is implied in ἐτάφη (etaphē, "he was buried") of 1 Cor 15:4. It is also possible that the empty tomb was not mentioned by Paul because it was not an object of faith but, rather, something that pointed to the nature of the resurrection of Jesus, that is, it was a corollary to the resurrection of Jesus but not yet an object of special attention. If Jesus was raised, then it was understood that his body had to be absent from the tomb. The evangelists and Paul do not say simply that the "activity" or "cause" of Jesus continued beyond Good Friday but that Jesus himself, who was put to death, survived the grave, was still alive, and had revealed himself to his disciples. That the nature of the event was not lost in obscurity is clear even in Paul, where the sequence of 1 Cor 15:3–5 places the resurrection after "he was buried" and, at the least, implies that the resurrection of Jesus was from the grave.

The majority of scholars who accept the resurrection of Jesus as an event of history agree that the appearances of Jesus took place in Galilee. Pannenberg says that there was no knowledge of the empty-tomb tradition in the appearance stories that took place in Galilee and the disciples would only have learned of it when they returned to Jerusalem. Because the empty-tomb tradition agreed with their encounter with the risen Jesus, he says, they incorporated it into the resurrection tradition.[80] This view presumes that the disciples left Jerusalem before the discovery of the tomb and returned to Galilee. Along this line, Pannenberg asks why there are no references in the passion narratives to their witness of the crucifixion and why they did not take part in the burial of Jesus if the disciples remained in Jerusalem.[81]

The likely answer to Pannenberg's questions is found in the fleeing of the disciples after Jesus' arrest. They were afraid for themselves (John 20:19) but were also, no doubt, quite confused and discouraged, having witnessed the arrest of the one whom they had believed would usher in the eschatological kingdom of God. Also, if the disciples had already departed for Galilee, what would be the purpose of the women telling the disciples to go to Galilee (Mark 16:7; Matt 28:7, 10)? All four evangelists tell of the command to the women (by the angels or Jesus) to report their findings at the tomb to the disciples who were in Jerusalem. Such multiple attestation suggests that the disciples did not depart from Jerusalem without knowledge of the empty tomb. Along with this, as we have seen, is the evidence of the story of the disciples' visit to the tomb in Luke 24:12, 24 and John 20:3–8, even though John overlays the tradition with another motive.

Mark 16:7 presupposes the disciples' return to Galilee, but the fact that the women are told to report the angelic message of the resurrection of Jesus to them (all four Gospels agree on this) also shows that the journey to Galilee was after the Sabbath. How soon they departed for Galilee or how quickly they returned to Jerusalem, however, cannot be established with any precision on the basis of the existing witnesses. Acts 2 indicates that the disciples at least returned to Jerusalem by the time of the Pentecost festival, though there is no indication in Acts that the disciples ever went back to Galilee.

Furthermore, if Luke's and John's stories concerning the Jerusalem appearances are correct, it is not easy to fit in a Galilean appearance of Jesus before the Jerusalem appearances. Luke 24:13 and John 20:19 seem to forbid this. A later Galilean appearance is also troubling, since for Luke everything concludes at the end of the first day with a command to remain in Jerusalem (24:49). It is possible that further Galilean appearances could be fitted in at the end of John's story about Thomas (20:24–29), but does 20:30–31 ("Now Jesus did many other signs in the presence of his disciples, . . . But these . . .) make room for such? If they were added at this juncture, they would serve no purpose. For John, the resurrection appearances of Jesus show that Jesus was exalted and glorified. In them Jesus gives to the disciples the Holy Spirit and visible proof of his exaltation and charges them with their mission. It is difficult to see what further

appearances in Galilee would have added to this. If the unlikely scenario is true—that Jesus originally intended that the disciples should go to Galilee but, because of their unbelief and unwillingness to go, he had to appear to them in Jerusalem in order to get them to Galilee—it is not clear what more would be revealed in Galilee that was not revealed in Jerusalem in the appearances referred to by Luke and John, especially since Matthew's missionary charge in Galilee (28:19) is not unlike Luke's missionary charge in Jerusalem (Luke 24:45–48; Acts 1:8).

For these reasons, the harmonization of such texts seems strained and fails to appreciate what may have been at the heart of the evangelists' intentions. There is no indication in the Gospels that harmonization is possible. Perhaps the earliest attempt to bring together the Jerusalem and Galilee traditions is found in the Johannine "appendix" (ch. 21), but it is awkward, and questions are still left unanswered. For example, if the disciples are with the risen Jesus in ch. 20, why do they not recognize him in ch. 21? If Jesus sees Peter in ch. 20, why is there no attempt to reconcile with him until ch. 21? More troubling, if Jesus commissions the disciples in 20:22–23, why are the disciples back fishing in ch. 21 rather than carrying out their commission? The difficulty one faces in bringing these two traditions together enhances the notion that more than a geographical problem is involved in the evangelists' choice for the location of the appearances. It is difficult to imagine that nothing other than geography presented itself to Luke in his choice of Jerusalem and his neglect of Galilee, especially in light of 24:6, where he evidently shows his awareness and rejection of Galilean appearance traditions (cf. Mark 16:7).

The above complex of explanations for the differences in the location of the appearances shows that there are few proposals for harmonization that have commended themselves. Each attempt has its own problems. In every case, a harmony seems impossible without doing damage to other parts of the resurrection narratives. This is so even if we account for the variations on the basis of the visionary nature of the appearances, since this would not solve the apparent contradictions in the narratives. Should we accept one tradition as more reliable than another, say, Mark instead of Luke, given that Mark was written first? This begs the question concerning Luke's purpose in accepting the tradition that was also followed by John and subsequently altered in the "appendix" to John's Gospel. Not enough information is available for us to decide. As the narratives stand, there are discrepancies, but is there a missing factor that could bring the two traditions together? In their accounts, do Luke and John reject the possibility that any appearances took place in Galilee? Do Mark and Matthew intend to exclude any appearances to the disciples in Jerusalem? (Matthew does have an appearance of Jesus to the women at the tomb but not to the disciples.)

Perhaps a view not yet advanced would do justice to the theological motives existing in, or leading to, the choice of location by each of the evangelists. As mentioned above, Paul, in 1 Cor 15:5–8, speaks of appearances to Peter, then to the Twelve, then to "more than five hundred brothers and sisters at one time," then to James, then to all of the apostles, and finally to Paul. The appearance to the "five hundred brothers and sisters" may be a reference to appearances in Galilee, where Jesus did most of his ministry. Von Campenhausen may be right in saying that this appearance was in Galilee, since Jesus appeared only to the disciples in Jerusalem and there would have been no place available in Jerusalem for Jesus to have appeared to such a large crowd. Only in Galilee, where he had a longer tenure of ministry, would Jesus have had five hundred disciples. His relatively brief tenure of ministry (one week) in Jerusalem would not suggest large numbers of followers.[82] The same could be said of the appearance to James (and possibly to "all of the apostles"), since James (also of Nazareth) was not one of the original Twelve and probably would not have traveled to Jerusalem with Jesus. Paul indicates that James also received an appearance that presumably led to his faith and that was likely in the region of Galilee. Because the thrust of Jesus' ministry was in Galilee, it is probable, therefore, that some of the appearances took place there, even though Luke and John only mention appearances to the disciples in Jerusalem. A large gathering of five hundred followers of Jesus is more likely to have occurred in Galilee than in Jerusalem not only because of the concentration of most of Jesus' ministry in that area but also because the atmosphere there would have been less hostile than in Jerusalem. The Pharisees, who were among Jesus'

strongest opponents in Jerusalem, had very little influence in Galilee.[83]

The earliest form of the church was in Jerusalem and was recognized as such in Acts 15 (the first council takes place there) and by Paul in Gal 2:1–10. Since the death and resurrection of Jesus occurred there, as well as the earliest Christian missionary activity, perhaps Luke and John chose to emphasize the Jerusalem appearances in their Gospels to stress the missionary activity to which Jesus had called the disciples. Jerusalem, the city of promise and fulfillment, became the place where the Jesus movement was established. On the other hand, it may be that since Jesus' preaching ministry had been primarily in Galilee and the majority of his followers were most likely still in that area in the early stages of the church's growth, Mark and Matthew wanted to emphasize the Galilean appearances.

What is needed in all of this is the missing link that can bring the two traditions together without diminishing the individual messages of either. At present, aside from positing differing theological motives, no one seems to have found such a connecting link, nor have they identified precisely what theological motives may have been present in the minds of the evangelists. These are still matters of debate, with no consensus emerging on the horizon. The location of the appearances of Jesus continues to be an important hindrance in any harmonized reconstruction of the events of Easter.

For this and the following discussions, refer to table 6-3, which compares the postresurrection appearances of Jesus in the Gospels.

B. To Whom Did Jesus First Appear?

Matthew says that Jesus first appeared to the women (Matt 28:9–10), while John indicates that the first appearance was to Mary alone (John 20:14–18). Mark and Luke, however, have no such appearance of Jesus to women only; they report instead the appearance of the interpreting angel or angels, who told the women that Jesus would appear in Galilee to his disciples and to Peter (Mark 16:7; Luke 24:4–7). Whether Mark intends that Peter would be the last to see Jesus in Galilee ("tell his disciples and Peter," 16:7) cannot be determined, but Peter is singled out for special mention. Whether this means that he would be the first to see Jesus is not disclosed (or prohibited either). Luke makes no

TABLE 6-3

A COMPARISON OF POSTRESURRECTION APPEARANCES OF JESUS IN THE GOSPELS

	Matthew 28	Mark 16	Luke 24	John 20
Location	In Jerusalem to the women at the tomb and later to the disciples on a mountain in Galilee	Promise is given (v. 7) to the women of the appearance in Galilee	In Jerusalem to two disciples on the road to Emmaus and later to the Eleven, both on Easter evening	In Jerusalem to Mary and later, after his ascension, to all of the disciples except Thomas during a meal
				One week later to Thomas
The touch	Women clasp Jesus' feet			Mary is told not to touch because his ascension has not yet happened
				Thomas is invited to touch Jesus one week later
Message of the appearances	To the women: Do not be afraid, go and tell my brethren to go to Galilee; there they will see me. To the disciples: Go, make disciples, baptize, and teach to observe the commandments; a promise to remain with disciples	Appendix, v. 15: Call to mission	Jesus engages in talk, denounces their lack of faith and shows from Scripture that Christ should suffer Jesus meets with the rest of the disciples and calls them to mission with the promise of the Spirit	Jesus calls Mary by name, forbids her to touch him, tells her of his ascension, and calls her to go and tell the disciples Jesus appears to the disciples, greets them with "peace," calls them to ministry, and gives them the Holy Spirit Later Jesus invites Thomas to touch him and believe, then says that those who have not seen yet believe are blessed
Responses	Disciples worship Jesus, but some still doubt after the appearance. A polemic against the church: the body was stolen, but the disciples tell of the guard		After Jesus breaks bread with them, the disciples on the road to Emmaus have their eyes opened. After Jesus' ascension, the disciples are filled with joy and blessing	Mary worships Jesus, and Thomas in belief cries out, "My Lord and my God!"

mention of an appearance of Jesus to the women, but he has two angels appear to tell them of the importance of the empty tomb. The women evidently believed their story and reported it to the unbelieving disciples (24:4–11). Luke instead reports an appearance to the two disciples on the road to Emmaus; it was *they* who then told "the eleven" that Jesus had risen and "appeared to Simon" (Luke 24:34). Exactly when the appearance to Peter occurred is not answered in Luke, but evidently it was before the appearance to the two disciples, and the implication is that such an appearance was mentioned to them by the risen Jesus. Luke here seems to be following the Pauline tradition (1 Cor 15:5) or one in common with Paul. All four Gospels mention the angelic appearance to the women but differ on who received the first appearance. Mark implies that it was the disciples and Peter (16:7 [note the order]), Matthew says the women (28:9), John says Mary Magdalene (20:14–18), and Luke says Peter (24:34).

Perhaps the solution to the problem might be found in the brevity of Mark's Gospel: if his Gospel had continued, he may have included a story of an appearance of Jesus to the women. Both Matthew (28:9–10) and John (20:11ff.) say that the appearance of Jesus to Mary or the women came immediately after the angelic appearance, as they (or Mary) were walking away from the empty tomb. Whether the original text of Mark would have included an appearance of Jesus to the women here is, of course, speculation and based on an elusive argument from silence. But since Matthew, who elsewhere seems to have followed Mark rather closely, has such an appearance and since John, who followed another tradition, agrees with him, this supposition may not be far-fetched.

If this speculation is true, however, we must ask why Luke fails to mention the appearance of Jesus to the women. What purpose would he have in omitting this first appearance if it had indeed occurred? An answer to this may be that Luke is trying to set forth the best defense he can for his Gospel and may have seen the mention of women in the story as a weakness in his argument. Nevertheless, in Acts 1:3 he presents his case for the resurrection in summary form, stating that there were "many proofs" (πολλοῖς τεκμηρίοις, *pollois tekmēriois*) of Jesus' aliveness after his death. Perhaps this is also the reason Paul does not mention

the appearance to the women in his list in 1 Cor 15. Women were not deemed competent to testify under Jewish law (see *m. Roš Haš.* 1:8),[84] and this may have figured into Luke's omission of the appearance to the women in his presentation of the case for Christianity.

On the other hand, von Campenhausen argues that there were no appearances to the women on the "third day," and he appeals to the silence of Mark and Luke for support.[85] Nevertheless, with the problem of women's credibility among the Jews at that time, it does not seem likely that such stories of appearances to women would have been readily accepted into the resurrection traditions of John and Matthew, two very Jewish Gospels, had there not been some perceived element of reliability in them. What motive could be advanced for the inclusion of an appearance to women in such an important tradition in these ancient patriarchal documents? It seems more reasonable to believe that such stories would be excluded, as they perhaps were in the case of 1 Cor 15:3–8, rather than added to the Gospel traditions. Peter's prominence in the formation of the early church would probably lead to special priority for him in the accounts, rather than the women who had also claimed to have a resurrection appearance. Matthew's and John's lack of special reference to Peter (Matt 28:10; John 20:17) may indicate that their sources at this point are earlier than Mark's or Luke's sources. A good reason can be suggested for adding Peter's name to the resurrection traditions or giving special priority to him but not for deleting references to him. Conversely, apologetic reasons could be found for omitting the story of an appearance to women (i.e., the lack of credibility given to the witness of women) but not for introducing it.

C. The Ascension and the Forbidding of Mary to Touch Jesus

One of the more intriguing and also complicated passages in the resurrection narratives is John 20:17, in which Jesus forbids Mary to touch him because he had not yet ascended to his Father and God. The intrigue increases when, in vv. 24–29, he invites Thomas to touch him. What happened in the meantime? According to one interpretation of John's Gospel, it was the ascension of Jesus to his Father. For many readers, part of the difficulty in understanding this passage is that they tend to understand "ascension" from the perspective of Luke, as the final appearance of Jesus to the disciples before he returns to heaven (see Luke's story in sec. D, below). C. F. Evans claims that the force of this Johannine passage is to emphasize the exaltation of Jesus to the Father as the fulfillment of the whole Gospel of divine sonship (see John 1:11–12). He argues that for John the ascension of Jesus took place on Easter morning before the appearances took place, and concludes that the early church always understood the resurrection appearances as the resurrection of the exalted and ascended Lord.[86] In the following discussion, we will look at various interpretations of this passage before examining a number of issues in order to make some sense of it.

At the time when the words of John 20:17 were spoken to Mary, the resurrection of Jesus had already occurred, but for John the ascension was still to come. Ramsey argues that John held that the ascension or exaltation to glory was separate from the resurrection, and maintains that the Acts account (1:9–11) shows that the ascension was considered from an early stage to be a separate and subsequent event to the resurrection of Jesus (though he admits that this is not always clearly seen in other passages of the NT).[87] He believes that John introduces the "touch me not" story to emphasize the importance of the ascension or exaltation of Jesus, which, though important to the resurrection of Jesus, is nevertheless subsequent to it. He admits that his interpretation here is difficult to square with other NT passages that link the exaltation of Jesus to his resurrection to indicate that by means of the resurrection from the dead, Jesus has been exalted or glorified.[88]

Dodd connects this story not so much with exaltation as with John's picture of the high priest going into the holy of holies to offer his sacrifice. Only after this offering for the people has been made will Jesus, the high priest, be touchable.[89] But if this is the case, John uses this particular story to emphasize a point that he nowhere else explicitly makes. Another view, drawing out the linguistic elements of the account, is that John sees Jesus as exalted but still moving toward ascension. In John 20:17 Jesus says that Mary is not to touch (ἅπτου, *haptou*) him since he is not yet in an ascended state (ἀναβέβηκα, *anabebēka*), but to tell the

disciples that he is in the process of ascending (ἀναβαίνω, *anabainō*), something that occurs after the Gospel story. The contrast is between a process begun by the resurrection and its culmination in the ascension.[90] Another interpretation of the passage requires that considerable theological and ecclesiastical meaning be poured into the term "cling" (or "touch"). It suggests that Jesus is saying to Mary that she may no longer cling to his earthly existence but must look for another way of experiencing his presence. As interesting as this view might be, especially because it recognizes that the passage intends to say much more than what a mere physical touch might suggest (there is no problem in the women touching Jesus in Matt 28:9), it seems unjustified and foreign to the context. Its proponents may be correct in arguing that v. 17 is a later Johannine redaction introduced for the purpose of adding a charge to go and tell the disciples, as we see elsewhere in Matthew and Mark, but there appears to be something more important than this in the passage.[91] John evidently uses the appearance stories to make clear that Jesus has entered a completely new mode of existence and is now exalted. By this reckoning, the ascension in John takes place before Jesus' appearance to the disciples in 20:19. After that, it is appropriate for Thomas to touch him (v. 27), even though the passage does not actually say that he did. The implication from the passage is that Jesus ascended between the first and second appearances, between vv. 17 and 19.

Elsewhere in the Gospel (10:11–18; 11:49–53;[92] cf. 18:12; 12:32–33), John seems to make the exaltation of Jesus synonymous with his crucifixion and gives more attention to the significance of the death of Jesus than do the synoptic evangelists and Acts 2:22–23. Not unlike John, Paul also emphasizes the importance of the death of Jesus for sins (cf. John 10:11, 15) followed by his exaltation (Phil 2:6–11). Paul isolates the proclamation of the death of Jesus from his resurrection in 1 Cor 1:22–24 and 2:2, even though he, like John, knew the importance of Jesus' resurrection (1 Cor 15:3–5, 12–20). The author of Hebrews also is aware of the resurrection (6:2), but because many of his readers were returning to Judaism and abandoning their faith, he emphasizes the superiority of Jesus' priesthood over that of Aaron and, with it, the exaltation of Jesus in his death as going into the holy of holies

(2:5–11; 9:11–14; 10:12–13; 12:2). For John, exaltation may come for Jesus through the cross, but this exaltation is not seen or acknowledged except through the resurrection. Faith comes in John not at the cross (though the redactor of 19:35 shows that it was possible) but only in Jesus' resurrection. John 20 was not a late appendage attached to the Gospel of John by a final redactor but was an integral part of it. According to John, at the arrest of Jesus, the disciples feared for their lives and fled. Peter denied he knew Jesus, and the others scattered. At his death, there was no faith but pain and despair. Besides the beloved disciple (discussed above), who "believed" at the grave site when he saw the grave clothes and empty tomb, Mary believed on the basis of Jesus' appearance to her (vv. 17–18; "I have seen the Lord"). Thomas was distraught and disbelieving until he saw the risen Lord (v. 27). Although John paves the way for understanding the exaltation of Jesus on the cross, that exaltation was not perceived apart from the resurrection of Jesus. The cross did not disclose its meaning to the disciples apart from the resurrection, and faith was not born at the cross, as some scholars have taught.[93]

O'Collins observes that identifying the exaltation of Jesus with his crucifixion opens the door to the docetic notion that only the spirit of Jesus ascended into heaven, leaving the body behind.[94] Brown accepts the notion of exaltation by way of the cross in John and acknowledges that the resurrection of Jesus does not easily fit within this scheme. Since it was such a firm part of the Christian tradition when John wrote his Gospel, he had to make it fit into the process of Jesus' passing from this world to the Father. If that is the case for John, then, according to Brown, the crucifixion of Jesus becomes a part of his further glorification. He says that John "dramatizes the resurrection so that it is obviously part of the ascension," using the appearance to Mary Magdalene as a vehicle to explain that only after the ascension, of which the resurrection is a part, can the enduring presence of Jesus in the Spirit be given. He notes that in 7:39 John says that only after Jesus' glorification could there be the gift of the Spirit. Consequently, when Jesus offers the Spirit in 20:22, Brown claims that John is saying that Jesus had already been exalted and glorified, that is, he had already ascended to the Father. It was therefore only the ascended and thereby

glorified Jesus who appeared to the disciples. As to whether John means that the appearance to Mary took place before the ascension and the appearance to the disciples took place after the ascension, Brown rightly concludes that, taken at face value, a positive answer to this would deny that the resurrection is the same event as the ascension. It would also imply that the appearance to Mary was of an inferior status.[95] Brown is aware that these inconsistencies in his view are difficult to overcome.

There is the further difficulty that John, unlike Luke, does not have an ascension at the end of the earthly appearances of Jesus; rather, it is implied to have happened as they began. Brown believes that an understanding of John's technique provides a solution to these questions. He maintains that John is

> fitting a theology of resurrection/ascension that by definition has no dimensions of time and space into a narrative that is necessarily sequential. If John's purpose is forgotten, the attempt to dramatize in temporal scenes what is *sub specie aeternitatis* [in the category of eternal] creates confusion. When the risen Jesus has to explain to Mary Magdalene that he is about to ascend, the emphasis is on the identification of the resurrection and the ascension, not on the accidental time lag. In Johannine thought there is only one risen Jesus, and he appears in glory in all his appearances.[96]

For Brown, the controlling interest of John is not the temporal sequence of events but, rather, his theological motive for explaining the meaning of the resurrection and the fact that the disciples were given the continuing presence of the Spirit by the risen Jesus. This interest or theme in John's resurrection narrative is the intimate connection between the ascension of the Son of Man and the giving of the Spirit. He recalls that in 16:7 Jesus says, "if I do not go away, the Advocate will not come to you; but if I go, I will send him to you." Brown concludes that this is fulfilled in John immediately after Jesus' death, as 20:17 and 22 show by associating the resurrection, the ascension, and the giving of the Spirit.[97]

According to John, the disciples abandoned Jesus at his arrest, and Peter even went so far as to deny him. From the time of the arrest (18:1–19:42) to the discovery of the empty tomb, there is no note of victory in John.[98] Although John finds the death or the manner of the death of Jesus a fulfillment of Scripture (19:24, 37), the sound of joy or triumph found in 20:18 ("I have seen the Lord") and 20:29

("My Lord and my God") is completely lacking in his story of the passion of Jesus. In his passion and resurrection narratives, the exaltation (or glorification) of Jesus is set forth only after the resurrection.

The ascension in John is a part of the resurrection story—a part that, from a temporal point of view, takes place somewhat awkwardly between the appearance of Jesus to Mary and the appearance to the rest of the disciples. As with the story about the disciples' visit to the tomb (20:3–10), John has made use of the story of the appearance to Mary Magdalene to point to a very important theological matter—the presence of the Spirit and the exaltation (glorification) of Jesus in his resurrection. This will become clearer in the next section.

D. What Was the Ascension?

One of the strange aspects about the ascension of Jesus is that it is only mentioned or referred to in the NT in John and Luke–Acts (John 20:17; Luke 24:50–53; Acts 1:9–11). Because the ascension, according to Luke and the church's traditional way of viewing this event, was the final appearance of Jesus before his exaltation, we discuss it here under the appearance stories. As we noted above, John apparently places the ascension of Jesus in a different sequence than does Luke (that is, between the first and second appearances, instead of as the last appearance). On the other hand, while Luke and John mention an ascension of Jesus, Matthew closes his Gospel emphasizing Jesus' abiding presence (28:20; cf. 1:23). Mark, in the extant form of his Gospel, abruptly ends in 16:8 with no mention of an ascension or a resurrection appearance. It is possible that, since Matthew draws so freely upon Mark, the original conclusion of Mark, if we had it, would be similar to Matthew's conclusion, but this is speculation. At any rate, there is no ascension story in Matthew, and it would not have added to his own theological emphasis on the abiding presence of the risen Christ with his church.

Regarding the nature of the ascension, Lampe argued that there was a growing tendency in the early church to make the resurrection of Jesus more of a physical event than the spiritual one that, he claims, it in fact was. This tendency naturally led to the question of the ultimate end of the body of Jesus: after it was raised from the dead and seen, what happened to it? He believes that, early

on, the resurrection of Jesus came to be thought of in terms of OT materialistic notions of resurrection. From this perspective it was natural to believe that the tomb was empty, just as we find in the Easter traditions of the Gospels. Because of the belief in the material resurrection of Jesus, according to Lampe, the ascension story naturally developed to answer the question of what happened to Jesus' body of flesh and bones.[99]

Lampe does not discuss the various possible meanings of the ascension in Luke and John, nor does he observe that John makes no mention of the final state of Jesus' resurrection body after the appearances. This was simply not a question that John entertained, and it is not the motivating factor behind his inclusion of the ascension story. Luke, on the other hand, may have had several meanings behind his story: the final completion of the appearances (Luke 24:50–53), the exaltation of Jesus (Acts 1:9–11; 13:30–39), and/or the introduction to the coming of the Holy Spirit (Luke 24:49; Acts 1:8).[100] Ramsey notes that there is nothing unusual or out of line in the idea that Jesus gave a parting appearance to his disciples at the close of a series of appearances: "There is nothing incredible in an event whereby Jesus assured the disciples that the appearances were ended and that His sovereignty and His presence must henceforth be sought in new ways."[101] John and Luke more likely used a well-known tradition in the early church, each modifying it in his own way, to point to the exaltation of Jesus in his resurrection (see John 20:24–27; Luke 24:51–53).[102] Any attempts to bring John and Luke together on the chronology of the ascension appear futile, but it is not an insignificant question to ask how each writer understood the ascension of Jesus.

Through the story of the appearance of Jesus to Mary at the tomb John is apparently trying to present an additional theological truth, that the exaltation of Christ is to be seen through a pattern of death, resurrection, and the giving of the Holy Spirit. John may also have been trying to answer an issue raised by the Docetists, who favored Christ's ascending into heaven at the moment of Jesus' death on the cross. John is opposed to such a view, since for him Jesus is the Christ who experienced death and was exalted or glorified in his resurrection before the giving of the Spirit. John has already said that only after the glorification of Jesus could the Spirit be given (7:39), and this followed the resurrection (20:19–23). Brown is probably right when he claims that the difficulty of an unglorified appearance of Jesus to Mary (before his ascension) does not come up in John because, in light of John's intention to show that the exaltation of Jesus to the Father came by way of the cross and resurrection, no appearance of Jesus was from an unexalted Lord, even if not from an ascended one. Brown's argument is supported by Mary's second report to the disciples in John 20:18 that she had "seen the Lord."[103]

If the exaltation (glorification) in John can be equated with Jesus' resurrection, then all of the appearances are by the exalted Lord, because the Holy Spirit can come only after the exaltation (or glorification) of Jesus (7:39; 20:17–23). This is also true for Luke. In Luke 24:49, the promise of the Father—the "power from on high"—is given with the purpose of enabling the disciples to witness. After this promise is given, Luke depicts the departure or ascension of Jesus in the familiar OT imagery of Elijah in 2 Kgs 2:11. Shortly after the departure of Jesus, the Holy Spirit comes. In both John and Luke, the exaltation of Jesus is conveyed through the ascension, and, for both, the giving of the Holy Spirit occurs as a result. In the rest of the NT, Jesus' resurrection is indistinguishable from his exalted status, nor is there any support for making two separate events out of the resurrection and the exaltation of Jesus. For example, in Acts 2:32–33 and 5:30–31, Rom 8:34, Col 3:1, Phil 2:8–9, Eph 1:19–20, 1 Tim 3:16, and 1 Pet 3:21–22 there is a linking together of Christ's resurrection with his exaltation.[104]

The ascension of Jesus, especially in Luke, is meant not so much to account for the location of Jesus' resurrection body, as Lampe would have it, as to illustrate graphically that in the resurrection Jesus had been exalted and the promise of the Spirit had been assured. While elsewhere in the NT, the exaltation appears to be interchangeable with the resurrection of Jesus, in Luke and John there is a theological rather than a historical difference between resurrection and ascension.

Yet another question concerns the time of the ascension in Luke. This has to do with the apparent discrepancy between Luke 24 on the one hand, where the ascension takes place late on the same day as the resurrection, and Acts on the other, where the giving of the Holy Spirit occurs only after "forty days" of repeated appearances. The number forty is a special "holy" number that is probably not to be taken literally. Notice, for instance, the many times in the Scriptures where this number is found: the "forty days and nights" of rains on the earth in the days of Noah, Moses' "forty days" on Mount Sinai, the Israelites' "forty years" in the wilderness, Elijah's "forty days" at Mount Horeb, and the "forty days" of Jesus' temptation in Luke. The recurrence of these numbers throughout the Scriptures suggests that something more than a literal forty days is intended. Anderson finds theological significance in the forty days, which according to him represent for Luke a special "holy interval" in sacred history, in which the apostles would be prepared by the coming of the Holy Spirit for their forthcoming task of witness.[105] O'Collins, however, believes that the mention of the forty days in Acts 1:3 is Luke's attempt, like John's and Paul's, to link the resurrection of Christ and the coming of the Holy Spirit: "His 'forty days' helps to ensure that his readers will understand Pentecost as the extension of Easter and the manifest outpouring of the Holy Spirit as the gift of the risen Christ."[106] But if this is so, why does Luke stop at forty days? Why not fifty days to coincide with Pentecost? Anderson argues that the forty days mentioned in Acts 1:3 suggests that there was also a "specific and limited time for the Resurrection appearances."[107] After a period of time, however long it was, the kind of appearances experienced by the disciples terminated. This is supported by the Easter tradition in 1 Cor 15:3–8, in which Paul says that the kind of experiences that the earliest witnesses experienced ceased after a definite period of time, that is, with Paul's Damascus road experience. If the forty days are to be taken literally, then there is a clear discrepancy between Luke 24 and Acts 1 regarding the length of the appearances and the time of the ascension. But if the number forty is a holy number, as Anderson claims, we may be able to resolve the conflict. The number forty is not repeated in Acts in reference to the length of the appearances (see 10:41; 13:31), but since the presence and power of God are referred to in all the places where the number forty occurs in Scripture (even in the temptation story of Luke 4:1–2), this is also the likely intention of Luke in Acts 1:3.

Another explanation of the discrepancy between the length of the appearances in Luke 24 and that in Acts 1 may lie in a change of Luke's purpose in the two instances. In Luke 24, Jesus apparently offers a final appearance to the disciples, the purpose of which is to indicate the cessation of his resurrection appearances and to focus on his commission to the disciples. He then departs in a very graphic manner—he is "carried up into heaven." The point is that the appearances as such cease and that the disciples are to look forward to a new manifestation of the presence of God in their midst: "And see, I am sending upon you what my Father promised; so stay here in the city until you have been clothed with power from on high" (v. 49). In Acts 1:1–5, however, Luke gives a summary of the contents of the first volume of his two-volume work. He restates the climactic ending of his Gospel so the reader does not forget the point of the Gospel as he starts the second volume. The number forty in v. 3 probably indicates that Luke was focusing on the presence of God in the appearances, rather than upon their length. In vv. 6–11, Luke also describes the ascension as a means of terminating the appearances in order to prepare the way for the coming of the Holy Spirit, the evangelistic ministry of the church, and the future return of Christ to the earth to establish his kingdom. Luke has not eliminated the apocalyptic nature of the kingdom while emphasizing the ministry of the Spirit (or, rather, the "power from on high") to evangelize. The kingdom is still coming, but the timing of it is not for the disciples to know. They are assured of it, however, by the promise of the return of the risen Christ (v. 11). Elsewhere, Luke speaks of the temporary abeyance of the kingdom, not its elimination (Luke 19:11–27).

Luke teaches that the risen Jesus is the exalted Lord even before his final departure. The last appearance, described in Luke 24:51 and repeated in Acts 1:8–11, indicates the cessation of all such appearances and points to the new continuing presence and power of God in the church through the Holy Spirit and also to the importance of the church's mission. The dominant theme, however, is the exaltation of Jesus in the resurrection; the disciples, getting the idea, worshiped him in Luke 24:52.

The ascension story was essentially the early church's understanding of the meaning of the resurrection of Jesus. In his resurrection, he was exalted, glorified, and made worthy of worship and service. All of the appearances are of the exalted, glorified Lord. John's story of the ascension emphasizes that Jesus, the risen Lord, is glorified in his resurrection (7:39) and worthy of worship (20:17–28). Although John and Luke appear to place the ascension of Jesus in different positions (between the first and second appearances vs. after the last), they do—according to this reconstruction—agree on the broad sequence of the primary events of Easter: resurrection, ascension, and the giving of the Holy Spirit. The chronology and substance of the ascension story for both John and Luke are not as important as the fact that it points to the exaltation of Jesus in his resurrection.

E. The Nature of the Resurrection Appearances

One of the most significant problems regarding the post-Easter appearances has to do with the nature of these manifestations. An interesting sidelight in the resurrection narratives is John's view of the self-raising of Jesus. This is not clearly expressed in the other Gospels, but John is unambiguous in stating that Jesus raised himself from the dead (cf. 2:19, 21; 10:17–18). John is the first NT writer to present the resurrection of Jesus in this manner, as the earliest Christian preaching argues that he "has been raised" (1 Cor 15:20) and that it was God who raised him up (Acts 2:24, 32). The most important issue related to the appearances, however, is not whether Jesus was self-raised but what the nature of the resurrection appearances was. Were they subjective visions or hallucinations born out of the faith of the earliest disciples in their departed Lord (or their collective guilt), as some claim, or were they actually manifestations of one who had died and who then was raised from death to life a short time later? If the latter, was the nature of Jesus' aliveness after death one of physical dimensions, or was it primarily of a visionary or spiritual nature? Those who reject the possibility of the supernatural intervention of God in human affairs tend to highlight the confusing nature of the Easter narratives and conclude that it is not possible to know precisely what happened in the resurrection of Jesus. Was the idea of Jesus being raised only a manifestation of the apostles' faith? Did they have some strange hallucinations after his death? Most of what we will discuss here goes beyond the strict limitations of the historical method, but not beyond exegetical inquiry.

Lüdemann rejects the view that the tomb of Jesus was empty. He contends, rather, that the whole Easter experience was psychologically self-induced, first by a visionary experience of Peter in Galilee that led to an "incomparable chain reaction," then later by a similar experience of Paul. From these two primary visionary experiences, he claims that Easter faith began. Using A.D. 33 as the year of Paul's conversion, he locates all of the appearances between A.D. 30 (the time of the death of Jesus) and A.D. 33 (Paul's conversion).[108] From his own historical reconstruction, he is led, however, "to the insight that the structural characteristics of the Easter experience . . . of the forgiveness of sins, the experience of life, the experience of eternity, are contained in the words and story of Jesus. So we have to say that before Easter, everything that was finally recognized after Easter was already present."[109]

In fairness to those scholars who have dealt with the serious problems in the resurrection narratives, the majority have still affirmed the resurrection of Jesus as an event of history, but they have frequently given simple answers to what are often very difficult and complex questions. Some scholars, affirming the resurrection of Jesus, nevertheless deny that his body was raised from the grave. They continue to affirm that he was alive even after death but speak of "objective visions": Jesus was alive after his death and manifested his aliveness to his disciples in a way that was unmistaken to them, but his body decomposed somewhere in Palestine. They claim that his resurrection was of a different sort from the physical resurrection or resuscitation described in the Gospels, especially in Luke 24:39–43. They note that the terms used by Paul to describe his experience with the risen Christ are normally used to depict visionary experiences. Thus, if all the testimony that we have on the nature of the appearances came from Paul or the book of Acts, then we might well conclude that Paul's experience, which he puts on a par with that of the other disciples (1 Cor 9:1; 15:5–8), was a visionary one.

Before we look at this position, however, we must first note that the two verbs used most fre-

quently in the NT in reference to the resurrection of Jesus are ἐγείρειν (egeirein) and ἀνιστάναι (anistanai), both of which appear in earlier intertestamental literature. Ἐγείρειν was used very little in secular Greek for the resurrection of the dead, probably because most ancient Greeks did not believe in a bodily resurrection, and instead referred most often to an awakening (see Eph 5:14), lifting up, or raising. Ἀνιστάναι was sometimes also used for raising of the dead, but its use is not always clear. C. F. Evans believes that the NT understanding of resurrection is better conveyed by the words "to live," "to make alive," and "to glorify":

> The resurrection of Christ is a living after death, and the conquest of death, so that he has dominion over all men (Rom. 14:9), and being the conquest of sin is a life lived permanently to God (Rom. 6:13; 14:8f.; II Cor. 13:4; Phil. 1:21; Col. 3:1f.), and who will be "made alive" (see ζωοποιεῖ in John 5:21). Since the word "glory" is the biblical word which comes nearest to expressing the being and nature of God himself, it is inevitably connected with the thought of resurrection as entry into the divine life.[110]

A belief in the resurrection from the dead was not universally accepted by Jews in the time of Jesus. This is illustrated in the NT by the debates over the resurrection between the Pharisees and the Sadducees (Acts 23:7–8; see sec. 2, above). Still, there seems to have been a general understanding and acceptance of varying notions of the resurrection of the dead by a significant number of Jews during this time.

Paul's use of the verb ὤφθη (ōphthē, "appeared") in 1 Cor 15:5–8 has been judged by some scholars to be a technical term used primarily of a vision from God in biblical writings.[111] The term, if used in this technical sense, might, then, imply that what the early witnesses to the appearances experienced was a vision or some special revelation from God. When we compare other passages in Paul that do not emphasize the physical nature of the appearances (Gal 1:15–17; 1 Cor 9:1; Phil 3:8; 2 Cor 4:6; 12:2–4), it is understandable that some interpreters might conclude that the earliest appearances were visionary in nature and that only after the Gospels began circulating did this notion change. This interpretation allows for the body of Jesus to have decomposed somewhere in Palestine (the absence of the body from the tomb is explained in natural terms—someone stole the body, the disciples went to the wrong tomb—or its emptiness is denied altogether) yet still maintains that the disciples experienced something—a vision from God—that initiated their Easter faith.

Since Paul says that he, like all the apostles, experienced an appearance of the risen Lord (1 Cor 9:1), some scholars have argued that 1 Cor 15:3–8, the earliest verses in the NT on the resurrection appearances, indicates that the nature of all of the appearances of Christ was visionary. They claim that in later-developing traditions such as the Gospels, the church, because of its apologetic needs, recast the resurrection appearances in a more concrete form, as in Luke and John. The verb ὤφθη and its various forms, however, are not so much technical terms as neutral terms simply denoting sight. The use of this aorist passive indicative of ὁράω (horaō, "see") in both Matt 17:3 and Luke 9:31 leaves open the question of the form of seeing. There is no single kind of use of ὤφθη in biblical or extrabiblical literature, and it appears that any arguments on the nature or form of the appearances are unwarranted if based on this term alone. Even Bultmann, who believed that the disciples experienced hallucinations or subjective visions, writes that "neither vision nor objective fact can be deduced from the 'was seen.'"[112] Michaelis's summary of his investigation of the various uses of ὤφθη, especially in 1 Cor 15, is worthy of note:

It thus seems that when ὤφθη is used as a t.t. [technical term] to denote the resurrection appearances there is no primary emphasis on seeing as sensual or mental perception. The dominant thought is that the appearances are revelations, encounters with the risen Lord who herein reveals Himself or is revealed, cf. Gal. 1:16. . . . The relation of ὤφθη in I Cor. 15:5ff. to the act of 9:1 does not involve a simple replacing of the act by the corresponding form. If so, the significance attached to seeing would be the same in both instances. The important point about ὤφθη with the dative, however, is that the one who constitutes the subject is the one who acts, i.e., appears, shows himself, with no special emphasis on the resultant action of the person in the dative, namely that he sees or perceives. ὤφθη Κηφᾷ ["he appeared to Cephas"] etc., does not mean in the first instance that they saw Him, with an emphasis on seeing, e.g., in contrast to hearing. It means rather: παρέστησεν αὐτοὶ ἑαυτὸν ζῶντα ["he himself stood among them living"] (cf. Acts 1:3), or even better: ὁ θεὸς ἀπεκάλυψεν αὐτὸν ἐν αὐτοῖς ["God revealed him among them"] (Gal. 1:16). He encountered them as risen, living Lord; they experienced His presence. In the last resort even active forms like ἑόρακα in I Cor. 9:1 mean the same thing.[113]

Lüdemann, while agreeing with the "objective vision" view of scholars on the visionary nature of the appearances, rejects their objective nature. He claims that Paul's own writings indicate that the resurrection appearances were visionary experiences rather than a real sighting of a risen Jesus (Gal 1:15–16; Phil 3:8; 2 Cor 4:6; 12:1–10). He bases this conclusion on his interpretation of the visionary type of experiences mentioned in Acts (9:1–19; 22:4–16; 26:9–18), as well as those of Paul.[114] Lüdemann says that these visions were subjectively induced because of Paul's guilt over persecuting the followers of Jesus and an "inner personal inability which depth psychology has established to be a frequent cause of aggressive behavior."[115] He concludes the same for Peter. Peter was guilt-laden because of his denial of Jesus but, under the impact of Jesus' preaching and death and through an appearance of the "Risen Christ," accepted God's forgiveness, which was already present in the earlier ministry and activity of Jesus (e.g., Mark 2:5). The other visions (e.g., 1 Cor 15:5–8) were also produced through mass psychosis or hysteria. As a result, God must no longer be considered the author of these visions; rather, "they were psychological processes which ran their course with a degree of regularity—complete without divine intervention."[116]

Much of the confusion on the nature of the resurrection appearances stems from the fact that Paul does not describe his encounter with the risen Lord in the traditional concrete terms found in the Gospels and does not mention the empty-tomb tradition. Luke describes Paul's encounter with the risen Christ as a "light from heaven" (φῶς ἐκ τοῦ οὐρανοῦ, phōs ek tou ouranou; Acts 9:3; 22:6; 26:13) accompanied by a "voice" (φωνή, phōnē; 9:4; 22:7; 26:14) intelligible only to Paul. In Acts 26:19 this encounter is described as a "heavenly appearing" (τῇ οὐρανίῳ ὀπτασίᾳ, tē ouraniō optasia). The ὀπτασία (optasia) here is not necessarily a vision, since Luke's normal word for "vision" is ὅπταμα (hoptama; see Acts 10:17) and the normal understanding of ὀπτασία is of a nonvisionary appearance.[117] There is no justification, then, for basing an understanding of visionary appearances solely on the use of ὤφθη. Nevertheless, if all we had was the testimony of Paul regarding his experience with the risen Lord (Gal 1:14) and the witness of Acts (9:3; 22:6; 26:13), we would be hard pressed to speak of more than a visionary encounter with the risen Lord.

What, therefore, can we conclude about the nature or form of the resurrection appearances for Paul? His argument in 1 Cor 15:42–54 indicates that in the resurrection of the body there is a transformed corporeality. Although the presence of Christ in the appearances seems nonvisionary in the Gospels, there are, as Michaelis contends, no adequate categories of human seeing to explain them. He concludes that the appearances should be described as "manifestations in the sense of revelation rather than making visible."[118] There is no evidence that Paul either rejected a bodily resurrection of Jesus or believed that the resurrected body was to be simply equated with the physical body of flesh. Paul believed, rather, that the Christian's resurrection would be like that of Jesus the Christ (Rom 8:9–11; Phil 3:21), and he argued that it would be a transformed bodily resurrection for the believer (1 Cor 15:52–54).

One of the main objections to the "objective vision" proposal is that this understanding of the resurrection appearances reduces the basis of Christian faith to the testimony of a few individuals who experienced little more than a vision. It is often said in response that such objections result from a failure to understand the nature of Christian faith, that is, that it involves risk and cannot seek refuge in the security of demonstrable facts. These objections come from those who, according to Lampe, seek guarantees for faith; God, on the other hand, "makes his activity known to faith, and faith is not compatible with unmistakable proofs."[119] Faith is indeed faith rather than sight, and Christian faith cannot advance beyond the faith of the earliest Christian disciples, nor can it verify the validity of the testimonies of those disciples through historical methodology. But is the only alternative the one that Lampe has suggested?

It is true that Paul's experience with the risen Lord seems to be best described by the word "vision," as is indeed the case in Acts 26:19. But were all the appearances like this? Because the same term, ὤφθη, is used for all of the appearances in 1 Cor 15:4–8, does it follow that anything more than Paul's claim to have encountered the same Lord was intended? Could the disciples have experienced the risen Lord through a bodily appearance while Paul experienced a visionary one? Could Paul's ref-

erence to being like one "untimely born" in 15:8 indicate some difference in his encounter with the risen Christ? This explanation is mere speculation, of course, and in the rush to dissociate Paul's experience from that of the other disciples, making their experience more concrete, it may fail to recognize the character of the appearances of Jesus to the disciples even in the Gospels. It is interesting to note in passing that Paul lists more appearances than do the evangelists (1 Cor 15:5–8).

A few observations need to be made for another kind of experience on the part of those who first saw the risen Lord. First of all, in the Gospels there is the peculiar problem that some of the disciples fail to recognize Jesus in his appearances to them. It is quite possible that the revelatory nature of the appearances is the reason that among the disciples "some doubted" after they saw the risen Lord (Matt 28:17), even though Matthew does not mention directly any difficulty in recognizing the Risen One as Jesus of Nazareth. In Luke's story (24:30–34) about the appearance of Jesus to the disciples on the road to Emmaus, Jesus was not recognized by two of his followers until he broke bread with them and departed. Only then did they know who he was. In the following appearance to the rest of the disciples, Jesus had to demonstrate to them that he was not a ghost or a spirit but a real being made up of flesh and bones and able to eat fish (vv. 37–43). In John 20:14–16, Mary did not at first recognize Jesus until he spoke her name. The Johannine "appendix" is quite similar here as well; it is only after a miracle is performed that the beloved disciple recognizes that the one standing on the beach is Jesus the risen Lord (21:4–7). Even John's story of Jesus' appearance to the disciples, without Thomas, suggests the need for Jesus to show some sign to prove that he was the same as the one who was crucified (20:20).

Fuller believes that the witnesses' difficulty in recognizing Jesus is a sign that his appearances were not "this-worldly occurrences" but were of a revelatory nature, perceived only by those whose eyes were open to such things.[120] This is often overlooked by those who search for physical manifestations of the risen Lord in the Gospels. It is true that Luke takes the time to describe Jesus' resurrection appearances in a more physical way (24:37–42), but his purpose for doing so is to dispel the notion that Jesus was merely a spirit (vv. 37,

39). Jesus' ability to disappear (v. 31) and then to reappear (v. 36) might lead some early Christians to conclude that only a spirit was in their midst, but Luke emphasizes that this was not so; Jesus' new mode of existence was bodily but not limited by the physical realm of this-worldly existence. John, who along with Luke describes the resurrection of Jesus in a very concrete fashion, also depicts the risen Jesus as having no physical limitations in his bodily existence. In John 20:19 the disciples are huddled together in a house where "the doors were locked," yet Jesus comes in and stands in their midst, evidently passing through the walls or doors. This seems especially clear in the appearance to Thomas eight days later: "Although the doors were shut, Jesus came and stood among them" (v. 26). Yet it is only in the Thomas story that an invitation is given by Jesus to touch his hands and side. Evidently the new mode of existence of the resurrected Lord was not simply spirit but a new mode of bodily existence that was not governed by the limitations of the physical body, even though it could be identified with it (vv. 20, 27). In Matt 28:2–6, the stone is rolled away by the angel of the Lord not to let Jesus out but to let the women in! Jesus was already out, evidently having come through the walls of the tomb. On the other hand, Matthew shows that the risen Lord can be touched as well as heard (vv. 9–10). But even then, after receiving an appearance from the risen Jesus, "some doubted" (v. 17).

The problems of doubt, and the difficulties in the initial recognition of Jesus in some of the narratives, may be due to the revelatory and unique nature of the appearances. The resurrection of Jesus was a bodily one, yet beyond the normal understanding of that term. Doubt that Jesus was raised from the dead (see esp. Matt 28:17; Luke 24:11, 38–42; John 20:24–29; Mark 16:12–14) is a common theme in the appearance narratives. In Matthew's story, those who doubted did so after the appearance of Jesus, while John 20:26–29 points to Jesus' rebuke of those who refused to believe the reports that he was indeed alive. In Matthew, the doubt is not rebuked but is evidently dismissed with Jesus' reference to his own authority. Perhaps, as Anderson suggests, the "doubt" mentioned in Matthew reflects the questionings of the later church "about a new Easter certainty and conviction."[121] It is likely that the other narratives that mention this

element of doubt do so with the subsequent, developing church in mind. Thomas is probably representative of the doubting element in the church (John 20:24–29). Perhaps some of the many differences in the resurrection appearances should be understood in this context. Each of the evangelists, in his own way, seeks to establish continuity between the crucified Jesus and the risen Lord. He who died is the same as he who has appeared to his followers—but doubt lingers in some, and this may well be due to the revelatory nature of the appearances.

Some scholars, especially Bultmann, have argued that Paul's failure to mention the empty tomb in 1 Cor 15:3–8 demonstrates his ignorance of it, and this has led them to emphasize the discontinuity between the Gospel narratives and Paul. The argument is that since 1 Corinthians was written first and does not have a reference to an empty-tomb tradition, the later Gospel narratives, which do have such a story, must have added something to the original story that was more relevant to the needs of a later generation of Christians. But even if the Gospels seem to indicate that the appearances of Jesus were physical in nature, or at least bodily (Luke 24:39; John 20:26), they also point to the revelatory nature of those appearances. In the Gospels, as well as in Paul, we can see that the appearances of Jesus were not just physical manifestations but were of a different order than has been generally understood. It may also be suggested that since this is not as clear in the Gospels as it appears in Paul, the Gospels should be understood in light of Paul's commentary in 1 Cor 15 on the nature of the resurrected body (vv. 35–55). There the exegete is more aware of a new mode of bodily existence in the resurrection than is apparent in the Gospels by themselves. But even without 1 Cor 15, a careful look at the Gospels demonstrates that far more than a mere physical resuscitation was involved in the resurrection of Jesus.

The ascension story in Luke says that the appearances of Jesus ceased after a period of time and that, whatever their nature, they were encountered by only a select few. In Acts 1:21–25, the basis for the selection of an apostolic replacement was in part his being a witness to the appearances of Jesus. Paul determines that these kinds of experiences concluded with his encounter with the risen Lord (1 Cor 15:8). What is common in all of these stories is that the apostles experienced something that transformed their lives but also ceased to occur after a relatively short period of time.

Paul reflects a spiritual or revelatory encounter with the risen Lord, but he also speaks of the bodily nature of the resurrection of Jesus (see Rom 8:9–11; Phil 3:21). We have seen the same in the Gospels. The nature of the resurrected body and therefore the nature of the manifestations to the disciples were spiritual-bodily (transformed-bodily) appearances, of whatever sort that may be. In Paul, the "old body" of flesh was transformed and incorporated into the new. How this was done, or what the results were for Jesus or for his future followers, remains a mystery. It is significant that all of the NT information surrounding the Easter event coincides with the view of a transformed-bodily resurrection appearance. The empty tomb supports the conclusion that the resurrection was bodily, and the various reports of Jesus' going through doors or suddenly appearing and vanishing support the contention that the appearances were significantly more than mere physical manifestations. The reports on the locations of the resurrection appearances might also support this thesis. There were no contemporary parallels to this kind of a manifestation, nor indeed are there any today. The resurrection appearances of Jesus were unique and revelatory and are recorded as such in the NT. Transformed-bodily resurrection appearances appear to answer the questions about the nature of the event itself and may be the key to understanding their various locations (Jerusalem, Galilee, Damascus road). The appearances were not a product of the disciples' faith but, rather, of the activity of God; this best accounts for the many differences in the Easter traditions regarding the nature of Jesus' resurrection from the grave.

Despite Lüdemann's challenges,[122] it is generally agreed that a Christian confesses faith in the risen Christ, and one of the oldest confessions of faith in the NT, Rom 10:9, supports this claim. That confession may be stated more precisely by saying that a Christian confesses that Jesus of Nazareth, who is the Christ of faith, actually rose from the dead. The physiological, spiritual, or psychological nature of that event, however, is no clearer to the person of Christian faith than it is to the critical historian, since it now lies beyond the experience, knowledge, and scope of inquiry of each. The historian may claim that something happened, and the Christian may claim to know what that something was (a resurrection from the dead), but how it happened escapes both. Whatever a transformed-bodily resurrection is cannot be known, since it was a unique event of history and is without parallel in human experience. In the NT, this is a revelatory event without parallel, and though it is possible to speak of a transformed corporeality with regard to the resurrection of Jesus, it is by no means clear what exactly is meant by it. There are no adequate human expressions available for a description of this event, though for the Christian that inexperience of the "beyond" is only temporary (Rom 8:11; Phil 3:21).

F. A Summary of the Events of Easter

From our discussion of the Easter traditions, the following conclusions may be suggested. The evangelists are agreed that after Jesus was crucified, he was buried by Joseph of Arimathea in a tomb near the city of Jerusalem on the day of preparation (Friday) as the Sabbath was approaching. When the Sabbath was over, a group of women from Galilee (or perhaps just Mary) came to the tomb where Jesus was buried to pay final respects to their departed Lord. Upon reaching the tomb, however, it was found to be empty; this was reported by the women, perhaps with an assurance of the empty tomb's significance, to the disciples who were still in Jerusalem, possibly in hiding. Some of the disciples, or perhaps just Peter, examined the tomb after hearing the report and confirmed that the tomb was in fact empty. This caused questioning among the disciples, but as yet their faith was still uncertain, and so they returned to Galilee. It is not clear how soon after the discovery of the empty tomb they returned, but in Galilee Jesus appeared to the disciples, reestablishing their faith and giving them their call to missionary service. If there were no appearances in Galilee, it is difficult to understand why the disciples ever came back to Jerusalem, unless with Moule one is prepared to say that their return was due to the next pilgrim feast.[123] Regardless, it is likely that they returned to Jerusalem after experiencing in Galilee an appearance from the risen Jesus. Jesus' final appearance(s) to the disciples may have been in Jerusalem or just outside Jerusalem, but this is not certain. If the location of the appearances is not clear in the Easter narratives, the fact that Jesus was raised from the dead and appeared to the disciples is. Belief in Jesus' resurrection from the dead and the conviction that he had indeed appeared to the disciples after his resurrection became the primary thrust of the earliest Christian preaching.

There is no doubt about the earliest Christians' belief in the resurrection of Jesus, but the nature of his resurrection is still not clear. It is true that the empty tomb pointed to the mode of his resurrection, that it was bodily but not with the physical limitations characteristic of human beings. It is not yet possible to be dogmatic on the nature of the resurrection appearances. In the Gospels, the resurrected Jesus is seen walking through closed doors and appearing and disappearing at will, leaving an element of doubt in the ability of the disciples to recognize him. This, along with the manner in which the Acts describes Paul's encounter with the risen Lord on the Damascus road, as well as the language that Paul himself uses to describe that experience (1 Cor 15:5–8; Gal 1:15–16), suggests that the appearances were more than simple physical manifestations yet also more than mere visionary experiences. The multiplicity of these experiences in the NT indicates that there is much more to them than mere subjective experiences, mass hysteria or hallucinations. For these reasons, we conclude that the appearances of Jesus were "revelatory" or "revelational" and that thereby they retain something of the unique and mysterious character that surrounds them in the NT narratives.

G. Concluding Comments on the Easter Narratives

Although Luke records no appearance of Jesus to the women as do Matthew (28:9–10) and John (20:11–18), it is difficult to see what is disclosed in Matthew's and John's narration of such an appearance that is not discernible in Luke's story of the two angels at the tomb. Matthew's account of the appearance of Jesus to the women adds little to the story already told by the angel (28:5–7), unless its purpose is to indicate to the women that, in their ability to touch Jesus' feet, they were encountering a "real" person.[124] This point is also clear, however, in the angelic message, and it is difficult to see why Matthew adds this appearance unless there

was a strong tradition circulating in his region that Jesus had appeared to the women in Jerusalem. The similar passage in John where Jesus appears to Mary also seems to be a very early tradition. John completely negates the message of the angels to Mary in favor of having the disclosure of the meaning of the empty tomb come from the risen Lord himself.

Matthew and John agree that Jesus appeared to the women (or woman) at the tomb and even that they touched Jesus (Matt 28:9) or Mary attempted to do so (or did? cf. John 20:17). The basic difference is John's use of the tradition to illustrate a theological truth, the exaltation of Jesus in his resurrection from the dead. Nevertheless, Matthew's reference to the women worshipping the risen Christ (28:9) may not be far from John's focus. Could this be the same reason behind John's story of the grave clothes (20:3–10; cf. Luke 24:12)? In all four Gospels there are also references to an appearance of Jesus to the disciples, or at least the promise of an appearance to them (Mark 16:7), so there is little doubt that all of the evangelists accepted this tradition as true.

Dodd finds that the typical appearance pattern (see beginning of sec. 5, above) in John's and Luke's narratives probably suggests some mutual dependence upon a common tradition rather than upon each other.[125] He distinguishes this tradition from folklore and believes that the story shows itself to be original and "has something indefinably first hand about it," which he says is a "reflective, subtle, most delicate approach to the depths of human experience."[126]

An issue that is worthy of comment here is the Gospel references to the resurrection of Jesus as a fulfillment of Scripture, such as in Luke's and John's resurrection narratives (e.g., Luke 24:27, 46ff.; Acts 2:25–36; 13:32–37; John 20:9) and in the resurrection tradition in 1 Cor 15:3–4. Part of the difficulty here is determining which Scriptures each writer had in mind. The evangelists likely had in mind the texts most commonly used in the earliest Christian preaching. These include Deut 18:15 (the prophet like unto Moses), Psalms 22 and 69 (the Passion Psalms), Psalm 110 (the exaltation of Christ to the right hand of God), and Isa 42 and 53 (Jesus as the Servant of God).[127] These passages do not indicate that the early church expected the resurrection of Jesus because of its interpretation of the Scriptures. Rather, the resurrection of Jesus took them by surprise. The early Christians were concerned, Leaney concludes, "to find some scripture to fit a fact, and were far from inventing a fact to fit a scripture."[128] There is little doubt that Jesus powerfully influenced the early Christians' understanding of the Scriptures. The importance of the Scriptures in the thinking of all Jews probably encouraged the early Christians to establish the resurrection of Jesus securely in their Scriptures; conversely, the significance of the resurrection of Jesus for the early church drove it to the Jewish Scriptures to justify its claim that the risen Christ was the agent of God's redemption.

That Luke, John, and Paul appealed to Scripture, which they argued foretold the resurrection of Jesus, is more correctly seen as an indication that the early Christians' understanding of the Scriptures was radically altered by their encounter with the risen Christ. This apologetic use of Scripture existed well before Paul referred to it in 1 Cor 15:3–5.[129] Nevertheless, it was difficult for the church to find scriptural support for its understanding of the resurrection of Jesus, since, as C. F. Evans writes, "resurrection is certainly not something which could have been arrived at by reflection on the OT."[130] So vague are the references to resurrection in the OT that, apart from the resurrection of Jesus actually taking place, it is difficult to account for the centrality of the resurrection in the thinking of the early church. The early church's attempts to establish the resurrection of Jesus in its Scriptures point to the great significance that the event had in its community but also to the difficulty of locating the origins of resurrection faith in anything other than the Easter event itself. Apart from Christians' strong belief that Jesus had in fact been raised from the dead, there appears to be no good reason for such attempts to use the Scriptures in this matter, not even the significant role that they played in the early development of the church.

Finally, we have not discussed any of the so-called transposed resurrection narratives. It has long been supposed by some interpreters that the Gospel reports of Jesus' remarkable activity during his earthly ministry are nothing more than transposed resurrection stories. These passages include: (1) the miraculous draft of fishes (Luke 5:1–11), (2) the stilling of the storm (Mark 4:35–41), (3) the walking on the water (Mark 6:45–52), (4) the feeding of the multitude (Mark 6:32–44; 8:1–10), (5) the transfiguration (Mark 9:2–8), and (6) the "you are Peter" saying (Matt 16:17–19). The arguments for calling such passages resurrection encounters with the risen Jesus are not convincing, however. Not only do these supposed appearance stories fail to conform to the usual appearance pattern mentioned above, the motives of the evangelists in doing so are unclear. What different purpose would they serve by being transposed, as opposed to being where they are? The arguments of those who continue to make these assertions are unconvincing, and so we have omitted any significant discussion of them. Long ago Dodd effectively answered the arguments for such conclusions.[131]

6. CONCLUSION

While it is not possible to treat equally all of the many issues related to the resurrection of Jesus, we have given considerable attention to some of the most important. For those interested in pursuing further the study of the resurrection of Jesus, we offer these suggestions.

It is important to be mindful that the evangelists' theologies had a significant role in their selection and shaping of their Easter proclamations, just as their theologies shaped the rest of their Gospels. An examination of the phenomena occurring at the death and resurrection of Jesus—for example, earthquakes, the tearing of the temple curtain, bodies going through the streets of Jerusalem, confessions of faith, darkness over the land, the length of the appearances of Jesus after his resurrection, the ascension story in Luke and John—leads one to raise the question of the evangelists' intentions, and whether and to what extent those intentions helped shape the traditions that they received. In any study of the Gospels, just as it is important not to overtranslate the text and import foreign theology into the text, it is equally important to avoid undertranslation or saying less than the evangelists intended to say. Although many Christians can live with literal interpretations of the various phenomena that occurred at the death and resurrection of Jesus, it is obvious that the evangelists intended to say much more than what such literal interpretations are capable of saying. The evangelists all intended to say not only that Jesus of Nazareth who died is now alive but also that this fact has the greatest of significance for those who believe in him.

On the other hand, we also need to be cautious of a reductionist interpretation of the narratives. The resurrection narratives cannot be reduced to a new understanding of human existence, as some scholars have argued (Bultmann, Marxsen, C. F. Evans), or traced back to some psychological guilt in Peter and Paul (Lüdemann). The narratives are especially about the fate of the crucified Jesus, that he who died is now alive and that the mode of his existence is a bodily one, however we might interpret that.

In discussing the resurrection of Jesus, we are dealing with a sphere of knowing and understanding that moves beyond the historical, and this complicates our understanding of the ancient sources even more. As Johnson says, "Some sort of powerful transformative experience is required to generate the sort of movement earliest Christianity was, and to necessitate the sort of literature the NT is."[132] It was infinitely more than just a lightbulb going on in someone's head. It occurred in time and space, but also in a realm totally unfamiliar to traditional historical inquiry.

Finally, we offer a word of caution to those who seek to harmonize the resurrection narratives. There is a tendency in such reconstructions to minimize important distinctions in the narratives and to blur the theological motifs that guided each evangelist in producing his Gospel. Throughout its history, the church has seen the wisdom of maintaining the integrity of each evangelist's message and avoided the temptation to adopt a single harmonized Gospel such as the *Diatessaron* produced by Tatian (ca. A.D. 170).[133] Apart from the difficulty, if not impossibility, of harmonizing the Easter narratives, most such attempts have been based on hypotheses that have little historical, rational, or narrative support. It is better to look at the differences in terms of each evangelist's purpose and to allow each narrative to stand by itself except when there are obvious parallels that show dependence on another canonical source or an independent prior source.

BIBLIOGRAPHY

ANDERSON, H. *Jesus.* Englewood Cliffs, N.J.: Prentice-Hall, 1967.

_____. *Jesus and Christian Origins.* New York: Oxford University Press, 1964.

ANDERSON, H., and W. BARCLAY, eds. *The New Testament in Historical and Contemporary Perspective.* Oxford: Oxford University Press, 1965.

BARTSCH, H.-W., ed. *Kerygma and Myth.* Trans. R. FULLER. 2 vols. New York: Harper & Row, 1961.

BOCKMUEHL, M. *This Jesus: Martyr, Lord, Messiah.* Edinburgh: T. & T. Clark, 1994.

BODE, E. L. *The First Easter Morning: The Gospel Accounts of the Women's Visit to the Tomb of Jesus.* Rome: Biblical Institute Press, 1970.

BORNKAMM, G. *Jesus of Nazareth.* Trans. I. and F. MCLUSKY with J. M. ROBINSON. New York: Harper, 1960.

BROWN, R. E. *The Virginal Conception and Bodily Resurrection of Jesus.* New York: Paulist, 1973.

BULTMANN, R. *Faith and Understanding.* Ed. R. W. FUNK. Trans. L. P. SMITH. London: SCM, 1966.

DAVIS, S. T. *Risen Indeed: Making Sense of the Resurrection.* Grand Rapids: Eerdmans, 1993.

_____. "Was Jesus Raised Bodily?" *CSR* 14 (1985): 140–52.

DILLON, R. J. *From Eye-Witnesses to Ministers of the Word: Tradition and Composition in Luke 24.* AnBib 82. Chicago: Loyola University Press, 1978.

DODD, C. H. *More New Testament Studies.* Grand Rapids: Eerdmans, 1968.

DUNN, J. D. G. *The Evidence for Jesus.* Louisville: Westminster John Knox, 1985.

EVANS, C. A. "Mark's Use of the Empty Tomb Tradition." *Studia biblica et theologica* 8 (2, 1978): 50–55.

EVANS, C. F. "I Will Go before You into Galilee." *JTS* NS 5 (1954): 3–18.

_____. *Resurrection in the New Testament.* London: SCM, 1970.

FULLER, D. P. *Easter Faith and History.* London: Tyndale, 1968.

FULLER, R. H. *Formation of the Resurrection Narratives.* London: SPCK, 1972.

GALVIN, J. P. "The Origin of Faith in the Resurrection of Jesus: Two Recent Perspectives." *TS* 49 (1988): 25–44.

GOERGEN, D. J. *The Death and Resurrection of Jesus.* Wilmington, Del.: Michael Glazier, 1988.

GRASS, H. *Ostergeschehen und Osterberichte.* Göttingen: Vandenhoeck & Ruprecht, 1962.

HEBERT, G. "The Resurrection-Narrative in St. Mark's Gospel." *SJT* 15 (1962): 66–73.

HENAULT, B. W. "Empty Tomb or Empty Argument: A Failure of Nerve in Recent Studies of Mark 16?" *SR* 15 (1986): 177–90.

JANSEN, J. F. *The Resurrection of Jesus Christ in New Testament Theology.* Philadelphia: Westminster, 1980.

JOHNSON, L. T. *The Real Jesus: The Misguided Quest for the Historical Jesus and the Truth of the Traditional Gospels.* San Francisco: HarperSanFrancisco, 1996.

KÜNNETH, W. *The Theology of the Resurrection.* London: SCM, 1965.

LADD, G. E. *I Believe in the Resurrection of Jesus.* Grand Rapids: Eerdmans, 1975.

LAMPE, G. W. H., and D. M. MacKINNON. *The Resurrection.* London: Mowbray, 1966.

LILLY, J. L. "Alleged Discrepancies in the Gospel Accounts of the Resurrection." *CBQ* 2 (1940): 99–111.

LORENZEN, T. *Resurrection and Discipleship: Interpretive Models, Biblical Reflections, Theological Consequences.* Maryknoll, N.Y.: Orbis, 1995.

LÜDEMANN, G. *The Resurrection of Jesus: History, Experience, Theology.* Trans. J. BOWDEN. Minneapolis: Fortress, 1994.

_____. *What Really Happened to Jesus? A Historical Approach to the Resurrection.* Trans. J. Bowden. Louisville: Westminster John Knox, 1995.

McDonald, J. I. H. *The Resurrection: Narrative and Belief.* London: SPCK, 1989.

MARXSEN, W. *Jesus and the Church.* Trans. P. E. Devenish. Valley Forge, Penn.: Trinity Press International, 1992.

_____. *Jesus and Easter: Did God Raise the Historical Jesus from the Dead?* Trans. V. P. FURNISH. Nashville: Abingdon, 1990.

_____. *The Resurrection of Jesus of Nazareth.* Trans. M. KOHL. London: SCM, 1970.

MOULE, C. F. D. "The Post-Resurrection Appearances in the Light of Festival Pilgrimages." *NTS* 4 (1957): 58–61.

_____, ed. *The Significance of the Message of the Resurrection for Faith in Jesus Christ.* London, SCM, 1968.

NEYREY, J. *The Resurrection Stories.* Wilmington, Del.: Michael Glazier, 1988.

NINEHAM, D. E., ed. *Studies in the Gospels.* Oxford: Blackwell, 1957.

O'COLLINS, G. *The Easter Jesus.* London: Darton, Longman, & Todd, 1973.

_____. *What Are They Saying about the Resurrection?* New York: Paulist, 1978.

OSBORNE, G. F. *The Resurrection Narratives: A Redactional Study.* Grand Rapids: Baker, 1984.

PANNENBERG, W. *Jesus—God and Man.* Trans. L. L. WILKINS and D. A. PRIEBE. London: SCM, 1970.

PERKINS, P. *Resurrection: New Testament Witness and Contemporary Reflection.* Garden City, N.Y.: Doubleday, 1984.

PERRIN, N. *The Resurrection according to Matthew, Mark, Luke, and John.* Philadelphia: Fortress, 1977.

PERRY, M. C., ed. *Historicity and Chronology in the New Testament.* 6 vols. London: SPCK, 1965.

RAMSEY, A. M. *The Resurrection of Christ.* London: Collins-Fontana, 1966.

REISER, W. E. "The Case of the Tidy Tomb." *HeyJ* 14 (1973): 47–57.

RILEY, G. J. *Resurrection Reconsidered: Thomas and John in Controversy.* Minneapolis: Fortress, 1995.

ROBINSON, J. M. "Jesus: From Easter to Valentinus (or to the Apostles' Creed)." *JBL* 101 (1982): 5–37.

SAWICKI, M. *Seeing the Lord: Resurrection and Early Christian Practices.* Minneapolis: Fortress, 1994.

SCHWEIZER, E. *Jesus.* Trans. D. E. GREEN. London: SCM, 1968.

STANLEY, D. M. *Christ's Resurrection in Pauline Soteriology.* Rev. ed. AnBib 13. Chicago: Loyola University Press, 1976.

STEMBERGER, G. *Der Leib der Auferstehung: Studien zur Anthropologie und Eschatologie des palästinischen Judentums im neuestestamentlichen Zeitalter.* Rome: Biblical Institute Press, 1972.

VAN DAALEN, D. H. *The Real Resurrection.* London: Collins, 1972.

WEDDERBURN, A. J. M. *Baptism and Resurrection: Studies in Pauline Theology against Its Greco-Roman Background.* WUNT 44. Tübingen: Mohr–Siebeck, 1987.

WILCKENS, U. *Resurrection: Biblical Testimony to the Resurrection: An Historical Examination and Explanation.* Trans. A. M. STEWART. Atlanta: John Knox, 1978.

WILLIAMS, R. *Resurrection: Interpreting the Easter Gospel.* Harrisburg, Penn.: Morehouse, 1982.

pages 179–181

1. G. W. E. Nickelsburg, "Resurrection (Early Judaism and Christianity)," *ABD* 5:685–91; here 685.
2. Trans. E. Isaac, in *OTP* 1:26.
3. Trans. H. A. Anderson, ibid., 2:562, 564.
4. Nickelsburg, "Resurrection," 5:686–88.
5. J. I. H. McDonald, *The Resurrection: Narrative and Belief* (London: SPCK, 1989), 5–24.
6. Ibid., 16.
7. See D. J. Goergen, *The Death and Resurrection of Jesus* (Wilmington, Del.: Michael Glazier, 1988), 78–79.
8. Trans. H. Danby, *The Mishnah* (Oxford: Oxford University Press, 1980), 397.
9. For further examples, see Goergen, *Death and Resurrection of Jesus,* 71–85.
10. R. Bultmann, "New Testament and Mythology," in *Kerygma and Myth* (ed. H.-W. Bartsch; trans. R. H. Fuller; 2 vols.; New York: Harper & Row, 1961), 1:38.
11. Throughout this discussion the terms "discrepancy," "contradiction," "difference," and the like will be used to describe textual differences that resist harmonization. It is always a possibility, however, that the somewhat fragmentary nature of the sources available leaves us without all the facts on which to decide such matters, so the word "apparent" should be understood. The theologian must walk a delicate line between questioning the Scriptures and allowing himself or herself to be questioned by them. Where there could be a reasonable explanation of basic differences in the Gospels, we will generally favor such an explanation. When harmonizations are possible and do not stretch one's credulity to suggest them, then that will be our practice. Good biblical scholarship is not necessarily a negative attitude toward the biblical tradition, and there is always the possibility that certain "assured" results of critical investigation will be changed or discarded in light of subsequent research. On the other hand, simplistic explanations for complex issues are often merely attempts to justify one's prejudices about the matter. We also disapprove of this practice.
12. In an enlargement of Matthew's account, the author of this apocryphal gospel has the resurrection of Jesus take place in front of the guard at the tomb and the Jewish authorities. The author lays blame for the crucifixion at the feet of the Jews and abandons the eschatological focus of the Synoptic Gospels. This suggests a second-century dating of the gospel, as the flavor of the writing is close to, but not exactly parallel with, the gnostic teaching of the second century. For a description and translation of this gospel, see C. Maurer and W. Schneemelcher, "The Gospel of Peter," in *New Testament Apocrypha* (ed. W. Schneemelcher; trans. R. McL. Wilson; 2 vols.; Louisville: Westminster John Knox, 1991), 1:216–27.
13. Except in Mark 16:9–20, which is a later addition to the Gospel, Mark does not record postresurrection appearances, but it is also unlikely that the original ending of Mark's Gospel was at 16:8. As noted in ch. 8, below, on the Gospels, it is more likely that the original ending and the original introduction of Mark were lost or that Mark, because of unknown circumstances, was unable to finish it.
14. G. Lüdemann, *What Really Happened to Jesus? A Historical Approach to the Resurrection* (trans. J. Bowden; Louisville: Westminster John Knox, 1995), 134.

15. Although scholars vary on the date of the writing of Luke–Acts, we believe that the sources that Luke used to write the book of Acts reflect the nature and substance of early Christian preaching. See ch. 8, below, on Luke–Acts.

16. J. D. G. Dunn (*The Evidence for Jesus* [Philadelphia: Westminster, 1985], 77–78) has discussed the weakness of the view that the empty-tomb tradition was added by the church to deal with the gnosticizing or docetic tendencies at the end of the first century.

17. X. Léon-Dufour (*The Gospels and the Jesus of History* [ed. and trans. J. McHugh; London: Collins, 1968], 254) makes this observation. It is borne out in the writings of conservative scholars such as C. Pinnock, "On the Third Day," in *Jesus of Nazareth: Saviour and Lord* (ed. C. F. H. Henry; London: Tyndale, 1966), 147–55; "Defense of the Resurrection," *Christianity Today* 9 (1965): 6–8; but also in scholars such as R. Bultmann, *Theology of the New Testament* (trans. K. Grobel; 2 vols.; New York: Scribners, 1951–1955), 1:45.

18. J. L. Lilly, "Alleged Discrepancies in the Gospel Accounts of the Resurrection," *CBQ* 2 (1940): 99–111.

19. The tenses in Greek are not to be equated with temporal values—context must be considered in each instance, since temporal values that hold elsewhere may not be transferable. See ch. 11, below.

20. J. Jeremias, *New Testament Theology* (trans. J. Bowden; London: SCM, 1971), 17–18. For other references in Mark, cf. 1:32, 35; 4:35; 10:30; 13:24; 14:12; etc.

21. G. Hebert, "The Resurrection-Narrative in St. Mark's Gospel," *SJT* 15 (1962): 66ff.

22. R. E. Brown, *The Gospel of John*, vol. 2 (AB 29A; Garden City, N.Y.: Doubleday, 1970), 981.

23. Lilly, "Alleged Discrepancies," 105.

24. Jeremias, *Theology*, 304–5 n. 9. C. K. Barrett (*The Gospel according to St. John* [2d ed.; Philadelphia: Westminster, 1978], 563) also believes the οἴδαμεν is an example of the synoptic influence upon John, but is careful to mention that the word itself does not stem from that tradition. He admits, however, that no such report of the "stolen" body exists in the synoptic tradition.

25. R. Bultmann, *The Gospel of John* (ed. G. R. Beasley-Murray; trans. G. R. Beasley-Murray, R. W. N. Hoare, and J. K. Riches; Philadelphia: Westminster, 1971), 684.

26. Brown, *Gospel of John*, 2:984.

27. E. Schweizer, *Jesus* (trans. D. E. Green; London: SCM, 1968), 48.

28. E. L. Bode (*The First Easter Morning: The Gospel Accounts of the Women's Visit to the Tomb of Jesus* [Rome: Biblical Institute Press, 1970], 169; cf. 168–70) argues that the development of the tradition of the angelic appearance at the tomb came about because Jewish polemic against the resurrection of Jesus needed more support than the testimony of some women. He concludes that the angelic appearances are separate from, and secondary to, the historical nucleus of the empty-tomb narrative.

29. R. Bultmann, *The History of the Synoptic Tradition* (trans. J. Marsh; rev. ed.; 1963; repr., Peabody, Mass.: Hendrickson, 1993), 285. Jeremias (*Theology*, 304) agrees with Bultmann at this point. G. O'Collins (*The Easter Jesus* [London: Darton, Longman, & Todd, 1973], 21) also believes that the repetition of the names is a clear indication of an editorial hand involved in Mark 16:1–8 in an effort to link the passion and burial of Jesus to the resurrection narratives; he also sees Mark 16:7 as another attempt to do the same thing; see p. 40 for

pages 182–186

those elements in 16:1–8 that he believes are late additions to the passage.

30. Bultmann, *Synoptic Tradition,* 285.
31. C. F. Evans, *Resurrection and the New Testament* (London: SCM, 1970), 82.
32. Jeremias, *Theology,* 310.
33. Bultmann, *Gospel of John,* 681–84.
34. Brown, *Gospel of John,* 2:995.
35. Greek νεανίσκος, *neaniskos* (lit., "a young man") is used here, but the description of him leaves little doubt that an angelic figure was intended. He is wearing a white robe, the dress used elsewhere to refer to the glory of the wearer. Cf. Mark 9:3; Luke 9:29; 24:4; John 20:12; Acts 1:10. In Rev 3:18; 4:4; 6:11; 7:9, 14; and esp. 19:8, 14, white clothing refers to various inhabitants of heaven. Since angelic apparel is spoken of as white robes elsewhere in the NT—the two men of Luke 24:4 in dazzling apparel are understood to be angels in 24:23—Mark probably understood the young man dressed in a white robe (16:5) to be an angel. And it would be difficult to explain why the women were amazed (v. 5b) if the young man were in fact only a young man.
36. D. H. van Daalen, *The Real Resurrection* (London: Collins, 1972), 22.
37. W. Lillie, "The Empty Tomb and the Resurrection," in *Historicity and Chronology in the New Testament* (ed. M. C. Perry; 6 vols.; London: SPCK, 1965), 6:106–8.
38. See ch. 8, sec. 3.F, below, for a discussion of the ending of Mark's Gospel.
39. Bultmann, *Gospel of John,* 684.
40. Note that Luke 24:12 is well attested in the manuscript evidence, although it is classified as a so-called Western noninterpolation, that is, an instance where the Western manuscript tradition has not expanded a reading. See ch. 12, below.
41. Brown, *Gospel of John,* 2:1004–7. See also O. Cullmann, *Salvation in History* (trans. S. G. Stowers; London: SCM, 1967), 273.
42. W. E. Reiser, "The Case of the Tidy Tomb," *HeyJ* 14 (1973): 51.
43. Fuller, *Formation,* 73.
44. Evans, *Resurrection,* 85–86.
45. W. Marxsen, *The Resurrection of Jesus of Nazareth* (trans. M. Kohl; London: SCM, 1970), 46.
46. Dunn, *Evidence for Jesus,* 63–66.
47. Bode, *Easter Morning,* 166–70; quotation, p. 178.
48. Ibid., 178, 182.
49. U. Wilckens, "The Tradition-History of the Resurrection of Jesus," in *The Significance of the Message of the Resurrection for Faith in Jesus Christ* (ed. C. F. D. Moule; trans. D. M. Barton and R. A. Wilson; London: SCM, 1968), 74.
50. Lüdemann, *What Really Happened to Jesus?* 79–80.
51. Ibid., 134–35 (italics his).
52. See instead G. Delling, "The Significance of the Resurrection of Jesus for Faith in Jesus Christ," in *Significance of the Message of the Resurrection* (ed. Moule), 81–82, who believes that Paul probably was aware of the empty-tomb tradition as well as the corporeality of the resurrection of Jesus. Note the arguments on pp. 83–88.
53. See Dunn's arguments against this view in *Evidence for Jesus,* 77–78. See also ch. 8, below, on the origins of Mark's Gospel.
54. G. Lüdemann, *The Resurrection of Jesus: History, Experience, Theology* (Minneapolis: Fortress, 1994), 46.

pages 186–194

55. Mark 16:7 is a command for the women to tell the disciples about the resurrection of Jesus, even though the present ending of the Gospel does not indicate that they complied with the angelic command. It should be noted that this command, found in all four Gospels, would be superfluous if the disciples had already fled or departed Jerusalem. The fourfold testimony to tell the disciples implies, at the least, their presence in Jerusalem at the time of the discovery of the tomb.

56. Dunn, *Evidence for Jesus,* 63–66.

57. McDonald, *The Resurrection,* 5–16, 140–41; quotation, p. 141.

58. Ibid., 143 n. 2. See also J. C. O'Neill, "On the Resurrection as a Historical Question," in *Christ, Faith, and History* (ed. S. Sykes and J. P. Clayton; London: Cambridge University Press, 1972), 205–19.

59. S. T. Davis, *Risen Indeed: Making Sense of the Resurrection* (Grand Rapids: Eerdmans, 1993), 61.

60. Ibid. (italics his).

61. Ibid., 71.

62. T. Lorenzen, *Resurrection and Discipleship: Interpretive Models, Biblical Reflections, Theological Consequences* (Maryknoll, N.Y.: Orbis, 1995), 167–68, 171–73, 180–87.

63. C. H. Dodd, *The Founder of Christianity* (London: Collins, 1971), 165.

64. Cf. J. F. Jansen, *The Resurrection of Jesus Christ in New Testament Theology* (Philadelphia: Westminster, 1980), 43–44. See also his balanced discussion of the historicity of the Easter proclamation on pp. 31–75. For a careful interpretation of the resurrection narratives, along with their theological significance for early Christianity, see J. Neyrey, *The Resurrection Stories* (Wilmington, Del.: Michael Glazier, 1988).

65. Dunn, *Evidence for Jesus,* 68.

66. L. T. Johnson, *The Real Jesus: The Misguided Quest for the Historical Jesus and the Truth of the Traditional Gospels* (San Francisco: HarperSanFrancisco, 1996), 135–36.

67. C. H. Dodd, "Appearances of the Risen Christ: An Essay in Form-Criticism of the Gospels," in *Studies in the Gospels* (ed. D. E. Nineham; Oxford: Blackwell, 1957), 9–35.

68. Bultmann, *Synoptic Tradition,* 285–86.

69. E. Lohmeyer, *Galiläe und Jerusalem* (Göttingen: Vandenhoeck & Ruprecht, 1956), 34–42. See also H. A. Anderson, *Jesus and Christian Origins* (New York: Oxford University Press, 1964), 197–98.

70. O'Collins, *Easter Jesus,* 36.

71. Bultmann, *Synoptic Tradition,* 285–86.

72. O'Collins, *Easter Jesus,* 37.

73. W. Marxsen, *Mark the Evangelist* (Nashville: Abingdon, 1969), 83–92; see also *Resurrection of Jesus,* 141ff., 163–64.

74. Fuller, *Formation,* 63.

75. Moule, *Significance of the Message of the Resurrection,* 4–6.

76. Ibid., 5. See also C. F. D. Moule, "The Post-Resurrection Appearances in the Light of Festival Pilgrimages," *NTS* 4 (1957): 58ff.

77. Lilly, "Alleged Discrepancies," 103–4.

78. C. F. Evans, "I Will Go before You into Galilee," *JTS* NS 5 (1954): 3–18.

79. Marxsen, *Resurrection of Jesus,* 78.

80. W. Pannenberg, *Jesus—God and Man* (trans. L. L. Wiliness and D. A. Priebe; London: SCM, 1970), 104–5.

81. Ibid., 45.

82. H. von Campenhausen, *Tradition and Life in the Church* (trans. A. V. Littledale; London: Collins, 1968), 47–48. It may be that John's longer tenure of Jesus' ministry (some three years), which also includes sev-

pages 194–202

eral visits to Jerusalem, is more accurate than the synoptic accounts, which report only on Jesus' Galilean ministry for about a year.

83. See E. P. Sanders, *Jesus and Judaism* (Philadelphia: Fortress, 1985), 198 and n. 90.

84. Von Campenhausen (*Tradition and Life*, 75) presents a number of arguments for this.

85. Ibid., 85.

86. Evans, *Resurrection*, 123–24, 119, 140. Cf. Brown, *Gospel of John*, 2:992.

87. A. M. Ramsey, "What Was the Ascension?" in *Historicity and Chronology in the New Testament*, 139, 144.

88. Paul, for example, assumes that the glorification of Jesus took place in his resurrection, without any separate event such as the ascension (see Rom 1:4; Phil 2:9–11), and this understanding is paralleled in Peter's speech in Acts 2:36.

89. Dodd, "Appearances of the Risen Christ," 18–20. See also H. Anderson, "The Easter Witness of the Evangelists," in *The New Testament in Historical and Contemporary Perspective* (ed. H. Anderson and W. Barclay; Oxford: Oxford University Press, 1965), 52, who argues that Jesus became touchable only after completing his high-priestly sacrifice and his intercession for the people in the "holy of holies." Fuller, *The Formation of the Resurrection Narratives*, 138–39, also notes this interpretation.

pages 202–207

90. See S. E. Porter, *Verbal Aspect in the Greek of the New Testament, with Reference to Tense and Mood* (SBG 1; New York: Lang, 1989), 356.

91. See Fuller, *Formation*, 138. He also raises the question whether the first "father" (πατέρα, *patera*) of this passage should be followed by "my" (μου, *mou*), saying that there is also fairly good evidence for it to be excluded. Whether this element of doubt suggests other weaknesses in the originality of the passage is questionable, but it remains a point for consideration.

92. John reports this as a prophecy; that is, Caiaphas the high priest tells the people what the will of God is regarding the death of Jesus!

93. It is difficult to follow Lüdemann (*Resurrection of Jesus*, 180–82), who argues that everything that was finally proclaimed after Easter in the church was already contained in the sayings and history of Jesus. He, like Bultmann before him, finds the basis for the proclamation of the early church in a new understanding of the cross of Jesus. For him the decision of faith is focused on the historical person (Jesus), not on the risen Christ (see sec. E, below). He rejects the notion that the figure of the historical Jesus had to be "raised to that of the mythical Christ . . . in order to have the well-known great effect" (p. 252 n. 702). This goes against what the NT teaches. There is no theology of the cross in the NT that overcomes the scandal of the cross without the resurrection of Jesus from the dead.

94. O'Collins (*Easter Jesus*, 52) believes that John is best understood when the exaltation implied by Jesus being put on the cross (John 12:32–33) "was manifested by the reality of the resurrection and ascension."

95. Brown, *Gospel of John*, 2:992–94, 1011–17.

96. Ibid., 1015.

97. Ibid., 1015–16.

98. John 19:35 is considered by most scholars to be a redactional or authorial insertion, which seems obvious from the verse itself.

99. G. W. H. Lampe and D. M. MacKinnon, *The Resurrection* (London: Mowbray, 1966), 54.

100. D. P. Fuller, *Easter Faith and History* (London: Tyndale, 1968), 197–98.
101. A. M. Ramsey, *The Resurrection of Christ* (London: Collins-Fontana, 1966), 123.
102. The manuscript support for the reading of Luke 24:51 is clearly in favor of this verse being in the earliest form of the text.
103. Brown, *Gospel of John*, 2:1014.
104. Ramsey, *Resurrection*, 137–39.
105. H. Anderson, *Jesus* (New York: Oxford University Press, 1964), 232.
106. O'Collins, *Easter Jesus*, 87.
107. Anderson, *Jesus*, 232.
108. Lüdemann, *What Really Happened to Jesus?* 14–15.
109. Lüdemann, *Resurrection of Jesus*, 181–82. He tries to account for Paul's and Peter's experiences with the risen Christ in psychoanalytical terms of guilt on the part of both. See esp. his discussion, pp. 79–100, but also his conclusions, 174–75.
110. Evans, *Resurrection*, 126.
111. See Lampe and MacKinnon, *Resurrection*, 36; and H. Grass, *Ostergeschehen und Osterberichte* (Göttingen: Vandenhoeck & Ruprecht, 1962), 186–232.
112. R. Bultmann, *Faith and Understanding* (ed. R. W. Funk; trans. L. P. Smith; London: SCM, 1966), 83.
113. W. Michaelis, "ὁράω," *TDNT* 5:358.
114. Lüdemann, *What Really Happened to Jesus?* 102–28. See also his more complete discussion of the visionary nature of the appearances to Paul in his *Resurrection of Jesus*, 47–87, and for Peter, 84–108.
115. Ibid., 128–30.
116. Ibid., 130.
117. See Michaelis, *TDNT* 5:353, 357, 372. An exception to this is in the plural ὀπτασίας, *optasias* ("appearances"), in 2 Cor 12:1, but as Michaelis shows, the usage is different from that of the singular (p. 357).
118. Ibid., 359.
119. Lampe and MacKinnon, *Resurrection*, 37.
120. Fuller, *Formation*, 75.
121. Anderson, *Jesus*, 224.
122. Lüdemann, *What Really Happened to Jesus?* 131–37.
123. Moule, "Post-Resurrection Appearances," 58–61.
124. Dodd argues this point in "Appearances of the Risen Christ," 12.
125. Ibid., 10–11, 12, 18–19.
126. Ibid., 19.
127. Fuller, *Formation*, 76.
128. A. R. C. Leaney, "Theophany, Resurrection, and History," in *SE V* (ed. F. L. Cross; Berlin: Akademie, 1968), 112.
129. For further discussion of this subject, see N. Clark, *Interpreting the Resurrection* (London: SCM, 1967), 44–58.
130. Evans, *Resurrection*, 14.
131. Dodd, "Appearances of the Risen Christ," 9–35.
132. Johnson, *The Real Jesus*, 136.
133. See J. H. Hill, *The Earliest Life of Christ Ever Compiled from the Four Gospels, Being the* Diatessaron *of Tatian* (Edinburgh: T. & T. Clark, 1894).

pages 207–217

THE EMERGENCE OF EARLY CHRISTIANITY:
A Look at the First Christians

1. INTRODUCTION

The sacred literature of early Christianity was selected from a larger body of literature (see ch. 13, below) and was shaped, produced, and passed on in that community. In the first and second centuries A.D., the sacred authority of much of this Christian literature was recognized, and it began to be used in the worship and teaching of the church. It is essential, therefore, to know something of the context, growth, and development of early Christianity not only in the first century A.D. but also beyond that time, into the second century A.D. The expansion of the earliest Christian Scriptures (the OT) to include the Christian writings that eventually became known as the NT both affirmed and supported Christian preaching and teaching. The emergence of a Christian sacred Scripture came at a time when the separation of Christianity from Judaism became final. Many other factors were also involved in the growth and development of the early church, and we briefly sketch some of the most important of these developments in this chapter.

2. ORGANIZATION AND ORDER IN THE EARLY CHURCH

The earliest Christians believed that they had a call from the risen Lord to be a witness for him

A bronze coin of Agrippa I, struck in Caesarea Maritima in A.D. 43. The coin depicts Agrippa I and the city of the god, Caesarea. Greek inscriptions: "The Great King Agrippa, Lover of Caesar," and, on the opposite side, "Caesarea near the Harbor." Photo © Rohr Productions. Used with permission.

(Acts 1:8; Matt 28:19, 20). They proclaimed that in Christ Jesus there were forgiveness of sins and hope for the kingdom of God. In a strict sense, Jesus did not found a church, even though he probably envisioned a community of the renewed Israel that would enter the coming kingdom of God. It is accurate to say that he called his disciples to a mission, and it can certainly be inferred from the Gospels that Jesus intended to build a community of

A sixth-century mosaic in the church at Madeba in Jordan, depicting the ancient Jordan Valley with Jericho at the bottom center, a lion chasing gazelle in the upper center, and the Jordan River in the center.
Photo © Rohr Productions. Used with permission.

followers (Matt 16:18; 18:17ff.).[1] He chose *twelve* disciples, which suggests that he thought of a renewed Israel (that is, representing the twelve tribes of Israel), even though the names of the Twelve are not clearly given in the canonical sources. As noted above, it is not likely that the early church invented this number, since it was not continued in use in the development of church organization. Jesus, however, left no guidelines or commands related to the organization or even formation of the church. He gave no clear directions on how the new community was to be founded except that his followers were to be ready for the coming kingdom of God by abandoning their security in the things of this world and by putting their hope in God, who called them to a life of self-denial, love, and forgiveness.

The early Christians preserved no traditions from Jesus on how this new community of faith—the new Israel—should be structured, who its leaders should be, or what they should be called (deacons, bishops, elders, apostles, etc.), though presumably this new community included the ones he had chosen to follow him. He gave no membership rules or requirements. He gave his disciples a mission but not a blueprint for organization. This can help to explain why there is so much variation in the organization and development of church offices in the NT.

A. The Organization of the Early Church

Because of the highly complex nature of the issues involved, an exact description of the developing organization of the earliest churches is impossible. Still, some aspects of that order seem clear.

1. Simple Initial Organization

At first, the Christians were a very simple fellowship of the followers of Jesus (Acts 2:42–46)[2] with little or no organization. They continued to meet for worship in the temple, in the Jewish synagogues (Acts 3:1ff.), and in homes (Acts 2:2; 12:12;

20:7–8). They continued to keep the laws of Moses (Acts 21:16–21) and to meet together for prayer, common meals, and sharing of their possessions to help those among them who were in need. Because the early Christians expected the imminent return of the risen Christ, they apparently did not at first give much attention to the organization of the church.

2. The Organization Expands

Very soon, however (at least within the first five years of the church's life), the loosely organized society that characterized the beginning of the church began to experience conflict (Acts 6:1–6), and the need was felt for some kind of organization and structure to help in the ministry of caring for the people in its fellowship. The urgency for offices and leadership in the church, other than the office of apostle, first arose from conflict in the church over how to care for the needs of its people.

3. Elders

By A.D. 40–44, the office of elder (πρεσβύτερος, *presbyteros*) was introduced into the life of the church at Jerusalem (Acts 11:27–30). We know almost nothing of the background or the development of this office in the church, except that it probably had a similar function in the Jewish synagogue's organizational structure. By the time of the church council in Acts 15:1–29 (the Jerusalem Council, ca. A.D. 49), convened to determine the Gentiles' relation to the law, elders were participating in the decision making of the church, along with the apostles and James the brother of Jesus. Luke does not inform us how this development came about, but we know that the office of elder was a special office in the organization of the Jewish synagogue and was probably adopted and adapted by the Jerusalem church for its own use. This was not an uncommon feature of early Christianity, which adopted and adapted many non-Christian functions for its own use.

4. Apostles, Prophets, and Teachers

As the church grew outside Jerusalem, the primary focus of authority lay in the offices of the apostles (there were many more besides the Twelve; cf. 1 Cor 15:5–7), prophets, and teachers. This was especially true in the churches Paul had founded (cf. Acts 13–20; 1 Cor 12:27–31; Eph 4:11). These churches were charismatically oriented and were developed chiefly around the use of gifts of the Holy Spirit (cf. Rom 12:3–8; 1 Cor 12–14).

In Paul's ministry we also see references to the presence of bishops and deacons. In Phil 1:1 the terms "bishop" or "overseer" (ἐπίσκοπος, *episkopos*) and "deacon" (διάκονος, *diakonos*) are used, apparently for recognized church offices, and these offices are explicated in terms of their qualifications in 1 Tim 3. Although the term ἐπίσκοπος is used in Phil 1:1 along with the oldest Christian term for office, διάκονος, which is used elsewhere for Phoebe (Rom 16:1) and for both Paul and Apollos (1 Cor 3:5), "bishop" did not apparently have the same implications of absolute authority and power as it did later in the ministry of Ignatius (ca. 115). The term "elder" is mentioned in Acts (11:30; 15:2, 6, 22, 23), but it is not as common in the Pauline churches until later in the first century, where it is mentioned in Titus 1:5 along with "overseer" (Titus 1:7). This could signify the lack of any influence from Jerusalem in the leadership of the Gentile churches, although this is not certain. It is interesting that Paul, who was very proud of his apostleship and defends it on several occasions (Gal 1:1; 1 Cor 9:1–14; etc.), nevertheless uses the term "deacon" for himself in 1 Cor 3:5 and 2 Cor 6:4. Also, the NT elsewhere calls all Christians διάκονοι, *diakonoi* ("deacons"; cf. John 12:26; Mark 9:35; 10:43). In 1 Cor 12:28 Paul mentions the office or gift of administrator ("forms of leadership," κυβέρνησις, *kybernēsis*). There are close parallels here with the use of the term "bishop" in Phil 1:1. Also, Paul mentions in 1 Cor 12:28 the office or gift of helper or servant ("forms of assistance," ἀντίλημψις, *antilēmpsis*). This term is not at all unlike the role of the deacon mentioned elsewhere by Paul. Indeed, it appears to be a different term for the same function. Paul does not ask in this passage if all Christians are administrators or helpers, since these offices were elected in the early church and anyone could hold them, unlike the other functions mentioned in 1 Cor 12 (apostle, prophet, teacher, etc.).

5. The Use of the Office of Elder in the Pauline Churches

At the time of the writing of 1 Timothy (cf. 5:17), the term "elder" was being substituted for the term "overseer," and was interchangeable with it until around the end of the first century A.D. and possibly later, except in the troubled church of Antioch, where strong leadership was needed and "bishop" was the term used for that role. Even in Rome around A.D. 95–100, in *1 Clem.* 42–44, the two terms are interchangeable.

6. The Wandering Prophets

As the rest of the early Christian church developed in its organization, there was still a strong presence of wandering charismatic prophets and teachers in many Christian communities outside Jerusalem and especially outside Israel. They continued to minister, and by the end of the first century, there appears to have been a need to regulate their activities because of the excesses of some of them (cf. *Did.* 11.1–12; 15.1–4). It seems that the problems of heresy and false teaching by the prophets in some churches led to the decline of their role in the life of the church (cf. Matt 24:11, 24) and the consequent emergence of the bishop as a more powerful figure.

B. Organization in the Jerusalem Church

By A.D. 41–44, the Jerusalem church had become organized after the order of the Jewish synagogue, with James the brother of Jesus serving as its leader.[3] During the severe persecution of the Jerusalem church during A.D. 62–66, which included the death of James (Josephus, *Ant.* 20.200–203), it moved to Pella (just south of Galilee and east of the Jordan River). The leadership of the church stayed in the family of Jesus until after the turn of the first century. Jesus' cousins, his brother Jude, and Jude's nephews and grandsons continued to lead this predominantly Jewish-Christian community (see the writings of the ancient historians Hegesippus and, esp., Eusebius, *Hist. eccl.* 3.11, 19, 20, 22.) This was also the home of the apologist Aristo (ca. 140), who wrote his *Dialogue between Jason and Papiskos concerning Christ* from Pella around the middle of the

second century. The work was so well known that Celsus, the pagan philosopher, cited the work critically in his *True Discourse*, written in the last quarter of the second century.[4]

The missionary activity among the Gentiles was not the result of the vision of the church in Jerusalem, nor did the Jewish Christians there offer any generous gifts to fellow Christians to start churches among the Gentiles. Indeed, the church in Jerusalem at first objected to the Jewish Christians' having any contact with the Gentiles (cf. Acts 11:1–18; Gal 2:11–21) and only subsequently recognized that the gospel had gone to the Gentiles as well as to the Jews. The spread of the gospel outside Palestine among the Gentiles came primarily through the efforts of the Hellenistic Jewish Christians, who began their ministry rather unintentionally as a result of being persecuted and forced to leave Jerusalem (cf. Acts 8:1–4; 11:19–20). In this sense, the Jerusalem church cannot be called the "mother church," as has been assumed by many, even though the Christian church had its beginnings in Jerusalem. Antioch has more claim to this role, as it was the church that initiated the Gentile mission in early Christianity (Acts 13:1–2).

C. Conclusion

The NT appears to have at least four basic patterns of organizational structure. (1) The first may be called congregational in the sense that the congregation selected its own leaders and disciplined its members (e.g., 1 Cor 5:3–5; Matt 18:15–18; Acts 6:3–7). (2) The second, often termed presbyterial (from πρεσβύτερος), is found especially in the Jerusalem churches, which patterned themselves after the Jewish synagogue. In Acts 11:29–30 the elders took care of relief aid that was brought to the church in Jerusalem, and in Acts 15:6 and 22 they participated in the decision regarding the Gentiles' relationship to the law; but this did not preclude the whole church from deliberating and participating in the discussion before the decision was made with the consent of the whole church (15:22). (3) Later in the NT, one finds an episcopal type of organization (from ἐπίσκοπος), which had leaders in the church select other persons to roles of responsibility (2 Tim 2:2). (4) There also appears to have been something of a charismatic style of structure that focused on the exercise of the gifts of the Spirit.

The ministry of the church was organized in accordance with the abilities and gifts of the church's members (1 Cor 12:4–11, 27–28). Typically there were prophets and teachers in these congregations who acted on behalf of the church (Acts 13:1–3). Congregational decisions, however, appear to have been a part of all organizational patterns. In the *Didache* (ca. A.D. 70–90), for example, the people were called to "elect [χειρονήσατε, *cheironēsate*] therefore for yourselves bishops and deacons worthy of the Lord" (*Did.* 15.1). Paul exhorts the congregation at Corinth to make decisions (judge) about the continuing membership of a young man in the Christian community who had been having sexual relations with his stepmother (1 Cor 5:1–5, 9–13).

Since Jesus commanded no particular pattern to be followed, and as the church grew and more structure was needed, Christians followed those patterns most familiar and useful to them. At first this was undoubtedly the synagogue structure, which the Jewish Christians adapted to their own needs to enable them to accomplish their mission. The earliest non-Christian description of life in the church comes in a letter from Pliny the Younger, the governor of Bithynia (ca. A.D. 113), written to the Emperor Trajan. The letter is instructive on the life of the congregation in that area. After describing the punishments and even executions of Christians who refused to curse Christ and worship the statue of Trajan, Pliny writes:

> It was their habit on a fixed day to assemble before daylight and recite by turns a form of words to Christ as a god; and that they bound themselves with an oath, not for any crime, but not to commit theft or robbery or adultery, not to break their word, and not to deny a deposit when demanded. After this was done, their custom was to depart, and to meet again to take food, but ordinary and harmless food. (*Ep.* 10.96.7)[5]

The church began to face increasing frustrations and problems brought on by Jesus' not returning as the church believed he would; the death of apostles; increasing persecutions and forced resettlements of Christian communities; the continuing spread of the Christian faith into many diverse communities, with the consequent difficulty of communication between the churches; and the emergence of "heresy," which led to many conflicts in the church. It was therefore inevitable that the church would develop several measures to deal with these problems. It dealt with them first by developing a stronger episcopate—an organizational structure that depended on a strong leader—and by adopting creeds, which came to constitute the *regula fidei* ("rule of faith"). Eventually, the church also began to recognize the authority of many Christian writings to help it deal with these matters, and these writings became a fixed collection of sacred Christian Scriptures (the NT) (see ch. 13, below, on this process).

3. GALILEE AND EARLY CHRISTIANITY

Jesus and his disciples (except Judas Iscariot)[6] came from the region of Galilee, in the midst of the ten Hellenistic cities of the Decapolis.[7] Jesus grew up in this area, where he had his longest period of ministry. Early Christianity, however, is often silent about this area except for what we read in the Gospels, which largely focus on Jesus' ministry there. Little else is known about the followers of Jesus in this region after his ministry. Nothing is found in Acts, and not much in the other surviving literature of the first or second centuries. Nevertheless, it is certain that there were Christian communities in this region in the latter part of the first century and following. Jewish Christians began to leave Jerusalem after the Romans began to threaten the city (ca. A.D. 67), probably moving into Pella (Eusebius, *Hist. eccl.* 3.5.3–4; Epiphanius, *Pan.* 30.2.7–8), a Transjordanian Decapolis town just south of the Sea of Galilee, and into other communities both in the Decapolis and in Galilee. The evidence for Christians living in and around Galilee stems primarily from second-century sources and early church tradition.[8] While the evidence for large Christian communities in this region is inconclusive, their presence here is in harmony with the fact that Jesus and his disciples came from this region and ministered in small towns and villages there. Sepphoris may have been one of the places where Jewish Christianity flourished.[9]

A. The Population of Galilee

Four main groups of people lived in the region of Galilee. (1) The largest group of Galileans was located primarily in farming and fishing communities; a large number of these peasant people were

Recent excavations at Hazor on the Via Maris north of Galilee, the major travel route from the coast of Palestine to Damascus. Photo Lee M. McDonald.

focused on village life, with its closed patterns of family and community loyalty. Although perhaps not as directly influenced by Hellenistic culture and the changing empires as was Jerusalem to the south, they were still very much a part of the Greco-Roman world. By the first century A.D., Hellenism had widely influenced Judaism, and Hellenistic symbols have been found throughout the region, especially in the synagogues at Tiberias and at Sepphoris. (2) The rural proletariat included day laborers and itinerant craftsmen. They were peasants whose jobs were not very stable and who were especially conscious of the economic and social disparity in the land. In Jesus' parable of the workers and the owner of a vineyard in Matt 20:1–16, we see that the workers were at the mercy of the vineyard owner. (3) A third category of people was the class of lesser officials who grew up in the Hellenistic system. These individuals included judges, civil administrators, lesser tax collectors, and stewards of absentee landlords; none of them had great love for their social inferiors. The hostility of tenants for stewards and landlords can be seen in Jesus' parable in Mark 12:1–12 (cf. Luke 16:1–8, where the steward manipulates the tenants). Jesus' parable about the householder who goes away and leaves the stewards in charge to invest his money (Luke 19:11ff.) reveals common practices of the day in Galilee. (4) A fourth class of persons in this region included the Jewish aristocracy and officials of Rome, who lived in the large Hellenistic cities of the region, such as Tiberias, Scythopolis, and Sepphoris.

They owned vast estates, many of which had been taken or confiscated from the peasants, often for the purpose of settling heavy tax debts. These few individuals formed the urban elite of the region and owed much of their status to the Hellenistic urbanization of Palestine, but especially to Herod the Great, who had given many land distributions in 20 B.C. to the wealthy for their favors to him and for their support of his kingship. Their privileged status depended upon their continued support of Herod and his successors and of Roman interests in the region.

A mosaic in a Roman villa unearthed in 1987 at Sepphoris, the capital of Galilee in the time of Jesus. The woman is perhaps Aphrodite, the goddess of love, with the Eros figure over her shoulder. She is often referred to as the "Mona Lisa of Galilee." Photo Lee M. McDonald.

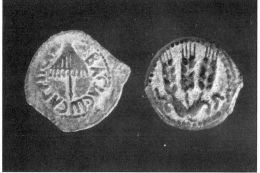

A coin of Agrippa I, struck in A.D. 42, depicting a canopy and, on the opposite side, three ears of barley. Greek inscriptions: "King Agrippa" and, opposite, "Year 6." See the reference to Agrippa I in Acts 12. Photo © Rohr Productions. Used with permission.

During the centuries before and after the birth of Jesus, one's social status largely depended upon birth and inheritance and less upon earned income and lifestyle. Generally speaking, privilege, wealth, and full civil rights belonged only to those persons born into a certain status, who in turn could pass it on to the next generation. The average Galileans were generally despised and ridiculed by the residents of Jerusalem as uncultured and unlearned peasants (e.g., Mark 6:2–3; John 7:41, 52; Acts 4:13). Their social status was, in large measure, imposed upon them by nonresident or absentee landlords.

B. Silence about the Church in Galilee

We noted above the strange silence in the rest of the NT about the church in Galilee after the resurrection of Jesus. All of the Gospel narratives, however, show that most of Jesus' ministry was in Galilee and that some of his resurrection appearances took place there as well (Matt 28:7–10, 16; Mark 14:27–28; 16:7; John 21). It is strange, therefore, that we never again hear of Galilee in the NT. Why? Luke says nothing of the Galilean appearances of the risen Christ mentioned in Mark's Gospel (Mark 14:28; 16:7). After Easter, Galilee evidently did not fit into Luke's literary plans. Was this for theological reasons? Was he trying to veil the Galilean background, which was generally looked down upon, as he tried to present his Gospel? If that were

so, why would he not take out all references to Galilee in his Gospel? Luke probably wanted to show that the church began in Jerusalem and that the original leaders of the church were the twelve companions of Jesus who witnessed his resurrection appearances there. More than one scholar has raised the question whether any conclusions should be drawn from the early disappearance of the twelve apostles from Acts and the omission of any discussion of Galilee. Are the two items related? Did the Twelve who came from Galilee with Jesus to Jerusalem eventually return to that region shortly before or after the Acts 15 council in Jerusalem? Their presence in the church at Jerusalem seems negligible after this council, and even there they do not appear to have as much to say in matters as do the elders and James.

As we discussed in the previous chapter, in 1 Cor 15:6 Paul mentions that the risen Christ "appeared to more than five hundred brothers and sisters at one time." One needs to ask where the most likely place would be for Jesus to have some five hundred followers, if not Galilee, where he had spent most of the time of his ministry. Since most of Jesus' ministry in Galilee centered around Capernaum, it is possible that many of his followers were from this area. It should be noted, however, that Jesus' ministry in Galilee may have been a failure, which would explain why he set out for Jerusalem. See, for example, his pronouncements of woe against some of the villages around Galilee in Matt 11:23; Luke 10:15.

Luke's interest in Jerusalem and his consequent neglect of Galilee seem obvious and could well stem from the fact that he is trying to present Christianity as a universal faith that originated in Jerusalem with Jesus and his companions. Is Galilee neglected by Luke because it is not considered to be the place of fulfillment in the Jewish tradition that Jerusalem was? Would Luke have agreed with the disparaging remark of Nathanael, "Can anything good come out of Nazareth?" (John 1:46). Conclusive arguments and answers are lacking.

Whatever the reason, Luke, who wrote the only document in the NT that purports to tell of the origin and early development of the church (Acts), completely omits any discussion of Galilee or the apostles after Acts 16:4. After that, James the brother of Jesus is clearly in charge of the church in Jerusalem, and the apostles are no longer mentioned. It may be argued, however, that since the appearances of the risen Lord to his followers were foundational for the initiation of their ministry and since Matt 28:16–20, Mark 16:7, and John 21:1–6 all indicate that Jesus appeared to his disciples in Galilee, there is reason to believe that (1) a Christian community existed there after the appearances and that (2) the original companions of Jesus may well have had something to do with the establishment of Christian communities there. The silence of the rest of the NT about Galilee and any Christian communities there is indeed strange, but the already noted references to Jesus' appearances in that region suggest that there may have been Christian churches there, possibly shortly after the emergence of Christianity.

4. GROWTH AND DEVELOPMENT IN EARLY CHRISTIANITY (A.D. 30–100)

A. The Composition of the First Christian Community

The earliest followers of Jesus appear to have included wandering preachers (or charismatic prophets) and their sympathizers, who later became their supporters, especially in Galilee. As the church developed in and around Jerusalem, it is clear that those who became members of the early church were from five basic categories of people. These categories are not intended as rigid distinctions (since several important early Christians, such as the apostle Paul, would belong to several groups) but as useful indicators of the complexity of early Christianity.

1. Aramaic/Hebrew-Speaking Jews

The earliest converts to Christianity came from a group of Palestinian Jews who practiced the Jewish law and accepted as their sacred literature the OT books, though they were not limited to these books alone (see ch. 13, below). Most of them spoke Aramaic (the merchants, if not most Jews in the region, probably also knew some Greek), and some may even have read their sacred Scriptures in Hebrew. By and large, they were cautious toward Jews who spoke only Greek, but were especially suspicious of Gentiles. Some of their group were undoubtedly among the so-called Judaizers who accepted Jesus as their Messiah but continued in the keeping of the law and in the observance of the many traditions about the law that developed in Palestine (e.g., the keeping of many dietary laws and requirements related to the Sabbath; cf. Mark 7:1–23). Among these Jews were some who believed that obedience to the law was essential for all followers of Jesus, including the Gentiles. Some believed that the Gospel was only for Jews or for those who had converted to Judaism. A good example of this attitude is found in the objections from the Christians in Jerusalem to Peter's having eaten with Gentiles in Caesarea (Acts 11:1–18).

2. The Hellenists

A large number of Jews living in Palestine spoke Greek; many of these had been born outside Palestine (e.g., Barnabas; Acts 4:36) and were very much at home with the Greco-Roman culture common throughout the Roman Empire. They tended to be among the more educated Jews in Palestine, and many of them had ties with Roman officials, whom the Aramaic/Hebrew-speaking Jews largely despised. Among these Jews were some who were less impressed with Jewish traditions, especially those developed in Palestine, and who were not convinced that the presence and activity of God were permanently tied to temple worship in Jerusalem (Acts 7:48–50; Heb 8:1–8). Some of them were also not convinced of the permanence of the law of Moses (Heb 8:7–8). When they became Christians, they were among the first to make concerted efforts to evangelize the Gentiles (Acts 11:19–26; 13:1–12), believing that the Gospel should be preached to all people. They rejected the require-

The amphitheater on a hillside of Pergamum (Bergama, Turkey). Remains of the temples of Dionysus and Trajan are in the upper right. Photo © Rohr Productions. Used with permission.

ment that a Gentile had to become a Jew in order to become a Christian; that is, they did not require Gentiles to be circumcised or to keep the law. In the NT, Stephen (Acts 6–7), Paul, Barnabas, and the author of the book of Hebrews are the primary representatives of this group, even though Paul himself was a Pharisee before his conversion. The Christians in this category were the most responsible for making the Christian faith a universal religion, open to all.

3. The Dispersion Jews

A large number of Jews lived outside Palestine and mostly only returned to Israel for special festivals and religious holidays, if at all. They were among the wealthier and more educated Jews of the first century. Acts 2:5–11 lists some of the coun-

tries where many of these Jews came from and notes that some of them were converted to Christianity on the day of Pentecost (Acts 2:37–42). The Epistle of James may well have been sent to Christian Jews scattered throughout the Roman Empire (Jas 1:1), some of whom had been converted at Pentecost in Jerusalem.

4. Gentiles Attracted to Judaism

Many of the Godfearers mentioned in Acts had followed the teachings of Judaism and later were drawn to the Christian message (Acts 2:10; 8:26–39; 10:1–7; 13:43; 17:1–4), perhaps because they were freed from the obligations of the law, especially circumcision, and from their second-class status within Judaism.[10] These Gentiles had been attracted to Judaism, had practiced the religious piety of the Jews, and had followed the law and the religious traditions surrounding the law. Some of them were also circumcised. The Ethiopian in Acts 8:26–40 and Cornelius in Acts 10:1–2 fall into the category of the Godfearers.

5. The Gentiles

Most of the Gentiles who became Christians in the first century had not been sympathetic to Judaism nor adopted its religious practices. They first learned the Christian message through Paul, Barnabas, and others who were active in pioneer missions. They came directly to the Christian faith and were often held in suspicion by the Judaizers of the Jerusalem church (Gal 2:11–21).

B. The Names of the Earliest Christians

The earliest followers of Jesus referred to themselves neither as "Christians" nor as the "Church"; these names came later.[11] Some of the more common names for the early church, however, warrant some explanation.

1. The Way

One of the earliest names accepted or selected by the followers of Jesus was "the Way" (Acts 9:2; 19:9, 23; 22:4; 24:14, 22), which may have come from Jesus' reference to himself as "the way" in John 14:6. This designation likely shows that the church thought of itself as a community of those who had found the way to God or were on the way to God through Jesus Christ.

2. Christian

The term "Christian" was first used in Antioch of Syria sometime around A.D. 40 (Acts 11:26), but its origins are obscure. We do not know whether the Christians gave themselves this name or the pagan community assigned it to the followers of Jesus, who subsequently accepted it. Jewish followers of Jesus probably did not use the term "Christian" to refer to themselves. If the pagan community coined this term, as is more likely, it is unclear whether it had positive ("little Christs") or negative connotations, although it perhaps functioned as a nickname. It may have referred to Christians as members of a political, social, or secretive club or association.[12]

3. Assembly of God (ἐκκλησία τοῦ θεοῦ, ekklēsia tou theou)

This is one of the most familiar terms for the church in the writings of Paul, who uses the neutral Greek term for a gathering or assembly, ἐκκλησία, and qualifies it for the Christian community (1 Cor 1:2; 2 Cor. 1:1; etc.; but note also how he does not qualify it in Gal 1:2 except by location). It has been plausibly argued that Jesus himself first used the term for an assembly of Christian believers, although many critical scholars doubt this.[13] It is likely that this term was chosen instead of the more common συναγωγή ("synagogue") because "synagogue" was already used by the Jewish community. Some Jewish Christians did use the latter term in reference to their gatherings (Jas 2:2), and in Sepphoris a Jewish Christian synagogue has been discovered.

4. Church

The origin of the word "church" to refer to gatherings of Christians is obscure. A number of different words began to be used regularly in Christian communities around the late second and early third centuries, but the same ones did not catch on in all Christian communities. The Latin countries of southern Europe, for example, continued to use

words (e.g., église, iglesia, chiesa) derived from the NT term ἐκκλησία (through Lat. ecclesia) to refer to the community of the followers of Christ. Derivations from the Greek word κυριακόν, kyriakon (e.g., "church," "kirk," Kirche) are more widely used in northern European countries. The root of κυριακόν is κύριος, kyrios ("Lord"), the title given to Jesus by the church. The last three letters of κυριακόν indicate possession in the Greek; thus the term means "belonging to the Lord." Κυριακόν in this sense is not found in the NT, but its derivatives have been used in English and German translations of the NT for ἐκκλησία. Ἐκκλησία is found in the NT as a designation for the Christian community and was used in some churches at least as early as the time of the Apostle Paul, though usually qualified with the words "of Christ" or "of God"; that is, the early Christians thought of themselves as "the gathering (or assembly) of God" (see no. 3, above). On one occasion in the NT (Jas 2:2), the Greek term συναγωγή is used to refer to the Christian community. Both ἐκκλησία, which is the most frequent term translated "church" in the NT, and συναγωγή mean much the same thing. Perhaps Christians chose ἐκκλησία in order to distinguish themselves from the Jews. It is also possible that the term κυριακόν came to be used by Christians sometime around the end of the second century A.D. in order to make clearer who its members were, namely, those who belonged to the Lord, although this is uncertain.

5. Other Names

There are several other names for the followers of Jesus in the NT, and each helps to explain how the early believers understood themselves and how they believed they were to live in relation to God or Christ. One of those terms is "saint" or "holy" (ἅγιος, hagios), a frequent designation for the Christian in Paul's writings (Rom 1:7; 1 Cor 1:2; 2 Cor 1:1; Phil 1:1; etc.) that refers to the follower of Jesus as a person separated unto God for a special calling or purpose. In the Johannine writings (esp. 1, 2, 3 John), we find another term for the followers of Jesus. John prefers the terms "children," "children of God," or "little children," all of which show the Christian community in tender and special relationships with God and with one another.

C. The Church toward the End of the First Century

The church existed in more places in Palestine than simply Jerusalem, Caesarea, and Galilee, and we are also certain that it existed in more places outside Palestine than the churches Paul founded, visited, or wrote to in his letters (e.g., Pontus, Cappadocia, Asia, Bithynia). It is possible that the author of Hebrews, on the basis of his style of writing and some of the Greek forms he employs, was from Alexandria, Egypt, or that vicinity. There are numerous old church traditions about missions being established in India, Spain, Africa, Armenia, and other regions. But our knowledge of the time between A.D. 65 and 95 is very limited. This period is sometimes called the "tunnel" of early church history because so little is known about it. We do know that there were many different kinds of Christian communities developing during this time—for example, the Ebionites, a rigidly Jewish-Christian community that tried to maintain an observance of the Mosaic law as well as faith in Christ; a community, addressed by the author of Hebrews, that perhaps tried to hold onto Judaism, with continued focus on Christ as the Son of God, so that some members gradually drifted back into Judaism; and the rather different community, addressed by John in 1, 2, and 3 John, in which some believed that Christ only appeared to be a man and did not take upon himself human flesh—a tendency known as "docetic." There were groups beginning to emerge that saw Jesus as an angel, and still others

that portrayed him as a spirit or even the divine Logos (Gk. for "Word"). These and other factors began to affect the church at the end of the first century A.D., and caused significant changes in the life of the Christian community as a whole.

1. Emergence of Heresy

After the earliest followers of Jesus began to die, few witnesses were left who had seen the risen Lord and who could report anything firsthand about the Christian faith. In a sense, there was a vacuum of authority in the early church. So-called heresies began to emerge, and it was difficult to find a voice in the church that was recognized by all Christians as authoritative. The most popular kind of heresy at the end of the first century was Docetism (from the Gk. δοκέω, *dokeō*, "seem," "appear"), which believed that flesh, and in fact all matter, was evil. To preserve Jesus from contact with what was evil, the Docetists taught that Jesus only "appeared" like a man or "seemed" to have human flesh; they believed that, as God, he could not have also been human. The first Christian document to call this teaching into question is 1 John (cf. 1 John 4:1–3). Ignatius later (ca. A.D. 115) also strongly condemns this heresy in his letters to the Ephesians (*Eph.* 7.1–2), to the Trallians (*Trall.* 10.1), and to the Smyrnaeans (*Smyrn.* 2–7). The roots of Docetism were in early forms of Gnosticism, to be discussed below.

2. Gnosis, Gnosticism, and Early Christianity

Among those Greco-Roman religions that believed in some form of salvation was Gnosticism, which held that salvation was through a savior on whom the obedient follower would depend.[14] For the gnostics, this salvation came through a special knowledge (Gk. γνῶσις, *gnōsis*) that revealed the secrets of the universe. It included knowledge of God's actions in the universe, of one's true self, and especially of how one might find escape from this world (salvation). The sources for the study of Christian Gnosticism are twofold. The first is the Christian antignostic writings of the second-century church fathers, especially Irenaeus of Lyons but also Epiphanius and Hippolytus of Rome, who

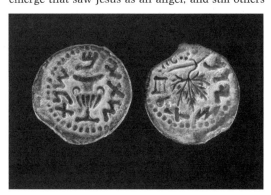

A bronze Jewish coin struck in the midst of the siege of Jerusalem in A.D. 67. Hebrew inscriptions: around the vase, "Year 2," and, around the vine leaf, "Freedom of Zion." Photo © Rohr Productions. Used with permission.

The Roman aqueduct at the site of ancient Pisidian Antioch (Yalvaç, Turkey). See Acts 13:13–52; 14:21–23.
Photo © Rohr Productions. Used with permission.

referred to a few of the Christian gnostics of the second century (Valentinus, Basilides, Cerinthus) but always in a negative light, denying that the gnostic expressions of Christian faith were valid. For centuries our only information about gnostic Christians came from these opponents, who called gnostic teachings anti-Christian heresies. The second source includes both Christian and non-Christian gnostic Coptic documents originally written in Greek and discovered near the Egyptian town of Nag Hammadi, sixty miles south of Luxor, in 1945. These texts, comprising fifty-two tractates in all, have taken us closer to the spirit of Gnosticism than what we could discover earlier in the anti-gnostic works of the early church fathers. The Nag Hammadi collection of documents contains forty-nine religious treatises dating variously over a long period of time, including many thought to have been written in the second century A.D. in Greek, with a few possibly in the first century A.D., although scholars disagree on the dating of these materials.

The roots of the gnostic movement are somewhat obscure, but it appears to have begun with the combination of pre-Christian Hellenistic notions about matter (the body), evil, and life after death and Jewish apocalyptic dualism of the second and first centuries B.C., but especially the failed apocalyptic eschatology of the late first century A.D. Gnosticism may owe some of its roots to Iranian dualism, some of the Jewish Wisdom literature, such as that found at Qumran, and the oriental mystery religions of Asia and Egypt. Christian Gnosticism appears to be a second-century A.D. phenomenon, but many of the ideas expressed in it are certainly pre-Christian. Whether there were developed pre-Christian gnostic systems is doubted by many scholars, but non-Christian gnostic views are found in the Nag Hammadi documents. At the root of Christian Gnosticism is a belief in the evil nature of matter and that the evil, malicious god who created the universe (the Demiurge), who is the God of the OT, is not the God of Jesus, the God of love. Generally speaking, the savior is seen to be the

The theater and a general view of the southwest across the ancient harbor of Miletus (western Turkey),
which is now silted up. Paul stopped here and met with the Ephesian elders (Acts 20:15-38).
Photo © Rohr Productions. Used with permission.

Christ who merged with Jesus at his baptism and then departed from him at his crucifixion. For the gnostics, then, Christ only appeared to die, while in Docetism, Jesus only appeared to have a body of flesh. The salvation of humanity is to be found in the acquiring of a secret esoteric knowledge that can free the soul of its imprisonment in the material world. There were various behavioral manifestations of this philosophy. Some, for example, saw themselves as "set free" to manifest any kind of physical expression they chose, since the body and its appetites, being evil, would someday perish and therefore it does not matter how one acts in these areas. The other side of Gnosticism, especially Christian Gnosticism, however, focused on ascetic withdrawal of oneself from the world. This asceticism took the form of withdrawal from sexual expressions, the world's pleasures, or even, in some cases, participation in the world system, which was deemed to be opposed to God. There were many expressions of gnostic belief in the ancient world, and for this reason there is a lot of confusion about how

to interpret what it was that the gnostic Christians believed or practiced. The special knowledge received by the gnostics was believed to free them from the bondage to this evil world and prepare them for the life to come, in which the soul would return to the sphere of the πλήρωμα (*plērōma*), the "fullness" of the divine. Gnosticism was especially concerned with the origin of evil and with knowledge as a means of escape or salvation from the material world.

Some of the keys to this system of thought are the prevalent Hellenistic views concerning the duality of spirit and matter, life after death, and the relationship of God to the universe. There was a widespread view that the body was the captor of the soul and that the soul needed to be freed from the body. Such views conflicted with early Christian preaching, such as when Paul spoke in Athens of a resurrected Lord in Acts 17:30–34. The notion of a God who would become a part of the human race was also counter to the most widely held views among the Greeks and the Romans. Whatever else the gods were, they were always remote and had a lack of concern (ἀπαθεία, *apatheia*) for human affairs. These views normally ran counter to Jewish thought, even though some Jews (generally the wealthier and more educated) had been able to accommodate themselves to the Hellenistic perspectives of the Greeks. Judaism, like early Christianity, focused on the activity of God in human history. For both Christianity and Judaism, God was a benevolent Creator, and for Christianity, God raised Jesus bodily from the grave. Many of the gnostic views found in the second century were current in Palestine in the century before the birth of Christ, when many of the Greek ideas were assimilated by some of the wealthy and influential Jews of Palestine and by many Jews of the Diaspora, who outnumbered those in Palestine by three or four to one. Recently scholars have differentiated between gnosis and Gnosticism. The former is "knowledge of divine mysteries reserved for an elite group," whereas Gnosticism is that fully developed gnostic system in the second century.[15] The ideas that Gnosticism assimilated informed the many different levels or kinds of gnostic thought up through the Mandaeans and later the Manicheans.[16]

Among the differing strands of Gnosticism, Valentinian Gnosticism was the best-known expression, though Gnosticism had several other voices. The following proponents of Gnosticism had their greatest influence in the church of the second century A.D.

a. Simon Magus (Acts 8:9–24) is credited (probably spuriously) with the *Gospel of the Four Points of the Compass*. The church fathers often credit him as the source of all heresy in the church.

b. Cerinthus (fl. ca. 100) taught that the Christ descended on Jesus at his baptism and departed before his crucifixion. The Alogi of Asia Minor in the last half of the second century claimed that Cerinthus wrote both the Gospel of John and the book of Revelation (see Eusebius, *Hist. eccl.* 3.28).

c. Basilides (fl. ca. 120–140) wrote extensively; all his works, including a Gospel commentary and twenty-four books of *Exegetica*, are now lost. He refused to believe that Christ was crucified, and said that Simon of Cyrene was crucified in Jesus' place. He held that salvation was such a spiritual matter that the sins of the flesh are of no consequence be-

cause they are of a different realm and thus not a concern to God.

d. Valentinus (fl. 140) was born in Alexandria, Egypt, but taught mostly in Rome from 136 to 165. Highly influential, he propounded an order of beings, or "aeons," who were arranged in pairs yoked together ("syzygies"), whose ultimate product was the Demiurge, the God of the OT. Like Basilides, he argued that the aeon Christ united with Jesus at his baptism and departed from him at the crucifixion. This Christ imparted to persons the true spiritual understanding (gnosis), which enabled them to enter the highest sphere, the πλήρωμα. His teaching may be represented in the *Gospel of Truth*, which was discovered at Nag Hammadi.

e. Ptolemy (fl. 140) is famous for his interesting depiction of the Mosaic law and how to understand it, in a work that he wrote to a woman named Flora. He attributes most of the Mosaic law to the Demiurge. He does not reject the OT outright, as did later gnostics, but tries rather to interpret it carefully.

f. Heracleon (fl. 145–180) wrote the earliest known commentary on the Gospel of John; it is quoted in Origen's commentary on John.

g. Marcion (fl. ca. 140, d. ca. 160) taught that the God of the OT (the Demiurge) was not the God of Jesus. Jesus (not, in Marcion's thought, a separate entity from Christ) came to reveal a God of love. Marcion rejected the OT, instead setting forth one of the earliest collections of Christian Scriptures, which included ten of Paul's epistles (he omitted the Pastoral Epistles—1, 2 Tim; Titus) and a truncated form of Luke's Gospel, which he believed originated with Paul (probably taking Paul's reference to "my gospel" to mean one that he had written). It is difficult to say for sure whether Marcion was a gnostic, though he did have similar views on the God of the OT. He did not, however, produce a collection of the more esoteric and fanciful documents that have become characteristic of the gnostics.

Some of the best-known gnostic writings include the *Gospel of Thomas, Gospel of Philip, Gospel of Mary, Gospel of Peter,* and *Apocryphon of John*. The longest gnostic document is the *Pistis Sophia*. Some scholars (see ch. 4, above) still debate whether the *Gospel of Thomas* should be dated to the late first century—possibly before the canonical Gospels—or perhaps considerably later. It is very difficult, however, to establish an early date.

3. Growth of the Church

By the end of the first century, because of the rapid growth of the Christian community throughout the Roman Empire, the Christians numbered somewhere around a hundred thousand.[17] This growth and wide dissemination of the Christian message made communication among the churches much more difficult. The number of Christians at the end of the first century was still, however, relatively small compared to the six to seven million Jews, approximately one-seventh to one-tenth of the entire population of the Roman Empire. Of this number, it is estimated that between one and two million Jews lived in Palestine.[18] As a result of the distance between churches, the writing of letters or epistles and their circulation by couriers, though difficult at best, became more and more common and enabled Christians to find out what was going on elsewhere. The letters were also used to teach and instruct new converts in the faith and to help maintain some sense of unity among the churches. By the third and fourth centuries some Christian leaders were regularly circulating or publishing their letters (e.g., Cyprian and later Athanasius). From probably the first century, besides the letters of the Apostle Paul, at least some of the General or Catholic Epistles in the NT (James, 1 Peter, and 1 John) were circulated among the churches (although some of these letters—2 Peter, 2, 3 John, and Jude—may have been written after the first century and not circulated until the late second century or even later). In the late first and early second centuries, letters were also written by Clement of Rome, Ignatius, and Polycarp and were well received and circulated widely in churches.

4. The Delay of the Parousia (Christ's Return)

By the end of the first century and in the early part of the second century, the delay of Christ's return to establish his kingdom upon the earth had begun to cause a change in outlook among Christians. The apocalyptic message of the earlier disciples, which had focused upon the imminent return of Christ and the violent overthrow of all existing kingdoms on the earth, was no longer as appealing to Christians as it had been. Jesus had not returned, and some Christians were losing patience. Some writings of that period and even later continued the apocalyptic message, urging Christians to steadfastness, patience, and preparation for the coming day of Christ's return (Rev 1:3; 3:10–11; 22:20; 2 Pet 3:3–7), but as time went on, this message had less attraction. By the turn of the century, Christians were generally settling in for a long wait before Christ's return. John's Gospel, for example, has almost no references to the coming apocalyptic kingdom of God as found in the Synoptic Gospels (see John 3:3; 5:25–29 for references to this kingdom). The primary message in John is about the eternal life that has already begun in Jesus (John 10:10; 1 John 5:11–13) and about becoming the children of God at the present time (John 1:11–12). This emphasis on the present and the eternal and the move away from the focus on the apocalyptic coming of the Son of Man have some parallels in the rise of the gnostic Christian message in the early second century. The delay of the coming (or return) of the expected Christ was difficult for many Christians. How the church was supposed to speak to its believing community at the end of the first century, when Jesus had not yet come after more than sixty years, was an issue that had to be addressed. Some late first- or second-century Christians had begun emphasizing a "realized" (already present) eschatology, and there was conflict over the matter of the time of the return, when the promises that the Christians had eagerly awaited would be fulfilled (cf. 2 Tim 2:16–18; 2 Pet 3:3–4).

5. A Vacuum of Authority and the Developing Structure of the Church

The deaths of the apostles and the decline of the prophetic voice in the church led to the gradual collection of Christian writings and their eventual recognition as Scripture. While there was a live voice in the church who had witnessed the activity of God in Christ, the church preferred the living witness over written documents, as Papias stated in the first third of the second century (Eusebius, *Hist. eccl.* 3.39.4).[19] Although the writings of Paul were likely gathered and circulated in Asia Minor by the end of the first century A.D., there is little to show that they were viewed as Scripture by that time. The vacuum, if we may speak of one, was eventually filled in the first decades of the second century A.D., when the office of bishop (earlier the title was still interchangeable with that of presbyter or elder) began to acquire more and more prominence in the church, and there was a recognized need for more organization, authority, and control in the church. This strong organizational structure under the leadership of the bishop was accompanied by creedal formulations, by which it sought to rid itself of heretics, and by a collection of Scriptures, which at first included the writings of the OT, various apocryphal and pseudepigraphal writings, and eventually several Christian writings. The inclusion of these writings in a biblical canon was a much later development in the church. (See ch. 13, below, on the formation of the Christian biblical canon.)

The other main causes of this increased tendency toward a hierarchical organization were the growth of heresy in the church, which threatened to sever it into many splinters, and the rapidly growing and expanding church, with large distances separating the various Christian communities. As the role of the wandering charismatic preachers or prophets within the church diminished, perhaps because of abuse of privilege, it gave way to the more stable role of the bishop and teachers in the church. *Didache* 11–13 offers an interesting look at the problem of the wandering prophets, how they were dealt with, and the conflict in the church over the reception of such individuals, some of whom were believed to be deceitful and were not to be received (2 John 7–11), while others were more acceptable and were to be received (3 John 5–10) (see sec. E.4, below). It was thought that the best way to deal with each of these problems, as well as others, was to increase the power of the local church officers. An improvement in the relations between the churches generally—though not always—resulted from having strong leaders or bishops over them. The notion of a central, overarching bishop (such as the position later occupied by the bishop of Rome) did not manifest itself in the early life of the church, but the idea of a powerful episcopate did take hold in Asia Minor, especially in the teaching and example of Ignatius of Antioch (died ca. A.D. 115). Ignatius's major concerns were unity among the churches and dealing with heretics within the churches. By the vesting of power in the bishop or overseer of the congregation, authority was assigned to deal with matters affecting the church. This authoritative, hierarchical structure cited as its authority the apostolic writings and creeds that emerged out of the "apostolic deposit" of teaching passed on in the churches (the *regula fidei*), and this appeal to authority enabled the church to deal more effectively with the threats to its unity and integrity as a community of followers of Jesus.

6. The Scriptures of the Early Christian Church

Along with OT writings and some writings commonly called the apocrypha and pseudepigrapha, a collection of Christian Scriptures was also eventually incorporated into the authoritative writings of the church to deal with the problems and issues that it faced in its social life, for catechetical needs, and for worship. The OT and some of the other books continued to be used in the churches of the first two centuries A.D., but primarily as prophetic books that pointed to Jesus and not generally as a list of laws and regulations to follow. The OT Scriptures were interpreted almost entirely as a prophetic document, that is, allegorically and typologically for practical application and for Christian apologetic. Many in the church had to deal with the problem of how to accept the OT as Holy Scripture without accepting its call to obey the law. This question was first addressed in a serious manner in the church by Paul in Gal 3–4 and Rom 3–6 and subsequently by Justin in the mid–second century.

The primary authority in the early Christian church at the end of the first century was, without question, the teachings of Jesus and examples drawn from his life. His death and resurrection formed the foundation for Christian preaching and teaching and was at the core of early Christian hope for forgiveness and reconciliation with God. The Gospels (perhaps only one or two of them at first) and the letters of Paul, whose theology was formulated around the death and resurrection of Jesus, were the primary Christian writings and received the earliest recognition in the churches. Among the earliest Christian writings to affect the church's life and worship were the Gospels, and this continued to be true throughout the second century even when other Christian writings were also being added to that collection. Paul's letters and his contributions will be discussed more fully in chs. 9 and 10, below.

D. Worship in the Early Church

Our study here will focus only on worship in the NT and the developing church after the death of the apostles. We note, however, that the use of OT Scriptures and the practices of first-century Judaism were the primary models for most worship in the early Christian church.[20]

1. Terms

There is no single word in the NT to describe all the dimensions of what appears to constitute NT worship. The terms most often used for worship are the following: (a) προσκυνέω (*proskyneō*). This is only found a few times in the NT, but its primary focus is adoration, veneration, and submission. The word means "kiss," "become prostrate," or even "bend" or "bow down," and these actions may well have originally been among acts of worship (see Matt 14:33; Mark 5:6; Luke 24:52; John 4:20, 1 Cor 14:25; etc.). (b) γονυπετέω (*gonypeteō*). This term, which means literally "bend the knee," is found in adoration texts such as Luke 22:41 and Matt 17:14. (c) λατρεία, λατρεύω (*latreia, latreuō*). This noun and cognate verb indicate service, as to a god, perhaps the offering of sacrifice and service without regard for reward. In the NT they emphasize service and dedication of one's life to God (see Acts 7:7, 42; Rom 1:9; 9:4; 12:1; Heb 9:1). (d) λειτουργία, λειτουργέω (*leitourgia, leitourgeō*). These are also terms of service, but they tend to be used of a ritual service, as in the case of "ministry" rendered to or for God (see Luke 1:23; Acts 13:2; 2 Cor 9:12; Heb 9:21; 10:11). The word "liturgy" comes from this term.

2. The Meaning of Worship

In the ancient Jewish and pagan world, worship consisted mainly of animal sacrifice. In the NT, however, the emphasis is upon self-sacrifice in honor and adoration of Christ because of his death/sacrifice on the cross (Mark 8:34–36). Worship appears to be the response of grateful persons to the grace of God that has come in the work of Jesus Christ

(see Rom 12:1, 2). It does not take place when a priest makes a sacrifice on one's behalf but, rather, when persons individually or corporately offer praise and service to God. In Christ the whole church has become a priesthood and a temple inhabited by the Holy Spirit or the presence of God (see 1 Cor 6:19; Eph 2:19–22; 1 Pet 2:9). From a NT perspective, worship is incomplete without personal participation in the giving or sacrificing of oneself to God. The author of Hebrews, however, underscores the assumption that Christ is our sacrifice (cf. 1 Cor 5:7) and that no other sacrifice need be performed. According to the author, the blood of bulls, goats, or other animals cannot accomplish what Christ's sacrifice accomplished (Heb 10:4–11; cf. Ps 40).

3. Elements of Worship and Ritual

Whatever ritual acts are involved in worship, from a NT perspective it is essentially spiritual in nature (see 1 Pet 2:5; Rom 12:2)—primarily an internal attitude, rather than the practice of external rituals. This emphasis is also found in Isa 1, 6 and Ps 51. Three rituals connected with worship are frequently mentioned in the NT, and two others less frequently. Explicit instruction on how to practice them is not given in the NT; this came much later in the early church, when there were many variations. They include the following: (a) Baptism. In its earliest form, baptism was administered by immersion after faith in Christ ("baptism" comes from the Gk. βαπτίζω, *baptizō*, "immerse") and was accompanied by a reference to Jesus, that is, in his name (e.g., Acts 2:38). Matthew 28:19 alone in the NT mentions baptism in the name of the Father, Son, and Holy Spirit. (b) Communion, Eucharist, or Lord's Supper. This is the only ritual regularly practiced by the early church. It apparently consisted of a simple meal of bread and wine over which a blessing and prayer of thanksgiving were pronounced (1 Cor 10:16; 11:26). The Greek term εὐχαριστία, *eucharistia* (verb εὐχαριστέω, *eucharisteō*), from which the word "eucharist" comes, means "thanksgiving," "giving thanks," and focuses upon the fact that thanksgiving was offered before partaking of the bread and wine. The term "mass," used later to denote this act, comes from the Latin *missa*, "sent." The origins of the use of this term for the Eucharist or communion are unknown, but it dates back at least to the fifth century A.D. in Vienne.

(c) Laying on of hands. This was associated primarily with the receiving of the Holy Spirit (Acts 8:17) but also with commissioning persons to Christian service (Acts 13:1–3). (d) Lifting up of hands. The practice of lifting up one's hands to God was already a common practice among the Jews (see Pss 134:2; 143:6) and other ancient peoples, including the Egyptians. To lift up the hands in worship probably symbolized one's submission to God and a reaching toward God. It was also the sign for pronouncing a blessing upon persons (see Lev 9:22; also Luke 24:50; 1 Tim 2:8). (e) Foot washing. Although this activity is described in John 13:5–17, it was not generally practiced by the early church, which apparently saw it not so much as a command to follow as an attitude to have, that is, one of submission.

4. Worship Services

The early church patterned much of its worship service after that of the Jewish synagogue service. The service was characterized by prayers (Acts 2:42), reading of Scriptures (1 Tim 4:13), exposition or explanation of the Scriptures (Rom 12:8), singing of spiritual songs (Eph 5:19–20), and contributions for those in need (see 1 Cor 16:2; also Acts 2:42–46; 4:32–35). The Christians apparently regularly shared in communion (see no. 3.b, above).

Many of the Christian worship services were characterized by joy and celebration (Acts 2:47; 1 Thess 5:16–18) as well as a corporate sharing of the gifts of ministry resident in the members of the congregation (1 Cor 14:26; Acts 4:32–37). Although at first Christians seemed to gather daily in the temple for prayers (Acts 2:46), the time of regular worship services seems first to have been on the Sabbath—Saturday—but by the middle of the first century, many Christians were gathering regularly on the first day of the week (see 1 Cor 16:2; Acts 20:7; Rev 1:10), probably in honor of the day Jesus was raised from the dead (see Justin, 1 Apol. 67, below).

The earliest known description of a Christian worship service outside the NT is found in Justin Martyr's 1 Apology (ca. A.D. 160). Its geographical setting is Rome, and he describes what usually took place when the Christians there gathered together for worship:

After these [services] we constantly remind each other of these things. Those who have more come to the aid of those who lack, and we are constantly to-gether. Over all that we receive we bless the Maker of all things through his Son Jesus Christ and through the Holy Spirit. And on the day called Sunday there is a meeting in one place of those who live in cities or the country, and the memoirs of the apostles [the Gospels] or the writings of the prophets [perhaps all or most of what we now call the OT] are read as long as time permits. When the reader has finished, the president in a discourse urges and invites [us] to the imitation of these noble things. Then we all stand up together and offer prayers. And, as said before, when we have finished the prayer, bread is brought, and wine and water, and the president similarly sends up prayers and thanksgivings to the best of his ability, and the congregation assents, saying the Amen; the distribution, and reception of the consecrated [elements] by each one, takes place and they are sent to the absent by the deacons. Those who prosper, and who so wish, contribute, each one as much as he chooses to. What is collected is deposited with the president, and he takes care of orphans and widows, and those who are in want on account of sickness or any other cause, and those who are in bonds, and the strangers who are sojourners among [us], and, briefly, he is the protector of all those in need. We all hold this common gathering on Sunday, since it is the first day, on which God transforming darkness and matter made the universe, and Jesus Christ our Saviour rose from the dead on the same day. For they crucified him on the day before Saturday, and on the day after Saturday, he appeared to his apostles and disciples and taught them these things which I have passed on to you also for your serious consideration. (Justin, 1 Apol. 67)[21]

5. Other Features of Early Christian Worship

Several other important features of early Christian worship, which are seen especially in the Pauline tradition, include the fact that the services were: (a) Charismatic. The offering of enthusiastic praise, service, and prayer under the influence of the Holy Spirit was characteristic of early church worship. This was done through normal speech (1 Cor 14:19) as well as tongues or ecstatic speech (1 Cor 14:2, 6–25). To each person was given a manifestation of the Spirit for the common good (1 Cor 12:7). (b) Didactic. The early Christians were a teaching community, giving instruction in their time of worship (see Acts 2:42–47; 1 Cor 12:8; 14:26; Eph 4:11; 1 Tim 3:2; 4:13; 5:17). (c) Eucharistic. They were a community conscious of the need to give thanksgiving to God (Eph 5:19). (d) Communal. The Greek term κοινωνία (koinōnia) means "sharing"—the kind of giving that builds up the whole fellowship of Christ and that includes but is not limited to the sharing of meals. This is the focus of 1 Cor 12:1–7.

6. Music in the Early Church

There is no question that the early Christians lifted their voices in praise to God. The NT frequently mentions the corporate singing that took place in worship. Some of the hymns used in worship include 1 Cor 14:26–33, Eph 5:19–20, and Col 3:16. Some scholars also think that examples of early Christian hymns can be found in Eph 5:14, 1 Tim 3:16, Phil 2:6–11, Col 1:15–20, and Heb 1:3. Besides these there are nativity hymns or hymns that are part of exaltation of the birth of Jesus: Luke 1:46–55 (Magnificat); 1:68–79 (Benedictus); 2:14 (Gloria in Excelsis); 2:29–32 (Nunc Dimittis, "Master, now you are dismissing your servant in peace, according to your word"). Other examples of hymns in the NT may well be found in John 1:1–14; 1 Pet 1:18–21, 2:21–25, 3:18–22; and Rev 5:9–12, 12:10–12, 19:1–3, 6–8. All of these hymns relate to the person and mission of Christ: sometimes his preexistence, how he became a man, or how he accomplished redemption or salvation for the world through his suffering and death. The dominant motif in NT hymns is that Christ is victorious over all his enemies and even death itself and is rightly to be worshipped as the image of the one who is God over all.

7. Early Christian Creeds in Worship

The use of creeds in the early church helps us to see that there was an agreed body of "sound doctrine" circulating in the churches that was widely—though not universally—accepted as representing the beliefs of the church. Scholars believe that several passages can be identified as early creedal statements, many exceptionally early—perhaps dating to the A.D. 40s or 50s. Evidence of the focus on teaching is found in Acts 2:42; Rom 6:17; Phil 2:16; 1 Tim 4:16; 2 Tim 1:13, 4:3; and Titus 1:9. Examples of creedal formulations are also found in Rom 10:9; 1 Cor 15:3–5; Phil 2:11, 16; and 2 Tim 2:15. Many of what have been listed as early Christian hymns (see no. 6, above) may better be described as creedal formulas. These statements often have sets of parallel expressions that encapsulate and make memorable essential early Christian belief.

5. WANDERING PREACHERS IN THE EARLY CHURCH

The book of Acts is strangely silent about many things, not the least of which is what took place during ten years of Paul's life after his conversion and what happened in the ministries of the Twelve after Acts 15.[22] Strangely, only Peter, Stephen, and Paul get much attention in Acts; the others receive only a few fleeting comments, mostly as a group. Some argue that another important omission is the story of some of the earliest followers of Christ, wandering charismatic preachers called "prophets," who proclaimed Jesus as the Christ after his resurrection. Paul indicates that prophets were at the very foundation of the other offices in the church (1 Cor 12:28; Eph 4:11), although it is not certain that these charismatic prophets are the ones that Paul has in mind. These prophets were a diminishing breed in the church by the middle of the second century A.D., but many believe that they were still quite active in the ministry of most churches at the end of the first century. Because many of these prophets were known for their excesses and because some charlatans were practicing the role of prophet, there were clear warnings in the early church to be alert and to test the ministry of the prophets (Matt 15:20; 24:11; Rev 2:20). *Didache* 11–13, written A.D. 70–90, offers a method for testing the genuineness of these prophets and teachers as well as of apostles (these terms were probably interchangeable at this time):

> Whosoever then comes and teaches you all these things aforesaid, receive him. But if the teacher himself be perverted and teach another doctrine to destroy these things, do not listen to him, but if his teaching be for the increase of righteousness and knowledge of the Lord, receive him as the Lord. And concerning the Apostles and Prophets, act thus according to the ordinance of the Gospel. Let every Apostle who comes to you be received as the Lord, but let him not stay more than one day, or if need be a second as well; but if he stay three days, he is a false prophet. And when an Apostle goes forth let him accept nothing but bread til he reach his night's lodging; but if he ask for money, he is a false prophet (*Did.* 11.1–6 [Lake, LCL]).

The excesses in the ranks of these charismatic preachers made it necessary for the church to distinguish the good prophets from the bad, often a very difficult task (2 John 7–11; 3 John 5–10).

Luke speaks of prophets in the church in Jerusalem (Acts 11:27; 21:10), at Antioch (Acts 13:1), and after the Acts 15 council meeting in Jerusalem (Acts 15:32–35). The office of prophet was essentially replaced by the office of teacher in the church by the end of the second century. The prophets do not, at first glance, appear to have done more in the churches than teach, though in Acts 13:1–2 they participate in the sending of Paul and Barnabas on a missionary journey to evangelize the Gentiles. In Jerusalem, the prophets do not seem to have played a very significant role in leadership decisions. They were evidently supported by sympathizers (Matt 10:11), but as time went on and the return of Christ did not occur, their "ethical radicalism"—their homelessness, lack of family and possessions, and lack of self-protection—was gradually tempered and eventually gave way to a more moderate and

settled lifestyle. Around A.D. 130–140 Lucian, the pagan satirist and philosopher, wrote a scathing satire against a self-proclaimed prophet in the church, by the name of Proteus Peregrinus, who defrauded a church in Asia Minor of much money before moving on to other opportunities. (See sec. 7.F, below, for Lucian's description of Peregrinus.)

6. THE SEPARATION OF CHRISTIANITY FROM JUDAISM[23]

A. When Christians Ceased Being Jews

Most scholars agree today on the following points: (1) Christianity began as a sect of Judaism in the first century A.D., but it ceased being a Jewish sect (2) when the church became predominantly Gentile in character and composition and ceased ob-

The Mosque of Abraham (Haram el-Khalil = Tomb of the Patriarchs) at Hebron was built by Herod the Great around the Cave of Machpelah to honor the patriarchs. The current walls and pavement within are Herodian, but portions of the structure may go back to the time of Solomon. Some parts of the structure were added by the Moslems, especially the top of the wall and the two minarets. Many Jews and Moslems believe that Abraham, Sarah, Isaac, Jacob, Rebecca, Leah, and Joseph were buried here, and some Moslems contend that Adam left his footprint when he prayed here.
Photo © Rohr Productions. Used with permission.

St. Catherine's Monastery at the base of Mount Sinai. Photo © Rohr Productions. Used with permission.

serving Jewish practices, especially circumcision and obedience to the law, and (3) when Jesus had been elevated to a position higher than that of any other intermediary person from the history of ancient Judaism.[24]

At the beginning, the church did not distinguish itself from the larger body of those adhering to the practice of Judaism. Nevertheless, Christianity generally ceased to be a part of what survived as mainstream Judaism well before the end of the first century A.D. The complete separation followed the Bar Kokhba rebellion of A.D. 132–135. What led to this separation? As stated, it was nearly complete when the church generally ceased observing the law, the practice of circumcision, the celebration of special holy days when Jesus was venerated as divine, and when there was widespread acceptance of Gentiles into the church's midst without observance of the above practices. The separation began very early with the Hellenistic Christian mission to the Gentiles, especially in Antioch, and also with the missionary endeavors of the apostle Paul, and it was confirmed by the ways in which Chris-

tians were treated by the Romans. The church did not necessarily wish for this break, nor did it advocate such a position. Even Paul saw himself within the mainstream of what true Judaism was all about (Rom 2:25–29). He was brokenhearted that most of his fellow Jews could not see that his gospel was well within the boundaries of Judaism (Rom 10:1–13). But his emphasis on the freedom of the Gentiles from the normativeness of the law and the constantly increasing number of Gentile converts continued the pressure for the separation to become final.

Although Jewish Christians continued their worship in the temple in Jerusalem until they departed for Pella because of persecution ca. A.D. 62 and although many continued to meet in the synagogues well into the second century, their participation in the mainstream of Judaism became increasingly more difficult much earlier. From before the time of the Jamnia (Jabneh) conference (ca. A.D. 90) until shortly after the Bar Kokhba rebellion (A.D. 132–135), there was a rapidly growing intolerance toward the Jewish Christians within

Aaron and Moses icons in St. Catherine's Monastery at Mount Sinai.
Photo © Rohr Productions. Used with permission.

mainstream Judaism. This intolerance of Christians was probably heightened by Jewish Christians' failure to support the nationalistic messianic movement of Bar Kokhba. More and more, however, the Gentile congregations saw themselves as having taken the place of the Jews in the plan of God, and this supersession, which was in effect a formal separation from Judaism, was set in motion in a direction from which the church never returned. Often this process was justified by such NT texts as Rom 11:17–24, but Paul himself shuddered at the thought of the church replacing the Jews in the plan of God. To him the setting aside of the Jews from receiving God's salvation in Jesus Christ was only a temporary measure, and he believed that all Jews would eventually convert to faith in Jesus Christ (Rom 11:25–32).

The vituperative language against the Jews by many of the early church fathers from the second to the fifth century, and even later, demonstrates the pain of that fateful separation of Christianity from Judaism. The process was often filled with hate, anger, and even violence from both Jews and Christians. The Christians, who saw themselves as the legitimate heirs of the Jewish religious traditions, were at pains to demonstrate that they had superseded the Jews. They called into question the Jewish inheritance as the people of God, their ability to interpret their own Scriptures, their method of interpretation, and even their future as the people of God (Origen, *Hom. Judic.* 8.2 [GCS 7.510.14]). They claimed as their own the antiquity and traditions of the Jews as the people of God, including the prophets, who were called believers in Christ and were appropriated into the Christian tradition. Ignatius of Antioch, for example, claims that the "Prophets also do we love, because they have announced the Gospel, and are hoping in him [Christ] and waiting for him, by faith in whom they also obtain salvation, being united with Jesus Christ, for they are worthy of love and saints worthy of admiration, approved by Jesus Christ, and numbered together in the Gospel of the common hope" (*Phld.* 5.2 [LCL]).

The Christians began to teach that the Scriptures themselves became the sole possession of the

Christians because only they could properly understand them and their fulfillment was only found in Christ (Clement of Alexandria, *Misc.* 6.28.1). According to Justin, the Christians had become the "true spiritual Israel" because the Jews had despised and forsaken the law of God and his holy covenant and had hardened their hearts, refusing to see and perceive the will of God given to them through the prophets (*Dial.* 11, 12). Along with many other Christian writers, starting with the Gospel of John (see 8:29–41a), Justin argued from the example of Abraham for the inclusion of the Gentiles and for the exclusion of the Jews (cf. *Dial.* 110). In Rom 11:25–27 Paul speaks of a temporary situation that allowed for the inclusion of the Gentiles while maintaining the Jews as the elect people of God. He uses the example of Abraham in Gal 3:6–9, 13–14 and Rom 4:1–18 not to exclude the Jews but to include the Gentiles. In time, however, the inclusion of the Gentiles was viewed as also excluding the Jews. Siker has noted similarly that Deut 7:1–6 was used by the Jews as a way of including the Jews and excluding the Gentiles.[25] Justin

Martyr, however, may be the first Christian writer to argue specifically that it is the Christians who are the "true spiritual Israel," who have replaced the Jews (*Dial.* 1, 123, 135).[26] Such arguments by Christians would obviously be met with strong opposition by the Jews. In this context, a battle ensued for the traditions and heritage of the Jewish tradition that the church laid claim to, contested between Christians and the survivors of first-century Judaism, rabbinic Judaism.

Under such titles as *Adversus Judaeos* (Against the Jews) and *Altercatio cum Judaeo* (A Debate with a Jew), the early church fathers produced many harsh polemical writings against the Jewish people. The frequency and intensity of this phenomenon are accompanied by the strange contradiction of its presence in *Christian* literature. The vast majority of these criticisms are religious in nature, that is, they are anti-Judaistic, but they also oppose those who followed the precepts of Judaism. The criticisms are not racial in their orientation, but many of the writings are unusually intense, even to the point of condemning the Jewish people as a whole

A portion of a chapel mosaic in St. Catherine's Monastery, Mount Sinai, depicting St. Peter at the Mount of Transfiguration. Photo © Rohr Productions. Used with permission.

and in some cases even suggesting or encouraging hostilities toward the Jews. Anti-Jewish sentiment was nothing new when the church was born, but the Christian anti-Judaic rhetoric was different from that of the Greco-Roman world, even though it may have been influenced by it. What at times may appear in the church fathers to be a reference to race, that is, Jews being condemned as a people or nation, is most often a reference to their *religious* identity rather than to their ethnic origins. A "religious" anti-Judaism, however, could be just as hostile and dangerous to the Jews as a bias based on race. Unfortunately, in that respect religious anti-Judaism was not unlike racial anti-Semitism, especially during the late patristic and medieval times. From the church's perspective, as Marcel Simon argues, "a Jew was characterized by his religion. If he was converted, he ceased to be a Jew, and the ultimate aim [of the church] was just that, the conversion of Israel."[27] In the *Dialogue of Timothy and Aquila,* for example, after Aquila (the Jew) converted to the Christian faith and was renamed Theognostos, he was then described as one who "became the receptacle of the Holy Ghost—*he who was once a Jew,* but now a Christian by [the grace of] God; he who was once a wolf, but now had become Christ's sheep."[28]

Although the NT contains negative comments about the Jews, there is not the invective in which the Jews are completely rejected by God and permanently replaced by the Christians. As mentioned, Paul understood the displacement of the Jews as a temporary matter and longed for their conversion (Rom. 11:11, 15, 23–24). There is little doubt that "theological anti-Judaism"[29] had its origins in the NT writings, especially those of John, where "the Jews" are seen as those who oppose Jesus (John 5:10–18; 6:41–59; 7:1, 10–13; 8:48–59), and even of Paul (Rom 11:17–30; Gal 3–4; 1 Thess 2:14–16). The anti-Jewish comments in Paul (who, it must not be forgotten, was himself a Jew) are more focused, however, on religious matters such as the law, its ritual, and the failure of the Jews to convert to the Christian faith than they are on the Jews themselves. The charges against the Jews of obduracy, blindness, crimes committed against the prophets, and finally the crucifixion of Jesus are all part of the Christian tradition from its beginning. For instance, the charge of blindness is found in the Jesus tradition in Matt 23:16 (cf. Mark 12:37–40),

which included judgment from God for killing the prophets in 23:29–36. The charge of obduracy among the Jews is similar to the charge in Acts 28:25–29, in which the author grounds his judgment in Isa 6:9–10. The charge of deicide against the Jews by Melito in Sardis ca. A.D. 180 is not far removed from the words of Paul in 1 Cor 2:8. Observing these charges, Ruether has raised the question whether anti-Judaism is essential to Christian theology. She contends that John gives the "ultimate theological form to that diabolizing of 'the Jews' which is the root of anti-Semitism in the Christian tradition," and concludes that there is no way to eliminate anti-Judaism from Christianity without overhauling its christological hermeneutic.[30]

The charges against the Jews in the writings of the church fathers, though similar and often parallel with those in the NT, are intensified and expanded to include God's ultimate and final rejection of the Jews. Among some of the church fathers there appears to have been a shift from an anti-Judaic stance to one that was more anti-Jewish; that is, instead of opposing the tenets of Judaism as a means of salvation, they began to reject the Jewish people themselves.[31] Some of the most intense Christian writers against the Jews (Aphraates, Ephraem, Chrysostom, Cyril of Alexandria, and even Augustine of Hippo) are from the fourth and fifth centuries. In time this language led to outright hostilities against the Jews, as in the case of Cyril of Alexandria (ca. A.D. 414), who tried to get the Christians to throw the Jews out of the city.[32] His success in this is not known, but his language against the Jews is. He calls them "the most deranged of all men," "senseless," "blind," "uncomprehending," and "demented" (*In Lucam,* Homily 101). John Chrysostom accused the Jews of being "bandits," "killers of the Lord," "licentious," "possessed by demons," and the like (Homily 8, *Against Jews* [PG 48:927–942]). Tertullian argued that God's grace had ceased working among the Jews because they had despised and rejected Jesus as their Messiah with impiety, which was foretold about them in the Scriptures (*Ag. Jews* 13).

The separation of the church from Judaism, which by all accounts was not a peaceful one, left many bitter feelings in its wake. By the end of the fifth century, the vast majority of the Christian literature that mentioned the Jews at all did so, with

Inside the Arch of Titus in the Forum at Rome. The arch celebrates Titus's victory over the Jews with the fall of Jerusalem in A.D. 70. Photo © Rohr Productions. Used with permission.

A menorah taken by the Romans from the temple in Jerusalem, depicted inside the Arch of Titus. Photo © Rohr Productions. Used with permission.

a few exceptions, in a negative manner.[33] In time, partly as a result of the Jews' opposition to the church and partly as a result of their failure to convert to Christianity, many of the church fathers encouraged Christians to take hostile actions against them. For example, when Christians in Callinicum in Asia, led by their bishop, burned down a Jewish synagogue, the local governor required them to rebuild the synagogue at the bishop's own expense. Ambrose, bishop of Milan (c. 339–397), hearing of this decision, appealed the sentence to the emperor, Theodosius the Great, and publicly refused him communion until he reversed the governor's sentence (Ambrose, *Ep.* 40, 41). The obvious implication drawn from Ambrose's actions was that it was all right to do such things to the Jews.[34]

B. The Causes of the Separation and Hostilities

The factors that led to the complete separation of Christianity from Judaism are in many respects very clear. The most important reason for the separation of the two religious groups was a difference in the Christians' understandings of the person of Jesus and of the nature and role of the Torah.

From the very beginnings of the Christian movement, the Jews stumbled over the notion of a crucified Messiah (1 Cor 1:23).[35] The christological formulations about Jesus, that he was Lord and Christ, were also considered incompatible with the Jewish understanding of the person and role of the Messiah.[36] It was also impossible for the Jews to square the Gentile Christian attitude toward the law with their own understanding of Torah and the responsibility of living within God's covenant.[37] The eventual separation of Christianity from Judaism therefore seems inevitable, even though a significant number of Jewish Christians, who were called Ebionites, Elkesaites, Cerinthians, and Nazarenes, did not see this as necessary.[38]

It is hard to imagine how the two groups could have stayed together long given their differences on these major issues. This still does not account for the level of vindictive rhetoric and eventual hostilities between them or for their negative preoccupation with each other for hundreds of years.[39] What moved the relations from debate and separation to open hostilities? Several factors played a role.

1. The Failure of the Jews to Convert to Christianity

Early Christians had three major expectations that did not materialize in the way they had hoped: (1) that Jesus would soon return to the earth and establish his kingdom, (2) that the city of Jerusalem would become the capital of the Christian faith, and (3) that the nation of Israel would soon come to accept Jesus as the promised Messiah.[40] This last point proved to be quite frustrating for the early church, which became preoccupied for centuries with concern for the Jews. How could those who had received the promises of God, were the interpreters of the Law and the Prophets, and were the heirs of Israel's traditions have failed to recognize that Jesus was the promised Messiah? Paul shared this frustration but, as mentioned, was convinced that the Jews would eventually come to faith in Christ (Rom 9–11). No one in the earliest church believed that Israel's rejection of Jesus as Messiah would continue for long.

The church attempted to deal with this problem in two ways. (1) They made many attempts to convert the Jews, believing that God had not re-jected them (see, e.g., the Petrine sermons in Acts 2:38–41, 3:17–26; Paul's argument in Rom 1:16, 10:1, 11:1–2, 23–32; and the thrust of many of the early and late *Dialogues*, which call upon the Jews to convert to Christ). (2) When these efforts did not prove successful and, as time went on, fewer and fewer Jews became Christians, especially after the Gentiles became a majority of the Christian community,[41] many Christians began to raise the question whether the Jews had been rejected by God, seeing that they were no longer able either to interpret the Scriptures because of their spiritual blindness and hardness of heart or to understand God's salvation in Christ. It was further argued, as we have already seen, that the church took the place of Israel and indeed had become the "new Israel." The problem facing those who held this view was that the "old Israel" not only continued to exist some four hundred years after the formation of the church but that it was also prospering and offering a viable alternative to the Christian faith. The failure of the Jews to convert, therefore, constituted a major theological problem for the early Christians, who called into question Israel's existence and religious heritage. The church's claim to have inherited Israel's promises and traditions could only bring it into sharp conflict with the Jews, who continued to have a vibrant and influential community of faith for centuries after the church had announced this claim.

2. Christian Apologetic Needs

The Christian apologies to the pagans and the Christian attacks on the various heresies and heretics within the church, for example, Marcion, often cast aspersions against the Jews. Tertullian had more criticism of the Jews in his treatment of Marcion and other heretics (*Prescr.* 8; *Ag. Marc.* 3.23.1–2; 4.14, 15) than when dealing specifically with the Jews in his *Against the Jews*. Their pagan opponents asked the Christians why they did not obey the law, practice circumcision, or observe the Sabbath if they truly had accepted the Hebrew Scriptures as their own. How can the Hebrew Scriptures be normative for the church when the church does not obey the law it promotes? These and other criticisms against Christianity were raised by Celsus (e.g., Origen, *Cels.* 1.55; 2.76–78; 3.10; 4.77). Porphyry wrote some fifteen books against the Christians, severely criticizing their religion and denouncing them for having abandoned their religious heritage, Judaism (see Eusebius, *Hist. eccl.* 1.2.1–4; 1.3.1). The Christian response came at the expense of the Jews. It was because of the Jews' hardness of heart and their many crimes that God first instituted the law, and because of their continuing obduracy that he changed the whole scheme of redemption, abolishing the necessity of the law. His new people, the church, was now under a new dispensation of God's grace and therefore no longer under the law. When the Jews were removed as the people of God and the church was made the new Israel, a new day in God's economy began. The Hebrew Scriptures could no longer be understood literally but only spiritually, since the Spirit was now resident in the new community of faith.

3. The Attractiveness of Judaism to Christians

Many Christians in the fourth and fifth centuries were anguished over the fact that Gentile Christians and many pagan Gentiles were finding Judaism more attractive than Christianity. Many were attending Jewish festivals regularly and even converting to Judaism. Large numbers of them sought physical healing from the Jews through their prayers and incantations and the wearing of Jewish amulets. The successes of the Jewish missionary efforts can be seen in the fact that Chrysostom felt obliged to warn Christians against converting to Judaism some twenty-three years after the death of Emperor Julian near the end of the fourth century.[42] The author of the *Apostolic Constitutions and Canons*, writing near the end of the fourth century and probably from Syria, shows that not just the laity but also the church's leaders were tempted toward Judaism. He stipulates what treatment should come to those who follow Jewish practices and orders that "if any bishop, or any other of the clergy, fasts with the Jews, or keeps the festivals with them, or accepts of the presents from their festivals, as unleavened bread or some such thing, let him be deprived; but if he be one of the laity, let him be suspended" (*Apos. Con.* 8.47.70 [*ANF*]). In another place, after he has enumerated the crimes of the Jews, including their blindness and hardness of heart, he commands that the Christians no longer "keep the feast with the Jews, for we have now

no communion with them" (*Apos. Con.* 5.3.16–17 [*ANF*]). In similar circumstances, John Chrysostom in 387 warned Christians against being attracted to Judaism and to do all that was necessary to bring a "defector" (one who had left the church and converted to Judaism) back to the Christian fold, even if it involved the use of force. He supported these measures by focusing on the enormity of the crimes of the Jews and told his audience to ask the defector, "Tell me, do you agree with the Jews who crucified Christ and who blaspheme him to this day and call him a transgressor of the law? Surely he will not dare say—if he is a Christian, and even if he has been judaizing countless times—'I agree with the Jews' " (Homily 8, *Against Jews* [PG 48:934]).[43] Such invective reveals that Judaism, far from vanishing from the scene, was in fact flourishing in the latter half of the fourth century.

4. The Intimidation Factor

As mentioned, by the turn of the first century, those who counted themselves among the Christians were probably fewer than a hundred thousand throughout the Roman Empire, while the Jewish population was somewhere between six and seven million. By any estimate, in their first two hundred years and probably longer, the Christians were greatly outnumbered and probably intimidated not only by the number of Jews in the empire but also by their large buildings, such as those at Sardis, and their long-standing influence and protected privileges in the Greco-Roman world. In the century following the conversion of Constantine, there is no certain evidence on whether the Christians significantly outnumbered the Jews.

Besides, there were many Gentile Godfearers, who had accepted several of Judaism's basic tenets, and an even larger number who accepted aspects of Judaism but did not convert to it.[44] Conversion to Judaism consisted of accepting the God and Torah of the Israelites and being accepted into the Jewish community. Before the destruction of the temple in A.D. 70, conversion to Judaism entailed circumcision, sacrifice, and the keeping of the law, but afterwards, along with circumcision, it always stressed the essential tenets of Torah as taught by Judaism's teachers of the law.[45] Many Gentiles throughout the empire had adopted some of the most common Jewish practices, such as Sabbath and holiday observance, attendance at the synagogue, and the veneration of God. John Chrysostom, for example, condemned Christians in Antioch who were observing with the Jews the first two of these practices.[46]

So powerful was the influence of the Jews in the empire that the Christians could not be certain even in the fourth and fifth centuries that the gains they had acquired under Constantine would not be overturned. In order to understand the Christians' fear, one need only recall the actions of the emperor Julian, who tried to return the empire to its former pagan ways. After rejecting his Christian upbringing, he attempted to reverse the gains of the Christians by promoting the welfare of the Jews over the Christians and by trying to rebuild the temple in Jerusalem. Twice earlier, during the reigns of Hadrian and Constantine, the Jews attempted to rebuild their temple but were unsuccessful. Had Julian's attempt succeeded, one of the Christians' most enduring arguments against Judaism would have been blunted. They had long claimed that the destruction of the temple and the expulsion of the Jews from Jerusalem under Hadrian were evidence of God's rejection of the Jews and proof of the consequent election of the Christians to take their place. So common was this claim that one can scarcely believe that Julian, who was raised in the Christian religion, was unaware of it.[47] Socrates Scholasticus, the church historian (ca. A.D. 380–450), tells of Julian's promotion of, and financial support for, the Jews to rebuild the temple in Jerusalem and describes in detail the supernatural intervention of God by an earthquake and fire to prevent it from happening. By emphasizing that Cyril, bishop of Jerusalem, had predicted the demise of the structure, Socrates denotes divine intervention in the matter. As a consequence of this divine activity, he says, many Jews "confessed that Christ is God: yet they did not his will" even after a cross miraculously appeared on their garments afterwards (*Hist. eccl.* 3.20). Whatever happened in Jerusalem to terminate Julian's plan, his early death from wounds received in battle in the east brought a cessation to any further plans for rebuilding the temple. Christians saw all this as proof of God's rejection of the Jews and validation of the Christian claims. Sozomen (ca. 425–430), affirming a divine role in this event, reports that after the destruction of Julian's temple

in Jerusalem, "many [Jews] were hence led to confess that Christ is God, and that the rebuilding of the temple was not pleasing to Him" (*Hist. eccl.* 5.22). Whether there is any truth to his claim—there is a tendency in ancient histories to be self-serving—one can at least see that the failure to rebuild the temple was important for Christian apologetics.

5. Jewish Polemic and Hostilities against Christians

Given the level of Christian anti-Judaic rhetoric, it is inconceivable that the Jews did not respond in some way to the Christian polemic against them. But therein lies a major problem. Very few Jewish sources from the earliest days of the church document such a response from the Jews. If the Jews did produce polemical writings against the church, how is it that so few of them currently exist? Moore suggests that the answer probably lies in the fact that such literature was expunged from the Jewish community after the Christian triumph over the empire,[48] but Meagher maintains that vilification of Jesus was infrequent in Jewish writings because, for the Jews, the real issue against the Christians was the law and not Jesus himself.[49] He argues that Christians, like Stephen in Acts, were persecuted because they abused the law, not for their views about Jesus' messiahship. He further adds that when the Christians retaliated against Jewish persecution, they eventually gained the upper hand.[50] Whatever the reasons for the scarcity of Jewish rhetoric against the Christians, the Christian writings themselves offer abundant evidence for the circulation of Jewish polemic against the church in the Roman Empire. In Origen's *Contra Celsum*, an unknown but thoroughly conservative Jew, who shows considerable awareness of the Christian faith, feeds Celsus with many substantial objections to the Christian faith (*Cels.* 2.4.1–2; 2.9.1; 2.13.1ff.; 2.18, 26, 28, 34, 39, 41; etc.). Porphyry also was aware of similar Jewish criticisms against the Christians and made wide use of them in his arguments against the Christian religion.

Part of Ambrose's argument to the emperor Theodosius, that Christians should not be forced to rebuild the Jewish synagogue destroyed by the Christians in Callinicum, was that the Jews themselves had destroyed several Christian churches. Complaining about the Roman laws that required that Christians assume responsibility for rebuilding of the synagogue, Ambrose asks, "Where were those laws when they [the Jews] set fire to the domes of the sacred basilicas [Christian churches]?" (*Ep.* 40 to Theodosius). Hence, nothing was done about reparations to the synagogue. Similar evidence comes from Cyril of Alexandria, who tried to have the Jews expelled from the city because of their hostilities against the church, which resulted in the deaths of several Christians.[51]

Although it has been popular since Harnack to question whether the Christian treatises against the Jews reflect a genuine attempt to deal with real objections by the Jews against the Christians, more recently some scholars are concluding that there were many contacts between the Jewish and Christian communities throughout the first five centuries and that the Christian writings do reflect many of the issues raised by the Jews, though not in an unbiased manner.[52]

The evidence from Judaism for a Jewish polemic against the Christians is slim but worth noting. The first is found in the *Birkath ha-Minim*, the benediction (or malediction) against heretics, in the twelfth of the Eighteen Benedictions, also called the *Shemoneh Esreh*, which forms the basic prayer of the Jewish liturgy. It states, "And for the separatists and for the heretics [*minim*] let there be no hope; and let all wickedness perish as in an instant; and let all thy enemies be cut off quickly; and mayst thou uproot and break to pieces and cast down and humble the arrogant kingdom quickly and in our days. Blessed art thou, O Lord, who breakest enemies and humblest the arrogant" (PB 50 [48]).[53]

The issue here is whether the *Birkath ha-Minim* contains a direct reference to the Christians. It may not have been so intended in its earliest formulations, but the question is when *minim* became a normal Jewish designation for Christians. Some versions of the twelfth benediction dating from the fourth century contain the word *noserim* (or *nozrim*), "Nazarenes." It is possible that this was strictly a reference to Jewish Christians, but Tertullian, for example, indicates that this term was used by the Jews as a reference to all Christians. Explaining the meaning of the word, he states that "the Christ of the Creator had to be called a *Nazarene* according to prophecy; whence the Jews also designate us, on that very account, *Nazarenes* after Him" (*Ag. Jews*

4.8.1 [*ANF*]). Though Flusser offers a detailed history of the origin and use of the *Birkath ha-Minim*, he rejects the notion that it was ever used of all Christians, claiming that it was instead directed first against the Essenes and then only much later against "Nazoraeans," whom he believes were *Jewish* Christians.[54] Segal is probably correct when he says that the term *minim* was a reference in the benedictions that included, but was not limited to, all Christians.[55] Justin appears to substantiate this when he refers to a curse directed against all Christians. Explaining for Trypho some of the reasons for the calamities that had befallen the Jews (probably the events surrounding A.D. 66–70 and 132–135), he writes, "Accordingly, these things have happened to you in fairness and justice, for you have slain the Just one, and His prophets before him; and now you reject those who hope in Him, and in Him who sent Him—God the Almighty and Maker of all things—*cursing in your synagogues those that believe on Christ.*" Referring to their persecutions of the Christians, he continues, "For you have not the power to lay hands on us, on account of those who now have the mastery, *but as often as you could, you did so*" (*Dial.* 16.4 [*ANF*] [italics added]; see also 16, 47, 96, 137).[56]

Along with the *Birkath ha-Minim*, the Palestinian Talmud and the subsequent *Toldoth Yeshu* offer an anthology of talmudic references put together for use against the Christians. C. A. Evans has collected a sample of texts in the talmudic literature that give clear indication of the tensions between Jews and Christians. In the Babylonian Talmud, he has shown that aspersions are cast against the mother of Jesus, Mary, who is sometimes also confused with Mary Magdalene; Mary is described as "one who was the descendent of princes and governors, played the harlot with carpenters [Joseph]" (*b. Sanh.* 106a). Jesus is said to be excommunicated and condemned for worshipping an idol (*b. Sanh.* 107b; *Soṭa* 47a). Jesus' practice of healing is described as sorcery: "Jesus the Nazarene practiced magic and led Israel astray" (*b. Sanh.* 107b; see the interesting parallel in Mark 3:22). Jesus' crucifixion is described in similarly negative terms in both the Babylonian and Jerusalem Talmuds: "On the eve of Passover they hanged Jesus the Nazarene. And a herald went out before him for forty days, saying: 'He is going to be stoned, because he practiced sorcery and enticed and led Israel astray. Anyone who knows anything in his favor, let him come and plead in his behalf.' But, not having found anything in his favor, they hanged him on the eve of Passover" (b. Sanh. 43a; cf. t. Sanh. 10.11; y. Sanh. 67a; y. Sanh. 7.16). Even the reports of Jesus' resurrection are spoken of disparagingly, for he is called a magician: "He then went and raised Jesus by incantation" (b. Giṭṭ. 57a, MS M); "Woe to him who makes himself alive by the name of God" (b. Sanh. 106a).[57] Rokeah's conclusion that "the Jews clearly had no hand in the persecutions of Christians by the imperial authorities: Jews neither informed on Christians nor turned Christians over to the Roman authorities"[58] cannot be substantiated by any fair treatment of the primary sources, both Jewish and Christian.[59] Equally unfounded is his contention that the Christian polemic and persecutions directed against the Jews were caused only by Christian frustration over the failure of the Jews to convert to Christianity.[60] He does not give sufficient weight to the long list of references in the patristic writers, who give ample evidence not only of Jewish rhetoric against the Christians but also of their persecution of them as well (see, e.g., Justin, Dial. 16, 17, 32, 34, 117, 131, 133, 136, 137; Irenaeus, Haer. 4.21.3; Hippolytus, Comm. Gen. 49.86, who also says that Jews joined with pagans against the Christians in Comm. Dan. 1.29.21; cf. Mart. Pol. 13.2, 17.2, 18.1, which tells of the Jews' complicity in the death of Polycarp; Origen, Hom. Gen. 13.3). If Jewish participation in Christian suffering did not occur, as Rokeah argues, then we are without an adequate cause for the hateful intensity of the Christian polemic against the Jews. Johnson has shown that Jewish polemic against pagans was common in ancient times and that some of the very language later used by Christians against the Jews was also used earlier by the Jews against their pagan enemies.[61] There are numerous references in Josephus to Jewish violence and hostilities, including Josephus's own use of malicious terms—plentiful in Against Apion—to describe his opponents and the enemies of the Jews.[62]

Johnson is right when he says that in today's world, perhaps to overcompensate for past injustices, theologians treat first-century Jews as if they were pacific in their relations to Jesus or the early Christian church and that they treat "uncritically" the Pharisaic traditions' own self-portrayal and "dismiss any possibility of frailty." As proof of Jewish culpabilities, he lists twenty-one references from Josephus showing that the Jews were often fanatical and violent.[63] Numerous parties from the ancient world made use of such language. Understanding this can rob an ancient polemic of much of its disproportionate force.[64] All of this is not to relieve Christians from any responsibility for their own actions but, rather, to balance the picture and remind us that the Jews were not beyond irresponsible and unkind acts in ancient times any more than were the Christians.

C. Conclusion

The church went to great lengths in its earliest years to maintain the unity of the God of the Hebrew Scriptures with the God of Jesus and the apostles, and also to stress that its roots were firmly in the Jewish religious tradition. The first Christians did not seek to leave Judaism or its synagogues, but this was eventually imposed upon them by the leading voices of Judaism that emerged out of the first century. Unfortunately, the recognition of Christian indebtedness to the Jewish heritage did not prevent Christians and Jews from their extreme and sometimes hostile competition over who was the rightful heir to that heritage. There is no question that a large body of angry anti-Jewish rhetoric exists in the writings of the early church fathers and that the rhetoric became even more intense in the fourth and fifth centuries. Whether this was in response to Jewish persecution and the Jews' polemic against the church or whether, inversely, the Christian polemic against the Jews led to persecution by Jews and the rise of the Jewish polemic against the Christians may be debated; the fact of Jewish opposition to Christianity, however, which is seen first in the NT and then in the church fathers, is established.[65] Jewish opposition to Christianity, we have pointed out, resulted from the church's christological perspective[66] as well as its teaching on the role of the law and its ritual. When Christianity was small, Judaism could largely ignore it—though there is no evidence that it did—but with the church's significant growth in the second and subsequent centuries, the Christian faith was seen as a threat to Judaism and drew serious Jewish reaction. On the other hand, the survival of Judaism posed a threat to Christianity's argument that the church had replaced Judaism and had become heir to its antiquity and Scriptures. It is diffi-

The great basilica at Hierapolis (Pamukkale) dates from the second century and was used as a church from the fifth to the eleventh century. Photo Lee M. McDonald.

cult to imagine how the two groups could have stayed together long given their differences. The breaking out of hostilities between them unfortunately damaged hope for reconciliation and adversely affected the ability of either group to listen to and appreciate the other. This does not mean that there would not have been such a separation if there had been more toleration and understanding at first, but it could have been a much better separation without the hostilities that engendered so much distrust.

7. HOW OTHERS SAW THE CHRISTIANS

The Christian faith was not born in a historical vacuum but, rather, in the midst of an empire that stretched around the Mediterranean world. Many who first heard about the Christians were unsettled by the things reported to them. Christians were generally held in suspicion by the Roman government as well as by the philosophically educated. Paul said that there were not many mighty or noble individuals or persons of means among the Christians (1 Cor 1:26); this fact was also recognized by others. The Christians' regard for sinners, the lowly, and the despised was considered distasteful by some. Many false rumors circulated that were misunderstandings of what the Christians were practicing. For example, they were accused of cannibalism when they partook of the body and blood of Christ in the communion meal. They were even accused of eating children.[67] Because they expressed love toward all and because everyone was a brother or a sister and used such terms as "love feast," the Christians were often accused of incest and immorality (called "Oedipodean intercourse," from the classical story of Oedipus of Thebes marrying his own mother). Their denial of the validity and reality of the state divinities, as well as their refusal to worship the emperor, led to the accusation of atheism (see esp. Athenagoras, *Leg.* 3; Minucius Felix, *Oct.* 9.) These and many other charges were brought against the Christians, and resentment against their witness was considerable, leading to many of the persecutions

The martyrium of Philip the Evangelist at Hierapolis (see Col 4:13), home of the
early church father Papias. Photo Lee M. McDonald.

that the Christian community suffered with greater or lesser intensity for its first three centuries. The following collection of quotations from antiquity gives some sense of how the Christians were perceived and received by state officials, prominent philosophers, and competing propagandists.[68]

A. Suetonius

Suetonius (Gaius Suetonius Tranquillus, ca. A.D. 69–140) was a friend of Pliny the Younger and a government official under the emperor Hadrian. He wrote *Lives of Illustrious Men,* some of which has survived, and also *Lives of the Caesars,* which portrays the Caesars from Julius to Domitian. Suetonius describes the Christians' punishment by Nero as follows: "Punishment was inflicted on the Christians, a class of men given to a new and mischievous superstition" (*Nero* 16.2 [LCL]). Again, speaking of the expulsion of the Jews from Rome by Claudius in A.D. 49, he writes, "Since the Jews constantly made disturbances at the instigation of Chrestus [Christ?], he expelled them from Rome" (*Claud.* 25.4 [LCL]).[69]

B. Tacitus

Tacitus (Cornelius Tacitus, ca. A.D. 55–120) was a major Roman historian. Among his better-known writings are the *Historiae* and the *Annales,* as well as *Agricola* and *Germania.* He describes the great fire at Rome in A.D. 64 and Nero's blaming of the event on the Christians. Although he agrees that the Christians perpetuate a "hideous and shameful" religion and constitute a "deadly superstition," he does not believe that the Christians were guilty of the fire:

But all human efforts, all the lavish gifts of the emperor, and the propitiations of the gods, did not banish the sinister belief that the conflagration [the burning of Rome] was the result of an order. Consequently, to get rid of the report, Nero fastened the guilt and inflicted the most exquisite tortures on a class hated for their abominations [*flagitia*], called Christians by the populace. Christus, from whom the name had its origin, suffered the extreme penalty during the reign of Tiberius at the hands of one of our procurators, Pontius Pilate, and a deadly superstition, thus checked for the moment, again broke out not only in Judea, the source of the evil, but also in Rome, where all things hideous and shameful from every part of the world meet and become popular. Accordingly, an arrest was first made of all who confessed; then, upon their information, an immense multitude was convicted, not so much of the crime of arson, as of hatred of the human race. Mockery of every sort was added to their deaths. Covered with the skins of beasts, they were torn by dogs and perished, or were nailed to crosses, or were doomed to the flames. These served to illuminate the night when daylight failed. Nero had thrown open his gardens for the spectacle, and was exhibiting a show in the circus, while he mingled with the people in the dress of a charioteer or drove about in a chariot. Hence, even for criminals who deserved extreme and exemplary punishment, there arose a feeling of compassion; for it was not, as it seemed, for the public good, but to glut one man's cruelty, that they were being destroyed. (*Ann.* 15.44.2–8)[70]

C. Pliny the Younger

An educated member of the Roman aristocracy and governor of Bithynia, Pliny (A.D. 61–114) wrote ten books of letters for publication that are valuable historical documents covering the period of Trajan's reign as Roman emperor (A.D. 98–117) and include an early reflection of attitudes toward the Christians by the emperor. Evidently, being a new governor, Pliny had not yet experienced any trials of the Christians, and he wrote Trajan to obtain help on how to deal with them and to tell the emperor what his practice with Christians had been. Some persons had reported to him that certain individuals were Christians, and upon investigating the matter, he found that there were three kinds of persons coming before him: (1) those who freely confessed that they were Christians and refused to deny their faith, who were consequently executed; (2) those who denied that they ever were Christians, who were given the opportunity to perform a pagan religious act (probably pouring out a libation to the gods and/or the emperor) and to curse Christ, upon which act they were released with no recriminations; and (3) those who had been Christians but turned away from the Christian faith and returned to pagan practices, who confirmed it by worshipping the pagan images of the gods and cursing Christ and were then released. The following is Pliny's letter to Trajan with his three questions of the emperor:

> It is my custom, lord emperor, to refer to you all questions whereof I am in doubt. Who can better

guide me when I am at a stand, or enlighten me if I am in ignorance? In investigations of Christians I have never taken part; hence I do not know how the crime is usually punished or investigated or what allowances are made. So I have had no little uncertainty whether there is any distinction of age, or whether the very weakest offenders are treated exactly like the stronger; whether pardon is given to those who repent, or whether a man who has once been a Christian gains nothing by having ceased to be such; whether punishment attaches to the mere name apart from secret crimes [*flagitia*], or to the secret crimes connected with the name. Meanwhile this is the course I have taken with those who were accused before me as Christians. I asked them whether they were Christians, and if they confessed, I asked them a second and third time with threats of punishment. If they kept to it, I ordered them for execution; for I held no question that whatever it was that they admitted, in any case obstinacy and unbending perversity deserve to be punished. There were others of the like insanity; but as these were Roman citizens, I noted them down to be sent to Rome.

Before long, as is often the case, the mere fact that the charge was taken notice of made it commoner, and several distinct cases arose. An unsigned paper was presented, which gave the names of many. As for those who said that they neither were nor ever had been Christians, I thought it right to let them go, since they recited a prayer to the gods at my dictation, made supplication with incense and wine to your statue, which I had ordered to be brought into court for the purpose together with the images of the gods, and moreover cursed Christ—things which (so it is said) those who are really Christians cannot be made to do. Others who were named by the informer said that they were Christians and then denied it, explaining that they had been, but had ceased to be such, some three years ago, some a good many years, and a few even twenty. All these too both worshipped your statue and the images of the gods, and cursed Christ.

They maintained, however, that the amount of their fault or error had been this, that it was their habit on a fixed day to assemble before daylight and recite by turns a form of words to Christ as a god; and that they bound themselves with an oath, not for any crime, but not to commit theft or robbery or adultery, not to break their word, and not to deny a deposit when demanded. After this was done, their custom was to depart, and to meet again to take food, but ordinary and harmless food; and even this (they said) they had given up doing after the issue of my edict, by which in accordance with your commands I had forbidden the existence of clubs. On this I considered it the more necessary to find out from two maid-servants who were called deaconesses, and that by torments, how far this was true; but I discovered nothing else than a perverse and extravagant superstition. I therefore adjourned the case and hastened to consult you. The matter seemed to me worth deliberation, especially on account of the number of those in danger; for many of all ages and every rank, and also of both sexes are brought into present or future danger. The contagion of that superstition has penetrated not the cities only, but the villages and country; yet it seems possible to stop it and set it right. At any rate it is certain enough that the almost deserted temples begin to be restored, and that fodder for victims finds a market, whereas buyers till now were very few. From this it may easily be supposed, what a multitude of men can be reclaimed, if there be a place for repentance. (Ep. 10.96)[71]

D. Trajan

When Trajan (Roman emperor, A.D. 98–117) replied to Pliny, he gave a timely report on the legal status of Christians in the empire:

You have adopted the proper course, my dear Secundus, in your examination of the cases of those who were accused to you as Christians, for indeed nothing can be laid down as a general ruling involving something like a set form of procedure. They are not to be sought out; but if they are accused and convicted, they must be punished—yet on this condition, that whoso denies being a Christian, and makes the fact plain by his action, that is by worshipping our gods, shall obtain pardon on his repentance, however suspicious his past conduct may be. Papers, however, which are presented unsigned ought not to be admitted in any charge, for they are a very bad example and unworthy of our time. (Pliny, Ep. 10.97)[72]

E. Graffiti

That Christianity was held up to ridicule and slander is seen in the graffiti on a stone in a guardroom on the Palatine Hill in Rome. Its precise date is difficult to establish, though it is probably from the middle to late second century. The etching depicts a man with the head of an ass hanging on a cross. Next to the figure is a man, of whom nothing is known, standing by the cross with his head raised in a gesture of adoration. The inscription reads, "Alexamenos worships his god."[73]

F. Lucian of Samosata

Lucian of Samosata (ca. A.D. 120–180), a man who wrote satires about religious and philosophical thought, did not hesitate to make biting comments about individuals with whom he had differences. Among his many writings is the story De

morte Peregrini, a satirical depiction of the life and death of a charlatan, Proteus Peregrinus, who lived in the early to middle second century A.D. and deceived, among others, a group of Christians and took them for their money (see sec. 5, above, on wandering preachers). Some scholars believe that he was writing about the life of Polycarp, who was martyred about the same time as Peregrinus died. They point to some obvious parallels to the Christian story of the Martyrdom of Polycarp, but aside from these interesting but not exact parallels, there is little to support this conclusion. Of special interest, however, is Lucian's detailed description of a wandering charismatic taking advantage of the early Christians and their response. Lucian had no respect for the Christians and speaks of them as simple and gullible people. Concerning Proteus Peregrinus, Lucian writes:

It was then that [Proteus] learned the wondrous lore of the Christians, by associating with their priests and scribes in Palestine.[74] And—how else could it be?—in a trice he made them all look like children; for he was prophet, cult-leader, head of the synagogue, and everything, all by himself. He interpreted and explained some of their books and even composed many, and they revered him as a god, made use of him as a lawgiver, and set him down as a protector, next after that other, to be sure, whom they still worship, the man who was crucified in Palestine because he introduced this new cult into the world.

Then at length Proteus was apprehended for this and thrown into prison, which itself gave him no little reputation as an asset for his future career and the charlatanism and notoriety-seeking that he was enamoured of. Well, when he had been imprisoned, the Christians, regarding the incident as a calamity, left nothing undone in the effort to rescue him. Then, as this was impossible, every other form of attention was shown him, not in any casual way but with assiduity; and from the very break of day aged widows and orphan children could be seen waiting near the prison, while their officials even slept inside with him after bribing the guards. Then elaborate meals were brought in, and sacred books of theirs were read aloud, and excellent Peregrinus—for he still went by that name—was called by them "the new Socrates."

Indeed, people came even from the cities in Asia, sent by the Christians at their common expense, to succour and defend and encourage the hero. They show incredible speed whenever any such public action is taken; for in no time they lavish their all. So it was then in the case of Peregrinus; much money came to him from them by reason of his imprisonment, and he procured not a little revenue from it. The poor wretches have convinced themselves, first and fore-

The Roman theater at Hierapolis. Photo Lee M. McDonald.

most, that they are going to be immortal and live for all time, in consequence of which they despise death and even willingly give themselves into custody, most of them. Furthermore, their first lawgiver [Jesus] persuaded them that they are all brothers of one another after they have transgressed once for all by denying the Greek gods and by worshipping that crucified sophist himself and living under his laws. Therefore they despise all things indiscriminately and consider them common property, receiving such doctrines traditionally without any definite evidence. So if any charlatan and trickster, able to profit by occasions, comes among them, he quickly acquires sudden wealth by imposing upon simple folk.

However, Peregrinus was freed by the then governor of Syria, a man who was fond of philosophy. Aware of his recklessness and that he would gladly die in order that he might leave behind him a reputation for it, he freed him, not considering him worthy even of the usual chastisement. (*Peregr.* 11–14 [LCL])

The passages quoted up to now, from Suetonius to Lucian, show, among other things, that the early Christians were often persecuted for their faith, that by and large they did not draw on the wealthy and learned classes, that they worshiped Jesus as a divine being, and that they cared for those of their number who were imprisoned by reason of their witness. Further, there was a perception on the part of the non-Christian world that many of the Christians were not afraid to face the consequences (imprisonment or death) for being Christians and that their eschatological hope was a primary source of encouragement to them. This supports the NT witness in these matters. The excerpt from Lucian also notes that the interpretation of their Scriptures by a prophet inspired by the Spirit was commonplace and that they were generous in their giving.

G. Celsus

Compared to the other critics of Christianity, Celsus (fl. ca. A.D. 178–180) shows more understanding of what the Christians believed, taught, and practiced than do his contemporaries. He seems to have read a number of Christian writings instead of merely listening to the rumors being spread about them. His arguments against the Christians, which were the most serious of the second century and even later, were examined in detail and answered fifty years later by Origen in *Contra Celsum*. Celsus, like Lucian, objected to the simplicity of the Christians and criticized their choice of faith over reason. He also objected to their doctrine of the incarnation of Christ, that is, God becoming a human being. According to Origen, from whom we know of Celsus,

> Celsus urges us to "follow reason and a rational guide in accepting doctrines" on the ground that "anyone who believes people without so doing is certain to be deceived." And he compares those who believe without rational thought to the "begging priests of Cybele and soothsayers, and to worshippers of Mithras and Sabazius and whatever else one might meet, apparitions of Hecate or of some other demon or demons. For just as among them scoundrels frequently take advantage of the lack of education of gullible people and lead them wherever they wish, so also," he says, "this happens among the Christians." He says that "some do not even want to give or to receive a reason for what they believe, and use such expressions as 'Do not ask questions; just believe,' and 'Thy faith will save thee.'" (*Cels.* 1.9 [*ANF*])

Origen claims that Celsus further charges that the Christians are unprofitable members of society who are weak, women, and slaves:

> Their injunctions are like this. "Let no one educated, no one wise, no one sensible draw near. For those abilities are thought by us to be evils. But as for anyone ignorant, anyone stupid, anyone uneducated, anyone who is a child, let him come boldly." By the fact that they themselves admit that these people are worthy of their God, they show that they want and are able to convince only the foolish, dishonorable and stupid, and only slaves, women, and little children.
>
> Those who summon people to the other mysteries make this preliminary proclamation: "Whoever has pure hands and a wise tongue." And again, others say: "Whoever is pure from all defilement, and whose soul knows nothing of evil, and who has lived well and righteously." Such are the preliminary exhortations of those who promise purification from sins. But let us hear what folk these Christians call. "Whosoever is a sinner," they say, "whosoever is unwise, whosoever is a child, and in a word, whosoever is a wretch, the kingdom of God will receive him."
>
> He asks, "Why on earth this preference for sinners?" (Ibid., 3.59 [*ANF*])

Celsus had no better attitude toward Jesus: "He was brought up in secret and hired himself out as a workman in Egypt, and after having

tried his hand at certain magical powers he returned from there, and on account of those powers gave himself the title of God" (ibid., 1.38 [LCL]). He even accuses Jesus of practicing sorcery (ibid., 1.6, 68). Celsus shows an obvious lack of knowledge about Jesus in these texts, but he had a good understanding of the low economic and educational status of the Christians and the simple outline of their faith.

H. Marcus Aurelius

Writing around A.D. 170, Marcus Aurelius (Roman emperor, A.D. 161–180), in his *Meditations*, alludes to the Christians' obstinacy in choosing death over conformity. At that time Christians were known as those who were willing to face death for their religious convictions, and to do so with dignity and resolve, not with public displays for self-glorification. Aurelius, however, only mentions the Christians once by name, and that in a passage that probably contains a later Christian interpolation:

> How admirable is the soul which is ready and resolved, if it must this moment be released from the body, to be either extinguished or scattered or to persist. This resolve, too, must arise from a specific decision, not out of sheer opposition *like the Christians*, but after reflection and with dignity, and so as to convince others, without histrionic display. (*Med.* 11.3)[75]

I. Galen

A Greek from Pergamum, Galen (ca. A.D. 129–199) rose from being a gladiators' physician to being the physician of Marcus Aurelius's court. He wrote not only about human anatomy and physiology but also about philosophy. He was an ardent monotheist, and so it is not surprising that he wrote about both the Jews and the Christians. His comments about the Christians are the most favorable found in the second century A.D. by a non-Christian:

> One might more easily teach novelties to the followers of Moses and Christ than to the physicians and philosophers who cling fast to their schools.
>
> . . . in order that one should not at the very beginning, as if one had come into the school of Moses and Christ, hear talk of undemonstrated laws, and in that where it is least appropriate.

A temple site at Pergamum (see Rev 2:12–17). Photo © Rohr Productions. Used with permission.

. . . If I had in mind people who taught their pupils in the same way the followers of Moses and Christ teach theirs—for they order them to accept everything on faith—I should not have given you a definition.

. . . Most people are unable to follow any demonstrative argument consecutively; hence they need parables, and benefit from them—and he [Galen—adds the editor who preserved this extract from a lost work] understands by parables tales of rewards and punishments in a future life—just as now we see the people called Christians drawing their faith from parables (and miracles) and yet sometimes acting in the same way as those who philosophize. For their contempt of death (and of its sequel) is patent to us every day, and likewise their restraint in cohabitation. For they include not only men but also women who refrain from cohabitating all through their lives; and they also number individuals who have reached such a point in their control regarding their daily conduct and in their intense desire for rectitude that they have in fact become not inferior to those who are true philosophers.[76]

J. Josephus

Flavius Josephus (ca. A.D. 37–120), the well-known Jewish general and historian, was born of royal descent from the Hasmonean line and was also a priest who supported the Pharisees. As an educated member of the aristocracy, he was in charge of the defense of Galilee at the outbreak of the Jewish revolt in A.D. 66. After surrendering to Vespasian, he prophesied that Vespasian would become the emperor. When that in fact happened, he was treated well by Vespasian. He took the name Flavius from his Roman patrons and wrote a number of literary works to defend the Jewish people. He is the principal historian of the Jewish people in the first century A.D. and an essential source for the history of early Christianity in Palestine. Scholars generally recognize that some of the comments in his writings about Jesus and the early Christians were probably introduced into his writings by the Christians themselves. Still, with care, much that is original can be discerned in his writings. Three primary texts have bearing on this topic. His references to John the Baptist have a number of similarities to the NT:

He was a good man and exhorted the Jews to lead righteous lives, practice justice towards one another and piety towards God, and so to join in baptism. In his view this was a necessary preliminary if baptism was to be acceptable to God. They must not use it to gain pardon for whatever sins they committed, but as a consecration of the body, implying that the soul was thoroughly purified beforehand by the right behavior. When many others joined the crowds about him, for they were greatly moved on hearing his words, Herod feared that John's great influence over the people would lead to a rebellion (for they seemed ready to do anything he might advise). Herod decided therefore that it would be much better to strike first and be rid of him before his work led to an uprising, than to wait for an upheaval, become involved in a difficult situation and see his mistake. Accordingly John was sent as a prisoner to Machaerus, the fortress mentioned before, because of Herod's suspicious temper, and was there put to death. (*Ant.* 18.117–119 [Feldman, LCL])

Josephus also provides important information about the death of James, the brother of Jesus, and he mentions in a noncommittal fashion that Jesus was called the Christ. Concerning James he says,

> Possessed of such a character, Ananus thought that he had a favorable opportunity because Festus was dead and Albinus was still on the way. And so he convened the judges of the Sanhedrin and brought before them a man named James, the brother of Jesus who was called the Christ, and certain others. He accused them of having transgressed the law and delivered them up to be stoned. Those of the inhabitants of the city who were consid-

ered the most fair-minded and who were strict in observance of the law were offended at this. (Ibid., 20.200–203 [LCL])

The third passage from Josephus, the one that purportedly tells about Jesus, seems to have been altered or interpolated by Christians, who were the primary preservers of Josephus's works after the eleventh century. In *Comm. Matt.* 10.17, Origen states that Josephus did not become a Christian, but in the following passage it appears that he did. It is therefore highly doubtful that the statements "He was the Messiah," "He appeared to them on the third day," and "holy prophets had foretold this" are genuine. Nevertheless, he could well have written the rest of this passage, which refers to Jesus:

> At about this time lived Jesus, a wise man, *if indeed one might call him a man.* For he was one who accomplished surprising feats and was a teacher of such people as accept the truth with pleasure. He won over many Jews and many of the Greeks. *He was the Messiah.* When Pilate, upon an indictment brought by the principal men among us, condemned him to the cross, those who had loved him from the very first did not cease to be attached to him. *On the third day he appeared to them restored to life, for the holy prophets had foretold this and myriads of other marvels concerning him.* And the tribe of the Christians so called after him has to this day still not disappeared. (Ibid., 18.63–64 [LCL])[77]

8. AN OUTLINE OF THE EARLY CHURCH'S DEVELOPMENT

The following is a brief overview or outline of the historical context of the emerging church in the first and second centuries.

A. TIMELINE

1. Apostolic Period (A.D. 30–65)
   The beginnings of the church until the death of its major leaders: Peter, Paul, and James.

2. Postapostolic (or Subapostolic) Period (A.D. 65–95)
   The primary time for the writing of the Gospels, the emergence of heresy (Docetism, Gnosticism), and the growth of hierarchy in church structure.

3. Apostolic Fathers (A.D. 95–160)
   The growth of "heresy" (christological controversies), disobedient congregations and the stabilized hierarchical structure of the churches, and early appeals to apostolic writings in worship and teaching in the churches.

4. Roman Priority (A.D. 160 and after)

The emergence and growth of "orthodoxy" as a response to docetic and gnostic teaching.

B. NOTEWORTHY EVENTS AND WRITINGS

1. Major Periods of Persecution
   a. A.D. 64–66: Rome, by Nero (local persecution)
   b. A.D. 85–95: Asia Minor, by Domitian (local persecution)
   c. A.D. 110–160: Rome, Asia Minor, and Palestine, allowed occasionally by several emperors (mostly local persecutions)
   d. A.D. 250–313: Empirewide, led by several emperors, especially Decius (ca. 250), Diocletian (fl. ca. 284–305), and Galerius (fl. ca. 304–311), until just after Constantine's Edict of Milan in February 313

2. The Apologists (A.D. 117–)

   Apologetic defenses of Christianity were made against the
   a. Jews (ca. A.D. 130–): Barnabas, Justin Martyr, the *Dialogues*, the *Adversus Judaeos* tradition
   b. Greeks (A.D. 117–): Quadratus (117–138), Aristides (138–147), Justin Martyr (160), Tatian (170), Athenagoras (177), Melito of Sardis (175), Apollinarius (175), anonymous *Diognetus* (possibly by Justin, ca. 160–180), Theophilus of Antioch (180), and many third-century writers who responded to Greco-Roman criticisms

3. Major Developments in the Second Century
   a. Increase in the "institutionalization" of the church (the growth in office and organization)
   b. Increase in creeds (early form of Apostles' Creed [old Roman creed, possibly as early as A.D. 100] emerges)
   c. Christian literature begins to be recognized as "Scripture" and used alongside the OT Scriptures
   d. Important issues:
      (1) Early heresies:
         (a) Docetism: see Ignatius and possibly 1 John
         (b) Gnosticism: probably developed out of the crisis (failure) of Jewish apocalyptic eschatology
         (c) Marcionism: the church's roots in Judaism were challenged
      (2) Persecutions (mostly local)
      (3) Problems of division in the churches, persecution, and expansion
      (4) Problem of authority: the emergence of an episcopate and a broadly accepted canon of beliefs *(regula fidei)* addressed this issue
      (5) Apologists and the *Adversus Judaeos* tradition, the growth of anti-Judaistic sentiment
      (6) Emergence and flourishing of religious sects of Christianity (Ebionites, Elkasites, Marcionites, Montanists, Gnostics, Alogi)
      (7) Development of early Christologies (angel and Spirit Christologies)
      (8) Problem of eschatology: the delay of the return of Jesus the Christ
      (9) Women of the Roman Empire increasingly active in the church

As Christianity grew out of its exclusively Jewish context and into its universal appeal to both Jews and Gentiles, becoming a predominantly Gentile church, there are important questions about what Christianity retained from its earliest Jewish heritage and what it left behind. What shifts in theological emphasis were made between the earliest community of followers of Jesus and the church of those of the late second and early third centuries? How are these shifts reflected in the sacred literature that the church of that era left behind? These questions require more discussion than is possible here; some will be examined in ch. 13.

BIBLIOGRAPHY

AUNE, D. E. *The New Testament in Its Literary Environment*. LEC. Philadelphia: Westminster, 1987.

_____. *Prophecy in Early Christianity and the Ancient Mediterranean World*. Grand Rapids: Eerdmans, 1983.

BALCH, D. L., E. FERGUSON, and W. A. MEEKS, eds. *Greeks, Romans, and Christians: Essays in Honor of A. J. Malherbe*. Minneapolis: Fortress, 1990.

BARRETT, C. K. *The New Testament Background: Selected Documents*. 2d ed. New York: Harper & Row, 1987.

BARTCHY, S. S. *First-Century Slavery and 1 Corinthians 7:21*. SBLDS 11. Atlanta: Scholars Press, 1973.

BAUER, W. *Orthodoxy and Heresy in Earliest Christianity*. Ed. R. KRAFT and G. KRODEL. Philadelphia: Fortress, 1971.

BENKO, S. *Pagan Rome and the Early Christians*. Bloomington: Indiana University Press, 1984.

BROX, N. *A History of the Early Church*. London: SCM, 1994.

BRUCE, F. F. *New Testament History*. Garden City, N.Y.: Doubleday, 1971.

CAIRD, G. B. *The Apostolic Age*. London: Duckworth, 1955.

CALLAN, T. *Forgetting the Root: The Emergence of Christianity from Judaism*. New York: Paulist, 1986.

_____. *The Origins of Christian Faith*. New York: Paulist, 1994.

CAMPBELL, R. A. *The Elders: Seniority within Earliest Christianity*. Studies of the New Testament and Its World. Edinburgh: T. & T. Clark, 1994.

COHEN, S. J. D. *From Maccabees to the Mishnah*. LEC. Philadelphia: Westminster, 1987.

CONZELMANN, H. *History of Primitive Christianity*. Trans. J. E. STEELY. Nashville: Abingdon, 1973.

DAVIES, A. T. *Anti-Semitism and the Foundations of Christianity*. New York: Paulist, 1979.

DUNN, J. D. G. *The Partings of the Ways between Christianity and Judaism and Their Significance for the Character of Christianity*. London: SCM, 1991.

EVANS, C. A., and D. A. HAGNER, eds. *Anti-Semitism and Early Christianity: Issues of Polemic and Faith*. Minneapolis: Fortress, 1993.

FERGUSON, E. *Backgrounds of Early Christianity*. Rev. ed. Grand Rapids: Eerdmans, 1993.

FILORAMO, G. *A History of Gnosticism*. Cambridge, Mass.: Blackwell, 1990.

FREND, W. H. C. *The Rise of Christianity*. Philadelphia: Fortress, 1984.

GAGER, J. *The Origins of Anti-Semitism: Attitudes toward Judaism in Pagan and Christian Antiquity*. New York: Oxford University Press, 1983.

GOPPELT, L. *Apostolic and Post-Apostolic Times*. Trans. R. A. GUELICH. New York: Harper, 1970.

GRANT, R. M. *Early Christianity and Society*. New York: Harper & Row, 1977.

_____. *A Historical Introduction to the New Testament*. New York: Simon & Schuster, 1972.

HARNACK, A. *The Mission and Expansion of Christianity in the First Three Centuries*. Trans. J. MOFFATT. London: Williams & Norgate, 1908.

HARRISON, E. F. *The Apostolic Church*. Grand Rapids: Eerdmans, 1985.

HENGEL, M. *Judaism and Hellenism: Studies in Their Encounter in Palestine during the Early Hellenistic Period*. Trans. J. BOWDEN. 2 vols. Philadelphia: Fortress, 1974.

HORSLEY, G. H. R., and S. LLEWELYN, eds. *New Documents Illustrating Early Christianity*. 8 vols. to date. North Ryde, N. S. W., Australia: Ancient History Documentary Research Centre, Macquarie University, 1981–.

HORST, P. W. van der. *Hellenism–Judaism–Christianity: Essays on Their Interaction.* 2d ed. Leuven: Peeters, 1997.

HULTGREN, A. J., and S. HAGGMARK. *The Earliest Christian Heretics: Readings from Their Opponents.* Minneapolis: Fortress, 1996.

JEREMIAS, J. *Jerusalem in the Time of Jesus.* Trans. F. H. CAVE and C. H. CAVE. Philadelphia: Fortress, 1969.

JOHNSON, L. T. "The NT's Anti-Jewish Slander and the Conventions of Ancient Polemic." *JBL* 108 (1989): 421–41.

KOESTER, H. *Introduction to the New Testament.* 2 vols. FFNT. Philadelphia: Fortress, 1982; 2d ed. of vol. 1, 1995; vol. 2, 2000.

LANE FOX, R. *Pagans and Christians.* Perennial Library. New York: Harper & Row, 1987.

LEANEY, A. R. C. *The Jewish and Christian World.* Cambridge: Cambridge University Press, 1984.

LEYTON, B. *The Gnostic Scriptures.* Garden City, N.Y.: Doubleday, 1987.

LOGAN, A. H. B. *Gnostic Truth and Christian Heresy: A Study in the History of Gnosticism.* Peabody, Mass.: Hendrickson, 1996.

LOHSE, E. *The New Testament Environment.* Trans. J. E. Steeley. Nashville: Abingdon, 1976.

LÜDEMANN, G. *Heretics: The Other Side of Early Christianity.* Trans. J. BOWDEN. Louisville, Ky.: Westminster John Knox Press, 1996.

MACMULLEN, R. *Christianizing the Roman Empore, A.D. 100–400.* New Haven: Yale University Press, 1984.

MACMULLEN, R., and E. N. LANE, eds. *Paganism and Christianity, 100–425 C.E.: A Sourcebook.* Minneapolis: Fortress, 1992.

MALHERBE, A. J. *Social Aspects of Early Christianity.* 2d ed. Philadelphia: Fortress, 1983.

MEEKS, W. A. *The First Urban Christians: The Social World of the Apostle Paul.* New Haven: Yale University Press, 1983.

MEEKS, W. A., and R. L. WILKEN. *Jews and Christians in Antioch in the First Four Centuries of the Common Era.* Missoula, Mont.: Scholars Press, 1978.

MEYER, B. F. *The Early Christians: Their World Mission and Self Discovery.* Good News Studies 16. Wilmington, Del.: Michael Glazier, 1986.

NEUSNER, J. *Jews and Christians: The Myth of a Common Tradition.* Philadelphia: Trinity Press International, 1991.

_____. *Judaism in the Matrix of Christianity.* Philadelphia: Fortress, 1986.

NICKELSBURG, G. W. E., and G. W. MACRAE, eds. *Christians among Jews and Gentiles.* Philadelphia: Fortress, 1986.

PAGELS, E. *The Gnostic Gospels.* New York: Vintage, 1979.

_____. *The Gnostic Paul: Gnostic Exegesis of the Pauline Letters.* Philadelphia: Trinity Press International, 1975.

PARKES, J. *The Conflict of the Church and the Synagogue.* Cleveland: World Publishing, 1961.

PERELMUTER, H. G. *Siblings: Rabbinic Judaism and Early Christianity at Their Beginnings.* New York: Paulist, 1989.

REICKE, B. *The New Testament Era: The World of the Bible from 500 B.C. to A.D. 100.* Trans. D. E. Green. Philadelphia: Fortress, 1968.

RICHARDSON, P., and D. GRANSKOU, eds. *Paul and the Gospels.* Vol. 1 of *Anti-Judaism in Early Christianity.* 5 vols. Waterloo, Ont.: Wilfrid Laurier University Press, 1986.

ROBINSON, J. M., ed. *The Nag Hammadi Library in English.* 3d ed. San Francisco: Harper & Row, 1987.

ROBINSON, J. M., and H. KOESTER. *Trajectories through Early Christianity.* Philadelphia: Fortress, 1971.

RUDOLPH, K. *Gnosis: The Nature and History of Gnosticism.* San Francisco: Harper & Row, 1983.

RUETHER, R. *Faith and Fratricide: The Theological Roots of Anti-Semitism.* Minneapolis: Seabury, 1974.

SANDERS, E. P., ed. *The Shaping of Christianity in the Second and Third Centuries.* Vol. 1 of *Jewish and Christian Self-Definition.* 3 vols. London: SCM, 1980.

SCHLATTER, A. *The Church in the New Testament Period.* Trans. P. P. Levertoff. London: SPCK, 1955.

SEGAL, A. F. *Rebecca's Children: Judaism and Christianity in the Roman World.* Cambridge: Harvard University Press, 1986.

SIKER, J. S. *Disinheriting the Jews: Abraham in Early Christian Controversy.* Louisville: Westminster John Knox, 1991.

SIMON, M. *Verus Israel.* Trans. H. MCKEATING. New York: Oxford University Press, 1986.

STAMBAUGH, J. E., and D. L. BALCH. *The New Testament in Its Social Environment.* LEC. Philadelphia: Westminster, 1986.

WALSH, M. *The Triumph of the Meek: Why Early Christianity Succeeded.* San Francisco: Harper & Row, 1986.

WILDE, R. *The Treatment of the Jews in the Greek Christian Writers of the First Three Centuries.* Washington, D.C.: Catholic University of America Press, 1949.

WILKEN, R. L. *The Christians as the Romans Saw Them.* New Haven: Yale University Press, 1984.

_____. *Judaism and the Early Christian Mind.* New Haven: Yale University Press, 1971.

WILLIAMS, A. L. *Adversus Judaeos.* Cambridge: Cambridge University Press, 1935.

WILLIAMSON, C. M., and R. J. ALLEN. *Interpreting Difficult Texts: Anti-Judaism and Christian Preaching.* London: SCM, 1989.

YAMAUCHI, E. M. *Pre-Christian Gnosticism: A Survey of the Proposed Evidences.* London: Tyndale, 1973.

pages 226–229

1. Some attribute these key passages not to the historical Jesus but to the early Christian community that Matthew addressed. However these passages may be interpreted, it is clear from Matthew that Jesus intended that a community should follow him, even though the specifics of how that community should be organized are not found in any of his teachings. All the evangelists stress, however, that those who follow Jesus will obey his will, demonstrate love even for the unlovely, and freely seek reconciliation through forgiveness and love based on grace, not on merit. This does not, of course, speak about the organization of such a community but about its character.

2. There is no doubt that Luke presents a simplistic picture of early Christianity—perhaps an idealized church, as some have argued—but it is still appropriate to speak of an initially simple organizational pattern that gradually becomes more complex. Allowances made for the summarizing nature of these passages, which have led some to think that there were no problems in the earliest church, do not nullify the simplicity found in the initial stages of the church, especially when many of its adherents believed that the Parousia, or coming of Christ, would be quite soon.

3. There are some parallels between the Jerusalem church and the organization of the Qumran community. Qumran had a board of twelve laymen who governed their community, and they were led by three priests. The overseer, who was called a *mebaqqer*, watched over the community's life and brought the new initiates into the fellowship.

4. See J. Quasten, *The Beginnings of Patristic Literature*, vol. 1 of *Patrology* (3 vols.; Utrecht: Spectrum, 1950), 195–96.

5. Trans. J. Stevenson, *A New Eusebius* (London: SPCK, 1957), 14. For a complete copy of the letter from Pliny, as well as Trajan's response, see H. C. Kee, *The New Testament in Context: Sources and Documents* (Englewood Cliffs, N.J.: Prentice-Hall, 1984), 44–45; and *The Letters of Pliny* (trans. B. Radice; 2 vols. LCL; Cambridge: Harvard University Press, 1969), 2:285–93. A larger context of the letter is presented in sec. 7.C, below.

6. R. E. Brown (*The Death of the Messiah* [2 vols.; New York: Doubleday, 1994], 2:1410–15) raises the question whether Judas came from the Galilee region.

7. On Galilee, see L. I. Levine, ed., *The Galilee in Late Antiquity* (New York: Jewish Theological Seminary, 1992); R. A. Horsley, *Galilee: History, Politics, People* (Valley Forge, Penn.: Trinity Press International, 1995); idem, *Archaeology, History, and Society in Galilee: The Social Context of Jesus and the Rabbis* (Valley Forge, Penn.: Trinity Press International, 1996).

8. For example, a growing number of scholars believe that the so-called Q source, the collection of sayings of Jesus in Matthew and Luke not found in Mark, was produced in Galilee. See S. Freyne, "Christianity in Sepphoris and Galilee," in *Sepphoris in Galilee* (ed. R. M. Nagy, C. L. Meyers, E. M. Meyers, and Z. Weiss; Winona Lake, Ind.: North Carolina Museum of Art/Eisenbrauns, 1996), 67–73.

9. E. M. Meyers, E. Netzer, and C. L. Meyers, in *Sepphoris* (Winona Lake, Ind.: Eisenbrauns, 1992), 15–17, show the presence of a Chi-Rho monogram at the end of a text of a Greek inscription in a synagogue in Sepphoris dating from the Roman period. They also report second-century sources claiming that a certain Jacob discussed Jesus with

Rabbi Eleazar, a notable Jewish sage of the second century said to have healed the sick in Jesus' name. There is no other clear mention of Christians at Sepphoris, however, until after the time of Constantine.

10. On the Godfearers, see M. De Boer, "God-Fearers in Luke–Acts," in *Luke's Literary Achievement: Collected Essays* (ed. C. M. Tuckett; JSNTSup 116; Sheffield: Sheffield Academic Press, 1995), 50–71; I. Levinskaya, *The Book of Acts in Its Diaspora Setting* (vol. 5 of *The Book of Acts in Its First Century Setting;* ed. B. W. Winter; Grand Rapids: Eerdmans, 1996), 51–126.

11. See H. J. Cadbury, "Names for Christians and Christianity in Acts," in *The Acts of the Apostles,* part 1 of *The Beginnings of Christianity* (ed. F. J. Foakes Jackson and K. Lake; 5 vols.; London: Macmillan, 1920–1933; repr., Grand Rapids: Baker, 1979), 5:375–92.

12. See Cadbury, "Names for Christians," 383–86; cf. E. A. Judge, "Judaism and the Rise of Christianity: A Roman Perspective," *TynB* 45 (2, 1994): 363–64, who uses the events surrounding the name (a tacit concession of Christ as Messiah) to indicate an early parting of the ways between Judaism and Christianity.

13. See S. E. Porter, "Vague Verbs, Periphrastics, and Matthew 16:19," *FN* 1 (1988): 171–72, for a discussion.

pages 233–239

14. Most of the following information is found in E. Ferguson, *Backgrounds of Early Christianity* (rev. ed.; Grand Rapids: Eerdmans, 1993), 282–95; and A. R. C. Leaney, *The Jewish and Christian World* (Cambridge: Cambridge University Press, 1984), 203–7.

15. H. Conzelmann and A. Lindemann (*Interpreting the New Testament: An Introduction to the Principles and Methods of New Testament Exegesis* [trans. S. S. Schatzmann; Peabody, Mass.: Hendrickson, 1988], 149) make this distinction.

16. The Mandaeans are a gnostic sect that began east of the Jordan in the late first or second century A.D. They taught that the body imprisoned the soul but that the soul would be set free by the redeemer, *Manda da Hayye,* who personified knowledge of life and defeated the powers of darkness on earth. Frequent baptisms and the laying on of hands by the priest were practiced to help in this struggle for freedom. Both knowledge and ritual were the vehicles for salvation. See K. Rudolph, "Mandaeism," *ABD* 4:500–502. Some Mandaeans still exist in modern Iraq near Baghdad. The Manicheans were a gnostic sect that originated with Manes (ca. A.D. 216–276), who was born near the Persian capital. He changed the views of the Jewish-Christian sect in which he was raised into a complete gnostic scheme of salvation through asceticism and knowledge. Their influence was felt especially in North Africa but also was known in Rome and even in southeast China. St. Augustine himself was converted to orthodox Christianity out of this sect. See P. A. Mirecki, "Manichaeans and Manichaeism," *ABD* 4:502–11.

17. L. T. Johnson, "The NT's Anti-Jewish Slander and the Conventions of Ancient Polemic," *JBL* 108 (1989): 423, gives this count of the Christians.

18. The size of the Jewish community in the first century A.D. varies in scholarly writings, but generally speaking, the above numbers are considered valid. Scholars of this period agree that the Jews were a sufficiently large community and significantly outnumbered the Christians in the first three centuries. See H. G. Perelmuter, *Siblings: Rabbinic Judaism, and Early Christianity at Their Beginnings* (New York: Paulist, 1989), 18, and W. A. Meeks, *The First Urban Christians* (New

Haven: Yale University Press, 1983), 34, who estimate that there were five to six million Jews in the first century; Poliakov, *Anti-Semitism*, 5, also puts the figure at three to four million Jews living in the Diaspora and one million in Palestine.

19. Cf. H. Y. Gamble, *Books and Readers in the Early Church* (New Haven: Yale University Press, 1995), 30–32.

20. There is no evidence that all churches cited all of the current OT Scriptures at this stage of the church's development. See ch. 13, below.

21. Trans. C. C. Richardson, *Early Christian Fathers* (New York: Macmillan, 1970), 287–88.

22. On this period, see M. Hengel and A. M. Schwemer, *Paul between Damascus and Antioch: The Unknown Years* (trans. J. Bowden; Louisville: Westminster John Knox, 1997).

23. This section is discussed in a more complete form in L. M. McDonald, "Anti-Judaism in the Early Church Fathers," in *Anti-Semitism and Early Christianity: Issues of Polemic and Faith* (ed. C. A. Evans and D. A. Hagner; Minneapolis: Fortress, 1993), 215–52.

24. See J. D. G. Dunn, *The Partings of the Ways between Christianity and Judaism and Their Significance for the Character of Christianity* (London: SCM, 1991), with necessary correctives in J. Lieu, "'The Parting of the Ways': Theological Construct or Historical Reality?" *JSNT* 56 (1994): 101–19; Judge, "Judaism and the Rise of Christianity," 355–68. G. Boccaccini's belief is that Christianity is one of the two main voices of ancient Judaism, the other being rabbinism, which survived the first century (*Middle Judaism: Jewish Thought, 300 BCE to 200 CE* [Minneapolis: Fortress, 1991], 16–18).

25. J. S. Siker, *Disinheriting the Jews: Abraham in Early Christian Controversy* (Louisville: Westminster John Knox, 1991), 254 n. 13.

26. It is not clear that this was Paul's intention in Gal 6:18, especially in light of his strong affirmation of the Jews as God's elect in Rom 11:28–29, but clearly Justin could have taken that text in Galatians to justify his claim. Matthew comes close to this position and in Matt 21:42–43 perhaps paves the way for it in Justin's interpretation.

27. M. Simon, *Verus Israel* (trans. H. McKeating; New York: Oxford University Press, 1986), 398.

28. Trans. A. L. Williams, *Adversus Judaeos* (Cambridge: Cambridge University Press, 1935), 78. The text is translated by Williams from *The Dialogue of Timothy and Aquila*. Original author is vague and debated. It is Christian propaganda.

29. L. Poliakov, *The History of Anti-Semitism* (trans. R. Howard; New York: Vanguard, 1962), 23, uses this term to describe what he calls the strictly "doctrinal" disputes that the church had with Judaism.

30. R. Ruether, *Faith and Fratricide: The Theological Roots of Anti-Semitism* (Minneapolis: Seabury, 1974), 116.

31. See S. J. Cohen, *From the Maccabeees to the Mishnah* (LEC; Philadelphia: Westminster, 1987), 46; and Simon, *Verus Israel*, 395–400, for a discussion of anti-Judaism and anti-Semitism. Cf. also W. Klassen, "Anti-Judaism in Early Christianity: The State of the Question," in *Paul and the Gospels*, vol. 1 of *Anti-Judaism in Early Christianity* (ed. P. Richardson and D. Granskou; 5 vols.; Waterloo, Ont.: Wilfrid Laurier University Press, 1986), 5–12. As these writers show, it is unlikely that anti-Semitism was present at all in the ancient world. Racial overtones, which are more commonly connected with modern times, are almost totally absent in ancient rhetoric; it was the Jewish religion and manners that were called into question by the ancient pagan world.

pages 239–248

pages 248–250

32. R. L. Wilken describes in detail the circumstances surrounding hostilities in Alexandria in *Judaism and the Early Christian Mind* (New Haven: Yale University Press, 1971), 9–38.

33. Eusebius claimed Philo in Alexandria had not only met some Christians but also "welcomed, revered, and recognized the divine mission of the apostolic men of his day" (*Hist. eccl.* 2.17.2 [LCL]). This could be Eusebius's fantasy or based on some tradition handed on to him, but it does show that not all Jews were considered diabolical by the Christians. It should also be noted that these "apostolic men" were, in the words of Eusebius, "of the Hebrew origin, and thus still preserved most of the ancient customs in a strictly Jewish manner" (ibid.). See R. Wilde, *The Treatment of the Jews in the Greek Christian Writers of the First Three Centuries* (Washington, D.C.: Catholic University of America Press, 1949), 80–82, 173–77, 192–98, 212–16, who gives several examples of favorable comments about the Jews in the church fathers.

34. Similar harsh comments can also be found in Ign. *Magn.* 8–10; Ign. *Phld.* 5–6; *Barn.* 2–3, 4.6–8, 6.6–8; *Diogn.* 3–4; Melito, *On the Passover* 259–279, 732–747; Tertullian, *Ag. Marc.* 2.19.1, 3.23.1ff., 5.4.1ff.; and others. Some of these writers evidently had frequent contacts with the Jews and maintained dialogue with them well into the fourth and fifth centuries even after the church had won a prominent role in the Roman Empire.

35. In Justin, *Dial.* 10.3, Trypho objects to the Christians' hope of the blessing of God because they are "resting their hopes on a man that was crucified." Justin overcomes this objection with an argument on the resurrection and the second advent of Jesus; cf. 32.1–3.

36. A. F. Segal, *Rebecca's Children: Judaism and Christianity in the Roman World* (Cambridge: Harvard University Press, 1986), 154–60; and Lazare, *Anti-Semitism,* 31, stress the importance of Christology as a significant factor in the separation of Christianity from Judaism, even though it does not take the prominent place in the polemic, as Simon, *Verus Israel,* 157, observes. D. Flusser's discussion of the problem a high or divine Christology posed for Judaism is worth consideration. Cf. his *Judaism and the Origins of Christianity* (Jerusalem: Magnes Press, 1988), 620–25, in which he stresses that even those Jews who were prepared to accept Jesus' messiahship were less prepared to accept him as the divine Son of God.

37. Segal, *Rebecca's Children,* 143, 156, 161.

38. The best source for determining the theology of early Jewish Christianity is the NT—e.g., the books of Matthew, James, Hebrews—but also the *Didache.* The fourth-century *Clementine Homilies* and *Recognitions (Pseudo-Clementines),* which depend on the late-second-century *Preaching of Peter,* provide us with our best post-second-century understanding of conservative Jewish Christianity. These are the Jewish Christians who eventually survived the first century, but their theological stance is much debated. Most agree that their christological formulations were incompatible with Gentile orthodox positions on the divinity of Jesus. See T. Callan, *Forgetting the Root: The Emergence of Christianity from Judaism* (New York: Paulist, 1986), 27–52, 65–66, for a summary of the Jewish-Christian theological stance.

39. Notice in *Did. apost.* 5.14.23 (3d cent.) that the chief reason for celebrating Easter was not only to observe the passion of Jesus but also "to obtain forgiveness for the guilty and unfaithful Jews."

pages 250–253

40. See S. Neill, *Jesus through Many Eyes* (Philadelphia: Fortress, 1976), 32–37, who discusses these disappointments and their consequences in the Christian community.

41. The dialogue genre, which purported to convince the Jews to convert to faith in Christ, continued in the churches well into the Middle Ages. There are numerous examples of a call for the Jews to convert to faith in Christ throughout the patristic period and even later. See Clement of Alexandria, *Misc.* 2; Hippolytus, *Demonstrations to the Jews* (PG 10:787–794), who makes such a call but sees no hope for it. So also Origen, *Hom. Jerem.* 5 and *Comm. Rom.* 8:9 and his *Did. apost.* 5.14.15, whose goal is the conversion of the Jews. Evagrius's *Dialogue between Simon and Theophilus* (ca. 400) shows continued interest in the conversion of the Jews and, like Justin, evidences more respect for the Jew (Simon) than do some of the other *Dialogues,* even though the Jew is still a straw man in the discussion.

42. See W. A. Meeks and R. L. Wilken, *Jews and Christians in Antioch in the First Four Centuries of the Common Era* (Missoula, Mont.: Scholars Press, 1978), 83–126, for a translation of the first and eighth of these homilies of Chrysostom. Eusebius reports that ca. A.D. 200 a certain Domnus had also "fallen away from the faith of Christ, at the time of the persecution, to Jewish will-worship" (*Hist. eccl.* 6.12.1).

43. Trans. Meeks and Wilken, *Jews and Christians,* 115.

44. Cohen, *Maccabees to the Mishnah,* 55. See also Wilkens, "Judaism," 313–18, who notes that many of the impressive gains by the Jews in the Roman Empire, especially between A.D. 135 and 425, were during the very years the polemical language by the Christians was most intense.

45. Cohen, *Maccabees to the Mishnah,* 50–59. He also indicates that women converted to Judaism by marriage to a Jew but that there were no generally accepted guidelines for a woman to convert. Cf. pp. 53, 54.

46. See ibid., 57.

47. Examples of this argument in the Christian tradition are found in Justin, *1 Apol.* 47, 53; *Dial.* 117; Irenaeus, *Haer.* 4.4.1–2, 4.13.4; Origen, *Cels.* 7.20 and *Hom. Jerem.* 14.13. The Jews themselves even gave this as evidence of God's judgment of them but not, of course, as evidence that God had replaced them in favor of the Gentiles; cf. Justin, *Dial.* 16, 40, 92. In the introduction to his *Ecclesiastical History,* Eusebius indicates that one of the purposes of his work is to "add the fate which has beset the whole nation of the Jews from the moment of their plot against our Saviour" (*Hist. eccl.* 1.1.2 [LCL]). He describes in detail the destruction of Jerusalem and the temple (2.6.3–7; 3.5–6), concluding that "such was the reward of the iniquity of the Jews and of their impiety against the Christ of God" (3.7.1 [LCL]). Ruether, *Faith and Fratricide,* 144–45, gives several other examples of this argument.

48. G. F. Moore, "Christian Writers on Judaism," HTR 14 (1921): 200. See also Segal, *Rebecca's Children,* 147.

49. J. C. Meagher, "As the Twig Was Bent," in *Anti-Semitism and the Foundations of Christianity* (ed. A. T. Davies; New York: Paulist, 1979), 19–20.

50. Ibid., 20–21.

51. Socrates Scholasticus, *Hist. eccl.* 7.13, relates this story. He does not hesitate to criticize Cyril for his behavior, but the Jews receive severe prejudicial treatment. This is reflected elsewhere in his history; cf. 3.20; 5.22.

52. Cf. Wilken, *Judaism,* 35–53, 229, and "Judaism," 327–28; and Simon, *Verus Israel,* 143ff.

53. Trans. H. Maccoby, *Early Rabbinic Writings* (Cambridge: Cambridge University Press, 1988), 208.

54. Flusser, *Judaism,* 637–43.

55. Segal, *Rebecca's Children,* 150.

56. Origen, *Hom. Jerem.* 10.8.2, Epiphanius, *Pan.* 29.9.1, and Jerome, *Ep.* 112.13 to Augustine, all saw the *Birkath ha-Minim* as a curse against the Christians. See also Justin, *1 Apol.* 131, in which he accuses the Jews of cruel punishments and even of killing the Christians.

57. Trans. C. A. Evans, *Non-canonical Writings and New Testament Interpretation* (Peabody, Mass.: Hendrickson, 1992), 113–15. He has included many other references to Jesus in ancient rabbinic literature that are also illustrative of the point made here. See also Segal, *Rebecca's Children,* 147–58; and Simon, *Verus Israel,* 178–201.

58. D. Rokeah, "Behind the Appearances," *Explorations* 3 (1989): 2–3.

59. See, e.g., references in *Mart. Pol.* 12.2; 13.1; 17.2; 18.1 to the Jews' participation in exciting the anger of the crowds to kill Polycarp and even desecrate his body by not allowing a proper burial. There is no reason to reject the essential reliability of this report, that the Jews incited the crowds against the Christian community.

60. Rokeah, "Behind the Appearances," 4.

61. Johnson, "Anti-Jewish Slander," 434–41. He observes rather crude language in Philo's *On the Embassy to Gaius,* where he describes his Alexandrian neighbors as "promiscuous and unstable rabble" (18.120) and, again, states that the Egyptians were a "seed bed of evil in whose souls both the venom and temper of the native crocodiles and wasps are reproduced" (26.166). Other similar examples are found in his *On the Contemplative Life* and in the earlier author of the Wisdom of Solomon (ca. 1st cent. B.C. in Alexandria).

62. See Johnson, "Anti-Jewish Slander," 422, 434–35, for several of these references.

63. Ibid., 421–22. He also cites examples of Essene hostilities against all outsiders (p. 439).

64. Ibid., 441.

65. While J. Gager, *The Origins of Anti-Semitism: Attitudes toward Judaism in Pagan and Christian Antiquity* (New York: Oxford University Press, 1983), 117–20, is correct in arguing that much of the NT focus against the Jews and Judaism in fact refers to Gentile Judaizers, this still does not account for all the anti-Jewish statements (e.g., 1 Thess 2:14–16; Acts 28:17–31).

66. Flusser, *Judaism,* 619–25, makes a good case for this. See also Segal, *Rebecca's Children,* 154–60, for a discussion of the christological issues that divided Christianity and Judaism.

67. On this and related issues, see S. Benko, *Pagan Rome and the Early Christians* (Bloomington: Indiana University Press, 1984), esp. 54–78.

68. For a more detailed study of such responses, see R. L. Wilken, *The Christians as the Romans Saw Them* (New Haven: Yale University Press, 1984).

69. Although many NT scholars take this as a reference to Christ, classical scholars are often dubious that it is Christ whom Suetonius is describing.

70. Trans. Stevenson, *New Eusebius,* 2–3.

71. Ibid., 13–14.

72. Ibid., 16.

73. See Ferguson, *Backgrounds,* 561.

pages 258–262

74. This is a probable confusion of Christianity with Judaism, since Christians did not have officeholders called priests or scribes in their churches. The term "priest" was not adopted by the church until much later, after the time of Lucian.

75. Trans. A. S. L. Farquharson, *Marcus Aurelius, Meditations* (Oxford: Clarendon, 1944). See the index to *Marcus Aurelius* (trans. C. R. Haines; LCL; Cambridge: Harvard University Press, 1916) for other, indirect references to Christians.

76. Trans. R. Walzer, *Galen on Jews and Christians* (London: Oxford University Press, 1949), reprinted in R. M. MacMullen and E. N. Lane, eds., *Paganism and Christianity, 100–425 CE: A Sourcebook* (Minneapolis: Fortress, 1992), 168.

77. The italicized portions of this text were probably supplied by Christians.

THE GOSPELS AND THE ACTS OF THE APOSTLES

1. INTRODUCTION TO THE GOSPELS

The word "gospel" (εὐαγγέλιον, *euangelion*) was first applied in the NT to the good news that was proclaimed about Jesus the Christ (Mark 1:1) and subsequently to the genre of writings we call Gospels.[1] The canonical Gospels were written well before the term "gospel" was applied to them in the second century A.D., but perhaps the first writing to call itself a "Gospel" is the writing called the *Gospel of Thomas*, which may be as early as the late first or early second century A.D. The word, however, was not invented by the early Christians but already had a long history of use in the OT and the pagan world before the time of Jesus.

In the LXX, the verb was used, for example, in both the second and the third parts of Isaiah (40:9; 52:7 [see Rom 10:15]; 61:1, which is cited by Jesus in Luke 4:18), and the noun is found in 2 Kgs 4:10, 18:22, 25. In these cases the focus of the verb is upon bringing news or a message, and the noun stresses primarily that a message or news was present. (The feminine form, εὐαγγελία, *euangelia*, is found in LXX 2 Kgs 18:20, 27; 2 Chron 7:10.)[2] When Mark began his Gospel with the words "The beginning of the gospel of Jesus Christ, the Son of God,"[3] he was not referring to a book but, rather, to the coming of the kingdom of God through the life, ministry, passion, and resurrection of Jesus that was already being proclaimed in the early churches long before he began writing his book.

The use of this term in a number of Greco-Roman documents indicates that the NT use seems more in line with that of the pagan community than with the OT writers'. It was not uncommon for Christians to borrow from their pagan counterparts language that had vivid significance among their contemporaries, in order to convey more effectively their Christian proclamation. The plural form εὐαγγέλια (*euangelia*) was used, for example, to announce a victory or great event in the life of an emperor. The earliest, and perhaps best-known, use of "good news" regarding the emperor is found in an inscription, dating from 9 B.C., found at Priene in Asia Minor. It celebrates the birthday of Augustus (Octavian), whom divine providence has sent as a "savior" to bring the wars to an end and, consequently, peace to the whole world. Not only does this language seem to be reflected in the opening of Mark 1:1, where the Gospel writer proclaims the beginning of the good news of Jesus Christ; it may well have inspired Luke as he wrote his story of the birth of Jesus in Luke 2:10–11. Part of the Priene inscription reads as follows:

> Everyone may rightly consider this event as the origin of their life and existence. Providence has mar-

velously raised up and adorned human life by giving us Augustus . . . to make him the benefactor of mankind, our saviour, for us and for those who will come after us. But the birthday of the god [Augustus] was for the world the beginning of the joyful messages [εὐαγγελίων] which have gone forth because of him.[4]

The Christian writings that we know by the name Gospels were intended by the earliest Christian communities and those that passed them on to others to proclaim that there was "good news" about the exalted Jesus Christ rather than about the emperor. Paul uses the term similarly when he says in Rom 1:1, 2 that he is set apart for the "good news" of God, promised beforehand through his prophets regarding his son. Paul expands use of the term to designate also the specific oral Christian tradition shared in the Christian communities not only about God's activity in the death and resurrection of Jesus (1 Cor 15:1–5) but also about his coming or παρουσία, *parousia* (1 Cor 15:23–28).[5] The preaching of the early church focused on Jesus, his deeds, and the presence of the kingdom of God in his words and deeds. When Mark began his Gospel, which was the first written, he was using the term in a wholly new sense in which the story of Jesus was understood as "good news." Many who followed Mark agreed that the life and teaching of Jesus, as well as his death, resurrection, and return, constituted that good news. Some thirty other gospels were written after Mark, many of which are now known only in fragmentary form or in brief quotations from the early church fathers; they purport to tell the story of Jesus or focus on his teachings or portions of his life, such as the infancy narratives listed in ch. 14, below.

The most indispensable sources we have today for reconstructing the events and teaching of Jesus are the canonical Gospels in the NT, even though recent studies are increasingly debating the importance of extrabiblical literature in helping us to be more informed about the historical Jesus. The most important extrabiblical sources cited by some critical scholars today include the *Gospel of Thomas*, P. Egerton 2, and the *Dialogue of the Savior;* also included are passages in a number of the early church fathers that continue some fairly early traditions, especially those found in *1 Clement*, and some of the fragmentary and apocryphal sources.[6] To this we add the agrapha, more than two hundred purported sayings of Jesus not found in the ca-

nonical Gospels, though their value for understanding Jesus is strongly debated (see ch. 14, sec. 3, below).

Nevertheless, the most valuable sources for reconstructing the life of Jesus are still the canonical Gospels. To say that the Gospels offer a complete reconstruction of the story of Jesus is, however, overly optimistic, since even a casual reading of them shows that a full biography was not the intention of the writers. There are numerous gaps in the life of Jesus, and only two evangelists show any interest in the story of Jesus before the beginning of his ministry. Only Matthew and Luke tell us anything of Jesus' birth, and only Luke reports anything about Jesus' childhood (Luke 2:39–52), sharing but one brief instance of his visit to the temple. The Gospels do not tell the whole story of Jesus and are obviously quite selective, having a primary interest only in his ministry, teachings, death, and resurrection. Also, only a very simple outline of the story of Jesus is discernible in the Gospels, and many of the details of his ministry are not in the same sequence in each of the Gospels.

As we compare the first three Gospels, we see not only their significant differences but also where they overlap in substance and verbal usage. We must, therefore, ask about their reliability for reconstructing the story of Jesus. Through a careful study of these sources, can we discover with some degree of probability the actual life and teachings of Jesus? The scholarly community does not agree on what precisely can be known about Jesus from the Gospels, and some even debate whether the canonical Gospels are the best or primary witnesses for examining the life of Jesus. Many scholars argue that the Gospels are more reflections of the life of the early Christian community than they are of the life of the historical Jesus. Recent scholarship has posed the question whether the writers of the Gospels were so self-serving, or so intent on serving the interests of their communities, that they actually obscured the true picture of the historical Jesus.

This question is not easily resolved, especially when, upon closer examination, we see that though all four Gospels treat essentially the same person and time frame—the ministry, passion, and resurrection of Jesus—John stands alone in his reconstruction of these events, not only in their sequence but also in many of the details. In the other three Gospels, though striking similarities have given rise to various views about interdependence, there are also significant differences, especially in the passion and resurrection narratives (see chs. 5 and 6, above) but also in the birth narratives and elsewhere. Details, for example, of the sequence of the events of Jesus' ministry do not appear to be significant to the evangelists, and some of the other differences probably reflect a matter of theological preference, as in the location of the appearances of Jesus in either Galilee (Matthew and Mark) or Jerusalem (Luke and John) (see ch. 5, above).

If we want to understand the story of Jesus, our first obstacle is to establish the essential reliability of our primary sources, the Gospels. In many churches today, such questions are not normally asked and are even considered inappropriate because of their impact on already well-established doctrines of biblical inspiration. Such notions, however, seriously hinder careful biblical inquiry. It is sometimes argued that if these Gospels are God's Word, they must therefore be reliable and completely accurate; the problem consequently lies with those who interpret the Gospels rather than with the Gospels themselves. Although there is an element of true piety in such statements, those who hold to them tenaciously seldom make significant advances in our understanding of the message of the evangelists. Indeed, such notions obscure the message of the Gospels when those who investigate them are forced to harmonize them into a single whole rather than allow the message of each Gospel to emerge in its own right.[7] Any careful investigation of the message of the biblical writings must determine the historical setting and message of these writings and deal with such issues as date, authorship, occasion, and how each writer handles the materials he used to produce his Gospel. The student must also look for theological motives that may account for some of the differences in the Gospels.

This study begins by focusing on the relationships among the first three Gospels, then considers the primary introductory material for each of them, and finally looks briefly at the Gospel of John and its value in recovering the story of Jesus' life and teachings. Because the volumes of Luke and Acts were written by the same person and in relatively the same time frame, introductory matters related to Acts will be treated at the same time as the Gospel of Luke.

2. THE SYNOPTIC PROBLEM: RELATIONSHIPS AND DIFFERENCES

A. *Introduction to the Synoptic Problem*

The first three Gospels have been called the Synoptic Gospels because they offer a similar picture of the events of Jesus' life. This similarity has resulted in the practice of arranging their texts in parallel columns to form a synopsis so that they may be viewed together. The problem of accounting for their parallel relationships as well as for their divergences is commonly known as the "synoptic problem." Throughout most of church history, a large portion of the attention given to Gospel research has focused on trying to harmonize the differences in the canonical Gospels. Toward the end of the nineteenth century, however, and especially in the first half of the twentieth, considerable interest was directed to accounting for the many similarities in the Gospels. More recently, and for completely different reasons, the focus has again shifted back to accounting for the differences in order to understand the peculiar theological perspectives of each evangelist (see ch. 2, sec. 3.E, above, on redaction criticism). There is little or no attempt now to harmonize the narratives; rather, the effort is to understand how such differences emerged and what they tell us about both the perspective of the writer and the community he was addressing with his narrative.

A revolution in Gospel criticism occurred in the nineteenth century when it was concluded that the Synoptic Gospels were not written independently of one another. While this in itself was a significant conclusion in Gospel studies, with roots going back at least to the time of Augustine or even earlier, other important considerations followed from this, namely, the widely held contemporary views that Mark was the first Gospel written and that Luke and Matthew made considerable use of Mark in producing their Gospels. Further, because of the many parallels between Matthew and Luke that are not found in Mark, many scholars concluded that both Matthew and Luke used a common source, which is commonly referred to as Q (from the German *Quelle,* "source") or the Sayings Source. Whether this Q source was a written document, a common oral tradition, or a combination of both is a matter about which scholars still disagree (see ch. 4, above).

In antiquity, the answer to the question about the many similarities among the Synoptic Gospels was answered by asserting Matthean priority; that is, it was claimed that Matthew was written first and that his Gospel was used by the other evangelists. Augustine argued that Mark simply abbreviated Matthew (*Harm.* 1.2.4 [PL 34.1044]). Origen earlier came to the conclusion that since the Spirit gave perfect memory to each of the Gospel writers, the differences between them were because of the "theological purposes" of Mark and Luke, which were often highly subtle in nature (see *Comm. Matt.,* frg. of bk. 2 [preserved in *Philoc.* 100.6]; 11.2–3, 6; *Princ.* 1, preface, 8).[8] In the eighteenth century, various theories about the relationships among the canonical Gospels began to emerge. In 1764, H. Owen argued that Matthew was written first, that Luke used Matthew, and that Mark, which was written last, used both Matthew and Luke.[9] In this way, the tradition of Matthean priority was maintained. This view was essentially followed by J. J. Griesbach of Germany in 1783 and is now known as the Griesbach hypothesis.[10] By the nineteenth century, however, long-established beliefs about the priority of Matthew began to change, and the view that Mark wrote the first Gospel gained widespread acceptance among biblical scholars. B. F. Westcott advanced the theory that each of the four canonical evangelists appealed to oral and written traditions independently of one another,[11] but this view did not prevail. Chief among the early proponents of Markan priority, that is, the idea that Mark wrote the first Gospel and that Matthew and Luke depended upon his work, were K. Lachmann and H. J. Holtzmann.[12] Lachmann, in a variation of the Westcott thesis, contended that Mark made use of more primitive sources or narratives in constructing his Gospel than did Matthew and Luke and that his Gospel was thus closer to the original narrative. This led others, notably Holtzmann, to conclude that Mark was the first Gospel written and that Matthew and Luke depended upon Mark in the areas that they have in common. He argued that an early form of Mark (*Ur-Markus*) was used by both Matthew and Luke independently of one another, in addition to the source that has come to be known as Q. Aside from minor modifications, Holtzmann's position has held sway among biblical scholars. With a few notable exceptions today,[13] it is generally held that Matthew and Luke made use of Mark, expanding it to some degree for their own theological and catechetical purposes, and that they also used a tradition, whether oral or written, designated Q. This is generally known as the two-document hypothesis.

The major work on the Synoptic Gospels in recent years has, however, been concerned equally with the problem of explaining the mutual relationships and differences between the Gospels, with the goal of seeing the individual theological and practical concerns each evangelist had in writing his Gospel. This has been one of the primary emphases of the redaction-critical approach to the Gospels. The explanations for these agreements and variations have been legion, and the debate about them continues. Long ago Westcott tabulated the parallel relationships between the Gospels, and his results are still quite useful today in understanding the overall situation (see table 8-1).[14]

TABLE 8 - 1		
PARALLEL RELATIONSHIPS BETWEEN THE GOSPELS		
Gospel of	**Peculiarities**	**Coincidences**
Mark	7%	93%
Matthew	42%	58%
Luke	59%	41%
[John	92%	8%]

The coincidences are not always exact verbal agreements, but they so approximate each other that most scholars agree that a close relationship is likely.

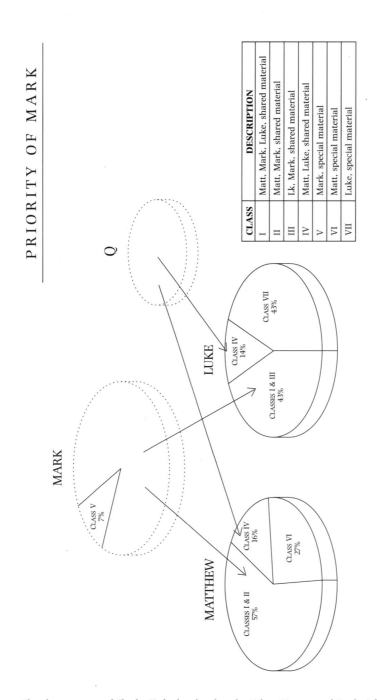

PRIORITY OF MARK

CLASS	DESCRIPTION
I	Matt, Mark, Luke, shared material
II	Matt, Mark, shared material
III	Lk, Mark, shared material
IV	Matt, Luke, shared material
V	Mark, special material
VI	Matt, special material
VII	Luke, special material

Q

LUKE

CLASS IV 14%

CLASS VII 43%

CLASSES I & III 43%

MARK

CLASS V 7%

MATTHEW

CLASS IV 16%

CLASS VI 27%

CLASSES I & II 57%

This chart courtesy of Charles Hedrick, taken from his When History and Faith Collide, *p. 86.*

The most commonly accepted explanation for these close affinities, called the four-source theory, suggests that (1) Mark wrote the first Gospel, which Matthew and Luke used and even altered for their own purposes, and that (2) Matthew and Luke also used another source(s), Q, which is not found in Mark. The verbal and sequential parallels between Matthew and Luke in the so-called Q passages are not as close as in the portions they have in common with Mark, but they are sufficiently close to call for either dependence of one evangelist upon the other or the more likely conclusion that both drew upon a common source, Q. It is further argued that (3) the unique portions of Matthew and Luke, that is, the genealogies and birth narratives and the sixteen parables in Luke that are not found elsewhere, come from Matthew's peculiar source or sources (commonly designated M) and Luke's peculiar source or sources (commonly designated L).[15] These relationships, together with the terms used to describe the material in the Synoptic Gospels, are the most widely accepted views held by biblical scholars today. The source relationships among the Synoptic Gospels are diagrammed in table 8-2.

If the Gospel of Mark was written before the other Gospels and used and expanded by them, then, historically and critically speaking, Mark's Gospel should be accepted as the primary witness to the events of Jesus' life, ministry, teaching, passion, and resurrection. The assumption here is that the closer a report is to an event, the more reliable it must be, containing fewer additions to the story. This is not necessarily the case in all situations, but the point is not without merit. So, though the earliest witness to an event is not always the most reliable, in this case, the value of Mark's report is clearly enhanced by its closer proximity to the events it describes. The other side of this assumption is that subsequent reports tend to expand the stories they report for their own purposes. A case in point might be the resurrection narratives, which are considerably longer in Matthew, Luke, and John than they are in Mark. Are the longer narratives less reliable than Mark's because they were expanded in the later traditions for their obvious catechetical value to the later growing Christian community? Although this issue cannot be settled here, it cannot be ignored. The question is not whether the Gospels were written with the

emerging Christian communities in view and the story of Jesus altered to meet the needs of these communities but whether these perspectives (alterations) distorted the story of Jesus beyond recovery and beyond credibility, as some scholars have claimed.

The question that still remains is, Was Mark the first Gospel? What evidence is there for this conclusion? Several factors point to Markan priority and the dependence of Matthew and Luke upon his Gospel.

1. By comparing all three Gospels, we find that, with the exception of three short reports (Mark 4:26–29; 7:31–37; 8:22–26) and three short narratives (Mark 3:22ff., 9:49; 14:51ff.), the whole of Mark's Gospel is found in Matthew and Luke. It is easier to explain the absence of these in Matthew and Luke than why Mark would omit the vast sections of Matthew and Luke that include such matters as the genealogy of Jesus, the expanded baptism stories, the additions made to the temptation narratives, and the Sermon on the Mount or Plain in Matthew and in Luke, which includes the Lord's Prayer. Why would Mark dismiss these and other reports about Jesus and his teaching ministry? Such selectivity makes little sense, but why Matthew and Luke may have omitted the portions of Mark that they did does make sense. Considering vocabulary statistics, Kümmel has shown that, in the sections that are common between Mark and Matthew and/or Luke, 8,189 of the 10,650 words of Mark are found in the two other Gospels: Matthew employs 7,768 of them, and Luke employs 7,040. Kümmel further notes that Matthew and Luke coincide extensively with Mark in the material they have in common, and argues that this phenomenon cannot be explained by Mark's omission of vast sections of Matthew's or Luke's Gospel.[16]

2. The sequence of the narratives also argues for the priority of Mark. For example, in the material that is common to all three Synoptics, Matthew and Luke agree with each other in sequence only so far as they agree with Mark, but where Matthew and Luke disagree with Mark's order, they also diverge from any common sequence of events among themselves. This strongly suggests Matthew's and Luke's sequential dependence on Mark, while their Q material is in a different sequence. Matthew's Sermon on the Mount (Matt 5–7) is only partially reproduced, in a different sequence, in Luke 6, but much of the rest of the material of Matthew's Sermon on the Mount appears in various other locations throughout Luke.

Table 8-3 lists materials that Matthew and Luke have in common (Q material) but not in the same sequence; the initial numbering indicates the sequence in that Gospel.

T A B L E   8 - 3

THE Q SOURCE MATERIAL[17]

Luke		Matthew
1. 3:7–9, 16–17	John's Preaching	1. 3:7–12
2. 4:2–13	Jesus' Temptation	2. 4:2–11
3. 6:20–23, 27–30, 32–36	Sermon on the Plain 1	3. 5:3–6, 11–12, 39–42, 45–48
4. 6:37–38, 41–49	Sermon on the Plain 2	7. 7:1–5, 16–21, 24–27
5. 7:1–10	Centurion from Capernaum	9. 8:5–13
6. 7:18–35	John's Question; Jesus' Reply	13. 11:2–19
7. 9:57–60	Nature of Discipleship	10. 8:19–22
8. 10:1–12	Sending-Out Discourse	11. 9:37–10:15
9. 10:13–15, 21–22	Cries of Woe and Joy	14. 11:21–23, 25–26
10. 11:1–4	Lord's Prayer	5. 6:9–13
11. 11:9–13	Concerning Prayer	8. 7:7–11
12. 11:14–23	Beelzebub Controversy	15. 12:22–30
13. 11:24–26	Return of the Evil Spirit	17. 12:43–45
14. 11:29–32	Against Sign Seeking	16. 12:38–42
15. 11:33–35	Sayings on Light	4. 5:15; 6:22–23
16. 11:39–52	Against the Pharisees	19. 23:4, 23–25, 29–36
17. 12:2–10	Exhortation to Confession	12. 10:26–33
18. 12:22–34	Anxiety and Possessions	6. 6:25–33, 19–21
19. 12:39–46	Watchfulness	22. 24:43–51
20. 13:18–21	Mustard Seed and Leaven	18. 13:31
21. 13:34–35	Lament over Jerusalem	20. 23:37–39
22. 17:22–37	Parousia Discourse	21. 24:26–28, 37–41
23. 19:11–28	Parable of the Talents	23. 25:14–30

3. Kümmel also argues that the linguistic or literary changes and variations in subject matter in the Synoptics are "decisive" in pointing to Markan priority. He has shown that there is strong agreement in wording among the Synoptics in the material common to all three, even though there is a tendency in both Matthew and Luke to change the simpler Greek of Mark to a more sophisticated Greek and correct oversights, such as where Mark attributes to Isaiah a quotation from Mal 3:1 (Mark 1:2; cf. Matt 3:3; Luke 3:4).

An interesting exception to this may be the several places where Matthew and Luke agree *against* Mark when they are dealing with the same event or teaching of Jesus. Comparing Mark 1:8 with Matt 3:11 and Luke 3:16; Mark 1:10 with Matt 3:16 and Luke 3:22; Mark 8:29 with Matt 16:16 and Luke 9:20; and Mark 15:46 with Matt 27:60 and Luke 23:53 demonstrates this phenomenon quite well.

We can also note the changes in grammar; for instance, the so-called historical present tense (where the present tense is used in a past narrative setting, such as "he says" [λέγει, *legei*] for "he said" [εἶπεν, *eipen*]), upon which Mark relies, is changed to a more usual narrative tense by Matthew and Luke (cf. Mark 2:12 with Matt 9:7 and Luke 5:25; Mark 4:10 with Matt 13:10 and Luke 8:9; Mark 16:8 with Matt 28:8 and Luke 24:9). Changes of subject are also quite striking—for example, in Matt 3:16 compared with Mark 1:10, and Matt 14:1 compared with Mark 6:14 regarding the title of Antipas.[18] It is much easier in these cases to understand why Matthew and Luke would have made their changes than it is to understand why Mark would change their two texts. C. A. Evans also discusses literary improvements and the argument of sequence. He adds to these the issue of propriety— that is, Mark's seeming lack of propriety in relating the weaknesses of the disciples (compare Mark 4:38 with Matt 8:24), Jesus' family's concern about his mental stability (Mark 3:21), and the seeming disrespect showed by Jesus to his family in Mark 3:33–34 (cf. Matt 12:49 and Luke 8:21 to see how the focus is toned down). It is more logical to postulate that Matthew and Luke removed these potential embarrassments than to say that Mark substituted more favorable comments about Jesus with less refined comments. Evans also observes that whereas Jesus is simply called "teacher" in Mark, he is called "Lord" in Matthew and "Master" in Luke (Mark 4:38; Matt 8:25; Luke 8:24).[19]

This brief summary of some of the arguments for Markan priority is in no way exhaustive, but these are some of the more suggestive arguments. The many arguments against Markan priority have not been discussed here, but they do not adequately address the above issues.[20] Further discussion of the Gospel of Mark—date, authorship, and reliability—appears below.

B. The Existence of Q

Besides the material that Matthew and Luke have in common with Mark, there are a number of λόγια *(logia)*[21] that are common to Matthew and Luke but are not found in Mark—for example, Matt 3:11, 12 and Luke 3:16, 17. Before the nineteenth century, it was generally agreed that such parallels were due to Luke's dependence upon Matthew's Gospel, but more recently it has been argued that another source existed that both Matthew and Luke freely employed for their own purposes.[22] As mentioned, this alleged document, known to both Matthew and Luke, has been called the Q document or the Sayings Source. Some of the scholars who accept the existence of such a document admit that its precise contents are still vague and cannot be determined with any assurance, but others think that the document's parameters are completely known, since they believe that it was fully incorporated into the Gospels of Matthew and Luke. If we assess the material that is common to Matthew and Luke alone, it appears that Q was, with just two exceptions, a collection of Jesus sayings or reports without a passion or resurrection story. It might be objected that this would not form a meaningful tradition, let alone a "Gospel" in early Christianity, but there may be some credibility to this view when we consider the existence of the *Gospel of Thomas*, which is nothing more than a string of apparently disconnected sayings of Jesus, unlike the canonical Gospels (see the earlier discussion of Q in ch. 4, sec. 3, above).

The Q material is, in scholarly convention, placed in the Lukan sequence and referred to by the Lukan verse references. References to this material are often grouped together on a thematic basis. Kee, for example, groups the passages under the categories of (1) discipleship—its privileges and trials, (2) the prophet as God's messenger, (3) repentance or judgment, and (4) Jesus as revealer and agent of God's rule.[23]

Many things about this alleged document are not known; we do not know who wrote it, where it was written, its complete contents (since no copies exist), the date of its composition, and the nature of its composition (oral or written). Though scholars disagree on all these issues, the general opinion is that (1) besides the sayings, Q contained narrative material, such as the temptation story and the story of the centurion at Capernaum; (2) Q was not a Gospel, since it has no passion narrative, but was a book or source for the edification of the church; (3) the ordering of the logia of Q was not random but was done with a distinct purpose in mind; (4) Q contained no passion narrative or passion kerygma (proclamation); (5) its place of origin and date are unknown, though some scholars are beginning to assign it to the region of Galilee around or before the time of the writing of Mark (ca. A.D. 65–70); and (6) it is not clear whether Mark knew or used such a source, that is, whether such a source stands behind the places where Mark, Matthew, and Luke agree.[24] Some have argued that, since it was probably a collection of sayings that were most likely not connected to an Easter story, just as we see in the *Gospel of Thomas*, then it must have been written early, before Mark. This is not conclusive evidence, however, since Matthew and Luke may have preferred the passion and resurrection narratives of Mark over that of Q. It is also possible that much of this information existed in oral form, which might account for the lack of an Easter tradition.[25] The most important objections to a written form of Q are that (1) Q may have been a fluid layer of oral tradition because the wording of the sayings postulated to have come from Q vary considerably between Matthew and Luke and (2) both Matthew and Luke take up and incorporate the Q material into their Gospels in a different sequence (see the Sermon on the Mount in Matt 5–7 and the Sermon on the Plain in Luke 6). Conzelmann counters these concerns with four important points: (1) in spite of the differences there are substantial agreements in word order in the Gospels; (2) if Q were nothing more than scattered oral tradition, it is amazing that there is so much in common from this tradition in both Matthew and Luke; (3) the Q material has *generally* been adopted in the same order in both Matthew and Luke, though not com-

pletely; and (4) the several "doublets" of sayings of Jesus in Matthew and Luke have their origin in their writers' selecting, almost mechanically, from the same source (compare, e.g., Luke 8:16–18 with Mark 4:21–25; then compare this with the doublet in Luke 11:33, which is also found in Matt 5:15).[26] The majority of scholars today contend, therefore, that Q did exist in written form, though the precise boundaries of that document are not known.

What other explanations are possible for the material common to both Matthew and Luke? Basically there are just the two that have been presented above: that Luke drew freely upon Matthew for his Gospel or that both Matthew and Luke made use of a common sayings source, generally designated Q. Robert Grant suggests two reasons against Luke's dependence upon Matthew:

> (a) In Matthew many sayings of Jesus have been assembled into a collection called the Sermon on the Mount (Matt. 5–7); in Luke these sayings are scattered over a number of chapters, in different contexts. Would Luke have felt free to treat Matthew this way? (b) Many sayings of Jesus are connected to one another by verbal association in both Matthew and Luke; but in about seventeen instances the word used for the association by Matthew differs from the word used by Luke. This proves that both Matthew and Luke drew independently upon a common stock of oral tradition.[27]

Again, the close following of Mark's sequence, the employment of most of his words by both Matthew and Luke, and their own significant differences in both sequence and verbal association strongly suggest that Matthew and Luke were not directly dependent upon one another.

Nevertheless, Grant concludes from the above that a Q document probably never existed, and suggests instead that the points of agreement came from common oral tradition that was available to both Matthew and Luke, some of which may have existed in written form but surely not all of it. His reasoning is supported by the way Matthew and Luke seem to handle the material. For example, if Matthew and Luke were using a written Q document, one would expect them to use it with the same consistency as they employed in using Mark's Gospel, but such is not the case. He concludes from this two possibilities: either Matthew and Luke did not use Q in the same way they used Mark, with no apparent reason for the change, or no such written source was in existence. Grant concludes the latter.[28]

Kee disagrees with Grant, suggesting that the best way to account for the verbal similarities that exist between Matthew and Luke is to conclude that they both drew upon a common written source, Q. He is much more optimistic about the existence of the Q document and even suggests its original order and a dating of it to as early as A.D. 50.[29] Kümmel is also optimistic about the existence of Q and believes that it originated in Palestine, very possibly around the year A.D. 68 but no later than 70.[30]

Some synoptic scholars argue for more of an oral tradition behind the current Gospels but at the same time contend that the postulated oral stage of transmission was not as fluid as scholars earlier supposed. Although direct dependence has not been clearly established, the use of rabbinic techniques for transmission of the oral tradition by the early Christian teachers has been asserted.[31] Those who suggest such a parallel claim that the use of oral tradition in the early Christian church was well defined, as in rabbinic Judaism, which eventually, in the late second century A.D., codified the oral tradition that had continued from the first and second centuries A.D. and, in some instances, probably before. Early Christians may well have learned similar principles of transmission in their catechetical training, involving repetition and memorization of short, well-organized thoughts. Theissen has argued that such parallels are also found in the classical world, which had a strong emphasis on oral tradition, especially noticeable in Socrates' method of training. Theissen shows the value of the oral tradition in early Christianity by highlighting the well-known quotation from Papias (ca. A.D. 140), who prefers the oral traditions about Jesus over the written (Matthew and Mark). Theissen cites the examples of Matt 28:19–20 and Luke 10:16 to show that Jesus' teaching was passed on orally at first rather than in written form. He also cites examples from Paul indicating that Paul knew of and used church oral tradition about Jesus (see 1 Cor 7:10–11; 9:1–14; 11:23–26).[32] Much of this tradition probably existed in small units that were apparently seen as detachable and applicable to different contexts, such as the teaching of the "first and the last" in Matt 19:30, 20:16 and Luke 13:30, two very different settings.

For those who accept Markan priority, the existence of Q is an essential component. Although the debate continues over whether Q ever existed as a written document or whether it was primarily an oral tradition, we will use Q to designate the non-Markan material that is found in both Matthew and Luke. Whether this source was written or oral would not affect its value as an early source for knowledge of the teaching of Jesus.

The earlier Pauline Letters make no mention of existing written sources or Gospels. Paul only acknowledges oral traditions (e.g., 1 Cor 11:23; 15:3), and there is not much other evidence for the existence of written traditions before the writing of Paul's letters. The fact that he appealed to tradition (παράδοσις, *paradosis*) passed on to him (1 Cor 15:3–7) or to his own encounter with the risen Christ as the source of his gospel (Gal 1:11–12, 15–16), rather than to any written sources, is an argument against the existence of written Gospels before or during Paul's ministry. If the canonical Gospels were written before the end of Paul's life, there is no evidence that they were in general circulation, so that reference could be made to them, but that some sources did exist from earlier times is implied in Luke 1:1–4. The precise nature of the sources that the evangelists used in their Gospels cannot be determined with any accuracy, although it seems fairly clear that Matthew and Luke made extensive use of Mark. Whether Q, M, and L were written or oral traditions available to the Gospel writers and whether other traditions may also have influenced the Gospel writers cannot be determined with certainty, but the verbal parallels between Matthew and Luke in the Q material suggest that they may have referred to a written tradition. But again, Luke does mention that others had undertaken to do what he himself was about to do when he began writing his Gospel (Luke 1:1–4).

C. Events Giving Rise to the Gospels

Jesus left no writings of his own and did not occupy any official position of the sort that would have caused an official record of his actions or speeches to be kept. His life and teachings were remembered by his followers not primarily out of historical interest but because, after his resurrection, these things seemed much more important for the life and witness of the church, especially for its worship and teaching ministries. It is difficult to understand how the early Christians could or would have perpetuated simply the story of a crucified, despised, humiliated, and rejected religious leader. These things became important for the faith and growth of the early community of believers only after the emergence of belief in Jesus' resurrection. As the early Christians remembered the events and teachings of Jesus, they used them in their worship and instruction, and these traditions were handed on in a manner that would meet the liturgical and instructional aims of the early community of believers.[33] Regardless of the argument stating that the *Gospel of Thomas*, whose author/collector gathered sayings of Jesus into a "gospel," has no clear reference to his passion and resurrection and thus is unconcerned with such matters, it is difficult to understand how any early Christian writers could continue to pass on traditions about Jesus without at least the assumption of his resurrection from the dead or his glorification and triumph in some manner. For this reason alone, it is difficult to give the *Gospel of Thomas* priority over the canonical Gospels. Rather, it probably belongs to some later time, when the Easter tradition could be taken for granted or when its absence could be accounted for in terms of the gnostic teaching of the second century. Although a few scholars have denied it, *Thomas* is, of course, a gnostic gospel. Further, Paul tied his understanding of the gospel to that of the earliest followers of Jesus (Gal 2:1–10), and stating that all of the earliest leaders of the church acknowledged the essence of the gospel (1 Cor 15:3–8), he concluded with the words "so we proclaim and so you have believed" (1 Cor 15:11). That a Christian community ever existed without a passion or resurrection tradition does not seem possible, and such a community is never referred to even polemically in any part of the NT writings. That oral and written traditions about sayings and activities of Jesus existed from early on (before A.D. 50), we do not deny. But we do question the notion that there ever existed in the first century a community of followers of Jesus who did not know about the death and resurrection of Jesus.

What historical events would have provided occasions for the writing down of this oral tradition about Jesus? The growth of the Gentile mission, the decline in the Jewish mission when the church moved from Jerusalem to Pella, and no doubt the destruction of Jerusalem in A.D. 70 all had important impacts upon the church, and this led to the writing down of its traditions. The most important catalyst, however, was probably the death of some of the key leaders in the church—Peter, Paul, and James—since the church's proclamation was based primarily upon their memories of Jesus and his teachings (1 Cor 15:5–8; Acts 1:21–22). Grant suggests that the persecution of Roman Christians in A.D. 64, when some of the leading apostles were probably put to death, and the execution of James the brother of Jesus in the year A.D. 62 in Jerusalem had to have been important motivations for the Christians to write down what had been circulating orally. When the eyewitnesses began to die, whether by persecution or old age, it became necessary to commit their teachings to writing. Following this line of reasoning, Grant concludes that Gospel writing probably began around A.D. 60, when the apostles and original eyewitnesses were growing old and were coming increasingly under persecution.[34]

Filson adds that, as this tradition was passed on in oral form, most of the actual historical sequence was probably lost beyond recovery, except for the broad outline of Jesus' ministry, which included his baptism, his initial preaching, his strong appeal to the crowds of people, the growing hostility from Jewish leaders, and, finally, his arrest, trial, crucifixion, and resurrection.[35] Within this general and fairly trustworthy outline, many of the events reported in the Gospels could have occurred either early or late in Jesus' ministry. Notice, for example, where the cleansing of the temple and Jesus' predictions about it are located in the Synoptics (late) and in John (early). Filson is probably correct when he says that the exact time and place of all these events did not fit into the needs of the early church and were therefore not given serious attention. Except in this broadest of outlines of Jesus' ministry, which was fairly well established in the traditions of the early church, the actual sequence of the events and teachings of Jesus was not of significant importance to the church, which therefore did not go to great lengths to preserve it.

The above suggestions about the origins and writing down of the Gospel traditions cannot be conclusively proved. The authorship and origins of these works, together with the uncertain limits of the sources employed, remain a mystery. The writing of these Gospels, however, took place when a stable form of the gospel tradition was needed—

one that could resist continuing change—but also when eyewitnesses to these events were still available to ensure against the fabrication and undue expansion of the tradition that might occur, especially if the written documents recorded material contradictory to the large amount of oral tradition circulating in the churches. It is not likely that any of the Gospels would have received widespread approval if eyewitnesses had discredited their reports. For this reason, when the evangelists wrote about the life, death, resurrection, and teaching of Jesus, it is likely that they were using traditions that had long been accepted by the earliest community of believers and been passed on by the church, first in oral and later in written form, with the approval of many persons who had been eyewitnesses and who were still living at the time of the writing. There is no need to conclude, as some form critics do, that these traditions were more products of the needs of the early church than they were reports of events that actually took place in the life of Jesus. This is not an either-or situation. The interpretation and development of these traditions in the early church does not necessarily mean that Christians greatly expanded them.

Metzger believes that the Gospel traditions reported what actually occurred. He contends that the reinterpretation and development that took place in the church need not have involved a fabrication of the events reported in the Gospels. He holds that the Gospel reports may be entirely "homogeneous with the original meaning, whose full vitality is thus unfolded for the benefit of the whole Church."[36]

D. Conclusion

The synoptic problem is to determine the relationships among the Synoptic Gospels, accounting for the similarities between them as well as their differences. This entails an examination of not only the oral and written sources (to the extent they are known) used by the evangelists but also the individual contributions of the evangelists themselves. Although biblical scholars have expended considerable energy accounting for the similarities in the synoptic tradition, they are also concerned to account for the sometimes significant differences in the parallel accounts. Can these differences be attributed to the particular theological biases of the evangelists, or to the specific needs of the congregations they addressed, or to some combination of these?

3. THE GOSPEL OF MARK

A. Introduction

There has hardly been an assertion made about the Gospels in recent years that has not been seriously questioned by NT scholars. The following comments about the Gospel of Mark are no exception. This brief summary of the background information on Mark is by no means final, and we freely acknowledge that there are alternative positions.

Until the turn of this century, Mark was the most neglected of all four canonical Gospels. But Mark was familiar to, or was used by, several second-century writers, including Papias (of whom we will say more presently), the author of the *Gospel of Peter*, Hermas, Tatian, Clement of Alexandria, Irenaeus, and also later authoritative church figures from the third, fourth, and fifth centuries, including Tertullian, Origen, Eusebius, and Jerome. Still, Mark was never put first in any of the collections of Christian writings, and there was no commentary on Mark that we know of until the fifth-century volume by Victor of Antioch. After Mark's incorporation into the fourfold Gospel canon by Irenaeus in the late second century, its use in the church diminished in the following centuries, and it was largely neglected.[37] Today, however, Mark has become the most studied Gospel of the Synoptics, because it is believed to have been the first written, thereby providing the *primary* source of information on the life of Jesus. Its stated purpose in writing is straightforward—to tell the story of Jesus in such a way as to call forth faith in the reader or hearer.

B. Authorship

The Gospel of Mark, as with the rest of the Gospels, has been handed down as an anonymous work. The current superscription, "The Gospel according to Mark" (εὐαγγέλιον κατὰ Μάρκον, *euangelion kata Markon*), comes from the fourth century, though the Gospel itself was attributed to Mark, the companion and interpreter of Peter, as early as the first half of the second century. The earliest and most important ancient source attributing the work to Mark is that of Bishop Papias of Hierapolis, writing around A.D. 140, as preserved by the church historian Eusebius (ca. A.D. 325):

> In the same writing he [Papias] also quotes other interpretations of the words of the Lord given by the Aristion mentioned above and traditions of John the presbyter. To them we may dismiss the studious; but we are now obliged to append to the words already quoted from him a tradition about the Mark who wrote the Gospel, which he expounds as follows. "And the Presbyter used to say this, 'Mark became Peter's interpreter and wrote accurately all that he remembered, not, indeed, in order, of the things said or done by the Lord. For he had not heard the Lord, nor had he followed him, but later on, as I said, followed Peter, who used to give teaching as necessity demanded but not making, as it were, an arrangement of the Lord's oracles, so that Mark did nothing wrong in thus writing down single points as he remembered them. For to one thing he gave attention, to leave out nothing of what he had heard and to make no false statements in them.'" This is related by Papias about Mark, and about Matthew this was said, "Matthew collected the oracles [τὰ λόγια] in the Hebrew language, and each interpreted them as best he could." (*Hist. eccl.* 3.39.14–16 [Lake, LCL])

On the basis of this testimony, it has traditionally been concluded that John Mark, onetime companion of Paul and Barnabas and subsequently of Peter (see Acts 13:5, 13 [John = John Mark]; 1 Pet 5:13), was the author of the Gospel bearing his name. Currently, however, there is no agreement among scholars on the authorship of the Gospel of Mark. Marxsen, who calls the statement by Papias "historically worthless," argues that the separate pericopes in Mark cannot be attributed to the preaching of Peter and claims that Papias is simply appealing to the authority of a great apostle in order to help him combat the Gnosticism of his day. Since by that time, or even earlier, Mark was considered to be the author of this Gospel and since separate testimony shows that he was an associate of Peter (1 Pet 5:13), this Gospel was an appropriate source available to Papias to help him in his defense of the gospel message.[38]

Essentially, the arguments against John Mark, a Jewish resident of Jerusalem and later the companion of Paul and also of Peter, writing this Gospel are that he does not appear to be familiar with the geography of Palestine in the first century (Mark 7:31; 11:1) or with Jewish customs, overgeneralizes about the Jews (7:3–4), from whom he seems to distance himself, and does not reflect the theology of either Paul or Peter as a companion might (Phlm 23; cf. Col 4:10; 2 Tim 4:11).[39]

Even though many other scholars today have called into question the tradition from Papias that Mark adapted the teaching of Peter to meet his hearers' needs, this tradition, as Martin argues, makes three very important claims: (1) the sources of the tradition in Mark were traced to Peter, (2) Mark himself had no firsthand knowledge of the words and deeds of Jesus, a statement that gives credibility to Mark instead of taking away from his report, and (3) Mark functioned as Peter's secretary (or interpreter, ἑρμηνεύτης, *hermēneutēs*), which squares with a late-second-century (or fourth-century) anti-Marcionite prologue to Mark that calls Mark Peter's interpreter.[40]

Although we cannot give conclusive answers to all of the objections raised against Markan authorship, the objections are not insurmountable, and there does not seem to be sufficient reason to deny the early church tradition that the Gospel of Mark was compiled by John Mark. Gundry, for example, gives considerable credence to Papias's tradition about Markan authorship and argues at length for this being an early tradition (A.D. 108–110) in the church.[41] It is perhaps going too far, however, to say that this Gospel consists simply of the reminiscences of Jesus as told by Peter to his friend John Mark, even though the Gospel of Mark may still contain much of Peter's testimony. Although form criticism claims that the Gospel of Mark also contains much of the early church's teaching, it is possible, and even likely if the book were written by the John Mark mentioned in the NT, that in the Gospel there are some traditions stemming from Peter himself, just as Papias stated. One tradition that may have come from Peter is Mark's reference to the failure of Peter and the rest of the disciples, which, as we noted above, was downplayed in Matthew and Luke but likely came from an eyewitness who was anxious to be candid about what happened.[42]

Because of this conflict, the value of authorship is disputed among some scholars. Marxsen, for example, states quite unambiguously that Markan authorship is immaterial: "This assumption does not really help us very much, for whatever name we assume to be that of the author does not make the work any more or any less than it is in its anonymous form."[43] Guelich, who acknowledges the weakness of the case in favor of Mark the companion of Paul as the author of the Gospel of Mark, also concludes that the matter of authorship is not of great importance.[44] We cannot agree here with Marxsen or Guelich, since Markan authorship would surely imply a close connection to an eyewitness of the events that Mark describes in his Gospel, and would make Mark the earliest and closest witness to the life and testimony of Jesus. If in the Gospel of Mark one is presented with testimony from Peter, it follows that Mark's testimony is more likely to reflect the views of earliest Christianity, including the eyewitness reports of Peter himself (1 Pet 5:1 says Peter witnessed the passion of Jesus). Although it is impossible to be dogmatic about authorship, we can scarcely deny the importance of the Gospel's possibly being written by a companion of Peter.

As we have mentioned, that Mark only wrote "reminiscences" coming from Peter, however, is too much to plead (as Conzelmann and Lindemann, Gundry, and Guelich agree). Filson is correct in questioning the veracity of Papias's statement that Peter was Mark's sole source of information. He believes that Mark also knew the oral tradition of the church and so would have used it in his writing.[45] Further, since this Gospel, unlike the *Gospel of Thomas,* which purports to come from an apostle, does not make a claim to apostolic authorship and all of the earliest testimony points to the authorship of Mark (who was clearly not an apostle), it is not likely that such a tradition would have been introduced without substantial support for it. If the name was fabricated by someone in the early church, a nonapostolic person was selected as the fictitious author, rather than, say, Peter himself, which is what happened in the case of the apocryphal *Gospel of Peter* (and many of the other apocryphal gospels). This is an especially important argument, since in the Gospels themselves there is nothing special about Mark that would lend any credibility to his report. In Acts, he is reported to have given up on Paul and Barnabas's first missionary endeavor (Acts 13:13), and Paul, no doubt as a result of this, subsequently had no confidence in Mark and would not take him on his second missionary journey (Acts 15:37–39). These are hardly credentials to commend the name of Mark to the early church, even with his recovery from this initial timidity and with his later profitable ministry (see 2 Tim 4:11; 1 Pet 5:13). The point here is obvious: it simply does not make sense to fabricate the name of Mark as the author of the Gospel, because he was not an apostle or an eyewitness to the story of Jesus. It would make much more sense to choose an apostolic name, as in the several apocryphal gospels (and possibly Matthew and John). Tertullian (ca. A.D. 200) gave the apostles themselves *(apostoli)* priority over their followers *(apostolici)*: "Of the apostles, therefore, John and Matthew first *instill* faith in us; while of the apostolic men, Luke and Mark *renew* it afterwards. These all start with the same principles of faith" *(Ag. Marc.* 4.2.2 *[ANF]*; adapted, italics added).

If Papias's testimony is to be trusted, however, we are then confronted with the difficult problem of trying to decipher which is the testimony of Peter and which are layers of tradition on top of it, a very challenging task that will not here be pursued.

C. Date

As with authorship, it is impossible to be certain about the dating of Mark's Gospel. Cranfield has noted that, according to the anti-Marcionite prologue for Mark and the testimony of Irenaeus, the Gospel of Mark was written after the death of Peter.[46] Irenaeus is the oldest and clearest evidence we have on this matter, and he claims that "after [Peter's and Paul's] death, Mark, the disciple and interpreter of Peter, transmitted to us in writing what was preached by Peter" *(Haer.* 3.1.1). It is probable that Peter died as a martyr during the Neronian persecution (ca. A.D. 64); if the tradition is correct about the time of Peter's death, this would place the writing of Mark sometime around A.D. 64–70.[47] Other than this, there is little evidence to give us guidelines for dating. Also, considering the impact upon the church from the destruction of Jerusalem and the temple and the relocation of the Jerusalem church to Pella, the lack of any clear reference to the destruction of Jerusalem and the temple in Mark is taken by some as an indication that Mark was written before A.D. 70.[48] Whether the reference to the impending destruction of Jerusalem in Mark 13:1–2 is a *vaticinium ex eventu* (a prophecy after the event has taken place, that is, a fabrication of a prophecy) is debated among scholars.[49] C. A. Evans has observed that such pessimism is unwarranted and that before the fall of Jerusalem and the destruction of the temple a number of persons had predicted that the temple would be destroyed.[50] Jesus' prediction fits well within the context of his day, when, because of the moral failure of the people and of the leadership of the nation, others also were predicting the destruction of the temple.

The early church fathers' apologetic use of the destruction of Jerusalem to support their view that they had inherited the Jewish role as the people of God points to the significance of this event for early Christianity. If it had already occurred, we would expect to see clearer references to it in Mark. The writing of Mark, therefore, was most probably sometime after the death of Peter and Paul but before the destruction of Jerusalem, in A.D. 66–70.

D. Influence and Reliability

Most scholars today believe that Mark's Gospel is the earliest of the four canonical Gospels and that it formed the basic pattern the other Gospel writers followed. Again, it is very doubtful that Mark himself composed the units of tradition in his Gospel solely upon the basis of Peter's reminiscences, but what does seem to be peculiar to Mark is his initiation of the Gospel genre itself. It appears that Mark set the pattern and scope of the Gospel narrative extending from the baptism of Jesus to his ministry, death, resurrection, and finally his recognition as the exalted Lord. This pattern is common to all four of the canonical Gospels.

Because Mark was the first Gospel to be written and because it was used by at least two other Gospel writers, it is inevitable that one should consider Mark as the primary source of information about Jesus.[51]

If Mark is the earliest Gospel, however, we must further ask whether he was faithful to his sources, leaving us with reliable information about Jesus. Did he pass his information on in the way he received it, or did he feel free to expand his sources and smooth out difficulties in and between his sources? Cranfield offers several reasons to support the contention that Mark was indeed a faithful and reliable witness, among them (discussed in detail above) that Mark's speech has been softened by Matthew and Luke and that his terms of address for Jesus have also been changed by Matthew and

Luke. Another reason Cranfield offers is that Mark did not create the vivid details in his Gospel if they were lacking in his sources. For example, there are numerous places where he could easily have invented detail in order to present a more vivid story (3:13–19; 6:6b–16; 6:30–34; 6:53–56), in comparison with his reports in 5:1–20, 9:14–29, and 10:17–22, where he seems to know more of the context. This comparison suggests that when Mark did not have details, he did not invent them. It must not be concluded from this that Mark lacked imagination but, rather, that he was a conscientious author, not an inventor or fabricator. Cranfield says that this reflects a "real reverence for the sacredness of historical events which he believed to have been the very deed of God."[52] Perhaps following this rule of self-restraint a little too closely, Mark seems to lack sufficient connecting links between the various sections in his Gospel. It seems that when Mark received a tradition in isolation without reliable information about its historical context, he was evidently hesitant to supply the missing historical links. On the other hand, Matthew and Luke often supply the missing links in places where Mark has none (compare, e.g., Luke 5:33 with Mark 2:18, and Matt 14:13 with Mark 6:30–31). For these reasons, Cranfield believes that a good case can be made for the basic reliability of Mark's handling of his sources. Another argument for the priority of Mark is that it is easier to understand why Matthew and Luke would have added these details than why Mark would have omitted them if he knew of them or had been using either Matthew or Luke as one of his primary sources.

In light of the integrity and careful manner with which the author of Mark handled his sources, it remains to be determined whether the sources he possessed and used in the compilation of his Gospel were reliable. Cranfield again suggests several reasons for the essential reliability of Mark and his sources. (1) The survival of many eyewitnesses, both hostile and friendly, throughout the oral-tradition transmission period would have limited the possibility of introducing fabricated stories into the Gospel traditions. (2) The prominence of such words for "witness" as μάρτυς (martys), μαρτυρεῖν (martyrein), μαρτυρία (martyria), and μαρτύριον (martyrion, which later came to refer to martyrdom) may show that the early Christian community was aware of its obligation to tell the truth, as the word *martys* in the ancient world referred especially to a witness in court. (3) The main outline of the events of Jesus' career and passion were often repeated in the early church (see, e.g., Acts 2:22–36; 1 Tim 3:16) in its preaching and worship and were thus kept clear in the memory of the early church. (4) The church's awareness and use of the oral tradition of the Jewish community, which was known for its painstaking care in passing on its traditions in considerable detail, and the similar fashion in which the church passed on its traditions (see 1 Cor 15:3–8; Rom 10:9–10) argue for the limitation of undue expansion of the primary traditions about Jesus during its formative years. (5) Along this same line, the manner in which Jesus taught (through parable, aphorism, and epigram) made it easy to pass on the tradition without significant loss. (6) Cranfield also observes that the use of Mark by the later evangelists would be strange if he were not considered to be reliable by them in the framing of their own Gospels. (7) There are a number of explicit Semitisms or Aramaisms in the Gospel of Mark—words or phrases in Aramaic carried over into the Greek—found in the sayings of Jesus and in many of the narratives (e.g., "Talitha cumi," or "little girl, get up," in Mark 5:41; "Abba," or "Father," in 14:36). The presence of these phrases argues against the notion, advanced by some scholars, that later Hellenistic influences considerably altered the traditions in Mark. (8) The fact that Mark freely shares traditions that discredit Peter and the other apostles and even mentions the ignorance of Jesus regarding the time of his second coming (13:32) strongly suggests the general reliability of the way Mark handled his sources and conveyed his message about Jesus.[53]

E. Basic Characteristics and Message

Mark was probably motivated to care for a community that was going through difficult times, and his Gospel contains two primary discourses from Jesus that appear to address such a circumstance. The first is in 4:1–34, a discourse on parables, and the second is the apocalyptic discourse on an imminent *eschaton* in ch. 13. The sayings material in Mark is significantly increased in both Matthew and Luke with the Q material.

Of importance also is the so-called messianic secret in Mark, in which the identity and signifi-

cance of Jesus are both hidden (from the main characters of the story) and revealed (to the readers of the book) (see 1:25, 34, 44; 3:12; 5:43; 7:36; 8:30; 9:9; cf. 5:19; 16:7).[54] Why did Mark not want the characters of his narrative to identify Jesus as the Son of God, especially when he begins the composition with such a declaration in 1:1? On the other hand, Jesus is identified as God's "beloved son" at his baptism in 1:11, at his transfiguration in 9:7, and by one of his executioners at his crucifixion in 15:39. Mark, like Matthew, also has a strong inclination toward sets of three. For example, he puts together three seed parables (4:3–32), three common opinions about John the Baptist (6:14–15), three common understandings of Jesus (8:27–28), three predictions of his passion (8:31; 9:31; 10:33–34), three occasions of the disciples falling asleep in the garden (14:32–42), and three denials of Jesus by Peter (14:66–72).[55] It appears that the messianic secret was maintained in order to make sure that Jesus' appointed time of suffering was not interrupted. Jesus as the suffering Son of Man is at the heart of the Gospel (chs. 8–10), along with the suffering of the disciples (Mark 8:31–32, 34–38). In these narratives the cost of discipleship is presented: those who wish to follow Jesus will have to take up a cross, deny themselves, and follow selflessly after Jesus, imitating the example that he has given. None of this, however, should override our recognition of Mark's primary concern to present Jesus as the Son of God—the overarching theme of the book. The significance of his message for his readers, who were facing an uncertain future and perhaps going through various trials for their faith, is obvious. That Jesus has triumphed over all his enemies, even at the point of abandonment by his closest friends and endurance of a cruel death on a cross, would have been highly significant for a community of faith that was uncertain of its future. Such a community's hope would have been related to its recognition of God's activity in Jesus and of his identification with the presence of the kingdom of God in his life and ministry.

F. Outline of the Gospel of Mark

Prologue to the Gospel (1:1–13)
The ministry in Galilee and nearby
(1:14–8:26)
The preparation for his passion (8:27–9:13)

The journey to Jerusalem (9:30–10:52)
The ministry in Jerusalem (11–13)
The passion of Jesus (14:1–15:47)
The resurrection of Jesus (16:1–8)
Markan appendix (16:9–20)

G. Postscript

Although most NT scholars today recognize that Mark 16:9–20 is a late addition to the Gospel, not all agree that 16:8 was the original ending of Mark. It certainly was unusual in ancient Greek to conclude a work with a conjunction, such as is found in Mark 16:8: ἐφοβοῦντο γάρ, *ephobounto gar* ("for they were afraid"). Indeed, a parallel case is found only in the first-century Pseudo-Demetrius's *Formae epistolicae,* which ends with ὀφείλω γάρ, *opheilō gar.* Fuller believes that there were no appearance stories in the original Easter tradition and that originally there were only proclamations of his resurrection. He sees no problem with concluding the Gospel with 16:8.[56] On the other hand, it seems strange to end a Gospel about the triumph of Jesus on a note of fear and fleeing. It is more likely that the original ending—and possibly the original introduction of the Gospel—has been lost, either because of extended use of the manuscripts or damage to the manuscripts during a time of persecution. It is also difficult to imagine why Mark would have left the appearance stories out of his Gospel if such were known. The earliest Easter tradition is found in 1 Cor 15:3–8, where Paul includes a list of appearances of the risen Lord to the disciples. All the other early Easter traditions include appearances, and they are supported indirectly in the story of the selection of Judas Iscariot's successor (see Acts 1:21, 23). Although some scholars prefer to have Mark conclude with the strange words "they said nothing to anyone, for they were afraid," this does not fit in with Mark's purpose of presenting Jesus as the Son of God. The other evangelists all recorded that the story of Jesus continued through the Easter appearances.

The current long ending of Mark (16:9–20) is not original to Mark but was added later by Christians who were concerned with the abrupt ending of this Gospel. The passage is not found in the oldest manuscripts of the Gospel but may nevertheless contain early traditions, some of which are parallel to, and probably summations of, the conclusions of

the other canonical Gospels. They perhaps preserve early sources upon which the early church drew. Most of the contents of this section are found in the other Gospels, as the following parallels show:

Parallels in Mark's Longer Ending	
Mark 16:11	Lack of belief (Matt 28:17)
Mark 16:12–3	Two on the road (Luke 24:13–35)
Mark 16:14	Reproach for unbelief (John 20:19, 26)
Mark 16:15	Great commission (Matt 28:19)
Mark 16:16	Salvation/judgment (John 3:18, 36)
Mark 16:17	Speaking in tongues (Acts 2:4; 10:46)
Mark 16:18a	Serpents and poison (Acts 28:3–5)
Mark 16:18b	Laying hands on the sick (Acts 9:17; 28:8)
Mark 16:19	Ascension (Acts 1:2, 9)
Mark 16:20	General Summary of Acts[57]

If Mark 16:9–20 was a late addition and 16:8 was not the original conclusion, what happened to Mark's original section? What accounts for the disappearance of this important conclusion, which almost certainly included appearances to the disciples in Galilee, as is promised in both 14:28 and 16:7, and which was probably closely followed and/or adapted by Matthew? A possible explanation for the loss of the original conclusion concerns the form in which the Gospel was first circulated, namely, the codex (or book) form, as opposed to a scroll. In a codex, the last page would include the final appearance story. Is it possible that the ending of Mark was lost and that the reason Mark 16:9–20 and several other conclusions were added to Mark 16:8 is the ancient church's recognition of this? As it stands, the conclusion of the Gospel at 16:8 with the words "they said nothing to anyone, for they were afraid" is hardly a way to speak of the certitude of faith that developed and that issued forth in the establishment of the church. It would be difficult to construct the logic of the good news from this kind of conclusion. The original conclusion may well have been lost, and the church supplied what was missing by offering a brief digest of the conclusions of the other canonical Gospels and portions of Acts.

4. THE GOSPEL OF LUKE AND THE ACTS OF THE APOSTLES

A. *Introduction*

Because of their theological congruity and the similarity in their introductions and their language patterns, quite early in the history of the church it was concluded that both Luke and Acts had the same author. This is so although both volumes were circulating separately as early as A.D. 140, when Marcion included the Gospel of Luke in his collection of Christian Scriptures but did not include Acts. The most important evidence that the two volumes came from the same author is found in their introductions. Acts (1:1–2) picks up on the introduction to Luke (1:1–4), noting not only the same addressee but also that Acts is the second volume of a two-volume work.

In terms of focus, the author clearly has universal ambitions for the gospel of Christ and is concerned about the missionary zeal of the earliest church in both Jewish and Gentile communities. For Luke, the mission of Jesus to Israel is extended in the church, in its worldwide mission to the Jews and the Gentiles. At any rate, the Luke–Acts corpus is commonly recognized as two volumes by the same author, who sought to trace Christianity from its origins to its spread throughout the Roman Empire, especially to Rome.[58] The author of Luke–Acts does not alter Mark's arrangement of the life of Jesus as much as Matthew does, nor does he make his account subservient to the five-discourse scheme that Matthew's Gospel follows. As Bultmann has noted, the author of Luke–Acts continues the method developed by Mark because "he is interested in an historically continuous and connected presentation, whose demands of course he realizes much more comprehensively than Mark."[59] The writer's purpose in his composition seems to be obvious from the introduction to the Gospel. He states that he seeks to explain carefully the origins of Christianity in the life, death, and resurrection of Jesus, as well as its growth and development from Jerusalem to Rome. The author shows himself to be one who is very interested in history and in presenting the historical events carefully and precisely (see, e.g., Luke 2–3), but with an evangelistic purpose. He was not an unbiased historical reporter but one with strong theological motives for writing his history of the origins of salvation and its early proclamation. The author of these two volumes can in no way be seen as an unbiased or unprejudiced historian seeking only the facts (if such a person has ever existed). He is completely involved in the story he is trying to relate, and has a special concern to share the universalistic appeal of the Christian message, making it known that salvation is not only for the Jews but also for the Gentiles. This can be seen in passages such as Luke 2:32, 3:6, 4:14–27, 13:29, 15:11–32, 24:7, and Acts 10:34–43, as well as in the remainder of Acts, in the Gentile mission of Paul, and also in that of Peter in Acts 10. The writer is obviously not interested solely in the "cold facts" of history but, rather, in the facts about Jesus the Christ that call individuals to faith.

Despite these facts, the corpus of Luke–Acts is one of the most controversial compositions in the NT. With few exceptions, Luke–Acts has been the center of more debate than almost any of the other books in the NT. Today the most contested issues continue to be matters related to authorship, date, the purpose of writing, the view of history, the speeches of Acts, the reliability of the two volumes as a historically reliable picture of the early church, and the accuracy of the author's reflection of Paul. Long ago W. C. van Unnik called the Luke–Acts corpus "a storm center in contemporary scholarship,"[60] an opinion that still holds true.

The following observations are summary discussions of some of the more important problems scholars deal with today, together with a few conclusions that we can draw from the two-volume work.

B. *Authorship*

Since the author's name is not attached to either of the books, the problem of authorship is somewhat complicated. Traditionally the "we" passages of Acts (cf. 16:10–17; 20:5–15; 21:1–18; 27:1–29; 28:1–16) have been used to argue that Luke, the companion of Paul, wrote both volumes. The oldest discussion available on this question comes from Irenaeus (ca. A.D. 180), who accepted the "we" sections as conclusive evidence that Luke wrote Luke–Acts. Arguing for the closeness of Luke to Paul in his journeys, unlike Mark and Barnabas, Irenaeus concludes:

> As Luke was present at all these occurrences, he carefully noted them down in writing, so that he cannot be convicted of falsehood or boastfulness, because all these [particulars] proved both that he was senior to all those who now teach otherwise, and that he was not ignorant of the truth. That he was not merely a follower, but also a fellow-laborer of the apostles, but especially of Paul . . . (*Haer.* 3.14.1 [*ANF*]; cf. 3.13.3)

Irenaeus's argument was intended to confirm a prior belief about Luke and Acts rather than introduce a new understanding of its authorship. In the list of Paul's missionary companions, only Luke and Jesus called Justus appear to be candidates for authorship; all early church tradition supports the former. A common view—and probably the strongest evidence in favor of Lukan authorship of Luke–Acts—has been that the author intended the "we" passages to show that he was a participant in some of the journeys of Paul and was not simply using the conventional "we," as some have argued. Acts and other ancient historical writings make use of the first-person plural in narrations of journeys often, though not always, to indicate participation (see esp. Polybius, *Hist.* 36.12, 12.27.1–6; Lucian, *Hist. conscr.* 47; Homer, *Od.* 12.402–425). Nevertheless, some scholars have questioned this conclusion. They have seen the "we" passages as part of a convention for ancient sea-voyage narratives, although this has been fairly well refuted. More plausible is the theory that the author relied upon an earlier, continuous source that has been interpolated throughout the larger narrative, marked by the retention of the use of "we," especially since the "we" passages have an outlook and theology that is distinctive when compared to the rest of the Acts narrative.[61] Kümmel, who denies Lukan authorship of Luke–Acts, contends that the compiler of the two-volume work found the "we" passages in the traditions he used to compile his work and simply left them in the final form of the work.[62] Kümmel notes further that were the author of Acts a companion of Paul, he would probably have shown a greater awareness of Paul's major teachings, Paul's epistles, and the fact that Paul used the title of apostle to describe himself, a title that is sel-

dom attributed to Paul in Acts (see 14:4, 14). The tendency of the writer of Acts to smooth out the differences in the early church, especially making Peter and Paul alike in regard to Gentile freedom from the law (cf. Gal 2:11–14), has caused some scholars to question its reliability. Such doubts have resulted in the hypothesis that the book of Acts is a form of novel or ancient romance.[63] Acts does share some of the characteristics of an ancient romance—such as depiction of the adventures of a hero, who travels and encounters various dangers—but there are also significant differences. It is important to remember that, just because Acts may be a tale well told, holding its reader's attention, this does not necessarily mean that it is unreliable, and certainly not that it is fiction.

The full title ascribed to Acts (ca. A.D. 150) suggests that the book was about the apostles, but after the early chapters Luke shows little interest in the apostles as a group. Although not original to the document, the title is nevertheless important evidence, from the second century, of the church's quest to root faith in apostolicity. Acts, however, concentrates its narrative around Peter (chs. 1–12) and Paul (chs. 9, 13–28). The first part of the book tells the story of the early church in Jerusalem and Palestine/Syria from the resurrection of Christ until the departure of Peter from Jerusalem. Peter serves as the transition and authentication of the Gentile mission of the church, principally carried out by Paul. The career of Paul is structured in three missionary journeys to the west from Antioch and Palestine/Syria, with a final journey as a prisoner to Rome. A feature of the contents of Acts is the frequent inclusion of speeches that summarize early Christian preaching and teaching (e.g., chs. 2, 3, 7, 13, 20, 22, 26).

Although the author aimed at providing an "orderly account" of the birth and development of the Christian movement for his patron Theophilus (Luke 1:3–4), he was also a zealous advocate for the Christian faith. He viewed the early Christians as models for conduct and wanted to show how the Christian movement, which began as a Jewish sect in Palestine, evolved in its identity and grew to have universal appeal to both Jews and Gentiles. The author likewise stresses that the church and the Roman government were not in conflict. Because of the length of Luke–Acts, the books were probably first published in two separate volumes,

Pools on the travertine cliffs at Hierapolis, formed by the calcareous concretions and mineral deposits from the local thermal springs, where the Romans built elaborate baths. Photo Lee M. McDonald.

or scrolls, of papyrus sheets, making it possible to circulate one without the other. Acts was viewed as a book separate from the Gospel and circulated in a codex, or booklike form, at least by ca. A.D. 140, when an edited form of Luke became part of Marcion's collection of Christian Scriptures along with ten of Paul's epistles. Acts was not used by Marcion probably because he was unaware of it. Since he edited the Gospel and since the largest focus in Acts is on the inclusion of the Gentiles into the church, it is difficult to know what in Acts would have so offended him that he could not also have expurgated it. Whatever it might have been, Marcion could just as easily have used the editor's pen to delete unwanted material, as he did in Luke's Gospel.

Although some verbal parallels exist between Acts and *1 Clement, Barnabas,* Polycarp, the *Didache,* and the *Shepherd of Hermas,* this may be evidence only of a vocabulary that was common in early Christian writings. Justin Martyr in the second century (ca. A.D. 160) has apparent citations from Acts

(compare Acts 1:8 with *1 Apol.* 50.12; Acts 17:23 with *2 Apol.* 10.6). Irenaeus was the first writer to mention Acts by name and also ascribe it to Luke, the companion of Paul. He also cited it in his attacks against Marcion, as noted above (e.g., *Haer.* 3.1.1; 3.10.1; 3.12.1–5). Acts is mentioned in an anti-Marcionite prologue of Luke (possibly as early as ca. 160–180 but probably later), which notes that Luke was a Syrian of Antioch, a disciple of the apostles who later followed Paul and who served the Lord as a single man until his death in Boeotia (Bithynia?) at the age of eighty-four. Clement of Alexandria frequently cites Acts in a scripturelike (i.e., authoritatively) manner (e.g., *Misc.* 3.6.49; 7.9.53). Origen makes use of several texts from Acts but is vague about its scriptural status (*Or.* 12.2; 13.6). Tertullian, like Irenaeus, appeals to Acts to refute Marcion (*Ag. Marc.* 5.1–2) and adds that those who did not accept Acts as Scripture were not of the Holy Spirit (*Prescr.* 22). After the book of Acts, some five known apocryphal Acts were written—Acts of Peter, Paul, John, Thomas, and

Andrew—in the late second and early third centuries in Asia Minor and Syria. All were modeled after the NT Acts, but unlike Acts, they are almost entirely fictional.

The book of Acts does not fit easily into any ancient pattern of historiography, although the author shows some acquaintance with the historian's craft and has a working knowledge of Greek rhetoric. Acts itself is neither a biography nor a history after the usual ancient patterns, although the author uses both in his own way to underscore the validity of Christianity. There is no question that the author of Acts made use of sources for his work, but he has so completely rewritten them that they are hardly distinguishable, except for the "we" source. He shares this practice with many ancient historians, such as Tacitus, Josephus, Dionysius of Halicarnassus (*Ant. rom.* 5, 8), and Lucian (*Hist. conscr.* 47), who, though they claim to have neither added nor deleted anything, appear to have completely rewritten their sources.[64]

Since Irenaeus, there have been other arguments put forward defending the traditional view that Luke, the companion of Paul, was the author of Luke–Acts. One of the most popular arguments for Lukan authorship around the end of the last century and the early decades of the twentieth came from William K. Hobart, who held that the "medical terms" used by the author of Luke–Acts proved that the work was written by Luke, the physician and companion of Paul.[65] Hobart argued that since Luke was a physician (Col 4:14; Phlm 24), he should display medical language in his writings. Hobart made a study of the language of Luke–Acts, concluding that the corpus was written by a physician, more precisely, Luke the physician. Hobart's work gained credence when it was later supported by the notable Adolf Harnack, who reinforced Hobart's arguments. Harnack was convinced that the medical language in Luke–Acts supported the view that Luke was the author of the entire work. He stressed emphatically that "the evidence is of overwhelming force; so that it seems to me that the third gospel and the Acts of the Apostles were composed by a physician." He concluded that "the result of our investigation is that the book is Lukan in style and vocabulary. . . . St. Luke, therefore, has manufactured this document."[66]

Henry Cadbury, together with many others after him, has taken exception to Hobart's and Harnack's position, explaining that the so-called medical terms attributed to Luke the physician were also used by others who were in no way connected with the medical profession. Cadbury argued that the "medical terms" cited by these authors, as such, did not exist.[67] The result of Cadbury's and other scholars' work on this question is that the argument based on medical language has seldom been used since, and then certainly not with the previous confidence. Vincent Taylor, for example, was much less dogmatic than Harnack about the "medical terms" and only argued that they "tend to confirm the ancient tradition" but they do not prove it.[68]

The classic argument against Lukan authorship and a first-century dating of the corpus was set forth by F. C. Baur in 1845.[69] Baur held that Acts was written far into the second century as an apology trying to bring together two opposing parties of the church, namely, Gentile Christianity (represented by Paul) and Jewish Christianity (represented by Peter). He noted that these groups were opposed to each other, especially over their understanding of the role and observance of the law in the church.

Baur is best known for his application of the Hegelian dialectical philosophy of history to early Christianity and using it in dating the NT writings.[70] He interpreted the conflict between the earliest strands of Jewish Christianity, represented by James (and in the book of Acts by Peter), which he considered the "thesis" form of early Christianity, and Gentile Christianity, represented by Paul, which he considered the "antithesis"; and he viewed Acts as the "synthesis" that attempted to bring these two opposing sides together. This synthesis was seen by Baur to represent the catholicizing tendencies of the second-century church. He argued that the unity of Acts consisted in its "tendency" (hence, Ger. *Tendenzkritik*) to represent the difference between Peter and Paul as unessential and trifling. He said that there was a tendency in Acts to make Peter appear like Paul, as when Peter went to the house of Cornelius in Acts 10 and defended Gentile rights in the church in Acts 11 and 15. Baur maintained that Paul, on the other hand, was made to look like Peter, as when Paul circumcised Timothy (Acts 16:3), cut his own hair at Cenchreae at the conclusion of a Jewish vow (Acts 18:18), and then joined with four Jewish Christians in a weeklong temple ritual of purification, meditation, and offering (Acts 21:23–26). Since Paul was the apostle of freedom and proclaimed freedom from the law—that a person was justified by faith alone apart from the works of the law (see Gal 2–3)—whereas Acts tries to view Paul as obedient to the law, it was clear to Baur that Acts was written late by an author trying to bring the two main elements in the church into harmony by covering up the differences between Paul and Peter. To Baur, the theology of Acts was foreign to Paul's theology, which was best seen in Paul's four undisputed Epistles—Romans, Galatians, and 1 and 2 Corinthians (see ch. 10, below). Baur's hypothesis is commonly known as the Tübingen theory, which also initiated the long-standing Tübingen school.

Although Baur had a major impact on the investigation of Luke–Acts for over a century, few scholars today accept his conclusions about Acts, especially those based on his Hegelian approach to early Christianity, but most still agree with him that there is a significant difference between the theology of Luke–Acts and the theology of Paul. This conclusion calls Luke's authorship of the two volumes into question. Kümmel, as mentioned above, maintains that the author of Luke–Acts either was not acquainted with Paul or did not accept Pauline theology.[71] Marxsen holds that the events of Acts depict a picture of the church at the end of the first century, not during the life of Paul.[72] Harrison, on the other hand, argues that the ecclesiastical and sacramental matters in Acts are very primitive in comparison to the early second century's more developed views, observable in Clement of Rome and especially in Ignatius. The primitive nature of Acts, for him, argues against a late dating of the work but in favor of Lukan authorship, just as the early church maintained.[73]

In general, as with the authorship of Mark, those who deny Lukan authorship of Luke–Acts must explain the unlikely attribution of the work to a nonapostolic person. On the other hand, those who accept Lukan authorship must explain the alleged differences in the theology and events in Acts with those described by Paul in his epistles. We are inclined to accept Lukan authorship, but not without some reservation, because of the differences in theology between Luke and Paul. The chief differences concern Paul's view of the significance of the death of Jesus "for our sins" (1 Cor 15:3; Rom 4:25),

compared with the emphasis on the resurrection (Acts 2:22–36; 3:13–16) by Luke, who only says that the death of Jesus was in the plan of God (Acts 2:23; 3:18). While the speech attributed to Paul in Acts 20 refers to the death of Jesus for sins (v. 28), the point is still that Luke's focus on the death of Jesus is not the same nor emphasized to the same degree as it is in Paul. Similarly, Paul's major emphases on reconciliation, redemption, and justification by faith, the use of "apostle," his favorite designation for himself, and any reference to Paul's letters are all missing in Acts. Although the "we" passages, in many scholars' minds, go a long way toward maintaining the traditional view of authorship, the most important question is the overcoming of the different theological perspectives between Luke and Paul.

C. Date

Harnack insisted on a date in the early 60s for the composition of Luke–Acts, partly because there is no mention of the death of Paul, the primary hero of Acts. For Harnack, it did not make sense that the writer should follow the ministry of Paul so closely, only to omit any mention of his death, unless it had not yet occurred by the time this work was completed.[74] Most estimates of the time of Paul's death (and all early traditions agree) place it during the Neronian persecutions in Rome in A.D. 64–65. On the other hand, O'Neill attempts to date Luke–Acts to a post–New Testament era, between A.D. 115 and A.D. 130, because of Acts' lack of direct awareness of Paul's thought and because the work was still not well known by the time of Justin (ca. A.D. 160), as presumably a first-century work would be.[75] Many scholars today object to O'Neill's conclusions, suggesting an earlier dating around A.D. 70–90, but agree with him that it was not written by Luke, the companion of Paul.

The argument for an early dating of Luke–Acts based on the failure to mention the death of Paul (or Peter, for that matter) is not used by many scholars today because this would push earlier the date of the composition of Mark.[76] More specifically, if Luke depended upon Mark and if Luke–Acts was written about A.D. 60–61 before the death of Paul, then Mark must be placed about A.D. 59–60 at the latest. This dating procedure is unacceptable to most because it forces Mark to a date that early tradition will not easily allow (see sec. 3.A, above).

Paul's death, though clouded over with mystery, could have occurred in the latter part of Nero's rule, as late as around A.D. 67. This is possible if we accept the early tradition that Paul was released from prison in Rome, went to Spain, was subsequently arrested in Rome, and put to death.[77] Since Paul did not go to Spain before his imprisonment in Rome (according to Acts, which has Paul arriving in Rome around A.D. 61–62), it has been argued that Paul was released from prison and rearrested later. In Rom 15:28 Paul speaks of his plans to visit Spain, and in 2 Tim 4:7 (disregarding the issue of authorship of the Pastorals for the moment) it is claimed that Paul had "finished his course," implying that his proposed journey had taken place.

If Paul was released from prison in Rome (it is by no means certain that he was), then Luke–Acts could have been composed between the time of Paul's two arrests in Rome, while he was on a visit to Spain and the Aegean area or traveling in the eastern Mediterranean (as 1 Timothy and Titus seem to indicate). If that was the case, Paul's final arrest and subsequent death could have been as late as A.D. 67, though few scholars would put his death this late. If Luke–Acts was composed during this intermediate phase of Paul's ministry, then the two volumes could have reasonably been written around A.D. 65–67. At any rate, a date of A.D. 70 or later is very unlikely, not just because there is no mention of Paul's or Peter's death but also because there is no mention of the fall of Jerusalem, which took place in A.D. 70 and had a significant impact upon the church. There is nothing whatever in Acts to suggest that Jerusalem had fallen or that its temple had been destroyed.

Bruce, however, comments, "The attitude to Roman power throughout Acts makes it difficult for some readers to believe that the Neronian persecution of ca. A.D. 65 had taken place." He also notes that throughout Acts Paul's appeal to Rome appears to be in anticipation of a favorable hearing. Had Luke been writing at a time when Nero had already begun his attack on Christians, it is doubtful whether Luke would have portrayed such an optimistic picture. In favor of an early dating of Acts, Bruce explains, "Prominence is given in Acts to subjects which were of urgent importance in the church before A.D. 70, but which were of less moment after that date. Such were the terms of Gentile admission to church fellowship, the coexistence of Jews and Gentiles in the church, the food requirements of the apostolic decree [ch. 15]."[78] For these reasons, an early dating of Luke–Acts—for instance, between A.D. 64 and 67—seems possible, even though the work may not generally have become known in the early church until twenty or twenty-five years later.[79]

We should briefly add that some scholars who date Luke–Acts after A.D. 70 or thereabouts do so on the basis of the prophecies of the Gospel of Luke, which speak of the fall of Jerusalem and the destruction of the temple and strongly suggest images of the Jewish war (see Luke 17:22–36; 21:20–28; 23:28–31). There are no adequate grounds, however, for assuming that all predictions must have occurred after the events to which they refer took place. Bruce is correct when he contends that "it is, indeed, quite uncritical to assume that every prediction which comes true is a *vaticinium ex eventu* [a prediction after the fact], quite apart from the consideration that these were the predictions of the Messiah Himself. The prediction of wars and sieges and sacking of cities is a common place of history."[80]

D. The Importance of Authorship for Interpretation

The establishment of Lukan authorship is far more important than the dating of Luke–Acts because of Luke's personal connection with Paul. Luke was acquainted with Paul and his ministry and with that of many of the other early church authorities, including Timothy, possibly Peter, Barnabas, James, and others. If the author was Luke, his sources for the life of Jesus and his history of the spreading of the Gospel by the earliest community of Christians would have a more direct and reliable connection to early eyewitness accounts of the events he describes, thereby making Luke–Acts more valuable for reconstructing the events of the early church. It is also precisely this issue that divides scholars—the Gospel of Luke's seeming lack of awareness of the major themes of Paul's preaching.

An early dating and Lukan authorship of Luke–Acts (ca. A.D. 64–67) would support the idea that the tradition about Jesus was not a late notion, originating in the needs of a community of Christians in answer to problems that arose in the church. This is especially true of the Gospel, but also of Acts. Lukan authorship and an early dating obviously would not *prove* that Paul was well acquainted with the teaching of the life and ministry of Jesus, but they would argue strongly for Luke's awareness of a common early tradition about Jesus that circulated both inside and outside Palestine.

The basic questions about the authorship and dating of Luke–Acts have clearly not been resolved and must remain open for future study and more substantial argumentation. The preceding discussion has, it is hoped, set forth possibilities for continued investigation. Even those scholars who are most skeptical about the traditional dating and authorship of Luke–Acts continue to appeal to the corpus as a source for NT church history. Indeed, it is impossible to formulate any coherent understanding of the early church, from whatever perspective or stance one has regarding authorship and date, without considerable dependence upon Luke–Acts.[81]

E. Outlines of the Gospel of Luke and the Acts of the Apostles

1. The Gospel of Luke

Prologue (1:1–4)
Birth of John and Jesus, Jesus' childhood (1:5–2:52)
Baptism, ancestry, and temptation (3:1–4:13)
Galilean ministry (4:14–9:50)
Journey to Jerusalem (9:51–19:27)
Last week of ministry (19:28–21:39)
Death and resurrection of Jesus (22:1–24:53)

2. The Acts of the Apostles

Prologue and ascension (1:1–14)
Spread of the gospel in Jerusalem (1:15–8:3)
Spread of the gospel to Samaria and the coastal regions (8:4–11:18)
Spread of the gospel to Gentiles—triumph and conflict (11:19–15:35)
Interlude: death of James, escape of Peter, death of Herod (12:1–23)
Spread of the gospel to western Asia and Greece (15:36–19:20)
Spread of the gospel from Jerusalem to Rome by Paul (19:21–28:31)

5. THE GOSPEL OF MATTHEW

A. Introduction

In the earlier discussion of the synoptic problem, we argued that the writer of Matthew used Mark as his primary source, besides a written or oral tradition known also to the writer of Luke and conveniently called Q. Along with Mark and Q, Matthew probably also used other traditions (or perhaps his own perspective on the issues he discusses), either written or oral, to compile his Gospel, traditions we call M.

Matthew, more than any other evangelist, relates the OT and issues in contemporary Judaism to the story of Jesus. This Gospel is not legalistic though it does at times lean in that direction, as can be seen in the writer's orderly way of arranging the teaching of Jesus and what he expects from his disciples (Matt 5–7). Matthew appears to have been written primarily for teachers in the church. The widespread use of Matthew—far more than any other Gospel—in the second century testifies to the church's perception of its reliability. Matthew, along with the Epistle of James and the *Didache*, is one of the primary expressions of the concerns of Jewish Christianity in the first century, but an important question is whether Matthew, or the author of the first Gospel, was a Jew or Gentile. Further, when was the Gospel written, and where? These are important questions, since they impact on the credibility of the writer, as we will show below.

B. Authorship

The obvious dependence of the first Gospel (Matthew) on Mark suggests that the Gospel was not written by an apostle but, rather, by a writer who knew how to use his sources well.[82] The traditional view that Matthew the apostle was the author has been considered highly suspect among most NT scholars for a considerable time. Most today consider that the author was a Hellenistic-Jewish Christian, but several notable scholars of late are wondering if the author of Matthew was Gentile instead.[83]

The evidence for all of these positions is both internal and external: there is evidence from an examination of the Gospel itself, and evidence from the oldest external evidence, the early church fathers' witness to the authorship. The primary external evidence for Matthew the apostle dates back to a statement from Bishop Papias of Hierapolis (ca. 140), who was quoted by Eusebius (*Hist. eccl.* 3.39.16). The critical part of the passage, for our purposes, comes after Eusebius concludes Papias's words about Mark's Gospel and then focuses on Matthew: "This is related by Papias about Mark, and about Matthew this was said, 'Matthew collected the oracles [or sayings, τὰ λόγια] of Jesus in the Hebrew [Aramaic?] language, and each [teacher?] interpreted [or translated; ἡρμήνευσεν, *hērmēneusen*] them as best he could' " (*Hist. eccl.* 3.39.16 [LCL]) (the full text is reproduced in sec. 3.B, above). Probably a misunderstanding of what Papias intended led early Christians such as Irenaeus, Tertullian, Origen, and especially Eusebius to argue that *logia* comprised a Gospel. Whether Papias himself explicitly drew this conclusion is not certain, but he does say earlier in the passage attributed to him that Mark gathered "the Lord's oracles" (τῶν κυριακῶν λογίων, *tōn kyriakōn logiōn*) but not in any particular order. The parallel is not exact, but close enough to raise the question whether Papias meant that Matthew wrote a Gospel. If the external tradition is to be trusted, then we must say yes. It is possible, however, that Matthew, though not composing a Gospel, did collect sayings of Jesus and wrote them in Hebrew or Aramaic. Irenaeus (ca. 180), however, claims that Matthew wrote his Gospel in the Hebrew dialect while Peter and Paul were preaching the Gospel in Rome (*Haer.* 3.1.1; cf. Eusebius, *Hist. eccl.* 5.8.2). Eusebius also reports a story from Pantaenus (ca. 170), the director of the school in Alexandria taken over by his student, Clement of Alexandria, that Matthew wrote a Gospel in Hebrew that was taken as far east as India and was left there in its Hebrew letters by Bartholomew (*Hist. eccl.* 5.10.3). Jerome (ca. 390–395) claimed to have seen and copied the Hebrew form of Matthew's Gospel (*Vir. ill.* [PL 23:643]), but only a few scholars give much credibility to his testimony. It is still very doubtful, however, that the Gospel of Matthew, as it now stands, ever existed in Hebrew or Aramaic. Thus far, no attempts at putting it back into Hebrew or Aramaic have been successful or gained approval among Matthean scholars. Harrington, who claims that the canonical Gospel of Matthew is and always has been in Greek, nevertheless adds that a complete copy of Matthew's Gospel in Hebrew appears in a fourteenth-century Jewish polemical treatise called *Even Bohan* ("The Touchstone"). Study of this document is still at an early stage, but he notes that it makes Judaism and Christianity more compatible than does the canonical version, and offers a higher estimation of John the Baptist.[84]

Since all of the ancient external testimony on this matter apparently depends on Papias, or a misreading of Papias, should it be discounted? Clement of Alexandria, Irenaeus, Origen, and Eusebius were all Greek speakers and wrote extensively in Greek, and they believed that Matthew was a translation from the Hebrew into Greek,[85] but can we trust their conclusions? Surely their expertise in the Greek language should give them an advantage in knowing; still, it is not clear how Matthew wrote in Hebrew but incorporated a Greek Gospel (Mark) into his work and allowed it to determine the material he presents. This is especially strange if the writer were an eyewitness and an apostle. It is also strange that an apostle would borrow the text of someone not an eyewitness to recount his own calling to follow Jesus (compare Matt 9:9–11 with Mark 2:14)! Why would he need to use another source about his own calling?[86] The external evidence points to a Palestinian Jew named Matthew; the internal evidence, however, points to one who was well versed in Hellenism and may have been a Jew, but most likely not Matthew the apostle.[87]

The internal evidence may also point to a Gentile writer. Meier has noted that the final redactor of the Gospel may well have been a Gentile rather than a Jew. This does not discredit the view that an earlier form of the Gospel may be attributed either to Matthew or to a Jewish Christian, but Meier's arguments are not easily dismissed. He reasons as follows: (1) The author is certainly well acquainted with the Jewish perspective, but unlike Paul, who was a religious zealot who converted to the Christian faith and wanted his fellow countrymen to convert to the same faith, Matthew denounces the Jewish nation and claims that it accepted the blood of Jesus on itself and its children (Matt 27:25). Instead of the religious leaders inciting the crowd, in Matthew it is "the people as a whole" who denounce Jesus. (2) If the writer was a Jew, he made a blunder in interpreting a Jewish document (Zech

9:9) when he had Jesus riding into Jerusalem on two donkeys (Matt 21:2, 7; cf. the same story with Mark 11:1–7; Luke 19:29–35; John 12:14–15).[88] This is hardly understandable if it comes from a well-educated and intelligent Jew. (3) Matthew did not understand the Jewish situation before A.D. 70, in particular the beliefs of the Sadducees. For example, Matt 16:11–12 on Jesus' warnings about the leaven of the Pharisees and Sadducees shows the author's ignorance of the teaching of the Sadducees, which could in no way be confused with that of the Pharisees. By contrast, Mark 8:14–21 says that Jesus warned his disciples against the leaven of the Pharisees and the *leaven of Herod*, without reference to Sadducees. Again, this observation does not preclude that the original Gospel was written by a Jewish Christian but only argues that the final redactor/editor of the work was likely a Gentile. (4) Mark uses far more Semitisms (Greek words with a Semitic origin) and Semitic words than Matthew, who drops many of the Semitisms in Mark and improves the Semitic Greek of Mark into more acceptable Greek. This suggests to Meier that Matthew is a Gentile Christian who has considerable appreciation for the Jewish-Christian traditions of his Antiochene church.[89]

Davies and Allison, offering a detailed discussion of the Gospel author's awareness of the issues of Judaism in his own day and before and of his knowledge of the Hebrew language, point out that there are many Semitisms in Matthew as well as in Mark, and many Jewish features in the special material peculiar to Matthew (M).[90] They conclude that the author was a Jewish Christian familiar with the Hellenistic world but whose Greek, though better than Mark's, was still far from the quality found in other treatises produced in Greek by Jewish authors whose native tongue was Aramaic (e.g., Josephus, who was a contemporary of the author of Matthew's Gospel). Meier, on the other hand, contends that the author was a Gentile from the church in Antioch of Syria and was trying to address a mixed community of both Christian Jews and Gentiles.

It is possible that Matthew the apostle may have composed some of the sayings in the Gospel that bears his name, but the Gospel of Matthew contains much more than simply sayings *(logia)* of Jesus, as the Papias tradition suggests: there is also a great deal of narrative material as well. The later

church fathers assumed without question that Matthew, who collected the sayings and who also was a disciple of Jesus, must have been the first evangelist to write. F. C. Grant says that one of the oversights of the later church fathers was that they forgot that Papias, as quoted by Eusebius, discusses Mark before he discusses Matthew, which may well be an early suggestion of Markan priority.[91] It does not therefore seem likely that the Gospel of Matthew, as we now have it, was the product of the Apostle Matthew. It is possible, however, that Matthew, the disciple of Jesus, could have produced a list of Scriptures that Jesus had fulfilled, together with a record of the sayings or teachings of Jesus, and that these, with Matthew's interpretation of them, could have been incorporated into the Gospel that now bears his name. Could it be that Matthew also composed the Q material in Hebrew or Aramaic and that a later form of it in Greek was taken up into the Gospel itself? T. W. Manson and many others have urged this position, and Davies and Allison suggest that it is possible.[92]

Perhaps all that can be said about the author of this Gospel is that he was a Jewish Christian, seemingly more familiar than the other evangelists with the geography of Palestine, and possibly, on this basis, a teacher in the church. Because of the overlapping of Judaism and Christianity in Matthew, it is likely that the Gospel was written to a Christian community that was experiencing tension between the two.

C. Date, Location, and Occasion

There is no way to date the Gospel of Matthew with any precision, but there are parameters. Matthew's date is determined broadly by its use of Mark (it therefore could not have been written before A.D. 60–70), by the possible references to it in the book of Revelation (not later than A.D. 90–100), and by allusions to it in *Did.* 8 (ca. A.D. 75–90) and the letters of Ignatius (ca. A.D. 110–115; see *Smyrn.* 1.1; *Pol.* 2.2; *Eph.* 19.2). From the internal allusions to the destruction of Jerusalem in Matt 22:7 (cf. 21:41; 27:25), a likely date is A.D. 80–90, but this cannot be suggested with any finality. It seems reasonable not to date Matthew much before the early 80s because Matt 24 mentions many "signs" of the "end of the age," which his readers may have felt they were experiencing during the reign of Domitian.

These references could have been an encourage-ment and a means of strengthening the many Jew-ish Christians who had survived the destruction of Jerusalem and moved to a safer community (Antioch of Syria) in the midst of continued threats to their security and to that of the Gentile Christians in the time that followed. J. A. T. Robinson claims that no literature of the NT was written after A.D. 70, be-cause there are no clear references to the destruc-tion of the temple and Jerusalem—events that had an enormous impact on the early Christian community—in the NT, including the Gospel of Matthew.[93] Few scholars have, however, accepted his conclusions.

Since Matthew was produced in Greek, it is less likely that it would have been produced in Judea or anywhere in Palestine. The lack of knowledge of the teaching of the Sadducees (see Meier's argu-ment above) also suggests a place outside Pales-tine. The Gospel is obviously Jewish in much of its focus, yet it has an attitude of openness to a Gentile mission (Matt 28:19–20). This suggests that the Matthean community had a large Jewish-Christian population but was open to Gentiles coming to faith in Jesus without the requirements of the law and its traditions (21:33–46). This community could have been in one of the Decapolis cities in Pales-tine, where both Greek and Aramaic were spoken and there was a considerable understanding of the Jewish traditions. Ladd suggests as a possible loca-tion for its composition Syria, where there was a significantly mixed community of both Jewish and Gentile believers.[94] Filson believes that the Gospel suggests that it was written by a Jewish Christian somewhere in Syria (maybe Antioch), but also pos-sibly in Phoenicia or even Palestine.[95] Antioch of Syria is one of the most familiar Gentile cities of the NT; it had a large number of Hellenized Jewish Christians, but the community was also open to ac-cepting Gentiles into its fellowship without the re-quirement of circumcision and other Jewish tradi-tions. In support of Antioch as the provenance of the Gospel and the center of hellenized Jewish Christianity is the fact that this Gospel alone was used in early Jewish Christianity up until the early fourth century A.D. The first clear references to Matthew's Gospel also come from Ignatius, the bishop of this community, about thirty years after its composition. Despite this evidence, we simply cannot be certain of the precise date or the location of the writing of Matthew.

We know, however, that the Judaisms that re-mained after the destruction of Jerusalem were vying for direction, survival, and the clarity of their mission. The primary sect of Judaism surviving the catastrophe of the 70s was led by the Scribes and the Pharisees and eventuated in the rabbinic Juda-ism of the second century and following. Matthew seems to write in this context to let his community (a large Jewish-Christian and Gentile-Christian community) know that their faith was in harmony with the Jewish traditions and Scriptures from which they had emerged and that they inherited (21:43) when the Christian Jews were separated from the synagogue. It is difficult to imagine that the comments found in Matt 6:1–5, 10:16–18, and 23:6–10, 34 could be said while the community of Matthew was still connected to the synagogue. The departure of these Christians from the synagogues was evidently under less than pleasant circum-stances and even with hostility (see ch. 7, sec. 4, above). Some scholars have asked whether the au-thor of Matthew was a Gentile, because of the strongly negative language against the Jewish leaders and, eventually, against the whole nation (21:41–43; 22:7); this language contrasts signifi-cantly with that of Paul, who, though abused by his fellow countrymen (1 Thess 2:13–16), desired their conversion (Rom 9:1–5; 10:1–4; 11:1–5, 23–27). The context had changed considerably by the end of the first century, and many no longer saw the conversion of Israel as viable. This language, how-ever, is not anti-Semitic but, rather, anti-Judaic. As Harrington points out, by the end of the first cen-tury, the Christians believed that there were three classes of people—Jews, Gentiles, and Christians. What Matthew apparently opposed was the surviv-ing Judaism that did not accept Jesus as the prom-ised Messiah, together with those who led its op-position to Christianity. When Jews were converted to Christ, they were no longer considered Jews (see ch. 7, sec. 4, above). Harrington is correct in con-cluding that Matthew and his fellow Jewish Chris-tians "still considered themselves Jews and sought to show that their identity as followers of Jesus was compatible with their Jewish heritage. Matthew and his church still lived within the framework of Judaism."[96]

D. Basic Characteristics and Message

Like Mark, Matthew wrote his Gospel to set forth his own understanding of the life and meaning of Jesus for those living in his own day, rather than merely try to set forth a historical record for subsequent generations. The understanding of Jesus in Matthew stands in continuity with expectation of the coming Christ, who would free Israel from its bondage and establish the kingdom of God. This concept of royalty is also seen in the birth narratives, in which royalty (the magi) come to see Jesus in a house and offer gifts fit for a king (see ch. 5, sec. 2, above). The kingship of Jesus is asserted not only in the genealogy and birth story but also in Herod's fear that a successor might replace him as king of Israel. Joseph and Mary flee to Egypt to fulfill the prophecy in Hosea, originally about Israel, that out of Egypt God would call his son. The Son of God motif, also quite pronounced in Matthew, speaks of Jesus' unique and special relationship with the heavenly Father. Matthew's understanding of Jesus' identity and activity provides a high Christology for his readers and is one of the central themes of his Gospel. He begins in 1:1–17, stating openly the identity of Jesus as the Messiah (Christ) who is also the son of David and, consequently, the legitimate heir to the throne of David. At times, "son of David" appears to be another term for the long-awaited Messiah in Matthew (9:27; 12:23; 15:22; 20:30–31; 21:9, 15; notice in the latter instances that the chief priests and scribes were angry because the crowds used this title in reference to Jesus). In several places in Matthew, Jesus is acknowledged to be the expected Messiah of Israel (1:1, 16, 17, 18; 11:2; 16:16–20; 22:42–45; Jesus' self-designation in 23:10). He is also acknowledged or recognized as the Son of God (4:2–6 and 8:29 by Satan and demoniacs; 14:33 by his disciples after Jesus calmed the storm). By far the two most common designations for Jesus in Matthew, however, are Son of Man and Lord. The former is the favorite term of Jesus for himself. Although in a few cases it may be only a reference to his humanity, the preponderance of its use is as a divine title that speaks of more than a human being (9:1; 12:8; 13:37–41; even 26:24 has this flavor of one about whom the Scriptures speak), and many instances refer to the apocalyptic one who will come at the end of the ages to establish God's kingdom (10:23; 16:27–28; 17:9; 19:28; 24:27, 30, 37–39, 44; 25:31;

26:64). Along with these titles, Matthew's use of "Lord" in reference to Jesus may be nothing more than "sir" in many places, but several of the instances may also betray the later church's most common title for Jesus after his resurrection—Lord, in the sense of his divine nature. This is often apparent where there is a combination of the title with other messianic terms such as "son of David" but also in other places (cf. 3:3; 7:21–22; 8:1, 5, 8, 21, 25; 9:28; 12:1; 14:28–30; 15:22, 25–27; 16:22; 17:4, 15; 18:21; 21:3, 9; 22:43; 23:39; 24:42). When these titles are combined with the opening comments to Joseph about who Jesus is, namely, "God is with us" (1:23), and with the closing of the Gospel, when Jesus says that he is "with you always, to the end of the age" (28:20), there is little doubt about who Matthew thinks Jesus is. He is the presence of God among humanity. This is a very high Christology even at the end of the first century (A.D. 80–90), when Matthew probably wrote.

Matthew is also interested in the continuity of ancient Judaism and its sacred Scriptures with the activity of Jesus and his followers. More than any other evangelist, he emphasizes the prophecy-and-fulfillment motif and seeks to show that, from Jesus' birth to his betrayal, the Scriptures had foreseen the story of Jesus. Jesus was also the one who most clearly understood the Law, came to fulfill its essential meaning (5:17) and all of the antitheses of 5:21–48, and was its most capable interpreter (12:1–8).[97] Those who follow Jesus, Matthew says, are also connected to a long-standing Jewish tradition, which has been turned over to the Christians because of the faithlessness of the leaders of Israel (21:33–46, esp. vv. 43–46). In the parable of the Vineyard, the vineyard is Israel (Isa 5:1–7), and the murdered son is Jesus, but the new tenants are the Christians (followers of Jesus), who are made up of Jews and Gentiles (28:19–20).

Matthew also has a significant interest in the theme of righteousness. Throughout his Gospel, Matthew expresses Jesus' interest in ethical behavior, which conforms to the will of God in Scripture. For example, he emphasizes in 5:20 that the righteousness of the followers of Jesus must exceed that of the scribes and the Pharisees. He urges the followers of Jesus to a higher ethical standard than that of the larger group from which they have separated.[98] This theme is especially prominent in the Sermon on the Mount in chs. 5–7. What is surprising is that Mark never uses the noun "righteousness" and Luke only uses it once (Luke 1:75), but Matthew uses it seven times to refer to God's ethical demands of disciples (see Matt 5:6, 10, 20; 6:1, 33; by inference in 5:16, where "good works" is equivalent to "righteousness").[99] It is probable that Matthew introduces this motif into the story of Jesus in order to deal with a particular problem in the community of faith for which he wrote, namely, the problem of unethical behavior especially among the new Gentile converts to his church. This is not to say that Jesus did not teach about ethical behavior but, rather, that Matthew probably heightened this teaching, stressing those aspects most relevant to his situation (*Sitz im Leben*). As stated, Meier claims that the Gospel of Matthew originated in Antioch, which had many Christian Jews but also a large number of Gentile Christians with little background in ethical behavior.[100] Their conduct may stand behind the inclusion of much of the material on morality and ethical behavior. For Matthew, ethical behavior entails the keeping of the law. In 5:17, Matthew's perspective is that Jesus did not come to destroy or abandon the law but to fulfill it. In 5:18–19, Matthew has in mind that all Christians should obey the law, even exceeding others (scribes and Pharisees) in their obedience to it.

Two other important themes in Matthew, discipleship and church, need some comment. Harrington has observed that whereas in Mark the disciples frequently misunderstand Jesus, in Matthew they generally understand and serve as models for the Matthean community (see 13:52; 16:12; but also 6:30; 8:26; 14:31; 16:8, 17–19; 17:20). Indeed, the disciples share in the power of the risen Lord and faithfully convey the teaching of Jesus; all who follow Jesus are to be taught how to become disciples (28:19–20).[101] This is, in fact, the church's mission in the world, to make disciples. The church also is a special theme in Matthew, the only Gospel that uses the word "church" (16:18; 18:17). Israel, by participating in the death of Jesus (27:25), has rejected its place in the coming kingdom, and it has been transferred to the church (21:43). There is no reference in Matthew to how the church should be ordered or organized, but some of its early leaders were prophets (10:40–41), wise men and scribes (13:52; 23:34), with Peter as the foundational leader (16:18–19) and the power of Jesus as his strength to lead it. Members of this church are also concerned with matters of discipline, the goal being reconciliation, but they also are invested with the same authority given to Peter to excommunicate if discipline is not accepted (18:15–18).[102]

E. Historical Reliability

The reliability of Matthew's witness to the Jesus tradition is more important than the question of authorship or the time of the Gospel's composition, though these are not insignificant. This question can only be settled by a careful look at the sources Matthew has employed in writing his Gospel. We have already argued that the Gospel was composed by an author who used as his primary sources the Gospel of Mark, Q, and possibly also a list of OT Scriptures that he believed Jesus fulfilled—M—which may have originated with Matthew himself or even with Jesus (see Luke 24:44–48, where Jesus reveals himself to the disciples from the OT Scriptures). The last of these sources, M, could have been written as early as A.D. 50 or a decade or two later, and it may have circulated in oral form for years before its incorporation into Matthew's Gospel.[103] If so, then Matthew relied heavily on early traditions circulating in the primitive churches and is therefore worthy of serious consideration in establishing the story of Jesus.

F. Outline of the Gospel of Matthew

Ancestry and birth (1:1–2:23)
Baptism and temptation (3:1–4:11)
Initiation of Galilean ministry and call of the disciples (4:12–25)
Message of the kingdom in Jesus' Galilean ministry (5:1–16:20)
Journey to Jerusalem and passion predictions (16:21–20:34)
Ministry in Jerusalem: the last week (21:1–25:46)
Passion and resurrection (26:1–28:15)
Epilogue for the future (28:16–20)

6. THE GOSPEL OF JOHN

A. Introduction

For more than a century NT scholarship has tended to ignore the Gospel of John as a valid source for the life and ministry of Jesus. This was due not only to the vast differences between John's Gospel and the three Synoptic Gospels but also to the widely held view that John's Gospel reflected more concern for theological than for historical interests and had stronger Hellenistic and gnostic tendencies than were believed present in the historical context of Jesus in the early first century.[104] Rather than interpreting this Gospel in a strictly Hellenistic context, scholars are now interpreting it in terms of its first-century Jewish background, which was also influenced by Hellenism.

There are many perplexing questions about this Gospel, including its authorship, date, provenance, theological stance, historical value, and the relationships between John and the Synoptic Gospels. The only consensus is that it is one of the most perplexing and intriguing books of the NT, although in recent years there has been a resurgence of interest in its reliability as a source for the historical picture of Jesus. Although most scholars continue to be cautious about their use of John, some maintain that there is more reliable history in John than was believed a generation ago.

B. Distinctive Features

Some ninety-two percent of John's Gospel is unique in comparison with the Synoptics. These differences have led some scholars to ask if John's Gospel comes from the same literary genre as the Synoptics. John has many peculiarities in vocabulary and style, a number of which are worth recounting. John has the only examples of a double "amen" on the lips of Jesus (1:51; 10:1; 12:24) and frequently has Jesus use the "I am" formula (6:35, 41, 48, 51; 8:12, 24–28, 58; 9:5; 15:5; etc.) to speak of his special relationship with God or his mission. Unlike the Synoptic Gospels, John seldom uses the terms "kingdom" (of God or of heaven), "Sadducees," "scribes," "forgive," "demons," and "tax collectors."[105] In the Synoptics there are few long discourses by Jesus (Matt 5–7, e.g., is made up of short sayings, some of which are complete in themselves), but in John there are several long discourses, which are sometimes repetitive (see John 14–16). Some terms are found far more frequently in John than in the Synoptics combined, for example, "love" (the verb ἀγαπάω, *agapaō*), "truth," "I am," "life," "Jews," "world," "witness," "remain,"

and "father."[106] Without question, however, the most distinctive features of John's Gospel are his high Christology, which acknowledges the divinity of Jesus during his ministry, and his emphasis on present eternal life that comes from God through Jesus the Christ.

C. John and the Synoptics

John is dramatically different in tone and substance from the first three canonical Gospels. As mentioned, John and the Synoptics overlap in only about 8 percent of the material found in the Synoptics, including the basic broad outline of Jesus' ministry and death. A careful reading of John shows many striking differences from the Synoptic Gospels, differences that include a willingness to use more laudatory and postresurrection designations for Jesus during his lifetime than do the Synoptics (Word, Lord, Son of God, Lamb of God, etc.). Bultmann has argued that one of the most important differences between John and the Synoptics is that the faith and the general picture of the earliest church—that is, its *Sitz im Leben*, or social setting—can be detected in the Synoptics but not in John. He explains that "while in the synoptics the vicissitudes, the problems, and the faith of the earliest church are reflected, scarcely anything of the sort can any longer be discovered in John."[107] Besides this, we also see that John has a different chronology of events from that found in the Synoptics and he makes the length of Jesus' ministry about three years rather than the one or two years implied in the Synoptics.[108] It is also apparent that the scene of most of Jesus' activity is shifted in John from Galilee to Judea, especially Jerusalem.

These differences notwithstanding, scholars have seen for years that the most noticeable differences between John and the Synoptics concern the content and form of Jesus' teaching:

> The parables, similes, and short prophetic utterances are gone, and in their place we find long discourses on recurring themes. These are not the familiar themes of the Synoptic Gospels: the kingdom of God, righteousness, repentance, forgiveness, and so forth. Rather they are themes of eternal life, light, truth, blindness, darkness, sight, and glory. John prefers symbolical language, and he gives words and events double meaning. In two series of sayings, one introduced by the words "I am," and the other by the words "Verily, verily, I say unto you," Jesus makes striking pronouncements about himself and his mission. He

explicitly affirms his divine Sonship in terms that never occur in the Synoptic Gospels.[109]

Other considerable differences between John and the Synoptics lead us to ask important questions. Why, for instance, would John not mention that Jesus was baptized by John, or omit that Jesus was tempted in the wilderness, or fail to include the parables of Jesus, especially when he records several extended discourses by him? Why is the cleansing of the temple early in John's Gospel (2:13–21) but late in the Synoptics, where it is introduced as a factor in Jesus' arrest and trial? Further, why does John not specifically say that Jesus experienced a transfiguration of which he was a witness according to the Synoptics, or that he instituted the Lord's Supper? In John, why are "signs" (e.g., 2:11; 4:54; 9:16; 10:41; 11:47; 12:18, 37; 20:30) indicators of the identity of Jesus, unlike in the Synoptics, where the signs or wonders are indicators of the arrival of the reign of God that Jesus announced?[110] Most important, why do Mark and John appear to disagree on the key factor that led to Jesus' arrest (compare Mark 11:18 with John 11:53)?[111]

All of these factors raise the question whether John knew of the other Gospels and, if so, whether he rejected them or tried to correct, modify, or interpret their presentation of Jesus.[112] This continues to be a matter of debate. John's high Christology suggests that he wrote later than the other canonical Gospels, that he depended upon them, especially Mark, and that he wrote to correct the picture Mark presented. Martin Hengel, for instance, insists that John knew and presupposed the Synoptic Gospels, making use of Mark and Luke while largely ignoring Matthew, when he set out to write a more accurate Gospel.[113] Barrett argues cogently that John was familiar with Mark and, to a lesser extent, also with Luke. He believes that the Johannine passion story is an edited version of Mark's Gospel into which John introduced fresh material.[114] Smith claims that the scholarly consensus about John's independence from the Synoptics can only be confined to the origin of the Johannine tradition or the original Gospel and cannot be uniformly applied to the Gospel in its present canonical form. He observes that both Bultmann and Brown in their respective commentaries on John (see the bibliography at the end of this chapter) argued that "evidence in the Gospel of John of knowledge of the Synoptics

[is] at a late, redactional stage. Neither ascribed that knowledge to the evangelist himself but rather to a later and final redactor."[115] Smith notes that at the beginning of this century scholars assumed John's knowledge of the Synoptics but from around 1955–1980 they began to argue that John was both ignorant and independent of the Synoptics. Smith concludes that "we have now reached a point at which neither assumption is safe, that is, neither can be taken for granted. Any exegete must argue the case afresh on its merits. . . . Apart from its ancient canonical setting, John's independence is obvious enough. The problem is how to understand and articulate it."[116]

The similarities between John and the Synoptics are considerably fewer than, and not as striking as, those between the Synoptics, but they also present a complex puzzle to interpreters of John. John, for example, agrees chronologically with the Synoptics in the broad outline of Jesus' life and ministry, including his coming to John the Baptist while he was baptizing (John 1:29–34), the beginning of his ministry in Galilee (1:43–2:1), having a last supper with his disciples, and his arrest, crucifixion, burial, and resurrection. Some of this may have been simply a common tradition that circulated among the churches, was incorporated by all of the evangelists, and included the broad outline of the ministry of Jesus. In addition, John and Luke agree on the general location of Jesus' resurrection appearances (Jerusalem), the number of angels at Jesus' tomb (two), and that Jesus ascended to the Father, albeit in a somewhat different sequence. Harrison notes that at least three other very important similarities are found in all four evangelists, namely, the aim of producing Jesus' self-testimony as the Son of God and the Son of Man, the presentation of the passion story, and the importance given to the Gentiles.[117]

Smith, following B. H. Streeter, agrees that there are six striking verbatim agreements between John and Mark (Mark 6:37 = John 6:7; Mark 14:3, 5 = John 12:3, 5; Mark 14:42 = John 14:31; Mark 14:54 = John 18:18; Mark 15:9 = John 18:39; Mark 2:11–12 = John 5:8–9). Smith also observes that when John agrees with the Synoptics, he also tends to agree with Mark's order.[118] Barrett concludes from this evidence that "where Mark and John agree closely together, as occasionally they do, there is no simpler or better hypothesis than that John drew his material from Mark, not in slavish imitation, but with the frequent recollections which a well-known and authoritative source would inspire."[119] On the other hand, knowing Mark as a source and using it as such are two different things. Whether or not John used the Synoptics as sources, did he at least have them in mind as he produced his Gospel? The evidence is not strong enough to conclude with certainty.[120]

D. Authorship and Date

The external testimony for the authorship of the fourth Gospel is mixed, but predominantly in favor of John the apostle and son of Zebedee. For example, Theophilus of Antioch (ca. 180) quotes from the fourth Gospel, calling it Scripture, and ascribes it to John the apostle, who published the work from Ephesus (*Autol.* 2.2). Irenaeus (*Haer.* 3.1.1) also agrees that John was the "beloved disciple" ("the disciple whom Jesus loved"; see John 13:23–26; 19:25–27; 20:2; 21:7, 20, 23, 24) or the "other disciple" (18:15–16; 20:3–4). From the third century onward, starting with Origen, no one seems to have doubted that John the apostle was the beloved disciple who also wrote the fourth Gospel. (The first commentary on John was written by the Valentinian gnostic teacher Heracleon [ca. 160], but it is not certain that he attributed it to John the apostle.)

Some of the external traditions, however, are not favorable to Johannine authorship of the fourth Gospel. The Alogi, a second-century Christian group in Asia Minor who rejected the divinity of Christ, attributed the Gospel of John to Cerinthus, a gnostic writer who they also said wrote the book of Revelation. Their rejection of Jesus as the divine Word (λόγος, *logos*) earned for them the name Alogi, perhaps first attributed to them by Epiphanius (*Pan.* 51). The Alogi's rejection of Johannine authorship of the Gospel may have been for theological rather than historical reasons, since Jesus' divinity, origins, and relationship to God are affirmed in the Gospel. Their rejection of John as the author, however, is supported by the lack of any reference to John by Ignatius (ca. A.D. 115) in his letter to the Ephesians in the early second century. Since he mentioned Paul's connection with them, it is strange that John was not mentioned, especially if the tradition that he lived and died there is true.

Since John lived there longer and more recently than Paul, if the tradition is correct, one would expect some word from Ignatius on John, but there is none. Also, a contemporary of Ignatius, Polycarp, who died ca. A.D. 155 and lived in the nearby city of Smyrna, never quotes the Gospel of John even though he quotes 1 John, and he says nothing of John in Ephesus. Further, Justin Martyr, who speaks of the "memoirs of the Apostles" (the canonical Gospels), never attributes the fourth Gospel to John or even mentions John in connection with a Gospel. Whether much can be made from these "arguments from silence" is debatable, but the external evidence that attributes the Gospel to John the apostle comes from the latter part of the second century and is not overwhelming.

From an internal perspective, the author does not identify himself as John the son of Zebedee. It has been argued, however, that the Gospel points in that direction, since internally it is attributed to the disciple whom Jesus loved, who is also the "other disciple" (see John 20:2), in 19:35 and 21:24.[121] The problem here is the identity of this beloved disciple. His name is nowhere given in the Gospel itself, unless that person is Lazarus (11:3). It is also possible that John was martyred quite early, as one may surmise from Mark 10:38–39. Could he have been put to death with James in Acts 12:2, since he is not mentioned by name after that (the situation in Gal 2:7–10 probably predates the Acts 12 situation, but not necessarily)? Whether in fact John, the son of Zebedee and disciple of Jesus, wrote this Gospel cannot be settled here. Few scholars today believe that the work represents that of an eyewitness, even though this has the testimony of responsible teachers of the late second century.[122] The evidence, however, is not telling enough for one to be certain. It remains a possibility that John the apostle wrote this Gospel, but it also remains a strong possibility that he did not and that the work was written instead by a disciple of John or by John the elder (cf. 2 John 1; 3 John 1). Most scholars today recognize that the vocabulary, style of writing, and even the theology of the three epistles attributed to John are very similar to that of the author of the fourth Gospel. Since the author of 2 and 3 John calls himself an elder (πρεσβύτερος, *presbyteros*) in the opening verse of each letter, it is possible that the author of the fourth Gospel and 1 John was an elder and not an apostle. It is especially doubtful whether an apostle would prefer to call himself an elder over the more prestigious title of apostle (2 John 1; John 1:1).[123] Hengel discusses the frequency of the name John in the ancient Jewish world and notes that there were many people with this name, not just John the son of Zebedee. He posits that the John who wrote the Gospel was John the elder, who was likely a contemporary with Jesus and the apostles and who in his later years was highly regarded as "the disciple whom Jesus loved" by the community he addressed in Asia Minor. Only later did the church identify him as the son of Zebedee.[124] The John who authored the Apocalypse (the book of Revelation) does not identify himself as an apostle. Since the vocabulary and style of that book are so different from the other Johannine literature, it is unlikely that John the apostle wrote it—or at least that the author of the Gospel was the author of Revelation—and probably best to say that many had the name of John in the early church.

Kee notes that in order for John the apostle to be seriously considered as the author of the Gospel that bears his name, several assumptions must be true: "that a certain John the Elder who was in residence in Ephesus in Asia Minor in the first quarter of the second century is identical with John the son of Zebedee . . . that John the disciple is the same as the beloved disciple mentioned in the last third of John . . . that the disciple wrote the gospel we now call by the name of John." He goes on to say that all three of these assumptions are unlikely and that the late-second-century claims about the authorship of the Gospel tell us more about the value the Christians of that time attached to apostolicity than about the author of John.[125] Solving the problem of authorship does not appear to be a possibility for biblical scholars today. Although most deny that the Gospel was written by John the apostle, there is no agreement on who its author might have been.

As for the date of the Gospel's composition, the most commonly accepted view among scholars today is that it was written sometime during the last decade of the first century. The earliest evidence of its use in the church comes from Egypt, where probably the earliest biblical papyrus fragment was found. Now housed in the John Rylands Library of the University of Manchester, England, this fragment (P.Ryl. Greek 457, also known as $\mathfrak{P}^{52}$), which con-tains parts of John 20, gives further evidence that John's Gospel was written sometime in the last decade of the first century. The Gospel was known in gnostic circles by no later than A.D. 130. Although it is still possible that John was written in or near Ephesus near the end of the first century, it also could have been written somewhere in Palestine, since the Hellenistic flavor found in the Gospel has also been found in some of the Essene writings from Qumran.[126] Antioch of Syria was suggested as an alternative location for its writing by the early-fourth-century church father Ephraem the Syrian, who in the Armenian version of his commentary on Tatian's *Diatessaron* claimed that "John [presumably the apostle] wrote that [Gospel] in Greek at Antioch, for he remained in the country until the time of Trajan [ca. 112]."[127] It has also been asserted that it was written in Alexandria, because of the heavy reliance on it by the gnostics of Alexandria in the second century and because of the commentary on John by Heracleon of Alexandria. For the most part, however, by the third century most early Christian writers attributed the fourth Gospel to John the apostle, who wrote it in or near Ephesus.[128] Although there is no consensus on either the authorship or the origins of the fourth Gospel, most scholars today agree that it was written in the last decade of the first century.

For some time it has been common to speak of the Gospel of John as the "Greek" or "Hellenistic" Gospel that reflected the Hellenistic and even gnostic tendencies of some second-century Christians. It played no major role in Christian gnostic circles, however, before Valentinus (ca. A.D. 140–150). While subsequent gnostic communities within the Valentinian school (those of his followers, such as Theodotus, Ptolemaeus, Heracleon, Florinus, and Marcus) made full use of this Gospel, probably because of its dualism (e.g., light and dark) and present (instead of future) eschatology, it is not clear that the many themes of later Gnosticism are found in John. Indeed, a strong argument can be made to the contrary.[129]

In recent studies of the Essene community at Qumran, scholars have noted far more parallels there with John's Gospel than with any of the other literature of the NT. Now it is not uncommon to hear such scholars as Charlesworth speak of John as "the gospel most clearly engaged with Judaism." Although no one is arguing by this that the Gospel of John has any direct connection with the Dead Sea Scrolls, several scholars suggest a "Palestinian origin and Jewish character of the Johannine tradition. The Gospel of John is perhaps the most Jewish of the canonical gospels."[130] The features that are considered most typical of gnostic dualism in the Gospel of John—the focus on ethical and eschatological dualism, the contrasts between light and darkness, and truth and falsehood—are more consistently parallel with the Dead Sea Scrolls than with the Philonic Judaism of Alexandria or the later gnostic (Mandaean) documents. Brown contends that "one can no longer insist that the abstract language spoken by Jesus in the Fourth Gospel *must* have been composed in the Greek world of the early second century A.D."[131] If a non-Palestinian origin of the fourth Gospel is maintained, it was likely either Alexandria, where there was a large Essene population, or Ephesus, which may well have had an Essene community in the first century A.D.[132]

E. Purpose and Historical Origins

The purpose of John's Gospel is clearly stated at the end, in 20:30–31, but is also illustrated throughout. Its readers are presented with the opportunity of having eternal life, or the light of God in their lives, through Jesus, who has a special relationship with the Father (e.g., John 1:4, 7–9; 3:15–21, 36; 4:14, 36; 5:21–24; 6:40; 10:10; etc.). Unlike the Synoptics, where the primary focus is on the coming kingdom of God, in John the future, with its gifts from God and the eternal life that it brings, is available now (3:16–18; 5:24; 10:10; 11:25–26). The giving of the Spirit (7:39; 14:3; 16:7; 20:22–23) suggests the realization of the future in present experience. On the other hand, the future is not totally realized now and a final *eschaton* still awaits those who believe in Jesus (5:25). It may be that the author of John wanted to correct a heavy emphasis on the future that lacked the needed concern for the present. It is easy to see how a time of many crises, such as that occurring at the end of the first century in Asia Minor during the Domitianic persecution, may suggest when John was written, but this is not certain.

More difficult to determine is the context in which this book was produced. Many suggestions have been put forward over the years, but none has gained widespread approval. Interpreters of John have long recognized, however, that other concerns were pressing the community that John addressed, among them the threat of persecution, the docetic heresy (see ch. 7, sec. 4, above), and conflict over authority in the community.

A current view that has received wide support claims that the Gospel was written to undergird a Christian community that had been recently expelled from the Jewish synagogue. This is supported by three references to expulsion from the synagogue, in 9:22, 12:42, and 16:2. Do these references reflect the circumstance of the historical Jesus or of the author of John and his community? Could they reflect both, and could the author have included them to give encouragement and understanding to the community that he was addressing at a later time? Jesus' high claims for his relationship with God, seen in such passages as 3:16, 5:18, 6:41–65, and especially 10:7–18, 22–34, may have contributed to the community's expulsion from the synagogue. These passages may have a veiled reference to a dialogue within the synagogue of the Johannine community before their exclusion over the identity of Jesus.[133] The fact that John uses the term "Jews" (Ἰουδαῖοι, *Ioudaioi*) more often than any other Gospel writer (66 or 67 times, compared to 16 in all the Synoptics combined), with several of these in pejorative contexts (9:18; 10:31; 18:12, 36–38; 19:12; etc.), lends credibility to this view. Kysar also mentions that the superiority of the Christian to Judaism is expressed a number of times (1:18; 6:49–50, 58; cf. 2:1–22) and gives further credence to the notion that John is writing from a polemical context in which Jewish Christians were being excluded from the synagogue. He posits that the most appropriate context for this expulsion was the time following the destruction of the temple in A.D. 70, when the dominant surviving Judaism that remained (Pharisaism) was seeking to establish its identity in light of that event.[134]

F. History and the Gospel of John

There is little reason to doubt that the author of the Gospel of John believed that the events he narrated actually happened, and that the conclusions he drew about the identity of Jesus were correct. Although he packs his narratives full of symbolical and theological meaning (e.g., Jesus' words to the woman at the well in Samaria in 4:10–14), there is nothing to suggest that he had little or no interest in the facticity of the events he presented in his Gospel (that is, Jesus had a Samaritan ministry, even if John used theological symbols to tell that story [4:1–42]). The chronology of John is different from that of the Synoptic Gospels, but it does not necessarily follow that John's chronology is wrong. Although traditionally John has been accepted as the "spiritual Gospel" (Clement of Alexandria seems to have been the first to call it that; see Eusebius, *Hist. eccl.* 6.14.7)—and that is certainly a fair description of it—this does not mean that John, for the sake of spiritual teaching, necessarily invented the events he reports. Ladd has observed, for instance, that John contains one of the most meaningful historical references found in any of the Gospels: "The comment in John 6:15, lacking in the Synoptics, that after the miracle of the feeding of the five thousand the people wanted to force Jesus to assume the role of messianic King, is one of the soundest and most meaningful historical references in all four Gospels."[135]

Scholars, nevertheless, have almost unanimously preferred the historical witness of the Synoptics, led by Mark, over the Johannine account of the story of Jesus. John as the spiritual Gospel, they believed, was uninterested in the actual history of Jesus. More recently, however, and partly as a result of the findings of redaction criticism, a growing number of interpreters of the Synoptics have concluded that the Synoptics also, like John, were heavily influenced by theological concerns. Kysar observes that scholars of the fourth Gospel now generally conclude that it is rooted in a primitive tradition in the early church, just like the Synoptics. In particular, he lists several features of John that are now considered to be more historical than was earlier believed: (1) the three-year length of Jesus' ministry, (2) the focus—unique to John—on Jesus' ministry to the Samaritans in 4:1–42, and (3), in the discourses, words of Jesus that may be authentic, even if they are filtered through the Johannine community's concerns. Kysar concludes that the value of John's Gospel for understanding the historical Jesus, as with the other Gospels, must be "critically mined for what might be historical, and each individual saying and each feature of every narrative must be evaluated. It may well

be that something of the historical Jesus can be discerned amid the Johannine narratives and discourses."[136]

John may also preserve the older and more reliable account of an earlier ministry of Jesus in and around Jerusalem that parallels the ministry of John the Baptist but is omitted in the Synoptic Gospels, except for a possible allusion to it in Matt 4:12. For this reason, there is more interest today in the sources that the author of John employed in producing his Gospel. He probably used a passion and resurrection narrative, a signs or miracle tradition, and possibly also a revelation discourse tradition as sources. Most scholars agree on at least this much, but some also find other sources in John.

The lack of smooth transitions between several of the passages of John suggests that the final author of the Gospel used several sources yet remained loyal to these sources by not inventing transitional phrases to smooth out his Gospel. For example, most agree that the sequence of chs. 5 and 6 probably should be reversed because they show in a rather clumsy way that Jesus traveled to and from Jerusalem too much. Indeed, from the end of ch. 4 (4:43ff.) to the end of ch. 8, it is very difficult to bring together in a coherent sequence the travels of Jesus. This problem may stem from a rather hurried assembly of the sources for John's story of Jesus or from too many secondary hands in reshaping the Gospel. The same difficulty arises in ch. 20, which meshes the visit of Mary and the visit of the disciples to the empty tomb. It has been suggested that the reason for the evidently disarranged text is that the author did not write it all at once and that when it was finally put together, the separate pieces of papyrus became disarranged before they were copied on a separate papyrus role, which was then made into a codex (or book form).[137] Whatever its cause, many scholars today agree that the chapters are out of order and that an editing of the Gospel of John took place after its initial writing. They only disagree on the number of editors who participated in the final product and the number of sources that were used. Many also agree that the "appendix" in ch. 21 (the Gospel concluded at 20:31)[138] is from an editor who wanted not only to bring the resurrection appearances into harmony with the witness of Matthew and Mark but also to deal with Peter's restitution and the tradition about the death of the "other disciple." The original writer may have been an eyewitness, or at least purports to be, and in 19:35 this personal witness is emphasized not only by the writer but also by a secondary editor. It may be that all of 19:35 comes from that second hand. Kysar argues that there were at least four stages of development in the Gospel of John,[139] but the arguments to support this have not been widely accepted.

It is clear that John's overall motivation for writing, however, was not so much his interest in simply recording the historical details of the life of Jesus, or even correcting the synoptic tradition, but, rather, in presenting the theological concerns that the story of Jesus addressed, concerns that were also pressing issues for his hearers at the time of his writing. He does not seem to be interested in setting forth the facts of Jesus' life to the same extent as Luke, or the other Gospel writers for that matter, but he is uniquely interested in the subject of eternal life and how this is to be found in Jesus. It should be stressed again, however, that even though his purpose seems throughout to be more theological than historical, there is no reason to suppose that the writer denied the historicity of the events he described. History does not yield to theological interpretation in John but instead becomes a vehicle for conveying it. This is especially true in his account of the death of Jesus, which C. H. Dodd maintains is worthy of serious historical consideration. He believes that John's passion narratives should be accepted as representing, like Mark's, a separate and important line of tradition, which may be inferior to Mark's in some respects and superior in others.[140]

The reliability of John as a historical source of information on the life and ministry of Jesus continues to be debated, but it remains a strong possibility that much of the Johannine source material had early origins and even predated the writing of the other Gospels, as well as their sources. Although this is acknowledged as possible by many scholars today, few of them rely upon John's Gospel. If current interest is any guide—and there has been an enormous amount of literature published on John in recent years—then future Gospel studies may well give considerably more weight to John as a separate and possibly equal source of information for our historical understanding of Jesus.

G. *Outline of the Gospel of John*

Prologue (1:1–18)
Book of Signs (1:19–12:50)
   A. Jesus gathers his disciples, begins his ministry (1:19–4:54)

      1. Jesus acknowledged as Messiah, Son of God (1:19–51)

      2. The beginning of Jesus' miracles (2:1–11)

      3. Early encounters in Jerusalem, Samaria, and Galilee (2:12–4:54)

   B. Disputes over Jesus' identity (5:1–12:50)

      1. Healing and discourse in Jerusalem (5:1–47)

      2. Further signs and discourses in Galilee (6:1–71)

      3. Jesus at the feast of Tabernacles (7:1–8:59)

      4. Further healing and teaching (9:1–10:42)

      5. Death and resurrection of Lazarus (11:1–57)

      6. Close of the public ministry in Jerusalem (12:1–50)

Book of Glory: Jesus Returns to the Father (13:1–20:31)
   A. Last Supper (13:1–17:26)
   B. Passion of Jesus (18:1–19:42)
   C. Resurrection of Jesus (20:1–29)
   D. Original conclusion of the book (20:30–31)
Johannine Appendix/Supplement (21:1–25)[141]

7. CONCLUSION

Although we have presented here some of the main characteristics of the canonical Gospels, this is only an introduction to the nature and scope of the issues involved, and one is encouraged to consult the volumes listed in the bibliographies for more complete information and discussion.

We have adopted a moderate approach to the traditions regarding the questions of the authorship, date, and essential reliability of the canonical

Gospels. Because many of the eyewitnesses to the events described in the Gospels were still alive when the traditions began to circulate in the churches and because their subject matter was important to the churches, we do not believe that the canonical Gospels contain any major departures from the received traditions about Jesus. Nothing was changed in them that would significantly alter Christian faith or rob it of its historical foundations in Jesus. We take for granted that these traditions grew and that some of the traditions were later added to the oral stage of development, but not in any significant way that would seriously affect their essential reliability. It does not seem possible, for example, that anything could have been introduced calling into question either the original and often radical teaching of Jesus or the historical facts about his life, ministry, death, and resurrection. An example of an expansion of the early traditions about Jesus might well be the story in Matt 27:51–53, which describes the return to life of those who were buried outside Jerusalem and their walking through the streets of the city. These verses suddenly appear and then are left without interpretation or parallel in the other Gospel traditions. This is the type of expansion that may have crept into the Gospels for the purpose of clarifying the significance of Jesus' death—in this instance, clarifying that with his death came the end times proclaimed by the prophets of old—but it does not seriously alter the essential message of the evangelist. Indeed, this example may help us to understand how, for Matthew, history is at times used as a vehicle for communicating theological truth. It is worth noting also, for example, that only Matthew has a story of the earthquakes at the death and resurrection of Jesus, as we saw in ch. 6, above. Just before those events in the Gospel (Matt 24:7–14), Jesus speaks of earthquakes at the beginning of the last days. Could it be that Matthew was trying to say or communicate with this story that in the death and resurrection of Jesus the future kingdom of God had arrived?

When, therefore, does history give way to theological interpretation, or when does it become merely the vehicle for conveying that truth? These complex questions cannot be completely answered here. The answer, for now, will undoubtedly be found in our use of the principles of multiple attestation and coherence and in a careful interpretation of the traditions themselves. If a story is repeated in other traditions and if it coheres with other facts that we have been able to establish about Jesus, then from a historical perspective we can make a case for its authenticity as a genuine part of the earliest traditions about Jesus. We can say further that in the case of Christianity's most important events—the death, resurrection, and glorification of Jesus—though many of the details surrounding them in the Gospels may differ, their essential message is the same: Jesus of Nazareth who died is now alive, he is worthy of our faith, and this has great significance for all who will receive it. There can be no doubt that the Gospels contain three basic layers of tradition: the level of the life of Jesus himself, the level of the early church, which transmitted the traditions both orally and in written form, and the level of the teaching of the evangelists themselves.[142]

The question of the authorship of the Gospels is more significant in the cases of Mark and Luke–Acts, but there is no consensus among scholars on these two Gospels. The arguments in favor of Mark's authorship of the Gospel are not insignificant, but they are also not conclusive. The case for the authorship of either Matthew or John, on the other hand, is not as important as it is with Mark or Luke–Acts, nor as sure. Matthew and John offer valuable information regarding the historical Jesus, and both contribute heavily to the commonly accepted tradition about Jesus in the earliest church. Agreements in three or four evangelists speak strongly in favor of the authenticity of an event or tradition. When applied to the Gospel tradition, this method of attestation shows that the evangelists offer a generally reliable story of the ministry and message of Jesus.

The reason certain traditions are held in question by some Gospel scholars often has less to do with the criteria discussed in ch. 4, above, than with their view of history. If God's remarkable activity in history is rejected in principle, that is, if anything supernatural or miraculous mentioned in the Gospels is ruled out of court in advance, then the criteria for authenticity (multiple attestation, embarrassment, coherence, dissimilarity) are of little value. Our understanding of history will often have as much to do with how we interpret the NT and the conclusions we draw from our sources as any criteria or critical tools employed.

Dunn claims that the kinds of tradition about Jesus that we would expect to be preserved are the very ones preserved in the Synoptic Gospels. In this limited sense, the Gospels are biographies, even though not the kind that we are used to today.[143] This memory of Jesus molded the thinking of the writers and participants of the early Christian church. This influence existed long before this tradition was put in written form. As the tradition emerged in written form, no doubt certain modifications were made to meet the needs of the church. The issue of how much modification was made is at the heart of much scholarly debate.

The earliest Christians were concerned to preserve the memory of Jesus in the church and to pass it on to new converts. They were more concerned, however, with the substance and meaning of what Jesus had said and done than with verbal meticulousness. The substance of the Gospels was undoubtedly a living tradition in the earliest churches before it was produced in written form. It is important that we understand the evangelists' interest in historicity on their own terms, not with those we impose on them.[144]

BIBLIOGRAPHY

A. General Bibliography on the Gospels

BROWN, R. E. *An Introduction to the New Testament.* ABRL. New York: Doubleday, 1997.

BROWN, S. *The Origins of Christianity: A Historical Introduction to the New Testament.* Oxford: Oxford University Press, 1984.

CONZELMANN, H., and A. LINDEMANN. *Interpreting the New Testament: An Introduction to the Principles and Methods of New Testament Exegesis.* Trans. S. S. SCHATZMANN. Peabody, Mass.: Hendrickson, 1988.

EPP, E. J., and G. W. MACRAE, eds. *The New Testament and Its Modern Interpreters.* The Bible and Its Modern Interpreters. Atlanta: Scholars Press, 1989.

FREYNE, S. *Galilee, Jesus, and the Gospels: Literary Approaches and Historical Investigations.* Philadelphia: Fortress, 1988.

GRANT, R. M. *A Historical Introduction to the New Testament.* 2d ed. New York: Simon & Schuster, 1972.

GREEN, J. B., S. MCKNIGHT, and I. H. MARSHALL, eds. *Dictionary of Jesus and the Gospels.* Downers Grove, Ill.: InterVarsity, 1992.

GUNDRY, R. H. *A Survey of the New Testament.* 3d ed. Grand Rapids: Zondervan, 1994.

JOHNSON, L. T. *The Writings of the New Testament: An Interpretation.* Revised edition. Minneapolis: Fortress, 1999.

KEE, H. C. *Understanding the New Testament.* 5th ed. Englewood Cliffs, N.J.: Prentice-Hall, 1993.

KOESTER, H. *Introduction to the New Testament.* 2 vols. FFNT. Minneapolis: Fortress, 1982; 2d ed. of vol. 1, 1995; vol. 2, 2000.

KÜMMEL, W. G. *Introduction to the New Testament.* Trans. H. C. KEE. 17th ed. Nashville: Abingdon, 1975.

PERKINS, P. *Reading the New Testament: An Introduction.* 2d ed. New York: Paulist, 1988.

SPIVEY, R. A., and D. M. SMITH. *Anatomy of the New Testament: A Guide to Its Structure and Meaning.* 5th ed. New York: Macmillan, 1995.

STANTON, G. N. *The Gospels and Jesus.* OBS. Oxford: Oxford University Press, 1989.

THEISSEN, G. *The Gospels in Context: Social and Political History in the Synoptic Tradition.* Trans. L. MALONEY. Minneapolis: Fortress, 1991.

B. Synoptic Problem

BELLINZONI, A. J., ed. *The Two-Source Hypothesis: A Critical Appraisal.* Macon, Ga.: Mercer University Press, 1985.

FARMER, W. R. *The Synoptic Problem.* New York: Macmillan, 1964.

_____, ed. *New Synoptic Studies: The Cambridge Gospels Conference and Beyond.* Macon, Ga.: Mercer University Press, 1983.

JACOBSON, A. D. *The First Gospel: An Introduction to Q.* Sonoma, Calif.: Polebridge, 1992.

JOHNSON, S. E. *The Griesbach Hypothesis and Redaction Criticism.* SBLMS 41. Atlanta: Scholars Press, 1991.

KLOPPENBORG, J. S. *The Formation of Q.* Philadelphia: Fortress, 1987.

KOESTER, H. *Ancient Christian Gospels: Their History and Development.* Philadelphia: Trinity Press International, 1990.

MILLER, R. J., ed. *The Complete Gospels.* Sonoma, Calif.: Polebridge, 1992.

MOULE, C. F. D. *The Birth of the New Testament.* 3d ed. San Francisco: Harper, 1982.

NEVILLE, D. J. *Arguments from Order in Synoptic Source Criticism.* Macon, Ga.: Mercer University Press, 1994.

SANDERS, E. P. "The Argument from Order and the Relationship between Matthew and Luke." *NTS* 15 (1969): 249–61.

TUCKETT, C. M. *The Revival of the Griesbach Hypothesis.* SNTSMS 44. Cambridge: Cambridge University Press, 1983.

VAN SEGBROECK, F., et. al., eds. *The Four Gospels, 1992.* BETL 100. Leuven: Leuven University Press/Peeters, 1992.

C. Gospel of Mark

ANDERSON, H. *The Gospel of Mark.* NCB. Grand Rapids: Eerdmans, 1976.

CRANFIELD, C. E. B. *The Gospel according to St. Mark.* Cambridge: Cambridge University Press, 1959.

GUELICH, R. A. *Mark 1–8:26.* WBC 34A. Dallas: Word, 1989.

GUNDRY, R. H. *Mark: A Commentary on His Apology for the Cross.* Grand Rapids: Eerdmans, 1993.

HURTADO, L. *Mark.* NIBC 2. Peabody, Mass.: Hendrickson, 1989.

LANE, W. L. *The Gospel according to Mark.* NICNT. Grand Rapids: Eerdmans, 1974.

NINEHAM, D. E. *Saint Mark.* PNTC. New York: Penguin, 1969.

PERKINS, P. *The Gospel of Mark: Introduction, Commentary, and Reflections.* NIB. 12 vols. Nashville: Abingdon, 1995. 8:508–733.

SCHWEIZER, E. *The Good News according to Mark.* Atlanta: John Knox, 1970.

TAYLOR, V. *The Gospel according to St. Mark.* 2d ed. London: Macmillan, 1966.

D. The Gospel of Luke and the Acts of the Apostles

1. Luke

CREED, J. M. *The Gospel according to St. Luke.* London: Macmillan, 1930.

CULPEPPER, R. A. *The Gospel of Luke: Introduction, Commentary, and Reflections.* NIB. 12 vols. Nashville: Abingdon, 1995. 9:1–490.

ELLIS, E. E. *The Gospel of Luke.* Rev. ed. NCB. Grand Rapids: Eerdmans, 1974.

EVANS, C. F. *Saint Luke.* Philadelphia: Trinity Press International, 1990.

EVANS, C. A. *Luke.* NIBC 3. Peabody, Mass.: Hendrickson, 1990.

FITZMYER, J. A. *The Gospel according to Luke.* 2 vols. AB 28, 28A. Garden City, N.Y.: Doubleday, 1981–1985.

JOHNSON, L. T. *The Gospel of Luke.* SP 3. Collegeville, Minn.: Liturgical, 1991.

LUCE, H. K. *The Gospel according to S. Luke.* Cambridge: Cambridge University Press, 1933.

MARSHALL, I. H. *Commentary on Luke.* NIGTC. Grand Rapids: Eerdmans, 1978.

NOLLAND, J. *Luke.* 3 vols. WBC 35A, B, C. Dallas: Word, 1989–1993.

SCHWEIZER, E. *The Good News according to Luke.* Atlanta: John Knox, 1984.

2. Acts

BARRETT, C. K. *A Critical and Exegetical Commentary on the Acts of the Apostles.* 2 vols. ICC. Edinburgh: T. & T. Clark, 1994–1998.

BRUCE, F. F. *The Acts of the Apostles: The Greek Text with Introduction and Commentary.* 3d ed. Grand Rapids: Eerdmans, 1990.

_____. *Commentary on the Book of Acts: The English Text with Introduction, Exposition, and Notes.* Rev. ed. NICNT. Grand Rapids: Eerdmans, 1988.

CONZELMANN, H. *Acts of the Apostles.* Hermeneia. Philadelphia: Fortress, 1987.

FITZMYER, J. A. *The Acts of the Apostles.* AB 31. New York: Doubleday, 1998.

FOAKES-JACKSON, F. J. *The Acts of the Apostles.* MNTC. London: Hodder & Stoughton, 1931.

FOAKES-JACKSON, F. J., and K. LAKE, eds. *The Acts of the Apostles.* Part 1 of *The Beginnings of Christianity.* 5 vols. London: Macmillan, 1920–1933. Repr., Grand Rapids: Baker, 1979.

GASQUE, W. W. *A History of the Criticism of the Acts of the Apostles.* Grand Rapids: Eerdmans, 1975.

HAENCHEN, E. *The Acts of the Apostles: A Commentary.* Philadelphia: Westminster, 1971.

HEMER, C. J. *The Book of Acts in the Setting of Hellenistic History.* Ed. C. H. Gempf. WUNT 49. Tübingen: Mohr–Siebeck, 1989. Repr., Winona Lake, Ind.: Eisenbrauns, 1990.

JOHNSON, L. T. *The Acts of the Apostles.* SP 5. Collegeville, Minn.: Liturgical, 1992.

MARSHALL, I. H. *Acts.* TNTC. Grand Rapids: Eerdmans, 1980.

NEIL, W. *The Acts of the Apostles.* NCB. Grand Rapids: Eerdmans, 1973.

WALLACE, R., and W. Williams. *The Acts of the Apostles.* London: Duckworth, 1993.

WILLIAMS, C. S. C. *The Acts of the Apostles.* HNTC. New York: Harper & Row, 1964.

WILLIAMS, D. J. *Acts.* NIBC 5. Peabody, Mass.: Hendrickson, 1989.

WINTER, B. W., ed. *The Book of Acts in Its First Century Setting.* 6 vols. Grand Rapids: Eerdmans, 1993–1996.

E. Gospel of Matthew

BEARE, F. W. *The Gospel according to Matthew.* New York: Harper & Row, 1981.

BORING, M. E. *The Gospel of Matthew: Introduction, Commentary, and Reflections.* NIB. 12 vols. Nashville: Abingdon, 1995. 8:87–505.

DAVIES, W. D., and D. C. ALLISON, Jr. *A Critical and Exegetical Commentary on the Gospel according to Saint Matthew.* 3 vols. ICC. Edinburgh: T. & T. Clark, 1988–1997.

GREEN, H. B. *The Gospel according to Matthew.* New Clarendon Bible. Oxford: Oxford University Press, 1975.

GUNDRY, R. H. *Matthew: A Commentary on His Literary and Theological Art.* Rev. ed. Grand Rapids: Eerdmans, 1994.

HAGNER, D. A. *Matthew.* 2 vols. WBC 33A, B. Dallas: Word, 1993–1995.

HARRINGTON, D. J. *The Gospel of Matthew.* SP 1. Collegeville, Minn.: Liturgical, 1991.

HILL, D. *The Gospel of Matthew.* NCB. Grand Rapids: Eerdmans, 1972.

MCNEILE, A. H. *The Gospel according to St. Matthew.* 1915. Repr., Grand Rapids: Baker, 1980.

MOUNCE, R. H. *Matthew.* NIBC 1. Peabody, Mass.: Hendrickson, 1989.

SCHWEIZER, E. *The Good News according to Matthew.* Atlanta: John Knox, 1975.

F. Gospel of John

BARRETT, C. K. *The Gospel according to St. John: An Introduction with Commentary and Notes on the Greek Text.* Rev. ed. Philadelphia: Westminster, 1978.

BEASLEY-MURRAY, G. R. *John.* WBC 36. Waco, Tex.: Word, 1987.

BROWN, R. E. *The Gospel according to John.* 2 vols. AB 29, 29A. Garden City, N.Y.: Doubleday, 1966–1970.

BRUCE, F. F. *The Gospel of John.* Grand Rapids: Eerdmans, 1983.

BULTMANN, R. *The Gospel of John: A Commentary.* Trans. G. R. BEASLEY-MURRAY et al. Philadelphia: Westminster, 1971.

CARSON, D. A. *The Gospel according to John.* Grand Rapids: Eerdmans, 1991.

LINDARS, B. *The Gospel of John.* NCB. Grand Rapids: Eerdmans, 1972.

MORRIS, L. *Commentary on the Gospel of John.* NICNT. Grand Rapids: Eerdmans, 1971.

O'DAY, G. R. *The Gospel of John: Introduction, Commentary, and Reflections.* NIB. 12 vols. Nashville: Abingdon, 1995. 8:491–875.

SCHNACKENBURG, R. *The Gospel according to St. John.* 3 vols. New York: Crossroad, 1968–1982.

pages 274–280

1. The Greek noun for Gospel is εὐαγγέλιον, *euangelion*, meaning "good news," and its verb form εὐαγγελίζομαι, *euangelizomai*, means "preach or proclaim good news or glad tidings."

2. See H. Koester, *Ancient Christian Gospels: Their History and Development* (Philadelphia: Trinity Press International, 1990), 1–4.

3. There is some dispute whether the words "Son of God" are part of the earliest manuscripts. Most scholars think that they are.

4. Trans. E. Charpentier, *How to Read the New Testament* (trans. J. Bowden; New York: Crossroad, 1984), 18. See also A. Deissmann, *Light from the Ancient East* (trans. L. R. M. Strachan; 1927; repr., Peabody, Mass.: Hendrickson, 1995), 366–67, who cites several other similar inscriptions and papyri. The entire Greek text of the Priene inscription is printed in *OGIS* 458 (2.48–60).

5. Koester, *Ancient Christian Gospels*, 4–6. For a discussion of the origins and use of the term "gospel" in antiquity and its use in designating a literary genre of the NT, see also pp. 6–23.

6. A useful recent collection of these sources is J. K. Elliott, *The Apocryphal New Testament: A Collection of Apocryphal Christian Literature in an English Translation* (Oxford: Clarendon, 1993), esp. 3–163.

7. It is significant that the early Christian community resisted the temptation to harmonize the Gospels when they did not accept as Scripture Tatian's attempts in the late second century to write a single Gospel using the four canonical Gospels and the *Gospel of Peter*. By not accepting Tatian's *Diatessaron*, in its own wisdom the church rejected the temptation toward a unified whole in favor of allowing the voice of each evangelist to be heard. Such attempts at harmony run the risk of obscuring the message of each Gospel.

8. R. M. Grant (*An Historical Introduction to the New Testament* [New York: Harper & Row, 1972], 110) has commented upon the astuteness of this observation.

9. H. P. Owen, *Observations of the Four Gospels* (n.p., 1764).

10. J. J. Griesbach, *Commentatio qua Marci Evangelium totum e Matthaei et Lucae commentariis decerptum esse monstratur* (1789), translated in *J. J. Griesbach: Synoptic and Text-Critical Studies, 1776–1976* (ed. and trans. J. B. Orchard and T. R. W. Longstaff; Cambridge: Cambridge University Press, 1978).

11. B. F. Westcott, *An Introduction to the Study of the Gospels* (6th ed.; London: Macmillan, 1881).

12. K. Lachmann, "De ordine narrationum in Evangeliis synopticis," *ThStKr* 8 (1835): 570–90; H. J. Holtzmann, *Die synoptischen Evangelien: Ihr Ursprung und geschichtlicher Charakter* (Leipzig: Engelmann, 1863).

13. W. R. Farmer, *The Synoptic Problem: A Critical Analysis* (New York: Macmillan, 1964), and *New Synoptic Studies: The Cambridge Gospels Conference and Beyond* (ed. W. R. Farmer; Macon, Ga.: Mercer University Press, 1983); and M. Goulder, *Luke—a New Paradigm* (2 vols.; JSNTSup 20; Sheffield: JSOT Press, 1989), 1:3–26.

14. Westcott, *Introduction to the Study of the Gospels*, 196.

15. The term *Sondergut* (Ger. "special material") is often used of the material that is peculiar to each Gospel.

16. W. G. Kümmel, *Introduction to the New Testament* (trans. H. C. Kee; Nashville: Abingdon, 1975), 57.

17. Ibid., 65–66. Note the Matthean order in the right column. *The Complete Gospels: The Annotated Scholars Version* (ed. R. J. Miller; rev. ed.; San Francisco: Harper, 1994), 253–300, is more complete; see also the introduction to this material (pp. 248–52).

18. Kümmel, *Introduction,* 46–48. Kümmel gives many other examples.
19. C. A. Evans, *Mark 9–16* (WBC 34B; Dallas: Word, forthcoming).
20. A good collection of arguments against Markan priority is found in Farmer, *Synoptic Problem,* which calls into question not only the priority of Mark but also the existence of any Q document. His work is commanding because of its extensive detail, but his arguments have had little influence on the majority of NT scholars today. J. A Fitzmyer, "The Priority of Mark and the 'Q' Source in Luke," in *Jesus and Man's Hope* (ed. D. G. Miller; 2 vols.; Pittsburgh: Pittsburgh Theological Seminary, 1970), 1:181–90, offers strong arguments against Farmer's work on the subject. In favor of Matthean priority, see also B. C. Butler, *The Originality of St. Matthew: A Critique of the Two-Document Hypothesis* (Cambridge: Cambridge University Press, 1951); A. M. Farrer, "On Dispensing with Q," in *Studies in the Gospels: Essays in Memory of R. H. Lightfoot* (ed. D. E. Nineham; Oxford: Blackwell, 1955), 55–86; A. J. McNicol, D. L. Dungan, and D. B. Peabody, eds., *Beyond the Q Impasse—Luke's Use of Matthew* (Valley Forge, Penn.: Trinity Press International, 1996); and D. L. Dungan, "Two Gospel Hypothesis," *ABD* 6:671–79. For a discussion of what is at stake in the matter, see W. F. Farmer, *The Gospel of Jesus: The Relevance of the Synoptic Problem* (Louisville: Westminster John Knox, 1994).
21. The *logia,* lit. "sayings," are Jesus' sayings or teachings.
22. It should not be concluded that Lukan dependence upon Matthew is no longer accepted. This view is still held by Farmer, Goulder, and others.
23. H. C. Kee, *Understanding the New Testament* (5th ed.; Englewood Cliffs, N.J.: Prentice-Hall, 1993), 89–90. For a different grouping, see P. Perkins, *Reading the New Testament* (rev. ed.; New York: Paulist, 1988), 64–65, who classifies these materials under the categories of narrative, ethical exhortation, eschatological warning, eschatological conflict, eschatological promise, eschatological discipleship, eschatological parables, and "Jesus brings eschatological salvation."
24. For a more complete discussion, see H. Conzelmann and A. Lindemann, *Interpreting the New Testament: An Introduction to the Principles and Methods of New Testament Exegesis* (trans. S. S. Schatzmann; Peabody, Mass.: Hendrickson, 1988), 57–59.
25. Grant (*Historical Introduction,* 113–14) gives several reasons to doubt the existence of a completely written document such as Q and maintains that Matthew and Luke drew upon a common reservoir of oral tradition, though some may have been in written form. Farrer ("On Dispensing with Q") has perhaps leveled some of the strongest arguments against the existence of Q and claims that Luke used Matthew's Gospel. He maintains that it is easier to assume the use of a known source, namely Matthew, than to accept the existence of an unknown source, Q. Following Farrer, see Goulder, *Luke—a New Paradigm,* 1:3–26. T. R. Rosche ("The Words of Jesus and the Future of the 'Q' Hypothesis," *JBL* 79 [1960]: 210–20), on the other hand, accepts the priority of Mark but not necessarily the existence of Q. In his brief but quite detailed study of Q, he concludes that the evidence for its existence is very weak.
26. Conzelmann and Lindemann, *Interpreting the New Testament,* 55–57.
27. Grant, *Historical Introduction,* 113.
28. Ibid., 115–116.
29. H. C. Kee, *Jesus in History* (New York: Harcourt, Brace & World, 1970), 64–66. T. W. Manson suggests that Matthew the apostle was the author of the Q document, a theory similar to the one that first

suggested the idea of Q: Papias's statement regarding the *logia* of Jesus being collected by Matthew led to the concept of Q (Eusebius, *Hist. eccl.* 3.39.16) (see sec. 5, below). Cf. T. W. Manson, "Studies in the Gospels and Epistles," in *In Search of the Historical Jesus* (ed. H. K. McArthur; London: SPCK, 1970), 32.

30. Kümmel, *Introduction,* 50–57.

31. See B. Gerhardsson, *Memory and Manuscript: Oral Tradition and Written Transmission in Rabbinic Judaism and Early Christianity* (2d ed.; trans. E. J. Sharpe; ASNU 22; Lund, Sweden: Gleerup, 1964; repr., Grand Rapids: Eerdmans, 1998); R. Riesner, *Jesus als Lehrer: Eine Untersuchung zum Ursprung der Evangelien-Überlieferung* (3d ed.; WUNT 2.7; Tübingen: Mohr–Siebeck, 1988).

32. G. Theissen, *The Gospels in Context* (trans. L. M. Maloney; Minneapolis: Fortress, 1991), 3–4.

33. F. V. Filson, *A New Testament History* (London: SCM, 1971), 80.

34. Grant, *Historical Introduction,* 108.

35. Filson, *New Testament History,* 80–81.

36. B. M. Metzger, *The New Testament: Its Background, Growth, and Content* (New York: Abingdon, 1965), 87. Cf. also G. N. Stanton, *The Gospels and Jesus* (OBS; New York: Oxford University Press, 1989), 163.

37. Cf. R. P. Martin, *New Testament Foundations: A Guide for Christian Students* (2 vols.; Grand Rapids: Eerdmans, 1975–1978), 1:177–78.

38. W. Marxsen, *Introduction to the New Testament: An Approach to Its Problems* (trans. G. Buswell; Philadelphia: Fortress, 1968), 143.

39. See, e.g., Conzelmann and Lindemann, *Interpreting the New Testament,* 218–19, who contend that Mark was a Gentile Christian otherwise unknown; cf. also B. L. Mack, *Who Wrote the New Testament? The Making of the Christian Myth* (San Francisco: Harper, 1995), 152–53, who concludes that the Gospel was attributed from the second century to a legendary figure named Mark; and B. Ehrman, *The New Testament: A Historical Introduction to the Early Christian Writings* (New York: Oxford University Press, 1997), 70, who questions Mark's understanding of several Jewish customs and suggests that the Gospel was written by a Gentile. R. Brown, *An Introduction to the New Testament* (ABRL; New York: Doubleday, 1997), 158–61, is not as skeptical as others, but also allows that the author may not have been the companion of Paul, the cousin of Barnabas (Col 4:10), or the companion of Peter (1 Pet 5:13), and may instead have been an otherwise unknown Mark who "was subsequently amalgamated with John Mark" (p. 160).

40. Martin, *New Testament Foundations,* 1:211. See L. M. McDonald, "Anti-Marcionite (Gospel) Prologues," *ABD* 1:262–63.

41. R. H. Gundry, *Mark: A Commentary on His Apology for the Cross* (Grand Rapids: Eerdmans, 1993), 1026–45. U. Schnelle, *The History and Theology of the New Testament Writings* (trans. M. E. Boring; Minneapolis: Fortress, 1998), 199–200, believes that the tradition of Mark writing the Gospel is quite old on the basis that few would attribute such a work to a Christian who did not belong to the original circle of Jesus' disciples, but Schnelle maintains that the work belongs to an otherwise unknown Mark who was a Greek-speaking Gentile Christian who had command of Aramaic and was a native of Syria.

42. G. R. Beasley-Murray, "Introduction to the New Testament," in *A Companion to the Bible* (ed. T. W. Manson and H. H. Rowley; Edinburgh: T. & T. Clark, 1963), 93, long ago made this observation, which still has merit today.

43. Marxsen, *Introduction,* 143.

pages 283–287

44. R. A. Guelich, *Mark 1–8:26* (WBC 34A; Dallas: Word, 1989), xxv–xxix.
45. Filson, *New Testament History*, 83.
46. C. E. B. Cranfield, "Mark, Gospel of," *IDB* 3:271–72.
47. See Brown, *Introduction*, 163–64. The first document that speaks of Peter's and Paul's deaths is *1 Clem.* 5–6, but the details are not clear. The *Acts of Peter*, which was circulating in the last half of the second century, perhaps ca. A.D. 180–90, indicates that Peter died during the persecutions of Nero in Rome. The death of Paul is also described in a late-second-century document that depends on the *Acts of Peter*. The *Acts of Paul* 11.1–7 gives a detailed description of the martyrdom of Paul and dates it to the reign of Nero. Although the stories presented have numerous fabrications and some sensationalism, few doubt the basic premise that both Peter and Paul were put to death during the Neronian persecutions of the Christians ca. A.D. 64–65.
48. Marxsen, *Introduction*, 113, believes that the references in Mark 13:7 and 14 to signs (v. 4) and "rumors of wars" indicate that the time of writing was during the period of the Jewish war (A.D. 66–70) but before the destruction of Jerusalem in A.D. 70. He suggests the date of its composition sometime between A.D. 67 and 69.
49. See G. R. Beasley-Murray, *Jesus and the Future* (London: Macmillan, 1954), passim but esp. 251–52.
50. C. A. Evans, "Predictions of the Destruction of the Herodian Temple in the Pseudepigrapha, Qumran Scrolls, and Related Texts," *JSP* 10 (1992): 89–147. He concludes that Jesus, like many others of his day and before, predicted the destruction of the Herodian temple, employing the classical prophets' (especially Jeremiah's and Ezekiel's) predictions. Because of the corruption of the leadership of the temple and the widespread peasant resentment of how that leadership operated the temple, Evans concludes that, because Herod himself had built the temple and because it was operated by the corrupt and non-Zadokite priestly families, it was believed by many of that day to face certain destruction (pp. 146–47).
51. It cannot be determined with any certainty whether Mark's Gospel had much or any influence upon the writer of John's Gospel, since John does not follow the sequence of events in Mark and, although only the broad outline of Jesus' ministry is similar to that of Mark, even that is significantly altered. The differences between these two Gospels will be spelled out more in the discussion of the Gospel of John. It is a distinct possibility that later apocryphal gospels made use of Mark and other canonical-Gospel traditions.
52. Cranfield, "Mark," 3:272.
53. Ibid., 3:271.
54. W. Wrede, *The Messianic Secret* (trans. J. C. C. Greig; Cambridge, England: J. Clarke, 1971).
55. For more discussion of this, see L. T. Johnson, *The Writings of the New Testament: An Interpretation* (Philadelphia: Fortress, 1986), 151–53.
56. See R. Fuller, *The Formation of the Resurrection Narratives* (London: SPCK, 1972), 64–67. See also R. H. Lightfoot, *The Gospel Message of St. Mark* (Oxford: Oxford University Press, 1950), 80- 7.
57. Evans, *Mark 9–16*, forthcoming.
58. The formulation Luke–Acts is attributable to H. J. Cadbury, *The Making of Luke–Acts* (London: Macmillan, 1927). For a recent discussion of views of authorship, see I. H. Marshall, "Acts and the 'Former Treatise,' " in *The Book of Acts in Its Ancient Literary Setting* (ed. B.W.

pages 287–291

Winter and A. D. Clarke; vol. 1 of *The Book of Acts in Its First Century Setting;* ed. B. W. Winter; Grand Rapids: Eerdmans, 1993), 163–84.

59. R. Bultmann, *The History of the Synoptic Tradition* (trans. J. Marsh; 2d ed.; 1972 repr. Peabody, Mass.: Hendrickson, 1993), 363.

60. W. C. van Unnik, "Luke–Acts, a Storm Center in Contemporary Scholarship," in *Studies in Luke–Acts* (ed. L. E. Keck and J. L. Martyn; New York: Abingdon, 1966), 15–32.

61. See S. E. Porter, *The Paul of Acts: Essays in Literary Criticism, Rhetoric, and Theology* (WUNT 115; Tübingen: Mohr–Siebeck, 1999), chs. 2 and 3.

62. Kümmel, *Introduction,* 131–32. One need not deny Lukan authorship of Acts to believe that the "we" passages derive from another source.

63. See R. I. Pervo, *Profit with Delight: The Literary Genre of the Acts of the Apostles* (Philadelphia: Fortress, 1987).

64. For further study on this issue, see entries in the concluding bibliography and Keck and Martyn, *Studies in Luke–Acts;* M. Hengel, *Acts and the History of Earliest Christianity* (Philadelphia: Fortress, 1980); and D. E. Aune, *The New Testament in Its Literary Environment* (LEC; Philadelphia: Westminster, 1987).

65. W. K. Hobart, *The Medical Language of St. Luke* (London: Longmans, Green, 1882).

66. A. Harnack, *Luke the Physician* (New York: Putnam, 1907), 175–98 (quotations, pp. 198, 223), originally published in German in 1906. His subsequent work on Acts supported the same conclusions; cf. *The Acts of the Apostles* (London: Williams & Norgate, 1909).

67. H. J. Cadbury, *The Style and Literary Method of Luke* (Cambridge: Harvard University Press, 1920), 39–72; cf. "Lexical Notes on Luke–Acts. II. Recent Arguments for Medical Language," *JBL* 45 (1926): 290–309.

68. V. Taylor, "Gospel of Luke," *IDB* 3:180.

69. F. C. Baur, *Paul, the Apostle of Jesus Christ, His Life and Work, His Epistles, and His Doctrine* (2 vols.; trans. A. Menzies; London: Williams & Norgate, 1876).

70. Hegel's philosophy of historical development revolved around the presupposition that thought developed by means of thesis, antithesis, and synthesis. The perhaps best known utilizer of Hegelian method was Karl Marx.

71. Kümmel, *Introduction,* 149–50.

72. Marxsen, *Introduction,* 168–70.

73. E. Harrison, *Introduction to the New Testament* (2d ed.; Grand Rapids: Eerdmans, 1971), 228.

74. A. Harnack, *The Date of Acts and of the Synoptic Gospels* (London: Putnam, 1911).

75. J. C. O'Neill, *The Theology of Acts in Its Historical Setting* (London: SPCK, 1970), 40–42; also 43–53 for the tables that illustrate his point.

76. This raises the logical problem of rejecting a conclusion on the basis of its implications. We will not address this question here, although it is one that should be faced.

77. This tradition includes *1 Clem.* 5.5–7 (ca. A.D. 95), the Muratorian Fragment (ca. A.D. 350 according to one of the authors of this volume and possibly second century according to the other author—see ch. 13, below, for discussion of this document), the apocryphal *Acts Pet.* 1.3 (ca. A.D. 180–200), and Eusebius, *Hist. eccl.* 2.25.5–8 (ca. A.D. 325–330).

78. F. F. Bruce, *The Acts of the Apostles: The Greek Text with Introduction and Commentary* (3d ed.; Grand Rapids: Eerdmans, 1990), 14, 17.

pages 291–296

79. In the first edition of his Acts commentary (1951), Bruce uses these points to argue that the time of the writing of Luke–Acts was ca. A.D. 60–61. More recently he appears to have moderated his view, allowing that the book could have been written later: "If, then, a date in the late 70s or 80s of the first century (say, in the principate of Titus or early in that of Domitian) is assigned to Acts, most of the evidence will be satisfied" (*Acts*, 3d ed., 18). But he still seems to prefer a date in the 60s.

80. Ibid., 16.

81. Some aspects of this section are found in L. M. McDonald, "Acts of the Apostles," *EEC* 14–17.

82. Because of its place in the biblical canon, that is, in the first place of the four Gospels, Matthew is often referred to as the "first Gospel." We will use that description from time to time without any reference to priority of origins. Although tradition has ascribed this work to the Apostle Matthew, most NT scholars today reject this view, but for convenience sake they continue to refer to the work by its traditional name. We will also follow this practice here.

83. Davies and Allison have noted that in the last hundred years only seven scholars have accepted Matthew the Apostle as the author of the work that bears his name. Most agree that the author was a Jewish Christian, but some eleven scholars have concluded that a Gentile writer produced the work. Cf. W. D. Davies and D. C. Allison, Jr., *A Critical and Exegetical Commentary on the Gospel according to Saint Matthew* (3 vols.; ICC; Edinburgh: T. & T. Clark, 1988–1997), 1:10–11.

pages 296–300

84. D. J. Harrington, *The Gospel of Matthew* (SP 1; Collegeville, Minn.: Liturgical, 1991), 4. Cf. W. Horbury, "The Hebrew Text of Matthew in Shem Tob Ibn Shaprut's *Eben Boḥan*," in Davies and Allison, *Commentary on Matthew*, 3:729–38.

85. Davies and Allison (*Commentary on Matthew*, 1:12–13) make this point.

86. Only Matthew gives the name Matthew to the tax collector who followed Jesus, while the other evangelists mention only Levi (Mark 2:14; Luke 5:27). Also, in their list of Jesus' disciples they never mention Matthew as being a tax collector (Mark 3:18; Luke 6:15). Meier has suggested that the prime example of a sinner in the Gospels is the tax collector and that Matthew may have made a play on the Greek words, since the Greek term for a disciple or learner is μαθητής, *mathētēs* (verb μαθητεύω, *mathēteuō*) and it sounds very much like Matthew. This would indicate that a prime example of a sinner could become a disciple. J. P. Meier, "Matthew, Gospel of," *ABD* 4:627.

87. Davies and Allison, *Commentary on Matthew*, 1:9.

88. See ch. 5, sec. I, above, for a discussion of the use of Zech 9:9.

89. Meier, "Matthew, Gospel of," 4:625–27.

90. Davies and Allison, *Commentary on Matthew*, 1:17–21, 25–27, and esp. 80–85, list the many supposed Semitisms in Matthew.

91. F. C. Grant, "Gospel of Matthew," *IDB* 3:303.

92. T. W. Manson, "The Gospel of St. Matthew," in *Studies in the Gospels and Epistles* (ed. M. Black; Edinburgh: T. & T. Clark, 1962), 68–104; and Davies and Allison, *Commentary on Matthew*, 1:17.

93. See J. A. T. Robinson, *Redating the New Testament* (Philadelphia: Fortress, 1976).

94. G. E. Ladd, *The New Testament and Criticism* (Grand Rapids: Eerdmans, 1967), 133.

95. Filson, *New Testament History*, 83–84.

96. Harrington, *Gospel of Matthew*, 21.
97. Ibid., 17.
98. See Stanton, *Gospels and Jesus*, 69–75, for a more complete discussion of this theme.
99. Ibid., 70–71.
100. Meier, "Matthew, Gospel of," 4:624.
101. Harrington, *Gospel of Matthew*, 19.
102. Meier, "Matthew, Gospel of," 4:639; see his more complete discussion of these matters, pp. 637–40.
103. It should be noted that Filson, *New Testament History*, 364, along with T. W. Manson, *The Teaching of Jesus* (Cambridge: Cambridge University Press, 1937), 27–28, held that Matthew could have been the author of the Q document, which could account for his name being attached to this Gospel quite early by the church fathers.
104. H. K. McArthur, introduction to *In Search of the Historical Jesus*, 3–20; here 9.
105. These observations come from R. Kysar, "The Gospel of John," *ABD* 3:912–31; here 914.
106. See C. K. Barrett, *The Gospel according to St. John: An Introduction with Commentary and Notes on the Greek Text* (rev. ed.; Philadelphia: Westminster, 1978), 5–6, for a complete listing of these terms in Greek and also for common synoptic expressions that are rare or missing in John.

pages 300–305

107. R. Bultmann, *Theology of the New Testament* (2 vols.; New York: Scribners, 1951–1955), 2:5.
108. Manson, *Teaching of Jesus*, 23, notes that the order of events in John's Gospel could have been written as a corrective to Mark's order of events, which Papias says was not correct.
109. H. C. Kee and F. W. Young, *Understanding the New Testament* (Englewood Cliffs, N.J.: Prenctice-Hall, 1957), 385.
110. These observations are made by Kysar, "The Gospel of John," 3:914–15.
111. Barrett, *Gospel according to John*, 47, discusses this issue.
112. See the discussion of R. A. Spivey and D. M. Smith, *Anatomy of the New Testament* (4th ed.; New York: Macmillan, 1989), 159–61.
113. M. Hengel, *The Johannine Question* (trans. J. Bowden; Philadelphia: Trinity Press International, 1989), 75–76, 194 n. 8.
114. Barrett, *Gospel according to John*, 15–21.
115. D. M. Smith, *John among the Gospels: The Relationship in Twentieth-Century Research* (Minneapolis: Fortress, 1992), 183–85.
116. Ibid., 189.
117. Harrison, *Introduction*, 134–35.
118. Smith, *John among the Gospels*, 3; cf. B. H. Streeter, *The Four Gospels: A Study of Origins* (London: Macmillan, 1936), 397–99.
119. Barrett, *Gospel according to John*, 15–16.
120. See G. R. Beasley-Murray, *John* (WBC 36; Waco, Tex.: Word, 1987), xxxv–xxxvii, who agrees with this conclusion.
121. See J. H. Charlesworth, *The Beloved Disciple: Whose Witness Validates the Gospel of John?* (Valley Forge, Penn.: Trinity Press International, 1995), who defends the beloved disciple as the author of the Gospel and as John the son of Zebedee.
122. Irenaeus, who became bishop of Lyons in A.D. 177, says that he heard Polycarp (who was martyred in A.D. 155) relate what he had heard from John and the other disciples about Jesus. Irenaeus also says that John composed the Gospel in Ephesus: "Afterwards [he has just mentioned the other three Gospels], John, the disciple of the

Lord, who also leaned upon His breast, did himself publish a Gospel during his residence at Ephesus in Asia" (*Haer.* 3.1.1 [*ANF*]). Eusebius, on the authority of Irenaeus, adds that Papias, bishop of Hierapolis (ca. A.D. 140), was a hearer of both John and Polycarp (*Hist. eccl.* 3.39).

123. For further information on the arguments concerning authorship, see Harrison, *Introduction,* 207–14, who lists the arguments in favor of John the apostle writing the Fourth Gospel; and Kümmel, *Introduction,* 165–74, for arguments against Johannine authorship of the Gospel.

124. For a discussion of this, see Hengel, *Johannine Question,* 102–35. See also J. L. Price, *Interpreting the New Testament* (2d ed.; New York: Holt, Rinehart & Winston, 1971), 579–80.

125. Kee, *Understanding the New Testament,* 160–61.

126. Spivey and Smith (*Anatomy,* 161) raise this as a possibility.

127. Trans. Beasley-Murray (*John,* lxxix), who notes that this tradition of Antiochene origin is attributed to the Armenian version of Ephraem's commentary, but few scholars give this tradition much credibility. The theory apparently goes back to F. C. Conybeare, "Ein Zeugnis Ephraims über das Fehlen von C.1 und 2 in Texte des Lukas," *ZNW* 3 (1902): 193, but also to F. C. Baur (so Kümmel, *Introduction,* 247 n. 224). The tradition of the Antiochene origin of the Gospel, however, continues to have widespread acceptance in the scholarly community because of parallels with the *Odes of Solomon,* which may have originated in Antioch; the close affinities with Syrian Gnosticism; and the writings of Ignatius of Syrian Antioch. This tradition is supported by Kümmel, *Introduction,* 246–47. Beasley-Murray, *John,* lxxix–lxxxi, raises the possibility that the Gospel arose in Palestine because of the similarities with the Judaisms of the first century or at least was written by someone who felt at home in Palestine, even if it was later taken to Antioch and from there to Ephesus.

128. For a recent defense of this position, see S. van Tilborg, *Reading John in Ephesus* (NovTSup 83; Leiden: Brill, 1996).

129. Beasley-Murray, *John,* lv–lviii.

130. J. H. Charlesworth, ed., *John and the Dead Sea Scrolls* (New York: Crossroad, 1990), xiii, xv.

131. R. E. Brown, "The Dead Sea Scrolls and the New Testament," ibid., 8.

132. For the arguments for an Alexandrian origin, see W. H. Brownlee, "Whence the Gospel of John?" ibid., 188–89. For those for Ephesus, see M.-E. Boismard, "The First Epistle of John and the Writings of Qumran," ibid., 156–65, who argues only for 1 John but whose comments are also relevant to the origins of the Gospel. Boismard draws attention to the parallels between John the Baptist and Qumran and argues that John the apostle was a follower of John the Baptist and that John the Baptist had disciples doing missionary work in Ephesus during the time of Paul's ministry (Acts 19:12–16).

133. Kysar, "The Gospel of John," 3:918.

134. Ibid.

135. Ladd, *New Testament and Criticism,* 137.

136. Kysar, "The Gospel of John" 3:930.

137. W. F. Howard, "The Gospel according to John: Introduction and Exegesis," *IB* 8:442.

138. It is accepted among many NT scholars today that John 21 is a later addition to the original Gospel, which seems to end at 20:31. The continuation of the story in ch. 21 is, in some respects, apparently

pages 306–308

contradictory to the preceding chapter: Jesus had already appeared to the disciples in Jerusalem in ch. 20 and had commissioned them, but in ch. 21 the disciples are not evangelizing but are back fishing in Galilee and apparently do not even recognize him when he comes to them again. Thus, ch. 21 in part seems to be an attempt to harmonize the location of the appearances of Jesus with Matthew and Mark, but this harmony causes more problems than it solves. This chapter, therefore, may well not be an original part of John's Gospel but may have been added in the second century.

pages 309–311

139. See R. Kysar, *The Fourth Evangelist and His Gospel: An Examination of Contemporary Scholarship* (Minneapolis: Augsburg, 1975), 38–54.

140. C. H. Dodd, "Some Considerations upon the Historical Aspect of the Fourth Gospel," in *In Search of the Historical Jesus* (ed. McArthur), 89; see also pp. 82–92 for more support of this claim.

141. This outline, in large part, is an adaptation of Perkins's outline of John in her *Reading the New Testament*, 247. We find her analysis of the text quite useful.

142. In this conclusion we have simply reversed the sequence of Stanton's assessment of what is in the Gospel tradition. See his *Gospels and Jesus*, 152.

143. J. D. G. Dunn, *The Living Word* (Philadelphia: Fortress, 1988), 30–31.

144. See ibid., 43.

THE PAULINE TRADITION

1. WHO WAS PAUL? HIS IMPORTANCE IN EARLY CHRISTIANITY

What transformed a Jew who persecuted Christians (Phil 3:6; Acts 8:1; 9:1–2; 22:4–5; 26:9–12) into perhaps the single most important follower of Jesus Christ of his (or any) time—as theologian, writer, missionary, preacher, and church planter? No complete study of the early church can neglect Paul and his writings. The story of his life and ministry is intriguing and enigmatic, and it continues to be so as scholars vigorously debate many of its important issues, such as the most significant influences on his pre-Christian life and on his turning to belief in Jesus as the Christ, and especially the meaning and value of his letters.[1]

A. The Value of Paul for the Early Church

Paul's value for the study of the NT can be summarized in three major points. First, Paul is probably the earliest writer of the NT. Some might put the book of James prior to Paul's letters (see ch. 11, below, for a discussion of the book of James). Even if Paul was not the earliest, however, he certainly made the most sizable contribution at an early date. Paul is therefore the closest to early

Christianity in terms of its most significant early events, such as the death and resurrection of Jesus Christ, which had a crucial role in the formulation of his theology. At times, Paul is concerned to make sure that his readers know that his gospel is his own and was not simply derived from others (see Gal 1:16–17), but he also makes it clear that his gospel is in continuity with that of the other apostles (e.g., Gal 2:1–10 and 1 Cor 15:3–11) (see below on Paul's status as an apostle). Earliest Christianity—that is, the Christian belief and practice most closely tied to Christianity's formative events—has always occupied a privileged place in Christian history and belief, and Paul has pride of place in this hierarchy.

Second, Paul is rightly known as the apostle to the Gentiles. He was instrumental in carving out a Gentile Christianity free from the strictures of Judaism, including obedience to the OT law, especially as it was manifested in circumcision, Jewish forms of worship, the practice of food laws, and the celebration of certain feasts. Christians today still live in the light of Paul's thinking on such a vital issue as the relation of Christian belief to its roots in Judaism. Paul was able to carve out this Gentile ministry through the course of a number of highly interactive missionary ventures that took him well beyond Palestine, across Asia Minor, and into Europe (Macedonia and Achaia in Greece, then Italy

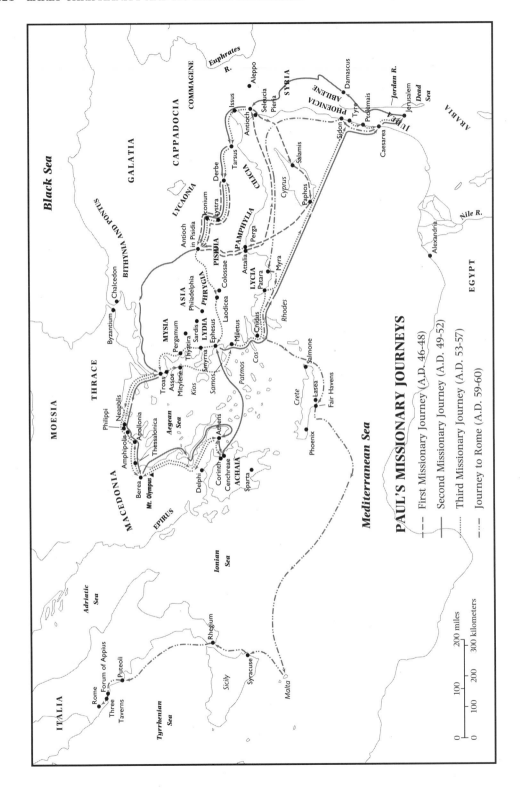

PAUL'S MISSIONARY JOURNEYS

First Missionary Journey (A.D. 46-48)
Second Missionary Journey (A.D. 49-52)
Third Missionary Journey (A.D. 53-57)
Journey to Rome (A.D. 59-60)

and possibly even Spain). These ambitious adventures were instrumental in establishing and maintaining a foothold for Christianity in Europe and afforded an opportunity for Paul to compose a number of letters that, although not written primarily as works of timeless theology, are still seen to be relevant in addressing issues in contemporary Christianity.[2]

Third, Paul was the first and perhaps the greatest Christian theologian. He has long been called the second founder of Christianity,[3] a comment indicative of the crucial role that his thinking and writing played in formative Christianity. In some senses, however, it is exactly right. Paul was not the only one involved in early Christian missionary endeavors (at the commencement of his first missionary journey he was apparently under the authority of Barnabas, according to Acts 13), but he was certainly the most successful and is now the best known. He played a sizable role in transforming Christianity from a regional religious sect of Judaism, confined to certain areas of Palestine, into a genuine world religion, and this all within his own lifetime. It is not an understatement to say that Christianity today is essentially Pauline Christianity, at least in the west.

The importance of such an individual would lead us to believe that there should be an abundance of material about him available for assessment. But this is simply not the case. There are two primary sources of evidence for Paul's life and ministry—his letters and the book of Acts (although many would minimize the importance of Acts)—though some other later sources from church history are also important. Among his letters, certainly his major letters are important sources of information about him and his thinking, but it must be remembered that they were written to specific church situations and so must be interpreted before they can be used for historical reconstruction. Within any particular context, there is no compelling reason why Paul should have revealed everything about himself or the totality of what he thought about a given topic or issue. One would only expect him to state what he thought was appropriate for the situation.[4] There is the further issue, to be discussed below, of how authorship of the letters is to be evaluated. The second source of information regarding Paul, the book of Acts, has been evaluated in a number of ways, from a radical (and rather simpleminded) skepticism that doubts the author's integrity at every turn, to an almost naive acceptance of everything that it says. The discussion in this chapter places primary emphasis on Paul's letters, but we will also refer to Acts where appropriate as an important secondary source on the mission of Paul.

B. Paul the Man

On the basis of his image and abiding importance in the church, one would expect Paul to cut a dashing and impressive figure. Little is actually known, however, about what Paul looked like, even though there has been some speculation. On the one hand, he is described as a young man at the death of Stephen (Acts 7:58), probably between eighteen and thirty years old. On the other hand, he refers to himself as an old man in Phlm 9, probably between forty and sixty.[5] In either case, these figures are compatible with Paul being born sometime early in the first century (A.D. 5–15), probably in the first decade. This would mean that he was only a slightly younger contemporary of Jesus himself.

An early Christian text, the *Acts of Paul* (2d cent. A.D.) refers to Paul as a small man, bald, bow-legged, ruddy in complexion, knit-browed, with a slightly long nose (§3; the text also says that sometimes he appeared as a man but at other times he had the face of an angel).[6] This text is a fairly late one for providing a "snapshot" of Paul (it claims to be based on a description by Titus), but there is some confirmatory biblical evidence that Paul was not the most imposing of physical figures. In Acts 14:8–18, after performing a healing at Lystra, Paul and Barnabas are worshipped by the crowd—Barnabas as Zeus and Paul as Hermes. Zeus, the primary god of the Greek pantheon, had lightening and thunder at his disposal and would have been seen as an awe-inspiring and authoritative figure. Hermes, on the other hand, was the messenger god. There was apparently genuine respect for Hermes in this area of Asia Minor, and Paul, as spokesman, was probably rightly seen as the messenger of the group; nevertheless, Hermes was not as elegant or magnificent a god as Zeus. He was also known as the god of the rock pile, an "earthy" god not of the first rank but, rather, of the second rank of Greek gods.[7] This scene perhaps indicates that not only by function but also by personal appearance Paul was the less physically imposing of the two.

Evidence from Paul's letters also implies that he cut a less than overwhelming physical figure. In 2 Cor 10:10, Paul cites his adversaries as depicting him as a good writer but as physically unimpressive and not a good speaker. There may be some rhetorically strategic reasons why Paul characterizes himself in such a dichotomous way, but his troubles at Corinth with adversaries and his initial failure to win the Corinthians over may give evidence that, in person, he was not as impressive as he would have liked to be or as many expected him to be as a public speaker. Furthermore, in Gal 4:13–14, Paul refers to a physical ailment. Scholars have long debated what this ailment was, especially in the light of 2 Cor 12:7–9, which refers to Paul's thorn in the flesh. This affliction may be some form of spiritual disability, since Paul refers to it as a messenger of Satan that torments him. In Gal 4:15, however, Paul refers to the Galatians as at one time willing to tear their eyes out for him, perhaps indicating that Paul's physical disability was bad eyesight.[8] In any case, apparently Paul was plagued by physical problems from fairly early on in his ministry, since Galatians is probably one of his earliest letters. These physical ailments came in conjunction with a number of other afflictions that Paul was made to suffer. In 2 Cor 11:23–28, Paul recounts a litany of abuses he suffered in the course of his ministry. Since he concludes by mentioning his concern for the churches and since this is in a context of creating a counterboast to his Corinthian opponents, there may well be some rhetorical embellishments here. The kinds of things he recounts, however, are compatible with what is known from Paul's other letters and especially from Acts. Such experiences as receiving thirty-nine lashes, being stoned and shipwrecked, and being imprisoned all must have taken a terrible physical toll on him over the years.

C. Paul and His Upbringing

When Paul first appears in Acts (Acts 8:1), involved in the stoning of Stephen, he is already an adult; and his letters are the products of his ministry after his conversion. Paul, however, had a life before adulthood. But where was it, and what was it like? Paul does not mention his birth or upbringing in his letters, but there are a number of retrospective statements in his letters, as well as Acts, that can be drawn upon. It is not to be seriously doubted that Paul was born in Tarsus, a significant city in the region of Cilicia (Acts 21:39; 22:3; cf. Strabo, *Geog.* 14.5.13). Tarsus, a city with a long history, probably was founded sometime in the late third or early second millennium B.C. It was saved by Alexander the Great from destruction by the retreating Persians in 333 B.C. The Romans gave it increased privileges, including political self-rule, and it had established itself as an important cultural center. Tarsus was a university town just slightly behind the class of such cities as Alexandria and Athens as centers of learning. It was especially flourishing at the time of Paul's youth, although it apparently declined later in the century. Well-known rhetoricians and philosophers made their way to Tarsus, but we do not know if Paul ever heard any of them speak. As a Greco-Roman city, Tarsus would have had a Greco-Roman educational system. This consisted of three major stages. Elementary education extended from ages seven to fourteen, when the student learned how to read, write (including some letter writing), and do basic mathematics. The second stage of education, from ages fourteen to eighteen, was conducted by the *grammaticus*, or grammar teacher, and consisted of reading and memorizing the major classical authors, especially Homer and Euripides. At this stage the student would learn grammar and how to compose essays and letters, besides studying other subjects, such as geometry and music. The final stage of education took place in the gymnasium, where the student studied rhetoric under the guidance of philosopher-teachers, for the purpose of becoming a good citizen.[9]

It is difficult to know the extent of Paul's exposure to this educational system. Scholars have argued everything from Paul having left Tarsus before participating in any of the Greek educational system to Paul having completed the entire course of education all the way through to the gymnasium. There is evidence that Paul had some education in Greek thought, but it is also possible that he received this in Jerusalem, since Palestine was a part of the larger Greco-Roman world and had access to Greek thinking and education (it was only in the second century A.D. and beyond that Judaism renounced connections with Greek culture and

A coin of Vespasian, struck in Rome in A.D. 71. Latin inscription: "Emperor Cae[sar] Vespasianus Aug[ustus], High Priest, Power of Tribune, father of Nation, Consul for the Third Time." © Rohr Productions. Used with permission.

The opposite side of the coin above, celebrating the capture of Judea. Translated Latin inscription: "Judea Captured." © Rohr Productions. Used with permission.

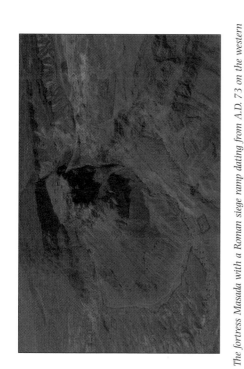

The fortress Masada with a Roman siege ramp dating from A.D. 73 on the western side. See also the Roman campsites in the square remains around the mountain. © Rohr Productions. Used with permission.

The Arch of Titus in the Roman Forum. © Rohr Productions. Used with permission.

language).[10] The rabbinic rules concerning education correspond surprisingly well with the Greek system. In light of the precedence of the Greek sources and the Hellenistic influence on Palestine before the development of even the antecedents of rabbinic Judaism, it is possible that the prescribed system of Jewish education took its formative influence from the Greek system.[11] The Jewish educational system apparently consisted of two major stages. From ages five to twelve the student began the study of Scripture, then of the legal traditions (*m. ʾAbot* 5:21). Josephus notes that the law and the traditions were taught in every city to Jewish boys "from our first consciousness" (*Ag. Ap.* 2.18), as does Philo (*Embassy* 210). At age thirteen, the boy became a *bar mitzvah,* or "son of the commandment," and took upon himself the full obligation of the law. The more promising youths would have been sent to Jerusalem to study under more advanced teachers, since there is no evidence of any advanced instruction equivalent to what became the rabbinic school in any city but Jerusalem before A.D. 70. That Paul may have been educated in such a way has been posited on the basis of Paul's argument in Rom 7, where he speaks of an age of innocence (Rom 7:9), followed by one of knowledge (7:9–11), and then one of responsibility (7:15–21), corresponding to the periods outlined above.[12] It is difficult to substantiate from this passage that Paul was educated in this way. Many who emphasize Paul's Jewish education, however, believe that it may have been at the age of thirteen that Paul went to Jerusalem to continue his education under Gamaliel, possibly living with his own married sister there (Acts 23:16).[13]

The question of where Paul was educated is raised directly in Acts 22:3. How this verse is rendered influences drastically how this question is answered, however. There are three ways in which this verse has been translated, depending upon how one understands the word "this" and the word "and" or "but" at the beginning of the second clause. The first interprets it to have Paul saying he is a Jew, "born in Tarsus of Cilicia, brought up in this city, educated at the feet of Gamaliel," with three separate clauses, the second of which is left ambiguous. This solution does not answer the question. The author of Acts may intentionally have left the passage ambiguous because he did not know where or when Paul was educated, but this

is not the most likely way that he would have communicated this. The second interprets the sentence to have Paul saying he is a Jew, "born in Tarsus of Cilicia, *but* brought up in this city [Jerusalem], educated at the feet of Gamaliel," with perhaps Paul physically pointing to his surroundings, Jerusalem. This is the most common understanding, reflected in the translations of the NIV, NRSV, etc. The third interprets the sentence to have Paul saying he is a Jew, "born in Tarsus of Cilicia *and* brought up in this city [Tarsus], educated at the feet of Gamaliel."

Is either of the last two interpretations more likely? Most scholars agree that Paul probably grew up in Jerusalem, although the exact age of his arrival in the city is unknown. The arguments for this position are several. The first is that the grammar of Acts 22:3 seems to indicate this, with the second interpretation seen by most scholars to be the most convincing. The second is that Paul's speech here in Acts is delivered in a context where there is a conscious effort being made to identify Paul with Jerusalem. He has just been taken into Roman custody but has been allowed to address the crowd, which had accused him of taking a Gentile, Trophimus, into the temple. It is in Paul's best interests to make sure that the Jerusalem rioters see him as identified with Jerusalem, so it is understandable that, in this speech, there is a downplaying of his ties with Tarsus and the possible corrupting influence of Gentile culture.

Some have questioned, however, the consistency of Acts' depiction of Paul as having been reared in Jerusalem—how is it that Paul had such a different approach to religiosity than did Gamaliel, his teacher in Jerusalem? Acts 23:3 is the only place in the NT where Paul is said to have been a student of Gamaliel; his clear Pharisaical ties (Phil 3:5–6), however, make this likely.[14] Unfortunately, not much more is known of Gamaliel from biblical or extrabiblical sources. What is known indicates that, early in the rise of the Christian movement, Gamaliel was quite tolerant of it. Acts 5:38–39 reveals Gamaliel, a member of the Sanhedrin, taking a conciliatory position, apparently in keeping with the Pharisaic doctrine that God triumphs over human actions (*m. ʾAbot* 4:14; 3:19; cf. Josephus, *Ant.* 13.172; 18.13). He recommends a tolerant attitude, because—so his reasoning goes—if this new movement is of God, one would not want to stand against it and hence against God himself. If it is not of God, it will fail anyway. This is a very different attitude from that of Paul, his supposed pupil, who was an active persecutor of Christians.[15] Several factors must be considered regarding Paul's relation to Gamaliel. The first is simply the difference in temperament or insight between the two men. It is entirely possible that Paul, perhaps because of his youthful enthusiasm or a natural kind of zeal, believed that he saw the situation more clearly than his older, more mature, and, at least in his eyes, overly cautious teacher.[16] The second factor is whether Paul's persecution was directed at the same group that Gamaliel is addressing in Acts 5. Gamaliel's attitude concerns Palestinian-Jewish Christians such as Peter and the other apostles. But there is good evidence Paul directed his persecution against Hellenistic Jewish Christians (as indicated by his role in the stoning of Stephen in Acts 8:1 and by his traveling outside Jerusalem to Damascus to persecute followers of "the Way" in Acts 9). Perhaps Paul retrospectively saw them as like those Diaspora Jews he had left when he came to Jerusalem to be educated, believing that their form of Judaism was tainted and corrupt. After all, Paul presents himself as a legalist before his conversion (Phil 3:6), one who wanted to keep the law in its totality and not be seen in any way as accommodating to those who would do otherwise. The third factor to consider is whether Gamaliel and other Jewish leaders underwent a change of heart regarding the early Christian movement.[17] When Gamaliel made his pronouncement in Acts 5, Christianity was a new movement still essentially confined to Jerusalem. By the time of Paul's persecution of believers, however, the movement had already shown signs of spreading, perhaps resulting in a change of attitude among the Jewish hierarchy.

The evidence for Paul's having had a Jewish education is minimal; nevertheless, there is some evidence for Paul's having at least some Greco-Roman education. An example is his use of the Greek letter form. This is not clear evidence of formal training in a Greek school system, however, since the letter form was widely known and used by many who never attended school, and amanuenses or scribes were frequently employed in the production of letters.[18] Paul took full advantage of this as well (see, e.g., Rom 16:22, where Tertius is mentioned by name), so he himself would not have required formal training beyond the elementary level. A second form of evidence would be his quotation of extrabiblical authors.[19] Here there is a surprising lack of explicit primary evidence from Paul's letters. Paul is quoted as citing the fourth-century B.C. poet Aratus in Acts 17:28 (*Phaen.* 5; cf. Cleanthes, *Hymn to Zeus*, line 4) and the sixth-century B.C. poet Epimenides in Titus 1:12. The only quotation in a major Pauline letter, however, is that from the play *Thais* by the third-century B.C. dramatist Menander, cited at 1 Cor 15:33. But this quotation is generally thought to have been part of the shared common knowledge of the time, much like "To be or not to be"—from Shakespeare's *Hamlet*—which many people might quote without having studied (or even read) any of Shakespeare's plays. Or it may have been one of many individual quotations contained within a quotation book used in elementary education.[20] A third piece of evidence for Paul's Greek education might be his use of forms of classical rhetoric (see ch. 2, sec. 3.G, above, for important definitions of terms). This is a topic of widespread discussion in current NT scholarship. A number of scholars argue that Paul avails himself of the full range of tools available to a rhetorician of the time, so that his Letter to the Galatians, as an example, is a form of either deliberative or judicial rhetoric, like a speech delivered by an ancient rhetorician, such as Demosthenes (4th cent. B.C.). There are two questions that can be raised regarding the rhetorical hypothesis, however. The first is whether this kind of rhetorical analysis of letters was something that was even known to the ancients. There is good evidence that the categories of rhetoric were used not for the analysis and examination of speeches or any other writings, including letters, but only for the creation and formulation of speeches. The second question is how accessible this knowledge was to those who did not reach the higher levels of the educational system. Paul does make use of several rhetorical conventions, including especially the diatribe style (e.g., Rom 1–14; 2 Cor 10–13), but this was probably not due to formal rhetorical training but because this was the way in which teachers and philosophers created arguments and carried on discussion in the ancient world.[21] In all, the evidence of Paul progressing very far in the Greco-Roman educational system is lacking. Nevertheless, he may well have acquired the basics, including a highly functional use of the Greek language, before proceeding to formal religious training.

Springs that help form the Jordan River near Tel Dan at the base of Mount Hermon.
© Rohr Productions. Used with permission.

A mosaic in St. Catherine's Monastery, depicting the transfigured Jesus flanked by Elijah (left of center)
and Moses with John, Peter, and John. © Rohr Productions. Used with permission.

D. Paul and the Roman Empire

Whether Paul was a Roman citizen is complicated by two considerations.[22] The first is how one defines citizenship. The other is that explicit claims to Roman citizenship by Paul only appear in Acts, never in his letters. There were several different levels of citizenship in the Roman Empire: one could, for example, be a citizen of the Roman state, a citizen of a particular city, a member of one of the orders or "tribes" of citizens. The word Paul uses to describe his being a citizen of Tarsus in Acts 21:39 is one that could refer to any one of these levels. In Acts 16:38 and 22:25 Paul makes the explicit claim to being a Roman citizen. Recent work on Acts argues that it is not a historically based account but, rather, a literary creation (perhaps like an ancient romance), designed to create an image of Paul as a hero of the early church.[23] As a result, many have come to doubt Paul's citizenship of Tarsus and his Roman citizenship. For example, Lentz concludes that Acts is designed to depict Paul as the ideal Greco-Roman man.[24] In a more detailed survey of the ancient evidence, Rapske shows the plausibility of a person being a citizen of a city such as Tarsus, a citizen of Rome, and a devout Jew all at the same time. What he cannot prove absolutely is that Paul was such a person, although the probabilities weigh clearly in that direction.[25] It is perhaps surprising that in Paul's letters, even with his ministry to the Gentile world, he does not mention his origin in Tarsus, his citizenship of Tarsus, or his Roman citizenship. Nevertheless, it seems probable, especially in light of the way this evidence is used in Acts, that he was a full citizen of Tarsus and of Rome on the basis of his family origins.

How was it that Paul's family secured Roman citizenship? The two most illustrative passages in Acts regarding Paul's citizenship are Acts 16:37–39 and 22:25–29. In the first, after being imprisoned overnight in Philippi and then released, Paul raises the question whether his treatment has been legal for a Roman citizen. In the second, after Paul has been taken into Roman custody in Jerusalem and the commander has ordered that he be beaten, Paul raises the question whether it is legal for a Roman citizen to be treated in such a way. When the commander arrives to sort out this potential difficulty, his discussion with Paul reveals that the commander purchased his citizenship, while Paul claims to have inherited his. At the time of these episodes, there had been a general expansion of Roman citizenship. By the middle of the first century B.C., the entire population of the Italian peninsula had been made Roman citizens. By the middle of the next century, there was a sizable number of citizens throughout the empire, and in A.D. 212 an edict was issued that made all free inhabitants of the empire citizens.[26] In the course of this expansion, there were several ways in which Roman citizenship could be acquired: it could be given to slaves who were manumitted, be bestowed for various reasons, including performing valuable services to the empire militarily or otherwise, be purchased for a large sum, or be inherited from a father who was a citizen.[27] Some have thought that, being in the tent-making business, Paul's father or grandfather may have performed valuable service to the Roman Empire and been awarded citizenship that Paul inherited; others speculate that one of Paul's relatives had purchased citizenship. But it simply cannot be said for certain how Paul's citizenship was secured.[28]

Simply invoking his citizenship, however, did not necessarily mean that Paul would immediately receive special treatment. It was more difficult in the ancient world to carry substantial proof of citizenship, especially when a person was away from a place where he or she may have been known or where family archives were kept. Paul may have carried some form of passport that citizens possessed, perhaps the kind of document that would have been found among Paul's scrolls. Citizens often carried small tablets that specified their status. As can be imagined, documentation indicating Roman citizenship would have been valuable in the Roman world, so there were many incidents of forgery, with severe penalties if discovered. A wise commander would not have necessarily accepted the documentation at face value but would probably have tried to secure some proof that the documents were genuine by, for example, intensively interrogating Paul. Being a Roman citizen entailed a number of privileges, including the right to a public accusation and trial, exemption from certain kinds of punishment—in most instances including crucifixion—and protection against summary execution. A Roman citizen had the right of appeal, although in times of civil unrest this right may have been abrogated. It does not appear that a citizen necessarily had the right to appeal to Caesar to have his case heard. In any event, an appeal probably would not have been heard by Caesar but, rather, by some judicial official appointed by him.[29]

The Roman citizenship of Paul's family raises the question whether his family performed Roman religious rites, such as worship of the emperor as a god. Would this account for Paul's leaving Tarsus? Several factors must be considered here. First, one must recognize that Diaspora Judaism was a complex and diverse phenomenon, in many ways integrated into the surrounding religio-cultural milieu. This does not mean that the Jews were not in many instances respected for their high moral standards and their belief in God, as the existence of Godfearers in Acts bears witness (10:2, 22, 35; 13:16, 26, 43, 50; 16:14; 17:4, 17; 18:7), but Judaism in the larger Greco-Roman world was merely one of a number of religious and cultural minorities, with various levels of acculturation and assimilation.[30] Second, the institutionalization of Roman emperor worship as something that was compelled of citizens did not occur until the second century. Augustus was cautious in his tolerance of the emperor cult, allowing those in the east to engage in it more freely than those in the west, where Romans would have been less willing to proclaim the deity of the emperor. At the time of Christ's birth, this kind of worship would probably have been, at most, optional, so there would have been no compelling reason for the Jews to have performed these kinds of rituals. In any event, Jews had previously served foreign military leaders on several occasions. During the period of Seleucid rule, they were hired on a few occasions as mercenaries, and Jewish officers had served various rulers. Third, the Jews in Greco-Roman cities may have been separated into their own order or tribe (the citizenry of a Greco-Roman city were divided into orders for management of the city's affairs). This would have meant that they had a degree of autonomy and self-government that allowed them to follow some of their own religious practices. Despite the last two considerations, Paul might have perceived moral and religious laxity among Jews in Tarsus, and this may have been a factor compelling him to go to Jerusalem to train to be a Pharisee under Gamaliel. Since

Jerusalem was the religious center, he might have viewed it as free from the perceived corruption of the Diaspora.

E. Paul's Occupation

There is abundant evidence that Paul worked as some form of craftsman or leather worker (Acts 18:3; 1 Cor 4:12; cf. 1 Thess 2:9; 2 Cor 12:14).[31] This has traditionally been taken to mean that he was a tent maker, but this may be too restrictive. Someone of his trade probably worked with all sorts of materials, making not only tents but sails for boats, canopies for theaters, and various forms of military equipment. A person in this line of work was probably considered to be skilled and hence above the social level of the general populace, which was engaged in menial or physical labor on the land. Some scholars have suggested that Paul worked as a craftsman because he was a Pharisee and every Pharisee was required to have a usable trade, but the evidence for such a pharisaic practice is not strong (cf. *m. ʾAbot* 2:2; *t. Qidd.* 1.22). A more likely explanation is that learning a skill was typical of both Jews and others throughout the Greco-Roman world. People would spend time learning a skilled trade for two or three years as an apprentice, then continue it throughout their adult lives. A skill was not only useful to Paul for providing for his material needs; it served a useful function in his missionary strategy. Paul would travel from city to city using his trade as a way of maintaining himself in his travels (as did other craftsmen and even other itinerant teachers) and of establishing and maintaining his apostolic credibility. He would often stay in the home of a convert (Acts 16:15, 40; 17:5–7; Phlm 22), working there or in a local shop (Acts 18:3, 11). Rather than be a financial burden on a local church and be mistaken for one of those disreputable itinerant teachers in the ancient world who would exploit their listeners for financial gain and then leave (cf. Lucian, *Peregr.* 11–14; *Merc. cond.* 20, 37), Paul was able to point to his working with his hands instead of being a burden on the local congregation (1 Thess 2:9). He was an early practitioner of a lifestyle evangelism in which he was able to inspire his listeners with his own willingness to work in his own support (1 Thess 4:10–12).

F. Paul's Religious and Ethnic Background

At several places in his letters, Paul chronicles his ethnic and religious background in Judaism (e.g., Phil 3:5–6; 2 Cor 11:22; Gal 1:13–14; Rom 11:1). Seeing how Paul conceived himself helps us to understand better his conversion and his subsequent Christian experience.

With Phil 3:5–6 as a framework,[32] the following elements of his past are worth recounting. First, Paul says that he was circumcised on the eighth day, the day that was prescribed by Jewish law (Gen 17:12; Lev 12:3). Hence, Paul clearly lays claim to having been Jewish by birth and by outward sign. Second, he says that he was of the race of Israel—that is, a physical descendant from the line that led directly back to the patriarchs. Third, and more specifically, he claims to have been of the tribe of Benjamin, a troublesome tribe to be sure, but considered part of Judah since the division of the two kingdoms, the tribe within whose ancestral territory Jerusalem was located. Because of the Babylonian captivity, Jews in Paul's time, especially those of the Diaspora, were not all able to trace their genealogy to establish their tribal descent (Neh 11:7–9, 31–36). Not all scholars are convinced of this genealogy; many note that Paul was named after the most famous member of the tribe of Benjamin, King Saul. Saul would have been Paul's Jewish name, with Paul being his *cognomen*, or personal name. (Most Romans had three names, including not only a *cognomen* but also a *praenomen*, or family name, and *nomen*, or surname. Paul's other two names are unknown, a phenomenon not unique to Paul, for this is the case even when it comes to well-known people of the ancient world.)[33] Fourth, Paul is said to be a Hebrew of Hebrews. References to Israel and the tribe of Benjamin provide racial and ethnic distinctions, but Paul's specification of himself as a Hebrew of Hebrews is probably a linguistic distinction, meaning more than simply being Jewish. In Acts 6:1, a distinction is made between Hellenists and Hebrews, probably differentiating between Palestinian Jews who spoke Greek and those who spoke a Semitic language—probably Aramaic—as their native language and could worship in this language or Hebrew. (Philo, *Dreams* 2.250 and *Abraham* 28, makes a similar distinction.)[34] Paul here identifies with the Aramaic-speaking branch of the Jewish people, making the claim that even though he may be a Diaspora Jew, he is a native speaker of Aramaic, as probably were his parents. This would have distinguished him from the vast majority of Diaspora Jews, who did not know Aramaic or Hebrew and were thus obligated to attend Greek-speaking synagogues and use the LXX as their Bible. Paul is depicted as using Aramaic on several occasions (Acts 21:40; 22:2; 26:14). Of course, this does not mean that Paul did not have native competence in Greek as well; he did, as is clearly evidenced in the ease with which he moved in the Greco-Roman world, as well as the facility he demonstrates in his letters.

Fifth, Paul identifies himself with the Pharisees (cf. Acts 26:5) (see ch. 3, sec. 3, above). The Pharisees were characterized by a theology that mixed determinism and free will, with an emphasis on application of the law to daily life.[35] In Acts 23:6, Paul reportedly calls himself a son of a Pharisee, which may mean that his father was a Pharisee, although it is more likely that this means that he had a Pharisee in his family line or that he had been the student of a Pharisee (i.e., Gamaliel). Sixth, Paul refers to his zeal being evidenced in persecuting the church (cf. Gal 1:13–14). It is difficult to substantiate where exactly such persecution took place, since the only direct evidence of Paul's participation in persecution seems to be his relatively minor role in the stoning of Stephen. In Acts, he refers to persecuting in Jerusalem and casting his vote against those who were put to death (Acts 26:10). Since the apostles seem to have been relatively unaffected by such persecution even though they were in and around Jerusalem (or perhaps chose to remain in spite of it), Paul's persecution was probably not of Palestinian-Jewish but of Hellenistic-Jewish Christians, such as Stephen and his group. Thus, it was while he was going to Damascus, probably for the first time to pursue Hellenistic-Jewish Christians, that he had his "conversion" experience. He was otherwise unknown to those in Damascus.[36] Seventh, Paul says that as to legalistic righteousness, he was faultless. This verse has been variously interpreted. Earlier in this century it was not uncommon for scholars to see Paul as being psychologically ill at ease with being a Jew, which contributed to the formulation of his theology as a Christian.[37] But there is no evidence here of Paul's being troubled by guilt, stress, doubt, or depression over his failure to keep the law. This verse does not state

The forum and cardo (main north-south street) through Gerasa (modern Jerash). Paul likely went through this city on his way to Damascus. Photo Lee M. McDonald.

that Paul considered himself "righteous" on the basis of keeping the law. He is stating instead that, so far as the demands of the law were concerned, he did what the law demanded and was faultless so far as this requirement could be met.

G. Paul's Conversion

The commencement of the persecution of Hellenistic-Jewish Christians (Acts 8:1) led to their fleeing to areas outside Judea.[38] There may have been some sort of extradition policy in effect, whereby breakers of the law, even though they broke the law outside Palestine, could be returned to Jerusalem to be punished under Jewish law. Such a policy was apparently originally instituted in 142 B.C. but had been redefined by Julius Caesar in 47 B.C. In his persecuting zeal, Paul undertook his journey to Damascus to bring back Christians to Jerusalem. If the document Paul carried with him did not go so far as to give him legal authority, apparently it would at least have implored the cooperation of the

synagogue leaders there.[39] This implies that there were already Christians in Damascus only a few years after Jesus' death. It also provides further evidence that Paul was persecuting primarily Hellenistic-Jewish Christians who had had some direct or indirect contact with Jerusalem.

Paul's conversion is mentioned three times in Acts (9:3–6; 22:6–11; 26:12–18; the first time a recounting of events in narrative sequence and the other two times descriptions in Pauline apologetic sections), once explicitly in Gal 1:15–16, and less directly in 1 Cor 9:1; 15:8.[40] Recent discussion has questioned whether this singular and significant event in Paul's life ought to be referred to as a conversion, since the term *conversion* seems to imply a change from no religion to religion, or a change from one religion to another. In either case, Paul had been a religious person before his conversion and continued to be one after, viewing his conversion as something that developed naturally from, and was in many essential ways in harmony with, his previous belief. As a result, some have wanted

Acco (Ptolemais) with a view to the north across the modern city of Acre. Paul visited this city on his third missionary journey (Acts 21:7). © Rohr Productions. Used with permission.

Joppa (Jaffa) with a view to the northwest across the ancient city (see Acts 9:36; 10:5–23). © Rohr Productions. Used with permission.

to refer to Paul's experience as a calling akin to that of some OT prophets (e.g., Isaiah or Jeremiah; see Isa 6; Jer 1:4–19), others as a visionary or ecstatic experience similar to those in other religious traditions, and still others as a revelatory event.[41]

As Segal has shown, however, regardless of the other elements that may have been present in Paul's Damascus road experience (including a vision similar to that of an OT prophet), "conversion" is entirely appropriate to describe what happened to Paul, since his experience had affinities with conversion experiences in Judaism of the time. The characteristics of conversion that Segal cites are the identification by the convert of a lack in his previous existence that is remedied by the new group (Phil 3:7–8), a restructuring of reality by the convert according to the presuppositions of the new group, and a resulting integration of the old perspective in the new.[42] Although Paul saw himself in continuity with essential Judaism after this crucial event and used it as the basis of his thought (see sec. 2, below), he came to see that the work of Christ superseded Jewish practice and belief. A distinct element in contemporary Judaism endorsed works as a means of entering and retaining one's covenantal status, but Paul placed his emphasis on the justifying work of God through Christ. Whereas Jews thought of themselves as obligated to keep the law with the hope of attaining and maintaining righteousness before God, Paul saw the law as totally ineffective in this quest and hence as having already accomplished its purpose. Judaism had rejected Jesus as Christ or the Messiah, but for Paul, Jesus was the Christ. In this respect, Paul's experience may well be characterized as conversion.

Paul's experience on the Damascus road nevertheless included a series of events similar to the calls of the prophets Isaiah and Jeremiah, in which God singled out these specific individuals and called them to fulfill his intended purpose. When these prophets were called, they were given a message to preach. It is unclear whether Paul saw his entire message at the time of his conversion, but what is clear is that by the time he wrote Gal 1:15–16 (a retrospective view compatible with conversion), he saw that an essential part of his calling was wrapped up

The recently excavated stadium/hippodrome at Gerasa. Photo Lee M. McDonald.

with being the apostle to the Gentiles.[43] So far as actual physical signs are concerned, both sight and sound attended his call. In his letters, Paul mentions that he saw Jesus (1 Cor 9:1; 15:8; Gal 1:16). The fact that Paul believed that he received his commissioning as apostle to the Gentiles at this time gives credence to the idea that he heard a voice, as is recorded in all three accounts in Acts (9:4–6; 22:7–8; 26:14–18). It is, however, possible that references to the voice are Luke's extrapolations from what is said in the Pauline Letters. As for Paul, he treats the appearance as an actual and valid revelation of Jesus Christ, one that conveyed authority for his missionary endeavors.

H. Acts and Paul

It is not often recognized how much of what is tacitly assumed to be reliable knowledge of Paul is dependent upon the book of Acts. For example, a clear statement of Paul's conversion experience on the Damascus road, the itinerary of his several missionary journeys, the Hellenistic side of his background and experience, including his coming from Tarsus and his Roman citizenship—all of these are found primarily, if not exclusively, in Acts, not in the Pauline Letters. Consequently, critical scholarship has often raised questions about whether these are accurate depictions of Paul. There are a number of other items related to Paul's life and experience that are only known from Acts and that critical scholarship doubts even more seriously, such as his numerous public speeches—for example, at Athens (Acts 17:22–31). This raises several important questions regarding the relationship between the Paul of Acts and the Paul of his letters.

The traditional view of Acts' authorship is that it is the second of two volumes composed by a traveling companion of Paul, Luke the physician. This authorship is attested since the second century in church tradition (see ch. 8, sec. 4, above). This tradition is reasonably early, but it must be recognized that the Gospel and Acts are formally anonymous, and so certainty regarding authorship cannot be established. Scholars have debated the evidence for and against the traditional view, recognizing various amounts of credibility in Paul's references to Luke among Paul's faithful companions (Col 4:14; 2 Tim 4:11; Phlm 24). Nevertheless, the majority of scholars would probably give more credibility to the traditional view of Lukan authorship. Further support for Lukan authorship is often found in the "we" passages of Acts (16:10–17; 20:5–15; 21:1–18; 27:1–29; 28:1–16).

Critical scholarship of the last hundred years, however, has called this traditional authorial attribution into question. The thought that the author of Luke–Acts was a physician can no longer be definitively supported from the text itself, since the so-called medical language found in Luke–Acts is typical of Luke's level and style of writing, and the majority of references to Luke as Paul's traveling companion are found in what are frequently called deuteropauline books, that is, books that were not necessarily written by Paul but, quite possibly, significantly later (these books often include 1, 2 Timothy and Titus [the so-called Pastoral Epistles], Ephesians, Colossians, and 2 Thessalonians; see sec. 6, below, and ch. 10 under the individual letters). Furthermore, there are a number of ways of explaining the use of the "we" passages, and the firsthand account is only one of them. These passages have been viewed as a fictional device to tell of a sea voyage or as an indication of the redactional activity of the author, and they have been thought to point to the incorporation of a source document or the author's own firsthand account. Even if they are thought to represent a firsthand account (the language does not necessarily mean an eyewitness), the most that can be argued is that another source is being used. It does not resolve the issue of authorship.[44]

Important for the relation of Paul to Acts are a number of questions regarding the accuracy and reliability of Acts in relation to what is known about Paul through his letters. A number of elements seem to some scholars to be so at odds with the picture of Paul gained through his own letters as to raise the question whether the person who wrote Acts could possibly have been a firsthand witness or close acquaintance:

1. Paul's literary contribution to the NT is only as a letter writer, but the author of Acts never depicts Paul as a letter writer. Nowhere in Acts is Paul seen carrying on the kind of ministry that is depicted in his letters, that is, maintaining and guarding his relationships with his churches through his epistolary correspondence. Paul certainly is depicted in Acts as being pastorally concerned for his churches (e.g., Acts 15:36, 41), but this does not include the sending of letters. Furthermore, the author of Acts, regardless

St. Catherine's Monastery, where many valuable biblical manuscripts were discovered, most notably Codex Sinaiticus.
© Rohr Productions. Used with permission.

of his possible knowledge of Paul's writing activities, does not use the letters in any clear way.

2. In the letters, Paul never explicitly mentions his missionary strategy as including visiting synagogues, but in Acts it is clear that Paul begins many of his preaching ministries in cities by attending the synagogue (e.g., Salamis in 13:5, Pisidian Antioch in 13:14, Iconium in 14:1, Thessalonica in 17:1–2, Beroea in 17:10, Athens in 17:17, Corinth in 18:4, and Ephesus in 18:19). Paul's statement that he was flogged five times (2 Cor 11:24) indicates that during this time he placed himself under the rules of the synagogue.

3. According to his own words in his letters, Paul apparently was not able to convince his audiences with his speeches on several occasions (e.g., 2 Cor 10:10, but with due care in interpreting this passage), even though in Acts Paul is portrayed as a highly convincing rhetorician (Acts 13:9–11, 16–41; 14:15–17; 17:22–31; 22:1–21; 24:10–21; 26:2–26), whose speeches have elicited analysis from a rhetorical perspective.[45]

4. Paul never mentions his Roman citizenship in the letters, but in Acts his citizenship is a crucial item of information that he cites at several significant junctures, especially when his safety is being threatened by what he sees as unjust charges (e.g., at Philippi in 16:37, at Jerusalem in 22:25, and at Caesarea in 25:11).

5. One would not be able to gather from Acts that Paul jealously guarded his apostleship with regard to the Corinthian church, warranting the kind of epistolary exchange that we find in the letters themselves (e.g., 1 Cor 9:1–18; Gal 1:1; 1:11–2:10).

These kinds of contrasts can be overdrawn, however. In Acts, we see Paul, for example, establishing the churches in Asia Minor on the outward portion of his first missionary journey and then visiting these same churches on the return journey (Acts 13:13–14:25). The second missionary journey is said in Acts to have come about from a desire by Paul to revisit the churches he had founded earlier (Acts 15:36). Acts does not depict the nature of the conflict at Corinth, but Acts does depict Paul in conflict at times—for instance, at Ephesus (Acts 19). And since Acts was written, by all accounts, after the conflict with the Corinthian church had been resolved sufficiently for Paul to write Romans from there, in all likelihood, only a year later, perhaps the author—who admittedly emphasizes Paul's triumphs—thought it unnecessary to retain this disappointing memory. This tendency to idealization perhaps accounts for the difference in depicting Paul's rhetorical skills—the author of Acts sees Paul's ultimate triumphs, whereas Paul himself, in the middle of his conflicts, or perhaps even for rhe-

torical reasons, downplays his abilities (e.g., 2 Cor 10:10).[46] It is probably fair to say that Acts emphasizes the Hellenistic side of Paul more than the letters, which in many ways, at least regarding personal details of his life, emphasize the Jewish side.

Second, the emphases of Acts and Paul's letters are different. For example, in Acts Paul has frequent contact with Romans, so it is appropriate to discuss his citizenship in the context of his arrest and their safeguarding him. In several of his letters, Paul is keen to emphasize his role as an apostle to groups of Christians. For example, his conflicts with the Judaizers of Galatia and with the opponents at Corinth revolve around his calling as an apostle. Paul clearly sees himself as an apostle in his letters and uses that term (see, e.g., Rom 1:1; 11:13; 1 Cor 1:1; 4:9; 9:1, 2; 15:9; 2 Cor 1:1; 11:5; 12:11, 12; Gal 1:1; etc.). This is not an emphasis in Acts, although Acts does not deny his apostolic calling (see Acts 13:4; 14:4, 14). It is noted by some that in Acts the depictions of Paul's conversion are all different from each other in some essential details—for example, concerning what his traveling companions saw or heard, or the lack of an emphasis on Paul's seeing Christ, items found in his letters (see 1 Cor 9:1; 15:8; Gal 1:15–16).[47] The problem whether Acts is internally consistent is, of course, not directly a problem of the Pauline Letters. Regarding these depictions in Acts, one must clarify what it means when they say that Paul saw a light and whether it was not possible for this experience to have been interpreted by him as his vision of Christ. It seems very likely that it was.

Third, there appear to be several differences in theological emphasis in Acts and the Pauline Letters. For example, it has been noted that in Acts Paul uses arguments from natural theology on several occasions, as in his speeches to the philosophers on the Areopagus (Acts 17:22–31) and to the people of Lystra, who wanted to worship Paul and Barnabas as gods (Acts 14:15–17). A negative example is the lack of emphasis in Acts on Christ's death, which is a major theological emphasis in the Pauline Letters. Paul makes Christ's death foundational for his theology, but it does not appear to be one of his major emphases in Acts. In his letters, Paul sees a relationship between the law and sin (Gal 3:19; Rom 4:13–16; 5:20; 1 Cor 15:26; 2 Cor 3:6), but in Acts, Paul is seen as performing some legalistic rituals—circumcising Timothy (Acts 16:1–3;

but cf. Gal 5:2), taking a vow and cutting off his hair (Acts 18:18), and performing acts of purification in the temple (21:26). These differences in emphasis, however, do not necessarily mean that Acts contradicts the Pauline Letters. Luke's theology may simply have been different from Paul's. In addition, Paul does use a naturalistic argument in Rom 1:18–32, where he depicts the general depravity of humanity, and this argument is foundational to the entire discussion in Romans. Finally, references to the death of Christ, though few in Acts, are not unknown; Acts 20:28, for instance, refers to the blood of Christ.

Fourth, it seems that the major difficulties between Acts and Paul's letters revolve around the chronological and historical details, which do not seem to match up. For example, there is no "painful visit" (2 Cor 2:1) from Ephesus to Corinth recorded in Acts during Paul's lengthy stay in Ephesus (Acts 19). Paul's stay in Arabia (Gal 1:15–17) is not developed in Acts. Galatians (1:18; 2:1) mentions only two visits to Jerusalem after his conversion, whereas Acts records three (9:26; 11:30 with 12:25; 15:2–30). It is highly debated how the Jerusalem Council of Acts 15 fits in with the events recorded in Gal 2. Some argue that the visit of Gal 2 is the one recorded in Acts 15, while others contend that it is the visit of Acts 11:30 and 12:25. Paul mentions that he suffered (2 Cor 1:8; 11:23–28) in ways that the book of Acts does not mention. Acts closes with Paul concluding a two-year imprisonment, apparently looking forward to release. This and his imprisonment for two years in Caesarea (Acts 23–26), together with a night in a Philippian jail (Acts 16:22–39), are his only imprisonments recorded in Acts. This raises the question of how to fit the so-called Prison Epistles into this chronology. Five of Paul's letters can be categorized as imprisonment letters—Colossians, Philemon, Ephesians, Philippians, and 2 Timothy—although even by a traditional view of authorship and chronology they are not all apparently from the same imprisonment. A traditional position is that Colossians, Philemon, Ephesians, and probably Philippians were written from a Roman imprisonment. (The view that Paul was imprisoned in Ephesus, the next most likely, does not have an explicit episode to point to in the account in Acts.) This leaves the question of where in the chronology to place the Pastoral Epistles, as 2 Timothy is also apparently an imprisonment epistle. This has suggested a second imprisonment theory, according to which Paul was released from his Roman imprisonment after Acts ends (after Acts was written?) and then began another itinerant ministry before a second Roman imprisonment and execution under Nero (after A.D. 64) (Eusebius, *Hist. eccl.* 2.22.1–8). In another historical difference between Acts and Paul's letters, Paul's stay in Arabia (Gal 1:15–17) is not mentioned in Acts, but it must be said that this is not an important detail in the letters either. Perhaps of greater interest is the account of various sufferings in 2 Cor 11:23–28, which finds no correlatives in Acts.

Many of these points are items of curiosity where it would be desirable to have more details, but they do not necessarily bring Acts into contradiction with the Pauline Letters. They provide a challenge to the interpreter to weigh the evidence fairly from the several sources and to construct a reasonable chronology (see sec. 3, below).

2. THE PRIMARY TEACHINGS AND THOUGHT OF PAUL

A. The Background to Paul's Thought

In considering the formative influences on Paul's thought, we must remember the nature of the ancient Greco-Roman world. This world was not one in which Judaic and Greco-Roman culture stood side by side as equals. It was a huge world, primarily as a result of Alexander's conquests, with surprisingly dense communication and trade holding it together. Alexander the Great had been instrumental in establishing Greek as the lingua franca, or common language, of the Hellenistic world through his ambitious program of conquest, which extended from Greece proper down to Egypt and east toward India. Where the language of the conquerors went, so did their social institutions and culture, since language is the single most important tool in the establishment of society and the spread of culture. Even though he was not able to consolidate his rule after his spectacular conquests, and his empire was divided among four generals soon after his death at thirty-three (323 B.C.), Alexander's love of Greek culture (Aristotle had been his teacher) had a lasting effect. Wherever he went, Greek culture and influence followed, and they had a pervasive influence on the conquered as the indigenous people strove to establish useful relationships with the conquerors. In linguistic terms, Greek was the "prestige" language, spoken by soldiers, merchants, traders, and anyone who wanted to profitably coexist or even thrive with them. Jews were involved in most avenues of Hellenistic life; they even served as mercenaries in the armies of the Hellenistic world (see 1 Macc 11:41–51; cf. 10:36), besides being actively engaged in various forms of business. Not only did Alexander leave the legacy of Greek language on these disparate peoples; he left a strong cultural heritage, including the organization of cities and government.[48]

The Hellenistic world was one of great accomplishments in many areas. For example, important philosophical schools developed, such as Stoicism; a huge amount of literature was written; genuine literary scholarship was practiced in Alexandria, centered upon its tremendous library; and theoretical science developed such things as geometry, whereby the circumference of the earth was calculated (the calculation was in error but only because one of the factors was inaccurate). The Greek educational system was emulated throughout the Hellenistic world. A gymnasium was built near the temple in Jerusalem in the second century B.C. To give some idea of the influence of Greek culture even upon the Jews, since exercise in the gymnasium was done naked and since the Greeks and Romans considered circumcision to be a form of bodily mutilation, some Jews reportedly attempted to have their circumcision surgically masked (called epispasm; 1 Macc 1:14–15). The Hasmoneans had been, essentially, local Hellenistic rulers, and this acceptance of Greek culture by the bulk of the Jewish population continued for several centuries, including under the Herodian rulers. It was only after the Bar Kokhba revolt of A.D. 132–135 that Judaism turned decisively away from Hellenism. The ancient world before the time of Alexander had been, for the most part, less well unified; now people could conceivably be citizens of the world, not simply citizens of a particular city. But this expansiveness also brought a backlash in the form of an emphasis upon the individual, as many people felt alienated and

The temple of Artemis (Diana) at Gerasa dates from the second century A.D. Photo Lee M. McDonald.

insignificant in such a vast and incomprehensible world. Partly as a result, the Greco-Roman world was dominated by superstition and syncretism, in which numerous kinds and ways of belief were often indiscriminately joined together by people as they sought spiritual meaning. It was within this larger context, dominated by Greek and Roman culture and religion, that Judaism existed as just one form of belief among many. In many ways, Jews were respected by others for their system of belief, and hence there were those who wished to emulate Jewish morality and theology. This did not keep the Jews above suspicion, however, not only in Palestine, where the Romans and the Greeks before them had always had trouble with rebellion and insurrection, but in other places in the empire as well, such as Rome, where the Jews were expelled en masse probably in A.D. 49 by an edict of the Emperor Claudius, and Alexandria, where similar conflicts arose. As a result, it is unfair to evaluate Paul's thinking in terms of a simple either/or regarding Hellenistic and Jewish elements. Indeed, the more the topic is explored, the more it must be recognized that the Judaism of the turn of the era was Hellenistic Judaism, even the forms practiced in Palestine. When we turn to Paul's writings, such a balance is certainly found.[49]

1. Hellenistic Elements in Paul's Writings

Greek was one of Paul's first languages (the other was Aramaic). He probably spoke Greek not only at home but also in his dealings outside his own home while he lived in Tarsus. After all, Greek was the language of communication of even Diaspora Judaism during the Hellenistic period. The translation of the Hebrew Bible into what became known as the Septuagint (LXX) was begun in Egypt during the third century B.C. out of recognition that most of the Jews living there were linguistically incapable of understanding, or meaningfully worshipping in, their religious language, Hebrew. So the largest and most ambitious translation project of the Greek and Roman world was begun, extending over the next two centuries; the entire translation was completed probably sometime in the first century B.C.[50] Some Diaspora Jews may have been able to worship in Hebrew or Aramaic, but the vast majority worshipped in Greek. Even though there was more Aramaic spoken in Pales-

tine by Jews than elsewhere, it is estimated that, of the Jewish population of Jerusalem itself, a minimum of 15–20 percent spoke Greek as their first language (this says nothing of the non-Jewish population, which would have almost certainly spoken Greek), and many more than this would have had a secondary bilingual capacity, acquired in order to conduct business and commerce with the dominant surrounding Greco-Roman culture. In other regions of Palestine, such as the Decapolis or many of the truly Hellenistic cities, such as Caesarea, Tiberias, or Sepphoris in Galilee, Greek would have been predominant, even for Jews. Other areas of the Roman east, such as Arabia, witnessed significant usage of Greek. Jewish funerary inscriptions give substantial evidence of the influence of Greek language upon the Jewish population worldwide. Fully 75 percent of the extant Jewish tombs in Rome from the first century B.C. to the fourth century A.D. use Greek for their epitaphs. In Palestine, 55–60 percent of the extant tomb inscriptions, from mostly the first to fifth centuries A.D., are written in Greek; roughly 40 percent of those in Jerusalem itself are in Greek.[51]

Paul was born and reared in this Hellenistic world. It is therefore not surprising that all of Paul's writings are in Greek. Since Greek was the lingua franca, Paul had the reasonable expectation that wherever he wrote in the world of his time, he could communicate if he wrote in Greek. Perhaps a similar instance is found in a letter written by an associate of the Jewish rebel Bar Kokhba to several of his deputies regarding supplies. He writes in lines 11–15 that "[the letter] is written how[ever] in Greek because th[e de]sir[e *or* th[e oppo]rtuni[ty (?) was not to be f[ou]nd in Hebrew to w[rit]e."[52] This rebel of the Jewish cause against Rome wrote here in Greek rather than Hebrew, implying that it was more effort, or there were fewer people available, to write in Hebrew. The writer had every expectation that the readers would be able to understand his letter. Even though Jewish literature was not read extensively outside their own circles, Jewish writers often wrote in Greek, even for their religious literature. Ben Sira reputedly translated his grandfather's work from a Semitic language into Greek in Egypt; parts of the *Testaments of the Twelve Patriarchs* were composed in Greek; in Palestine, additions to Daniel and Esther were made in Greek; and 1 Esdras and 2 Maccabees are thought to have been originally

Caesarea-Philippi (Baniyas, Banias, Paneas, Syria), at the foot of Mount Hermon (Mark 8:27), was the site of a major battle between the Ptolemies and the Seleucids in 198 B.C. that gave control of Palestine to the Seleucids. It was also the home of Herod Philip. © Rohr Productions. Used with permission.

composed there in Greek. A number of Jewish works, including *2 Esdras* and *Judith*, have survived predominantly in Greek, although they were probably originally composed in Hebrew.[53]

Besides writing in Greek, Paul utilized one of the common literary forms exploited by the Hellenistic world: the letter. The Hellenistic letter, like the letter of today, had established forms, which consisted of various sections and various formulae used in these sections. Paul qualifies as one of the great masters of the Hellenistic letter form, adapting the set form to his particular purposes. He wrote personal letters (e.g., to Philemon), but he also apparently originated and developed the ecclesiastical letter, the letter to a church. Although there were standard forms of address, Paul developed his own formula, which theologizes the standard letter opening—"grace and peace." He also used two other sections of the letter—the thanksgiving and the parenesis (= admonitory material)—as a way of emphasizing Christian ethical standards. (More is said about the letter form in section 4, below.)

Within the letter form, Paul also made use of several other well-known literary conventions of the time. Two in particular are worth noting: the diatribe, and vice and virtue lists.

The diatribe is a communication technique, or possibly even a literary genre, that was developed by Cynic and Stoic philosophers during the Hellenistic period.[54] It is a dialogical form in which a teacher and student(s) engage in a verbal question-and-answer exchange in order to learn more about the subject being discussed. Along with this basic dialogical format, there are a number of other linguistic features, such as hortatory forms ("let us . . .") to create pleas to action; particular connective words, including strong contrastive ones ("but"); antithetical and parallel statements; rhetorical questions; and words of direct address. A number of ancient authors used the diatribe, the most famous perhaps being the ex-slave and philosopher Epictetus.[55] His diatribes have obviously been put into literary form in his writings (perhaps by Arrian, who wrote his teaching down), but they appear to reflect, at several points, actual conversations. Probably the form originated in philosophical literature, reflecting a classroom or instructional environment, and then was taken over in the synagogue for pedagogical purposes.

Paul has several sustained sections of diatribe, in particular Rom 1–11 and sections in 1 and 2 Cor.

In his writings, the discussion may reflect genuine questions being asked by those in the churches to which he writes, but his diatribes are not transcriptions of actual conversations. Paul creates his opponent, who raises crucial questions and objections to which his narrative voice profitably responds. Paul often addresses this literary creation as "man" or "you," with the single individual often standing for a group that thinks or acts similarly. As an example, here is Rom 3:1–8 laid out in diatribe fashion (Q = Paul's dialogical partner; P = Paul's narrative response):[56]

> Q: What therefore is the advantage of being a Jew, or what is the advantage of circumcision?
>
> P: Much in every way! First, they have been entrusted with the words of God.
>
> Q: But what if some do not have faith? Their lack of faith won't nullify God's faithfulness, will it?
>
> P: Certainly not! Let God be true and every man a liar—as it is written: "So that you may be justified in your words and will prevail in your judging."
>
> Q: But if our unrighteousness establishes God's righteousness, what shall we say? The God who brings his wrath is not unjust, is he? (I am using a human argument.)
>
> P: Certainly not! How will God then judge the world? "If the truth of God by my falsehood multiplies into his glory, why am I still condemned as a sinner?" Why not—as we are being slandered and as some claim that we say—"Let us do evil things so that good things may come about"? Their condemnation is deserved.

The form of the diatribe is well illustrated by this reconstructed dialogue, all written by Paul himself.

Paul also makes use of vice and virtue lists. Such lists were especially used by Stoic philosophers in moral exhortation to catalogue or inventory personal vices and virtues.[57] They were not meant to be comprehensive lists of all of the instances of a particular category, but give representative examples as a means of focusing on the particular subject. Sometimes the lists are of character traits; other times they are personified. In either case, the effect is designed to be the same. Their use by Paul is in keeping with Stoic philosophy, by which the world is seen to function according to rational principles and the goal of human life is to align oneself with the divine rational spirit. Instances of virtue lists in the letters attributed to

The Agora of Athens with a view to the Acropolis, crowned by the Parthenon. Photo Lee M. McDonald.

Paul are found in 2 Cor 6:6–7, Phil 4:6–9, and Eph 4:2–3. Examples of vice lists are found in Rom 1:29–31, 13:13; 1 Cor 5:10–11; Eph 4:31–32, 5:3–5; 1 Tim 1:9–10, 6:4–5; and Titus 1:7–10. A good example of the use of a vice list and a virtue list together is in Gal 5:19–23:

> Now the works of the flesh are obvious: fornication, impurity, licentiousness, idolatry, sorcery, enmities, strife, jealousy, anger, quarrels, dissensions, factions, envy, drunkenness, carousing, and things like these. I am warning you, as I warned you before: those who do such things will not inherit the kingdom of God. By contrast, the fruit of the Spirit is love, joy, peace, patience, kindness, generosity, faithfulness, gentleness, and self-control. There is no law against such things. (NRSV)

Paul not only uses Greek literary forms and conventions; his thought also illustrates well some of the principles of Hellenistic thought. In the early twentieth century, emphasis was placed on how Paul's thinking was similar to that of a variety of Greco-Roman mystery religions.[58] Mystery religions are not well understood because, by definition, they were private religious cults that apparently prac-

ticed secretive initiation procedures in which the initiates became in some way intimately involved with the god, often through a ritual that may have included some sort of a baptismlike practice. Our best-known source is the Hermetic Corpus, but this is much later than the NT and was probably influenced by the NT rather than the other way around. There is little basis for claiming that Paul was in any way influenced by these religious practices, although some of the writings attributed to Paul may reflect a response to them. For example, in Eph 5:18, the author implores his readers not to be drunk with wine but to be filled with the Holy Spirit. This language is similar in ways to that in Euripides' *Bacchae* (line 281, but cf. 278–301; cf. Plutarch, *Def. orac.* 40.432E) about Dionysus, the god of wine, one of the most widely read texts of the Greco-Roman world and instrumental in several religious cults. The author of Ephesians, however, may merely be countering a tendency in the Ephesian church to engage in indulgent practices.

More can be made of parallels in thought between the Stoics and Paul. This is not because Pauline

Mount Sinai and St. Catherine's Monastery. © Rohr Productions. Used with permission.

thought is Stoic in orientation but because Paul and Stoic (and other) philosophers were concerned with similar kinds of issues. If the account in Acts 17 is historical (and there is good reason to think that it is),[59] then there is direct evidence that Paul engaged in philosophico-religious discussion with philosophers of the day, including Stoics and Epicureans, and that many—though not all—of his concerns would have found a sympathetic ear. The speech in Acts 17 is crafted in such a way that it begins from the kind of argument that would have found general apologetic acceptance with these philosophers. It is only when resurrection is mentioned that objections are raised. As mentioned above, Stoic thought was concerned with how one lived a life aligned with the pervasive divine rational force. In Stoic thought there is also a tension between divine necessity and human responsibility, well captured in Cleanthes' *Hymn to Zeus*, lines 26–29. These are the kinds of topics that any religious system must come to terms with, and as did the Stoics, so did Paul. There are several examples where similarities of thought are present. For example, in Rom 7:15 Paul struggles aloud with the dilemma of fighting against one's own will: "I do not understand my own actions. For I do not do what I want, but I do the very thing I hate." The Stoic Epictetus (*Diatr.* 2.26.4) speaks of a similar human dilemma: "What he wants he does not do and what he does not want he does." In 1 Cor 14:25, Paul speaks of God being within or among human beings. Seneca reflects similar thought when he says, "God is near you, he is with you, he is in you" (*Ep.* 41.1) and, "A holy spirit resides within us" (*Ep.* 41.2). In Rom 9:1, Paul speaks of the human conscience confirming the truth of what he is saying. Again, Seneca says, "Nor can I consent to such things with a clear conscience" (*Ep.* 117.1).[60]

With such philosophical thinking in the air, it is not surprising to see reflections about what constitutes the virtuous person. In Greek thought, and later in Roman, there was persistent speculation about what virtues (ἀρεταί, *aretai*) characterized the virtuous person. These virtues gave grounds for boasting. Paul appears to have been influenced by such debate, but he has transformed it into its negative form, downgrading the convention of boasting in one's virtues and emphasizing what would have been looked down upon in contemporary society as virtueless. For example, in 2 Cor 10–13 (see

also Phil 3:4–6), Paul turns traditional claims to fame on their head when he begins by characterizing himself as meek and gentle (10:1). Paul defends his apostolic ministry by recounting what distinguishes his ministry, including his litany of abuses in 11:22–29. He begins in 11:21 by rhetorically stating, "But whatever anyone dares to boast of—I am speaking as a fool—I also dare to boast of that." And he concludes in 11:30 by declaring, "If I must boast, I will boast of the things that show my weakness." Similarly, in Rom 5:3–5, Paul states a progressive and climactic series of Christian virtues that distinguish the believer: "we also boast in our sufferings, knowing that suffering produces endurance, and endurance produces character, and character produces hope, and hope does not disappoint us, because God's love has been poured into our hearts through the Holy Spirit that has been given to us."[61]

Paul's logic and means of argumentation are also full of Hellenistic features (see also on the diatribe, above). Two of them will be selected here for special mention: his literary style and his literary imagery. As mentioned above, there is varied opinion among scholars regarding the influence of classical rhetoric upon Paul. Some scholars come very close to arguing that Paul was in essence a Greek rhetorician or speechwriter who committed his work to paper, but this is probably not the best explanation of his work. It is certainly true that Paul's letters are persuasive, but this is probably less because he used rhetoricians' genres or forms of organization or development than because he simply knew how to create a convincing argument that utilized the logical capacity of language.[62] For example, the logical outline of the book of Romans gives good evidence of how Paul's mind worked. Within the body of the letter he begins by describing the human predicament that requires God's response (1:18–3:20)—a treatment divided into three sections, progressing from a general indictment of humanity, to an implication of the moral person, and finally even to condemnation of the Jew. Then Paul presents the solution to a person's legal problem of incurring the wrath of God (3:21–4:25). Paul moves from there to dealing with a person's legal and personal relationship with God, which he characterizes as reconciliation, and which brings a person full circle by overcoming the legal and personally alienating effects of Adam's sin through

Christ's work on the cross (5:1–21). Paul then discusses the implications of this changed status by discussing more fully what it means to participate in a personal relationship with God, characterized as life in the Spirit (6:1–8:39).[63] He concludes the body of the letter by selecting one crucial example, that of Israel, to illustrate the faithfulness of God to his promises of election. This logical pattern provides what many have found to be a compelling argument, but the pattern does not conform to any of the established patterns of classical rhetoric, even though it makes significant use of a number of features of persuasive discourse, including the exemplum or paradigm (4:1–25 on Abraham; 5:12–21 on Adam) and the diatribe (chs. 1–11).

Paul also utilizes various stylistic features: parallelism (e.g., Rom 3:21–26); metaphor and simile (1 Cor 12:12ff.; 2 Tim 4:6); synecdoche and metonymy, where a part or related item stands for the whole (Rom 5:9, where Paul uses "by his blood" as a metonym for death; and 2 Cor 3:15, where Moses stands for the entire Pentateuch); antonomasia, where a substitute name is used (Rom 5:14, where "the one who was to come" describes Christ); irony (Phlm 9); litotes, a form of understatement (Rom 1:16); apostrophe, or direct address (Rom 7:1, etc.); and many others.[64] This is not to deny that Paul also uses some of the other means seen in the rhetoricians for creating and structuring an argument. But he does not do so in a systematic way that would distinguish him as a classical rhetorician, any more than any other persuasive writer of the time. For example, as a means of proving his argument, Paul appeals to his character (ἦθος, ēthos), as in Philemon, especially vv. 8–9. Paul also will appeal to emotion (πάθος, pathos) should the occasion warrant it, as in Gal 1:6–9. Of course, he also uses reason or logic (λόγος, logos)—for instance, in the exemplum, or example (Rom 4:1–25; 5:12–21); the syllogism, a form of argument with major and minor premises (1 Thess 4); and various forms of definition.[65]

To substantiate points, Paul frequently appeals to various institutions of the Hellenistic world, showing his connection to the culture around him and illustrating the relevance of what he is saying to the world in which the churches he addresses live. Without going into significant detail, we can mention a few of these images: Greek political terminology (Phil 1:27; 3:20; Eph 2:19), Greek games (Phil

2:16; 3:14; 1 Cor 9:24–27; 2 Cor 4:8–9; 2 Tim 4:7), Greek commercial terminology (Phlm 18; Col 2:14), Greek legal terminology (Gal. 3:15; 4:1–2; Rom 7:1–3; 13:6), the slave trade (1 Cor 7:22; Rom 7:14), and Hellenistic celebrations in honor of the emperor (2 Cor 2:15–16; 1 Thess 2:19; Col 2:15; cf. Josephus, *War* 7.132–133, 148–157).

2. Jewish Elements in Paul's Writings

Paul was a Jew, as emphasized above, but he was a Diaspora Jew, and so several of the characteristics of his approach to theological matters may almost seem as much Hellenistic as they do Jewish. Nevertheless it is worth noting a number of features of Paul's thinking that seem to reflect Jewish thought and influence.

The single most noticeable Jewish influence upon Paul's thinking and writing is clearly the OT. There are two major ways in which the OT informs Paul's thinking. The first is through direct quotation,[66] and the second is through allusion and indirect quotation, in which the OT becomes a part of the framework of Paul's thinking.[67] He directly quotes the OT numerous times, including eighty-eight direct quotations in Romans, 1 and 2 Corinthians, and Galatians alone. Romans has fifty-three direct quotations.

There are two important factors to consider with regard to Paul's quotation of the OT. The first is that Paul does not hesitate to quote the OT even when he is writing to churches that are predominantly or even perhaps almost exclusively Gentile in composition. It is true that there probably were some Jews in virtually all of the Pauline churches, except perhaps the one at Philippi (Acts 16:13 may indicate, however, the presence of a synagogue in that city), but it is still significant that the use of the OT figures large in his thinking. There are several possible explanations for this. Some scholars think that there was perhaps more Jewish presence in some of these churches than has been traditionally thought. There is significant discussion, for example, concerning the composition of the church in Rome (see ch. 10, sec. 2.F, below). But when it is considered that the major sections citing or alluding to the OT are almost indisputably addressed to the Gentile faction (see Rom 9–11; 14:1–15:13), this explanation seems insufficient. A second explanation is that the Jewish Scriptures were so influential even in the non-Jewish world that Paul could count on the Gentile population's familiarity with them. This explanation would make better sense if it could be shown that most of Paul's Gentile converts were members of the group called the Godfearers, those Gentiles who had respect for Jewish moral and theological life but were unwilling to commit themselves to full membership as proselytes (which required circumcision). There were almost assuredly some Godfearers among the converts, but the evidence (or lack of it) from the Pauline Letters leaves this explanation short of substantiation. Perhaps the most likely explanation has less to do with Paul's audience than it does with Paul himself. It seems more likely that Paul's mind and theological attitude were so suffused with biblical thinking—since much of what we now call the OT was the Bible of both Judaism and Christianity at this time—that he often simply could not construct an argument without exploring its theological and hence biblical basis and implications. For just one small example, when it came to defining God's mercy, even though he was addressing primarily Gentiles whom he had not met (and therefore whose biblical literacy he did not know), Paul cited the OT—Hos 2:23, 1:10, Isa 10:22–23; 1:9—in Rom 9:25–29 (see ch. 10, below, on the founding and nature of the Roman church). Paul relies upon the OT to substantiate what he is arguing, even if the text would have been unfamiliar to his readers.

The second major factor to consider is that the version of the OT that Paul seems to cite the most is what we call the LXX. In some instances, it is difficult to know which version Paul may be citing, since he apparently felt free to adapt the text to his particular context or may have been using another version entirely; generally speaking, however, the Greek version is the basis of his citations. A good example of the potential difficulty in sorting out Paul's use of the OT is found at 1 Cor 15:54–55, where Paul combines versions of Isa 25:8 and Hos 13:14. For the most part, the citation is a composite of the LXX and the Hebrew version of the OT, except for the word "victory," which Paul seems to have introduced if it was not from a source now unknown to us. Paul apparently felt free to provide his interpretation of the text in a nonrigid way, creating one continuous, well-structured quotation.[68] In this use of the OT Paul is unlike a number of his contemporary Jewish interpreters of Scripture, who tended to base their interpretation upon specific wording or phrasing, sometimes in a quite literalistic way (there are perhaps some similarities with Qumran exegesis), and he is more like a number of secular Hellenistic writers of the time, who felt free to embellish and alter their citations of classical sources.

Among scholars, one of the most intriguing and yet still unsettled issues in NT study focuses upon the use of the OT in the NT, now often referred to as intertextuality, that is, the way in which various texts are related and speak to each other.[69] In Pauline studies, this difficulty is as prevalent as it is with any other writer. There are at least five major means of OT interpretation used by Paul.[70] (1) In one, the typological, the author, Paul, draws an explicit correlation between a person or event in the OT (the type) and its correlative in the work of Jesus Christ (the antitype). The emphasis does not lie on any preconceived idea in the mind of the original author how this person or event might find some kind of fulfillment in the work or ministry of Jesus; this correlation is drawn by Paul. A good example is Paul's use of Ps 112:9 in 2 Cor 9:9, where he finds in the image of scattering abroad a model of generosity to be emulated by Christians at Corinth. (2) Pesher interpretation is named after the kind of OT interpretation practiced at Qumran, in which what was spoken of in the OT was seen to be fulfilled in the contemporary circumstances of the faith community. In a number of passages, Paul makes a similar equation, seeing what was foretold in the OT as specifically fulfilled in the NT era. For example, in 2 Cor 6:2, he sees the day of salvation referred to in his quotation of Isa 49:8 as having arrived in God's gracious work in Christ. (3) Allegorical interpretation resembles typological interpretation in that Paul finds explicit points of correlation between the OT antecedent and its NT fulfillment, with the difference that the points of comparison are more numerous and extended. The classic example is the use of Sarah and Hagar in Gal 4:21–31, with reference to Gen 16:15; 21:2. Paul helps the reader to see what he is doing by labeling this as allegorical interpretation.[71] In an extended comparison, Hagar represents the current Jerusalem bound or enslaved to the law of Mt. Sinai, and Sarah represents the new Jerusalem from above, free from enslavement to the law. In several ways, Paul's use of the allegorical method resembles the kind of interpretation found in the contemporary Hellenistic Jewish philosopher Philo of Alexandria. Scholars are divided on how closely Paul conforms to Philo's allegorical method, although it is fair to say that there is more than passing resemblance, especially in his treatment of such figures as Abraham. (4) In a running commentary, another means of interpretation, a number of passages may be cited and briefly commented on as the author develops his theme. An excellent example of this technique is in Rom 9–11, where Paul is developing his theme of God's faithfulness despite Israel's rejection. Paul marshals scriptural texts from throughout the OT in order to develop the various stages in his argument, which includes, for example, an elucidation of God's justice and election by citing a number of texts from Exodus and the Prophets; a substantiation of Israel's guilt and rejection by citing numerous passages from Deuteronomy and the Prophets; and a concluding description of God's faithfulness by citing a few passages from Deuteronomy and Psalms. (5) A fifth means of interpretation is midrash. Sometimes midrash is used as the generic label to describe any form of interpretation of the OT, but here it is distinguished as a means of interpretation that was commonly found among Paul's Jewish contemporaries. This method is difficult to characterize but is typified by the quotation of a passage and then a detailed commentary upon it, often including specific treatment of individual words. Paul avails himself of midrash on several occasions. He seems to make use of this technique in Gal 3:16, where he cites the specific use of the singular "seed" in Gen 12:7, 13:15, and 24:7 to point to Christ.

If these methods of interpretation are valid as applied to Paul, one cannot limit his use of the OT to a single model or category. He displayed the kind of creative flexibility that takes a given text and sees the full possibilities of it for his argument, not bound by any one model or method.

Besides Paul's explicit use of the OT, mention should be made of his allusions or indirect references to Scripture. It is difficult to define an allusion or indirect quotation; nevertheless, it is hard to deny that they exist.[72] These take a variety of forms in Paul, but the most common is probably his citation of OT figures. Frequently, as in the Gal 3 or Rom 4 discussions of Abraham,[73] these occur in conjunction with OT quotations (see above). But at other times, Paul simply mentions the figure, apparently with the expectation that his readers either know something of the person or can glean enough from the context to make the allusion useful. A number of OT figures were generally known in the Greco-Roman world. Moses, probably the best known, was thought of as a native or Jewish inhabitant of Egypt who was a lawgiver of an inferior law.[74] In 2 Cor 3:7–18, to draw a contrast with believers who are able to look directly at the radiance of the Spirit, Paul appeals to the incident recorded in Exod 34:29–35, where Moses covered his face with a veil after being in God's presence and the Israelites were not able to look on him. This well illustrates Paul's interpretive freedom in using the OT, because he moves from the veil to the unbelief of the Israelites, saying that this emblem of lack of spiritual perception remains to the current day. Paul also uses the figure of Adam, especially in 1 Cor 15 and Rom 5.[75] In Rom 5:12–21 he draws a series of contrasts between what Adam accomplished through his singular sin and the surpassing accomplishments of Christ. Although knowledge of Adam's sin enhances appreciation of the contrast, Paul apparently includes sufficient information in the context for even a person uninformed about the specifics of Adam's sin to make sense of what Paul says regarding the greatness of Christ's work on the cross. In another form of indirect quotation or allusion, Paul refers to OT passages or even words of Jesus. He only explicitly cites words of Jesus on a few occasions (e.g., 1 Cor 7:10; 9:14), which has raised questions in a number of scholars' minds. What is frequently overlooked, however, is how much Paul appears to allude to the words of Jesus, in addition to the essential facts of his life, death, and resurrection. As Wenham has pointed out, there is extensive verbal and thematic allusion in Paul's letters to the thoughts and ideas of Jesus. For example, in Rom 13:8–10 Paul apparently alludes to Jesus' words about loving one's neighbor (Mark 12:31 and parallels).[76]

Another Jewish influence in Paul is his use of forms of rabbinic argumentation and logic (t. Sanh. 7.11).[77] Contemporary rhetoricians debate the origin and development of these principles, since most of the so-called rabbinic forms of argumentation seem to have been derived from Greek sources on rhetoric as well. Some of these have been mentioned above. It is not entirely clear when the rab-

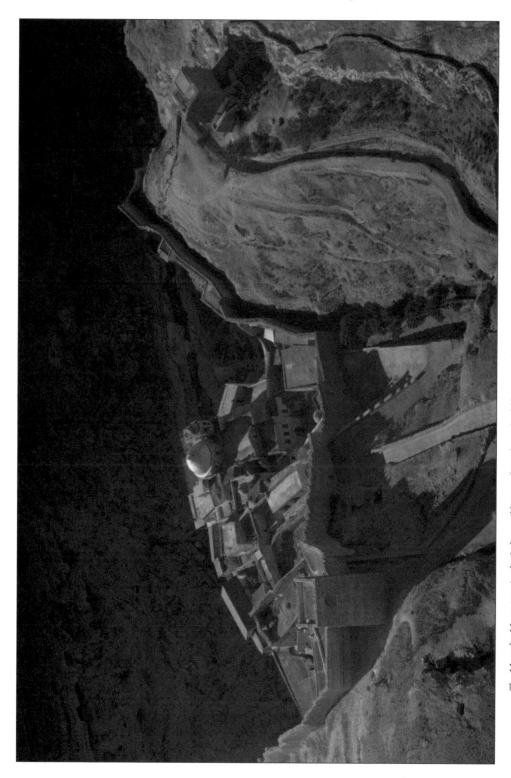

The Marsaba Monastery in the Judean wilderness dates from the fifth century but was reconstructed in the nineteenth. It is home to a dozen monks and the site of the supposed discovery of the Secret Gospel of Mark by Morton Smith. © Rohr Productions. Used with permission.

binic principles of interpretation became formulated, but even if they were later than the writing of Paul's letters, there is evidence that the principles themselves may well have been used earlier than their written codification, since they are found in Jesus' teaching also. In two of the most common of these principles used in Paul there is a logical movement from the greater to the lesser or from the lesser to the greater instances. For example, in Rom 5:10, Paul says, "If while we were enemies, we were reconciled to God through the death of his Son, much more surely, having been reconciled, will we be saved by his life." The implication is that, if humans could be made to be at peace with God while they were completely at odds with him, then once they have been brought into relation with him, it is a relatively easy thing to think of their salvation. Paul uses the opposite kind of logic as well. In 1 Cor 9:9–11, he cites the example of not muzzling an ox while it is treading grain (Deut 25:4), using this relatively trivial example as proof that if this kind of rule holds in an insignificant case, then how much more can we expect in the significant case of a preacher such as Paul getting his due.

The last influence on Paul worth mentioning is the synagogue. The history of the synagogue is difficult to reconstruct, and a great portion of the evidence for its physical plan and layout is only found in later archaeological remains.[78] Nevertheless, the synagogue had an important function in Paul's ministry, according to the book of Acts. A crucial part of Paul's missionary strategy was apparently to take advantage of the presence of a Jewish synagogue in the cities he visited on his missionary journeys. It is unfortunate that Paul does not mention his synagogal preaching in his letters, since a comparison could then be made with what he is recorded as saying in Acts—for example, in Acts 13:16–41, when he preached in Pisidian Antioch. This omission is a little surprising in light of how many Jewish references there are in Paul's letters, especially regarding his personal background. On the other hand, perhaps he fails to mention it not because he did not preach in the synagogue but because, for the most part, his practice was of short duration and/or ended in disaster. Even after a first successful sermon in Pisidian Antioch, by the next week the Jews were talking abusively against Paul (Acts 13:45). Several of the most disappointing epi-

sodes occurred in Iconium (Acts 14:1–7), Thessalonica (Acts 17:1–9), and Corinth (Acts 18:1–6). Indeed, his sizable successes in the synagogue were few. Consequently, when Paul wrote to a church founded in a city where he is recorded in Acts as having first preached in the synagogue, he may have felt that the productive result of his ministry had little to do directly with this contact. Still, it seems that Paul liked to enter a city in this way and establish at least a connection with the Jews who worshipped there.

B. Major Pauline Beliefs

Pauline beliefs are usually treated in theology volumes as all existing on the same conceptual level, as if they all were of equal importance. This is not the way that Paul's major theological beliefs come across in his letters, however. For example, as the letter structure makes clear (see sec. 4, below), material is presented in the letter form in varying places, and these places help to determine the nature of the assertions being made. Something similar appears to be going on in Paul's mind when he thinks theologically. On the one hand, Paul holds a number of essential beliefs, and he does not spend much time justifying them. Consequently, when he deals with ideas related to these, he merely invokes these concepts and does not argue for their existence. On the other hand, there are also a number of beliefs that Paul does not hold as foundational but that he clearly believes are worth arguing for. For the most part, these are beliefs that, so far as can be determined from the biblical evidence, are primarily Pauline in orientation and development. The fundamental beliefs probably would have been held by a number of Christian believers, and some of them by any person who may have had a religious orientation toward life. But Paul seems to think that the developed beliefs need to be argued for, often at some length. In the treatment that follows, the beliefs are divided into these two categories. Along the way, we will attempt to determine the origin or conceptual background of these beliefs.

A number of developed beliefs originated in Hellenistic thought, and a number originated in Jewish thought. There are others whose origin it is difficult to determine. Identification of the origin of these beliefs may well have a bearing on how they are understood and interpreted, but for the most part Paul gives sufficient explication so that interpreters have at least a basic understanding of what he is asserting.[79]

1. Fundamental Beliefs

Paul's theological and expositional method consists of applying the implications of his theologically fundamental beliefs to various situations. The following are some of the most important of Paul's fundamental beliefs.

a. God. The concept of God has been seen by at least one new Testament theologian as the center of Paul's thought.[80] Despite Paul's close ties to Hellenism, as described above, Paul never wavers in his monotheistic belief in the God of the OT.[81] Thus he is probably citing the Shema (Deut 6:4) in 1 Cor 8:6 as a Christian affirmation (Paul's language is very similar to that of the LXX). He assumes that the God of Judaism and of the OT, that is, the God of Abraham (Rom 4:3 and passim), is also the God of the NT, the Father of the Lord Jesus Christ (2 Cor 1:3) and the Father of a new people of God (Rom 9:6–9). For Paul it is God who stands behind all of the important salvific and soteriological actions of the NT. Thus God demonstrates his love for us in Christ's death (Rom 5:8), predestines, calls, justifies, glorifies (Rom 8:29–30), and judges (Rom 2:16). Paul uses the word "God" (θεός, *theos*) approximately 550 times, fully 40 percent of all the uses of this word in the NT, more than his corpus would warrant. It is difficult to specify all that he attaches to this word, which is not the only indicator in Paul's thinking about God. Nevertheless, the statistics tend to indicate how foundational the belief was for Paul.

b. Jesus Christ. In the OT there were many messiahs,[82] or many people appointed for particular divine purposes (see ch. 3, sec. 2.H, above). In other words, there was not any one conception of the Messiah. Messianic figures in the OT include kings (1 Sam 16:6; 2 Sam 1:14), priests (Exod 30:30), prophets (1 Kgs 19:16), and even Cyrus the Persian king (Isa 45:1). During the so-called intertestamental period, with the return from exile, the rule of the Greek kings—in particular the Seleucids—the Hasmonean revolt, and subsequent domination by Rome, a variety of messianic expectations formed among the Jews. It was into this environment that Jesus the Christ was born. Several of these messianic expectations included a political figure who would free the Jews of Roman tyranny, while others were expecting more of a prophetic figure. In many ways, although Jesus was pressured to fulfill a variety of messianic expectations, he did not fully satisfy the demands of any particular group. Nevertheless, in the light of his resurrection, Christianity came to accept Jesus as the Christ, or God's anointed one. The Pauline writings use the word "Christ" approximately 380 times, or over 70 percent of the times that it is used in the NT. In the vast majority of instances it appears in conjunction with Jesus' personal name (i.e., Jesus Christ). The question for biblical scholars is how Paul viewed these two names when used together. There are three options. Some say that "Christ" has become, in Paul's mind, simply a part of who Jesus is, so that it becomes another proper name for him. Others say that "Christ" always retains its titular sense whenever it is used by Paul. A third group argues that the word order is determinative for its meaning: when the order is "Christ Jesus," the titular sense is paramount (as in Rom 1:1), whereas when the order is "Jesus Christ," the word is used as a name. It is difficult to solve this issue, except to say that even though Paul probably does not make a theological claim every time he uses the wording "Jesus Christ," he clearly accepts that Jesus was God's anointed Messiah, as evidenced through his death, resurrection, and exaltation (Phil 2:6–11; 1 Cor 15:20–25). It is one of the unargued assumptions of his theological belief.

Paul goes further, however, and depicts Jesus Christ in terminology that is clearly meant to ascribe to him divine actions and existence; that is, he is seen as God or the Son of God (Rom 1:4). This is apparent in two major ways. First, in a number of Pauline passages Jesus Christ is described in terms of divine characteristics. The most important of these statements is Phil 2:6–11 (see ch. 10, below). Some have wished to see in this passage an equation of Christ with Adam, but the force of the passage is to depict Christ as in the very form of God but not retaining his equality with God. Similarly, Col 1:15–20 (see ch. 10, sec. 3.B, below) depicts Christ in terms of divine characteristics and actions, such as creation. The passage says that the universe was created in, through, and for him.[83]

The Byzantine city wall with its eastern gate at Nicaea (Iznik, Turkey) in the ancient province of Bithynia in northwestern Asia Minor.
© Rohr Productions. Used with permission.

There are two even more explicit passages, where the very words "God" and "Christ" are explicitly, grammatically linked. Despite controversy over Rom 9:5, Murray Harris has shown that the best understanding of this verse is that Christ is being described as God blessed forever. Even though this is the only explicit statement of its kind in the acknowledged Pauline Letters, in light of Jewish divine-enthronement language (Psalms 2, 110) and Greco-Roman emperor cult language, it is highly plausible, especially in a book such as Romans, that in this passage Paul is depicting Christ as God. Similarly, in Titus 2:13 Christ is called "our great God and savior."[84] The second way in which Paul describes Jesus in divine terms is the citation of OT passages that explicitly refer to God in the OT but are used by Paul to refer to Christ. Even though the term "Lord" (κύριος, *kyrios*) is used consistently in the OT to render the name of God, several Pauline passages refer to Christ by quoting an OT passage that uses "Lord." For example, in Rom 10:13, referring to Jesus Christ, Paul says, "Everyone who calls on the name of the Lord shall be saved" (Joel 2:32). In Rom 14:11, Paul writes that the Lord, probably meaning Christ, says that everyone will confess to God (Isa 45:23). Also, 1 Cor 1:31 and 2 Cor 10:10, citing Jer 9:24, speak of boasting in the Lord, and 1 Cor 2:16, quoting Isa 40:13, asks who has known the mind of the Lord, and then goes on to say that we have the mind of Christ.[85]

In conjunction with Paul's basic belief in Jesus as the Christ is his use of the phrase "in Christ" (or similar phrases, such as "in him"). Paul uses the phrase "in Christ" 165 times to describe the foundational relationship that the believer has with Christ. Defining exactly how Paul saw this relationship, however, is more problematic, since Paul does not state what he means by a person being "in Christ." Two of the older but still persistent viewpoints take the language more or less literally. For example, the German scholar Deissmann spoke of a "mystical union," in which Christ's work results in a spiritual union between Christ and the believer. Deissmann's focus on a Christian mystical element in Paul's belief is often neglected in contemporary thinking.[86] Nevertheless, while this view has an attractive emphasis upon the sense of unity between the believer and Christ, noting especially the reciprocal language in which Christ is said to be in the believer and the believer in Christ, it fails to explain how

this relationship functions. A second view, which has had great influence over the last fifty years or so, emphasizes the corporate unity between Christ and the believer. This unity verges on a physical unity in which Christ is said to indwell the believer.[87] Unfortunately, this perspective is fundamentally flawed in its reliance upon an inaccurate assessment of the concept of corporate personality in biblical thinking. It was once thought that Jews of the OT and NT did not differentiate between the individual and the group and hence saw a solidarity between believers and Christ. But the ancient Israelites, while believing in corporate responsibility (i.e., that an individual could be responsible for the group), did not have trouble differentiating individuals from the group. The most likely explanation of what Paul means by being "in Christ" is that one falls within the sphere, power, or control of Christ. As 1 Cor 15:22 and Gal 1:22 make clear, to be "in Christ" is to be in Christ's sphere of influence, especially when Paul differentiates between earthly existence, under the control of the Adamic nature, and redemptive existence, under the control of Christ. This understanding also helps to explain how this terminology becomes virtually synonymous with what it means to be called a Christian (Rom 16:7) and, in a possible instrumental sense (1 Cor 1:2), what it means to be controlled by Christ.[88]

c. Holy Spirit. The Holy Spirit plays a more significant role in Paul's teaching than many scholars have recognized.[89] Part of the neglect is probably caused by the potential ambiguity of the Greek word for spirit (πνεῦμα, *pneuma*), which can be used not only for the Holy Spirit but for any number of other spirits, thereby making some contexts ambiguous (e.g., Rom 1:9). It is difficult to know whether the spirit referred to in Phil 1:27 is a divine or a human spirit. There is also the further question whether the spirit of God and the spirit of Christ in Rom 8:9 (cf. 8:14) are meant to be treated synonymously, although it seems that they should be. For Paul, the Holy Spirit is God's means of communicating with believers since Jesus Christ left the earth (Rom 8:16, 26), and is the abiding presence of God that governs the life of the believer (Rom 8:1–17). The doctrine of the Trinity was not formulated until long after the NT was written, but the question is frequently raised regarding what assumptions Paul made about the relationship among the members of the godhead. In Paul, there are several passages where his treatment of the three members points to his belief that they function on a similar level, if not in the same way. For example, in Rom 8:9, Paul first mentions the spirit as an independent being and then as the spirit of God and the spirit of Christ, as if the spirit as an independent being is in some way an emissary for these other beings. In Rom 1:1–4, Paul mentions the functions of the three again: this time God is the originator of the gospel, the Son is the subject of the gospel message, and the spirit of holiness (assuming that this is the Holy Spirit; this is debated by commentators) is the one who declared the Son to be the Son of God with power. In 2 Cor 13:14, at the close of the letter, Paul gives the grace benediction, invoking different though parallel functions for the Lord Jesus Christ, God, and the Holy Spirit.

d. Grace. In the Pauline Letters, the word "grace," which in its noun (χάρις, *charis*) and verb (χαρίζομαι, *charizomai*) forms appears approximately a hundred times, refers to God's love or unmerited favor toward humanity. The significance of grace is illustrated in Rom 1:5, where it is seen as something to be received through Jesus Christ our Lord, almost as if it is salvation itself. In Eph 2:8 (cf. 2:5), the single most noteworthy usage of the word may rely upon the formulation by an early Pauline interpreter, but it captures well the sense in which Paul uses the term: "By grace you have been saved through faith." In the salutation of all the Pauline Letters, the "grace and peace" invocation (χάρις καὶ εἰρήνη, *charis kai eirēnē*) is part of the greeting. This usage departs from the opening of the typical Hellenistic letter in that it includes a double wish and uses noun forms in verbless clauses rather than the infinitive. What kind of theological weight should be given to such differences? Too much weight should not be given to this feature of the letter, although these differences are worth noting, since the introductory wording is formulaic for Paul. The Greek χάρις has several derived forms as well, including χάρισμα, *charisma* (1 Cor 12:4ff.), sometimes simply transliterated "charisma" or translated "grace gift." For Paul, this represents a special endowment of the Holy Spirit for work in the church.

e. Faith. The distinction traditionally drawn between the Hebrew and the Greek concepts of faith elevates the Hebrew idea as a religious one in which belief and trust are paramount and denigrates

the Greek as a nonreligious and more philosophical and rhetorical concept related to persuasion.[90] Like so many of these Greek-versus-Hebrew disjunctions, in the light of further investigation this one is shown to be in error. It now appears that in classical Greek there was an early religious use of words in this group, especially verbs, to refer to belief in gods. The LXX, in rendering its Hebrew source, maintains a similar kind of meaning, one that is further developed in Hellenistic Greek. The NT writers, including Paul, use it in a technical sense to refer to one's proper orientation of putting trust or having faith in God. The noun (πίστις, *pistis*), verb (πιστεύω, *pisteuō*), and adjective (πιστός, *pistos*) appear over 225 times in Paul's letters, virtually always with the sense specified above, except in some of the disputed letters, where, especially in the Pastoral Epistles, the noun is regularly used to refer to "what is believed" (see, e.g., Titus 1:2; Eph 4:5) rather than belief itself. Some have taken the latter meaning as an indication of later development in the meaning of this word group, in which belief as an act came to represent the content of that belief as Christianity moved toward doctrinal development.[91] But the similar use of "faith" in Phil 1:27 shows that Paul could use the word in this way in the undisputed letters (cf. also Col 2:7).

Recently, scholars have debated whether Paul's use of the phrase "faith of Jesus Christ" (πίστις τοῦ Ἰησοῦ Χριστοῦ, *pistis tou Iēsou Christou*; e.g., Rom 3:22; Gal 2:16) refers to faith or belief directed toward Jesus Christ (the objective genitive in Greek), or to the faith or faithfulness of Jesus Christ (the subjective genitive). Without denying the faithfulness of Jesus Christ or the weight of the arguments for this interpretation, we maintain that Paul appears to be referring to the faith or belief that a believer directs toward Jesus Christ. The genitive construction here is apparently shorthand for the Greek phrase "to believe in . . ." This explanation seems to make the best sense of several factors in Paul's argumentation, including his use of the verb phrase speaking of belief (Rom 3:22), and his general theological orientation.[92]

This covers most of the essential Pauline beliefs, which can be found anywhere in his letters, since they provide the basic framework for his view of life. Paul does not attempt to argue for these beliefs but, rather, assumes them, and he seems to think that his readers will as well. But these are not all that Paul wishes to convey theologically. Indeed, a good number of Paul's beliefs count among his developed beliefs.

2. Developed Beliefs

This title is not meant to imply that these beliefs in some way are less important than, or secondary to, Paul's essential beliefs. To the contrary, these developed beliefs have preoccupied scholars more than the essential beliefs, not least because they are treated at relatively greater length in Paul's letters and present plenty of material to which to respond. Whether these elements constitute the theological center of Paul's belief is frequently debated. Discussion concerning them has taken several different turns in recent scholarly publication. Earlier in this century it was common to posit what constituted Paul's theological center; recent discussion shuns the very concept of a theological center, choosing instead to emphasize the contingent nature of each of Paul's letters and hence making it difficult to conceive of a single idea, even if a complex one, constituting an essential belief. Most of the following beliefs merit attention, but it is probably fair to say that a single idea cannot be seen to stand at the center of Paul's thinking; rather, a number of these beliefs have great importance in his thinking. The following list is not meant to be complete, and the discussion is not detailed.

a. Justification by Faith. Since the time of the reformer Martin Luther, who saw the heart of the gospel expressed in this idea, justification by faith has been one of the most important theological categories for discussing Paul.[93]

On the basis of both OT and Greek usage, justification language has traditionally been defined in legal or forensic terminology, the idea being that the sinner stands before God, the righteous judge, who renders a verdict concerning him or her. When evaluated against the righteous standards of God's character, every human being is found to be a sinner and inadequate (Rom 1:18). For Paul, law-centered religion cannot be a substitute for this required righteousness (Gal 5:3ff.). On the basis of faith or belief in Jesus Christ (this phrase is an abbreviated way of referring to the death of Jesus Christ on the cross), the human can be justified by God.[94] Several modern interpreters, however, have

rejected the legal terminology and opted for eschatological language instead, in which God's righteousness is equated with his power and sovereignty. What God does in justifying sinners is a divine, regal fiat, announcing a new day when past failures are put away, debts are canceled, and guilt is removed (see Rom 1:17; 3:21, where revelatory or epiphanic language is used). God delivers the promise of a new world in which his power reaches out to capture the entire universe for his sovereignty (Rom 3:24–25).[95]

There are several questions raised by these analyses.[96] One is whether this righteousness refers to the inauguration of a new relationship with God or the restoration of an old relationship. Another concerns the time when this justification occurs in the life of the believer, which is related to its status or nature. Traditionally, justification has been used to speak of the establishment of a new relationship with God. Recent analysis of Paul and this concept, however, has tended toward seeing justification more in terms of God's relationship to his covenant community, Israel. In this sense, if the language is borrowed from OT thinking according to which God's people are expected to uphold God's righteous standards, then the thought about justification might have in mind the restoration of a previous relationship. But when Paul introduces justification in his two most significant writings on the topic, Galatians and Romans (but cf. 1 Cor 6:11; Phil 3:9), he does so in terms of the story of Abraham. He refers to Abraham believing in God and this being accounted to him as righteousness (Gen 15:6; cited in Rom 4:3, 22; Gal 3:6). The force of these discussions seems to speak of the institution of a new relationship between God and humanity, one that precedes any performance of righteousness or fulfillment of the law.

The question when this justification occurs has been an item of significant debate. Sometimes it is posited that since Paul uses several different verb tenses to speak of justification, he apparently thinks that it is something past, present, and future.[97] But since the verb tenses in Greek are not essentially time-based,[98] this argument is of little value in answering the question. When justification is discussed, however, what kind of status is this righteousness the sinner is said to have? For those who adopt the legal terminology, differentiation is often made between acquittal or exoneration and amnesty or pardon. The idea of acquittal or exoneration is probably to be rejected in light of Paul's view of sin, since they seem to imply that the sinner might well not have committed the offense for which the charge of guilt is brought. There are no innocent defendants in Paul (Rom 4:5; cf. Rom 3:24). The language of amnesty is better suited to the Pauline analysis, in which a divine pardon is offered to the undeserving.[99] But what is the status of this pardon? This is a topic that verges on the categories of systematic theology. For several scholars earlier in this century, saying that righteousness is imparted to the sinner smacked of a "legal fiction," in which the sinner is viewed as righteous when it is known full well from human experience that the individual continues to sin. This also calls into question the value of the divine decree, since it seems to be ineffectual. Others have viewed righteousness in terms of a declared or imputed righteousness, in which righteous status is given in anticipation of actual righteousness in the age to come. One's status before God is treated as if it were true, even though it will not become so until the *eschaton.* Although this view might avoid the problem of God's divine decree of righteousness, it does not mitigate the problem of God's apparently pretending to treat as righteous those who still are not.

Perhaps the best solution is to view justification in relational terms. God is seen to have established a right relationship with humans, so that a new attitude of humans to God as well as of God to humans is established. Some scholars have therefore preferred to use the invented word "rightwize" instead of "justify." Human recovery and renewal are begun, and their ultimate goals are totally righteous behavior and eternal life with a righteous God.

b. The Law. The law has probably been the single most discussed topic in recent Pauline studies, since it has implications for understanding how Paul characterizes his own Jewish background and for the nature of the Judaism he defines and confronts in his epistles.

The traditional and widely held view was that Paul saw Christianity as a religion of faith but that Judaism was a religion of works, in which one attempted (wrongly in Paul's eyes) to establish a right relationship before God by keeping the law rather than by faith. For Paul this was impossible, and so he opposed the works-righteousness of Judaism with faith in Jesus Christ.

In recent years, a number of scholars have argued for a revision of the traditional view of Paul, and consequently what he was opposing, especially in Galatians and Romans. This brief discussion will attempt to outline the issues and indicate why the traditional view is more tenable than this recent view.

In 1977, E. P. Sanders published his *Paul and Palestinian Judaism,* a discussion that was supplemented and expanded in *Paul, the Law, and the Jewish People* in 1983.[100] In these books, he redefines the Judaism of the first century and Paul's reaction to it. Sanders's work has resulted in a thorough rethinking of the Judaism of the time and Christian response to it. He has been followed by many others, the two most important probably being H. Räisänen[101] and J. D. G. Dunn.[102] The positions of these three merit examination before a response is proposed.

Räisänen has argued that the traditional view is exactly what Paul thought, that is, that Judaism saw salvation as a human achievement through works, but that Paul was wrong on this point, primarily because he is internally inconsistent in his thinking. For example, at times Paul sees the law functioning differently for Jews and Gentiles (Rom 2:12), but at other times he holds that all humans are held accountable by it (Rom 3:13–14). Sometimes Paul seems to believe that some Gentiles have fulfilled the law (Rom 2:27), but this requires a narrow view of law not applied elsewhere, where all humans are seen to be violators of the law (Rom 3:20). Sometimes Paul seems to think that the law is valid, but at other times he sees its function as having been ended. Sometimes he views sin as having been caused by the law (Rom 7:7–11), but at other times he views the law as God's response to sin (Rom 5:20; 7:14). Räisänen rightly brings to the interpreter's mind the complexity of Paul's thought regarding the law, and several of his analyses merit consideration. But his failure to appreciate the larger context of Paul's argument (e.g., differentiating several major functions of the law in Paul's thought) and his questionable juxtaposition of certain passages (e.g., verses in Rom 7) leave his reinterpretation of Paul unsatisfactory.[103] Most scholars do not, however, go so far as Räisänen.

Offering a more consistent program of interpretation, Sanders claims that "covenantal nomism"[104] provides the fundamental theological concept underlying the Jewish thinking of the first century. By covenantal nomism he means that an Israelite's place in God's plan is determined by God's gracious covenant, with obedience to the law as a response. Salvation, therefore, is not a strict weighing and evaluation of transgressions but depends, rather, upon divine mercy. The righteous Jew is not necessarily the one who can keep all of the commandments but one who accepts and remains within the covenant community. This is the form of Judaism that Paul would have known, not one in which salvation was founded upon works. Indeed, according to Sanders, Paul's thinking as a Christian is not significantly different from Jewish thinking, except that he saw salvation as resident in Jesus Christ. The problem with Judaism for Paul, according to Sanders, was that it was not Christianity. Starting from the assumption that the work of Christ had changed the basic human condition (rather than working from the human dilemma to the solution), Paul worked back to the human problem of sinfulness. For Paul, the problem with Judaism was its thinking that it had special privileges it alone was able to pursue, whereas Paul saw the same grace available to Jews and Gentiles.

Dunn, in his "new perspective" on Paul, begins from Sanders's thinking but believes that Sanders does not go far enough in his estimation of the Jewish law. For the Jew, according to Dunn, the law was an identity or boundary marker, which became a part of Jewish national consciousness as a distinctive people. Circumcision, food laws, and Sabbath observance gave the Jews a sense of privilege at being chosen by God and favored with the law and covenants. For Paul, then, for example in Rom 2, "works of the law" refers to reliance upon these boundary issues. Paul argues against the Jews' use of the law as a boundary marker for their nationalist zeal.

Several other proposals regarding "works of the law" have also been put forward. For example, it has been argued that this phrase means "works which the law does"; emphasis is put upon the law as the performer of the action.[105] But for Paul, human performance of the law is what is meant, as Rom 3 and 4 illustrate. It has also been argued that "works of the law" refers to "legalism," a distortion

of the Jewish law into an attempt to bribe God.[106] But at several points in Paul's writings, "works of the law" is treated synonymously with "law" (Gal 2:16, 21; Rom 3:20, 21, 28) and opposed to faith (Rom 4:1–6), and thus seen not as negative in and of itself, though not to be relied upon for right status with God.

Sanders and Dunn's new or revised perspective on Judaism, Paul, and the law has met with many supporters. At the least it has made all interpreters more sensitive to issues of Pauline interpretation, even though it has not, in our minds, proved convincing. Nevertheless, Sanders and Dunn do not see fundamental issues in this discussion in the same way. For example, Dunn criticizes Sanders for taking "works of the law" as a synonym of "law," but this equation of the two is exactly what Paul seems to be making. At several places, since Paul equates "works of the law" with "law," Paul cannot simply be talking about the law taken in its restrictive sense, as Dunn believes (see Gal 2:16 vs. 2:21; 3:11; 5:4; Rom 3:20, 28 vs. 3:20, 21). "Works of the law" has something to do with the Mosaic law in its origin, nature, and function, or so it seems to be treated by Paul, as Rom 3:20–28 illustrates, where the commandments referred to appear to be from the Decalogue, which is cited above at Rom 2:21–22. Such specialization of meaning as Dunn requires is also unwarranted in the light of Paul's discussion of Abraham and his "works" preceding the giving of the law.

With respect to Sanders's and similar analyses, there are several further lines of criticism that could be pursued but that will only be summarized here.[107] First, there is serious question whether the Jewish evidence has been correctly interpreted. Sanders attempts to characterize a pattern of religious belief, but this pattern has struck many interpreters as being fairly selective. For example, the OT evidence itself is more works-oriented than Sanders admits. Numerous passages, such as Lev 18:3–5 and passages in Deuteronomy (e.g., 4:1; 5:33; 6:24–25; 8:1; 11:26–28), equate keeping God's commandments with life, and disobedience with condemnation and death. Furthermore, the rabbinic evidence he cites is admittedly late (i.e., second century A.D. and later), and his attempts to argue for early traditions are not always convincing. There is also some special pleading when, to deny the value of evidence that seems to speak of works in the rabbinic sources, he claims that these references assume the covenantal context that he presupposes. For example, after examining an important passage regarding the belief of the rabbi Akiba, one scholar has concluded, "Careful exegesis of *m. Aboth* 3:16–17 demonstrates that the traditional view of first-century rabbinic soteriology as based on works-righteousness is not completely based upon pseudo-scholarship as claimed by Sanders."[108] Recent analysis has also argued that in a number of texts roughly contemporary with the period of the NT there is a works-oriented scheme clearly evident, such as in the *Psalms of Solomon* (e.g., 10:4) and in 1 Macc 2:51–52: "Remember the deeds of the ancestors, which they did in their generations; and you will receive great honor and an everlasting name. Was not Abraham found faithful when tested, and it was reckoned to him as righteousness?" Several Qumran documents seem to attest to similar belief, such as the *Manual of Discipline* (e.g., 1QS XI, 3, 12). Especially notable is the recently published Qumran document *Miqsat Maaseh ha-Torah* (4QMMT), which probably dates to a little earlier than the time of the NT.[109] This text explicitly states that "works of the law" (a phrase apparently unparalleled in other extrabiblical Jewish literature, except for a possible disputed reading in 4Q174) will be accounted as righteousness, probably citing Gen 15:6 with reference to Abraham, the very text that Paul cites in Rom 4 and Gal 3, when he says that Abraham's faith was counted to him as righteousness. *Miqsat Maaseh ha-Torah* states, "We have written to you of some of the works of the law . . . for your good and for [that] of your people. . . . And this will be accounted to you for righteousness, because you are doing what is right and good before Him (4Q398 2 II)." The word for "works" is cognate to the verb "doing," and the wording regarding accounting righteousness is very similar to that of Gen 15:6 in the Hebrew Masoretic Text. *Miqsat Maaseh ha-Torah* therefore seems to establish that there were Jews around the first century who thought of works as leading to righteousness. Thus, not only has Paul rightly understood this segment of Judaism; he uses the same OT texts in support of his discussion of the Law, but concluding exactly the opposite. *Miqsat Maaseh ha-Torah* equates doing "works of the law" with righteousness, but Paul states that it is apart from "works of the law"—by faith—that one is

made righteous. The traditional understanding of Paul's view of righteousness in Judaism is apparently vindicated.

Second, Sanders's reading of the Pauline texts is subject to severe scrutiny. Besides the fact that Sanders is addressing Palestinian Judaism—and Diaspora Judaism may have been different—Sanders's framework has a legalistic element to it, in which staying in the covenant is predicated upon works, as he admits. Even if the evidence were to indicate that the Jews believed in covenantal nomism as Sanders outlines it (and this is debatable, as the evidence shows), it appears that Paul did not envision such a combination of mercy and deeds but grace alone (e.g., Gal 5:4; Rom 9:30–31; 11:20–21, where faith, not works, is the issue). Paul did not think in terms similar to those of a covenantal nomism of Judaism, at least as Sanders relates them. Sanders contends that Paul's complaint against Judaism was that it was not Christianity, that Paul believed that salvation was in Jesus Christ, and that he worked back from this conclusion to the problem (from solution to plight). But, as Sanders must admit, in Rom 1–3 Paul works from plight to solution.[110] Furthermore, in Sanders and Dunn's reckoning, there was a role for the law in salvation, but this does not seem to conform to Paul's view when he categorically excludes the role of the law (e.g., Rom 4:13–16). For Paul, it is not the law of the OT that Christians are to follow but a new law of love, or love of Christ (Gal 5:14, 22–23). At least in Paul's mind this does not seem to be nomism, since Paul at several points contrasts his view of how one gets right with God by faith with a justification that comes about by law.

Furthermore, for Paul, one's relationship is not covenantal, at least as this is understood by Sanders in terms of an entire community of people. For Paul, one's gracious standing before God on the basis of faith is apparently personal (Rom 3:28, and the instance of Abraham). This is not to deny the element of grace in Judaism (this has perhaps been overemphasized in recent thought) but only to suggest that, at least in Paul's eyes, Judaism would at best be characterized as a system that depended upon grace *and* works. For Paul, this was not good enough, since God's grace mediated through faith must constitute the sole basis for justification (Rom 4:13–16), even if good works (not necessarily doing the law) followed from this through the work of the Spirit (Rom 8:1–11).[111]

Paul rightly thought that at least some, if not most, of the Judaism of his time believed that salvation was intimately connected with works, and he rejected this in affirming that salvation was only by God's grace through faith. Consequently, statements in the Pauline writings that reject the doing of the law and assertions that justification is on the basis of the death and resurrection of Christ (e.g., Gal 2:21) are not simply rejections of the markers that gave Israelites their identity and pride, nor simply christological statements, but also descriptions of the futility of attempts to secure justification through human actions.

The difficulty in defining Paul's thinking regarding the law (νόμος, *nomos*)—in large part caused by misguided linguistic analysis—has been recently overcome, at least in part, by the application of principles of modern linguistics to the analysis of the terminology.[112] The traditional approach began with the assumption that "law" means something specific (often on the basis of the noun appearing with the article) and often means one thing, or primarily one thing. Thus Paul was usually seen to be referring to the Jewish law, or at least to one of its forms, such as the Mosaic law in its entirety or the law specifically in its demands or requirements that must be kept. It might be useful to define "law" first in terms of its sense within the Greek language, and then in terms of what it might denote in the real world of Paul's day, before seeing how Paul uses it to refer to specific instances of law. The word νόμος has the sense of any standard, guide, or control on behavior or conduct. It might, then, be used to denote a variety of natural and human laws, such as the laws of nature and the laws or customs of specific societies and organizations. Paul seems to use it to refer, in many instances, to the Jewish law or various permutations of it (e.g., Romans and Galatians), but also to other human laws (Rom 7:23), specific principles of conduct (Rom 2:14), the law seen generically (Rom 4:15), and even principles by which the world functions (Rom 3:27; 8:2). In other words, it is impossible to use a single understanding of "law" to understand the variety of Paul's use of this single term.

c. Reconciliation. Traditionally justification has been seen as the center of Paul's theology; some recent interpreters, however, have instead seen reconciliation as the central idea.[113] Justification language appears frequently in the main Pauline Letters, but the language of reconciliation (verb καταλλάσσω, *katallassō;* noun καταλλαγή, *katallagē*) or peace (εἰρήνη, *eirēnē*) occurs relatively infrequently. Justification language has ties to OT language, but reconciliation language owes its origins almost exclusively to the Hellenistic world. Reconciliation language is treaty language, in which parties at enmity, including God and humanity, have their hostility overcome and peaceful relations restored. For Paul, this can only occur through the work of Christ.[114]

Four passages are important for understanding Paul's thought about reconciliation. The first is 2 Cor 5:18–21, in which Paul proclaims what God has done through Christ. Some think that this passage is supplemented by traditional material (sayings that were already in use in the early church), but this is unlikely, especially since there is little evidence for previous theological usage of reconciliation terminology, and no precedent for the way Paul uses it here. In 2 Cor 5:18–19 God is the one who effects reconciliation "through Christ." In a difficult phrase, probably best rendered, "God was reconciling the world to himself through Christ," Paul, by using the active voice form of the verb, is the first extant author to speak of the offended party (i.e., God) initiating reconciliation. So it is God who reconciles "us" or "the world" to himself, through the work of Christ on the cross. Similar thought is conveyed in Rom 5:8–11, in which Paul establishes a clear (though difficult to define) relationship between justification and reconciliation (note the parallel phrasing in Rom 5:1 and vv. 9, 10). In Rom 5:1, 10, peace with God and reconciliation are explicitly equated. The sense is that of an objective well-being, in which harmonious relations are established between God and humanity, who are clearly said to be enemies. The means of reconciliation are emphasized in Rom 5, where "through our Lord Jesus Christ" is used three times (vv. 1, 11, 21; cf. v. 10).

Reconciliation language is also found in Col 1:20–22. Understanding of this passage is often linked with interpretation of the so-called hymn in 1:15–20 (it is difficult to prove the "hymn's" pre-Pauline existence). In Col 1:20, 22, both God and Christ are apparently seen as the agents or initiators of reconciliation. This indicates a shift in Paul's thinking from seeing God as the sole initiator to seeing Christ as the coinstigator of reconciliation with him. Nevertheless, this pattern is consistent with the depiction of Christ in Col 1. As in the other reconciliation passages, in Col 1 the agent of reconciliation is Christ, or the work of Christ on the cross (Col 1:20, 22), but the goal of reconciliation here is also Christ (the end for which reconciliation is accomplished), who is reconciling all things, including things upon the earth and things in heaven. This cosmic reconciliation has aroused significant discussion, since it leaves open a universalism not found elsewhere in Paul. What is probably meant here, however, is that God's reconciling activity is a general principle that encompasses the entire cosmos. Ephesians 2:14–17 is the fourth and final reconciliation passage (cf. Eph 1:9-10). Colossians 1 introduces cosmic reconciliation (the idea that the entire cosmos is in some way reconciled), but Eph 2 addresses the relationship of Jews and Gentiles. Paul states that, through reconciliation, Jews and Gentiles are said to become "one new person" and that the dividing wall of hostility between them is torn down.[115] Thus, reconciliation unites humanity and then reconciles humanity to God. Christ is said to be the agent of this reconciliation, with God as its goal, again effected by the work of Christ on the cross.

d. Sanctification or Holiness. Paul uses a number of different words and phrases to describe sanctification or holiness. This is an important category for him because it includes both soteriological status and ethical and eschatological perfection.[116] In other words, this concept describes a condition of those who are followers of Christ, instructing them in the importance of the consequential actions of salvation. Paul desires holy and pure behavior by followers of Christ, even though he realizes that complete attainment in this life is not possible.

Like many of Paul's theological ideas, sanctification overlaps with some other categories of his thought (e.g., 1 Cor 6:11), and his letters are often concerned to define the differences and similarities. On the one hand, in 1 Thess 3–4, sanctification appears to be the consequence of justification. Having finished the body of his letter in ch. 3, Paul turns to ethical instruction in ch. 4. He says that God's will for the Thessalonians is their sanctification (1 Thess 4:3, 7), and he defines this in terms of purity, especially with regard to sexual morality. On the other hand, in Rom 6:19–23 (part of the body of the letter), sanctification appears to overlap with justification, but without being equated with it. The difference is that, in this instance, it appears that sanctification has more of a soteriological than an ethical dimension. In Rom 6:19–23, in the context of Paul's theological argument of Rom 1–8, especially the theme of "life in the Spirit" (Rom 6:1–8:39), he speaks of sanctification as the goal of justification. If justification is the initiatory salvific experience, sanctification may well include this initiation as well as look forward to the end of the entire process, eternal life.

e. Salvation. Salvation in Paul's thinking seems to overlap with a number of other beliefs.[117] Words with the idea of saving—including "salvation" (σωτηρία, *sōtēria*), "save" (σώζω, *sōzō*) and "savior" (σωτήρ, *sōtēr*)—which are used approximately sixty times in Paul, can be used by him to refer to a number of divine acts with respect to the human. For example, salvation terminology in Rom 5:9–10 seems to overlap with both justification and reconciliation. Salvation for Paul includes being delivered from sin, from death, and from this age, with the goal of eternal life (Rom 8:23–24). Thus, salvation is seen to be in keeping with the "secular" concept of savior as benefactor, in which one has, in some sense, a personal or moral obligation to look out for and take care of an inferior, who may well depend upon the beneficence of the superior. In several of the Pauline contexts salvation is seen to constitute an inclusive term that spans the extent of God's saving activity—for example, in Phil 2:12. For another example, in Rom 1:16–17, salvation is defined in three ways, in terms of (1) justification as an initiatory event, corresponding perhaps to salvation as deliverance from sin and death in other contexts (Rom 3–4); (2) reconciliation as a sustaining event, corresponding to God as benefactor (Rom 5); and (3) sanctification as a life preparatory for eternity (Rom 6–8). In Eph 2:5, 8, salvation is the capstone for describing the process by which humanity is brought into right relationship with God.

f. The Triumph of God. Recent thought has emphasized Paul as an apocalyptic thinker.[118] By this is meant that Paul looked forward to certain endtime occurrences with cosmic, universal, and definitive implications, such as universal judgment, which is to be brought about as a result of the death, resurrection, and return of Christ. This thought is, at many points, consistent with contemporary Jewish apocalyptic thinking and characterized by God's vindication of his covenantal promises made to Israel and the nations (see Rom 9–11). This implies a type of universalism, in which universal salvation was held out as a hope by Paul for those who heard the gospel and responded in obedience and faith. Paul is not as dualistic a thinker as many of his Jewish contemporaries, in that he does not make a rigid distinction between this age and the age to come but, rather, sees a continuum (Rom 8:29–30). Instead, Paul sees the church as living in this tension between the ages, between the first and second comings of Christ, as well as between the powers of life and death. For Paul, this end of time had an imminency to it, but an imminency increasingly tempered by the reality that Christ's return might not be in Paul's own lifetime. In 1 Thess, Paul depicts an imminent return with nothing to impede it (see 1:9–10; 4:13–5:8). But by the time of writing Romans (e.g. 1:17–18), Paul also sees righteousness and wrath as apocalyptic terms, using them in anticipation of Christ's return, in hope for what is not yet seen or fulfilled. By the time of writing Philippians (e.g., 1:21–24; 2:17), Paul fully considers the possibility of his own death before Christ's return.

g. The Gospel. The term often translated "gospel" or "good news" is used approximately eighty times by Paul in its noun (εὐαγγέλιον, *euangelion*) and verb (εὐαγγελίζομαι, *euangelizomai*) forms. There is ongoing debate on how much Paul knew about the earthly Jesus, since he does not cite many incidents from his earthly life.[119] Paul shares, in common with other NT writers, especially those of the Gospels themselves (in particular Matthew and Luke), the perception that Jesus' work on the cross constituted a turning point in humanity's relation to God. Paul seems to use this terminology of good news in at least three ways (see ch. 8, sec. 1, above). In the first, he refers to the gospel as good news that runs contrary to competing secular good news. The same Greek terminology was often used to refer to a significant secular event, such as the birth of a son to the emperor or the celebration of the emperor's birthday. There cannot help but be more than a little irony in Paul's mind, for example, when he refers to himself in a letter addressed to the church in the capital of the Roman Empire as a servant of Christ Jesus, an apostle, and one set apart for God's good news (not the em-peror's or any other human's) (Rom 1:16–17). For Paul, God is the origin or source of this good news, not some secular authority (see ch. 3, sec. 4.B, above, on the emperor cult).[120] Paul's good news directly confronts the Roman view of the emperor as savior or benefactor when he sees God at work in bringing the good news through the death and resurrection of his son (see Rom 5:7). Second, Paul views the good news in terms of its objective accomplishments. Jesus Christ's death on the cross and resurrection constitute the content of the gospel (Rom 1:3–4; cf. 1 Cor 15:3–4). Consequently, for Paul, the gospel then becomes shorthand for, or a statement of, essential Christian belief, that is, the belief that leads to life or condemnation and is to be obeyed (Gal 2:5, 14; Rom 2:16; 10:16). Third, Paul views the good news in terms of a personal motivational factor. For Paul, the gospel was integral with his calling as an apostle to the Gentiles, not only as the substance of his belief but as a very real part of who he was. Paul claims that he received his gospel from the risen Christ, not from any human source, and to be opposed to it is to be accursed (Gal 1–2; Rom 15:15–20).

h. The Church. The church forms an important backdrop to Paul's thinking, and in this sense constitutes one of the basic assumptions of his thinking and writing. He specifically addresses several of his letters to the churches located in Corinth, Galatia, and Thessalonica (Paul, however, uses more than simply the Greek word ἐκκλησία, *ekklēsia*, to refer to this concept of "church"). Even though he does not address specific churches in some others of his letters, in these an ecclesiastical setting is still understood (e.g., Philemon, Romans, Ephesians, Colossians, and the Pastorals, where church order and structure are debated). Consequently, there are numerous references in Paul's writings to a specific church or to specific churches—the group of believers that probably met together within house churches in a given city to worship (see, e.g., 1 Cor 11:18; 16:19; Gal 1:22). Paul assumes the existence of these churches, quite frequently addressing his letters to issues that have obviously arisen in the conduct and administration of these local bodies of believers.

This is not all that Paul says regarding the church, however. He also uses the term "church" in a more widespread sense to refer to the community of believers that exists without reference to the confines of a given city or local community. When referring to believers joined by their common faith, Paul uses a number of different analogies or metaphors. The most important (and certainly the most widely debated) is the analogy of the body.[121] In 1 Cor 12:12–28, Paul speaks of believers in terms of a body where there are numerous parts, some that are traditionally held to be more important or useful and some that are regarded as less important or even trivial. Paul's point is that just as the body has many parts, some of which are more highly regarded than others but all are vitally necessary for constituting the body, so it is with the body of believers. This body of believers is called the body of Christ, with the implication that the church constitutes Christ's body or is to be equated with Christ in his spiritual existence. The apostles, prophets, teachers, miracle workers, and so forth form a hierarchy within this body.

Similar, though not identical, language is used in Eph 5:22–32, where the analogy of the body is also used. In this context, the church is equated with Christ's body, and Christ is depicted as the head of the church. There has been significant debate among scholars whether these analogies can be made to correlate. On the one hand, in the Corinthian analogy the entire church is equated with Christ, and no specific differentiation of the head is made, with the implication that the various positions of leadership within the church are to be equated with the head, the hands, and so on as valuable parts of the body. On the other hand, in the Ephesian analogy, the differentiation is explicitly between the church as the body and Christ as the head having a position of authority over it. Whatever one decides regarding Ephesian authorship, it is clear that the basis of both passages is a Pauline vision of the church and its relation to Christ, whether or not Paul himself expanded or made more explicit the analogy with Christ as the head.

Paul also uses a number of other terms to speak of the church. These have proved of less significance so far as scholarly discussion goes, but their appropriateness to the individual letters in which they are found has literary and epistolary significance. For example, in Gal 6:10, Paul speaks of the church in terms of a household or family. This is entirely appropriate in the context of the controversy in Galatia, in which there were Christians who threatened to disrupt the familial unity of the Galatian church. In Phil 3:20, Paul speaks of members of the church as enjoying a common citizenship in heaven. It is likely that the Philippian church, for the most part enjoying Paul's praise, in light of its privileged position as an independent city populated by Roman citizens, came to put undue pride in its political privileges and opportunities. Paul takes this occasion to remind them that their citizenship is not primarily earthly but, rather, one that they enjoy in a heavenly realm. In 1 Cor 1:9, Paul speaks of God having called the believers of Corinth into fellowship with his Son Jesus Christ. Again he has used an appropriate metaphor for the situation of his readers, as he is responding to a church that has found difficulty with unity, threatening to be divided and factionalized by various groups claiming to owe allegiance to various leaders or figures.

i. Jesus' Death and Resurrection. The last concept in this brief summary of Paul's major teachings concerns Christ's death and resurrection. It has been mentioned above at several points (see, e.g., the discussions of justification and reconciliation in secs. a and c, above) that Paul believes that the work of God through Christ for believers is predicated upon the death and resurrection of Jesus Christ. In this sense, Paul's belief in the death and resurrection of Jesus Christ is not something that he argues for but something that he assumes. He does, however, at several places treat Christ's death and resurrection in terms of a theological framework that shows their special significance (e.g., 1 Cor 15:3–8; 1:18–25). This salvation-historical view of redemptive history is worth noting in Paul's thought. Paul was obviously not the first to link these two events together or to see them as fundamental to Christian belief. For example, in 1 Cor 15:3–4, possibly citing a passage formulated early on in the church and used to encapsulate the essence of Christian confession, Paul says that he passed on to the Corinthians what he received as of first importance: that Christ died for sins, was buried, and was raised on the third day. There are similar formulations elsewhere in the Pauline corpus (see, e.g., 1 Thess 4:14; 1 Tim 3:16).

There are at least two other noteworthy elements to Paul's view of Christ's death. First, he puts an emphasis upon the crucifixion or the cross of Christ. Eighteen times he refers to the cross or crucifixion in his letters, not as a heroic or commendable event but as one that was ignominious and disgraceful.[122] For example, in 1 Cor 1:18, he refers to the message of the cross as foolishness for those who are perishing (cf. 2:2), and in Gal 3:13, he cites Deut 21:23 and its reference to the curse upon anyone who is crucified. This ignominy, however, is a part of what Paul sees as a very important element of the progress of salvation history, one that Christ fulfilled in his death and resurrection. Second, Paul sees the death of Christ as sacrificial, involving the shedding of blood. There is repeated debate regarding how Paul depicts Christ as a "sacrifice of atonement" in Rom 3:25 (whether Christ is seen as the seat of mercy or simply the means by which sins or God's wrath is turned away, this reference involves OT sacrificial imagery), where his blood is depicted as the means by which this process is conducted (see also Rom 5:9). Third, Paul sees the resurrection as a necessary extension of Christ's death. In Paul's mind the death was crucial, but the resurrection was a confirmation of what God was seen to be doing in Christ (Rom 4:25). Paul says that the resurrection marks the point at which God's son was seen to be the Son of God with power (Rom 1:4) and that the resurrection is the confirmation of the validity of faith. Without the resurrection to confirm the validity of Christ's death, humans remain in their sinful condition (1 Cor 15:17).[123]

These events are part of a larger framework that Paul seems to work from, one in which the plan of God is depicted as being redemptive, with Christ's death and resurrection the climactic event in God's dealings with humanity. First of all, Paul speaks of the electing or predestining purposes of God that find their fulfillment in the work of God in Christ. For example, in Rom 8:33, Paul asks who will bring a charge against one of God's elect, since Christ, the one who died and was raised, is seated at God's right hand interceding (see also Rom. 9:11; cf. Eph 1:4, 5, 9). Second, Paul at various places mentions significant individuals who formed a crucial part of God's redemptive plan. The first was Adam, who established the sinful human condition. It was his disobedience that required a suitable and concomitant response by God to redeem humans from their condition, having been constituted sinners after Adam (Rom 5:12–21; cf. 1 Cor 15:22; 1 Tim 2:13–14). Christ, as the last Adam, undid the effects of Adam's sin.[124] Next in Paul's chronology is apparently Abraham, the father of

Israel, who was justified or reckoned righteous before God not on the basis of works or any accomplishment (certainly not the fulfillment of the law, which did not come for over four hundred years) but through his faith. Paul shows that the means of redemption for humanity has always been the same, through faith (Rom 4; Gal 3). Another figure, one more enigmatic for Paul's progress of salvation history, is Moses. Moses was revered as the one who brought God's law to the people of God (Paul may have believed that the law had been mediated by heavenly beings and did not come directly from God; this may explain his negative view of it: see Gal 3:20), and was one of the few Jewish heroes respected or even known by non-Jews. In Paul's eyes, he too points toward the work of Jesus Christ. When Moses had been with God, he had a radiance that could not be looked upon by the Israelites, who were living under the old covenant. Those who live under the new covenant reflect the unmediated glory (2 Cor 3:7–8). In Christ, the mystery of God, that is, his redemptive work through Christ's death and resurrection, has been revealed. The term "mystery" is used slightly differently in its several instances in the Pauline writings, but it seems to center on what God has done in Christ, whether it involves believers seen as a whole or Jews and Gentiles (see 1 Cor 2:7 and frequently; cf. Col 2:2; Eph 6:19).

Although other topics could well be introduced regarding Paul's teachings—and there are many, such as prophetic criticism, adoption, and various images of Christ[125]—those discussed above provide a sufficient enough introduction to his thought to enable the reader to grasp several of his major ideas and emphases.

3. PAUL'S MISSION AND MINISTRY: AN OUTLINE

Any reconstruction of Paul's missionary ministry must be extrapolated from the available literary texts, even when the book of Acts is used as one of the sources in this reconstruction. Nowhere does Acts label Paul's several journeys as "missionary" journeys, and it is even disputed whether there were three. As the chronologies below try to illustrate, there are a number of ways to construe the evidence regarding Paul's travels, and anywhere from three (the standard number) missionary journeys to five (some combine what we have called the second and third journeys into a single endeavor) can be counted—assuming that they are to be given such a label. Paul's missionary journeys have often been understood as well-planned, organized, and sponsored ventures, but this is perhaps not the best way to think of them.

A stairway to the Tombs of the Kings, Jerusalem, burial site of Helena, queen of Adiabene in the first century A.D. She was a convert to Judaism and chose to be buried here. She cared for the people of the city during the famine (Acts 11:27–30). See Josephus, Ant. 20.17-53, 92-96; and Eusebius, Hist. eccl. 2.12.1–3. Photo Lee M. McDonald.

As for organization, the church at Antioch seems to have been central in planning and supporting several of the ventures (Acts 13:1–3; 15:1–2; 15:35–16:1). Even this is shrouded in some mystery: even though Paul seems to have begun from Antioch on several occasions, very little is known about what role the church played apart from its commissioning Paul and Barnabas for the first venture into Asia Minor. Some have argued that, after Paul's confrontation with Peter, mentioned in Gal 2:11–21, Paul was no longer welcome in Antioch.[126] In fact, it is not proper, according to the account in Acts, to speak of *Paul* and Barnabas on even the first missionary venture, since the indication in Acts is that this first expedition, on which John Mark also went, was led by Barnabas, at least in its early stages (Acts 13:1). Nor did the journeys always return to Antioch; several of these journeys ended up in Jerusalem (Acts 21:17). At least Paul's third trip to Jerusalem—during which he was apparently falsely accused and arrested[127]—was his own idea, insti-

gated by his desire to bring the collection from the Gentile churches to Jerusalem (it is unknown how large the collection was or whether it got to Jerusalem and into the proper hands, since it is not mentioned in the account in Acts 21).[128] There are other factors to consider in plotting the Pauline chronology as well. One is how to describe Paul's ministry before he appears to take a prominent part in Acts and before he began his letter writing. Another is how to characterize his ministry on the way to Rome, at Rome, and possibly (see the chronology below) after his release from imprisonment in Rome (if in fact he was released before being rearrested and killed under Nero). All of these questions merit some comment as we reconstruct the Pauline chronology and try to gain some insight into the strategy of Paul's mission.

Scholars continue to debate the merits and validity of using Acts in the reconstruction of a Pauline chronology. That offered below relies heavily upon what is offered in Acts and considers its contribution to constitute an important and indispensable supplementation to what is revealed in only sketchy form in Paul's letters.[129] Besides legitimate dispute over the ordering of the chronology itself, there is also much discussion about the exact dates of these events and about how the dates of composition of the Pauline Letters fit within this chronology. Thus, the following chronology is offered with the recognition that much of the dating is tentative, even though we have attempted to make it as accurate as possible.

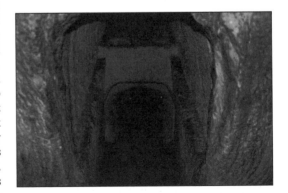

Queen Helena's tomb inside the Tomb of the Kings in the mid–first century was hidden in a secret section of the tombs to protect the burial site from thieves. It was only discovered in the last century. Photo Lee M. McDonald

A. Paul's Conversion and the Early Years (ca. A.D. 33–47)

1. Conversion (Gal 1:15–16; Acts 9:3–7; cf. Acts 22:3–16, 26:12–18)
   A.D. 33–34. There are apparent discrepancies between the accounts of Paul's conversion, but the basic account of his encounter on the road to Damascus when he was on his way to persecute the church is consistent.

2. Damascus (Acts 9:8–22)
   Paul spent several days in Damascus, apparently before being compelled to leave because of a plot to kill him (Acts 9:23; 2 Cor 11:32–33).

3. Arabia (Nabatea) (Gal 1:17a) and Damascus (Gal 1:17b–18)
   A.D. 33–37. Recorded in Galatians, though not in Acts, are Paul's three-year stay in the Arabian desert and his return to Damascus. It is uncertain whether the attempt to kill him took place in his first or second visit to Damascus, although the dates for the rule of the ethnarch of King Aretas are probably A.D. 37–40, in-dicating the second visit (Acts 9:23; 2 Cor 11:32–33).

4. Jerusalem (Gal 1:18–20; Acts 9:26–29)
   A.D. 37. This is Paul's first visit to Jerusalem, where he stayed for at least fif-teen days, speaking with the apostles and debating with the Greek Jews until they tried to kill him.

5. Syria and Cilicia (Gal 1:21; Acts 9:30)
   A.D. 37–47. Paul apparently spent ten years in the Tarsus area of Syria.

6. Antioch (Acts 11:25–26)
   Barnabas sought Paul out and brought him to Syrian Antioch, where they met with the church and taught together.

7. Jerusalem (Gal 2:1–10; Acts 11:27–30, 12:25)
   A.D. 47. This is probably Paul's second visit to Jerusalem, the so-called famine visit to bring aid to the church in Judea. It apparently occurred fourteen years (less likely seventeen years) after Paul's conversion, referred to in Gal 1:23. Many would disagree, however, that these passages are referring to the same meeting (see ch. 10, below, on Galatians).

B. First Missionary Journey (Acts 13–14; A.D. 47–49)

1. Antioch (Acts 13:1–3)
   Barnabas and Saul were sent on the first missionary journey from the church at Syrian Antioch. They departed from the port at Seleucia for the first leg of their journey to Cyprus (Acts 13:4).

2. Cyprus (Acts 13:4–12)
   a. Salamis (Acts 13:5). Barnabas and Paul preached in the synagogue and were accompanied by John Mark.
   b. Paphos (Acts 13:6–12). At Paphos, Elymas the false prophet was blinded, and as a result, the proconsul believed.

3. Asia Minor (Acts 13:13–14:26)
   a. Perga (Acts 13:13). Paul and his companions sailed to Perga in Pamphylia, where John Mark left them.

b. Pisidian Antioch (Acts 13:14–50). Paul preached in the synagogue at Pisidian Antioch in Phrygia, but the Jews stirred up the people so that Paul and Barnabas were forced to leave.

c. Iconium (Acts 13:51–14:6). Paul and Barnabas went to the synagogue and preached with success in Iconium in Phrygia, but unbelieving Jews stirred up the people against them, and they had to flee.

d. Lystra (Acts 14:6–20). After performing a healing, Paul and Barnabas were mistaken by those in Lystra in Lycaonia for the gods Hermes and Zeus. When agitators from Iconium and Antioch arrived, Paul was stoned and left for dead.

e. Derbe (Acts 14:20–21). Paul and Barnabas preached in Derbe in Lycaonia and then returned by way of Lystra, Iconium, and Pisidian Antioch, strengthening the churches as they went (14:21–23).

f. Perga (Acts 14:24–25). In the region of Pamphylia, they preached in the city of Perga.

g. Attalia (Acts 14:25–26). From the port of Attalia in Pamphylia, Paul and Barnabas sailed back to Syrian Antioch.

4. Syrian Antioch (Acts 14:26–28)

At Antioch, Paul and Barnabas gave a report of all that God had done, and stayed with the disciples.

Galatians? A.D. 49. Some place Galatians much later (see ch. 10, below), but on the basis of the lack of reference to the Jerusalem Council (Acts 15), the equation of Gal 2:1 with Acts 11:27–30, and the Roman regional nomenclature at the time, it is most likely that Galatians was sent to the churches in Pisidian Antioch, Iconium, Lystra and Derbe, that is, the Phrygian Galatian region, evangelized on Paul's first missionary trip. (The South Galatia theory is discussed in ch. 10, sec. 2.A, below.)

5. Jerusalem (Acts 15:1–35)

A.D. 49. According to Acts, Paul and Barnabas represented the position of the Antioch church at a meeting in Jerusalem. Many critical scholars doubt that such a meeting took place. Others think that Paul's mentioning of going to Jerusalem in Gal 2:1–10 is a reference to this meeting (see ch. 10. below, on Galatians).

C. Second Missionary Journey (Acts 15:36–18:22; A.D. 50–52)

1. Antioch (Acts 15:36–40)

After a split with Barnabas over John Mark, who had left the pair at Perga in Pamphylia, Paul took Silas and departed on the second missionary journey.

2. Syrian Cilicia (Acts 15:41)

Paul traveled through the region of Cilicia in the province of Syria, strengthening the churches.

3. Phrygian Galatia—Derbe and Lystra (Acts 16:1–6)

Paul preached in the area (and possibly sent emissaries to Colossae), circumcising Timothy in Lystra, whose father was a Greek but whose mother was a Jewess. Paul and his companions were forbidden by the Spirit from entering Bithynia (Acts 16:7–8).

Galatians? A.D. 50–52. Galatians may have been written at this time, which would coincide with either the southern or the northern hypothesis discussed in ch. 10, below.

4. Troas (Acts 16:8–10).

    In Troas in Asia, Paul had a vision of a man of Macedonia calling him and his companions to Macedonia. They traveled from Troas to Samothrace and to Macedonian Neapolis, and then to Philippi (Acts 16:11).

5. Philippi (Acts 16:12–40).

    In Philippi, the leading city of the district of Macedonia, Lydia was converted, and Paul and Silas were imprisoned for exorcising a slave girl and depriving her owners of their means of profit (her owners were paid for her prophecies). An earthquake released them, leading to their jailer's conversion. Here Paul utilized his Roman citizenship.

6. Thessalonica (Acts 17:1–9).

    After passing through Amphipolis and Apollonia, they arrived in Thessalonica in Macedonia, where Paul preached in the synagogue. As a result, there was an attack on his host, Jason.

7. Beroea (Acts 17:10–14)

    After preaching in the synagogue, Jews from Thessalonica stirred up the crowd in Macedonian Beroea against Paul, who was then forced to leave.

8. Athens (Acts 17:15–34)

    While Paul was waiting for Silas and Timothy, he engaged in dialogue in the synagogue and addressed the philosophers in a speech on Mars Hill in Athens, which is located in Achaia.

9. Corinth (Acts 18:1–18)

    Autumn A.D. 50–spring A.D. 52. During his one-and-a-half-year stay in Corinth, Paul appeared before Gallio, the Roman proconsul of Achaia. There he met Priscilla and Aquila, who had fled from Rome in response to Claudius's edict of A.D. 49;[130] *later, after being opposed in the synagogue, he taught in the house of Titius Justus.*

    1 and 2 Thessalonians. A.D. 50–52. It is generally agreed that 1 Thessalonians and 2 Thessalonians (if the latter is authentically Pauline; see ch. 10, sec. 2.C.1, below) were written during Paul's stay in Corinth; see 1 Thess 3:1.

10. Ephesus (Acts 18:19–21)

    This was Paul's first visit to Ephesus in Asia, where he left Priscilla and Aquila. He began his ministry here by preaching in the synagogue.

11. Caesarea and Jerusalem (Acts 18:22)

    Acts says that Paul landed at Caesarea and went up and greeted the church; this probably refers to going up to Jerusalem.

12. Antioch (Acts 18:22)

    Paul closed this missionary journey by returning to Antioch.

D. Third Missionary Journey (Acts 18:23–21:17; A.D. 53–57)

1. Antioch (Acts 18:23)

    Paul began his third missionary journey from Antioch.

2. Galatia and Phrygia (Acts 18:23)

Paul is said to have visited Galatia and Phrygia, which, as in Acts 16:6, probably refers to the Phrygian region of the Galatian province and would have included the cities of Pisidian Antioch and Iconium.

3. Ephesus (Acts 19:1–41)

Spring or autumn A.D. 53–55/56. After recounting the arrival of Apollos, a Jew from Alexandria, in Ephesus, Acts says that while Apollos was in Corinth, Paul arrived at Ephesus. Sometime either before arriving in Ephesus or early in his stay, Paul probably wrote his first letter to the Corinthians (now lost). Here he baptized the Ephesians into the name of the Lord Jesus, and they received the Holy Spirit. Paul stayed in Ephesus for two years and three months. During this time, Paul spoke in the synagogue for three months before opposition forced him to preach in a room owned by a certain Tyrannus. He also performed miracles (Acts 19:11). Apparently at the end of the period, the silversmith Demetrius caused a riot because the trade in idols of Artemis had diminished as a result of the success of Paul's preaching. During this time Paul also probably made what is known as the "painful visit" to Corinth, traveling by boat across the Aegean Sea (2 Cor 2:1).

Galatians? Spring or autumn A.D. 53–summer A.D. 55. Galatians may have been written at this time, which would coincide best with a northern hypothesis, discussed in ch. 10, sec. 2.A, below.

1 Corinthians. Spring A.D. 55. It is generally agreed that Paul wrote from Ephesus his second letter to the Corinthians (what we call 1 Corinthians; 1 Cor 16:8), and then, after his "painful visit" to them, his third, the "severe letter" (also probably lost, although some think fragments in 2 Corinthians [actually the fourth letter; see below], such as 2 Cor 10–13, might be part of it).

Philippians? A.D. 55. For those suggesting an early date for Philippians, this would be the most likely time of composition.

4. Troas (2 Cor 2:12–13)

Upon leaving Ephesus, Paul traveled to Troas, where he waited to no avail for Timothy's word on how the Corinthians received his "severe letter." When Timothy did not meet him there, he proceeded to Macedonia.

5. Macedonia (Acts 20:1–2)

Paul traveled through the area, probably visiting Philippi and Thessalonica (perhaps Beroea) and possibly getting as far as Illyricum in Dalmatia (Rom 15:19–20). This traveling may have taken up to a year.

2 Corinthians. A.D. 56. Second Corinthians (or at least chs. 1–9), the fourth and final letter to the Corinthian church, was probably written during this time, probably from Philippi.

6. Greece (Acts 20:2–3)

A.D. 56 or 57. Paul stayed three months in Greece, almost certainly in Corinth. Because of a plot by the Jews, he did not sail for Syria.

Galatians? A.D. 56 or 57. Galatians may have been written at this time because of its similarities to Romans, according to a version of the northern hypothesis.

Romans. Spring A.D. 56 or 57. Romans was probably written from Corinth during this time (Rom 15:14–29).

7. Macedonia, including Philippi (Acts 20:3–6)

Passover A.D. 57. Accompanied by many traveling companions, Paul made his way back to the east through Macedonia, including Philippi.

8. Troas (Acts 20:6–12)

During Paul's seven days in Troas, he preached the sermon during which Eutychus dropped off to sleep and fell three floors to the ground.

9. Miletus (Acts 20:13–38)

Traveling by way of Assos and other cities on the coast of Asia, Paul and his companions arrived at Miletus, where he spoke to the elders of the Ephesian church, who tried to talk him out of going to Jerusalem because of his prediction of danger.

10. Tyre (Acts 21:3–7)

Passing through several ports, Paul and his companions arrived on the coast at Tyre. He met with disciples who tried to dissuade him from going to Jerusalem, and then sailed on to the port of Ptolemais, from which they proceeded to Caesarea.

11. Caesarea (Acts 21:8–14)

In Caesarea, a prophet named Agabus came from Judea and attempted to dissuade Paul from going to Jerusalem.

12. Jerusalem (Acts 21:15–23:32)

Pentecost A.D. 57. Paul agreed to perform a vow to demonstrate that he had not abandoned the law. While in the temple area, a number of Jews from Asia (possibly Ephesus?) stirred up the crowd to accuse Paul of opposing the law of Moses (antinomianism) and bringing Greeks into the temple area. When a riot ensued, he was taken into the custody of the Romans. Paul was interrogated, kept in protective custody, and appeared before the Sanhedrin. When a plot against his life was uncovered, he was transferred to Caesarea.

E. Paul in Roman Custody (A.D. 57–62)

1. Paul's Caesarean Imprisonment (Acts 23:33–26:32)

A.D. 57–60. Paul was in Roman custody in Caesarea under two Roman procurators, Felix and Festus. He also made a defense before Agrippa before having his case referred to Rome.

2. Paul's Travels to Rome (Acts 27:1–28:15)

A.D. 60–61. Paul sailed to Rome under the custody of a centurion named Julius. Passing by Cyprus, Cilicia, and Pamphylia, the ship landed at Myra in Lycia. Then they boarded an Alexandrian ship for Rome. While sailing by Crete, a storm came up that finally shipwrecked them on Malta. After three months, they again set sail and arrived at Puteoli, on the Italian coast.

3. Paul's Roman Imprisonment (Acts 28:16–31)

A.D. 61–62. Paul was imprisoned in Rome for two years in a private house. Philippians, Colossians, Philemon, and Ephesians. A.D. 61–62. If these letters were written from a Roman imprisonment and they are all genuinely Pauline (see ch. 10, sec. 3, below, for a discussion of authorship), they would have been written during this time. Establishing the order of their writing is difficult; some put Philippians at the beginning of this period, and others put it at the end. Other views of the imprisonment would put the letters earlier (see sec. 4, below).

F. Paul's Possible Release from Prison and Later Reimprisonment (A.D. 62–65)

If Acts does not record the closing period of Paul's life, the following is a possible scenario of what happened after his release.

1. Paul's Travels in the Mediterranean Area

Acts apparently does not record these travels to such places as Macedonia and possibly Ephesus (1 Tim 1:3), probably Crete (Titus 1:5), Nicopolis (Titus 3:12), Troas (2 Tim 4:13) and Miletus (2 Tim 4:19).

1 Timothy and Titus. A.D. 64–65. These two letters, if they are authentically Pauline, and most scholars do not believe that they are, would most likely have been written during this period of freedom.

2. Pauline Reimprisonment (2 Tim 1:16–17, 4:6)

A.D. 64–65. Paul, according to this view, was reimprisoned and died during the Christian persecutions by Nero (possibly as late as A.D. 67).

2 Timothy. A.D. 64–65. If this letter is authentically Pauline, and most scholars do not believe that it is, it would most likely have been written during this final imprisonment of Paul.

4. PAUL'S IMPRISONMENTS

That Paul was imprisoned is not a matter of dispute. The question is not even how many times he was imprisoned. What is important is that it appears that during one of his imprisonments he wrote at least two letters (Philippians and Philemon) and possibly more (Colossians and Ephesians, and possibly 2 Timothy). Traditionally Philippians, Colossians, Philemon, and Ephesians are attributed to the same imprisonment, while 2 Timothy is attributed to a later imprisonment. What is the evidence regarding these various imprisonments, and what bearing do these facts have upon discussion of the Prison Epistles? The evidence is inconclusive, but as Wansink has recently shown, it is important to understand Paul's imprisonment in terms of both the physical conditions that he would have been subject to and the influence these may have had upon how he devel-

oped various themes in his letters. We do not have space to develop the influence of imprisonment upon Paul's writings. It is, nevertheless, worth recounting the evidence for the various imprisonments.[131]

The Church of St. Paul at Pisidian Antioch, built on the remains of a synagogue that dates back to the first century A.D. It may be where Paul first preached in this ancient city. Photo Lee M. McDonald.

A. Paul the Prisoner

That Paul was imprisoned is attested in several different ways. First, numerous references in his letters witness to his imprisonment: Phil 1:14; Col 4:10; Eph 6:20; Phlm 1, 23; 2 Cor 11:23; 2 Tim 1:8. Second, there are references to Paul's imprisonments elsewhere in the NT, particularly in Acts: 16:23–26, in Philippi for one night; chs. 23–26, in Caesarea for roughly two years; 28:30–31, in Rome for two years. Third, there are references in extrabiblical sources, the most notewor-

Ruins of the temple of Augustus in Pisidian Antioch (Acts 13:13–52; 14:1, 21). Photo Lee M. McDonald.

The cardo *leading from the theater and temple at Pisidian Antioch. Photo Lee M. McDonald.*

thy being Eusebius (*Hist. eccl.* 2.22), who reports that Paul was imprisoned for two years in Rome before being released, later reimprisoned, and killed during this last imprisonment. The evidence is conclusive and decisive—Paul was in prison on several occasions. But where might he have been in prison when he wrote the Prison Epistles?

B. The Places of Imprisonment

Four major locations are suggested for the imprisonment during which Paul wrote the Prison Epistles (the number of letters may be fewer, depending upon one's view of the Pauline authorship of several of the letters). J. A. T. Robinson has made a commendable attempt to place the Pastoral Epistles into what is known of the Pauline chronology from Acts, but his scheme has generally been rejected by scholars.[132] He raises some important issues, but generally the differences in the letters—granted, many of these have been overdrawn—seem to require that they be treated separately, either as pseudonymous compositions or as products of a period of writing that extends beyond the end of Acts (a period suggested by Eusebius, cited above). The four major places of imprisonment during which letter writing could have occurred are, in decreasing order of probability, Rome, Ephesus, Caesarea, and Corinth.[133]

1. Rome

The Roman imprisonment is the traditional and still the majority view regarding the place of

Paul's imprisonment during the composition of the Prison Epistles. As was noted above, Eusebius says that Paul was brought to Rome and that with him was Aristarchus, whom he calls a fellow prisoner in Col 4:10 (cf. also Acts 27:2, where Aristarchus is said to be accompanying Paul). Paul's imprisonment at Rome was "without restraint" (so says Eusebius), which is compatible with the kind of freedom mentioned at the end of Acts (28:30) and consistent with—and even necessary for—the kind of ministry, including writing and receiving people, that seems to go on in the Prison Epistles. For example, Timothy is said to be the coauthor or cosender of all of the prison letters, and in all of these letters, Paul mentions people who have come to him, including Epaphroditus, Epaphras, and Onesimus, to name only a few (e.g., Phil 2:25; Col 4:10–12, 14). It is likely, according to this view, that Onesimus fled (or traveled) to the capital of the empire in order to escape detection. Rome was a city of 750,000 to 1,000,000 people at this time, fully half of them slaves. It is understandable that an escaped slave wishing to go undetected would have selected Rome as a city in which he could live unnoticed.

When the Roman imprisonment is compared with other possible places mentioned in the sources cited above, it appears to be the only viable option. So far as hard evidence is concerned, the half-night imprisonment at Philippi is clearly inadequate, and even the Caesarean imprisonment, though it lasted for two years (Acts 24:27), seems to have involved a different situation, in which Paul's movements and the possibility even of receiving people and writing letters would have been more restricted,

An unexcavated mound at ancient Lystra, where Paul and Barnabas planted a church (Acts 14:6–20), in Turkey. Photo Lee M. McDonald.

The ruins of the gateway to Troas, the location of Paul's Macedonian vision (Acts 16:8–10). Photo Lee M. McDonald.

especially if there were fear of a plot against his life (Acts 23:16). The last piece of evidence for the Roman imprisonment is the thought reflected in the Prison letters. The great theological themes of the major letters, such as justification apart from works, do not seem to be emphasized in these letters. While this might point to a period earlier than the time of composition of the main letters, this is not a serious option, and hence would seem to indicate a later date. This later date is supported by the fact that these letters discuss several topics in which there is a more developed theology in terms of the church as the body of Christ, and by the orderliness that has become more predominant in these churches (compare the Corinthian letters with Phil 1:1 and the household codes [Ger. *Haustafeln*], which specify mutual submission between members of the household, in Colossians and Ephesians).[134]

Even though there is significant evidence for the Roman imprisonment, not all have been convinced. There are two major objections to the Roman hypothesis. The first concerns the Pauline chronology as established by Acts. If it is thought desirable to fit all of the Pauline Letters into this chronology, it appears very difficult to do so, apart from Robinson's scheme mentioned above. The second concerns the distance between Rome and the cities involved in the prison correspondence. The distance between Colossae and Rome is approximately a thousand miles. If it is assumed that Onesimus ran away from Philemon in Colossae, he would have been required to travel a considerable distance both by land and by boat. The increased danger of traveling by boat lay in the fact that if he

had been detected, there would have been no way to escape, short of attempting to swim the Mediterranean! Furthermore, there are other trips involved in this scenario. Besides Onesimus, Epaphras and Epaphroditus came to Paul, although the latter traveled a shorter distance from Philippi. Then Tychicus and Onesimus returned to Colossae with the two letters Colossians and Philemon. Such long journeys seem to be treated in a rather casual way in the letters, considering the distances involved. Nevertheless, this is not atypical for papyrus letters in general, in which safety is more important than distance (cf. Phil 2:25–29 regarding Epaphroditus). Finally, the reference that Paul makes in Phlm 22 to his intention to visit Colossae and to have a bed prepared for him may seem a bit difficult to understand in the light of both his intention to travel to the west from Rome (Rom 15:24, 28) and the distance involved.

The reconstruction of the Stoa of Attalus in the Agora of ancient Athens now serves as a museum. Photo Lee M. McDonald.

2. Ephesus

There is no record of an Ephesian imprisonment in Acts or Paul's letters, but there is explicit mention in *Acts Paul 6*. Consequently, an argument for Ephesian imprisonment would depend on inference and late evidence, but a plausible case has been made for it, nonetheless. According to this position, first argued by Deissmann, who was followed by a significant number,[135] Paul was imprisoned in Ephesus during one of his two trips to the city, perhaps during his first visit on his second missionary journey (Acts 18:19–21) or, more likely, during his third missionary journey after the incident with Demetrius, who convinced his fellow idol makers that Paul was hurting their business (Acts 19:23–41). He then wrote Philippians, Colossians, and Philemon; the composition of Ephesians was reserved for a later period (if it was written by Paul). There is no direct reference to this imprisonment, but there are several lines of indirect evidence, including the plausible scenario just

The Forum in Rome. Photo Lee M. McDonald.

outlined. Included in this evidence is the fact that Paul, in 2 Cor 11:23, testifies that he was imprisoned many times and that he had troubles in Asia, including fighting with wild beasts in Ephesus (1 Cor 15:32), having severe trials (2 Cor 1:8), and Priscilla and Aquila risking their lives for him (Rom 16:3, 4). The Marcionite prologue lists Ephesus as the place of origin of the Letter to the Colossians.[136] Ephesus was situated only a hundred miles from Colossae, a short distance for Onesimus to travel after fleeing Colossae. Ephesus was known to have a slave underground into which Onesimus could have hoped to be integrated. This location seems to make better sense of Paul's reference in Phlm 22 to prepare for his visit.

In spite of the case that has been made for an Ephesian imprisonment, it has still failed to displace the Roman imprisonment theory. There are several possible reasons for this. First, though there are references in Paul's letters to various troubles in Asia, in particular Ephesus, including his fighting with beasts (1 Cor 15:32),[137] none of these references is clearly a reference to an imprisonment. Few, if any, would take the reference to fighting with wild beasts as something that happened during an imprisonment, for the simple reason that Paul would almost assuredly not have been around to talk of this event if it had literally happened (and was not a metaphorical reference to conflict with humans). Furthermore, there is no evidence that such punishment was used on Christians at this early date. Even though 2 Cor 11:23 refers to other imprisonments, it does not specify an Ephesian imprisonment. It is doubtful that so significant an imprisonment would be completely overlooked by the author of Acts, especially since he mentions Paul's

The temple of Athena (6th cent. B.C.) at Assos. From 347 to 344 B.C. Aristotle made his home at Assos, and Paul stopped here on his last missionary journey (Acts 20:13–14). Photo Lee M. McDonald.

being in Ephesus on several occasions, as well as the trouble that he had with Demetrius. It is not impossible that Onesimus fled to Ephesus, but the distance is perhaps too close for an escaped slave to expect to be able to blend in, especially since his master probably would have started his search in that very city. Furthermore, there is no evidence that a praetorian guard, which is mentioned in Phil 1:13, was located in a senatorial province.[138] Finally, the significance of Phlm 22 is probably being missed. It is not that Paul would have been likely to drop in but, rather, that Paul is making use of the convention of the "apostolic presence," in which he would use his authority as a way of creating leverage for his requests.

3. Caesarea

The Caesarean imprisonment theory, although Acts refers to an imprisonment there, has never been a particularly strong position to maintain or defend.[139] It has been argued that Aristarchus's sharing of Paul's imprisonment (Col 4:10) can be harmonized with Paul's imprisonment in Caesarea (Acts 24:23) and Tychicus's going on to Colossae (Col 4:8) just as easily as with the Roman imprisonment. Indeed, it is claimed, in light of the distances of Rome and Ephesus from Colossae, the one being too far and the other too close, Caesarea is the most likely place for Onesimus to have gone, especially since he would have had to travel only by land, not by sea. The request for accommodation in Phlm 22 came more likely, this position maintains, from Caesarea, before Paul appealed to Caesar, when there was still hope that he would be freed from there. His heading from Caesarea to Colossae would have been part of his westward movement, which was anticipated when he wrote Romans (15:24).

Even though what is said of Caesarea may be compatible with the evidence in Acts and Colossians, it is highly unlikely that Paul's Prison Epistles were written there. Caesarea was a very Roman city of approximately fifty thousand inhabitants and with the headquarters of the Roman procurator, so it is highly unlikely that Onesimus could have hoped to blend in there as an escaped slave or that so much missionary activity could have gone on there as required (see Col 4:3, 4, 11).

4. Corinth

It has also been suggested that Paul was imprisoned in Corinth,[140] probably when he appeared before Gallio after the Jews made accusations against the Christians regarding worshipping in illegal ways (Acts 18:12–17). The polemic of, for example, Phil 3:1–11 is said to be consistent with other Pauline writings of this time (e.g., 2 Corinthians), and the distance would have been suitable for communication with those in Asia. Although this position is based upon inference, the argument is that there was a period of imprisonment after the charges were brought against Paul and before his case was heard before Gallio, even though it was immediately dismissed. The time would have been sufficient for production of the Prison Epistles, since Paul was in Corinth during this stay for over a year. This would move the composition of letters written during this imprisonment to around A.D. 50–52.

This view has little to commend it. Not only does it require an imprisonment that is not mentioned in Acts, Paul's letters, or any other source even though it would have been literarily important; it also requires a complete rethinking of the theological development of Paul's letters. That some of Paul's great doctrines, such as justification, are not major topics in the Prison Epistles is not the chief problem. The problem is that Paul appears to have a more developed view of the church as body in several of the Prison Epistles than he does in the major epistles (compare Eph 4:15–16, 5:29–32 with 1 Cor 12:12–31; Philippians may not show the same degree of development, perhaps suggesting a date different from the other Prison Letters). This kind of development does not make sense. It is understandable that Paul would choose not to emphasize certain beliefs in subsequent letters, but it is difficult to account for an underdevelopment of ideas compared to the major letters. Furthermore, the atmosphere reflected in the Prison Epistles does not seem to be the same as that of the Corinthian situation, where Paul is surrounded by friends engaged in active ministry.

In conclusion, it is clear that the Roman imprisonment still has the most to commend itself, even if one cannot be dogmatic about this conclusion. Although the distances involved are great, they are not insurmountable in the light of what we know of travel in the Greco-Roman world. If the conditions were favorable, it was possible for a person to make a trip from Rome to a place on the eastern Mediterranean in about four to seven weeks.[141] There is the further possibility that Onesimus may have been sent on a trip by his master, a trip that may have taken him to the vicinity of Paul, even Rome itself. Rightly understood as the invocation of apostolic authority that it is, Phlm 22 presents no difficulty to this position. Nor does Paul's possible decision after his release to travel around the eastern Mediterranean rather than head to Spain present a difficulty (such travels do not preclude a trip to Spain). Paul's statements in Romans describing his intended program are not determinative.

5. THE PAULINE LETTER FORM[142]

A. The Letter in the Hellenistic World

The Hellenistic period was a letter-writing age, and Paul was a letter writer. As the great classical scholar Gilbert Murray says of Paul, "He is certainly one of the great figures in Greek literature"[143] because of the importance of his letters. The joining together of the world surrounding the Mediterranean, which began during the time of Alexander the Great, not only brought a sense of extended unity to the entire region but also created the need for communication between people who were sometimes removed by great distances from each other. As a result, the letter became a very important form of communication. The postal system was for official letters, so the vast majority of

correspondence was private, carried by whoever would agree to do so.[144]

Thousands upon thousands of letters from the Greco-Roman period have been found among a huge quantity of papyrus documents from the ancient world.[145] Papyrus was essentially the paper of the Hellenistic world, a writing material manufactured when the papyrus plant, split into lengths, was pressed together and dried into flat sheets. The vast majority of these papyrus documents have been found in Egypt, in such areas as the Fayyum region and near the ancient city of Oxyrhynchus. The major discoveries occurred in the mid-nineteenth and early twentieth centuries. As James Hope Moulton titled his book about the importance of these discoveries—*From Egyptian Rubbish-Heaps*[146]—they were literally discovered in the old city dumps of these cities. The favorable atmospheric conditions and their use in the packing of various mummies ensured that thousands of these texts could one day be discovered. Some of them are relatively large sheets of writing in good condition, while many are simply small fragments. The kinds of documents found include the range of things that one might expect: wills, land surveys, reports, receipts for various financial transactions, contracts for especially agriculture and related services, personal letters, a variety of judicial, legal, and official documents and letters, and numerous literary and theological works.[147]

As a part of the Hellenistic world, early Christianity was also a letter-writing religion. Of the twenty-seven books found in the NT, twenty-one

The ancient harbor at Assos (Behramkale, Turkey) (Acts 20:13–14). Photo Lee M. McDonald.

The Mamertine Prison adjacent to the Forum in Rome is believed by some to be the place where the Apostles Peter and Paul were incarcerated just before their death. Photo Lee M. McDonald.

The Roman fortress of Antipatris. Photo © Rohr Productions. Used with permission.

have been identified as letters of various forms: letters to individuals (such as Philemon), letters to various groups or churches (such as Romans and 1 Peter), letters meant to circulate to various groups (such as Galatians), and anonymous letters (such as Hebrews if it is a letter; see ch. 11, below). Even the book of Revelation, if it is not itself a letter, contains letters (chs. 2–3). The same pattern was continued by the Apostolic Fathers; twelve of the fifteen texts by the nine authors are letters, such as *1 Clement*.[148]

At first, the discovery of the papyri did not have a significant influence upon NT scholarship. The German scholar Deissmann was one of the foremost pioneers in recognizing the importance of ancient Greek letters for understanding the NT. He tells how, during a chance trip through the Marburg library, he noticed an unbound volume of papyri and, on one page, the words "son of god," which led to his excited investigation of their language.[149] To him, it resembled that of the NT, and he proceeded to undertake some of the most important lexical studies of the Greek of this period. He was followed by a number of other important

scholars, including Moulton. (See ch. 13, below, on the language of the NT.)

One of the most important of Deissmann's findings concerned the nature of the Christian letter, including the letters of Paul. Deissmann noted that the letters from Egypt tended to be short, ranging in length from only a few words to approximately 300, the average being around 275. The letters of the NT, however, are significantly longer than these letters, with the exception of Philemon, which, at 335 words, is slightly longer than the average Egyptian letter. On the other hand, there are a number of letters by literary figures, including those attributed to Plato, Isocrates, Demosthenes, Cicero (who reputedly wrote 931 letters), and Seneca. As a result of his studies, in conjunction with his analysis of the sociological makeup of the early church, Deissmann distinguished the "true letters" of the papyri from "literary letters" or "epistles." His analysis concluded that Paul's letters were true letters (except for the Pastoral Epistles), since they were addressed to a specific situation and specific people, reflected Paul's genuine and unaffected thoughts and ideas, and were written in the language of the people of the day, rather than in some artificial literary style.[150] This was in keeping with Deissmann's conclusion regarding the nature of the early church, that it was essentially a group of people connected with the lower economic levels of the times, of which Paul was a part. Most studies of the letters of the NT are responses to Deissmann's classifications.

The general conclusion of later studies is that a variety of factors must be considered, rather than simply length and supposed genuineness. Better than seeing a disjunction between letter and epistle is the idea that there is a continuum, which depends on at least the following factors: language, whether the letters have a formal or informal style; content, whether their subject matter is one of business, personal recommendation, praise or blame, or instruction; and audience, including whether the letters are public or private. There are other factors to consider in analyzing Paul's letters. Unlike most true letters, his are not private in the conventional sense; at the same time, they are not for any and all who might be interested in reading them. They are for groups of followers of Christ, or churches, hence the frequent use of the second-person-plural form of address. His letters are significantly longer than the average papyrus letter, and they have some unique features of organization, discussed below. The body of the Pauline letter is recognizably that of the ancient personal letter, the major difference being that the topics are not usually personal commendations but, rather, instructions in the Christian faith. In many respects, Paul's style is that of the everyday language, but he was also a linguistic innovator. He used certain words in ways that were previously unknown (e.g., the use of the verb "reconcile" [καταλλάσσω, *katalassō*] in the active voice, with the offended party, God, as subject; see 2 Cor 5:18, 19 and sec. 2, above), and he shaped his language to meet the needs of the churches he was addressing.

B. The Purposes of Letters

Letters in the ancient world seem to have functioned very similarly to the way they do in the modern world. There were at least three major purposes of letters in the ancient world, all of which are exemplified in Paul's letters. First, letters were used to establish and maintain relationships. They were seen as a means of bridging the distance between the correspondents. For example, a husband might write from Alexandria to his wife back in Oxyrhynchus, maintaining contact by informing her how his job in Alexandria is going and when he is expecting to return home (e.g., P.Oxy. 744). Or Paul writing to the Philippians includes thanks for their generosity (Phil 4:10–20). For a relationship that has not been recently maintained, or maintained as one party thinks it should have been, the letter could also be used to revive the relationship (e.g., P.Oxy. 119, where a peevish boy writes to his father, who has gone to Alexandria without him; BGU 3.846, a letter from a prodigal son wishing to return home). One of the challenges of letter writing is that between the parties there is not only a physical but also a temporal distance, both of which must be overcome. As a result, the recipient of a letter is often written to as if present. In this sense, the letter is a substitute for the personal presence of the writer. This is a very important function of the Hellenistic letter, but it is not the only function.

The second purpose of a letter in the ancient world was to provide a form of dialogical interchange. The letter formed one side of a conversation, perhaps conveying various types of information. This information could give instructions, for example, regarding some function to be performed by the recipient, such as buying or selling an animal, or make requests, such as to send money (e.g., P.Tebt. 40 regarding land management). It could convey information—for instance, the condition of life of the one initiating the conversation. The content of the letter could vary depending upon the nature of the correspondence; Paul uses 1 Corinthians to respond to particular issues raised by those at Corinth.

The third purpose was to provide a permanent record of some form of interaction between the sender and receiver. This is often the case with the legal texts found in the papyri. Receipts and acknowledgments of legal and other transactions bear witness to the kinds of dealings these people had (e.g., P.Eleph. 1 is a marriage contract). The recording of it in a letter provides a record of this transaction for future reference. Paul's Letter to Philemon provides a good example of this kind of letter. A number of official letters also bear witness to governmental correspondence and decrees. These letters were meant to promulgate the decrees

The Flavian amphitheater at Rome, commonly called the Colosseum because of the colossal statue of Nero once adjacent to it. Begun by Vespasian and completed by Domitian (A.D. 81–96), it seated 50,000 people, and the walls reflect the three primary patterns of Greek architecture (Doric, Ionic, Corinthian) in its three stories. A fourth level added in the third century increased its capacity. Countless thousands of slaves, Christians, and others considered to be enemies of Rome were killed here in gladiatorial combat or slaughtered by beasts at the pleasure of the Romans (see 2 Tim 4:17).
Photo Lee M. McDonald.

and ensure that there was a record of the terms of the order. The Letter to the Romans may well be categorized as recording a set of Paul's beliefs in similar fashion.

C. The Form of the Letter

The ancient Greek letter is usually said to have three formal parts: the opening, the body, and the closing. Often at the beginning of the body of the letter there is a thanksgiving, in which the writer gives thanks to a god or the gods for the health and safety of the recipient. It is this form that Paul seems to have adapted to his own purposes. Scholars are divided over whether Paul's letters fall into three, four, or five parts.[151] The question revolves around whether two of the parts are seen, on functional grounds, to be separate and distinct units within the letter or whether these are subsumed in the body of the letter. Without wishing to distance Paul's letters from those of the Hellenistic world, especially in light of how Paul enhanced the letter form, we believe that it is appropriate to expand the traditional form-based three-part structure and, using functional categories as well, talk in terms of five parts to the Pauline letter form: opening, thanksgiving, body, parenesis, and closing. This is not, however, to say that each of the Pauline Letters has all five of these forms. As the outlines of the letters in ch. 10, below, indicate, in some there are fewer than five parts. Nevertheless, when one of these sections is missing, it is worth asking whether there is a reason for this departure from his standard form. The outlines in ch. 10 depart from the outlines usually found in commentaries and other introductions because the former utilize the ancient epistolary form as the standard rather than the usual thematic, theological, or subject-oriented approach.

1. Opening

The usual (though certainly not unvarying) opening of a letter in the ancient world included three elements: the sender, the recipient, and a word of greeting, often in the form "A to B, greetings [χαίρειν, *chairein*]." This was the standard form from the third century B.C. to the third century A.D., although the form "To B from A, greetings" was also found.

Paul includes all three elements in his standard opening, with several modifications. Three are worth noting. The first is that Paul more times than not includes others as coauthors or cosenders of his letters. Only Romans, Ephesians, and the Pastoral Epistles do not include a cosender. First Corinthians also lists Sosthenes; 2 Corinthians, Timothy; Galatians, all the brothers (though not a specific designation); Philippians, Timothy; Colossians, Timothy; 1 and 2 Thessalonians, Silas and Timo-

Inside the Colosseum. Notice the underground network of rooms and corridors for animals and gladiators. Photo Lee M. McDonald.

thy; and Philemon, Timothy. The question is why he does this. Are these people also authors? Should the corpus be known as the Pauline and other authors' letters (especially Timothy)? Since a distinctive Pauline voice comes through the Pauline Letters, most scholars do not wish to see these people as coauthors on an equal footing with Paul. Instead, they may best be seen as cosenders. Paul, by including these colleagues, such as his long-standing companions Timothy and Silas, perhaps shows that his gospel is not his alone, that what he is saying comes from a Christian community to another Christian community. Since Timothy is also seen frequently as a letter carrier in Acts and the Pauline Letters, the specification at the beginning of the letter probably helped to establish the authority of the letter carrier, who may well have been responsible for reading the letter to the audience. There were some who read to themselves, but for the most part reading was done out loud in the ancient world, so most reading had the character of a public activity (Col 4:16). Since, at most, only

15–20 percent of the men were literate,[152] virtually all of the writings of the NT, including the letters, would have been read out loud to their churches. It is worth noting that Romans and Ephesians do not have cosenders, perhaps because these letters were sent under different circumstances than the other Pauline Letters, the first to a church that Paul had never visited and that was located outside his immediate sphere of influence (Paul had probably not been to Colossae either, but it was within his sphere of influence), and the second perhaps to no specific church but to a number of churches in Asia. The Pastorals also include no cosender, but if they are authentic and if they were sent to Timothy and Titus, two of Paul's close associates, they would have no need of a cosender.

The second feature of the Pauline opening is that he often expands the specification of the sender or recipient. For example, in Rom 1:1–6 Paul expands the designation of the sender. His designation of himself as set apart for the gospel of God leads to a lengthy expansion on the nature of this

The theater at Ephesus (Acts 19:28–32), with a seating capacity of 25,000. Photo Lee M. McDonald.

gospel, focusing upon its relation to Jesus Christ. In 1 Cor 1:2, there is expansion of the designation of the recipient, defining the church of God in Corinth in terms of those who are sanctified and called to be holy. Whereas designation of the title or position of the sender or recipient in a letter was known in the ancient world, this kind of expansion is virtually unknown before the time of Paul.

The third feature of the Pauline opening is that Paul has apparently modified the word of greeting. All of Paul's letters include not the verb "greetings" (χαίρειν) but the words "grace" (χάρις) and "peace" (εἰρήνη), with the word "mercy" (ἐλεημοσύνη, eleēmosunē) added in 1 and 2 Timothy. There has been persistent scholarly interest in why Paul adds the word "peace." The word for "grace" is cognate to the word "greetings," so it is easy to see that Paul is playing upon the standard convention for greeting. Some have suggested that Paul includes "peace" as a translation of the Hebrew word for

peace, *shalom,* and that this reflects his integration of Greek and Jewish elements into his letter, thus reflecting the very nature of Paul's ministry as apostle to the Gentiles, bringing the message of the crucified and resurrected Christ. Since this greeting is not found in any other Jewish letters of the time in Greek *(shalom)* is found in Hebrew characters, but not "grace and peace"), it is not certain that this is what Paul is doing. This is not to minimize the fact that Paul has theologized or christianized the letter opening, however. Grace is God's beneficent favor upon sinners, and peace is the condition of sinners being reconciled to God. In any case, the Pauline letter opening is distinct and provides an entry point into the thinking of the apostle.

2. Thanksgiving

After the opening, many Greco-Roman letters then proceeded to the health wish, in which a prayer or word of thanks was offered for the well-being of the addressee. In the Egyptian papyri, this was often addressed specifically to one of the Egyptian gods, such as Serapis. Like these thanksgivings, Paul uses a formula in which a verb of thanksgiving (εὐχαριστῶ, *eucharistō*) is addressed to God with a reason for Paul's thanks.[153] Paul has again taken the convention of the Hellenistic letter form and adapted it to his purposes, further developing the thanksgiving section. He might include within a letter such things as a prayer formula, in which he states that intercession is being made for his recipients (Rom 1:9–10; Phil 1:9–11), or a memorial formula, in which he states that he is keeping his recipients in his memory (Phil 1:3; Phlm 4), but these are contained within the thanksgiving section. In this section, Paul, instead of giving thanks to the gods, gives thanks to God for his recipients and for the blessings that they have received and for the blessings that they are to him. The thanksgiving is present in all of the church letters of Paul except Galatians. The lack of a thanksgiving in Galatians provides for a jarring transition from the opening to the body of the letter, in which Paul expresses his astonishment that they have so quickly deserted their calling. By contrast, 1 Thessalonians is full of thanksgiving by Paul for the Thessalonian Christians. Some scholars have gone so far as to say that 1 Thessalonians is one large thanksgiving, estimating that as much as three-fifths of the letter is thanksgiving (see ch. 10, below). It is not surprising that Paul utilizes formulas that express joy or rejoicing in this portion of his letters (e.g., Phil 1:3–6; 1 Thess 1:2–10).

Two features of the Pauline thanksgiving are worth mentioning here. The first is that many scholars believe that Paul not only takes and adapts the convention of the health wish to a Christian thanksgiving but also utilizes this portion of the letter for the very important purpose of forecasting the topics that are to be discussed in the letter. There is some truth in this analysis, but it has limitations as well. For example, taking 1 Thessalonians again, in the thanksgiving proper (1 Thess 1:2–10) Paul mentions, among other things, the Thessalonians' work and what it produced, the fact that they were imitators of him and the Lord, that they became a model to all of Macedonia and Achaia, and that they were waiting for the return of Christ. All of these ideas are developed in various ways in the rest of the letter: their work in 1 Thess 2:1–16, their being imitators in 3:6–10, their being models in 4:1–12, and the return of Christ in 5:1–11. On the other hand, 1 Cor 1:7 mentions spiritual gifts and eschatology, but these are only two of the many themes discussed in 1 Corinthians.[154] There is perhaps a rough correlation, but certainly not a complete matching, leaving some topics to be introduced within the body of the letter. It is probably more accurate to say that the thanksgiving provides a general orientation to the relationship between Paul and the particular church and this relationship is then developed in the rest of the letter. The second feature of the Pauline thanksgiving is the shift from giving thanks for the gods and what they have done in preserving the health of the recipients to giving thanks to God for the faithfulness of the congregation (e.g., Phil 1:3–8). Intercession on behalf of the recipient church also tends to occur in the thanksgiving (e.g., Col 1:3).

3. Body

The body of the Pauline letter has been the least studied part in terms of its relation to the Hellenistic letter form, perhaps because the Hellenistic letter body has also not been heavily studied. Since the body of the letter could be called upon to perform a large number of purposes, it is perhaps inevitable that less has been done about its formal or functional features. For Paul, the body of the letter tends to concern one or both of two general subjects. The first is what might be called Christian doctrine. The bodies of such letters as Romans, Galatians, and 1 Corinthians tend to outline and develop important Pauline theological categories, such as the sinfulness of humanity, justification, reconciliation, Christian unity, and the roles of the law, faith, and grace. The second general subject, reflecting similarities to the friendship letter of the Hellenistic world, is Paul's own situation, especially in relation to the church to which he is writing. Philippians provides a very good example of this kind of letter, as do 1 and 2 Corinthians. In Philippians, Paul discusses his own situation of imprisonment, how he views his personal ministry, especially in terms of his own personal background, and how the Philippians should react. This letter also develops important theological ideas (e.g., 2:6–11), but in terms of Christ as a model to imitate, a model that Paul himself has been trying to exemplify (3:14).

The body of the Pauline letter, like other ancient letters, can be divided into three parts: the body opening, the body middle or body proper, and the body closing. All of these portions concern the matter of the letter body, but they serve various functions in introducing and concluding this matter. Paul relies upon a number of formulas both to mark the various portions of the body and to draw attention to the significance of various ideas. In the body opening, for example, Paul makes use of several formulas. One is the request or appeal formula, with a form of the verb "beseech" (παρακαλῶ, *parakalō*). Paul uses this verb in a formula nineteen times in his letters (e.g., 1 Cor 4:16; 16:15; Phlm 8, 10), often for a transition from the thanksgiving to the body of the letter (e.g., 1 Cor 1:10) but sometimes for other kinds of transitions. Paul also uses disclosure formulas, found in other kinds of Hellenistic letters as well. Disclosure formulas typically have phrasing such as "I want you to know" or "I don't want you to be ignorant," marking some idea that the sender believes the recipients should know. Often disclosure formulas occur near the beginning of the body of the letter (see, e.g., Rom 1:13; 2 Cor 1:8; 1 Thess 2:1; Phil 1:12; Gal 1:11). In addition, Paul uses expressions of astonishment (e.g., Gal 1:6). The disclosure formula indicates that the sender expects that the recipients already know the information to be stated, while the expression of astonishment indicates that the sender completely objects to what the recipients are doing or saying (usually in relation to what is being disclosed). Paul also utilizes compliance formulas, in which he restates something that places an obligation of action upon the recipients (e.g., Gal 1:9, 13–14).

The body closing also has a number of formulas. Whereas those of the body opening are designed to introduce or reintroduce already known or assumed information, the body closing formulas are designed to help the sender tie the argument of the body together and to close this portion of the letter. For example, Paul frequently uses a confidence formula, in which he expresses confidence that his recipients will understand what he has said and will act appropriately upon it (e.g., Rom 15:14; 2 Cor 7:4, 16; 9:1–2; Gal 5:10; 2 Thess 3:4; Phlm 21). He also uses an eschatological conclusion, which places what Paul has been saying in a

larger framework, in which all the actions of both sender and recipients are seen in the light of the imminent return of Christ (e.g., Rom 8:31–39; 11:25–26; 1 Cor 4:6–13; Gal 6:7–10; Phil 2:14–18; 1 Thess 2:13–16). Paul appeals to early Christian belief in the imminent return of Christ as a serious motivation for proper Christian action and belief because one would not want to be caught deviating from these at Christ's return. Paul also employs a travelogue near the close of the body portion of his letter (e.g., 1 Thess 2:17–3:13). This has been characterized by Funk as the "apostolic parousia" or apostolic presence.[155] Paul indicates his reason for writing or his intention to send an emissary or even pay a personal visit to his recipients. In effect, the letter is a temporary substitute for the apostle's (or his designated representative's) presence. This imposes a certain amount of subtle pressure upon the recipients to be concerned for their belief and behavior in the light of an impending visit of the

A view of the Celsus Library at Ephesus from the upper part of Curetes Street. Ephesus was the home of Paul's ministry for an extended period (Acts 19). 2d cent. A.D.). The beauty and enormity of this city was evident in the first century A.D., but it developed well past the second century. A major church council was held here in A.D. 431–432. Photo Lee M. McDonald

The statue of the god Hermes (3d cent. A.D.) located on Curetes Street in Ephesus. Notice that he is holding a ram by its horns in his right hand and a caduceus (wand), which was his symbol, in the other. Hermes has wings on his feet, and the wand, a symbol of healing, is surmounted by two wings and entwined with two serpents—still the primary medical symbol today. Photo Lee M. McDonald.

apostle himself or his representative. The travelogue outlining the plans of the apostle usually occurs near the end of the body or even the parenesis (Rom 15:14–33; Phlm 21–22; 1 Cor 4:14–21; 1 Thess 2:17–3:13; 2 Cor 12:14–13:13; Gal 4:12–20; Phil 2:19–24), but it is not necessarily only found at the close (see Rom 1:10; 1 Cor 4:21; Phil 2:24).

4. Parenesis

The parenetic part of the Pauline letter concerns Christian behavior, whereas the body of the letter concerns dogma or doctrine or a discussion of the fortunes of the apostle himself. The parenesis often specifies what is proper Christian behavior, using various traditional forms of moral instruction, including moral maxims, vice and virtue lists, and household codes (e.g., Eph 5:21–6:9; Col 3:18–4:1). Paul draws upon material from a variety of sources, including the OT, contemporary Jewish thinking, Greco-Roman thought, and Hellenistic moral traditions. His best-known parenetic sections are Rom 12:1–15:13, Gal 5:13–6:10, and 1 Thess 4:1–5:22.

5. Closing

In the closing of the letter, Paul is perhaps less bound to the Hellenistic letter form than he is anywhere else. The typical Hellenistic letter would express a health wish, often in terms of a closing imperative, a word of farewell, and the word "goodbye" (ἔρρωσο or pl. ἔρρωσθε, *errōso* or *errōsthe*).

The Pauline closing might consist of any number of the following elements. He typically greets a number of people or conveys greetings to the recipients from those who are with him. The longest list of greetings is found in Romans (16:3–23), but there are lists of greetings in most of his letters (1 Cor 16:19–21; 2 Cor 13:12–13; Phil 4:21–22; 1 Thess 5:26; Phlm 23–25). Paul also frequently includes a doxology at the end of his letter (one might be included earlier as well, as in Gal 1:5). These doxologies often contain exalted language of praise and glory to God (e.g., Rom 16:25–27, but see ch. 10, below; Phil 4:20; 1 Thess 5:23). Paul also includes a benediction, which can take several different forms, depending upon whether it is a grace or a peace benediction. In either case, it (1) begins by conveying grace or peace upon the recipients, (2) continues by attributing a blessing to God, and (3) concludes by directing the blessing to the recipients (Rom 15:33; 16:20; 1 Cor 16:23; 2 Cor 12:14; Gal 6:18; Phil 4:22; 1 Thess 5:28; Phlm 25). Paul also occasionally speaks of greeting each other with a holy kiss (Rom 16:16; 1 Cor 16:20; 2 Cor 3:12; 1 Thess 5:26).[156]

Recently it has been argued that, like the thanksgiving, the closing also contains a brief recapitulation of the major themes or ideas of the letter. Whereas it is often true that some of the ideas and themes presented in the letter are also summarized in the closing, this does not seem to be the best description of the function of the closing. The closing of the letter is simply a way of concluding the correspondence, often not by adding to or even recapitulating what has already been said but by providing suitable words of closing. These words are similar to those used in other Hellenistic letters, but Paul has again theologized and christianized the closing, leaving his recipients with a bidirectional closing: on the one hand, praise and glory are ascribed to God (Rom 16:25–27, but see ch. 10, below, on textual difficulties with this closing); on the other, grace or peace is wished upon the recipients (2 Cor 13:14).

D. Paul's Use of the Amanuensis

Amanuenses, or scribes, were widely used in the ancient world for the writing of both public and private documents.[157] Their training and competence varied, one's ability to pay often dictating the quality of service received. Since a good many people simply were unable to write, some papyri have what is called an illiteracy formula attached: at the close of the papyrus, the scribe, who has written the letter, states, "X wrote because Y does not know letters."[158] There were, however, other reasons for using a scribe. The cost of writing materials (such as papyrus) made it highly desirable to have a scribe who could write carefully and use as little papyrus and ink as possible. The difficulty of writing on the uneven papyrus surface, which varied with the quality of the papyrus and depended on whether one was writing on the recto (with the grain running horizontally) or the verso (with the grain running vertically), made professional scribes very useful.

There are clear indications that Paul, like other writers in the ancient world, used a scribe. Romans 16:22 contains an explicit reference to the scribe, Tertius, who sends his greetings to the Christians in Rome. Other passages have more indirect references to Paul's use of a scribe. Even though he used a scribe, Paul, who was literate, took the pen in his own hand as a way of authenticating that the letter was written and sent under his authority. Galatians 6:11 seems to indicate that Paul used a scribe, though scholars differ about when the scribe handed the pen over to Paul. The verse draws attention to the fact that Paul's hand, that of an untrained writer or perhaps someone whose eyesight was failing, was much larger than that of

the professional scribe (see also 1 Cor 16:21; 2 Thess 3:17; Col 4:18, and Phlm 19).

What was the exact role of the scribe? There is evidence from the ancient world that scribes performed a number of functions. One function was to take dictation, virtually word for word. There is fairly strong evidence that a form of shorthand was developed in the Hellenistic world that would allow scribes to take down what was being said so that they could transcribe it later in longhand (see P.Oxy. 724). Second, scribes were also capable of editing a writer's work, by using a rough draft or taking down the sense of what the author wished to say and then working out the individual wording. This might be one explanation of the composition of Ephesians, a letter whose authorship in the Pauline corpus is highly disputed. Because of its similarities to Colossians, as well as a number of distinctive features, it is possible that a scribe was instructed by Paul to compose the letter following the pattern of Colossians but emphasizing particular themes (is 1 Pet 5:12 similar?). Third, the scribe might simply be instructed to write a letter, without being given the exact or full sense of what was to be said. The scribe then composed the actual wording and came up with the sense of the correspondence. An example is found in Cicero's instructions to Atticus to write letters to anyone he had forgotten (Cicero, *Att.* 3.15.8). This might be considered a form of coauthorship. In other words, the range of scribal functions was considerable, and it is difficult from the extant evidence to be more specific regarding what a scribe might or might not do or in what contexts certain roles would be appropriate.

Even though we know that Paul used scribes, almost assuredly quite frequently, this still does not answer the question how much the scribe did in a particular situation. Most scholars recognize a distinctive Pauline voice running through the letters, at least the main letters. This militates against the scribe being given virtually free rein to compose the letter. Nevertheless, a number of scholars have found considerable linguistic and even theological differences between the so-called disputed and undisputed letters. A possible explanation of these differences is that a scribe was employed whose language did not match that of the Pauline voice. The scribal hypothesis is a very attractive one to explain a number of the issues regarding Pauline au-

The Herodian harbor at Caesarea Maritima with the Crusader citadel.
Photo © Rohr Productions. Used with permission.

thorship, but it cannot be used uncritically because of the lack of proof. From the evidence at hand, there is no way to prove the roles that scribes played in the composition of the Pauline Letters. What is certain, however, is that, for any author, including Paul, once the letter was signed by the sender, the letter became the product and responsibility of the one who instituted the correspondence, regardless of whether the exact wording was his conscious choice.

E. Summary

Although Paul's letters are part of the corpus of letters from the Greco-Roman world, they are also distinct and merit examination in their own right. Paul's letters were less formulaic than those of his contemporaries who were writing letters, with more freedom of expression and variation. The content is uniquely Paul's and is rich with theological meaning as he addresses complex relations among church members with the common language of the day.

He had dynamic and changing relations with his churches, and he took the opportunity to address their situations with his authority as a leader of the church. This sense of authority comes through in his letters. Paul's style is not that of the typical papyrus, nor the florid and polished language of the literary letter. His is a living language for contemporary church situations.

This raises the question of how and why Paul's letters were kept. It seems that, fairly early on, Paul's letters received recognition as being of special worth (2 Pet 3:16), but we apparently do not have all of them (see Col 4:16 regarding the reading of the now unknown Laodicean letter, and note 1 Cor 5:9 and the several letters to the Corinthians). What kinds of efforts were taken to gather together Paul's letters, which had been sent to various places in the Mediterranean world? And when were they collected? Three theories seem to be the most prevalent.[159] The first is that they were gradually collected as their enduring value was realized. The letters would have first circulated in the regions to which they were addressed (Asia Minor, Rome, Macedonia, Achaia/Greece), then these regional collections would have been joined together. The evidence for this position, however, is slight, and the difficulties—such as what or who compelled the regional collections to be joined together—are great. In the second theory, a number of scholars have followed Goodspeed in arguing that Paul's letters were collected around A.D. 90 when, after a lapse of interest, there was a revival of interest in Paul's letters after publication of Acts (Goodspeed's theory that Ephesians was written as a type of cover letter for this collection has been less widely received).[160] The difficulty with Goodspeed's hypothesis is the lack of evidence that interest in Paul's letters lapsed. The third proposal is that Paul himself may have been involved in collecting together his letters. On the basis of analysis of NT canonical lists, the letter collections that we have in the early papyri and codices, and other collections of writings by ancient authors, Trobisch has argued that Paul was responsible for at least instigating collection of his letters, beginning with the first four—Romans, 1 and 2 Corinthians, and Galatians.[161] Perhaps Paul's scribe had kept a wax writing tablet with a rough draft, or a second copy was made for correction or reference. The entire corpus was gathered in three stages, according to Trobisch. Ephesians to 2 Thessalonians were gathered in the second stage (in this sense Trobisch's theory is similar to Goodspeed's, with Ephesians as the first letter of this collection), and the Pastorals and Philemon were gathered in the third, with Paul decreasingly involved in the effort. Trobisch notes that although the letters are placed in order roughly according to length in words, Ephesians is actually longer than Galatians, and 1 Timothy longer than 1 or 2 Thessalonians. These differences indicate to him the literary seams formed in the assembling of the corpus. Although there is some merit to Trobisch's view, especially about the *possibility* that Paul was involved, at least in the early stages, in collecting his own corpus of letters, the partial return to Baur's hypothesis on the authentic four letters is untenable (see ch. 10, below). At most, Trobisch's evidence points to Paul's possible involvement in the initial stages of gathering together the entire collection of what we call the Pauline letter corpus.

6. PSEUDONYMITY AND THE PAULINE LETTERS

In dealing with authorship in the NT, and especially Paul's letters, the question of pseudonymity must also be discussed.[162] There are a number of formally anonymous works in the NT, such as all four Gospels, Acts, Hebrews, and the Johannine Epistles, but so far as pseudonymous works are concerned, only those with explicit claims to authorship can be considered pseudonymous.[163] These potentially include the Pauline Letters (i.e., 2 Thessalonians, Colossians, Ephesians, and the Pastoral Epistles) and the Petrine Letters.[164]

There is a tendency to look at the question of pseudonymity as if it were a problem only of the biblical and related literature (e.g., apocalyptic literature such as 1 Enoch), when it was actually an issue throughout the ancient world. In fact, this is such a large topic that a thorough analysis cannot be offered here. Pseudonymous writings existed in the ancient world, and these included letters. The evidence for this can be seen in at least two ways: there are comments in the ancient writers, including those of the early church, regarding writings that are known to have false authorship; and there are a number of writings, especially of a literary type, such as the Platonic and Cynic letters, that have been determined to be pseudonymous.[165] The issue here is whether pseudonymous writings exist in the NT, in particular whether certain Pauline Letters such as the Pastorals are pseudonymous.

Before addressing this, it is worth noting how pseudepigraphal literature was handled in the ancient world and the early church. Discussions of pseudonymity often note that ancient secular writers were aware that some of the writings they were dealing with were pseudonymous. For example, among nonbiblical writers, Suetonius described a letter of Horace as spurious, Galen took only thirteen out of the sixty or eighty Hippocratic texts as genuine and was concerned that his own works were being infiltrated by those he did not write, Philostratus disputed a work by Dionysius, and Livy reported that, when discovered, pseudonymous books attributed to Numa were burned. One of the most complex questions in the ancient world was the corpus of Lysias's speeches. Over 420 were ascribed to him, but many ancients knew that many were not genuine, and they formulated various lists attempting to determine those that were genuine. For example, one list includes as many speeches as possible but questions the authenticity of a third of them.[166]

A similar situation apparently held in Christian circles. There may have been instances where ancient writers commented favorably upon the possibility of pseudonymous writings in their midst unknown to them, but these instances are certainly few, if any, and this was not the usual response. The general, if not invariable, pattern was that if a work was known to be pseudonymous, it was excluded from any group of authoritative writings. For example, Tertullian (*Bapt.* 17) in the early third century tells of the author of "3 Corinthians" (mid–2d cent.) being removed from the office of presbyter.[167] Bishop Salonius rejected Salvian's pamphlet written to the church in Timothy's name.[168] The best-known example is the instance where Serapion, bishop of Antioch, in ca. A.D. 200 reportedly rejected the *Gospel of Peter*. According to Eusebius, after Serapion discovered the *Gospel of Peter* being read, he wrote to the church at Rhossus in Cilicia, "We receive both Peter and the other Apostles as Christ; but as experienced men we reject the writings falsely inscribed with their names, since we know that we did not receive such from our fathers" (*Hist. eccl.* 6.12.1–6 [LCL]). Despite initial tolerance because of its seeming innocuousness, the *Gospel of Peter* was rejected through a complex process that involved especially theological and ecclesiastical issues.

Admittedly, in the ancient world, including that of Christianity, the several means and reasons by which pseudepigrapha were exposed and excluded from authoritative collections are diverse. One of the common arguments cited for pseudepigraphal writings being included in any canon is the so-called noble lie—that it is in the best interests of the readers that they not know or are deceived regarding authorship by someone other than the purported author. Donelson points out the shortcomings of this approach: the noble lie is still a lie, with all of the attendant moral implications.[169] Kiley rightly claims that this gives valuable insight into pseudepigraphers' motives.[170] Nevertheless, when they were detected, their work was discredited, no matter how noble the motive. As Donelson observes: "No one ever seems to have accepted a document as religiously and philosophically prescriptive which was *known to be forged.* I do not know a single example."[171] He includes both Christian and non-Christian documents in this assessment.

Contrary to some recent discussion, it is not so simple to establish pseudonymous authorship of any of the letters of the Pauline corpus simply by appealing to other NT letters that are disputed or even highly doubted, such as the Pastoral Epistles, Ephesians, possibly 2 Thessalonians and Colossians, or 2 Peter. Such an appeal simply introduces a circularity to the argumentation, which can only be solved by discovery of some sort of external criteria to adjudicate the issues. But this poses difficulties in several respects. There are apparently no known explicit statements from the first centuries of the Christian church that someone knew that any of the Pauline Letters were pseudonymous, so this line of inquiry does not resolve the issue. Nor is it sufficient to cite noncanonical Jewish or especially Christian documents as examples of pseudonymous literature, as if this proves its existence in the NT.[172] The fact that these documents are noncanonical is apparently confirmation of the fact that documents found to be pseudonymous did not ultimately find a place in the canon, even if this process of "discovery" took some time.[173] If anything, it might constitute a prima facie argument that, at least for the sake of discussion at the outset, all of the Pauline Letters should be considered authentic, since they all survived scrutiny and now are in the canon. Since, in the discussion of the biblical books, issues such as style, language, and theology are inconclusive and highly contentious, argumentation must be utilized that does not appeal to the body of primary texts in dispute.

Meade has put forward a suggestion that has been fairly widely accepted.[174] His supposition is that, within the OT, there is a tradition of pseudonymous literature, in which traditions were supplemented, interpreted, and expanded in the names of earlier authors. He gives three major traditions: the prophetic, the wisdom, and the apocalyptic. The only one with direct relevance to the NT is the prophetic tradition.[175] Particularly in Isaiah, Meade sees this tradition developed by anonymous writers whose writings were attached to the earlier authentic Isaiah. Hence, Second Isaiah is not by the historical Isaiah who is attested in First Isaiah itself and elsewhere in the OT, but it can still only be understood in terms of First Isaiah.[176]

Several factors need to be considered further before this pattern can be applied to the NT, however. It is easy to think that Meade's argument has a parallel in the Pauline Letters, since there was a pattern of attributing writings to a recognized figure, possibly and even probably after the person's death, and that this practice was known to the audience. But this is only a superficial similarity. First, the type of literature is different. Isaiah is anonymous literature, better compared with, for example, the Gospels. The Pauline Letters are directly attributed to a known author. Second, the process of literary production is different. In the Isaianic writings the tradition was expanded and compiled and the document itself grew. In the Pauline Letters, the argument would have to be that the tradition grew by adding new documents to the corpus, not merely by expanding those in the corpus. This would imply that the corpus had already been gathered together—something not sufficiently established to be used as evidence in this discussion—and that the theology of the added letters posed no problem when placed side by side with the authoritative Pauline Letters.[177] If such a process truly occurred, inclusion must have been early, since attestation of many, if not most, of the now disputed Pauline Letters in the church fathers ranges from possibly as early as *1 Clement* to the third quarter of the second century (see ch. 10, below, for evidence regarding the various letters). Third and most problematic for his theory, Meade himself admits that one cannot use the tool that he has devised for *discovering* the pseudonymous origins of a given piece of literature.[178] His schema, according to his own analysis, is devised to explain the possible development of the tradition once it has been shown that the material is pseudonymous. In other words, his proposal does not solve the issue being considered here. To our knowledge, there has been no scheme proposed that circumvents the difficulties raised above.

Before drawing out the implications for canon, it is important to discuss the issue of deception in pseudonymous literature. This has been a particularly sensitive issue. Apart from Donelson and only a few others, there are few scholars who apparently want to admit that deception may have had a role to play in canonical formation and acceptance of any of the books in the NT: "We are forced to admit that in Christian circles pseudonymity was considered a dishonorable device and, if discovered, the document was rejected and the author, if known, was excoriated."[179] There were, nevertheless, all sorts of encouragements for skillful pseudepigraphal writing, including pietistic motives prompting those in the church to speak for an earlier figure,[180] and self-serving motives, such as the money paid by libraries for manuscripts by particular authors.[181] This all occurred in the context of the apparently guaranteed exclusion of any document from an author's corpus upon discovery of its pseudonymous nature. This forces Donelson to conclude that the only way to speak of the Pastoral Epistles, with which he is concerned, is that they were produced and consequently accepted into the canon in conjunction with deception.[182] The same would presumably apply to any of the other supposedly pseudonymous Pauline Letters. Of course, he is assuming that these letters are not genuinely Pauline. He goes further, however, claiming that eighteen of the twenty-seven books of the NT are pseudepigraphal and were included under deceptive means.[183] He has apparently joined anonymity with pseudonymity at this point.

Donelson's analysis needs to be considered further, however. This can be conveniently done in terms of the circumstances surrounding the production of the Pastoral Epistles, in particular their personal features and the original audience or receivers of the letters. Many scholars have struggled with the difficulties in the circumstances of these letters if they are authentic. The same questions must arise, however, regarding pseudonymous authorship. As Meade has recognized, if they are pseudonymous, there is a "double pseudonymity" of both author and *audience.*[184] What sort of situations were at play when these letters were received into the church? It is undecided, even by those who take the Pastoral Epistles as pseudonymous, when the letters were written and/or regarded as authoritative; dates range from an early date of A.D. 80–90 to the last half of the second century. In any case, the original audience would almost assuredly have known that Paul was dead. Were the letters simply introduced as new letters from Paul, or at least inspired by the situations such that Paul would have said these things had he been there? Many have argued that these pseudonymous writings are transparent fictions that no one would have thought were actually written by Paul. This reasoning, however, encounters this problem: why were they acknowledged in the first instance, in light of the apparently universal response by the early church to known pseudepigrapha, which, as we have demonstrated, were consistently rejected? Also, this theory does not account satisfactorily for three important features of the Pastoral Epistles that have parallels in most of the disputed Pauline Letters: (1) the specific selection of Timothy and Titus as the recipients of the letters, two men who would also by then have been dead or who would have been themselves in some sense literary creations; (2) the need for inclusion of very personal and arguably unnecessary details, especially in 2 Timothy regarding Paul's own life; and (3) the acceptance and endorsement of their developed theology.

An explanation might be that perhaps the letters were not simply introduced as what Paul would have said but were in some way subtly integrated into a collection of Paul's letters or slipped undetected into a collection that was being put together. What could have accounted for such an action? It is easy to say that only the best motives would have governed this behavior, in the sense that the person who wrote them was a follower of the great apostle and thought that he had been inspired to pass on words that the apostle would have conveyed to a serious situation. The person—and ultimately we must speak of a person or, at the least, a very small group of confederates—must have known that to come forward and say that the letter was not by Paul would have meant its rejection (and ecclesiastical trouble for that person); otherwise the efforts taken for its acceptance would not have been necessary. To extend this further, the same person may not have slipped the document into the system but may have discovered the document one day in a pile of the Pauline Letters and, upon reading it, realized that this was Paul's word to a particular situation. This hypothesis encounters three difficulties requiring explanation. (1) Again, the endorsement of the recognizably developed theology of the Pastoral Epistles presents a problem (see ch. 10, below). (2) The time lag between writing and discovery must have been relatively short, since some of the letters appear to have been at least known and possibly acknowledged, if not accepted, fairly soon (see ch. 10, below, for discussion of individual letters). The pseudepig-

raphal letters would have needed to penetrate Pauline churches to trade on the force of pseudepigraphal authorship, and the fact that we have Pauline Letters attests to the early respect given to his writings. This means that the risk of detection must have been even greater, with less time elapsing between the time of the apostle's life and the writing of the pseudepigraphal letters. (3) This scenario simply pushes back the deception a little further; the deception must have been perpetrated by someone earlier than the one discovering the letters. In any case, deception becomes a part of the process. In this instance, it would be a successful deception, since the church apparently accepted the letters as genuine.

In his commentary on Ephesians, Lincoln recognizes—if only in passing—several of these issues. At the end of his discussion, however, he says that pseudonymity does not affect canonicity or detract from the validity or authority of the particular pseudonymous document as part of the NT canon. He argues that to worry about such a thing is committing what he calls the "authorial fallacy," which he defines as setting more store by who wrote a document than by what it says.[185] This argument requires further scrutiny. The question of authorship does have serious implications, even if it may not (and this is a very debatable point) affect our understanding of what a document says. First of all, each of the Pauline Letters in the NT is ascribed to a particular author, one who is well known in the NT. These letters are not anonymous, without any line of definite connection. Why would a pseudepigrapher have selected Paul as his pseudonym if authorial ascription were not important? (See ch. 14, below, for other possible reasons why pseudepigraphy occurred.) The convention of pseudepigraph writing seems to demand ascription to an important and illustrious figure. Second, even if one may have some sense of how to read a letter but not know who the author is, for Ephesians—as well as any other disputed Pauline letter—authorship does make a difference. Authorship is important for determining whether the situation being addressed is one in the 50s or the 180s, whether one is reading a letter confronting problems at the beginning of the Christian movement or developed problems of, for example, church order.[186] Third, one evaluates whether any disputed Pauline letter is pseudonymous by comparing it with the undisputedly authentic Pauline letters; otherwise there would be no issue at all. If Lincoln really believes that authorship makes no difference, then perhaps even asking the question of authorship at all is unnecessary or committing the "authorial fallacy," for these as well as any other books of the NT. Fourth, the Pauline authorial question has consequences regarding the canon. Lincoln is probably not implying that the canon should still be open and that documents that say the right things, whoever wrote them and whenever, should be included. He seems to be saying that the documents being considered are part of the accepted canon of documents of the church and hence should not be deleted but, rather, continue to be interpreted within this group. What is missing, however, is a recognition of how the church's canon came to be, especially the collection of Pauline Letters. It is doubtful that Lincoln would say that the canon was given directly by God one day and had no more historical process to it than that (see ch. 13, below). He could say with others that canonical formation involved a complex process intertwining various authorial, historical, theological, and interpretive issues, some of which have been raised above.

With regard to canonicity, a number of factors must be weighed concerning the authorship of the Pauline Letters. The internal evidence on the authorship of the disputed Pauline Letters is so ambiguous that the issue cannot be decided simply on the basis of these factors (see ch. 10, below, on the various letters). The only reasonably strong basis for doubting the authenticity of the disputed letters is the developed theology thought to be found in each (e.g., changes in eschatological perspective, developed church order, views of personal relationships) and seen by many to be out of harmony with the authentic Pauline Letters. The fact that theological issues are the most distinguishing features of these letters (see ch. 10, below) and yet all of the letters were accepted without demur, as far as we know, prompts the thought that there must have been other important factors at play if any of the letters are not Pauline. If they are not authentically Pauline, one must face certain implications for these books as part of the NT canon. The question of implications regarding canonicity cannot simply be dismissed.

For some, an authoritative canon is completely outmoded. This does not mean that the questions raised in this section are unimportant, however.

The process of canonical formation in the early church, regardless of our not knowing as much as we would like, is important for both historical and theological reasons.

For those who are concerned about an authoritative canon of Scriptures, other issues are brought into prominence if some of the Pauline Letters are not by Paul. First, in light of theological development and possible pseudepigraphal authorship, the disputed or pseudonymous Pauline Letters should not be used in establishing Pauline theology. Pauline theology is here a slippery term, but one that must be defined at least in part. For some, it may simply mean a theology of all of the letters attributed to Paul, whether genuine or not, because they are in the canon. The disputed letters would constitute evidence for the diversity of early Pauline theology so defined. For those concerned with trying to establish a Pauline theology based on what Paul may have actually thought and written, pseudonymous letters, of course, cannot be used to create a Pauline theology in this sense. They are instead part of a record of how some people responded to Paul, how others developed his thought, how some people applied his ideas to later situations, or even how some people wished Paul could have spoken—each such letter can never be more than only one interpretation among many others. The fact that they were included in the canon has enhanced their authority and may mean that they represent the most influential or powerful followers of Paul, but it does not raise their level of authenticity. They are still not authentically Pauline and thus should not be used to formulate a Pauline theology.[187]

Second, we must come to terms with the question of deception in the NT, in particular concerning the Pauline Letters. Is it so difficult to believe that the early church was in some way fooled into accepting these letters? As Donelson says, "We are further forced to admit . . . that the disreputable practice [of pseudepigraphy] was extremely common in early Christianity."[188] If the letters are not authentic, this must be the answer, since there is no clear record of objection to their acceptance. It seems likely, if any of the letters are inauthentic, that someone tried to ensure their acceptance by various means, including use of the Pauline letter form, inclusion of personal details, imitation of the Pauline style, and, especially, direct attribution to Paul. The writers apparently went to such lengths to include these items in the disputed letters because these "faithful" disciples, knowing that exposure as a forger would have meant trouble for themselves and their writings, were using every means possible to create as plausible a deception as possible. Their motives for writing may well have been noble, including finding a way for Paul to speak to their communities, but deception it was nevertheless.

It may even be postulated that the early church rightly accepted some of these writings, even if it was for the wrong reasons and under the wrong circumstances. This raises a new set of questions. For example, have certain documents been excluded from the canon simply because they were exposed as pseudonymous, when their motives for being written may have been no worse (and in fact better) than those of others and their content may well have been perfectly orthodox, perhaps even more edifying than some others? Why should these documents have been excluded simply because they were unable to escape detection? Why should the successfully deceptive document be privileged over the others, simply because of tradition, lack of perception, historical precedent, or having the proper content? These and related issues must be given due consideration in light of recent scholarship on pseudonymy and the authorship of books in the NT (see chs. 13 and 14, below, for further discussion).

The implications of such an analysis can be seen in the discussion above regarding the essence of Paul's theology. Most of the major categories discussed rely most heavily upon the undisputed major letters. But many of the categories are also enhanced by reference to significant passages in Paul's other letters as well. A factor not as fully appreciated as it might be, especially by students first coming to terms with the message of the NT, is the difference that the issue of authorship makes for determining Paul's theology. A similar situation is found in the individual treatment of Paul's letters, as in the following chapter. The character and description of the corpus is affected by authorship.

BIBLIOGRAPHY

A. Introductions to Paul and His World

BARRETT, C. K. *Paul: An Introduction to His Thought.* London: Chapman, 1994.

BORNKAMM, G. *Paul.* London: Hodder & Stoughton, 1969.

BRUCE, F. F. *Paul: Apostle of the Heart Set Free.* Grand Rapids: Eerdmans, 1977.

DEISSMANN, A. *Paul: A Study in Social and Religious History.* 2d ed. Trans. W. E. WILSON. 1927. Repr., New York: Harper, 1957.

GLOVER, T. R. *Paul of Tarsus.* London: Methuen, 1925.

ELLIS, E. E. *Paul's Use of the Old Testament.* 1957. Repr., Grand Rapids: Baker, 1981.

HAGNER, D. A., and M. J. HARRIS, eds. *Pauline Studies: Essays Presented to F. F. Bruce.* Grand Rapids: Eerdmans, 1980.

HAYS, R. B. *Echoes of Scripture in the Letters of Paul.* New Haven: Yale University Press, 1989.

HENGEL, M., with R. DEINES. *The Pre-Christian Paul.* Trans. J. BOWDEN. London: SCM, 1991.

HENGEL, M., and A. M. SCHWEMER. *Paul between Damascus and Antioch: The Unknown Years.* Trans. J. BOWDEN. Louisville: Westminster John Knox, 1997.

HOCK, R. F. *The Social Context of Paul's Ministry: Tentmaking and Apostleship.* Philadelphia: Fortress, 1980.

HOWELLS, E. B. "St. Paul and the Greek World." *GR* 11 (1964): 7–29.

JEWETT, R. *Dating Paul's Life.* London: SCM, 1979.

KNOX, W. L. *St. Paul and the Church of the Gentiles.* Cambridge: Cambridge University Press, 1939.

_____. *St. Paul and the Church of Jerusalem.* Cambridge: Cambridge University Press, 1925.

LÜDEMANN, G. *Paul, Apostle to the Gentiles: Studies in Chronology.* Trans. F. S. JONES. Philadelphia: Fortress, 1984.

NOCK, A. D. *St. Paul.* London: Butterworth, 1938.

OGG, G. *The Chronology of the Life of Paul.* London: Epworth, 1968.

RAMSAY, W. M. *St. Paul the Traveller and Roman Citizen.* London: Hodder & Stoughton, 1895.

RIESNER, R. *Paul's Early Period: Chronology, Mission Strategy, Theology.* Trans. D. STOTT; Grand Rapids: Eerdmans, 1998.

ROETZEL, C. J. *The Letters of Paul: Conversations in Context.* 3d ed. Louisville: Westminster John Knox, 1991.

SCOTT, C. A. A. *Christianity according to St. Paul.* Cambridge: Cambridge University Press, 1939.

SOARDS, M. L. *The Apostle Paul: An Introduction to His Writings and Teaching.* New York: Paulist, 1987.

STANLEY, C. D. *Paul and the Language of Scripture: Citation Technique in the Pauline Epistles and Contemporary Literature.* SNTSMS 74. Cambridge: Cambridge University Press, 1992.

WALLACE, R., and W. WILLIAMS. *The Three Worlds of Paul of Tarsus.* London: Routledge, 1998.

ZIESLER, J. *Pauline Christianity.* Oxford: Oxford University Press, 1983.

B. Paul's Thought

BASSLER, J. M., ed. *Thessalonians, Philippians, Galatians, Philemon.* Vol. 1 of *Pauline Theology.* Minneapolis: Fortress, 1991.

BEKER, J. C. *Paul the Apostle: The Triumph of God in Life and Thought.* Philadelphia: Fortress, 1980.

DAVIES, W. D. *Paul and Rabbinic Judaism: Some Rabbinic Elements in Pauline Theology.* 4th ed. Philadelphia: Fortress, 1980.

DUNN, J. D. G. *The Theology of Paul the Apostle.* Grand Rapids: Eerdmans, 1998.

_____. *Unity and Diversity in the New Testament: An Inquiry into the Character of Earliest Christianity.* Philadelphia: Westminster, 1980.

FEE, G. D. *God's Empowering Presence: The Holy Spirit in the Letters of Paul.* Peabody, Mass.: Hendrickson, 1994.

FITZMYER, J. A. *Paul and His Theology: A Brief Sketch.* 2d ed. Englewood Cliffs, N.J.: Prentice Hall, 1989.

GRAYSTON, K. *Dying, We Live: A New Enquiry into the Death of Christ in the New Testament.* London: Darton, Longman & Todd, 1990.

HAY, D. M., ed. *1 and 2 Corinthians.* Vol. 2 of *Pauline Theology.* Minneapolis: Fortress, 1993.

KIM, S. *The Origin of Paul's Gospel.* WUNT 2.4. Tübingen: Mohr–Siebeck, 1981. Repr., Grand Rapids: Eerdmans, 1982.

LONGENECKER, R. N. *Paul, Apostle of Liberty: The Origin and Nature of Paul's Christianity.* 1964. Repr., Grand Rapids: Baker, 1976.

MORRIS, L. *The Apostolic Preaching of the Cross.* 3d ed. Grand Rapids: Eerdmans, 1965.

_____. *New Testament Theology.* Grand Rapids: Zondervan, 1986.

MUNCK, J. *Paul and the Salvation of Mankind.* Trans. F. CLARKE. Atlanta: John Knox, 1959.

PORTER, S. E. Καταλλάσσω *in Ancient Greek Literature, with Reference to the Pauline Writings.* Estudios de filología neotestamentaria 5. Córdoba: El Almendro, 1994.

PORTER, S. E., and C. A. EVANS, eds. *The Pauline Writings: A Sheffield Reader.* Bib Sem Sheffield: Sheffield Academic Press, 1995.

REUMANN, J. *Variety and Unity in New Testament Thought.* OTM. Oxford: Oxford University Press, 1991.

RIDDERBOS, H. *Paul: An Outline of His Theology.* Trans. J. R. DE WITT. Grand Rapids: Eerdmans, 1975.

SANDERS, E. P. *Paul, the Law, and the Jewish People.* Philadelphia: Fortress, 1983.

SCHOEPS, H. J. *Paul: The Theology of the Apostle in the Light of Jewish Religious History.* Trans. H. KNIGHT. Philadelphia: Westminster, 1959.

SEGAL, A. F. *Paul the Convert: The Apostolate and Apostasy of Saul the Pharisee.* Princeton: Princeton University Press, 1990.

WESTERHOLM, S. *Israel's Law and the Church's Faith: Paul and His Recent Interpreters.* Grand Rapids: Eerdmans, 1988.

WHITELEY, D. E. H. *The Theology of St. Paul.* 2d ed. Oxford: Blackwell, 1974.

ZIESLER, J. A. *The Meaning of Righteousness in Paul: A Linguistic and Theological Enquiry.* SNTSMS 20. Cambridge: Cambridge University Press, 1972.

C. Paul and His Literary Forms

AUNE, D. *The New Testament in Its Literary Environment.* LEC. Philadelphia: Westminster, 1987.

_____, ed. *Greco-Roman Literature and the New Testament.* SBLSBS 21. Atlanta: Scholars Press, 1988.

BAILEY, J. L., and L. D. VANDER BROEK. *Literary Forms in the New Testament.* London: SPCK, 1992.

DEISSMANN, A. *Bible Studies.* Trans. A. GRIEVE. 1901. Repr., Peabody, Mass.: Hendrickson, 1988.

_____. *Light from the Ancient East.* Trans. L. R. M. Strachan. 4th ed. 1927. Repr., Peabody, Mass.: Hendrickson, 1995.

Donelson, L. R. *Pseudepigraphy and Ethical Argument in the Pastoral Epistles.* HUT 22. Tübingen: Mohr–Siebeck, 1986.

Doty, W. G. *Letters in Primitive Christianity.* Philadelphia: Fortress, 1973.

Meade, D. G. *Pseudonymity and Canon: An Investigation into the Relationship of Authorship and Authority in Jewish and Earliest Christian Tradition.* WUNT 39. Tübingen: Mohr–Siebeck, 1986.

Murphy-O'Connor, J. *Paul the Letter-Writer: His World, His Options, His Skills.* Wilmington, Del.: Michael Glazier, 1995.

Richards, E. R. *The Secretary in the Letters of Paul.* WUNT 2.42. Tübingen: Mohr–Siebeck, 1991.

Stowers, S. K. *The Diatribe and Paul's Letter to the Romans.* SBLDS 57. Chico, Calif.: Scholars Press, 1981.

_____. *Letter Writing in Greco-Roman Antiquity.* LEC. Philadelphia: Westminster, 1986.

Trobisch, D. *Paul's Letter Collection: Tracing the Origins.* Minneapolis: Fortress, 1994.

White, J. L. *Light from Ancient Letters.* FFNT. Philadelphia: Fortress, 1986.

pages 323–328

1. For an overview of Paul's world, see R. Wallace and W. Williams, *The Three Worlds of Paul of Tarsus* (London: Routledge, 1998).
2. See J. M. Scott, *Paul and the Nations: The Old Testament and Jewish Background of Paul's Mission to the Nations with Special Reference to the Destination of Galatians* (WUNT 84; Tübingen: Mohr–Siebeck, 1995), esp. 1–180, where he defines Paul's concept of "nations" in terms of fulfillment of the Abrahamic promise (Gen 12:3).
3. W. Wrede, *Paul* (London: Longman Green, 1907), 179.
4. On methodology in reading the Pauline Letters, see N. T. Wright, *The Climax of the Covenant: Christ and the Law in Pauline Theology* (Edinburgh: T. & T. Clark, 1991), esp. 4–13; cf. V. P. Furnish, "On Putting Paul in His Place," *JBL* 113 (1994): 3–17.
5. As P. van der Horst, *Ancient Jewish Epitaphs: An Introductory Survey of a Millennium of Jewish Funerary Epigraphy (300 BCE–700 CE)* (Kampen, Netherlands: Kok Pharos, 1991), 73–84, has indicated on the basis of grave inscriptions in Palestine, the average age of demise of a Palestinian Jewish man in the first century A.D. was about twenty-nine. Therefore, anyone over thirty would have been considered old.
6. See R.A. Lipsius and M. Bonnet, *Acta Apostolorum Apocrypha* (Leipzig: Mendelssohn, 1891), 237, for the text. See J. Bollók, "The Description of Paul in the Acta Pauli," in *The Apocryphal Acts of Paul and Thecla* (ed. J. Bremmer; Kampen, Netherlands: Kok Pharos, 1996), 1–15, with a translation, p.1.
7. See W. Burkert, *Greek Religion* (trans. J. Raffan; Cambridge: Harvard University Press, 1985), 156–59; cf. W. K. C. Guthrie, *The Greeks and Their Gods* (Boston: Beacon, 1950), 87–94.
8. G. Harrop, *The Strange Saints of Corinth* (Hantsport, N.S.: Lancelot, 1992), 62–63.
9. On Greco-Roman education, see D. L. Clark, *Rhetoric in Greco-Roman Education* (New York: Columbia University Press, 1957), 59–66; S. F. Bonner, *Education in Ancient Rome: From the Elder Cato to the Younger Pliny* (London: Methuen, 1977); W. V. Harris, *Ancient Literacy* (Cambridge: Harvard University Press, 1989), 233–48.
10. See M. Hengel, *Judaism and Hellenism: Studies in Their Encounter in Palestine during the Early Hellenistic Period* (trans. J. Bowden; Philadelphia: Fortress, 1974), the classic work on this topic; supplemented by *Jews, Greeks, and Barbarians: Aspects of the Hellenization of Judaism in the Pre-Christian Period* (trans. J. Bowden; London: SCM, 1980); *The "Hellenization" of Judaea in the First Century after Christ* (trans. J. Bowden; London: SCM, 1989). On Paul as a Diaspora Jew (although perhaps not as accurate regarding Paul's acculturation and accommodation to Hellenization), see J. M. G. Barclay, "Paul among Diaspora Jews: Anomaly or Apostate?" *JSNT* 60 (1995): 89–120.
11. In a related area, rhetoric, D. Daube, "Rabbinic Methods of Interpretation and Hellenistic Rhetoric," *HUCA* 22 (1940): 239–64, has shown that rabbinic methods of interpretation derived from Hellenistic rhetoric.
12. See W. D. Davies, *Paul and Rabbinic Judaism: A Comparison of Patterns of Belief* (4th ed.; Philadelphia: Fortress, 1980), 23–31; assessed by S. E. Porter, "The Pauline Concept of Original Sin, in Light of Rabbinic Background," *TynB* 41 (1, 1990): 9–13.
13. On Paul's pre-Christian past, see M. Hengel with R. Deines, *The Pre-Christian Paul* (trans. J. Bowden; London: SCM, 1991), esp. 59–66, including discussion of Acts 23:3.

14. See K. Lake and H. J. Cadbury, "English Translation and Commentary," in *The Acts of the Apostles,* part 1 of *The Beginnings of Christianity* (ed. F. J. Foakes-Jackson and K. Lake; 5 vols.; London: Macmillan, 1920–1933; repr., Grand Rapids: Baker, 1979), 4:278–79.

15. There is a later rabbinic tradition of an unnamed pupil of Gamaliel who disputed with him. Some have thought that this was Paul, but there is no way of knowing who it was (*b. Šabb.* 30b).

16. See T. R. Glover, *Paul of Tarsus* (London: SCM, 1925), 57.

17. See R. Longenecker, "Acts," in *The Expositor's Bible Commentary* (ed. F. E. Gaebelein; 12 vols.; Grand Rapids: Zondervan, 1981), 9:100.

18. See E. R. Richards, *The Secretary in the Letters of Paul* (WUNT 2.42; Tübingen: Mohr–Siebeck, 1991).

19. See, e.g., E. B. Howells, "St. Paul and the Greek World," *GR* 11 (1964): 7–29, who deals with explicit and implicit quotations, among other evidence of Paul's Greek education.

20. These quotation books are known from copies of exercises that we have on papyrus and from references by authors, such as Quintilian.

21. On Paul and ancient rhetoric, see S. E. Porter, "Paul of Tarsus and His Letters," in *Handbook of Classical Rhetoric in the Hellenistic Period, 330 B.C.–A.D. 400* (ed. S. E. Porter; Leiden: Brill, 1997), 533–85.

pages 328–332

22. On Roman law in general, see A. Watson, *The Law of the Ancient Romans* (Dallas: Southern Methodist University Press, 1970); on the social context, see J. E. Stambaugh and D. L. Balch, *The New Testament in Its Social Environment* (Philadelphia: Westminster, 1986).

23. See R. Bauckham, "The Acts of Paul as a Sequel to Acts," in *The Book of Acts in Its Ancient Literary Setting* (ed. B. W. Winter and A. D. Clarke; vol. 1 of *The Book of Acts in Its First Century Setting;* ed. B. W. Winter; Grand Rapids: Eerdmans, 1993), 105–52.

24. J. C. Lentz Jr., *Luke's Portrait of Paul* (SNTSMS 77; Cambridge: Cambridge University Press, 1993).

25. B. Rapske, *Paul in Roman Custody* (vol. 3 of *The Book of Acts in Its First Century Setting;* ed. B. W. Winter; Grand Rapids: Eerdmans, 1994), 72–90. Many Roman historians have little trouble believing that Paul was a Roman citizen. See, e.g., E. T. Salmon, *A History of the Roman World from 30 B.C. to A.D. 138* (6th ed.; London: Routledge, 1968), 196 n. 1; R. Wallace and W. Williams, *The Acts of the Apostles* (London: Duckworth, 1993), 10; and the classic and still valuable studies by A. N. Sherwin-White, *Roman Society and Roman Law in the New Testament* (Oxford: Clarendon, 1963), 144–93, and *The Roman Citizenship* (2d ed.; Oxford: Clarendon, 1973), 273, who provides much documentation on this issue.

26. See Wallace and Williams, *Acts of the Apostles,* 25; Watson, *Law of the Ancient Romans,* 29.

27. The money did not actually go toward the purchase of citizenship but to paying off various officials in the process. The amount of 500 drachmae apparently was common according to some later sources, roughly the equivalent of two years wages for an average worker.

28. See Rapske, *Paul in Roman Custody,* 72–90.

29. See F. F. Bruce, *Paul: Apostle of the Heart Set Free* (Grand Rapids: Eerdmans, 1977), 363–67, for documentation of the above statements. In fact, Nero had made it clear that he would not himself hear cases (Tacitus, *Ann.* 13.4.2).

30. See J. M. G. Barclay, *Jews in the Mediterranean Diaspora: From Alexander to Trajan (323 BCE–117 CE)* (Edinburgh: T. & T. Clark, 1996), for a thorough and detailed study. He notes that there are only five locations of Diaspora Judaism with sufficient evidence for detailed study:

Egypt, Cyrenaica, the province of Syria, the province of Asia, and Rome (p. 10). Although he notes some very telling religious phenomena, such as apparent worship of Pan by Jews at El-Kanais in Egypt (pp. 99–100), there is further evidence worth considering, including praise to "the gods" in a Jewish papyrus from Egypt (C.Pap.Jud. I 4 = P.Cair.Zen. I 59076 [257 B.C.], reprinted in J. L. White, *Light from Ancient Letters* [FFNT; Philadelphia: Fortress, 1986], no. 16, pp. 39–40). See also a Dacian bilingual curse tablet (*NewDocs* 2:12).

31. See R. F. Hock, *The Social Context of Paul's Ministry: Tentmaking and Apostleship* (Philadelphia: Fortress, 1980), esp. 11–25.

32. See P. T. O'Brien, *The Epistle to the Philippians* (NIGTC; Grand Rapids: Eerdmans, 1991), 368–81; S. Kim, *The Origin of Paul's Gospel* (WUNT 2.4; Tübingen: Mohr–Siebeck, 1981; repr., Grand Rapids: Eerdmans, 1982), 32–50.

33. See C. J. Hemer, "The Name of Paul," *TynB* 36 (1985): 179–83.

34. See H. A. Brehm, "The Meaning of Ἑλληνιστής in Acts in Light of a Diachronic Analysis of ἑλληνίζειν," in *Discourse Analysis and Other Topics in Biblical Greek* (ed. S. E. Porter and D. A. Carson; JSNTSup 113; Sheffield: Sheffield Academic Press, 1995), 180–99.

35. On the Pharisees, see G. Porton, "Diversity in Postbiblical Judaism," in *Early Judaism and Its Modern Interpreters* (ed. R A. Kraft and G. W. E. Nickelsburg; Philadelphia: Fortress, 1986), 69–72, with bibliography.

pages 332–339

36. See Hengel with Deines, *Pre-Christian Paul*, 65–79.

37. E.g., A. Deissmann, *Paul: A Study in Social and Religious History* (2d ed.; trans. W. E. Wilson; 1927; repr., New York: Harper, 1957). In Acts 26:14, when the Lord is quoted as saying, "It hurts you to kick against the goads," this does not imply Paul's living in a state of rebellion but is an aphoristic statement forbidding opposition to God. See L. T. Johnson, *The Acts of the Apostles* (SP 5; Collegeville, Minn.: Liturgical, 1992), 435.

38. This persecution by ca. A.D. 44 was aimed also at non-Hellenistic Jews. See Acts 12:1–5.

39. For the evidence of this, see Bruce, *Paul*, 72–73.

40. See A. D. Nock, *Conversion: The Old and the New in Religion from Alexander the Great to Augustine of Hippo* (Oxford: Oxford University Press, 1933); A. F. Segal, *Paul the Convert: The Apostolate and Apostasy of Saul the Pharisee* (New Haven: Yale University Press, 1990), 72–114.

41. See Kim, *Origin*, 55–56.

42. Segal, *Paul*, 75, 117–49.

43. See R. Y. K. Fung, "Revelation and Tradition: The Origins of Paul's Gospel," *EvQ* 57 (1985): 25–34; cf. M. Winger, "Tradition, Revelation, and Gospel: A Study in Galatians," *JSNT* 53 (1994): 65–86.

44. Issues related to Acts are conveniently discussed in Foakes-Jackson and Lake, *The Acts of the Apostles*; Winter, *The Book of Acts in Its First Century Setting*.

45. See M. L. Soards, *The Speeches in Acts: Their Content, Context, and Concerns* (Louisville: Westminster John Knox, 1994).

46. See D. Litfin, *St. Paul's Theology of Proclamation: 1 Corinthians 1–4 and Greco-Roman Rhetoric* (SNTSMS 79; Cambridge: Cambridge University Press, 1994), who emphasizes Paul's proclamation over his rhetoric.

47. See I. Jolivet Jr., "The Lukan Account of Paul's Conversion and Hermagorean Stasis Theory," in *The Rhetorical Interpretation of Scripture: Essays from the 1996 Malibu Conference* (ed. S. E. Porter and D. L. Stamps; JSNTSup180; Sheffield: Sheffield Academic Press, 1999), 210–20.

48. See W. Tarn and G. T. Griffith, *Hellenistic Civilisation* (3d ed.; London: Edward Arnold, 1952), esp. 210–38.

49. On the above, see C. G. Starr, *A History of the Ancient World* (3d ed.; New York: Oxford University Press, 1983), 359–625; Hengel, *Judaism and Hellenism;* idem, *"Hellenization" of Judaea;* F. Millar, *The Roman Near East, 31 B.C.–A.D. 337* (Cambridge: Harvard University Press, 1993), 27–79, 337–86; T. R. Glover, *Paul of Tarsus;* idem, *The Conflict of Religions in the Early Roman Empire* (2d ed.; London: Methuen, 1909); J. D. Newsome, *Greeks, Romans, Jews: Currents of Culture and Belief in the New Testament World* (Philadelphia: Trinity Press International, 1993); M. Grant, *Herod the Great* (London: Weidenfeld & Nicolson, 1971); M. E. Stone and D. Satran, eds., *Emerging Judaism: Studies on the Fourth and Third Centuries B.C.E.* (Minneapolis: Fortress, 1989); and T. Engberg-Pedersen, ed., *Paul in His Hellenistic Context* (Edinburgh: T. & T. Clark, 1994).

50. See S. P. Brock, "The Phenomenon of the Septuagint," in *The Witness of Tradition* (ed. A. S. van der Woude; OS 17; Leiden: Brill, 1972), 11–36.

51. See van der Horst, *Ancient Jewish Epitaphs.*

52. The complete text with translation is found in S. E. Porter, "The Greek Papyri of the Judaean Desert and the World of the Roman East," in *The Scrolls and the Scriptures: Qumran Fifty Years After* (ed. S. E. Porter and C. A. Evans; JSPSup 26; RILP 3; Sheffield: Sheffield Academic Press, 1997), 315–16, with discussion on pp. 298–308; cf. J. A. Fitzmyer, "The Languages of Palestine," in *The Language of the New Testament: Classic Essays* (ed. S. E. Porter; JSNTSup 60; Sheffield: JSOT Press, 1991), 142. There is a major question whether "desire" or "opportunity" (or other words) is the best reading in the text, however.

53. The above evidence is discussed in S. E. Porter, "Jesus and the Use of Greek in Galilee," in *Studying the Historical Jesus: Evaluations of the State of Current Research* (ed. B. Chilton and C. A. Evans; NTTS 19; Leiden: Brill, 1994), 123–47.

54. See S. K. Stowers, *The Diatribe and Paul's Letter to the Romans* (SBLDS 57; Chico, Calif.: Scholars Press, 1981); "The Diatribe," in *Greco-Roman Literature and the New Testament* (ed. D. E. Aune; SBLSBS 21; Atlanta: Scholars Press, 1988), 71–83.

55. His works are conveniently found in *Epictetus* (trans. W. A. Oldfather; 2 vols.; LCL; Cambridge: Harvard University Press, 1925–1928).

56. Trans. S. Porter. Cf. S. K. Stowers, "Paul's Dialogue with a Fellow Jew in Romans 3:1–9," *CBQ* 46 (1984): 707–22, for a different arrangement of the dialogue.

57. See D. E. Aune, *The New Testament and Its Literary Environment* (LEC; Philadelphia: Westminster, 1987), 194–96; A. J. Malherbe, *Moral Exhortation, a Greco-Roman Sourcebook* (LEC; Philadelphia: Westminster, 1986), 138–41, with examples.

58. A classic study is W. Bousset, *Kyrios Christos: A History of the Belief in Christ from the Beginnings of Christianity to Irenaeus* (trans. J. E. Steely; Nashville: Abingdon, 1970). More balanced is the conclusion of G. H. C. Macgregor and A. C. Purdy, *Jew and Greek: Tutors unto Christ—the Jewish and Hellenistic Background of the New Testament* (London: Ivor Nicholson & Watson, 1936), 273–91: "Striking resemblances there admittedly are, but they are in vocabulary and outward form rather than in essential thought and content" (p. 289).

59. The reasons for this include the way Paul is depicted and his form of naturalistic argumentation, fundamental to Rom 1:18–32.

pages 341–347

60. A convenient summary of Stoic and Pauline parallels is found in E. D. Freed, *The New Testament: A Critical Introduction* (Belmont, Calif.: Wadsworth, 1991), 232–34, used here; and D. A. deSilva, "Paul and the Stoa: A Comparison," *JETS* 38 (1995): 549–64. There are discussions of the influence of Stoic thought on a number of individual passages. See, e.g., J. W. Martens, "Romans 2.14–16: A Stoic Reading," *NTS* 40 (1994): 55–67; T. Engberg-Pedersen, "Stoicism in Philippians," in *Paul in His Hellenistic Context* (ed. Eugberg-Pedersen), 256–90; W. Deming, *Paul on Marriage and Celibacy: The Hellenistic Background of 1 Corinthians 7* (SNTSMS 83; Cambridge: Cambridge University Press, 1995). On the influence of popular philosophy on Paul, see A. J. Malherbe, *Paul and the Popular Philosophers* (Minneapolis: Fortress, 1989).

61. See W. Meeks, *The Moral World of the First Christians* (LEC; Philadelphia: Westminster, 1986).

62. See D. L. Stamps, "Rhetorical Criticism of the New Testament: Ancient and Modern Evaluations of Argumentation," in *Approaches to New Testament Study* (ed. S. E. Porter and D. Tombs; JSNTSup 120; Sheffield: Sheffield Academic Press, 1995), 129–69.

63. See S. E. Porter, "A Newer Perspective on Paul: Romans 1–8 through the Eyes of Literary Analysis," in *The Bible in Human Society: Essays in Honour of John Rogerson* (ed. M. Daniel Carroll R., D. J. A. Clines, and P. R. Davies; JSOTSup 200; Sheffield: Sheffield Academic Press, 1995), 366–92.

pages 347–350

64. See Porter, "Paul of Tarsus and His Letters," 576–84.

65. See F. Young, "The Pastoral Epistles and the Ethics of Reading," *JSNT* 45 (1992): 115.

66. See C. D. Stanley, *Paul and the Language of Scripture: Citation Technique in the Pauline Epistles and Contemporary Literature* (SNTSMS 74; Cambridge: Cambridge University Press, 1992).

67. For a chart of indirect quotations, see UBS^2 897–920. The issue of indirect quotations or allusions is one that has not been fully explored in scholarly research. See M. B. Thompson, *Clothed with Christ: The Example and Teaching of Jesus in Romans 12.1–15.13* (JSNTSup 59; Sheffield: JSOT Press, 1991), 28–36.

68. See Stanley, *Paul and the Language of Scripture*, 209–15.

69. The term was first used for Pauline studies apparently by R. B. Hays, *Echoes of Scripture in the Letters of Paul* (New Haven: Yale University Press, 1989).

70. See J. D. G. Dunn, *Unity and Diversity in the New Testament: An Inquiry into the Character of Earliest Christianity* (Philadelphia: Westminster, 1977; repr., Valley Forge, Penn.: Trinity Press International, 1990), 81–102, on whom this discussion depends. There are many other treatments of this subject worth examining.

71. In apparent backlash against the convoluted allegorism of medieval interpretation, some modern interpreters wish to resist allegorical interpretation in the NT at almost any cost, even by ignoring the text.

72. See S. E. Porter, "The Use of the Old Testament in the New Testament: A Brief Comment on Method and Terminology," in *Early Christian Interpretation of the Scriptures of Israel: Investigation and Proposals* (ed. C. A. Evans and J. A. Sanders; Studies in Scripture in Early Judaism and Christianity 5; JSNTSup 148; Sheffield: Sheffield Academic Press, 1997), 79–96.

73. On Abraham, see Stowers, *Diatribe*, 171–73.

74. See J. G. Gager, *Moses in Greco-Roman Paganism* (SBLMS 16; Nashville: Abingdon, 1972).

75. On Adam, see J. R. Levison, *Portraits of Adam in Early Judaism* (JSPSup 1; Sheffield: JSOT Press, 1988).

76. See D. Wenham, *Paul: Follower of Jesus or Founder of Christianity?* (Grand Rapids: Eerdmans, 1995); cf. A. J. M. Wedderburn, ed., *Paul and Jesus: Collected Essays* (JSNTSup 37; Sheffield: JSOT Press, 1989); and F. Neirynck, "The Sayings of Jesus in 1 Corinthians," in *The Corinthian Correspondence* (ed. R. Bieringer; BETL 125; Leuven: Leuven University Press/Peeters, 1996), 141–76.

77. See C. A. Evans, *Noncanonical Writings and New Testament Interpretation* (Peabody, Mass.: Hendrickson, 1992), 117–18.

78. See J. Gutmann, ed., *Ancient Synagogues: The State of Research* (BJS 22; Chico, Calif.: Scholars Press, 1981).

79. We approach Paul's letters as the primary source of information about the theology of Paul. We are less concerned to argue for a theology of the Pauline Letters, as if this could exist apart from the man. On some of these issues, see J. D. G. Dunn, "Prolegomena to a Theology of Paul," *NTS* 40 (1994): 407–32. See also J. D. G. Dunn, *The Theology of Paul the Apostle* (Grand Rapids: Eerdmans, 1998).

80. L. L. Morris, *New Testament Theology* (Grand Rapids: Zondervan, 1986), ch. 1. This volume is used throughout this section. Cf. N. Richardson, *Paul's Language about God* (JSNTSup 99; Sheffield: Sheffield Academic Press, 1994).

81. See L. W. Hurtado, *One God, One Lord: Early Christian Devotion and Ancient Jewish Monotheism* (London: SCM, 1988).

82. See R. Hess, "Images of the Messiah in the Old Testament," in *Images of Christ: Ancient and Modern* (ed. S. E. Porter, M. A. Hayes, and D. Tombs; RILP 2; Sheffield: Sheffield Academic Press, 1997), 22–33.

83. See S. E. Fowl, *The Story of Christ in the Ethics of Paul: Analysis of the Function of the Hymnic Material in the Pauline Corpus* (JSNTSup 36; Sheffield: JSOT Press, 1990), 49–154; contra J. D. G. Dunn, *Christology in the Making: A New Testament Inquiry into the Origins of the Doctrine of the Incarnation* (Philadelphia: Westminster, 1980), 98–128, 163–212.

84. See M. J. Harris, *Jesus as God: The New Testament Use of Theos in Reference to Jesus* (Grand Rapids: Baker, 1992), 143–72, 173–85. Cf. M. Hengel, *The Son of God* (trans. J. Bowden; London: SCM, 1976); repr. in *The Cross of the Son of God* (London: SCM, 1986), esp. 7–15.

85. See D. B. Capes, *Old Testament Yahweh Texts in Paul's Christology* (WUNT 2.47; Tübingen: Mohr–Siebeck, 1992), esp. 115–49; cf. L. Hurtado, "Lord," *DPL* 563–64; S. E. Porter, "Images of Christ in the Pauline Letters," in *Images of Christ* (ed. Porter, Hayes, and Tombs), 101–5.

86. See Deissmann, *Paul,* 297–99.

87. See, e.g., C. F. D. Moule, *The Phenomenon of the New Testament* (London: SCM, 1964), 29–42.

88. On "in Christ," see K. Grayston, *Dying, We Live: A New Enquiry into the Death of Christ in the New Testament* (London: Darton, Longman & Todd, 1990), 382–94, for a recent summary of the issues; S. E. Porter, *Idioms of the Greek New Testament* (2d ed.; Biblical Languages: Greek 2; Sheffield: JSOT Press, 1994), 159, for a defense of the spherical solution; cf. idem, "Two Myths: Corporate Personality and Language/Mentality Determinism," *SJT* 43 (1990): 289–99.

89. For a comprehensive treatment of the Holy Spirit, see G. D. Fee, *God's Empowering Presence: The Holy Spirit in the Letters of Paul* (Peabody, Mass.: Hendrickson, 1994).

90. See J. L. Kinneavy, *Greek Rhetorical Origins of Christian Faith* (New York: Oxford University Press, 1987); cf. R. Bultmann, "πιστεύω, κτλ," *TDNT* 6:217–19.

pages 350–356

91. See D. R. Lindsay, "The Roots and Development of the pist- Word Group as Faith Terminology," *JSNT* 49 (1993): 103–18.

92. For a summary of the issues in the light of recent debate, see J. D. G. Dunn, "Once More, Pistis Christou," *SBLSP* 30 (1991): 730–44; responding to R. B. Hays, "Pistis and Pauline Christology: What Is at Stake?" *SBLSP* 30 (1991): 714–29.

93. See, e.g., Luther's declaration, printed at the beginning of *A Commentary on St. Paul's Epistle to the Galatians* (ed. J. P. Fallowes; trans. E. Middleton; London: Harrison Trust, n.d.), xi–xvi.

94. See J. A. Ziesler, *The Meaning of Righteousness in Paul: A Linguistic and Theological Enquiry* (SNTSMS 20; Cambridge: Cambridge University Press, 1972); and M. A. Seifrid, *Justification by Faith: The Origin and Development of a Central Pauline Theme* (NovTSup 68; Leiden: Brill, 1992), who also surveys recent developments. See also M. T. Brauch, "Perspectives on 'God's Righteousness' in Recent German Discussion," in E. P. Sanders, *Paul and Palestinian Judaism* (Philadelphia: Fortress, 1977), 523–42.

95. E. Käsemann, "'The Righteousness of God' in Paul," in *New Testament Questions of Today* (trans. W. J. Montague; Philadelphia: Fortress, 1969), 168–82.

96. This subject is also related to discussion of the new perspective on Paul. See sec. b, below, for discussion of that topic.

97. Something like this is found in G. B. Caird, *New Testament Theology* (ed. L. D. Hurst; Oxford: Clarendon, 1994), 118.

98. See Porter, *Idioms of the Greek New Testament*, esp. 20–45, where the issue of time and tense is discussed.

99. See W. Sanday and A. C. Headlam, *A Critical and Exegetical Commentary on the Epistle to the Romans* (5th ed.; ICC; Edinburgh: T. & T. Clark, 1902), esp. 30.

100. E. P. Sanders, *Paul, the Law, and the Jewish People* (Philadelphia: Fortress, 1983).

101. See H. Räisänen, *Paul and the Law* (WUNT; Tübingen: Mohr–Siebeck, 1983; repr., Philadelphia: Fortress, 1986); *Jesus, Paul, and Torah: Collected Essays* (trans. D. E. Orton; JSNTSup 43; Sheffield: JSOT Press, 1992).

102. J. D. G. Dunn, "The New Perspective on Paul," *BJRL* 65 (1983): 95–122; repr. in *Jesus, Paul, and the Law: Studies in Mark and Galatians* (London: SPCK, 1990), 183–206; *Romans*, vol. 1 (WBC 38B; Dallas: Word, 1988), lxiii–lxxii; *The Theology of Paul's Letter to the Galatians* (New Testament Theology; Cambridge: Cambridge University Press, 1993), esp. 75–92.

103. On Räisänen's interpretation of the law in Paul, see J. A. D. Weima, "The Function of the Law in Relation to Sin: An Evaluation of the View of H. Räisänen," *NovT* 32 (1990): 219–35.

104. "Covenantal nomism" is defined by Sanders (*Paul and Palestinian Judaism*, 75) as "the view that one's place in God's plan is established on the basis of the covenant and that the covenant requires as the proper response of man his obedience to its commandments, while providing means of atonement for transgression."

105. L. Gaston, *Paul and the Torah* (Vancouver: University of British Columbia Press, 1987).

106. E. DeW. Burton, *A Critical and Exegetical Commentary on the Epistle to the Galatians* (ICC; Edinburgh: T. & T. Clark, 1921).

107. For criticism of the new perspective drawn upon here, besides Seifrid, *Justification by Faith*, see S. Westerholm, *Israel's Law and the Church's Faith: Paul and His Recent Interpreters* (Grand Rapids: Eerdmans,

1988), esp. 105–97; cf. also H. Hübner, *Law in Paul's Thought* (Edinburgh: T. & T. Clark, 1984); Wright, *Climax of the Covenant;* T. R. Schreiner, *The Law and Its Fulfillment: A Pauline Theology of Law* (Grand Rapids: Baker, 1993); F. Thielman, *Paul and the Law: A Contextual Approach* (Downers Grove, Ill.: InterVarsity, 1994). An excellent assessment is found in M. A. Seifrid, "Blind Alleys in the Controversy over the Paul of History," *TynB* 45 (1, 1994): 73–95.

108. C. L. Quarles, "The Soteriology of R. Akiba and E. P. Sanders' *Paul and Palestinian Judaism*," *NTS* 42 (1996): 185–95; quotation, p. 195.

109. This text is published in E. Qimron and J. Strugnell, *Qumran Cave 4. V. Miqsat Ma'ase Ha-Torah* (DJD 10; Oxford: Clarendon, 1994), 62–63, but better translated in R. Eisenman and M. Wise, *The Dead Sea Scrolls Uncovered* (Shaftesbury: Element, 1992), 200, which is the translation cited here.

110. On this terminology, see F. Thielman, *From Plight to Solution: A Jewish Framework for Understanding Paul's View of the Law in Romans and Galatians* (NovTSup 61; Leiden: Brill, 1989).

111. See M. Hooker, "Paul and 'Covenantal Nomism,' " in *Paul and Paulinism: Essays in Honour of C. K. Barrett* (ed. M. D. Hooker and S. G. Wilson; London: SPCK, 1982), 47–56.

112. See M. Winger, *By What Law? The Meaning of* Νόμος *in the Letters of Paul* (SBLDS 128; Atlanta: Scholars Press, 1992).

113. See, e.g., R. P. Martin, *Reconciliation: A Study of Paul's Theology* (Atlanta: John Knox, 1981).

114. See S. E. Porter, "Peace, Reconciliation," *DPL* 695–99; Καταλλάσσω *in Ancient Greek Literature, with Reference to the Pauline Writings* (Estudios de filología neotestamentaria 5; Córdoba: El Almendro, 1994), esp. 125–89.

115. This almost assuredly refers to the wall that separated Gentiles from the Jewish precincts in the temple in Jerusalem. Inscriptions stating the death penalty for infringement of this separation have been found. See A. Deissmann, *Light from the Ancient East* (trans. L. R. M. Strachan; 4th ed.; 1927; repr., Peabody, Mass.: Hendrickson, 1995), 80.

116. See S. E. Porter, "Holiness, Sanctification," *DPL* 397–402.

117. See Morris, *New Testament Theology*, 32–35.

118. See J. C. Beker, *Paul the Apostle: The Triumph of God in Life and Thought* (Philadelphia: Fortress, 1980); *Paul's Apocalyptic Gospel: The Coming Triumph of God* (Philadelphia: Fortress, 1982); L. J. Kreitzer, *Jesus and God in Paul's Eschatology* (JSNTSup 19; Sheffield: JSOT Press, 1987); M. C. De Boer, *The Defeat of Death: Apocalyptic Eschatology in 1 Corinthians 15 and Romans 5* (JSNTSup 22; Sheffield: JSOT Press, 1988); G. Vos, *The Pauline Eschatology* (Princeton: Princeton University Press, 1930; repr., Grand Rapids: Baker, 1979); A. T. Lincoln, *Paradise Now and Not Yet: Studies in the Role of the Heavenly Dimension in Paul's Thought with Special Reference to His Eschatology* (SNTSMS 43; Cambridge: Cambridge University Press, 1981). For a critique of these kinds of studies, see R. B. Matlock, *Unveiling the Apocalyptic Paul: Paul's Interpreters and the Rhetoric of Criticism* (JSNTSup 127; Sheffield: Sheffield Academic Press, 1996).

119. It is dubious, however, to claim with R. Bultmann, *New Testament Theology* (trans. K. Grobel; 2 vols.; New York: Scribners, 1951–1955), 1:292, on the basis of 1 Cor 2:2 (cf. 2 Cor 5:16), that Paul knew nothing about Jesus.

120. See L. R. Pearson, *The Divinity of the Roman Emperor* (Middletown, Conn.: American Philological Association, 1931; repr., Atlanta:

pages 360–363

Scholars Press, n.d.), esp. 267–83, for the evidence from the inscriptions and papyri regarding the emperor cult.

121. See, e.g., J. D. G. Dunn, "'The Body of Christ' in Paul," in *Worship, Theology, and Ministry in the Early Church* (ed. M. J. Wilkins and T. Paige; JSNTSup 87; Sheffield: JSOT Press, 1992), 146–62.

122. See M. Hengel, *Crucifixion* (trans. J. Bowden; London: SCM, 1977); repr. in *The Cross of the Son of God,* 93–185.

123. See B. H. McLean, *The Cursed Christ: Mediterranean Expulsion Rituals and Pauline Soteriology* (JSNTSup 126; Sheffield: Sheffield Academic Press, 1996), although McLean argues that an apotropaic function or the removal of human sin was not able to account for the means by which sin was removed. Cf. also A. T. Hanson, *The Paradox of the Cross in the Thought of Paul* (JSNTSup 17; Sheffield: JSOT Press, 1987), 25–37. See also R. B. Gaffin Jr., *The Centrality of the Resurrection: A Study in Paul's Soteriology* (Grand Rapids: Baker, 1978); M. J. Harris, *Raised Immortal: Resurrection and Immortality in the New Testament* (Grand Rapids: Eerdmans, 1983).

124. See C. K. Barrett, *From First Adam to Last: A Study in Pauline Theology* (London: A. & C. Black, 1962), the classic treatment of this topic.

125. See Porter, "Images of Christ in Paul's Letters," 95–112, for a survey.

126. See N. Taylor, *Paul, Antioch, and Jerusalem: A Study in Relationships and Authority in Earliest Christianity* (JSNTSup 66; Sheffield: JSOT Press, 1992), 123–39. Cf. J. D. G. Dunn, "The Incident at Antioch (Gal. 2:11–18)," *JSNT* 18 (1983): 3–57, soundly critiqued by J. L. Houlden, "A Response to J. D. G. Dunn," *JSNT* 18 (1983): 58–67, and D. Cohn-Sherbok, "Some Reflections on James Dunn's: 'The Incident at Antioch (Gal. 2:11–18),' " *JSNT* 18 (1983): 68–74.

127. The narrative in Acts 21 leaves open the strong possibility that Paul was treated duplicitously by the leaders of the Jerusalem church. Their asking Paul to participate in the purification ritual seems like an unnecessary test, and they had to know that Paul might have caused some stir in the temple. See S. E. Porter, *The Paul of Acts: Essays in Literary Criticism, Rhetoric, and Theology* (WUNT 115; Tübingen: Mohr–Siebeck, 1999), 172–86.

128. On the collection, see D. Georgi, *Remembering the Poor: The History of Paul's Collection for Jerusalem* (Nashville: Abingdon, 1992).

129. The following discussion is similar in approach to that of C. J. Hemer, "Observations on Pauline Chronology," in *Pauline Studies: Essays Presented to F. F. Bruce* (ed. D. A. Hagner and M. J. Harris; Grand Rapids: Eerdmans, 1980), 3–18; cf. G. Ogg, *The Chronology of the Life of Paul* (London: Epworth, 1968); J. C. Hurd Jr., *The Origin of 1 Corinthians* (New York: Seabury, 1965), esp. 3–42; K. P. Donfried, "Chronology: New Testament," *ABD* 1:1016–22; L. C. A. Alexander, "Chronology of Paul," *DPL* 115–23, D. A. Carson, D. J. Moo, and L. Morris, *An Introduction to the New Testament* (Grand Rapids: Zondervan, 1992), 223–31. R. Riesner, *Paul's Early Period: Chronology, Mission Strategy, Theology* (trans. D. Stott; Grand Rapids: Eerdmans, 1998), esp. 3–32; and S. E. Porter, "New Testament Chronology," *Eerdman's Dictionary of the Bible* (ed. D. N. Freedman; Grand Rapids: Eerdmans, forthcoming).

130. There has been much debate recently whether the edict of Claudius took place in A.D. 49 or A.D. 41. See G. Lüdemann, *Paul, Apostle to the Gentiles: Studies in Chronology* (trans. F. S. Jones; Philadelphia: Fortress, 1984), esp. 164–70.

131. See C. S. Wansink, *Chained in Christ: The Experience and Rhetoric of Paul's Imprisonments* (JSNTSup 130; Sheffield: Sheffield Academic

pages 364–372

pages 373–378

Press, 1996), esp. 27–95, on the conditions of imprisonment. Cf. also Rapske, *Paul in Roman Custody*, esp. 195–422, for Paul's imprisonments in Acts.

132. See J. A. T. Robinson, *Redating the New Testament* (Philadelphia: Westminster, 1976), 31–85, esp. 84.

133. See Hurd, *1 Corinthians*, 14, 330, for representatives of the various positions.

134. The differences in treatment of these issues only become a problem if one assumes that churches in different cities had similar organizational structure and development. This is an assumption that many NT scholars seem to make, but it may not have been the case.

135. Deissmann, *Paul*, 17 n. 1; G. S. Duncan, *St. Paul's Ephesian Ministry: A Reconstruction with Special Reference to the Ephesian Origin of the Imprisonment Epistles* (London: Hodder & Stoughton, 1929); cf. F. J. Badcock, *The Pauline Epistles and the Epistle to the Hebrews in Their Historical Setting* (London: SPCK, 1937), 54–71.

136. See B. M. Metzger, *The Canon of the New Testament: Its Origin, Development, and Significance* (Oxford: Clarendon, 1987), 97–99. The Marcionite prologues are brief introductions found in a number of Latin manuscripts. Many think that they go back to Marcion. They are published in A. Souter, *The Text and Canon of the New Testament* (rev. C. S. C. Williams; London: Duckworth, 1954), 188–91.

137. See Malherbe, "The Beasts at Ephesus," in *Paul and the Popular Philosophers*, 79–89; H. Koester, "Ephesos in Early Christian Literature," in *Ephesos: Metropolis of Asia* (ed. H. Koester; Valley Forge, Penn.: Trinity Press International, 1995), 120–24, esp. 120.

138. See M. Silva, *Philippians* (Chicago: Moody, 1988), 7.

139. See Robinson, *Redating the New Testament*, 57–80.

140. See R. P. Martin, *Philippians* (NCB; Grand Rapids: Eerdmans, 1976), 44–45, for an assessment of this position.

141. See Silva, *Philippians*, 6 n. 4.

142. For a fuller treatment of the Pauline letter form, see S. E. Porter, "Exegesis of the Pauline Letters, Including the Deutero-Pauline Letters," in *Handbook to Exegesis of the New Testament* (ed. S. E. Porter; NTTS 25; Leiden: Brill, 1997), 539–50 followed here.

143. G. Murray, *Five Stages of Greek Religion* (London: Watts, 1935), 164.

144. See S. Llewelyn, "Sending Letters in the Ancient World: Paul and the Philippians," *TynB* 46 (2, 1995): 339–49.

145. Convenient introductions to the papyri and their uses in scholarship can be found in E. G. Turner, *Greek Papyri: An Introduction* (2d ed.; Oxford: Clarendon, 1980); and R. S. Bagnall, *Reading Papyri, Writing Ancient History* (London: Routledge, 1995).

146. J. H. Moulton, *From Egyptian Rubbish-Heaps* (London: Kelly, 1916). See also W. F. Howard, *The Romance of New Testament Scholarship* (London: Epworth, 1949), 111–37, for a discussion of the discovery of the papyri.

147. Convenient collections of these letters, with relevance to NT study, can be found in a variety of places. See esp. *Select Papyri* (trans. A. S. Hunt and C. C. Edgar; 3 vols.; LCL; Cambridge: Harvard University Press, 1932–1934); G. H. R. Horsley and S. Llewelyn, eds., *New Documents Illustrating Early Christianity* (8 vols. to date; North Ryde, N.S.W., Australia: Ancient History Documentary Research Centre, Macquarie University, 1981–); White, *Light from Ancient Letters*.

148. These are conveniently found in *The Apostolic Fathers* (trans. K. Lake; 2 vols.; LCL; Cambridge: Harvard University Press, 1924).

149. See Deissmann, *Light from the Ancient East*, 346 n. 4.

150. See esp. A. Deissmann, *Bible Studies* (trans. A. Grieve; 1901; repr., Peabody, Mass.: Hendrickson, 1988), 1–59. For a critique of Deissmann's hypothesis and a discussion of recent research in Greek epistolography, see S. K. Stowers, *Letter Writing in Greco-Roman Antiquity* (LEC; Philadelphia: Westminster, 1986), 17–26.

151. The three-part letter is ably defended by J. L. White, "Ancient Greek Letters," in *Greco-Roman Literature* (ed. Aune), 85–105, esp. 97; the four-part by J. A. D. Weima, *Neglected Endings: The Significance of the Pauline Letter Closings* (JSNTSup 101; Sheffield: JSOT Press, 1994), 11; and the five-part by W. G. Doty, *Letters in Primitive Christianity* (Philadelphia: Fortress, 1973), 27–43, who is followed below.

152. See Harris, *Ancient Literacy*, 16–46.

153. On the Pauline thanksgiving and other thanksgivings, see J. T. Reed, "Are Paul's Thanksgivings 'Epistolary'?" *JSNT* 61 (1996): 87–99; cf. G. P. Wiles, *Paul's Intercessory Prayer: The Significance of the Intercessory Prayer Passages in the Letters of Paul* (SNTSMS 24; Cambridge: Cambridge University Press, 1974), who analyzes prayers in the thanksgiving, as well as the other parts of the letter.

154. See J. Bailey and L. D. Vander Broek, *Literary Forms in the New Testament* (London: SPCK, 1992), 24.

155. R. W. Funk, "The Apostolic Parousia: Form and Significance," in *Christian History and Interpretation: Studies Presented to John Knox* (ed. W. R. Farmer, C. F. D. Moule, and R. R. Niebuhr; Cambridge: Cambridge University Press, 1967), 249–68. Whereas Funk tries to identify a formal category, the apostolic presence is better seen as a functional convention. Cf. M. M. Mitchell, "NT Envoys in the Context of Greco-Roman Diplomatic and Epistolary Conventions: The Example of Timothy and Titus," *JBL* 111 (1992): 641–62, who questions some of Funk's conclusions.

156. On features of the Pauline letter closing, see H. Gamble Jr., *The Textual History of the Letter to the Romans: A Study in Textual and Literary Criticism* (SD 42; Grand Rapids: Eerdmans, 1977), 56–83; Weima, *Neglected Endings*.

157. See Richards, *Secretary in the Letters of Paul*, who supplies much of the evidence in the discussion below; and J. Murphy-O'Connor, *Paul the Letter-Writer: His World, His Options, His Skills* (Wilmington, Del.: Michael Glazier, 1995), 8–37.

158. See Harris, *Ancient Literacy*, 141.

159. See A. G. Patzia, *The Making of the New Testament: Origin, Collection, Text, and Canon* (Downers Grove, Ill.: InterVarsity, 1995), 80–83.

160. See E. J. Goodspeed, *New Solutions of New Testament Problems* (Chicago: University of Chicago Press, 1927), 1–20; developed further by J. Knox, *Philemon among the Letters of Paul* (1935; repr., London: Collins, 1960); C. L. Mitton, *The Formation of the Pauline Corpus of Letters* (London: Epworth, 1955).

161. D. Trobisch, *Paul's Letter Collection: Tracing the Origins* (Minneapolis: Fortress, 1994).

162. This section draws upon S. E. Porter, "Pauline Authorship and the Pastoral Epistles: Implications for Canon," *BBR* 5 (1995): 105–23; cf. also "Pauline Authorship and the Pastoral Epistles: A Response to R. W. Wall's Response," *BBR* 6 (1996): 133–38; Porter, "Exegesis of the Pauline Letters," 531–39.

163. Here genuine authorship is taken to include writing by a scribe or by someone under the direct authority of the ascribed author. K. Aland has made a virtue of pseudonymity by arguing that it derives from anonymity. See his "The Problem of Anonymity and Pseudonymity

in Christian Literature of the First Two Centuries," *JTS* 12 (1961): 39–49; repr. in *The Authorship and Integrity of the New Testament* (London: SPCK, 1965), 1–13. The fact that school exercises and even fiction were written under pseudonyms does not enter into the equation, since they were part of an accepted convention whereby readers understood what was being done. Nevertheless, they were part of an environment in which pseudepigrapha were written.

164. The book of Revelation is not included here because, although it claims to be written by a person named John, it does not make a clear claim to a particular John. See ch. 11, sec. 6, below.

165. See L. R. Donelson, *Pseudepigraphy and Ethical Argument in the Pastoral Epistles* (HUT 22; Tübingen: Mohr–Siebeck, 1986), esp. 9–23, 23–42. It may be true that there is less evidence of Christian pseudepigraphal letters (see Carson, Moo, and Morris, *Introduction,* 367–68), but as the argument below explores, that may only mean that there was less detection.

166. See M. Kiley, *Colossians as Pseudepigraphy* (Biblical Seminar; Sheffield: JSOT Press, 1986), 18 and nn. 9, 10, 11, 12; cf. pp. 17–23, for reference to, and citation of, primary sources for the above; B. M. Metzger, "Literary Forgeries and Canonical Pseudepigrapha," *JBL* 91 (1972): 6 and passim, who discusses many instances of exposed pseudepigrapha; and K. J. Dover, *Lysias and the Corpus Lysiacum* (Berkeley: University of California Press, 1968).

167. See Carson, Moo, and Morris, *Introduction,* 368–69, who also cite the example of the letter to the Laodiceans, which, according to the Muratorian Fragment, was clearly rejected by the early church along with a letter to the Alexandrians (see G.M. Hahneman, *The Muratorian Fragment and the Development of the Canon* [OTM; Oxford: Clarendon, 1992], 196–200).

168. Donelson, *Pseudepigraphy and Ethical Argument,* 20–22; E. E. Ellis, "Pseudonymity and Canonicity of New Testament Documents," in *Worship, Theology, and Ministry in the Early Church* (ed. Wilkins and Paige), 218.

169. Donelson, *Pseudepigraphy and Ethical Argument,* 18–22. The noble lie refers to Plato's acceptance of a lie that is useful for the one to whom the lie is told (see *Rep.* 2.376e–382b, 3.389b, 414ce). The question might well be raised whether the noble lie was involved in efforts for acceptance of Hebrews. The fact that Hebrews is anonymous removes it from discussion here.

170. Kiley, *Colossians,* 21.

171. Donelson, *Pseudepigraphy and Ethical Argument,* 11 (italics ours). Donelson (p. 18) notes that *Apos. Con.* 6.16 accuses certain books of being forgeries while itself being pseudepigraphal. But this fourth-century (or later) document only had limited acceptance for a short period of time. It may not have been known to be pseudepigraphal during this time.

172. A. T. Lincoln, *Ephesians* (WBC 42; Dallas: Word, 1990), lxx–lxxi.

173. This includes the Jewish works 2 Esdras and *1, 2 Enoch* and the Christian works *Didache, 2 Clement, Barnabas,* etc. Admittedly, some of these documents floated on the edges of various corpora of authoritative writings for some time.

174. D. Meade, *Pseudonymity and Canon* (WUNT 39; Tübingen: Mohr–Siebeck, 1986), esp. 17–43. His position has been accepted by, e.g., Lincoln, *Ephesians,* lxviii.

pages 388–389

175. The wisdom tradition in the OT is essentially confined to anonymous literature, and the apocalyptic tradition is confined to Daniel, for whom there is no tradition of being an illustrious hero.

176. For a discussion of the growth of the Isaiah tradition, see Meade, *Pseudonymity and Canon,* 26–42.

177. On the assembling of the Pauline corpus, with Paul possibly involved in the process at least for the first four letters, see sec. 5, above.

178. Meade, *Pseudonymity and Canon,* esp. 16.

179. Donelson, *Pseudepigraphy and Ethical Argument,* 16.

180. It is questionable whether this motive can be considered an innocent one. See Donelson, *Pseudepigraphy and Ethical Argument,* 10.

181. See also M. L. Stirewalt Jr., *Studies in Ancient Greek Epistolography* (SBLRBS 27; Atlanta: Scholars Press, 1993), 31–42.

182. Donelson, *Pseudepigraphy and Ethical Argument,* 54–66.

183. Ibid., 16, citing M. Rist, "Pseudepigraphy and the Early Christians," in *Studies in New Testament and Early Christian Literature* (Festschrift P. Wikgren; ed. D. E. Aune; Leiden: Brill, 1972), 89.

184. Meade, *Pseudonymity in the New Testament,* 127.

185. Lincoln, *Ephesians,* lxxiii.

186. A clear case in point is Hebrews. Since so little is known of such issues as authorship, date of composition, addressees, and situation, the range of proposals is very wide. See ch. 11, below.

187. This raises the issue of a canon within a canon. On this issue, see E. Käsemann, "The Canon of the New Testament Church and the Unity of the Church," in *Essays on New Testament Themes* (trans. W. J. Montague; London: SCM Press, 1968), 95–107.

188. Donelson, *Pseudepigraphy and Ethical Argument,* 16.

THE PAULINE LETTERS

1. INTRODUCTION

There have been several major periods in the discussion of the Pauline Letters. After the period during which the canonical group was recognized (see ch. 13, below, on the origins of the Christian Bible), the first is the period of the full Pauline corpus. Acceptance of Hebrews as Pauline appears to have been early, as reflected in the important second-century papyrus text $\mathfrak{P}^{46}$, where the Pauline corpus is arranged generally according to length, with Hebrews following Romans and preceding the Corinthian letters. In several other early manuscripts, Hebrews is also found in the Pauline corpus.[1] This acceptance persisted in the West until the time of the Reformation, when a number of scholars, including Luther, finally decided against its Pauline authorship. The Pauline canon that resulted remained intact until the time of the Enlightenment.

During the nineteenth century in particular, a number of biblical scholars undertook a virtually complete reassessment of the shape of the Pauline corpus. We can now see that an unwarrantably radical skepticism was expressed toward a number of the Pauline Letters, although many of the results of this reformulation are still with us. Led by Baur and by others who undertook similar independent investigations in continental Europe, there was a reevaluation of the history of earliest Christianity.[2]

Baur contended that there was far more contention among rival factions in the early church than is revealed in the documents of earliest Christianity, particularly Acts (see ch. 8, above). According to Baur, Acts was a second-century composition that attempted to rewrite the history of earliest Christianity so as to conceal the major unresolved conflict between the Pauline, or antinomian (that is, rejecting the Mosaic law), and Jerusalem (or legalistic) Christian factions. In the course of Baur's and others' subsequent investigation, the number of unquestionably authentic Pauline Letters was narrowed down from the canonical thirteen to four main, or pillar, epistles (often called the *Hauptbriefe*, "main letters"). These are Romans, 1 and 2 Corinthians, and Galatians. Even so, this does not mean that these letters were considered by Baur and others to have been written as single letters, as discussion below illustrates, only that they consist mostly of authentic Pauline material. The major criteria for this assessment, which will be summarized and evaluated later in this chapter, focused upon matters of theology, historical situation, and language.

These criteria have continued to constitute the major criteria for evaluation of the letters. One criterion is whether the theological perspective of a given book is consistent with what is thought most plausibly to represent Paul's thought. Thus, when 1 and 2 Thessalonians discuss eschatology, it is asked what their perspectives are, whether these perspectives are consistent with the kind of Jewish eschatology current during this time, whether the eschatological perspectives are consistent with each other, whether the eschatology is consistent with that of Paul's undisputed letters, and whether the language used to express these thoughts is consistent with Paul's standard vocabulary. For a further example, when the Pastoral Epistles (1 and 2 Timothy and Titus) discuss various positions of church leadership, it is asked whether these positions are plausibly found in the churches of the A.D. 60s, where these letters would fit within the Pauline chronology, especially his imprisonments, and whether the vocabulary (e.g., how he uses words related to "faith" and "belief") and content (e.g., salvation and church order) are consistent with his usage elsewhere (see ch. 9, sec. 2, above).

Since the nineteenth century, there has been a steady reassessment of the conclusions of Baur, his contemporaries, and his successors. Scholars differ on numerous details and even on some of the major points of evidence and how they are to be evaluated, but it appears that seven of the Pauline Letters can conveniently be placed into the category of undisputed letters (Romans, 1 and 2 Corinthians, Galatians, Philippians, 1 Thessalonians, and Philemon). This does not mean that every scholar believes that these were written by Paul, or that he wrote them alone or in their entirety as they stand in the canon, but that, generally speaking, these books constitute the basic corpus of Paul's authentic writings in the NT. The other six letters can be categorized as the disputed or deuteropauline letters (Ephesians, Colossians, 2 Thessalonians, 1 and 2 Timothy, and Titus). Again, this does not mean that every scholar believes that these were not written by Paul, or that they do not contain authentic Pauline material, or, certainly, that they were written under Paul's name to deceive an ancient audience. But generally speaking, it cannot be assumed in scholarly discussion that Paul is their author. In some circles, the authenticity of these books is still being debated. This is less true of the Pastoral Epistles, whose authenticity is so widely doubted that authenticity is often not even a subject of discussion. There is more debate about the authenticity of Colossians, Ephesians, and 2 Thessalonians.

In this chapter, the undisputed and disputed letters of Paul will be discussed together, according to the reconstructed Pauline chronology in the preceding chapter (see ch. 9, sec. 3, above). They are therefore divided into the Main Epistles, the Prison Epistles, and the Pastoral Epistles. Here the evidence for and against their authenticity is presented, along with discussion of the possible historical and theological contexts in which they were written. Although we do take positions and draw conclusions, the purpose of this chapter is not so much to convince the reader of any one position as to present each reader with sufficient data to arrive at a personal decision. Along with the evidence for authenticity will be presented a suitable and plausible scenario for how the letter fits in with the Pauline chronology.[3] Along with the evidence against Pauline authorship will be presented suitable alternatives for the writing of the letter. Comments in this chapter on the circumstances and purpose of composition, along with discussion of Paul's opponents in the churches where relevant, should be combined with the dimensions of Pauline belief discussed in chapter 9 to determine the particular theological contribution of each of the letters. No attempt is made at being complete in every aspect. Pauline studies is one of the most fruitful and productive areas of biblical scholarship, and these issues continue to generate lively and informative discussion. A more thorough and complete analysis of each of the issues can be found in volumes devoted to these topics. The theories that seem to us to be the most potentially enlightening will be discussed.[4]

2. THE MAIN EPISTLES

A. Galatians

"The Epistle to the Galatians is spiritual dynamite, and it is therefore almost impossible to handle it without explosions," says Cole in his short commentary on Galatians.[5] The book has indeed caused all sorts of explosions, from its earliest times up to the present. Not only does it appear to have caused a number of debates within the early church; it has been an important book in recent discussion of the nature of Judaism and Paul's characterization of it (see ch. 9, above).

1. Authorship

The opinion of Kümmel is the consensus regarding authorship of Galatians: "That Galatians is a real, genuine letter is indisputable."[6] Apart from a very few eccentric critics through the ages, Galatians has been considered authentically Pauline. For Baur, to whom we owe a good portion of our enduring critical discussion regarding such issues as authorship, Galatians, along with Romans and 1 and 2 Corinthians, as mentioned above, was one of the four pillar epistles. As with 2 Corinthians, Philippians, and even Romans, however, this does not mean that all believe that every portion of the letter was written by Paul, or even at the same time. O'Neill has questioned the authenticity of portions of Galatians, arguing that there were later interpolations.[7] But his questioning of particular passages does not call into question the integrity and authorship of the bulk of the letter. In any case, he has not been followed in his view.

2. Destination and Date

The authorship of the letter is not seriously questioned, but a number of critical issues continue to be debated with regard to Galatians. Two of the most important are its destination and its date of composition.

a. Destination: North or South Galatia? One of the major debates over the last hundred years regarding Galatians is whether the letter was addressed to the North Galatians, that is, those living in the ancient ethnic area of the Galatians, or Gauls, who settled in Asia Minor in the fourth century B.C. from Europe, or to the South Galatians, that is, those living in the southern part of the Roman province of Galatia. There are several implications for this discussion. If the destination was North Galatia, the epistle almost assuredly had to be written after Paul's second missionary journey, with Gal 2:1–10 being a Pauline account of the Jerusalem Council in Acts 15 (or, in the minds of some, possibly the source for writing or creating the account in Acts 15). If the destination was South Galatia, then the letter could have been written as early as the end of Paul's first missionary journey, before the meeting of the Jerusalem Council. This would not preclude it from being written later, however. If the letter was written as early as the

end of the first missionary journey, then Gal 2:1–10 could be Paul's account of the so-called famine visit to Jerusalem of Acts 11:27–30 and 12:25 or a private meeting not mentioned in Acts.

The history of discussion of this issue is surprisingly recent. The early church, from the second century on, took the North Galatia, or ethnic, view, since the region of Lycaonia had apparently separated from the province of Galatia and united with Cilicia, thus putting several of the churches founded by Paul on his first missionary journey (e.g., Lystra and Derbe) in a separate province from Galatia. By the fourth century, the Roman province of Galatia had been reduced to its original, smaller size, thus eliminating evidence of the larger territory. The North Galatia view was generally accepted until the nineteenth century, when William Ramsay, as a result of firsthand exploration, concluded that the South Galatia, or provincial, view (first raised in the mid–eighteenth century) was more plausible.[8] Scholars have been divided on this issue ever since.

(1) North Galatia Hypothesis. The North Galatia view has been held by many important scholars, including the renowned J. B. Lightfoot (who wrote before Ramsay's discoveries and provides the classic discussion of the North Galatia view), Moffatt, Kümmel, Betz, and Martyn.[9] The main lines of argument for this position are as follows.

(a) The term "Galatia," from the Gauls or Celts (Γαλάται, *Galatai*; Κέλται, *Keltai*) who migrated from Europe into Asia Minor in the fourth century B.C., referred not to the political province but to the people who had been subdued by the Romans. Use of the term "Galatians" in Gal 3:1 in a racial sense would seem to support this interpretation.

(b) Acts 16:6 and 18:23 illustrate the geographical sense of the term "Galatia," since the author also mentions Phrygia, which was another territory in that area. The emphasis should be on the word "and" in both verses.

(c) In Acts 16:6, Paul and his companions "passed through" Phrygia and Galatia because they "had been forbidden" from preaching in the province of Asia. This implies that they went north to the Galatian region.

(d) Luke does not refer to Galatia when he mentions Paul going to Lystra and Derbe during the first missionary journey (Acts 14:6, 20, 21); he mentions instead Lycaonia, a different province, in which these cities were located.

(e) In Gal 4:13, the use of "former" (πρότερος, *proteros*) implies two former visits, those recorded in Acts 16:6 and 18:23. (This datum could, however, also be used to argue for a later date with the South Galatia view.)

(f) Since the style and subject matter of Galatians seem to be most compatible with Romans, the dates of their composition must have been very close to each other. It is difficult to take Galatians, with its discussion of law, as Paul's first letter, to be followed by the Thessalonian letters, which do not even mention the law. (This argument again only supports a later date of composition, not necessarily the North Galatia hypothesis.)

(g) The temperament of the Galatian Christians seems to reflect racial stereotypes of the period concerning the Galatians as a people—fickle, superstitious, and unsophisticated (Gal 3:1).

(h) By this view, Gal 1:21 refers to the first missionary journey in Acts 13–14.

(2) South Galatia Hypothesis. The South Galatia hypothesis has been held by Ramsay, Burton, Bruce, Martin, and Longenecker, among others,[10] although all scholars do not agree about the time of writing (see below). The major arguments for the South Galatia hypothesis are as follows.

(a) The phrase "Phrygia and Galatia" in Acts 16:6 and 18:23 contains the use of Phrygia in an adjectival sense, thus referring to Phrygian Galatia, the area of the Galatian province that includes the region of Phrygia. Ramsay was not able to provide an exact parallel of this usage, but he found similar kinds of modification that indicated this pattern was acceptable usage.

(b) The North Galatia view requires an unnatural detour in Acts 16, in which the normal trade routes along the borders of the province of Asia would not have been followed. Paul tended to follow the main roads and centers of communication in Roman provinces (that is, from Syria to Cilicia to Iconium and then to Ephesus). The southern side of the Anatolian plateau, which consisted of low hills with an adequate water supply, was far more important than the north, which was very difficult to get to. It is true that Lystra and Derbe were "backward" places, by Ramsay's own admission, but at least these cities were in the area in which Paul was traveling and so did not require a radical detour.[11]

(c) Paul is not precise in every instance, but unlike Luke, he normally uses Roman provincial titles, especially for areas where churches are located. Hence he uses Achaia or Greece rather than Hellas, which Luke uses.[12]

(d) In Acts 16:6, the aorist participle translated "forbidden" (κωλυθέντες, *kōlythentes*) is best taken as indicating that the forbidding took place not before Paul and his companions passed through Phrygia and Galatia but at the same time or after. Hence the verse is best translated, "they passed through Phrygian-Galatia, then were forbidden to speak the word in Asia," probably referring to Ephesus. In Greek, this sequence is determined by the word order (the participle follows the main verb) rather than by the tense of the participle.[13]

(e) Acts mentions only Paul's time in South Galatia, never recording a North Galatian ministry.

(f) Acts 20:4 refers to people from South Galatia (Gaius of Derbe, Timothy of Lystra) as involved in the collection, but no one from the north. No one from Corinth is mentioned either, but this is a different kind of omission in light of Paul's travel itinerary.

(g) The mention in Gal 2:1, 9, and 13 of Barnabas is better explained if Paul founded on the first missionary journey the churches to which he refers, since this was the only missionary journey on which Barnabas went with Paul.

(h) In light of the subject matter of Galatians, including debate over the Jewishness of Gentiles, it is difficult to believe that Paul would not mention the meeting in Jerusalem in Acts 15 if that meeting had already occurred (if it really did take place). As will be discussed below, however, though the South Galatia hypothesis does allow for greater flexibility regarding the date of composition of the letter, if the letter was written before the Jerusalem Council, it had to be written to the South Galatia churches.

(i) There is the possibility that the reference in Gal 4:14 and 6:17 to Paul being received as an "angel of God" by the Galatians or receiving the marks of Jesus coincides with the identification of Paul with Hermes and Barnabas with Zeus by the Lystrans in Acts 14:11–18, and with references to physical harm in Acts 14:19.

There are arguments for both sides, but it seems that the evidence for the South Galatia hypothesis has the greatest strength. During the first century, the province of Galatia was a large one that included many regions that brought together ethnic groups of all different sorts. One Latin inscription of the Roman period, recording the full title of a governor of Galatia, illustrates this diversity: he is described as governor "of Galatia, of Pisidia, of Phrygia, of Lycaonia, of Isauria, of Paphlogonia, of Pontus Galaticus, of Pontus Polemoniacus, of Armenia."[14] With the evidence that is at hand, it is more plausible to think that the letter was addressed to the churches at Lystra, Derbe, Iconium, and Antioch—churches that we know Paul visited and that were located in an area known in Roman times as Galatia—rather than conjecture about a different destination far removed from these in location. As Wallace and Williams add, "How could Paul have addressed the Christians in these four cities collectively except as Galatians?"[15]

b. Date[16]

(1) North Galatia. There are three possible dates for those who hold to the North Galatia hypothesis. The first is sometime after the first possible visit by Paul to North Galatia (Acts 16:6), sometime during his second missionary journey (i.e., A.D. 50–52). The second, held by Betz and others, is early in Paul's Ephesian ministry in Acts 19:1–41 (i.e., A.D. 53–55), taking the word "quickly" of Gal 1:6 literally with reference to the Galatians' abandoning the faith. Paul had visited the churches of Galatia in Acts 16:6 and 18:23 and then gone to Ephesus, where, according to this view, he must have written to them upon hearing of immediate danger. The third possible date is sometime after leaving Ephesus, giving a little bit of time between Paul's visit and his need for writing. Lightfoot dated the letter after the Corinthian letters, since there is no reference to the problem with Judaizers in the Corinthian correspondence, but before Romans—perhaps written in Macedonia—because of the theological similarities but less developed thinking (i.e., ca. A.D. 56–57).

(2) South Galatia. For those who hold to the South Galatia hypothesis, there are two possible time frames for composition. The later time of composition correlates with any of the dates suggested by the North Galatia hypothesis.[17] In this case, the "quickly" of Gal 1:6 indicates the quickness of their turning away rather than the length of time from

their conversion. The earlier date of composition posits that Paul wrote to the churches after his first missionary journey but before the Jerusalem Council of Acts 15 (i.e., A.D. 49?). In this case, Gal 4:13 refers to the two visits on his first missionary journey.

3. Paul's Visits to Jerusalem in Acts and Galatians

The discussion concerning the date of the composition of Galatians can be further clarified if reference is made to the visits to Jerusalem that are mentioned in Galatians and in Acts.[18] There are two major schemes for understanding the relationship between the Jerusalem visits of Paul according to Galatians and Acts. The following scheme assumes that the Jerusalem Council of Acts 15—or something like it in its essential subject matter—actually happened. Ever since Baur, there has probably been unnecessary skepticism over whether the council of Acts 15 took place. The oddness of the council's conclusions compromising Christian freedom—which Paul seems to take fairly lightly in his subsequent ministry—are sufficient to make a plausible case for its historicity; there is little motivation for the author to introduce potentially divisive issues on no historical grounds.

One reconstruction of the events of Galatians and Acts follows.

T A B L E   1 0 - 1
PAUL'S VISITS TO JERUSALEM I

Galatians		Acts	
1:18–20	Paul sees Cephas and James	9:26–29	Barnabas takes Paul to the apostles
1:21	Paul visits Syria and Cilicia	9:30	Paul departs for Tarsus
2:1–10	Paul and Barnabas, along with Titus, meet James, Peter, and John	15:2–29	Paul and Barnabas with the apostles and elders at the council

In this scheme, there are various explanations of Acts 11:27–30, the famine visit.[19] Some argue that the episode in Acts 11 is not historical and that Paul therefore does not mention it. Others argue that the two accounts in Acts 11 and 15 are duplicates that the author of Luke–Acts perhaps found in two separate sources, not realizing it was the same story. A third explanation is that the meeting of Acts 11, which appears to be a private meeting in which the apostles are not mentioned, is passed over in Galatians, since the challenge to which Paul is responding in Galatians concerns his relationship to the apostles.

A second reconstruction of the events in Galatians and Acts follows.

T A B L E   1 0 - 2

PAUL'S VISITS TO JERUSALEM II

Galatians		Acts	
1:18–20	Paul sees Cephas and James	9:26–29	Barnabas takes Paul to the apostles
1:21	Paul visits Syria and Cilicia	9:30	Paul departs for Tarsus
2:1–10	Paul and Barnabas, along with Titus, meet James, Peter, and John	11:27–30, 12:25	Paul and Barnabas bring famine relief
		15:2–29	Paul and Barnabas meet with the apostles and the elders

There are still some difficulties with this second equation. Most notably, the apostles and Titus are not mentioned in Acts 11, and it seems that Paul receives confirmation of his message to the Gentiles, even though this precedes his first missionary journey, which would have been the first test of his message. Nevertheless, the second solution is still a more plausible one. First, there is a place for Acts 11 and 15, without resorting to discrediting Luke's

account. Second, the meetings of Acts 11 and Gal 2:1–10 (see esp. v. 2) both look like private meetings. Third, Paul appears to be giving a strict chronology, so it would be surprising if he left out an important incident. This also raises the question of when the incident of Gal 2:11–14, Paul's confrontation with Peter (probably at Antioch), would have occurred. Some scholars think that Paul emerged unsuccessful from this confrontation, though this is probably not correct.[20] Most likely this meeting occurred before the events of Acts 15; otherwise the results of the meeting would have been reported in Galatians.

4. Galatian Opponents, the Occasion of the Letter to the Galatians, and Its Purpose

The occasion of a Pauline letter is defined as the specific circumstance or circumstances in force at the time of writing—for example, the audience's composition as a church, the history of its contact with Paul, and any relevant details regarding positive accomplishments or problems surrounding this contact. The purpose of a letter, on the other hand, is defined as the reason standing behind the composition of a letter, so far as this can be reconstructed from the letter itself. There is often not an easy or clear line of connection between the occasion and the purpose of a letter.

a. The Evidence. The evidence for Paul's opponents at Galatia includes the following features: People had visited this mission field (1:7; 5:10, 12), possibly coming from James in Jerusalem (2:12), bringing another teaching and questioning Paul's authority and apostleship (1:9, 10–11). They are characterized as troublemakers (1:7; 5:10) or agitators (5:12), and are seen as imposing requirements of Jewish law, especially circumcision (5:3, 11) and the observance of special days (4:10; 2:16; 3:2, 21b; 4:21; 5:4).

b. Paul's Response. Paul's response to the threat in the Galatian churches is vitriolic, evidencing his passion for the gospel. He characterizes the opponents' teaching as a perversion of the gospel (1:7) that represents a turning from God (1:6; 5:8), a falling from grace (5:4), and a denial of the promise of the Spirit (3:25). They have substituted a false message for the true one (1:8–9), a message that Paul received through revelation and that was later approved by those in Jerusalem (1:12; 1:13–2:10), exposing the opponents to judgment (5:10). In effect, their teaching is contrary to justification by faith (2:21), attempts to make the law a means of justification (3:11), and undermines Christ's death (2:21).

c. Definition of the Group(s) Involved.[21]

(1) A view held since the second century through Luther to the present, and still the majority view, is that the opponents in Galatians are Judaizers, a radical Jewish-Christian group of opponents of Paul from Jerusalem (perhaps sent by the Jerusalem apostles, as Baur speculated; see 2:12).[22] They penetrated the churches that Paul founded and attempted to persuade the Gentile Christians to accept circumcision and adopt the Jewish law as a necessary part of their belief in Christ, probably referring to Abraham's circumcision as his first great act of faith.[23] The fact that they have apparently come from outside the Galatian church is supported by Paul's use of the third person to refer to these groups (cf. 1 and 2 Corinthians [e.g., 1 Cor 5:1–2; 2 Cor 7:2–4], where the second person is used for insiders).[24] These legalists, however, may also have some proto-gnostic tendencies (Gal 4:9–10), in which their lack of regard for the earthly sphere results in libertinism (see 6:1).[25] It is more likely, however, that the references to freedom and indulgence (see 5:13, 16; 6:1, 8) can be explained as simply part of the message of the Judaizers, to which Paul responds by saying that though it may seem that they are free to do these things (using an inversion of Paul's own message?), there is a limit to their freedom.[26]

(2) A modification of the first position has argued that the opponents are Jewish Christians who have accepted circumcision and want to convince others to do the same.[27] The reason for this is that, supposedly, zealot activity in Jerusalem increased and Jewish Christians were trying to persuade Gentile Christians to accept circumcision so that the Jewish Christians would avoid persecution for association with Gentiles, arguing that God required it of them. Since the language of the letter is concerned with strictly Jewish practices and beliefs such as the law (ch. 3), circumcision (5:6; 6:15), and the calendar (4:10) and the opponents are characterized in terms of those who are not followers of Christ, this view is unlikely.

(3) A third position is that there are possibly two opponents, the Judaizers (see above) and libertine pneumatics, or those emphasizing life in the Spirit (6:1), who were attacking Paul's claim to apostleship. But the libertine dimension to the opponents can be explained simply as a part of the teaching of the Judaizers under the Judaizer hypothesis above. Since Paul seems to address his opponents as one cohesive group, it is not necessary to posit two sets of opponents.

5. Outline of Galatians

A. Opening (1:1–5)
  1. Sender (1:1–2a)
  2. Addressee (1:2)
  3. Greeting (1:3)
  4. Doxology (1:5)
(B. Thanksgiving—none)
C. Body: In defense of the apostle (1:6–5:12)
  1. Body's opening: A contrary gospel (1:6–9)
  2. Paul's authority (1:10–2:14)
  3. Paul's defense (2:15–5:12)
  4. Body's close on Christian freedom
D. Parenesis (5:13–6:10)[28]
  1. Love fulfills the law (5:13–15)
  2. The Spirit overcomes the flesh (5:16–26)
  3. The law of Christ is to help one another (6:1–10)
E. Closing (6:11–18)
  1. Pauline authority (6:11–17)
  2. Benediction (6:18)

B. 1 Thessalonians[29]

1. The City of Thessalonica

The city of Thessalonica was technically a part of the ancient kingdom of Macedonia, the home of Alexander the Great and his father, Philip.[30] But since that time (mid–4th cent. B.C.), with the influence that Philip and Alexander exerted upon restructuring this portion of the world, Macedonia had been considered part of the wider sphere of Greek influence, and for all intents and purposes Thessalonica was considered a Greek city. For a time, this northern portion of Greek territory, extending well into Macedonia proper, had existed independently as one of the Diadochian kingdoms after the dissolution of Alexander's empire following his death in 323 B.C., but with Roman expansion across the Adriatic Sea, it was inevitable that Macedonia would engage in conflict with Rome. After several wars, Macedonia was finally incorporated into the Roman Empire, first as four separate republics, with Thessalonica the leading city of the southernmost of these republics, and then finally as the one large province of Macedonia in 148 B.C.

The city of Thessalonica itself was founded in 315 B.C., and soon became an important city, as it lay on what became a major thoroughfare (known in Roman times as the Via Egnatia, or Egnatian Way) from the Adriatic Sea to Philippi and on to Byzantium. After a hundred years of Roman provincial rule, in 42 B.C. Thessalonica became a free city: its citizens enjoyed self-governance, under the authority of a person with the title of politarch or under some other form of governor. The accuracy of the account in Acts 17:6 used to be questioned, since it was the only literary text to record the title of politarch. In the twentieth century, however, several inscriptions bearing witness to the title have been discovered, even though the exact function of this official is not entirely clear.[31]

Recent excavations of the Roman forum in Thessalonica. Paul would have stayed in this area as a guest of Jason (Acts 17:6–7). Photo Lee M. McDonald.

The city seemed to consist of a mixed population, not untypical of numerous cities of the Roman Empire. According to Acts 17:2, there was a Jewish community in the city, since they had a synagogue where they worshiped. Christianity came to Thessalonica during Paul's travels in approximately A.D. 50–52, on what is sometimes referred to as his second missionary journey. He began his ministry in this city by preaching in the

synagogue, and it is reasonable, on the basis of what we find in the letter itself, to conclude that the account in Acts, which says that there were converts, is accurate. According to Acts, the converts were both Jews and Godfearers—Gentiles who respected the moral, ethical, and theological disposition of Judaism but resisted full proselytization, which would have involved circumcision.[32]

2. Paul in Thessalonica

The account in Acts 17 says that Paul went to the synagogue for three Sabbaths before the Jews were aroused to jealousy, formed a mob, and started a riot that forced Paul to leave the city. In light of the nature of the correspondence with the Thessalonians, especially the way it evidently adds to teaching on a number of issues that Paul apparently discussed with them, many scholars have inquired exactly how long Paul was in Thessalonica. A number have concluded that he must have been in the city longer than Acts states. Ramsay argued that Paul was in Thessalonica for approximately six months.[33] Some have determined that it is possible to posit a significantly longer period of time in the city, with the reference to three Sabbath days perhaps only describing his initial discussion or the length of time he attended the synagogue before he had converts.[34] Of course, there is also the possibility that the Acts account here does not accurately or completely record all that happened in Thessalonica.

From Thessalonica, Paul went on to Beroea, where he was followed by troublemakers from Thessalonica (Acts 17:13). He then went to Athens (17:16–33) and then to Corinth (18:1–18), where he stayed for one and a half years, according to Acts (see ch. 9, sec. 3, above). This occurred during the reign of Gallio and provides one of the reasonably certain dates for establishing the Pauline chronology. Paul was apparently in Corinth from ca. A.D. 50 to 52, and it was during this time that he probably wrote his letter to the Thessalonian church known as 1 Thessalonians (the authenticity of 2 Thessalonians is discussed below; if 2 Thessalonians is authentic as well, it was probably written soon after 1 Thessalonians from Corinth). Mention in 1 Thessalonians of Philippi (2:2), Macedonia and Achaia (1:7–8), and Athens (3:1) matches what Acts tells us of Paul's itinerary during this trip through Asia Minor and Greece. This occasion to write seems to have arisen fairly soon after Paul left the city, when he followed up on a number of the issues that he had apparently discussed with them during his time there. Perhaps the time Paul spent in Thessalonica is not as long as some scholars have thought necessary; a number of the issues raised in the letter appear to be ones that Paul would have reasonably discussed with them if he had been with them for a significant amount of time, such as the destiny of Christians who have died before the return of Christ.

Did Paul ever revisit the city, for which he had so many good things to say? He may well have done so on what is called his third missionary journey, probably about five years later (ca. A.D. 56), as is recorded in Acts 19:21 and 20:1–3. On this journey, Paul went to and from Greece through Macedonia and may well have passed through Thessalonica, possibly on his outward journey. On the basis of Paul's statement in Rom 15:19 regarding the spread of the gospel from Jerusalem all the way to Illyricum, some have speculated that Paul may have traveled west on the Via Egnatia into the territory of Illyricum. He may have had the intention of crossing over the Adriatic Sea to Rome, or even of traveling into a Latin-speaking territory in preparation for a future trip to Rome or Spain. This cannot be established with any certainty and in fact is probably unlikely, since the phrasing in Romans may well only refer to the spread of the gospel from Jerusalem as far as (or up to) Illyricum.

3. Authorship

The authorship of 1 Thessalonians is generally not disputed.[35] It is widely accepted as genuinely Pauline, except by a very small number of the most negative of critics, several of whom wrote during the nineteenth century during a particularly skeptical period of continental European criticism. The external testimony to Pauline authorship of 1 Thessalonians is well established and includes Marcion (Tertullian, *Ag. Marc.* 5.15; mid–2d cent.) and the Muratorian Fragment. Irenaeus, in the third century, also quotes it directly (*Haer.* 5.6.1; 5.30.2).[36] The internal witness is confirmatory as well, since there are several distinctive markings of Pauline authorship. The first is the opening of the letter, which claims to have come from Paul, Silas (or Silvanus), and Timothy. (The discussion of

pseudonymity and the Pauline Letters in ch. 9, above, suggests that epistolary pseudonymity was a more widespread phenomenon in the ancient world than many more conservative scholars wish to recognize. A plausible case for the pseudonymity of this letter cannot, however, be made in light of the other criteria for authenticity.) Second, there is evidence of an early date for 1 Thessalonians in 5:12, where Paul, referring to church organization, mentions "those who . . . have charge of you." This seems to imply that at this point there was not a formal title for those in positions of leadership within local congregations of believers. That such titles apparently were developed quite early is confirmed by Phil 1:1, but that letter was probably written ten years later. (Acts 14:23, which mentions the appointment of elders on Paul's so-called first missionary journey, does not necessarily contradict this, since the author of Luke–Acts may be retroactively ascribing titles developed by the time of his writing.)[37]

Also confirmatory of an early date is the issue of the Parousia, or return of Christ. The author may well have had the expectation—or at least was open to the possibility—of being alive at the time of the return of Christ (4:17). This is an unlikely stance for a later author to take, especially if it were known that Paul was dead, and it introduces an unnecessary hypothesis in light of what is known about the early eschatology of the church, with its expectation regarding Christ's return. The evidence is sufficiently ambiguous even among the undisputed Pauline Letters that we would not want to posit too strongly what Paul's definitive position on Christ's imminent return was. But it is fair to say that he was at least open to this possibility, even if it was not, in his mind, as strong a likelihood later on (as 2 Corinthians and Philippians, both later letters, seem to confirm). The scene regarding expectation of the Parousia painted in this letter is consistent with the portrait of Paul drawn in Acts and makes it entirely likely that Paul would have written a letter of this sort to the Thessalonian church.

In spite of this substantial evidence regarding Pauline authorship, there has still been some debate over the integrity of the letter. Two passages—2:13–16 and 5:1–11—have been suggested to be later interpolations.[38] The first passage has been questioned on the grounds that it appears to be anti-Semitic, reflecting not only an un-Pauline theological perspective (cf. Rom 11:25–26) but also events after the destruction of Jerusalem. Hence, according to this view, it may well be a post–70 interpolation reflecting later Jewish-Christian tensions. This proposal has been rejected on many fronts: (1) it fails to appreciate the early tensions between Jews and Christians, at least from the time of Paul; (2) the kind of hyperbole found in this passage is well within the parameters of Paul's argumentative style; and (3) there is no good reason for this interpolation.[39] Arguments that 5:1–11 is non-Pauline stem from the premise that the author was correcting Paul's mistaken view of the Parousia. Used in support of this premise are changes in wording (παρουσία ["coming"], used elsewhere in this letter, gives way here to "day of the Lord") and parallels with passages that do not express eschatological imminence. This position has also found few supporters, since the kinds of contrasts that it depends upon do not seem justified.[40] Despite arguments that draw attention to problems in the text and features of the language, these theories have not convinced most scholars, so that it is fair to say that the letter can be treated in its entirety as authentically Pauline. (Redactional and partition theories are discussed in sec. C, below.)

4. 1 Thessalonians and Acts

Disregarding this evidence for coherence between 1 Thessalonians and the picture of the early church in Acts, a number of apparent discrepancies between 1 Thessalonians and Acts are still worth mentioning (in addition to how many Sabbaths Paul spent in Thessalonica; see sec. B.2, above). The first concerns the composition of the Thessalonian church. In the letter itself, the author appears to be addressing Gentiles, since he mentions that they turned from idols to serve God (1:9), they have suffered from their own countrymen, just as other churches suffered from the Jews (2:14), and they now are unlike the heathen (4:5). The problem for some scholars arises from the account in Acts, where no emphasis is placed upon converts from paganism. It must be kept in mind, however, that the perspective of Acts may well be different from that of the letter, especially since, in several of Acts' brief accounts of Paul's visits to cities, a far from complete list of events is recorded.

More to the point is the fact that Acts' account does record that Paul's converts included Jews and Godfearers. There has been sustained controversy regarding the category of Godfearers. A number of scholars, most recently led by Kraabel, have argued that this category is an invention by the author of Luke–Acts and has no factual basis to describe a group in the religious climate of the ancient world.[41] It appears that Acts understands these people as Gentiles who found the moral, ethical, and theological disposition of Judaism commendatory and commensurate with their own inclinations. Recent publications drawing upon inscriptions give credence to the Acts account.[42] Acts does not say what proportion of Christian converts came from each category, but it is not unreasonable to conclude that the majority may well have been Gentiles, with most of these Godfearers.

A second point of contention revolves around the coauthorship of Timothy and Silas in light of the evidence in Acts. Acts 18:5 says that these companions rejoined Paul at Corinth, while 1 Thess 3:1–2 says that Timothy was in Athens. How can these data be made to square with the coauthorship of 1 Thessalonians and what we know of Pauline chronology? The solution may well be that there was a journey—not recorded in Acts—by Silas and Timothy from Athens to Macedonia and then to Corinth. The chronology would be that Silas and Timothy waited in Beroea while Paul went to Athens (Acts 17:14), from which he traveled to Corinth (Acts 17:16). Silas and Timothy arrived in Athens, but they were sent off again by Paul to Macedonia and then arrived in Corinth. This may well have provided the source of information from the church in Thessalonica to Paul, its apostle, who had so recently departed, apparently in some hurry, and was unable to impart anything close to all the teaching that the church required or that he would have been able to give bit-by-bit as situations arose. After Silas and Timothy rejoined Paul at Corinth and conveyed information from the church to him, he began his correspondence with it (Acts 18:5). Admittedly, this reconstruction is speculative, but its reading of the evidence must be considered.

5. Occasion and Purpose

It is important to establish the occasion and purpose of 1 Thessalonians. Timothy apparently brought back a good report after his visit (posited in sec. B.4, above, but not stated in Acts) regarding the faith and love of the church at Thessalonica (1 Thess 3:6). According to Acts, Paul apparently had to leave Thessalonica in a hurry once the Jews were aroused to jealousy; it is not known how long Paul was in Thessalonica (Acts mentions three Sabbaths), and it is possible that he was there longer than Acts records, perhaps even as long as six months (see sec. B.2, above). Since he probably did not bring a number of issues to a satisfying conclusion because of his apparently speedy departure, perhaps some made accusations against Paul regarding his character. They may have chosen to depict him in a light similar to that of other itinerant teachers and philosophers in the ancient world, who entered a city and spoke publicly so long as they were well received and well rewarded by the people but who took advantage of these same people and then fled when trouble began.[43]

Paul therefore wrote to the Thessalonians with apparently a twofold purpose. The first was to express his general satisfaction with the believers in Thessalonica, and the second was to answer the charge that his motives might be suspect. He ends up answering a number of questions that Timothy evidently brought with him and that were being asked by the Thessalonian Christians, but his placement of these in the parenetic section of the letter suggests that these were not initially at the forefront of his thinking or his purpose in writing.

Paul expresses satisfaction over the progress of the Christian community, using the thanksgiving of the letter (1:2–10) to express his thanks to God for their response to his message. He singles out their faith, love, and hope (1:3)—note his use of a rhetorically forceful list of three, the same list used in 1 Cor 13—as qualities that have produced results. God has chosen them because the gospel came not only in words but in power and in the Holy Spirit (1:5). The Holy Spirit was the one who brought the message that they had received, the verification of which is their having become imitators of Paul and the compatriots of both himself and the Lord despite severe suffering. This may constitute an incidental reference to the persecution that some of the Christians at Thessalonica received when the Jews became hostile toward Paul. Later in the letter, Paul again encourages their perseverance in the face of opposition, this time from

their own countrymen, that is, Gentiles (2:13–16). This section, too, expresses Paul's thanksgiving regarding the Thessalonians. The thankful tone is so pronounced and interspersed throughout the first part of the letter that it has been proposed that 1 Thessalonians is less a letter following the Pauline structure and more an expanded thanksgiving running throughout most of the first two chapters, possibly to 3:13, if not further.[44] In any case, the Thessalonians have become a model to all the believers in Macedonia and Achaia, and their faith is known everywhere (1:8–10). We would expect thankful expressions in the thanksgiving part of the letter. But it is also clear that Paul does not hesitate to withhold thanksgiving and commendation where they are not warranted, as in the Letter to the Galatians. Indeed, there are few letters in the Pauline corpus, if any, where heartfelt thanks are more readily and freely given than in these opening verses of 1 Thessalonians.

Paul answers at some length in the body of the letter (2:1–12; 2:17–3:5) the apparent charges against him that he was self-seeking, cowardly, and mercenary in his dealings with the Thessalonians, as confirmed by his failure to return to see them. The body of this letter, like other Pauline Letters, is devoted not only to spiritual concepts but to a defense of his own ministry to the church (see the Corinthian correspondence and Galatians). He points out that he is not unaccustomed to opposition and even suffering, having come from Philippi, where he also suffered. The reason for his defense, he says, is that his motives are not erroneous or impure, and certainly not based upon trickery. He is not trying to please humans but, rather, God, who tests human hearts and stands as his witness. For further proof of his sincerity, he points out that whereas his position as an apostle might have warranted some form of financial entitlement provided by the church, this was not his or his followers' approach. Not only did they share the gospel with the Thessalonians; they shared in a common physical existence as well. For Paul, this means that he engaged in physical work to help support himself (2:8–9; see ch. 9, above, on Paul and his profession). Paul does confine his statements to his own position of leadership, however. Seeing in these accusations a potentially larger implication about the leadership of the church, he tells the Thessalonians that they owe their current leaders the same kind of respect (5:12–13). As to the second prong of the attack on his character—why he had not returned to see the church again—Paul seems aware of the difficulty this might have caused; he admits that his first visit was curtailed but assures them that he had made efforts to visit them again. When he was not successful—he attributes it to Satan stopping him and his coworkers—he sent Timothy, who had brought back the good report.

More space and attention in 1 Thessalonians are devoted to the issue of the Parousia (4:13–18) and the day of the Lord (5:1–11) than to any other topic. But regardless of the space given it in the letter and the important role it has played in certain contemporary circles that have become preoccupied with biblical eschatology, the issue is not of primary significance for the *purpose* of the letter. This becomes evident when one considers the letter's structure. As the following outline indicates, the body of the letter (2:1–3:13) is concerned with Paul's relationship with the Thessalonian Christians. The purpose is clearly to commend the Thessalonians in their behavior and to provide a rationale for his behavior with them and since. The material on the Parousia falls within the parenetic section of the letter (4:1–5:22). Although it is not unimportant material (see below), it is simply not as central to the purpose of the letter as other topics.

Paul discusses a number of important theological issues in this letter, but certain ones stand out as unique and significant. Because of the contingent nature of the Pauline Letters and the fact that 1 Thessalonians expresses only a portion of a complex relationship between Paul and the Christians at Thessalonica, it is difficult to establish the proportional significance of the topics discussed. For example, throughout this letter, Paul assumes without argumentation the conceptual framework of several theological beliefs. Thus Paul does not argue for, but rather supposes, the existence of the "living and true God" (1:9), who is the Father of his Son, Jesus Christ, whom he raised from the dead (1:10). To Christ himself is ascribed the exalted status of being present with God, having died for believers (1:1; 5:10). Likewise, the Holy Spirit is seen as empowering believers to proclaim the gospel (1:5), giving joy (1:6) and helping them to be holy (4:8).

In two other areas, however, Paul does offer significant teaching. These occur in the parenetic section of the letter, probably indicating that the material is presented with the idea of being less doctrinal than exhortatory (although there is a distinctive exhortatory sense about the whole letter)[45] and that it is designed to enhance the quality of the believer's life rather than to establish its theological basis. The first topic concerns Christian living (4:1–12), sanctification. This has already been treated regarding Paul's primary teaching (see ch. 9, above), but the way he treats it in this letter warrants further discussion. Underlying Paul's discussion with the Thessalonians is the apparent assumption that believers, both Paul and the Thessalonians themselves, are to display or live out a life in harmony with the gospel. Paul commends the Thessalonians for displaying lives that are worthy of imitation by other Christians because they are imitators of Paul and of the Lord. Paul apparently addresses these words to a church that had experienced persecution from fellow Gentiles, just as Paul had experienced persecution from Jews when he was in Thessalonica. Love, honesty, and good works are to characterize the Christian life, even when one is enduring trials and persecution. The goal, Paul says, is to be holy at Christ's coming. This theme is excellent for illustrating how Paul links the body of the letter with the parenesis. He closes the body of the letter, as he often does, with one of his travelogues (2:17–3:13), which comes to an eschatological climax (3:11–13), where, in a doxological format, he wishes that God might present the Thessalonians blameless and holy at Christ's return. Then, in the first parenesis of the letter (4:1–12), Paul discusses the theme of living to please God, introduced by an exhortatory formula (παρακαλῶ, *parakalō*, "entreat"). After telling the Thessalonians of the ideal, he now instructs them how to live. What he desires for them is holiness or sanctification (4:3–8) in the area of sexual and personal ethics and that they exemplify brotherly love (4:9–12). Christian sexual ethics came into direct conflict with pagan sexual ethics. Sexual practices often played a part in the religious cults of the time, to say nothing of their role in the general culture, where sexual immorality was common. Perhaps Paul realized or had heard that for many of the Gentiles in the church at Thessalonica, it was difficult to change earlier practices. Paul, however, clearly considers Christian morality to be categorically different from pagan morality (4:4 is a difficult verse, meaning either "to gain mastery over his body" [NEB] or "to take a wife for himself" [RSV]; each has merit).[46]

The second issue on which Paul spends time is the Parousia, or coming of the Lord. This is not the place to try to solve the many enigmas of this passage, but a few observations are warranted. Paul's comments here apparently follow up on instructions he gave them when he was in Thessalonica regarding the return of Christ, but perhaps his premature departure curtailed his teaching. The singular difficulty appears to have concerned the fate of believers who died before the return of Christ. Notice, however, how much Paul seems to assume they already know—for example, the resurrection of the dead (since this is what those who have "fallen asleep" are thought to miss out on [4:14]), the living believers' being caught up to heaven (4:15), and the nearness of the end (4:16). To comfort those concerned about dead friends or relatives, Paul conveys a useful chronology in which the living have no advantage over the dead, since the same spectacular events are to occur to both groups. The sequence he describes is for the dead in Christ first, and then the living (4:16–17), to be caught up to "meet the Lord in the air"; "meet [the Lord]" is a term used elsewhere of a delegation going outside a city to meet an important dignitary.[47] In 5:1–11, the transition in v. 1 can indeed indicate a shift in topic, but here it appears to indicate a logical shift, from the comforting facts regarding the return of Christ to the question of when this is supposed to occur. Again, Paul indicates that he does not need to write to the Thessalonians because they know a sufficient amount already. Instead he contrasts those who are awaiting Christ's return with those who are going to be caught unprepared. For the latter it will come like a thief in the night, so he instructs the Thessalonians to be sons of light and sons of the day, prepared so as not to suffer wrath but, rather, experience salvation. The imagery Paul uses in this section is apocalyptic. Apocalyptic imagery is characterized by the otherworldly intervention of God in a situation where his followers are persecuted and despair of society being transformed from within. As depicted in works of apocalyptic literature, the translation from this world to another through a heavenly journey is the kind of experience the redeemed can expect.

Many commentators have taken 4:15, 17, where Paul speaks of being alive at the Parousia of the Lord, to indicate that he believed that the return of Christ would occur during his own lifetime. Others, however, believe that in light of such passages as 2 Cor 5:1–10 and Phil 1:20–24, Paul was not necessarily teaching this belief. Positions claiming that Paul develops in his thinking from one position to another have also been argued. Scholarly opinion generally sees Paul as living with a tension between Christ's already being present and his expected return.[48] While it is not entirely certain that Paul believed that he would be alive at that time, since he uses the first person plural throughout 1 Thessalonians, apparently sometimes referring to himself (e.g., 1 Thess 3:1) and sometimes referring to other believers as well (e.g., 1 Thess 2:1), there is a sense of imminence conveyed in the letter. It comes through in this section in the similar treatment of both the dead and the living at Christ's coming. Paul could well have thought that a number of those alive at the time of his writing would still be alive at Christ's return; otherwise he would have responded in a different way, instructing his readers that the resurrection of those asleep would be the fate of all. But this is not what he says. Elsewhere in the letter, the sense of imminence also comes through with the emphasis on right living in the expectation that Christ could return and catch someone failing to live a holy life. It is possible to conceive of Paul believing at the outset of his ministry in the imminent return of Christ but being forced to moderate his optimism in subsequent writings in light of the increasing evidence that he himself would die before Christ's return. In any event, the sense of imminence is evident. (Comparison of the eschatological teaching of this letter with 2 Thessalonians has led many scholars to call into question the authenticity of 2 Thessalonians.)

6. Outline of 1 Thessalonians

   A. Opening (1:1)
      1. Sender (1:1)
      2. Addressee (1:1)
      3. Greeting (1:1)
   B. Thanksgiving (1:2–10)
   C. Body: Paul's relationship with the Thessalonians (2:1–3:13)
      1. Body's opening: Paul's defense (2:1–12)
      2. Further thanksgiving (2:13–16)

3. Pauline travelogue: Paul's relationship with the Thessalonians (2:17–3:13)
D. Parenesis (4:1–5:22)
  1. Living to please God (4:1–12)
  2. The coming of the Lord (4:13–5:11)
  3. Final exhortations (5:12–22)
E. Closing (5:23–28)
  1. Doxology (5:23)
  2. Greetings (5:26)
  3. Benediction (5:28)

C. 2 Thessalonians

1. Authorship and Authenticity

Many scholars seriously question the authenticity of 2 Thessalonians. There has been some question about Pauline authorship since the nineteenth century, but this dispute has arisen most strongly within the last twenty-five years, with the vast majority of scholars before 1970 arguing for authenticity. If, at the end of the discussion below, the evidence seems to weigh for the reader in favor of Pauline authorship, then the situation in Thessalonica noted above and its probable correlation with the evidence presented in Acts will need to be consulted.

When arguments regarding the Pauline authorship of 2 Thessalonians are presented, the following seem to carry the most weight.

a. External Evidence. Although external evidence from the church father Justin is not decisive (*Dial.* 32, 110, 116), 2 Thessalonians is found in Marcion's collection and the Muratorian Fragment, is cited in Polycarp (*Phil.* 11.3 [1:4]; 11.4 [3:15]), Tertullian (*Scorp.* 13; *Res.* 24), Irenaeus (*Haer.* 3.7.2; 5.25.1), and Clement of Alexandria (*Strom.* 5.3), and is possibly referred to in Origen (*Cels.* 2.65). It may be cited in *Barnabas* as well (18.2 [2:6]; 4.9 [2:8]; 15.5 [2:8, 12]).[49] Thus the external evidence and attestation for 2 Thessalonians is stronger than that for 1 Thessalonians and for most of the other disputed epistles.

b. Internal Evidence. The most detailed argument against Pauline authorship of 2 Thessalonians was made in 1972 by Trilling. Trilling's work has had widespread influence, but it has also garnered severe criticism.[50] In what follows, an evaluation is made of the major arguments that Trilling and others have made against Pauline authorship. The internal evidence can be evaluated in several different spheres: attestation of the letter itself, tone, apparent audience, similarities of circumstances to 1 Thessalonians, and teaching and theology.

(1) The attestation of the letter clearly points to Paul as at least the ostensible author. Like 1 Thessalonians, the letter purports to have been written by Paul, Silas (or Silvanus), and Timothy (1:1). Second Thessalonians does not refer directly to 1 Thessalonians, but it has an indirect reference to the author having previously corresponded with the recipients (2:15). This statement is possibly to be interpreted in conjunction with the implication suggested by 2 Thessalonians that it was sent in response to some other inauthentic letter (2:2; 3:17). The author also claims to be Paul in 3:17, where he claims to affix a final greeting in his own hand, something that distinguishes his letters. The fact that Paul affixes his signature to this letter but not to 1 Thessalonians raises intriguing questions regarding authenticity; some speculate that this is an attempt by the pseudonymous author to convince the recipients that the letter is authentic. This issue is discussed below (sec. C.3) in relation to the order of composition of the letters.

(2) As noted above, it is virtually unanimously accepted that 1 Thessalonians was written with an almost overwhelming sense of thanksgiving to the Christians in Thessalonica, but many perceive a change of tone in 2 Thessalonians. The warm and friendly tone of 1 Thessalonians is, according to some, exchanged for a more formal and frigid tone in 2 Thessalonians. Whereas 1 Thess 1:2 says that "we always give thanks," 2 Thess 1:3 and 2:13 state that "we must always give thanks," as if there is some impediment to the same kind of thanksgiving. By most accounts of those who argue for authenticity, 2 Thessalonians was written very soon after 1 Thessalonians, thus making this change in tone perplexing. This purported change, however, may not be as severe as some have thought. Paul refers in 2 Thessalonians to the readers as "brothers and sisters" (3:1), asks for prayer from them (3:1–2), and is polite in dealing with the problem of idleness, one already raised in 1 Thess 5:14. A possible change in circumstances for Paul or his readers—including a failure by the Thessalonians to take note of Paul's teaching—might make some change in tone warranted, especially if the Thessalonians still failed to understand his comments on eschatology.

The temple of Hadrian on Curetes Street in Ephesus. © Rohr Productions. Used with permission.

Egirdir Lake, near Pisidian Antioch in Turkey. © Rohr Productions. Used with permission.

(3) While the audience of 1 Thessalonians appears to be of Gentile composition, it has been argued that the readers of 2 Thessalonians appear to be Jewish, or at least know the thought of the OT better than the audience of the first letter (see 2 Thess 1:6–10 on retribution) and are more familiar with the imagery often associated with Jewish apocalyptic writings (2:1–12). But the fact that there are no direct quotations of the OT in 2 Thessalonians raises the question whether there is any imagery or thinking in the letter that would not be readily understood in context. Furthermore, the composition of the church, as discussed in 1 Thessalonians, included a large number of Gentiles, but many of these Gentiles came apparently from the ranks of the Godfearers; they therefore probably would have been very familiar with the thought and even language of the OT.

(4) Another question often raised about the authenticity of 2 Thessalonians concerns the similarities between the two letters: why would Paul have written two letters so similar to each other within such a short space of time? First and 2 Thessalonians are linguistically the two most closely linked of the Pauline Letters. This can be illustrated not only by the use of particular vocabulary items but by repeated instances of parallel phrasing as well (2 Thess 1:1–2 and 1 Thess 1:1; 2 Thess 1:3 and 1 Thess 1:2; 2 Thess 1:11 and 1 Thess 1:3; 2 Thess 1:8 and 1 Thess 4:5; 2 Thess 2:14 and 1 Thess 5:9; 2 Thess 3:8 and 1 Thess 2:9; 2 Thess 3:10 and 1 Thess 3:4).[51] One must be careful with such an argument against authenticity, however. All sorts of situations can be suggested that might warrant such a procedure. For example, if the author believed that the situation warranted discussion of similar issues once more, would he not tend to use similar language? The short space in time could argue in favor of similar language, since it appears less likely that the author would undergo a radical shift in style in so short a time. This argument, in its present form, is simply untenable. One can envision a similar argument being made for non-Pauline authorship if the books were dissimilar in language. This raises the very important question of what constitutes differences and similarities in language and how such differences are weighed. In other words, how dissimilar or similar can or should they be? How is this usable as a test for authenticity?

(5) The final issue often raised in discussion of authenticity concerns the teaching and theology of the letter, especially its eschatological teaching. Eschatological teaching is part of Paul's parenetic directives in 1 Thessalonians, but it constitutes the body of the letter of 2 Thessalonians. Perhaps even more noticeable, however, is the supposed change in perspective. First Thessalonians has a sense of imminence, but this appears to be far less intense in 2 Thessalonians because the author states that certain events have to take place before the coming of the Lord can occur (2:1). The characterization of the man of lawlessness, furthermore, appears to draw upon other NT writing or some form of apocalyptic thinking. The man of lawlessness, it has been claimed, appears to be another way of describing the anti-Christ, quite possibly copied from Rev 13:1–9 (or even 1 John), making the letter obviously derivative and later than the time of Paul. Speculation regarding such a figure, especially in light of Paul's own life, also provokes thoughts about whether this is a depiction of the Nero myth. (There apparently grew up speculation in apocalyptic circles that Nero, the cruel persecutor, had not died but would return to resume once more his oppression.) Some scholars have proposed, however, that one need not look to the Nero myth for an explanation of the man of lawlessness, since the idea is found in intertestamental Jewish literature (e.g., *1 En.* 85–90; *Jub.* 23:16–32; *Sib. Or.* 3:388–400) and might well be used to refer to a pseudomessianic figure.[52]

Other theological ideas are sometimes cited as not being as important in 2 Thessalonians as they are in 1 Thessalonians. For example, the Spirit (2 Thess 2:2, 8, 13), the death and resurrection of Christ (cf. 1 Thess 4:14), and God do not seem to be as significant to the author of 2 Thessalonians as they are to the author of 1 Thessalonians. It does appear that some of these ideas are not as extensively mentioned in 2 Thessalonians as they are in the other letter, but one must be careful how this evidence is handled. For example, the Spirit and God are two of the Pauline theological assumptions, ideas that he does not appear to believe he needs to justify, and seems to simply assume (see ch. 9, above). We must be cautious, therefore, how much weight we attach to theological ideas that even in Paul's undisputed letters he does not believe he must argue for. The failure to mention these ideas cannot constitute a sufficient argument to establish non-Pauline authorship. Nevertheless, it is noteworthy that 1 and 2 Thessalonians both equate Christ with God, with similar phrasing used in each (e.g., 2 Thess 2:13 and 1 Thess 1:4).

2. Explaining the Difficulties in Pauline Authorship

If a traditional estimation of Pauline authorship is rejected despite the evidence that 2 Thessalonians was sent to the entire church at Thessalonica—then how, why, and by whom was the letter composed? The number of scenarios has been significant, covering a full range of options.

Several explanations wish to retain the idea of Pauline authorship while still addressing the differences between the two letters.[53] For example, several proposals revolve around the intended audiences of the letters. Thus Harnack proposed his divided-church theory, according to which 1 Thessalonians was addressed to the Gentiles of the church and 2 Thessalonians was addressed to the Jewish Christians at Thessalonica.[54] This theory takes account of several features noted above regarding the sense gained from each of the letters (at least by some scholars) about the primary audience. Dibelius proposed that 1 Thessalonians was addressed to the small group of leaders of the church while 2 Thessalonians was for public reading; conversely, Ellis proposed that 2 Thessalonians was addressed to Paul's coworkers in the city to deal with the problem of idleness induced by eschatological thinking whereas 1 Thessalonians was addressed to the church as a whole. A number of problems with these solutions, however, make them seem unlikely to most scholars (besides the solutions' being, in some instances, contradictory). The evidence of a divided church is slender according to internal and external evidence. In 1 Thess 2:13–16, the Judean church is held up to the Thessalonians as an example to be followed—unlikely if the letter is only addressing the Gentiles of the Thessalonian church. The similarities of the letters in so many regards, which are addressed to the same church and which both mention idleness, also argue against the kind of distinction that these theories require. The instruction of 1 Thess 5:27 that the letter be read aloud certainly argues against its being a private letter.

An idea first suggested in the nineteenth century and recently revived is that the material found in 1 and 2 Thessalonians is perhaps more than two letters. Therefore, a number of partition theories have been proposed. The most well known, by Schmithals, goes a long way toward providing a defense of Pauline authorship, taking note of several of the difficulties about the structure of 1 and 2 Thessalonians. These include the apparent second major thanksgiving in 1 Thessalonians, closing at 3:11. Schmithals proposed four letters—compiled into the canonical two letters—each epistle ending with a section introduced by "May the Lord/God" (2 Thess 3:16; 1 Thess 5:23; 2 Thess 2:16; 1 Thess 3:11): Thessalonians A = 2 Thess 1:1–12; 3:6–16; Thessalonians B = 1 Thess 1:1–2:12; 4:2–5:28; Thessalonians C = 2 Thess 2:13–14; 2:1–12; 2:15–3:3 (or 3:5); 3:17–18; and Thessalonians D = 1 Thess 2:13–4:1.[55] The unfortunate problem with this idea (and others like it), as creative and sensitive as it purports to be with handling the textual difficulties, is that there is no text-critical evidence that the letters were ever arranged in this way. There is no external evidence that the letters were ever circulated in anything other than the form in which they are found canonically. All of the textual changes must have been made before the writing of our extant NT manuscripts. This could have happened, but it cannot be proven from the evidence that we have. This theory is also dependent upon 2 Thessalonians being written before 1 Thessalonians, a theory that is far from proven (see below). The dilemma that haunts this and other partition theories is that, on the one hand, it is asserted that Paul's words were venerated in the early church and thus preserved, while, on the other hand, it must be admitted that sections of the original forms of these letters—such as the Pauline openings and closings, as well as possibly other major portions—were excised and lost.

It has also been proposed that 2 Thessalonians was sent to another church in Macedonia—not the one at Thessalonica, which received 1 Thessalonians. The letters were sent at about the same time. Some of the suggestions for the original destination of 2 Thessalonians include Beroea and Philippi, cities with which Paul had significant contact during his second missionary trip (Acts 16:12–40; 17:10–15). Beroea is the city that he visited right after leaving Thessalonica in a hurry when jealous Jews

The interior of the western theater at Gerasa (Jerash, Jordan). © Rohr Productions. Used with permission.

A colonnade at the Asklepion near the theater in Pergamum. © Rohr Productions. Used with permission.

reportedly rioted. Philippi is the most significant city visited before Thessalonica; there Paul had a successful ministry, not even excluding his night in jail. This theory certainly can account for the two letters being written close together and using similar language. It has difficulty, however, explaining the textual evidence—that there is no extant text of 2 Thessalonians bearing witness to a destination other than Thessalonica. There are, furthermore, the supposed significant differences in theology, especially regarding eschatology. If the theologies are in conflict, it is unlikely that Paul was responsible for sending these letters with two different perspectives to these cities.

Another explanation has not been as seriously considered as it probably should be—that 2 Thessalonians departs from the standard Pauline letter because of coauthorship or the role of an amanuensis. According to this theory, 2 Thessalonians (or 1 Thessalonians) may have been composed by Timothy (who is mentioned in the opening salutation of six other Pauline Letters) or Silvanus (Silas). Reconstructing the exact circumstances that would have warranted this involvement from a coworker or even an unnamed scribe is nearly impossible, other than what we know of the obvious impediments to Paul himself writing: the need to make a living, difficult physical circumstances, or other commitments. Even if one or both of the cosenders or another person was involved, Paul's name was clearly attached to it in 1:1 and 3:17. This would be due to Paul's status in the Thessalonian community as its founding apostle and his active involvement in, and concern for, the church there, as illustrated by his first letter to it. This would warrant the second letter being called Pauline as well. Such a solution solves a number of problems, including the evident similarities of the letters and the shift in tone, but there are other problems it does not solve. For example, if the eschatology is different between 1 and 2 Thessalonians, it is difficult to account for Paul's putting his name to both letters. There is the further problem of quantifying such a theory. Apart from the several names included in 2 Thess 1:1, there is no specific evidence for it.

The most plausible explanation for those who dispute Pauline authorship of 2 Thessalonians is that the letter is pseudonymous—that is, that it was written some time later than 1 Thessalonians

by a sympathetic follower of Paul using his name. It has sometimes been asked whether a church that had received one genuine letter would be willing to accept a second letter not by the same author. This presumes, however, that the pseudonymous letter was sent to the Thessalonian church during the time when the recipients of the first letter were still alive. Especially in light of the contents of the first and the second letters, and the language of 2 Thessalonians regarding the second coming of Christ, the evidence points away from such an audience. The theories on the circumstances of this composition vary; some propose that the letter was written around the turn of the first and second centuries to a church experiencing a problem similar to that of the original Thessalonian church, perhaps a problem made even more acute by the still delayed return of Christ.[56] Why the author would have included a reference to Paul's signature at 3:17 can be answered in several ways—for instance, the literary convention of including realistic and evidentiary statements, not to deceive but to indicate the relationship of the letter to its apostolic precursor.

3. Order of Composition of 1 and 2 Thessalonians

For those who believe that both epistles are sufficiently Pauline that they could have arrived in Thessalonica one soon after the other (any number of the proposals mentioned above could be compatible with this situation), there is still the question of which was sent first. The traditional view is that Paul wrote 1 Thessalonians first and then 2 Thessalonians soon afterwards, probably within the same year. Recently, this position has been questioned by a number of scholars (e.g., Wanamaker, in a recent English-language commentary on the Greek text).[57]

Arguments employed to establish that 2 Thessalonians preceded 1 Thessalonians and is therefore the earlier of the two follow, with brief responses. (1) The traditional order is apparently based upon length (e.g., $\mathfrak{P}^{45}$ has the Pauline Letters arranged according to length), not chronological order, thus opening up at least the possibility that 2 Thessalonians was written first. But does this indicate that 2 Thessalonians *should* be first? The argument does not directly address that issue. (2) Second

Thessalonians 2:5 and 3:10 give reasons for a misunderstanding that Paul tries to solve, opening up the possibility that the more settled tone of 1 Thessalonians indicates that the problem is now resolved. This is a matter of judgment. These passages may just as easily indicate Paul's continuing frustration that the Thessalonians are still having difficulties despite his previous letter to them. (3) Some contend that the eschatology in 2 Thessalonians is more primitive and that 1 Thessalonians reflects Paul's later realization that Christ would not return as soon as he had thought. It is debatable that this is the way to read these two letters, since 2 Thess 2:7 talks of "the one who now restrains" and 1 Thess 4:17 talks of "we who are alive." (4) It has been argued that 2 Thessalonians indicates trials that are being endured or are still ahead (1:4, 5) while 1 Thessalonians says that trials are over (2:14). There are several responses to this. First, one should not overstress the temporal values of the verb tenses in an English translation, since Greek tenses are not time-bound. Second, it is difficult to know the exact nature of the troubles in Thessalonica. Are there new troubles? Has Paul spoken with assurance to encourage the Thessalonians, even though they may be experiencing more troubles? This cannot be known. (5) Second Thessalonians 3:11–12 seems to speak of difficulties with idleness in the congregation as if this was a new development, but these difficulties seem familiar in 1 Thess 5:14. Similarly, it appears to some that 1 Thess 4:10–12 needs 2 Thess 3:6–15 to be understood. But it could be argued in the opposite way that Paul's more general statements in 1 Thessalonians were not clear enough and needed fuller exposition in 2 Thessalonians for an abiding problem. (6) The same kind of logic appears in the argument that 1 Thess 5:1 is more understandable if 2 Thess 2:1–12 is already known to the church. By this reckoning, however, 1 Thess 5:2 should not be included; yet it is. (7) First Thessalonians 4:9 and 5:1, with "now concerning," seem to indicate the discussion of topics already broached, and it is posited that 2 Thess 3:6–15 and 2:1–12 may be these topics. But they may also have been topics brought to Paul by Timothy, who is introduced before the "now concerning" passages (1 Thess 3:6). (8) Second Thessalonians 3:17 contains a personal reference to Paul's writing in his own hand; it is argued that such a statement is only important in a first letter. But if spurious Pauline letters had been sent to the church, as 2 Thess 2:2 suggests, there might well be the need for an authentic sample of handwriting. In all, these reasons are not convincing to establish that 2 Thessalonians was written before 1 Thessalonians, and the traditional order seems to be acceptable.

Besides this lack of convincing arguments against the priority of 1 Thessalonians, there are several reasons in support of it: (1) the problems of 1 Thessalonians seem to have deepened in 2 Thessalonians, especially concerning eschatological expectation and the accompanying tendencies toward idleness; (2) 2 Thess 2:2, 15 and 3:17 appear to refer to a previous letter, possibly (and probably) 1 Thessalonians; and (3) the personal references of 1 Thess 2:17–3:6 seem to precede 2 Thessalonians, where there are no personal greetings.

4. Occasion and Purpose

The occasion and purpose of 2 Thessalonians are closely related to those of 1 Thessalonians (see sec. B.5, above). In light of the discussion above, that there is no convincing argument that 1 Thessalonians follows 2 Thessalonians, we work from the hypothesis that 2 Thessalonians was written after 1 Thessalonians when Paul learned that 1 Thessalonians had not been as effective as it might have been. It is possible that there had also arrived at the church in Thessalonica a false letter arguing that the coming of Christ had occurred (2 Thess 2:2). If the church at Thessalonica had misunderstandings regarding the second coming, they may simply have been increased by its own thinking on the matter. In any case, Paul attempts to clarify the signs of the coming of Christ by specifying a number of events that indicate this has not occurred: since the apostasy or rebellion (2 Thess 2:3) and the coming of the man of lawlessness (2 Thess 2:3) have not yet happened, because they have been restrained (2 Thess 2:7), the day of the Lord has not yet come. Because of this misunderstanding about the impending coming of the Lord, it appears that some in the congregation may have given up work. Paul reprimands them (2 Thess 3:6, 11–12) with the admonition that they should not be idle but should earn the bread that they eat, rather than depend upon others to support them.

5. Outline of 2 Thessalonians

A. Opening (1:1–2)
    1. Sender (1:1)
    2. Addressee (1:1)
    3. Greeting (1:2)
B. Thanksgiving (1:3–12)
    1. The Thessalonians' faith (1:3–4)
    2. God to judge their afflictors (1:5–10)
    3. Intercession formula (1:11–12)
C. Body: The Parousia (2:1–12)
    1. The topic: The Parousia and being gathered to him (2:1)
    2. Words of comfort (2:2–4)
    3. Signs to be seen (2:5–7)
    4. Christ's triumph (2:8–12)
D. Parenesis (2:13–3:15)
    1. Thanksgiving for the Thessalonians (2:13–15)
    2. Doxology (2:16–17)
    3. Paul's request for prayer (3:1–5)
    4. Paul's instructions to follow his example (3:6–15)
E. Closing (3:16–18)
    1. Doxology (3:16)
    2. Personal signature (3:17)
    3. Benediction (3:18)

D. 1 Corinthians

1. Authorship

Kümmel says that "the genuineness of I Cor is not disputed."[58] First Corinthians constituted one of Baur's pillar epistles, and its authorship continues to be undisputed among scholars, although some seriously question elements of its integrity.

2. The City of Corinth

Corinth has been described by Fee as "the New York, Los Angeles and Las Vegas of the ancient world."[59] By this he probably means that it was a financial and commercial center, a city full of the upwardly mobile, and a center of religion and entertainment, much of it far from virtuous. This opinion can be substantiated from what is known of the city from the ancient records (esp. Strabo, *Geog.* 8.6.20–23 and Pausanias, *Description of Greece*, book 2).[60] The potential is great for overstatement about the city, however, since some of the records used to characterize Corinth probably refer to the time before 146 B.C. rather than Greco-Roman times.

Corinth was located at the land bridge between the Greek mainland and the Peloponnese. Because boats could be taken from one side of the land bridge to the other, it had two harbors, Cenchreae on the east and Lechaeum on the west. Thus, it was strategically located to become a center of trade and travel, and hence commerce of all sorts.

The cardo of ancient Corinth. Acrocorinth ("hill" or "mountain" of Corinth) is in the background, which supposedly had a Greek temple of Aphrodite on top. Photo Lee M. McDonald.

The ancient city of Corinth flourished in classical times until it was destroyed in 146 B.C. after joining with other cities of the area against the growing power of Rome. The city was rebuilt in 44 B.C. by Julius Caesar as a Roman colony, however, and then became capital of the Roman senatorial province of Achaia, so that those citizens living there enjoyed the rights of citizens as if they lived in Rome. Since Corinth was partly populated by freedmen, it tended toward a lower economic level, at least in the early Roman days. Because of its location, there was· an influx of people—both the wealthy and those who wished to be wealthy—who were involved in various forms of commerce and trading, and this development increased the city's material prosperity. By the time of the NT, however, many of these people, together with others attracted to the opportunities that it created, had attained significant wealth, so that a patronage or benefaction system seems to have been firmly in place. As a result, Corinth was arguably the most important city in the province of Achaia. The church probably reflected the mix of socioeconomic levels within the city, which perhaps led to many of the difficulties within the church, such as disputes

The ruins of the spring of Peirene at Corinth, dating to the Roman imperial period and elaborately developed as a bath in the second century A.D. Photo Lee M. McDonald.

over communion meals.[61] It has even been posited that the Erastus of Rom 16:23, who is said to be "the city treasurer," may be the Erastus who is mentioned in a first-century Corinthian inscription as responsible for laying a pavement.[62] Although the identification of Erastus cannot be established, his title of city treasurer indicates that at least one person of high social standing was a member of the Corinthian church.

In natural resources, Corinth enjoyed many advantages. Because of its location, the city not only had the benefit of trade and travel by sea towards the east and the west; it also stood at the intersection of land travel between the Peloponnese and the Greek mainland. The city had an adequate water supply and natural defenses from Acrocorinth, a mountain of 1,857 feet overlooking a hill upon which was built a temple to the goddess Aphrodite. The city was the host to the Isthmian Games, an athletic competition comparable to the rival Olympian Games. In light of Paul's use of athletic imagery

(e.g., 1 Cor 9:24–27; Phil 3:12–16), it is possible that Paul may have even been in the city when the games were going on.[63] The structure of the surrounding area also lent itself to the natural acoustics of a large amphitheater. This was appropriate

The Doric Temple of Apollo at Corinth. Photo Lee M. McDonald.

A colonnaded Roman street in Gerasa. This town was on the primary route from Jerusalem to Damascus in the time of Paul (Acts 9:1–19) © Rohr Productions. Used with permission.

for a city of perhaps a hundred thousand, the estimated population of Corinth.

There is widespread disagreement about what kinds of religious practices can be substantiated in Corinth during the Roman period. What is known is that the population included a mix of races and, with it, a mix of religions, virtually all of them pagan (except for the Jews and then later the Christians, as noted below). The temple of Aphrodite was only one of several religious institutions, for there were other temples as well; Pausanias describes twenty-six religious sites.[64] Aphrodite was the Greek goddess of love and life, and according to Strabo (*Geog.* 8.6.20), the temple had a thousand cult prostitutes. This information is highly questionable in light of recent archaeological discoveries from Corinth, which indicate that Strabo was either exaggerating or referring to pre-146 B.C. practices. There is no substantive evidence of cult prostitution during this time in Greece.[65] Associated with the reputation, if not the reality, of Corinthian religious and sexual life was its contribution to literary "culture." The verb "to Corinthize" (κορινθιάζεσθαι, *korinthiazesthai*) was used by Aristophanes to mean "to fornicate" (frg. 354). Plays by Philetaerus and Poliochus were entitled *The Whoremonger* (Κορινθιαστής, *Korinthiastēs*) (Athenaeus, *Deipn.* 7.313C, 13.559A), and a "Corinthian girl" (Κορινθία κόρη, *Korinthia korē*) was a prostitute (Plato, *Rep.* 404d). To be fair, reference was also made to "Corinthian style or workmanship," which referred to artistic (e.g., the Corinthian capitals on columns, with their ornate decoration) and literary accomplishments in Corinth. Despite exaggeration regarding religious practices in Corinth, we do know that the trade in idol meat was large and was responsible for the vast amount of meat available for sale. This meat was offered in idol sacrifice and then sold by the priests.[66]

There was a Jewish population in Corinth, attested by the remains of the lintel of a synagogue with an inscription.[67] The Jewish presence would be natural in such an accessible center, although Pausanias does not refer to the synagogue. Although all of the legal issues are not clear, it is possible that the Jews in Corinth had certain protected rights, including the right to assemble, permission to send the temple tax to Jerusalem, and exemption from certain kinds of activities on the Sabbath. According to Acts 18:4, Paul reasoned with the Jews every Sabbath in the synagogue.

The Roman proconsul would have held legal hearings in the city, since it became the capital of Achaia in 27 B.C. Since the territories that they governed were often quite large (e.g., Galatia), the Roman proconsuls often made regular tours of their territory to hear cases and render judicial verdicts, as this was their main function. Gallio, according to what can be made of the Gallio inscription (see ch. 9. sec. 3, above), was proconsul in A.D. 51/52, and it was before him that Paul appeared (Acts 18:12–17). Gallio was probably hearing cases at this time, and according to Acts he considered the charges made against Paul to be a matter of Jewish law, not one that concerned him.

3. The Corinthian Situation

A number of difficulties concerning the Corinthian situation revolve around such issues as how many letters Paul sent to the Corinthian church and how many of these we have in our NT, either in whole or in part. In other words, what is the relationship between the composition of the letters that we do have, 1 and 2 Corinthians, and the original letters that were sent to the Corinthians? How do the record of Acts and what is said in 1 and 2 Corinthians help to establish Paul's travel itinerary? These are difficult questions that have important implications for reading 1 and 2 Corinthians, so an attempt at reconstructing the surrounding events must be made.[68] The following is one possible scenario.

a. Paul's planting of a church on his second missionary journey, autumn A.D. 50–spring A.D. 52 (Acts 18:1–18). Paul stayed in Corinth for a year and a half on this occasion, including his appearance before the proconsul Gallio, who dismissed the charges against him. Gallio probably either directly or through his verdict helped to guarantee Paul's safety in Corinth (1 Cor 3:6; 2 Cor 1:19). Paul began his ministry there by preaching in the synagogue. When there was resistance, he went to the house of Titius Justus. Upon leaving Corinth, Paul finished his second missionary journey by returning to Antioch by way of Ephesus, Caesarea, and Jerusalem. During his time in Corinth, he probably composed at least 1 Thessalonians, and 2 Thessalonians as well if it is considered authentically Pauline.

b. Paul's stay at Ephesus (Acts 19:1–41). In the earlier part of his third missionary journey, sometime during spring A.D. 53–summer A.D. 55, Paul sent his first letter to the Corinthian church from Ephesus after "Chloe's people" informed him of problems in the church (1 Cor 1:11). Some scholars still think that 2 Cor 6:14–7:1 is part of the lost letter. Recent work, however, has plausibly shown that this is probably not the lost letter (see sec. E, below).[69] At nearly the same time, Paul apparently received a letter from the church asking for advice on a number of issues (see 1 Cor 5:1; 7:1). To this letter, Paul responded with 1 Corinthians, possibly delivered by Titus (2 Cor 12:18), who then returned to Paul (if Titus carried the "severe letter," discussed below, he probably did not deliver 1 Corinthians). Timothy was then sent on a special mission to Corinth (1 Cor 4:17; 16:10), where he discovered that there was a crisis, which included attacks being made on Paul's authority (2 Cor 2:5–11; 7:8–12). Timothy was unable to deal with the crisis and returned to Ephesus to tell Paul. Paul, upon hearing of these difficulties, visited Corinth briefly to deal with these issues in person, but he was rebuffed. This is later referred to by Paul as the "painful visit" (2 Cor 2:1; 12:14; 13:1, 2), which is not recorded in Acts. After his visit, Paul sent a powerful letter in response, probably carried by Titus, to deal with this crisis concerning his apostleship. This letter is referred to as the "tearful" or "severe" letter (2 Cor 2:4; 7:8–12). Some scholars have maintained that 2 Cor 10–13 is a part of this letter. The reasoning for this is based on, among other things, the use of the verb tenses in the different sections. For example, there are some pairs of verbs where the so-called present tense is found in 2 Cor 10–13 but a so-called past tense is found in 2 Cor 1–9, with the implication (at least in some scholars' minds) that the events described in the past tense occurred before those in the present tense (see 10:6 and 2:9; 13:2 and 1:23; 13:10 and 2:3). Unfortunately for this theory, as we have seen several times already, since the verb tenses in Greek do not refer primarily to time, they will not sustain such an argument. For this and other reasons, most scholars probably would claim that this third letter to the Corinthians is now lost.[70]

c. Macedonia and Philippi (Acts 20:1–2). After writing this third letter to the Corinthians, Paul left Ephesus and went toward Macedonia (1 Cor 16:5–9).

He was delayed along the way by a visit to Troas, where he waited for Titus but could not find him (2 Cor 2:12–13). He went on to Macedonia, where he met Titus, who said that the worst of the crisis in Corinth was over (2 Cor 7:6–16). Second Corinthians was written from Macedonia and sent by means of Titus and other "brothers" (2 Cor 9:3, 5); some think that 2 Cor 10–13 may have been sent separately from the rest of the letter—probably later if they were separate.[71] The relation of 2 Cor 10–13 to the rest of the letter, especially in terms of a perceived shift in tone, is discussed in the next section, on 2 Corinthians.

d. Corinth (Acts 20:3). Paul traveled on to Corinth, from which, within a year, he wrote the Letter to the Romans, apparently without any difficulties in Corinth. This indicates the likelihood that the Corinthian crisis was resolved in Paul's favor.

The following chart lays out what has been said above.

T A B L E 1 0 - 3	
Events	**Letters**
Paul founds Corinthian church	
Paul stays at Ephesus	
Paul responds to information from Corinth	First Letter to Corinth (2 Cor 6:14–7:1?)
Paul receives a letter from Corinth	1 Corinthians
Timothy visits Corinth Paul's "painful visit" to Corinth	Third Letter to Corinth, so-called tearful or severe letter (2 Cor 10–13?)
Paul goes to Macedonia	
Titus reports that the crisis is over	2 Corinthians

4. Textual Integrity of 1 Corinthians

The vast majority of scholars accept that 1 Corinthians is virtually intact; nevertheless, there are

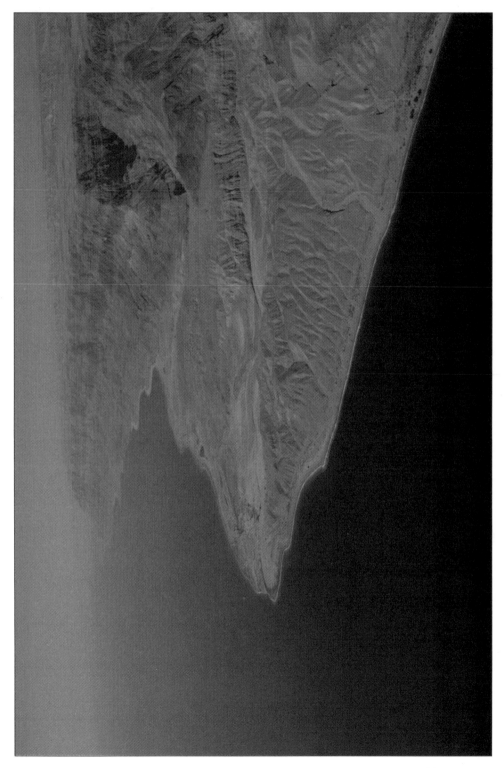

A view of the northwest side of the Dead Sea. © Rohr Productions. Used with permission.

two textual issues to discuss. The first is the hypothesis of, for example, Hurd and Trobisch that 1 Corinthians is a composite document of various smaller Pauline units; the second issue is that there are a number of passages that may not be part of the original letter.

The major reason for the past speculation regarding the textual integrity of 1 Corinthians was the perception of differences in tone between passages that are restrictive in nature and those that are more lenient. Thus, passages such as 1 Cor 10:1–22 on food offered to idols, 6:12–20 on the avoidance of immorality, and 11:2–34 on the veiling of women and on conduct of the Lord's Supper were all placed together as taking a more restric-

The bema seat at Corinth. The Apostle Paul stood here before Gallio, the proconsul of Achaia (Acts 18:12–17). Photo Lee M. McDonald.

tive tone than other passages in 1 Corinthians. These passages, together with 2 Cor 6:14–7:1 and sometimes 1 Cor 9:24–27, were thought by some to constitute Paul's first letter to the Corinthians. The remainder of 1 Corinthians, except chs. 1–4, was thought to be a second letter, and chs. 1–4 were often suggested to be the third letter, the second and third letters being sent on separate occasions, though close in time. As Hurd states, however, "Most scholars and the present writer, while recognizing the above points, do not believe that this evidence is strong enough to support the burden of proof which this kind of theory must always bear."[72] Scholars of previous generations often spent time discussing these hypotheses, but they do not merit significant discussion in recent commentaries. The general thought is that tensions between these various passages, such as between ch. 8 and ch. 10 on food offered to idols, can be resolved when the character of the letter as responding to a number of problems in the church is considered.[73] Recent work on the structure of the letter has shown that patterns of argumentation may well account for the shape of the letter as we have it.[74]

The second issue concerns a few select passages that are often thought to be non-Pauline interpolations. The first is 1 Cor 1:2, where not only the church of God in Corinth is addressed but "all those who in every place call on the name of our lord Jesus Christ." The argument is that this is too inclusive a statement for a letter addressed to a series of specific problems in the church at Corinth. But in light of how Paul saw himself as apostle to the Gentiles and not simply as apostle to the Corinthians,

The Corinth Canal, begun by Nero in the first century but completed only in the late nineteenth century. In antiquity, small ships and cargo were dragged across the isthmus on the Diolkos, a paved slipway, between the Gulf of Corinth and the Saronic Gulf to save time and avoid the rough waters around the southern end of the Peloponnese.
Photo Lee M. McDonald.

A view of the Diolkos. Photo Lee M. McDonald.

Ruins of Cenchreae, the harbor of Corinth (Acts 18:18; Rom 16:1–2). Photo Lee M. McDonald.

together with the problems in the Corinthian church, which may well have stemmed from the self-conceit of some Corinthians as categorically superior to others because they followed certain individuals, the opening of the letter is not inappropriate at all. Indeed, one might argue that this is just the kind of opening needed for a letter to a church with such problems. In this sense, Paul may have intended for this letter, like Colossians, to be read widely, and the introduction would have included that possibility. Also, there is no substantive textual evidence for the exclusion of this verse.[75]

The second textual problem is at 1 Cor 14:33b–35. Fee summarizes the position for those who believe that these verses are non-Pauline: "Although these two verses are found in all known manuscripts, either here or at the end of the chapter, the two text-critical criteria of transcriptional and intrinsic probability combine to cast considerable doubt on their authenticity."[76] It is ironic that Fee dismisses

Conzelmann's desire to include vv. 33b and 36 as Pauline by stating that there is "no textual warrant" for this theory when, as he admits, there is no textual warrant for his position either. The most that is at issue is whether the verses belong at their traditional place or after v. 40 (see UBS[3] for the options), not whether they should be excised.

5. Occasion and Purpose

There has been debate recently regarding the dispute in Corinth that brought forth the series of correspondence. The traditional view has been fairly well established over the years, but recent work by Fee has called this into question. Both views will be briefly discussed.

a. Disunity. The traditional view of the issue at Corinth has been that it was about unity and disunity. There are indications that the church was divided, possibly into a variety of factions, with various controversial issues or practices that warranted a series of comments from the apostle.

(1) Inquiries about Issues. It is clear that 1 Corinthians was not the first letter that Paul wrote to the church at Corinth (1 Cor 5:9). Since the first letter, Paul had apparently received two forms of communication from the church. Members of Chloe's household (1:11) had orally communicated to him, apparently about various quarrels and divisions within the church (1:10–17). He had also received written communication (7:1; probably 5:1), likely carried by Stephanas, Fortunatus, and Achaicus (16:16), about specific issues in the church that had divided it into various factions.

Many scholars begin their analysis of the major problems in the church with 7:1, but 5:1 is probably a better place. At this point, as the outline below indicates, Paul turns from the brief body of his letter, regarding the issue of unity in the church, to a lengthy parenetic section in which he deals specifically with issues in the Corinthian church. He treats them in serial fashion, usually giving an indication that he is switching topics by use of the phrase περὶ δέ, *peri de* (7:1, 25; 8:1; 12:1; 16:1), but this is not the only connective that he uses.[77] The following issues appear to be important. First, there seem to have been some sexual problems. The church had tolerated a Christian man immorally engaged with his stepmother (5:1–13). The rationale for the church's tolerant behavior is not stated, but it appears that it reflected either accommodation to the surrounding sexual ethics of the city or a view of the body that made self-indulgence tolerable because it was thought to have no consequences (perhaps similar to later gnostic ideas). There were also problems related to prostitutes (6:12–20). Some in the Corinthian church were apparently using Christian freedom as freedom to indulge their sexual appetites. The reason for this behavior also is not stated. Paul rejects such encounters on the basis that, unlike other sins, they constitute a sin against one's own body. A third dimension of the sexual difficulties at Corinth seems to have been problems with asceticism (7:1, 28).[78] Paul takes the occasion to address the issue of marriage in a Christian context. He is apparently directly responding to some within the Corinthian church who considered marriage to be sinful. In light of Paul's eschatology of imminence (7:29–31), he may agree that staying in one's present condition of singleness is preferable (7:24), but he does not take an ascetic's position.

A second major set of difficulties seems to have concerned pagan practices, especially food offered to idols. Only a small portion of an animal used in pagan sacrifice was burned, with the remaining amount usually being sold. This was the largest and cheapest supply of fresh meat for people to purchase. The majority of those who could afford such meat were of some financial wealth, indicating that the church included a range of people from various social and economic strata.[79] There seems to have been a controversy within the church between those who were scrupulous in not eating food that may

have been offered to idols and those who held no scruple at eating this meat in places where it was known to be served (8:10; 10:27–28). Paul must tread a fine line between the argument that the pagan gods do not exist and the fact that there was in his mind an evil spirit world, and he must consider the believers who might stumble by seeing such behavior. This kind of contact with the institutions of the surrounding culture may also have accounted for Corinthian Christians' engagement in court cases with each other (6:1–11). Paul dismisses such involvement by saying that the church should appoint the lowliest of its members to judge these cases. The same kind of social division appears to have crept into the celebration of the Lord's Supper, where the wealthier members were taking advantage of the situation by turning what should have been a communal meal into an occasion for gluttony, so that the poorer members were not able to participate in the eating (11:17–34). Paul makes abuse of the ceremony a very serious matter: sinning against the body and blood of the Lord.

There also appears to have been some difficulty within the church about practices of worship, since there was a general spirit of disorder. For instance,

The theater (4th cent. B.C., expanded in the 2d cent. B.C.) at Epidaurus seats 14,000 persons and is one of the best-preserved theaters of antiquity. It is located near the site of an Asclepion where thousands of persons came for healing. As a part of the treatment, theatrical performances were believed to purge or cleanse the spectators. Smaller theaters have been found at Pergamum and at Corinth, both of which also were centers of healing in antiquity. Asclepia were located all over the Greco-Roman world, including two found in Jerusalem.
Photo Lee M. McDonald.

apparently a number of women were particularly vocal during the service, and undue emphasis was put on the charismatic gifts, in particular speaking in divine or heavenly languages. Paul tells the women that they should show appropriate respect, including asking their husbands at home if they have questions about what is said in the service. And comparing the use of tongues with prophecy (1 Cor 12, 14), Paul makes a general plea for order.

The last matter of concern for Paul is the issue of the resurrection (ch. 15). It has been debated whether the Corinthian church held to a view that the resurrection of Christ had not occurred or whether it was experiencing a dispute over whether there would be a resurrection of believers, especially if some of the members believed that they had already entered the close of the age (the *eschaton*). In any case, Paul reestablishes the importance of Christ's resurrection as the guarantee of a future human resurrection, but as part of a larger scheme of Christ vanquishing death and ruling the world.

The question that emerges from this brief discussion of the various problems in the Corinthian church is, What may have provided the basis for this kind of tension within the community? In other words, what best accounts for the disunity within the community? The views have been many and varied.[80] In his classic essay, Baur expressed his belief that Paul's opponents were representatives of Jewish Christianity, the Petrine wing of the church.[81] This was based upon Baur's idea of a fundamental clash between Jewish and Gentile sections of the church in its earliest days. What evidence there is for a Petrine opposition in Corinth is being explored by Goulder, who shows that what many have thought are random comments in the letter can be read as part of a structured opposition to a Petrine legalistic position (see 3:4–5, 22; 4:6).[82] There apparently was contact between the Corinthian church and Jerusalem (1:12; 3:22), but there does not seem to be an indication, at least in 1 Corinthians (cf. 2 Corinthians below), that the opposition is seen as coming from outside.[83]

(2) Gnostics. A second hypothesis, one that has tended to dominate discussion of 1 Corinthians, is that there were Jewish-Christian gnostics in the church.[84] Reflecting the kind of dualism that typifies gnostic thought, they disparaged the earthly and the fleshly and elevated esoteric knowledge (see references to "knowledge" in 1:18–2:16; 3:18–23)

and the spiritual realm. The result may well have been overindulgence (see, e.g., 5:1–6:20; 11:17–34). These Jewish-Christian gnostics were concerned to mediate the otherworldly to this world, but it raised some direct questions regarding their Christology, seen most clearly in Paul's response in ch. 15. If Christ was God, how could he also be a man? Their position would have tended toward what became known as a docetic view, in which Christ's humanness would have been merely an appearance of being human.

Responses to the gnostic hypothesis have been several. One is the recognition that there is a difference between proto-gnostic tendencies and full-blown Gnosticism as it emerged in the second and third century with its myth of the heavenly redeemer, full of all sorts of emanations and manifestations. The most that can be argued is that there were at Corinth some proto-gnostic tendencies in which heavenly knowledge had an exalted place over the earthly, but none of the gnostic Christology or worldview.[85] A second response to the gnostic hypothesis is that often what is cited as gnostic may reveal other influences, such as Jewish wisdom thought, rather than Gnosticism.[86]

(3) Overrealized Eschatology. A somewhat related view is that the major problems at Corinth stemmed from an overrealized eschatology.[87] All the practices that those in the church were engaged in, such as baptism and the Lord's Supper, seem to have had, in the minds of the Corinthians, a mystical or magical element to them. Those practicing them thought quite highly of their spiritual status and depreciated earthly things; they thought of themselves as already having entered the *eschaton*, and lived accordingly. This kind of thinking may well have derived from some form of Hellenistic thought, including wisdom speculation. Many have thought that Hellenistic Judaism was responsible for these influences, but the focus must be on Hellenistic thought in general, of which Jewish thought was a component. The emphasis was upon general exaltation of esoteric knowledge, perhaps in conjunction with the kind of rhetorical teaching that was part of the Hellenistic Second Sophistic, a philosophical movement influenced by Platonic thought.[88] Besides the criticisms raised above regarding possible gnostic influences, it is questionable that the Corinthian church was so influenced by the normal categories of rhetoric associated with the Sec-

An excavated site at Khirbat Qumran near the northwestern shore of the Dead Sea. The Dead Sea Scrolls were mostly found adjacent to this site. © Rohr Productions. Used with permission.

ond Sophistic that one can claim that this was the background to the movement.[89] It is also precarious to try to create a divide between Hellenistic Judaism and Hellenism, since Judaism was thoroughly immersed in Hellenistic culture and thought.

(4) Divisive Groups. Others have argued that there was a wide variety of divisive groups in the Corinthian church, none of which was preeminent, even though some may have thought of themselves as such. For example, some were libertines (5:1–13; 6:12–20) who had misunderstood Christian freedom to have no concern for propriety or the thoughts of those Christians who may not have had the same view of Christian freedom; for them it became an excuse for excessive indulgence. Others were ascetics, who had opted for the opposite approach to Christian behavior, a very rigid one in which Christians were forbidden from engaging in such activities as marriage, because it was viewed as sinful (7:1–28). Still others were ecstatics who were allowing spiritual experience to lead to disorderly behavior in the church (ch. 14). Some of these may have had a realized eschatology, in which they thought that they had already attained the *eschaton* and that this justified their behavior. Each of these groups may have been associated with a particular individual or recognizable group in Corinth, or there may also have been, besides the groups named above, a number of people who sided with various individuals, including the Paul group, the Apollos group, the Cephas group, and the Christ group (1:12).[90]

b. Paul's Apostolic Authority. The characterizations of the opponents tend to emphasize the internal struggles within the Corinthian church, but Fee has argued that the major problem at Corinth was between the church and its founder, Paul.[91] The crisis seems to have been over Paul's authority and the nature of the gospel. In 1 Cor 9:1–14, Paul engages in a rigorous defense of himself, rejecting the Corinthians' judgment of him and any perceived vacillation on his part. In response to their letter to him, in which they took exception to several of his positions in his previous letter (5:9), Paul reasserts his authority (3:5–9; 4:1–5). Paul corrects the Corinthians as a whole church—hence his use of the second person—in three crucial passages (1:10–12; 3:4–5; 11:18–19). Contrary to most reconstructions of the situation, Fee thinks that there is no evidence of outside opposition having come into

the church (so "opponents" may even be the wrong term); he believes instead that the problem stems from anti-Pauline sentiment in the church, probably started by a few who had eventually infected the whole church. These people considered themselves wise and thought that Paul's preaching was "milk" compared to their mature teaching (2:8; 3:1). His behavior was seen to be weak or vacillating on such issues as food offered to idols (8:1–11:1). When Paul emphasized that he was writing on spiritual things (14:37), it was in response to people who thought of themselves as "spiritual" and did not so consider Paul, since they had experiences to back their claims (chs. 12–14). Their spiritual endowment was related to their knowledge and wisdom (chs. 1–4, 8–10). In fact, they went further, contending that they were already experiencing the Spirit in full measure; their number probably included some eschatologically inclined women who thought they had entered the new age (chs. 7, 11), contrary to the weak Paul, who had not.

Fee's position is to be commended, in that it provides a unified depiction of the problem and rightly focuses upon the apostle Paul and his defense of his apostleship (9:1–14); it has not, however, garnered support from many scholars. The predominant position seems to be one that sees Paul responding to thinking in the Corinthian church that originates with influences from the surrounding Hellenistic world.

6. Outline of 1 Corinthians[92]

    A. Opening (1:1–3)
      1. Senders (1:1)
      2. Addressee (1:2)
      3. Greeting (1:3)
    B. Thanksgiving (1:4–9)
    C. Body: Church unity (1:10–4:21)
      1. The problem of disunity (1:10–17)
      2. The gospel contradicts human wisdom (1:18–2:5)
      3. God's wisdom comes by the Spirit (2:6–16)
      4. Divisiveness (3:1–23)
      5. Paul as Christ's servant (4:1–21)
    D. Parenesis (5:1–16:12)
      1. Questions of morality (5:1–6:20)
      2. Questions of marriage (7:1–40)
      3. Questions of food sacrificed to idols (8:1–11:1)

E. 2 Corinthians

1. Authorship

As with 1 Corinthians, Kümmel states, "The authenticity of II Cor as a whole is uncontested."[93] Nevertheless, as we have seen, there is ongoing discussion of whether the entire book was written at the same time. It is probably accurate to say that although there are a number of strong advocates of a unified 2 Corinthians, the majority of scholars would argue that 2 Corinthians is in some sense a composite letter. In any case, the essential Pauline authenticity of the letter is not disputed.

2. Unity of 2 Corinthians

The question of the unity of 2 Corinthians revolves around several significant passages.[94] They are not all equally disputed; nevertheless, they merit discussion, since many of the issues that they raise are among those recurring most often in discussions about the nature and shape of the Pauline Letters.

a. 2 Corinthians 6:14–7:1. The problems regarding this short passage in the body of the letter are three: (1) many see an abrupt change in tone from 6:13 to 6:14; (2) 6:13 seems to be a suitable introduction to 7:2, and when 6:14–7:1 is removed, the flow of the letter's argument is improved; and (3) the subject matter and style are seen to be inconsistent with the rest of the Corinthian correspondence.[95] For example, 1 Cor 5:9 says that one is *"not to associate with sexually immoral people,"* but 2 Cor 6:14–7:1, according to some interpreters, deals with the relations of believers and unbelievers; and 2 Corinthians is described as a letter of reconciliation (see esp. 5:18–21), but 6:14–7:1 seems to argue for exclusivism. Several major solutions have been proposed for these difficulties.

(1) Interpolation hypothesis. The first solution offered is that this small section is part of the first letter to the Corinthians (now lost), interpolated into 2 Corinthians. It is possible, according to this view, that Paul's strong language of 2 Cor 6:14–7:1 favoring dissociation from the pagan world, sent as part of his first letter to the Corinthians, was misunderstood and interpreted to mean that there should be absolutely no contact whatsoever. Perhaps 1 Cor 5:10–11 then shows Paul clarifying his original statement, hence his correction that believers are "not to *associate* with sexually immoral people."

This interpolation theory raises several questions, however. First, some have responded that the shift in tone from 2 Cor 6:13 to 6:14 is not as severe as others have postulated, especially if the language is seen in terms of establishing degrees of exclusivism and association. For example, in 6:1–13, Paul makes common cause with the Corinthians as fellow workers and says that there is nothing he has done to discredit the ministry. After recounting a number of trials and triumphs, he repeats that as he has been open to the Corinthians in all his affection, they, too, are to be open and generous in theirs. In 6:14–7:1, however, Paul addresses the relations of Christians and non-Christians, stating that they should not be mismatched—the Greek word is a term for unevenly yoking animals to pull a plow. Paul supports this by several quotations of the OT (Lev 26:12; Isa 52:11; 2 Sam 7:14; Hos 1:10), all of which support the idea that God's people are separate from everything incompatible with his holiness. Second, composition over a space of time might well account for the shift in tone, even if gradual. Third, why would part of the lost first letter have been inserted at this place in 2 Corinthians, the fourth letter? Other places would have been just as likely, and there is apparently no evidence in the textual tradition of its absence in the earliest extant manuscripts. Many scholars at one time held that this passage was a fragment of the first letter, but this view is not widely held today.

(2) Qumran fragment. The second major solution proposed is that a non-Pauline fragment from Qumran was placed here. The reasons for this are several: (1) nine terms are found in this passage that are found nowhere else in Paul;[96] (2) the extreme exclusiveness is out of character for Paul; (3) there are similarities of thought with the Qumran community, such as its dualism and emphasis

Khirbet Qumran. The first Dead Sea Scrolls were found in this location. The Qumran community itself was located in the upper right of the photo. © Rohr Productions. Used with permission.

A burial chamber for Jews at Beth Shearim. It was used by the Jews after their conflict against Rome in A.D. 135 when Hadrian, because of the Bar Kokhba rebellion, refused to allow them to bury their dead on the Mount of Olives. © Rohr Productions. Used with permission.

upon the temple; and (4) the words "flesh" and "spirit" are used in a non-Pauline way. These reasons have indicated to some that 6:14–7:1 is non-Pauline and that the fragment may well have come from a group that reflected such exclusivity and emphasis upon the temple, that is, the Qumran covenanters.

In response to this suggestion, however, it has been pointed out that an argument based upon hapax legomena (terms used in a given author or book only one time) is not precise, especially here, since many of the terms found in this "fragment" have cognates in Paul's letters (e.g., μετοχή [metochē] is not found elsewhere in Paul but μετέχω [metechō], the verb for "share," is). Furthermore, 2 Cor 6:3–10 also has several unique words, but this passage is not suspected of being non-Pauline. Second, Pauline outbursts of various sorts often have unique words in them (e.g., 1 Cor 4:7–13 with six unique words, and 2 Cor 6:3–10 with four unique words), but they are not automatically suspected of being non-Pauline. Third, it is argued that one must pay attention to what is Pauline and what is quoted from the OT in this fragment. According to this position, it is the OT quotations that are largely responsible for the exclusivistic sense of the passage, not the surrounding Pauline material. Fourth, it has been argued that this supposed fragment is not at odds with established Pauline thought and that many of the ideas are found not only at Qumran but in other circles as well (e.g., Greek dualism).

(3) Preformulated material. A third proposal is that though this passage may have been preformulated or borrowed in some way, Paul was the one who incorporated it into his account. This view attempts to accommodate the perceived change of tone and content and at the same time retain the integrity of the passage's Pauline composition. But as noted above, there is no external textual witness to a textual difficulty, certainly not in the sense that the passage was incorporated. It would have to have been incorporated very early, before the extant texts were copied, but such an occurrence is difficult to prove without any extant evidence. This view encounters a number of other problems. There may be a perceived shift in tone or content, but the passage can easily be seen to fit its context. If the subject of 6:1–7:16 is the nature and degree of Christian relationships, 6:14–7:1 fits well as the second of its three sections. The first describes Paul

and the Corinthians as fellow workers (6:1–13), emphasizing their common cause and mutual openness. But this openness does not imply compromise (6:14–7:1). Rather, it is predicated upon not taking advantage of each other (7:2–16). If Paul has used a preformulated or prewritten section, he has utilized it within his letter in such a way that he has made it his own.

b. 2 Corinthians 10–13[97]

(1) The Problems. There are essentially five problems with 2 Cor 10–13. (a) It has been argued that chs. 1–9 are full of praise for the Corinthian believers but chs. 10–13 are characterized by condemnation, making it difficult to see how these two portions of the letter fit together in one integral composition. (b) The vocabulary regarding boasting and Paul's commending himself is used differently in the two major portions of the letter, implying that the letter is not a unity but a composition of at least two letters. The problem is seen most clearly in how a common word for boasting (καυχάομαι, kauchaomai) is used positively in chs. 1–9 but negatively in chs. 10–13. For example, 5:12 implies that Paul has commended himself, while in 10:13 Paul says that he will not boast. (c) Scholars have noted a number of passages in chs. 10–13 that appear to be forward looking while chs. 1–9 appear to be looking backwards. Some examples are 10:2 and 8:2 on confidence, 10:6 and 2:9 on obedience, 12:16 and 4:2 on trickery, 12:17 and 7:2 on fraud, 13:2 and 1:23 on sparing the Corinthians, and 13:10 and 2:3 on travel. It has been observed on the basis of this evidence that chs. 1–9 seem to be looking back at a situation that is now resolved while chs. 10–13 seem to be looking forward to resolution. (d) To the minds of many scholars, there appears to be a set of contradictions between chs. 1–9 and 10–13. For example, in 1:24 Paul sees the Corinthians as "firm in the faith," while in 13:5 he admonishes them to see if they are "in the faith." Furthermore, in 7:16 he expresses confidence in them, while in 12:20–21 he is afraid of them. These attitudes seem to reflect different sets of circumstances at Corinth. (e) According to some scholars, Paul's reference to wanting to preach "beyond" Corinth (10:16) makes sense in terms of Rome and Spain if chs. 10–13 were written from Ephesus as the third Corinthian letter (since Rome and Spain are west of Ephesus and Corinth), but not from Macedonia as part of the fourth letter, since a southward geographical

trajectory from Macedonia to Corinth would reach across the Mediterranean to Africa.

(2) Solutions. There have been many solutions proposed regarding the relationship of 2 Cor 1–9 and 10–13. They can be divided into essentially two possibilities: either the two represent two separate documents or they are part of the same document.

(a) Chapters 10–13 written and sent separately from chs. 1–9. On the basis of the apparent discrepancies between the two portions, it has been argued that this evidence points to the two portions being parts of separate letters. Many who argue for separate letters claim that chs. 10–13 constitute the "severe letter" sent by Paul as the third letter to the Corinthian church, soon after his disastrous visit to them. This would supposedly make sense of the general tenor of the differences noted above: chs. 10–13 look forward to resolution, and chs. 1–9 reflect a later resolution; chs. 10–13 treat boasting as a negative quality, probably reflecting Paul's antagonism to what he encountered in Corinth, but in chs. 1–9, after resolution of the difficulties, he allows himself to boast of the Corinthians; in chs. 10–13, Paul questions the faith of the Corinthians and reflects continuing fear of them, but in chs. 1–9 he knows that they now have faith and he has confidence in them. In a variation on this, a small group of scholars argues that chs. 1–9 and 10–13 were written and sent as separate letters, with chs. 10–13 sent after chs. 1–9, possibly even very soon after. The latter formulation apparently rests upon either seeing differences between the two sections (even though they are unavoidably close in content) or positing a new set of (now unknown) circumstances in the Corinthian church (after the apparent difficulties had been resolved). Because of obvious difficulties in making such distinctions, this variation has had far fewer adherents.

In response to these alternatives, it is important to note that several of the apparent difficulties may not be quite as pressing as is sometimes argued. For example, the apparent shift in tone may not be so great or severe as is sometimes thought. The formulation is often in terms of chs. 1–9 reflecting a settled situation and chs. 10–13 reflecting uncertainty. It must be noted, however, that chs. 1–9 refer to continuing opposition as well (e.g., 2:6, 17; 4:2–5; 5:11–13), even if the overall tone is more conciliatory. This may well indicate that even if the majority of the church at Corinth has been con-

vinced by Paul's argument, there remains a minority that is still to be won over. Similarly, chs. 10–13 do not categorically reflect opposition to Paul but only some opposition to his authority (e.g., 10:2, 7, 11–12; 11:5, 12–13, 18, 20; 12:11, 21; 13:2). Furthermore, the internal references within chs. 1–9 and chs. 10–13 may not necessarily reflect a relationship only between these two parts of the letter. There are several other possibilities. For example, the backwards references in chs. 1–9 could be referring to the second letter, our canonical 1 Corinthians, instead of chs. 10–13. In another plausible scenario, Paul may have received word from Titus that there had been widespread positive response in the Corinthian church to his ministry but that it might not have been complete, especially if a new group of outsiders arrived (see below); thus, he still had grounds to hope for further necessary improvement. Consequently, Paul's comments in chs. 1–13 might well reflect an appreciation for what had been done (chs. 1–9), together with a hope for further response (chs. 10–13).

It is fair to say that the vast majority of the supposed contradictions are, in fact, not formal contradictions but are merely discrepancies that can be relatively easily explained. For example, the reference to "beyond" in 10:16 is not a great difficulty when it is noted that, for Paul, "beyond" means beyond the confines of the eastern Mediterranean, and thus Rome and Spain, no matter from which direction he may be writing. Regarding commending himself in 3:1 and 5:12, Paul is referring to using letters of recommendation, and he compliments the Corinthian church as being his letter of recommendation. In chs. 10–13, it is true that Paul disparages boasting, but he is addressing his opponents, not the Corinthians as a whole—he takes pride in the Corinthians (10:13–14; 11:16–21; cf. 1:12–14).

A further contradiction is actually introduced if chs. 10–13 are taken as the "severe letter." In 12:18 there is reference to Titus, who delivered the "severe letter" and who now delivers 2 Corinthians (7:6–8; 8:6, 16–18). This could not be a reference to Titus as the deliverer of the "severe letter" if this *is* that letter, and the interrogative language of the passage indeed seems to be referring to the "severe letter." Thus, even if chs. 10–13 were written at a different time than chs. 1–9, they would not be the "severe letter," unless the references were added later for some unaccountable reason.

Finally, there is no manuscript authority for dividing the letter into parts. This may seem to be a point not worth making, but there are some implications for the larger discussion. If there were two or more letters contained in the one letter (see the discussion of Philippians on this same issue), it has the implication that the original openings and closings, as well as other portions, of the genuine letters were deleted. We may not understand the full situation, but this is different from such cases as the letter to the Laodiceans, where the entire letter is no longer extant (though this may be Ephesians; see the discussion in sec. 3.D, below). It is quite different to say that part of a letter was valued and retained but other portions of the same valued letter were excised and not retained. There seems to be an inherent contradiction between retention of Paul's writings as valuable and instructive, and expunging some portions. By today's standards we may think that openings and closings (and other portions now unknown to us?) are not as important, but this merely begs the question: can we say that they were not important for the early church, especially with the innovative Pauline opening, the occasionally theologically expanded description of the sender or addressee, and the benedictions and grace formulas? This is doubtful.

(b) Chapters 10–13 as part of 2 Corinthians. The second solution is that regardless of the difficulties above, 2 Corinthians 10–13 is part of the original letter. As noted, the shift in tone and other supposed contradictions, combined with the manuscript evidence, do not leave grounds for clearly arguing for two or more letters. Indeed, there are several other lines of evidence that point away from separate letters and toward textual integrity. First, if chs. 10–13 are a separate letter, these chapters do not seem to address the issue that was being confronted at Corinth. In 2 Cor 2:1–4 and 7:12, the reason for the "severe letter" was an individual who had in some way offended Paul. If this is the case, it is noteworthy that chs. 10–13 make no mention of this but address the Corinthians as a church. Paul's defense of himself in 2 Corinthians (e.g., 12:1, 11–15) is not focused upon individual difficulties but the situation in the church. This is, however, consistent with the rest of 2 Corinthians (as well as 1 Corinthians, e.g. 1 Cor 9:1–14, which

focused on apostolic authority in relation to church difficulties). Second, the exhortation formula of 10:1 (with παρακαλῶ) is consistent with the exhortative stance of the parenetic section of a letter. The parenetic section, by definition, implies a different tone than the body of the letter, although one need not overdraw this contrast. Nevertheless, a somewhat similar shift can be found in the relation of Rom 14:1–23 to the rest of Romans. Paul apparently does not hesitate to introduce strongly worded instruction even if he is concerned with his personal relationship with a church. Such instruction might be especially appropriate if new opposition to Paul was introduced into the Corinthian situation (see below).

There are other possible solutions to this supposed change of tone. For example, the process of literary composition in the ancient world was quite different from the one used today, in which word processors are available to ensure speed and consistency of content and presentation. The writing of a letter as lengthy as any of the major Pauline Letters would have been a sizable undertaking, involving a scribe, the availability of writing materials, and a certain amount of time. Perhaps the letter or at least sections of the letter were written first in draft on a wax tablet before being copied onto the papyrus for sending. Reusable wax tablets used in the Greco-Roman world for such writing purposes have been found. In the course of this writing, editing and copying, there would be plenty of opportunity for any number of developments, including a change of mind by Paul on what he wanted to express and how he wanted to say it, the receipt of new information regarding the Corinthian church, circumstances requiring that Paul be away from the letter for a period of time before returning to it in a different frame of mind, or even (Lietzmann's now famous idea) a night of insomnia after ch. 9 that resulted in Paul's cranky attitude in ch. 10 and subsequent chapters.[98] A number of plausible solutions can therefore account for the perceived change of tone, some of them requiring the supposition of separate letters and others not.

(c) 2 Corinthians 8 and 9.[99] The questions regarding these two chapters concern whether they were independent of 2 Corinthians 1–7, or whether one or more was separate, and if so, what was the order in which they were sent. The arguments for the independence of chs. 8 and 9 are five: (1) 9:1

has a connective phrase that separates it from ch. 8 and indicates the possibility of a new letter; (2) chs. 8 and 9 duplicate information regarding the collection, emissaries, etc.; (3) 8:1–5 and 9:1–2 seem to be addressed to different groups, both out of character with the audience in ch. 7; (4) chs. 8 and 9 list different purposes for those Paul is sending, comments remarkably lacking from ch. 7; and (5) there are contradictions in details from ch. 8 to ch. 9— for example, Paul introduces the collection in 9:1 as superfluous when he has already been discussing it (8:1–5). A last reason is sometimes given: the rhetorical structure found in each chapter supposedly points to unity and independence. This argument should not be given much credence, for several reasons. The first is that rhetorical criticism is used in various ways, depending upon the interpreter, sometimes to prove unity of a letter and sometimes to prove unity of a subsection, thus making it difficult to show how it can be used to prove either. The second is that it has not been shown that the categories of ancient rhetoric, designed for the creation of speeches, are applicable to the analysis of ancient letters. All indications, in fact, are that they are not. Nevertheless, on the basis of such reasoning, several proposals have been put forward. Some have argued that chs. 1–8 or chs. 1–7, 9 were units, with the remaining chapter sent separately. Others have argued that chs. 8 and 9 were independent of chs. 1–7 and of each other, some claiming that ch. 8 was sent first (probably to Corinth) and others that ch. 9 was first (probably as a circular letter to a wider area of Achaia).

The reasons cited for positing one or more interpolations in chs. 8 and 9 raise important questions about the composition of the letter but are far from conclusive proof that the letter is a composite of these once independent chapters. The first reason they are not conclusive is that there are no external text-critical indicators that the letter ever was known or circulated in anything other than a single form. These textual alterations may have occurred, but they had to occur earlier than our text-critical evidence can support. Second, the use of the connective phrase in 9:1 περὶ μὲν γάρ (*peri men gar*), rather than indicating separation of the chapter, indicates connection and continuation (cf. Acts 28:22). It is neither the equivalent of the transitional markers that Paul uses in 1 Corinthians (see sec. D.3.2, above) nor a formula to introduce new material. Third, one does not want to overemphasize the amount of duplication between the two chapters. Similar topics are raised, but they are treated in different ways, with ch. 9 adding information not found in ch. 8. Fourth, the argument that 8:1–5 refers to Macedonia as a model for the Corinthians but 9:2 refers to the Corinthians as a model for the Macedonians is not as contradictory as it first appears. Paul commends the Macedonians to the Corinthians in ch. 8, but he uses the Macedonians as a witness to what the Corinthians should be doing in ch. 9. Fifth, reference in 9:3, 5 to those Paul is sending is introduced in 8:16–24, the one clarifying the other. Sixth, concerning the seemingly superfluous mention of the collection in 9:1, perhaps the most difficult of the problems to explain, there are a number of possible explanations other than simply positing a separate letter. One is that the verse may be saying nothing more than that it is unnecessary for him to go on with the writing he is engaged in (so that "write" [τὸ γράφειν, *to graphein*], with the Greek article and the present-tense infinitive, refers to what has already been said).

The tendency has been to separate either ch. 8 or ch. 9 or both from chs. 1–7, but this is not necessary to make sense of these chapters. The connections of ch. 8 with chs. 1–7 are strong, and some of the information in ch. 9, such as the identity of the "brothers" (9:3, 5), seems to require ch. 8, thus arguing strongly for the unity of the chapters.

3. Occasion and Purpose

The problems addressed by 1 Corinthians seem to have been a variety of disunifying factors in the Corinthian church, but in the process of Paul's confrontation with the church, there seems to have been a development of the situation and the entry of new opponents. If the occasion that prompted the first couple of letters to the Corinthians was the possible fragmentation of the church, in 2 Corinthians it seems that the disunity has been largely overcome, at least to the point that apparently a minority of people were personally attacking Paul— probably a new group of outsiders (from Jerusalem? 11:5, 13, 23; 12:11) questioning Paul's apostolic authority in a potentially persuasive way. Consequently, the opponents that elicited 2 Corinthians can be characterized in terms of the nature of their

The base of the altar of Zeus at Pergamum. The altar itself has been reconstructed and placed in the Pergamum museum in Berlin. © Rohr Productions. Used with permission.

attack. Paul vigorously opposed them, and it appears that the fourth letter to the Corinthians (no matter how much of it is found in our 2 Corinthians) dealt sufficiently with the problem so that Paul could consider the threat overcome. This reinforces the view that these opponents represent a minority position that was finally rejected by the church at Corinth.

a. Personal Attack against Paul. The nature of the attack against Paul seems to have consisted of a number of wide-ranging and not entirely fair accusations brought by these outsiders. These include accusations of his instability—as evidenced by a change of plans and vacillation (1:15–18)—lack of clarity in what he meant (1:13–14), ineffectiveness (10:10), tyrannical words (10:8), abandonment of the Corinthians (2:1; 13:2), failure to make his gospel clear (4:3), and pitiful speech (10:11; 11:6), probably indicating that he was not trained in rhetoric as some of them may have been. Concerning his claim to being a representative of Christ or an apostle, Paul was apparently denigrated for a number of reasons: he had no formal letters of recommendation, as perhaps did other itinerant preachers and teachers (3:1; 4:2); his claims about belonging to Christ were apparently seen as unsupported, perhaps because he had not actually seen Christ (10:7, with its emphasis on seeing); he arrived in Corinth without a clear mandate (10:13–14); and he was said to be inferior to the "super-apostles." The latter were probably those who claimed authority from the church at Jerusalem (11:5; 12:11), a position that Paul himself may well have indirectly endorsed because he placed himself in a less exalted position by refusing financial support from the congregation (11:7–9). All of this may well have indicated to some that Paul was not even to be considered an apostle (12:12, 14) and that Christ was not speaking through him (13:3). More than this, Paul may well have been accused of having a deleterious effect upon the congregation because his behavior seemed to be offensive, including his praise of himself (3:1, 5; 4:5; 5:11–15; 6:3–5; 10:2, 8; 11:16–18; 12:1, 11). It was perhaps said that he was working duplicitously for gain (7:1; 12:17–18), even using the collection (8:20–21), that he was a coward (1:23; 8:2; 10:1, 10; 11:32–33), and that he ended up harming the Christian community by abandoning the Corinthians (2:1; 13:2) and exploiting the situation for his own benefit (7:2; 12:16).

b. Minority Accusations. To Paul's mind, at least as reflected in 2 Corinthians, the kinds of attacks made against him seem to have originated with a minority of people connected with the Christian community in Corinth, quite possibly Jewish Christians from Jerusalem, as already mentioned. Paul had to find a suitable tone in the letter and make his perspective clear. For example, he says that they were a minority (2:6; 10:2) who were paid—implying that they, as opposed to Paul, readily accepted financial compensation (2:17; 11:20), something he did not seek though he believed he was entitled to it (1 Cor 9:3–11)—and who had gained entrance into the church by letters of recommendation and self-commendation (3:1; 10:12, 18). They apparently did not hesitate to boast of their own excellence (5:12; 11:12, 18), to emphasize ecstatic experience that Paul counters with his own (5:13; 12:1–6), and overtly to claim both the apostolic office (11:5, 13; 12:11) and superiority to Moses (3:4–11), but without making known their own Jewish heritage (11:22). In response to such claims, Paul says that they in fact were preaching another gospel (11:4), had encroached on others' missionary territory (10:15–16), were immoral (12:21; 13:2), were boastful (10:12–13), and were led by a particular person (2:5; 7:12; 11:4). The result, to Paul's mind at least, was that they were Satan's servants (11:13–15). By contrast, Paul regarded himself as an apostle (1:1), and the proof of this lay in the Corinthians themselves (3:2–3), among whom he had done mighty things (12:12), reflecting his appointment from God (3:5, 6; 4:7).

Is it possible to characterize these false preachers more definitively?[100] Scholars have engaged in endless speculation, often focusing upon ch. 11, especially v. 4. Some, such as Baur, Barrett, and Gunther, have characterized them as Judaizers (Gal 1:6–9), on the basis of their emphasis upon their Jewish heritage (3:4–7; 11:22).[101] But even though the problem in Corinth is serious, Paul's response does not seem to be of the same kind as found in Galatians, hence making this perhaps not the best explanation. A second proposal comes from Bultmann and Schmithals, who claim that the opponents are "gnostics."[102] These scholars note the willingness to trade on ecstatic experience, but this position would require a fuller development of Gnosticism than is likely for the first century. This is not to say that there were not some gnostic tendencies, especially in their taking pride in the possession of "true knowledge," but a formalized Gnosticism does not seem to be the case. A third idea, by Georgi, is that these were Hellenistic Jews who were making claims regarding their miraculous powers.[103] This is the theory of the "divine man" (θεῖος ἀνήρ, *theios anēr*)—the man of God was expected to be some sort of miracle worker—for which there is not significant evidence before Christianity had taken firm root; consequently, the best parallels come from the third century and later. It is possible that these false preachers were followers of Apollos and reflected the Hellenistic Judaism of Alexandria.[104] They therefore may well have been educated and articulate spokesmen who were formidable opponents for Paul. There is merit in this suggestion, especially in light of 1 Corinthians (e.g., 1:12, 18–31; 2:1–5), but the ways in which Paul seems to handle the two situations are quite different: he is more conciliatory in 1 Corinthians but more confrontative in 2 Corinthians. This may well be because the situation had escalated, even though it is hard to form a hard line of connection between the two. The most likely explanation is that this group of false preachers originated in Palestine, possibly as emissaries (whether legitimate or renegade) of the Jerusalem leaders or "super-apostles," or as itinerant preachers who claimed to have been with Jesus. This is not to say that the Jerusalem leaders necessarily were directly opposing Paul at Corinth, but one must not dismiss the degree of suspicion that apparently existed between the Jerusalem and Antiochian missionary efforts (see Acts 15:1–5; 21:20–21). The "super-apostles" may be the leaders in Jerusalem, and Paul's opponents in Corinth may have been claiming the authority of the Jerusalem church, whether they had it or not.[105] In response, Paul suggests that the Corinthians have been too quick to accept the false preachers' claims to have the authority and endorsement of the "super-apostles," whereas he asserts his equal standing and authority with any apostles, including those in Jerusalem. Anyone who says otherwise is a false apostle (2 Cor 11:5, 12–15).

4. Outline of 2 Corinthians

A. Opening (1:1–2)
   1. Sender (1:1)
   2. Addressee (1:1)

   3. Greeting (1:2)
B. Thanksgiving (1:3–7)
C. Body: Paul's ministry to the Corinthians (1:8–9:15)
   1. Formal opening (1:8–11)
   2. Paul's explanation of his recent conduct (1:12–2:13)
   3. Paul's apostolic ministry (2:14–7:16)
   4. The collection for Jerusalem (8:1–9:15)
D. Parenesis (10:1–13:10)
   1. Paul's personal appeal regarding his apostolic authority (10:1–12:10)
   2. Pauline travelogue (12:11–13:4)
   3. Final exhortation (13:5–10)
E. Closing (13.11–14)
   1. Call to unity (13:11)
   2. Greetings (13:12–13)
   3. Benediction (13:14)

F. Romans

"The principal and most excellent part of the NT . . . a light and a way in unto the whole Scripture. . . . No man verily can read it too often or study it too well; for the more it is studied the easier it is; and the more it is chewed the pleasanter it is, and the more groundly it is searched the preciouser things are found in it, so great treasure of spiritual things lieth hid therein!" Apart from the archaic form of the language, this passage could have been written by Luther, Wesley, Augustine, or even Barth, but it was actually penned by William Tyndale in his 1534 introduction to the NT.[106] The significance of the book of Romans, not only to the giants of the church mentioned above but to Christianity as a whole, is seen in the observation by Bruce that Romans has been tied to every major Christian awakening.[107]

1. Authorship

Romans is yet another letter about which Kümmel expresses confidence: "The authenticity and homogeneity of Rom 1–15 are subject to no serious doubt."[108] We will turn to the question of ch. 16 below, but this statement expresses concisely and accurately the consensus that there is no serious critical doubt regarding Pauline authorship of this letter. Of late there have been two related discussions worth noting, however, if only because

The theater and stoa at the Asklepion in Pergamum. © *Rohr Productions. Used with permission.*

of their unusual and aberrant character. The first is the kind of criticism seen in the commentary on Romans by O'Neill, who raises questions of authorship for certain sections and suggests that several of the most important passages and some of the most distinctively Pauline wording may not be authentic.[109] Nevertheless, he does not deny Pauline authorship of the letter, and few have followed his text-critical speculation. A second analysis is that of Schmithals, who divides the letter into two major letters plus some fragments. His claims regarding the two letters are not convincing, but even so, he does not deny Pauline authorship of the two letters and the fragments that he thinks went into the composition of the book.[110]

So far as the evidence from the early church is concerned, the external witness is unanimous. Writings and writers who bear witness to Romans are *1 Clem.* 32.2 (Rom 9:4–5), 33.1 (Rom 6:1), 35.4–6 (Rom 1:29–32), 36.2 (Rom 1:21), 47.7 (Rom 2:24), 61:1 (Rom 13:1); Ign. *Eph.* 9, 19.3; *Magn.* 6.2, 9.1; *Trall.* 9.2; Marcion; Origen; and the Muratorian Fragment.[111] There are also many parallels to Galatians as confirmatory evidence.

2. Date

The precise date of Romans is determined by what one does with Rom 16 (see below). If ch. 16 is seen as authentic to the letter, it allows for a fairly precise dating. If ch. 16 is not seen to be authentic, the dating can still be established within a one-year period.

On his third missionary journey, with his ministry in Ephesus ended after a stay of two years and three months, Paul decided to visit Macedonia and then Greece before going to Jerusalem to bring them the collection that he had been taking (Acts 18:23–21:17, in particular 20:1–3, 19:21; Rom 15:22–26, with reference to the collection being complete). If ch. 16 is original to the letter, then it is almost certain that Paul wrote Romans to the Roman Christians while he was in Corinth on his third missionary journey (Acts 20:3). The evidence overwhelmingly points in this direction. The passage in Acts does not refer specifically to Corinth, but Rom 16:1 speaks of Phoebe, a deaconess of the church at Cenchreae, the eastern port of Corinth, being commended to the church at Rome, with the idea that she is the one carrying the letter to the church. Romans 16:23 mentions Gaius and Erastus. A Gaius, who in Romans sends greetings, is said to have been baptized by Paul in 1 Cor 1:14, and an Erastus, who also sends greetings, is said to have remained in Corinth in 2 Tim 4:20.[112] Even if ch. 16 is not original to the letter, it is still virtually certain that Paul wrote the Letter to the Romans either during his travels throughout Macedonia (Acts 20:1–2) or, more likely, during his stay in Corinth. This is established through the content of the letter, in which Paul states that he intends to visit Rome after he has delivered to the church at Jerusalem the collection that he has gathered in Macedonia and Greece (Rom 15:24–26). This closely matches his traveling itinerary in Acts 20.

Depending upon the date of the third missionary journey, the date of the composition of Romans is likely between A.D. 55 and 59, with a date around A.D. 56 or 57 very probable.

3. Audience

Establishing that Paul wrote the Letter to the Romans and that he wrote it during his third missionary journey still does not solve the problem of his audience. He singles out the addressees of the letter with the words "To all God's beloved in Rome" (Rom 1:7). This probably indicates that he has in mind all of the believers in that city—but who are those believers?

a. Rome during the Time of Paul. Rome of the first century was a large city, with probably somewhere around one million inhabitants.[113] Of these, perhaps forty to fifty thousand of them were Jews, which was a fairly high concentration.[114] Jews first came to Rome apparently with Pompey when he brought them back as slaves from Palestine in 63 B.C. Synagogues were formed; eleven to fifteen Jewish synagogues are known from sepulchral inscriptions to have been in Rome in the first century. One was called the synagogue of the olive tree (cf. Rom 11:17), and another the synagogue of the Hebrews, even though Aramaic would have been the language used by this Jewish population for worship (and Greek for daily life).[115]

In A.D. 41, the emperor Claudius (A.D. 41–54) was crowned. Not a strong-willed man, he was governed by others, including his wives. He was apparently poisoned by his wife, Agrippina, who had persuaded him to appoint her son Nero (A.D. 54–68) to succeed him. It was during Claudius's reign that the Jews were expelled from Rome. There are three controversial issues regarding this event: its cause, its precise date, and the date the expulsion order was lifted. The Roman historian Suetonius says that "since the Jews constantly made disturbances at the instigation of Chrestus, he expelled them from Rome" (*Claud.* 25.4 [LCL]). The majority of NT scholars have interpreted this to mean that there were a number of disputes among the Jews, probably Jewish Christians and non-Christian Jews, over the nature and identity of Jesus Christ. "Chrestus," therefore, is taken as a variant or mistaken spelling of "Christ" by Suetonius. He appears to have thought that this Chrestus was a contemporary person who was stirring up the Jews in Rome. If this scenario is correct, it is more likely that the issue of the resurrection was causing an uproar among the Jewish population there. It is disputed by some NT scholars and classical scholars, however, that Suetonius is talking about such a scenario. It is perhaps more likely, according to this view, that there actually was a person named Chrestus who had caused the Jews to riot. With a slave population of approximately half the population of Rome, the Romans always feared uprisings. As Pliny stated when one slave owner was attacked by his slaves, "No master can feel safe because he is kind and considerate; for it is their brutality, not their reasoning capacity, which leads slaves to murder masters" (*Ep.* 3.14 [LCL]).[116] During 139–133 B.C. in Sicily, slave revolts had been put down with great violence and bloodshed, and there was no wish to repeat them. So apparently Claudius issued an edict that forced the Jews to leave Rome, though it seems not to have resulted in the confiscation of their property (see Acts 18:1–3). The second dispute concerns the date of Claudius's edict. The vast majority of scholars have accepted a date of A.D. 49, on the basis of the Christian writer Paulus Orosius (5th cent. A.D.), who dates the event to the ninth year of Claudius's reign (*Hist. pag.* 7.6.15). Some, however, have argued that the date was A.D. 41 (or 43), on the basis of Dio Cassius's report of Claudius's edict forbidding Jews to meet (*Rom.* 60.6.6).[117] Claudius apparently was hostile toward Jews from the beginning of his principate (there are other edicts of his regarding the Jews, especially in Egypt; see P.Lond. 1912

[printed in *Select Papyri* 2:212]), perhaps resulting in his initially forbidding them to meet together. Nevertheless, the later date is probably still correct for the expulsion. The third and last issue is when and how the edict would have expired. An edict such as this would have been decreed by the emperor to last in perpetuity, but in fact, such a decree would only have been in force so long as an emperor wished it. Consequently, if a new emperor came to power, he would have had the option of continuing to keep it in force or of allowing it to expire.[118] Apparently, Nero did not enforce the decree (if Claudius himself had in fact enforced it for so long), so that the Jews were allowed to return to Rome.

At first, Nero may have appeared to be an emperor concerned with justice and proper procedures, but by A.D. 65, Christians in Rome were being martyred by him.[119] He found the Christians easy victims to blame for a number of disasters and difficulties that he had in Rome, including a devastating fire in A.D. 64. As part of his "sport," Nero reportedly used Christians as human torches at his parties, all of which eventually led to sympathy for Christians (Tacitus, *Ann.* 15.44.2–5, esp. 4).[120] It was likely during the persecution of Nero in A.D. 64/65 that Paul and perhaps Peter were martyred in Rome (*1 Clem.* 5.4). Nero's reign came to an ignominious end when, insane, he died in a pathetic attempt at suicide. The scholar of Roman religion T. R. Glover reportedly said that little did the emperor suspect in his condemnation of Paul that "there would come a time when men would name their dogs Nero and their sons Paul."

b. The Christians at Rome. The founder of the Christian community at Rome is unknown. But by A.D. 49, when the Jews were expelled from Rome, there were apparently Jewish Christians among those who were compelled to leave (see Acts 18:2). How did those first Christians get to Rome? There is no record of any sort of apostolic visit, even by Peter or Paul, until long after there was a Christian presence in Rome. This has led to widespread speculation regarding the early spread of Christianity, and several possible scenarios are worth considering. On the one hand, Rome was the center of the Roman Empire, and in literal and figurative senses, all roads led to Rome. So it is entirely possible that a Christian or a few Christians, in the course of their travels, would have come to Rome, perhaps to settle or at least to conduct business. During the course of their time there, they perhaps set up a Christian community. On the other hand, it is just as possible that Christianity made its way to Rome soon after the events at Pentecost. Acts 2:10 says that there were visitors from Rome in Jerusalem on that day. Perhaps some of those converted were from Rome and returned there soon after, taking their newfound belief in the risen Christ with them. In any event, by the time Paul wrote to the Christians in Rome, Christianity could have been there for over a decade and become well established.[121]

If the church was well established in Rome, this does not mean that it was without problems and tensions, however. Some of the major problems would probably have been caused by the edict of Claudius and the subsequent return of the Jews after the edict expired under Nero.

There is widespread debate regarding the composition of the Christian community at Rome. The four major positions are that the church was predominantly Jewish Christian, predominantly Gentile Christian, a fairly evenly divided mixed group, or an aggregation of separate, independent churches. Minear and, more recently, Watson (the two on different grounds and in different ways) have argued for the last position, claiming that the Christian community at Rome consisted of multiple independent churches. In his reconstruction of the situation at Rome, Minear claimed to have found five major church groups, each referred to by Paul in Romans and thus able to be characterized in a particular way.[122] In his assessment of Romans, Watson used the specific references in Rom 14:1–15:13 to the "weak" and "strong" to argue that there were two major church groups in Rome.[123] These views have highlighted the potential sociological conflicts in the Roman Christian community, but neither view has garnered widespread support. The major problem with this kind of reconstruction is that it appears to be both too literalistic and too interpretative. Minear must differentiate these various groups on the basis of a number of incidental comments, but even so, he must do a fair amount of speculative synthesis. Why this number of groups and not more or less? Watson is almost certainly correct that there was some sort of difficulty in the Roman church(es), but to take these, at best, interpretatively obscure references as clear indicators of two distinct churches is too literalistic and requires more extrapolation than is justified by the text.

More likely the church was composed of Jewish and Gentile Christians, although it is difficult to know what the mix was or how many churches there were.[124] A number of scholars have argued that the church was composed of mostly Jewish Christians. The evidence often used for this position consists of passages that refer directly to the Jews or appear to allude to Jewish institutions and conventions. For example, in 2:17, Paul refers directly to those who bear the name "Jew"; in 3:1–2, he asks what advantage the Jew has over the Gentile; and in 16:3, 7, 11, he greets the Jewish coworkers Priscilla and Aquila and his "relatives." In ch. 4, using "Abraham, our ancestor" (4:1), as an example of someone who was saved by faith, not by works, Paul relies upon an implicit OT chronological argument in which the statement that he was reckoned righteous (Gen 15:6) preceded his circumcision (Gen 17). In Rom 9–11, there is a heavy reliance upon OT quotations, often strung together and interwoven with OT imagery (e.g., God as the potter and the people as the clay; Rom 9:20–23, citing Isa 29:16; 45:9). In Rom 15:7–12, there seems to be reliance upon OT quotations that are addressed specifically to the Jews, rather than to the Gentiles. One of the most important pieces of evidence in this reconstruction is the widespread use of the language of "law" (esp. chs. 3–4), which refers in most of these instances to the Jewish law, or Torah.

Nevertheless, this position, regardless of how popular it has been in the past, is probably not the most likely scenario, for two reasons. The first is historical. If the Jews were expelled from Rome in A.D. 49 and had not begun to return until A.D. 54 at the death of Claudius or slightly before and if Romans was written around A.D. 57 (which is the scholarly consensus),[125] it would be difficult to suppose that a sufficient number of Jewish Christians had returned to become the dominant force in the church. The Gentile Christians, it must be kept in mind, would probably not have been expelled from Rome (except possibly those who followed the Jewish law and customs), and so they would have been responsible for maintaining the church during the intervening years. It seems most likely that they would have continued to be the predominant force at the time of Paul's writing to the Romans. The second reason for disputing the Jewish-Christian hypothesis is the interpretation of the passages that are often cited in support of the position. For example, Rom 2:17 occurs in the midst of a section that is describing the sinfulness of all of humanity, not only of Jews. It is not clear that, even in 2:17 and following, the Jews emerge as the specifically addressed group. This could be said of most passages cited above, especially chs. 9–11. Although, because of their use of the OT, these chapters may seem to have a distinctively Jewish feel about them, the references in this section make it clear that the exposition has Gentiles in mind. For example, 9:3–4 appears to have Paul speaking about a group other than his primary audience when speaking of the Jews. The same is true in 10:1–3 and even 11:1–2. Most significant, perhaps, is 11:13, where Paul specifically states that he is speaking to those who are Gentiles, since he is the apostle to the Gentiles. And Paul's use of the Abraham story does not depend upon one's being Jewish to understand it—in fact, it may well be addressed to Gentiles.

Because of this, a second group has argued for the predominantly Gentile composition of the church. The argument for this rests not only upon the historical scenario mentioned above—the expulsion and return of the Jewish Christians to Rome—but upon passages in Romans pointing to a Gentile audience. For example, in 11:13–32 Paul not only addresses the Gentiles directly (v. 13) but, at the end of the section, speaks of the Jews being regrafted onto the olive tree, and he uses "you" to speak to the Gentiles in the course of his argument. Throughout Romans, Paul heralds his position as apostle to the Gentiles—for instance, in 1:5–6, chs. 9–11, and 15:15–16. If ch. 16 is part of the original letter and hence addressed to the church at Rome (see below for a defense of this position), it is worth noting that most of the names used in the greetings of Rom 16:3–25 are Greek, not Jewish.[126] If there were many Jews in Rome, Paul apparently (according to this evidence) did not know them.

Nevertheless, this view has perhaps also overlooked significant evidence: although the Jews may not have been predominant in the church at Rome, the framework of Paul's argument is predicated upon a Jewish understanding. It is possible that this is simply the way Paul thought and wrote; but it is at least as likely that Paul continued to use this way of structuring his argument—in a way that he does not use in his other letters—because of his knowledge of the significant Jewish population of the church at Rome (it is also worth noting that

many Jews of this time had Greek names, making the argument from Romans 16 doubtful). First, the issue of law continues to be an important issue throughout the letter. The only other Pauline letter where this issue looms so large is Galatians, where Paul is apparently confronting Judaizers, who argue that in order for Gentiles to become Christians, they must become Jews also. Paul is apparently not confronting Judaizers in Rome, but he at least appears to be arguing from a framework that the Jews would understand. Second, Paul relies heavily upon the OT. Of the eighty or so direct OT quotations in the Pauline Letters, over fifty of these appear in Romans. It is perhaps not so striking that Paul, being a Jew, would choose to rely so heavily upon the OT, certainly if he realized that there would be an audience that could appreciate his use of the Jewish Scriptures.

In conclusion, it is probably best to argue that the church at Rome was a mixed group, including both Jews and Gentiles. This is the view of the majority of commentators on Romans. If one were to venture a guess as to the predominance of one group or another, there were probably more Gentiles in the church than Jews. It certainly appears that the Gentiles were the predominant force, since Paul seems to identify with them in 15:1. A plausible scenario, based upon the above evidence, is that the Jews had returned to the church in Rome to find that their positions had been taken by Gentiles and that this had resulted in, if not overt conflict, some tension regarding the roles and relationships of the two groups (see Rom 14:1–15:13). The Jews may have believed that they had a privileged position and that they were at least owed a greater role than they were currently exercising (2:17–24), and the Gentiles may have lost sight of the fact that the Jews had certain distinguishing practices that needed to be shown respect (3:1; 14:13–23), even if they were not to dominate the church any longer. It was probably to such a church environment that Paul wrote.

4. Occasion and Purpose[127]

a. Occasion. The circumstances that elicited the Letter to the Romans seem to be encapsulated in a number of important passages that occur at the beginning and the end of the letter. Paul states in Rom 1:13–15 that he planned to come to Rome and that he is eager to preach the gospel to them, even though he has been prevented from doing so. In 15:22, he clarifies why he was prevented—he has been preaching in the eastern part of the Mediterranean. Now that he has preached from Jerusalem all the way to Illyricum (15:19) and has no place further to preach in the east (15:23), he sets his sights on Spain (15:24, 28). In conjunction with that journey, he intends to visit the church in Rome (15:23, 28–29), even though first he has to go to Jerusalem to deliver the collection that he gathered from the churches in Macedonia and Greece (15:26). There has been speculation about whether Paul ever got to Spain. *First Clement* 5.7 has been interpreted to imply that he did, but this is not certain, especially in light of what appears to have been his travels as represented in the Pastoral Epistles (on the authorship of the Pastorals see sec. 4, below). There is the further question of whether Paul knew Latin, since the western part of the Roman Empire had begun to become Latin speaking in the first century B.C., a process apparently largely completed during the first century A.D. Paul mentions that he had spread the gospel as far as Illyricum (or Dalmatia), but Illyricum was also a Latin-speaking area, so it is possible that Paul knew Latin and hence was fully prepared for a preaching mission to Spain, whether or not he ever got there.[128]

b. Purpose. The occasion of Paul's proposed visit to Rome was part of the westward expansion of his preaching mission. But the purpose or motivation for his writing the Letter to the Romans is not so clear and has elicited an immense amount of debate.[129]

In recent discussion, the contingency of the Pauline Letters has become important: Paul is a writer who is addressing in each letter a unique set of circumstances that warrants a response to that particular situation. Beker has emphasized this contingency,[130] which is undeniable. When the Pauline Letters are examined, however, it also becomes clear that there is a consistent personality standing behind Paul's letters (this is true of whatever corpus is accepted as genuine, usually by virtue of the criterion of consistency by which these corpora are defined). There is a transcontingent, or more universal, set of beliefs that must also be considered when analyzing Paul's letters. Some wish to say that Paul is hopelessly contradictory, even

within a given letter (and many of these comments refer to Romans), but such deconstructive criticism neither forms a sound interpretive model nor is borne out by the evidence at hand. It usually reflects a half-hearted effort to come to terms with the complexities with which Paul deals. In light of the ongoing discussion regarding Romans, however, there are at least eight proposals regarding purpose worth mentioning.

(1) Compendium of the Christian Religion. The traditional view of Romans, summarized in Melanchthon's phrase that Romans is a compendium of the Christian religion, is that the letter is as close to a systematic theology as is found in Paul's writings. The contention is that Paul has taken the occasion—writing to a church that he has not visited but that figures importantly in his future travel plans—to set out the major tenets of Christian belief, and he does so in a highly systematic and organized way, but within the letter form. This position tends to minimize the contingent elements of Paul's presentation, including the relevance of specific contextual factors, and emphasizes the major doctrines that constitute the Pauline gospel, including justification by faith, human sinfulness, the role of Adam and Christ, sanctification, reconciliation, the relations of Jews and Gentiles, and the role of the state. This position was virtually unchallenged until the work of Baur in the early nineteenth century,[131] and still has enduring currency. It is reflected most recently perhaps in Moo's commentary on Romans and in the work of Wright.[132] Wright has combined it with Paul's missionary motive, in the sense that Paul's mission is founded on his theology—the two are seen to be inseparable.

There are two major objections to this position: (1) it appears to minimize the context or the circumstances to the point that it appears this letter could have been written to virtually any Christian community anywhere at any time; and (2) many of what some scholars would consider major Christian doctrines are lacking in Romans, making it at best an incomplete (and hence flawed?) compendium. Some of the subjects often cited as lacking are eschatology, Christology, the doctrine of the church, the Lord's Supper or Eucharist, and marriage. These two objections are not, however, strong. Romans has spoken to widely varying Christian communities throughout the last two millennia, probably more so than any other Pauline letter and even any other NT book. Besides, there is nothing inherently contradictory in saying that a work can be written with full consideration of a particular situation and, at the same time, with larger theological motives in mind. The second objection cannot be taken too seriously. One only needs to look at the list presented above to see that there are two major objections to it. The first is that it is not an accurate characterization of Romans. In what sense can it be said that Christology is not a major concern of the book?[133] It is clear from Paul's argumentative line that he predicates all of Christian existence—justification, reconciliation, and sanctification—upon the work of Christ (e.g., 1:3–4) and Christ's ongoing ministry through his Spirit (8:36–39). For example, in ch. 5, where Paul speaks of reconciliation, he states explicitly three times (vv. 1, 11, 21) that it was accomplished "through our Lord Jesus Christ"; these statements frame the entire chapter. The second objection is that the importance of many of these missing doctrines is a matter of dispute. The lack of any particular doctrine in Romans may be significant, but this does not necessarily reveal a deficiency in Romans. Several of the doctrines mentioned above have only limited relevance in the other Pauline Letters as well (e.g., the Lord's Supper, which is only discussed in 1 Corinthians).[134]

(2) Manifesto of Paul's Deepest Convictions. Manson has argued a position that, in some ways, addresses one of the major objections to the first position, the letter as a compendium of the Christian religion. He claims that Romans was sent originally to the churches at both Rome (chs. 1–15:23 or 33) and Ephesus (chs. 1–16) and reflects not a full-blown compendium of all major Christian doctrine but, rather, the ideas that were deepest in Paul's thought.[135] Paul had first to go to Jerusalem, but he was also going to Rome on the way farther west. Unable to visit Ephesus, he sent this letter to both, in a larger form for the Ephesians. This would account for the names in ch. 16 that seem to be associated with Ephesus and for the fact that, in some manuscripts, the Roman destination is missing (see sec. 5, below, on the text-critical issues). Thus, the letter is expanded in its scope from being a letter addressed to a single church to a type of circular letter.

The objections to this position are several, however. The first is that, in light of extant exter-nal textual evidence, there is not a strong case to be made for the text circulating in a form that only included chs. 1–15. Besides, this would make for a somewhat abrupt and truncated close and an unnatural Pauline ending. The second objection questions why Paul would convey his deepest convictions to the church at Rome. It is understandable that a revised form would be sent to the church at Ephesus (the textual difficulties remain, however), but why Rome and not Corinth, or Antioch, or another church closely associated with him? Paul had never been to Rome, so why would he send a meditation upon his deepest convictions to a church other than one he had founded? It is more understandable that he would send a compendium of Christian belief to a church that he anticipated visiting, rather than an exposition of his deepest beliefs.

(3) Last Will and Testament. Bornkamm has argued that Paul was facing an unknown future on his contemplated journey to Jerusalem with the collection from the churches in Greece and Macedonia.[136] If the record in Acts 21:17–26 is to be trusted at this point (and it seems very likely that it is, since it creates a very plausible course of events in which the Jerusalem church is implicated in Paul's arrest; see ch. 9, sec. 3, above), Paul had every reason to wonder about the reception that would await him in Jerusalem (Rom 15:31). His missionary ventures had been closely watched, and his proclamation of the gospel had aroused suspicion. For whatever reason, perhaps Paul had some sense or direct warning regarding the Jerusalem church; after all, he had been the center of controversy before (see Acts 15:1–5; Gal 2:1–10). In anticipation of the troubles that may have been awaiting him, Paul took this occasion of writing to the Christian community at Rome to provide a permanent record of his message, as a forecast of the preaching and missionary ministry he wished to continue. Consequently, there is a balance maintained in the letter that reflects one of his persistent battles and perhaps one of the issues to be faced in Jerusalem—legalism and antinomianism (opposition to the law). He had been accused of being an antinomian, but he was anxious to show that neither he nor the Christian faith was either antinomian or legalistic. There is insight to be gained from consideration of this view, especially in light of the circumstances that befell Paul.

Nevertheless, several other objections must be considered. First, why did Paul choose to write this kind of letter to Rome, a church that he had never visited? Bornkamm tries to make it clear that this is not the last will and testament of a person who anticipates he will not be able to carry on his ministry. If that is true, then in what sense is it a *last* will and testament? Furthermore, if it were to be his last, Paul may well have poured out his theological heart to his friends, certainly to one of the churches that could have been expected to maintain the Pauline mission. Second, does the kind of situation that Bornkamm posits appear in the letter? Does it reflect the unsettled state upon which this sort of view is predicated? To be sure, there are references to uncertainty regarding the church at Jerusalem (Rom 15:31), but this is offset by Paul's conviction that he is determined to make his way to Rome on his way to Spain after visiting Jerusalem (15:24). By comparison, Romans has none of the gloom found in passages such as 2 Cor 10–13 or especially 2 Tim 4:6–7 (which Bornkamm considers deuteropauline), where Paul seems genuinely exhausted and concerned regarding the future.

(4) Apology to Jerusalem. It has been argued (though probably inaccurately) that the distinguishing mark of all of the genuine Pauline Letters is mention of the collection (e.g., 1 Cor 16:1–4; 2 Cor 8:1–9:15).[137] This seems to be predicated upon a presumption about which letters are authentic. The point is still well taken that the collection is important in Paul's thinking. Consequently, it has been posited that Romans, though addressed to the Roman churches and apparently formally directed towards them, is in fact a letter that is "addressed to Jerusalem."[138] That is, it was written with Jerusalem in mind, as if it were being overheard by that church, so that it would accept Paul's ministry along with his collection and so that he could overcome any possible objections it may have had to what he had been teaching in his missionary journeys. It is even possible that what he was writing in the letter was a dress rehearsal for the kind of speech that he would deliver to the leaders of the church in Jerusalem.

As seen above, Paul's concern regarding his reception in Jerusalem was valid; nevertheless, it is dubious that Romans is best seen as an apology to Jerusalem. There are three objections. (a) This letter provides only an indirect way of offering an apology to the Jerusalem church for his belief and behavior, since it is sent in the completely opposite direction, that is, to Rome. Jerusalem is not mentioned in the letter in any way that would indicate that Paul is concerned that the letter he is sending to Rome might reach those in Jerusalem (the reference in Rom 15:31 is completely insufficient to suggest that). Furthermore, there is material in the letter that would hardly appeal to Jews, especially an audience that Paul was trying to please (see Rom 4, 11). (b) The collection, while it might provide a suitable occasion for writing the letter, hardly constitutes a sufficient purpose for writing such a lengthy and involved letter. This is clear when one notes that references to the collection are minimal. (c) It is unclear how this letter would help Paul achieve his apologetic purpose with Jerusalem, even if the letter were forwarded or served as a commendation on his behalf.

(5) Letter of Self-Introduction. Perhaps a more realistic option is that Paul wrote this letter as a letter of self-introduction, possibly verging on an apologetic letter.[139] According to this theory, Paul wrote to the Roman Christians so that they would welcome him and speed him on his way to Spain (1:11–15; 15:24, 28). A certain amount of rapport was needed with members of that church so that they would be receptive to him and his gospel, since he might well be in need of financial support (prepared by his mention of the collection and his work on behalf of the church in Jerusalem). In the letter, Paul displays many of the features one would expect from a teacher or an apologist. For example, he uses the diatribe, a dialogical form of persuasion used by philosopher-teachers in the Hellenistic world (see ch. 9, sec. 2). In the epistolary convention, Paul of course writes both sides of the dialogue, but he raises issues, explains ideas, raises objections, and responds to them, all as a way of leading his audience through his argument. Whether one characterizes this as teaching the essentials of the Pauline gospel or as an attempt to provide an apologetic for Christian faith, Paul is seen as creating a useful platform for the continuation of his missionary work in the west. Just as Corinth, Ephesus, and Antioch had provided platforms for his work in the eastern Mediterranean, he envisioned Rome as his platform for moving farther west.

Appreciation of Paul's literary and philosophical techniques is crucial to understanding the way in which he promotes his gospel; nevertheless, there are some legitimate objections to this position. (a) Paul seems to be engaging in too heavy a theology for just a simple attempt to say hello and introduce himself to the Romans. Would he not risk an adverse response by the Roman Christians if he touched on some disputed issue or if he, an outsider, delved into the issue of Jewish and Gentile relations? The counterargument is that it is not like Paul to change his approach or be overly concerned with offending his audience. This is one of his great points of consistency. (b) This kind of approach is not consistent with what Paul does elsewhere: he does not lay out his gospel for others to examine for approval. The church at Rome, however, was unique in Paul's experience. Even though he had possibly not visited the church at Colossae, he had at least been instrumental in its evangelization. And although he used other churches as bases, he had either been sent from them or been responsible for bringing the Christian message to them (e.g., Corinth and Ephesus). Now Paul was entering a new phase in his ministry, and perhaps it is a tribute to his abilities that he was able to adjust to the new situation. (c) It is difficult to believe that Paul was so unknown to the church at Rome that it warranted such an extended introduction, unless he had been misrepresented to the Romans by others and felt a need to clarify his gospel. If he were that unknown, it seems likely that he would have needed more than simply the Letter to the Romans to serve as an introduction. (d) The references to his visit to Rome are, at best, vague (1:11–13; 15:24, 28). Indeed, his plans seem to center more on Spain and less on Rome. Rome appears only incidental as a place that he would be visiting as he passed through to the west.

(6) Providing the Roman Church with an Apostolic Grounding. Klein has argued that Paul wrote Romans as a letter to refound the church so that it would have an apostolic grounding to which it could point.[140] According to this position, Paul views some churches as full and complete, and others he does not. Paul says in 15:20 that he does not build upon another's foundation, but this can be reconciled with 1:15 and his eagerness to preach in Rome if it is seen that the church does not in fact have the kind of foundation that he sees as necessary for an apostolic church.

There are several substantive objections to this position, however. (a) It is difficult to quantify what exactly the Roman church would lack by not having an apostolic foundation such as outlined by Klein. For example, Paul says in the letter that they are full of knowledge, capable, and proclaimers of the faith (1:6–16; 15:14–23). In fact, in 1:6, Paul characterizes the Romans as being "among" the Gentiles who have become obedient to the faith, making it unlikely that he is distinguishing them in any meaningful way. (b) Even if it could be proven from Romans that Paul is forcefully asserting his apostolic authority (which he does not appear to be emphasizing; see 1:12), this would not necessarily mean that he is doing so to found or refound the church there. The evidence of such a refounding is absent. (c) No other situation such as Klein's reconstruction—where a church has no apostolic founding and is seen to have some form of liability or detriment as a result—is found in the NT.

(7) Gentile and Jewish Relations. There are two major theories that the purpose of Romans is tied up with Gentile and Jewish relations.

(a) The first depends upon the scenario suggested by Baur about the divide in early Christianity between Petrine, or Jewish, and Hellenistic, or Pauline, elements.[141] This position argues that the letter was the earliest support for this great Gentile church in Rome, opposing the Jewish Christians there. According to this theory, Paul wanted to be able to deliver the picture of a unified Gentile Christianity when he presented his collection in Jerusalem, so this letter has nothing to do with Rome per se but with Rome as a church of Gentiles to which Paul can point as a noteworthy and significant success in support of his position as representative of the Hellenistic side of the equation.

As much truth as there may be to the conflict between Jewish and Hellenistic elements in the early church, there are limitations to this position. (1) There are too many specific references in the letter for it to be unconcerned with the church at Rome (see, e.g., 1:8–15; 13:1–7; chs. 14–15). (2) There are also too many references to the Jews, including lengthy discussion in chs. 9–11, for a letter that is merely designed to present a unified picture of Gentile Christianity. (3) No other letter does this, making it difficult to posit that Romans figures into a strategy for which it is the only evidence. (4) If the dispute in the early church is primarily an ethnic one, why is the issue not addressed in this way? There is far too much that is comprehensive in scope, including description of Jews and Gentiles in religious terms, to provide an argument that this letter is concerned only to promote the Hellenistic side of the argument.

(b) The second theory holding that Romans concerns Gentile and Jewish relations is represented by Minear and Watson and has already been discussed above regarding the balance between Jews and Gentiles in the Roman church. This position argues that divergent communities are being addressed, possibly the weak (Jewish) and the strong (Gentile), according to Watson, or groups differing in status, according to Minear. This theory takes seriously the conditional and contingent nature of the Pauline writings, and the specific references within the letter, especially those in the parenetic section. According to this position, Paul perhaps gives something to each side in the dispute. For example, the Jews are allowed to retain pride in Abraham, while the Gentiles can see themselves as grafted onto the tree that Israel once solely occupied. The goal is to establish unity "in Christ," in that even though all are sinners, they share the same gospel.

There are two major objections to this reconstruction (besides those noted above regarding the composition of the church). (1) This theory does not seem to offer help in understanding Romans until chs. 14–15. Interpreting the weak and the strong as referring to Jews and Gentiles leaves the vast bulk of the letter unexplained. (2) It is not clear that the weak and the strong are being addressed as divergent communities. The issue of what it means to be "in Christ" is addressed, but not enough is known of the composition of the church to make firm equations with particular groups.

There is no consensus regarding the purpose of Paul's writing the Letter to the Romans; nevertheless, several important points must be kept in mind. First, its status as a letter—a real letter written to a genuine Christian community—must be maintained. This is important for studying any of the letters, but Romans in particular, since so little is known of the relationship between the church and Paul. Second, one cannot avoid the confrontation with major theological categories in this letter. Not all of Paul's theology may be discussed in it, but much important theology is. Apparently, since the letter reflects beliefs that he considers very important, he structures his argument differently from any of his other letters. By doing so, he does come close to systematically presenting his theology.

5. Textual Issues

As noted in the above discussion, there are several issues of textual criticism that have direct bearing on understanding Romans.

a. Romans 15 and 16. Romans 15 and 16 are in nearly every manuscript of Romans, but the question is whether they belong there (e.g., a Latin summary of Codex Amiatinus does not describe 15:1–16:24; Tertullian's *Against Marcion* seems to imply that Marcion did not know chs. 15 and 16; and the descriptions of some other manuscripts seem to imply that ch. 16 was missing).[142] The difficulty is suggested by the placement of the doxology, which is usually found in 16:25–27 but is also sometimes found in other places in various manuscripts (e.g., after ch. 16 only; after chs. 14 and 16; after ch. 14 only, with and without ch. 16; and after ch. 15 only). Its movable placement suggests that there were different versions of the letter, to which other chapters may have been added. The textual debate concerns how to account for versions that may have had only chs. 1–14 or chs. 1–15, if in fact they ever existed. (This textual issue is considered by some as the most complex in the entire NT.) Compounding the difficulty is the content of ch. 16, which includes a surprisingly large number of people to be greeted, especially since Paul had never been to the church at Rome. How would Paul know these people? Usually he does not greet those he does not know. Who are these people? There is speculation regarding a few of them, but for the most part, they are unknown, even though some of the names were popular in the Hellenistic world.[143] Paul had not been to Rome, but he had spent a long time in Ephesus (over two years according to Acts 19). Indeed, Priscilla and Aquila, mentioned in Rom 16:3, are last seen in Ephesus in Acts 18:19, and Paul calls Epaenetus in Rom 16:5 the "first convert in Asia" (Ephesus was capital of the Roman province of Asia). These points of connection have suggested a relationship of Rom 16 to Ephesus (see the views of Manson and others in sec. 4, just above).

The textual evidence in Romans suggests a number of possible forms of the original letter.[144]

(1) Romans 1–16 as the Entire Letter. In a lengthy and informative treatment of the issues, Gamble maintains that a recent consensus has been reached that chs. 1–16 constitute the Letter to the Romans,[145] although some say that the doxology found at 16:25–27 was added later, perhaps by Marcion, to supply a suitable ending. This is the position that we find most convincing and from which our analysis is taken.

(2) Romans 1–16 Abbreviated to a Circular Letter of 1–14 or 1–15. This view maintains the integrity of the original letter (chs. 1–16), as in the first position above, but argues that a later circular letter was created, which consisted of either chs. 1–14 or chs. 1–15.[146] This would account for the problems at 1:7 and 15 in a few late manuscripts, where "Rome" is omitted. The problem with this position is that it would mean ending the letter at 14:23, in the middle of an argument that goes all the way to 15:13. Another problem is that it overlooks specific references in 1:8–15 that are picked up near the end of ch. 15. Romans 15:33 is a somewhat better place to end the letter, but then there is no epistolary closing, which it would have been necessary to attach and for which there is no external textual evidence.

(3) Romans 1–14 as a Circular Letter. It has been argued that chs. 1–14 were originally written as a circular letter and then ch. 15 was added later when the letter was sent to Rome.[147] The support for this supposedly comes from the general nature of the letter apart from chs. 1 and 15–16. But the question is raised why this letter would consist of chs. 1–14, since the letter breaks off in the middle of an argument that goes to 15:13, as noted above about the second position. Furthermore, there is no alternative address to suggest any other recipients. In addition, there is the problem of ch. 16 and where it came from. Was it a letter addressed to Ephesus (see 4th position)?

(4) Romans 1–15 as a Circular Letter. This theory holds that chs. 1–15 were originally written as a circular letter, to which ch. 16, addressed to Ephesus, was attached. According to this position, there are two alternative scenarios. In the first, ch. 16 was the entire letter to the Ephesians, a small letter that accompanied and served as a cover letter for the larger Romans 1–15.[148] But is it possible that an entire Pauline letter was made up essentially of a list of greetings and other names? The second scenario—one with widespread appeal earlier in this century—is that ch. 16 was part of a larger letter to the Ephesians and was later attached to Romans.[149] The problem with this theory is that there is no other reference to any other letter (as there is in Col 4:16 regarding the letter to the Laodiceans), and it would be extremely odd for only this part of an Ephesian letter to be kept. This position seems to work too hard to establish the Ephesian connection, on the basis of fairly slender evidence. Paul had many acquaintances, and they were not necessarily confined to Ephesus (especially since similar names have been found in Rome). It is entirely possible that Priscilla and Aquila had returned from Ephesus to Rome, since they apparently traveled quite a bit (Acts 18:18). In addition, why would such extensive descriptions of the individuals have been provided in the posited letter to the Ephesians, whom Paul would have already known? The elaborate nature of the chapter seems to point away from an Ephesian reception. And again, there is the problem that Rom 15:33 is not the most natural close for a Pauline letter (see 2d position).

(5) Romans 1–14 as a Marcionite Letter. Sanday and Headlam, followed by Bruce, argued that Marcion, the second-century Roman heretic who was excommunicated in A.D. 144, in arguing for a radical form of Christianity with a severe dichotomy between faith and law, may have edited the Letter to the Romans.[150] The result of other Marcionite editing appears to have been the exclusion of significant portions of the NT that emphasized the OT. The result was a corpus that consisted of an edited form of the Gospel of Luke and ten Pauline Letters, excluding the Pastorals and Hebrews. Perhaps Marcion cut ch. 15 because it had too much OT in it, besides objectionable passages (e.g., 15:4, 8). As tempting as this theory is, there is simply too little knowledge of the situation to substantiate it thoroughly, even though Origen states that Marcion abridged Romans at 14:23 (Comm. Rom. 14:23 [PG 14:1290]). There are other texts with no Marcionite influence that have shorter readings. Nevertheless, since many of the early church fathers, such as Tertullian, do not cite chs. 15 and 16, this has continued to be a very attractive explanation.[151]

(6) Romans 1–15 as Catholic Generalization. This theory argues that the abbreviated form of the

letter was a conscious revision done for legitimate purposes of catholic or universal instruction.[152] Because of the more specific Roman content of the final chapter, this theory holds that to use the letter in the wider church without losing valuable material, a shorter form was made for instructional purposes. There are two major problems with this position. The first is that there is little substantive proof that the letter was in fact used in this way. The second is that other Pauline letters with material specific to their intended audiences have not been abbreviated.

b. Doxology. The placement of the doxology (16:25–27) has proved very important in textual criticism of Romans. The fact that the doxology appears in a variety of places in different manuscripts has given rise to speculation regarding the original integrity of the entire letter.[153] In many of the best and earliest manuscripts (including $\mathfrak{P}^{61}$ ℵ B C and many others), the doxology is found at the end of ch. 16. It is printed there in almost all English Bibles; in the rest, it is printed at the end of ch. 14. The text-critical evidence for its placement in the latter location is very weak, consisting of mostly late manuscripts (Y and the Majority Text). A few manuscripts have it at the end of both chs. 14 and 16 (A P and others). A third place for the doxology is at the end of ch. 15, as in $\mathfrak{P}^{46}$ (ca. 200), the early Alexandrian papyrus. This is the earliest manuscript with the doxology, but it also includes 16:1–23 after the doxology; it is unclear what this indicates. The fourth alternative is for the doxology to be omitted altogether, but this apparently occurs only in a few late manuscripts (F G 629) and in what we know of Marcion's text from Origen's comments on 16:25–27 in his commentary on Romans.

6. Outline of Romans

A. Opening (1:1–7)
  1. Sender (1:1–6)
  2. Addressee (1:7)
  3. Greeting (1:7)
B. Thanksgiving (1:8–17)
  1. Paul's thoughts for the Roman church (1:8–15)
  2. Summary statement of the basis for thanksgiving: Justification and sanctification (life) equal reconciliation (1:16–17)

C. Body (1:18–11:36)
  1. The human predicament revealed (1:18–3:20)
  2. Justification as the solution to the human sinful (legal) condition (3:21–4:25)
  3. Reconciliation as the fulfillment of justification and the anticipation of sanctification (5:1–21)
  4. Sanctification for the Christian believer (6:1–8:39)
  5. God's faithfulness despite Israel's rejection (9:1–11:36)
D. Parenesis (12:1–15:33)
  1. Individual behavior (12:1–13:14)
  2. Group behavior (14:1–15:13)
  3. Apostolic presence (15:14–33)
E. Closing (16:1–27)
  1. Commendation and greetings (16:1–16)
  2. Closing warning (16:17–20)
  3. Personal greetings (16:21–23)
  4. Doxology (16:[24]–27)

3. THE PRISON EPISTLES

A. Philippians

1. The City of Philippi

Philippi was located in the eastern part of the Roman province of Macedonia.[154] It was not, properly speaking, a Greek city (as Greece was in the Roman province of Achaia), but because Macedonia and Greece proper had been under common control since the time of Alexander the Great's father, Philip II of Macedon, it was seen as Greek.

The city was named after Alexander the Great's father, who began the campaigns that led to his son's massive conquests. It was built upon the site of a small market town called Krenides, which may mean "well" or "spring." In 356 B.C., Philip captured Krenides and renamed it after himself. This became a greatly expanding city on what became the Via Egnatia, with gold mines forming the basis of a prosperous economy (Strabo, *Geog.* 7 frg. 34). In 42 B.C., Antony and Octavian (who became Augustus Caesar in 27 B.C.) defeated Brutus and Cassius at Philippi, and from that time retired Roman soldiers were routinely settled there (Strabo, *Geog.* 7 frg. 41).[155]

This settlement continued after Octavian defeated Antony and Cleopatra at the battle of Actium in 31 B.C. The population of the city was composed of a mix of native Macedonians, Greeks, and the Romans who had emigrated to Philippi. As an Augustan colony (Acts 16:12), Philippi was one of the four most important in the region, and by the third century A.D. was under the *jus italicum*, the law that gave the colony the same rights as those in Italy. The strong Roman presence is indicated by the fact that 85 percent of the inscriptions found at Philippi from around the first century A.D. are in Latin, and only 15 percent in Greek. This is unusual for a Greco-Roman city of the time, because Greek was the lingua franca in Philippi as elsewhere, at least in most of the eastern part of the empire (Greek inscriptions are better represented in Jerusalem than they are at Philippi!). This may indicate that Paul had some facility in Latin before traveling to Illyricum in Dalmatia, a major Latin-speaking area of the empire (see Rom 15:19). Nevertheless, when writing to the Philippian Christians, Paul used Greek.

The religious climate of Philippi was syncretistic, as one might expect in a city that drew its population so widely from the surrounding Roman world. There is inscriptional and historical evidence for a variety of cults. These include those of the traditional Greek gods, various oriental cults such as Serapis and Isis, and the imperial cult.[156] Acts' account of Paul's visit to the city makes no mention of Paul beginning his missionary efforts by visiting a synagogue, although Acts 16:13 refers to a "place of prayer" (προσευχή, *proseuchē*) where women congregated. There is widespread debate on whether to understand the "place of prayer" as a synagogue. Some scholars have argued that the "place of prayer" was the way that Diaspora Judaism referred to its formal gatherings, while other scholars have argued that the place was simply a place of prayer, possibly because there were insufficient men to convene a synagogue.[157] There is other evidence that there was a significant amount of henotheism in Philippi,[158] which may have made Paul's message more attractive to some of the city's inhabitants.[159] The incident in Acts with the fortune-telling slave girl (16:16–24) may give some indication of the kinds of superstitious belief present in the city.

The Via Egnatia between Kavalla (Neapolis) and Philippi (Acts 16:11-40). The primary Roman road extending east to west across Macedonia, it enabled Paul to accomplish his mission with greater ease of movement. Photo Lee M. McDonald.

The church at Philippi was founded on Paul's second missionary journey (Acts 16:11–40) as a result of his vision in which a man of Macedonia begged him to come to Macedonia to help its inhabitants (Acts 16:9). Paul's entry into Macedonia marked the beginning of his missionary endeavor in what we now call Europe. It is difficult to determine whether Paul was the first missionary in Europe, but this may have been the case (see sec. 2.F, above, on the founding of the Roman church). In any event, this marked the beginning of Paul's efforts outside Asia Minor and was a significant turning point in the growth of the Christian movement into a worldwide religion. On his first visit to Philippi, Paul saw results from his preaching, especially in the conversion of Lydia, originally from Thyatira in Asia Minor (see Acts 16:11–15; cf. Rev 2:18–29). She is described as a seller of purple. Purple dye was in great demand as a color indicating success and status, and therefore it appears that she was a successful businesswoman. It is not unlikely that Paul's missionary endeavor appealed to the business and professional element of society (see discussion in sec. 2.D, above, on Corinthians).

The evidence is uncertain, but Paul probably visited Philippi two more times on his travels, both on his third missionary journey. The second of the three times came as he traveled on the outward leg of his journey, which ended up in Greece, probably Corinth. Acts 20:1–2 does not state that Paul actually visited Philippi, but it does say that he traveled through Macedonia. Since Philippi was the major

The Roman forum at Philippi with the Via Egnatia in the foreground. Most of these ruins date after Paul's ministry here. Photo Lee M. McDonald.

city he had previously visited in the area, it makes sense to think that he again went to Philippi, if only briefly, on this trip. The final time Paul visited Philippi was on the return leg of his third missionary journey. Acts 20:3 says that Paul decided to go back through Macedonia, and 20:6 indicates that he stopped off at Philippi.[160] Nothing more is said of Paul's second and third visits to Philippi, but the evidence from the Letter to the Philippians indicates that Paul's relationships with the church there continued to be warm and close, with the Philippian church taking an active concern in his ministry (see 4:10–20 on its gift to Paul).

2. Authorship

Although questioned by Baur, the authorship of Philippians is no longer widely disputed. Philippians is one of the seven undisputed letters of Paul. Its authenticity can be seen in the way the apostle describes himself (3:5–6), the way the letter conforms to what we know of the Pauline chronology (see Acts 16:11–40; 20:1–2, 6), the Pauline style and epistolary form, and the letter's conformity with Pauline thought.

Nevertheless, even for those who attribute the letter to Paul, not all are agreed that the entire letter was written by Paul to the Philippians at the same time.[161] Consequently, various interpolation and multiple-letter hypotheses are often suggested regarding the letter.

Besides these theories, however, there are many who debate whether the so-called Philippian hymn

at 2:6–11 is authentically Pauline or an early Christian tradition that Paul employed. The supposed hymn, one of the most widely discussed NT passages, has a number of words that are unique in the Pauline or NT vocabulary, and its pronounced structure and style are not typically Pauline. Some theories posit that Paul incorporated a preformed hymn after adding several portions to conform its theology to his own, such as the reference to death on the cross (2:8). The current debate is inconclusive. Unfortunately, debate over the hymn's origins has diverted attention from the major issue: how does Paul use the hymn in Philippians?[162]

3. Literary Integrity

There have been numerous reconstructions of the letter or letters,[163] some of which are outlined below (one author has analyzed over twenty proposals regarding the multiple-letter hypothesis.)[164] Commentaries and other introductions often refer to the longstanding debate (beginning as early as 1803) about integrity, but this is misleading, since writers in the early nineteenth century were not as quick to find divisions in the text as some modern scholars are. Since 1950, discussion has increased dramatically.

a. Evidence for Disunity. There are at least nine pieces of evidence to consider for possible disunity.

(1) Philippians 1:27–28 seems to refer to an impending danger without apparent knowledge of a specific threat, but 3:2 seems to have a particular group in mind and so uses a stronger admonitory tone.

As will be discussed below, however, trying to determine the concerns and composition of the so-called opponents in the church at Philippi is not easy. We will see that the evidence is diverse and that it is difficult to characterize it in a straightforward description. As a result, many have probably rightly decided that Paul is not responding to a threat to his apostleship but, rather, to various interests within the church that may well have threatened its unity. In light of this, it is difficult to posit literary divisions in the letter simply on the basis of statements that may imply various degrees of reality in a danger. Not much more can be drawn out of these two passages.

(2) Philippians 4:10–19/20, in which Paul thanks the Philippians for money, is thought to be too late in the letter to be considered an expression of sincere and heartfelt thanks. Paul had apparently received a significant monetary gift from the Philippian church, a church that he had founded. The thought here is that the understated way in which he addresses the Philippians without actually saying "thank you" is inappropriate.

There are several responses to this argument: (a) This word of thanks indicates that this is not the first or only communication of thanks by Paul. Paul could have sent oral thanks with Epaphroditus as the letter carrier, or he may have sent some earlier communication (e.g., 2:26). (b) Paul's word of thanks is not as brief as some have posited, and would not have been delayed if Epaphroditus had not fallen ill. But since he did fall ill, it is only now possible for Paul to respond to the gift of the Philippians. (c) Paul is in fact offering thanks to the Philippian church in a way generally consistent with social conventions for gratitude in the Greco-Roman world.[165] One must be careful not to judge Paul by modern standards. There was a consistent disparagement of overt and bombastic verbal thanks among the ancients. The papyrus letters that address the issue of thanks attest that thanks between friends should be like for like, not simply in words. This evidence indicates not that Paul was neglecting his duty of thanking the church at Philippi but that the level of friendship was very close between the two parties, further evidenced by the amount of help that Paul offers in kind to them through his apostolic foundation and continued apostolic teaching and concern.

(3) The use of "finally" (τὸ λοιπόν, to loipon) in 3:1 and 4:8 is thought to be a clear indicator of division in the letter, implying that the material that comes next is the "final" word to be said. The spacing of these words of finality, especially in 3:1 combined with the word "rejoice," indicates to some that this is the conclusion to each of two letters (see schemas below).

It is not certain, however, that Paul or other ancient writers always used the word "finally" to close part of a letter (the papyri illustrate usage similar to Philippians).[166] For example, sometimes it appears that "finally" means no more than "then," other times "finally, so far as this point or topic is concerned" (e.g., 1 Thess 4:1; 2 Thess 3:1)—often

considerably earlier than the letter's conclusion—and other times simply "from now on."[167]

(4) There is an abrupt change of tone at 3:2. Translations vary in how forcefully they render this verse, but most use strong words of warning about what is typically seen as possible opponents in the church. For example, the NIV renders 3:2 as "Watch out for those dogs, those men who do evil, those mutilators of the flesh." This word of warning is seen to be particularly strong in contrast to the mild tone of 3:1.

There have been several explanations of the strong transition at 3:2. (a) Some have argued that the words themselves should not be so strongly rendered. Kilpatrick claims that the verb used should be rendered "consider."[168] While this may be true, there is still the problem of the way in which the opponents are characterized, in terms of dogs, evil-workers, and mutilators. By almost all accounts, these are unflattering and disparaging terms, probably being used to characterize Jewish opponents. (b) Lightfoot thinks that a possible explanation for the transition is that there was some sort of break between 3:1 and 2.[169] But our standard chapter and verse divisions are often misleading and unhelpful; it is possible that if the chapter division took place between 3:1 and 2, the transition implied would not arouse the same kind of critical interest. Lightfoot's point, however, was that perhaps something Paul heard from a new messenger brought to his attention a more pressing situation at Philippi than he had at first envisioned. Perhaps this led to a change of mind on how to respond to the Philippians' situation. (c) There are similar abrupt transitions in other letters, but multiple-letter hypotheses are not suggested to explain them (Rom 16:17; 1 Cor 15:58; Gal 3:1; 4:21; 5:12). Furthermore, the supposed change in tone is not as long-lasting as some have thought. Philippians 3:4 and following seem to return to the more relaxed tone of the earlier part of the letter. This also raises a further question: how could an editor have left such a rough seam if it is as abrupt as is often speculated? (d) It has been argued that 3:1b is stating that Paul is going to repeat the topics of 1:12–2:18 or even what he had previously told them in person; this would account for any duplication in ch. 3 of what is said earlier in the letter.[170]

(5) Philippians 2:19–24 relates Paul's travel plans. It is sometimes argued that travel plans are usually

and better kept for the end of Pauline letters. Since they occur at 2:19–24, they may well indicate that this is in fact near the end of the letter.

What is overlooked in this supposition is the fact that Paul places his travel plans in a variety of places in his letters. For the most part, they occur in the body of his letters, as does their mention in 2:19–24 (see the outline below), but this is not always the case. For example, in Romans, Paul unusually mentions his travel plans in the thanksgiving portion of his letter (1:11–15), besides at the end (15:23–29).

(6) The word translated "rejoice" (χαίρετε, *chairete*) (3:1; 4:4) is said to be used often at the beginning of papyri, but also at the conclusion in the sense of "farewell." The appearance of these words in 3:1 and 4:4 in conjunction with "finally"—arguably similar to the way that it is used in 2 Cor 13:11—supports the idea that the closings of two letters have been reached.

Forms of this word are used in the openings of papyrus letters, but there is relatively little evidence for their use in this way at the end of letters. It is also a word that can be used in a variety of other ways as well. As will be seen below, one of the motifs of Philippians is that of joy and rejoicing. The use of this word is one way to express this idea, so it is not surprising to find it at various places throughout the letter. Its usage within Philippians is entirely idiomatic and consistent with this motif. Second Corinthians 13:11 is also better explained as use of the word in its more usual sense of "rejoice."

(7) A scholar has recently argued that the letter to the Laodiceans confirms that there were at one time independent Pauline letters to the church at Philippi.[171] It is not argued that the Laodicean letter that we have is actually a Pauline letter but that it reflects knowledge of the earlier textual tradition. The letter to the Laodiceans is a fourth-century Latin letter, quite clearly derivative from passages especially in Philippians, but also in Galatians. The letter supposedly quotes canonical Philippians in order, but in its citations, according to one reconstruction of the multiple-letter hypothesis, it only cites one of the letters. Thus, the failure to cite more than this one letter supposedly shows that there were independent letters at a stage earlier than our textual evidence.

Textual criticism as usually employed in NT studies does not know any evidence of multiple Philippian letters, since all of the manuscripts in which the letter appears have only the one Philippian letter. It is also important to note that the earliest Pauline nonfragmentary manuscript, $\mathfrak{P}^{46}$ (ca. A.D. 200), includes a single Philippians. While one might hypothesize that the significant textual changes took place before this time, this is difficult to prove because of our limited external textual evidence before this time. More to the point here is that if a different hypothesis on the content of the original letters is used, the letter to the Laodiceans is seen to be citing at least two, if not three, of these letters; thus the theory not only fails to prove what it claims but supports the integrity hypothesis by attesting to early knowledge of most parts of Philippians.

(8) In 2:25–30 it seems to have been a long time since Epaphroditus was away, but in 4:18 it seems that he recently arrived. This would be consistent with a view that 4:10–20 was part of the first letter and 2:25–30 part of a later letter (this does not fit well with the two-letter hypothesis, however).

This theory only works with a view that sees three or more letters; it may not even be a clear argument for such a position, however, since 4:18 hardly supports such a hypothesis.

(9) Polycarp (A.D. 70–156) refers to "letters" of Paul (*Phil.* 3.2). In this hypothesis, Polycarp, as an early writer, had clear knowledge of several letters to the Philippians and conveys that information.

In another reading of Polycarp, however, it is not clear that this is what Polycarp is saying. The statement is sufficiently ambiguous that Polycarp may mean multiple letters to the Philippians; or our canonical letter together with letters to other churches; or the contents of our single letter. Polycarp does not indicate the content of these letters. He may be referring not to letters addressed only to the Philippians but to all of the Pauline Letters, since by this time Paul's letters could have been gathered into a letter collection available to the various Pauline churches.

b. Hypotheses of Composition. Because of the kinds of arguments covered above, several hypotheses have been put forward regarding the number of letters that lie behind the single book of Philippians in the NT. The multiple-letter hypotheses are numerous. Some have suggested up to five letters, but two or three letters are the normal number. Several of the more prominent hypotheses are summarized in Table 10–4 on p. 468.

Recent work in the areas of literary structure and rhetoric has attempted either to prove or to disprove the multiple letters of Philippians. Those who utilize the principles of literary and rhetorical analysis (see ch. 3, above) argue that Philippians exemplifies literary and rhetorical unity (e.g., consistently mentioned themes or a clear rhetorical structure) that indicate that the letter as we have it was composed as a unified and integral whole.

Studies by Watson, for example, have perhaps aided our understanding of particular passages in Philippians,[172] but his work is far from proving that Philippians was originally written as a unity. Such methods encounter two major problems. First, the critical tools being employed may not be appropriate to the task for which they are being used. It is not certain that the principles of literary criticism can and should be applied to letters as they would be to modern literature, and there is sustained and recurring criticism of applying the principles of ancient rhetorical criticism to the epistolary genre, since rhetoric was designed with persuasive *oral* discourse in mind. Indeed, when comparison is made of other letters in the ancient world, one sees that they are often quite incoherent in shape and structure according to the principles of literary and rhetorical criticism employed. Second, attempts to discover the literary or rhetorical unity may be doing nothing more than establishing the literary and rhetorical competence of the redactor or redactors of the letters, not the original author. Hence, these tools may be able to produce a unified reading of Philippians, but they cannot be used to establish integrity.

In recent criticism, discourse analysis has made a major contribution to the study of the NT, and so principles of discourse analysis have been employed to analyze the Letter to the Philippians. The results have, however, been ambiguous. On the one hand, Wolfgang Schenk, utilizing its principles in his commentary on Philippians, has confirmed his analysis that the letter is composite.[173] On the other hand, Black, also utilizing these principles, has discovered that it is a unity.[174] This divided opinion is not true of all discourse analysis; for the most part, discourse analysis works from the premise that discourses are cohesive, and the task of the analyst is to examine the text and show how the text coheres and how it is structured to bring certain ideas into prominence. One cannot begin with the idea of literary unity or disunity and then claim to prove

this. All that can be claimed is that the analytical tool has provided criteria for judging integrity. But the criteria themselves do not establish integrity; this must be established on other grounds.[175]

Since there is no external textual attestation that many letters were written and sent by Paul to Philippi, there is the question of motivation for bringing the letters together. It is not difficult to imagine that there was a church, possibly at Philippi, that had a keen desire to retain the Pauline letters and would oversee their consolidation into a single letter. But why? First, this consolidation must have occurred extremely early. To some extent the date of consolidation depends upon when the Pauline letter collection was made. If the collection was made around the turn of the first century, then the consolidation must have occurred between Paul's death and ca. A.D. 100, a fairly narrow window of opportunity. But if Paul himself had something to do with the collection of his letters (this has not been proved but is worth considering), it is almost impossible that there was a window of opportunity for the consolidation (unless Paul perhaps did it himself). Second, one must ask what kind of compulsion there was to consolidate the letters. The Pauline corpus as we have it has several examples of multiple letters to various churches—Corinth, Thessalonica, and Colossae (with Philemon)—and to Timothy. The authorship of several of these has been questioned, and there is a multiple-letter hypothesis regarding 2 Corinthians as well, but prima facie there is no compelling reason why the letters would have to be united. The church at Philippi may not have known of these multiple letters to other churches, however. Nevertheless, its members must have known that they had multiple letters, and even if only they knew this, it is still unclear why they would have consolidated them. Third, several opposing factors apparently compete to explain why these letters would have been united. On the one hand, the argument would have to hold that the church at Philippi was uniting the letters together out of some sense of reverence for the writings of Paul. This makes perfect sense in light of what is known about reverence for Paul's writings in the early church (2 Pet 3:16)[176] and about the gathering of the Pauline corpus. On the other hand, in order to consolidate the letters, the church would have had to delete certain portions of the apostle's words. We do not know what the original letters included, but it is a virtual certainty that we would not have all of the two or three letters (even aside from the deleted openings and closings). When the individual hypothetical letters are examined for length, they are seen to be shorter in length than any of Paul's other letters to churches. If 4:10–19/20 constitutes a single letter, its only rival is Philemon, a personal letter. This would mean that the individual letters, at least as they are reconstructed, would be very uncharacteristic of the Pauline letter. This is either an argument against multiple letters or an argument that some portions of these letters have been excised and now lost. At the least, the openings and closings of the letters, except for one, have been edited out. Furthermore, it can be argued that the editor himself must have been working at cross-purposes. On the one hand, it was considered important to edit the various individual letters into a single whole, yet the editor did his job relatively badly, leaving several tell-tale signs that this was done (e.g., 3:1 and 2, and placement of 4:10–20). In conclusion, there are good reasons to read Philippians as a single document, especially as arguments for the multiple-letter hypothesis—as interesting and provocative as they are—remain unproved.

4. Opponents and Occasion

Determining the opponents and the occasion of the Letter to the Philippians has proved exceedingly difficult. The reasons are the diversity of evidence within the book itself and the lack of knowledge about the situation that warranted the letter's being written. Definitive answers are far from certain; the following survey will give some idea of the options.

a. The Evidence for the Opponents. There are four main passages to consider in trying to determine the nature of the opponents or problems at Philippi.[177]

(1) Philippians 1:15–18. In this passage, Paul mentions that the gospel is being preached but not always out of the same good motives. Apparently this refers to some rivalry between Paul and other Christian groups. The question of importance here, however, is whether it refers to a problem in Philippi. Some have thought that Paul may be opposing a group of Christian missionaries who had a "divine man" theology—as mentioned earlier, a theology in which the man of God was expected to be some

sort of miracle worker—and that Paul as a prisoner did not conform to this image.[178] By all accounts, Paul stood opposed to this characterization of a man of God because he endorsed humility, meekness, and suffering (e.g., 1:13–14, 20–24; 3:12–13). Perhaps these opponents questioned whether Paul was a legitimate apostle.

There are three problems with this position. (a) The language does not make it clear that this was a problem at Philippi. (b) This view has difficulty harmonizing with the other evidence of opponents at Philippi, since the problem in 1:15–18 would seem to indicate an internal church problem, not one with external opponents. (c) "Divine man" theology is probably a later development, not one of the first century (see sec. 2.E.3, above). It is possible that the preachers with bad motives were part of one of the other groups of opponents (see the other options), but this is only a hypothesis. Paul mentions these preachers in his opening section of the letter, in which he is discussing the general advancement of the gospel despite his own imprisonment (1:12–18). It is therefore unlikely that in 1:15–18 he is referring to specific opponents at Philippi, and certainly not to a situation that threatens the church there.

(2) Philippians 1:27–30. In this section, Paul admonishes the Philippians to stand firm in the faith and not to be frightened by those who oppose them. Paul goes on to draw a contrast between the opponents' impending destruction and the Philippians' salvation, but affirms that part of their calling has been to suffer. These statements are vague, and it is difficult to know whether they are made in reference to theologically based opponents or general adversity

Inside the ancient prison at Philippi, where arguably Paul and Silas were imprisoned. Photo Lee M. McDonald.

in Philippi. That the suffering they are undergoing or can expect to undergo may not be from religious conflict but, rather, from general life in society is perhaps supported by Paul's saying that they are going through the same struggle he had gone through (1:30). The idea here may be that Paul is in prison because of the Roman authorities and it is the Roman authorities who are in some way causing trouble for the Philippians. In this case, the passage would not be a reference to some form of religious opponents, even if Paul's response reflects his own theological position.

(3) Philippians 3:2–4. Paul here enjoins the Philippians to "beware of the dogs, beware of the evil workers, beware of those who mutilate the flesh." The first two characterizations could be general. In light of 3:3–6, however, where Paul continues on about circumcision (there is an apparent play on the words "mutilation" [κατατομή, *katatomē*] and "circumcision" [περιτομή, *peritomē*]) and emphasizes his Jewish background, it is likely that 3:2–4 is a characterization of either Jewish or Jewish–Christian opponents. It is generally agreed that Jews did not try to compel Gentiles to be circumcised and conform to their laws, so it is probable that Jewish Christians are in view here. In other words, Paul has in mind opponents similar to those who threatened the Galatians. He uses strong language to characterize these possible Judaizers, but it is noticeably more restrained than what he

TABLE 10-4

MULTIPLE-LETTER HYPOTHESES FOR PHILIPPIANS

Two-letter hypotheses		
	Material	**Content**
Hypothesis 1	3:2–4:23 (or 20)	Thanks for the gift
Hypothesis 2	1:1–3:1 (and 4:21–23)	Letter sent with Epaphroditus
Three-letter hypotheses		
	Material	**Content**
Hypothesis 1	4:10–20	Thanks for the gift
	1:1–3:1; 4:2–9, 21–23	Letter sent with Epaphroditus
	3:2–4:1	Interpolation warning readers
Hypothesis 2	4:10–20	Thanks for the gift
	1:1–2.30; 4:21–23	Letter sent with Epaphroditus praising him
	3:1–4:9	Paul facing death
Hypothesis 3	1:1–2; 4:10–20	Thanks for the gift
	1:3–3:1; 4:4–9, 21–23	Letter sent with Epaphroditus
	3:2–4:3	Warning regarding Judaizers

used in Galatians (Gal 2:11–3:5, esp. 2:21–3:1); this has caused some to doubt the identification. There are several possible responses, however. One is that Paul, in his experience and age, has mellowed in his approach to such problems. A second is that although the opponents are similar, the threat is not seen to be as strong, possibly because the Jewish population in Philippi was at best quite small. These Judaizers could have come from outside Philippi, but in any case, no significant Jewish presence has been discovered at Philippi, making it difficult to believe that significant numbers were involved.

(4) Philippians 3:18–19. In these verses (cf. also 3:11–16), Paul draws attention to those who live lives as enemies of the cross, whose god is their stomach and whose glory is in their shame. Their minds are on earthly things. Paul is apparently addressing those with libertine tendencies, who indulge their appetites in an unhealthy way. The emphasis is perhaps upon gluttony and nudity. Some have suggested that this indicates that the opponents in Philippi were some form of proto-gnostics or those with an overrealized eschatology (they believe that the *eschaton* had already begun), such as were also possibly found at Corinth. Some people who had gnostic tendencies became ascetics, but others took an opposite turn and became overly indulgent. The probable reasoning was that since earthly substance was illusory and hence ultimately did not matter, indulgence was a viable option with no enduring consequences. Similarly, if those to whom Paul refers had an overrealized eschatology, they may well have believed that they had already entered into the *eschaton* and that therefore their spiritual situation was secure, with the result that they could indulge with impunity. Fee, however, points out that this group is mentioned nowhere else in the letter than in this tearful description and may better serve as a general description of those Paul has previously told them about, but not present opponents.[179]

b. Occasion and Purpose. In light of the proposals above, describing the occasion and purpose of composition may well involve the following factors.

(1) Paul's Assessment. Paul wished to offer an assessment of his current situation to the church at Philippi, one that had recently demonstrated its continued concern and support for his work by giving a helpful gift (4:10–19/20). To this gift, Paul appears to have responded in a way that was fitting for close personal friends (see sec. 3.a.3, above, of this discussion of Philippians regarding reciprocal thanks). Furthermore, he wishes to tell them why Epaphroditus and not Timothy is returning to them. It is because of this close friendship and concern that Paul addresses several other issues. By informing the Philippian church of his own suffering yet joyful attitude (1:12–26; 2:24)—expecting release yet desiring the benefits of heaven—Paul is able to teach them the importance of remaining joyful even amidst adversity. He commends himself and Christ as examples. He acknowledges that there has been opposition to his ministry in various quarters, some taking advantage of his imprisonment for their own selfish gains, but he is willing to accept this as long as the gospel is preached.[180]

(2) Paul's Opponents. For the most part, Paul is concerned with commending the Philippians for their unity, for their good thinking, and for being a source of joy to him (1:5; 2:2; 1:19; etc.). But he is also aware that other influences may have crept into the church that might threaten their unity and their having the mind of Christ (4:2–3). Here he offers words of warning regarding the opponents. Recent research has emphasized the possibility and even likelihood that the situation in Philippi was a complex one that involved several competing interests.[181] One of these appears to have been the influence of Judaizers. They probably were only a small group within Philippi, or a group of outsiders who were arguing that the Philippian Christians needed to participate in Jewish rituals. The influence of this group was not as pronounced or as advanced as it had been in Galatia, and so Paul did not respond as forcefully. The influence of this group of Judaizers may have been aided by the situation in Philippi. As mentioned above, Philippi was a Roman colony, in which Roman law was clearly exercised and where the emperor cult was probably beginning to grow (see ch. 3, sec. 3). Even if the Jews did not have special rights as a "recognized religion" *(religio licita)* within the Roman Empire, being a Jew did permit them a certain amount of latitude regarding participation in certain rituals of Roman religion, especially in a world as religiously complex as the Roman. Gentiles who decided to become followers of Christ, however, would not have had as much latitude and may have found themselves forced to make a decision how to respond to the pressures of pagan religion. This would have raised questions of what it meant to be a "good citizen"

of Philippi and of heaven. The Judaizers would have been offering a way to continue being Christians and to resist some of the pressures of pagan worship. To this Paul responds in two ways. First, he informs them that their status as believers is determined by a spiritual or internal transformation, not by outward signs. Second, he reminds them that their citizenship and duty to be good citizens are defined in terms of what is required of them as followers of Christ. His response was formulated in language similar to that of the Stoics regarding appropriate behavior.

5. Date and Place of Writing

A more detailed treatment of the issue of the Pauline imprisonment can be found in ch. 9, above. This section draws attention to issues that relate specifically to Philippians.

If Paul wrote Philippians during an Ephesian imprisonment, he would have written the letter either in A.D. 52/53 during his first Ephesian visit or, more likely, somewhere between A.D. 53 and 55 during his lengthy two-year stay. If Paul wrote Philippians during his Cesarean imprisonment, he would have written the letter in A.D. 57–60. If he wrote it during his Roman imprisonment, he would have written it in A.D. 61–62.

According to the discussion of imprisonment in ch. 9, above, Paul most likely wrote the Prison Epistles during the Roman imprisonment, but several other factors internal to Philippians point in this same direction.

a. Praetorian Guard. In Phil 1:13, Paul mentions the praetorian guard. This was a special detachment of soldiers assigned to the emperor. Since being the emperor of the Roman Empire was a precarious occupation (half of the emperors of the first century were murdered or died under mysterious circumstances), in part because of the political intrigue in which the emperor had to participate to maintain his status, the emperors maintained a special group of soldiers to try to ensure their protection. It is possible that other cities may have had detachments of the praetorian guard (and it appears that Philippi had such a detachment), especially cities visited frequently by the emperor, but a reference to the praetorian guard would most likely mean the guard in Rome, since it is known for certain that they were there.

b. Those of Caesar's Household. Reference to Caesar's household in 4:22 has often been misinterpreted. It probably does not mean that some close to Caesar had become followers of Christ but that some persons within the vast expanse of Caesar's household were followers. They could have included lowly servants and slaves and even individuals higher up. Caesar's household encompassed all those in the employ of Caesar for domestic and administrative duties. It is likely that some of his household were in other cities where Caesar maintained residences, but the largest contingent was in Rome.

c. Historical and Personal Context. Paul was in prison but possibly nearing release (1:7, 19–27; 2:24). His references to a possible release make the most sense in terms of a Roman imprisonment, for he is confident that due process will result in his release and that there is no higher authority to which appeal against accusations can be made.

6. Outline of Philippians[182]

A. Opening (1:1–2)
  1. Sender (1:1)
  2. Addressee (1:1)
  3. Greeting (1:2)
B. Thanksgiving (1:3–11)
  1. Thanksgiving proper (1:3–8)
  2. Prayer/intercession (1:9–11)
C. Body: Living Christ's example (1:12–2:30)
  1. Formal opening: The advance of the gospel (1:12–18)
  2. Paul's situation (1:19–26)
  3. Living the Christian life worthy of Christ's gospel (1:27–2:18)
  4. Pauline travelogue (2:19–30)
D. Parenesis (3:1–4:20)
  1. Introduction: Repetition as a safeguard (3:1)
  2. Opponents not to be followed (3:2–6)
  3. Summary of Paul's theology (3:7–11)
  4. Striving for perfection (3:12–4:1)
  5. Exhortation to unity and joy and peace in personal relations (4:2–9)
  6. Word of thanks for the Philippians' gift (4:10–19)
E. Closing (4:20–23)
  1. Doxology (4:20)
  2. Greetings (4:21–22)
  3. Grace benediction (4:23)

B. Colossians

1. The City of Colossae

Colossae was the least important church to which any of Paul's letters is addressed.[183] The city was located in the Lycus Valley in the western part of the Roman province of Asia, near the more important cities of Laodicea and Hierapolis (Col 2:1; 4:3, 15–16), in the region of ancient Phrygia, and was known for its cold-water supply, which fed various surrounding cities. It was near the Meander River, of which the Lycus River is a tributary, approximately a hundred miles east of Ephesus.

Herodotus mentions Colossae as a "great city of Phrygia" (*Hist.* 7.30.1), though he is inaccurate in his description of its location; this reference attests to its antiquity and early greatness. Xenophon, too, says that it was populous, wealthy, and large (*Anab.* 1.21.6). The city suffered varied political fortunes under the Seleucids, however, until the Romans had the entire region given to them in 133 B.C. Commentaries frequently include comments about a period of decline for Colossae in the first century B.C., and Strabo refers to it as a small town (*Geog.* 12.8.13). This decline is true but may not be the entire story. According to O'Brien, on the basis of inscriptional evidence, Colossae continued to exist well into the first century A.D. It was in the midst of an area given to wool production, and was very well known for a very fine quality of dark red dyed wool, called Colossian or in Latin *colossinus* (see Strabo, *Geog.* 12.8.16; Pliny, *Nat.* 21.51).[184] A major difficulty in gaining knowledge about Colossae is the fact that the site has never been excavated.

Laodicea, a more recently founded city, was located near Colossae. Laodicea had been founded under the Seleucid king Antiochus II in 261 B.C. and was named after his wife, Laodice. It was the center of the judicial circuit, had a Roman cohort stationed there, and was the center of the financial and banking industries. In contrast to the modest financial wealth of Colossae, it is reported that after a particularly bad earthquake in A.D. 60/61 (Pliny, *Nat.* 5.105; according to Strabo, Laodicea and its environs were known to have numerous earthquakes), the city was sufficiently wealthy to be able to afford rebuilding itself with its own money (it is unknown whether or how Colossae was affected by this earthquake). Hierapolis, or "holy city," located a few miles northwest of Colossae, was also a Seleucid

city, founded either in 281–261 B.C. or 197–160 B.C. It was known for its hot mineral springs.

The Jewish settlement at Colossae probably originated sometime in the early second century B.C. when Babylonian Jews were brought into the area (according to Josephus, *Ant.* 12.147–153), although it is possible some Jews settled there a little earlier. These Babylonian Jewish settlers may well have originally been sent as military troops, the terms of service being no taxes for ten years and the right to live under their own laws. There was a tradition (2 Macc 8:20) that these Diaspora Jews were particularly good fighters. On the basis of accounts that record a dispute in 62/61 B.C. about the temple tax (the Roman governor Flaccus tried to prevent the sending of the temple tax, but he was removed from office for this; see Cicero, *Flac.* 28.68) and about whether money could be sent from one region to another, scholars have tried to estimate the number of Jews in the area. The debates over the temple tax indicate that a large number of Jews, possibly even as many as 11,000, lived in the Laodicea and Hierapolis area.

It is difficult to determine the origin of the Christian population of Colossae. There are two major alternatives. The first is that those from the surrounding area were responsible for bringing the gospel to Colossae. Acts 2:10 says that Phrygians were in Jerusalem on the day of Pentecost; they may have been responsible for bringing Christianity to the area upon their return home. The second alternative is that the city was evangelized by Paul but perhaps not directly, even though he evangelized elsewhere in Phrygia-Galatia (Col 2:1), but by one of his fellow missionaries, such as Epaphras (Col 1:7, 4:12, 13), probably at the time of Paul's stay in Ephesus during his second missionary journey (Acts 19:10). In either case, it appears that the area had been evangelized by Christians within twenty-five years of Christ's death. The church may have turned away from Christianity for a while, quite possibly because of the problems addressed in the letter (see also 2 Tim 1:15), but it appears to have remained faithful for at least a few years after the letter was written.[185]

2. Authorship

The majority of critical scholars now reject Pauline authorship of Colossians, but the percentage

Small Byzantine fortress and prison at Kavalla. The town dates back to the sixth century B.C. The city is at the eastern end of the Via Egnatia and was the port city that serviced Philippi. Paul came through here on his way to and from Philippi. Photo Lee M. McDonald.

is not lopsided. The first serious doubts about Pauline authorship of the letter were raised by the German scholar Mayerhoff in 1838, and they were more rigorously pursued by Baur and his followers.[186] The debate concerning authorship has been lively and ongoing ever since, and, along with discussion of the Colossian opponents, is one of two major critical issues regarding Colossians.[187]

a. Arguments against Pauline Authorship. The major arguments against Pauline authorship revolve around the issues of vocabulary, style, and theology.

(1) Vocabulary. Scholars who argue against Pauline authorship frequently draw attention to the absence of many of the favorite Pauline words and expressions, such as "salvation," "righteousness," and "justification." Colossians contains thirty-four words found nowhere else in the NT, such as the words translated "visible" (τὸ ὁρατόν, *to horaton;* 1:16) and "the record" (τὸ χειρόγραφον, *cheirographon;* 2:14). More than this, Colossians also contains a number

of unusual expressions not used by Paul elsewhere in his writings, such as the phrase "the blood of his cross" (τὸ αἷμα τοῦ σταυροῦ αὐτοῦ, *to haima tou staurou autou;* 1:20), "evil deeds" (τὰ ἔργα τὰ πονηρά, *ta erga ta ponēra;* 1:21), "the forgiveness of sins" (ἡ ἄφεσις τῶν ἁμαρτιῶν, *hē aphesis tōn hamartiōn;* 1:14), and "the fullness of deity" (τὸ πλήρωμα τῆς θεότητος, *to plērōma tēs theotētos;* 2:9).

(2) Style. Many scholars have drawn attention to the rough Greek style of Colossians, wording uncharacteristically less refined and polished than the sentences of the main letters of Paul. For example, 1:9–12 and 1:24–27 constitute one sentence each in the Greek text, what some would argue are overly long and convoluted sentences. Another element of the letter's style that often incites comment is the redundancy found in such phrases as "praying . . . asking" (1:9), "wisdom and understanding" (1:9), "endurance . . . with patience" (1:11), "securely established and steadfast" (1:23), "teach and admonish" (3:16), and "psalms, hymns, and spiritual songs"

(3:16). A further characteristic of the style of Colossians is the linking of several modifying phrases (phrases using modifying words in the Greek genitive case). Some of these phrases end up forming chains of expressions whose sense is difficult to understand. Some of these include "all the riches of the fullness of knowledge" (2:2) and "of the knowledge of the work of God" (2:12).

(3) Theology. The major arguments against Pauline authorship concern theology. The general tenor of such arguments is that the theology of Colossians has developed to a sufficient degree to indicate non-Pauline authorship. The arguments take several forms. One is that there are a number of theological arguments that cannot be found in the other Pauline Letters. For example, in 1:24, Paul depicts himself as in some way a vicarious sufferer on behalf of Christ, by some means filling up what is lacking in Christ's afflictions. In light of the emphasis upon justification apart from works in the major Pauline Letters, especially Galatians and Romans, the notion that there may be something that Christ has not accomplished that Paul can in some way fulfill comes as a fairly radical departure. Furthermore, the major letters depict the fulfillment of the Christian life as in process or still not complete, but in Colossians, it is argued, that sense of urgency or constraint is missing. In Colossians, the end is seen as already present (1:28), a form of realized eschatology. There is none of the apocalyptic urgency of the earlier authentic letters, with their apocalyptic woes or discouragement regarding human behavior. Instead, God has already delivered believers from the realm of darkness (1:13), so that they are buried and raised with Christ (2:12, 13), and the estranged are now reconciled (1:22). Hope is not something looked forward to (see Rom 8:24–25), but is already stored up in the heavenly realms as a symbol of assurance and confidence (1:5). Lastly, imagery regarding the church is more developed. In 1 Cor 12:12–27, Christ is equated with the body of believers, with the emphasis upon the unity within the church body; in Colossians, the church is the body of Christ of which he is its head as a cosmic, universal figure (1:15–20, 24)(see sec. b, below, of this discussion of authorship). The church has expanded from a local body of believers to a universal spiritual entity that is part of Christ's universal reconciliation. Church order has developed with this body imagery. The use of the word trans-lated "minister" or "servant" (διάκονος, *diakonos;* 1:7, 23, 25, 4:7) differs from its use in the main letters. In Colossians, it is closer to particular vocations in the church, as in 1 Tim 3:8, 12 and 4:6.

On the basis of this evidence, those who dispute Pauline authorship of Colossians usually argue for pseudonymous authorship.[188] The salutation of Col 1:1 indicates the possibility of dual authorship by Paul and Timothy, and it is known that Paul used a scribe on several occasions (Rom 16:22; Gal 6:11–16), but this solution has not commended itself to those who dispute Pauline authorship. Most of Paul's letters, especially other letters attributed to Paul and Timothy (such as Galatians), have some sort of joint attribution, but the style and subject matter of Colossians are still thought to be sufficiently different from the undisputed letters. The issue of the use of a scribe in the ancient world is a very difficult one. Even though the scribes Paul used for Galatians and Romans were probably different from the scribe he used for Colossians, the distinctive Pauline voice comes through well enough in those major letters that those who dispute Pauline authorship of Colossians note that this same voice is not to be found in Colossians. The result is that a later date for composition, by some writer who pseudonymously represents himself as Paul, must be posited, probably some time in the last quarter of the first century.

b. Arguments for Pauline Authorship. In spite of these rather skeptical comments, there are still valid arguments for Pauline authorship. In assessing the issue of authorship, one must be careful not to be misled by some of the evidence and argumentation. For example, Freed claims that the view of baptism is very different in Col 2:11–12, where baptism and circumcision are equated, from elsewhere in Paul's letters, such as Rom 6.[189] According to Freed, circumcision is a "meaningless Jewish rite" for Paul! First of all, however, Paul is not quite so negative about circumcision. To be sure, circumcision has no redemptive value for Paul, but the word itself is used in several different ways, sometimes in a metaphorical sense, as in Rom 2:28–29, where circumcision of the heart is positive. Second, Freed must admit that there is some correlation between Col 2:11, regarding circumcision without hands, and Rom 2:29, and between Col 2:13–14 and Rom 6:3–5. This kind of argumentation does not clarify the issue of authorship.

When more substantial arguments are considered, the case for non-Pauline authorship of Colossians is less clear. There are four lines of evidence to consider: external evidence, word statistics, lexicography and grammar, and theology.

(1) External evidence. The claim for Pauline authorship has been supported by various kinds of external evidence.[190] Several important church fathers, such as Ignatius (*Eph.* 2; *Magn.* 2; *Phld.* 4; *Smyrn.* 1.2; 12; *Trall.* 5.2), Irenaeus (*Haer.* 3.14.1), Tertullian (*Prescr.* 7), and Clement of Alexandria (*Misc.* 1.1), and the Muratorian Fragment, endorse Pauline authorship of Colossians, and none of them entertain any doubts about this attribution. The connection of Colossians with Philemon must also be considered, since the links between the two are very strong. Both contain Timothy's name with Paul's in the salutation (Col 1:1; Phlm 1), and greetings are sent from some of the same people in both letters, including Aristarchus, Mark, Epaphras, Luke, and Demas (Col 4:10–14; Phlm 23–24; only Jesus/Justus is excluded in Philemon). In Phlm 2, Archippus is called a "fellow soldier"; in Col 4:17, he is directed to fulfill his ministry. In Col 4:9, Onesimus, the slave of Philemon, is mentioned as being sent with Tychicus. The lines of connection between Colossians and Philemon are so strong that if Colossians is not authentically Pauline, there was a distinct effort to deceive the early church into accepting it as Pauline (see ch. 9, sec. 6, above, on pseudonymous Pauline literature).

(2) Word statistics. Word statistics are not always clear, and one must be careful in drawing conclusions from them. For example, Galatians has thirty-one unique words, roughly the same number as Colossians, but this causes no one to raise any doubts as to whether Galatians was written by Paul. More to the point, even the counting of supposedly unique words is difficult. For example, ἀνταναπληρόω (*antanaplēroō*, "fill up") in 1:24 is often cited as a unique occurrence in Colossians, but προσαναπληρόω (*prosanaplēroō*) in 2 Cor 9:12 is the same basic verb but with a different prefix. As most recent work with vocabulary statistics indicates, this is not a firm criterion for disputing authorship.

(3) Lexicography and grammar. It is often noted that the author of Colossians uses a different word for "reconcile" (ἀποκαταλλάσσω, *apokatallassō*) than Paul uses in Rom 5:10 and 2 Cor 5:19 (καταλλάσσω, *katallassō*). Freed claims that this makes a "slight difference in the concept of reconciliation," but he

does not say what that difference is.[191] The form in the Romans and Corinthian passages is not prefixed with a preposition as it is in Colossians. The words are in separate entries in a standard lexicon, but they clearly overlap in form and in sense.[192] Not too much should be made of these differences. It may well be that the style has been adapted to suit the subject matter, with twelve of the thirty-four new vocabulary items in Colossians appearing in possible descriptions of or responses to opponents (e.g., 1:10–20; 2:16–23) or in distinctively liturgical style (e.g. 1:15–20).

(4) Theology. The so-called hymn of Col 1:15–20 raises interesting questions regarding authorship. This passage has aroused discussion in three areas: authorship, origin, and use.[193] Many scholars believe that this hymn was written by someone other than the author of the Letter to the Colossians, that it became part of the liturgy of the early church and was included here by the author because it was thought appropriate. Other scholars, however, are not convinced that such is the case. Some grant that it may have been written by the author, quite likely Paul, on another occasion than the composition of the letter, but they note that nothing prohibits the author of such a passage as 1 Cor 13 from having written this passage as well. Some of those who posit that the hymn was written independently of the letter have suggested a form of Semitic precursor, while others have suggested a Greek original. All these attempts to characterize the hymn, however, have the same problem: the supposed hymn, as it appears in Colossians, cannot be convincingly shown to reflect known forms of either Semitic or Greek poetry. Indeed, it is highly difficult to outline this passage as a hymn, even when the two relative pronouns in 1:15 and 18 are used as markers of hymnic structure (but cf. 1:13 as well). Various reconstructions have divided it into two, three, and four stanzas, with interpolations posited at significant points. Some have suggested that a form of either Semitic wisdom Christology or Greek-based proto-gnostic theology rests behind the hymn (the gnostic theory has fallen on hard times lately—see below). In both cases, Christ is seen as the creator of all things (1:16), with three different prepositions (in [ἐν, *en*], through [διά, *dia*], and to/for [εἰς, *eis*]) used to describe his creative function. Christ is depicted in the hymn as the firstborn of all creation (1:15), which has been variously in-

The mound in the right of center is Colossae, an unexcavated site that was destroyed by an earthquake in A.D. 64. Photo Lee M. McDonald.

terpreted as first in a temporal sequence (e.g., Prov 8:22, regarding Wisdom) or as first in rank or priority (Ps 89:27). This is admittedly a very high Christology, but it probably should not be seen as having its origins either in wisdom theology or in proto-gnostic thought.[194] Gnosticism did not develop the idea of the heavenly redeemer figure until later, probably under the influence of Christianity. What is said here of Christ goes well beyond the subordinate role given to Wisdom in Wisdom literature. This is seen in the fact that Christ is recognized by language that elsewhere is reserved for God in his function as creator and sustainer of the universe. Even more, the hymn goes on to depict Christ as the head of the church on the basis of his resurrection (1:18). All the fullness of God is said to dwell in Jesus. If this is proto-gnostic language, the author is usurping it for his own purposes, because he goes on to say that complete reconciliation of all things is through Christ, meaning his death (cf. 1:23). This passage causes a dilemma for those who argue against Pauline authorship. If the passage is either non-Pauline or not written by the author of this book, it cannot be used as evidence for the non-Pauline authorship of the book. If it was part of an earlier liturgical or creedal statement used by the church, then the argument of the overly developed theology is dissipated. For if the passage existed earlier (and it is difficult to say how much earlier), it must have been early enough to be formalized and passed down.

Philosophers of the Greco-Roman world depicted various organizations in terms of the analogy of the body—e.g., Maximus of Tyre, *Or. 15.4–5*).[195] Regarding the church as the body of Christ, there is no doubt that Colossians seems to have a more developed understanding of this metaphor or analogy than other letters commonly accepted as Paul's (see sec. a, above, of this discussion of authorship). One question to be asked is whether a plausible line of connection can be created from the acknowledged authentic Pauline use of this imagery to the imagery in Colossians. If it appears that the development is too far removed or cannot be accounted

Gates to the ancient city of Laodicea. Photo Lee M. McDonald.

for on this basis, we must ask how the early church was led to believe that such a stretched and strained metaphor could have come from Paul. The church's depiction as the body of Christ is a common Pauline metaphor (Rom 12:4–5; 1 Cor 12:12–30; Gal 3:28). The metaphor is essentially the same in Colossians; what is new is that now Christ is the head of the church in the analogy of the body (Col 1:18, 24). This lies along a very plausible conceptual (though not necessarily temporal) trajectory: it began with the church depicted as a body (Rom 12:4–5), then this body was equated with Christ's body (1 Cor 12:12–27), and finally this body was given a head, Christ (Col 1:15–20). Indeed, it would have been surprising if the analogy had not been developed in this way. Since the first two stages are found in writings acknowledged as authentically Pauline, it is plausible that the third is authentically Pauline as well.

(5) Conclusions. Colossians is either Pauline or non-Pauline in authorship. Since the letter purports to be by Paul, non-Pauline authorship would mean that the letter is pseudonymous (see ch. 9,

sec. 6, above). To claim Pauline authorship raises the issues of the role played by the coauthor, in this case Timothy, and the possible role of a scribe. It has recently been argued again that Timothy may have been the actual author of the letter, possibly writing somewhat independently of Paul.[196] Since none of these theories can be quantified in any meaningful way, it is very difficult to factor this scribal or coauthorship hypothesis into the equation. On the basis of the other evidence cited above, however, even though there are some recognizable differences in Colossians from the other Pauline Letters, a plausible case for Pauline authorship remains.

3. Imprisonment

Colossians is one of the four letters often referred to as the Prison Epistles (see ch. 9, above). Ephesus, Caesarea, and Corinth have been suggested as possible places of authorship, but the traditional view of the Roman origin of the letter still commands the greatest degree of probability and scholarly support.

4. Opponents, Occasion, and Purpose

Trying to determine the occasion that elicited Colossians—the second most important critical issue regarding the letter—has aroused significant discussion but led to no scholarly consensus. One of the difficulties is the issue of authorship. If the letter is non-Pauline and thus probably written at the end of the first century, if not later, it is even more difficult to establish the situation to which it is addressed, since little can be known of the actual author, situation, or audience.[197] Consequently, the discussion below assumes Pauline authorship.

a. The opponents. There are six important views about the opponents.

(1) Hooker has argued against the traditional criteria used in most discussions of the opponents, noting that nowhere is there a formal exposition of any heresy that the author disputes.[198] So far as her reading is concerned, the only comments made in the letter argue against the readers' conformity to the beliefs and practices of their Jewish and their pagan neighbors. Hooker chooses to stress the positive statements that Paul makes rather than the negative. One of her complaints against most historical reconstructions of the situation behind the NT is that there is a circular reasoning at play, in which a heresy is posited and then this heresy is read out of the evidence.

Hooker's approach is a welcome one in many ways, not least because it brings to mind many of the pitfalls and implied assumptions of historical reconstruction. Most scholars have not responded positively to the challenge that her work presents, however. The familiar evidence in Colossians dealing with the opponents includes the following.

(a) Colossians appears to be confronting some form of philosophy (2:8) based upon tradition (2:8) and designed to impart knowledge or wisdom (2:23).

(b) Some of the characteristic beliefs of these opponents are endorsement of some kind of entrance into a realm of further knowledge or understanding (2:18), an entrance that might require a form or procedure of worship involving humility and harsh treatment of the body (2:23). What is worshipped is somehow connected with what are perceived to be the fundamental or basic principles of the universe, or with angelic beings (2:8, 20).

(c) Paul appears to be quoting, or at the least paraphrasing, some of his opponents' own language, including such phrases as "all the fullness" (1:19; 2:9), "self-abasement and worship of angels" (2:18), and "Do not handle, Do not taste, Do not touch" (2:21).

(2) In light of this evidence,[199] one of the most popular and enduring positions has been that this is a form of Gnosticism. Lightfoot, for example, proposed that Paul was responding to a form of Jewish Gnosticism.[200] According to Lightfoot, there were elements of Judaism that Paul was opposing (such as Sabbath rules and dietary restrictions), but they were gnostic in nature, including an emphasis upon an intellectual elite who took pride in wisdom, cosmological speculation (accounting for the "fullness" language), asceticism, mysteries, and various regulations that followed the calendar. Bornkamm refined this by proposing a syncretistic gnostic Judaism with pagan elements, which came to be identified with Essene Judaism. This theory combined elements of Judaism with Gnosticism and various other eastern pagan cults. Lightfoot's position dominated thought for the seventy-five years after he put it forward, but there are two major problems with it. First, it is unclear that Essene Judaism was in fact gnostic, and there is considerable doubt about how much Gnosticism is found in the first century. This objection has jeopardized all gnostic understandings of the Colossian problem. Second, some of the distinctive features of Essene Judaism, such as ritual washings, are not mentioned at all in Colossians.

Dibelius later emphasized the gnostic elements further in terms of a mystery religion, citing the use of the word for "entering into [mysteries]" (ἐμβατεύω, *embateuō*) (2:18) as meaning initiates' entrance into the sanctuary to consult the oracle on completion of a rite, and the "basic principles" (στοιχεῖα, *stoicheia*) (2:20; NRSV: "elemental spirits") as meaning the powers to whom the worshippers were devoted.[201] Dibelius's analysis draws attention to some important terminology, but one of the problems with pagan mystery cults is that they were highly secretive. Various forms of often syncretistic mystery religions flourished in the empire, including Mithraism, but only the initiates were allowed in to experience the mysteries. This secrecy makes it very difficult to establish any sort of systematic understanding of their beliefs or practices, and it must have been an obstacle even for Paul to obtain enough knowledge to argue against them.

(3) In light of the discovery of the Dead Sea Scrolls, Lyonnet has proposed the existence of a syncretistic Judaism that combined beliefs of the Essenes, perhaps as represented at Qumran, with various other Jewish beliefs.[202] This theory saw supposedly gnostic characteristics paralleled in other Greek thinking, and such important concepts as the "elemental spirits," "worship of angels," and entrance into the mysteries were all reinterpreted. The problem with this solution is the challenge to find where syncretistic Jewish belief of this sort existed, apart from a reconstruction of the Colossian situation.

(4) Jewish mysticism has also been seen to be the origin of the Colossian problem. Francis proposed an ascetic and mystical kind of Judaism, similar to apocalyptic Judaism. According to this position, the opponents advocated observance of a number of practices (such as dietary restrictions, calendar observance, and circumcision [2:11]) to prepare the person for a mystical vision and journey with angels to worship God. This has become a very popular position of late, and it has been significantly bolstered by recent work on the apocalyptic dimensions of the contemporary Judaism.[203] The major problem with this position is the interpretation of the Greek phrasing. For example, the phrase "worship of angels" is taken as indicating worship alongside angels, which is not the most likely interpretation of the phrase, especially in light of the study of extrabiblical texts.[204]

(5) Some form of Hellenistic philosophy has been cited by a number of recent scholars as the most likely explanation of the Colossian opposition. For example, Schweizer contends that the statements concerning eating, the ascetic statements, and the issue of the "basic" or "fundamental principles" do not indicate a Jewish element but, rather, the concerns of Greco-Roman philosophical circles. Neo-Pythagorean teaching dealt with these kinds of issues; according to it, humanity strives through various ascetic practices to escape this lower realm of existence. More recently, Troy Martin has argued that Hooker is correct that Colossian Christians are responding to the beliefs and practices of their neighbors, which include elements of Cynic philosophy. Important features are asceticism, bodily humiliation, criticism of others, viewing oneself as an inhabitant of the cosmos, and the human will.[205] The emphasis upon Hellenistic elements is a useful redress of the imbalance of previous scholarly emphasis upon Jewish elements, but one must question whether this provides the best interpretation of the factors involved. There is no doubt that early Christianity came into contact with various Hellenistic philosophies, but it is unproven that either of the two suggested above had a strong influence upon the Colossian Christians.

(6) The final proposal, that the Colossian opponents were syncretistic, has taken various forms. For example, DeMaris, emphasizing 2:8, 16–23, especially vv. 16–19, as the polemical core of essential texts requiring interpretation, argues that there is a "distinctive blend of popular Middle Platonic, Jewish, and Christian elements that cohere around the pursuit of wisdom."[206] In his focus upon these passages, DeMaris's study is like the others noted above, even though he contends that his analysis recognizes the diversity of evidence. Middle Platonism was the later, mystical expansion of Plato's thought, and its elements include the order of the cosmic elements (2:8, 20), the asceticism that liberates the investigative mind (2:18, 23), and the intermediary figures (2:18). A recognizable weakness of such a hypothesis is in finding a group that actually held to such beliefs, apart from the Colossians. Arnold has argued for a similar syncretistic solution, invoking local evidence to characterize the philosophy. Distinguishing between polemic (2:4–8, 16–23) and theology (1:15–20; 2:9–15) and drawing upon a wide array of inscriptional and papyrological evidence, Arnold concludes that "the beliefs and practices of the opponents at Colossae best cohere around the category of what might loosely be called folk religion."[207] This theory has the advantage of comprehensiveness but the disadvantage that it cannot be proved true or false. Virtually every feature of this syncretistic belief can be found in a parallel text of some sort and, by definition, can be included within the structure of the set of syncretistic beliefs.

b. Paul's Response. Paul's response to the opponents of Colossians, whoever or whatever they were, takes a three-pronged approach: Christology, apostolic teaching and tradition, and the importance of Christian freedom.[208]

(1) Christology. Paul relies upon a high and developed Christology in Colossians (problems that this raises for authorship are discussed above). The opponents are seen as threatening this supremacy of Christ, who is the head of the church (2:19). In-

stead, Christ is depicted in Colossians as taking a cosmic and universal role as creator (1:15–17) and reconciler of both heaven and earth (1:19–23). While some of the opponents may have created the role of intermediaries, and even placed Christ in that role, for Paul there is no role for intermediaries, and even Christ is not to be seen in this position, for it is in him and only him that the fullness of divinity dwells (2:9; 1:19). The consequences for this preeminence of Christ are seen in his position of authority over all creation, including the cosmic forces (1:18, 2:10). Nevertheless, Paul, along with his view of the exalted Christ, sees this position of exaltation predicated upon the humanity of Christ. This includes the reality of the incarnation (1:22; 2:9, 11–12) and the fact that redemption was on the basis of the cross, where Christ's blood was shed (1:20) and suffering occurred (1:24).

(2) Apostolic tradition and teaching. In Colossians, Paul opposes the traditions and teachings of the opponents with the apostolic tradition. Repeating a theme that he also emphasizes in Galatians (1:16–17), Paul makes it clear that the tradition that he is conveying is antithetical to human tradition (2:8, 22). The Colossians learned from Epaphras of God's grace (1:7) and heard the gospel preached (1:5), which they accepted by faith in Christ Jesus (1:4). Paul admonishes them to continue to walk in this tradition, which they have received (2:6), and to bear fruit and grow in it (1:6).

(3) Christian freedom. On a more practical level, Paul opposes what is being taught at Colossae because it impinges upon Christian freedom. The imposition of regulations by the opponents constitutes a threat to Christian freedom (2:8), since the Colossians were called to live Christian lives without these false regulations and restrictions (2:22). Rather than enlightening them, which can only come from Christ's power (3:1–3; 1:12), in which they have participated in Christ's work of conquering demonic forces (2:20), these false regulations impose darkness upon them (2:17). Their old nature has died to self, and they now have a new nature from Christ (2:11–13; 3:9–12). Christ, as head of the church, has transformed all of their previous relations and standards of behavior (ch. 3, esp. vv. 5–11 on the earthly passions and vv. 18–4:1 on social relations in the Christian household). They are now one body (3:5), joined together by Christian love and peace (3:14–15).

It is difficult to say what the exact situation was at Colossae. It seems to have been related to competition from some form or forms of religious belief—quite possibly with ties to Judaism or some other group with tendencies toward, or interest in, mysteries—which threatened to substitute such religious practices for belief and worship of Christ. Paul seems to be concerned not only to exalt the position of Christ but to ensure that there is no belief or practice in the Colossian church that could in any way displace the rightful role of Christ.

5. Outline of Colossians

A. Opening (1:1–2)
  1. Sender (1:1)
  2. Addressee (1:2)
  3. Greeting (1:2)
B. Thanksgiving (1:3–12)
  1. Thanksgiving proper (1:3–8)
  2. Intercession (1:9–12)
C. Body: The superiority of Christ (1:13–2:15)
  1. Formal opening: Deliverance and redemption through Christ (1:13–14)
  2. Christ, the supreme being (1:15–23)
  3. The work of Paul for Christ (1:24–2:5)
  4. Christ Jesus as Lord (2:6–15)
D. Parenesis (2:16–4:9)
  1. Do not submit to false regulations (2:16–23)
  2. Rules for living a holy life (3:1–17)
  3. The Christian household (3:18–4:1)
  4. Christian behavior as seen by others (4:2–6)
  5. Travelogue of Tychicus (4:7–9)
E. Closing (4:10–18)
  1. Greetings (4:10–17)
  2. Benediction (4:18)

C. Philemon

Philemon is by far the shortest of the Pauline Letters. In several ways, as will be noted below, it is uncharacteristic of the Pauline corpus. Instead of causing problems, however, this has helped to endear the letter to readers and has also helped it to endure and even avoid some of the controversy that has attended other Pauline Letters. Nevertheless, within the space of only twenty-five verses, it manages to raise a number of provocative issues.

1. Authorship

The Letter to Philemon is a truly personal letter, one of few such not only in the Pauline corpus but also in the NT. Apart possibly from the Pastoral Epistles (see below), only Philemon and 3 John in the NT appear to be written as personal letters. The form of the letter seems to be that of a letter from the apostle to a person or persons about a personal matter, rather than about a matter of concern to a local church. This is not to say that the issues raised in the letter do not have and have not had implications for the church, especially regarding the issues of authority and slavery. But this letter follows very closely the form of a letter of commendation or petition, which was widely used in the ancient world. In a letter of commendation, the author commended another person, often in conjunction with some sort of petition or request. This is exactly what Paul seems to be doing in this letter. His commendation concerns the escaped or runaway slave Onesimus, and Paul, in an indirect way, makes fairly specific petitions of Onesimus's owner, Philemon. As Kümmel states regarding authorship of Philemon: "Only tendenz-criticism could doubt the authenticity of this letter, which was already included in Marcion's authoritative writings. The letter, which of all Paul's letters stands closest in form to ancient private letters, displays in its personal features the signs of a genuine true-to-life quality."[209]

Philemon appears to be a personal letter, and the content is the discussion of a personal matter, but the form of the letter does not entirely support this analysis. This is seen in two ways. First, the letter is said to be from Paul and Timothy. This follows the form of all the other Prison Epistles except Ephesians and reflects the general Pauline epistolary convention that a letter comes from Paul and a cosender, often Timothy, his traveling companion and fellow missionary. Second, the letter is addressed to Philemon, Apphia, and Archippus and the church that meets in "your" (singular) house. The letter begins with the plural address, but the rest of the letter continues in the second person singular, "you." This will be discussed further below, when alternative reconstructions regarding Philemon are introduced. But it appears, and will be the view taken here, that the letter was addressed primarily to Philemon, but with the idea that others in the church at Colossae, in particular Apphia and Archippus, would be interested in how Philemon responded to the apostle's letter.

As mentioned earlier (ch. 9, sec. 5, above), the average papyrus letter in the ancient Greco-Roman world, of which Egypt was representative, would have been somewhere around 275 words in length; but the Letter to Philemon is around 335 words, hence slightly longer than the usual personal letter. The letter is surprisingly similar in form to that of the ancient Greco-Roman letter as well. As noted, the typical Pauline letter has a five-part structure, including the opening, thanksgiving, body, parenesis, and closing, an expansion of the typical three-part structure of the Greco-Roman letter. Philemon, however, departs from this structure in that it does not have a parenetic section. Since the parenesis appears to have been one of the distinctives of the Pauline letter, at least insofar as he developed this into a major section of his letters, perhaps its absence is not surprising in a personal letter, especially one that conforms so closely to the ancient Greco-Roman form. These letters often had a prayer of thanksgiving to the gods at the close of the greeting or at the beginning of the body (depending upon how one analyses the letter form). The only other Pauline letter that follows Philemon's form is 2 Timothy (cf. 1 Peter and 2 John).

2. Date and Place of Composition

The Letter to Philemon has a close connection to Colossians, and so, to some extent, its dating depends upon this connection. As mentioned in the discussion of Colossians above, of the six companions of Paul who send greetings in Colossians (4:10–14), five of these (Jesus/Justus is missing) send greetings to Philemon (23–24). Onesimus is referred to as one of the Colossians in Col 4:9.

The letter was written during Paul's imprisonment (Phlm 23), in either Rome, Ephesus, Caesarea, or Corinth, with Rome being the most likely (see ch. 9, sec. 4). It was probably sent by means of Tychicus (Col 4:7), who took the letter to Colossae, along with Onesimus, who was returning to Philemon. If the Roman imprisonment is the correct one, then the letter was probably written in A.D. 61–62, with Paul's attitude possibly indicating that it was near the end of this time.

3. Occasion and Purpose

The occasion and purpose of the Letter to Philemon are usually closely tied together, but here the two will be separated.

a. Occasion

(1) Traditional view. The traditional view is that Philemon was a member of the Colossian church.[210] Apparently he was converted under Paul (Phlm 9), though it is not known how or when this took place. Philemon had a slave named Onesimus, who had either fled from his master's control, possibly taking money or valuables, or simply not returned when he had been sent on a task for his master. Onesimus somehow came into contact with Paul, probably in Rome. If Onesimus had been on a trip for his master, it may have taken him directly to where Paul was; this would obviate the difficulty of the distance between Colossae and Paul's place of imprisonment. Indeed, the trip may have taken Onesimus to Rome itself, if he had been a particularly well-trusted slave, possibly even sent to minister to Paul. Nevertheless, even if he had fled from Colossae, a thousand miles from Rome, he could have made the trip in five weeks, so this is not an insuperable difficulty for the Roman imprisonment hypothesis. We do not know how Onesimus came into contact with Paul. He may have stumbled onto him by accident, or perhaps he was pointed in Paul's direction by someone Onesimus knew or had met. Onesimus may even have known Paul from when they had both been in Asia. In any event, Onesimus had apparently become a Christian through Paul (Phlm 10) and had served him for a short while. Now he is being returned to his master, Philemon, accompanied by this letter.

(2) The Knox hypothesis. John Knox had an alternative view of the historical occasion of Philemon and its consequences.[211] His theory was that Philemon was the overseer of churches in the region of Colossae and Laodicea. Archippus—not Philemon—who lived in Colossae and in whose house the church met, owned the slave Onesimus, who was sent to Paul. Paul was sending Onesimus back, but by returning him by means of Philemon, with this letter, to Laodicea (for Knox, this is the lost Laodicean letter). Paul did not know the owner (Col 4:16) and requested that Onesimus be released for Christian service. The two letters, Colossians and what we call Philemon, were to be read out at Colossae when Philemon and Onesimus arrived. Archippus's ministry (Col 4:17) was the task of receiving back his slave. In the early second century A.D., a letter of Ignatius (*Eph.* 1.3; cf. 2.2) refers to an Onesimus as bishop, and this Onesimus, according to Knox, was responsible for gathering the Pauline Letters. This accounts for why this letter was kept.

The Knox hypothesis raises several interesting issues and attempts to solve them, but most scholars reject this theory for several good reasons.[212] (a) Archippus is the third addressee in the letter, making it unlikely that he was its intended primary recipient. (b) The "church in your house" most likely refers to Philemon's house, as he is mentioned first, not to Archippus's. (c) Archippus's "task" of Col 4:17 is probably more than simply the matter of receiving his slave, since this would be a very obscure reference at best. It might also imply that Paul did know that Archippus was the slave's owner. (d) Paul seems to know the slave's owner, as Phlm 19 makes clear. (e) The text is not explicit that Onesimus was a runaway slave, but this is probably a more likely scenario.[213] (f) It is difficult to believe that this is the letter to the Laodiceans (Col 4:17) and that this was the letter to be read out. The statement in Colossians seems to imply an exchange of equal letters, but the Letter to Philemon is out of balance in almost every way with Colossians.

b. Purpose of Philemon.
The purpose of Philemon appears straightforward. Paul requests that his friend, whom he converted, receive his slave Onesimus back. Philemon must recognize, however, that the situation has changed. Onesimus is no longer to be treated as a slave but, rather, as a fellow servant of Christ and Philemon's partner in the spread of the gospel.

Several important features show how Paul attempts to effect this change in relationship.[214] For example, Paul tries to maintain two levels of status in relation to Philemon. On the one hand, he plays on his own hardship by depicting himself as a prisoner (Phlm 1, 10) and an old man (10; this may mean simply "elder"). On the other hand, he maintains the position of being at least Philemon's equal (17) and an apostle (22; understanding this as invocation of the apostolic presence). In depicting Philemon and Onesimus, Paul uses the language of family and social relations; for example Onesimus is his son (10) and his very heart (12), and is Philemon's brother (16). A second feature is that Paul, through indirect means, makes it clear that he expects Philemon to treat Onesimus as an equal as well. Paul recognizes that Onesimus has done wrong, probably in stealing from Philemon, but he also provides a means for him to be forgiven. Paul, playing upon Onesimus's name, which is cognate with the word for "useless," states that in Onesimus's new condition of being a follower of Christ, he is a "useful" person both to Paul and to Philemon. At the beginning of the letter, Paul commends Philemon because he has heard of his faith and his love for all of the saints (5, 7). Paul appeals to Philemon's love as the basis for his treatment of Onesimus as an equal in Christ. He points out that Onesimus had served in Philemon's stead while Paul was in prison. He does not describe what he expects Philemon to do, but at the least he counts on him to welcome Onesimus as he would welcome Paul himself (17). And if there is a debt owed—and here we see Paul tighten the screws—he instructs Philemon to charge it to Paul's account, but remembering that Philemon owes his Christian life itself to Paul, a difficult debt ever to repay (18). As a final gesture to guarantee compliance, Paul instructs Philemon to prepare a guest room for Paul (22).

On the one hand, Paul is complying with the law, which required him to return a slave. Harboring a slave would have incurred punishment equivalent to the loss of income the owner could have gained per day from the work of the slave.[215] On the other hand, Paul is apparently instigating a subtle yet significant change in the social system, at least insofar as Christian treatment of slaves is concerned. As Bruce says: "What this letter does is to bring us into an atmosphere in which the institution could only wilt and die. When Onesimus is sent to his master 'no longer as a slave, but as a dear brother,' formal emancipation would be but a matter of expediency, the technical confirmation of the new relationship that had already come into being."[216] To call for widespread manumission of slaves, however, would have incurred the wrath of the Roman government and an oppression of Christians that could well have proved fatal to the cause. As Martin says: "It is sometimes alleged that since the NT never explicitly condemns slavery it is defective at a crucial point. But part of the answer to this is that Paul does not advocate a social philosophy which countenances revolution and violence. Given the social structures of the Roman Empire of Paul's day, slavery could have been overthrown only by vio-

lent means; and the apostle will be no party to class hatred or violent methods (cf. Rom. 12:17–21)."[217]

4. Outline of Philemon

   A. Opening (1–3)
      1. Sender (1)
      2. Addressee (1–2)
      3. Greeting (3)
   B. Thanksgiving (4–7)
   C. Body: Commendatory or petitionary letter (8–22)
      1. Formal opening: Paul's request (8–14)
      2. Basis for the request (15–21)
      3. Pauline presence (22)
   (D. Parenesis—none)
   E. Closing (23–25)
      1. Greetings (23–24)
      2. Benediction (25)

D. Ephesians

Ephesians has been called the "quintessence of Paulinism" by Bruce.[218] By this he means that it contains the concentrated essence of genuine Pauline teaching; other scholars have taken the view that Ephesians may well give the essence of Paul, but an essence written later by a close follower and disciple of the great apostle. This is only one of several critical questions about this book.

1. Authorship and Date

The issue of the authorship and date of Ephesians is highly complex, and one that has divided critical scholars. There is a fairly even divide on the authorship of Colossians, but for Ephesians, those who hold to Pauline authorship are in a distinct minority, even though some recent work is reasserting the argument that Paul may be the author. In the current debate, three major views are argued: (1) the traditional view, which maintains Pauline authorship; (2) the majority view, which maintains pseudonymous authorship; and (3) various mediating positions, which posit the influence of a colleague, such as Luke. The discussion of authorship will raise many other related issues.

a. Pauline Authorship. The traditional view is that the apostle Paul was the author. Many scholars still maintain that the letter was originally sent to the church at Ephesus, but more now dispute this (see below); the destination of the letter, however, does not have a necessary bearing upon the issue of authorship. Scholars with such diverse opinions as Guthrie and Goulder have argued for Pauline authorship of the letter. There are at least five reasons in defense of Pauline authorship.[219]

(1) The Epistle's Self-Claims. The author of this letter clearly claims to be Paul, with his apostolic authority (1:1; 3:1). The other Prison Epistles are said to be coauthored with Timothy, but Ephesians (like Romans, even though a scribe was involved; Rom 16:22) has the singular claim of having been written only by Paul. This claim to authorship is reinforced by regular use of the first person singular throughout the letter (1:15, 16; 3:3–4, 7, 13, 14–15; 4:1, 17–18; 5:2; 6:19, 21, 22). One would expect this to be the case if the letter were written by Paul; if it is not by Paul, either directly or indirectly, the issue of pseudonymity is introduced (see ch.9, sec. 6, above).

(2) External Evidence. It appears that Ephesians was written before the turn of the first century and was in widespread circulation by the mid–second century. The letter is clearly cited by Clement (1 Clem. 64 [Eph 1:3–4], 46.6 [4:4–6], 36.2 [4:18], 59.3 [1:18]), who wrote in ca. A.D. 96, as well as by the Didache (4.10–11), Ignatius (Pol. 1.2, 5.1; Smyrn. 1.1; Eph. 1.1, 10.3), Polycarp (Phil. 1.3, 12.1), and the Shepherd of Hermas (Mand. 3.1.4; Sim. 9.13.17).[220] The Muratorian Fragment, line 51, also lists the letter. On the basis of this external evidence, one might be able to date Ephesians to A.D. 80–95 but still not require Pauline authorship. Another factor to consider is the apparent assumption in the letter that the temple in Jerusalem is still standing. When the author speaks of the reconciling activity of Christ as destroying the dividing wall (2:14), he is probably referring to the wall of the temple dividing the holy of holies from the outer areas, and to make the analogy understandable, assumes that this wall is standing.[221] Taking the dividing wall metaphorically of some other division between Jew and Gentile is possible, but not likely in light of the context, which seems to place the scene in Jerusalem around the death of Jesus.

(3) Letter Form. The letter itself follows the standard outline of a Pauline letter, with the five major sections: opening (1:1–2), thanksgiving (1:3–23), body (2:1–3:21), parenesis (4:1–6:20), and closing (6:21–24). Indeed, in some ways it forms the archetypal Pauline letter, showing a balance of proportion not found in others.

(4) Language. Differences of style in Ephesians have been noted since the time of Erasmus, but there are also several typical Pauline characteristics in the language. These include the vocabulary, which for the most part is more in harmony with the language used in Paul's earlier letters than any other of the letters falling into this later period (see below). The author makes use of paradoxical antitheses (6:15, 20), typical of the main Pauline Letters, and relies upon citation of the OT, typical only of the main Pauline Letters, in particular Romans.[222] Not only does he cite the OT (4:8–11); he makes use of OT imagery (1:22; 2:13, 17; 4:25; 5:2; 6:1–3). A number of objections have been raised to other features of the language of Ephesians. The most important of these is the use of strings of modifying phrases. Opponents of Pauline authorship often cite numerous examples in Ephesians where modifying phrases, often using words in the genitive case, are strung together, arguably without a clear sense of modification (e.g., 1:18, literally: "the riches of the glory of his inheritance"), as we saw above in Colossians. In his recent work on the opponents in Ephesians (which he takes to be the letter to the Laodiceans), Goulder points out two things. First, in Paul's letters, including his main letters, one of his common techniques is to cite his opponents' claims but gloss them with his own rebuttal (e.g., 1 Cor 2:6–7; 2 Cor 3:1–3, 7; 4:4; etc.). And second, when Paul responds, he often does so in terms of what he believes has been accomplished in Christ. Thus a mammoth single sentence such as Eph 1:3–14 makes good sense of its repeated use of "in Christ" phrasing when opponents with a subordinate view of Christ are concerned (see also 3:16–17). As Goulder says: "Once one is aware of this tendency, the loose trailing on of clauses and genitival phrases is seen to be no more un-Pauline in Ephesians than in 2 Cor. 4.4. The denial of Pauline authorship is the consequence of the widespread temptation to substitute counting for thinking."[223]

(5) Theology. There are numerous theological similarities between the approach of Ephesians and the other Pauline Letters. Included among these are references to God as glorious (1:17), powerful (1:10–20), merciful (2:4–10), and predestining (1:5–14). Christ is seen to have a high and exalted

position, witnessed not only by the repeated use of "in Christ" language noted above (e.g., 1:3, 10, 11) but also by the function he is given of reconciling humanity to God and humans to each other by means of the cross (2:13–16). Christ is also the one who triumphs over all other powers (1:21–22). The Holy Spirit serves as an agent of revelation (2:18; 3:5) and as a unifying force in the Christian community (4:3; 5:18). The church has been brought together or reconciled by Christ so that Jew and Gentile form one new creation (2:13–16).

b. Non-Pauline Authorship. The majority of scholars deny that Paul wrote Ephesians. Hence, any references to Paul as writer must be taken as pseudonymous references and not historically accurate. There are three reasons for this.[224]

(1) Point of View. The point of view in Ephesians seems to reflect a period later than that of Paul. This is seen in two ways. First, Paul is treated with a high amount of dignity unbefitting his writing the letter himself (3:1–13) but more in keeping with a later follower or disciple of Paul writing with reverence and respect for the former apostle to the Gentiles, as if he were still speaking to the Christian community. Second, and in keeping with the first, the letter seems to refer to the apostles as if they were a closed group (2:20; 3:5). If Paul were one of the apostles, it is unlikely that he would refer to the group as a separate and distinct foundational group that the current church had been constructed upon (cf. 1 Cor 12:28, where there is closer integration of apostles with others in the church, reflecting the tone of 1 Corinthians).

(2) Language and Style. There are forty *hapax legomena*, or words not found elsewhere in the NT (there are fifty-one words not found in the undisputed letters of Paul), including the words translated "tossed to and fro" (4:14; κλυδωνίζομαι, *klydōnizomai*) and "lost all sensitivity" (4:19; ἀπαλγέω, *apalgeō*). There are other words used in a new sense, such as "mystery" (5:32; μυστήριον, *mystērion*), "plan" or "commission" (e.g., 1:10; 3:2, 9; οἰκονομία, *oikonomia*), and "fullness" (1:23; πλήρωμα, *plērōma*). Many have seen the language of Ephesians reflecting the language not of the early Pauline Letters but of the Apostolic Fathers, indicating a date in the late second century.[225] When words that are Pauline are found in Ephesians, it is not uncommon to find that they have been compounded or that they are strung together

in large phrases and expressions (1:3–14, 15–23; 2:1–10)—often highly repetitious ones such as "great love with which he loved us" (2:4) or "holy and blameless" (1:4). Colossians and Ephesians are quite similar in arrangement and subject matter (see below), and by the traditional chronology and views of authorship, they must have been composed at very close to the same time. They are sufficiently different in their language and style, however, to raise questions. Some might posit the greater involvement of a scribe or secretary in composition, but this would mean that the secretary had sacrificed Paul's language for that of another.

(3) Theology. In Ephesians, certain doctrines seem to have either faded from prominence or been replaced by other doctrines. For example, to some it appears that the stress on the death of Christ and the theology of the cross have faded from view in Ephesians. The cross is only mentioned at 2:16, and Christ's death only at 1:7 and 5:2, 25. While the earlier Pauline Letters seem to reflect a futuristic eschatology (1 Thess 4:13–17; 2 Thess 2), Ephesians seems to reflect a realized eschatology in which believers are already seated in the heavens with Christ (2:6), although there is a current battle with evil powers (2:2; 6:12). Concerning marriage, it appears that the author of Ephesians is making concessions regarding the strong position exemplified in 1 Cor 7. First Corinthians 7 has a firm but egalitarian posture. Ephesians 5:22–33 alters that stance, however, by imposing a subordinationist position on women and moves the discussion away from considerations of actual life to a spiritualized sense in which husband-wife relations are related to Christ and the church. The church, instead of being built on Jesus Christ (cf. 1 Cor 3:11), is now seen to be built on the "apostles and prophets" (Eph 2:20) and is the replacement of Israel, an idea hinted at in the main Pauline Letters only in Gal 6:16.

In spite of this recognizably strong evidence, there are two major problems with the view that Ephesians is not by Paul. First, the evidence tends to be negative (e.g., regarding language and style)—finding problems with the traditional view but not concerned to explain the evidence at hand. For example, most would argue for a date of A.D. 80–90 if the letter is not by Paul, even though some of the evidence used to establish non-Pauline authorship claims that the language dates to the late second century. Second, there are the historical and theological problems, as with all pseudonymous-letter theories. Since the letter is clearly attributed to Paul, it means that some later writer who was not Paul used the apostle's name. This raises important issues regarding the nature of the Pauline corpus (see ch. 9, sec. 6, above). Nevertheless, many scholars still maintain that Ephesians was written as a letter for the Pauline churches of Asia Minor after the apostle had died, since he had left followers, possibly a school, who perpetuated his tradition through written letters.

c. Modified View. The modified position, represented by Martin, recognizes the weight of the evidence for Pauline authorship.[226] He notes the kinds of similarities in language and thought mentioned above, as well as the external evidence. But he also recognizes that there are persistent difficulties and problems in accepting the letter as Pauline, in the same sense that other letters are accepted as Pauline, such as Philippians. The solution he proposes is that the teaching, while authentically Pauline and originating with the apostle, has been compiled and published by a faithful follower. This person must have been someone familiar with Paul's thinking, one who could be entrusted to represent what Paul had to say, but adapt it to the situation being addressed. For Martin, the logical choice of writer is Luke. In support of such a hypothesis is the fact that of the words found in Ephesians but not in Paul's main letters, twenty-five are found in Luke–Acts, and ten of these are found nowhere else in the NT; in addition, some phrasing seems Lukan. Further support is found in parallels between Ephesians and Paul's meeting with the Ephesian elders recorded in Acts 20:17–38—for example, the discussion regarding the Holy Spirit (Acts 20:23, 28; Eph 3:5; 4:3–4).

If Martin is correct and Luke was the actual "writer" of Ephesians, that is, the one who took Paul's thinking and applied it to the situation at Ephesus and committed this to writing, several difficulties are overcome. First, this would account for stylistic differences between Ephesians and the major Pauline Epistles. It would even account for the fact that Ephesians is often seen not to be as personal a letter, since only Tychicus is personally greeted at the end of the letter (Eph 6:21). Second, the portrayal of Paul's apostleship as unique and authoritative (3:1–13) would make sense if the writer or compiler of the letter were someone such as Luke, a longtime traveling companion and follower of the great apostle. Third, such a view of authorship would make sense of some of the modifications in thought from other letters, such as the waning of expectation regarding the Parousia (3:20–21) or the view of the church in terms of a new creation, with racial boundaries abolished (especially if the writer were a Gentile such as Luke).

Martin's idea has much to commend it, but it encounters two sets of difficulties. One concerns particular items of his comparisons. For example, Mitton raises the discrepancy that Acts does not know of Paul's letters, while Ephesians—supposedly written by Luke—knows of Acts 20.[227] The second set of difficulties concerns what constitutes evidence and how the hypothesis can be proved true or false. On the one hand, similarities between Ephesians and the Lukan writings become evidence for Luke's involvement because Ephesians is already seen to be under Luke's influence. On the other hand, anything that does not conform to Paul's style or thinking can be attributed to Luke as well. It is difficult to know what would constitute proof that Luke—or almost any other writer—was involved in the writing process. Furthermore, so little is known about the traveling companions of Paul, including Luke, that it is difficult to attribute such writing activities to them or know the nature of any involvement by them.

In conclusion, the critical issues above—especially the Lukan hypothesis and the negative, rather than positive, evidence regarding non-Pauline authorship—are highly problematic and difficult to prove. Since the arguments for Pauline authorship at least address the major problems, authentic Pauline authorship is as reasonable a choice as the alternatives.

2. Relation of Colossians and Ephesians

The complex relation of Colossians to Ephesians is important regardless of the view one takes of authorship. For those who hold to Pauline authorship, it indicates composition of the letters at a similar point in Paul's ministry—while being held prisoner, probably in Rome. It suggests that Paul wrote one of the letters, probably Colossians first, and then used some of the same ideas, and occasionally even the same wording, when writing Ephesians. A comparison of Colossians and Ephesians may suggest something similar for those who hold to the modified view of Pauline authorship, according to which the writer—whether he was Luke or not is unimportant at this stage—likely used Colossians in some way as a template for his composition. For those who hold to non-Pauline authorship of Ephesians, the picture may well have been similar, except that there was an interval between the writing of Colossians by Paul—if in fact it was by Paul—and its use by someone to create a letter to a fellow church in Asia. The purpose of this section is not to argue for a particular view of Ephesians' relation to Colossians but, rather, to present the similarities so that they can be appreciated in studying the two letters.

It has been estimated that 34 percent of the words of Colossians reappear in Ephesians. Or if the movement was the other way, 26.5 percent of Ephesians appears in Colossians.[228] Despite this significant amount of overlap, very few extended passages are paralleled. The one important exception is Col 4:7–8 and Eph 6:21–22, which have extended verbal agreement of twenty-nine words. In all other parallel passages, five to seven words at most are the same from one letter to another. Perhaps more noticeable than the verbal parallels, however, are similarities not only in the epistolary form but also in the topics. These are set out in Table 10–5, on p. 490. One must be careful with such a chart, however. As Lincoln points out, there are also a number of differences in content. And certain organizational features (e.g., the opening) regularly appear in set places in the Pauline Letters, thus minimizing some of the similarities of these two letters.

3. Origin, Purpose, Occasion, and Destination

Determination of the origin of Ephesians depends upon one's view of authorship. If the letter is Pauline or by a close associate, such as Luke, it originated during his imprisonment in either Rome, Ephesus, Caesarea, or Corinth, with Rome being the most likely (see ch. 9, sec. 4). If the letter is non-Pauline, it is impossible to determine the origin or destination of the letter.

The destination, purpose, and occasion of the letter are closely interconnected. These will be treated together in light of the difficulty with the opening of the letter. There is serious debate regarding the destination of the letter in Eph 1:1 because all of the

best and earliest manuscripts ($\mathfrak{P}^{46}$ ℵ B, among others) lack the words "in Ephesus." If the words "in Ephesus" are taken out, as they almost assuredly should be, the Greek phrasing is not only awkward but unparalleled,[229] indicating that at some time there must have been some city or destination listed in the manuscript. Unfortunately, the manuscript tradition lists no city but Ephesus. Origen, the church father, attempting to explain the opening without a destination, speculated that the opening "the saints who are" refers to those called into existence by God, who is Being himself. Others have tried to explicate "the saints who are" and the "faithful" as Jewish and Gentile Christians respectively. None of these proposals has proved satisfactory. Other solutions are more enlightening.[230]

a. Letter to the Ephesians. For those who maintain Pauline authorship of the letter, some might still maintain that it was originally addressed to the church at Ephesus, even if it was addressed to other churches as well. This position recognizes that, despite the dispute over the destination of the letter, Ephesus is nevertheless the only one recorded in the textual tradition, including the church fathers.[231]

This view of Ephesus as the destination still encounters several objections, especially if Paul is the author of the letter. The letter gives the idea that the author does not know the congregation (Eph 1:15; 3:2–3; 4:21), but Paul spent several years ministering in Ephesus (see Acts 19). Furthermore, as mentioned, there are no personal references in the letter, apart from the mention of Tychicus (and this is a commendation), and no apparent firsthand knowledge of the situation in Ephesus. The letter appears to be addressed to Gentiles, but there were also Jewish Christians in Ephesus. This evidence seems to indicate that either Paul was addressing only one faction of the congregation or the traditional destination is not accurate and must be reassessed.

b. Circular Letter. The view that the letter is a circular letter can take at least two forms. Some have argued that the letter is authentically Pauline but was not addressed to only one church, that it was a circular letter, quite possibly taken by Tychicus at the same time he carried to Colossae the letters to the Colossians and Philemon. This would account for the blank in the early manuscripts, since it was left to the reader of the letter in a given city to fill in the name of that city; for the lack of formal greetings and the more distant tone; and, in the view of certain scholars, for the letter's assemblage of some of Paul's essential thoughts. Later, possibly because a copy of the letter remained in Ephesus, the letter became associated with that city. One problem with the circular-letter hypothesis is that besides the place of destination, "Ephesus," the word "in" is missing from the earliest manuscripts. One might expect the inclusion of this word to indicate where to insert the destination (i.e., "in . . ."). Others have argued that the letter was a circular letter that is not authentically Pauline. Written in the spirit of an authentic Pauline letter, it was designed to disseminate his message to a number of churches in Asia. This view has similarities to Goodspeed's hypothesis regarding the origin of the Pauline Letters corpus (see below).

c. Safeguard Letter against the Colossian Heresy. This view, tied to the circular-letter hypothesis, argues that the letter was not written to the Ephesians alone but, rather, to the larger surrounding community of Christians in Asia to provide a safeguard against the spread of the Colossian heresy (see the sec. 3.B, above, on Colossians for a discussion of the possible opponents). This theory would explain why the letter uses or reveals dependence upon Colossians, since it was designed to provide a more general statement that a large number of churches could read with profit. According to this view, Tychicus probably carried this letter as well and set it in circulation when he arrived in the area.

d. Letter to the Laodiceans. Colossians 4:16 states that after the Letter to the Colossians has been read, it is apparently to be exchanged with a letter to the Laodiceans so that the latter can be read to the Colossian church. There have been many attempts to locate the letter to the Laodiceans, but several hypotheses aside, no letter has been found (a fourth-century letter in Latin, cited in discussion of the Letter to the Philippians, is certainly not that letter).[232] Goulder argues that Ephesians must be the letter to the Laodiceans if it is authentic (which he believes it is), for several reasons: the associating of the Colossians with the Laodiceans (Col 2:1), the linkage between the two letters, the problems about the identification of the addressee, and Marcion's purported attribution of Ephesians to a Laodicean origin (Tertullian, *Ag. Marc.* 5.17.1; note also that there is a Marcionite prologue for a letter to the

Laodiceans but not one for the Ephesians).[233] The evidence cited plausibly points in the direction of the Laodicean letter, but it is still not in the manuscript tradition. Goulder argues that when the Laodicean community became anti-Pauline (Rev 3:14–22), the original letter was destroyed but a copy survived at Ephesus; the ancient evidence commends this view.

e. Ephesians and the Pauline Corpus. Goodspeed proposed that the Pauline Letters were gathered together at around the turn of the first century, after waning in importance since the death of the apostle. Interest in Paul's writings revived, and the letter we know now as Ephesians was written as a cover letter for this collection.[234] In Goodspeed's view, a devoted follower of Paul, writing it for those who were unfamiliar with Paul's writings, used the opportunity to summarize what he thought was important and enduring in Paul's thought. The collection of the Pauline Letters would have circulated to various churches, with the addressee conceivably changing according to the church in receipt of it.

The problems with this view are several. Since recent rethinking about the formation of the Pauline letter collection does not recognize a time when Paul's letters were under a threat of being forgotten, this theory is less plausible than ever. The major problem is that there is no trace that Ephesians was ever at the head of any collection of the Pauline corpus. One would expect to find some collection in which this order of assemblage is reflected, but no set of manuscripts or manuscript list shows this. There are also further difficulties. How do we explain the reference to Tychicus if he were not involved in the letter's dissemination? And why was Colossians, of all letters, chosen as the letter to imitate in Ephesians, especially when Romans has traditionally been seen to serve the function of introducing the major Pauline teachings?

f. Summary. The occasion for Ephesians is, in many ways, one of the most difficult to determine because of the factors mentioned above. It is clear that the letter was addressed to a Gentile church (2:11; 3:1), quite possibly under some form of threat from a group of Judaizers, Jewish Christians who were arguing for the continued practice of the law (2:11). Paul's response was to assert that the Jewish practices had been abolished (2:15) and that both Jew and Gentile are on equal footing with God (2:13–16), since salvation is by grace through faith

(2:8), thus creating one unified church (5:18–21). Goulder has argued that there was a problem with Jewish visionaries promoting an apocalyptic Jewish-Christian theology that compromised the position and preeminence of Christ.[235] One does not need to go as far as Goulder, however, to appreciate the situation that the letter addresses, one that Paul encountered elsewhere in his missionary endeavor (e.g., Galatians).

4. Outline of Ephesians[236]

A. Opening (1:1–2)
  1. Sender (1:1)
  2. Addressee (1:1)
  3. Greeting (1:2)
B. Thanksgiving (1:3–23)
  1. Thanksgiving proper (1:3–14)
  2. Intercession (1:15–23)
C. Body: Unity in Christ (2:1–3:21)
  1. Salvation by grace to do good works (2:1–10)
  2. Incorporation of Gentiles into one Christian faith (2:11–22)
  3. Paul as minister of the mystery (3:1–13)
  4. Concluding prayer and doxology (3:14–21)
D. Parenesis (4:1–6:20)
  1. Living a worthy life (4:1–6)
  2. Responding to God's grace (4:7–16)
  3. Living the Christian life (4:17–5:20)
  4. Submission in household relationships (5:21–6:9)
  5. Being strong in the Lord (6:10–17)
  6. Praying in the Spirit (6:18–20)
E. Closing (6:21–24)
  1. Tychicus (6:21–22)
  2. Benedictions (6:23–24)

4. THE PASTORAL EPISTLES

"Although these letters purport to be written by Paul, . . . most scholars believe they are post-Pauline—even later than Colossians, Ephesians, and 2 Thessalonians."[237] The Pauline origin of these letters was apparently not disputed from their earliest attestation until the early part of the nineteenth century,[238] but today the broad consensus among most critical scholars is that the Pastoral Epistles were not written by Paul but, rather, by some later followers of Paul using his name. Hence they are pseudonymous. This scenario raises a number of very intriguing and

difficult questions for discussion, since there are a number of factors that must be taken into account (see ch. 9 on the problem of pseudonymity and ch. 13 on the formation of the biblical canon).

A. Timothy and Titus

One of the clear things about the Pastorals is that they are written as if they are personal letters addressed to single individuals. The personal nature of the letters is widely disputed; most scholars consider them to be church or community documents (in line with comments in the Muratorian Fragment). This is not entirely clear from the way the letters present themselves, however. It was not until the early eighteenth century that 1 and 2 Timothy and Titus were first referred to as the Pastoral or Shepherd Letters,[239] apparently appearing to most to be personal letters, even if they address issues of interest within a larger church setting.

A number of personal characteristics are worth noting. For example, Timothy is a very important minor character in the NT. The son of a Jewish mother named Eunice and a Greek father (Acts 16:1–2), he was an associate of Paul (Acts 17:14–15; 18:5; 19:22) and is at least given credit for coauthorship in the NT by being included in the salutation of a number of Paul's letters (1 and 2 Thessalonians, 2 Corinthians, Philippians, Philemon, and Colossians). Indeed, he is mentioned in all but three of the traditional Pauline Letters (Galatians, Ephesians, and Titus). In the Pastoral Epistles, he is shown remaining at Ephesus at the time of Paul's supposed release from his first Roman imprisonment (1 Tim 1:2, 3) and is still there when Paul is back in prison in 2 Tim 1:18 (cf. 4:9ff.). He did important missionary work at Thessalonica (1 Thess 3:2) and Corinth (1 Cor 4:17), although he appears to have had a timid personality, such that he may have been easily intimidated by others at Corinth and Ephesus.

Less is known about Titus, who is mentioned twelve times in the NT. He was a Greek and remained uncircumcised (Gal 2:3). He apparently had a bolder personality than Timothy and consequently undertook several difficult tasks for Paul, especially at Corinth (2 Cor 7:6, 7, 13–15; 8:6; 12:18), including taking the "severe letter" and 2 Corinthians to the church there and reporting to Paul when the crisis was apparently over. Titus was—according to the book with his name—left at Crete by Paul (Titus 1:5ff.), and then rejoined Paul at Nicopolis (3:12); at the end of Paul's life he was in Dalmatia (2 Tim 4:10).

It is appropriate that the Pastoral Epistles—whether authentically Pauline or pseudonymous—are addressed to these historical figures involved in various ways in the ministry and mission of the historical Paul.

B. Critical Difficulties

The four major critical difficulties regarding the Pastoral Epistles concern the epistolary form, the style and content, the Pauline chronology, and the use of these letters in the early church.[240]

1. Epistolary Form

The Pastoral Epistles purport to be addressed to individuals. But it has been plausibly argued that the letters are in fact community or church letters, like virtually all of the other Pauline Letters (the apparent exception being Philemon). One reason for this position is the amount of material in the letters concerned with such things as the faith or Christian belief, the administration of the church—including its officers and those who serve in it—and social issues that the early church confronted, such as the responsibility for widows. Another reason given is that the personal elements, typical of Paul's personal letters, have supposedly receded into the background as church interests emerge. But which personal letters are these that would provide suitable examples for comparison? Philemon, addressed to Philemon, Apphia, Archippus, and the church? Some would say that Philemon is the only authentic personal letter in the Pauline corpus, while others would question whether even Philemon is a genuine personal letter. If this is the case, it is difficult to categorically deny, on the basis of aberrant epistolary form, that the Pastoral Epistles are personal letters, since there is only one or no authentic Pauline personal letter for true comparison.

According to Dibelius and Conzelmann, 2 Timothy best fits the picture of the Pauline letter, because the personal element is "strongly emphasized." Titus holds an intermediate position, since addressing instructions to a person where there is not an established church order is at least understandable.

First Timothy, however, "affords the most difficulties. For here, personal elements fade into the background."[241] But how does one determine this fading of the personal elements? Subject matter alone is not a sufficient criterion, since it does not compromise the integrity of a personal letter to discuss matters that affect those other than the primary person(s) involved (as the nonliterary papyri amply attest—e.g., when one writes to another about a third party). There would need to be some formal characteristic in the language of the letter to establish this fading of the personal. But there is no instance, for example, of second person plural verb forms, only second person singular, and no instance of second person plural pronouns, only second person singular, apart from the formulaic closing in 6:21.[242] So far as formal criteria are concerned, it is not clear how one could establish the features of personal address in 1 Timothy more clearly.

2. Style, Content, and Theology

The question here is whether differences in content can be explained by the nature of the letters, or whether they point to non-Pauline authorship. Debate regarding style falls essentially into two areas: vocabulary and style proper. There have been numerous statistical studies undertaken to show how un-Pauline the vocabulary and style of the Pastorals are on the basis of a high number of singular occurrences of certain terms (*hapax legomena*), varying word or word-class frequencies, and more regular and less varied sentence structure. There have likewise been a number of studies that have countered these claims by showing flaws in the calculations regarding vocabulary and arrangement; by configuring the vocabulary items counted in different ways in relation to the other Pauline Letters, the rest of the NT, and other bodies of literature; and by arguing that differences of context and subject matter require modified word choice and sentence structure.[243] There are two unresolved issues here.

The first is the size of the appropriate sample for study. In Neumann's recent discussion of the issue, he includes a survey of the numbers proposed. These range from 85 to 3,500 words in recent studies, and as high as 10,000 words in earlier studies. What is evident is that there is no agreed-upon number of words for a sample. Thus Neumann apparently almost arbitrarily decides that 750 words will be his sample size, not on the basis of a reasoned argument but only so that the Pauline Letters can be included. Even so, Titus, with its 659 words, is still too small.

The second consideration regarding style is what exactly is being determined and how significant the findings must be before it can be decided that something is or is not Pauline. The methods used to determine authorship are almost as varied as the scholars doing the calculations, with very little control on what criteria are being used and what would count as an adequate test of the method. Furthermore, aside from the appearance of scientific accuracy, one must still interpret the results. What does it mean that one of the early church fathers' writings satisfies certain statistical tests and is placed close to the authentic Pauline Letters, whereas one of the disputed Pauline Letters is further away? What does it mean that one of the supposedly authentic Pauline Letters is further away? In other words, how much variety is tolerable in the statistical outcome before one questions authorship? This has not been determined.[244] These two major difficulties make it extremely difficult to use statistics to determine Pauline authorship of the Pastoral Epistles.

Formalization of church order is often mentioned as a criterion for authorship.[245] In many scholars' minds, the Pastoral Epistles appear to be referring to an established church structure. This structure has formal offices (elders, overseers/bishops, deacons), with people who occupy these positions having authority over the other members of the community. The charisma of the Spirit, according to this view, has been curtailed and has been replaced by an orderly succession through the laying on of hands. Furthermore, the church finds itself responding to a form of thinking (1 Tim 6:20) that advocates asceticism and a kind of legalism (1 Tim 1:7; 4:3, 8; Titus 3:9) in the context of a realized eschatology (2 Tim 2:17–18). This is all seen to reflect an "early catholicism," typical of what appears in writings of the second century and later, especially those influenced by Gnosticism.[246] In

T A B L E 1 0 - 5	
COLOSSIANS AND EPHESIANS	
Parallels of Outline and Content[247]	
Opening	Col 1:1–2; Eph 1:1–2
Thanksgiving, intercessory prayer	Col 1:3–14; Eph 1:3–14, 15–23
Readers' alienation but now reconciliation	Col 1:21–23; Eph 2:11–22
Paul as a suffering apostle and minister of mystery	Col 1:24–29; Eph 3:1–13
Head-body relation	Col 2:19; Eph 4:15–16
Old and new person	Col 3:5–17; Eph 4:17–5:20
Household code	Col 3:18–4:1; Eph 5:21–6:9
Exhortation to prayer	Col 4:2–4; Eph 6:18–20
Tychicus commended	Col 4:7–9; Eph 6:21–22
Benediction	Col 4:18; Eph 6:23–24

order to back up this theory, however, one must successfully deal with several issues. The first is how to explain the fact that Phil 1:1 uses the terms "bishops/overseers" and "deacons,"[248] singling them out in the very order in which they appear in 1 Tim 3. They are not defined in Philippians, but they probably reflect an early form of institutional structure already present in the Pauline churches. (Incidentally, the author of Luke–Acts may know something of this in Acts 14:23, which refers to elders being appointed in the Pauline churches.) The second issue concerns the form of opposition being confronted in the Pastoral Epistles. The tendency is to place the opponents in the second century, but there is still some question whether any of the practices or apparent beliefs mentioned in the Pastorals are totally unfamiliar to the authentic Pauline Letters (e.g., 1 Cor 7:1; 8:1–3; 15:17–19; Gal 4:8–10; cf. also Col 2:20–22).[249]

Regarding the theology of the Pastoral Epistles, certain terminology that occurs in the authentic Pauline writings is used in different ways. Thus the concept of faith, which, in the authentic Pauline Letters, seems to be a subjective or obedient response to God, takes on the more objective sense of a common body of belief or virtue, or even Christianity itself (e.g., 1 Tim 1:2, 5, 14, 19; 2:7, 15; 3:9; 4:1, 6, 12; 5:8, 12; 6:10, 11, 12, 21; 2 Tim 1:5; 2:22; 3:8, 10; Titus 1:4, 13; 2:2; 3:15). This tradition is to be received, protected, and passed on.[250] Righteousness, which, in the authentic Pauline Letters, signifies the state of being in right relation with God, seems to take on the more neutral and objective sense of justice in the Pastoral Epistles (e.g., 1 Tim 6:11; 2 Tim 2:22; 4:8; Titus 1:8). Love, which is a key virtue in the authentic Pauline writings, is seen as one virtue among others in the Pastoral Epistles, often side by side with faith (e.g., 1 Tim 1:14; 2:15; 4:12; 6:11; 2 Tim 1:7, 13; 2:22; 3:10; Titus 2:2). The Pauline phrase ἐν Χριστῷ, *en Christō*, which has been variously interpreted but seems to indicate some sort of relation in which believers find themselves within the sphere of Christ's control, seems to have taken on a more technical sense of "existence within the Christian community" in the Pastoral Epistles (e.g., 1 Tim 1:14; 2 Tim 1:2, 9, 13; 2:1, 10; 3:12, 15). In the Pastoral Epistles, God is called Savior, in six of the eight times that such phrasing appears in the NT (1 Tim 1:1; 2:3; 4:10; Titus 1:3; 2:10; 3:4; cf. Phil 3:20; Eph 5:23). In the

Pastoral Epistles the conscience of members of the community is either good and pure or soiled and seared, rather than strong or weak (e.g., 1 Tim 1:5, 19; 3:9; 4:2; 2 Tim 1:3; Titus 1:15), just as teaching is now either healthy or sick, rather than holy or unholy (1 Tim 1:10; 4:6; 2 Tim 4:3; Titus 1:9; 2:1, 7). A few ideas are unique to the Pastoral Epistles and are often related to the use of unique words or phrases. An example would be "The saying is sure" (e.g., 1 Tim 1:15; 3:1; 4:9; 2 Tim 2:11; Titus 3:8), for which there is no true parallel in the authentic Pauline Letters.[251] And 1 Tim 1:13, which says that Paul was shown mercy by God because of his previous ignorance and unbelief, may reflect non-Pauline thought. Still, ideas unique to the Pastoral Epistles are admittedly few. Nevertheless, there are perceivable theological differences, at least in their context of usage. In other words, ideas are present, for the most part, in the authentic Pauline Letters, but there has been a development whose nature is unclear. Is it complementary development, and hence still possibly Pauline, or is it contradictory, and hence probably non-Pauline?[252] The latter kind of development, which would be necessary to establish the distinctiveness of the Pastoral Epistles, would also raise the further question of how and why these writings were incorporated into the canon.

3. Pauline Chronology

The third major issue concerns how these letters fit in with the Pauline chronology as established in Acts and the other Pauline Letters. If there were a number of so-called Prison Epistles written during an imprisonment in Rome, such as the one recorded in Acts 28:29–31, then where do the Pastorals fit in? This is made more acute by the fact that 2 Tim 1:17 indicates that it was written from Rome. Most consider it highly unlikely that it was written from Rome during the same imprisonment. This suggests a second Roman imprisonment, for which there is no other attestation. A further difficulty is that although Paul states his intention in Rom 15:24, 28 to visit Rome on the way to Spain, the Pastoral Epistles have him traveling in the eastern Mediterranean. First Timothy is apparently written from Macedonia (1 Tim 1:3), the book of Titus to Crete, where there is apparently an established Pauline church (Titus 1:5), and 2 Timothy from imprisonment in Rome (2 Tim 1:16–17). It is not apparent how these fit together. Neverthe-less, Paul was in, or had every intention of going to, Macedonia several times during his travels, as his undisputed letters state (1 Cor 16:5; 2 Cor 1:16; 2:13; 7:5; Phil 4:15). There is no other record of Paul's visiting Crete, apart from his shipwreck there on his way to Rome (Acts 27), but Titus 1:5 may not be saying that Paul actually left Titus there, only that he left him to his task, Paul being elsewhere,[253] and he was imprisoned several times, again according to his authentic letters (2 Cor 6:5; 11:23; Phlm 1, 9). So 1 Timothy and Titus could eas-ily be placed within the Pauline letter chronology. Does 2 Tim 4:16 imply a previous imprisonment, as some have argued, or only a previous defense, which the language could well mean? Since we do not know all of Paul's travels from the letters (the key example is Paul's so-called painful visit to Cor-inth from Ephesus in the midst of his correspon-dence with them; see sec. 2.E, above), there is the possibility that he made a significant trip to Mace-donia. Neither Paul's letters nor Acts gives a com-plete chronology of Paul's life and travels; hence, it is impossible to solve the chronological issues in the Pastoral Epistles.

4. Use in the Early Church

Most scholars consider the evidence of use of the Pastorals in the early church to be weak. The most common arguments are that evidence of use of the Pastorals by Ignatius and Polycarp is incon-clusive at best and perhaps indicates instead that the Pastorals used these church fathers, that Marcion does not include them in his canon, and that the early and important papyrus text of the Pauline Letters, $\mathfrak{P}^{46}$ (ca. 200), does not include them.[254] This evidence warrants consideration in the attempt to arrive at an estimation of author-ship. For the most part, however, this purportedly negative evidence is at best ambiguous, while other important evidence is slighted.[255] For example, evi-dence of the literary dependence of Ignatius and Polycarp upon the Pastorals is stronger than often thought. According to White, there appear to be at least five clear instances in Ignatius, and three in Polycarp, of literary dependence on the Pastoral Epistles.[256] Marcion does not include the Pastorals, but Tertullian in *Ag. Marc.* 5.21 states that he is "surprised . . . that he [Marcion] rejects the two to

Timothy and the one to Titus." Tertullian's state-ment may be apologetic and not in fact prove that Marcion rejected them. But as Kümmel points out, Marcion's failure to include them does not mean that these letters were not in existence.[257] The lack of the Pastorals in $\mathfrak{P}^{46}$, while important to note, cannot prove that they were not in existence, since there are several possible explanations for this lack. These include the scribe's difficulty in calculating how many pages of the papyrus codex were left (it is incomplete at both beginning and end), further adjustments the scribe may have made in writing the letters when he realized he was possibly run-ning out of room, because he wanted to fit them in (the scribe already shows an increase from twenty-six to thirty-two lines per page), and our lack of knowledge regarding the purpose of this particular papyrus collection of writings. Not only are the Pastorals missing from $\mathfrak{P}^{46}$; it breaks off in 1 Thessa-lonians and lacks the rest of 1 Thessalonians, 2 Thessalonians, and Philemon as well. Two other fragmentary papyri, however, have been dated to approximately the same time as $\mathfrak{P}^{46}$: $\mathfrak{P}^{32}$, a frag-ment of Titus (1:11–15; 2:3–8), and $\mathfrak{P}^{87}$, a fragment of Philemon (13–15, 24–25).[258] There also seems to be a literary relationship between the Pastoral Epis-tles and *1 Clement*.[259] Some have seen the Pastorals as dependent upon *1 Clement*, but a trajectory be-ginning with the Pastorals is also a possibility.

C. Proposed Solutions to the Problems of the Pastoral Epistles

With so many problems raised by the Pastoral Epistles, it is not surprising to find a number of so-lutions as well.

1. Pseudonymity

In light of the manifest difficulties raised above, it has been suggested by a number of scholars—and is clearly the scholarly consensus today—that the Pastoral Epistles are pseudepigrapha.[260] This position argues that the letters were written after Paul's death, quite possibly in the second century, in response to some form of threat to the Pauline churches, and that they were written to express what Paul himself would have said if he were ad-dressing these issues. It must also follow from this view that the events and personal references in the Pastoral Epistles, including the very personal references in 2 Tim 4 and the mention of Rome, were artificially created by the author or authors of these letters to enhance the likelihood that the letter would be accepted in Paul's. If so, whoever did this would have been creating a literary deception.[261] On the other hand, if pseudepigrapha were a common convention of the early church (as has been argued), then such references would have been unnecessary and served no legitimate purpose. This raises the question why it would have been necessary to write pseudepigrapha at all. The position that the Pastoral Epistles are pseudepigrapha helps explain the apparent contradiction that advice regarding behavior and church order were given to Timothy, a very close companion of Paul, although he would apparently have known Paul's thinking on such issues, since he was a traveling companion and coauthor of so many letters. If the letters are pseudepigraphal, then the writers borrowed the name of Timothy, but they needed to have this redundant information declared to Timothy as if for the first time so that they could explicitly state it for their contemporary church situation.

2. Fragmentary Hypothesis

The fragmentary hypothesis, proposed earlier in this century by Harrison and later followed by others, claims that there are certain authentic sections within the Pastoral Epistles.[262] Harrison performed several analyses upon the letters, later revising his first findings. The major sections Harrison discerned were the following: Titus 3:12–15; 2 Tim 1:16–18; 3:10–11; 4:1, 2a, 5b–8, 9–15, 20, 21a, 22b and the ascription "Paul." A variation on this hypothesis is that another person in a Pauline church produced this literature and, in so doing, also shared something of what happened to Paul with his readers: people in Asia turned against him, he died in Rome full of faith, and others abandoned him while he was in prison. In other words, authentic traces of Paul in the Pastorals may not mean that Paul necessarily wrote them; instead, they tell a true story, and there was no other reason to include these authentic details. The conclusion of such a hypothesis is that the Pastorals are Pauline in a strictly limited sense, with the latter

form of the hypothesis virtually indistinguishable from the pseudepigraphal hypothesis (see above). One noticeable shortcoming of the traditional fragmentary hypothesis is that it still does not explain the origin of 1 Timothy, since there are no purportedly authentic fragments found in it; neither does it explain the necessity of three letters rather than a single one. How and why were these particular fragments determined to be authentic, other than that they tend to be those concerned with personal matters? One might contend that there is no reason for these portions to be passed on unless they are authentic and that there was no reason to fabricate them, because they did not otherwise significantly add to the message of the book. Precisely because these are such ordinary bits of information, no one can find an occasion for which they might be created for the church of a later generation. All of these contentions, however, seem to work from the assumption that the letters are inauthentic, and they try to find an explanation of the fragments instead of starting from the letters and determining the fragments from that direction. In any event, this view of authorship recognizes the problem with the personal elements if the letters are not Pauline, but it does not then adequately explain the rest of the letters. It seems highly unlikely that elaborate letters concerning a number of issues were constructed around such personal matters, certainly when the personal matters do not suggest the subjects of the rest of the letters. When these particular fragments of personal information are examined more closely, however, it is surprising to find that such fine judgments are made by scholars regarding several quite ordinary pieces of information. In this case, a bad job has been done of creating plausible letters around the preserved fragments of authentically Pauline material. To claim that the author incorporates authentic Pauline tradition into his letters in order to clarify the tradition is a more plausible explanation why so little material is preserved, but it does not address the question why the letters were written in the first place, since the message of the letters suits a later stage in the development of the church rather than the context of the authentic Pauline Letters and Acts. The concerns of the letters themselves are more comfortable in a subsequent generation when faith was waning, Christ had not returned, and the temptation to leave the church was greater. One still wonders, however, if the only basis for the fragmentary hypothesis is the similarities of the fragments with authentic Pauline material.

3. Amanuensis

It is an undeniable fact, as Richards has clearly shown, that the use of scribes was widespread in the ancient world.[263] As was discussed in ch. 9, sec. 5.D, above, these scribes or amanuenses performed a wide range of functions, from taking straight dictation to serving a creative role similar to that of modern personal assistants given responsibility for composing letters sent under their bosses' names. It is also known that Paul used scribes, as is seen in Rom 16:22, which refers to Tertius, and Gal 6:11–16, where Paul apparently takes up the writing instrument himself. A recurring problem in Pauline studies is the role that the Pauline scribe played (see sec. 3.D and ch. 9, above). The view of most scholars is that Paul probably allowed for only a limited amount of scribal creativity, since there is an overwhelming consistency of presentation in his major letters in both content and style. There is the possibility that he always used the same scribe (perhaps Timothy's role should be given larger credit?), but it is thought more likely that he used different scribes but his rhetorical skills dominated the correspondence. Such a scenario allows for the possibility that, on another occasion, a scribe was given the opportunity to write a letter on Paul's behalf with a degree of freedom not previously given. It has been suggested that such a writer would be Luke, the reputed author of Luke–Acts, and possibly the traveling companion of Paul.[264] He is referred to in 2 Tim 4:11 as the only one left with Paul, and could be considered one of Paul's most enduring companions. In support of this hypothesis are certain similarities in vocabulary between Luke–Acts and the Pastoral Epistles. There are also some difficulties with this position, however, since the Pastorals actually share more words in common with the other Pauline Letters than with the Lukan writings. Furthermore, if the Lukan hypothesis is to explain authorship of the Pastorals and Ephesians, one would expect them to have significant similarities. It has been argued that the Pastoral Epistles have important similarities to Paul's speech to the Ephesian elders (Acts 20:17–38),[265] a passage often thought to resemble

the style of Ephesians, but the evidence does not clearly point to common authorship of the Pastorals and Ephesians.

4. Pauline Authenticity

a. Paul's Life after Acts 28:31. The fourth proffered solution to the problem of authorship suggests that the story of Paul's life does not end with the account found in Acts and that he composed the letters after his release from a first Roman imprisonment.[266] Some reason for optimism for his release is found in both Acts and the Pauline Letters themselves, as well as in extrabiblical writings (e.g., Eusebius, *Hist. eccl.* 2.22.2–8; Muratorian Fragment, lines 38–39). Acts makes it clear throughout that the Roman authorities had no legitimate complaint against Christians, including Paul, and that the Jews were mainly responsible for the troubles, as recognized by such Roman officials as Gallio. In Phil 1:25–26, 2:14 and Phlm 22, Paul himself seems optimistic that his release is imminent. Philemon 22 also suggests that Paul will be traveling east from Rome (if he is imprisoned in Rome, as we suggest that he is) to Colossae. If Paul did eventually suffer martyrdom under Nero, this could have occurred at the earliest in A.D. 64. If the chronology of Acts for Paul's missionary journeys is accurate and this imprisonment occurred somewhere around A.D. 61–62, then two more years must be accounted for. Eusebius (*Hist. eccl.* 2.22.2–8) speaks of two imprisonments of Paul, stating that, in the interim, he traveled to the various places recorded in the Pastoral Epistles. It is possible, of course, that Eusebius obtained this information from the Pastorals and created his own scenario, but it is at least as likely that if he had known another scenario, he would have presented it. There is thus a reasonable basis for the hypothesis of two Roman imprisonments, with a span of approximately two years for Paul to carry out the traveling and correspondence suggested by the Pastoral Epistles.

b. Paul's Life before Acts 28:31. J. A. T. Robinson suggests a different scenario.[267] The personal references are fewer in 1 Timothy, but on the basis of 1 Tim 1:3, which states that Timothy was urged to stay on at Ephesus when Paul was heading toward Macedonia, Robinson posits that 1 Timothy was written on the third missionary journey, perhaps from Corinth after Paul had left Ephesus and traveled through Macedonia into Greece. On the basis that Titus had left Corinth (he is not mentioned in the greetings of Rom 16) and had been sent off to Crete to deal with the church there (Titus 1:5), Robinson suggests that Titus was written on Paul's journey to Jerusalem, possibly from Miletus (noting the similarities with the speech in Acts 20). The similarities in the names mentioned in 2 Timothy and Colossians and Philemon, together with the sense of desperation, compel Robinson to argue that 2 Timothy was written during Paul's imprisonment in Caesarea, where his future was still in doubt, after an assassination attempt against him in Jerusalem. As mentioned in ch. 9, sec. 4, most scholars do not accept Robinson's reconstruction, but it is unwise, and probably unfair, to be too dogmatic on the non-Pauline origins of the letters.

D. The Evidence

The following gives a brief summary of the evidence often marshaled in discussion of the Pastoral Epistles. There are some inherent dangers in this approach—that is, discussing all of the letters together—since it runs the risk of blurring their distinctives. Still, if they are pseudonymous, they were probably written by the same person over a short amount of time.

1. The Opponents

Two kinds of evidence are often marshaled regarding the opponents in these letters: Jewish elements and gnostic or proto-gnostic elements. The Jewish elements include the claim by the opponents to be teachers of the law (1 Tim 1:7), disputes over the law (Titus 3:9), and the reference to those of the circumcision (Titus 1:10). They were concerned with various fables and genealogies (1 Tim 1:4; Titus 1:14; 3:9), perhaps connected to Genesis (see 1 Tim 2:13–14), and were ascetics (1 Tim 4:3; 2:15?; 5:23), but they were not Judaizers, at least of the kind that Paul had to combat earlier in his ministry. The gnostic or proto-gnostic elements of this group are indicated by some of the same evidence of Jewish elements: attention to fables and genealogies (1 Tim 1:4; Titus 1:14; 3:9), concern for knowledge (1 Tim 6:20), and a view of the world as evil (1 Tim 4:4). On the contrary, Paul puts forward a view of God as "one" (1 Tim 2:5), the creator (1 Tim 4:3–4), and the savior (1 Tim 1:1; 2:3; Titus 1:3; 2:10; 3:4). The only mediator between God and the world is Christ (1 Tim 2:5). The letters dispute that the readers have already experienced the resurrection (2 Tim 2:17–18), as they seem to have been promoting.

When could such a mix of these two kinds of elements have arisen in the early church? Two major solutions are usually put forth. One is that the opponents were second-century gnostics who believed in access to the heavenly realm through emanations and ascetic practice.[268] The major problem with this position is that our knowledge of Gnosticism is incomplete. It is now commonly recognized that fully developed Gnosticism did not emerge until the second century at the earliest, even though many of the elements of Gnosticism have their roots in Hellenistic and even classical philosophy and in Jewish apocalyptic thought. This makes it difficult to establish a clear beginning point for gnostic influence, as distinct from proto-gnostic influence. A further difficulty is that, from what we do know, the emanations were never called genealogies, a link that some have thought necessary in order to find this important gnostic doctrine in the Pastorals. One would really have expected a more sharply defined criticism of such a movement were it really behind this letter. Besides, this position does not explain the Jewish elements apparently present.

A second proposal—perhaps as likely as any other—is that the author has sensed in several of these churches a movement with a set of beliefs very similar to those opposed at Colossae. Perhaps it represents a syncretistic form of Judaism with some ascetic and legalistic elements peculiar to its beliefs. In conjunction with this, there may have been problems of church organization—posited by some as reflecting early catholicism—or concerning widows, including the question of egalitarianism (equal status) for various groups of women.[269] This movement does not constitute the kind or degree of threat that some other sets of opponents would, so the author responds in more general terms, reaffirming essential belief regarding

God and Christ—comments that could have been directed to any belief system that was highly syncretistic.

2. Theology

There is no denying that many elements of the theology of the Pastorals are consonant with the theology found in the main Pauline Letters.[270] These include the affirmations that God's mercy has been revealed in Jesus Christ (1 Tim 1:12–17; Titus 3:3–7) and that salvation depends upon God's grace (2 Tim 1:9; Titus 3:5) through faith in Christ (1 Tim 1:16), who is the redeemer, ransomer, and justifier for sinners (1 Tim 2:5–6; Titus 3:7). Eternal life is the goal of the Christian life, but there is a sense in which something of the joy of that existence is experienced now (1 Tim 6:12; cf. 2 Tim 1:1; Titus 1:2; 3:7). Besides the more formally theological elements, a number of moral issues are also addressed, such as "second" marriages (1 Tim 3:2, 12; 5:9), slaves (1 Tim 6:1), and the state (1 Tim 2:1–4).

In addition to these elements of commonality, however, there are a number of elements that have struck many, if not most, scholars as representing differences from established Pauline theology. First, several major concepts are not found in the Pastoral Epistles. For example, it is often said that the notion of faith as a "justifying principle" is missing in the Pastorals, that instead faith has taken on the idea of a body of belief, that is, "orthodoxy" (1 Tim 3:9; 4:1; Titus 1:13; 2 Tim 4:7). Faith as the justifying principle is, however, represented in 1 Tim 1:4, 16 and Titus 3:8. The kind of semantic expansion found in the Pastorals is perfectly legitimate to find within one author, especially one who wrote over a number of years. Also, Jesus as "Son" is not found in the Pastorals. This is true, but it is likewise not found in Philippians and Philemon and only once in 2 Corinthians; so perhaps this is not a legitimate criterion.

Second, some scholars state that certain terms are used radically differently in the Pastorals than in the other Pauline Letters. An example of this is the concept of love, which is said not to be as key a virtue in the Pastorals as it is, for instance, in Rom 5:5. But the importance of love, for Paul, as a cardinal virtue in motivating God's action is probably not as great as some have argued. In addition, in 1 Tim 1:5, the author says at the outset of the letter that love from a pure heart is the goal of our in-

struction, an idea that is not totally foreign to the authentic Paul. Others have argued that "in Christ" is synonymous with what it means to be a Christian in the Pastorals, not with the mystical union of believers to Christ as in the authentic Pauline Letters. But the sense of mystical union has been overdrawn in discussing "in Christ" language in Paul (see the synopsis of Pauline theology in ch. 9, sec. 2, above), and besides, there is the use of similar language in the Pastorals, for example in 2 Tim 1:13, which says that faith and love are "in Christ Jesus."

A third supposed theological difference concerns the way doctrine and orthodoxy themselves are viewed in the Pastoral Epistles. According to some scholars, what distinguishes the Pastorals is the treatment of Christian doctrine as something entrusted to believers (1 Tim 6:20) that is to be handed on (2 Tim 1:13–14; 2:2; 3:14); that is, it takes on the status of tradition, consistent with a later date of writing. The only problem with such an analysis (and it is not to be denied that there is this sense of Christian doctrine as something to be handed on to subsequent believers) is that a similar idea is found in the other Pauline Letters, such as 1 Cor 15:1–3, where Paul says that he has passed on to the Corinthians what he himself first received. Not only are the concepts traditional; so is the means of formulation: Paul cites what is perhaps early church tradition already formulated in a memorable creedal statement (1 Cor 15:3–8).

3. Language and Style

It has been argued that a number of words and phrases, many of them prominent, are not found in the other Pauline Letters but are found in the Pastorals. It is true that a number of crucial terms appear to be unique to the Pastorals. Examples include words often translated "to be healthy" or "sound" (ὑγιαίνω, hygiainō; 1 Tim 1:10; Titus 1:9, 13; 2:1, 2; 2 Tim 4:3; 1 Tim 6:3; 2 Tim 1:13), "self-controlled" (ἐγκρατής, enkratēs; Titus 1:8), and "piousness" or "godliness" (εὐσεβεία, eusebeia; 2 Tim 3:5; Titus 1:1).

As mentioned in ch. 9, sec. 6, above, in the discussion of pseudepigraphy, the questions that this evidence raises are these: How different must the results of a stylistic and lexicographical analysis be before serious doubt is thrown on the idea of two works sharing a common author? And how divergent must such results be before it becomes implausible to entertain works as authentically Pauline?[271] At the end of the day, the results are mixed for the Pastoral Epistles. Romans has the same percentage of unique words as do 2 Timothy and Titus, yet it is hardly doubted that Romans is Pauline.[272] In light of the small corpus available and the uncertainty of the results of such tests, perhaps it is better not to rely upon them as the deciding factor, especially when there are available other explanations for the deviance, such as the occasion and audience (that is, whether the letters are personal or to churches), the role of an amanuensis, or the possibility of a trusted compatriot as author (such as Luke).

E. Authorship

As with Colossians and Ephesians, there are only two real conclusions regarding authorship of the Pastoral Epistles: pseudonymous or authentic Pauline authorship. The pseudonymous explanation must answer a number of questions, including the following: (1) Why are there three letters and not one or two? The point here is that similarities among the three letters indicate common authorship at roughly the same time, and the question is why three letters would have been necessary to accomplish what one well-constructed letter could do. It is unlikely that there were several pseudepigraphers, one following another, at various times and in various locales. (2) Why are there so many personal details, especially in 2 Timothy? If the personal details are included to try to convince the reader of Pauline authorship, is there not the issue of deception to face? That is, was the early church deceived into believing that these letters were by Paul? This also raises the question whether 1 Timothy should be seen as plausibly Pauline. The answer to this last question may well be affirmative, in many scholars' minds.

If the author of the Pastoral Epistles was Paul, several difficulties are resolved. First, the opponents are consistent with those found in other Pauline Letters, such as Colossians, so there is no need to speculate on a hypothetical scenario some time in the second century or even later. Authentic Pauline authorship allows the Pastorals to be read as they appear, that is, not as fiction but as real correspondence. It is difficult to account for the long personal sections unless they reveal a genuine set of circumstances; otherwise one has great difficulty accounting for the references to Hymenaeus and Alexander in 1 Tim 1:20. If Robinson's suggestion is not accepted about integrating the Pastoral Epistles into the Acts chronology (most do not accept it), then one must date Paul's release from Roman imprisonment sometime around A.D. 62. First Timothy would have been written from Macedonia to Ephesus, understandable in light of the church at Philippi and its support of Paul (1 Tim 1:3), although it is possible that Paul went first to Spain and then to Macedonia. In any event, he could have then gone to Crete (his reference in Titus 1:5 does not require his having gone there) after spending the winter in Nicopolis (Titus 3:13), but this is not known for sure. Paul was then arrested and taken to Rome, or arrested in Rome, probably after going to Troas (2 Tim 4:13), Miletus (2 Tim 4:20), and Corinth, and imprisoned a second time in Rome, where he died under Nero's persecution, beginning in A.D. 64/65.

F. Outlines of the Pastoral Epistles

a. 1 Timothy

A. Opening (1:1–2)
  1. Sender (1:1)
  2. Addressee (1:2)
  3. Greeting (1:2)
(B. Thanksgiving—none)
C. Body: Behaving as a leader in God's church (1:3–4:16)
  1. Formal opening: Refuting the false teachers (1:3–11)
  2. Paul's faithfulness to his calling (1:12–20)
  3. Instructions for church governance and behavior (2:1–3:16)
  4. Timothy's role in the church (4:1–16)
D. Parenesis? (5:1–6:19)
  1. Household duties (5:1–6:2)
  2. The return on false doctrine and godliness (6:3–10)
  3. Pursue what is righteous, etc. (6:11–19)
E. Closing (6:20–21)
  1. Closing words to Timothy (6:20–21)
  2. Grace benediction (6:21)

b. 2 Timothy

A. Opening (1:1–2)
    1. Sender (1:1)
    2. Addressee (1:2)
    3. Greeting (1:2)
B. Thanksgiving (1:3–5)
C. Body: Serving Christ (1:6–4:8)
    1. Formal opening: God gives a spirit of power (1:6–14)
    2. Some have not been faithful (1:15–18)
    3. Endurance is for long-term service (2:1–13)
    4. False teaching is to be resisted (2:14–26)
    5. Eschatological climax (3:1–9)
    6. Apostolic charge (3:10–4:18)
(D. Parenesis—none)
E. Closing (4:19–22)
    1. Greetings (4:19–21)
    2. Benediction (4:22)

c. Titus

A. Opening (1:1–4)
    1. Sender (1:1–3)
    2. Addressee (1:4)
    3. Greeting (1:4)
(B. Thanksgiving—none)
C. Body: Leading the church (1:5–16)
    1. Qualifications for elders (1:5–9)
    2. Response to false teachers (1:10–16)
D. Parenesis (2:1–3:14)
    1. Teaching sound doctrine (2:1–15)
    2. Living under rulers, authorities, and others (3:1–7)
    3. Avoiding divisiveness (3:8–11)
    4. Personal comments (3:12–14)
E. Closing (3:15)
    1. Greetings (3:15)
    2. Grace benediction (3:15)

BIBLIOGRAPHY

A. Introductions and Discussions of Paul's Language

BADCOCK, F. J. *The Pauline Epistles and the Epistle to the Hebrews in Their Historical Setting.* London: SPCK, 1937.

BRUCE, F. F. *Paul: Apostle of the Heart Set Free.* Grand Rapids: Eerdmans, 1977.

CARSON, D. A., D. J. MOO, and L. MORRIS. *An Introduction to the New Testament.* Grand Rapids: Zondervan, 1992.

CHILDS, B. S. *The New Testament as Canon: An Introduction.* Philadelphia: Fortress, 1985.

FULLER, R. H. *A Critical Introduction to the New Testament.* London: Duckworth, 1966.

GUTHRIE, D. *New Testament Introduction.* Downers Grove, Ill.: InterVarsity, 1970.

JOHNSON, L. T. *The Writings of the New Testament: An Interpretation.* Philadelphia: Fortress, 1986.

KENNY, A. *A Stylometric Study of the New Testament.* Oxford: Clarendon, 1986.

KOESTER, H. *Introduction to the New Testament.* 2 vols. FFNT. Philadelphia: Fortress, 1982; 2d ed. of vol. 1, 1995.

KÜMMEL, W. G. *Introduction to the New Testament.* Trans. H. C. KEE. 17 ed. Nashville: Abingdon, 1975.

MARTIN, R. P. *New Testament Foundations: A Guide for Christian Students.* 2 vols. 2d ed. Grand Rapids: Eerdmans, 1986.

MOFFATT, J. *An Introduction to the Literature of the New Testament.* 3d ed. Edinburgh: T. & T. Clark, 1918.

MORTON, A. Q., and J. MCLEMAN. *Paul, the Man and the Myth.* New York: Harper & Row, 1966.

NEUMANN, K. J. *The Authenticity of the Pauline Epistles in the Light of Stylostatistical Analysis.* SBLDS 120. Atlanta: Scholars Press, 1990.

ROBINSON, J. A. T. *Redating the New Testament.* Philadelphia: Westminster, 1976.

B. Galatians

BETZ, H. D. *Galatians: A Commentary on Paul's Letter to the Churches in Galatia.* Hermeneia. Philadelphia: Fortress, 1979.

BRUCE, F. F. *The Epistle to the Galatians: A Commentary on the Greek Text.* NIGTC. Grand Rapids: Eerdmans, 1982.

BURTON, E. DeW. *A Critical and Exegetical Commentary on the Epistle to the Galatians.* ICC. Edinburgh: T. & T. Clark, 1921.

DUNN, J. D. G. *The Epistle to the Galatians.* BNTC. Peabody, Mass.: Hendrickson, 1993.

LIGHTFOOT, J. B. *The Epistle of St. Paul to the Galatians.* 1865. Repr., Peabody, Mass.: Hendrickson, 1993.

LONGENECKER, R. N. *Galatians.* WBC 41. Dallas: Word, 1990.

LÜHRMANN, D. *Galatians: A Continental Commentary.* Trans. O. C. DEAN Jr. Minneapolis: Fortress, 1992.

LUTHER, M. *A Commentary on St. Paul's Epistle to the Galatians.* Ed. J. P. FALLOWES. London: Harrison Trust, n.d.

MARTYN, J. L. *Galatians.* AB 33A. New York: Doubleday, 1997.

MATERA, F. J. *Galatians.* SP 9. Collegeville, Minn.: Liturgical, 1992.

RAMSAY, W. M. *A Historical Commentary on St. Paul's Epistle to the Galatians.* London: Hodder & Stoughton, 1899.

C. 1 and 2 Thessalonians

BEST, E. *A Commentary on the First and Second Epistles to the Thessalonians.* BNTC. Peabody, Mass.: Hendrickson, 1977.

BRUCE, F. F. *1 and 2 Thessalonians.* WBC 45. Waco, Tex.: Word, 1982.

FRAME, J. E. *A Critical and Exegetical Commentary on the Epistles of St. Paul to the Thessalonians.* ICC. Edinburgh: T. & T. Clark, 1912.

MARSHALL, I. H. *1 and 2 Thessalonians.* NCB. Grand Rapids: Eerdmans, 1983.

MENKEN, M. J. J. *2 Thessalonians.* London: Routledge, 1994.

MORRIS, L. *The First and Second Epistles to the Thessalonians.* 2d ed. NICNT. Grand Rapids: Eerdmans, 1991.

PLUMMER, A. *A Commentary on St. Paul's First Epistle to the Thessalonians.* London: Robert Scott, 1918.

_____. *A Commentary on St. Paul's Second Epistle to the Thessalonians.* London: Robert Scott, 1918.

RICHARD, E. J. *First and Second Thessalonians.* SP 11. Collegeville, Minn.: Liturgical, 1995.

WANAMAKER, C. A. *The Epistles to the Thessalonians: A Commentary on the Greek Text.* NIGTC. Grand Rapids: Eerdmans, 1990.

D. 1 and 2 Corinthians

BARNETT, P. *The Second Epistle to the Corinthians.* NICNT. Grand Rapids: Eerdmans, 1997.

BARRETT, C. K. *The First Epistle to the Corinthians.* 2d ed. BNTC. Peabody, Mass.: Hendrickson, 1971.

_____. *The Second Epistle to the Corinthians.* BNTC. Peabody, Mass.: Hendrickson, 1973.

BULTMANN, R. *The Second Letter to the Corinthians.* Ed. E. DINKLER. Trans. R. A. HARRISVILLE. Minneapolis: Augsburg, 1985.

CONZELMANN, H. *1 Corinthians: A Commentary on the First Epistle to the Corinthians.* Hermeneia. Philadelphia: Fortress, 1975.

FEE, G. D. *The First Epistle to the Corinthians.* NICNT. Grand Rapids: Eerdmans, 1987.

FURNISH, V. P. *II Corinthians.* AB 32A. Garden City, N.Y.: Doubleday, 1984.

HUGHES, P. E. *Paul's Second Epistle to the Corinthians.* NICNT. Grand Rapids: Eerdmans, 1962.

MARTIN, R. P. *2 Corinthians.* WBC 40. Waco, Tex.: Word, 1986.

ORR, W. F., and J. A. WALTHER. *1 Corinthians.* AB 32. Garden City, N.Y.: Doubleday, 1976.

PLUMMER, A. *A Critical and Exegetical Commentary on the Second Epistle of St. Paul to the Corinthians.* ICC. Edinburgh: T. & T. Clark, 1915.

QUAST, K. *Reading the Corinthian Correspondence.* New York: Paulist, 1994.

ROBERTSON, A., and A. PLUMMER. *A Critical and Exegetical Commentary on the First Epistle of St. Paul to the Corinthians.* 2d ed. ICC. Edinburgh: T. & T. Clark, 1911.

THRALL, M. E. *A Critical and Exegetical Commentary on the Second Epistle to the Corinthians.* 2 vols. ICC. Edinburgh: T. & T. Clark, 1994–.

WITHERINGTON, B., III. *Conflict and Community in Corinth: A Socio-Rhetorical Commentary on 1 and 2 Corinthians.* Grand Rapids: Eerdmans, 1995.

E. Romans

BARRETT, C. K. *A Commentary on the Epistle to the Romans.* 2d ed. BNTC. Peabody, Mass.: Hendrickson, 1991.

BLACK, M. *Romans.* NCB. Grand Rapids: Eerdmans, 1973.

BRUCE, F. F. *Romans.* Rev. ed. TNTC. Grand Rapids: Eerdmans, 1985.

CRANFIELD, C. E. B. *A Critical and Exegetical Commentary on the Epistle to the Romans.* 2 vols. ICC. Edinburgh: T. & T. Clark, 1975–1979.

_____. *Romans: A Shorter Commentary.* Grand Rapids: Eerdmans, 1985.

DODD, C. H. *The Epistle of Paul to the Romans.* MNTC. London: Hodder & Stoughton, 1932.

DUNN, J. D. G. *Romans.* 2 vols. WBC 38A, B. Dallas: Word, 1988.

FITZMYER, J. A. *Romans.* AB 33. New York: Doubleday, 1993.

KÄSEMANN, E. *Commentary on Romans.* Trans. G. W. Bromiley. Grand Rapids: Eerdmans, 1980.

LEENHARDT, F. J. *The Epistle to the Romans: A Commentary.* Trans. H. KNIGHT. London: Lutterworth, 1961.

MOO, D. *The Epistle to the Romans.* NICNT. Grand Rapids: Eerdmans, 1996.

MORRIS, L. *The Epistle to the Romans.* Grand Rapids: Eerdmans, 1988.

MURRAY, J. *The Epistle to the Romans.* 2 vols. in 1. NICNT. Grand Rapids: Eerdmans, 1968.

SANDAY, W., and A. C. HEADLAM. *A Critical and Exegetical Commentary on the Epistle to the Romans.* 5th ed. Edinburgh: T. & T. Clark, 1902.

SCHLATTER, A. *Romans: The Righteousness of God.* Trans. S. S. SCHATZMANN. Peabody, Mass.: Hendrickson, 1995.

STUHLMACHER, P. *Paul's Letter to the Romans: A Commentary.* Louisville: Westminster John Knox, 1994.

ZIESLER, J. *Paul's Letter to the Romans.* London: SCM, 1989.

F. Philippians

BEARE, F. W. *A Commentary on the Epistle to the Philippians.* BNTC. Peabody, Mass.: Hendrickson, 1959.

COLLANGE, J.-F. *The Epistle of Saint Paul to the Philippians.* Trans. A. W. HEATHCOTE. London: Epworth, 1979.

FEE, G. D. *Paul's Letter to the Philippians.* NICNT. Grand Rapids: Eerdmans, 1995.

HAWTHORNE, G. F. *Philippians.* WBC 43. Waco, Tex.: Word, 1983.

LIGHTFOOT, J. B. *St. Paul's Epistle to the Philippians.* 1913. Repr., Peabody, Mass.: Hendrickson, 1995.

MARTIN, R. P. *Philippians.* NCB. Grand Rapids: Eerdmans, 1976.

O'BRIEN, P. T. *The Epistle to the Philippians.* NIGTC. Grand Rapids: Eerdmans, 1991.

PLUMMER, A. *A Commentary on St. Paul's Epistle to the Philippians.* London: Robert Scott, 1919.

SILVA, M. *Philippians.* Chicago: Moody, 1988.

G. Colossians and Philemon

ABBOTT, T. K. *A Critical and Exegetical Commentary on the Epistles to the Ephesians and to the Colossians.* ICC. Edinburgh: T. & T. Clark, 1897.

BARTH, M., and H. Blanke. *Colossians.* AB 34B. New York: Doubleday, 1994.

BRUCE, F. F. *The Epistles to the Colossians, to Philemon, and to the Ephesians.* NICNT. Grand Rapids: Eerdmans, 1984.

CALLAHAN, A. D. *Embassy of Onesimus: The Letter of Paul to Philemon.* Valley Forge, Penn.: Trinity Press International, 1997.

DUNN, J. D. G. *The Epistles to the Colossians and to Philemon.* NIGTC. Grand Rapids: Eerdmans, 1996.

HARRIS, M. J. *Colossians and Philemon.* Exegetical Guide to the Greek NT. Grand Rapids: Eerdmans, 1991.

LOHSE, E. *Colossians and Philemon.* Hermeneia. Philadelphia: Fortress, 1971.

LIGHTFOOT, J. B. *St. Paul's Epistles to the Colossians and to Philemon.* 1897. Repr., Peabody, Mass.: Hendrickson, 1995.

MOULE, C. F. D. *The Epistles to the Colossians and to Philemon.* CGTC. Cambridge: Cambridge University Press, 1957.

O'BRIEN, P. T. *Colossians, Philemon.* WBC 44. Waco, Tex.: Word, 1982.

POKORNÝ, P. *Colossians: A Commentary.* Trans. S. S. Schatzmann. Peabody, Mass.: Hendrickson, 1991.

SCHWEIZER, E. *The Letter to the Colossians: A Commentary.* Trans. A. Chester. Minneapolis: Augsburg, 1976.

WRIGHT, N. T. *Colossians and Philemon.* TNTC. Grand Rapids: Eerdmans, 1986.

H. Ephesians

ABBOTT, T. K. *A Critical and Exegetical Commentary on the Epistles to the Ephesians and to the Colossians.* ICC. Edinburgh: T. & T. Clark, 1897.

BRUCE, F. F. *The Epistles to the Colossians, to Philemon, and to the Ephesians.* NICNT. Grand Rapids: Eerdmans, 1984.

BARTH, M. *Ephesians.* 2 vols. AB 34, 34A. Garden City, N.Y.: Doubleday, 1974.

KITCHEN, M. *Ephesians.* London: Routledge, 1994.

LINCOLN, A. T. *Ephesians.* WBC 42. Dallas: Word, 1990.

MITTON, C. L. *Ephesians.* NCB. Grand Rapids: Eerdmans, 1973.

ROBINSON, J. A. *St. Paul's Epistle to the Ephesians.* 2d ed. London: Macmillan, 1904.

SCHNACKENBURG, R. *The Epistle to the Ephesians: A Commentary.* Trans. H. HERON. Edinburgh: T. & T. Clark, 1991.

I. Pastoral Epistles

DIBELIUS, M., and H. CONZELMANN. *The Pastoral Epistles.* Hermeneia. Philadelphia: Fortress, 1972.

FEE, G. D. *1 and 2 Timothy, Titus.* NIBC. Peabody, Mass.: Hendrickson, 1988.

GUTHRIE, D. *The Pastoral Epistles.* Rev. ed. TNTC. Grand Rapids: Eerdmans, 1990.

HANSON, A. T. *The Pastoral Epistles.* NCB. Grand Rapids: Eerdmans, 1982.

KELLY, J. N. D. *A Commentary on the Pastoral Epistles.* BNTC. Peabody, Mass.: Hendrickson, 1963.

KNIGHT, G. W., III. *The Pastoral Epistles.* NIGTC. Grand Rapids: Eerdmans, 1992.

LOCK, W. *A Critical and Exegetical Commentary on the Pastoral Epistles (1 and II Timothy and Titus).* ICC. Edinburgh: T. & T. Clark, 1924.

PARRY, R. St. *The Pastoral Epistles.* Cambridge: Cambridge University Press, 1920.

QUINN, J. D. *The Letter to Titus.* AB 35. New York: Doubleday, 1990.

SIMPSON, E. K. *The Pastoral Epistles.* London: Tyndale, 1954.

pages 409–412

1. See D. Trobisch, *Paul's Letter Collection: Tracing the Origins* (Minneapolis: Fortress, 1994), 6–27. These early manuscripts include Codices Sinaiticus, Alexandrinus, and Vaticanus.

2. On the history of the discussion, see W. G. Kümmel, *The New Testament: The History of the Investigation of Its Problems* (trans. S. McL. Gilmour and H. C. Kee; Nashville: Abingdon, 1972), esp. 133–37; S. Neill and T. Wright, *The Interpretation of the New Testament 1861–1986* (2d ed.; Oxford: Oxford University Press, 1988), 20–29.

3. Reference will be made to our knowledge of the various cities to which Paul writes. A useful further guide is S. E. Johnson, *Paul the Apostle and His Cities* (Wilmington, Del.: Glazier, 1987).

4. For a more complete discussion of the various views of the Pauline opponents, see J. J. Gunther, *St. Paul's Opponents and Their Background: A Study of Apocalyptic and Jewish Sectarian Teaching* (NovTSup 35; Leiden: Brill, 1973); E. E. Ellis, "Paul and His Opponents: Trends in the Research," in *Prophecy and Hermeneutic in Early Christianity: New Testament Essays* (WUNT 18; Tübingen: Mohr–Siebeck, 1978; repr., Grand Rapids: Eerdmans, 1978), 80–115; and the methodological statements found in J. L. Sumney, *Identifying Paul's Opponents: The Question of Method in 2 Corinthians* (JSNTSup 40; Sheffield: JSOT Press, 1990), esp. 75–12; and J. M. G. Barclay, "Mirror-Reading a Polemical Letter: Galatians as a Test Case," *JSNT* 31 (1987): 73–93. Not all of the letters involve opponents in a combative sense.

5. R. A. Cole, *The Epistle of Paul to the Galatians* (TNTC; Grand Rapids: Eerdmans, 1965), 11, cited in R. P. Martin, *New Testament Foundations: A Guide for Christian Students* (2 vols.; 2d ed.; Grand Rapids: Eerdmans, 1986), 2:145.

6. W. G. Kümmel, *Introduction to the New Testament* (trans. H. C. Kee; 17th ed. Nashville: Abingdon, 1975), 304. See J. B. Lightfoot, *The Epistle of St. Paul to the Galatians* (1865; repr., Peabody, Mass.: Hendrickson, 1993), 57–62, for evidence of its use in the church.

7. J. C. O'Neill, *The Recovery of Paul's Letter to the Galatians* (London: SPCK, 1972).

8. See W. M. Ramsay, *The Church in the Roman Empire before A.D. 170* (4th ed.; London: Hodder & Stoughton, 1895), 97–111; *A Historical Commentary on St. Paul's Epistle to the Galatians* (London: Hodder & Stoughton, 1899); and "Galatia," *HDB* 2:81–89. Ramsay's view has been strongly endorsed by S. Mitchell, "Galatia," *ABD* 2:870–72, esp. 871; C. Breytenbach, *Paulus und Barnabas in der Provinz Galatien: Studien zu Apostelgeschichte 13f.; 16,6; 18,32 und den Adressaten des Galaterbriefes* (AGJU 38; Leiden: Brill, 1996), 99–173, with excellent plates; and J. M. Scott, *Paul and the Nations: The Old Testament and Jewish Background of Paul's Mission to the Nations with Special Reference to the Destination of Galatians* (WUNT 84; Tübingen: Mohr–Siebeck, 1995), esp. 181–215, who shifts the debate to reflect an OT understanding of who the Galatians were.

9. See Lightfoot, *Galatians*, 18–35; J. Moffatt, *An Introduction to the Literature of the New Testament* (3d ed.; Edinburgh: T. & T. Clark, 1918), 90–101; Kümmel, *Introduction to the New Testament*, 296–98; H. D. Betz, *Galatians* (Hermeneia; Philadelphia: Fortress, 1979), 3–5; J. L. Martyn, *Galatians* (AB 33A; New York: Doubleday, 1997), 15–17.

10. E. DeW. Burton, *A Critical and Exegetical Commentary on the Epistle to the Galatians* (ICC; Edinburgh: T. & T. Clark, 1921), xxix–xliv; F. F. Bruce, *The Epistle to the Galatians* (NIGTC; Grand Rapids: Eerdmans, 1982), 3–18; Martin, *Foundations*, 2:148–52; R. N. Longenecker,

Galatians (WBC 41; Dallas: Word, 1990), lxi–lxxii, who provides an excellent summary of the issues.

11. We should also note that Lystra and Derbe were visited by Paul after being chased out of Iconium (Acts 14:6).

12. On this terminology, see T. Mommsen, *The Provinces of the Roman Empire from Caesar to Diocletian* (trans. W. P. Dickson; 2 vols.; London: Macmillan, 1909), 1:252–56.

13. See S. E. Porter, *Verbal Aspect in the Greek of the New Testament, with Reference to Tense and Mood* (SBG 1; New York: Lang, 1989), 385–87.

14. R. Wallace and W. Williams, *The Acts of the Apostles* (London: Duckworth, 1993), 23, citing no. 1017 from H. Dessau, *Inscriptiones latinae selectae* (Leipzig: Weidmann, 1892–1916).

15. Wallace and Williams, *The Acts of the Apostles*, 74–75.

16. On the dating of Galatians, see J. C. Hurd, *The Origin of I Corinthians* (New York: Seabury, 1965), esp. 18 for a useful chart.

17. R. H. Fuller, *A Critical Introduction to the New Testament* (London: Duckworth, 1966), 26; M. Silva, *Explorations in Exegetical Method: Galatians as a Test Case* (Grand Rapids: Baker, 1996), 129–39.

18. On the issue of Pauline autobiography in Galatians, see G. Lyons, *Pauline Autobiography: Toward a New Understanding* (SBLDS 73; Atlanta: Scholars Press, 1985).

19. See D. Guthrie, *New Testament Introduction* (Downers Grove, Ill.: InterVarsity, 1970), 458–65, for discussion of these issues.

20. See N. Taylor, *Paul, Antioch, and Jerusalem: A Study in Relationships and Authority in Earliest Christianity* (JSNTSup 66; Sheffield: JSOT Press, 1992), 139.

21. See Longenecker, *Galatians*, lxxxviii–c; and J. D. G. Dunn, *The Theology of Paul's Letter to the Galatians* (New Testament Theology; Cambridge: Cambridge University Press, 1993).

22. See M. Luther, *A Commentary on St. Paul's Epistle to the Galatians* (ed. J. P. Fallowes; trans. E. Middleton; London: Harrison Trust, n.d.); Lightfoot, *Galatians*, 29–30; C. K. Barrett, *Paul: An Introducton to His Thought* (London: Chapman, 1994), 26–33; cf. J. Munck, *Paul and the Salvation of Mankind* (Atlanta: John Knox, 1959), 87–134, who contends that the problem was Gentile Judaizers. See also G. F. Howard, *Paul: Crisis in Galatia—a Study in Early Christian Theology* (SNTSMS 35; Cambridge: Cambridge University Press, 1979), 1–20, who argues that the Judaizers were not opposed to Paul, although he was to them.

23. See G. W. Hansen, *Abraham in Galatians: Epistolary and Rhetorical Contexts* (JSNTSup 29; Sheffield: JSOT Press, 1989).

24. Cf. Bruce, *Galatians*, 24–25.

25. Cf. W. Schmithals, *Paul and the Gnostics* (trans. J. Steely; Nashville: Abingdon, 1972), 13–64, who concludes that Paul's opponents were Jewish-Christian gnostics. This position has not been widely accepted.

26. See J. M. G. Barclay, *Obeying the Truth: A Study of Paul's Ethics in Galatians* (Edinburgh: T. & T. Clark, 1988).

27. See R. Jewett, "The Agitators and the Gentile Congregation," *NTS* 17 (1970–1971): 198–212; accepted by Martin, *Foundations*, 2:154–56.

28. See F. J. Matera, "The Culmination of Paul's Argument to the Galatians: Gal. 5.1–6.17," *JSNT* 32 (1988): 59–91.

29. For a thorough annotated bibliography of work on Thessalonians, see J. A. D. Weima and S. E. Porter, *An Annotated Bibliography of 1 and 2 Thessalonians* (NTTS 26; Leiden: Brill, 1998).

30. See H. L. Hendrix, "Thessalonica," *ABD* 6:523–27.

31. See G. H. R. Horsley, "The Politarchs," in *The Book of Acts in Its Graeco-Roman Setting* (ed. D. W. J. Gill and C. Gempf; vol. 2 of *The*

pages 412–416

Book of Acts in Its First Century Setting; ed. B. W. Winter; Grand Rapids: Eerdmans, 1994), 419–31; *NewDocs* 2:34–35.

32. On the Godfearers, see M. C. De Boer, "God-Fearers in Luke–Acts," in *Luke's Literary Achievement: Collected Essays* (ed. C. M. Tuckett; JSNTSup 116; Sheffield: Sheffield Academic Press, 1995), 50–71. See no. 42, below.

33. W. M. Ramsay, *St. Paul the Traveller and the Roman Citizen* (London: Hodder & Stoughton, 1895), 228.

34. See L. Morris, *The First and Second Epistles to the Thessalonians* (rev. ed.; Grand Rapids: Eerdmans, 1991), 3.

35. See R. Jewett, *The Thessalonian Correspondence: Pauline Rhetoric and Millenarian Piety* (FFNT; Philadelphia: Fortress, 1986), 3.

36. See Moffatt, *Introduction,* 69–70.

37. Paul's reference to himself as a servant in 1 Cor 3:5 and 4:1 may also show a stage of development in this terminology, although the contexts of these passages are not parallel to the more technical uses in the examples above.

38. The question of how evidence is evaluated regarding interpolations is ably raised by W. O. Walker Jr., "The Burden of Proof in Identifying Interpolations in Pauline Letters," *NTS* 33 (1987): 610–18.

39. A recent defense of the authenticity of 1 Thess 2:14–16 is C. J. Schlueter, *Filling up the Measure: Polemical Hyperbole in 1 Thessalonians 2.14–16* (JSNTSup 98; Sheffield: Sheffield Academic Press, 1994).

40. See Jewett, *Thessalonian Correspondence,* 36–42; I. H. Marshall, *1 and 2 Thessalonians* (NCB; Grand Rapids: Eerdmans, 1983), 11–13.

41. A. T. Kraabel, "The Disappearance of the 'God-Fearers,' " *Numen* 28 (1981): 113–26.

42. P. W. van der Horst, "A New Altar of a Godfearer?" in *Hellenism–Judaism–Christianity: Essays on Their Interaction* (2d ed.; Leuven: Peeters, 1998), 65–71. See also De Boer, "God-Fearers in Luke–Acts."

43. See A. J. Malherbe, " 'Gentle as a Nurse': The Cynic Background to 1 Thessalonians 2," in *Paul and the Popular Philosophers* (Minneapolis: Fortress, 1989), 35–48. On Paul's relation to the church in Thessalonica, see A. J. Malherbe, *Paul and the Thessalonians: The Philosophic Tradition of Pastoral Care* (Philadelphia: Fortress, 1987).

44. See E. Best, *A Commentary on the First and Second Epistles to the Thessalonians* (2d ed.; BNTC; Peabody, Mass.: Hendrickson, 1977), 33–34, for a survey of the opinions.

45. See A. J. Malherbe, "Exhortation in First Thessalonians," *NovT* 25 (1983): 238–56.

46. F. F. Bruce, *1 and 2 Thessalonians* (WBC 45; Waco, Tex.: Word, 1982), 83.

47. Ibid., 102–103. Cf. M. R. Cosby, "Hellenistic Formal Receptions and Paul's Use of ΑΠΑΝΤΗΣΙΣ in 1 Thessalonians 4:17," *BBR* 4 (1994): 15–33; response by R. H. Gundry, "A Brief Note on 'Hellenistic Formal Receptions and Paul's Use of ΑΠΑΝΤΗΣΙΣ in 1 Thessalonians 4:17,' " *BBR* 6 (1996): 39–41.

48. See P. T. O'Brien, *The Epistle to the Philippians* (NIGTC; Grand Rapids: Eerdmans, 1991), 135–37.

49. See Moffatt, *Introduction,* 82.

50. W. Trilling, *Untersuchungen zum zweiten Thessalonicherbrief* (Leipzig: St. Benno, 1972), accepted by, e.g., H. Koester, *Introduction to the New Testament* (2 vols.; FFNT; Philadelphia: Fortress, 1982; 2d ed. of vol. 1, 1995), 2:241–46; rejected, e.g., by Marshall, *Thessalonians,* 29–45. An excellent summary and evaluation is found in Jewett, *Thessalonian Correspondence,* 10–18. As Jewett clearly indicates, not all of the arguments are worth considering.

pages 416–422

51. See Best, *Thessalonians*, 51.
52. See Bruce, *Thessalonians*, 179–88; G. C. Jenks, *The Origins and Early Development of the Antichrist Myth* (BZNW 59; Berlin: de Gruyter, 1991), for surveys of the positions.
53. See Marshall, *Thessalonians*, 26–27, who lists the following positions.
54.. A. Harnack, "Das Problem des zweiten Thessalonicherbriefes," *SPAW.PH* 31 (1910): 560–78.
55. Schmithals, *Paul and the Gnostics*, 212–13, refuted by Best, *Thessalonians*, 45–50.
56. See B. Childs, *The New Testament as Canon: An Introduction* (Philadelphia: Fortress, 1985), 371.
57. Wanamaker, *Thessalonians*, 37–45.
58. Kümmel, *Introduction*, 275.
59. G. D. Fee, *The First Epistle to the Corinthians* (NICNT; Grand Rapids: Eerdmans, 1987), 3.
60. These texts and others are cited in J. Murphy-O'Connor, *St. Paul's Corinth: Texts and Archaeology* (Wilmington, Del.: Michael Glazier, 1983); cf. also his "Corinth," *ABD* 1:1134–39.
61. On the social structure of Corinth, especially concerning financial issues, see P. Marshall, *Enmity in Corinth: Social Conventions in Paul's Relations with the Corinthians* (WUNT 2.23; Tübingen: Mohr–Siebeck, 1987); J. K. Chow, *Patronage and Power: A Study of Social Networks in Corinth* (JSNTSup 75; Sheffield: JSOT Press, 1992); D. W. J. Gill, "In Search of the Social Élite in the Corinthian Church," *TynB* 44 (2, 1993): 323–37; and A. D. Clarke, *Secular and Christian Leadership in Corinth: A Socio-historical and Exegetical Study of 1 Corinthains 1–6* (AGJU 18; Leiden: Brill, 1993).
62. D. W. J. Gill, "Erastus the Aedile," *TynB* 40 (2, 1989): 293–301.
63. See K. Quast, *The Corinthian Correspondence: An Introduction* (New York: Paulist, 1994), 20.
64. See ibid., 21, for descriptions of some of these.
65. H. Conzelmann, *1 Corinthians* (Hermeneia; Philadelphia: Fortress, 1972), 12.
66. See W. L. Willis, *Idol Meat in Corinth: The Pauline Argument in 1 Corinthians 8 and 10* (SBLDS 68; Chico, Calif.: Scholars Press, 1985); P. D. Gooch, *Dangerous Food: 1 Corinthians 8–10 in Its Context* (Waterloo, Ont.: Wilfrid Laurier University Press, 1993).
67. A. Deissmann, *Light from the Ancient East* (trans. L. R. N. Strachan; 4th ed.; 1927; repr., Peabody, Mass.: Hendrickson, 1995), 16.
68. Discussion of the issues regarding the Corinthian letters in an exegetical context is found in S. E. Porter, "Exegesis of the Pauline Letters, Including the Deutero-Pauline Letters," in *Handbook to Exegesis of the New Testament* (ed. S. E. Porter; NTTS 25; Leiden: Brill, 1997), 512–23 followed here.
69. See M. E. Thrall, *A Critical and Exegetical Commentary on the Second Epistle to the Corinthians* (2 vols.; ICC; Edinburgh: T. & T. Clark, 1994–), 1:25–36.
70. See Thrall, *Second Corinthians*, 5–18.
71. See ibid., 18–20.
72. Hurd, *1 Corinthians*, 47.
73. See Gooch, *Dangerous Food*, 57–58.
74. See, e.g., A. C. Wire, *The Corinthian Women Prophets: A Reconstruction through Paul's Rhetoric* (Minneapolis: Fortress, 1990).
75. See Fee, *First Corinthians*, 33.
76. See ibid., 699.

pages 424–436

77. See M. M. Mitchell, "Concerning PERI DE in 1 Corinthians," *NovT* 31 (1989): 229–56. Paul also uses conditional clauses (1 Cor 7:17; 13:1; 15:12), a knowledge formula (10:1), a strong adversative (15:35), and an emphatic cataphoric pronoun (11:17; 15:50).

78. See V. L. Wimbush, *Paul, the Worldly Ascetic: Response to the World and Self-Understanding according to 1 Corinthians 7* (Macon, Ga.: Mercer University Press, 1987); cf. W. Deming, *Paul on Marriage and Celibacy: The Hellenistic Background of 1 Corinthians 7* (SNTSMS 83; Cambridge: Cambridge University Press, 1995).

79. See W. A. Meeks, *The First Urban Christians: The Social World of the Apostle Paul* (New Haven: Yale University Press, 1983), 98.

80. For a recent survey, see J. D. G. Dunn, *1 Corinthians* (NT Guides; Sheffield: Sheffield Academic Press, 1995), 27–89.

81. F. C. Baur, "Die Christuspartei in der korinthischen Gemeinde, der Gegensatz des petrinischen und paulinischen Christentums in der alten Kirche, der Apostel Petrus in Rom," *Tübinger Zeitschrift für Theologie* 4 (1831): 61–206; repr. in *Historisch-kritische Untersuchungen zum Neuen Testament* (Stuttgart: Frommann, 1963), 1–146. See also F. C. Baur, *The Church History of the First Three Centuries* (trans. A. Menzies; 2 vols.; London: Williams & Norgate, 1878–1879), esp. 1:44–152.

82. M. D. Goulder, *Early Christian Conflict at Corinth* (Peabody, Mass.: Hendrickson, forthcoming).

83. See J. Painter, "Paul and the Πνευματικοί at Corinth," in *Paul and Paulinism: Essays in Honour of C. K. Barrett* (ed. M. D. Hooker and S. G. Wilson; London: SPCK, 1985), 239–40.

84. See, e.g., W. Schmithals, *Gnosticism in Corinth: An Investigation of the Letters to the Corinthians* (trans. J. E. Steely; Nashville: Abingdon, 1971).

85. R. McL. Wilson, "Gnosis at Corinth," in *Paul and Paulinism* (ed. Hooker and Wilson), 102–14; cf. also Painter, "Paul," 240–46.

86. See B. A. Pearson, *The Pneumatikos-Psychikos Terminology* (SBLDS 12; Missoula, Mont.: Scholars Press, 1973).

87. See A. C. Thiselton, "Realized Eschatology at Corinth," *NTS* 24 (1977–1978): 510–26, for the standard discussion of this issue.

88. See G. W. Bowersock, ed., *Approaches to the Second Sophistic* (University Park, Penn.: American Philological Association, 1974).

89. Cf. D. Litfin, *St. Paul's Theology of Proclamation: 1 Corinthians 1–4 and Greco-Roman Rhetoric* (SNTSMS 79; Cambridge: Cambridge University Press, 1994), esp. 109–34.

90. C. K. Barrett, "Christianity at Corinth," in *Essays on Paul* (Philadelphia: Westminster, 1981), 3–6.

91. Fee, *First Corinthians*, 6.

92. Cf. L. L. Belleville, "Continuity and Discontinuity: A Fresh Look at 1 Corinthians in the Light of First-Century Epistolary Forms and Conventions," *EvQ* 59 (1987): 15–37, esp. 23–24.

93. Kümmel, *Introduction*, 287.

94. See Thrall, *Second Corinthians*, 3–49, for a survey of opinions, with a tabulation on pp. 47–49.

95. Besides Thrall (*Second Corinthians*, 25–36), who surveys opinion, for a bibliography see J. A. Fitzmyer, "Qumran and the Interpolated Paragraph in 2 Cor. 6.14–7.1," *CBQ* 23 (1961): 271–80; P. B. Duff, "The Mind of the Redactor: 2 Cor. 6:14–7:1 in Its Secondary Context," *NovT* 35 (1993): 160–80; W. J. Webb, *Returning Home: New Covenant and Second Exodus as the Context for 2 Corinthians 6.14–7.1* (JSNTSup 85; Sheffield: JSOT Press, 1993); M. D. Goulder, "2 Cor. 6:14–7:1 as an Integral Part of 2 Corinthians," *NovT* 36 (1994): 47–57.

pages 437–441

96. "Mismatched, unequally yoked" (ἑτεροζυγέω, *heterozygeō*), "partnership, share" (μετοχή, *metochē*), "fellowship, harmony" (συμφώνησις, *symphōnēsis*), "Beliar," "agreement" (συγκατάθεσις, *synkatathesis*), "walk" (ἐμπεριπατέω, *emperipateō*), "welcome, receive" (εἰσδέχομαι, *eisdechomai*), "almighty" (παντοκράτωρ, *pantokratōr*), and "defilement" (μολυσμός, *molysmos*).

97. Besides Thrall (*Second Corinthians*, 5–20), who surveys opinion, for a bibliography see L. L. Welborn, "The Identification of 2 Corinthians 10–13 with the 'Letter of Tears,' " *NovT* 37 (1995): 138–53.

98. H. Lietzmann with W. G. Kümmel, *An die Korinther I–II* (HNT; Tübingen: Mohr–Siebeck, 1923), cited in Martin, *Foundations*, 2:182.

99. Besides Thrall, who surveys opinion, see J. M. Gilchrist, "Paul and the Corinthians—the Sequence of Letters and Visits," *JSNT* 34 (1988): 47–69, esp. 50–51; V. D. Verbrugge, *Paul's Style of Church Leadership Illustrated by His Instructions to the Corinthians on the Collection* (San Francisco: Mellen Research University Press, 1992), esp. 100–104; S. K. Stowers, "Per men gar and the Integrity of 2 Cor. 8 and 9," *NovT* 32 (1990): 340–48; D. A. DeSilva, "Measuring Penultimate against Ultimate Reality: An Investigation of the Integrity and Argumentation of 2 Corinthians," *JSNT* 52 (1993): 41–70.

100. See Sumney, *Identifying Paul's Opponents*, esp. 13–73 for a summary of the positions noted below, and 187–91 for his own conclusions.

pages 441–451

101. Baur, "Die Christuspartei," passim; C. K. Barrett, "Paul's Opponents in 2 Corinthians," 60–86, and "ΨΕΥΔΑΠΟΣΤΟΛΟΙ (2 Cor. 11.13)," 87–107, in *Essays on Paul*; Gunther, *St. Paul's Opponents*, 1–94.

102. R. Bultmann, *The Second Letter to the Corinthians* (trans. R. A. Harrisville; Minneapolis: Augsburg, 1985); Schmithals, *Gnosis in Corinth*.

103. D. Georgi, *The Opponents of Paul in Second Corinthians* (Philadelphia: Fortress, 1986); contra C. Holladay, *Theios Aner in Hellenistic-Judaism: A Critique of the Use of This Category in New Testament Christology* (SBLDS 40; Missoula, Mont.: Scholars Press, 1977).

104. For a survey of opinion, see R. Pickett, *The Cross of Christ: The Social Significance of the Death of Jesus* (JSNTSup 143; Sheffield: Sheffield Academic Press, 1997), 39–74.

105. Cf. R. P. Martin, "The Opponents of Paul in 2 Corinthians: An Old Issue Revisited," in *Tradition and Interpretation in the New Testament: Essays in Honor of E. Earle Ellis* (ed. G. F. Hawthorne with O. Betz; Grand Rapids: Eerdmans, 1987), 279–87.

106. F. F. Bruce, *Romans* (rev. ed.; TNTC; Grand Rapids: Eerdmans, 1985), 56–58.

107. Ibid., 9. For an interpretation that questions this use of Romans, see S. K. Stowers, *A Rereading of Romans: Justice, Jews, and Gentiles* (New Haven: Yale University Press, 1994).

108. Kümmel, *Introduction*, 314. Kümmel goes further in n. 30, saying that claims that there are "individual interpolated sections" such as Rom 13:1–7 (he cites P. N. Harrison, C. H. Talbert, E. Barnikol, and J. Kallas; others could be cited as well) are unproved.

109. See J. C. O'Neill, *Paul's Letter to the Romans* (Harmondsworth, England: Penguin, 1975), 264–71, for the reconstructed letter.

110. W. Schmithals, *Der Römerbrief als historisches Problem* (StNT 9; Gütersloh: Mohn, 1975), esp. 180–211.

111. See Moffatt, *Introduction*, 148–49.

112. Even if 2 Timothy is not authentically Pauline, it is possible that the Erastus mentioned is the same one and that the early church remembered where he lived.

113. See J. S. Jeffers, *Conflict at Rome: Social Order and Hierarchy in Early Christianity* (Minneapolis: Fortress, 1991); cf. J. F. Hall, "Rome," *ABD* 5:830–34.

114. See Georgi, *Opponents*, 83, who says that there were anywhere from four to six million Jews in the Roman world, approximately one-seventh of the total population of the empire. Three times as many lived in the Diaspora as lived in Palestine.

115. See H. J. Leon, *The Jews of Ancient Rome* (rev. ed.; Peabody, Mass.: Hendrickson, 1995), esp. 135–66; cf. W. Wiefel, "The Jewish Community in Ancient Rome and the Origins of Roman Christianity," in *The Romans Debate* (ed. K. P. Donfried; 2d ed.; Peabody, Mass.: Hendrickson, 1991), 85–101.

116. See K. R. Bradley, *Slaves and Masters in the Roman Empire: A Study in Social Control* (New York: Oxford University Press, 1987), 113 n. 1, who cites other evidence as well: Tacitus, *Ann.* 14.42–45; Pliny, *Ep.* 8.14.

117. See G. Lüdemann, *Paul, Apostle to the Gentiles: Studies in Chronology* (trans. F. S. Jones; Philadelphia: Fortress, 1984), 164–71, among others.

118. Bruce, *Romans*, 17.

119. See A. N. Sherwin-White, *Roman Society and Roman Law in the New Testament* (Oxford: Clarendon, 1963), 110–12; Jeffers, *Conflict at Rome*, 16–17; E. T. Salmon, *A History of the Roman World from 30 B.C. to A.D. 138* (6th ed.; London: Routledge, 1968), 175–82, part of a chapter on Nero.

pages 451–455

120. See B. Reicke, *The New Testament Era: The World of the Bible from 500 B.C. to A.D. 100* (Philadelphia: Fortress, 1968), 245–51.

121. Martin, *Foundations*, 2:34–35, 138–41.

122. P. S. Minear, *The Obedience of Faith: The Purpose of Paul in the Epistle to the Romans* (London: SCM, 1971).

123. F. Watson, *Paul, Judaism, and the Gentiles: A Sociological Approach* (SNTSMS 56; Cambridge: Cambridge University Press, 1986), 94–98.

124. See C. E. B. Cranfield, *A Critical and Exegetical Commentary on the Epistle to the Romans* (2 vols.; ICC; Edinburgh: T. & T. Clark, 1975–1979), 1:17–22. Those connected with the predominantly Jewish view are—according to Cranfield—Baur, Zahn, and W. Manson, and those connected with the predominantly Gentile view are Sanday and Headlam, Denney, Barrett, and Kümmel. See also A. J. Guerra, *Romans and the Apologetic Tradition: The Purpose, Genre, and Audience of Paul's Letter* (SNTSMS 81; Cambridge: Cambridge University Press, 1995), 22–42, who argues for predominantly Jewish Christians, but because of the protreptic literary genre (see no. 5, below); J. C. Walters, *Ethnic Issues in Paul's Letter to the Romans: Changing Self-Definitions in Earliest Roman Christianity* (Valley Forge, Penn.: Trinity Press International, 1993), 56–66; and M. D. Nanos, *The Mystery of Romans: The Jewish Context of Paul's Letter* (Minneapolis: Fortress, 1996).

125. Contra Lüdemann, *Paul*, 262, who dates Romans to A.D. 51/52. See J. D. G. Dunn, *Romans*, vol. 1 (WBC 38A; Dallas: Word, 1988), xliii-xliv, for the consensus.

126. See P. Lampe, "The Roman Christians of Romans 16," in *Romans Debate* (ed. Donfried), 216–30.

127. For these issues treated in an exegetical context, see Porter, "Exegesis of the Pauline Letters," 524–31.

128. On the spread of Latin, see M. Cary, *A History of Rome down to the Reign of Constantine* (2d ed.; London: Macmillan, 1967), 463, 587. Ramsay has been followed by many in his hypothesis that Paul spoke Latin (*St. Paul the Traveller and the Roman Citizen*, 225).

129. See the summary of various positions in A. J. M. Wedderburn, *The Reasons for Romans* (Edinburgh: T. & T. Clark, 1988); L. A. Jervis, *The Purpose of Romans: A Comparative Letter Structure Investigation* (JSNTSup 55; Sheffield: JSOT Press, 1991); R. Morgan, *Romans* (Sheffield: Sheffield Academic Press, 1995), 60–77.

130. J. C. Beker, *Paul the Apostle: The Triumph of God in Life and Thought* (Philadelphia: Fortress, 1980), 23–36; "Paul's Theology: Consistent or Inconsistent?" *NTS* 34 (1988): 364–77.

131. F. C. Baur, "Über Zweck und Veranlassung des Römerbriefs und die damit zusammenhängenden Verhältnisse der römischen Gemeinde," *Tübinger Zeitschrift für Theologie* 3 (1836): 59–178; repr. in *Historisch-kritische Untersuchungen zum Neuen Testament*, 147–266, esp. 153–66. See also his *Paul the Apostle of Jesus Christ: His Life and Work, His Epistles and His Doctrine* (2 vols.; 2d ed.; London: Williams & Norgate, 1876), 1:331–65.

132. D. J. Moo, *The Epistle to the Romans* (NICNT; Grand Rapids: Eerdmans, 1996), esp. 22–24; N. T. Wright, *The Climax of the Covenant: Christ and the Law in Pauline Theology* (Edinburgh: T. & T. Clark, 1991), 234.

133. J. A. Fitzmyer ("The Christology of the Epistle to the Romans," in *The Future of Christology* [ed. A. J. Malherbe and W. A. Meeks; Minneapolis: Fortress, 1993], 81–90) shows that it clearly is a major concern.

134. See A. J. B. Higgins, *The Lord's Supper in the New Testament* (SBT 6; London: SCM, 1952), 64–73.

135. T. W. Manson, "St. Paul's Letter to the Romans—and Others," in *Romans Debate* (ed. Donfried), 3–15. Possible support is now provided by Trobisch, *Paul's Letter Collection*, 72–73. See also H. Koester, "Ephesos in Early Christian Literature," in *Ephesos: Metropolis of Asia: An Interdisciplinary Approach to Its Archaeology, Religion, and Culture* (ed. H. Koester; Valley Forge, Pa.: Trinity Press International, 1995), 122–24.

136. G. Bornkamm, "The Letter to the Romans as Paul's Last Will and Testament," in *Romans Debate* (ed. Donfried), 16–28.

137. M. Kiley, *Colossians and Pseudepigraphy* (Sheffield: JSOT Press, 1986), 46.

138. J. Jervell, "The Letter to Jerusalem," in *Romans Debate* (ed. Donfried), 53–64.

139. F. F. Bruce, "The Romans Debate—Continued," ibid., 175–93; A. J. M. Wedderburn, "Purpose and Occasion of Romans Again," ibid., 195–202; P. Stuhlmacher, "The Purpose of Romans," ibid., 231–42. On the apologetic or protreptic letter, see Guerra, *Romans and the Apologetic Tradition*, following D. E. Aune, "Romans as a *Logos Protreptikos*," in *Romans Debate* (ed. Donfried), 278–96.

140. G. Klein, "Paul's Purpose in Writing the Epistle to the Romans," in *Romans Debate* (ed. Donfried), 29–43.

141. Various forms of this view are held by R. Jewett, "Following the Argument of Romans," ibid., 265–77; W. S. Campbell, "Romans III as a Key to the Structure and Thought of Romans," ibid., 251–64, repr. in his *Paul's Gospel in an Intercultural Context* (Studies in the Intercultural History of Christianity 69; Frankfurt: Lang, 1992), 25–42; K. P. Donfried, "False Presuppositions in the Study of Romans," in *Romans Debate* (ed. Donfried), 102–24.

142. See Moo, *Romans*, 6, who includes a chart of the major manuscripts; cf. Bruce, *Romans*, 26–27, who quotes the ending of Codex Amiatinus.

143. See Lampe, "Roman Christians," 222–29.

144. See H. Gamble Jr., *The Textual History of the Letter to the Romans* (SD 42; Grand Rapids: Eerdmans, 1977), 127–42, esp. 141, who summarizes the various positions and their advocates.

pages 455–460

145. A recent advocate is J. A. Fitzmyer, *Romans* (AB 33; New York: Doubleday, 1993), 55–67, with bibliography.
146. J. B. Lightfoot, "The Structure and Destinaton of the Epistle to the Romans," in *Biblical Essays* (London: Macmillan, 1893), 287–320, 352–74, esp. 315–20; and, more recently, Gamble, *Textual History*, 115–24.
147. See K. Lake, *The Earlier Epistles of St. Paul: Their Motive and Origin* (London: Rivingtons, 1911), 350–70, who includes a detailed discussion of alternative hypotheses.
148. Manson, "St. Paul's Letter to the Romans," 5–14, followed by some more recent advocates, such as Martin, *Foundations*, 2:194–96.
149. E.g., Moffatt, *Introduction*, 135–39.
150. W. Sanday and A. C. Headlam, *A Critical and Exegetical Commentary on the Epistle to the Romans* (5th ed.; ICC; Edinburgh: T. & T. Clark, 1902), lxxxv–xcviii, esp. xcvi–xcviii; Bruce, *Romans*, 29.
151. See C. E. B. Cranfield, *A Critical and Exegetical Commentary on the Epistle to the Romans* (2 vols.; ICC; Edinburgh: T. & T. Clark, 1975–1979), 1:6–7, who cites the church fathers. Tertullian does not appear to know these two chapters in any of his writings.
152. Bruce, *Romans*, 29–30.
153. See Gamble, *Textual History*, 131, for a chart of various manuscripts and the placement of the doxology.

pages 460–463

154. See D. W. J. Gill, "Macedonia," in *Graeco-Roman Setting* (ed. Gill and Gempf), 397–417, esp. 411–13; R. P. Martin, *Philippians* (NCB; Grand Rapids: Eerdmans, 1976), 2–9; H. L. Hendrix, "Philippi," *ABD* 5:313–17; and P. Pilhofer, *Philippi. I. Die erste christliche Gemeinde Europas* (WUNT 87; Tübingen: Mohr–Siebeck, 1995), esp. on the inscriptional evidence.
155. On the army, see J. B. Campbell, *The Emperor and the Roman Army, 31 B.C.–A.D. 235* (Oxford: Clarendon, 1984).
156. See, e.g., an inscription from Neapolis, the seaport of Philippi (IGR 3.137), conveniently reprinted with other texts in L. R. Taylor, *The Divinity of the Roman Emperor* (Middletown, Conn.: American Philological Association, 1931; repr., Atlanta: Scholars Press, n.d.), 272.
157. See J. Gutmann, "Synagogue Origins: Theories and Facts," in *Ancient Synagogues: The State of Research* (BJS 22; Atlanta: Scholars Press, 1981), 3; I. Levinskaya, *The Book of Acts in Its Diaspora Setting* (vol. 5 of *The Book of Acts in Its First Century Setting*; ed. B. W. Winter; Grand Rapids: Eerdmans, 1996), 207–25. Some pertinent inscriptions are published in W. Horbury and D. Noy, eds., *Jewish Inscriptions of Graeco-Roman Egypt* (Cambridge: Cambridge University Press, 1992).
158. Henotheism is the worship of one god, recognizing that there may be other gods, as opposed to monotheism, which is the belief in the existence of only one god.
159. See C. J. Hemer, *The Book of Acts in Its Hellenistic Setting* (WUNT 49; Tübingen: Mohr–Siebeck, 1989; repr., Winona Lake, Ind.: Eisenbrauns, 1990), 231.
160. The reference to the days of Unleavened Bread appears to be an indication of the time of year. It is too vague to provide evidence of Jews at Philippi.
161. Kümmel, *Introduction*, 332.
162. See R. P. Martin, *Carmen Christi: Philippians 2:5–11 in Recent Interpretation and in the Setting of Early Christian Worship* (rev ed.; Grand Rapids: Eerdmans, 1983), who argues for pre-Pauline origins, for a survey of research; G. D. Fee, "Philippians 2:5–11: Hymn or Exalted Pauline Prose?" *BBR* 2 (1992): 29–46, who defends Pauline composi-

tion; S. Fowl, *The Story of Christ in the Ethics of Paul: An Analysis of the Function of the Hymnic Material in the Pauline Corpus* (JSNTSup 36; Sheffield: JSOT Press, 1990), 49–76, who emphasizes its ethical function over its compositional history.

163. For a concise summary of the issues and an argument for unity of 1:1–4:9, see J. T. Reed, "Philippians 3:1 and the Epistolary Hesitation Formulas: The Literary Integrity of Philippians, Again," *JBL* 115 (1996): esp. 63–90; cf. his *A Discourse Analysis of Philippians: Method and Rhetoric in the Debate over Literary Integrity* (JSNTSup 136; Sheffield: Sheffield Academic Press, 1997), 124–52.

164. D. E. Garland, "The Composition and Unity of Philippians: Some Neglected Literary Factors," *NovT* 37 (1985): 155 n. 50.

165. See G. W. Peterman, "'Thankless Thanks': The Epistolary Social Convention in Philippians 4:10–20," *TynB* 42 (2, 1991): 261–70; *Paul's Gift from Philippi: Conventions of Gift Exchange and Christian Giving* (SNTSMS 92; Cambridge: Cambridge University Press, 1997), esp. 212–61; cf. also B. J. Capper, "Paul's Dispute with Philippi: Understanding Paul's Argument in Phil 1–2 from His Thanks in 4.10–20," *TZ* 49 (1993): 193–214; and K. L. Berry, "The Function of Friendship Language in Philippians 4:10–20," in *Friendship, Flattery, and Frankness of Speech: Studies on Friendship in the New Testament World* (ed. J. T. Fitzgerald; NovTSup 82; Leiden: Brill, 1996), 107–24.

166. See, e.g., P.Oxy. 2149.5 (2d–3d cent. A.D.) and 1480.13 (A.D. 32), cited in Reed, "Philippians 3:1," 83 n. 82.

167. Cf. M. E. Thrall, *Greek Particles in the New Testament: Linguistic and Exegetical Studies* (NTTS 3; Leiden: Brill, 1962), 25–30, whose grammatical analysis, however, is influenced by her epistolary analysis; Gamble, *Textual History*, 146.

168. G. D. Kilpatrick, "ΒΛΕΠΕΤΕ, Philippians 3:2," in *In Memoriam Paul Kahle* (ed. M. Black and G. Fohrer; Berlin: Töpelmann, 1968), 146–48.

169. J. B. Lightfoot, *St. Paul's Epistle to the Philippians* (1913; repr., Peabody, Mass.: Hendrickson, 1993), 69–70, 143.

170. See T. Engberg-Pedersen, "Stoicism in Philippians," in *Paul in His Hellenistic Context* (ed. Eugberg-Pedersen; Edinburgh: T. & T. Clark, 1994), 258 n. 5.

171. P. Sellew, "Laodiceans and the Philippians Fragments Hypothesis," *HTR* 87 (1994): 17–28.

172. See D. Watson, "A Rhetorical Analysis of Philippians and Its Implications for the Unity Question," *NovT* 30 (1988): 57–88.

173. W. Schenk, *Die Philipperbriefe des Paulus: Ein Kommentar* (Stuttgart: Kohlhammer, 1984).

174. D. A. Black, "The Discourse Structure of Philippians: A Study in Textlinguistics," *NovT* 37 (1995): 16–49.

175. For an assessment of these issues, see Reed, *Discourse Analysis of Philippians*, esp. 34–122 on method.

176. Regardless of the date of 2 Peter (see ch. 11, sec. 4, below), it does give testimony to the regard—which probably began very early, as evidenced by the number kept by churches—for the Pauline Letters.

177. See G. F. Hawthorne, *Philippians* (WBC 43; Waco, Tex.: Word, 1983), xliv–xlvii, for a concise discussion of the passages; and V. Koperski, *The Knowledge of Christ Jesus My Lord: The High Christology of Philippians 3:7–11* (Kampen, Netherlands: Kok Pharos, 1996), esp. 113–32.

178. See R. Jewett, "Conflicting Movements in the Early Church as Reflected in Philippians," *NovT* 12 (1970): 362–90.

179. G. D. Fee, *Paul's Letter to the Philippians* (NICNT; Grand Rapids: Eerdmans, 1995), 9, 366–75.

pages 463–469

pages 469–477

180. See L. G. Bloomquist, *The Function of Suffering in Philippians* (JSNTSup 78; Sheffield: JSOT Press, 1993).

181. See M. Tellbe, "The Sociological Factors behind Philippians 3.1–11 and the Conflict at Philippi," *JSNT* 55 (1994): 97–121; B. W. Winter, *Seek the Welfare of the City: Christians as Benefactors and Citizens* (Grand Rapids: Eerdmans, 1994), 81–104.

182. Cf. L. Alexander, "Hellenistic Letter-Forms and the Structure of Philippians," *JSNT* 37 (1989): 87–101; R. Russell, "Pauline Letter Structure in Philippians," *JETS* 25 (1982): 295–306.

183. See C. J. Hemer, *The Letters to the Seven Churches of Asia in Their Local Setting* (JSNTSup 11; Sheffield: JSOT Press, 1986), 178–86; J. B. Lightfoot, *St. Paul's Epistles to the Colossians and to Philemon* (1879; repr., Peabody, Mass.: Hendrickson, 1993), 1–72, with references to the ancient sources; and C. Arnold, "Colossae," *ABD* 1:1089–90.

184. P. T. O'Brien, *Colossians, Philemon* (WBC 44; Waco, Tex.: Word, 1982), xxvi–xxvii.

185. See Lightfoot, *Colossians*, 41ff., on the Colossian church.

186. See Guthrie, *New Testament Introduction*, 551–52, for a discussion.

187. See R. DeMaris, *The Colossian Controversy: Wisdom in Dispute at Colossae* (JSNTSup 96; Sheffield: JSOT Press, 1994), 11–12, for a summary of the discussion of authorship. Two important studies are W. Bujard, *Stilanalytische Untersuchungen zum Kolosserbrief: Als Beitrag zur Methodik von Sprachvergleichen* (SUNT 11; Göttingen: Vandenhoeck & Ruprecht, 1973); and G. E. Cannon, *The Use of Traditional Materials in Colossians* (Macon, Ga.: Mercer University Press, 1983). The standard commentaries discuss these issues; see, e.g., E. Lohse, *Colossians and Philemon* (Hermeneia; Philadelphia: Fortress, 1971), 84–91; and M. Barth and H. Blanke, *Colossians* (AB 34B; New York: Doubleday, 1994), 114–26.

188. See, e.g., Kiley, *Colossians as Pseudepigraphy*.

189. E. D. Freed, *The New Testament: A Critical Introduction* (Belmont, Calif.: Wadsworth, 1991) 305–6.

190. See Moffatt, *Introduction*, 154.

191. Freed, *New Testament*, 306.

192. See S. E. Porter, Καταλλάσσω *in Ancient Greek Literature, with Reference to the Pauline Writings* (Estudios de filología neotestamentaria 5; Córdoba: El Almendro, 1994), 172–85.

193. See Fowl, *Story of Christ*, 103–54; Porter, Καταλλάσσω, 163–69; C. E. Arnold, *The Colossian Syncretism: The Interface between Christianity and Folk Belief at Colossae* (WUNT 2.77; Tübingen: Mohr–Siebeck, 1995), 246–51.

194. There is the possibility of origins in Mithraism, a syncretistic cult based upon worship of the sun. Mithraism had conceptual and theological similarities with Christianity (e.g., a heavenly mediator) and thrived in the Roman Empire. It was not, however, particularly strong in Asia Minor. See A. S. Geden, ed., *Select Passages Illustrating Mithraism* (London: SPCK, 1925).

195. See A. J. Malherbe, *Moral Exhortation, a Greco-Roman Sourcebook* (LEC; Philadelphia: Westminster, 1986), for examples of this and other texts.

196. J. D. G. Dunn, *The Epistles to the Colossians and to Philemon* (NIGTC; Grand Rapids: Eerdmans, 1996), 35–39, who admits, however, that his view may be very close to forms of scribal or Pauline authorship.

197. This has not stopped scholars from speculating, however. See Koester, *Introduction to the New Testament*, 2:261–67. Much of the argument, however, is not concerned with authorship.

198. M. D. Hooker, "Were There False Teachers in Colossae?" in *Christ and Spirit in the New Testament* (ed. B. Lindars and S. S. Smalley; Cambridge: Cambridge University Press, 1973), 315–31.

199. See DeMaris, *Colossian Controversy*, 18–40.

200. Lightfoot, *Colossians*, 73–113. See R. Yates, "Colossians and Gnosis," *JSNT* 27 (1986): 49–68; and M. Goulder, "Colossians and Barbelo," *NTS* 41 (1995): 601–19, who argues for Jewish-Christian Gnosticism.

201. M. Dibelius, "The Isis Initiation in Apuleius and Related Initiatory Rites," in *Conflict at Colossae* (ed. F. O. Francis and W. A. Meeks; rev. ed.; SBLSBS 4; Missoula, Mont.: Scholars Press, 1975), 61–121.

202. S. Lyonnet, "Paul's Adversaries in Colossae," ibid., 147–61.

203. F. O. Francis, "Humility and Angelic Worship in Col. 2:18," ibid., 163–95; T. J. Sappington, *Revelation and Redemption at Colossae* (JSNTSup 53; Sheffield: JSOT Press, 1991).

204. See C. Rowland, "Apocalyptic Visions and the Exaltation of Christ in the Letter to the Colossians," *JSNT* 19 (1983): 73–83, for references.

205. E. Schweizer, *The Letter to the Colossians: A Commentary* (trans. A. Chester; Minneapolis: Augsburg, 1982), 127–33; T. W. Martin, *By Philosophy and Empty Deceit: Colossians as Response to a Cynic Critique* (JSNTSup 118; Sheffield: Sheffield Academic Press, 1996), esp. 106–13.

206. DeMaris, *Colossian Controversy*, 17.

207. Arnold, *Colossian Syncretism*, 5. Arnold may, however, misrepresent DeMaris as taking a philosophical position, when it is better described as syncretistic.

208. See Martin, *Foundations*, 2:214–16.

209. Kümmel, *Introduction*, 349–50.

210. See Bruce, *Paul*, 393–406; cf. B. M. Rapske, "The Prisoner Paul in the Eyes of Onesimus," *NTS* 37 (1991): 187–203; C. S. Wansink, *Chained in Christ: The Experience and Rhetoric of Paul's Imprisonments* (JSNTSup 130; Sheffield: Sheffield Academic Press, 1996), 175–99. On slavery, see J. A. Harrill, *The Manumission of Slaves in Early Christianity* (HUT 32; Tübingen: Mohr–Siebeck, 1995); D. B. Martin, *Slavery as Salvation: The Metaphor of Slavery in Pauline Christianity* (New Haven: Yale University Press, 1990).

211. J. Knox, *Philemon among the Letters of Paul* (rev. ed.; London: Collins, 1960); original edition published in 1935.

212. For discussion of these issues, see B. W. R. Pearson, "Assumptions in the Criticism and Translation of Philemon," in *Translating the Bible: Problems and Prospects* (ed. S. E. Porter and R. S. Hess; JSNTSup 173; Sheffield: Sheffield Academic Press, 1999), 253–80.

213. See J. G. Nordling, "Onesimus Fugitivus: A Defense of the Runaway Slave Hypothesis in Philemon," *JSNT* 41 (1991): 97–119; contra S. C. Winter, "Paul's Letter to Philemon," *NTS* 33 (1987): 1–15; and Wansink, *Chained in Christ*, 174–99.

214. See N. Petersen, *Rediscovering Paul: Philemon and the Sociology of Paul's Narrative World* (Philadelphia: Fortress, 1985).

215. See C. F. D. Moule, *The Epistles to the Colossians and to Philemon* (Cambridge Greek Testament Commentary; Cambridge: Cambridge University Press, 1957), 34–37, who cites a very instructive papyrus (P.Par. 10), which asks for help regarding return of a slave.

216. Bruce, *Paul*, 401. Cf. J. M. G. Barclay, "Paul, Philemon, and the Dilemma of Christian Slave-Ownership," *NTS* 37 (1991): 161–86.

217. Martin, *Foundations*, 2:313.

218. Bruce, *Paul*, 424, following A. S. Peake, "The Quintessence of Paulinism: A Lecture," *BJRL* 4 (1917–1918): 5–31.

pages 477–483

219. See Guthrie, *New Testament Introduction*, 479–82. An instructive op-position of positions is found in two essays: J. N. Sanders, "The Case for the Pauline Authorship," in *Studies in Ephesians* (ed. F. L. Cross; London: Mowbray, 1956), 9–20; and D. E. Nineham, "The Case against the Pauline Authorship," ibid., 21–35.

220. See Moffatt, *Introduction*, 394; cf. T. K. Abbott, *A Critical and Exegetical Commentary on the Epistles to the Ephesians and to the Colossians* (ICC; Edinburgh: T. & T. Clark, 1897), ix–xiii.

221. See M. Barth, *Ephesians* (AB 34; 2 vols.; Garden City, N.Y.: Doubleday, 1974), 1.283–87.

222. On use of the OT, see T. Moritz, *A Profound Mystery: The Use of the Old Testament in Ephesians* (NovTSup 85; Leiden: Brill, 1996).

223. M. D. Goulder, "The Visionaries of Laodicea," *JSNT* 43 (1991): 21.

224. See A. T. Lincoln, *Ephesians* (WBC 42; Dallas: Word, 1990), lix–lxxiii.

225. Cf. C. L. Mitton, *The Epistle to the Ephesians: Its Authorshp, Origin, and Purpose* (Oxford: Clarendon, 1951), 111–58; cf. 279–315, where Mitton finds that Ephesians draws heavily upon the other Pauline Letters in its wording, as well as upon 1 Peter.

226. Martin, *Foundations*, 2:230–33.

227. C. L. Mitton, *Ephesians* (NCB; Grand Rapids: Eerdmans, 1973), 17.

228. See Lincoln, *Ephesians*, xlviii. An excellent synopsis of the two books is provided in Moffatt, *Introduction*, 375–81.

229. See F. Blass and A. Debrunner, *A Greek Grammar of the New Testament and Other Early Christian Literature* (trans. R. W. Funk; Chicago: University of Chicago Press, 1961), § 413(3).

230. See E. Best, "Recipients and Title of the Letter to the Ephesians: Why and When the Designation 'Ephesians'?" *ANRW* 2.25.4 (1987): 3247–79; Lincoln, *Ephesians*, 1–4; D. A. Carson, D. J. Moo, and L. Morris, *An Introduction to the New Testament* (Grand Rapids: Zondervan, 1992), 309–11.

231. See F. J. A. Hort, *Prolegomena to St. Paul's Epistles to the Romans and the Ephesians* (London: Macmillan, 1895), 86–98. On Ephesus, see G. H. R. Horsley, "The Inscriptions of Ephesos and the New Testament," *NovT* 34 (1992): 105–68; R. E. Oster Jr., "Ephesus," *ABD* 2:542–49; Koester, *Ephesos: Metropolis of Asia*.

232. See J. K. Elliott, *The Apocryphal New Testament* (Oxford: Clarendon, 1993), 543–46.

233. Goulder, "Visionaries of Laodicea," 16 n. 1.

234. E. J. Goodspeed, *New Solutions of New Testament Problems* (Chicago: University of Chicago Press, 1927), chs. 1 and 2.

235. Goulder, "Visionaries of Laodicea," esp. 37–39.

236. See Lincoln, *Ephesians*, xliii.

237. Freed, *New Testament*, 440.

238. Kümmel, *Introduction*, 371.

239. Ibid., 367.

240. See S. E. Porter, "Pauline Authorship and the Pastoral Epistles: Implications for Canon," *BBR* 5 (1995): 107–13; and M. Davies, *The Pastoral Epistles* (NT Guides; Sheffield: Sheffield Academic Press, 1996), for a recent treatment of the issues involved.

241. M. Dibelius and H. Conzelmann, *The Pastoral Epistles* (Hermeneia; Philadelphia: Fortress, 1972), 11.

242. J. T. Reed, "To Timothy or Not: A Discourse Analysis of 1 Timothy," in *Biblical Greek Language and Linguistics: Open Questions in Current Research* (ed. S. E. Porter and D. A. Carson; JSNTSup 80; Sheffield: JSOT Press, 1993), 106.

pages 483–489

243. See K. J. Neumann, *The Authenticity of the Pauline Epistles in the Light of Stylostatistical Analysis* (SBLDS 120; Atlanta: Scholars Press, 1990), esp. 23–114, for a survey of research and a bibliography; and A. Kenny, *A Stylometric Study of the New Testament* (Oxford: Clarendon, 1986), esp. 80–100.

244. See B. M. Metzger, "A Reconsideration of Certain Arguments against the Pauline Authorship of the Pastoral Epistles," *ExpT* 70 (1957–1958): 94.

245. See, e.g., J. D. G. Dunn, *Unity and Diversity in the New Testament* (Philadelphia: Westminster, 1977), 341–45; Kümmel, *Introduction,* 378–82.

246. "Early catholicism" is the increased institutionalization of the church in the light of fading hope of the return of Christ, resulting in the faith taking on fixed forms. See Dunn, *Unity and Diversity,* 341–66, following E. Käsemann, "An Apologia for Primitive Christian Eschatology," in *Essays on New Testament Themes* (trans. W. J. Montague; Philadelphia: Fortress, 1964), 169–95. But cf. I. H. Marshall, "'Early Catholicism' in the New Testament," in *New Dimensions in New Testament Study* (ed. R. N. Longenecker and M. C. Tenney; Grand Rapids: Zondervan, 1974), 217–31.

247. See Lincoln, *Ephesians,* xlix.

248. F. Young, *The Theology of the Pastoral Letters* (New Testament Theology; Cambridge: Cambridge University Press, 1994), 107. Cf. Schenk, *Die Philipperbriefe,* 78–82, who takes this reference as a later interpolation. The textual evidence cannot be made to show this.

249. Johnson, *Writings of the New Testament,* 384.

250. This, too, is often seen as a reflection of "early catholicism."

251. As G.W. Knight III admits (*The Faithful Sayings in the Pastoral Letters* [Amsterdam: Kok, 1968; repr., Grand Rapids: Baker, 1979], 1).

252. Cf. P. Pokorný, *Colossians: A Commentary* (trans. S. S. Schatzmann; Peabody, Mass.: Hendrickson, 1991), 6–7 and table 2, who notes that the theology of the Pastoral Epistles is a relatively logical development from Paul's authentic writings and only appears so divergent when compared with other supposedly deutero-Pauline writings, such as Colossians and Ephesians.

253. Paul's absence may well clarify why Paul has to explain why he left Titus to his task, since, if he had actually left him, it is plausible to think that he would have told him why at that time. See Johnson, *Writings of the New Testament,* 383.

254. See Dibelius and Conzelmann, *Pastoral Epistles,* 1–2, for this line of argument.

255. Cf. B. Weiss, *A Manual of Introduction to the New Testament* (trans. A. J. K. Davidson; 2 vols.; London: Hodder & Stoughton, 1887), 1:201–6.

256. See Ign. *Magn.* 8 (Titus 1:14; 3:9), 2 (2 Tim 4:5; 2:5; 1:10; 1:5, 12), 3 (2 Tim 2:12), 4 (1 Tim 6:1, 2), and 6 (2 Tim 2:4), plus other possible instances; and Pol. *Phil.* 4 (1 Tim 6:7, 10), 9 (2 Tim 4:10), and 12 (1 Tim 2:2; 4:15), plus other references. These are cited in N. J. D. White, "The First and Second Epistles to Timothy and the Epistle to Titus," in *Expositor's Greek Testament* (ed. W. R. Nicoll; 5 vols.; 1897; repr., Grand Rapids: Eerdmans, 1980), 4:77–79.

257. Kümmel, *Introduction,* 370.

258. See Trobisch, *Paul's Letter Collection,* 16, for information on 𝔓⁴⁶ and the above.

259. See *1 Clem* 2 (Titus 3:1; cf. also *1 Clem* 34 and 2 Tim 2:21; 3:17), 7 (1 Tim 2:3, 4), 29 (1 Tim 2:8), 32 (Titus 3:5–7), 37 (1 Tim 1:18; cf. 2 Tim 2:3, 4; 2 Cor 10:3), 45 (2 Tim 1:3; cf. 1 Tim 3:9), and 55 (2 Tim 2:1),

pages 490–492

among others. See White, "First and Second Epistles," in *Expositor's Greek Testament*, 4:76–77; cf. J. B. Lightfoot, *The Apostolic Fathers* (2 vols.; 1889–1890; repr., Peabody, Mass.: Hendrickson, 1989), vol. 1, part 2, pp. 19, 104, 113, 138, 180.

260. See L. R. Donelson, *Pseudepigraphy and Ethical Argument in the Pastoral Epistles* (HUT 22; Tübingen: Mohr–Siebeck, 1986).

261. See Davies, *Pastoral Epistles*, 105–18, esp. 113–17, who raises the question of the ethical dilemma in pseudepigraphy and its possible implications for the canon.

262. P. N. Harrison, *The Problem of the Pastoral Epistles* (Oxford: Oxford University Press, 1921); cf. also R. Falconer, *The Pastoral Epistles* (Oxford: Clarendon, 1937), 1–30. Some similarities to this view are to be found in J. D. Miller, *The Pastoral Letters as Composite Documents* (SNTSMS 93; Cambridge: Cambridge University Press, 1997).

263. See E. R. Richards, *The Secretary in the Letters of Paul* (WUNT 2.42; Tübingen: Mohr–Siebeck, 1991), passim.

264. See J. N. D. Kelly, *A Commentary on the Pastoral Epistles* (BNTC; Peabody, Mass.: Hendrickson, 1963), 21–27, who describes a possible scribe; C. F. D. Moule, "The Problem of the Pastoral Epistles: A Reappraisal," *BJRL* 47 (1965): 430–52, who argues that Luke composed the letters during Paul's lifetime; F. J. Badcock, *The Pauline Epistles and the Epistle to the Hebrews in Their Historical Setting* (London: SPCK, 1937), esp. 114–33, who argues for the possibilty of Luke using Paul's notes after Paul's death, so that the letters are authentically Pauline (he also argues that 2 Timothy is composed of two letters); and S. G. Wilson, *Luke and the Pastoral Epistles* (London: SPCK, 1979), who argues for composition by the "Luke" who wrote Luke–Acts but was not a companion of Paul (he does not apparently know the work of Badcock).

265. See W. Lock, *A Critical and Exegetial Commentary on the Pastoral Epistles (I & II Timothy and Titus)* (ICC; Edinburgh: T. & T. Clark, 1924), xxiv–xxv.

266. For a recent summary of this position, see G. W. Knight III, *The Pastoral Epistles* (NIGTC; Grand Rapids: Eerdmans, 1992), 21–45.

267. See. J. A. T. Robinson, *Redating the New Testament*, esp. 67–85. See also M. Prior, *Paul the Letter-Writer and the Second Letter to Timothy* (JSNTSup 23; Sheffield: JSOT Press, 1989).

268. See, e.g., Kümmel, *Introduction*, 378–79.

269. See C. K. Barrett, "Pauline Controversies in the Post-Pauline Period," *NTS* 20 (1973–1974): 229–45; E. Käsemann, "Paul and Early Catholicism," in *New Testament Questions of Today* (trans. W. F. Bunge; Philadelphia: Fortress, 1969), 236–51; Koester, *Introduction to the New Testament*, 2:300–305. Cf. B. Holmberg, *Paul and Power: The Structure of Authority in the Primitive Church as Reflected in the Pauline Epistles* (Philadelphia: Fortress, 1978).

270. See P. H. Towner, *The Goal of Our Instruction: The Structure of Theology and Ethics in the Pastoral Epistles* (JSNTSup 34; Sheffield: JSOT Press, 1989).

271. The example of Hebrews is not germane here, since the book is formally anonymous and there is a long history of discussion of authorship in the early church regarding it, discussion not to be found regarding the Pastoral Epistles.

272. See Knight, *Pastoral Epistles*, 40–45; cf. D. Guthrie, *The Pastoral Epistles* (rev. ed.; TNTC; Grand Rapids: Eerdmans, 1990), 224–40.

pages 492–497

HEBREWS, THE GENERAL EPISTLES, AND REVELATION

1. INTRODUCTION

Hebrews, the General Epistles, and Revelation constitute their own category of writings in the NT, not because they have many features in common but because they do not fit conveniently into the other categories. Although Hebrews was placed within the Pauline corpus early in church tradition, since the Reformation it has not been thought to belong there (see sec. 2.B, below). As a result, Hebrews now stands at the forefront of a number of writings about which relatively little is known for certain. All of these writings except Revelation are in the rough form of letters, or are thought to have been letters at one time, although whether these books are in fact letters is highly debated. Eusebius (*Hist. eccl.* 2.23.24–25) was apparently the first to speak of James, 1 and 2 Peter, 1, 2, and 3 John, and Jude as the "seven catholic letters." By this was meant that they had a breadth and generality to their contents that were intended to speak to the universal church. As will be seen below, however, this is not an entirely accurate characterization of the letters, since at least 1 Peter and 2 and 3 John might well have been sent to particular people, churches, or areas.[1] James, 2 Peter, 2 and 3 John, and Jude are also in the category of "disputed" (ἀντιλεγόμενα, *antilegomena*) writings, those writings Eusebius says were not accepted by all (*Hist. eccl.* 3.25.2–3), as will be discussed below.

2. HEBREWS

A. Introduction

Concerning Hebrews, little is known of background issues, such as authorship, date, and audience, despite their admitted importance in trying to determine the meaning and significance of various dimensions of a biblical text. As will be noted below, since there is a range of proposals about each of these elements—and others besides—one must wonder how much is and can be known about this book called "to the Hebrews."

Because of the dearth of certain knowledge in these areas, larger questions are raised regarding the canonicity of Hebrews, most of them by the very fact that the book is in the NT and survived the canonizing process. For those who take the NT as canonical Scripture, the word of God for the church, it raises further questions about the criteria for canonicity, such as the apostolicity, antiquity, and nature of a given document's teaching. Apparently it was suspected from the outset that this book was not written by an apostle, but it seems that Pauline authorship was attached to the book fairly early, perhaps as a means of solidifying its place within the canon. The book was written at least as early as the second century, but it apparently had trouble establishing its importance in the western church, even though its position was secured earlier in the eastern church. There may not be many ideas, if any, that are unorthodox or contradictory to what eventually was recognized as orthodoxy, but there is certainly a very different feel about the book, in terms of both form and content, that suggests an unknown writer—certainly not Paul. The author is also writing to an unknown church situation, using various forms of argumentation and example that are not usually found or developed elsewhere in the NT.

B. Authorship

The book of Hebrews is formally anonymous; that is, there is no extant opening that makes an explicit (or even an implicit) claim to identify an author by name, and there is no other indication throughout the rest of the book.[2] Even though the book is often referred to as a letter or an epistle, it does not begin with anything resembling an epistolary opening: there is no sender, no addressee, and no word of salutation. The book simply begins almost in medias res (in the midst of the action). The ending of the "letter" (Heb 13:22) has some characteristics of a Pauline letter closing, including reference to "our brother Timothy," prompting the suggestion that it may have been added in an attempt to give it a Pauline resemblance, and hence a more secure place in the canon. Whatever one thinks of the ending, however, there is nothing in it that leads us to suspect that Paul wrote it.

1. Paul

The eastern or Alexandrian church appears to be the first that attributed the book of Hebrews to Paul. The earliest extant text of Hebrews is found in $\mathfrak{P}^{46}$, a papyrus document probably from ca. A.D. 200, although this date is debated by many, with some arguing (unconvincingly) for a first-century date and others claiming a third-century date. In $\mathfrak{P}^{46}$, Hebrews is placed after Romans and before the other Pauline Letters. This document clearly appears to be a collection of the Pauline Letters (2 Thessalonians, Philemon, and the Pastoral Epistles, however, are not included—see the discussion on pseudonymity in ch. 9, sec. 6, above). The writings are arranged roughly according to length, and it seems clear that those who assembled the biblical books in $\mathfrak{P}^{46}$ believed that Hebrews was the second largest of the Pauline Letters (although it is actually slightly shorter than 1 Corinthians and longer than 2 Corinthians).[3] Hebrews is included in several such fourth- and fifth-century groupings of the Pauline corpus, although its position varies (see, e.g., ℵ B and A).

Clement of Alexandria (A.D. 150–215) believed that Paul wrote Hebrews (Misc. 5.10.62; 6.7.62), and says that Paul wrote it as the apostle to the Gentiles (Eusebius, Hist. eccl. 6.14.4). Origen, ambivalent on Pauline authorship, notes that the language of the book is different in style and tone, but also says that the thoughts and teachings are the apostle's (Eusebius, Hist. eccl. 6.25.11–13). Differences in the Greek style, however, prompted various attempts to retain Pauline authorship and at the same time account for the obvious differences from Paul's established letters. Clement of Alexandria proposed that Paul wrote the book of Hebrews in Hebrew but Luke translated it for the Greeks (Eusebius, Hist. eccl. 6.14.2–3), a view that has attracted a number of scholars in the past.[4] This proposal is inadequate for at least three reasons: (1) there are no other letters or any other kind of writing known to have been composed by Paul in Hebrew or Aramaic; (2) it is doubtful that Luke, or at least the author of Luke–Acts, knew Hebrew, or any other Semitic language, well enough to translate it, and it is probable he only spoke Greek (evidenced by his use of the LXX); and (3) there is no evidence that Hebrews was ever written in Hebrew.[5] Origen also suggested that one of Paul's disciples wrote the book from Paul's notes, possibly Luke or Clement of Rome, the likely author of 1 Clement (Eusebius, Hist. eccl. 6.25.14). While possible, this is unprovable. This scenario has also been advanced for several of the Pauline Letters, especially Ephesians and the Pastoral Epistles. Luke, who might have been Paul's coauthor of these books, is commonly suggested as an author of Hebrews. In support of this theory is the fact that Luke's Greek and that of the author of Hebrews stand as some of the best in the NT. As already discussed (see ch. 9, above), authors in the ancient world used scribes for various functions, ranging from taking word-for-word dictation to writing relatively free compositions. It is difficult, however, to establish the exact degree of involvement of an ancient scribe. Like today's secretary, this may have

Mound at Meggido opposite the site of the apocalyptic battlefield of Armageddon in Rev 16:16. This was a strategic military fortification from 1500 B.C. until the fourth century B.C. It has been dormant since. © Rohr Productions. Used with permission.

The reconstructed Herodian theater at Caesarea Maritima. © Rohr Productions. Used with permission.

depended on the relationship of the scribe to the author and also the scribe's ability. Since Paul seems to have been an overwhelming literary presence, it is difficult to argue here that someone composed Hebrews from Paul's notes despite Paul's use of several different scribes.

Unlike the eastern churches, which accepted Pauline authorship of Hebrews, the western or Latin churches were skeptical until the latter part of the fourth century (see Eusebius, *Hist. eccl.* 3.3). Jerome (*Vir. ill.* 5.59) and Augustine (*City* 16.22) helped to shift the opinion in the west. However, as Westcott has shown, the evidence from Jerome and Augustine is ambiguous, sometimes endorsing Pauline authorship and other times simply endorsing the authoritative status of the book.[6] Nevertheless, from the early fifth century on, belief in Pauline authorship of Hebrews persisted until the Reformation, when the question of authorship was reexamined by Calvin and Luther, the former arguing for Clement or Luke and the latter for Apollos.[7] Some interpreters continue to argue for Pauline authorship, but after an examinination of the book from all angles—vocabulary, sentence structure, letter form, conceptual world, and theology—it is highly unlikely that Paul was the author, at least not directly.

2. Alternatives to Pauline Authorship

Besides the views that try to retain some element of Pauline authorship, a number of other proposals have been made about the authorship of Hebrews.

a. Clement of Rome. As noted above, Origen, according to Eusebius, appears to have known of Clement of Rome as a proposed author of Hebrews, a view accepted by others, including Jerome, and some more recent authors. Clement does cite or allude to Hebrews at several places (*1 Clem.* 17.1, 5; 21.9; 27.2; 31.3; 36.2–5). Despite some apparent linguistic similarities between *1 Clement* and Hebrews and similar citation of the OT, their fundamental categories regarding Christ, his supremacy, and his uniqueness as high priest are opposite. Whereas *1 Clem.* 32.2 uses Heb 7:14 to justify establishment of a Christian hierarchy patterned after Judaism, the author of Hebrews rejects this (e.g., Heb 7:11–28).

b. Luke. As mentioned, Luke was suggested early on as the author of Hebrews, often in conjunction with a mention of Clement, but the idea has little support. Although both Luke and Hebrews know and utilize the LXX and possess a developed Greek style, there are a number of conceptual differences, even where they share the same vocabulary. A major difference is Hebrews' reliance upon the depiction of Jewish institutions, something not prominent in Luke's writings.

c. Barnabas. The authorship of Barnabas, possibly first proposed by Tertullian (*Modesty* 20), has become popular again in critical discussion. For example, Badcock argues that Barnabas was the author, probably in conjunction with a visit to Paul while he was in prison in Caesarea.[8] Barnabas is said in Acts 4:36 to be a Levite from Cyprus; hence he would have been a Jew with a Hellenistic perspective, thought by some to be appropriate for the author of Hebrews. He closely collaborated with Paul and recruited Paul for their first missionary journey from Antioch (Acts 13–14). This close working relationship may well account for any similarities in content or expression found in the book and for the reference to Timothy, one of Paul's most important later fellow workers, at the end of the book. More speculatively, Barnabas is referred to in Acts 4:36 as "son of encouragement," and the phrase "word of encouragement" appears in Heb 13:22, using the same word for "encouragement." Some have thought that the latter reference is Barnabas using his signature epithet, although this is a very slender thread to tie up this argument. Against this view, however, is the likelihood that *Barnabas* was not written by the same person (and it was not written by Barnabas), as the clear differences in content and style indicate. Without any sure sample of writing by Barnabas (since *Barnabas* is pseudepigraphal), it is difficult to argue this case more strongly than as a hypothetical reconstructed scenario.

d. Priscilla and Aquila. Harnack first proposed Priscilla as a possible author of the book of the Hebrews, but he has convinced few.[9] Following the presentation of Priscilla as the more important of Priscilla and Aquila in the book of Acts, it is claimed that the interchange of "we" and "I" in Hebrews (e.g., 13:18 vs. 13:19) can be accounted for as a switch from Priscilla writing alone to Priscilla writing with help from her husband, Aquila. It is clear from Acts 18:26 that Priscilla and Aquila were knowledgeable in the faith, since they taught Apollos.

The failure to mention the author by name may well have been the result of bias against women, such that it would have detracted from the authority of the book if she had mentioned her name. Besides the problem of Heb 11:32, where the masculine singular participle is used, this hypotheis suffers from two problems. The first is that the use of "I" is relatively infrequent compared to "we," which seems to be a literary usage for a single author.[10] The second is the difficulty in establishing what evidence could count for or against the hypothesis, since there is no writing from either Priscilla or Aquila for comparison.

e. Apollos. Luther proposed that Apollos was the author, a position argued more recently by Manson and Hugh Montefiore.[11] In Acts 18:24, Apollos is called an "eloquent man, well-versed in the scriptures." He was from Alexandria, to which, on the basis of $\mathfrak{P}^{46}$, the earliest text of Hebrews, the book of Hebrews was connected early on. Apollos, too, had some connections with Paul and his mission (Acts 18:24–28; 1 Cor 1–4), although they may not always have been congenial, at least among their followers at Corinth (see 1 Cor 1:12). Manson speculates that Hebrews was written from Corinth to the Lycus Valley in Asia Minor and sent along with a letter to Paul in Rome, thus accounting for the relation between Hebrews and Paul at an early date. As Manson admits, such a position is highly speculative and no more than a set of assumptions.

f. Others. Other proposals, less likely even than those above, include Peter, or Silas as Peter's amanuensis, for which there is very little support, even with the few clear parallels between Hebrews and 1 Peter; Jude, even though the letter by this name has a very different tone because of its apocalyptic dimension; Stephen, because of similarities between Acts 7 and Heb 11; Philip the deacon, mentioned after Stephen in Acts 6:5, a man involved in serving others and possibly engaged in reconciling factions in the early church; Aristion, by making a circuitous connection between the long ending of Mark and Hebrews; Mary, on the basis of a tenuous connection between the Lukan infancy narrative and Hebrews; and Epaphras, so that Hebrews is the letter to the Laodiceans of Col 4:16.[12]

g. Summary. As stated above, none of these proposals or any others have proved conclusive regarding the authorship of Hebrews. The book is anonymous, and authorship will probably stay unknown barring further discoveries. As Origen finally concludes about the authorship of Hebrews, "God only knows the truth" (Eusebius, *Hist. eccl.* 6.25.13).

C. Date, Audience, and Destination

The date, destination, and audience of Hebrews are almost as uncertain as that of authorship.[13] At the end of the discussion, one is forced to conclude that despite the heavy speculation there is not much certainty regarding many of the subissues. Indeed, because some of the proposals are almost diametrically opposed to each other, it is very difficult to determine specifically what is being addressed in the letter.

1. Date

The question of Hebrews' date is one of the most complex in the NT, and much of the confusion is caused by failure to appreciate the issues involved. It appears that the book was written not to the first but to the second generation of Christians. This can be seen from Heb 2:3 (cf. also 13:7), which says that certain things spoken by the Lord were confirmed to the author's generation by those who had heard these words. There is also some indication that the book is addressed to those who have been Christians for some time (Heb 3:12; 5:12; 6:1). If these passages have direct bearing, a date of probably no earlier than A.D. 60 is suggested as the earliest possible date of composition. It appears that *1 Clement* quotes the letter (see sec. B.2.a, above, for references). If the date of composition of *1 Clement* is ca. A.D. 96, as most scholars believe (though certainly not all; some place it earlier), then this provides the latest possible date of composition. Thus, the span is from approximately A.D. 60 to 96.

Many scholars suggest that the destruction of the temple is important for dating the book of Hebrews more precisely. In theory, this would merit closer attention, especially since we are speaking about a book that is concerned with Jewish themes (including the temple, sacrifice, the tradition of the OT heroes, the relation of Christ to these heroes, such as Melchizedek, etc.). On a number of occasions, the author of Hebrews uses Greek present-tense verbs to speak of various rituals often associated in

The Hebrew University, the Israel Musuem, and the Knesset (Parliament)
(the square building right of center) in Jerusalem. © Rohr Productions. Used with permission.

The "upper" Herodian aqueduct just north of Caesarea Maritima. © Rohr Productions. Used with permission.

Judaism with the temple, which was destroyed in A.D. 70.[14] Passages often cited include Heb 5:1–4; 7:28; 8:3–5; 9:6–7, 9, 13, 25; 10:1, 8; and 13:10–11. A number of proposals have been made for the date of Hebrews on the basis of these data. (a) A number of scholars have argued that since the present-tense verb indicates present time, these passages show that the book was written while the Jerusalem temple ritual was still being performed.[15] This explanation, however, fails on several counts. (1) The Greek present tense is often contrasted by these commentators with supposed Greek past tenses, but there is no single Greek past tense but a number of tenses, the present tense included, that can be used to speak of the past. "Present tense" is a name given to one of the Greek tenses, but in a significant number of instances it clearly does not indicate present time (although at other times it certainly can). Indeed, one cannot rely on the present or any other tense to indicate any particular temporal sphere. (2) More problematic for this position, other ancient Greek authors, writing after the fall of the temple in Jerusalem, used the present tense in reference to the temple.[16] The present tense was used in such contexts probably because it is more emphatic than some others and draws attention to the particular events being described, rather than indicating when they occurred. (b) Others have taken the use of the present tense to indicate a "timeless" (Lane) or "literary" (Bruce) description of these events.[17] The timeless explanation comes up short, however, because it provides no direct help in establishing the date of composition of Hebrews. The present tense can be used timelessly, that is, to speak of the truths of theology or mathematics, but it is doubtful that this is how Hebrews is using it. The literary explanation recognizes the range of uses of the present tense, as well as the literary dependence upon the OT in Hebrews, but it still does not help in determining the date of composition. (c) The third explanation is that, on the basis of the parallels from extrabiblical authors who write about the temple in the present tense after its destruction, the present tense is being used to speak of this past event. But the present tense cannot simply be equated with past time, either. More explicit criteria seem to be necessary for determining the date of composition of Hebrews than the use of the present tense. Without explicit indicators in the book as to when it was written, a plausible scenario can be made for composition sometime between A.D. 60 and 70. Although the author is not expressly interested in the Herodian temple per se, he is concerned that Christ be seen as the new high priest and that the rituals associated with the tabernacle, in some way continued by the temple ritual, be seen as completely superseded. If the book had been written after the destruction of the temple, one might legitimately have expected the author to use the destruction as some kind of an object lesson to confirm his perspective. The lack of such a statement leads us to believe that when the book was written, the temple in Jerusalem was still standing (see Heb 10:1–3, where the point seems to depend upon the temple standing).[18]

2. Audience

Hypotheses regarding the recipients of Hebrews are also numerous. At least five proposals merit attention. These diverse proposals make evident the difficulty of knowing much about the original audience, in light of so little data in the text.

a. Christians in General. The first proposal is that the book was written for Christians in general, especially those being urged to continue their confession of Christ (Heb 3:4, 6, 14; 4:14; 6:4–6, 9; 10:23, 26; 12:22–24). Although there is perhaps little overtly objectionable regarding this proposal, the supposed audience fails to be specific enough to be of much help. Furthermore, it does not address several apparently important issues, such as why there is so much OT and related imagery in the book. It appears that the group must have had some Jewish ties to appreciate the importance of the language, which may account for the title "to the Hebrews."

b. Jewish Christians. The second proposal, therefore, is that the book was written to Jewish Christians in particular. They were apparently in danger of abandoning Christianity and going back to Judaism. Perhaps they had been disowned by their fellow Jews who had not recognized Christ as the promised one (Heb 10:32–36), and they were now facing persecution. Consequently, they were rethinking their choice to follow Christ. This explanation certainly accounts for the use of OT ideas and concepts, but it, too, is not specific enough, since Jewish

Christians may have come from Palestine or Diaspora communities.

c. Greek-Speaking Jewish Christians. This position refines the above position and argues that the projected audience was not Aramaic-speaking but Greek-speaking Jewish Christians, whether from Palestine or the Diaspora. The overwhelming use of the LXX for the OT quotations (approximately twenty-nine citations and over seventy allusions, none of which is clearly dependent on the Hebrew text)—quotations that need to be explained—and the elevated Greek style argue for native Greek speakers. Nevertheless, the attention to ritual and liturgy points in the direction of those who worshipped in the temple or possibly Diaspora Jews who had visited Jerusalem or paid the temple tax.

d. Gentile Christians. A fourth proposal is that the book is addressed to Gentile Christians. Although the OT connections are undeniable, the way in which they are treated and discussed has prompted some to argue that the book was written to Gentiles who are being introduced to the Christian faith with the hope that they will progress beyond basic knowledge (Heb 6:1–2). The use of the OT, it has been argued, is similar to the allegorical interpretation found in Philo of Alexandria's writings.[19] That is, various elements of the OT are given a spiritual significance so that the Gentile converts can appreciate the OT foundations of the faith, understanding more fully its Christian spiritual dimensions. If the audience was Gentile, it has been suggested that the letter may have been sent to Rome, since the earliest associations of the letter are with Rome (*1 Clement*). "Those from Italy" in Heb 13:24 would then mean those who were formerly from Italy and now live elsewhere. This proposal may still be too vague to be helpful, however.

e. Jewish Sect. Finally, it has been suggested that the book was written for a special segment of Judaism. There is a difference of opinion what this segment may have been, however. Some have proposed that it was former members of the Qumran community, others that it was former priests of Judaism, and others still that it was former Essenes.[20] Each of these variations could be argued on the basis of the book's OT and Jewish imagery, but this approach is too specific and not well enough supported to be convincing.

f. Summary. None of the above proposals is entirely satisfying. Many scholars argue that the book is addressed to Jewish Christians of some sort, quite possibly those who were Greek-speaking (option c above), and this is perhaps the best explanation in light of the admonishments to the audience not to return to Judaism. Nevertheless, the proposal that the book was written to Gentile Christians has some merit to it as well. Some have therefore suggested a mixed audience of Jewish and Gentile Christians.

D. Literary Genre

In light of the above discussion, it is not surprising that the inability to specify the authorship and audience of Hebrews has led to ambiguity regarding its literary genre. Not only has the genre proved problematic; the proposed structure of the work itself differs widely from commentator to commentator. George Guthrie surveys five basic approaches to the structure of Hebrews: structural agnosticism, conceptual or thematic analysis, rhetorical criticism, literary or rhetorical analysis, and linguistic analysis or text linguistics.[21] He illustrates well that the criteria for determining the structure of the book vary according to the analyst and the framework in which the analysis is done. Guthrie's proposal is to utilize a form of discourse analysis or textlinguistics on the book of Hebrews (see ch. 2, sec. 3, above, on linguistic criticism). Discourse analysis is an attempt to describe and explain the meaning of linguistic patterns in a text. Guthrie's results are an attempt at a quantifiable means of discussing structure, through defining units of discourse and their interrelations. Nevertheless, even though lines of connection (cohesive ties) may be established by such a method, the question of genre still persists. In recent discussion there are four proposals to consider.

1. Letter

Traditionally, Hebrews has been regarded as a letter, and this view was probably predominant until fairly recently.[22] It is based on the closing (Heb 13:20–25), which is epistolary and seems even Pauline in nature. But the Pauline nature of the closing, and the fact that there is an epistolary closing and no opening, has suggested to many that the closing was added later and hence may not provide much, if any, evidence that the book was originally a letter. There is no epistolary opening to the letter, although the very abrupt beginning has also raised questions. The speculation is that there was at one time an epistolary opening as well but it has been lost. In this case, it may well have been a fairly lengthy opening, perhaps something like the opening of Romans (1:1–7). Nevertheless, as tempting as it is to speculate on the epistolary opening, it is mere speculation. In addition, there are theological content and moral exhortation in Hebrews, but they are not arranged in a way that resembles other (genuine) letters in the NT, usually with doctrine followed by pareenesis. In Hebrews, this material is more closely intertwined, with exhortation following directly from precept. Specific problems are addressed in the letter, such as concern about falling away (Heb 6; 10:2–3) or for those facing hardship (10:32–39). But much of the letter gives the impression that it is not actually addressed to specific problems or situations in a contemporary church. At best, Hebrews would resemble a form of literary letter—that is, some form of philosophical or religious treatise presented in the form of a letter. That Hebrews may be not an actual letter but some other form of address has prompted several other proposals that are taken more seriously in current discussion.

2. Homily or Sermon

The best-known and still most popular theory is that Hebrews is a homily or set of homilies—that is, a long sermon or possibly a set of sermons brought together in one document.[23] There are several indications that the book may have originated in this form. For instance, the writing refers to itself as a "word of exhortation" (Heb 13:22). Also, at several points in the book, a stance is taken that is reminiscent of one that a preacher might take. For example, the audience is regularly addressed as "brothers and sisters" (3:1, 12) or "you" (5:11–12; 12:4–5), and the writer often refers to himself (or herself, if Priscilla is the author) as a speaker, the way a preacher might (2:5; 5:11; 6:9; 8:1). Furthermore, the author's exegetical and homiletical approach is that of giving scriptural quotations and then explaining them, possibly also making use of midrashic technique (see below on midrash and Psalm 110).

3. Midrash

The fact that OT Scripture is so important in Hebrews has suggested to some that it is not necessarily a sermon but perhaps an exercise in biblical exegesis, that it is a midrash on Psalm 110.[24] A midrash in Jewish writing was an extended explanatory commentary on a biblical passage. NT scholars debate the influence of midrash upon the NT writers. Some argue that entire books are examples of midrash and hence that it was a recognized genre the NT writers adopted, while others argue that it is more appropriately described as an exegetical technique, found to varying degrees in the writers of the time, to elucidate and explain biblical passages and incidents.[25] The first group would perhaps posit that Hebrews not only utilizes midrashic technique but is itself a form of the genre of midrash. For example, in Heb 7:11–28, the author, taking up the idea that Christ is a priest forever after the order of Melchizedek, elucidates Ps 110:4, which is quoted or alluded to five times. It would be claimed that the entire book is a midrash upon the various portions of this psalm. As Hay has shown, however, Psalm 110 is not discussed throughout Hebrews in the extended way typical of midrash. The explication of the psalm plays an important role in a detailed discussion, but the ideas of such a discussion, especially regarding Melchizedek, are only a small part of the author's entire message regarding the preeminence of Christ.[26]

4. Oration

Recent analysis of Hebrews has argued for the rhetorical structure of the book, that it is in the style of an ancient oration (see ch. 2, sec. G, above, on rhetorical criticism).[27] This idea was apparently first suggested in the sixteenth century and has been revived in several commentators and monographs. The assumption is that there are a number of rhetorical features in Hebrews that point to its construction as a form of early Christian oratory, to be delivered orally. To some commentators, these features have indicated that the author was knowledgeable in classical rhetorical conventions and may even have been educated in a rhetorical school. Although these commentators agree on the rhetorical nature of Hebrews, they are divided over whether it is deliberative or epideictic rhetoric.[28] Deliberative rhetoric is concerned with persuasion or dissuasion about some future action (the writer is trying to convince his audience to cling to their faith and not abandon it), while epideictic rhetoric reinforces beliefs already held by the audience (the writer seeks to reinforce the beliefs of the group regarding what Christ has accomplished). The use of rhetorical categories raises a number of questions. While it is plausible that the author of Hebrews constructed the book in conformity with classical rhetorical precepts, establishing its type of rhetoric is problematic. Perhaps the safest conclusion is that the author avails himself of dimensions of classical rhetoric, especially stylistic features, while concentrating upon his theological purpose.

E. Basic Characteristics and Message

The view one takes on the issues noted above—in particular, audience, destination, and literary genre—will have a direct bearing on how one interprets the features found in the book of Hebrews.

The basic content of Hebrews is an almost apologetic defense of who God's Son is. As the outline below makes clear, the book first establishes who God's Son is, and then develops the implications of this identity for those who wish to enter into the new covenant. Hebrews begins rather abruptly with the declaration that God has chosen to speak through his Son in this age (Heb 1:2). The author then notes how this Son is superior to all other beings, including those of significance in Judaism: angels; other human beings; such notables as Moses and Joshua; those important to the Jewish cultus, such as the high priest and Melchizedek; and any elementary teaching, such as was found in Judaism (1:5–7:28). Making a transition to discussion of the new covenant, the author of Hebrews speaks of the Son as a substitute for various dimensions of the old covenant (8:6, 7, 13). The Son, instead of serving as an earthly high priest, serves in a heavenly sanctuary. In this capacity, he replaces the old with the new, including a new convenant and new sacrifices. On the basis of this new high priesthood, entrance into the new covenant is possible for those who persevere, have faith, endure, practice graciousness, and are obedient (10:19–13:19).

The book of Hebrews provides an interesting mixture: Jewish imagery presented in Greek form. The Jewish elements, many of them already noted above, are highly suggestive of OT religion, including especially the practices of the Jewish cult. But there are other indications, as discussed above, that the first recipients of this letter may not have been native to Palestine and would have appreciated the imagery as a symbolic or perhaps analogical representation of spiritual realities. It has been suggested that this imagery is very similar to the kind of imagery and exegetical technique used by the Alexandrian Jewish writer Philo, who paraphrased and interpreted the OT in terms of its Neo-Platonic, or at least analogical, characteristics. The overall purpose of this language in Hebrews is clearly to exhort the book's readers not to abandon their Christian faith, whether they are being tempted to return to a form of Judaism or even possibly being lured for the first time into a Judaism filled with impressive but now defunct ritual.

Scholars will continue to discuss the imagery of Hebrews, especially in terms of how comparisons are made between the OT traditions and those of Christianity. No passage in the book is perhaps as highly contested as 6:4–6, however. The debate concerns the theological issue of whether those who have been enlightened by the Christian faith but commit apostasy can repent and be restored to fellowship within the community of faith. Most of the interpretations of this passage depend upon whether one believes that the situation is an actual instance or a hypothetical one and, if hypothetical, whether it is offered as a warning or as a real possibility.

F. Outline of Hebrews[29]

A. God speaks through his Son (1:1–4)
B. The Son superior to other beings (1:5–7:28)
   1. To angels (1:5–2:4)
   2. To other humans (2:5–18)
   3. To Moses and Joshua (3:1–4:13)
   4. To the high priest (4:14–5:10)
   5. To any elementary teaching (5:11–6:20)
   6. To Melchizedek and any other priest (7:1–28)

Ruins of a Hasmonean fortress guarding Jerusalem's western approach (late 2d cent. B.C.).
© Rohr Productions. Used with permission.

The Church of the Ascension, built in 1886 near the summit of the Mount of Olives in Jerusalem to commemorate the place
where some believe Jesus ascended to heaven. A minaret and a mosque from the early seventeenth century are next to the small
chapel, which supposedly has the footprint of Jesus in the center of the floor. © Rohr Productions. Used with permission.

C. The Son the new high priest of the new covenant (8:1–10:18)

    1. He serves in heaven (8:1–13)

    2. He replaces the earthly with a heavenly sanctuary (9:1–14)

    3. He replaces the old covenant with a new covenant (9:15–22)

    4. He replaces the old sacrifices with new sacrifices (9:23–10:18)

D. Entrance into the new covenant (10:19–13:19)

    1. Perseverance (10:19–39)

    2. Faith (11:1–40)

    3. Endurance (12:1–13)

    4. Graciousness (12:14–29)

    5. Obedience (13:1–19)

E. Closing (13:20–25)

    1. Benediction (13:20–21)

    2. Epistolary closing (13:22–25)

3. JAMES

A. Introduction

The book of James has been surrounded by controversy from its beginnings, through the Reformation, and into the present. The reasons have varied and include disputes over its authorship, the nature and quality of its content, and the implications of its message.

Whether James appears to be known by church writers of the late first and the second century has been a major issue in discussion of the epistle. Mayor marshalled an overwhelming amount of evidence that James was known early on; this position was rejected by Ropes but accepted in part by Moffatt, but again it was doubted later by Davids. The conclusions of these scholars regarding authorship and dating are closely related to their evaluation of the early testimony. Although it appears that, in the late first and second centuries, a number of authors show some familiarity with the book of James, including *1 Clement* (23.2–3 [1:8; 4:8]), the *Shepherd of Hermas* (*Mand.* 5, 9, 12, among others), the *Didache* (4.4), and *Barnabas* (19.5), James was not generally accepted by the eastern churches as Scripture until the third century, when Origen appears to have been the first to acknowledge it as such (*Comm. Jo.* 19.6). Widespread acceptance of James in the western churches did not come until the fourth century. In the east,

Eusebius classified it as one of the disputed books (*Hist. eccl.* 3.33).[30] With such a late acceptance, it is almost inevitable that the book would cause continued controversy (or perhaps continued controversy over the book led to its late acceptance). Luther, denigrating the book's failure to proclaim Christ clearly enough for him, called it an "epistle of straw," and while admitting that there were many good sayings in it, he consigned it to the back of his edition of the NT. Erasmus and Calvin had reservations as well.[31]

B. Authorship

The book of James purports to have been written by a person named James.[32] Since there are many by that name in the NT, it is difficult to pinpoint which James claims to have written the book (Jas 1:1). Five are worth mentioning here. The first, James the son of Zebedee and brother of John, was purportedly killed by Herod in A.D. 44, according to Acts 12:2 (cf. also Matt 4:21; 10:2; 17:1; Mark 10:35; 13:23; Luke 9:54). The second, James the son of Alphaeus, was one of the disciples (Matt 10:3; Mark 3:18; Luke 6:15; Acts 1:13). The third, James the Less, was the son of Mary the wife of Clopas (Matt 27:56; Mark 15:40; John 19:25). The fourth, James the father of Judas, was one of the disciples (Luke 6:16; Acts 1:13). There is no evidence that any of these four was the author of the book. The fifth and most likely choice, based upon the NT evidence, is James the brother of Jesus, mentioned in Gal 1:19; 2:9, 12 and Acts 12:17; 15:13; 21:8. Although he does not seem to have been at all connected with, or involved in, the ministry of Jesus, he appears later as a leader of the church in Jerusalem. Besides his prominent profile in the early Jerusalem church, other factors are often cited as indicating that the letter was written by James the brother of Jesus.[33] There appear to be a number of similarities in language between Acts 15:13–21, a speech delivered by James at the so-called Jerusalem Council, the following letter in Acts 15:23–29, and the book of James. These include the standard epistolary greeting, χαίρειν (*chairein*, "greeting"; Jas 1:1; Acts 15:23), used in only three places in the NT (see also Acts 23:26), and numerous peculiarities of phrasing (Acts 15:17, Jas 2:7; Acts 15:13, Jas 2:5; Acts 15:14, Jas 1:27; Acts 15:19, Jas 5:19, 20; Acts 15:29, Jas 1:27; etc.).[34] A number of apparent allusions to the teaching of Jesus in the so-called Q material, such as the Sermon on the Mount (Matt 5–7), are also in James, especially ch. 4 (e.g., vv. 3, 8, 10, 11, 12).[35] And lastly, there are a number of Jewish features in the letter; for example, it is addressed to the twelve tribes of the dispersion (possibly indicating Palestinian origin) and expresses its concern for works in relation to faith (Jas 2:14–26; see below).

Rather than pointing to James as the author of this book, however, the parallels between James and the Q material raise four major questions.[36] (1) The Greek of James, including its syntax and vocabulary, seems to be of too high a standard for one brought up with Jesus in Galilee. Most scholars are now willing to admit that knowledge of Greek in Palestine was more widespread than previously thought,[37] but they are still not convinced that such a polished literary creation could be produced by James the brother of Jesus (e.g., there is a possible Greek hexameter line of poetry—a line with six accented metrical feet—in Jas 1:17).[38] (2) The notion of "the perfect law, the law of liberty" (Jas 1:25) is out of harmony with what is known of James's more legalistic mind (see Acts 15, 21; Gal 2:12). On the other hand, Jas 2:14–26, which is often interpreted as contradicting Paul, supports the picture we see of James in Acts and Galatians. (3) There is a minimum of Christology in the letter. James 1:1 and 2:1 are the only explicit christological statements. (4) Recognition of the status of this letter by the church was slow in coming. While a few scholars are convinced that the letter was cited in *1 Clement* and by the *Shepherd of Hermas*, widespread reference to it did not appear until much later. If the letter was known to be written by the brother of Jesus, such neglect is more difficult to explain than if it was not. Consequently, the attribution of authorship to James, the brother of Jesus, appears more complex than earlier thought.

Two other suggestions need to be considered. Some of those wishing to retain James the brother of Jesus as the author have argued, in light of the linguistic and other difficulties, that the letter, as we have it now, is a collection of his edited sermons.[39] According to this theory, the production of the book of James took place in two stages, first as a series of sermons that came from James the brother of Jesus, then as a later redaction of these sermons into a letter, possibly by James himself but more probably by someone else. As is noted in our discussion of Hebrews, the sermon hypothesis is frequently suggested for this category of disputed writings in the NT. This proposal is designed to handle the range of evidence, which suggests that the book has not only features indicating an early composition (such as items of local Palestinian color and links between the speeches of James in Acts and the letter) but also features suggesting a late composition (such as the kind of Greek used). One of the major features of the letter that indicates its sermonic nature is the use of commands regarding behavior. There are approximately sixty imperatives in the book of James, and this is thought to be consistent with the exhortatory style of sermon, in which the preacher, in this case James, is trying to motivate his audience. According to this hypothesis, the essential sermon(s), including its subject matter and dependence upon the words of Jesus, is the product of James. It was then rendered into good Greek by an editor, since James would have been a relatively uneducated Palestinian Jew, probably much more at home in Aramaic. Although it has the merit of retaining the traditional authorship while addressing the questions raised, this proposal has several severe limitations. These include the difficulty of proving or disproving the theory, since any evidence can easily be categorized as either early or late. Any supposedly primitive or Palestinian elements can be attributed to James, while any other elements are attributed to the redactor. The span of time between the sermons and the final letter could have been quite long, which would introduce a new set of problems regarding the retention and transmission of these documents, if in fact they were written documents.

Because of the problems mentioned above, the vast majority of scholars have come to believe that the book of James is a pseudonymous work written by an unknown Christian in the name of James. Further reasons to doubt the traditional view of authorship are the failure of the author to identify himself as Jesus' brother and his apparent utilization of a Greek version of the Sermon on the Mount. If James had explicitly heard the Sermon from his brother Jesus, one might have expected his rendition of the Sermon to indicate more clearly that he had heard an Aramaic version, not that he relied upon a translation passed on by others. The author's use of Greek versions of the Sermon on the Mount may suggest an orientation toward the

Excavations on the south end of the temple wall in Jerusalem. El Aqsa Mosque is in the upper left.
© Rohr Productions. Used with permission.

The Lions' Gate and the Muslim Quarter on the northern side of the Temple Mount in Jerusalem. See also the pool of Israel from the Herodian period and the beginning of the traditional Via Dolorosa. © Rohr Productions. Used with permission.

Tombs of members of the Sanhedrin, the supreme legal body of Second Temple Judaism. Twenty-one graves are here.
© Rohr Productions. Used with permission.

The Church of the Holy Sepulcher in Jerusalem, begun by the mother of Constantine in the fourth century. At the time of its construction, it was the largest such edifice in the world.
© Rohr Productions. Used with permission.

A forest near Jerusalem forest where the tomb and ossuary box of Caiaphas, the high priest was recently discovered.
© Rohr Productions. Used with permission.

A modern view of Jerusalem, the city of David, below the Herodian Temple Mount.
© Rohr Productions. Used with permission.

Greek-speaking Jewish Christians, rather than toward the predominantly Aramaic-speaking Christians of the Jerusalem church. This Greek-speaking audience would also account for the more legalistic position on the relation of works and law in Jas 2:14–26. If James and Paul had had contact on several occasions, including especially their meeting in Jerusalem reflected in Acts 15 (cf. Gal 2:9–10)— where Paul's opinion on the relationship of Jews and Gentiles concerning the law apparently triumphed and was endorsed by James—it is difficult to understand why now James pits himself against Paul.[40]

In conclusion, at least some of the material in the letter appears to be early (see sec. D, below), possibly reflecting firsthand acquaintance with Paul's teaching. But it is our opinion, against the majority of scholars, that the letter is probably not pseudonymous, since it could easily have been written by someone named James in the early church, even if it cannot be determined precisely who that James was (but see sec. D, below). Indeed, the book's own lack of specificity about authorship and the abundance of people named James make pseudonymous authorship a less likely solution than authorship by someone named James. Further discussion of who this James might be is presented below.

C. Literary Genre

There have been at least three proposals regarding the literary genre of the book of James. Although determination of literary genre is important, as is seen in this section and the next, it is only part of an overall understanding of the book.

1. Genuine Letter

The first proposal is that it is a genuine letter written and sent by James or by someone sending the letter in his name. The letter opens with the standard epistolary greeting (χαίρειν), as mentioned above, and develops in the standard format of the NT letter, with a two-part structure (chs. 1–2, 3–5).[41] Within this structure, a number of particular issues are addressed that are typical of the genuine NT letter (e.g., wealth and poverty, testing, law and grace, and eschatology).[42] It is addressed not to a specific audience but, rather, to a wide-

spread group ("the twelve tribes in the Dispersion"), implying that it was probably a circular, not a personal, letter. The letter was perhaps addressed to Jewish Christians dispersed throughout a region of the Greco-Roman world.

2. Sermon

The second proposal is that the book is essentially a sermon or set of sermons (see sec. B, above). Nevertheless, these sermons were eventually put into the form of a letter.

3. Literary Letter

A third proposal is that James is a literary letter, that is, not written as a real letter but as a form of public statement. This hypothesis is based upon several factors. The opening is the only one among any of the letters of the NT (apart from quotations in Acts 15:13 and 23:26) that includes the standard Greco-Roman epistolary greeting χαίρειν, immediately after the opening. The letter then takes on the character of an exhortatory discourse (see sec. B, above, on the sermon) and concludes with no epistolary closing and no personal elements typical of a genuine letter. Also lacking are such personal elements as greetings, the travel plans of the author, and prayer requests or benediction.

There are two major variants on the theory that this is a literary letter, each attempting to describe the literary force or function of the letter's contents. Ropes emphasizes that the letter displays the features of the Hellenistic diatribe.[43] Diatribe was a dialogue-based literary form typically used by philosophers and other teachers of the Hellenistic world. In a written text such as this, there is a fictitious dialogue established between the author and a supposed hearer. This is especially found in James at 2:14–26 and 4:1–10, although there are other diatribal elements throughout the book (parallelism, rhetorical questions, antitheses). A second factor is the presence of numerous commands in the space of the relatively short book, as mentioned earlier. They are strung together in such a way as may indicate an attempt at ethical instruction, possibly resembling that of protreptic literature, an ancient hortatory form. Lastly, there is the general applicability of what is said. It has frequently been noted that apart from 1:1 and 2:1, there are few, if any, specific Christian references in the book.

The second variation on the theory of the literary letter was proposed by Dibelius, who saw the letter as parenetic and pointed to several features. One is its eclectic nature, drawing upon analogies from all kinds of situations (nature, social structures, etc.). A second is the lack of continuity; various ideas are juxtaposed, often linked by word associations (1:4–5, 12–13, 26–27; 2:12–13; 3:17–18; 5:9–12, 19–20).[44] There have been various theories on the origins of the parenetic material, including a wisdom tradition such as is found in other Jewish parenetic literature (e.g., Proverbs, Qoheleth/Ecclesiastes, ben Sira, and even the Q tradition). This has led to further speculation that the book took up a non-Christian ethical tract and applied it in only a loose way to a Christian situation, in which economic and class distinctions were apparently being made in the church. Indeed, the kind of situation envisioned is not unlike that found in many urban settings in the ancient Greco-Roman world.

Without agreeing that the book is based upon a non-Christian ethical tract, it seems clear to us that moral exhortation exerts a heavy influence upon the letter. As Johnson has shown, this book probably has some connections with the Greco-Roman moralistic tradition but more basis in the OT, especially the wisdom tradition (e.g., Proverbs), other Jewish literature, and even a number of Christian writings (e.g., the Sermon on the Mount in Q, Didache, Barnabas).[45]

D. Date

Because of uncertainty over the authorship of the book of James and our lack of knowledge about its early history, it is difficult to be precise about the date of its composition. At least three dates merit serious consideration. Some scholars state categorically that it is the earliest writing of the NT, perhaps in the early or middle 40s, clearly pointing to authorship by James the brother of Jesus. Factors in support of this include the emergent nature of its Christian theology and ethics. Others, while retaining the authenticity of the letter, place it near the end of his life, around A.D. 60. This gives enough time for conflict to develop between James and Paul and for problems to develop within the church over such issues as wealth. For those who do not hold to

authorship by James the brother of Jesus, the date could extend into the second century, perhaps just before the Bar Kokhba revolt of A.D. 132, which marked a significant turning point in Jewish-Christian relations.[46]

One passage has often been cited as a means of establishing the date of the book—Jas 2:14–26.[47] These verses are well known because of their supposed endorsement of works as equal to faith and, consequently, their apparent opposition to the teaching of Paul on the same subject. The author addresses the issue of faith and works by seeing faith through works; that is, a person is justified by works. Suggestions regarding this passage and its relation to Paul include the claim that James represents genuine diversity in the NT, in that this passage is in unharmonizable conflict with Paul's teaching. James argues for faith and works, while Paul argues for faith alone, the former representing the legalistic interests of early Jewish Christians and the latter the law-free interests of Gentile Christians.[48] One scholar proposes that James has misunderstood Paul's position on the issue of justification as advocacy of moral laxity.[49] Others suggest that the two writers can be harmonized according to one's understanding of the concept of justification. Perhaps James uses "justify" to indicate vindication before people, while Paul refers to justification before God, or perhaps James refers to vindication at the Last Judgment, while Paul speaks of initial salvation.[50] Finally, some argue that the two authors are simply speaking of different things. Both assume the importance of faith, but Paul opposes those who say that faith comes from works, while James endorses works as demonstrating one's faith.[51]

These findings have implications for the date of the composition of the letter. Ropes has argued that the book of James was written later than Paul's writings (others would argue very late, especially if it is pseudonymous), as a response to Paul's teaching. It may be that the author of James sees Paul as a libertine, that is, one who sees no role and purpose for the law, and as one who is endorsing a life freed from any obligation of personal responsibility for actions.[52] Consequently, they say, the book of James is written to defend the role and purpose of works in the Christian life. With this hypothesis, however, there is always the possibility that the author of James may have misunderstood

Paul or may have failed to appreciate fully his emphasis on works. It is clear from virtually all of Paul's letters, especially in the parenetic sections concerned with proper Christian behavior, that Paul has a very strong emphasis on proper Christian conduct (e.g., Rom 12:1–15:33; 1 Cor 5:1–16:12). It may well not be equated by him with justification, but it is vital to holy Christian living (e.g., 1 Thess 4:1–12).

A few have argued for an early date on the basis of Jas 2:14–26. The argument is that James was written when Paul's teaching was only beginning to have an impact on the church. Consequently, at that time, the author either did not know Paul's teaching or had not had enough time or exposure to it to understand exactly what Paul was saying. By this reckoning, some might even argue that the book of James was written before James and Paul met, thus probably before Gal 1:19 and certainly before the events of Acts 15.[53]

There is room for further discussion of the authorship, date, and purpose of James. The vast majority of scholars opt for pseudonymous authorship, probably near the end of the first century or into the early second century, but the evidence above suggests that the letter may have been written as early as ca. A.D 50. The evidence for this position is not, however, overwhelming.

E. Basic Characteristics and Message

The book of James has long been considered one of the most practical and applied books of the NT. The reasons for this are several. First, the explicit theology, especially the overtly Christian content, is often said to be minimal. Some have even gone so far as to say that there is little to nothing distinctively Christian about the book of James. A second reason is the exhortatory nature of the book. There is a high concentration of command language in the book (see above), giving the impression that it was consciously intended to motivate readers to action. Third is the emphasis upon the role of faith, as discussed above. Fourth is the language of wisdom, designed to offer those who are being addressed a basis for the action that they are exhorted to do. Fifth and finally, the readers seem to be facing a situation of adversity, not only outside but within the church, that calls for such instructive language and wise behavior.

Whether James is a genuine or a literary letter, it seems to be structured after the typical Greco-Roman letter form, with one notable variation. Although the letter opens with a form of address closer to that of the Greco-Roman letter than any other of the letters in the NT, the audience is not a specific one but simply those of the Diaspora (see above). From the outset, the thanksgiving section addresses the fact that the faith community is experiencing trials and tests. The author exhorts them to have joy in the face of these trials because they produce endurance. Wisdom in handling this situation comes from God, and the relations between, for example, tested and testers can be reversed if wisdom is not heeded. The person who endures, however, will be blessed by God for doing what he or she ought, not simply hearing without acting. These opening exhortatory words lead to the body of the letter, which explicates further what it means to live the wise or Christian life. Living the Christian life is framed in terms of various "works" that one should do toward fellow Christians. Some of these are positive actions, but others are negative. The author betrays a certain amount of frustration, perhaps at those who have failed to heed his advice. For example, he states that forms of favoritism among the community are to be excluded and that faith, if it really is faith, will result in good works. The writer therefore seeks to instill, for instance, the realization that speech has its consequences, both for good and for bad, as does wealth. Throughout the book of James, doing the wise thing, that is, wisdom, is equated with doing what God would want one to do. The author closes with a series of exhortations regarding patience, swearing, prayer, and repentance. The letter does not have a formal closing but instead a general word of admonition about the virtue of bringing a sinner to repentance.

The book of James, perhaps above all others in the NT, offers the example of a work addressed to the practical realities of life in the early church. Rather than offer a beatific depiction of the early Christian communities, James addresses the hard realities of a Christian church that included believers who came from all walks of life. Their repentance did not necessarily remove them from the pressures of daily life, and these problems apparently had done more than silently creep into various Christian communities. The author therefore apparently felt the need to address these practical realities in terms of proactive Christian behavior rather than rehearse theological truths.

F. Outline of James[54]

A. Opening (1:1)
  1. Sender (1:1a)
  2. Addressee (1:1b)
  3. Greeting (1:1c)
B. Thanksgiving (1:2–27)
  1. Joy in the face of trials (1:2–11)
  2. Blessed is the one who endures (1:12–27)
C. Body: Doing the Christian life (2:1–5:6)
  1. Favoritism is excluded (2:1–13)
  2. Faith produces works (2:14–26)
  3. Speech has consequences (3:1–12)
  4. Wisdom produces peace (3:13–18)
  5. One must submit to God (4:1–10)
  6. Inaccurate speech has dire results (4:11–17)
  7. Misuse of wealth brings condemnation (5:1–6)
D. Closing exhortations (5:7–20)
  1. Patience (5:7–11)
  2. Swearing (5:12)
  3. Prayer for others (5:13–18)
  4. Repentance (5:19–20)

4. THE PETRINE LETTERS AND JUDE

A. Introduction

Numerous problems attend to the Petrine Letters and Jude. These include (1) the differences between the two Petrine Letters in light of their supposed common apostolic authorship, (2) 2 Peter's seeming use of Jude, a literary dependence that moves in the opposite direction to what might be expected if 2 Peter is an apostle's writings, and (3) issues regarding the growth and development of early Christianity.

B. 1 Peter

Essentially two major issues arise concerning 1 Peter: the authorship, date, and destination of the letter; and its literary form and character. From an examination of them, lesser issues come into sharper focus.

1. Authorship, Date, and Destination

The traditional view is that 1 Peter was written by the Apostle Peter sometime before A.D. 62 and certainly before A.D. 64/65, when, according to tradition, he was martyred under Nero in Rome (see Eusebius, *Hist. eccl.* 2.25.5). The traditional view has been defended along several lines. The first is internal evidence that includes the clear ascription of the letter to "Peter, an apostle of Jesus Christ," in 1:1. Several other passages point in the direction of Peter as well. For example, in 5:1 the author claims to be a "witness of the sufferings of Christ," which appears to be a claim to be an eyewitness to the life and death of Jesus. This is perhaps further strengthened by 2:20–25, which is thought to reflect Peter's situation, especially as he watched Christ suffer and then rejected him at the first sign of trouble though he himself had not suffered at all. It has further been noted that there is abundant phrasing in 1 Peter similar to some of Peter's sermons in Acts (e.g., Acts 2:23 and 1 Pet 1:2, 20; 2:4, 5; Acts 2:33 and 1 Pet 1:12; 3:22; 4:1; Acts 2:36 and 1 Pet 1:11; 3:15; 4:12; Acts 2:38 and 1 Pet 3:22; Acts 10:42 and 1 Pet 4:5). External evidence includes a possible reference in 2 Pet 3:1 and clear acknowledgment of the letter in Polycarp (*Phil.* 1.3; 2.1, 2; 6.3; 7.2; 8.1–2; 10.2–3), Eusebius (*Hist. eccl.* 2.15.2), Irenaeus (*Haer.* 4.9.2; 5.7.2), Tertullian (*Scorp.* 12), Clement of Alexandria (*Tutor* 1.6; 3.11, 12; *Misc.* 3.12; 4.18, 20), and Origen (according to Eusebius, *Hist. eccl.* 6.25.8). This evidence prompts Michaels to state that "aside from the four Gospels and the letters of Paul, the external attestation for 1 Peter is as strong, or stronger, than that for any NT book. There is no evidence anywhere of controversy over its authorship or authority."[55]

Regardless, several doubts about Petrine authorship of 1 Peter still persist among a wide range of scholars. These doubts have been raised by at least four issues, to which advocates of Petrine authorship have given responses.[56]

a. Use of Greek. The first is the excellent Greek that is used in 1 Peter. Even if one acknowledges that a fisherman from the Galilee area would have had to know Greek in order to conduct his business (and this is very likely),[57] it is highly unusual and unlikely that this fisherman would have known Greek to the standard found in 1 Peter and, especially, have been able to write as accomplished a

This beautiful mosaic in the Dome of the Rock celebrates Moslem victories in battle.
© Rohr Productions. Used with permission.

Ruins of the pool of Bethsaida (Bethesda) (John 5:2–13) in Jerusalem. It was also the site of an Asklepion,
where persons received medicinal baths hoping to be healed. © Rohr Productions. Used with permission.

literary piece as this. In many scholars' estimation, the quality of Greek in 1 Peter rates among the three or four most highly literate works in the NT (along with Hebrews, James, and Luke–Acts). On the other hand, 1 Pet 5:12 may provide the answer to this problem. There the author says that "through Silvanus . . . I have written this short letter to encourage you."[58] There is thus the possibility that while the letter is attributed to Peter and he stands behind its authority, Silvanus may have served as a scribe, an amanuensis, or even a commissioned author responsible for the writing of the Greek. If this Silvanus is Silas, the traveling companion of Paul (see Acts 15:40–18:5) and coauthor/cosender of 1 and 2 Thessalonians (parallels between the Thessalonian letters, 1 Peter, and Acts 15:22–32 have been contended), it may well provide an explanation of the Greek problem. Consequently, many argue for Petrine authorship and acknowledge the use of Silvanus/Silas to explain the literary quality of the letter.[59]

b. Theology. The second problem is that the theology of 1 Peter appears to be too dependent upon Pauline theology. For example, Jesus' death is seen as atoning for sins (1:18–19; 2:24), suffering with Christ is endorsed (4:13; 5:1), obedience to authorities is commanded (2:14–15), and believers are said to be "in Christ" (3:16; 5:10, 14). As a result, some have thought that 1 Peter is more Pauline than the Pastoral Epistles.[60] This apparent dependence is thought to be unexplainable in light of Peter's having been a disciple and very close follower of Jesus during his earthly ministry. Nevertheless, a number of other considerations must be kept in mind. First, if Silvanus/Silas, the traveling companion of Paul, had a hand in the composition of the letter, he no doubt came under the influence of Paul's thinking and may have reflected this thinking when writing for Peter. A subsidiary factor is that Peter and Paul had had confrontations over theological issues before, most notably the one reflected in Gal 2:11–21. There is dispute over whether Paul or Peter prevailed in this confrontation, but it is quite possible that the encounter left a mark on Peter's theology. Lastly, by the time Peter wrote this letter, probably from Rome, the Roman church already was in receipt of Paul's Letter to the Romans, which could well have had a profound effect on the thinking of Peter.

c. Jesus' Life. A third question about the authorship of 1 Peter concerns the lack of concrete evidence for the author's knowledge of events in Jesus' life. This is surprising in light of Peter's close association with Jesus during his ministry and, in particular, his place in the inner circle of disciples, which, for example, enabled him to be present at the transfiguration. This lack of reference is more understandable for the Pauline writings, since Paul does not make a claim to have been with the earthly Jesus. Apart from the fairly allusive comments in 1 Pet 2:20–25, mentioned above, there are no specific references to the events in Jesus' life. But the question is whether this proves anything.

d. Persecution. The fourth objection to Petrine authorship is that the passages that refer to persecution—1:6; 3:13–17; 4:12–19; 5:9—may refer to a time late in the first century (under Domitian) or early in the second century (under Trajan), when persecution of Christians supposedly became more widespread and organized in the Roman Empire. (These persecutions may reflect the fact that Christianity was no longer viewed as part of Judaism.) Nevertheless, it is difficult to judge when the persecution these passages describe would have taken place. While there is no evidence of widespread systematic persecution until the mid–third century (under Decius), there is evidence of incidental or local persecution, persecution that could be directly relevant to that reflected in these passages (e.g., the persecution of Christians by Nero in Rome in 64–65). Furthermore, other comments in 1 Peter make it difficult to believe that the letter originated in a time of sustained persecution by the Roman authorities, whether under Domitian, Trajan, or Decius. In 2:13–14, 17, there is a favorable view taken of civil authorities, for Christians are told to submit to those in such positions, including the emperor. The passage is highly reminiscent of Rom 13:1–7 but not as well developed logically. This passage may not only indicate a close tie in thought between the author of 1 Peter and Paul; it also perhaps indicates a time before Christians ran into serious trouble with the Roman authorities, other than in individual incidents.

e. Summary. The majority view today is that 1 Peter is pseudonymous, written by a later Christian or Christians as part of a Petrine school.[61] He was writing under the name of Peter, possibly from Rome (if "Babylon" in 5:13 refers to Rome), to churches in Asia Minor that were suffering persecution. The reasons for this position include the belief that the difficulties raised above are clearly insuperable for the traditional view, even if modified to include the role of a scribe, amanuensis, or coauthor. In recent discussion, pseudonymous authorship is often associated with authorship by a Petrine community or a composite authorship, since close interconnections in language and content exist among 1 and 2 Peter and Jude. The later date of composition implied by such a position (A.D. 65 on) is consistent with the status of 1 Peter in the early church (see above).

2. Literary Form and Character

There are many questions about the literary form of 1 Peter, and their number continues to increase because of the difficulty in establishing its literary form. Examination of these questions gives insight into the content and character of 1 Peter. The first proposal is usually suggested by those who think that the letter was written by Peter or an amanuensis, or possibly by later followers of a Petrine school. Other proposals regarding the original form of 1 Peter tend to reflect a Petrine community school or composite view of authorship.[62]

a. Genuine Letter. This proposal holds that the letter is a genuine letter just as it purports to be. For example, 1 Pet 5:12 refers to writing, which seems to indicate epistolary composition. It is more difficult to establish the exact nature of this letter. On the one hand, some have proposed that it was originally meant as a circular letter, addressed to "the exiles of the Dispersion in Pontus, Galatia, Cappadocia, Asia, and Bithynia" (1:1). The wide expanse covered by this address suggests that the letter was written to be circulated in the numerous churches located in Asia Minor.[63] On the other hand, there are a number of noteworthy personal references in the letter as well, including those to friends (2:11; 4:12) and elders (5:1–4) and probably to the church in Rome and to Mark (1 Pet 5:13).

b. Cultic Function. Several suggestions point to a cultic function for the letter, proposing that 1 Peter may have been some form of baptismal document, possibly a baptismal sermon in whole or in part. Although there have been numerous variations on this analysis, F. L. Cross's is perhaps the most important.[64] As the letter does not have many specific references to people and places, has a highly polished style, begins with an impressive opening in 1:3–12, concludes with a doxology and an "Amen" in 4:11, and includes a number of hymnic passages (e.g., 1:20; 3:18–22), it has been argued that the bulk of the letter (1:3–4:11) was a transcript of an actual baptismal service or at least the words of address to a group of those recently baptized. In this case, 4:12–5:11 could be a supplemental portion, perhaps attached later, reflecting on a more serious situation involving persecution. Cross was even more specific, claiming that the letter reflects an Easter paschal baptismal liturgy. This elaborate set of hypotheses has not proved convincing, however, especially when it is considered that the word "baptism" occurs only in 1 Pet 3:21 (but cf. allusions in 1:3, 23; 2:2). If Cross were right, one might well expect a clearer reference to the occasion. Instead, other subjects unrelated to baptism, such as suffering, are discussed (e.g., 3:13–22).

c. Parenesis. The parenetic hypothesis has been the most enduring in discussion of the nature of 1 Peter. The most important work establishing this hypothesis was that of Selwyn even though he argued that baptismal material lay behind the catechetical emphasis.[65] According to this position, 1 Peter as parenesis reflects a form of literature commonly known in the ancient Near East and used to give practical moral instruction through exhortation and admonition designed to reinforce the audience's beliefs or influence their behavior. Some parenetic analyses have focused upon the ethical dimension of 1 Peter, while others have focused on its theology. Whereas most parenetic analysis of 1 Peter, following Selwyn's example, has concentrated on describing the *origins* of this material, concentrating upon either the kerygma or the fear of punishment as its basis, recent work has attempted to focus on the *motivation* for the parenesis, utilizing insights from rhetorical study.[66]

d. Apologetic Tract. In light of the letter's emphasis on suffering, some have argued that 1 Peter is an apologetic tract explaining the readers' trials in order to encourage them. Although some more traditional interpreters have taken this line, much of this perspective has been argued by those using social-scientific models. For example, in his commentary, Goppelt argued that the audience's

Inside Dome of the Rock on the Temple Mount. This is the probable site of sacrifices from ancient temples of Solomon and Herod the Great and it is also believed by Moslems to be the site of the ascension of Mohammed to heaven. © Rohr Productions. Used with permission.

The Chapel of Dominus Flevit on the Mount of Olives, believed by some to be the place where Jesus wept over Jerusalem (Luke 19:41). Several ossuary boxes dating from the first century A.D. were also discovered here. © Rohr Productions. Used with permission.

situation is "characterized decisively by conflict with society." For Christians, suffering is of the essence of their existence; therefore the author encourages and exhorts them to behave properly. John Elliott argues that 1 Peter addresses Christian social groups who are characterized as "resident aliens," that is, poor rural inhabitants in social conflict with the established urban culture of Asia. The "household" of God is a sociological institution providing a home for the homeless against the strains of estrangement. Balch argues that 1 Peter is an attempt to integrate Christianity into Greco-Roman society, which was highly suspicious of foreign religions. The household codes of early Christianity, including 1 Pet 2:13–3:8, were designed to stress harmony so that households would not be divided. Thus the code's apologetic function is to respond to outside criticism.[67] Martin is correct that these proposals put too much stress upon the sociological dimension, neglecting the theological dimension, which remains paramount in 1 Peter.[68]

e. Homiletical Midrash. Schutter has recently concluded that over half of the material in 1 Peter is from the OT. This includes forty-six direct quotations, plus allusions. He argues that the author uses what he calls homiletical midrash (similar to the interpretation at Qumran) to emphasize that the church is the temple community (see 2:4–8, 9–10; 3:15–16; 4:12–17). This is an attempt at early Christian self-identification, which perhaps underscores the recognizably Jewish character of the letter.[69] This theory draws attention to the eschatological dimension of the book in the coming of Christ (1:10–13). The eschatological and apocalyptic dimensions have also been emphasized in other recent interpretation.[70] This position, while it draws attention to the use of the OT, has the shortcomings of many midrashic interpretations in that it is difficult to establish what exactly is meant by the term and whether it is a viable category for describing a book of the NT.

f. Summary. These proposals highlight the important mix of material in 1 Peter. The writer places clear emphasis upon offering encouragement and exhortation to a people undergoing times of suffering and persecution. According to one's understanding of the letter's character, the author might do this by appealing to one of their fundamental practices, such as baptism, or by discussing social

relations (2:11–20; 3:1–12). But mostly the writer chooses to emphasize the importance of holy living (1:13–2:3) on the basis of a renewed life through the resurrection of Jesus Christ from the dead (1:3–9). This is the foundation that allows the believer to endure persecution and to endure the various adverse circumstances that will inevitably come (3:13–22; 4:12–5:5).

C. 2 Peter and Jude

Scholarship has recently experienced a revival of interest in 2 Peter and Jude because they raise a number of issues regarding the shape and formation of the NT.

1. Authorship of 2 Peter

a. Pseudonymous Authorship. The majority of scholars believe that 2 Peter is pseudonymous. Six major factors point in this direction.[71] (1) Second Peter is apparently dependent on Jude. A synopsis of 2 Peter and Jude shows that 2 Peter has apparently borrowed and/or adapted nineteen of the twenty-five verses of Jude (Jude 4–13, 16–18 in 2 Pet 2:1–18; 3:1–3).[72] This may not be problematic in itself, but Peter was supposed to be one of the closest disciples of Jesus. If this is so and if Peter is the apostle who stands behind Mark's Gospel (illustrating that his memory was perfectly capable of recounting what had happened earlier in his life), it is difficult to understand his dependence upon Jude (see below on Jude). (2) Second Peter's style is very different from that of 1 Peter and, indeed, any other book in the NT. There is a larger proportion of *hapax legomena*—words appearing only one time—in 2 Peter than in any other book of the NT, and also a number of elaborate constructions. Some have therefore maintained that the style of 2 Peter resembles the so-called Asiatic style, a kind of Greek that originated in some rhetorical circles and, although characterized by an aspiration to lofty thoughts, seems to have ended up merely with inflated and unwieldy syntax and archaic and unnatural vocabulary.[73] Second Peter's style makes it very difficult to accept that 1 and 2 Peter are both authentically Petrine and to link 2 Peter with any other possible author in the NT. (3) The third objection to Petrine authorship concerns the reference in 3:15–16 to Paul's letters as Scripture (his statement that they are difficult to understand is simply an early confirmation of what many still think). This seems to imply that Paul's letters had already been collected together, something that scholars have until very recently considered unlikely until sometime late in the first century at the earliest. It also implies a recognized authoritative status for the Pauline Letters, something that many scholars do not consider to have been given until well into the second century. Such a late date of composition seems to be confirmed by references in 2 Peter to the apostles and fathers as "in the past," like the prophets (3:2, 4). (4) Second Peter seems to be a second-generation Christian composition, reflecting what has been called "early catholicism." That is, after the initial charisma wore off, Christians came to terms with the failure of Christ's imminent return through an increasing institutionalization and a crystallization of the faith into set forms—e.g., 1:19–21, concerned with regulating prophecy; 2:1–3, acknowledging that there are many false prophets present in the church; and 3:3–4, occasioned by Christians dying before Christ returns.[74] (5) That 2 Peter was a later pseudonymous composition may be confirmed by what appears to be relatively late initial acceptance of 2 Peter as authoritative Scripture. Although 2 Peter may have been known in the second century (*Apoc. Pet* 1 [2 Pet 2:1, 8], 21 [1:19], 22, 28 [2:2, 21], 30 [2:21; 3:2]), it probably was not widely used until the third or fourth century, when it began to be accepted as an authoritative writing. $\mathfrak{P}^{72}$, dated third or fourth century, is the earliest text referring to this document (cf. Justin, *Dial.* 82.1 [2:1]).[75] (6) In light of this evidence, it is generally posited that 2 Peter is not a personal letter but, rather, a genuine letter sent to churches familiar with 1 Peter and the Pauline Letters in the form of a "farewell speech" or "testament," a literary form familiar from intertestamental literature (e.g., *Testament of Moses, Testaments of the Twelve Patriarchs, Testament of Job, 1 En.* 91–104). The letter was probably written to encourage a later generation of Christians not to abandon the Christian faith because Jesus had not yet come. The letter indicates a context in the late first century, at the earliest, and probably well into the second century, when Christians were abandoning their early-held apocalyptic beliefs. This would explain the writer's motivation to encourage his people

and use the strongest name he could find, that of Peter, to underscore the importance of their holding fast to their hope that Christ would return again soon. This is the heart of 2 Pet 2–3. The fact that very few of the church fathers ever cite 2 Peter as an authority for the church indicates its lack of early reception as authoritative. The early church fathers were probably not fooled into thinking that it was written by Peter. This case for pseudonymous authorship has proved so convincing that there is little debate among most scholars over the authorship of 2 Peter.

b. Traditional Authorship. The traditional view of authorship of 2 Peter is that the book was written by Peter, the disciple of Jesus, around A.D. 62 or thereabouts, from Rome. This position is based upon a number of factors, not least that the book makes a direct claim to Petrine authorship (1:1). The author notes that his death is close (1:14) and that he was a witness to the transfiguration (1:16–18). There is furthermore the statement in 3:1 that this is the "second letter," 1 Peter being most likely the first. This raises important questions regarding the use of pseudonymity in the ancient world and, in particular, the early church. First, in light of 3:1, it is difficult to avoid the thought that the author was apparently attempting to have this work accepted as the second Petrine letter by making a specific reference to it as the "second letter." If this is not actually Peter writing, it is legitimate to raise the issue of motivation; in other words, through the use of personal references or details, did the author deliberately try to lead the original audience to accept the letter as from Peter? Second, if pseudonymity is transparent fiction, why could the letter not have gone out under the name of the actual author, since this person or group would have been known to the recipients? The test, it is often said, of a work in the early church was orthodoxy.[76] If this is true (it is subject to close definition), there is even less reason for the letter to attempt to make a claim of Petrine authorship, since it only needed to be judged sufficient on theological grounds. Further, why did personal details need to be used at all if the letter were a transparent fiction, since everyone would have known that the letter was not written by the purported author?

As a way of defending Petrine authorship, questions are often raised regarding the pseudepigraphal hypothesis to mitigate the force of the opposing arguments. This method does less to prove the case for Petrine authorship than to temper the assuredness of the pseudepigraphal hypothesis. Nevertheless, many valid questions can be raised, among them the following.

(1) Regarding literary dependence, as Knight rightly notes, there are five possibilities for the relationship between Jude and 2 Peter, each of them attracting advocates: (a) Jude is dependent upon 2 Peter, (b) 2 Peter is dependent on Jude, (c) one interpolated the other, (d) both are dependent on a common source, and (e) both have a common author.[77] Most scholars opt for the second, but as Neyrey says, "they have by no means proven it,"[78] since the evidence can be seen to support arguments on all sides. Indeed, some of the statistical information leaves the question of priority seemingly unprovable. As Donald Guthrie says of the relationships between the two writings:

> Verbal agreements are not impressive. If statistics are any guide, the following data may supply some indication. Out of the parallel passages comprising 2 Peter i. 2, 12, ii. 1–4, 6, 10–12, 15–18, iii. 2, 3 and Jude 2, 4–13, 17, 18, the former contain 297 words and the latter 256 words, but they share only 78 in common. This means that if 2 Peter is the borrower he has changed 70% of Jude's language and added more of his own. Whereas if Jude borrowed from 2 Peter, the percentage of alteration is slightly higher, combined with a reduction in quantity. Clearly there can be no question of direct copying or of editorial adaptation. It is also significant that out of twelve parallel sections, Jude's text is verbally longer than 2 Peter's on five occasions, showing that neither author can be considered more concise than the other. The passages showing the greatest verbal agreement are 2 Pet iii. 2, 3 and Jude 17, 18 (16 words). . . . Perhaps at this point the author relied on his "copy" rather than his memory. The only other passages where extended verbal agreement is found are 2 Pet. ii. 12 and Jude 10, 12a (14 words), the only passages incidentally where the order of the two Epistles slightly diverges (Jude 11 corresponds to 2 Pet. i. 15, 16).[79]

(2) Concerning style, it is incontrovertibly clear that there are differences between 2 and 1 Peter.[80] In light of the limited evidence, however, one must examine what bearing this has on Petrine authorship. If Silvanus was responsible for 1 Peter, then 2 Peter could have been written by someone else, even Peter, especially in light of the badly executed attempt at lofty style, such as someone trying too hard might well have done. If both letters reflect amanuenses (see Jerome, *Ep.* 120.11, on Peter's pos-

sible use of two interpreters), then the comparison is simply between various scribes and even more difficult to quantify in relation to Peter. The appeal to an amanuensis is not solid evidence, since so little is known of the particularities of scribal use by NT writers, but it at least raises further questions regarding authorship. Knight has suggested, however, that the differences are more than simply stylistic, that they are theological as well. For example, different eschatological wording is used (e.g., 1 Pet 1:7, 13 [2 Pet 3:4, 10]; 1 Pet 1:9 [2 Pet 1:11]). He also notes, however, that "1 Peter has a general application (1.1–2) while 2 Peter seems more obviously designed to meet a specific situation in an unnamed church."[81] Differences in circumstances could well account for differences in content, without resolving the issue of authorship.

(3) The exclusion of Petrine authorship on the basis of an appeal to the collected Pauline Letters as "scripture," indicating a date into the second century, cannot be easily mitigated, unless one is able to show that the use of γραφή (*graphē*) in the plural is not a technical term (as it appears to be virtually everywhere else in the NT) or that the Pauline Letters were gathered together and achieved authoritative status very early. Some have tried to show that the Pauline writings were gathered together very early, but this has yet to be proven. The author may in fact not know the entire Pauline corpus but be alluding merely to all the letters known to him at the time, and the Scriptures he is referring to may be what we now call the OT.

(4) As to 2 Peter reflecting "early catholicism," one must be careful in the use and definition of such terms. For, as Hengel has shown, one can argue that Jesus and Paul reflect characteristics of early catholicism, including various dimensions of church institutionalization.[82]

(5) Concerning acknowledgment and citation of 2 Peter in the early church, there is no denying the lack of early evidence of 2 Peter's existence and of early utilization. This bears on authenticity but is of more importance regarding authority.

(6) Concerning the testament as the most likely genre, Charles has recently attacked the premise of this literary form and the validity of the comparison. He questions the idea that the testamental literature provided a transparent fiction, and thus justifies its pseudepigraphal status without introducing the element of deception. He also doubts

that this is how the literary form of testament would have been applied in the case of 2 Peter, especially in light of the fact that the church apparently later forgot that 2 Peter was pseudepigraphal for a number of centuries. On the validity of equating 2 Peter with a testament, Charles notes that many of the features of the testament (e.g., apocalyptic elements, blessings and curses, the transference of authority, the lack of prominence of the author's death) are lacking in 2 Peter.[83]

For most scholars, debate over authorship of 2 Peter has been long resolved, however. The matters of content, style, language, historical references and context, and early church ignorance of it have led most to conclude that 2 Peter is not by the author of 1 Peter, and certainly not by the Apostle Peter.

2. Authorship and Date of Jude

The book of Jude begins with the claim that the author is the brother of James (Jude 1). Although there were several individuals named James in the early church (see sec. 3, above), the most likely here is James the brother of Jesus, who, although not mentioned in the accounts of Jesus' ministry, became the leader of the Jerusalem church (Gal 1:19; 2:9, 12; Acts 12:17; 15:13; 21:28) and is seen as the traditional author of the book with his name. There are also five Judes worth mentioning: Jude/Judas the brother of Jesus (Mark 6:3; cf. Eusebius, *Hist. eccl.* 3.19.1–3.20.7), Judas of Acts 9:11, Thomas known as Jude by Syrian Christianity, Judas Barsabbas (Acts 15:22, 26, 31), and Judas of James (*Apos. Con.* 7.46). In light of the ability to identify a Jude with a known James, the most likely traditional hypothesis is that this is Jude the brother of James and of Jesus.[84]

At this point, however, the traditional ascription of authorship encounters difficulty. Many scholars think that the ascription of authorship is an attempt to align the book with the family of Jesus. This falls afoul of several of the same problems that the traditional ascriptions of James and 1 Peter do, including the level of Greek, considered far too sophisticated for a typical Jew from Galilee. There are other questions as well. If this James is the brother of Jesus (and the author of the book of James according to the traditional view), it is more than passing strange that the author makes no explicit claim to be the brother of Jesus. If this James is other than

the brother of Jesus, then the author is making a claim to be the brother of an otherwise uncertain person in the NT. Others have argued that Jude shows signs of early catholicism—for example, in v. 3 about contending for "the faith." Thus, as Kümmel states, "Jude must be considered a pseudonymous writing. That is all the more fitting if Jude 1 contains a reference to a pseudonymous James."[85]

Many have not followed Kümmel in his judgment, however.[86] Since there is no explicit identification of who this Jude was, it is difficult to argue that the work is pseudonymous, because it could well be that there was some other Jude, the brother of a James, who was the author but is unknown to us now. Second, the work was cited frequently in the second and third centuries (e.g., Tertullian, *apparel.* 1.3; Clement of Alexandria, cited in Eusebius, *Hist. eccl.* 6.14) and perhaps even earlier (e.g., *Did.* 2.7 [Jude 22–23]; 3.6 [Jude 8–10]),[87] leaving even less time for a pseudonymous work to be written at a distance from the original author. It appears that questions only arose about the authority of Jude in the fourth century and beyond, when some had trouble accepting the author's citation of pseudepigraphal Jewish writings (see no. 3, below). Third, there is the further question of the plausibility of this being a pseudonymous writing. Why would someone wish to write in the name of a relatively obscure figure in the early church, since pseudonymous writings have the overwhelming tendency to be written in the name of well-known and identifiable figures (e.g., Paul, Peter, Enoch, Moses, the patriarchs)? This makes it relatively difficult to conceive of a situation that would have prompted someone to use Jude's name to construct a pseudonymous letter, and even more difficult to conceive of the church accepting such a letter as authoritative.

Even if Jude is authentic, however, reconstructing the situation of its composition is still difficult. The book is probably a genuine letter, perhaps written in a Jewish exhortatory fashion, to a group characterized as "those who are called." There seems to be some problem with antinomianism, addressed by appealing to apocalyptic Jewish writings. If the letter is genuine, it could have been written from around A.D. 50 to 80, since it shows no signs of early catholicism. If it is pseudonymous, it could have been written from A.D. 80 to anytime in the second century.[88]

The Kidron Valley, looking south with the Temple Mount on the right and the Mount of Olives on the left.
© Rohr Productions. Used with permission.

3. Jude and the Citation of Pseudepigraphal Sources

There have been a number of questions raised by Jude's apparent quotation of two pseudepigraphal writings and by what this may imply regarding his relationship to his community of faith, the development of the OT canon, and the concept of an authoritative body of Scriptures. This discussion is, of course, only a part of the larger topic of NT citation of the OT and other texts. Although there are no direct citations of the OT in Jude, recent interpreters have come to appreciate the author's apparent literary sophistication in employing biblical themes and topics to address the subjects discussed in the letter. For example, Charles has noted that the author uses a prophetic typology that draws upon nine subjects—unbelieving Israel (v. 5), fallen angels (v. 6), Sodom and Gomorrah (v. 7), Michael the archangel (v. 9), Moses (v. 9), Cain, Balaam, Korah (v. 11), and Enoch (vv. 14–15)—to counter those who pose a danger to his community of faith.[89]

Whereas the author alludes to biblical material in most of the examples, in vv. 9 and 14–15 he draws upon nonbiblical sources. It is possible that v. 9, through paraphrase and allusion, is citing the *Assumption of Moses* regarding a dispute between the archangel Michael and Satan, an episode unknown in any canonical text (but see Deut 34:1–6; Zech 3:2); it is difficult to make a strong case for direct quotation. Verses 14–15, however, appear to quote *1 En.* 1:9 concerning the Lord's coming with his holy or elect to judge the ungodly. First, the author sets the stage for the quotation by referring to Enoch, in the seventh generation from Adam, as the one who prophesied the words. Some think that the author believes that the words of *1 En.* 1:9 come from the canonical Enoch (Gen 5:24) when in fact *1 Enoch* is a pseudepigraphal work probably written between the early second century B.C. (190–180 B.C.) and, for some parts, the first century A.D. Second, the question is sometimes raised about the implications of citing a pseudepigraphal work in what is now a canonical document—a question prompted by a literalistic interpretation of the theological concept of inspiration. It also has implications for a number of other citations in the NT from extrabiblical writers, such as Aratus in Acts 17:28 and Menander in 1 Cor 15:33. Third and most important, the citation of *1 Enoch* raises the question

of the status of the Ketuvim, or Writings of the OT. This is not the place to debate the formation of the OT canon (see ch. 13, below), but the range of scholarly opinion on the time when such a process became formalized has extended in recent years from the fourth century B.C. into the first, second, or even fifth centuries A.D. According to one highly persuasive view, the author of Jude considered *1 Enoch*, and possibly the *Assumption of Moses*, to be a part of his authoritative writings.

Charles has attempted to show, however, that part of the literary artistry of the author of the book of Jude may be to emphasize the tension between the faithful and the ungodly. His prophetic typology is designed, according to this position, to reenforce the call to faithfulness by drawing upon types from the past. The same might be the case in the use of *1 En.* 1:9. Charles acknowledges that the writings of Enoch may have been held in high regard by the opponents of Jude. He glosses v. 14 as "For even (your own) Enoch . . . prophesied," which suggests to Charles that Jude adapted the quotation to suit his own theological and literary purposes. Rather than endorsing the text as authoritative, Jude is, then, acknowledging the authoritative status of the text for others.[90] This view would put Jude's perspective in line with Paul's citation of extrabiblical texts as well. Nevertheless, the difference between Paul's quotations of extrabiblical poets and Jude's statement that Enoch prophesied may well present a difficult barrier for Charles's position to overcome, since those who prophesied in a writing were considered to be prophets led by the Spirit of God to write. If true, it is perhaps the case that, for whatever reason, the author of Jude cited *1 En.* 1:9 as part of his authoritative writings.

D. Basic Characteristics and Message

These three letters, 1 and 2 Peter and Jude, have much in common, and much that separates them. Questions of authorship and dating have a direct influence on how one chooses to characterize their contents.

As an example, 1 Peter in many ways has a very different attitude toward the Christian life than does 2 Peter or Jude. Addressed ostensibly to those of the dispersion in Asia Minor, 1 Peter has an opening thanksgiving that exalts God for the blessings that he has provided to those who have been born anew to a living hope through the resurrection of Christ. The letter then develops the idea of what it means to live as the people of God in the midst of suffering. Even though the context is one of suffering, the letter concentrates upon the positive dimensions of the Christian experience. Suffering is not seen as something to be shunned or as a sign of God's disfavor. On the contrary, the readers are exhorted to holiness as God's chosen people. This holiness is to manifest itself in their personal relations, which could involve suffering for doing what is right and good, including suffering for being Christians. One of the most interesting passages in 1 Peter from the standpoint of modern interpretation is the apparent endorsement in 1 Pet 2:13–17 of being subject to the government, because it is God's will. This passage has been variously interpreted, as noted above (see sec. B.1), because it seems to provide evidence for early composition, and it has made for very difficult situations for Christians of later years who have wanted to follow these commands but are faced with tyrannical governments that seem to be doing anything but punishing evil and praising what is right. A second intriguing passage is found in 1 Pet 3:18–21, where the author speaks of Christ preaching to spirits in prison, those who formerly disobeyed. The language here is allusive, as well as elusive, as most commentaries attest. The author is probably alluding to the thought, related to that found in some intertestamental and apocalyptic documents, that Christ during the time he was in the tomb went to the underworld and pronounced a message of judgment on sinners from the time of Noah. Without getting overly concerned to exegete this passage, we can say that the point is that Christ's ultimate triumph through the resurrection is assured, and this constitutes part of the assurance of the letter.

Second Peter and Jude, on the other hand, as noted above, have much in common, however that commonality is explained. Whereas 1 Peter had a more moderate tone in the face of adversity, 2 Peter and Jude have a more strident tone. The apparently different contexts perhaps account for this. Second Peter reflects a situation in which the readers have been infiltrated by false prophets and teachers, who are introducing teaching that the author does not endorse. The author has very strong words to say about their behavior

and standards of conduct and about the punishment that awaits them. The readers are perhaps susceptible to their teaching because of disappointment about the return of Christ. The author of 2 Peter seems to be sensitive to the need to remind his readers of what they have been taught in the past and recognizes that the kinds of false teachers who have joined their group are to be expected and, in fact, were prophetically anticipated. In other words, God's sovereign power attests to his ultimate triumph when he judges those who are ungodly. The book of Jude continues this same theme, with its advocacy of the destruction of the ungodly and its exhortation to contend for the faith. A litany of those in Egypt, Sodom and Gomorrah, and elsewhere who have met with such previous destruction is offered. In support of his case, the author cites *1 En.* 1:9 as evidence of the judging power of God.

E. Outlines of 1 Peter, 2 Peter, and Jude

1. 1 Peter[91]

   A. Opening (1:1–2)
      1. Sender (1:1a)
      2. Addressee (1:1b–2a)
      3. Greeting (1:2b)
   B. Thanksgiving (1:3–9)
   C. Body: Living for God in the midst of suffering (1:10–5:11)
      1. The basis of salvation (1:10–12)
      2. Being the people of God in the midst of suffering (1:13–5:11)
   D. Closing (5:12–14)
      1. Greetings (5:12–14a)
      2. Benediction (5:14b)

2. 2 Peter

   A. Opening (1:1–2)
      1. Sender (1:1a)
      2. Addressee (1:1b)
      3. Greeting (1:2)
   B. Body: The sufficiency of God (1:3–3:10)
      1. Confirming one's faith (1:3–11)
      2. The need for a reminder (1:12–21)
      3. False teachers (2:1–22)
      4. The Day of the Lord (3:1–10)
   C. Parenesis (3:11–16)
   D. Closing (3:17–18)

The so-called Absalom's Pillar, or Absalom's Tomb, in the Kidron Valley dates from the first century B.C.
© Rohr Productions. Used with permission.

The Tombs of the Kings in Jerusalem, constructed by Queen Helena of Adiabene in the middle of the first century A.D.
She was buried here with her family (see Josephus, Wars 5:2; Ant. 20:4). © Rohr Productions. Used with permission.

3. Jude

A. Opening (1–2)
  1. Sender (1a)
  2. Addressee (1b)
  3. Greeting (2)
B. Body: The doom of the ungodly (3–19)
  1. Appeal to contend for the faith (3–4)
  2. Examples from the OT (5–13)
  3. Enoch (14–16)
  4. The apostles (17–19)
C. Parenesis (20–23)
D. Closing (doxology) (24–25)

5. THE JOHANNINE LETTERS

A. Introduction

A number of features particular to each of the Johannine Letters demand individual attention, but there are also a number of common features that allow the letters to be examined together here. Many scholars have grouped these three letters together with John's Gospel and Revelation even though the three letters were not always treated together in the early church (e.g., Eusebius, *Hist. eccl.* 3.39.17, where Papias seems to know only 1 John, or possibly did not use 2 and 3 John). Today many, if not most, scholars dispute that these five books have a common authorship and were written by an apostle.

B. Literary Genre

Although they are referred to as the Johannine Letters, there is considerable doubt over whether they are of the same genre. On the surface, 2 and 3 John appear to be genuine letters.[92] Their epistolary features include the following: a length similar to that of other letter papyri (ca. 250 words), an epistolary opening (2 John 1–3; 3 John 1), a thanksgiving/health wish (2 John 4; 3 John 2), addressing the recipients in the vocative case (case of address) (2 John 5; 3 John 2, 5, 11), a request formula (2 John 5–6; 3 John 5–6), the promise of a visit (2 John 12; 3 John 14), an epistolary closing (2 John 12–13; 3 John 13–14), and a mention of writing to the recipients (2 John 5, 12; 3 John 9, 13). Lieu has pointed out, however, that whereas 3 John follows the Hellenistic epistolary form very closely, 2 John seems to reflect features of the Pauline epistolary

form. Pauline features include an expanded greeting, a thanksgiving instead of a health wish, and a peace benediction. 2 John is also characterized by a number of impersonal statements (e.g., the reference to the "elect lady" in 2 John 1). Third John is clearly a genuine letter, and 2 John may be addressing a real situation as well. The possible Pauline influence may mean that 2 John has a theological emphasis not found in 3 John.

More problematic by far is determining the genre of 1 John. Evidence has been marshaled both for and against its being a genuine letter. The evidence against is very similar to the evidence often suggested for the books of Hebrews and James. As Westcott says, "It has no address, no subscription; no name is contained in it of person or place: there is no direct trace of the author, no indication of any special destination."[93] There are also no concluding remarks or epistolary closing. Nevertheless, as Westcott also points out, there is a personal tone to the writing, as the author seems to be reflecting on actual circumstances on the basis of personal experience. There are also a number of references within the letter to "writing" (1 John 2:1, 7, 12, 13, 14, 26) and the frequent use of the second person plural (e.g, 1:5; 3:1).

What can be concluded from this evidence? It is difficult to know what to think about 1 John. It is not entirely certain that it is a letter, or at least a genuine letter sent to a real epistolary situation. But even if one concludes that it is a letter, what kind of a letter is it? The following proposals are worth noting (similar proposals would apply to 2 and 3 John).[94] (1) Some have suggested that it is a pastoral letter, written by a leader to his church. Several references indicate the pastoral and personal involvement of the author with the congregation. These include addressing the recipients in terms of affection, such as "children" (1 John 2:1, 12, 14, 18, 28; 3:7, 18; 4:4), and other terms of close relation, such as "fathers" (2:13, 14). (2) Another view is that the letter was some form of sermon or informal tract. Striving to teach and instruct his congregation, the author addresses in a pastoral tone the crisis that has arisen in the church. With its use of the second person plural and direct address, 1 John has many of the characteristics of popular philosophy, such as the diatribe, known also in religious instructional material of the time. (3) Others have suggested that the letter was never meant as strictly a personal or pastoral letter but, rather, as an encyclical or general letter. Rather than respond to a crisis in a single local church, the author addresses the letter to a number of churches, although these would probably have to be seen as "Johannine" churches, that is, churches within the scope of the author's authority or influence. This view is consistent with the fact that this is the only NT letter to contain no single personal name and that it is not addressed to a specific church (but cf. Ephesians, which, though it is probably not a circular letter, mentions only one person, Tychicus, in 6:21). There is also no OT quotation in the book, with a quotation perhaps to be expected as providing a common theological basis for an encyclical letter. The only OT reference is to Cain in 3:12, but it is not certain how this may or may not help the view that the letter is circular or general. (4) Related to proposal 3 is the idea that 1 John was a general religious tract. Not written to a specific church or situation, it may have been written for the whole of Christianity, as a kind of manifesto of Christian belief regarding what it means to be a child of God in a world where God's love must survive amidst false witness. This view, however, probably overlooks some of the more specific features of the writing, such as the Johannine language and tradition and the reference to some who "went out" (2:19, 22). (5) A fifth proposal is that the book served a cultic or liturgical purpose. It may have been a baptismal or catechetical document, designed to teach recent converts. The moralistic and hortatory tone (see, e.g., 1:3, 4; 5:13 with commands for living the proper Christian life) creates a didactic emphasis in the letter. More particularly, the reference in 5:8 to the three that bear witness, "the Spirit and the water and the blood," is thought by some to reflect the three stages of Christian initiation, that is, reception of the Holy Spirit, baptism, and the Eucharist or first communion. Like all liturgical hypotheses, however, although there are a number of factors that perhaps can be interpreted in this way, it is difficult to prove that the document was written to conform to such a genre. (6) Lastly, some have proposed that there perhaps is not a specific genre to which 1 John conforms but that it is itself a kind of commentary on the Gospel of John. The letter is not addressed to the adversaries but, rather, to those of the Johannine commu-

nity, elucidating Johannine ideas that had perhaps been disputed or misinterpreted.

Although it cannot be decided to which genre 1 John belongs, the most convincing interpretations are those that recognize the writing is addressing a specific situation. Rather than intending a composition for universal Christianity, or even for a number of unnamed churches spread over a large area, it appears that the author has a particular situation in mind, even if it is one that may be relevant for more than a single church or a single community of believers. The failure to specify the author implies that the churches knew him, and the tone of address, including the terms of endearment, confirms a pastoral relationship.

The Church of St. John near Ephesus, built by Justinian I (483–565) in the sixth century. The four Byzantine columns in the center, at the nave of the church, are believed by many to mark the burial site of John the apostle. Photo Lee M. McDonald.

C. Reception, Authorship and Date, and Order of Composition

1. Reception

Scholars have debated whether instances of possible wording from the Johannine writings in a number of early writers are citations or merely reflect common theological language.[95] These passages include *1 Clem.* 49.5, 50.3 (1 John 4:18); 27.1, 60.1 (1 John 1:9); *Did.* 10.5 (1 John 4:18); *Barn.* 5.9–11 (1 John 4:2; 2 John 7); *Barn.* 14.5 (1 John 3:4, 7, 8); Pol. *Phil.* 7.1–2 (1 John 4:2; 3:8; 2:18; 2:22; 2 John 7); *2 Clem.* 6.9 (1 John 2:1); Herm. *Mand.* 3.1 (1 John 2:27); 12.3.5 (1 John 5:3); Herm. *Sim.* 9.24.4 (1 John 4:13); and *Diogn.* 10.2–3 (1 John 4:9, 19); 11.14 (1 John 1:1). More certain is direct reference by

Irenaeus, *Haer.* 16.3 (2 John 11), 16.5 (1 John 2:18–19, 21–22), 16.8 (2 John 7–8; 1 John 4:1–2; 5:1), and Eusebius. As mentioned above, Eusebius cites Papias as familiar with 1 John (*Hist. eccl.* 3.39.17) and Origen as familiar with 2 and 3 John, although he also notes that not all considered them genuine (*Hist. eccl.* 6.25.10). Clement of Alexandria, among later writers, offers plentiful evidence for 1 John (*Misc.* 2.15.66 [1 John 5:16–17]; 3.4.32 [1 John 1:6–7]; 3.5.42, 44; 3.6.45; *Salvation* 37.6 [1 John 3:15]; *Misc.* 4.16.100 [1 John 3:18–19; 4:16, 18]; 5.1.13 [1 John 4:16]; 4.18.113 [1 John 4:16]; *Salvation* 38 [1 John 4:18]). If the early references are citations of the Johannine writings, 1 John is far better attested than 2 and 3 John; and 2 John was apparently known earlier than 3 John, which was hardly known at all. The early references are most clearly to 1 John, but there is very little early evidence that is clear about the use of 2 or 3 John, especially the latter. The Muratorian Fragment only mentions two letters by John (which two is not certain, but few scholars believe the fragment refers to 3 John); thus, the evidence for all three Johannine writings being known is fairly late (third century on), with 2 and 3 John being disputed even at that time.

2. Authorship, Date, and Order of Composition

All three of the Johannine writings are formally anonymous. Second and 3 John are said to be written by the "elder," but without any designation of who this elder might be. Various views have been advocated: that they were written by one author, or that 1 John and 2 and 3 John were written by two different authors, or that they were written by three different authors. There is also the question whether the letters, especially 1 John, were written by the same author as the Fourth Gospel. The general scholarly opinion is that the three letters were written by the same author, although there is disagreement whether this was the same author as that of the Gospel.[96] Those who argue that the books share the same author do not usually believe that this was an apostolic author.

a. 1 John. The traditional view—that 1 John was written by the author of the Fourth Gospel, John the son of Zebedee, the disciple of Jesus—is based on a number of considerations. These include lin-guistic similarities: numerous phrases where similar, if not identical, wording is used (e.g., 1 John 4:6 and John 14:17: "the spirit of truth"); grammatical and stylistic features, such as failure to use the relative pronoun, the use of "that" or an equivalent (e.g., 1 John 3:11 and John 15:12), and the use of asyndeton; and similarities of vocabulary (including words for "sin" [ἁμαρτία, *hamartia*, etc.], "darkness" [σκοτία, *skotia*], "dead" [νεκρός, *nekros*], "savior" [σωτήρ, *sōtēr*], "world" [κόσμος, *kosmos*], and "live" and "life" [ζῶ, *zō*; ζωή, *zōē*]).[97] In conjunction with similarities in vocabulary are similarities in motifs, such as the polarities of light and dark, life and death, truth and life, love and hate, between which there is no middle ground.[98] It has also been argued that both 1 John and the Fourth Gospel share the "same divine purpose or scheme of salvation."[99] But this evidence, though consistently pointing to John as the author, tends, like the evidence for the Gospel, to be highly circumstantial—in other words, based upon the issues and perspective of certain types of early Christianity.

Arguments against the Johannine authorship of 1 John, that is, against associating the letter with the Gospel, tend to rely upon various negative factors.[100] (a) First is their formal anonymity. Although they have anonymity in common, it is extremely difficult to establish a line of connection between them, since there is no explicit claim to authorship in either document. (b) There are also numerous differences of style, such as 1 John's use of conditional sentences in ways unparalleled in the Gospel (e.g., 1 John 1:6, 8, 9; 2:1, 29; 5:9, 15). (c) Another factor is vocabulary. Despite many similarities, there are also numerous differences; for instance, the words for "glory" and "glorify" (δόξα, *doxa*; δοξάζω, *doxazō*), "grace" (χάρις, *charis*), "fullness" (πλήρωμα, *plērōma*), "heaven" (οὐρανός, *ouranos*), and "save" and "salvation" (σῴζω, *sōzō*; σωτηρία, *sōtēria*) are missing from 1 John. (d) The theological perspective is different in the two books. For example, 1 John looks to the near return of Christ (1 John 2:25, 28), whereas the Gospel has a realized eschatology. First John views the death of Christ as propitiatory (1 John 2:2; 4:10), whereas the Gospel sees his death as an exaltation and glorification. The concept of the Spirit in 1 John (e.g., 1 John 3:24; 4:6, 13; 5:6–8) is not as developed as in the Gospel, especially in John 14–16.[101] (e) If the Fourth Gospel was a community product (as many recent scholars believe) and if 1 John was related to a community within which there may have been a Johannine school (as some scholars believe on the basis of the use of "we" in the letters: 1 John 1:5; 3:11),[102] it would be exceptionally difficult to speak of a common author for the two works, or even of the concept of authorship in traditional terms. In this scenario, a later Johannine community, perhaps associated with Ephesus (see Eusebius, *Hist. eccl.* 3.31.3; 5.24.2; Irenaeus, *Haer.* 3.1.1), was responsible for continuing and developing the tradition of John. Whereas the Gospel might well be based upon some actual or early reminiscences of the apostle, an epistolary tradition, influenced by the Pauline missionary strategy, perhaps grew up around Ephesus. This would have entailed widespread letter writing (making plausible a composition date around A.D. 100, which could apply even if apostolic authorship for both writings is maintained). This speculation is plausible because the territories of Pauline and Johannine Christian groups could have overlapped and the Pauline epistolary strategy probably influenced other Christian movements.

b. 2 and 3 John. Like 1 John, 2 and 3 John are formally anonymous, in that there is no explicit claim to named authorship. The author calls himself the "elder," and this has elicited a number of interpretations.[103] One is that it is an explicit claim to authorship, most probably of John the disciple, as John was an "elder statesman of the church, that is, an apostle" (cf. 1 Pet 5:1). Another is that the elder is one who had a position of formal authority in a local congregation. A third theory is that the elder was a disciple of the original apostles, such as the John the Elder, or Presbyter, mentioned by Eusebius (*Hist. eccl.* 3.39.3–4), quoting Papias:

> I shall not hesitate to append to the interpretations all that I ever learnt well from the presbyters and remember well, for of their truth I am confident. For unlike most I did not rejoice in them who say much, but in them who teach the truth, nor in them who recount the commandments of others, but in them who repeated those given to the faith by the Lord and derived from truth itself but if ever anyone came who had followed the presbyters, I inquired into the words of the presbyters, what Andrew or Peter or Philip or Thomas or James or John or Matthew, or any other of the Lord's disciples, had said, and what Aristion and the presbyter John, the Lord's disciples were saying (Lake, LCL).

Eusebius (ibid., 3.39.5) offers an interpretation of this passage from Papias:

> It is here worth noting that he twice counts the name of John, and reckons the first John with Peter and James and Matthew and the other Apostles, clearly meaning the evangelist, but by changing his statement places the second with the others outside the number of the Apostles, putting Aristion before him and clearly calling him a presbyter. This confirms the truth of the story of those who have said that there were two of the same name in Asia, and that there are two tombs at Ephesus both still called John's. This calls for attention: for it is probable that the second (unless anyone prefer the former) saw the revelation which passes under the name of John (LCL).

Many think that Eusebius misinterpreted Papias and that the two Johns are the same, designated differently because John perhaps outlived the other apostles into the next era.

These may be tempting propositions, but none of them can be definitively proved, since the ascription in the Johannine Letters is only to the "elder," leaving the identification uncertain and the work formally anonymous. As noted above, the traditional view that the author of 2 and 3 John is John the disciple or apostle, the author of 1 John and the Gospel, is not directly supported by the text. There is certainly some linkage of 2 and 3 John to 1 John in vocabulary and themes, such as the attestation that Jesus Christ came in the flesh (2 John 7 and 1 John 4:2) and concern for the deceiver or antichrist (2 John 7 and 1 John 2:23). These parallels may well show that the books issued from a similar context, but they cannot establish authorship.

c. Order of Composition. Earlier in this century there were a number of proposals regarding sources of the Johannine Letters, but these have found little to commend them and are not often maintained.[104] More important for discussion is whether the letters were composed in their canonical order. All possible combinations have been proposed at one time or another. Some alter the canonical order because they consider 2 and 3 John suitable introductions to 1 John. In 2 John 9–11, it has been argued, the false teachers have not yet arrived, while in 1 John they clearly have, and the letter is a response to them (1 John 2:18, 22) and notes that they have gone out (1 John 2:19; 4:1–3). Brown raises the possibility that the statements in 2 John 10–11, about excluding false teachers, may have led to their formal secession mentioned in 1 John 2:19.[105] In spite of these arguments, the evidence is insufficient to establish the order of composition.

D. Situation and Content

The major themes of all three letters seem to reflect late-first-century and possibly second-century disputes in the church. Whereas later christological disputes in the third and fourth centuries focused upon the divine character of Jesus Christ, it appears that 1 John confronts dispute over the genuine humanity of Jesus.[106] This would be consistent with the rise of Gnosticism, or at least some form of teaching that differentiated between an immaterial, divine Christ-spirit and the physical, human Jesus. The divine spirit was seen to be good, while physical being was linked to inherently evil matter. It is possible that these letters were written in response to teaching that maintained that the Christ-spirit came upon the human Jesus, possibly at baptism, and left him at the crucifixion, the problem of Docetism. In response to this, the Johannine Letters assert the physical, fleshly reality of Jesus (1 John 1:1–3; 4:2–3; 5:6; 2 John 7). In conjunction with the false teaching may have been the thought that followers of Christ could attain earthly sinlessness (e.g., 1 John 3:4, 6, 8, 9; 5:18). The author appears concerned to tread a very fine line between recognizing the unavoidability of sin and not endorsing it. Although there are very serious statements in 1 John about the need to avoid sin, the author also points out that sin will occur but there is a provision for it in Christ (e.g., 1:8–10; 2:1).[107] The emphasis upon persecution, especially as it is related to eschatology, is also consistent with other writing in the late first century and with the atmosphere of Revelation (see sec. 6, below). That the church was suffering persecution is seen in the emphasis upon the many antichrists who are already in the world (1 John 2:18–28; 2 John 7), in anticipation of *the* antichrist (1 John 2:18). This sense of living in the final hours before the apocalyptic intervention is consistent with Revelation and relates the issue of authorship and date to both Revelation and the Gospel of John, with its realized eschatology.

E. Outlines of 1, 2, and 3 John

1. 1 John

A. Prologue on the word of Life (1:1–4)
B. Walking in the light (1:5–2:2)
C. Keeping God's commandments (2:3–17)
D. Warning against antichrists (2:18–27)
E. Being children of God (2:28–4:21)
F. Belief regarding Jesus (5:1–12)
G. Christian behavior (5:13–21)

2. 2 John

A. Opening (1–3)
  1. Sender (1a)
  2. Addressee (1b–2)
  3. Greeting (3)
B. Thanksgiving (4)
C. Body: Christ's command to love (5–11)
  1. The commandment of love (5–6)
  2. This teaching as the test of faith (7–11)
D. Closing (12–13)
  1. Writing (12)
  2. A hope to visit (12)
  3. Greetings (13)

3. 3 John

A. Opening (1)
  1. Sender (1a)
  2. Addressee (1b)
B. Health wish (2–4)
C. Body: Praise and blame (5–12)
  1. Praise of Gaius (5–8)
  2. Blame of Diotrephes (9–10)
  3. Praise of Demetrius (11–12)
D. Closing (13–15)
  1. Writing (13)
  2. A hope to visit (14)
  3. Peace benediction (15)

6. REVELATION

A. Introduction

In a title probably affixed to the book in the second century, what we now call the book of Revelation or the Apocalypse is given the title "Apocalypse of John" (ἀποκάλυψις Ἰωάννου, *apokalypsis Iōannou*).[108] The book itself, however, does not refer to itself as an apocalypse of John but, in 1:1, as an apocalypse of Jesus Christ (ἀποκάλυψις Ἰησοῦ Χριστοῦ, *apokalypsis Iēsou Christou*). And although the book is often referred to as an apocalypse, this is in fact the only time that the word "apocalypse" (ἀποκάλυψις, *apokalypsis*) appears in the entire book. The noun is also rare in literary Greek. Elsewhere in the NT, it means "revelation," sometimes of God (Rom 2:5) or of Christ (1 Cor 1:7), made to the church (Rom 16:25) and through the Spirit (Eph 1:17). In other words, it is not used in a technical sense, and certainly not of a kind of literature. In Rev 1:1, is the phrase "of Jesus Christ" a subjective or an objective genitive? In other words, is it a revelation that Jesus Christ *gave* or that had its origins in Jesus Christ (subjective genitive), or is it a revelation *about* Jesus Christ (objective genitive)? Revelation 1:11 and the letters that follow in chs. 2–3 from the Son of Man may indicate a subjective genitive, since the Son of Man gives these revelations. Furthermore, the wording, "which God gave to him [i.e., Jesus Christ]," in 1:1 also indicates that the construction is a subjective genitive. Thus, with the emphasis upon transmission by God and Jesus Christ, the opening words of the book are best seen as a description of the contents of the work, not a title of it per se. This is consistent with usage elsewhere in the NT.

B. Literary Genre

For the book of Revelation, three kinds of genre merit discussion: apocalypse, prophecy, and letter. Previous interpreters have tried to narrow the definition to one form, but recent interpreters argue that Revelation is a combination of the three and cannot be placed exclusively in any one category.[109]

1. Apocalypse

Since the revival of interest in apocalyptic literature in the 1940s, and especially in the 1970s, much attention has been given to defining what is meant by "apocalypse" and "apocalyptic," especially as a distinctively Jewish type of literature and perspective. Many previous definitions relied upon providing a list of significant literary and theological features and included a discussion of visionary accounts, symbolism and its interpretation, and es-

chatology.[110] There was a tendency not to distinguish between apocalypse as a literary genre, apocalyptic eschatology as a worldview, and apocalypticism as a social and religious movement.[111] Now a matrix view that takes these various features into account has been developed. The matrix approach to the discussion of apocalyptic literature differentiates three categories of data: literary features (genre), theology (content), and social setting (function). Apocalyptic literature, or the apocalypse as a literary genre, can be described as an autobiographical prose narrative of the author's visionary revelatory experiences. It is concerned to reveal transcendent and often eschatological perspectives, such as an opening of heaven to reveal the throne of God. The literature often concerns an oppressed people despairing of any kind of internal redemption of society but relying upon the intervention of God into the historical-sociological dimension of their situation. The apocalypse is also designed to legitimate such a socially transforming perspective through its presentation of otherworldly experience.[112] Thus, there is an appreciation of the literary character of the literature as revelatory, esoteric, dualistic, often pseudonymous, historically based, and exhortative, in addition to its eschatological theological dimension. Apocalyptic eschatology is concerned with the consummation of God's purposes and focuses upon such motifs as the belief in two ages, a sense of imminent expectation of the end, and a final cosmic catastrophe. Current scholarship places all this within a sociohistorical setting, for apocalyptic eschatology arose out of the tradition of prophetic eschatology, set in various oppressive political scenarios (e.g., under Antiochus IV Epiphanes in 165 B.C. or the Romans of the first century A.D. and following): the literature was written with particular crises in mind. The matrix approach has added a necessary flexibility to defining the boundaries of apocalyptic and provided a means for comparing within these broad categories of literary features, theology, and social setting.

The book of Revelation evidences features of apocalyptic literature in at least three major ways.[113] (1) The book is concerned to convey the disclosure of a transcendent perspective. (2) It has a prophetic dimension, in that it is concerned with a genuine historical situation, in this case apparently the oppression of Christians in Roman Asia Minor near the end of the first century. (3) It is concerned with the same kind of question as Jewish apocalyptic: Who, in light of oppressive circumstances, is in control of the world? Is it God, or is it the forces of evil?

In spite of these similarities, Revelation has a number of features that are not automatically part of the genre of the apocalypse.[114] First is the huge amount of visual imagery, as distinct from other forms of revelation, such as conversations (cf. 2 Esdras 3–10; *2 Bar.* 10–30). Instead of angels interpreting the visions, as they often do in other apocalypses, Revelation conveys them without interpretation. While other apocalypses often have many shorter visions, Revelation is in some ways one extended vision. Whereas most Jewish apocalypses are pseudepigraphal (e.g., *1 Enoch*), Revelation is not. Revelation includes the commissioning of a prophet (Rev 1:17–19; 10:8–11:2) as well as prophetic oracles (1:7, 8; 13:9–10; 14:12–13; 16:15; 19:9–10; 21:5–8) and oaths (10:5–7). Revelation also includes much liturgical language, including hymns (4:11; 5:9–14; 7:10–12, 15–17; 11:15–18; 12:10–12; 15:3–4; 16:5–7; 19:1–8) and a dirge (18:2–24). There are also lists of virtues and vices (9:20–21; 14:4–5; 21:8, 27; 22:14–15). The messages to the seven churches, together with the opening and closing, give the book the appearance of a personal message to local churches in Asia Minor, not of some grand-scale apocalypse. The book is less a reflection of a philosophy of history than an assertion of God's present reality. Instead of being strictly Jewish, the book of Revelation is, above all, a Christian book. Even though there are clearly close affinities between apocalypse and Revelation, most interpreters do not think that the appeal to other apocalyptic literature satisfactorily explains all of the material in Revelation.

2. Prophecy

The second category is prophecy. The author was apparently known as a prophet, as witnessed by his addressing the situation in a number of churches in his area and by his reference to the content of the book as prophetic (1:3; 22:6). In early Christian prophecy, prophets seem to have delivered their words from God before their congregations (see 1 Cor 12). The book of Revelation may well be prophecy, although the complexity of the imagery and the developed literary form would indicate that this prophecy goes well beyond what would normally have been delivered in person. Its type of prophecy is more than simply the conveyance of an oracle; it presents a complex set of images that contain oracles and much more. The OT is not cited explicity in Revelation, but the author is thoroughly immersed in biblical imagery (e.g., Dan 9–10) and apparently saw himself as in some way carrying forward the OT prophetic tradition. He even portrays himself as having a prophetic commissioning (Rev 10:8–11) similar to that of the OT prophets (Ezek 2:9–3:3). He also, as Bauckham points out, may see himself as at the climax of the OT prophetic tradition, as evidenced by the use of the OT passages against Babylon in his denunciations in Rev 18:1–19:8.[115]

3. Letter

The letters to the seven churches in Asia have figured heavily in discussion of Revelation. Whereas a number of interpreters cite the letters as simply contained within the larger book, in more recent thought it has been argued that the book of Revelation itself is a form of circular letter addressed to the churches in Ephesus, Smyrna, Pergamum, Thyatira, Sardis, Philadelphia, and Laodicea. It is possible that there is numerical significance to the selection of these seven churches, but on the basis of his study of the development of early Christianity in Asia, Ramsay argues that the churches were mentioned in the order in which the letter bearer would have visited them. They were the major Christian churches in the region and were arranged along trade routes that would have been conducive to visiting them in the order given.[116] Even though the book begins with a prologue (1:1–3) that describes its content, it follows with an epistolary opening (1:4), in which John specifically addresses the seven churches and then offers a salutation. The epistolary opening follows the Hellenistic letter convention ("John to the seven churches") with a verbless salutation ("Grace to you and peace") that is Pauline in form, not found otherwise outside Paul's letters in the earliest Christian writings (1 Pet 1:2 includes a verb). There is also a short epistolary closing (22:18–21). As Bauckham points out, however, our limited knowledge of circular letters in the ancient world indicates that such letters were general in orientation (e.g., 2 Peter), but this letter has particular information for each of these churches, besides the vast bulk of material for all of the churches in general.[117]

C. Date

There have been at least six proposals for the date of authorship of Revelation.[118] These are based upon the correlation of the known persecutions of the church by the Roman government with the kinds of events depicted in the book. Trying to establish these correlations is very complex because of the highly symbolic character of Revelation, which engages in all sorts of symbolism, numerology, and figurative language (some of it will be discussed below). The purpose of this symbolism appears to have been to provide a means of indirectly representing the situation in which the author and his church found themselves, in order to avoid further persecution. Any scheme that attempts to make clear correlations of these symbols with future events has a very difficult task on its hands and runs the risk of misinterpreting, if not completely distorting, the purpose and function of apocalyptic imagery. These symbols must be seen as highly context-specific to the social situation of the recipients of an apocalypse. The six proposals for dating Revelation follow, ordered according to their likelihood.

1. Domitian (A.D. 81–96)

The most likely date of composition of Revelation—and the traditional view (see Irenaeus, *Haer.* 5.30.3; cf. Victorinus, *Apoc.* 10.11; Eusebius, *Hist. eccl.* 3.18; Clement of Alexandria, *Salvation* 42; Origen, *Comm. Matt.* 16.6)—is during but probably late in the reign of the emperor Domitian. There are several strands of evidence to consider. (a) Although Domitian's reputation for cruelty may have been exaggerated by later Christian writers, it is true that Domitian strengthened the emperor cult. Although the origins of the emperor cult were much earlier, it grew in intensity during the first century and was an established part of Greco-Roman life by the second century A.D. Thus, it is possible that Revelation reflects a conflict between the worship of the emperor and the worship of Christ, in which Christians resisted worship of the

emperor and were persecuted for it. The book says that the beast demands universal worship (13:4, 15–16; 14:9–11; 15:2; 16:2; 19:20; 20:4), and Domitian appears to have been the first emperor to demand acclaim as a god. He issued a decree in the form of a circular letter that began, "Our lord and god orders . . ." (Suetonius, *Dom.* 13).[119] (b) Revelation depicts a situation of possible persecution: it appears to have been written in exile (Rev 1:9); Christians in Smyrna are warned of imprisonment (2:10); Christians have been killed at Pergamum (2:13); and there is mention of an hour of trial (3:10), martyrdom (6:9), and the harlot who is drunk with the blood of the saints (17:6; 18:24; 19:2), probably referring to Rome. Later Christian tradition describes Domitian as a persecutor of Christians, but the evidence from contemporary sources is lacking for widespread persecution, especially anything systematic. But Domitian apparently did kill one of his relatives and banish his wife, Domitilla, for sacrilege (Dio Cassius, *Rom.* 67.14),[120] and Clement refers to repeated troubles (*1 Clem.* 1.1). Although Rev 6:6 may allude to Domitian's order to destroy vineyards in the provinces in order to preserve the vineyards in Italy,[121] there is no substantial evidence of any persecution of Christians outside Rome. (c) Revelation may reflect knowledge of the Nero myth (Rev 13, 17; cf. Tacitus, *Hist.* 2.8–9; Suetonius, *Nero* 57). It appears that two forms of this myth were promulgated after A.D. 80. The earlier form claimed that Nero was not really dead (he committed suicide in A.D. 68) but had escaped to the east. The later, more developed, form claimed that he would return with Rome's enemies, the Parthians, against Rome itself. The reference in Rev 13:3 to the beast with the wound that heals might well allude to Nero's alleged recuperation from his fatal injury; the story has been changed from his physical return to his identification with the beast from the abyss (Rev 17:8).[122] There is the distinct possibility, however, that, by this time or later, the Nero myth had become a joke, not taken seriously by the vast majority of people (Tacitus, *Hist.* 1.1). (d) The references to the seven churches can be seen to support this date, for the mentioned deterioration of the churches at Ephesus, Sardis, and Laodicea is consistent with what is generally thought to have happened to these churches in Asia Minor. Since the church at Smyrna apparently did not come into existence until A.D. 60–64

This elaborate third-century gymnasium beside a large synagogue was operated by the Jewish community in Sardis (Sart, Turkey). See Rev 3:1–6. Photo Lee M. McDonald.

(according to a passage in Pol. *Phil.* 11.3), some would see this as the earliest date for composition; the Nicolaitans, active at Ephesus (Rev 2:6) and Pergamum (2:15), were by then a well-established sect.

2. Nero (A.D. 54–68)

Some argue that Revelation was written during the reign of the emperor Nero. There are several lines of evidence to consider here. (a) The first is the reference in Rev 17:9, 10 to seven hills—and thus the seven hills of Rome—and to seven kings, five of whom have already fallen and one who is yet to come, thus leaving the sixth the currently reigning king. The interpretation is that Nero was the sixth Roman emperor and that this is a cryptic way of mentioning him. In calculating the emperors, however, if one begins with Julius Caesar, it is difficult to see how Nero could be the sixth, because of the second triumvirate and the gap of seventeen years between Caesar's death (44 B.C.) and Augus-

tus's accession (27 B.C.). If one begins with Augustus (see Tacitus, *Ann.* 1.1; *Hist.* 1.1), then Nero was the fifth, so Rev 17:10 would apply only to Nero's death and the beginning of the short-lived reign of the insignificant Galba (A.D. 68). (b) It is sometimes proposed that the reference in Rev 13:18 to the number of the beast as 666 is a reference to Nero (there is a textual variant with 616, which throws off the numerical symmetry). The history of attempts to solve this difficulty is long and tedious. There are so many difficulties with most numerological proposals, especially those dealing with Hebrew, that the effort seems next to worthless. (c) There is clear evidence that Nero was involved in the persecution of Christians,[123] even if it was only on a local level. It is not inconceivable that the author received information of such a persecution and, because it was occurring in the center of the empire, foreboded doom. (d) The last evidence is what may be a reference to pre-siege conditions in Jerusalem. It is thought that Rev 11:1–2 implies that the Jerusalem temple was still standing. But since other writers refer to the temple similarly (see sec. 2.C, above)

Remains of the Trajan temple at Pergamum (see Rev 2:12-17). Photo Lee M. McDonald.

even though it was clearly not standing at the time of their writing (and the author of Revelation may well have been using previously written sources at this point), it is difficult to use this reference as support for this position. In any event, the persecution of Nero was local to Rome, but the situation of Revelation is Asia Minor, making correlation of the writing of Revelation with Nero's persecution difficult.

3. Trajan (A.D. 98–117)

A number of scholars believe that the situation reflected in Revelation occurred during the reign of Trajan. There are two reasons for this. (a) There is clear evidence of persecution of Christians in Asia Minor during his reign, as documented in the correspondence between him and Pliny (e.g., Pliny, *Ep.* 10.96–97, ca. A.D. 112). (b) This evidence also shows enforcement of the emperor cult, since Pliny's vexation over the spread of Christianity and other cults that may jeopardize the worship of the emperor causes him to write for advice from the emperor. As Court points out, since Trajan does not appeal to precedent in his response, this may be the first sustained attempt to deal with the problem of Christianity and other cults by enforcement of the emperor cult.[124]

4. Vespasian (A.D. 69–79)

A few scholars have argued that Revelation was written during the reign of the emperor Vespasian. If one begins with Augustus as the first emperor but skips the three short-lived emperors (Galba, Otho, and Vitellius), then Vespasian is the sixth (see Rev 17:9–10). This reconstruction is unlikely, however, since Vespasian did not take the idea of his divinity very seriously (see Suetonius, *Vespasianus*), and there is no known persecution of the church during his reign (cf. Eusebius, *Hist. eccl.* 3.17). In fact, his reign as emperor was a period of relative calm.

5. Four Emperors (A.D. 68–69)

Related to the fourth suggestion above is the recent idea of Moberly that the crisis of three emperors in one year (Galba, Otho, and Vitellius)

A colonnade at the entrance to the Asklepion in Pergamum. Photo Lee M. McDonald.

6. Titus (A.D. 79–81)

The reign of Titus also has been posited as the time of Revelation's composition for two reasons. (a) It was Titus who oversaw the destruction and burning of the temple in Jerusalem, while he was in command of the Roman troops in Judea (A.D. 70). This would have served as an indication of his religious intolerance and ruthlessness. (b) Titus's destruction of the temple has led some to suggest that he may have been the sixth emperor described in Rev 17:10, with Nero the first. Such speculation seems designed to avoid Titus's successor, Domitian, because there was no systematic or widespread persecution during Domitian's reign. This suggestion is unfounded, however, since, because of his short reign, Titus did not formally designate a successor; thus, seeing a line of connection between them is unwarranted. Titus's reign was characterized by generosity and beneficence, with little in the way of executions or other forms of oppression.

In conclusion, the traditional date of Domitian still seems to be the best founded, although the argument for a period under Nero or his immediate successors also has substantial merit. The nature of the evidence, including the references within Revelation itself, makes it difficult to be more precise or certain.

D. Authorship

Although the author of Revelation is explicitly stated to be "John" four times (1:1, 4, 9; 22:8), it is unclear who this John was, since many people in

A snake-figured column at the Asklepion of Pergamum. The snakes were a symbol of healing. Photo Lee M. McDonald.

and the imminent conflict between Vitellius and Vespasian, each of whom was backed by a number of Roman legions, gave rise to Revelation.[125] There are two arguments in favor of this position. (a) The sense of crisis and impending disaster in Revelation was well reflected in the atmosphere of contemporary Rome, which was experiencing unprecedented internal strife and turmoil. Vitellius could be counted as the sixth emperor (Rev 17:10) if one counted those who had been murdered or committed suicide; in recent times the pace of their extermination had quickened, with Nero quickly followed by Galba and Otho. (b) There is the chance that Nero's recent suicide and the fact that one of Nero's successors, Otho, allowed himself to be proclaimed "Nero" prompted the Nero myth to come into play. As the situation deteriorated and war between Vitellius and Vespasian became imminent, perhaps it provoked the thought that Nero would return, or had returned in the form of one of these emperors.

the early church were named John. The traditional view is that it was John the son of Zebedee, but this position apparently was first mentioned only in the second century by Justin Martyr (*Dial.* 81) and Irenaeus (*Haer.* 3.11.1; 4.20.11; 4.35.2), although from this time on the work was seen by many as apostolic. The book may well have finally been accepted into the biblical canon because it was believed that John the apostle wrote it.

There are many good arguments, however, against common authorship with the author of the Fourth Gospel (whether or not this was John the apostle): his advanced age if this work was written late in the reign of the emperor Domitian (see above); its language, which is very different from that of the Gospel or of any other Johannine writing; its apocalyptic eschatology, which is opposed by the realized eschatology of John's Gospel; and various theological peculiarities, including the interest only in Jesus' death as the Lamb, not the events of his life.[126] As recorded in Eusebius (*Hist. eccl.* 7.25.7–27), someone as early as Dionysius, the third-century bishop of Alexandria, argues against John the apostle as the author on the basis of its language and style being different from those of the Gospel, the lack of a claim to apostolic authorship in the book, and the construction and structure of the book in comparison with the Gospel. The widespread view of contemporary critical scholarship is that Revelation is not by John the apostle or the author of the Fourth Gospel.

The author appears to have been a Jewish-Christian prophet named John, but not an apostle, since the apostles are referred to in 18:20 and 21:14 as other than the author. The work was written, according to Rev 1:9, from the island of Patmos— off the coast of Asia Minor opposite Miletus—to seven known churches in Asia Minor.

Because of the inconclusive evidence on authorship, some have suggested that Revelation is pseudonymous. The reasons proposed for the book's use of pseudonymous authorship are varied and merit mention. For example, some believe that a pseudonym was used to protect the real author from detection and possible retaliation. Others have argued that it was a traditional, artificial, and conventional device copied from Daniel (assuming that Daniel is pseudonymous) or that it was a way to establish authority for the work during a period when prophecy was thought to have declined or

ceased. Some have posited that it involved a psychological or mythical identification of the actual author with the author who purportedly wrote the work, that an attempt was made to attribute or project the writer's experience onto an ancient hero, or that it was an attempt to enhance the prestige and authority of the work. Since the time of Charles, however, pseudonymous authorship has not been widely accepted.[127] There are two major reasons for this. (1) The invocation of pseudonymous authorship is misleading here, since the work is attributed to a person who already appears to have been known by his church. If there had been an effort to identify the author with some other figure, this identification could have been made much more clearly. One must not necessarily correlate the authorship of Revelation with the later traditional attribution of the Fourth Gospel, which is an anonymous work. (2) It is not clear that the use of an unspecified John would have enhanced the book's chances of acceptance by the church (even though the church later linked the book with the apostle), and there is certainly no clear indication that the book is being identified with some well-known hero of the church. Revelation, therefore, does not provide useful information in arguing for the presence of pseudonymity in the NT, despite what second- or third-century readers may have thought concerning its relationship to the Gospel.

If it is not clear that Revelation was written by John the apostle or that it is pseudonymous, one is left with a range of speculation regarding authorship. Some of those proposed are John the Elder (Eusebius, *Hist. eccl.* 3.39.4–5), a hypothetical John the prophet, John Mark (ibid., 7.25.15), and even John the Baptist.[128] The best explanation may simply be that we do not know who John the author of Revelation is.

E. Problems of Interpretation

Interpretation of the book of Revelation has been bedeviled by numerous problems, not all of them recent. Some of the problems are related to the apparent foreignness of the language used. But to some extent, this is a difficulty created by an unfamiliarity with types of extrabiblical literature that may be reflected in the book of Revelation, especially Jewish apocalyptic features. A number of the attempts to come to terms with the book merit mention.[129]

1. Chiliastic or Futurist Theory

A common and recurring interpretative framework for Revelation from its earliest interpreters (e.g., Justin Martyr, *Dial.* 81; Tertullian, *Ag. Marc.* 3.24; Irenaeus, *Haer.* 4–5) to the present has been the chiliastic or futurist interpretation. This may well have been one of the earliest forms of interpretation, seen in the belief in the literal and imminent return and reign of Christ,[130] and it is still found today in a number of literalistic interpreters of Revelation. Adherents of this position often argue that Rev 4:1–22:5 recounts a set of events that are to happen just before the cataclysmic end of the age, although some claim that these chapters recount all of human history leading up to the end of the age. One literalistic conception, that of the millennium (Rev 20:1–6), is often associated with a literal kingdom on earth of 1,000 years[131] and equates the beast of Rev 13 and 17 with a world ruler. This kind of literalistic reading has sometimes been applied to the rest of the book as well, with some interpreters going so far as to claim that the section on the seven churches in chs. 2–3 summarizes the so-called church age. The major problem with this position is that the two short chapters devoted to the church neglect the vast bulk of church history and certainly have very little to offer in the way of instruction. There is the further problem of knowing how the symbolism and imagery are to be interpreted, since many generations have seen themselves as living in the period just before the end.

2. Recapitulation Theory

Victorinus, the third-century writer, whose commentary on Revelation is the oldest surviving, saw the book as a recapitulative description of contemporary events in the world. Thus, rather than taking a sequential view of events, such that there was a progression from one set of events to another, this view held that the seven seals (6:1–8:1), the seven trumpets (8:2–11:19), and the seven bowls (15:1–16:21)—the major bulk of the descriptive portion of the book—all recapitulated the same set of events, although in different images. In some ways, this view has been revived in recent work.[132]

3. Historical View

With roots much earlier, this position was prominent especially during medieval times and has noticeable overlap with the chiliastic view mentioned above. According to the historical view, the apocalyptic imagery of the book is directly applied to contemporary events of the interpreters' time, such that they are convinced they are living in the final events of Rev 17–18, with the coming of wrath and judgment and the fall of Babylon. Forms of this view continue to be attractive to some popular theologians, in spite of continual and repeated disappointment. For example, it was thought by some in the eleventh century, calculating 1,000 years from the beginning of the church, that the end had come; despite this serious disappointment, some still read their newspapers with Revelation in mind. Joachim of Fiore (ca. 1132–1202) offered a detailed analysis of Revelation, dividing it into seven periods of church history, a period of rest, and then the final consummation. He equated his time with that of the conflict between the church and the degenerate Holy Roman Empire. Among some conservative or fundamentalistic Protestants there has often been an equation of the antichrist with the pope or some ecumenical movement that is seen to be debasing the integrity of the church (such as the World Council of Churches). These kinds of facile equations show how subjective such interpretation is and how only a very small portion of the book is seen by such interpreters to be relevant.

4. Eschatological View

Similar to the chiliastic theory, the eschatological view arose in the sixteenth century as a reaction to historical applications of the book (see no. 3, above). Protestants in particular had applied Revelation to the papacy and the Catholic Church, and Catholics, in reaction, saw the book as concerned with the end of the world and the signs heralding it, the last stages of history. In this interpretation, chs. 4–21 are all eschatological, and historical interpretation is not appropriate, apart possibly from some of the earlier images applying to the early church. The book becomes essentially a timeless document that cannot be applied directly to any contemporary situation. This position, which has been argued by contemporary biblical scholars, tends towards an idealist interpretation (see no. 8, below), in which the book describes an ultimate conflict between good and evil. Many would respond that this interpretation tends to neglect the book's historical context and original historical relevance, which demands a historical fulfillment.

5. Contemporary-Historical or Preterist View

Another reaction in the sixteenth and seventeenth centuries to the historical interpretation (see nos. 3 and 4, above) was the contemporary-historical view. The emphasis was on understanding Revelation solely in terms of recent events contemporary with the situation of the author. This was very much a rationalist interpretation of the book and tended toward an antisupernatural and antiprophetic bias. Thus, for example, in one interpretation, Rev 6:6 was seen to be reflecting the famine prices of A.D. 68 when the grain crop failed; 8:7 with the storms of A.D. 67, 68, and 69; 8:8 and 9:2 with the famous eruption of the volcano Vesuvius; 8:10 with the falling of a meteorite; 8:12 with the eclipse or storm of January 10, A.D. 69; and the ch. 11 witnesses with two members of the church. Ramsay held to this position, confirmed in his mind after his extensive firsthand research and travels in Asia Minor.[133]

6. Source Criticism

Source criticism, less concerned with interpreting Revelation as a whole than with tracing the compositional history of the book, reflects the interests of much nineteenth-century and early-twentieth-century scholarship. For example, in his commentary of 1920, Charles is concerned with the independent documentary sources and interpolated fragments that have been redacted in the book.[134] His view is that the editor was somewhat incompetent and thus left tell-tale signs of redaction that enable scholars to determine the various seams of the book and to reconstruct its original "logical" order. Although not all scholars would be as optimistic as Charles about their ability to detect the internal contradictions and conclude what the various sources were, this is a position that reflects modern higher-critical concerns. Tracing the origins of the sources and how they have been handled has been substituted for understanding the meaning of the text both when it was written and now.

7. Religions-History View

In the nineteenth and twentieth centuries, scholarship often became highly interested in the various religious and historically based traditions that were utilized in the growth and development of the biblical tradition. Consequently, scholars often tried to trace the various OT Jewish and Christian traditions that were involved in the construction of such an elaborate work as Revelation. For example, in the OT, they noticed the influence of the Daniel tradition and of the prophets Joel and Zechariah. This did not mean, however, that Revelation was simply an OT book in NT dress. There were also other extrabiblical Jewish traditions, such as the apocalyptic tradition as found in *1 Enoch*, that had influenced the writing of Revelation. On top of this, there was the influence of non-Christian traditions that needed to be considered as well. For example, in Rev 12, the description of the woman pursued by the dragon was often discussed in terms of the influence from various Greek and Babylonian myths.

8. Idealist View

The idealist perspective, while rejecting attempts to identify each of the images or events depicted in Revelation, claims that the symbolism about the nature and character of God is revelatory. The emphasis is upon the great revelatory themes regarding God's character, the nature of good and evil in the world, the timeless opposition of these forces, and the ultimate and final triumph of God. Without being confined to any given time or age, this position tends to cut the book of Revelation loose from time altogether, making it difficult to understand the context out of which it arose and to which it was written.

9. Summary

Some elements of insight are to be drawn from virtually all the positions outlined above, but they also have many limitations, especially those positions attempting to use Revelation as a road map for either our contemporary or some future situation. There is, however, a place for contemporary relevance; in his book on Revelation, Bauckham outlines several of these points.[135] For instance, Revelation, through its imagery and depiction of the structures of the universe, purges and refurbishes the Christian imagination. It emphasizes the truth of God; its picture of God at the center of existence confronts and triumphs over the political and economic structures of the world that tend to oppression and injustice; and it depicts Christians as vitally involved in this struggle, both by resisting evil in the world and by offering a prophetic word to the church.

F. Outline of Revelation

A. Opening (1:1–20)
  1. Prologue (1:1–3)
  2. Epistolary opening (1:4–8)
  3. Initial vision (1:9–20)

B. Letters to the seven churches (2:1–3:22)
  1. Ephesus (2:1–7)
  2. Smyrna (2:8–11)
  3. Pergamum (2:12–17)
  4. Thyatira (2:18–29)
  5. Sardis (3:1–6)
  6. Philadelphia (3:7–13)
  7. Laodicea (3:14–22)

C. The apocalypse (4:1–22:5)
  1. Introductory visions (4:1–5:14)
  2. Seven seals (6:1–8:1)
  3. Seven trumpets (8:2–11:19)
  4. Seven unnumbered visions (12:1–15:4)
  5. Seven bowls of wrath (15:5–16:21)
  6. Fall of Babylon (17:1–19:10)
  7. Seven unnumbered visions (19:11–21:8)

D. Epilogue (22:6–21)

BIBLIOGRAPHY

A. Hebrews

ATTRIDGE, H. W. *The Epistle to the Hebrews.* Hermeneia. Philadelphia: Fortress, 1989.

BRUCE, F. F. *The Epistle to the Hebrews.* Rev. ed. NICNT. Grand Rapids: Eerdmans, 1990.

ELLINGWORTH, P. *The Epistle to the Hebrews.* NIGTC. Grand Rapids: Eerdmans, 1993.

HUGHES, P. E. *A Commentary on the Epistle to the Hebrews.* Grand Rapids: Eerdmans, 1977.

LANE, W. L. *Hebrews.* WBC 47A, B. Dallas: Word, 1991.

MONTEFIORE, H. *A Commentary on the Epistle to the Hebrews.* BNTC. Peabody, Mass.: Hendrickson, 1964.

NAIRNE, A. *The Epistle to the Hebrews.* CGTSC. Cambridge: Cambridge University Press, 1917.

ROBINSON, T. H. *The Epistle to the Hebrews.* MNTC. New York: Harper & Brothers, n.d.

WESTCOTT, B. F. *The Epistle to the Hebrews.* London: Macmillan, 1889.

B. James

ADAMSON, J. B. *The Epistle of James.* NICNT. Grand Rapids: Eerdmans, 1976.

DAVIDS, P. H. *The Epistle of James.* NIGTC. Grand Rapids: Eerdmans, 1982.

DIBELIUS, M. *Commentary on the Epistle of James.* Rev. H. Greeven. Hermeneia. Philadelphia: Fortress, 1976.

HORT, F. J. A. *The Epistle of St. James.* London: Macmillan, 1909.

JOHNSON, L. T. *The Letter of James.* AB 37A. New York: Doubleday, 1995.

LAWS, S. *The Epistle of James.* BNTC. Peabody, Mass.: Hendrickson, 1980.

MARTIN, R. P. *James.* WBC 48. Waco, Tex.: Word, 1988.

MAYOR, J. B. *The Epistle of St. James.* 3d ed. London: Macmillan, 1913. Repr., Minneapolis: Klock & Klock, 1977.

MITTON, C. L. *The Epistle of James.* London: Marshall, Morgan & Scott, 1966.

MOO, D. J. *James.* TNTC. Grand Rapids: Eerdmans, 1985.

ROPES, J. H. *A Critical and Exegetical Commentary on the Epistle of St. James.* ICC. Edinburgh: T. & T. Clark, 1916.

ROSS, A. *The Epistles of James and John.* London: Marshall, Morgan & Scott, 1954.

C. 1 Peter, 2 Peter, and Jude

BAUCKHAM, R. J. *Jude, 2 Peter.* WBC 50. Waco, Tex.: Word, 1983.

BIGG, C. *A Critical and Exegetical Commentary on the Epistles of St. Peter and St. Jude.* 2d ed. ICC. Edinburgh: T. & T. Clark, 1910.

CRANFIELD, C. E. B. *The First Epistle of Peter.* London: SCM, 1950.

DAVIDS, P. H. *The First Epistle of Peter.* NICNT. Grand Rapids: Eerdmans, 1990.

GOPPELT, L. *A Commentary on 1 Peter.* Ed. F. HAHN. Trans. J. E. ALSUP. Grand Rapids: Eerdmans, 1993.

GRUDEM, W. *1 Peter.* TNTC. Grand Rapids: Eerdmans, 1988.

HORT, F. J. A. *The First Epistle of St. Peter I.1–II.17.* London: Macmillan, 1898.

KELLY, J. N. D. *A Commentary on the Epistles of Peter and Jude.* BNTC. Peabody, Mass.: Hendrickson, 1969.

MASTERMAN, J. H. B. *The First Epistle of Peter (Greek Text).* London: Macmillan, 1900.

MAYOR, J. B. *The Epistle of St. Jude and the Second Epistle of St. Peter.* 1907. Repr., Grand Rapids: Baker, 1979.

MICHAELS, J. R. *1 Peter.* WBC 49. Waco, Tex.: Word, 1988.

NEYREY, J. H. *2 Peter, Jude.* AB 37C. New York: Doubleday, 1993.

SELWYN, E. G. *The First Epistle of St. Peter.* 2d ed. London: Macmillan, 1947.

D. 1, 2, and 3 John

BROOKE, A. E. *A Critical and Exegetical Commentary on the Johannine Epistles.* ICC. Edinburgh: T. & T. Clark, 1912.

BROWN, R. E. *The Epistles of John.* AB 30. Garden City, N.Y.: Doubleday, 1982.

DODD, C. H. *The Johannine Epistles.* MNTC. London: Hodder & Stoughton, 1946.

MARSHALL, I. H. *The Epistles of John.* NICNT. Grand Rapids: Eerdmans, 1978.

ROSS, A. *The Epistles of James and John.* London: Marshall, Morgan & Scott, 1954.

SMALLEY, S. S. *1, 2, 3 John.* WBC 51. Waco, Tex.: Word, 1984.

STOTT, J. R. W. *The Epistles of John.* TNTC. Grand Rapids: Eerdmans, 1964.

WESTCOTT, B. F. *The Epistles of St. John.* 2d ed. London: Macmillan, 1896.

E. Revelation

AUNE, D. E. *Revelation.* 3 vols. WBC 52A, B, C. Nashville: Nelson, 1997–1998.

BEASLEY-MURRAY, G. R. *Revelation.* NCB. Grand Rapids: Eerdmans, 1974.

CAIRD, G. B. *A Commentary on the Revelation of St. John the Divine.* BNTC. Peabody, Mass.: Hendrickson, 1966.

CHARLES, R. H. *A Critical and Exegetical Commentary on the Revelation of St. John.* 2 vols. ICC. Edinburgh: T. & T. Clark, 1920.

FORD, J. M. *Revelation.* AB 38. Garden City, N.Y.: Doubleday, 1975.

LADD, G. E. *A Commentary on the Revelation of John.* Grand Rapids: Eerdmans, 1972.

METZGER, B. M. *Breaking the Code: Unlocking the Book of Revelation.* Nashville: Abingdon, 1996.

MOUNCE, R. H. *The Book of Revelation.* NICNT. Grand Rapids: Eerdmans, 1977.

SWETE, H. B. *The Apocalypse of St. John.* London: Macmillan, 1906.

WAINWRIGHT, A. W. *Mysterious Apocalypse: Interpreting the Book of Revelation.* Nashville: Abingdon, 1996.

pages 517–523

1. See R. H. Fuller, *A Critical Introduction to the New Testament* (London: Duckworth, 1966), 151.
2. See P. Ellingworth, *The Epistle to the Hebrews* (NIGTC; Grand Rapids: Eerdmans, 1993), 3–21, for a very complete survey of authorship options, relied upon in the following discussion.
3. See D. Trobisch, *Paul's Letter Collection: Tracing the Origins* (Minneapolis: Fortress, 1994), 16–17.
4. See J. Moffatt, *An Introduction to the Literature of the New Testament* (3d ed.; Edinburgh: T. & T. Clark, 1918), 433, 435.
5. See B. F. Westcott, *The Epistle to the Hebrews* (London: Macmillan, 1889), xxxii–xxxv.
6. Ibid., lxxii–lxxiv.
7. See D. A. Carson, D. J. Moo, and L. Morris, *An Introduction to the New Testament* (Grand Rapids: Zondervan, 1992), 395, who cite Calvin on Heb 13:23 as well as Luther's opinion, given in other introductions as well.
8. F. J. Badcock, *The Pauline Epistles and the Epistle to the Hebrews in Their Historical Setting* (London: SPCK, 1937), 182–201, although he entertains the idea that Luke and Philip the Evangelist were also present with Paul.
9. See A. von Harnack, *The Mission and Expansion of Christianity in the First Three Centuries* (trans. J. Moffatt; 1908; repr., New York: Harper & Brothers, 1962), 52–53 n. 1; cf. his "Probabilia über die Addresse und den Vergasser des Hebräerbriefes," *ZNW* 1 (1900): 16–41.
10. This is not the same situation as is faced in Acts with the "we" passages. In Acts, the alternation is between the remote third person (e.g., "he" or "they") and the inclusive first person plural ("we"). This represents a major shift in narrative stance from narrator noninvolvement (the so-called objective narrator) to some form of narrator involvement. In Hebrews, the shift is one of number only, from singular to plural.
11. T. W. Manson, "The Problem of the Epistle to the Hebrews (1949)," in *Studies in the Gospels and Epistles* (ed. M. Black; Manchester: Manchester University Press, 1962), 242–58; H. Montefiore, *The Epistle to the Hebrews* (BNTC; Peabody, Mass.: Hendrickson, 1964), 9–31.
12. See Ellingworth, *Hebrews*, 15–20.
13. For a discussion of many of the issues discussed below, from the standpoints of the individual authors, see L. D. Hurst, *The Epistle to the Hebrews: Its Background of Thought* (SNTSMS 65; Cambridge: Cambridge University Press, 1990); J. M. Scholer, *Proleptic Priests: Priesthood in the Epistle to the Hebrews* (JSNTSup 49; Sheffield: JSOT Press, 1992), esp. 13–81.
14. See S. E. Porter, "The Date of the Composition of Hebrews and Use of the Present Tense-Form," in *Crossing the Boundaries: Essays in Biblical Interpretation in Honour of Michael D. Goulder* (ed. S. E. Porter, P. Joyce, and D. E. Orton; BIS 8; Leiden: Brill, 1994), 295–313.
15. Westcott, *Hebrews*, xlii; P. E. Hughes, *A Commentary on the Epistle to the Hebrews* (Grand Rapids: Eerdmans, 1977), 30; J. A. T. Robinson, *Redating the New Testament* (Philadelphia: Westminster, 1976), 202.
16. See, e.g., Josephus, *Ant.* 3.151–178, 3.224–257; *Ag. Ap.* 2.193–198; *1 Clem.* 40.5, 41.2; *Diogn.* 3; Philo, *Spec. Laws* 3.131.
17. See W. L. Lane, *Hebrews*, vol. 1 (WBC 47A; Dallas: Word, 1991), lxiii; F. F. Bruce, *The Epistle to the Hebrews* (rev. ed.; NICNT; Grand Rapids: Eerdmans, 1990), 22.

18. See Ellingworth, *Hebrews*, esp. 33 n. 105, for a survey of opinion on the date; cf. Carson, Moo, and Morris, *Introduction*, 399–400.

19. On this topic, see R. Williamson, *Philo and the Epistle to the Hebrews* (ALGHJ 4; Leiden: Brill, 1970).

20. See D. Guthrie, *New Testament Introduction* (Downers Grove, Ill.: InterVarsity, 1970), 709–10; Ellingworth, *Hebrews*, 48–49.

21. See G. H. Guthrie, *The Structure of Hebrews: A Text-Linguistic Analysis* (NovTSup 73; Leiden: Brill, 1994); cf. H. W. Attridge, *Hebrews* (Hermeneia: Philadelphia: Fortress, 1989), 14–15.

22. See N. Turner, *Style*, vol. 4 of *A Grammar of New Testament Greek*, by J. H. Moulton (4 vols.; Edinburgh: T. & T. Clark, 1976), 113: "For all its oratory, Hebrews is no more than an epistle written in the exhortatory style, mingling theology and paraenesis in alternating sections, as distinct from Paul's method of keeping the theology and paraenesis apart. Nevertheless, Hebrews begins as a sermon and ends as an epistle."

23. See Moffatt, *Introduction*, 428–29; cf. S. Stanley, "The Structure of Hebrews from Three Perspectives," *TynB* 45 (2, 1994): 247–51.

24. G. W. Buchanan, *To the Hebrews* (AB 36; Garden City, N.Y.: Doubleday, 1971), xix. On Psalm 110, see D. M. Hay, *Glory at the Right Hand: Psalm 110 in Early Christianity* (SBLMS 18; Nashville: Abingdon, 1967).

25. See A. J. Saldarini, "Judaism and the New Testament," in *The New Testament and Its Modern Interpreters* (ed. E. J. Epp and G. W. MacRae; Atlanta: Scholars Press, 1989), 34–37, 40–42.

26. See also M. E. Isaacs, *Sacred Space: An Approach to the Theology of the Epistle to the Hebrews* (JSNTSup 73; Sheffield: JSOT Press, 1992), 127–78.

27. See Lane, *Hebrews*, lxxvi–lxxx, for an assessment of the use of rhetoric to examine Hebrews.

28. E.g., B. Lindars ("The Rhetorical Structure of Hebrews," *NTS* 35 [1989]: 382–406) classifies it as deliberative, while D. E. Aune (*The New Testament in Its Literary Environment* [LEC; Philadelphia: Westminster, 1987], 212) classifies it as epideictic. For an analysis of some of the rhetorical features, see Turner, *Style*, 107–108; M. R. Cosby, *The Rhetorical Composition and Functon of Hebrews 11: In Light of Example Lists in Antiquity* (Macon, Ga.: Mercer University Press, 1988).

29. For an analysis of various attempts at the structure of Hebrews, see Guthrie, *Structure of Hebrews*, 21–40; and Stanley, "Structure of Hebrews."

30. See J. B. Mayor, *The Epistle of St. James* (3d ed.; 1913; repr., Minneapolis: Klock & Klock, 1977), lxix–lxxxiv; J. H. Ropes, *A Critical and Exegetical Commentary on the Epistle of St. James* (ICC; Edinburgh: T. & T. Clark, 1916), 21–22; Moffatt, *Introduction*, 467–68; P. Davids, *The Epistle of James* (NIGTC; Grand Rapids: Eerdmans, 1982), 8.

31. See D. J. Moo, *James* (TNTC; Grand Rapids: Eerdmans, 1985), 18–19; but cf. A. Ross, *The Epistles of James and John* (London: Marshall, Morgan & Scott, 1954), 22, who says that Luther's 1522 statement was not reprinted in later editions of his Bible and in any event he made the comment in comparison with John, Romans, Galatians, and 1 Peter.

32. For a chart of positions on authorship (and date), see Davids, *James*, 4. Cf. F. F. Bruce, *Peter, Stephen, James, and John: Studies in Early Non-Pauline Christianity* (Grand Rapids: Eerdmans, 1979), 86–119; P.-A. Bernheim, *James, Brother of Jesus* (London: SCM, 1997).

33. See J. B. Adamson, *James: The Man and His Message* (Grand Rapids: Eerdmans, 1989), 3–52, for a recent defense of James the brother of Jesus as author.
34. See Mayor, *James,* iii–iv.
35. On this Q material, see P. J. Hartin, *James and the Q Sayings of Jesus* (JSNTSup 47; Sheffield: JSOT Press, 1991). See also chs. 4 and 8, above, for a discussion of Q.
36. See W. G. Kümmel, *Introduction to the New Testament* (17th ed.; trans. H. C. Kee; Nashville: Abingdon, 1975), 412–13; R. P. Martin, *James* (WBC 48; Waco, Tex.: Word, 1988), lxx–lxxiii; cf. Davids, *James,* 9–22. Martin and Davids respond to these objections as well.
37. See S. E. Porter, "Jesus and the Use of Greek in Galilee," in *Studying the Historical Jesus: Evaluations of the State of Current Research* (ed. B. Chilton and C. A. Evans; NTTS 19; Leiden: Brill, 1994), 129–47, on the widespread use of Greek in Palestine and environs.
38. See Adamson, *James,* 138–42, 119–38, although even those disputing authorship by James do not wish to overemphasize the qualities of the Greek (see Ropes, *James,* 24–27).
39. See Davids, *James,* 22–27; Martin, *James,* lxxiii.
40. See Ropes, *James,* 43–52.
41. Adamson, *James,* 53–65. But see the outline below for an alternative structure.
42. See Davids, *James,* 34–57; T. C. Penner, *The Epistle of James and Eschatology: Re-reading an Ancient Christian Letter* (JSNTSup 121; Sheffield: Sheffield Academic Press, 1996).
43. See Ropes, *James,* 10–16, 18; see also ch. 9, sec. 2, above, on Pauline diatribe.
44. See M. Dibelius, *James* (ed. H. Greeven; Hermeneia; Philadelphia: Fortress, 1975), 3–11.
45. The best treatment of literary relations of James with Greco-Roman and Jewish literature is in L. T. Johnson, *The Letter of James* (AB 37A; New York: Doubleday, 1995), 26–88; cf. S. E. Porter, "Is *dipsuchos* (James 1,8; 4,8) a 'Christian' Word?" *Bib* 71 (1990): esp. 475–76, 485–94.
46. E.g., see Robinson, *Redating the New Testament,* 130–31, for an early date in James's life; F. J. A. Hort, *The Epistle of St. James* (London: Macmillan, 1909), xiv–xv, for a late date in James's life; and Ropes, *James,* 47–49, for a date in the second century.
47. See A. Chester and R. P. Martin, *The Theology of the Letters of James, Peter, and Jude* (New Testament Theology; Cambridge: Cambridge University Press, 1994), 20–28; Penner, *Epistle of James and Eschatology,* 47–74.
48. See J. D. G. Dunn, *Unity and Diversity in Early Christianity* (Philadelphia: Westminster, 1977), 251–52.
49. Ropes, *James,* 35–36.
50. Carson, Moo, and Morris, *Introduction,* 419.
51. Hartin, *James,* 238–39.
52. See, e.g., M. Hengel, "Der Jakobusbrief als antipaulinische Polemik," in *Tradition and Interpretation in the New Testament* (ed. G. F. Hawthorne with O. Betz; Grand Rapids: Eerdmans, 1987), 248–78.
53. See, e.g., G. Kittel, "Der geschichtliche Ort des Jakobusbriefes," *ZNW* 41 (1942): 79–80.
54. This outline attempts to capture some of the epistolary features of the book of James without rigidly imposing the Pauline letter form. See Hartin, *James,* 245–46.

pages 528–534

55. J. R. Michaels, *1 Peter* (WBC 49; Waco, Tex.: Word, 1988), xxxiv, who cites the evidence given above.
56. See, e.g., Kümmel, *Introduction*, 423–24; and Carson, Moo, and Morris, *Introduction*, 422–23.
57. See Porter, "Jesus and the Use of Greek," 129–47.
58. Kümmel (*Introduction*, 423) contends that no one has proved that "write through" "can mean to authorize someone else to compose a piece of writing," but Turner (*Style*, 123) claims that "the word *through* can designate the actual writer, as when I Clement is referred to as *written through Clement*." Turner gets this point from C. Bigg, *A Critical and Exegetical Commentary on the Epistles of St. Peter and St. Jude* (ICC; Edinburgh: T. & T. Clark, 1902), 5.
59. See, e.g., E. B. Selwyn, *The First Epistle of St. Peter* (2d ed.; London: Macmillan, 1947), 9–17; and the modified view of P. H. Davids, *The First Epistle of Peter* (NICNT; Grand Rapids: Eerdmans, 1990), 5–7; L. Goppelt, *A Commentary on 1 Peter* (ed. F. Hahn; trans. J. E. Alsup; Grand Rapids: Eerdmans, 1993), 51–53.
60. Fuller, *Critical Introduction*, 157, although he admits that this could be caused by Silvanus's influence.
61. On the Petrine school, see Chester and Martin, *Theology*, 91–92.
62. Our analysis of these other proposals relies upon L. Thurén, *Argument and Theology in 1 Peter: The Origins of Christian Paraenesis* (JSNTSup 114; Sheffield: Sheffield Academic Press, 1995), 14–27; and Chester and Martin, *Theology*, 95–98.
63. See F. J. A. Hort, *The First Epistle of St. Peter I.1–II.17* (London: Macmillan, 1898), 157–84; C. J. Hemer, "The Address of I Peter," *ExpT* 89 (1977–1978): 239–43. On the destination as including Jewish and Gentile Christians in Asia Minor, see W. Grudem, *1 Peter* (TNTC; Grand Rapids: Eerdmans, 1988), 37–38.
64. F. L. Cross, *I. Peter: A Paschal Liturgy* (London: Mowbray, 1954).
65. See Selwyn, *1 Peter*, 18–23, 363–466.
66. See Thurén, *Argument and Theology*, 30–227.
67. Goppelt, *1 Peter*, 36; J. H. Elliott, *A Home for the Homeless: A Social-Scientific Criticism of 1 Peter, Its Situaton and Strategy* (Minneapolis: Fortress, 1990); D. L. Balch, *Let Wives Be Submissive: The Domestic Code in 1 Peter* (SBLMS 26; Atlanta: Scholars Press, 1981), esp. 81–116.
68. Chester and Martin, *Theology*, 97.
69. See W. L. Schutter, *Hermeneutic and Composition in 1 Peter* (WUNT 2.30; Tübingen: Mohr–Siebeck, 1989). But cf. G. L. Green, "The Use of the Old Testament for Christian Ethics in 1 Peter," *TynB* 41 (2, 1990): 276–89.
70. See Michaels, *1 Peter*, xlvi–xlix, who describes the book as "an apocalyptic diaspora letter to 'Israel' "; and Davids, *1 Peter*, 15–17, who emphasizes apocalyptic characteristics.
71. The most detailed discussion is found in R. Bauckham, *2 Peter, Jude* (WBC 50; Waco, Tex.: Word, 1983), 135–38, 141–54, 158–63.
72. See Moffatt, *Introduction*, 348–50; J. Kahmann, "The Second Letter of Peter and the Letter of Jude: Their Mutual Relationship," in *The New Testament in Early Christianity* (ed. J.-M. Sevrin; BETL 86; Leuven: Leuven University Press/Peeters, 1989), 105–21.
73. An advocate of this style for 2 Peter is D. F. Watson, *Invention, Arrangement, and Style: Rhetorical Criticism of Jude and 2 Peter* (SBLDS 104; Atlanta: Scholars Press, 1988), 144–46. On the style of 2 Peter, see J. B. Mayor, *The Epistle of St. Jude and the Second Epistle of St. Peter* (1907; repr., Grand Rapids: Baker, 1979), xxvi–lv; and L. Thurén, "Style Never Goes out of Fashion: 2 Peter Re-evaluated," in *Rhetoric,*

pages 534–539

Scripture, and Theology: Essays from the 1994 Pretoria Conference (ed. S. E. Porter and T. H. Olbricht; JSNTSup 131; Sheffield: Sheffield Academic Press, 1996), 345–53.

74. See Dunn, *Unity and Diversity*, 341–66, referring to the classic essay of E. Käsemann, "An Apologia for Primitive Christian Eschatology," in *Essays on New Testament Themes* (trans. W. J. Montague; Philadelphia: Fortress, 1964), 169–95. See also I. H. Marshall, "'Early Catholicism' in the New Testament," in *New Dimensions in New Testament Study* (ed. R. N. Longenecker and M. C. Tenney; Grand Rapids: Zondervan, 1974), 217–31.

75. Much of the ancient evidence is laid out by Bigg, *St. Peter and St. Jude*, 199–210.

76. On this criterion, as well as others, see L. M. McDonald, *The Formation of the Christian Biblical Canon* (rev. ed.; Peabody, Mass.: Hendrickson, 1995), 229–49, esp. 232–36.

77. J. Knight, *2 Peter and Jude* (NT Guides; Sheffield: Sheffield Academic Press, 1994), 20–22, with references to advocates of the various positions.

78. J. Neyrey, *2 Peter, Jude* (AB 37C; New York: Doubleday, 1993), 122.

79. Guthrie, *Introduction*, 926–27 n. 3.

80. Cf. G. H. Boobyer, "The Indebtedness of 2 Peter to 1 Peter," in *New Testament Essays: Studies in Memory of Thomas Walter Manson, 1893–1958* (ed. A. J. B. Higgins; Manchester: Manchester University Press, 1959), 34–53, who shows appreciable similarities between the two letters.

81. Knight, *2 Peter*, 23.

82. M. Hengel, *Acts and the History of Earliest Christianity* (trans. J. Bowden; London: SCM, 1979), 122: "The term 'early Catholicism,' so often misused, is inappropriate and does not add anything to our understanding of earliest Christian history. We would do better to avoid it altogether, as it leads us astray into a cliché-ridden approach to earliest Christianity, coupled with distorted judgments. If we want to, we can find 'early-Catholic traits' even in Jesus and Paul: the phenomena thus denoted are almost entirely a legacy of Judaism."

83. J. D. Charles, *Virtue amidst Vice: The Catalog of Virtues in 2 Peter 1* (JSNTSup 150; Sheffield: Sheffield Academic Press, 1997), 49–75. This volume is an excellent analysis of many of the issues surrounding the authorship of 2 Peter.

84. See Knight, *2 Peter*, 23–26. Cf. R. Bauckham, *Jude and the Relatives of Jesus in the Early Church* (Edinburgh: T. & T. Clark, 1990).

85. Kümmel, *Introduction*, 428.

86. See Bauckham, *2 Peter*, 14–16.

87. See Guthrie, *Introduction*, 905.

88. See ibid., 908–12.

89. See J. D. Charles, "The Use of Tradition-Material in the Epistle of Jude," *BBR* 4 (1994): 1–14, esp. 2; cf. E. E. Ellis, "Prophecy and Hermeneutic in Jude," in *Prophecy and Hermeneutic in Early Christianity: New Testament Essays* (WUNT 18; Tübingen: Mohr–Siebeck, 1978; repr., Grand Rapids: Eerdmans, 1978), 221–26, who discusses midrashic techniques.

90. See J. D. Charles, "Jude's Use of Pseudepigraphical Source-Material as Part of a Literary Strategy," *NTS* 37 (1991): 130–45, esp. 143–44. Cf. also his "'Those' and 'These' in the Use of the Old Testament in the Epistle of Jude," *JSNT* 38 (1990): 109–24.

91. See L. Thurén, *The Rhetorical Strategy of 1 Peter with Special Regard to Ambiguous Expressions* (Abo: Abo Academy Press, 1990), 88.

92. See J. Lieu, *The Second and Third Epistles of John: History and Background* (Edinburgh: T. & T. Clark, 1986), 37–51.

93. B. F. Westcott, *The Epistles of St. John* (2d ed.; London: Macmillan, 1886), xxix.

94. See R. E. Brown, *The Epistles of John* (AB 30; Garden City, N.Y.: Doubleday, 1982), 86–92.

95. See ibid., 5–13, for an informed discussion. A. E. Brooke (*A Critical and Exegetical Commentary on the Johannine Epistles* [ICC; Edinburgh: T. & T. Clark, 1912], lii–lviii) prints the passages cited below.

96. E.g., Kümmel (*Introduction* 445–51) argues for the same author, whereas C. H. Dodd (*The Johannine Epistles* [MNTC; London: Hodder & Stoughton, 1946], vi, lxviii–lxix) argues against. Although Dodd's opinion met strong resistance (see Turner, *Style*, 132–33, for a discussion of the history of debate), his conclusions have more recently been endorsed by Brown, *Epistles*, 22–23. For a discussion of the major issues, and endorsement of John the Elder as the author of all three letters and the Gospel, see M. Hengel, *The Johannine Question* (trans. J. Bowden; London: SCM, 1989), 24–73.

97. See Brooke, *Johannine Epistles*, i–xix; V. S. Poythress, "Testing for Johannine Authorship by Examining the Use of Conjunctions," *WTJ* 46 (1984): 350–69.

98. See Carson, Moo, and Morris, *Introduction*, 447.

99. J. R. W. Stott, *The Epistles of John* (TNTC; Grand Rapids: Eerdmans, 1964), 17–19.

100. See Dodd, *Johannine Epistles*, xlix–lvi, for many of these arguments.

101. On these issues, see D. A. Carson, "The Three Witnesses and the Eschatology of 1 John," in *To Tell the Mystery: Essays on New Testament Eschatology in Honor of Robert H. Gundry* (ed. T. E. Schmidt and M. Silva; JSNTSup 100; Sheffield: JSOT Press, 1994), 216–32.

102. Brown, *Epistles*, 94–97, following his *The Community of the Beloved Disciple* (London: Chapman, 1979), esp. 93–144, although he admits that his reconstruction is highly tentative.

103. For a summary of these views, see Lieu, *Second and Third Epistles*, 52–58. See also Ross, *Epistles of James and John*, 125–29; I. H. Marshall, *The Epistles of John* (NICNT; Grand Rapids: Eerdmans, 1978), 42–48.

104. See Marshall, *Epistles*, 27–30; Brown, *Epistles*, 36–46, both of whom give little credence to such ideas.

105. See Brown, *Epistles*, 28–30. See also J. C. Thomas, "The Order of the Composition of the Johannine Epistles," *NovT* 37 (1995): 68–75, for the order 3, 2, 1 John.

106. See Marshall, *Epistles*, 14–22, esp. 17–18.

107. Some translations are misleading on these verses about sin. They render verses speaking of the avoidance of sin with the Greek present-tense form as stating that Christians should not engage in the "practice" of sin; and they render verses with conditional statements about provision for forgiveness of sin (often with Greek aorist-tense verbs) as referring to singular acts of sin for which there is forgiveness. The issue is far more complex than this simple summary, not least because the Greek perfect tense is also used (1 John 1:10). A recent summary of the issues and possible (though not necessarily persuasive) solutions is found in R. B. Edwards, *The Johannine Epistles* (NT Guides; Sheffield: Sheffield Academic Press, 1996), 98–102.

108. See Justin, *Dial.* 81; Melito of Sardis according to Eusebius, *Hist. eccl.* 4.26.2; Irenaeus, *Haer.* 3.11.1; 4.20.11; 5.35.2; and Tertullian, *Ag. Marc.* 3.14.24; as well as the Muratorian Fragment, a second- or fourth-

century A.D. work, all of whom attribute Revelation to the Apostle John.

109. See R. Bauckham, *The Theology of the Book of Revelation* (New Testament Theology; Cambridge: Cambridge University Press, 1993), 1–17; G. R. Beasley-Murray, *Revelation* (NCB; Grand Rapids: Eerdmans, 1974), 12–29.

110. See, e.g., D. S. Russell, *The Method and Message of Jewish Apocalyptic, 200 B.C.–A.D. 100* (London: SCM, 1964); and L. Morris, *Apocalyptic* (Grand Rapid: Eerdmans, 1972).

111. See D. E. Aune, "The Apocalypse of John and the Problem of Genre," *Semeia* 36 (1986): 65–96, esp. 67.

112. The matrix position is represented in a number of important writings. See D. Hellholm, ed., *Apocalypticism in the Mediterranean World and the Near East* (Tübingen: Mohr–Siebeck, 1983); J. J. Collins, ed., "Apocalypse: The Morphology of a Genre," *Semeia* 14 (1979); J. J. Collins, *The Apocalyptic Imagination: An Introduction to the Jewish Matrix of Christianity* (New York: Crossroad, 1984).

113. Bauckham, *Revelation*, 5–9.

114. See J. M. Court, *Revelation* (NT Guides; Sheffield: JSOT Press, 1994), 83–84; Bauckham, *Revelation*, 9–12.

115. Bauckham, *Revelation*, 5. On the use of the OT in Revelation, see J. Fekkes III, *Isaiah and Prophetic Traditions in the Book of Revelation: Visionary Antecedents and Their Development* (JSNTSup 93; Sheffield: JSOT Press, 1994); S. Moyise, *The Old Testament in the Book of Revelation* (JSNTSup 115; Sheffield: Sheffield Academic Press, 1995); and G. K. Beale, *John's Use of the Old Testament in Revelation* (JSNTSup 166; Sheffield: Sheffield Academic Press, 1998).

116. W. M. Ramsay, *The Letters to the Seven Churches of Asia* (London: Hodder & Stoughton, 1904), 183. On the seven churches, see Hemer, *Letters to the Seven Churches*, 35–209.

117. Bauckham, *Revelation*, 13.

118. Helpful for the discussion that follows are Guthrie, *Introduction*, 949–61; Court, *Revelation*, 95–103; and Robinson, *Redating the New Testament*, 221–53. On the Roman emperors, see E. T. Salmon, *A History of the Roman World, 30 B.C. to A.D. 138* (6th ed.; London: Routledge, 1968), 175–236.

119. See J. N. Kraybill, *Imperial Cult and Commerce in John's Apocalypse* (JSNTSup 132; Sheffield: Sheffield Academic Press, 1996), 17, who sees Revelation as written to Christians of Asia Minor who are called upon "to sever or to avoid economic and political ties with Rome because institutions and structures of the Roman Empire were saturated with unholy allegiance to an Emperor who claimed to be divine (or was treated as such)."

120. See B. Reicke, *The New Testament Era: The World of the Bible from 500 B.C. to A.D. 100* (Philadelphia: Fortress, 1968), 295–302.

121. Moffatt, *Introduction*, 507.

122. R. H. Charles, *A Critical and Exegetical Commentary on the Revelation of St. John* (2 vols.; ICC; Edinburgh: T. & T. Clark, 1920), 1:xcv–xcvii.

123. See J. C. Wilson, "The Problem of the Domitianic Date of Revelation," *NTS* 39 (1993): 587–605.

124. Court, *Revelation*, 98.

125. R. B. Moberly, "When Was Revelation Conceived?" *Bib* 73 (1992): 376–93.

126. On the language of Revelation, see S. E. Porter, "The Language of the Apocalypse in Recent Discussion," *NTS* 35 (1989): 582–603. Despite many hypotheses regarding the Greek of Revelation (that it is a

pages 552–558

pages 558–560

form of Semitic Greek, translation Greek, or some form of Holy Ghost Greek), the best explanation is still that it is a reflection of the author's own Greek usage, or idiolect, full of nonstandard constructions.

127. Charles, *Revelation*, l:xxxviii–xxxix.

128. On these positions, see J. Gunther, "The Elder John, Author of Revelation," *JSNT* 21 (1981): 3–20; Charles, *Revelation*, l:xliii; J. M. Ford, *Revelation* (AB 38; Garden City, N.Y.: Doubleday, 1975), 3–37.

129. See J. M. Court, *Myth and History in the Book of Revelation* (Atlanta: John Knox, 1979), 1–19; and his assessment of contemporary ways of reading Revelation in *Revelation*, 9–20; cf. R. H. Charles, *Studies in the Apocalypse* (London: A. & C. Black, 1913), 1–78, for an older yet similar perspective.

130. Contra C. E. Hill, *Regnum Caelorum: Patterns of Future Hope in Early Christianity* (Oxford: Clarendon, 1992).

131. This neglects the fact that other numerical estimates are given in other Jewish literature (e.g., 400 years in 2 Esd 6:35–9:25), lending credence to the idea that the number is used to speak of a hoped-for time of great duration.

132. See J. W. Mealy, *After the Thousand Years: Resurrection and Judgment in Revelation 20* (JSNTSup 70; Sheffield: JSOT Press, 1992).

133. See Ramsay, *Letters to the Seven Churches*, esp. viii.

134. One of Charles's most telling examples is the relation between 1–20:3 and 20:4–ch. 22. Of 20:4–ch. 22, he says that the "traditional order of the text exhibits a hopeless mental confusion and a tissue of irreconcilable contradictions" (*Revelation*, 1:l-lv; cf. 1:144–54).

135. See Bauckham, *Revelation*, 159–64.

chapter 12

THE LANGUAGE, TEXT, AND TRANSMISSION OF THE NEW TESTAMENT

1. INTRODUCTION

The language, text, and transmission of the NT are essential areas of study for understanding the full meaning of the Christian proclamation and the writings of the NT. Each of these areas could be selected for extended treatment, but our comments here are designed to reflect the current status of discussion, with some indication of where future developments might lead. Though these issues are treated at the end of this volume, no one should conclude that they are therefore unimportant. The language, text, and transmission of the Bible are foundational for our understanding of the Christian faith and for our understanding the Bible itself. We will limit ourselves to the NT in this discussion, but the same is equally true for study of the OT. The first Christians generally spoke Aramaic; some even read the Hebrew Bible and could communicate in Hebrew. But a large percentage of the earliest Christians, Jesus' first followers, could also communicate in Greek (as we will discuss later). The fact that the whole of the NT, and even the apocryphal NT writings and the writings of the early church fathers, are all in Greek is an indicator of the significance of this language for exploring

the meaning of Christian faith. This fact alone should encourage all of us to be interested in learning more about the nuances of the language that clarifies for us the meaning of the Christian faith and the testament of writings that faith has presented to us. Since the writing of the NT texts themselves did not have the aid of printing presses and computer technology as we have today, the initial writing had to be followed up with the production of handwritten copies of these writings for dispatch to other churches. These churches in turn produced copies of these writings that were passed on from generation to generation. In the process, changes—some intentional and some unintentional (see sec. 3.D, below)—were made to the writings. Well-intentioned copiers, who wanted to make clear the meaning of difficult passages in the NT, often simply made changes that were considered appropriate. They also made changes when the passages were no longer as understandable to subsequent generations of Christians as they were to the first Christians. On occasion, some issues of later generations were pressing enough that the copiers introduced items into passages in order to allow the text to speak more meaningfully to these generations. For example, the note to John 3:13 in the NRSV translates a later addition—that Jesus is also in heaven while he is speaking on earth—to the original Greek text. Likewise the note to 1 John 5:7–8 translates an addition by a zealous copier hoping to make the Trinity more understandable. Many other such alterations—whether made by accident or by design—were retained and passed on from generation to generation. We therefore must ask what principles governed the textual transmission of these writings and what principles should be used in determining and establishing the texts today. When these sacred writings began to be translated for communities whose primary tongue was not Greek, how reliable were those translations? And as we look at the translations of the Bible today, how reliable are they?

2. THE LANGUAGE OF THE NEW TESTAMENT

A. Introduction

The NT is written in the Greek language.[1] As A. T. Robertson, the well-known American NT Greek grammarian, once wrote: "The Greek NT is the NT. All else is translation."[2] Translations are valuable tools in the study of the Bible (for those who do not know the original languages, they are indispensable guides), but they are nothing more than authorized or published individual or group interpretations of the Greek NT. This is not meant as a derogation of translations, just a call to recognition of their limitations. With all the available tools for discovering the meaning of the biblical text today, students can certainly get a good grasp on the meaning of the NT. But if they want to enter into serious dialogue with the text and be proficient in their interpretation, this must be accomplished through the original language, Greek. Robertson cites Erasmus, who wrote in his preface to his Greek NT, "These holy pages will summon up the living image of His mind. They will give you Christ Himself, talking, healing, dying, rising, the whole Christ in a word; they will give Him to you in an intimacy so close that He would be less visible to you if He stood before your eyes."[3]

The vast majority of those who read their Bibles will not have the luxury and, in some cases, the ability to learn all the languages that are necessary for scholarly study of the Bible. Since there are limitations to doing biblical interpretation without developing these skills, those who have not had the opportunity must rely on competent scholarly resources that can give insight into the text of the NT in its original language. For those who can (and most students of the Bible who have the time can do at least this much), it is important to learn the Greek symbols so that they may follow some of the best commentaries, dictionaries, and other tools available for study. One who learns only the symbols, however, is not thereby a Greek scholar; it is important to listen to the competent authorities on the text. The hope is that this discussion of the Greek language's development will prompt students of the Bible to have a new understanding of how the NT was written and an appreciation for the many unsung heroes of the church who have dedicated their lives to making its message available to as wide an audience as possible.

The Greek of the NT is not the Greek of such writers as Plato, Thucydides, or the tragedians Aeschylus, Sophocles, and Euripides but that of the Hellenistic world.[4] Although various dates are given for the Hellenistic period, the third century B.C. to the fourth century A.D. will suffice for purposes of discussion. The Greek language belongs to the group of languages called Indo-European. The earliest form of these languages, frequently called Proto-Indo-European (PIE), was not an actual language but is a hypothetical reconstruction by scholars attempting to describe the common origins of languages that share a family resemblance. Most of the languages of western Europe are Indo-European. Hebrew, on the other hand, is one of the Semitic languages, and although the Greek alphabet came from the Phoenician alphabet, which also provided the alphabet for Hebrew, the languages belong to two different language families.

The earliest language forms that we can recognize as Greek go back to the Mycenaeans, who came to occupy what are known today as the Greek islands and mainland. Mycenaean civilization reached great heights in the second millennium B.C. (on Crete and mainland Greece), and it is to this period that the great legendary heroes of classical Greece, such as Achilles and others in the Trojan War, likely belong. This great civilization declined or was destroyed by approximately 1100 B.C., however, throwing that region into what has been called a "dark age"—a period about which very little is known. In the nineteenth century, a number of tablets and other inscriptions were found, especially at the remains of a city called Pylos on the Greek mainland. What scholars today call Linear B was the script of the Mycenaeans. First deciphered in 1952, it is an earlier form of writing that is recognizably Greek.[5] Linear B is known from clay tablets discovered in the remains of virtually all the centers of Mycenaean civilization.

In approximately 800 B.C., the Greek islands emerged out of their dark age when various groups in the territory rediscovered writing, which resulted in the development of several different regional dialects on the Greek islands and mainland. There were four major regional dialects: Arcado-Cypriot, West Greek including Doric, Aeolic, and Attic-Ionic. The time from about 800 B.C. until the fourth century B.C. is called the dialect period of Greek language. It was during the sixth and fifth centuries B.C. that there emerged what is called the classical period; this term describes the ascendance of Athenian culture, literature, arts, and economy. During this very intriguing era of Greek history, a surprisingly large number of significant thinkers and writers congregated in Athens. Combined with the economic prosperity of Athens, this concentration of talent led to phenomenal achievements in the arts and literature. Because of Athenian dominance, its particular variety of the Ionic dialect of Greek came to be widely used, and much of the literature from this period is written in it. Comparisons of Greek texts from Herodotus and Thucydides illustrate some of the differences between Doric (Herodotus) and Attic (Thucydides). Some regional dialects differed in significant ways, but many of the differences were limited to matters of sound and spelling. When spoken, the dialects may have been unintelligible to each other in many instances, but it appears that the written forms of the languages were mutually understood without great difficulty (cf. Herodotus, *Hist.* 8.144.2, who says that the Greeks were of one blood and one tongue). The language of Athens (like all other languages) developed over the course of centuries, and the remains of this language come to us in the form of written texts. We obviously do not have any instance of the spoken language (e.g., recordings). What we do know of it is based upon reconstructions from various written texts, including inscriptions. The confusion in spelling of words, for example, gives us some idea of how certain letters were pronounced at the time.

Recent study has uncovered a number of facts that are important for study of the language of the NT. First, probably only 20 to 30 percent of the men of classical cities, at the most, could read or write, with much lesser percentages throughout the majority of the Greco-Roman world.[6] For the most part, people had to have the written inscriptions read to them. Second, it appears that the language spoken by the Athenians (and this would apply similarly to other varieties or dialects of the Greek language as well) was not the literary language of the best writers of the time but a variety not characterized by the same intricacies of syntax.[7] This is not to say that spoken language is necessarily simple but that it does not maintain the same artificiality as typifies much Athenian prose and certainly poetry of the time. This is consistent with what is known of the general relationships between written and spoken forms of the same language. Third, even though the dialects showed significant differences and their users struggled to maintain their identity, the process began fairly early (at least by the fourth century B.C.) of creating a standard form of language used in such contexts as inscriptions.[8]

All languages develop, but not according to some predetermined rate or pattern. A major turning point in the development of the Greek language was the rise to power of the Macedonian Alexander III (the Great).[9] One of the most influential people of any time in the ancient world, he was more responsible for the writing of the NT in Greek than probably any other single factor. Alexander was educated for two years by Aristotle, who was selected by Alexander's father, Philip II of Macedon, because of Philip's love for things Hellenic and his high regard for this thinker. Alexander was heavily influenced by a similar passion for things Greek.

When Alexander undertook his conquest of the Persians, he gathered an army of 50,000 Greek mercenaries. Thus Alexander instigated a very important linguistic movement at the same time he inaugurated his military campaigns. Wherever he went, he took the Greek language with him. As a result of his widespread conquests, Greek was established as the common language of communication, coming to dominate local and regional indigenous languages as various peoples were conquered and submitted to Alexander's rule. Through Greek's widespread dissemination, especially as it came into contact with a variety of other languages and as the dialects of soldiers and others mixed, the process of linguistic change was accelerated, moving Greek away from its many regional peculiarities to a more universally used common dialect. This pattern of development was consistent with other Hellenistic cultural dissemination. Greek city planning, Greek civil administration, and Greek cultural and social institutions were all exported from the Greek territories throughout the empire Alexander created and his successors, the Diadochi, continued. This pattern persisted under the four Hellenistic Greek kingdoms, including those of the Ptolemies and the Seleucids, and, in many ways, under the Romans. Although the Romans brought many new innovations, especially in the area of governmental administration, much of the Romans' culture depended upon their Greek predecessors.

The result was that a form of Hellenistic Greek became the prestige language of the Greco–Roman world and remained so even long after Latin established itself as a significant language of the empire in the second century A.D. Greek documents surviving antiquity outnumber Latin almost ten to one. In linguistic terms, this means that Greek was the language used by those who had cultural and economic superiority; and those who wished to attain such status or carry on effective interaction with these people had to know Greek. Greek is found in a wide range of authors and texts, from the most ephemeral business contracts and receipts, as recorded in papyri, to the numerous literary writers of the time (e.g., Polybius the Roman historian). Even though the works of a good number of the most famous and popular writers of the time have disappeared without much trace (e.g., Epicurus, whose 300 volumes have all vanished, surviving only in quotations by others), there is still an abundance of material to be examined.[10] In the second century A.D., a movement developed in which a few writers, rejecting what they perceived to be the corruption of the language, advocated a return to the standards of vocabulary and style of the best classical writers of Athens. This movement, called Atticism, did not have much influence

except on certain literary authors (including some later Christian writers). What is noteworthy and in some ways surprising about the linguistic situation of the first century is the significant consistency of the Greek language across the span of the Greco-Roman world. Even in Phrygia and Lycaonia, in the interior of Asia Minor, where regional dialects had a better chance of survival (and did in some remote places), Greek was the common language, although perhaps with some regional differences in pronunciation (see Acts 14:11). Palmer says of this common language that it "smothered and replaced the ancient local dialects": "Profound linguistic consequences might have been expected from the adoption of what was basically the Attic dialect by users of not merely non-Attic, but non-Greek speech. In fact the changes were remarkably slight."[11] It was in this language that the NT was written.

One of the best resources for the study of Hellenistic Greek is the abundance of papyrus documents from Egypt. Widespread discovery of these documents began in the middle of last century, and most of the major finds had been made by the first part of this century. Scholars are still deciphering and publishing these documents, in which there have been phenomenal discoveries. A number of literary texts among them (e.g., fragments from various known and even unknown authors, such as the Oxyrhynchus historian) have provided us with our earliest documents of some of the classical writers (e.g., Homer). Some apocryphal-gospel fragments have also been discovered among these (e.g., P.Egerton 2, held in the British Library), as well as the earliest fragment of the NT (P.Ryl. Greek 457 = $\mathfrak{P}^{52}$). By far the single most important discovery, however, is what has been learned about the common language through the examination of everyday documents. We find a man writing to his wife about how he will not be home for a while, since he is in Alexandria earning money for his family (P.Oxy. 744). We read a letter to his father from a petulant boy, upset because he has not been taken to Alexandria (P.Oxy. 119). We find records of various business and financial transactions—wills, marriage arrangements, and the like. From these close and firsthand glimpses of daily life in the Hellenistic period, we have gained phenomenal insights into the possible meanings of numerous words and grammatical constructions used in the Hellenistic world. Although some have resisted the claim that the Greek from Egypt is representative of the Greek in use throughout the Hellenistic world, this special pleading must be rejected. The Greek texts are too numerous and too consistent with each other to be overlooked. There has been no other Hellenistic Greek dialect found. Even though the vast majority of papyri have come from Egypt, since the late 1940s there have also been significant finds of Greek texts in other areas, including a number of letters and other documents from Palestine.[12] Greek documents were found even among the Jewish patriots of the Bar Kokhba rebellion of A.D. 132–135 (e.g., SB 8.9843, 8.9844).

In NT studies, two major questions about the Greek of the NT are often discussed. First, what kind of Greek is found in the NT, especially in the Gospels? Second, did Jesus speak Greek, and if so, how much? These questions have important implications for understanding the NT.

B. The Greek of the New Testament

The question of the kind of Greek found in the NT has gone through several stages of discussion, even in this century.[13] Because the Egyptian papyri had yet to be analyzed and appreciated, before the turn of this century there was a widespread belief in many circles that the language of the NT constituted a special dialect, biblical Greek, possibly even a divinely inspired or "Holy Ghost" Greek. This theory was not advanced in a highly systematic way but grew out of frequent significant differences between the Greek of the NT and the Greek found in the literary writers even of the Hellenistic period and certainly of the classical period. The periodic style of Thucydides, or even of Polybius, is not the style of the Greek NT. One of the leading Greek–English lexicons of the day had a list of several hundred words that supposedly had meanings in the Greek Bible that were unattested elsewhere.[14]

Two scholars were primarily responsible for showing the inadequacy of the view that the Greek of the NT was a special form of Greek, as emotionally and theologically appealing as that view was (and still is in some people's minds): Deissmann of Germany and Moulton of England, who discerned and disseminated the importance of the recent papyrological discoveries. After Deissmann's chance notice of the similarities between a papyrus text and the Greek of the NT, he undertook an investigation into the vocabulary of the NT. This resulted in several major books on the topic[15] that are still highly valuable tools for study. In them, Deissmann abundantly shows how the Greek of the papyri and inscriptions from the Hellenistic period help to elucidate the Greek of the NT. The lengthy list of words with supposedly unattested meanings has been reduced to a small handful, with every expectation that even these meanings may someday be discovered; if they are not, the perspective is that it is simply a quirk of history that some document does not contain them. Moulton undertook a lexicon to illustrate how the vocabulary of the Greek Bible could be elucidated by the papyri, but his even greater accomplishment was to show the grammatical significance of the papyri for understanding the Greek of the NT.[16] It has occasionally been argued that various constructions in the Greek of the NT are odd or unusual Greek or even heavily influenced by Semitic languages such as Hebrew and Aramaic, but the papyri have shown that most, if not virtually all, of these phenomena were possible, if not regular, constructions in the Greek of the first century A.D. For example, it has been claimed that the use of the present tense in John and Mark reflects their Aramaic origins. In fact, the frequency of this kind of tense usage within the Gospels falls within the parameters of its usage in other historical writers of the period who have no Semitic influence in their writings.[17]

Unfortunately, Moulton was killed during World War I by a German U-boat while crossing the Mediterranean on the way back from a missionary trip to India and so was unable to complete the major task of writing an entire grammar of the NT according to the principles illustrated above. To our minds, however, Deissmann and Moulton clearly established that the Greek of the NT is best understood as part of the common Greek of the Hellenistic world that is today frequently called Koine Greek.

After the deaths of Deissmann, Moulton, and others who had appreciated the importance of the papyri, there was a backlash against this position, to some extent because the ground was sadly left undefended by advocates of the hypothesis. In light of the Jewish origins of Christianity, it is perhaps understandable that a number of scholars assumed that the language of the NT—even though it is Greek—was also Semitic in some form. Several different Semitic hypotheses have been advanced to explain the Greek of the NT. In its earliest forms, this view is perhaps best illustrated by the work of Charles Torrey, who argued that the Gospels, the first half of Acts, and Revelation were all translated from Aramaic (some have argued that Hebrew was the original language of composition for some of the books of the NT, although this view is much more difficult to sustain).[18] While many have pointed out grammatical deficiencies in the Greek NT (many of these are simply failures to conform to the artificial standards of classical Greek as used by Athenian writers), Torrey took these as indications not of the texts' linguistic deficiencies but of their high status as translations. Instead of being sloppy or badly done, these translations, according to Torrey, were made with the intent of preserving the original meaning. This first generation of Semitic hypotheses came under severe attack, even by advocates of other forms of Semitic hypotheses. The major lines of criticism focused on the failure to show that supposed instances of translation were in fact best explained in this way, as opposed to being examples of common Greek. The next generation of Semitic language advocates made a much more modest set of claims regarding the Greek NT.[19] Rather than argue that the Gospels or other NT books were originally Aramaic documents, proponents conceded that they were Greek documents, but they maintained that these writings reflected authors whose native tongues were Aramaic or that they recorded words spoken by Jesus and others and translated out of Aramaic. This is not to say that the author of a writing simply made a wooden translation of the Aramaic words, but an Aramaic substratum lay behind these Greek texts. According to proponents, this is indicated not only by what is generally known about the linguistic character of Palestine at the time; occasional oddities in the wording or concepts also point to the Semitic original. This position is clearly correct in recognizing that at least some, if not most, of the original words of Jesus were in Aramaic. Nevertheless, it works from an improper estimation of the linguistic climate in Palestine. As noted above, the situation was not that of simply two languages, Aramaic and Greek, competing on an even footing. Greek was the prestige language of Palestine, and anyone wishing to conduct business on an extended scale, including successful fishermen from the region of Galilee and probably any craftsmen or artisans who came into contact with Roman customers, would have needed—indeed would have wanted—to know Greek. In such a situation, the nonprestige language will usually show the grammatical influence of the prestige language, not the other way around. Palestine was heavily influenced by the Greek of the first century A.D., much more indeed than was thought a generation ago. The evidence shows that Palestine, including the Jerusalem region, was part of the Greek-speaking Hellenistic world.[20]

A small but significant number of scholars have advocated that the confrontation between Aramaic and Greek led to the development of a special dialect of Greek.[21] For some this dialect was a temporary linguistic situation when the two came into initial confrontation, while for others this constituted an independent variety of Semitic Greek that continued to be used in the early church. This Semitic Greek hypothesis has not attracted a large number of followers, but its influence has been widely felt. It appeals to those who have a predisposition for wishing to find something special about the language of the NT, a position usually based on theological rather than linguistic criteria. It seems also to appreciate the Jewish background of Christianity while recognizing that all of its canonical documents were in Greek. The existence of this so-called Semitic Greek dialect has been argued by N. Turner, a well-known grammarian who was responsible for writing one of the few reference grammars of NT Greek. The shortcomings of this hypothesis, however, are numerous. First, there is little linguistic foundation for this theory. Such a composite Greek cannot be found any place outside the NT (the body of literature being examined), including the early church writings, which frequently tended toward Atticism in style. So it can hardly be used as the evidence to prove its own existence. There is thus no evidence that this phenomenon ever existed, and none that it continued. Second, the notion of a Semitic Greek dialect makes it difficult to understand why such a Greek would be used in the NT, especially in the Pauline Letters, which were written for widespread dissemination within the Hellenistic world with the full expectation that they would be understood by their readers, whether in Rome, Corinth, or Ephesus (to cite three very different locales).

In about the last twenty years, there has been a return to support of the Greek hypothesis of Deissmann and Moulton. Silva has been instrumental in this return because of his close attention to matters of linguistic method.[22] Aided by Horsley's recent work in the papyri, Silva has shown that the linguistic distinction between *langue* (the language system) and *parole* (a particular writer's use of it) clarifies the linguistic situation in Palestine in the first century. Although one's individual *parole* may have had peculiarities brought about through knowledge of a Semitic language, the *langue* in use was clearly Hellenistic Greek. Thus, for understanding the Greek of the NT, one needs to be most attentive not to the Semitic sources but to the Greek of the papyri and other contemporary writers. The Semitic sources are more valuable in discovering the context of early Christianity than in understanding the Greek language of the NT.

C. The Language of Jesus

Related to the issue of the Greek of the NT is the question whether Jesus spoke Greek. Although some have discussed the possibility that Jesus spoke Hebrew and there is some evidence from Luke 4:16–20 that he did, the vast majority of scholars believe that Jesus' primary language was Aramaic.[23] This hypothesis seems well founded. Jesus was born to a Jewish family and apparently was well versed in the institutions of the Jewish people, including the use of Aramaic, spoken by Jews since the return from the exile. Aramaic continued in use during the first century (contrary to some earlier hypotheses), as is well attested from the Dead Sea Scrolls, Targumim, and other related documents. Jewish worship during this time was often carried on in Aramaic, in the interpretative translation (Targum) of the biblical text. The Gospels support this scenario for Jesus; he is seen to be communicating on numerous occasions with members of the Jewish religious establishment and participating in various Jewish religious observances in Palestine, and he is recorded as using Aramaic on several different occasions (e.g., the direct quotations in Mark 5:41; 7:34; 15:34 = Matt 27:46). Thus it is reasonable to suppose that on many, if not the vast majority of, occasions when Jesus spoke or taught those who gathered around him, he probably used Aramaic and that the words of Jesus recorded in the NT, although rendered into Hellenistic Greek, were at one time translated out of Aramaic. Nevertheless, because of the difficulties of translation, for which it is rare to find word-for-word equivalence between languages, and because the words of Jesus are contextually placed within the sustained narratives of the Gospels, one must be cautious in attempting to reconstruct these Aramaic words. As Black, an advocate of the Aramaic hypothesis, states, in the majority of cases the " 'translation' is not literal but literary; in other words, it is doubtful if it can be justly described as translation at all in some cases. . . . The Evangelists, that is to say, are for the most part writing Greek Gospels, even where they are dependent upon sources."[24]

Jesus' use of Aramaic is virtually certain, but there is also good evidence for thinking that Jesus knew and used Greek, possibly even using it on occasions when he taught. Before examining the specific evidence in the NT, we must recognize that Jesus came from an area that had been highly influenced by Greek culture. He was from Nazareth, living close to an excellent example of a Greek city in Palestine, Sepphoris, where both Greek and Aramaic were spoken, and near the primarily Gentile Decapolis, ten Hellenistic cities or villages in the vicinity of Galilee. He was involved in a trade where, it is reasonable to assume, he would have had contact with other than simply his local townspeople, possibly Romans or Greek speakers. In the course of his itinerant ministry, Jesus also traveled into parts of Palestine where he may have had contact with people who spoke Greek. Indeed, several of his disciples, including Andrew and Philip, had Greek names despite being Jewish. When we turn to the Gospels, at least five episodes in the Gospels point to the conclusion that Jesus knew Greek.[25] The first and most important is in Mark 15:2–5 (= Matt 27:11–14; Luke 23:2–5; John 18:29–38), where Jesus is interrogated by Pilate. In the course of their conversation there is no indication of a translator present, and it is unreasonable to think that Pilate spoke Aramaic or that they conducted their conversation in Latin. The Roman prefect of this troublesome part of the empire would probably have scorned the idea of learning the indigenous language, especially when so many of the people spoke Greek (55–60 percent of all Jewish funerary inscriptions in Palestine are in Greek, including about half of the inscriptions found in Jerusalem itself),[26] and Latin itself was reserved for official Roman business (at least one Roman complained near the end of the first century that Greek was all that one heard spoken even in Rome!). On the basis of this evidence, of the Gospel criteria of multiple attestation (i.e., a tradition is found in two or more independent sources), and of redactional tendencies (i.e., a feature cannot be attributed to the editorial tendencies of a writer), it can be argued very convincingly that Jesus and Pilate spoke Greek to each other in their conversation. In the course of Pilate's questioning of Jesus, he asks him, "Are you the king of the Jews?" Jesus answers, "You say so." These sentences are not lengthy, but there is good reason to think that they are the actual Greek words of the conversation. In the four other passages, there is no evidence to establish the actual wording of Jesus (Mark 7:24–30; John 12:20–28; Matt 8:5–13 = Luke 7:2–10), but the scenarios and the linguistic characteristics suggest that on these occasions also Jesus spoke in Greek.

In conclusion, the widespread use of Greek created a fortuitous situation. On the one hand, it was a major force in uniting together a vast territory that had a wide variety of differing cultural, social, economic, and religious backgrounds. On the other, the conquest of Alexander and his introduction of things Greek into the wider Mediterranean world helped provide the basis for the later Pax Romana, the Roman peace of Augustus' reign, which was characterized by social, political, and economic stability in addition to linguistic stability and unity. It was into this Greco-Roman world that Jesus was born. Although he used Aramaic predominantly, he apparently employed Greek as well, and it was Greek that became the language of the early church. This linguistic unity helped create ecclesial unity. Paul and others wrote letters to churches located throughout the Greco-Roman world, with the full expectation that their members would be able to read and understand these letters. Although we have much evidence that the audiences did not always appreciate what was said in the letters, there is nothing to suggest that the problem was caused by a failure to understand the language in which the letters were written. It was in Greek that not only the NT writings but virtually all the apocryphal NT materials (see ch. 14, below, for a listing of these) were preserved. The earliest church fathers were Greek writers. It is therefore reasonable that one should learn something of both the Greek language, in which the NT was written, and the larger conceptual, intellectual, and linguistic world in which this language was used.

3. THE TEXT AND TRANSMISSION OF THE NEW TESTAMENT

Textual criticism has been described above (ch. 2), but it is appropriate here to discuss in more detail the principles and practices of textual criticism. The issues include (1) basic concepts about our texts of the NT, (2) the way manuscripts of the NT are often categorized and analyzed, (3) the criteria by which variant readings in the NT documents are adjudicated, and (4) basic principles of textual transmission.

A. Basic Concepts of Textual Criticism

Although most people realize that we do not have the original NT documents (or any original biblical manuscript, for that matter), they do not understand what textual criticism is and what it is designed to do. The goal of textual criticism is easy to explain but extremely difficult to accomplish. Simply stated, its goal is to reconstruct a text as close as possible to the original text from the pen of the author. At every point where there is a textual variant—where manuscripts present different readings, sometimes as small as a single letter (e.g., a long or short o in ἔχωμεν, ἔχομεν, echōmen, echomen, in Rom 5:1) and sometimes as large as a whole verse or even a whole passage (e.g., John 7:53–8:11 or Mark 16:9ff.)—the textual critic must decide which reading is closest to the original. It is unlikely that the reconstructed (or eclectic) text resulting from such a process would be identical to the original text, and it is virtually certain that the original text would not match any of our extant copies. All of the complete surviving manuscripts are several copy generations removed from the original writing.

From the study of manuscript readings, one can see that certain manuscripts seem to reflect the same textual traditions and tendencies in the way they vary. Manuscripts are arranged according to these broad resemblances, and certain types of manuscripts provide the basis for our modern editions. The so-called Alexandrian text type, reflecting texts that are thought to have originated in Alexandria, Egypt, from the second century on, forms the basis of most modern eclectic (reconstructed) editions. It is, however, thought inadvisable simply to follow the two major Alexandrian manuscripts, Codex Sinaiticus (א) and Codex Vaticanus (B). Even these early texts, already removed from the original by several generations, reveal numerous second and subsequent hands at work on the manuscript. In studying manuscripts it is often difficult to decide whether an alteration was a correction made at the time of writing or was added later. Some texts even cross their typological boundaries and influence each other.

St. Catherine's Monastery at the foot of Mount Sinai. It is the source of several important biblical manuscripts, including Codex Sinaiticus (א). Photo © Rohr Productions. Used with permission.

In pursuing the goal of textual criticism—reconstruction of the original text—one is faced with two kinds of evidence for establishing the text and deciding between variants. Internal evidence is concerned with the transcriptional probabilities that seemed to be in effect when an ancient manuscript was copied and recopied. For example, did the copyists tend to add or subtract material when they wrote? External evidence is concerned with the nature and kind of surviving manuscripts—not simply their numbers but how old they are and how they relate to each other (e.g., the various tendencies noted in the changes introduced into manuscripts provide the basis for classifying them). Scholars differ on how much weight to give to internal and external evidence, but there are at least three major groupings of opinions in this debate.[27]

1. Majority Text

The first grouping follows the so-called Majority Text.[28] The Majority Text is the text reflected in the Authorized or King James Version (KJV). More precisely, it is the text as reconstructed on the basis of the majority of manuscripts (the two, the KJV and the Majority Text, should be distinguished but are often confused or equated). This is not the place to debate the relative merits of the KJV, except to say that there has been far too much uninformed hyperbole, in terms of textual criticism, regarding its continuing merits or those of the text that stands behind it. There is no denying the beautiful language of the KJV, much of it reflecting the excellent translation of William Tyndale (1494–1536), the first English speaker to translate the NT from the original Greek (1534).[29] Previous translations, such as that of Wycliffe, had been from the Latin. The text behind the KJV, the Majority Text, however, is not as highly regarded by scholars today as it once was. The reason is that we now have available approximately five thousand surviving manuscripts of variously sized portions of the NT (far more than for any other ancient author or set of authors).[30] Most of these manuscripts come from the Byzantine period (fifth century A.D. and later), when, with the spread of Christianity, the need for more manuscripts increased. Numerous copies of manuscripts were produced, many of which are still extant. Textual decisions ought to consider the best manuscripts, however, without consideration of how many further copies of this manuscript there are. A recopied mistake is still a mistake, no matter how many copies of it have been made. In addition, there is often attached to a defense of the Majority Text a kind of belief in the virtual inspiration and divine preservation of the translation itself, a doctrine that has no foundation in Christian theology. Advocacy of the Majority Text clearly opts for external criteria (the sheer number of manuscripts) over internal criteria (e.g., how changes were made in manuscripts; see secs. C and D, below), which are often considered by defenders of the Majority Text as too subjective.

2. Rigorous or Thoroughgoing Eclecticism

There is a form of textual criticism with far more argumentative force and intellectual responsibility than advocacy of the Majority Text; it is sometimes called rigorous or thoroughgoing eclecticism.[31] This form, most recently vigorously defended by the late G. D. Kilpatrick and by J. K. Elliott, argues that internal criteria are all that ought to be considered in determining the correctness of a variant reading. The argument is that the nature of the external evidence makes it an unreliable guide to determining the correct reading in a given context, although the external evidence may well give some indication of the range of readings that are available for consideration. Instead, the advocates of this approach say that internal criteria alone should be used to evaluate each of the suggested variants, no matter its date or textual type, the idea being that even a very late text could preserve the original reading.

3. Reasoned Eclecticism

Most textual critics today reject the two methods presented above and settle on a model frequently called reasoned eclecticism.[32] Developed by the very important and foundational work of Westcott and Hort, especially in Hort's introduction to their critical text of the NT, reasoned eclecticism argues that there must be appreciation of both forms of criteria, internal and external.[33] On the one hand, due consideration must be given to the textual types and their relationships in establishing the viability of variant readings. The manuscripts are more than simply repositories of variant readings; comparison and analysis of the texts themselves can give insight into the probability of a given reading, and the date of the manuscript or text is also important, even if it cannot be the only criterion for judging (see sec. C, below). On the other hand, reasoned eclecticism argues further that due consideration must be given to internal criteria, since there seem to be established patterns by which manuscripts were transmitted. These internal criteria are fairly well established among modern textual critics (see sec. D, below). Finding the balance between these two criteria, however, has resulted in a number of different forms of reasoned eclecticism. For example, some give far higher priority to the major Alexandrian codices (codices were early forms of books especially used by Christians; see sec. 4, below), especially Sinaiticus (א) and Vaticanus (B), while others argue that the

papyri ought to be given far more weight than they usually are.[34] Debate of these priorities is still ongoing, but reasoned eclecticism seems to have prevailed in NT text-critical circles except among those textual critics noted above and a few others.

Manuscripts are numbered according to a complex system. Codices are given a number beginning with 0 (e.g., 029), with special codices given a letter as well (03 or B). Papyri are given a $\mathfrak{P}$ number (e.g., $\mathfrak{P}^{46}$). Minuscules, or lower-case texts, are given a simple number (e.g., 28, 33), while lectionaries are given an *l* and a number (e.g., *l* 47).

B. History of the Modern Critical Text

The history of the modern critical text of the Greek NT is a fascinating one. Erasmus, the Dutch scholar, published his text of the Greek NT in 1516, based on only five relatively late manuscripts (ca. A.D. 1300–1400). The so-called Received Text of Erasmus—the Textus Receptus[35]—provided the basis for subsequent texts and translations of the NT until the mid- to late 1800s, when two significant events took place. The first was the discovery and editing of a huge quantity of new biblical manuscripts. Although a number of significant scholars were involved in this enterprise, the most important was probably Constantin Tischendorf. Trained in Leipzig, and without much money, he was able to travel around Europe and the Mediterranean finding and editing biblical manuscripts out of a desire to establish and prove the reliability of the biblical text. In the course of his travels he discovered, in St. Catherine's Monastery in Sinai, Codex Sinaiticus, part of which is now housed in Leipzig and the rest in the British Museum after first being housed in Leningrad.[36] Tischendorf edited more biblical manuscripts than anyone else and was responsible for publishing multiple editions of texts of both the Greek Old and New Testaments. The second important event was one of the most important accomplishments of the nineteenth century: the publication of Westcott and Hort's edition of the NT and their introduction to textual criticism. The second volume gives what has now become the classic exposition of textual criticism, one that has set the standard for subsequent discussion. Virtually all textual critics reject Westcott and Hort's supposition of Codices Sinaiticus and Vaticanus as what they called a neutral text—the text closest to the original without corruption. Nevertheless, in practice these two early Alexandrian codices still constitute the foundation for the establishment of many, if not most, modern critical editions of the NT, along with major papyrus texts, such as $\mathfrak{P}^{46}$ for the Pauline Letters (ca. A.D. 200). As a result of textual criticism's discovery and use of many more ancient manuscripts, we are now able to get a thousand years closer to the time of the original writings than Erasmus.

The text currently used for most NT scholarship—an eclectic text (see sec. A, above) that does not exclusively follow any one particular text type as its base (although the Alexandrian text has been very important)—is patterned after that of Westcott and Hort. The standard editions are UBS[3] and UBS[4] (*The Greek New Testament*, United Bible Societies, 3d and 4th eds.) and NA[27] (*Novum Testamentum Graece*, 27th ed., by E. Nestle and his later editor, K. Aland).[37] These critical editions are the same so far as the text itself is concerned, but they differ in other respects. A major difference is in punctuation. The UBS edition tends to follow punctuation patterns reflecting English conventions, although this has been altered in its fourth edition, whereas the NA edition claims to reflect punctuation more in keeping with ancient Greek phrasing. Another difference is in the texual apparatus. The UBS edition was designed to be a text useful for translators, and supposedly in keeping with such a need, a smaller number of variants (approximately 1,400) are given, with more detailed listings of the manuscript evidence, as opposed to the NA edition, where a far larger number of variants are given (approximately 10,000), but with less full documentation. But it is unclear why translators would need reference to fewer variants with more extensive lists of manuscripts; the opposite appears to be the case. A feature of the UBS edition not found in the NA edition is a rating system in which each variant is assigned a letter grade from A to D in decreasing order of certainty. The first to third (corrected) editions of the UBS text were fairly consistent in their rating criteria and their distributions of ratings, but UBS[4] has experienced severe "grade inflation," with a disproportionately high number of elevated ratings.[38] For this reason, many scholars appear to be continuing use of the third (corrected) edition, since the text is the same, and to be consulting the fourth edition for the updating of

the witnesses to various ratings, although these are minimal. Editions of the Greek NT by Souter and Kilpatrick are also still used, the first done for the Oxford Classical Texts (OCT) series by a scholar known to be a fine textual critic in his own right, and the second for the British and Foreign Bible Society, reflecting Kilpatrick's rigorous eclecticism.[39]

C. Textual Types

The manuscripts used to be classified according to family, implying that one could establish clear lines of descent that, when traced backwards, would eventually lead to the original manuscript. As knowledge of manuscript kinds and relationships has increased, it has become increasingly difficult to identify clear family ties, and most scholars prefer today to refer to text types. The implication is that there is far less concern for the supposed ancestor of a manuscript than for the similarities and differences it may have in relation to other manuscripts.

There are three major manuscript types: Alexandrian, Western, and Byzantine, with the possibility of a fourth, the Caesarean.[40]

1. Alexandrian Text

The Alexandrian text type consists of manuscripts that were once thought to originate in Alexandria, Egypt, a major center of textual scholarship in the Hellenistic period. Indeed, textual studies (practiced then for the preservation of the ancient classical writers, such as Homer and the tragedians) seem to have originated among the scholars of the Alexandrian library. Manuscripts of the Alexandrian type are the earliest we have, and the vast majority of the papyrus texts seem to reflect the Alexandrian text type. The Alexandrian text type is generally agreed to have been prepared by careful and skillful editors in the tradition of Alexandria. The earliest texts in this group seem to point to their origin early in the second century. The Alexandrian texts are now generally favored by scholars as the most reliable, although each passage must be discussed independently. As mentioned above, Westcott and Hort used Codex Sinaiticus (א) and Codex Vaticanus (B) as their so-called neutral texts, believing that they showed the least evidence of having been affected by outside influences,

TABLE 12-1

ALEXANDRIAN MANUSCRIPTS

Proto-Alexandrian	Siglum	Name	Date
	$\mathfrak{P}^{45}$	Chester Beatty Papyrus	3d cent.
	$\mathfrak{P}^{46}$	Chester Beatty Papyrus	A.D. 200
	$\mathfrak{P}^{66}$	Bodmer Papyri	A.D. 200
	$\mathfrak{P}^{75}$	Bodmer Papyri	A.D. 200
	א	Codex Sinaiticus	4th cent.
	B	Codex Vaticanus	4th cent.
Later Alexandrian Gospels	L	Codex Regius	8th cent.
	T	Codex Borgianus	5th cent.
	W	Codex Freerianus (or Washingtonensis) Alexandrian portions Luke 1:1–8:12 and John 5:12–21:25	5th cent.
Acts	$\mathfrak{P}^{50}$		4th or 5th cent.
	A	Codex Alexandrinus[41]	5th cent.
Pauline Epistles	A	Codex Alexandrinus	5th cent.
Catholic Epistles	$\mathfrak{P}^{20}$	Oxyrhynchus Papyri	3d cent.
	$\mathfrak{P}^{23}$	Oxyrhynchus Papyri	early 3d cent.
	A	Codex Alexandrinus	5th cent.
Revelation	A	Codex Alexandrinus	5th cent.

although the concept of a neutral text is no longer widely used in textual criticism. Most of the papyrus fragments with Pauline texts follow what is often called the proto-Alexandrian, or early form of the Alexandrian, text type. Quotations in Clement of Alexandria and Origen and certain Coptic versions tend to be Alexandrian as well, since Clement and Origen lived in Alexandria, the primary location of the Coptic church.

Table 12-1 gives information on some of the important Alexandrian manuscripts (including the Chester Beatty papyri, mostly housed in Dublin; the Bodmer papyri in Oxford).

2. Western Text

The Western text type is so named because the earliest known forms of this manuscript type came from the western part of the Roman Empire, including Rome and northern Africa. This text type has undergone serious and repeated reevaluation in recent years. Its fortunes have changed from being highly revered for offering insight into the Jewish elements of the early church to being seen as merely reflecting corruptions that tended to expand the text. Scholars of late have settled on a middle position, noting that although the Western text type contains many expansions, in some instances it seems to preserve an earlier reading than the Alexandrian text type. The Western text type is thought by some to have been a deliberate revision of an earlier text, although most scholars believe its lack of homogeneity indicates the haphazard growth of a textual tradition. The book of Acts has a distinct Western text version (D), the relation of which to the Alexandrian tradition continues to interest scholars.[42] Several early church fathers are thought to have used the Western text type, including perhaps Marcion and probably Tatian, Irenaeus, Tertullian, and Cyprian, on the basis of their NT citations, and it had a wide geographical distribution. The Early Latin versions reflect the Western tradition as well. The following are important Western text manuscripts.

> ### T A B L E   1 2 - 2
>
> Gospels: D (Bezae Cantabrigiensis; 5th or 6th cent.); W (Mark 1–5:30; Washington; 5th cent.)
>
> Acts: $\mathfrak{P}29$ (Oxyrhynchus; 3d cent.); $\mathfrak{P}38$ (A.D. 300); $\mathfrak{P}48$ (late 3d cent.); D (Bezae Cantabrigiensis; 5th or 6th cent.)
>
> Pauline Epistles: D^p (Paris; 6th cent.); E^p (9th or 10th cent.); F^p (9th cent.); G^p (9th cent.)

3. The Byzantine Text

The Byzantine text type, which did not apparently emerge before A.D. 350, is considered the latest of the three major text types. It is so named because of its distribution throughout the Byzantine Empire. Since it comprises more than 80 percent of all of the manuscripts, it is also called the Majority Text. The Byzantine text type is characterized by relatively late manuscripts. It is a mixed text, resulting from editorial work in the fourth century to produce a "smooth, easy, and complete text."[43] The result is conflated and longer readings, generally held to be the furthest from the originals. The following are important Byzantine text manuscripts.

> ### T A B L E   1 2 - 3
>
> Gospels: A (Alexandrinus; 5th cent., the earliest Byzantine text); E (Basel; 8th cent.); F (9th cent.); G (9th cent.); K (9th cent.); W (Matthew; Luke 8:13ff.; John 1–5:12; Washington; 5th cent.)
>
> Acts: H^a (9th cent.); L^{ap} (9th cent.); P^a (9th cent.)
>
> Epistles: L^{ap} (9th cent.); 049 (9th cent.)
>
> Revelation: 046 (10th cent.)

4. Caesarean Text

Some scholars debate about a fourth text type, the Caesarean text. The Caesarean text, if it is a text type, is often identified with Origen, who lived in Caesarea. It probably originated in Egypt and was brought by Origen to Caesarea, then to Jerusalem. This text type includes a compromised mixture of Western and Alexandrian readings and a literary tendency toward elegance. Many lectionaries reflect the Caesarean text, as do citations in Origen and Eusebius, and the Old Armenian, Old Georgian, and some Old Syriac versions. Since it is today regarded as the least homogeneous of the major text types, there is doubt regarding its categorization as a text type.

> ### T A B L E   1 2 - 4
>
> $\mathfrak{P}45$ (Chester Beatty; 3d cent.); W (Mark 6ff.; Washington; 5th cent.); f^1 (collection of minuscules; 12–15th cent.); f^{13} (collection of minuscules; 11–15th cent.); 28 (minuscule; 11th cent.); q (9th cent. Old Latin version)

Some of the texts listed are mixed. For example, C (5th cent.) is a palimpsest (a manuscript that has been written over a previous text, with the text of interest having been rubbed out to make way for the new text) that combines all of the major text types. Codex A (5th cent.) is Byzantine for the Gospels and Alexandrian for the rest. Those interested in pursuing more precise definitions and boundaries of these categories should consult a standard reference tool, such as the Alands' or Metzger's introductions to their respective *Text of the New Testament*, to find the exact breakdown of the sections. Some of the manuscripts are in several sections housed in different places (e.g., $\mathfrak{P}^{46}$, with portions in Michigan and Dublin.

In judging the relative merits of a given reading found in these three or four major text types, one needs to consider several factors. The first is the age of the manuscript. An older manuscript has a higher probability of being closer to the original reading than does one much later. The second factor is the distribution of readings among the manuscripts. If all the readings come from the same type of manuscript, there is the suspicion that all these readings come from the same earlier manuscript, and there is little merit in the numbers alone. If a variant is distributed over several types of manuscripts, there is the increased chance that these are independent witnesses to an earlier reading.

Besides the manuscripts in Greek, there are three other major kinds of external evidence worth mentioning. These are the church fathers and other early church documents, the old translations, and lectionaries. This material has also aroused serious discussion of late as it has come into increasing prominence in recent textual criticism. Most of the writings of the church fathers[44] are at least as old as, or older than, most of the surviving manuscripts, and they can often be dated and located fairly precisely, so their quotation or even citation of a biblical passage can give some insight into at least the version of the various books of the Bible that was known in their Christian communities. In this sense, the Greek church fathers are easier to use than the Latin ones, since the factor of translation does not enter into the equation. Nevertheless, there are other problems to consider besides the obvious fact that we do not have the original texts of these Fathers (indeed, attempts are only now under way to establish critical texts for many of these Fathers through the same principles of textual criticism discussed here). For example, it is not always possible to tell when the church fathers are quoting

directly or simply paraphrasing and thus what the use of a particular passage might say about the reading that they had before them. Likewise, in some of the church fathers the same passage is cited several times in widely differing forms. What is the best course to take when a church father offers a reading that is significantly different? For example, Clement of Alexandria (ca. 170), one of the first Christian scholars, cites Matt 21:9 as stating that "the children" went forth (*Tutor* 1.5), something not found in any of our NT manuscripts, all of which are later than Clement. Should we include the reference to the children at this place in the NT text? For several reasons, including the tendency in a number of church fathers to introduce references to children where none are found in the biblical text, this reading should almost assuredly be rejected.[45] This illustrates that the church fathers have their own interests and are not necessarily to be relied upon as indicators of the best and earliest texts.

Besides passing down the textual tradition in Greek, a number of churches early on engaged in translation of the NT into their particular languages. For example, there are Syriac, Armenian, and Gothic versions, besides a wide range of Old Latin versions to consider, some of them in quite fragmentary form.[46] Again, besides the problem that we do not possess the original of any of these versions and hence textual criticism must be done here as well, there is the serious question of translation. The complexity of the issue is that these texts are in languages different from the original text of the NT and require not only the understanding of these languages but knowledge of the various principles of translation that may have been used in the course of their development. There is the further problem, exacerbated by the difference in languages, of determining which text was before the translator. The problems with these translations necessarily introduce the question whether they are good guides in establishing the original text of the NT. In some cases, however, they can help to clarify certain issues; for example, the Syriac Peshitta does not have John 21 (on the question whether John 21 belonged to the original Gospel, see ch. 8, above).

The third and final source to mention is lectionaries.[47] Lectionaries are collections of biblical passages that were used for liturgical purposes. The texts are often marked to indicate the units for liturgical reading. There are many possible insights to be gained from lectionaries, since they illustrate the most important texts of a particular church community. Nevertheless, there are limitations to this evidence. For example, only two lectionaries date to before the sixth century (*l* 1604 and *l* 1043); most are Byzantine and hence relatively late. Lectionaries are selective in their contents and organize their pericopes, or shorter texts, in a way that does not agree with the majority of later lectionaries, so, without the original text for comparison, it is difficult to know how to account for variations in a given text. Although lectionaries have been neglected, more attention has rightly been given to them in recent textual criticism. Nevertheless, their importance must still be established for a given variant.

D. Internal Criteria

Discussion of the internal criteria for determining an original reading can be divided into two different categories.[48] One way of discussing them is in terms of unintentional and intentional changes.[49]

Intentional changes are those introduced by a scribe for a variety of conscious reasons. Most of these changes were probably made with only the best of intentions in mind, the scribe attempting to correct a text that was perceived as in some way in need of alteration or change. In some cases, these were merely grammatical changes, such as the correction of the spelling of a word or the smoothing out of a sentence. These may seem relatively harmless; nevertheless, there are implications. For example, the Greek of the NT was originally written in a form of Greek typical of that used in the Greco-Roman world. Under various cultural and linguistic pressures, especially prevalent in the Alexandrian manuscript tradition with its emphasis upon textual propriety, more "proper," or Attic, spellings and phrasings were introduced. Other kinds of intentional changes were introduced as well, including alterations of content. For example, it is common to find one of the copyists apparently changing the wording of one of the Synoptic Gospels to conform it to the other two Gospels and thus bring them into full harmony. Or OT quotations in the NT may be changed so that they agree more closely with the OT text. Another alteration is apparent in

Mark 1:2, where some later manuscripts change "Isaiah the prophet" to "the prophets" because the text quotes Malachi in addition to Isaiah. There are also theological alterations, designed either to elucidate an obscure statement or to alter a statement that may have appeared to be out of character with the rest of the NT. In Mark 13:32 some manuscripts have excluded the reference to the "son" not knowing the day and hour because that would imply a limitation to Jesus' knowledge, something the church may not have wanted to promote. Some statements designed to clarify the text may well have never been intended to be part of the text but were written in the margin, only to be added later into the main text itself by another scribe. Many of these textual variations may have arisen before the text reached scriptural status, when some may have felt freer to improve, correct, or change the text. This probably happened more in the Gospels because of synoptic parallels.

Unintentional changes are those introduced through no predetermined effort or plan by the scribe involved in copying the manuscript; rather, they are the kinds of changes that would normally creep in during the process of writing out the manuscript. Many of these become readily understandable when it is realized that the earliest texts were written in continuous writing, that is, without a break between letters or words, in capital letters. For example, a scribe might write an incorrect letter (especially when so many of the Greek capital letters are written so similarly, such as ΓΤΙ or ΑΔΛ), mishear a vowel (since many of the vowels were pronounced in the same way, such as the omicron and the omega with short *o* and long *o* vowel sounds), skip a line or two between two words ending in the same letters (e.g., John 17:15 in Codex Vaticanus [B] reads, "I am not asking you to protect them from the evil one," leaving out "to take them out of the world, but"), or repeat the same material between words ending in similar letters.

The probable correctness of a given reading, with regard to whether it involves unintentional or intentional changes, can be judged against two sets of criteria. One concerns what a scribe might do in a given instance (transcriptional probabilities); and the other, broader linguistic and literary considerations of authors (intrinsic probabilities). Most of these criteria have a certain amount of innate sense to them, although they are not always recognized or heeded.

1. Transcriptional Probabilities

The first category of internal criteria is transcriptional probabilities. These kinds of readings can be accounted for by recognized scribal habits. The following transcriptional probabilities are some of the better known and more common ones.

a. The more difficult reading that still makes sense is generally to be preferred, especially when the sense appears at first glance to be in error but proves understandable on further analysis. The tendency appears to have been for a scribe to resolve difficult phrasing into simpler or more straightforward, possibly even expanded, wording. Hence the more difficult reading that is still comprehensible has more likelihood of being correct. A notorious example is how Rev 1:4 has been changed from the awkward grammar of nominative-case nouns following a preposition when the genitive case is required. In Mark 10:40, the Greek letters should probably be read as "for those," rather than one word, "for others," which does not make sense in the context.

b. The shorter reading is generally to be preferred, especially where it is clear that a scribe has duplicated material (dittography). The exception to the priority of the shorter reading would be where it is clear that the scribe has omitted material (haplography)—for example, by skipping over material (parablepsis) because words have similar endings (homoioteleuton), similar beginnings (homoioarcton, or similar middle sections (homoiomeson), or by excising material considered superfluous, harsh, impious, and so forth. These errors could have been made by a scribe reading out the text for others to copy. There are also errors caused by a scribe's faulty hearing. A classic example of haplography occurs at Luke 10:32, where Codex Sinaiticus omits the verse, probably because a scribe's eye jumped from the same verb at the end of 10:31 to 10:33.

c. The less well harmonized parallel passage is generally to be preferred. For example, in Mark 13:11 one variant includes both the verb from the parallel in Luke 21:14 ("prepare in advance") *and* the verb found in other Markan manuscripts ("worry beforehand").

d. The rougher or less refined Greek is generally to be preferred, since scribes often substituted more familiar words, altered grammatical expressions to the more refined Attic construction, or added words to make a smoother text. For example, the use of "and" in Rev 1:6 between the Greek participles in v. 5 and the finite verb "made" in v. 6 has been deleted by many Alexandrian texts.

2. Intrinsic Probabilities

Intrinsic probabilities look at larger linguistic and literary patterns as a guide to determining what an author may have done, whether intentionally or unintentionally. They are often taken into account in trying to decide the original reading, since they tend to indicate broad and consistent authorial tendencies.

a. One should consider the style and vocabulary of the author throughout the book, realizing that a fine balance must be maintained in recognizing the more difficult reading without adopting a variant reading that would be totally foreign to the author's vocabulary and style.

b. The immediate context must also be examined. In Col 1:23 some manuscripts have added a number of extra words to describe Paul, including "preacher" and "apostle," rather than leaving him simply as a "servant," which is more appropriate to the context and probably what the author wrote.

c. When one considers harmony with the author's usage elsewhere, and especially harmony with Gospel parallels, the less harmonious reading is generally to be preferred as what the author would have written. Thus Mark 10:7 in some manuscripts introduces the words "and he will be joined to his wife," which are found in Matt 19:5.

d. The possible linguistic backgrounds of the NT must also be considered. Concerning Paul, this almost assuredly means attention to the Greek linguistic context. Concerning the teaching of Jesus, for many textual critics this has often meant a predominant focus upon the Aramaic background of the Gospels and the early chapters of Acts. But the discussion above (see secs. 2.B, 2.C) should make clear that this cannot be assumed; the Greek background must be considered as well. Thus at Acts 2:30 "heart," found in some texts, is thought to represent an Aramaic source, and "belly" is from the LXX. Both are to be rejected for "loin" as what the author probably wrote.

e. One should consider the priority of Mark. The conclusion that Mark is the first Gospel is disputed in some circles and is certainly not as secure as it appeared to be earlier in this century. Nevertheless, the priority of Mark should still be given preference, since it is by far the most plausible explanation of the synoptic problem. Markan priority does not, however, solve all of the textual issues in a simplistic way.

f. The influence of the Christian community upon the formulation and transmission of a passage cannot be minimized. Passages that reflect later church accretions and explanations ought almost certainly to be rejected. For example, as emotionally and spiritually satisfying as the pericope of the woman caught in adultery may be (John 7:53–8:11), it is almost assuredly not original to the author of John's Gospel and should be rejected as part of the original text of the NT. To be rejected as well are the additional endings of Mark's Gospel. It is fairly easy to show how each of the verses of the longer ending finds its antecedent in some other verse in the other Gospels and Acts, revealing that this ending was constructed later, almost certainly to provide what some in the early church considered a more suitable conclusion than the abrupt ending at Mark 16:8 (see ch. 8, above).

E. Conclusion

The text-critical reading finally decided upon should be defensible both externally and internally.[50] One of the best tests of the plausibility of a solution to a textual difficulty is to create some sort of relationship among the variants, such that the original reading is able to account for the development of the other variant readings. If one is able to do this, there is a good chance that the solution arrived at gives at least a plausible explanation of the earliest reading and of the subsequent readings that were derived from it.

4. TEXTUAL TRANSMISSION AND BIBLE TRANSLATIONS

A. Ancient Writing and Its Materials

By the first century A.D., a number of writing materials were in use in the ancient world.[51] These included at least the following: stone, upon which were placed what are called inscriptions (writing on stone); clay and wooden tablets, often used in ancient writing, and fragments called potsherds (ostraca are potsherds containing writing); cured animal skin, called parchment; metal surfaces, such as copper, through etching (e.g., Qumran's *Copper Scroll* [3QTreasure or 3Q15]); and papyrus. By far the most common writing surface was papyrus,[52] made from the papyrus plant, a reedlike plant that grew abundantly in Egypt and later was grown in other regions. The plant was taken and cut into strips, which were laid out flat, with the grain running either horizontally or vertically, and bonded together. Sheets of off-white papyrus were then used for writing, either individually or joined together (an average sheet was 9.75 in. high and 7.4 in. wide). Papyrus was not particularly expensive in the ancient world, and as the abundant finds in the Egyptian rubbish heaps of the nineteenth and early twentieth centuries illustrate, sheets were not often reused for the sake of economy.

Papyrus was a very strong writing material, as its endurance through the centuries has well illustrated. The preferred side for writing is often called the recto, on which one writes with the horizontal grain. The back side is often called the verso, on which one writes with the vertical grain.[53] Papyrus was at first joined together end to end to form scrolls (the join was called a κόλλησις, *kollēsis*), with the verso side on the outside. Later all of the sheets were joined at one end into the codex (even if the sheets were made from joined sheets of papyrus and folded over). Parchment was made by scraping and smoothing the skins of animals down to a lower layer suitable for the reception of ink. The flesh side, as opposed to the hair side, is preferable for writing; but the hair side, being rougher and more absorbent, often preserves the text better. For example, the flesh side of P.Vindob. Greek 2324, a fifth-century lectionary (*l* 1043), is in many places virtually unreadable, but the hair side is still clear. Although at first papyrus was more important as a writing surface for the church, parchment later became far more important than papyrus, though the latter continued to be used. The reasons for the change from papyrus to parchment are not clear; it took place even in Egypt, where papyrus was in abundant supply.[54]

To write upon papyrus and parchment, scribes used various forms of writing nibs and inks. The writing tool of the Greco-Roman world was usually a relatively thick piece of reed with a point sharpened by a knife, but metal pens were occasionally used. Carbon- and metal-based inks were used. The carbon-based ink, from soot, was easier to use and quite enduring. It also had the advantage of being more easily corrected or even rubbed out. In general, carbon-based ink was used on papyri, and metal-based ink on parchment. The metal-based ink has proved destructive to the surfaces on which it was used. Many manuscripts today have only an outline of their previous lettering, since the metal-based ink has eaten its way through the surface. For example, on P.Oxy. 840, a small parchment written in metal-based ink, one must reconstruct many of the letters from their remaining outlines.

At first, the NT texts were probably originally written and also copied onto papyrus scrolls. The scroll, however, had a number of limitations as a writing surface. One is length. Over the years, the size of scrolls increased up to 19.7 feet, but with this increase came a growing unwieldiness. Not only were the scrolls difficult to handle; writing on them was also difficult. Second, since a scroll could only be so long, there was a limit on the amount of material that could be copied onto it. A third difficulty was accessibility. In order to find a passage, the reader had to unroll the scroll, possibly going all the way to the other end. If someone, for example, was using a scroll of Paul's letters and wanted to check a passage in Romans while reading 1 Thessalonians, the scroll had to be wound back to virtually the beginning. In any event, this had to be done at the end of a reading to prepare for the next.

Most scholars are now of the opinion that the Christian church had a significant early influence upon writing and its materials by its active use of the codex.[55] The codex was an early form of what we would today recognize as a book, developed probably in the first century. Instead of joining sheets of papyrus together end to end, with writing on one side only, the codex had sheets of papyrus or parchment folded in half and fastened on one end (this is called a gathering). The advantages of the codex are several. First, there was less limitation upon size, since extra sheets of writing material could be added to a gathering of pages, especially if one realized, before beginning to write, that extra length was needed (early on, however, scribes also realized that separate gatherings of pages could be added at the end of a codex). A second advantage was the increased economy and compactness of writing on both sides of the sheet (this was possible with scrolls also but, for some reason, was virtually never done)—thus doubling the usefulness of the writing material—and of putting individual texts together in one grouping. A third advantage was ease of use and access. A reader did not need to unwind an entire scroll to find a passage but simply turned pages until reaching the proper place. The fourth—and arguably most important—reason the church adopted and even promoted the use of the codex appears to have been the ability thus to imitate the sacred tablet in Judaism.[56] The church used both papyrus and parchment for its codices. In secular literature, the increased use of the codex was slow in coming, but in Christianity the codex became prominent very early on, so that the vast majority of early Christian texts are from codices rather than scrolls.

By the fourth century, the codex form had developed sufficiently so that all of the writings of the OT and NT could be collected into one large codex. Several of these large parchment codices have survived. For example, Codex Sinaiticus is a beautiful example of a parchment codex, with thin sheets of about 15.6 in. by 27.3 in. folded in half, and four columns per page in the NT.[57] It includes most of the OT, plus all of the books that we now include in our NT, plus *Barnabas* and portions of the *Shepherd of Hermas*. Codex Vaticanus also includes much of the OT and most of the NT, including *1 and 2 Clement*. These two codices probably date to the first half of the fourth century. The later Codex Alexandrinus (5th cent.) also contains most of the two Testaments, plus *1* and *2 Clement* and Canticles. There are also some pages of individual manuscripts that have page numbers on them, indicating that they were part of a larger collection. Nevertheless, even in the fourth and fifth centuries it was still apparently quite common for individual writings to circulate without being gathered into a single book of the Bible. Since so many of the extant manuscripts are fragmentary (i.e., only a small portion of a single sheet has been found), it is difficult to know the extent of the text of which the fragment is a part.

The first copies of the NT were written in Greek capital letters, called majuscule or sometimes uncial letters, with usually no space between letters and virtually no punctuation. All of the manuscripts designated as papyri (with a 𝔓 and a number) are written in these capital or majuscule letters, as are the codices with a letter or with a number beginning in zero. The quality of the writing of these manuscripts differs greatly. Some of the early ones are written in very small, tightly packed lines. 𝔓45 (3d cent. A.D.) is such a manuscript, with small thin letters written on a slight angle. Many of these early manuscripts were not written by professional scribes. By the middle to late fourth century, however, the quality of the writing had improved, since the church began to use better-trained scribes to make copies of its sacred texts. These later manuscripts are often quite beautiful, with writing on ruled lines and with a precisely calculated number of letters to a line and number of lines to a page. This kind of regularity is occasionally noted on other ancient manuscripts, and the study of the number of letters or syllables to a line and lines to a page is called stichometry.[58] It can be very helpful in attempting to reconstruct a manuscript, although some recent textual criticism seriously questions its value. If we know the number of characters to a line and lines to a page and there is writing on the back, we can attempt to calculate the size of a given page and hence determine whether a given variant reading may have been in a given manuscript.

Over time, a larger number of punctuation marks, section divisions, and even word separations began to be used in manuscripts. By the eighth to tenth centuries, these are fairly common, although not entirely systematically used. By the ninth and tenth centuries, some scribes began to use spaces between the words and write in lowercase letters. These manuscripts are called minuscules, used until the 1500s, when the printing press was invented. Some of these texts can be considered works of art, since they have been highly decorated with elaborated letters and pictures. These decorated manuscripts are called illuminated manuscripts, and they include not only biblical but other kinds of texts, such as devotional books.

The deciphering of manuscripts is quite difficult. The difficulties with majuscule manuscripts are particularly noteworthy, since they constitute the most important NT documents. These difficulties are caused by a number of factors. First is the poor state of preservation of many texts. Virtually every one of the papyrus biblical fragments was found in the sands of Egypt in the nineteenth or early part of the twentieth centuries. The earliest papyrus text found is P.Ryl. Greek 457 (= 𝔓52), a codex fragment of John's Gospel (18:31–33, 37–38) dated to around A.D. 125.[59] Most were part of texts that had been thrown out, and so preservation was not of importance. They show signs of deterioration, including drying out and damage from such elements as water and sand (nevertheless, they are surprisingly resilient to have lasted so long). A second difficulty is that the writing conventions for continuous capital letters do not make decipherment easy. It requires a trained eye to differentiate the various letters, especially as some of them may be incomplete, and then to divide them into their individual words. Often the ink has come off the papyrus, or the papyrus may be abraded or rubbed out at a particular spot, or it may even have a hole in it. A third difficulty is that the style of handwriting both is particular to a given scribe and changes over the centuries. One must learn the peculiarities of a given scribe—for example, whether that scribe uses any ligatures (characters composed of two connected letters) or writes letters in such a way that they are easy to confuse with others (e.g., A vs. Δ or M vs. N). Greek handwriting also developed over the centuries; this provides one of the means by which manuscripts are often dated. But the dating of manuscripts is not a precise science, with scholars often differing by several centuries in their estimates.[60] It is fair to say, however, that Byzantine writing, especially of the later periods, is significantly different from that of the Roman period. Copyists sometimes give some form of identification in a colophon either at the beginning of the manuscript or at the end of a book. A particularly beautiful example concludes the book of Baruch in Codex Alexandrius.[61] A fourth difficulty in the decipherment of manuscripts is that part of the convention of writing was to use various types of shortened forms of words.[62] In Christian scribal circles, special forms of the names "God" and "Jesus" and those of people, significant places in the Bible, and so forth were frequently employed. These are called *nomina sacra,* or "sacred names," and are often indicated in the manuscript with a line over the two or three letters used in the new form. For example, IHCOYC ('Ιησοῦς) might be written as I̅C̅. Minuscule manuscripts have their own peculiarities, as minuscule handwriting was often used as a form of shorthand with highly connected letters. The later manuscripts, both majuscule and minuscule, are often in better condition than those of the earlier period, but their value for textual criticism is often less, since they are further removed from the earliest forms of the manuscript tradition.

As a result of these difficulties, when scholars read papyri and parchment manuscripts, they use a set of conventions to indicate their readings.[63] One of the best procedures is for the textual critic first to write what is called a diplomatic text. This transcribes the text from the papyrus or parchment as closely as this can be done. Various degrees of certainty of the reading of a particular letter should also be indicated—for example, by use of dots under fairly clear but not absolutely certain letters, and of square brackets around letters that are introduced by the editor. A regularized text should then be produced. This is the Greek text written out with proper word divisions, accentuation, and restorations of incomplete words, and so forth, and still indicating what is certain and what is questionable in the transcribed text. Indicating the certainty of the scholar's readings is important so that other scholars will not later use the transcription and exegete what may only be the reconstruction of the scholar who read the text originally. There are numerous stories of how questionable readings have become part of a textual tradition. For example, the standard English versions of one of the apocryphal gospels, P.Vindob. Greek 2325, the so-called Fayyum fragment, translate a reading that was later abandoned by the first scholar reading it and then changed by later readings.[64]

B. Translations Ancient and Modern[65]

The LXX was one of the great translation projects of the ancient world.[66] From the third century B.C. portions of the OT began to be translated into Greek for the use of Jews in Alexandria, Egypt, who were not able to read their sacred literature in He-

brew. The value of this translation was readily acknowledged, and it was copied and used in Jewish communities throughout the Greco-Roman world (the Diaspora), apparently even in Palestine. In the second century A.D. the Jews began to make other Greek translations of their Scriptures (e.g., Theodotion), but the Christians continued to use the LXX. From almost the first days of Christianity, its sacred literature was translated into other languages. The earliest translations were the Old Latin, the Syriac, especially the Syriac Peshitta, and the Armenian. Work on some of these began in the second century.

For Christians of the west, the Latin version of the Scriptures, compiled by Jerome and called the Vulgate, essentially became the sacred text. The early translations of the Bible into English, such as that by John Wycliffe in 1480, followed the Vulgate. During the Reformation, Erasmus was the first to compile a Greek NT. As mentioned above, he did this on the basis of a limited number of later Byzantine minuscule texts (which constitute the majority of texts), since the most important codices and the papyri had not yet been discovered. His edition published in 1633 became known as the Received Text, or Textus Receptus, since it was the one received as the standard edition. Most of the translations of the Bible into English from that time until the early part of the twentieth century were based upon this so-called Majority Text. The KJV (1611) was based on such manuscripts. The KJV has been greatly venerated, but arguably much of its most memorable phrasing is from the earlier translation of William Tyndale (1534). For example, his translation of Matt 7:7 reads, "Ask and it shall be given you: seek and ye shall find: knock and it shall be opened unto you." Tyndale was the first person to translate the English Bible from the original languages, rather than the Latin.[67] The KJV prevailed until the early part of the last century, when a veritable explosion of English Bibles began to be produced.[68]

What is a translation of the Bible? The question is probably better put, What is the purpose of a given translation? Sometimes a distinction is made between a proper translation and a paraphrase, but this is not very useful. Much of the earlier thinking about translating tried to distinguish between more and less literalistic renderings of the original language, but it has been superseded by the work on translation by the United Bible Societies, especially under the influence of the linguist Eugene Nida.[69] A translation can be defined as a careful rendering of the words, phrases, and larger units of structure (e.g., paragraphs) of the Bible in their original languages into another language, taking into consideration the various nuances of the language, the cultural background, and idioms—all put into meaningful equivalents of another language. A paraphrase is not different in kind but in degree. Since no translation from one language to another can be made exactly word for word and still make sense (try to read the interlinear portions of an interlinear Greek NT), a translator attempts to arrive at the full sense of a unit of thought in one language and to translate it into similar meaningful units of thought in another language. Some translations are better than others in terms of their readability, their faithfulness to the original, and their theological orientations, and hence are suitable for various purposes. What follows is a brief categorization of some of the translations that are currently available on the market.[70]

A number of translations can be placed together as careful and serious renderings that are still fairly conservative in their decisions. These include the Revised Standard Version (RSV), the New Revised Standard Version (NRSV), New International Version (NIV), New English Bible (NEB), the recent Revised English Bible (REB), the Jerusalem Bible (JB), the New American Bible (NAB), and the New Jerusalem Bible (NJB).[71] Each of these, in various ways, provides a translation that can probably be used for study of the NT in both an academic and an ecclesiastical context. In other words, one can use it in private study of the text, often in conjunction with the original Greek, and in the corporate study and reading of Scripture, especially in liturgical contexts.

Several translations make better study aids for those working in the Greek text. These include the American Standard Version (ASV) and the New American Standard Bible (NASB). The first is encumbered by some archaic English, and the second

does not always find the most idiomatic English expression. But especially the second serves as a useful guide to the original Greek, even if it does not always provide a smooth English translation of the Greek.

Several translations are noted as excellent reading Bibles but are perhaps less well recommended for use with the Greek text. These are the Today's English Version (TEV, formerly the Good News Bible) and the Contemporary English Version (CEV). Both of these directly reflect the translational- or functional-equivalence theories of Nida. The first is very important in the history of Bible translation, since it marked a strong departure from traditional literalistic translation and the incorporation of principles of linguistics into Bible translation.[72]

Other translations may be less useful for ecclesiastical purposes than those above, although they may often provide insights in personal study. These include many of the personal translations, such as those by Phillips, Weymouth, Rieu, Lattimore, Berkeley, and Moffatt.[73] Other freer translations that are perhaps less useful include the Amplified Bible (because it loses the literary sense by including, for many of the translated words, numerous synonyms, most of which are not sensitive to the context of the passage); the Cotton Patch Version, reflecting a particular socioeconomic context; and the Living Bible, now recently revised as the New Living Translation.

For study purposes, it is, of course, best if a person utilizes the original languages, along with one or two of the translations recommended in the first two groupings above. But if a person is not able to use the Greek NT, consulting several of these translations, perhaps one that is more Greek-text-oriented and one that is a better English-reading Bible, is to be recommended. In any case, one should make a serious study of the issues of each passage, rather than seek first some translation that agrees with one's prejudice. By utilizing study and translations in a responsible way, the reader can gain insight into passages that require further consideration.

BIBLIOGRAPHY

A. Greek Language and Grammar[74]

BLASS, F., and A. DEBRUNNER. *A Greek Grammar of the New Testament and Other Early Christian Literature.* Trans. R. W. FUNK. Chicago: University of Chicago Press, 1961.

BROOKS, J. A., and C. L. WINBERY. *Syntax of New Testament Greek.* Lanham: University Press of America, 1979.

BURTON, E. D. W. *Syntax of the Moods and Tenses in New Testament Greek.* 3d ed. Chicago: University of Chicago Press, 1900.

CONYBEARE, F. C., and S. G. STOCK. *A Grammar of Septuagint Greek.* Boston: Ginn, 1905.

FANNING, B. M. *Verbal Aspect in New Testament Greek.* OTM. Oxford: Clarendon, 1990.

GOODWIN, W. W. *Greek Grammar.* London: Macmillan, 1879.

_____. *Syntax of the Moods and Tenses of the Greek Verb.* Boston: Ginn, 1889.

JAY, E. G. *New Testament Greek: An Introductory Grammar.* London: SPCK, 1965.*

MACHEN, J. G. *New Testament Greek for Beginners.* Toronto: Macmillan, 1923.*

MCKAY, K. L. *A New Syntax of the Verb in New Testament Greek: An Aspectual Approach.* SBG 5. New York: Lang, 1993.

MANDILARAS, B. G. *The Verb in the Greek Non-literary Papyri.* Athens: Hellenic Ministry of Culture and Sciences, 1973.

MOULE, C. F. D. *An Idiom Book of New Testament Greek.* 2d ed. Cambridge: Cambridge University Press, 1959.

MOULTON, J. H. *A Grammar of New Testament Greek.* 4 vols. Edinburgh: T. & T. Clark, 1908–1976.

MOUNCE, W. D. *Basics of Biblical Greek: Grammar.* Grand Rapids: Zondervan, 1993.*

PORTER, S. E. *Idioms of the Greek New Testament.* Biblical Languages: Greek 2. 2d ed. Sheffield: JSOT Press, 1994.

_____. *Studies in the Greek New Testament: Theory and Practice.* SBG 6. New York: Lang, 1996.

_____. *Verbal Aspect in the Greek of the New Testament, with Reference to Tense and Mood.* SBG 1. New York: Lang, 1989.

_____, ed. *The Language of the New Testament: Classic Essays.* JSNTSup 60. Sheffield: JSOT Press, 1991.

PORTER, S. E., and D. A. CARSON, eds. *Biblical Greek Language and Linguistics: Open Questions in Current Research.* JSNTSup 72. Sheffield: JSOT Press, 1993.

_____. *Discourse Analysis and Other Topics in Biblical Greek.* JSNTSup 113. Sheffield: JSOT Press, 1995.

ROBERTSON, A. T. *A Grammar of the Greek New Testament in the Light of Historical Research.* 4th ed. Nashville: Broadman, 1934.

SMYTH, H. W. *Greek Grammar.* Rev. G. M. MESSING. Cambridge: Harvard University Press, 1956.

SWETNAM, J. *An Introduction to the Study of New Testament Greek.* 2 vols. Rome: Pontifical Biblical Institute Press, 1992.*

THACKERAY, H. ST. J. *A Grammar of the Old Testament in Greek according to the Septuagint.* Cambridge: Cambridge University Press, 1909.

THRALL, M. E. *Greek Particles in the New Testament: Linguistic and Exegetical Studies.* NTTS 3. Leiden: Brill, 1962.

WALLACE, D. B. *Greek Grammar beyond the Basics.* Grand Rapids: Zondervan, 1996.

WENHAM, J. W. *The Elements of New Testament Greek.* Cambridge: Cambridge University Press, 1965.*

ZERWICK, M. *Biblical Greek Illustrated by Examples.* Trans. J. Smith. Rome: Pontifical Biblical Institute, 1963.

B. Lexicography

ABBOTT-SMITH, G. *A Manual Greek Lexicon of the New Testament.* 3d ed. Edinburgh: T. & T. Clark, 1937.

BAUER, W. *A Greek–English Lexicon of the New Testament and Other Early Christian Literature.* Trans. W. F. ARNDT, F. W. GINGRICH, and F. W. DANKER. Chicago: University of Chicago Press, 1979.

DEISSMANN, A. *Bible Studies.* Trans. A. GRIEVE. 1901. Repr., Peabody, Mass.: Hendrickson, 1988.

HORSLEY, G. H. R., and S. LLEWELYN, eds. *New Documents Illustrating Early Christianity.* 8 vols. to date. North Ryde, N.S.W., Australia: Ancient History Documentary Research Centre, Macquarie University, 1981–.

LIDDELL, H. G., and R. SCOTT. *A Greek–English Lexicon.* 10th ed. Oxford: Clarendon, 1996.

LOUW, J. P., and E. A. NIDA, eds. *Greek–English Lexicon of the New Testament Based on Semantic Domains.* 2 vols. New York: United Bible Societies, 1988.

MOULTON, J. H., and G. MILLIGAN. *The Vocabulary of the Greek Testament Illustrated from the Papyri and Other Non-literary Sources.* London: Hodder & Stoughton, 1914–1929. Repr. Peabody, Mass.: Hendrickson, 1997.

NIDA, E. A., and J. P. LOUW. *Lexical Semantics of the Greek New Testament.* SBLRBS 25. Atlanta: Scholars Press, 1992.

SILVA, M. *Biblical Words and their Meaning: An Introduction to Lexical Semantics.* Rev. ed. Grand Rapids: Zondervan, 1994.

THAYER, J. H. *A Greek–English Lexicon of the New Testament, Being Grimm's Wilke's Clavis Novi Testamenti.* New York: American Book Company, 1886.

C. Textual Criticism

ALAND, K., and B. ALAND. *The Text of the New Testament: An Introduction to the Critical Editions and to the Theory and Practice of Modern Textual Criticism.* Trans. E. F. RHODES. 2d ed. Grand Rapids: Eerdmans, 1989.

BRUCE, F. F. *The New Testament Documents: Are They Reliable?* 5th ed. Downers Grove, Ill.: InterVarsity, 1960.

CLARKE, K. D. *Textual Optimism: A Critique of the United Bible Societies' Greek New Testament.* JSNTSup 138. Sheffield: Sheffield Academic Press, 1996.

COMFORT, P. W. *The Quest for the Original Text of the New Testament.* Grand Rapids: Baker, 1992.

EHRMAN, B. D., and M. W. HOLMES, eds. *The Text of the New Testament in Contemporary Research: Essays on the Status Quaestionis.* SD 46. Grand Rapids: Eerdmans, 1995.

ELLIOTT, K., and I. MOIR. *Manuscripts and the Text of the New Testament: An Introduction for English Readers.* Edinburgh: T. & T. Clark, 1995.

EWERT, D. *From Ancient Tablets to Modern Translations: A General Introduction to the Bible.* Grand Rapids: Zondervan, 1983.

FINEGAN, J. *Encountering New Testament Manuscripts: A Working Introduction to Textual Criticism.* Grand Rapids: Eerdmans, 1974.

GREENLEE, J. H. *Introduction to New Testament Textual Criticism.* Rev. ed. Peabody, Mass.: Hendrickson, 1995.

GREGORY, C. R. *Canon and Text of the New Testament.* Edinburgh: T. & T. Clark, 1907.

KENYON, F. G. *Handbook to the Textual Criticism of the New Testament.* 2d ed. London: Macmillan, 1926.

———. *The Text of the Greek Bible.* 3d ed. Rev. A. W. Adams. London: Duckworth, 1975.

LAKE, K. *The Text of the New Testament.* Rev. S. New. 7th ed. London: Rivingtons, 1953.

METZGER, B. M. *The Text of the New Testament: Its Transmission, Corruption, and Restoration.* 3d ed. Oxford: Clarendon, 1992.

———. *A Textual Commentary on the Greek New Testament.* Rev. ed. London: United Bible Societies, 1994.

NESTLE, E. *Introduction to the Textual Criticism of the New Testament.* Trans. W. EDIE and A. MENZIES. London: Williams & Norgate, 1901.

MILLIGAN, G. *The New Testament and Its Transmission.* London: Hodder & Stoughton, 1932.

PORTER, S. E., and C. A. EVANS, eds. *New Testament Text and Language: A Sheffield Reader.* Bib Sem Sheffield: Sheffield Academic Press, 1997.

SOUTER, A. *The Text and Canon of the New Testament.* Rev. and ed. C. S. C. WILLIAMS. London: Duckworth, 1954.

VAGANAY, L. *An Introduction to New Testament Textual Criticism.* Trans. J. HEIMERDINGER. Cambridge: Cambridge University Press, 1991.

WESTCOTT, B. F., and F. J. A. HORT. *The New Testament in the Original Greek.* 2 vols. 2d ed. 1896. Repr. of vol. 2. Peabody, Mass.: Hendrickson, 1988.

1. A fuller form of much of the material in this section can be found in S. E. Porter, "The Greek Language of the New Testament," in *Handbook to Exegesis of the New Testament* (ed. S. E. Porter; NTTS 25; Leiden: Brill, 1997), 99–112.

2. A. T. Robertson, *A Grammar of the Greek New Testament in the Light of Historical Research* (3d ed.; Nashville: Broadman, 1934), xix.

3. Ibid., xix.

4. For a history and discussion of Greek, including a description of its various grammatical features, see L. R. Palmer, *The Greek Language* (London: Duckworth, 1980), esp. 3–198; G. Horrocks, *Greek: A History of the Language and Its Speakers* (London: Longman, 1997), esp. 32–127. See also P. W. Costas, *An Outline of the History of the Greek Language, with Particular Emphasis on the Koine and the Subsequent Periods* (Chicago: Ukranian Society of Sciences of America, 1936; repr., Chicago: Ares, 1979); R. Browning, *Medieval and Modern Greek* (2d ed.; Cambridge: Cambridge University Press, 1983), esp. 19–52.

5. See J. Chadwick, *Linear B and Related Scripts* (London: British Museum Publications, 1987); and, more technical, *The Decipherment of Linear B* (2d ed.; Cambridge: Cambridge University Press, 1967). For an excellent account of this and the subsequent period in Greek-language history, see L. R. Palmer, *Mycenaeans and Minoans: Aegean Prehistory in the Light of the Linear B Tablets* (London: Faber & Faber, 1961).

6. See W. V. Harris, *Ancient Literacy* (Cambridge: Harvard University Press, 1989), esp. 141, who discusses the levels of literacy throughout the Greek and Roman worlds.

7. See S.-T. Teodorsson, "Phonological Variation in Classical Attic and the Development of Koine," *Glotta* 57 (1979): 61–75, esp. 68–71. See B. F. Atkinson, *The Greek Language* (2d ed.; London: Faber & Faber, 1933), 264–306, with sample texts for comparison.

8. Palmer, *Greek Language*, 189–93.

9. See R. Lane Fox, *Alexander the Great* (London: Allen, 1989).

10. See K. J. Dover et al., *Ancient Greek Literature* (Oxford: Oxford University Press, 1980), 134–76, esp. 134–36.

11. Palmer, *Greek Language*, 175, 176.

12. See, e.g., N. Lewis, *The Documents from the Bar Kokhba Period in the Cave of Letters: Greek Papyri* (Jerusalem: Israel Exploration Society, 1989).

13. See S. E. Porter, ed., *The Language of the New Testament: Classic Essays* (JSNTSup 60; Sheffield: JSOT Press, 1991), for further bibliography (pp. 11–38) and for selections of major texts from the authors in the following discussion.

14. See H. Cremer, *Biblico-theological Lexicon of New Testament Greek* (4th ed.; Edinburgh: T. & T. Clark, 1895).

15. E.g., A. Deissmann, *Bible Studies* (trans. A. Grieve; 1901; repr., Peabody, Mass.: Hendrickson, 1988) esp. 61–267; idem, *Light from the Ancient East* (trans. L. R. N. Strachan; 4th ed.; 1927; repr., Peabody, Mass: Hendrickson, 1995). This tradition is being perpetuated through the work of G. H. R. Horsley and S. Llewelyn, eds., *New Documents Illustrating Early Christianity* (8 vols. to date; North Ryde, N.S.W., Australia: Ancient History Documentary Research Centre, Macquarie University, 1981–).

16. See J. H. Moulton, *Prolegomena*, vol. 1 of *A Grammar of New Testament Greek* (4 vols.; Edinburgh: T. & T. Clark, 1908). A handy conspectus of Moulton's views is contained in his "NT Greek in the Light of Mod-

ern Discovery," in *Essays on Some Biblical Questions of the Day: By Members of the University of Cambridge* (ed. H. B. Swete; London: Macmillan, 1909), 461–505.

17. See S. E. Porter, *Verbal Aspect in the Greek of the New Testament, with Reference to Tense and Mood* (SBG 1; New York: Lang, 1989), 134–36.

18. C. C. Torrey, *Our Translated Gospels: Some of the Evidence* (London: Hodder & Stoughton, 1936); *The Composition and Date of Acts* (HTS 1; Cambridge: Harvard University Press, 1916); *The Apocalypse of John* (New Haven: Yale University Press, 1958).

19. The best representative is perhaps M. Black, *An Aramaic Approach to the Gospels and Acts* (3d ed.; Oxford: Clarendon, 1967; repr., Peabody, Mass.: Hendrickson, 1998); see also "The Recovery of the Language of Jesus," *NTS* 3 (1956–57): 305–13; "The Semitic Element in the New Testament," *ExpT* 77 (1965–1966): 20–23.

20. See S. E. Porter, "Jesus and the Use of Greek in Galilee," in *Studying the Historical Jesus: Evaluations of the State of Current Research* (NTTS 19; Leiden: Brill, 1994), 134–47, for a summary and assessment of the evidence.

pages 575–579

21. See, e.g., H. Gehman, "The Hebraic Character of Septuagint Greek," *VT* 1 (1951): 81–90; N. Turner, "The Language of the New Testament," in *Peake's Commentary on the Bible* (ed. M. Black and H. H. Rowley; London: Nelson, 1962), 659–62; N. Turner, *Syntax*, vol. 3 of *A Grammar of New Testament Greek*, by J. H. Moulton (4 vols.; Edinburgh: T. & T. Clark, 1963), esp. 1–9; idem, *Grammatical Insights into the New Testament* (Edinburgh: T. & T. Clark, 1965), 174–88.

22. M. Silva, "Bilingualism and the Character of New Testament Greek," *Bib* 61 (1980): 198–219. See also G. H. R. Horsley, "Divergent Views on the Nature of the Greek of the Bible," *Bib* 65 (1984): 393–403; C. J. Hemer, "Reflections on the Nature of New Testament Greek Vocabulary," *TynB* 38 (1987): 65–92; and P. van der Horst, *Ancient Jewish Epitaphs: An Introductory Survey of a Millennium of Jewish Funerary Epigraphy (300 BCE–700 CE)* (Kampen, Netherlands: Kok Pharos, 1991), 24–32.

23. Still valuable on Jesus' use of Aramaic is G. Dalman, *Jesus–Jeshua: Studies in the Gospels* (trans. P. P. Levertoff; London: SPCK, 1929), esp. 1–37. See also J. A. Fitzmyer, "The Languages of Palestine in the First Century A.D.," in *Language of the New Testament* (ed. S. E. Porter), 126–62 (a corrected version of an article that first appeared in *CBQ* 32 [1970]: 501–31). On Hebrew and Jesus, see H. Birkeland, *The Language of Jesus* (Oslo: Dybwad, 1954).

24. Black, *Aramaic Approach*, 274. On translation from Aramaic, see L. D. Hurst, "The Neglected Role of Semantics in the Search for the Aramaic Words of Jesus," *JSNT* 28 (1986): 63–80.

25. See S. E. Porter, "Did Jesus Ever Teach in Greek?" *TynB* 44 (2, 1993): 223–35; cf. R. A. Horsley, *Archaeology, History, and Society in Galilee: The Social Context of Jesus and the Rabbis* (Valley Forge, Penn.: Trinity Press International, 1996), esp. 154–71.

26. See van der Horst, *Ancient Jewish Epitaphs*, 23–24.

27. For a brief history of the discussion, see J. N. Birdsall, "The Recent History of New Testament Textual Criticism (from Westcott and Hort, 1881, to the Present)," *ANRW* 2.26.1 (1992): 100–177.

28. See D. B. Wallace, "The Majority Text Theory: History, Methods, and Critique," in *The Text of the New Testament in Contemporary Research: Essays on the Status Quaestionis* (ed. B. D. Ehrman and M. W. Holmes; SD 46; Grand Rapids: Eerdmans, 1995), 297–320; cf. D. A. Carson, *The*

King James Version Debate: A Plea for Realism (Grand Rapids: Baker, 1979).

29. See W. Tyndale, *Tyndale's New Testament* (ed. D. Daniell; New Haven: Yale University Press, 1989).

30. See F. F. Bruce, *The New Testament Documents: Are They Reliable?* (5th ed.; Downers Grove, Ill.: InterVarsity, 1960), esp. 16–17.

31. See G. D. Kilpatrick, *The Principles and Practice of New Testament Textual Criticism: Collected Essays of G. D. Kilpatrick* (ed. J. K. Elliott; BETL 96; Leuven: Leuven University Press/Peeters, 1990); J. K. Elliott, *Essays and Studies in New Testament Textual Criticism* (Estudios de filología neotestamentaria 3; Córdoba: El Almendro, 1992); idem, "Thoroughgoing Eclecticism in New Testament Textual Criticism," in *Text of the New Testament in Contemporary Research* (ed. Ehrman and Holmes), 321–35.

32. This is the method associated with most of the well-known figures in textual criticism, including Vaganay, Colwell, Metzger, Epp, Fee, Birdsall, and the Alands. See the summary by M. W. Holmes, "Reasoned Eclecticism in New Testament Textual Criticism," in *Text of the New Testament in Contemporary Research* (ed. Ehrman and Holmes), 336–60.

33. See B. F. Westcott and F. J. A. Hort, *The New Testament in the Original Greek* (2 vols.; 2d ed.; 1896; vol. 2 repr., Peabody, Mass.: Hendrickson, 1988).

34. See E. J. Epp and G. D. Fee, *Studies in the Theory and Method of New Testament Textual Criticism* (SD 45; Grand Rapids: Eerdmans, 1993), for a discussion of these issues, among others. See also E. J. Epp, "The Papyrus Manuscripts of the New Testament," 3–21; D. C. Parker, "The Majuscule Manuscripts of the New Testament," 22–42; B. Aland and K. Wachtel, "The Greek Minuscule Manuscripts of the New Testament," 43–60, all in *Text of the New Testament in Contemporary Research* (ed. Ehrman and Holmes).

35. The designation ("the received text") is based upon a statement in the second edition of the text (1533) that referred to it as the text that we have received. On Erasmus's editions, see B. M. Metzger, *The Text of the New Testament: Its Transmission, Corruption, and Restoration* (3d ed.; Oxford: Clarendon, 1992), 98–103.

36. See C. Tischendorf, *Codex Sinaiticus: The Ancient Biblical Manuscript Now in the British Museum* (London: Lutterworth, n.d.), esp. 15–32; and *The Codex Sinaiticus and the Codex Alexandrinus* (London: British Museum, 1963).

37. K. Aland et al., eds., *The Greek New Testament* (3d corr. ed.; New York: United Bible Societies, 1983); B. Aland et al., eds., *The Greek New Testament* (4th ed.; Stuttgart: Deutsche Bibelgesellschaft, 1993); E. Nestle and K. Aland, eds., *Novum Testamentum Graece* (27th ed.; Stuttgart: Deutsche Bibelgesellschaft, 1993).

38. See K. D. Clarke, *Textual Optimism: A Critique of the United Bible Societies' Greek New Testament* (JSNTSup 138; Sheffield: Sheffield Academic Press, 1997), for a complete study of the UBS rating system. He effectively points out the unfounded nature of most of these elevated ratings.

39. See A. Souter, ed., *Novum Testamentum Graece* (2d ed.; OCT; Oxford: Clarendon, 1947); G. D. Kilpatrick, ed., Η ΚΑΙΝΗ ΔΙΑΘΗΚΗ (2d ed.; London: British and Foreign Bible Society, 1958).

40. Many of the standard volumes on textual criticism have descriptive lists of the manuscripts. The number of NT manuscripts is, however, constantly increasing. See Metzger, *Text of the New Testament*, 36–66,

pages 579–581

247–56; F. G. Kenyon, *The Text of the Greek Bible* (rev. A. W. Adams; 3d ed.; London: Duckworth, 1975), 63–111; K. and B. Aland, *The Text of the New Testament: An Introduction to the Critical Editions and to the Theory and Practice of Modern Textual Criticism* (trans. E. F. Rhodes; 2d ed.; Grand Rapids: Eerdmans, 1989), 72–184. The following discussion relies upon Metzger. See also J. K. Elliott, *A Bibliography of Greek New Testament Manuscripts* (SNTSMS 62; Cambridge: Cambridge University Press, 1989).

41. This is Codex Alexandrinus, named after its earliest known location, Alexandria, before being taken to Constantinople.

42. E.g., E. J. Epp, *The Theological Tendency of Codex Bezae Cantabrigiensis in Acts* (SNTSMS 3; Cambridge: Cambridge University Press, 1966). See also J. M. Wilson, *The Acts of the Apostles: Translated from the Codex Bezae with an Introduction on Its Lucan Origin and Importance* (London: SPCK, 1924); A. C. Clark, *The Acts of the Apostles* (Oxford: Clarendon, 1933); J. H. Ropes, "The Text of Acts," in *The Acts of the Apostles*, part 1 of *The Beginnings of Christianity* (ed. F. J. Foakes-Jackson and K. Lake; 5 vols.; London: Macmillan, 1920–1933; repr., Grand Rapids: Baker, 1979), vol. 4; and D. C. Parker, *Codex Bezae: An Early Christian Manuscript and Its Text* (Cambridge: Cambridge University Press, 1992).

43. Metzger, *Text of the New Testament*, 131.

44. See G. D. Fee, "The Use of the Greek Fathers for New Testament Textual Criticism," 191–207, J. L. North, "The Use of the Latin Fathers for New Testament Textual Criticism," 208–213, and S. P. Brock, "The Use of the Syriac Fathers for New Testament Textual Criticism," 224–36, all in *Text of the New Testament in Contemporary Research* (ed. Ehrman and Holmes).

45. E. C. Colwell, *The Study of the Bible* (rev. ed.; Chicago: University of Chicago Press, 1964), 44-45.

46. See B. M. Metzger, *The Early Versions of the New Testament: Their Origin, Transmission, and Limitations* (Oxford: Clarendon, 1977). All of these versions and more are discussed in a number of different essays in Ehrman and Holmes, eds., *Text of the New Testament in Contemporary Research*, 77–187.

47. See C. D. Osburn, "The Greek Lectionaries of the New Testament," in *Text of the New Testament in Contemporary Research* (ed. Ehrman and Holmes), 61–74.

48. See Metzger, *Text of the New Testament*, 186–206, from whom the following examples are often taken, among other volumes with similar information. On the transmission of extrabiblical texts, see L. D. Reynolds and N. G. Wilson, *Scribes and Scholars: A Guide to the Transmission of Greek and Latin Literature* (2d ed.; Oxford: Clarendon, 1974).

49. On the difference that dictation makes, see T. C. Skeat, "The Use of Dictation in Ancient Book-Production," in *Proceedings of the British Academy* 42 (London: Oxford University Press, 1956).

50. See J. Finegan, *Encountering New Testament Manuscripts: A Working Introduction to Textual Criticism* (Grand Rapids: Eerdmans, 1974).

51. An excellent treatment of this issue is T. C. Skeat, "Early Christian Book-Production: Papyri and Manuscripts," in *The West from the Fathers to the Reformation*, vol. 2 of *The Cambridge History of the Bible* (ed. G. W. H. Lampe; 3 vols.; Cambridge: Cambridge University Press, 1969), 54–79, which is drawn upon below.

52. Technical confusion is sometimes caused by the fact that "papyrus" is often used as the generic term for any kind of writing on perishable surfaces, such as tablets, potsherds, parchment, and papyrus.

pages 582–587

pages 587–590

For a recent discussion of the general field of papyrological studies and, in particular, how they can be used in historical reconstruction, see R. Bagnall, *Reading Papyri, Writing Ancient History* (London: Routledge, 1995). On papyrus, see M. L. Bierbreier, ed., *Papyrus: Structure and Usage* (British Museum Occasional Papers 60; London: British Museum, 1986), with bibliography.

53. These terms are problematic. See E. G. Turner, *The Terms Recto and Verso: The Anatomy of the Papyrus Roll* (Papyrologica bruxellensia 16; Brussells: Foundation Égyptologique Reine Élisabeth, 1978).

54. Useful descriptions of the varieties of manuscripts from the ancient world, with photographs, are found in E. G. Turner, *Greek Manuscripts of the Ancient World* (rev. P. J. Parsons; 2d ed.; Institute of Classical Studies Bulletin Supplement 46; London: Institute of Classical Studies, 1987).

55. On the codex, see the very important works of C. H. Roberts and T. C. Skeat, *The Birth of the Codex* (London: British Academy, 1983); and E. G. Turner, *The Typology of the Early Codex* (n.p.: University of Pennsylvania Press, 1977).

56. See Roberts and Skeat, *Birth of the Codex*, 57–61.

57. See T. S. Pattie, *Manuscripts of the Bible* (London: British Library, 1979), plate 11, for a photograph of the altered ending of John's Gospel, where a scribe appears to have added 21:25 to the book, which originally ended with 21:24.

58. The classic treatment of stichometry is J. R. Harris, *Stichometry* (London: Cambridge University Press, 1893).

59. See C. H. Roberts, *An Unpublished Fragment of the Fourth Gospel* (Manchester, England: Manchester University Press, 1935).

60. See C. P. Thiede, "Papyrus Magdalen Greek 17 (Gregory–Aland $\mathfrak{P}^{64}$): A Reappraisal," *TynB* 46 (1, 1995): 29–42, who raises these issues in reassessing the date of P.Magd. Greek 17.

61. See Pattie, *Manuscripts of the Bible*, plate 7.

62. See K. McNamee, *Abbreviations in Greek Literary Papyri and Ostraca* (BASPSup 3; Atlanta: Scholars Press, 1981).

63. An excellent guide is E. G. Turner, *Greek Papyri: An Introduction* (Oxford: Clarendon, 1968), esp. 54–73; the equivalent for the study of inscriptions is A. G. Woodhead, *The Study of Inscriptions* (2d ed.; Cambridge: Cambridge University Press, 1981), esp. 67–76. See also E. Maunde Thompson, *An Introduction to Greek and Latin Palaeography* (Oxford: Clarendon, 1912); and F. G. Kenyon, *The Palaeography of Greek Papyri* (Oxford: Clarendon, 1899).

64. See S. E. Porter, "The Greek Apocryphal Gospel Papyri: The Need for a Critical Edition," in *Akten des 21. Internationalen Papyrologenkongresses* (Archiv für Papyrusforschung Beiheft 43.2; Stuttgart: Teubner, 1997), 796–97.

65. See D. Ewert, *From Ancient Tablets to Modern Translations: A General Introduction to the Bible* (Grand Rapids: Zondervan, 1983), 85ff., for an excellent assessment of various translations, both ancient and modern.

66. See S. Jellicoe, *The Septuagint and Modern Study* (Oxford: Clarendon, 1968); the older treatment by H. B. Swete, *An Introduction to the Old Testament in Greek* (Cambridge: Cambridge University Press, 1902); and the recent treatment by M. Müller, *The First Bible of the Church: A Plea for the Septuagint* (JSOTSup 206; Sheffield: Sheffield Academic Press, 1996).

67. On the quality of Tyndale's translation, see D. Daniell, "Translating the Bible," in *The Nature of Religious Language: A Colloquium* (ed. S. E.

Porter; RILP 1; Sheffield: Sheffield Academic Press, 1996), 68–87. For a history of the English Bible before the modern period, see W. F. Moulton, *The History of the English Bible* (London: Kelly, n.d.), with plates of early translations.

68. See Ewert, *From Ancient Tablets*, 250–51, for a partial list of translations, and passim for discussion of the most important ones.

69. See, e.g., E. A. Nida, *Toward a Science of Translating with Special Reference to Principles and Procedures Involved in Bible Translation* (Leiden: Brill, 1964); and J. De Waard and E. A. Nida, *From One Language to Another: Functional Equivalence in Bible Translating* (Nashville: Nelson, 1986).

70. See B. Chilton, *Beginning New Testament Study* (London: SPCK, 1985), 95–119, for a discussion of various translations in terms of NT study.

71. On the process for a recent translation, see K. L. Barker, ed., *The NIV: The Making of a Contemporary Translation* (Grand Rapids: Zondervan, 1986).

72. See E. A. Nida, *Good News for Everyone: How to Use the Good News Bible (Today's English Version)* (Waco, Tex.: Word, 1977).

73. See E. H. Robertson, *The New Translations of the Bible* (London: SCM, 1961), 39–137.

74. Beginning-language texts are marked with an asterisk.

THE ORIGINS OF THE CHRISTIAN BIBLE

1. INTRODUCTION: THE NOTIONS OF SCRIPTURE AND CANON

The sacred literature of the early Christian church included, but was not limited to, what we now call the Old Testament (or "First Testament").[1] Eventually a number of Christian writings also began to take their place alongside these Scriptures of the early church and were used in worship, teaching, the church's apologetic, and its mission. Like the Scriptures of the First Testament, those of the New Testament ("Second Testament") were also incorporated into the life of the churches and offered identity and direction to them. What processes or circumstances led the churches to accept this literature as sacred Scripture? The question is significantly more complicated than some might suppose, in part because neither the processes nor the criteria employed to identify its sacred literature are described in detail anywhere in the early church fathers.

The processes by which the various books of the Bible came to be recognized as sacred Scripture and placed alongside other sacred books in a canon of Scripture have long been of special interest to the church.[2] The attention given to this subject in the last hundred years, however, is out of proportion to the attention it received before the end of the nineteenth century. There is much we do not

know about this subject, and it requires far more study than has been done to this point.

For both Judaism and Christianity the final authority for faith is, of course, God, but especially in the later stages of OT Judaism the belief arose that the revelation and will of God were disclosed not only in mighty acts through which Yahweh invades history, such as the exodus, but eventually also in written materials. In the Pentateuch, for example, the writing down of something was an important mark of revelation (Exod 24:12; 31:8; 32:15, 32; 34:1; Deut 4:13; 8:10; etc.). Just as Moses wrote down the commandments of the Lord in Exod 24:4 and 34:27, so also did Joshua in Josh 24:26 and Samuel in 1 Sam 10:25. In the book of Deuteronomy, which was probably written in its present form toward the end of the OT era, the king is called upon to write down for himself a copy of the law of God for reading all the days of his life to remind him of the statutes of God and to be humble in his dealings with his people (Deut 17:18–20). The people also are called upon to write the words of God on their doorposts (6:9; 11:20). By way of contrast, the Gospels do not indicate that Jesus wrote any books or letters; nor did he command others to write anything down.[3] Eventually, however, many Christian writings were recognized for their value in preaching and teaching in the ministry of the church, and subsequently their sacred status was also acknowledged in the Christian community. The literature that was recognized from both the OT and the NT was broad and varied, but it was eventually gathered into collections of sacred Scripture, and the limits of that collection were fixed. This is what became the Christian Bible.

Scripture is essentially a written revelation of the word and will of God communicated to his people. When a particular writing was believed by a religious body to have its origins in God and that community recognized its authority for the community, then the writing was elevated to the status of Scripture. This description, however, is only a part of an overall understanding of Scripture for the early church. Unlike in Judaism, the early church understood Scripture to be essentially eschatological; that is, there was the belief that the Scriptures had their primary fulfillment in Jesus (e.g., Matt 2:5, 17, 23; 3:3; 4:14; Mark 14:49; 15:28; Luke 4:21; Acts 1:16; John 17:12; 19:24, 28). Paul adds that this fulfillment is also found in the Christian community (see Rom 4:23; 15:4; 16:26; 1 Cor 9:10; 10:11), but he still sees Jesus the Christ as the norm for understanding and using the Scriptures (2 Cor 3:12–16). The church held that the OT writings were of unimpeachable authority (John 10:35; Matt 5:18) and that they had a christological fulfillment because they bear witness to Christ. Their authority is acknowledged insofar as they point to God's activity in Jesus Christ. There is no question that the OT (the limits of which were not yet fully defined in the time of Jesus) was authoritative in the early Christian churches (Matt 21:42; 22:29; 26:56; Luke 24:32, 44; John 5:39; 1 Cor 15:3ff.; etc.).

Distinguishing the notion of scripture from canon is not always easy to do. In some sense, they overlap in meaning because a biblical canon is also a normative guide for a religious community. Both terms are at this point interchangeable, but they are also distinguishable. While Scripture has to do with the divine status of a written document, a scriptural canon is a fixed collection of sacred writings that defines the faith and identity of a particular religious community. In this sense, all Scripture is canon, but a biblical canon is a fixed collection of Scriptures that compose the authoritative witness for a religious body.

The Greek κανών (*kanōn*) is derived from κάνη (*kanē*), a loan word from the Semitic *kaneh*, which means "measuring rod" or "measuring stick." Among the Greeks, "canon" came to mean that which is a standard or norm by which all things are judged or evaluated, whether the perfect form to follow in architecture or the infallible criterion by which things are to be measured. The term "canon" was used with a similar meaning as the authoritative guide in the fields of sculpturing, architecture, music, grammar, art, and even philosophy, as the criterion or canon by which one discovers what is true and false.[4] This is not unlike the way the biblical Scriptures have been understood and employed in the Jewish and Christian communities of faith.

James Sanders adds two other essential characteristics of canon, that is, adaptability and survivability. He has shown that the Jews were able to adapt their authoritative Scriptures to new and changing circumstances, and the very adaptability of these Scriptures allowed them to continue as authoritative texts within the Jewish community.[5] The same can be said for the Christian scriptural canon. Canons are by nature adaptable to the changing life of the believing community, and this explains how the biblical canon continues to function as such in churches. Literature that no longer speaks to the changing needs of a community of faith ceases being canon. In the case of both the Hebrew (OT) canon for the Jews and the NT canon for the Christians, in time certain writings that earlier had been considered sacred for a variety of reasons ceased functioning that way for the believing communities, and they simply dropped out of use.

2. THE PROBLEM OF DEFINITION: CANON 1 AND CANON 2

A large part of the difficulty in canonical studies concerns definitions. What is a biblical canon? Gerald Sheppard has shown two ways of understanding the notion of canon in the ancient world.[6] The first of these is what he calls "canon 1": something functions in an authoritative manner in a community, that is, as rules, regulations, or guides. Canon 1 is present wherever there is a respect for some authority within a community. It is also a flexible or fluid authority that is not yet fixed. The other understanding of canon, what he calls "canon 2," comes when these canon 1 authorities become more fixed in a given community. A canon 2 authority is one that becomes so well established in a given community that very little doubt exists about the authority of the text thereafter. There were many canon 1 texts in antiquity. Undoubtedly, for some in Israel and for some of the early Christians, this included the acceptance of apocryphal and pseudepigraphal writings as sacred authorities. In the case of the OT, only probably the Law and the Prophets fall under the category of canon 2 before the time of Christ. In the case of the NT, only a few writings were generally accepted in a canon 2 fashion before the end of the second century A.D.

When the Greek Old Testament (LXX) was produced (ca. 250–225 B.C.), only the Law was translated into Greek; the Prophets (circulating in a collection ca. 200–180 B.C.) and Writings (circulating in a looser form ca. 130 B.C. or later) were added only later. It is difficult to know the precise contents of the LXX in the first century B.C. or A.D., since no complete copies from that time survive, but that the LXX had expanded to include the Prophets and Writings is virtually certain. The NT writers use the LXX in more than 80 percent of their references to the OT, and these citations come from each of the three categories of the Hebrew Scriptures—the Law, Prophets, and Writings. The authority given to the LXX in antiquity is obvious from the sensational description of its translation in the legendary *Letter of Aristeas* (ca. 190 B.C.–A.D. 35).[7] For the author of this letter, the law of Moses was unquestionably accepted as canon 2. If the Prophets and Writings had already obtained that status when the LXX was started, it is puzzling that they were not also included in the initial translation.

3. THE OLD TESTAMENT CANON

Although a discussion of the formation of the OT biblical canon is normally reserved for OT introductions and separate works on the OT, we have included it here because its literature was the first primary sacred literature of the early Christian church. The designation "Old Testament" is a Christian term that appeared at the end of the second century in Irenaeus and Tertullian to distinguish the Christian writings from those sacred writings preceding them. This literature significantly influenced the writers of the Christian literature (of which the NT is the most important part)

and all subsequent generations of Christians. For example, Clement of Rome uses numerous references to the OT to support his teachings about Christian conduct in his letter to the Corinthians (*1 Clem.* ca. A.D. 90–95). There is scarcely a page of the NT that does not cite or use imagery from the OT. This brief section on the formation of the OT and its acceptance within the emerging Christian community necessarily involves some inquiry into the formation of the Hebrew Scriptures.

Until the time of the Reformation, the church generally had a much larger collection of OT Scriptures than we find now in Protestant Bibles. The process of recognizing the authority of the OT began prior to the NT era, but the finalization of that process (canon 2) was not settled, either for rabbinic Judaism or for the church, until probably well into the fourth or fifth centuries.

A. The Scriptures of Judaism and Early Christianity

There are numerous places in the OT where a prophet who spoke a word of admonition to ancient Israel could have strengthened his case considerably by citing a text from the Law. Amos, for instance, could have had a stronger argument for his reproof of the house of Israel had he enlisted texts from the Law to support his accusations against Israel (see Amos 2:6–16; 5:1–6:14; and the five visions in 7:1–9:15), but he did not. Similarly, Hosea might have intensified his argument against Israel had he cited sacred texts from the Decalogue about the Israelites' having no other gods before the Lord (Exod 20:4–6), but he did not. Nathan the prophet also could have been more specific about David's murder of Uriah and his adultery with Bathsheba violating specific commandments of the Law had he quoted "You shall not murder" or "You shall not commit adultery" from the Decalogue (Exod 20:13–14); instead he told David a parable about an injustice done to a disadvantaged man to reinforce his case against him (2 Sam 12:1–15). He tells David that he has broken the word of the Lord (12:9), but does not indicate what that word is. It is difficult to read into this passage a reference to a codified law that prohibited such conduct, since there are no other references to such laws in the rest of 1 and 2 Samuel. Even if the law of Moses did stand behind the prophet's message, citing a specific violation of the law would have greatly added to the impact of the writer's message on the writer's audience. Joshua appeals to keeping the "book of the law" (Josh 1:8), but this kind of reference is rare and not as obvious in Judges (see a reference to the word of the prophet in Judg 6:8–11, but with no clear recollection of a sacred text). There are many such examples of silence elsewhere in the OT. For some, this lack of citation of the Law raises the question whether the Law functioned as canon or absolute authority in Israel during this time. When did the OT take on canonical authority in Israel? Why did it not function as canon more prominently before the reforms of Josiah, where its use becomes explicit (2 Chron 34:14–33)?[8] At the end of the period of the first temple, there was a concerted effort to show the relevance of the law of Moses to the people, that is, to acknowledge them as canon 2. With the reforms of Ezra there is a clear call to observe and obey the law of Moses (Ezra 10:2–3; Neh 8:1–8).

In time, similar authority—but never equal authority—was conferred upon the Prophets, no doubt first upon those sometimes called the Former Prophets and later upon those called the Latter Prophets. Recognition of the Prophets, or at least some of them (Sir 49:8–10), appears to have taken place at the latest around 180 B.C. Our primary witness for this is Sirach, who shows an awareness of the books of Ezekiel, Job, and the Twelve Prophets (or Minor Prophets). Sirach may not be referring to a collection of the writings of the Prophets but to the heroes who were prophets. The passage in Sirach falls at the end of his "History of Famous Men" (Sir 44:1–50:24), throughout which he shows an awareness of the contents of some of the books of the Prophets as he tells the story of the famous persons or activists in his list.[9] Nevertheless, knowledge of the books of the Former and Latter Prophets and of the book of Job are obvious in the passage. Minimally there is a canon 1 recognition here.[10]

When Sirach's grandson, or someone else (authorship is uncertain), wrote the prologue for the book of Sirach (Ecclesiasticus) and translated it into Greek for those in Alexandria (ca. 130 B.C.), he described the literature that had already been translated for them as "the Law and the Prophets and the others that followed them." In a subsequent paragraph, while describing the difficulty of trans-

lation from Hebrew to Greek, he states that there are differences that remain in the translation of "the Law itself, the Prophecies, and the rest of the books," as well as in the translation of his grandfather's work. We do not know what these "other books" are for sure.[11] It is anachronistic to read back into ancient times circumstances and views that only later obtained widespread acceptance in Israel. We do see, however, the beginnings of a three- or four-part collection of sacred Scriptures emerging among the Jewish people. Philo (ca. A.D. 20–35), for example, mentions the holy books of the Therapeutae or Essenes, which they take with them into their sacred shrines or holy places in Egypt. These included "the laws and the sacred oracles of God enunciated by the holy prophets, and hymns, and psalms, and all kinds of other things by reason of which knowledge and piety are increased" (*Contempl. Life* 3.25).[12] It is impossible to conclude from these references that there were three specific and well-defined collections of sacred Scriptures, let alone what was in them. The fact that there were other books found at or near Qumran and placed in a sacred collection by an Essene community other than the Therapeutae in Egypt requires us to be cautious about equating these books with those that eventually made up the Hebrew Bible or the Protestant OT canon. In the recently translated Qumran text *Miqsat Maaseh ha-Torah* (4QMMT, c. 150 B.C.), there is also a reference to three or possibly four categories of sacred writings. The text reads in part, "surely, for your good we bring our words forward and we write [to] you to pay attention to the *Book of Moses and to the words of the prophets as well as to David and the day to day chronicles through the ages.*"[13] In this text, the third and fourth categories are vague. Does the third category, David, refer to the Psalter and the fourth category, the "day to day chronicles," refer to Chronicles, Ezra–Nehemiah, and possibly Esther? Neither Philo's text nor the halakic letter known as *Miqsat Maaseh ha-Torah* presents a clear statement about the contents of what is later identified in rabbinic writings as the Ketuvim or Hagiographa (the Writings). They do show us that both the Therapeutae in Egypt and those addressed by the *Miqsat Maaseh ha-Torah* text from Qumran had three or four categories of writings. But whether these are like the writings discovered later at Qumran or like the more precise threefold division of the Scriptures mentioned in Josephus (see sec. B, below) is uncertain. We must also be cautious in deciding whether, in either Philo or *Miqsat Maaseh ha-Torah*, the reference is to a closed collection of writings (canon 2) that possessed clearly defined boundaries.[14]

In the NT, Jesus is recorded as making reference to a three-part collection of Scriptures that includes "the law of Moses, the prophets, and the psalms" (Luke 24:44). Whether the last category should be taken to include all of what later came to be known as the Ketuvim is disputed. For some time, scholars have claimed that in several rabbinic writings the term "fifths" (Heb. *homashim*) sometimes refers not just to the five books of the Pentateuch but also to the five parts of the book of Psalms, and even to the whole of the Ketuvim.[15] If this is correct, and if it was also so understood in the first century, then it could be argued that Jesus endorsed the whole Hebrew biblical canon. That conclusion, however, goes beyond the evidence at present.[16]

We simply cannot be sure that texts dating considerably after the time of Jesus can clarify for us what Jesus, Philo, or *Miqsat Maaseh ha-Torah* meant by a reference to the "psalms." The problem here is that the terms "Ketuvim" and "Hagiographa" are not found in the first century as references to the third part of the Hebrew Scriptures, nor is the term "fifths" used in reference to any part of the biblical canon at that time. We cannot be sure that "psalms" in the first century ever referred to anything more than psalmic literature. Furthermore, it is not at all certain that the Ketuvim, the third section of the Hebrew Bible, began with the Psalms. At the end of the first century A.D., it is probable that only the Law and the Prophets were clearly defined and that the third section was still in need of definition. The references to the "psalms" in *Miqsat Maaseh ha-Torah*, Philo, and Luke probably refer only to the psalms that, along with the Law and the Prophets, composed most of what was generally recognized as canonical and fixed (canon 2) in the first century A.D.[17] The second-century A.D. Mishnaic tradition in *m. Yad.* 3:5 shows that Song of Songs and Ecclesiastes (or Qoheleth) were still being disputed in at least the rabbinic community, if not elsewhere among religious leaders in Israel.[18]

Thus, there is no first-century evidence that the Psalms stood for the whole of what later was called the Ketuvim. Although there is evidence that a third part of the Hebrew Scriptures was emerging in Israel even before the time of Jesus, there is no clear statement from the first century indicating what was in this third part. For most Jews of the first century, the third part of their Scriptures was still imprecise, and because it is likely that the early Christians acknowledged the same scriptural collection in the first century A.D., the full scope of the OT was also imprecise for them.

B. Josephus's Scriptural Canon

Some scholars argue that Josephus's well-known text in *Ag. Ap.* 1.37–43, which was written in defense of Judaism, demonstrates that all Jews in the first century A.D. accepted a three-part, twenty-two-book biblical canon. On the surface, the passage is one of the strongest arguments in favor of a closed biblical canon in the first century, as some scholars maintain. Ellis, for instance, argues that Josephus contradicts any views about an undetermined biblical canon in the first century, and says that this well-known passage was "a closely reasoned polemic against *inter alia* the work of an erudite Alexandrian grammarian, and he could not afford to indulge in careless misstatements that could be thrown back at him." He adds quickly that Josephus did not write for his own Pharisaic party but for all the Jewish people.[19] The most significant portion of this well-known text from Josephus is as follows:

> Our books, those which are justly accredited, are but two and twenty, and contain the record of all time. . . .

> We have given practical proof of our reverence for our own Scriptures. For, although such long ages have now passed, no one has ventured either to add, or to remove, or to alter a syllable; and it is an instinct with every Jew, from the day of his birth, to regard them as decrees of God, to abide by them, and, if need be, cheerfully to die for them. (*Ag. Ap.* 1.39–42 [Thackeray, LCL])

There are two important observations about this reference: first, not Josephus's twenty-two-book canon eventually obtained in Judaism but, rather, the twenty-four-book canon that was popular even in Josephus's own day (see 2 Esd 14:44–48); and second and more important, it is well known that Josephus was given to exaggeration. A number of scholars have questioned the reliability of Josephus's comments on the extent of the Jewish biblical canon at the end of the first century A.D. Leiman points out that the above passage was written in an apologetic context, that is, as "a vigorous rebuttal" not only against Apion but also against all who denied the antiquity of the Jews and their sacred literature. Therefore, he argues, Josephus is contending for the accuracy of the Hebrew Scriptures as reliable history, not arguing for them as Scripture. Leiman contends that Josephus's comment that "no one has ventured to add, or to remove, or to alter a syllable" is simply without justification, since "it is inconceivable that Josephus was unaware of the wide range of textual divergency that characterized the Hebrew, Greek, and Aramaic versions of Scripture current in first century Palestine." But how do we account for the exclusive language about the contents and inviolability of the Hebrew Scriptures in Josephus? Leiman argues that this rhetoric has several parallels in classical historiography, and concludes that Josephus need not be taken literally.[20] Feldman, even more critical of Josephus's reliability, cites several examples where he exaggerates and is given to propaganda, especially in the defense of Judaism, which is, of course, the context of *Against Apion*. Feldman reviews the prejudices and inaccuracies of Josephus and concludes that "he is far from infallible" in this regard. He believes that Josephus is generally reliable in the topography and geography of the land of Israel and also in matters of economics, but he is nonetheless a propagandist in the defense of Judaism against the pagan intellectuals of his day.[21] D. J. Silver claims that Josephus's twenty-two-book canon reveals his wish rather than the actual state of affairs regarding the biblical canon in his day, and maintains that there were many such texts circulating in that time with a claim to canonical authority, "with more appearing all the time."[22] Since Josephus claims that the succession of prophets (*Ag. Ap.* 1.41) ceased with Artaxerxes, the son of Xerxes, whom he identifies in *Ant.* 11.184 as Ahasuerus from the book of Esther, it is understandable why he concluded his biblical canon as early as he did, but this view was not the only view about prophecy among the Jews of the first century.[23]

Although Leiman acknowledges that Josephus frequently exaggerated in his writings, he still believes that Josephus presented a standardized biblical canon that could be verified: "He could hardly lie about the extent or antiquity of the canon; any Roman reader could inquire of the nearest Jew and test the veracity of Josephus' statement."[24] This assumes, however, that any Jew would know the contents of the biblical canon and would be interested in the question. Leiman further assumes that all Jews would agree on the matter. It is precisely this kind of questioning that Melito, bishop of Sardis at the end of the second century, could have done in his own community, where there was a large Jewish population, but evidently, he could not find sufficient awareness of the scope of the biblical canon in his own city. He therefore made a special trip to the east (Palestine) to discover the contents of the Hebrew Scriptures/Christian OT (Eusebius, *Hist. eccl.* 4.26.13–14). If the church had received a closed biblical canon from Jesus, it is odd that the bishop of a prominent church at the end of the second century did not know the books that made up his Bible. This would be strange indeed if the matter had been settled for a long period in the church, but not so strange if the matter was still uncertain.

Where did Josephus get his understanding of the biblical canon, if it was not widely held information in his day? Ellis and Beckwith have noted that a later version of *Jub.* 2:23–24 contains the first reference to a twenty-two-book scriptural canon, and may stand behind the reference in Josephus, *Ag. Ap.* 1.37–43.[25] The original text of *Jubilees* was probably written ca. 150 B.C. and was corrupted in transmission. Several versions of *Jub.* 2:23–24, including the Ethiopic text, have survived from antiquity.[26] The earliest form of the text that we possess, however, does not have the reference to the twenty-two-book collection. The later version may have been an insertion placed in the text during a time when the notion of a twenty-two-book canon had subsided in Israel, but the tradition of the twenty-two books was well known among the church fathers, who frequently referred to it.[27] They apparently passed on this canon in the church longer than it continued in the rabbinic traditions. It is likely, therefore, that the twenty-two-book canon did not originate with Josephus and that he may have depended on an earlier form of the text of *Jubilees*, but this is not obvious or certain. Whatever the source of this twenty-two-book canon, it is difficult to affirm by the available evidence that

Josephus's scriptural canon was as widespread and inviolable as he claims.

Some scholars continue to argue that the Hebrew Scriptures were completed no later than the second century B.C. and that they were endorsed by Jesus and accepted by the earliest Christian communities.[28] This does not seem to square with the attitude of the earliest followers of Jesus, however. They were informed in their thinking by the apocryphal writings and, in the case of Jude, a pseudepigraphal writing (Jude 14–15 citing *1 En.* 1:9).[29] A further difficulty with this position is the widespread use of the apocryphal and pseudepigraphal writings in the apostolic fathers and other church fathers after them. To account for this, we must argue, as some do, that the early church fathers simply lost the biblical canon that had been given to them by Jesus, that their understanding of the use of tradition was different from ours, or that a final biblical canon (OT) was never given to them in the first place. Since they were so keen to pass on the traditions of Jesus both orally and in written form and since they never mention that a biblical canon was handed on to them by Jesus or attribute one to him, it seems reasonable to say that they never received one from him. In light of this evidence, it appears that the OT as now constituted was not complete in the time of Jesus and that discussions of the contents of the biblical canon were not raised in the same way in that day. Had the contents of a biblical canon as we now know it been of interest to Jesus or his earliest followers, it seems reasonable that at least one tradition about its contents would have been preserved in the church.[30]

C. The Completion of the Old Testament Canon

Over the last eighty or more years, the most popular view regarding the completion of the OT canon has been that the third part of the Hebrew Scriptures was defined or closed at a "council" of rabbis that took place at Jamnia (Jabneh) at the end of the first century A.D.[31] This view is still held by some scholars today, but recent work has rejected its credibility. Some scholars assume that if the Jamnia theory is set aside, then the most reasonable time for finalizing the third part of the Hebrew Bible is sometime earlier than Jamnia. Leiman, for example, claims that the third part of the Hebrew Bible reached its present form no later than the time of Judas Maccabeus (ca. 165 B.C.), who collected the Hebrew Scriptures after the attempts of Antiochus Epiphanes to destroy them. Judas's collection of the scattered and remaining Scriptures provides the most obvious place of termination for the Hebrew Scriptures.[32] The passage cited in support of this position (1 Macc 1:56–57), however, only refers to the law being destroyed. Even though Leiman believes that "law" applies to all of the Scriptures of the Hebrew Bible, it is not clear from this passage how the third part of the Bible was completed as a result of Judas's activity. That conclusion cannot be drawn from the Maccabean literature. We suggest that the third part of the Hebrew Bible and the full scope of what is now the Christian OT did not come to finalization before the time of Jesus, or even in the early second century A.D. This occurred for some rabbinic Jews near the end of the second or early third century A.D., and even later for others. For the Christians, this final definition probably took place in the last half of the fourth century or following. Our reasons for this conclusion follow.

1. The rabbinic text *bar. b. B. Bat.* 14b, which is the first rabbinic text to identify specifically the books of the Hebrew Bible in Babylon, was a *baraita* written sometime toward the end of the second century A.D., and was not included in the accepted Mishnaic traditions at the end of the second century. It did not find acceptance in the late-second-century/early-third-century Mishnah of Rabbi Judah ha-Nasi. We do not dispute that some second-century sages held to the canon in *b. B. Bat.* 14b, but at that time this *baraita* was a minority position and did not occupy much interest in the rabbinic tradition. In the second century A.D., apart from Melito's similar but not identical list, published by Eusebius in the fourth century (see sec. B, above), of OT books, the *baraita* has no other parallels.

2. The apocryphal 2 Esd 14:44–48 (ca. A.D. 90–100) shows that, besides the twenty-four books of the Hebrew Bible that were acknowledged as holy books at the turn of the century and whose identity is unclear, seventy other books were also deemed to be inspired by God and authoritative. According to the tradition, these seventy other books were transmitted by God to Ezra and his scribes (2 Esd 14:19–48) and were reserved for wise

individuals, a reference to their special holy nature and spiritual insight. If they were not considered scriptural or inspired, would the author of 2 Esdras have indicated that they were transmitted by God (14:22–26) and were to be given only to the wise among them, "for in them [the seventy books] is the spring of understanding, the fountain of wisdom, and the river of knowledge" (14:47)? Many of the early Christians welcomed 2 Esdras into their sacred collections and even made significant additions to it by transforming parts of the legend into a Christian text. This would be strange indeed if their biblical canon had been settled before the time of Jesus.

3. Christians readily made use of many noncanonical writings in an authoritative manner soon after the time of Jesus. This suggests that their OT canon was not complete during his day. This point is hardly debatable, since the many references to noncanonical literature in the apostolic fathers is well known, some of them even referring to this literature as "scripture." If the Scriptures were already in a fixed form in the first century A.D., why is it that the first traditions that identify this canonical literature are in the late second century in Melito of Sardis and in the *bar. b. B. Bat.* 14b? Is it because it became necessary to construct such a list only later, when the scope of the biblical canon became blurred in the church as some scholars suggest, or is it because the matter had not yet been settled in the churches? More important, if the matter were settled earlier, in the time of Jesus or before, how is it possible that there are so many variations in the canonical lists of OT books that were drawn up by the Christians in the fourth, fifth, and sixth centuries?[33] If we must assume that the earliest Christians had a well-defined OT canon, we must also conclude that subsequent generations of Christians lost it![34] That is highly unlikely given their interest in preserving the tradition of Jesus and the apostles (the *regula fidei*, rule of faith).

4. When we try to establish the canon of Jesus by tabulating the Scriptures he cites (not an illegitimate procedure if we are mindful of the *way* he cites them),[35] what do we say about the Scriptures that he does not refer to—for example, Judges, Song of Songs, and Esther? Should we only use sources that Jesus quotes, or do we rely on the fact that he quoted passages from all three of the divi-

sions of the biblical canon, even if they were not well defined by the end of the first century even by Josephus? If we knew for certain the precise contents of the biblical canon at that time and if we were also certain of three well-defined collections of Scriptures, we might be able to argue this way. We simply cannot know this, however, either from the ancient testimony available inside and outside the Bible or from the references that Jesus made to his disciples. We do not know what the absence of a citation of a book means in terms of Jesus' canon. Since we have no complete record of all that he said (observe John 20:30) and since, for the most part, the sayings of Jesus that we do have are ad hoc (that is, he was responding to specific situations), how can we know for sure what his entire biblical canon was? As far as is known, no one ever asked Jesus the scope of his Bible and he did not say, so the argument from citations and quotations is two-edged—which is often not sufficiently considered by those who use it.

5. The lack of a precise definition of the biblical canon among the Amoraim, the rabbinic interpreters of the Mishnah (third century A.D. and later), is consistent with the fact that several of the Writings (Song of Songs, Ezekiel, Esther, Ecclesiastes, and Proverbs) were still disputed among the Jews during the fourth and fifth centuries A.D.[36] The dispute was never resolved by reference to an earlier time when these writings had been accepted or "canonized." Further, the acceptance of at least two noncanonical writings (Sirach and Wisdom of Solomon) was debated among the sages in terms of whether they "defiled the hands" (i.e., were sacred Scripture; see no. 7, below) (*y. Ber.* 11b; *y. Naz.* 54b; *Ber. Rab.* 91.3; *Koh. Rab.* 7.11; *b. Ber.* 48a). This debate shows that a precise definition of the contents of the Hebrew Bible was still lacking for some rabbis at this time. In the collection mentioned by Melito (Eusebius, *Hist. eccl.* 4.26.13–14), he omits Esther and includes Wisdom of Solomon without any discussion on whether such writings belonged or not. If Esther is missing and Wisdom is included, how fixed could this collection have been, especially among the Jews from whom he presumably got his list? Which Jews (or Christians?) gave this canon to him?

It is almost certain that the framers of the Mishnah were the same people who were involved in the finalization of the Hebrew Scriptures, but by the time such matters were being openly discussed at the end of the second century, there was already a move to include in their sacred collection, along with the OT, the Mishnah and eventually the Tosefta, *Genesis Rabbah, Leviticus Rabbah,* the two Talmudim (the Mishnah and the Gemara), and various midrashim of rabbinic Judaism. The expansion of the Torah-based canon to include not only the Hebrew Scriptures but also these other writings occurred when the myth of the oral Torah became a part of the sages' teaching. In the fourth century, when the sages mentioned the Torah, they no longer spoke of a scroll of the laws of Moses but of both the written and the oral teaching that were revealed to Moses at Sinai (the "whole Torah"). This eventually included all that the rabbis taught about the Law as well as the Law itself.[37] Thus the Scriptures of the Jews were expanding, not reducing in size, even though the apocryphal and pseudepigraphal writings, for the most part, had dropped from their sacred collections.

The framers of the Mishnah, however, do not appear to have been very interested in the scope of their Scriptures, since the matter occupies very little space in their second-century A.D. deliberations.[38] The framers of the Mishnah apparently felt no need to support with the Hebrew Scriptures their various prescriptions and proscriptions for holy living. This is not what one would expect from a community that was "willing to die" for its Scriptures, as Josephus had argued. Neusner calls this absence of references to Scripture in the Mishnah "writing *without* Scripture."[39] This all changed when the Amoraim supported the prescriptions of the Mishnah in their Talmud with references to the Hebrew Scriptures. This was the Amoraim's way of showing that both the written and the oral dimensions of Torah were the same and did not contradict each other. Neusner denies that the Hebrew canon was ever closed until after the two dimensions of Torah became one and the "whole Torah" became the canon of Judaism.[40] Kraemer may be more correct in saying that the basic contours of the Hebrew Bible were eventually defined in the late second century A.D.,[41] even though at the same time the canon of the rabbis was expanding, since the Amoraim supported nearly all of the passages of the Mishnah with texts from the Hebrew Scriptures. This practice has some parallels in the early church.

6. There was no significant discussion of the contents of the OT canon in the church, or even the notion of canonization as such, in the second or third centuries A.D. Only the canon or rule of faith, which was regularly employed to deal with the heretical challenges facing the church, was a matter of discussion. Both the OT and the NT were regularly cited by the church fathers to deal with heresies and crises that were confronting the church, especially in addressing questions about the nature of Christ, but there was no listing of the OT nor any long discussions about the contents of a scriptural collection at that time. The fact that Melito did not know the contours of the biblical canon suggests that this issue was not an important one to the church of his time and location. Furthermore, since only one Hebrew text in the second century mentions the contents of the Hebrew Scriptures (*bar. b. B. Bat.* 14b), it is not likely that this was an important item for rabbinic Judaism either.

7. Finally, the absence, both before and immediately after the time of Jesus, of an appropriate term to describe a collection of Scriptures should inform us that such a notion was not current then. In the second century A.D., the Jews employed a category called "defiling the hands" to describe and identify their sacred texts. It was then that the debate started about which books ritually "defile the hands."[42] It appears that only with the secularization of the scribal profession, which took place in Judaism in the second and third centuries A.D., did it become important to distinguish between sacred and secular in writings.[43] This began to happen in Judaism in the context of the Tannaitic writers of the late second century and following.[44] Christians never used the term "defiling the hands," but in the fourth and fifth centuries they also found a relevant term of their own that expressed the sacredness of their Scriptures: "canonical" or "encovenanted scriptures" (τῶν ἐνδιαθήκων γραφῶν, *tōn endiathēkōn graphōn*) (Eusebius, *Hist. eccl.* 5.8.1).[45]

D. Conclusion

A major problem for an early closure of the Hebrew biblical canon is how to account for the larger collection of writings circulating among the early Christians for several centuries and their free use of noncanonical writings in a Scripture-like manner.[46] If they received a closed and endorsed biblical canon from Jesus, they nowhere discuss it or show any awareness of it. The earliest Christians undoubtedly followed Jesus' lead in matters related to Scripture, but it is not clear that Jesus endorsed any fixed biblical canon. At least, no evidence that he did currently exists. If his followers had received a canon from him that approximates or is equal to our current Protestant OT canon, then they apparently lost it, since they never refer to it or to Jesus' endorsement of it. When the church fathers and church councils began to deliberate and recognize a canon of Scriptures in the fourth century, they never attributed any of their lists to a tradition from Jesus or to some other tradition passed on by him through the apostles. It appears, therefore, that early Christianity, like Judaism, was simply not interested in closed biblical canons the way that Christians were later in church history. Imposing such notions on individuals or churches of those times is anachronistic.

So how did the Christians arrive at the OT they possess? It is most likely that the first Christians received from the Jews of the first century the Scriptures that were recognized in much of Judaism before the time of their separation from the synagogues, namely, before A.D. 70. The prevailing collections of Scriptures at that time most naturally became the Scriptures of the first Christians. Portions of those Scriptures were fixed and well recognized, especially the Law and the Prophets, but final decisions about the Writings and the use of apocryphal and even pseudepigraphal writings had not yet been made for Pharisaic Judaism in the first century. Widespread parallels to, and use of, these writings in early Christianity are apparent, even in the NT. It is not inappropriate to say that the NT writings were informed by more than the canonical OT writings. As Metzger states: "For early Jewish Christians the Bible consisted of the Old Testament and some Jewish apocryphal literature. Along with this written authority went traditions (chiefly oral) of sayings attributed to Jesus."[47]

There was no normative Judaism in the time of Jesus with a universally fixed and accepted Scripture; rather, there were competing sects of Judaism, of which the Essenes, Pharisees, Sadducees, and Christians, as well as Samaritans, were all a part. Some recent scholars have tried to show that there was no essential difference among these sects in the scope of their scriptural canons,[48] but the evidence from Qumran, for example, suggests that the covenanters of Qumran recognized more than

the current OT canon (excluding Esther). This conclusion is based on the discovery of many more writings in the vicinity of Qumran than the OT writings. It is therefore unlikely that the current OT canons of the Protestant and Catholic churches can be equated with the canon of Scriptures of the first Christian community, even though there is considerable overlap. The early Christian community appears to have been informed by much more than the literature that is in our Bibles today.

There is a final important observation concerning the organization of the Christian OT and the Jewish Hebrew Bible.[49] The books that comprise the Protestant OT, and most of the books in the Catholic and Orthodox traditions (excepting their inclusion of the apocryphal/deuterocanonical writings), are the same as those in the Hebrew Bible. The ordering of the books, however, varies considerably between the Jewish and Christian collections. This ordering is a later development in both of these two religious traditions, and probably comes after the various books were selected to be a part of these collections. In other words, the recognition of the sacredness of these books was a prior step in their inclusion in the two different Bibles, and the location of the various books in those collections has significance for how those collections are interpreted.

The current Hebrew Bible (Tanak) begins with the books of the Law *(Torah)*, has the Former and Latter Prophets *(Neviim)* in the middle of its collection, and concludes with the Writings *(Ketuvim)*. In some forms of the Hebrew Bible (e.g. the Leningrad Codex) the order of books varies. The story line of the Hebrew Bible begins with Genesis and ends at 2 Kings with the defeat of the tribes of the north (Israel) and those of the south (Judah) at the hands of the Assyrians and Babylonians respectively. The Jews were, for the most part, exiled from their land. Even after the decree of Cyrus, who allowed the Jews to return to their land, most Jews did not return but either stayed in Babylon and its environs or immigrated to other lands. The Christian OT extends this time line considerably by inserting Ruth after Judges and making it a historical book. Chronicles are placed after Kings, and Ezra, Nehemiah, and Esther are also included in the time line. In Catholic and Orthodox Bibles, this time line is further extended to include Judith, Tobit, and Maccabees.

In the Jewish canon, the Latter Prophets, beginning with Isaiah, Jeremiah, and Ezekiel and including the Twelve Minor Prophets, follow the historical narrative to explain the tragedy that has come to the nation and why Israel is in its current condition given the earlier promises of God (Gen 12:1–3; 2 Sam 7:10–17). The Writings begin by emphasizing individual piety (the Psalms) and conclude by showing how Israel's history declined from its former glorious days, which peaked during the reign of Solomon into captivity and deportation. The final part of this canon appears to call each individual to personal faithfulness to Yahweh. This final collection maintains no significant focus on the coming kingdom or blessings of God or any other great promise for the nation of Israel. Given the devastating tragedy that befell the nation both in the A.D. 70 destruction of Jerusalem and in the brief messianic fervor that brought about the crushing of the Bar Kokhba rebellion of A.D. 132–135 by the Romans, there was very little belief in the rabbinic survivors of those disasters that caused the Jews to hope for any future of their nation. For the Jews, the Writings encourage persons to be obedient, to serve, and, above all, be faithful to God—this was an appropriate response of the Jews given their recent history.

The Christian OT, on the other hand, focuses on the future unfolding activity of God that was soon to break forth, Christians believed, in the activity of Jesus. The Christian canon contains four parts: the Pentateuch, the Historical Books, the Wisdom or Poetic Books, and the Prophets. Daniel, one of the Writings in the Hebrew Bible, becomes one of the Prophets in the Christian Bible. The Prophets' role in the Christian Bible was not so much to explain the adversity that had befallen Israel as it was to point to the gospel of Jesus Christ. By concluding the First or Old Testament with the Prophets, both Major (Isaiah, Jeremiah, Ezekiel, and Daniel) and Minor (the Twelve), the church saw that the prophetic literature pointed to hope for a new day in which those who were faithful to God would be blessed and judgment would come to the disobedient. Those days, according to this ordering of books, would be preceded by the coming of Elijah the prophet (Mal 4:1–6), who would prepare the people of God for the coming rule of the Lord. The next part of the Christian Bible, the NT, begins with the announcement of the coming of Christ by John the Baptist, who is believed by Jesus to fulfill the role of Elijah (Matt 11:7–15). As the first part of the Christian Bible ends, it anticipates a future that is described in the second part, the NT.

The following table comparing the two collections of Scriptures illustrates the different perspectives described above.[50]

TABLE 13-1
ORDER OF SCRIPTURE COLLECTION

HEBREW BIBLE (TANAK)	CHRISTIAN OT
Torah	**Pentateuch**
Genesis	Genesis
Exodus	Exodus
Leviticus	Leviticus
Numbers	Numbers
Deuteronomy	Deuteronomy
Prophets *(Neviim)*	**Historical Books**
Former Prophets	Joshua
Joshua	Judges
Judges	Ruth
1 and 2 Samuel	1 and 2 Samuel
1 and 2 Kings	1 and 2 Kings
Latter Prophets	1 and 2 Chronicles
Major Prophets	Ezra and Nehemiah
Isaiah	**Apocryphal/**
Jeremiah	**Deuterocanonicals**
Ezekiel	Tobit
Twelve Minor Prophets	Judith
Hosea	Wisdom of Solomon
Joel	Sirach (Ecclesiasticus)
Amos	Baruch
Obadiah	1 and 2 Maccabees
Jonah	**Poetic/Wisdom**
Micah	Job
Nahum	Psalms
Habakkuk	Proverbs
Zephaniah	Ecclesiastes
Haggai	Song of Solomon
Zechariah	**Prophets**
Malachi	Major Prophets
Writings *(Ketuvim)*	Isaiah
Psalms	Jeremiah
Proverbs	Lamentations
Job	Ezekiel
Five Megilloth Scrolls	Daniel
Song of Songs	Twelve Minor Prophets
Ruth	Hosea
Lamentations	Joel
Ecclesiastes	Amos
Esther	Obadiah
	Jonah
Daniel	Micah
Ezra and Nehemiah	Nahum
1 and 2 Chronicles	Habakkuk
	Zephaniah
	Haggai
	Zechariah
	Malachi

How the books of the Hebrew Bible and the Christian OT are ordered is very important for interpreting what each community was trying to say about this literature and what they believed God was doing in the respective communities. The Christians believed that they were living in the last days of fulfillment that were promised in their OT Scriptures, and that the blessings of the new age had descended upon them. The Hebrew Bible, on the other hand, has a much more sober perspective and focuses only slightly on the future of the nation. It appears from the ordering of its canon that such notions were no longer the object of the nation's hope. With the stabilization of the biblical texts in the second century A.D. and with the emerging use of the codex (book form) instead of the scroll, it became possible to fix the order of the books of the Hebrew Bible. This development and the context in which it occurred are important for understanding how these sacred texts were read in rabbinic Judaism. These circumstances were considerably different for the Christian communities, and their ordering of books reflects those differences.

4. THE NEW TESTAMENT CANON

The complexity of the origins and development of the OT canon is also true of the formation of the NT canon. It has become common to locate the origin and growth of the NT canon in the second century A.D., allowing for minor modifications and adjustments in its scope at a later time. The second century has largely been accepted as the context for the development of the NT canon by such scholars as R. M. Grant, Hans von Campenhausen, D. Farkasfalvy, W. Farmer, B. M. Metzger, F. F. Bruce, and Everett Ferguson (see bibliography at the end of the chapter). They have attempted to place in that century the factors that gave rise to that canon, often beginning with Marcion and concluding with the Montanists. When the basic assumption of a semiclosed biblical canon is examined in the context of the writings of the second-century Fathers, however, it becomes questionable whether such matters were ever discussed, let alone considered, in the second century. We will examine these and other assumptions below and offer the fourth century as an alternative context for the finalization of the NT canon.

A. Recognition of New Testament Writings as Scripture

When the writers of the NT were producing their manuscripts, as we observed above, with one possible exception (Rev 22:18–19), they were not consciously aware that they were producing inviolable or prophetic Scripture. Even though Paul, in his advice to the widows, considered his words authoritative (1 Cor 7:40), he does not claim the authority of an inviolable Scripture when he writes. His final authority is the testimony of Jesus (7:10, 17), although he frequently refers to the OT to support his positions (15:3–5). Paul, however, distinguishes his own words and authority from the words and authority of Jesus (7:12, 25; see also 11:23).[51]

When do these and other Christian writings begin to be recognized as sacred Scripture, and when do they begin to take their place in a fixed biblical canon? A number of important references to the Gospels and Paul appear in the writings of the Apostolic Fathers in the late first and early second centuries, and the Gospels and Paul also influenced subsequent Christian writers of the second century—especially in their teaching and preaching. Until the end of the second century, however, the NT was not generally called Scripture.[52]

The NT writings were at first employed to instruct the churches in doctrine.[53] When they began to be read alongside the OT Scriptures in the worship services of the Christians, as they were in the church that Justin Martyr describes in *1 Apol.* 67, then the recognition of the scriptural status of these writings had begun, even if those writings were not yet generally called Scripture. They were functioning in a canonical fashion (canon 1), even though there is no reference to a fixed form or collection (canon 2) of these writings.

B. Influences toward Canonization

What influences led to the canonization of the NT? No single factor can be isolated, but with the recognition of the usefulness of the NT writings for instruction and preaching, as well as the practice of reading them regularly in the churches, the acknowledgment of their scriptural status was just a matter of time. And that is the most important question: how much time? Once their scriptural status was accepted, their eventual inclusion into an authoritative collection of Christian Scriptures was also a matter of time. Those who accept a second-century context for this process account for its emergence in the events of the second century. On the other hand, those who see the final stages of the process more at home in the fourth century argue that it is not easy to establish the broad formative stages of the canon's development in the second century, even though the recognition of some Christian literature as Scripture was widespread at that time.

It is generally agreed that some of the first collections of Christian writings were of Paul's letters, probably already circulating at the end of the first century (and perhaps first collected during Paul's own lifetime). Bruce suggests that other collections of Christian writings were also circulating at that time and observes that the early Valentinian school of the first half of the second century also possessed and employed many of the NT writings. For example, the *Gospel of Truth*, which is probably the most important of their writings, alludes to several of the NT writings, including Matthew, Luke, John, 1 John, possibly Acts, ten of Paul's epistles (no Pastoral Epistles), Hebrews, and Revelation. In some cases, as Bruce has noted, there were allegorical interpretations of this literature, and this demonstrates the authoritative or Scripture-like standing it had among the Valentinian Christians.[54] On the other hand, although there is little doubt that the Valentinians used a large number of the NT writings, there is no focus in the *Gospel of Truth* on the formation of a canon, that is, a specific listing of a collection of Christian Scriptures, nor yet a limited or fixed number of NT writings. Like other Christian communities in the first half of the second century, however, the Valentinians were making use of the NT writings in their teaching and preaching.

A number of scholars contend that several second-century influences were the most important factors leading the church to formulate its own canon of Scriptures. We will examine the most important of these influences below.

1. Marcion

Several scholars have claimed that Marcion was the first to produce a canonical list of Christian

Scriptures and that the church responded to his action by producing one that better represented its life and faith.[55] If Marcion produced a biblical canon, so the argument goes, this would set a precedent for the existence of other such canons in the second century.

By the mid–second century, various Christian communities or churches were gradually recognizing the usefulness of a body of Christian literature for their life and worship, but it is difficult to establish a fixed normative Christian collection to which one could appeal at that time. Marcion saw the importance of a collection of authoritative Christian writings for use in worship and teaching in his community of churches, but his design was not so much to document an insight into the normative value of a few NT writings (an edited Paul and an abbreviated Luke)—that is, the recognition of a biblical canon or even Christian Scripture as such—as it was to effect a separation between Judaism and Christianity. His anti-Judaistic sentiment caused him to reject the use of the OT and all other Jewish influences in the Christian community.[56] Marcion recognized, perhaps more clearly than others of his day, the difficulty of accepting the OT as normative sacred writings for the church when vast segments of that literature were no longer seen to be binding upon Christians. This was especially true of the legal and moral codes and the traditions associated with keeping the law. Believing that he was following the correct teaching of Paul, he argued that Christians were free from the law and therefore they had no reason to give token allegiance to what had been rendered obsolete by faith in Christ. He rejected use of the most arbitrary means of interpreting the OT—the allegory or typology that many other Christians commonly employed to find meaning and guidance from the OT.[57] Marcion's rejection of the OT and of the allegorical interpretation of it stripped the church not only of its Scriptures but also of its prized claim to the heritage of Israel's antiquity and to being the religion of historical fulfillment.[58] The church responded by excommunicating him.

Marcion's collection of Pauline letters was probably not the first such collection, even though he may well have been the first to have both a limited number of Epistles and a Gospel in a collection. It is likely that his collection became available to him only because churches before him had first made use of Paul's writings and circulated them to other churches (e.g., Ephesians may have been or become a circular or encyclical letter intended to introduce other Pauline letters to churches [see discussion in ch. 10, above]; and Col 4:16 may refer to the Ephesian letter that was originally sent to Laodicea, since Marcionite Prologues mention a letter to the Laodiceans but not one to the Ephesians). It is safe to assume that several of Paul's writings were circulating in Asia Minor at the end of the first century, and even in Rome. Clement of Rome (ca. A.D. 95), for example, refers to four of Paul's epistles.

Marcion may have been an important catalyst in causing the church to come to grips with the question of which literature best conveyed its true identity and possibly also which literature could be called Scripture. Marcion's concern, however, was not so much with a NT canon of Scriptures as with eliminating Jewish influences that affected the life of early Christianity. Both Irenaeus and Tertullian strongly reacted against Marcion's rejection of the OT and of all the Gospel literature except Luke (Irenaeus, *Haer.* 4.29–34; Tertullian, *Ag. Marc.* 4.2), but they did not do so by establishing a canon of Scriptures. They responded with the church's sacred teachings, that is, its *regula fidei*, which was illustrated by a number of OT and NT Scriptures that only later became part of a fixed biblical canon. With Marcion, however, one finds the first clear reference to Luke—though not to Acts—and also to a collection of the writings of Paul (ten letters, excluding the Pastoral Epistles; his letter to the Laodiceans may have been what we call the Letter to the Ephesians). When Irenaeus introduced his four-Gospel canon, it may have come as a response to the teachings of Marcion, but more likely it was a response to the ignoring of the Gospel of John in the greater church or to Tatian's *Diatessaron,* which blurred the distinctions between the Gospels.[59]

It is much too strong to say with von Campenhausen, however, that Marcion was the "creator of the Christian holy scripture,"[60] but it is generally conceded that he was the first individual known by name to set forth a well-defined collection of Christian writings. Although his motive was anti-Judaistic, he may have had the effect of spurring the church into rethinking its understanding of its use of the OT. But this is considerably different from saying, as did Harnack, that Marcion was the cause

that led the church to adopt a broader NT canon. We do not know for certain how many other Christian writings were familiar to Marcion, but the churches that followed him felt free to edit his work and even admitted into their Scriptures verses from the canonical Gospels.[61] It is not possible to demonstrate that Marcion knew of all four canonical Gospels or other NT writings, but it is likely that he was at least aware of the Gospel of Matthew because of its widespread popularity in the second century. When we observe that Marcion's followers also added to his writings a collection of Psalms later rejected by the author of the Muratorian Fragment (see lines 83–84) and that the Armenian Marcionites probably accepted Tatian's *Diatessaron,*[62] it appears that, with Marcion, we are not yet talking about a closed biblical canon or perhaps even about a biblical canon at all. The writings in Marcion's collection no doubt functioned authoritatively (canon 1) in his communities, but there was no firmly fixed biblical canon at this time for him or for anyone else, and the church did not respond to him with a different canon of Scriptures but with a tradition of truth (the *regula fidei*) that had been handed down through the churches, and with the authoritative Christian writings that circulated in their communities.

2. *The Gnostics*

The gnostic Christians in the second century produced a vast amount of literature that they considered sacred. Although their roots are somewhat obscure, a significant amount of their literature has been found and is now preserved in the recently translated Coptic documents discovered in Nag Hammadi, Egypt, near the upper Nile in 1945.[63] These documents, which were originally written in Greek and were translated into Coptic, have enabled us to view gnostic Christianity from its own perspective. Before this discovery, all that was known about these people and their views came from their opponents, the "orthodox" Christians, especially Irenaeus (*Haer.* 1), who leveled the severest attacks against them (see ch. 7, above).

The widespread esoteric writings of the gnostics, along with their claims to secret revelations from the apostles, were rejected by Irenaeus, who argued instead for the legitimacy of the truth of the *regula fidei* that he contends was passed on in the church by apostolic succession through the bishops. Notice, for example, his famous line of reasoning: "For if the apostles had known hidden mysteries, which they were in the habit of imparting to 'the perfect' apart and privately from the rest, they would have delivered them especially to those to whom they were also committing the leadership of the churches themselves" (adapted from *Haer.* 3.3.1 [*ANF*]). One can scarcely deny Irenaeus's logic here. The presence of these gnostic writings at the end of the second century, however, did not lead the orthodox churches to define more precisely the boundaries or limitations of their Scriptures, as some have argued, but the Christian *regula fidei*, their understanding of the truth. It is difficult to find a direct relationship between the church's confrontation with gnostic heresy and the development of a canon of orthodox Scriptures.

3. The Montanists

Many canon scholars have emphasized the role of the Montanists in spurring the church into defining more precisely the limits of its sacred Scriptures. The Montanists, who emerged from Phrygia in the mid–second century, focused on the need for a "new prophecy," rigid asceticism, martyrdom, and the presence and power of the Holy Spirit.[64] It is reported that the Montanists produced a large number of prophetic documents (see Eusebius, *Hist. eccl.* 5.16.3–4). Those who most vigorously opposed the Montanists and their new prophecy in Asia Minor, the so-called Alogi (from their rejection of the divine Logos, or Word, in John's prologue), also rejected the Gospel of John and the book of Revelation, which were heavily used by the Montanists. The greater church also rejected the Montanist movement and was hesitant about the Gospel of John, because of its focus on the Paraclete, and the book of Revelation, because of its apocalyptic focus. Even Hebrews was called into question by the Alogi because it was linked with the Montanist crisis,[65] probably because of its view of the hopeless condition of the apostate Christian (see Heb 6:4–6; 10:26–31), a view that coincided with the Montanists' harsh penitential practice.[66] By the year 200, the Montanists had expanded their influence to Rome and North Africa, though their most significant influence was among rural communities.[67]

In their enthusiasm, the Montanists generated numerous "prophetic" books that they claimed were divinely inspired. In response, von Campenhausen says, the greater church felt the need to identify more precisely which literature was inspired and which was not and, consequently, which writings were authoritative in the church. But did the Montanists produce any "scriptural" literature? Scholarly opinion is divided on this question.[68] Tertullian defended this practice of producing inspired literature, since it is, he says, mere prejudice to heed and value only past demonstrations of power and grace: "Those people who condemn the one power of the one Holy Spirit in accordance with chronological eras should beware."[69] Von Campenhausen says that, for Tertullian, "it is the recent instances to which far higher respect ought to be paid; for they already belong to the time of the End, and are to be prized as a superabundant increase of grace."[70] Tertullian argues that these new writings were from God, who "in accordance with the testimony of Scripture, has destined [them] for precisely this period of time."[71] It is important that, however far along the canonical process was at this time (ca. 200), it had not so impressed Tertullian that he was willing to close off the possibility of new inspired literature to inform his Christian understanding.[72]

According to von Campenhausen, the mainstream churches rejected the Montanist prophecies essentially on the grounds that their prophecies were contrary to the earlier Christian writings (now called Scriptures).[73] He maintains, however, that, because of the Montanists, the church could no longer continue having a roughly defined canon of Scriptures. He therefore concludes that the Montanists and their production of numerous books were the primary factors that caused the church to define more precisely which books belonged to the NT and which did not.[74] It was at this point, von Campenhausen claims, that the last phase of the canonical process began, though it will become clear that this phase was apparently by no means complete as a result of a polemic against the Montanists.[75] On the contrary, if the church at large were interested in closing the NT canon at this time, one would expect to find some discussion in the church fathers of such a need or some description of a scriptural collection as we find later in

Eusebius; but this is precisely what is missing. As we noted above, in the second century, the criticism of the various fringe or "heretical" groups was not made with a canon of books but, rather, with a criterion of truth. As with Marcion and the gnostics, the second-century church responded to all such movements with an understanding of Christian truth that had been handed on in the churches through its bishops, not with a fixed canon of Christian writings. It also freely used the writings of the early Christian community to support its criticisms of such movements.

4. Irenaeus, Clement, and Origen

In the fourth century, Eusebius reported that Irenaeus (170–180) had recognized a canon of Scriptures (see *Hist. eccl.* 5.8.1–9), but this is not necessarily the case. We do not question that he had a *regula fidei* to which he regularly appealed (see *Haer.* 1.10.1; cf. 3.4.2) and that he supported with references to those to whom Christ had committed this "apostolic deposit," namely, the apostolic community and its writings (*Haer.* 4.15.2). It is not clear, however, that he produced a canon of Scriptures like those we see beginning with Eusebius in the fourth century. Irenaeus was one of the primary teachers in the church to deal with heresies in the Christian communities by appealing to the apostolic deposit of truth in the churches that was passed on in the church through the bishops (*Haer.* 3.4.1). He appeals in his writings to the OT and NT to argue his case against heresies, but there is no clear identification in his own writings of what were contained in those collections. Melito, a contemporary of Irenaeus, alone tried to discover the contents of the Hebrew Scriptures, but he was singled out by Eusebius (*Hist. eccl.* 4.26.13–14) because of his uniqueness in being concerned with the contents of this collection, not because he was typical. Irenaeus mentioned only a closed Gospel canon (*Haer.* 3.11.8, 9), but his unconvincing arguments (by today's standards) appear to have been a means of including recognition of the Gospel of John, which was under suspicion in many second-century churches. Why else would he give such a fanciful and forceful argument if everyone

was already in full agreement on the matter (see *Haer.* 3.11.8, 9)?

Clement of Alexandria was known for the many sources to which he referred in his writings and for his seeming inability to reduce the number of sources he used. He appealed to apocryphal writings and to those writers who were "Greek and barbarian alike" (Eusebius, *Hist. eccl.* 6.13.5), as well as to what Eusebius referred to as the "disputed" writings (Jude, but also *Barnabas* and the *Apocalypse of Peter;* Eusebius, *Hist. eccl.* 6.13.4–7). Although Eusebius called this literature "disputed" (*Hist. eccl.* 6.14.1), the Muratorian Fragment (lines 68–69) reported that Jude and the Epistles of John were recognized "in the catholic church"—something that is found at the end of the fourth century but generally not before then. It could well be argued that the use of this literature in an "undisputed" fashion in the Muratorian Fragment could speak for its early dating, although that would make this instance the first reference to this literature as a part of the Christian Scriptures. More likely, its undisputed appearance in such a list may provide evidence of a late origin of the Muratorian Fragment (see sec. D, below).

Origen, who refused to reduce his collection of OT Scriptures to the twenty-two or twenty-four books of the Hebrew biblical canon, simply acknowledged the scope of the biblical canon of the Jews (see Eusebius, *Hist. eccl.* 6.25.1–2); he does not himself appear to have had a precisely defined OT or NT (Eusebius, *Hist. eccl.* 6.25.3–14). His NT canon, if there was one, is unlikely to have been the same as that reported in Eusebius, which is probably no more than a select list of writings that Origen cited or quoted.[76] Was Origen actually focusing on or assuming a biblical canon when he freely cited earlier sources?[77] There is nothing that directly suggests this conclusion.

The primary arguments for establishing a widely recognized and largely closed biblical canon at the end of the second century are not convincing. It is more likely that there was a general recognition of something like an "open" biblical canon (canon 1) at the end of the second century, but it is not clear how widespread this recognition was, nor what the scope of such a collection was. At the end of the second century, apart from the term "Scripture," there were no generally accepted terms to identify this collection of Christian writings. The terms "Old

Testament" and "New Testament" had begun to be used in that century but had not gained sufficient recognition by that time.[78] The most that can be said is that there was a general recognition of the scriptural status of the four Gospels, Acts, and most of the Epistles of Paul at the end of the second century.

5. The Burning of Books

As a likely termination point for the recognition of which books were sacred in individual Christian communities, we have to consider the Diocletianic persecution (A.D. 303–313), when Christians were asked to turn over their sacred books to be burned by the authorities (see *Gesta apud Zenophilum* [CSEL 26]). The individual churches would certainly have made choices by that time regarding which books were sacred Scriptures (and should not be turned over) and which were not (and so could be turned over to the authorities). This does not presuppose, however, more than that individual churches and regions of churches had made such decisions; we cannot say at this time what the church at large was thinking on the matter, as the variations in the biblical canons of the late fourth century show. Further, the traditions that have survived about the book burning in the early fourth century do not tell us specifically which books were handed over to the authorities and which were burned. But decisions on which books could be turned over were undoubtedly made no later than this time, and this aspect of the Diocletianic persecution had to be a strong incentive for the churches individually at least to come to grips with the issue of which writings were deemed sacred.

6. Constantine and Eusebius

Whether Constantine, who called for unity in both the empire and in the church, had an influence upon the contents of the biblical canon of the church is difficult to determine, but his involvement in most major decisions of the church in the second quarter of the fourth century over matters of doctrine, leadership, and ecclesiastical harmony strongly suggests that he could have.[79] Along with this, his personal request of Eusebius to produce fifty copies of the Scriptures (*Vit. Const.* 4.36) for use in the churches in Constantinople, the New Rome, would result in, at the least, a strong influence by Eusebius on churches in that area, if not upon the whole of the empire. Whatever Eusebius sent and the emperor accepted would logically carry much weight in the churches, but as the canonical lists show, there was no unanimity on the scope of the sacred collection. If the copies produced were of all the NT Scriptures (rather than just the canonical Gospels, as Robbins claims),[80] then knowledge of their contents and their approval by the emperor would go a long way in commending them and their contents to other Christians. In any event, Eusebius's influence on others in terms of what he selected to go into those copies had to be considerable, and when we consider the fact that he is the first to produce or publish several canonical lists, including his own (*Hist. eccl.* 3.25.1–7), this production of NT Scriptures was probably quite important in the overall canonical development in the church. Around A.D. 320–330, when he wrote his *Ecclesiastical History*, he offered three categories of writings for consideration: the "recognized" writings (ὁμολογούμενα, *homologoumena*), the "disputed" writings (ἀντιλεγόμενα, *antilegomena*), and the "rejected" or "spurious" writings (νόθα, *notha*). Only the first category, the recognized books, which was composed of twenty-one or twenty-two books of the current NT canon, was Eusebius's canon.[81] The disputed books were not accepted by Eusebius, and by the end of the fourth century, there was no category remaining for these doubtful books. Writings then were either recognized or rejected in the sacred collections (even though the latter could be read privately by Christians). Eusebius therefore provides a very important bridge in the development of the biblical canon in the fourth century. Before the century was complete, several of the NT canons that emerged in the churches had the full twenty-seven books that are present in our current biblical canon, though even then there was not complete unanimity. When we add to these elements the probable involvement of Constantine, it is likely that these fourth-century factors fixed and defined the biblical canon of the church. It is difficult to deny that there was a push, led by the emperor himself, toward conformity in the churches in all matters.

With the council meetings in the churches in the fourth century and following, there was more of an opportunity for the churches together to speak specifically to the issue of the contents of the biblical canon. At that time, there was growing unity over the matter, but by no means complete agreement. The Syrian churches, for example, continued to prefer the use of Tatian's *Diatessaron* well into the sixth century. In the core of the NT, however, there was general agreement on the acceptance and recognition of the four canonical Gospels, Acts, Paul's letters (which at this time included the Pastorals and usually Hebrews), James, 1 Peter, and 1 John; there continued to be some doubt about Hebrews, 2 Peter, 2 and 3 John, Jude, and Revelation in some of the churches.

C. Criteria for Canonization

Perhaps more important than this brief survey of canonical influences are the criteria that the early church used to identify its sacred Scriptures. It is generally recognized that the church employed several criteria, often unequally, in order to determine the status of a particular writing. There were essentially four: (1) Apostolicity. If a writing was produced by an apostle or was believed to have been produced by an apostle, then it was accepted as an authoritative word of Scripture and was eventually included in the NT.[82] (2) Orthodoxy. The church also employed what became known as a *regula fidei*, or the criterion of "orthodoxy," to determine whether writings used in the church were to be included or excluded. Bishop Serapion's rejection of the *Gospel of Peter* was based on this criterion of truth (see Eusebius, *Hist. eccl.* 6.12.1–6).[83] If a writing was too far away from what was believed to be the core or central teaching handed on in the churches through the succession of the bishops, then it was rejected (see Eusebius, *Hist. eccl.* 3.25.7). (3) Antiquity. If a writing was believed to have been written after the period of the apostolic ministry, then it was rejected. This was obviously a criterion

The Ayasofya (formerly the church of Hagia Sophia [Divine Wisdom]) in Istanbul (Byzantium/Constantinople). When built by Justinian in the sixth century, this church was the largest enclosed space in the world. It remained so for almost a thousand years and was a prominent symbol of power for the Byzantine Empire. Photo Lee M. McDonald.

for the author of the Muratorian Fragment in his rejection of the *Shepherd of Hermas* (see lines 73–74). (4) Use. What probably was most determinative was the widespread use of a writing in the churches. Eusebius mentions the books "recognized" by churches when he cites his own canon (*Hist. eccl. 3.25.4–7*). More precisely, however, it mattered to the churches who was favorable toward the acceptance of a document and who was not. Athanasius and Epiphanius, for instance, would have had a greater influence on the church than many lesser-known figures. Also, churches in the larger areas, such as Antioch, Alexandria, Rome, and Ephesus, were more likely to have a greater influence on which books were included than were the smaller churches in rural areas. Inspiration, though often assumed to be a criterion for acceptance, was in fact more of a corollary to a writing's canonicity than a criterion. In other words, if a writing was accepted as Scripture and a part of the biblical canon, it was also assumed that the writing was inspired by God. Inspiration, however, was never limited by the early church to sacred writings but was extended to what was considered true, whether it was written or taught/preached orally.

One more factor can be mentioned here that is not so much described as assumed. The writings functioning as Scripture in the worship of churches and providing for them adequate catechetical instruction were those that were adaptable for use in the life and ministries of the churches. Some writings that were considered Scripture earlier in the church's history, such as *Barnabas*, *1 Clement*, the letters of Ignatius, the *Shepherd of Hermas*, and *Eldad and Modad* (a lost apocalypse), did not survive the criterion of usefulness. They fell into disuse, and were therefore eventually dropped from the Scripture collections. This was more likely to happen before the development of the size of the codex, which by the fourth century had improved enough to be able to contain the whole of the NT writings. Even then, however, some noncanonical writings continued to appear in various NT manuscripts and in lists of the church's Scriptures (e.g., *Barnabas* and the *Shepherd of Hermas* are in Codex Sinaiticus [ℵ], and *1* and *2 Clement* are in Codex Vaticanus [B]).[84]

More fundamental than the individual traditional criteria is the question of how legitimate these criteria are. If they are the appropriate crite-

ria, should they be reapplied today with the help of the modern critical and historical disciplines with which most biblical scholars are familiar? If we did reapply them, would all of the current books of the NT make it into our NT canon? Certainly Hebrews would not survive the criterion of apostolicity, nor, in some scholars' minds, would the Pastoral Epistles, 2 Peter, and Jude. Should these books, then, be left out of our Bibles? That might be the case if the above were our only criteria. In other words, can we continue to accept as a part of our biblical canon literature that was earlier ascribed to an apostle but that we now think was not written by an apostle? This question also raises the issue of pseudepigraphy in our NT canon. Should a writing remain if the basis of its original acceptance, apostolic authorship, can be proved false? Did a writing become a part of the NT solely because of its authorship, or was it also because of its contents? Hebrews was not written by the Apostle Paul, but its contents were clearly useful to the church in spite of who wrote it, and its contents continue to be a source of enrichment to the church of today. On the other hand, what about the usefulness of the *Didache*, *1 Clement*, Ignatius, *Barnabas*, and the *Shepherd of Hermas*? Compared to books such as 2 Peter, 2 and 3 John, and Jude, are they not more useful and just as orthodox? In the case of 2 Peter and possibly the Pastorals, some noncanonical writings may be as early as, if not earlier than, these writings (e.g., *Didache*, *1 Clement*, *Barnabas*, and *Shepherd of Hermas*). The reapplication of the traditional criteria today is a very important issue in canonical discussions, and it is here that the historian and the believer often part company. The impact of a particular writing on the history of the church and its recognized value for preaching and teaching must also be considered, but this is not an easy matter to identify, and there is seldom agreement on the value of all of the NT writings adopted by the church—the book of Revelation, for instance—let alone their authorship and occasion.

D. The Muratorian Fragment: A Fourth-Century Canonical List?

One of the pivotal issues in NT canonical studies today concerns the dating and provenance of the Muratorian Fragment. In 1738–1740, Lodovico Antonio Muratori discovered and edited in the

Ambrosian Library of Milan what many canon scholars believe is one of the most important documents for establishing a late-second-century date for the formation of a NT canon. The document he found in a codex is a seventh- or eighth-century fragment of a larger document that was poorly translated into Latin from the Greek, commonly called the Muratorian Canon or Muratorian Fragment. It is usually dated ca. A.D. 180–200, but more recently some scholars have called for a fourth-century dating. The document lists twenty-two NT writings, including Wisdom of Solomon (lines 69–70) and tentatively the *Apocalypse of Peter* (lines 71–72). Hebrews, James, one of the epistles of John, and 1 and 2 Peter are missing. The fragment consists of some eighty-five lines and is missing both the opening and concluding lines. Optimistically, the Muratorian Fragment has been hailed as "the oldest extant list of sacred books of the NT,"[85] and most scholars believe that it was written in Rome or in its vicinity.[86] For von Campenhausen, a second-century dating of the Muratorian Fragment originating from the west supported his view that the NT canon was largely formed in a polemic against the Montanists at the end of the second century.[87] A significant problem in dating the Muratorian Fragment to the second century is its lack of parallels and lack of any impact upon the church for more than 150 years.[88] Indeed, until the middle of the fourth century, there are no parallels to it in either the eastern or the western churches, and the most impressive parallels then come from the east, not the west.

In 1973, Sundberg made the first major challenge to the traditional dating and provenance of the Muratorian Fragment, and has been joined more recently by Hahneman, who has significantly advanced Sundberg's thesis.[89] They both argue for a fourth-century dating of the Muratorian Fragment and for an eastern origin. If this view is correct, it helps us to understand why Eusebius was still hedging about the scope of his canon in the first quarter of the fourth century. For example, Kalin and Robbins have reasonably argued that Eusebius himself rejected, or at least did not endorse, the so-called disputed books—James, Jude, 2 Peter, 2 and 3 John, and possibly Revelation and Hebrews.[90] Why would Eusebius have raised a question about some of these books if the matter had been settled for the church in the second century,

as a second-century dating of the Muratorian Fragment suggests, especially in regard to Jude, 2 and/or 3 John, and Revelation (*Hist. eccl.* 3.25.2, 4)? The growth and development of the biblical canon in the fourth century are seen in the fact that the three categories in Eusebius (recognized, disputed, and spurious) fade away by the end of the fourth century and only the recognized writings are included while the rejected writings are excluded. There is no disputed category by that time, and this is what we find in the Muratorian Fragment.

The reference to the General Epistles (lines 68–69) and the Pastoral Epistles (lines 59–60) in the Muratorian Fragment is unusual, since there is little evidence to show that they were either cited as Scripture or widely received as such in the late second century by the church. There are very few clear references to this literature in the second century, although, with Tertullian in the third century, there are several clear citations of Paul, including the Pastoral Epistles.[91]

More telling than this is the strange reference in the Muratorian Fragment (lines 69–70) to Wisdom of Solomon, an OT apocryphal writing, among the list of NT books. This is highly unusual and has its only parallels in the fourth century, in the east, in the writings of Eusebius, where he discusses Irenaeus's canon, which included, along with Wisdom, the *Shepherd of Hermas* (*Hist. eccl.* 5.8.1–8), and in Epiphanius, *Pan.* 76 (ca. 375–400), who added both Wisdom and ben Sira to his NT list. On the other hand, Melito, in the second century, includes Wisdom of Solomon in an OT list (*Hist. eccl.* 4.26.14). Wisdom of Solomon had more popularity in the east than in the west, though the document was referred to by western writers as well (Heb 1:3 citing Wis 7:25; *1 Clem.* 3.4; 7.5; 27.5; Tertullian, *Prescr.* 7; *Ag. Val.* 2).[92] The significance of this may be that the reference in the Muratorian Fragment also comes from the fourth century or later and from the east.[93] Although Wisdom of Solomon was excluded from OT lists in the fourth century, it was sometimes included in NT Scriptures or accepted as a secondary reading, as in Eusebius, Athanasius, Epiphanius, and Rufinus (*Symb.* 38).

The most common argument for a second-century dating of the Muratorian Fragment and its western provenance concerns the reference to the rejection of the *Shepherd of Hermas*, because it was written "quite lately [very recently] in our time"

(Lat. *vero nuperrime temporibus nostris*; lines 73–74).[94] Hermas lived and flourished roughly A.D. 100–145 and therefore was not from the apostolic era. The author of the Muratorian Fragment evidently separated the apostolic times from all other times. The statement that Pius, the brother of Hermas, was currently the bishop of Rome (line 73), suggests that "our time" is a reference to the second century and no later than A.D. 200,[95] but more likely A.D. 140–150. Hahneman, following Sundberg, claims that the words "quite lately in our time" most plainly mean that the *Shepherd of Hermas* was during the time of Pius's episcopacy (ca. A.D. 140–154?) and so the writing of the Muratorian Fragment came shortly after that. Sundberg, however, argues that the words, instead of referring to the lifetime of the composer of the fragment—namely, "within our lifetime"—simply express how the ancient churches distinguished the apostolic times from their own. "Our times," he concludes, is a reference to the postapostolic era, as opposed to the times of the apostles themselves (e.g., Ign. *Eph.* 3.2; Pol. *Phil.* 9.1, and especially Eusebius, *Hist. eccl.* 3.31.6). He gives several examples of this practice, including one from Irenaeus, who uses "our times" (*temporibus nostris*) of an event nearly a hundred years before him (the end of the reign of Domitian).[96] The problem with dating the Muratorian Fragment this early in the second century is that, at that time, there are even fewer parallels acknowledging Christian writings as Scripture, let alone as part of a fixed canon. The NT writings, of course, had to be called Scripture before they could be called canon, and they were only beginning to be called Scripture in the second century.[97] Ferguson grants the possibility that "in our times" could refer to anytime after the apostolic times, but he still says that it is compatible with a second-century dating of the document, claiming that "in our times" was not the usual way of distinguishing those times.[98]

It may be that the *Shepherd of Hermas* was written in the early part of the second century, as its widespread use in the latter part of that century is well known. The recognition and acceptance of the *Shepherd* continued up to the fourth century, even in the west. In the late second century, Irenaeus, for instance, calls the *Shepherd* "Scripture" (ἡ γραφή, *hē graphē*) (*Haer.* 4.20.2). Eusebius also knew of this reference and acknowledged Irenaeus's reception of the *Shepherd* (*Hist. eccl.* 5.8.7–8). This recognition

also came from Clement of Alexandria (*Misc.* 1.1.1, 1.85.4, and frequently; *Extracts* 45), who frequently quoted the *Shepherd* as if he was quoting other Scriptures from both the OT and the NT. According to Eusebius, Origen likewise included this work in his sacred collection (*Hist. eccl.* 6.25.10). It is also listed in Codex Sinaiticus (‭א‬) and Codex Claromontanus (D^p) even though, in the latter case, in a secondary position. Eusebius appears to be the first to place the *Shepherd* in a disputed category (*Hist. eccl.* 3.3.6), but he still recognized that many held it in high esteem (5.8.7). Later, Eusebius himself placed the book among the spurious (3.25.1–5). Athanasius called the book "most edifying" (ὠφελιμωτάτης, *ōphelimōtatēs*) in his *De incarnatione Verbi Dei* (ca. A.D. 318 or 328), but his famous *Festal Letter* 39 (A.D. 367) lists it not as part of the New Testament but as recommended reading for new Christians. Both Jerome and Rufinus also speak respectfully of the book, even though they place it in a secondary position, that is, not as a part of the NT canon.[99] Our point here is that the rejection of the *Shepherd of Hermas* seems much more at home in the fourth century and following than it does in the second century, where it was considered Scripture by the Fathers at the end of that century.

Further possible evidence of the Muratorian Fragment's later date is the listing of the four canonical Gospels without any defense, such as we find earlier in Irenaeus, and without reference to any rivals. This is evidence of their fixed status in the church and an argument against a second-century dating of the fragment. The closest contemporary writer from the west in the last quarter of the second century is Irenaeus, whose strange way of arguing for the four canonical Gospels suggests, as we have noted above, that not everyone in the second century was as convinced about their canonicity as he was (*Haer.* 3.11.8–9). On the other hand, Tatian's use in Asia of more than the four canonical Gospels in his *Diatessaron* and his preference for the Gospel of John would seem to show that not all of Irenaeus's contemporaries agreed that the Gospels should be limited to the four canonical Gospels, at least not as rigidly as Irenaeus proposed. Even if it was some of Tatian's followers who later inserted clauses from the *Gospel of the Hebrews* and from the *Protevangelium of James* into the *Diatessaron*, as seems likely, one still cannot find in Tatian the loyalty to the "inspired text" that one can find in possibly Rev 22:18–19, or in Irenaeus's defense of the four-Gospel canon. From the fragment of the *Diatessaron* that has survived, it is clear that much of the context, especially from the Synoptic Gospels, is omitted. Does this mean that the full canonical and "inspired" status of the four Gospels was not yet fully recognized by Tatian and by many of his other contemporaries? No doubt he saw them as responsible and faithful documents, but perhaps not as inviolable texts. Although it can be argued that Irenaeus's canon of Gospels was not universally accepted in his day—hence Irenaeus's need to provide a defense of the four—the same cannot be said about the Muratorian Fragment, in which the acceptance of four canonical Gospels is assumed without debate. As late as the early third century, Tertullian, who accepted the four canonical Gospels, still made a distinction between them, preferring Matthew and John over Mark and Luke because of the issue of apostolic authorship (*Ag. Marc.* 4.2.5). None of this ambiguity or division is reflected in the Muratorian Fragment, which suggests that it was produced at a later date, when such matters were largely settled in the church—namely, in the fourth century.

On the whole, since there are apparently no parallels to the Muratorian Fragment until after the time of Eusebius and from the east, the document arguably should be dated after the mid–fourth century, with its provenance in the east, though we cannot insist on the location.[100] The Muratorian Fragment is an important document for our understanding of the growth and development of the NT canon, but it is not as pivotal as many scholars have supposed. It seems to fit with the fifteen other canonical lists from the fourth and early fifth centuries, even though it is not identical to any of them. Ferguson has argued that the form of the Muratorian Fragment, unlike the lists of books without comment in the fourth century, shows that the Muratorian Fragment is out of step with the fourth-century canonical lists.[101] Although he correctly observes that no exact fourth-century parallels to the Muratorian Fragment exist, a factor that is true in regard to several lists, there are close enough parallels with Eusebius (*Hist. eccl.* 3.25). He lists his Scriptures with comment—not in a simple list—and his list is also without exact parallel in contents from the fourth century. There are no second-century parallels in form or style, but there are

several fourth-century parallels (see Eusebius's descriptions [*Hist. eccl.* 5.8.1–9; 6.25.3–14] of Irenaeus's and Origen's canons, which are similar in style to the Muratorian Fragment). The fourth century appears, then, to be the time when the Muratorian Fragment is most at home, and the only time it is comparable to any other lists. When Ferguson argues that the list would be strange in the fourth century because it attacks second-century heresies, we would agree, but we would add that this is precisely what Eusebius also does when he attacks the teachings of the Marcionites, gnostics, and Montanists, all second- and third-century heresies, in the fourth century. The closure or fixing of the NT canon is more at home in the fourth century, even though the process of canonization may have begun with the recognition and use of Christian literature as Scripture as early as the second century.

5. CONCLUSIONS ABOUT THE OLD AND NEW TESTAMENTS

There are a number of unresolved questions about how the biblical canon was formed, when it was formed, what factors led to its formation, and how to account for the divergencies within it. For those who are uncomfortable with "loose ends" here and there, especially the lack of a sharp definition where one might prefer precision, there may be a problem in accepting the current biblical canon. For those who can only accept a neatly designed collection of Scriptures that resulted from the application of clearly and widely accepted criteria that were evenly applied, disappointment will surely be their lot, or they will spend more than a considerable amount of time defending the canon in ways that it cannot be defended. There is a diversity throughout the biblical canon that defies any cleverly devised harmonizations. The traditional criteria do not account for everything in our Bible, and the care with which the ancient criteria were applied by the church is, in several instances, highly questionable. The formation of the NT was a long and arduous process that refuses simple explanations, but it is nevertheless clear that most of the Christian writers of the second century and following believed that their faith was identified and defined by the Gospels, Paul, and their OT Scriptures, which were larger in scope than the current

Protestant OT. Nevertheless, we are hard pressed to explain how a number of other writings were included in the NT (esp. 2 Peter, 2 and 3 John, and Jude). The church eventually agreed that these writings also clarified its identity in ways that are often not apparent to us today.

While such diversity is found in the biblical canon, it is clear that there were limits to the kind of diversity that was acceptable in the ancient church. The gnostics and Marcionites were not acceptable, nor were the Montanists, the Ebionites, or the Elkesaites. Eventually all of the Pseudepigrapha were excluded. The final determination was made for the Roman Catholics by a split vote at the Council of Trent (1545–1563) and for the Protestants during the Reformation, when the Apocrypha were also excluded.[102] Both the diversity in the specifics of the biblical canon and the broad general agreement that resulted in the churches are difficult to explain.[103] It is also surprising that the early Christians did not always insist on harmonizations of the sometimes divergent texts, as many Christians do today,[104] and we do the early church a disservice when we think that they might not have known of these differences, especially in the canonical Gospels. Why did they prefer the four Gospels over Tatian's *Diatessaron?* Regardless of their motive for opting for four distinct Gospel testimonies instead of one harmonious text, how can we today take seriously a biblical canon that has so much diversity in it? Is this not the root of much of the diversity within the church? Is it more appropriate to try to reconcile all the divergent texts, as some Christians are prone to do, or can we find a way to listen to their individual messages?

What are we to do with those texts that no longer seem relevant to the Christian community? Do we have the same right as the early church to reject that which we believe is no longer useful? Even though many have rejected in principle the notion of a canon within the canon, we nevertheless often function as if we had a more restricted biblical canon. In many seminaries, for example, priority is given to the Gospels and Paul over the General Epistles and Revelation. Indeed, students may go all the way through seminary without exposure to the so-called fringe books in our biblical canon.

The church has always depended on Jesus' teachings and the events that were pivotal in his life, namely, his death and resurrection, in order to guide it in its deliberations and mission. Writings that it believed most capably told the story of Jesus and his mission or predicted his coming and ministry (the OT) were at the center of its scriptural canon. In this sense, Jesus was always the canon of the church, long before there was an acknowledged scriptural canon to give it guidance. In the process of determining what literature best reflected the church's Lord as well as its true identity and mission, many writings that were appealed to as Scripture or authoritative sacred writings early in the church's history did not later obtain a position in our biblical canons (e.g., *Eldad and Modad, 2 Esdras, 1 Clement, Shepherd of Hermas, Barnabas*). We are always hard pressed to answer why some documents were included in our Bible and why other books were not. In some cases, the answer is obvious, but in others we are uncertain.

For those who do not require twentieth-century standards of precision in their Bibles and who appreciate the human element in the production of both the scriptural writings and their later collection, loose ends here and there do not pose so great a problem, especially when we look at the whole of the Scripture and use it in our worship and ministry without getting lost in its details or others' forced harmonizations. The resilience and adaptability of the church's Scriptures throughout history have demonstrated to the church the presence and activity of God at work in them. In one's humanness it is tempting to ignore or to excise those portions of the Bible that are embarrassing, but when one listens carefully to those texts, frequently even they can challenge an individual to a new understanding of faith and of obedience to the call of God. This is seldom possible for those who insist on a tidy biblical canon. For those who require that all of the ambiguities of faith be resolved before they can make free use of the church's Scriptures, the biblical canon will continue to be an enigma that will lead either to its rejection or to untenable hypotheses for reconciliation. On the other hand, for those who understand the Bible as the word of God, careful canonical inquiry will not remove the need for faith, nor will it remove the need for careful biblical study. Although faith cannot set aside the results of a reasonable historical inquiry into the origins of the Bible, it need not be displaced by such an inquiry either.[105]

BIBLIOGRAPHY

ACKROYD, P. R., and C. F. EVANS, eds. *The Cambridge History of the Bible.* 3 vols. Cambridge: Cambridge University Press, 1963–1970.

ALAND, K. *The Problem of the New Testament Canon.* Oxford: Mowbray, 1962.

ATTRIDGE, H. W., ed. *The Formation of the New Testament Canon.* New York: Paulist, 1983.

BARR, J. *Holy Scripture: Canon, Authority, Criticism.* Philadelphia: Westminster, 1983.

BARTHÉLEMY, D. "La critique canonique." *Revue de l'Institut catholique de Paris* 36 (1991): 191–220.

BECKWITH, R. T. *The Old Testament Canon of the New Testament Church.* Grand Rapids: Eerdmans, 1985.

BRUCE, F. F. *The Canon of Scripture.* Downers Grove, Ill.: InterVarsity, 1988.

CAMPENHAUSEN, H. von. *The Formation of the Christian Bible.* Trans. J. A. BAKER. Philadelphia: Fortress, 1972.

CHILDS, B. S. *Biblical Theology of the Old and New Testaments: Theological Reflection on the Christian Bible.* Minneapolis: Fortress, 1993.

_____. *The New Testament as Canon: An Introduction.* Philadelphia: Fortress, 1985.

ELLIS, E. E. *The Old Testament in Early Christianity: Canon and Interpretation in Light of Modern Research.* Grand Rapids: Baker, 1992.

EPP, E. J., and G. W. MacRAE, eds. *The New Testament and Its Modern Interpreters.* Atlanta: Scholars Press, 1989.

FARMER, W. R. *Jesus and the Gospel: Tradition, Scripture, and Canon.* Philadelphia: Fortress, 1982.

FARMER, W. R., and D. M. FARKASFALVY. *The Formation of the New Testament Canon.* New York: Paulist, 1983.

FELDMAN, L. H., and G. HATA, eds. *Josephus, the Bible, and History.* Detroit: Wayne State University Press, 1989.

FERGUSON, E. "Canon Muratori: Date and Provenance." Pages 677–83 in *Studia Patristica.* StPatr 17. Leuven: Peeters, 1982.

_____. Review of G. M. HAHNEMAN, *The Muratorian Fragment and the Development of the Canon.* JTS 44 (1993): 691–97.

_____, ed. *Encyclopedia of Early Christianity.* New York: Garland, 1990.

FREEDMAN, D. N. "The Symmetry of the Hebrew Bible." *StTh* 46 (1992): 83–108.

_____. *The Unity of the Hebrew Bible.* Ann Arbor: University of Michigan Press, 1991.

GAMBLE, H. Y. *The New Testament Canon: Its Making and Meaning.* GBS. Philadelphia: Fortress, 1985.

GRANT, R. M. *The Formation of the New Testament.* New York: Harper & Row, 1965.

HAHNEMAN, G. M. *The Muratorian Fragment and the Development of the Canon.* OTM. Oxford: Clarendon, 1992.

HAWTHORNE, G. F., and R. P. MARTIN, eds. *Dictionary of Paul and His Letters.* Downers Grove, Ill.: InterVarsity, 1993.

KALIN, E. R. "Re-examining New Testament Canon History: 1. The Canon of Origen." *CTM* 17 (1990): 274–82.

KÄSEMANN, E. *Essays on New Testament Themes.* London: SCM, 1968.

KLASSEN, W., and G. F. Snyder, eds. *Current Issues in New Testament Interpretation: Essays in Honor of Otto A. Piper.* New York: Harper & Brothers, 1962.

KOESTER, H. "Apocryphal and Canonical Gospels." *HTR* 73 (1980): 105–30.

_____. "Writings and the Spirit: Authority and Politics in Ancient Christianity." *HTR* 84 (1991): 353–72.

KRAEMER, D. "The Formation of the Rabbinic Canon: Authority and Boundaries." *JBL* 110 (1991): 613–30.

LAYMON, C. M., ed. *The Interpreter's One-Volume Commentary on the Bible.* New York: Abingdon, 1971.

LEIMAN, S. Z. *The Canon and Masorah of the Hebrew Bible: An Introductory Reader.* New York: Ktav, 1974.

_____. *The Canonization of the Hebrew Scripture: The Talmudic and Midrashic Evidence.* Hamden, Conn.: Archon, 1976.

LEWIS, J. P. "What Do We Mean by Jabneh?" *JBR* 32 (1964): 125–32.

LIGHTSTONE, J. N. "The Formation of the Biblical Canon in Judaism of Late Antiquity: Prolegomenon to a General Reassessment." *SR* 8 (1979): 135–42.

McDONALD, L. M. *The Formation of the Christian Biblical Canon.* 2d ed. Peabody, Mass.: Hendrickson, 1995.

_____. "The Origins of the Christian Biblical Canon." *BBR* 6 (1996): 95–132.

METZGER, B. M. *The Canon of the New Testament: Its Origin, Development, and Significance.* Oxford: Clarendon, 1987.

MEUER, S., ed. *The Apocrypha in Ecumenical Perspective.* Trans. P. ELLINGWORTH. UBS Monograph Series 6. New York: United Bible Societies, 1991.

MILLER, J. W. *The Origins of the Bible: Rethinking Canon History.* New York: Paulist, 1994.

MULDER, M. J., and H. SYSLING, eds. *Mikra: Text, Translation, Reading, and Interpretation of the Hebrew Bible in Ancient Judaism and Early Christianity.* Minneapolis: Fortress, 1990.

NEUSNER, J., with W. S. GREEN. *Writing with Scripture: The Authority and Uses of the Hebrew Bible in the Torah of Formative Judaism.* Minneapolis: Fortress, 1989.

PATZIA, A. G. *The Making of the New Testament: Origin, Collection and Canon.* Downers Grove, Ill.: InterVarsity, 1995.

REUSS, E. W. *History of the Canon of the Holy Scriptures in the Christian Church.* Trans. D. HUNTER. Edinburgh: R. W. Hunter, 1891.

ROBERTS, C. H. "The Christian Book and the Greek Papyri." *JTS* 50 (1949): 155–68.

RYLE, H. E. *The Canon of the Old Testament.* London: Macmillan, 1914.

SANDERS, J. A. "Cave 11 Surprises and the Question of Canon." *McCQ* 21 (1968): 284–317.

_____. *From Sacred Story to Sacred Text.* Philadelphia: Fortress, 1987.

SILVER, D. J. *The Story of Scripture: From Oral Tradition to the Written Word.* New York: Basic Books, 1990.

SUNDBERG, A. C., Jr. "Canon Muratori: A Fourth-Century List." *HTR* 66 (1973): 1–41.

_____. "The Old Testament: A Christian Canon." *CBQ* 30 (1968): 403–9.

_____. *The Old Testament of the Early Church.* Cambridge: Harvard University Press, 1964.

VANDERKAM, J. C., and J. T. MILIK. "The First *Jubilees* Manuscript from Qumran Cave 4: A Preliminary Publication." *JBL* 110 (1991): 243–70.

pages 600–603

1. Most of the information in this chapter is found in much more detail in L. M. McDonald, *The Formation of the Christian Biblical Canon* (Peabody, Mass.: Hendrickson, 1995). Some modified sections of what follows are in L. M. McDonald, "The Origins of the Christian Biblical Canon," *BBR* 6 (1996): 95–132.

2. There has never been complete agreement in the church at large on the scope of its sacred literature, however. The three most common Bibles are those of the Roman Catholic, the Greek Orthodox, and the Protestant churches. While there is considerable overlap, these Bibles differ in what is included and excluded (see below).

3. G. Schrenk, "γραφή," *TDNT* 1:744–56. The secondary text of John 7:53–8:11, even if genuine, would hardly qualify as a written document. The only NT exception is found in the book of Revelation, where the risen Christ commands the angels of the churches to put his message in written form (Rev 2:1–3:14).

4. See H. W. Beyer, "κανών," *TDNT* 3:596–602. An excellent treatment of the term is found in B. M. Metzger, *The Canon of the New Testament: Its Origin, Development, and Significance* (Oxford: Clarendon, 1987), 289–93.

5. J. A. Sanders, *From Sacred Story to Sacred Text* (Philadelphia: Fortress, 1987), 9–39, esp. 23–30.

6. G. T. Sheppard, "Canon," in *The Encyclopedia of Religion* (ed. M. Eliade; 16 vols.; New York: Macmillan, 1987), 3:62–69. The distinction of two kinds of canon, however, stems from the work of J. A. Sanders, "Canon," *ABD* 1:837–52, here 839.

7. It is difficult to establish the date of origin for the *Letter of Aristeas* with any precision. The latest possible date is A.D. 35, since it was referred to by Philo (*Moses* 2.25–44). But a date before the invasion of Egypt by Antiochus IV Epiphanes in 169 B.C. is preferable on the basis of internal evidence. See S. Jellicoe, *The Septuagint and Modern Study* (Oxford: Clarendon, 1968), 29–58.

8. J. Barr (*Holy Scripture: Canon, Authority, Criticism* [Philadelphia: Westminster, 1983], 6–8) argues that in the earlier stages of Israel's monarchy its religion was not yet the scriptural religion that it later became. It is also probable that only the Deuteronomic code is behind the reforms of Josiah.

9. H. M. Orlinsky, "Some Terms in the Prologue to Ben Sira and the Hebrew Canon," *JBL* 110 (1991): 483–90, here 487.

10. Sirach shows awareness of the books of Joshua (Sir 46:1–6), Samuel (46:13–47:11), and Kings (47:12–49:3), including important persons who are highlighted in them, namely, David and Solomon, and mentions Hezekiah and Isaiah (48:20–25), Josiah (49:1–4), Jeremiah (49:6), Ezekiel, Job, and the Twelve Prophets (49:9–10). This suggests that the twelve Minor Prophets were already circulating in one volume in Israel by this time (200–180 B.C.).

11. It is tempting to assume that they were the same as the third part of the twenty-two books that Josephus describes in *Ag. Ap.* 1.37–43 (see sec. B, below), or perhaps like those in the second-century A.D. *bar. b. B. Bat.* 14b (see sec. C, below). It may also be that the "other books" were something like the "seventy" books in 2 Esd 14:44–48 (see sec. C, below), but we do not know for sure.

12. Trans. C. D. Yonge, *The Works of Philo* (Peabody, Mass.: Hendrickson, 1993), 700.

13. Italics added. Trans. B. W. W. Dombrowski, *An Annotated Translation of Miqsat Ma'seh ha-Torah (4QMMT)* (Cracow: Enigma, 1993), 13–14.

Because of the poor condition of the text, several words have to be supposed. Nevertheless, the above translation is not unreasonable.

14. W. W. Klein et al. (*Introduction to Biblical Interpretation* [Dallas: Word, 1993], 57) point out that all of the books of the OT except Esther were found at Qumran and only one book of the Apocrypha (Tobit) was found there. This is not a complete picture, however, since other documents were also found at or near Qumran: the *Damascus Document* (CD), *Manual of Discipline* (1QS), *Rule of the Congregation* (1QSa), *Blessings* (1QSb), *War Scroll* (1QM and a number of fragments from Cave 4 and Cave 11), *Hodayot (Thanksgiving Hymns)* (1QH), *Genesis Apocryphon* (1QapGen), and *Temple Scroll* (11QTemple). Besides these, portions of Sirach, Epistle of Jeremiah, *Jubilees, Enoch,* and *Testaments of the Twelve Patriarchs* were also found at Qumran. How can one with any assurance say what the limits of Qumran's canon were? J. Neusner (*Midrash in Context: Exegesis in Formative Judaism* [Philadelphia: Fortress, 1983], 6), speaking of the other writings found at Qumran, observes that "those documents at Qumran appear side by side with the ones we know as canonical Scripture. The high probability is that, to the Essenes, the sectarian books were no less holy and authoritative than Leviticus, Deuteronomy, Nahum, Habakkuk, Isaiah, and the other books of the biblical canon they, among all Israelites, revered."

page 604

15. See R. T. Beckwith, *The Old Testament Canon of the New Testament Church* (Grand Rapids: Eerdmans, 1985), 438, also 111–14, who cites *Seper Torah* 2.3–4 and *Sop.* 2.4.

16. Beckwith (*Old Testament Canon,* 114–15; cf. 118–20) reasons that since Jesus also cited the book of Daniel (see, e.g., Dan 4:26 in Matt 4:17 and Dan 7:13 in Mark 14:62), which was a part of the Hagiographa, he must have intended the whole of the Hagiographa when he mentioned the "psalms" in this passage. See also F. F. Bruce, *The Canon of Scripture* (Downers Grove, Ill.: InterVarsity, 1988), 31, who agrees with him.

17. Bruce (*Canon,* 31) believes that he can detect the order of the Hebrew biblical canon from Luke 11:49–51, where Jesus spoke of the first prophet (Abel) and the last prophet (Zechariah) to be killed. Zechariah (ca. 800 B.C.; cf. 2 Chron 24:20–24) was the last canonical prophet to be killed, since Zechariah was the last prophet to die in 2 Chronicles, the last book in the Hebrew Scriptures. Bruce contends that Jesus' words in Luke 11:49–51 were intended by him to cover the whole of the Hebrew Scriptures from Genesis to 2 Chronicles. Beckwith (*Old Testament Canon,* 170 n. 29), however, acknowledges that Jerome's canon does not conclude with Chronicles and that he has only a twenty-two book canon. The most commonly cited Hebrew text today, the Aleppo text from which our current Masoretic Text is taken, places Chronicles at the *beginning* of the third division and Ezra–Nehemiah at the end. The concluding sentences of 2 Chron 34 are the same as the opening sentences Ezra 1. It would appear that the writer/editor of this collection of sacred books at least wanted to have Chronicles in first place and Ezra–Nehemiah in last place. Jerome's reference to the OT in the fifth century preserves the threefold division of the Hebrew Bible, but he has Job in first place in the third category and Chronicles in seventh place followed by Esdras (Ezra–Nehemiah), concluding with Esther. Although *bar. b. B. Bat.* 14b has Chronicles at the end of the collection, Ruth stands at the beginning, not the Psalms.

18. Orlinsky ("Some Terms," 490) stresses that the Alexandrian Jewish community, where Philo lived and wrote his *On the Contemplative Life* and to which the grandson of Sirach addressed the prologue to Sirach, produced the LXX but never had a clearly defined tripartite biblical canon.

19. E. E. Ellis, *The Old Testament in Early Christianity: Canon and Interpretation in Light of Modern Research* (Grand Rapids: Baker, 1992), 39; cf. 7–8. See also Bruce, *Canon*, 23, 32–34; and R. T. Beckwith, "Formation of the Hebrew Bible," in *Mikra: Text, Translation, Reading, and Interpretation of the Hebrew Bible in Ancient Judaism and Early Christianity* (ed. M. J. Mulder and H. Sysling; Minneapolis: Fortress, 1985), 50, who, acknowledging that there may be some exaggeration by Josephus in his account, dismisses the notion that Josephus may have misrepresented the actual state of affairs at the end of the first century A.D.; Beckwith also contends that Josephus reflects a long-standing tradition regarding the biblical canon within the Jewish community.

20. S. Z. Leiman, "Josephus and the Canon of the Bible," in *Josephus, the Bible, and History* (ed. L. Feldman and G. Hata; Detroit: Wayne State University Press, 1989), 51–53; quotation, p. 52. He notes that Maimonides (d. 1204) and Joseph Albo (15th cent.) have similar statements in an apologetic context.

21. L. Feldman, introduction, ibid., 3–47, here 46–47.

22. D. J. Silver, *The Story of Scripture: From Oral Tradition to the Written Word* (New York: Basic Books, 1990), 134; 2 Esd 14:44–48 is one such example.

23. See Leiman, "Josephus," 51.

24. Ibid., 54.

25. Ellis, *Old Testament in Early Christianity*, 10, 33; Beckwith, *Old Testament Canon*, 235–40.

26. Epiphanius (*Mens. et pond.* 22) mentions the twenty-two-book tradition in Israel. The early-ninth-century George Syncellus text is similar. It is not clear whether there was some relationship between these two texts. For a careful discussion of this passage and others in *Jubilees*, see J. C. VanderKam and J. T. Milik, "The First *Jubilees* Manuscript from Qumran Cave 4: A Preliminary Publication," *JBL* 110 (1991): 243–70, here 259–60 and 267–68. The Qumran form of this text does not include the twenty-two books.

27. For example, Origen referred to it, according to Eusebius, *Hist. eccl.* 6.26.1, 2. If the tradition were a late-first-century invention, it is easy to see how a reference to it by Josephus would impact Christian writers of the fourth century who had high respect for Josephus and continued to publish his works.

28. See Ellis, *Old Testament in Early Christianity*, 36; W. S. Lasor, R. Hubbard, and W. Bush, *Old Testament Survey* (Grand Rapids: Eerdmans, 1983), 17.

29. Metzger, *Canon*, 159. Metzger has observed that Tertullian (*Apparel* 1.3) cites Jude 14 to support the authority of Enoch!

30. D. N. Freedman ("The Earliest Bible," in *Backgrounds for the Bible* [ed. M. P. O'Connor and D. N. Freedman; Winona Lake, Ind.: Eisenbrauns, 1987], 29–37; "The Symmetry of the Hebrew Bible," *StTh* 46 [1992]: 83–108) argues that the OT was essentially complete by the early part of the fourth century B.C., which he bases on an elaborate symmetry of the Hebrew Bible. He argues that finalization of the Hebrew Scriptures, except for the book of Daniel, took place no later than between 400 and 350 B.C. but that the Law and the Former

pages 604–606

Prophets (Joshua–Kings) were completed in Babylon before the return of the Jews from exile in 538 B.C.

31. H. E. Ryle, *The Canon of the Old Testament* (London: Macmillan, 1914). Although this view may have originated with several earlier German scholars, it was apparently made popular by Ryle. See D. E. Aune, "On the Origins of the 'Council of Javneh' Myth," *JBL* 110 (1991): 483–90.

32. S. V. Leiman, *The Canonization of the Hebrew Scripture: The Talmudic and Midrashic Evidence* (Hamden, Conn.: Archon, 1976), 29. See also Beckwith, "Formation," 56–58.

33. These are listed in McDonald, *Formation*, 259–73.

34. Klein et al. (*Introduction to Biblical Interpretation*, 55) make this suggestion to account for the early church's use of the apocryphal literature.

35. For example, he cites Daniel in a Scripture-like manner in Matt 24:15. We disagree with the arguments that Jesus never made this statement, but this cannot be debated here. That Jesus held to an apocalyptic worldview is well established, and the reference in this passage illustrates the point made above, at least for the canon of the author of Matthew.

36. See Beckwith, "Formation," 58–60, who acknowledges this point, but argues that the disputes were among a minority of Jews when the majority had already accepted the contents of the Hebrew Bible as we have it today.

pages 606–608

37. For discussion, see D. Kraemer, "The Formation of the Rabbinic Canon: Authority and Boundaries," *JBL* 110 (1991): 613–30; J. Neusner, *Midrash in Context*, 135–36; idem, *Judaism and Christianity in the Age of Constantine: History, Messiah, Israel, and the Initial Confrontation* (Chicago: University of Chicago Press, 1987), 128–43; J. Neusner with W. S. Green, *Writing with Scripture: The Authority and Uses of the Hebrew Bible in the Torah of Formative Judaism* (Minneapolis: Fortress, 1989).

38. *m. Yad.* 3:4–5 hardly qualifies as a significant debate or inquiry into the issue, and at any rate it does not address all divisions or books of the Hebrew Bible but only whether the Song of Songs and Ecclesiastes (Qoheleth) "defile the hands" (or are sacred Scripture).

39. Neusner with Green, *Writing with Scripture*, 1–2.

40. Neusner, *Midrash in Context*, 135ff.

41. Kraemer ("Formation of the Rabbinic Canon," 626) disagrees with Neusner's view that there was no qualitative difference between the Hebrew Scriptures and the Talmudim, since both of the Talmudim "often seek to justify rabbinic traditions by reference to scriptural proof. Why do so if what is scriptural is not distinct and authoritatively superior?"

42. The meaning of this term is somewhat obscure, but apparently it refers to the fact that the books were considered holy. To touch them, according to D. J. Silver (*A History of Judaism: From Abraham to Maimonides* [2 vols.; New York: Basic Books, 1974], 1:217–18), was to "receive their holiness into one's hands and to accept a ritual obligation to wash off this holy residue before engaging in any mundane task. In this ceremonial way the divine inspiration of these books was made clear for all to see." See also *m. Yad.* 3:2–5 and 4:6 for a discussion of the term in the Mishnah.

43. This observation comes from M. Bar-Ilan, "Scribes and Books in the Late Second Commonwealth and Rabbinic Period," in *Mikra* (ed. Mulder and Sysling), 28, who cites several examples of the secular-

ization of the scribal profession. Since all scribal writing was held to be sacred, so he claims, there was a prohibition against writing down prayers, oral traditions, and legends until the third century A.D. When the prohibition ceased, the need was to distinguish between what was and what was not sacred.

44. The shift in the meaning of Torah from a scroll of the Pentateuch to all that the sages had to say about the Torah began during this time as well. By the fourth century the notion was complete that the Torah was twofold when given to Moses: what was written and what was oral or committed to memory. This change is significant, since it effectively and considerably expanded the Hebrew canon of authoritative writings.

45. For a discussion, see G. A. Robbins, "Eusebius' Lexicon of 'Canonicity,'" in *Studia Patristica* (StPatr 25; Leuven: Peeters; 1993), 134–41.

46. For examples of this, see E. Oikonomos, "The Significance of the Deuterocanonical Writings in the Orthodox Church," in *The Apocrypha in Ecumenical Perspective* (ed. S. Meurer; UBS Monograph Series 6; New York: United Bible Societies, 1991), 16–32, esp. 18–23.

47. Metzger, *Canon*, 72.

48. Bruce, *Canon*, 40, who concludes, "It is probable, indeed, that by the beginning of the Christian era the Essenes (including the Qumran community) were in substantial agreement with the Pharisees and the Sadducees about the limits of Hebrew scripture." See also Beckwith, *Old Testament Canon*, 86–93, for a similar view.

pages 608–612

49. See J. A. Sanders, "Spinning the Bible," *Brev* 14 (June 1998), 22–29, 44-45, who describes the importance of differences in the Jewish and Christian collections of Scriptures. These differences are often overlooked and their significance ignored in studies of canon formation.

50. This table is a modified form of the one found in ibid., 26. It should be noted that not all manuscript traditions in the Hebrew Bible follow this order (e.g., the Leningrad Codex).

51. The writer of 2 Pet 3:15–16 appears to recognize Paul's writings as Scripture, but this passage does not indicate what the "other scriptures" were (OT or NT), nor does this take away from the point that the writers of the NT were not consciously aware that they were writing sacred Scripture.

52. There are several examples where some of the NT writings were called or equated with Scripture in the early second century. These are summarized in Metzger, *Canon*, 39–73; and McDonald, *Formation*, 142–54. But this was not usually the case in the Apostolic Fathers.

53. See, e.g., *1 Clem.* 13.1–4; 46.7–8. Clement employs the writings of Paul to argue his points in *1 Clement*, and so do Ignatius (*Eph.* 5.2; 8.2; etc.) and the author of the *Didache* (5.1–2; 9.5; 10.6). They do not call these writings "Scripture," but they use them to establish their points, showing that the writings functioned authoritatively in Christian communities.

54. Bruce, *Canon*, 146–49. Bruce's point—that Marcion was not the first to circulate a collection of Christian writings—is well taken.

55. A. Harnack, *Marcion: Das Evangelium vom fremden Gott* (TU 45; Leipzig: Hinrichs, 1921; ET *Marcion: The Gospel of the Alien God* [trans. J. E. Seely and L. D. Bierma; Durham, N.C.: Labyrinth, 1990]), 210–15, was the first to make this claim, but it has been repeated frequently since his view first emerged. See, e.g., H. von Campenhausen, *The Formation of the Christian Bible* (trans. J. A. Baker; Philadelphia: Fortress, 1972), 163.

pages 612–613

56. Marcion believed that the Christian gospel was absolute love and that the gospel was completely contrary to the law. This belief led him to write his *Antitheses,* which rejected the OT altogether, along with the Judaistic influence upon Christianity, and he maintained that Christianity was something completely new. He stressed that the God of the law was a Demiurge, or "Craftsman" (δημιουργός)—Plato's term for the creator of the universe. Marcion argued that the God of the OT was not the same as the unknown God of the gospel and of Jesus. Therefore, he turned his attention toward effecting a separation of Christianity from its Jewish roots and influences.

57. Von Campenhausen, *Formation,* 148–72. Marcion's rejection of Judaism can be seen in the so-called Marcionite Prologues to the Epistles of Paul. See D. J. Théron, *Evidence of Tradition* (Grand Rapids: Baker, 1980), 79–83, especially the Marcionite prologues to Romans, 1 Corinthians, Galatians, Philippians, Colossians, 1 Thessalonians, and Titus. These and other prologues survive only in copies of the medieval Latin Vulgate manuscripts, and it is not clear how they managed to be included in the Scriptures of the orthodox community, but they are probably indicative of what is known of Marcion's feelings toward those with Judaizing tendencies in the church. For a brief discussion of what some scholars have argued were responses to Marcion's prologues, see L. M. McDonald, "Anti-Marcionite (Gospel) Prologues," *ABD* 1:262–63.

58. Von Campenhausen, *Formation,* 151. Marcion selected as his authoritative literature only the Gospel of Luke—from which he removed all OT influences and traces—and a freely edited collection of ten Pauline Letters. Tertullian wrote that Marcion had "interpolated" Paul's epistles, and claimed that "as our heretic is so fond of his pruning knife, I do not wonder when syllables are expunged by his hand, seeing that entire pages are usually the matter on which he practices his effacing process" (*Ag. Marc.* 5.18.1 [*ANF*]). See the whole context of *Ag. Marc.* 5.16–18 for examples of this. We have no evidence from Marcion that he specifically called his collection of writings "Scripture" or "canon," though it clearly functioned as Scripture later in his churches.

59. Justin probably used only the Synoptic Gospels, since the Fourth Gospel does not appear to have been read much in the western churches at this time, in spite of Irenaeus's fourfold Gospel canon shortly after Justin. What is more surprising is that Tatian, Justin's pupil, clearly preferred John's Gospel over the Synoptics in producing his *Diatessaron.*

60. Von Campenhausen, *Formation,* 163. Simple observance of the church fathers will show that some NT writings were called "scripture" or treated as such even before Marcion made his selection of writings from Paul and Luke. Marcion's writings have not survived, but what has in the writings of his critics and his own prologues will not permit von Campenhausen's conclusions.

61. See G. M. Hahneman, *The Muratorian Fragment and the Development of the Canon* (OTM; Oxford: Clarendon, 1992), 90–91, where Hahneman cites as evidence the Marcionite Marcus, who is said to have cited John 13:34 and 15:19, in Adamantius, *De recta in Deum fide.* 2.16, 20, and Tertullian, *Ag. Marc.* 4.5. Ephraem the Syrian claimed that the followers of Marcion had *not* rejected Matt 23:8 (*Hymni* 24.1). Also, in his *Comm. Matt.* 15.3, Origen quoted a Marcionite interpretation of Matt 19:12.

62. Hahneman (*Muratorian Fragment*, 92) cites here the conclusions of R. Casey, "The Armenian Marcionites and the Diatessaron," *JBL* 57 (1938): 185–94.

63. J. M. Robinson, ed., *The Nag Hammadi Library in English* (rev. ed.; San Francisco: Harper & Row, 1990). See also the translation in B. Layton, *Gnostic Scriptures* (London: SCM, 1987), xv–xxvii.

64. Around A.D. 170, a man (possibly a former priest of Cybele) by the name of Montanus was joined by two women, Prisca and Maximilla, who came to Phrygia in Asia Minor claiming to be inspired by the Paraclete (Holy Spirit) and announcing the Parousia, or coming of the Lord. Together they had a major impact upon the people of Phrygia and the rest of Asia Minor and were received with enthusiasm by many throughout the Mediterranean world, especially in North Africa. Their message was apocalyptic in focus, and they strongly advocated a special interpretation of the message of the book of Revelation.

65. R. F. Collins, *Introduction to the New Testament* (Garden City, N.Y.: Doubleday, 1983), 26.

66. So argues von Campenhausen, *Formation*, 232.

67. W. H. C. Frend, *The Rise of Christianity* (Philadelphia: Fortress, 1984), 256.

pages 613–616

68. There were "innumerable books" according to Hippolytus, *Elench.* 8.19.1. See von Campenhausen, *Formation*, 227–32; but cf. W. Schneemelcher, "Apocalyptic Prophecy of the Early Church," in *New Testament Apocrypha* (ed. E. Hennecke and W. Schneemelcher; trans. R. McL. Wilson; 2 vols.; Louisville: Westminster John Knox, 1991), 2:685 n. 2.

69. Tertullian, introduction to *Pass. Perp.*, 1.1–2. Trans. von Campenhausen, *Formation*, 229.

70. Von Campenhausen, *Formation*, 229.

71. Tertullian, *Pass. Perp.* 1.1. Trans. von Campenhausen, *Formation*, 229.

72. The fact that Tertullian joined the Montanists might have had an undue influence on his thoughts in this regard, however.

73. Von Campenhausen, *Formation*, 231. See Eusebius, *Hist. eccl.* 5.16.3–4.

74. Von Campenhausen, *Formation*, 231; cf. also Metzger, *Canon*, 106.

75. Von Campenhausen, *Formation*, 232.

76. Beckwith ("Formation of the Hebrew Bible," 46), following this same example, also determines a writer's biblical canon on the basis of quotations from, or references to, the OT. This argument fails when applied to the church fathers, especially Clement and Origen, and even later Athanasius, who has an OT canon different from that we use today.

77. Beckwith, ibid., 46, seems to say "yes" in every instance except where a NT writer cites a noncanonical writing, as in the case of Jude 14 citing *1 En.* 1.10.

78. The terms were still unfamiliar to large sections of the Christian community in the third and fourth centuries. See, e.g., how Origen speaks of the terms in his *Comm. Jo.* 5.4 and *Princ.* 4.11. See also Eusebius, *Hist. eccl.* 3.9.5, who shows, in his reference to the "so-called Old Testament," the lack of popularity of the terms in his own community. Further, the fact that Wisdom of Solomon could appear in NT lists in the fourth century (Eusebius, the Muratorian Fragment, and Epiphanius) speaks against the widespread understanding of the

pages 616–619

meaning of the term to identify a fixed collection of Scriptures in the second century.

79. On the scope of his involvement and insistence on unity and conformity in the church, see McDonald, *Formation*, 182–89. Constantine's presence within the church and his influence on its decisions were considerable.

80. G. A. Robbins, "Fifty Copies of Sacred Writings (VC 4.36): Entire Bibles or Gospel Books?" in *Studia Patristica* (StPatr 19; Leuven: Peeters; 1989), 91–98, although with questionable reasoning.

81. Revelation was somewhat doubtful to him, which shows that his canon of twenty-one or twenty-two books had an element of doubt. See Eusebius, *Hist. eccl.* 3.25.2, 4.

82. In Eusebius, *Hist. eccl.* 3.25.4–7, his argument against the apostolic authorship of the pseudepigraphal literature reflects the authority of the apostles that was acknowledged by all groups within the church.

83. Serapion (d. ca. 210) was asked by the church at Rhossus, to which he gave oversight, whether the *Gospel of Peter* could be read in their church (Eusebius, *Hist. eccl.* 6.12.1–2). He at first allowed it to be read but later reversed himself. The reason for his rejection of this book had nothing to do with its place inside or outside a collection of Scriptures. He used a criterion of truth, with no reference to a closed canon of NT scriptures (Eusebius, *Hist. eccl.* 6.12.3–6): the book did not conform to what was generally accepted as true in the churches. Serapion's initial willingness to accept the reading of the *Gospel of Peter* in his churches even when he was unaware of its contents is also instructive. Had there been a widely recognized and closed four-Gospel canon at that time, he might well have rejected the *Gospel of Peter* on such grounds. His decision also had little to do with whether the writing was by an apostle or even whether it dated from apostolic times and belonged to an accepted list of Scriptures. Even apostolicity and antiquity did not place as high in his criteria as did the criterion of truth.

84. See C. H. Roberts, "Books in the Greco-Roman World and in the New Testament," in *The Cambridge History of the Bible* (ed. P. R. Ackroyd and C. F. Evans; 3 vols.; Cambridge: Cambridge University Press, 1970), 1:48–66; McDonald, *Formation*, 223–25.

85. D. Farkasfalvy, "The Early Development of the New Testament Canon," in *The Formation of the New Testament Canon* (ed. H. W. Attridge; New York: Paulist, 1983), 161 n. 1.

86. Metzger, *Canon*, 193, and Bruce, *Canon*, 158–69, share this view, among others.

87. Von Campenhausen, *Formation*, 243–44, following Harnack.

88. A. C. Sundberg Jr., "The Bible Canon and the Christian Doctrine of Inspiration," *Int* 29 (1975): 362, has made the point that, if neither Irenaeus nor Origen had lists of canonical NT Scriptures, and there is no clear evidence that they did, the Muratorian Fragment has no parallels until the fourth century.

89. A. C. Sundberg Jr., "Canon Muratori: A Fourth Century List," *HTR* 66 (1973): 1–41; G. M. Hahneman, "More on Redating the Muratorian Fragment," in *Studia Patristica* (StPatr 18; Leuven: Peeters, 1988), 19–23; idem, *Muratorian Fragment.*

90. E. R. Kalin, "The Inspired Community: A Glance at Canon History," *CTM* 42 (1971): 541–49; Robbins, "Eusebius' Lexicon of 'Canonicity,' " 134–41.

91. See Tertullian, *Ag. Marc.* 5.1–21, where he defends Paul's epistles, including the Pastorals, and, as Metzger, *Canon*, 159, has noted, even cites Jude to support the authority of *1 Enoch* in his *Apparel* 1.3.
92. E. Ferguson, "Review of G. M. Hahneman, *Muratorian Fragment*," *JTS* 44 (1993): 679.
93. Hahneman, *Muratorian Fragment*, 200–201, also makes this point.
94. E.g., Metzger, *Canon*, 124; von Campenhausen, *Formation*, 242–46; and many others.
95. Metzger, *Canon*, 193–94.
96. Irenaeus, *Haer.* 5.30.3. See Sundberg, "Canon Muratori," 8–11.
97. Hahneman (*Muratorian Fragment*, 71–72) adds that the statement that Hermas is the brother of Pius, the bishop of Rome, is without foundation and unknown until the fourth century and that the poor transcription of the fragment makes the historical reference to Hermas and Pius suspect.
98. E. Ferguson, "Canon Muratori: Date and Provenance," in *Studia Patristica* (StPatr 17; Leuven: Peeters, 1982), 677–83, here 677–78.
99. Hahneman, *Muratorian Fragment*, 61–69.
100. The discovery of the document in the west, in spite of its origins in Greek and the lateness of its translation into Latin, suggests the possibility of a western origin, but again, the nature of the list itself appears to be eastern, as do many of the peculiarities within it. See the section on peculiarities ibid., 183–214, in which Hahneman contends for an eastern origin and a mid- to late-fourth-century date.
101. Ferguson, "Review of Hahneman," 696.
102. Note that the Eastern Orthodox have an even larger biblical canon that includes the apocryphal (or the deuterocanonical) books, 2 Esdras (LXX 1 Esdras), and 3 Maccabees, with 4 Maccabees in an appendix; the Russian Orthodox add *3 Esdras* (Vulg. *4 Esdras*) and omit 4 Maccabees. The Ethiopian biblical canon, which claims traditional roots back to the fourth century, contains eighty-one books.
103. For example, when it comes to the nature of Christ, does Matthew reflect the orthodoxy that prevailed in the early church, or is it better reflected in the Gospel of John?
104. For example, how often the cock crowed, the precise words of Jesus on the cross, the differences in the resurrection narratives. On the other hand, it is also clear that some NT writers changed some of the texts they used to improve their accuracy (e.g., Mark 1:2; cf. Matt 3:3; Luke 3:4).
105. We have not focused on the role of the Holy Spirit in illuminating the text or in helping the church to identify the biblical text, but this is not the job of the historian; it is a special task of theological inquiry. We have also not addressed adequately the problems of which text is the canonical text of Scripture for the church and whether we can isolate the reading of a text from its canonical position and read it in isolation from other texts, as its first recipients were able to do. These hermeneutical issues, beyond the scope of this section, are addressed in McDonald, *Formation*, 299–309.

pages 619–622

THE APOCRYPHA, PSEUDEPIGRAPHA, AND AGRAPHA

1. APOCRYPHA AND PSEUDEPIGRAPHA

The term "Apocrypha" (lit. "hidden" or "concealed") is commonly used to refer to those Jewish writings, dating mostly from the second century B.C. to around A.D. 90–100, that were included in early Christian lists of OT books but are excluded in Protestant Bibles today.[1] That same collection is now called the "deuterocanonical" books by the Roman Catholics to indicate that the books were recognized as canonical at a later date than the "protocanonical" books (the Jewish and Protestant OT), and they are included as authoritative literature (except for doctrine) in Catholic Bibles. Catholics now often use the term "Apocrypha" to refer to the books listed below as Pseudepigrapha.

Although not everyone agrees on which literature should be included, most scholars agree that the Apocrypha includes the following: 1 Esdras, 2 Esdras (= 4 *Ezra*), Tobit, Judith, additions to the book of Esther, Wisdom of Solomon, Sirach (= Ecclesiasticus), Baruch, the Epistle of Jeremiah, additions to the book of Daniel (Prayer of Azariah, Song of the Three Young Men, Susanna, Bel and the Dragon), Prayer of Manasseh, 1 Maccabees, and 2 Maccabees. As we will note later, many of these writings were produced by persons whose real identities are lost, as the works were perpetuated under the names of earlier heroes of antiquity (Jeremiah, Baruch, etc.) and most may technically be called pseudonymous writings.[2]

A pseudonym is a fictitious name or an assumed name, normally used by an author who, for various reasons, may want to conceal his or her real identity. The practice of writing under an assumed name was a common practice during the intertestamental period, when writers frequently made use of well-known names from the OT. The collection of writings called the Pseudepigrapha (lit. "false superscriptions") contains sixty-five documents, which are related to the OT and were written by both Jews and Christians from ca. 250 B.C. to A.D. 200. For a time, many Christians and Jews considered large portions of these writings to be given by God, and along with the OT, they were used in worship and instruction. Most of this literature was shaped and inspired by the language, metaphors, and symbols of the OT, and the authorship of many of these books is attributed to OT figures such as Enoch, Abraham, Shem, Moses, Levi, and other Hebrew patriarchs. Although the designation "Pseudepigrapha" is commonly used to refer to this collection, most scholars agree that the term is imprecise and somewhat misleading, since the original author is clearly identified in some of the literature. There is also, as

T A B L E   1 4 - 1

APOCALYPTIC AND TESTAMENTARY WRITINGS

Apocalyptic and related works

1 (Ethiopic Apocalypse of) *Enoch*	Jewish, ca. 200 B.C.–A.D. 50
2 (Slavonic Apocalypse of) *Enoch*	Jewish, ca. A.D. 75–100
3 (Hebrew Apocalypse of) *Enoch*	Jewish, present form from ca. 5th–6th cent. A.D.
Sibylline Oracles	both Jewish and Christian, ca. 2d cent. B.C.–7th cent. A.D.
Treatise of Shem	ca. near end of first cent. B.C.
Apocryphon of Ezekiel	mostly lost, original form ca. late 1st cent. B.C.
Apocalypse of Zephaniah	mostly lost, original form ca. late 1st cent. B.C.
4 Ezra	original Jewish form after A.D. 70, final Christian additions later
Greek Apocalypse of Ezra	present form is Christian ca. 9th cent. A.D. with both Jewish and Christian sources
Vision of Ezra	a Christian document dating from 4th to 7th cent. A.D.
Questions of Ezra	Christian, but date is imprecise
Revelation of Ezra	Christian and sometime before 9th cent. A.D.
Apocalypse of Sedrach	present form is Christian from ca. 5th cent. with earlier sources
2 (Syriac Apocalypse of) *Baruch*	Jewish, from ca. A.D. 100
3 (Greek Apocalypse of) *Baruch*	Christian utilizing Jewish sources, ca. 1st–2d cent A.D.
Apocalypse of Abraham	Jewish primarily, ca. A.D. 70–150
Apocalypse of Adam	Gnostic derived from Jewish sources from ca. 1st cent. A.D.
Apocalypse of Elijah	both Jewish and Christian, ca. A.D. 150–275
Apocalypse of Daniel	present form ca. 9th cent. A.D., but contains Jewish sources from ca. 4th cent A.D.

Testaments

Testaments of the Twelve Patriarchs	current form is Christian, ca. A.D. 150–200, but Levi, Judah, and Naphtali are Jewish and date before A.D. 70 and probably 2d–1st cent. B.C.
Testament of Job	Jewish, ca. late 1st cent. B.C.
Testaments of the Three Patriarchs	Jewish Testaments of *Abraham, Isaac,* and *Jacob* from ca. A.D. 100 which are linked with the Christian *Testament of Isaac* and *Jacob*
Testament of Moses	Jewish, from ca. early 1st cent A.D.
Testament of Solomon	Jewish, current form ca. 3d cent. A.D., but earliest form ca. A.D. 100
Testament of Adam	Christian in current form ca. late 3d cent. A.D., but used Jewish sources from ca. A.D. 150–200

Expansions of Old Testament and other legends

The Letter of Aristeas	Jewish, ca. 200–150 B.C.
Jubilees	Jewish, ca. 130–100 B.C.
Martyrdom and Ascension of Isaiah	has three sections, the first Jewish from ca. 100 B.C., and 2d and 3d sections are Christian. The second from ca. 2d cent. A.D., and the third, *Testament of Hezekiah,* ca. A.D. 90–100
Joseph and Asenath	Jewish, ca. A.D. 100
Life of Adam and Eve	Jewish, ca. early to middle 1st cent. A.D.
Pseudo-Philo	Jewish, ca. A.D. 66–135
Lives of the Prophets	Jewish, ca. early 1st cent. A.D. with later Christian additions
Ladder of Jacob	earliest form is Jewish dating from late 1st cent. A.D.; one chapter is Christian
4 Baruch	Jewish original but edited by a Christian, ca. A.D. 100–110
Jannes and Jambres	Christian in present form, but dependent on earlier Jewish sources from ca. 1st cent. B.C.
History of the Rechabites	Christian in present form dating ca. 6th cent. A.D., but contains some Jewish sources before A.D. 100
Eldad and Modad	very early, probably before the 1st cent. A.D., now lost, but quoted in *Shepherd of Hermas* ca. A.D. 140
History of Joseph	Jewish, but difficult to date

T A B L E   1 4 - 2

WISDOM AND PHILOSOPHICAL LITERATURE

Ahiqar	Jewish dating from late 7th or 6th cent. B.C. and cited in Apocryphal Tobit
3 Maccabees	Jewish, ca. 1st cent. B.C.
4 Maccabees	Jewish, ca. before A.D. 70
Pseudo-Phocylides	Jewish maxims attributed to 6th cent. Ionic poet, ca. 50 B.C.–A.D. 100
The Sentences of the Syriac Menander	Jewish, ca. 3rd cent. A.D.

T A B L E   1 4 - 3

PRAYERS, PSALMS AND ODES

More Psalms of David	Jewish psalms from ca. 3rd cent B.C. to A.D. 100
Prayer of Manasseh	sometimes in Apocrypha, Jewish from ca. early 1st cent. A.D.
Psalms of Solomon	Jewish, ca. 50–5 B.C.
Hellenistic Synagogal Prayers	Jewish, ca. 2nd–3rd cent A.D.
Prayer of Joseph	Jewish, ca. A.D. 70–135
Prayer of Jacob	mostly lost Jewish document from ca. 4th cent A.D.
Odes of Solomon	Christian but influenced by Judaism and Qumran, ca. A.D. 100

---

mentioned, a fair amount of pseudonymous literature in the apocryphal writings and, some would argue, in the biblical literature.

Charlesworth, who has cautioned that not all of this literature originates either from the same sources or from the same motives, has also identified five loosely defined categories of pseudepigraphal writings.[3]

Besides these, there are numerous Christian pseudepigraphal writings, including gospels, Acts attributed to or concerning various apostles, epistles, and apocalypses. This literature is mostly sectarian and appears to appeal to an apostle's name in order to find acceptance in segments of the Christian community. Most of this literature is described in detail in Edgar Hennecke and William Schneemelcher's *New Testament Apocrypha*,[4] but for our purposes we will list only the most commonly mentioned literature. In Table 14–4, Dennis MacDonald has conveniently listed some of the most important representatives of this collection, some of which currently exist only in fragments.[5]

There are also numerous other examples of pseudepigrapha in antiquity outside those produced within Judaism and early Christianity. Such classical writers as Lysias, Galen, Apollonius, Plato, Pythagoras, Socrates, and Xenophon had writings attributed to them by those who either succeeded them in office or position or came after them (see ch. 9, sec. 6, above).

The ethics of the practice of producing pseudonymous literature in the ancient Jewish and Christian communities is debated today among scholars. As yet, there is no agreement on why it emerged or which literature is properly pseudonymous, though awareness has grown that distinctions should be made in the kinds of literature falling into this category. For some Christians, the issue is how forged documents can serve as inspired and sacred literature for the church (see ch. 9, sec. 6, above). We will return to this question later.

Aune has noted that there are generally four explanations for the existence of pseudonymous literature: (1) it arose at a time when the biblical canon was already closed and well-known names were used to secure acceptance; (2) pseudonymity was used to protect the identity of the writer, who might be in danger if his true identity were known; (3) apocalyptic visionaries may have had visions from those figures to whom they attributed their work; and (4) the writer may have identified with a person of the past and written as his representative.[6] Aune believes that the first of these options is the most likely, but not without qualifications. As a device to legitimize a piece of literature, he argues, pseudonymous authorship was intended to accord the writing in question the esteem and prestige given to the earlier well-known figure. As Aune states, "Pseudonymity is functional only if readers accept the false attribution."[7]

TABLE 14-4

CHRISTIAN PSEUDEPIGRAPHICAL WRITINGS

Gospels[8]	*The Protevangelium of James* *The Infancy Gospel of Thomas* *The Gospel of Peter* *The Gospel of Nicodemus* *The Gospel of the Nazoreans* *The Gospel of the Ebionites* *The Gospel of the Hebrews* *The Gospel of the Egyptians* *The Gospel of Thomas* *The Gospel of Philip* *The Gospel of Mary*
Acts[9]	*The Acts of John* *The Acts of Peter* *The Acts of Paul* *The Acts of Andrew* *The Acts of Thomas* *The Acts of Andrew and Matthias* *The Acts of Philip* *The Acts of Thaddaeus* *The Acts of Peter and Paul* *The Acts of Peter and Andrew* *The Martyrdom of Matthew* *The Slavonic Act of Peter* *The Acts of Peter and the Twelve Apostles*
Epistles[10]	*Third Corinthians* *The Epistle to the Laodiceans* *The Letters of Paul and Seneca* *The Letters of Jesus and Abgar* *The Letter of Lentulus* *The Epistle of Titus*
Apocalypses[11]	*The Apocalypse of Peter* *The Coptic Apocalypse of Paul* *The First Apocalypse of James* *The Second Apocalypse of James* *The Apocryphon of John* *The Sophia of Jesus Christ* *The Letter of Peter to Philip* *The Apocalypse of Mary*

Although deception may have played a role in some pseudepigraphy, one cannot with certainty conclude that all of the writers of pseudepigrapha wrote for purposes of deception. Charlesworth notes seven different categories of pseudepigrapha in the literature of early Christianity, including that of the NT. Many would not accept that there are pseudepigrapha in the NT, but for those who do, the following list attempts to categorize some of their possible origins:

> (1) works not by an author but probably containing some of his own thoughts (Ephesians and Colossians); (2) documents by someone who was influenced by another person to whom the work is ascribed (1 Peter and maybe James); (3) compositions influenced by earlier works of an author to whom they are assigned (1 Timothy, 2 Timothy, Titus); (4) Gospels (eventually) attributed to an apostle but deriving from later circles or schools of learned individuals (Matthew and John); (5) Christian writings attributed by their authors to an Old Testament personality (*Testament of Adam, Odes of Solomon, Apocalypse of Elijah, Ascension of Isaiah*); (6) once-anonymous works (perhaps Mark, Luke, and Acts) now correctly or incorrectly credited to someone (some manuscripts attribute Hebrews to Paul); (7) compositions that intentionally try to deceive the reader into thinking that the author is someone famous (2 Peter).[12]

If some of the NT writings above are pseudepigraphal (see the comments in the chapters above regarding these books, and ch. 9, sec. 6, above), this literature may well have been produced with a view toward deception. And yet it is likely that some examples of it were written in the sincere belief that the pseudepigraph represented what the earlier hero, often a prophetic figure or an apostle, was known for or practiced. Many biblical scholars believe that pseudepigrapha are found in the biblical canon, though not all agree on which writings of the Bible are pseudonymous. For example, most agree that the OT book of Daniel is pseudonymous, even though a few scholars maintain that the earliest form of the book did in fact derive from the Hebrew prophet and that only its latest or final form stems from the mid–second century B.C. Some scholars question whether the Gospels of Matthew and John were written by these apostles, and many also dismiss Markan and Lukan authorship of the Gospels that have their name attached. This reveals imprecise thinking, however, since the canonical Gospels cannot be pseudepigraphal, as none of the original texts of these Gospels appear to

have had names attached to them. They are more appropriately designated "anonymous" literature, as Charlesworth notes above in his category 6. The earliest writer to claim apostolic authorship for his gospel is the writer of the *Gospel of Thomas* (ca. A.D. 90? at the earliest in its Greek form). Further, many scholars agree that Paul did not write all the literature that was later attributed to him. This includes especially the Pastoral Epistles (1 and 2 Timothy, Titus), possibly also Ephesians, Colossians, 2 Thessalonians, and certainly Hebrews (which also is formally anonymous and not actually pseudepigraphal). Many other writings not in our NT are also generally acknowledged as pseudonymous works, including the *Didache, 2 Clement,* the *Apostolic Constitutions and Canons, Barnabas,* the *Gospel of Thomas,* and many more. The practice of writing under an assumed name was apparently fairly common in the early church until the mid–second century, when its practice was called into question, as the example of the *Gospel of Peter* illustrates (Eusebius, *Hist. eccl.* 6.12.2–3; see ch. 9, sec. 6, and ch. 13, sec. 3, above) though the book was not finally rejected over issues related to authorship but, rather, because of theological irregularities.

It is also interesting that the *Apostolic Constitutions and Canons,* which themselves are pseudepigraphal, warn against Christians reading pseudepigraphal literature! First the producers of this writing claim to be apostles:

> On whose account also we, who are now assembled in one place,—Peter and Andrew; James and John, sons of Zebedee; Philip and Bartholomew; Thomas and Matthew; James the son of Alphaeus; Simon the Canaanite, and Matthias, who instead of Judas was numbered with us; and James the brother of the Lord and bishop of Jerusalem, and Paul the teacher of the Gentiles, the chosen vessel, having all met together, have written to you this Catholic doctrine for the confirmation of you, to whom the oversight of the universal Church is committed. (*Apos. Con.* 6.14 [*ANF*])

Then, two chapters later, they comment about those who produce such writings:

> We have sent all things to you, that you may know our opinion, what it is; and that you may not receive those books which obtain in our name, but are written by the ungodly. For you are not to attend to the names of the apostles, but to the nature of the things, and their settled opinions. For we know that Simon and Cleobius, and their followers, have compiled poisonous books under the name of Christ and of His

disciples, and do carry them about in order to deceive you who love Christ, and us his servants. And among the ancients also some have written apocryphal books of Moses, and Enoch, and Adam, and Isaiah, and David, and Elijah, and of the three patriarchs, pernicious and repugnant to the truth. The same things even now have the wicked heretics done, reproaching the creation, marriage, providence, the begetting of children, the law, and the prophets; inscribing certain barbarous names, and as they think, of angels, but to speak the truth, of demons, which suggest things to them (ibid., 6.16 [*ANF*]).

What this implies has been variously interpreted. One reading is that the standard applied to pseudepigrapha was orthodoxy. If a writing fit in theologically with what was acceptable to a particular Christian community, then it was acceptable even though it may have been written by someone other than the author listed. Another view, noted above, is that there was the assumption that any work written under the name of Christ and one of his disciples was by nature deceptive and hence one should not rely upon the attributed names to betray it but, rather, look at its unwholesome teaching, which was bound to reveal its deleterious nature. It is also worth noting that the concerns over the deceptive nature of pseudepigrapha come mostly from the fourth to the sixth centuries—not from the time when it was produced. Such literature may have been more acceptable at the time of its writing and less so at a later time (fourth century) when matters of canon were at issue.

Koch has noted that particular names were able to attract entire genres of literature. For example, all divine law came from Moses, wisdom from Solomon, and church regulations from apostles, as in the case of the *Didache* and the *Apostolic Constitutions and Canons*.[13] A typical justification of pseudonymous literature is that pseudonymous writings imply the writer's consciousness that "association with a tradition confers legitimacy." Koch explains that "in many cases the authors to whom the writings are ascribed are considered as alive in heaven and therefore still effective in the present. To this extent attribution of authorship to men of God is similar to ascribing it to God, Christ, or angels. Since what is involved is not the conscious use of an inaccurate name, the designation 'pseudonymous' should be used only with reservations."[14] Charlesworth agrees and warns against calling all such literature forgeries.[15] Whereas not all pseudepigrapha may have been intended to deceive read-

ers and the authors may have considered it acceptable to attribute a writing to one who had inspired them, not all scholars accept that the process of having such works accepted as canonical was straightforward. The fact that no work known to be pseudepigraphal was accepted into any writer's group of accepted writings in the ancient Greco-Roman world—this includes not only the NT but secular writers as well[16]—and if discovered to be such, a writing was rejected, indicates to some scholars that, despite perhaps good intentions, some potentially deceptive mechanism must have been in place to secure canonical acceptance (see ch. 9, sec. 6). By the fourth century, as we see in the writings of Eusebius (*Hist. eccl.* 3.25.4–7), any writing that was believed pseudonymous was rejected. Such discussions are very sparce before the fourth century, and many of the pseudepigraphal works were considered sacred Scripture among the church fathers before that time (e.g., Tertullian cited *1 Enoch* as Scripture to deal with women's attire in *Apparel* 1.3, and the pseudonymous *Barnabas* was in several collections of sacred books well into the fourth and fifth centuries A.D.). For NT questions, it is possible that some writings gained wide acceptance under the assumption that the writing was produced by an apostle—for instance, Hebrews. But when this book was later deemed nonapostolic, the church continued to retain it in its biblical canon, though not without hesitation on the part of many. When most of these pseudepigraphal writings were produced, discussions of the NT canon and pseudonymous writings were rare. The wide acceptance of much of this literature when it was first produced does not necessarily imply naivete in the first readers but may simply reflect different concerns and a different understanding of that genre of literature. Some scholars are not bothered by the idea that pseudonymous literature may have been included in the NT under these conditions; others find such conclusions unacceptable.

2. THE PROBLEM OF PSEUDONYMITY

There is an almost universal response of disbelief and disappointment among Christians who hear for the first time that the ascribed author of one of the biblical books did not actually write the work to which his name is attached. This is, no

doubt, because we live in an age in which both pla-
giarism and writing in another person's name are
looked upon as unethical, and it is easy to assume
unethical motivations in those who produced this
literature in the ancient religious communities. Although it may be true in many cases, other writings may have been written in honor of a particular hero of the prophetic or apostolic tradition. It is
not always easy to discover the motive of a writer
who produced such literature. Whether the reason
was to gain acceptance for a particular perspective
that the writer wanted others to accept but that
may not have been well received, or to give honor
to an earlier hero of the faith, or simply to deceive
in order to gain acceptance is not always easy to
determine. In the case of the *Letter of Aristeas,* it
seems clear that the author, probably a Jew, wanting to establish the divinely given status of both the
LXX and the temple, perpetuated a widely accepted
tradition that did just that. Whether the author of
the Pastoral Epistles (if he was not Paul) simply
wanted apostolic sanction for his views on church
organization and discipline and therefore attached
Paul's name to his own writings is not easy to determine, especially since there are probably authentic Pauline traditions in this collection—for
example, the rejection of Paul in Asia Minor, the
manner of the apostle's death, and many of the
closing comments to colleagues in 2 Tim 4:14–22.
Finding a satisfactory explanation for the presence
of authentic traditions within a pseudonymous
writing is overly optimistic and is not likely to satisfy those who believe that all such literature is deceptive. Other scholars, however, believe that some
authentic traditions may well survive in literature
produced in the name of an earlier hero. An example of this in the OT is the book of Daniel. Few
scholars today believe that the book, in its current
form, is the work of the biblical Daniel who was
taken into exile in Babylon, but many scholars
have argued that the story preserved in the current
form of the book contains authentic and historically reliable information from that period. Some
parts of the book best fit the context of the second
century B.C. (ch. 11), but other aspects about Daniel, the Babylonian leader, and the fall of Babylon
seem to reflect an earlier period. The *Acts of Paul*
(ca. 2d cent.) is acknowledged by all to be pseudonymous, but it may well contain some authentic traditions about Paul (this is the only ancient writing

that physically describes him), and much of the
story of Thecla is believed to have some basis in reality. This may be the case also in the Pastoral
Epistles, which almost certainly reflect some genuine traditions about Paul but may nonetheless be
pseudonymous writings or, better, pseudepigraphal. The tendency among scholars is either to accept the Pastoral Epistles completely as the work of
Paul or, as in the case of the majority of scholars,
to reject them as the work of Paul. There are other
alternatives to consider, however, including the
role of an amanuensis or scribe, current followers
of Paul (such as Luke), or even later followers (an
unknown author) helping produce them. What we
are suggesting here is that not all of the pseudonymous literature of the ancient world came out of
the same mold. Care should be taken in each instance to determine not only authorship, whenever
that is possible, but also motive and procedure in
producing the writing.

If one accepts that there are pseudonymous
writings in the NT, another question often arises:
How can a writing be maintained in our canon if
the work was not written by the one to whom it
was ascribed? How can its inspiration be legitimate
if it is a forgery, especially if that book was accepted
into the canon for the wrong reasons, that is, on
the basis of apostolic authorship? This matter cannot be completely solved here, but again it is appropriate to question whether all ancient pseudonymous writers' intentions were unethical or whether
all such literature was written with the same intention; it is also important to question the dependence of divine inspiration on apostolic authorship.
Is the writing inspired because it was written by a
particular writer or because the writing inherently
addresses the needs and circumstances of the
church to whom it was written, with a divine message that continues to have relevance for the
church today? There is nothing in antiquity that
suggests that only the apostolic witness was inspired and that all other voices were not. On the
contrary, the early church did not believe that the
role of inspiration was limited to the apostles or to
writings per se but that it was given to the whole
church in perpetuity. The church was in the age of
the Spirit, and there is no definite time when that
was perceived to have stopped. In the first five centuries of the church everything that was true was
also considered inspired of God. Only if it was un-

true was it considered uninspired. The apparent reason a book such as Hebrews was retained in our biblical canon, even though many of the early church fathers did not believe that Paul wrote it, was its useful message to the church. Although many of the church fathers may have accepted it because they thought Paul wrote it, the majority had serious questions about it and placed it in various places in their canons, noting their doubt about its authorship.[17]

But what about the acceptance of a writing because it was believed to have been written by an apostle when in fact it was not? If a writing only made it into the biblical canon because it was reputed to have been written by an apostle, should that writing be taken out of the canon if it can be reasonably shown that an apostle never wrote it? It is perhaps better to see how that writing speaks to the worship, needs, and mission of the church and to determine its inspiration based on this and on its faithfulness to the authentic witness of Jesus preserved in the early Christian literature. Our present canon is consciously and explicitly not limited to apostolic authorship (e.g., Mark, Luke–Acts, Jude), and the early church found, for a long period of time, some nonapostolic writings particularly helpful in worship and catechetical instruction (*1 Clement, Didache, Barnabas, Shepherd of Hermas*; see ch. 13, above). It is arguable that a similar case should be made for originally anonymous literature that, though earlier attributed to an apostle, has subsequently been determined by careful investigation to be otherwise (e.g., perhaps Matthew, John). Concerning Revelation, the writing is not anonymous, but which John wrote it is unknown, though historically it has been attributed to the Apostle John even if the book does not say this specifically.

The value of apocryphal and pseudepigraphal literature for a study of early Christianity cannot be overestimated. Along with the canonical literature, the apocryphal and pseudepigraphal literature presents as clearly as any other what Barnstone calls "a lucid picture of the life and ideals of the early Christendom."[18] Without it we have only a vague understanding of the emergence and growth of early Christianity. It shows us the great diversity—at a later time not tolerated—in the formative years of the Christian community. This body of literature is also invaluable in bringing some clarity to our understanding of many commonly used terms and ideas in the NT, especially Son of Man, angels, and the notion of apocalyptic eschatology, kingdom, messianic expectations, the NT's use of the OT, and many more topics of special interest. Most interpreters of Scripture today see the immense value of this literature for informing our understanding of the context of the NT.

3. THE AGRAPHA

Various sayings of Jesus circulated in the early Christian community, at first orally but then written down in works outside the canonical Gospels. They have been found in Christian apocryphal writings, in writings of the early church fathers, and even in some surviving manuscripts of the NT. These sayings, commonly called agrapha (ἄγραφα), were made popular by Jeremias in a small but important book that both lists and discusses these sayings.[19] Since this literature may have functioned in an authoritative manner in the early church, it becomes an important part of the ancient literature that informed early Christianity. This raises a significant question for the study of the biblical canon: should this literature also be added to it?

Scholars have known for some time that a large number of sayings of Jesus circulated in the early Christian community in its noncanonical literature. There are reportedly 266 of these sayings surviving outside the biblical literature, but scholars disagree on how many of them are authentic to Jesus.[20] They are found in the NT apocryphal sources, such as the *Gospel of Thomas* and the *Gospel of Peter*, but also in many other sources. Jeremias believes that, of the much larger list, only 18 of the sayings are authentic to Jesus. Hofius, on the other hand, argues that even Jeremias's conclusions were too generous. He claims that only 9 of the agrapha need be taken seriously and that, of these, only 4 or 5 are probably authentic to Jesus.[21] In the following selection of examples of agrapha, we follow Hofius's more conservative list of 9 sayings and note that he fully supports the authenticity of only the 5 sayings that are marked by an asterisk.[22]

1. "As you are found, so will you be led away [sc. to judgment]." (*Syriac Liber Graduum, Serm.* 3.3; 15.4)

2. "Ask for the great things, and God will add to you what is small." (Clement of Alexandria, *Misc.* 1.24.158)

3. "Be competent [approved] money-changers!" (*Ps. Clem. Hom.* 2.51.1; 3.50.2; 18.20.4)

*4. "On the same day he [Jesus] saw a man working on the sabbath. He said to him: 'Man, if you know what you are doing, you are blessed; but if you do not know, you are accursed and a transgressor of the law!" (Luke 6:5 Codex D).

*5. "He who is near me is near the fire; he who is far from me is far from the kingdom." (*Gos. Thom.* §82; Origen, *In Jer. hom.* lat. 3.3; Didymus, *In Psalm.* 88.8)

*6. "(He who today) stands far off will tomorrow be (near to you)." (P.Oxy. 1224 Fr. 2 recto col. i 5)

*7. "And only then shall you be glad, when you look on your brother with love." (*Gos. Heb.*, according to Jerome, *In Eph.* 5.4)[23]

8. "The kingdom is like a wise fisherman who cast his net into the sea; he drew it up from the sea full of small fish; among them he found a large (and) good fish; that wise fisherman threw all the small fish down into the sea; he chose the large fish without regret." (*Gos. Thom.* §8)

9. "How is it then with you? For you are here in the temple. Are you then clean? . . . Woe to you blind who see not! You have washed yourself in water that is poured forth, in which dogs and swine lie night and day, and washed and scoured your outer skin, which harlots and flute girls also anoint, bathe, scour, and beautify to arouse desire in men, but inwardly they are filled with scorpions and with [all manner of ev]il. But I and [my disciples], of whom you say that we have not [bathed, have bath]ed ourselves in the liv[ing and clean] water, which comes down from [the father in heaven]" (P.Oxy. 840 §2).

T A B L E 1 4 - 5	
APOCRYPHAL GOSPELS	
Apocryphon of James	preserved in Nag Hammadi Codex I
Dialogue of the Savior	preserved in Nag Hammadi Codex III
Gospel of the Ebionites	preserved in quotations by Epiphanius
Gospel of the Egyptians	preserved in quotations by Clement of Alexandria
Gospel of the Hebrews	preserved in quotations by various Fathers
Gospel of the Nazoreans	preserved in quotations by various Fathers
Gospel of Peter	preserved in a large fragment from Akhmim in Egypt (P.Cairo 10759) and P.Oxy. 2949 and possibly 4009
Gospel of Thomas	preserved in Nag Hammadi Codex II and P.Oxy. 1, 654, and 655
P.Egerton 2 and P.Köln 255	
P.Oxy. 840	
P.Oxy. 1224	
Protevangelium of James	preserved in a supposed letter of Clement of Alexandria
P.Vindob. Greek 2325	Fayyum Fragment

*10. "And never be joyful, save when you look upon your brother in love." (*Gos. Heb.* §5; compare Jerome, *In Eph.* 3 [on Eph 5:4]).[24]

Besides perhaps functioning authoritatively in the communities in which they were discovered, some of these extracanonical sayings may have circulated quite widely in the church, even though they never became a part of a fixed canonical collection in the developing Christian communities.

The question today is not so much whether authentic sayings of Jesus may have been preserved in the noncanonical sources but, rather, how to distinguish among them and what to do with those finally regarded as authentic. For our purposes, we may ask whether they should be added to the canonical scriptures of the Christian community if they are deemed to be original or authentic sayings of Jesus. Should they inform the theology of the church today as they did in ancient times, forming a part of the authoritative base for constructing the church's doctrinal teachings? Do they provide an independent tradition or source for scholars to reconstruct the life and teaching of Jesus? There is no agreement among scholars on these questions, but more and more, there is an acknowledgment that some authentic sayings of Jesus may well exist in the noncanonical sources. While there is no consensus on which of the many extracanonical sayings of Jesus are authentic, a growing number of scholars agree that they are an important resource for historical-Jesus research. They also raise important questions for the study of the biblical canon.

The most commonly cited apocryphal gospels which are employed in the more recent historical-Jesus research are those in Table 14–5.[25]

There is strong disagreement on the evaluative process to determine whether Jesus said any of the things attributed to him in these sources, and no one today seriously believes that everything contained in these sources was said or done by Jesus. But how do we decide among them? What criteria are employed to decide the matter? The same criteria that scholars use for evaluating the Gospels are often used to determine the authenticity of noncanonical sayings of Jesus. These are discussed in more detail in ch. 4, above.

As noted, when these criteria are applied to the agrapha, the number of purportedly authentic sayings is greatly reduced. But there is still this question: what are we to do with the sayings that

remain? In the *Gospel of Thomas*, for instance, of the perhaps twenty or so possibly authentic sayings of Jesus in that document, can they be explained as a conflation of the canonical Gospels, or is there more to them? Some scholars place remarkable confidence in these sources. Koester claims that the canonical Gospels were dependent upon noncanonical sources such as the earlier Sayings Source (Q), the *Gospel of Thomas*, the *Dialogue of the Savior*, the unknown gospel of P.Egerton 2, the *Apocryphon of James*, and the *Gospel of Peter*.[26] Crossan also depends heavily on the extracanonical literature for his portrait of Jesus as a Jewish peasant cynic philosopher, and he claims that much of this literature predates the canonical literature and offers authentic sayings of Jesus.[27] He also places the *Gospel of Peter* prior to the Synoptics and the Gospel of John (somewhere in the A.D. 50s). The questions related to the dating of these sources vary widely according to the many scholars who study them and cannot be settled here. Evans and Meier, strongly disagreeing with Crossan, conclude that the noncanonical sources do not constitute an important and independent source for the teaching of Jesus but, for the most part, are dependent on the canonical sources.[28] Meier claims that the rabbinic material, the agrapha, and the apocryphal gospels do not "offer us reliable new information or authentic sayings that are independent of the NT."[29] Meier's conclusion is worth repeating:

> For better or for worse, in our quest for the historical Jesus, we are largely confined to the canonical Gospels; the genuine "corpus" is infuriating in its restrictions. For the historian it is a galling limitation. But to call upon the *Gospel of Peter* or the *Gospel of Thomas* to supplement our Four Gospels is to broaden out our pool of sources from the difficult to the incredible.[30]

The strong differences in the scholarly community over these matters suggest that the final answers to the questions raised over the earliest and most authentic sources for the study of Jesus and his teachings, as well as the dependencies and relationships of these sources, have not yet been finally determined, at least not for some scholars.

Papias's comment (ca. A.D. 130–140) about the circulation of the oral teachings of Jesus—"For I did not suppose that information from books would help me so much as the word of a living and surviving voice" (Eusebius, *Hist. eccl.* 3.29.4 [LCL])—

confirms that the oral traditions that were passed on in the churches had more meaning or value for him (and probably for others) than those written in books (the canonical Gospels and others?). This witness may inform us of the significance that these sayings had in the life of the early church.

BIBLIOGRAPHY

AUNE, D. *Prophecy in Early Christianity and the Ancient Mediterranean World.* Grand Rapids: Eerdmans, 1983.

BARNSTONE, W., ed. *The Other Bible.* New York: Harper & Row, 1984.

CAMERON, R. *The Other Gospels: Non-canonical Gospel Texts.* Philadelphia: Westminster, 1982.

CHARLES, R. H. *The Apocrypha and Pseudepigrapha of the Old Testament.* 2 vols. Oxford: Oxford University Press, 1913.

CHARLESWORTH, J. H., ed. *The Old Testament Pseudepigrapha.* 2 vols. Garden City, N.Y.: Doubleday, 1983–1985.

_____. *Old Testament Pseudepigrapha and the New Testament.* Cambridge: Cambridge University Press, 1985.

CHILTON, B., and C. A. Evans, eds. *Studying the Historical Jesus: Evaluations of the State of Current Research.* NTTS 19. Leiden: Brill, 1994.

CROSSAN, J. D. *The Historical Jesus: The Life of a Mediterranean Jewish Peasant.* San Francisco: Harper, 1991.

DONELSON, L. R. *Pseudepigraphy and Ethical Argument in the Pastoral Epistles.* HUT 22. Tübingen: Mohr–Siebeck, 1986.

EVANS, C. A. *Noncanonical Writings and New Testament Interpretation.* Peabody, Mass.: Hendrickson, 1992.

ELLIOTT, J. K. *The Apocryphal New Testament: A Collection of Apocryphal Christian Literature in an English Translation.* Oxford: Clarendon, 1993.

HENNECKE, E., and W. SCHNEEMELCHER, eds. *New Testament Apocrypha.* Trans. R. McL. WILSON. 2 vols. Rev. ed. Louisville: Westminster John Knox, 1990.

KOESTER, H. *Ancient Christian Gospels: Their History and Development.* Philadelphia: Trinity Press International, 1990.

METZGER, B. M. *An Introduction to the Apocrypha.* 3d ed. New York: Oxford University Press, 1977.

_____. "Literary Forgeries and Canonical Pseudepigrapha." *JBL* 91 (1972): 3–24.

MEYER, M. *The Gospel of Thomas: The Hidden Sayings of Jesus.* New York: HarperSanFrancisco, 1992.

NOTES TO CHAPTER 14
THE APOCRYPHA,
PSEUDEPIGRAPHA, AND
AGRAPHA

pages 634–641

1. See C. A. Evans, *Noncanonical Writings and New Testament Interpretation* (Peabody, Mass.: Hendrickson, 1992), for further discussion of the topics covered in this chapter.
2. D. W. Suter, "Apocrypha, Old Testament," *HBD* 36–38. For an excellent discussion of the Apocrypha, see B. M. Metzger, *An Introduction to the Apocrypha* (3d. ed. New York: Oxford University Press, 1977).
3. J. H. Charlesworth, "Pseudepigrapha," *HBD* 836–40.
4. E. Hennecke and W. Schneemelcher, eds., *New Testament Apocrypha* (trans. R. McL. Wilson; 2 vols.; Louisville: Westminster John Knox, 1990).
5. D. R. MacDonald, "Apocryphal New Testament," *HBD* 38–39.
6. Ibid., 109.
7. Ibid., 110.
8. For a careful discussion of the apocryphal gospels, see J. H. Charlesworth and C. A. Evans, "Jesus in the Agrapha and Apocryphal Gospels," in *Studying the Historical Jesus: Evaluations of the State of Current Research* (NTTS 19; Leiden: Brill, 1994), 491–532; cf. also H. Koester, *Ancient Christian Gospels: Their History and Development* (Philadelphia: Trinity Press International, 1990), 20–31, 173–240.
9. Some would add here the canonical Pastoral Epistles and the Epistles of Peter.
10. The first five of these are called the Leucian Acts and were often circulated together.
11. "Apocalypse" is a transliteration of the Greek ἀποκάλυψις, *apokalypsis*, meaning "revelation" or "disclosure." D. E. Aune, *Prophecy in Early Christianity and the Ancient Mediterranean World* (Grand Rapids: Eerdmans, 1983), 108, defines this literary genre as "a form of revelatory literature in which the author narrates both the visions he has purportedly experienced and their meaning, usually elicited through a dialogue between the seer and an interpreting angel. The substance of these revelatory visions is the imminent intervention of God into human affairs to bring the present evil world system to an end and to replace it with an ideal one. This transformation is accompanied by the punishment of the wicked and the reward of the righteous."
12. J. H. Charlesworth, "Pseudepigraphy," *EEC* 2:961.
13. K. Koch, "Pseudonymous Writing," *IDBSup* 712–13.
14. Ibid., 713.
15. Charlesworth, "Pseudepigraphy," 766.
16. See L. R. Donelson, *Pseudepigraphy and Ethical Argument in the Pastoral Epistles* (HUT 22; Tübingen: Mohr Siebeck, 1986), 11.
17. See D. Trobisch, *Paul's Letter Collection: Tracing the Origins* (Minneapolis: Fortress, 1994), 20–21.
18. W. Barnstone, ed., *The Other Bible* (New York: Harper & Row, 1984), xix.
19. J. Jeremias, *The Unknown Sayings of Jesus* (London: SPCK, 1957; 2d ed., 1964). These are conveniently listed in Charlesworth and Evans, "Jesus in the Agrapha and Apocryphal Gospels," 483–91.
20. W. D. Stroker, *Extracanonical Sayings of Jesus* (SBLRBS 18; Atlanta: Scholars Press, 1989), offers the text of these 266 sayings without evaluating their contents or attributing authenticity or inauthenticity to them.
21. O. Hofius, "Unknown Sayings of Jesus," in *The Gospel and the Gospels* (ed. P. Stuhlmacher; Grand Rapids: Eerdmans, 1991), 336–60.
22. O. Hofius, "Isolated Sayings of the Lord," in *New Testament Apocrypha* (ed. Hennecke and Schneemelcher), 1:91.

23. Ibid., 1:91.

24. For other examples, see Hofius, "Unknown Sayings of Jesus," 336–60, and D. J. Théron, *Evidence of Tradition* (Grand Rapids: Baker, 1980), 96–99.

25. This list is essentially from Charlesworth and Evans, "Jesus in the Agrapha and Apocryphal Gospels," 480. See also S. E. Porter, "The Greek Apocryphal Gospels Papyri: The Need for a Critical Edition," in *Akten des 21. Internationalen Papyrologenkongresses Berlin* (ed. B. Kramer et al.; 2 vols.; Archiv für Papyrusforschung Beiheft 42.3; Stuttgart: Teubner, 1997), 2:795–803.

26. For a complete discussion, see Koester, *Ancient Christian Gospels*, 75–127, 173–240. Cf. also his "Apocryphal and Canonical Gospels," *HTR* 73 (1980): 105–30.

27. See, e.g., J. D. Crossan, *The Historical Jesus: The Life of a Mediterranean Jewish Peasant* (San Francisco: Harper, 1991), xi–xiii, xxvii–xxxiv, 332–40, 427–34. See also his *Four Other Gospels: Shadows on the Contours of Canon* (Minneapolis: Seabury, 1985), 144; and *The Cross That Spoke: The Origins of the Passion Narrative* (San Francisco: Harper & Row, 1988), 404, in which he argues that the Cross Gospel, which he locates in the *Gospel of Peter*, lies behind the passion narrative in all four canonical Gospels.

28. Charlesworth and Evans, "Jesus in the Agrapha and Apocryphal Gospels," 532–33; J. P. Meier, *A Marginal Jew: Rethinking the Historical Jesus* (3 vols.; ABRL; New York: Doubleday, 1991–), 1:112–66.

29. Meier, *A Marginal Jew*, 1:140.

30. Ibid., 1:140–41

pages 641–643

CHRONOLOGY OF EVENTS AND PERSONS RELEVANT TO THE HISTORY OF EARLY CHRISTIANITY (200 B.C.–A.D. 200)

1. CHRONOLOGY OF EVENTS IN THE WORLD OF THE NEW TESTAMENT AND THE EARLY CHURCH

The following dates, like all ancient dating methods, are approximate and often based on conflicting data or data that is interpreted variously by the scholars who investigate it. They are, however, among the most generally accepted dates for the major events affecting early Christianity. Scholars of this period agree that the majority of the dates listed below are always subject to change when more information comes to light. The double asterisk (**) signifies the firmer dates in New Testament chronology. The dates of rulers are those of their reigns. Those dates of others referring to the periods of their productivity (literary or otherwise) are marked "fl." ("flourished").

332–330 B.C.	Alexander the Great (356–323 B.C.) conquers Palestine
250–100 B.C.	Origins of the LXX translation in Egypt
198–142 B.C.	Palestine taken over by the Seleucid Dynasty. Ptolemy V defeated by Antiochus III ("the Great") at Panion (Caesarea-Philippi)
169 B.C.	Antiochus IV Epiphanes invades Egypt and ruthlessly subjugates Palestine
168–167 B.C.	Mattathias, a priest, emerges as the leader of the nation of Israel in its revolt against the Seleucid Dynasty
165 B.C.	Religious freedom won by Judas Maccabeus, "the Hammer," who carried on the revolt begun by his father Mattathias
159–142 B.C.	Jonathan Maccabeus succeeds as leader of the nation after the death of Judas Maccabeus
142 B.C.	Political independence from Seleucid Dynasty established by Jonathan and Simon Maccabeus
142–134 B.C.	Simon Maccabeus establishes the Hasmonean Dynasty
134–104 B.C.	John Hyrcanus I succeeds Simon and extends the borders of the nation

ca. 125 B.C.	Possible date of the establishment of the Essene community at Qumran. The Pharisee party comes into prominence
104–103 B.C.	Aristobulus has a short rule as a Hasmonean king
103–76 B.C.	Alexander Jannaeus rules the Jewish people
76–67 B.C.	Salome Alexandra succeeds her husband as ruler of the Jewish people
67–63 B.C.	Aristobulus II rules the Jewish people until Rome invades the nation and the Hasmonean Dynasty loses power
63 B.C.	Pompey invades Jerusalem
63–43 B.C.	Cicero fl.
63–40 B.C.	Hyrcanus II rules a part of the Jewish people, but with little power
58–44 B.C.	Julius Caesar fl.
41 B.C.	Octavian along with Mark Antony defeats Brutus and Cassius at Philippi
40 B.C.	Parthians invade Syria and help in the Hasmonean struggle in Jerusalem
40–37 B.C.	Antigonus Mattathias, son of Aristobulus II, serves as high priest until he is drowned by Herod the Great
37 B.C.	Herod the Great captures Jerusalem and begins his reign
32–31 B.C.**	Octavian defeats Mark Antony at Actium and unites the Roman Empire. Octavian becomes Caesar Augustus
30 B.C.–A.D. 10	Two leading rabbis, Shammai and Hillel, fl.
20–19 B.C.	Herod begins the rebuilding of the temple in Jerusalem
10 B.C.–A.D. 40	Philo in Egypt fl.
6–4 B.C.**	Birth of Jesus
4 B.C.**	Herod the Great dies
4 B.C.–A.D. 39	Herod's sons (Archelaus, Antipas, and Philip) rule Palestine
6 A.D.	Archelaus deposed and Judea ruled by Roman governors
A.D. 12–14	Coregency of Caesar Augustus and Tiberius
A.D. 14	Beginning of Tiberius's reign as Roman emperor
A.D. 26–27**	Beginning of John the Baptist's ministry
A.D. 26–36	Pilate is procurator of Judea
ca. A.D. 28–29	Beginning of Jesus' ministry
A.D. 29–30**	Death of Jesus in Jerusalem
A.D. 31–34	Stephen martyred
A.D. 32–34	Conversion of the Apostle Paul
A.D. 33–44	Paul in Tarsus for ten years, after which he goes to the church in Antioch with Barnabas
A.D. 40–65	Seneca of Rome fl.
A.D. 41–44	Herod Agrippa becomes king of Samaria and Judea
A.D. 44**	Peter imprisoned in Jerusalem; James beheaded
A.D. 44	King Herod Agrippa dies. Judea becomes a province again
A.D. 47–49	Paul's first missionary journey with Barnabas
A.D. 48–49	Jews (including probably Christian Jews) expelled from Rome (Acts 18:1–2)
A.D. 49–50	Jerusalem Council decides for Gentile freedom from the law (Acts 15)
ca. A.D. 49–62	Period of Paul's correspondence
A.D. 50	Paul's second missionary journey begins
A.D. 50–52**	Paul's ministry in Corinth
A.D. 53–55/56	Paul in Ephesus
A.D. 53–57	Paul's third missionary journey
A.D. 54–68	Nero the Roman emperor
A.D. 57–62	Paul's arrest in Jerusalem and imprisonment
A.D. 60–61	Paul goes to Rome as a prisoner (events of Acts end)
A.D. 62	Peter goes to Rome
A.D. 62**	James the brother of Jesus martyred in Jerusalem

A.D. 62–64**	The church leaves Jerusalem for Pella in the midst of persecution
A.D. 64	Rome burned probably by Nero, but Christians blamed. Persecution of Christians follows
A.D. 64–67**	Peter and Paul die in Rome under Nero's persecution (end of apostolic age)
A.D. 65–95	Post- or subapostolic age begins with the deaths of the primary apostles (Peter and Paul, and James, the leader of the church in Jerusalem)
A.D. 66–74**	First Jewish war. Jerusalem under siege and finally destroyed in 70. Temple worship is ended, along with the Sadducees' party; the demise of the Sanhedrin
A.D. 68–69	Turmoil in Rome; four Roman emperors in a year
A.D. 70	Rabbinical academy established at Jamnia (Jabneh) by Rabban Johanan ben Zakkai, son of Rabban Gamaliel (Acts 5:34)
A.D. 70–90	Often called the Tunnel period, since not much is known of events during this time. Pharisaism and the rabbis emerge as the dominant expression of Judaism. Also date of the production of the *Didache*
A.D. 73–74**	Masada, earlier fortified by Herod the Great, becomes the last stronghold of the Jews but falls to the Romans
A.D. 75	Josephus writes *Jewish War*
A.D. 81–96	Domitian rules the Roman Empire
A.D. 85–95	Outbreak of a persecution against the Christians
A.D. 90-95	Rise of heresy (Docetism; see 1 John 4:1–3) in the church
A.D. 90	Jews meet at Jamnia to deal with the reformation of Judaism, especially one without its temple cultus
A.D. 93	Josephus writes *Antiquities of the Jews*
A.D. 94–95	John the apostle dies on the Isle of Patmos, off the coast near Ephesus, during Domitian's persecution
ca. A.D. 95–100	Beginning of the period of the Apostolic Fathers. Clement of Rome writes *1 Clement*
A.D. 98–117	Trajan rules the Roman Empire
A.D. 100	Josephus dies
A.D. 115–117	Epistles and martyrdom of Ignatius
A.D. 117–138	Hadrian reigns as Roman emperor
A.D. 120	Shepherd of Hermas written
A.D. 125	Quadratus, earliest Christian apologist, fl.
A.D. 130	Basilides, gnostic writer, fl.
A.D. 132–135	Second Jewish War: the Bar Kokhba rebellion put down by Rome, the Jews expelled from Jerusalem by Hadrian, and Jerusalem named Aelia Capitolina after the emperor's mother
A.D. 135	Gnosticism flourishes
A.D. 140–160	Marcion and Valentinus begin their teaching. Marcion writes *Contradictions* and *Prologues*
A.D. 145	Aristides, second Christian apologist, writes
A.D. 150	Writing of *Epistle to Diognetus* (by Polycarp?)
A.D. 154	Polycarp goes to Rome
A.D. 156	Montanus begins his ministry
A.D. 160	Justin Martyr writes *Apologies* and *Dialogue with Trypho*
A.D. 160–200	Galen fl.
A.D. 166	Polycarp martyred
A.D. 170	Heracleon, the gnostic Christian, writes
A.D. 172–185	Montanist movement flourishes in Phrygia
A.D. 175–180	Catechetical school begun in Alexandria by Pantaenus and later (180–200) headed by Clement of Alexandria

A.D. 175–180	Tatian, producer of *Diatessaron*, fl.
A.D. 177–180	Athenagoras writes *Supplication for the Christians*
A.D. 178	Celsus writes *True Reason*, the first major reasoned attack on the Christian faith
A.D. 180	Theophilus of Antioch writes *To Autolycus*
A.D. 180–185	Irenaeus writes *Against Heresies*
A.D. 190	Clement of Alexandria writes *Miscellanies*
A.D. 190–220	Tertullian fl.
A.D. 195	A major controversy emerges between the churches in the east and those in the west on when to celebrate Easter. Irenaeus intervenes in Rome in what is called the Quartodeciman controversy

2. HASMONEAN DYNASTY (SECOND AND FIRST CENTURIES B.C.)

Mattathias (d. 166)
Judas Maccabeus (d. 160)
Eleazar (d. 163)
John (d. 159)
Jonathan (159–142)
Simon (142–134)
John Hyrcanus I (134–104)
Aristobulus (104–103)
Alexander Jannaeus (103–76)
Salome Alexandra (76–67)
Aristobulus II (67–63)
Hyrcanus II (63–40, d. 30)
Antigonus Mattathias (40–37), son of Aristobulus II

3. HERODIAN DYNASTY

Antipater (procurator of Judea, 55–43 B.C.)
Herod the Great (40/37–4 B.C.), married to Mariamne I (d. 29 B.C.), granddaughter of Hyrcanus II
Herod Archelaus over Judea, Samaria, and Idumea (4 B.C.–A.D. 6)
Herod Antipas over Galilee and Perea (4 B.C.–A.D. 39)
Herod Philip over Batanea, Auranitis, and Trachonitis (4 B.C.–A.D. 33/34)
Herod Agrippa I over Galilee (A.D. 40), over all Israel (A.D. 41–44)
Herod Agrippa II over territory of his father (ca. A.D. 50–100)

4. JEWISH HIGH PRIESTS

Joazar son of Boethus (4 B.C.)
Eleazar son of Boethus (4 B.C.–?)
Jesus son of See (?–?)
Annas (A.D. 6–15)
Ishmael son of Phiabi (A.D. 15–16)
Eleazar son of Annas (A.D. 16–17)
Simon son of Camithus (A.D. 17–18)
Josephus Caiaphas son-in-law of Annas (A.D. 18–36)
Jonathan son of Annas (A.D. 36–37)

Theophilus son of Annas (A.D. 37–?)
Simon Cantheras son of Boethus (A.D. 41)
Matthias son of Annas (A.D. 41–44)
Elionaeus son of Cantheras (A.D. 44–46)
Ananus son of Annas (A.D. 62)

5. ROMAN PREFECTS AND PROCURATORS OF JUDEA AND SAMARIA

Coponius (A.D. 6–9)
Marcus Ambibulus (A.D. 9–12)
Annius Rufus (A.D. 12–15)
Valerius Gratus (A.D. 15–26)
Pontius Pilate (A.D. 26–36)
Marcellus (A.D. 36–37)
Marullus (A.D. 37–41) (of all of Israel)
Fadus (A.D. 44–46)
Tiberius Alexander (A.D. 46–48)
Ventidius Cumanus (A.D. 48–52)
Felix (A.D. 52–60)
Porcius Festus (A.D. 60–62)
Albinus (A.D. 62–64)
Gessius Florus (A.D. 64–66)

6. ROMAN EMPERORS

Augustus/Octavian (30 B.C.–A.D. 14)
Tiberius (A.D. 14–37, or A.D. 12–37 if coregency with Augustus)
Gaius Caligula (A.D. 37–41)
Claudius (A.D. 41–54)
Nero (A.D. 54–68)
Galba (A.D. 68–69)
Otho (A.D. 69)
Vitellius (A.D. 69)
Vespasian (A.D. 69–79)
Titus (A.D. 79–81)
Domitian (A.D. 81–96)
Nerva (A.D. 96–98)
Trajan (A.D. 98–117)
Hadrian (A.D. 117–135)
Antonius Pius (A.D. 138–161)
Marcus Aurelius (A.D. 162–180)
Commodus (A.D. 180–192)
Four emperors (A.D. 193–194)
Septimus Severus (A.D. 193–211)

7. MESSIANIC CLAIMANTS AROUND THE TIME OF JESUS

Judas of Sepphoris, son of Hezekiah the "brigand chief" (4 B.C.)
Simon of Perea (4 B.C.)
Athronges the shepherd of Judea (4–2 B.C.)

Menahem (grand) son of Judas of Sepphoris (A.D. 66)
John of Gischala, son of Levi (A.D. 67–70)
Simon bar Giora of Gerasa (A.D. 68–70)
Lukuas of Cyrene (A.D. 115)
Simeon bar Koziba/bar Kokhba (A.D. 132–135)

8. JEWISH PROPHETS AROUND THE TIME OF JESUS

John the Baptist (A.D. late 20s)
The "Samaritan" (ca. A.D. 26–36)
Theudas (ca. A.D. 45)
The "Egyptian" Jew (ca. A.D. 56)
An anonymous "impostor" (ca. A.D. 61)
Jesus son of Ananias (A.D. 62–69)
Jonathan the Weaver, refugee of Cyrene (ca. A.D. 71)

Glossary of Critical and Historical Terms[1]

Abba. Aramaic form of "Father."

adoptionism. A form of early Christology that argued that Jesus became the son of God by adoption at his baptism ("you are my beloved son").

agrapha ("unwritten"). The sayings of Jesus not found in the canonical Gospels. The singular, agraphon, is used of individual sayings. Some of these sayings are preserved in the early church fathers, in certain biblical manuscripts, and in apocryphal writings such as the *Gospel of Thomas.*

amanuensis. A scribe or secretary who wrote out documents in the ancient world. Paul made use of such a person named Tertius (Rom 16:22).

Am Ha'arets ("the people of the land"). A term that was used of lower-class persons, possibly with contempt.

Amoraim (Heb. = amora, lit. a "teacher," "reciter"). The rabbinic teachers from A.D. 220 through the talmudic period, roughly the sixth century.

They composed the Gemara, or commentary on the Mishnah and the Hebrew Scriptures.

anacoluthon (Gk. = "not following"). The abandonment of one grammatical construction for another in the middle of a sentence.

antinomianism (lit. "being against law"). The belief that law, especially the Jewish law, is no longer binding.

aphorism. A short, pithy saying, often with memorable qualities. See also "apophthegm."

Apocalypse, apocalyptic (Gk. = "revelation"). The last book of the NT, or a specific genre of visionary literature that focuses on the end times, often using terms with hidden meanings and referring to hidden revelations of the "last days."

Apocrypha, apocryphal (Gk. = "hidden"). Sacred literature that was not accepted into the biblical canon but was highly valued in Jewish and early Christian communities. Often a reference to esoteric writings.

---

[1]Some of the terms in this list are adapted from those listed in the much longer collections of N. Turner, *Handbook for Biblical Studies* (Philadelphia: Westminster, 1982); and R. N. Soulen, *Handbook of Biblical Criticism* (Atlanta: John Knox, 1976). Other useful terms are found in R. F. Collins, *Introduction to the New Testament* (Garden City, N.Y.: Doubleday, 1983), 409–30; and H. Koester, *Introduction to the New Testament* (2 vols.; FFNT; Philadelphia: Fortress, 1982; 2d ed. of vol. 1, 1995) 2:349–52.

apophthegm, apotegm. A short, pithy saying. Often, in Gospel studies, referring to pronouncement stories or paradigms. See also *aphorism*.

Aramaism. In the Greek of the NT, wording that betrays a Palestinian Aramaic origin, for example, Abba (Mark 14:36; Rom 8:15).

asyndeton. Clauses or phrases that are linked together without connective words such as "but" or "and."

autograph. The original manuscript of a book. Normally, the biblical authors' original writings, none of which have survived.

baraita (Heb. = "external"; pl. *baraitoth*). A rabbinic tradition (writing) that was not included in the Mishnah by R. Judah ha-Nasi (*Nasi* = "Prince," "Chief," "President"). The extent to which this material was widely known or acknowledged as authoritative in the second century A.D. or before is not clear. Since this material was not included, it seems unlikely that its recognition was widespread.

berakah (Hebr. = "blessing"). A Jewish prayer of blessing and thanksgiving.

canon (Gk. = "measuring rod," "guideline"). Normally, a collection of literature that was considered by the Christian community to be sacred and authoritative. Also, any recognized group of authoritative writings.

catechesis. Oral instruction, often in conjunction with teaching given to candidates for baptism.

catena. A collection of biblical quotations found in the church fathers, used to interpret the Scriptures.

chiasmus, chiastic (from the Gk. letter chi [χ]). The practice, in ancient Greek writing, of reversing the subject and object of the first line in the second line. See Mark 2:27.

chiliasm, chiliastic (Gk. = "thousand"). Literature that focuses on an imminent eschatological kingdom of God. Often referred to as "millenarianism"; based on apocalyptic literature in the Bible (esp. Daniel and Revelation).

codex (pl. codices). Ancient manuscripts put together in the form of a book, unlike the more typical scroll. Christians were the first to use codices on a large scale to publish their sacred writings.

cognate. A word from the same root or family of words as another. For example, ἀγάπη ("love"), ἀγαπητός ("beloved"), and ἀγαπάω ("I love") are all cognates.

colophon (Gk. = "summit," "finishing touch"). A publisher's identification mark, normally on a title page or, in the case of older manuscripts, at the end of a book, giving the time and location of the publication.

covenantal nomism. A category of thought used in recent Pauline studies to describe what some see as the belief of the Jews regarding covenant and law. The Jews are said to be in a covenantal relation to God on the basis of grace, not law.

credo (Lat. = "I believe"), creed. A collection of teachings that is believed by a person or group.

Decalogue. The Ten Commandments.

Demiurge (Gk. = δημιουργός, "craftsman"). The gnostic term for the creator of the world, who is to be distinguished from the unknown God of Jesus.

demythologizing. A term made popular in the writings of Rudolf Bultmann, who tried to explain and interpret what he called the myth of the NT (miracle stories) in terms of human self-understanding. He intended the term to refer to reinterpreting myth, not eliminating it.

diachronic (lit., "through time"). Denoting historical change over a period of time. When sequence is prominent, the term "diachronic" is used. "Synchronic" is the opposite.

Diaspora (Gk. = "scattered"). The Jews who lived outside Palestine. Sometimes a reference to the Assyrian and Babylonian captivities of the Jews. See Jas 1:1 and 1 Pet 1:1.

Diatessaron (Gk. = "through four"). Term used by Tatian in the late second century to refer to his "Gospel made up of Four," a harmony of the four canonical Gospels and probably some non-canonical writings.

didachē (Gk. = "teaching"). Sometimes used of the teaching ministry of the early church, as opposed to the proclamation, or kerygma, of the church. The *Didache* was a late-first-century writing that summarized the teaching of the church; its longer title is "The Teaching of the Lord to the Nations by the Twelve Apostles."

Docetism (Gk. = "I seem," "I appear"). The belief of a group of Christians of the late first century and throughout the second century that Jesus only appeared to have a body. They taught that the Christ descended upon Jesus at his baptism and only appeared to have suffered on the cross, in fact ascending just prior to the cross. This is a gnostic belief that emphasized the corruptness of human flesh and sought to preserve the Christ from such corruption.

Ebionites. A Jewish sect of Christians who lived east of the Jordan in the second century and rejected the deity of Jesus. They had a "low" Christology.

ecclesiology. The study of the church, its doctrines and organization.

eclecticism. The process of selecting from a number of different sources. The term is especially used of the methods in textual criticism that draw, to varying degrees, on the range of readings offered by internal criteria (see rigorous or throughgoing eclecticism and reasoned eclecticism in ch. 12, sec. 3).

Eighteen Benedictions. A series of Jewish prayers called the *Shemoneh-Esreh*, used in the synagogue and in personal prayer. These come mostly from the late first century A.D., but also from the second century. Of special note to the Christian community is whether the twelfth benediction against heretics (Heb. *minim*) is against Christians ("let the Nazarenes [Christians?] and heretics perish in a moment").

ekklēsia (Gk. = "assembly," "gathering"). In the NT, the group of followers of Christ. It is often modified by "of God" or "of God in Christ," etc. The term itself is a neutral one but was quickly adopted by the Christian community. In meaning, it is not unlike the Greek term *synagōgē*.

encratite (Gk. = "self-controlled," "strengthened"). Used of Christian sects such as the Ebionites, Docetics, and gnostics, who were known for extreme asceticism that barred them from eating meat and from marrying.

epigraphy (Gk. = "writing upon," "inscription"). The study of inscriptions on stone, ostraca, and other writings on such surfaces.

epiphany (Gk. = "manifestation"). The manifestation of a deity. Some strong leaders of the ancient world adopted the term for themselves, such as Antiochus Epiphanes IV (165 B.C.).

eschatology, *eschaton* (Gk. = "last," "end"). The study of the end times of the ages. Eschatology focuses on the kingdom of God in the NT, which is also paralleled with a time of judgment. The *eschaton* is the final reality of the end times.

ethnarch (Gk. = "ruler of a nation," "ruler of a people"). A ruler or governor of a province or nation.

euangélion (Gk. = "good news"). The "good news" brought by the coming of Jesus Christ. Also translated "Gospel," to describe the first four books of the NT, and "gospel," to describe the message they and other books of the NT proclaim.

exegesis (Gk. = "explanation," "interpretation"). The interpretation of the biblical text, using all of the skills and disciplines related to lexicography, grammar, analysis of literature, and historical-critical inquiry in order to explain the original meaning. An exegete is an interpreter of a text. The opposite is called "eisegesis," often used disparagingly to label viewpoints one does not hold.

expiation (Lat. *expiare* = "to appease," normally by sacrifice). In the Bible, usually the atonement for one's sins through an offering (sacrifice) made to God.

florilegium (Lat. = "a gathering of flowers"). A collection of proof texts that were used by the early Christians in their apologies before skeptics and in their instructions to new converts.

Gattung (Ger. = "kind," "type"). A kind, style, or type of literature, art, etc. Used in biblical studies to distinguish forms of literature (parable, epigram, apothegm, etc.). See "genre."

Gemara (Aram. = "completion"). The Amoraim's additions to the Mishnah—explanations, further teachings, or interpretations of the Mishnah. The Mishnah and its Gemara make up the Talmud. There is both a Palestinian and a Babylonian Gemara to the Mishnah.

gematria. A method of interpreting ancient texts in terms of their numerical value. For example, the sevens of the book of Revelation refer to completion or perfection. It is not clear to what 666 (Rev 13:18) refers. Is the number forty in the Bible packed with additional meaning (the times of the flood on the earth, Moses at Sinai, Elijah at Horeb, Israel in the wilderness, Jesus' temptations and his appearances after the resurrection)? Because numbers were used to conceal meanings, there continues to be much speculation on such meanings in the biblical text.

genizah, geniza (Heb. = "a hiding place"). A room normally attached to a synagogue for the purpose of discarding and storing worn-out portions of holy writings and Scripture. Even heretical literature, if it contained the divine names, was discarded in a genizah out of respect for the divine names; often only the divine names in heretical literature were stored here.

genre (French = "kind," "type"). A kind, style, or type of literature, art, etc. Used in biblical studies to distinguish types of literature (gospel, letter, apocalypse, etc.).

Geschichte (Ger. = "history"). Although no substantive distinction is made in normal German usage between *Geschichte* and *Historie* (both mean "history"), in theology the terms have come to refer to the actual event *(Historie)* and its significance *(Geschichte)*. The question has been raised regarding events of the NT: are they *Historie* or *Geschichte?* Bultmann spoke both of the cross as *Historie* and of its significance *(Geschichte)*, which was revealed to the disciples of Jesus.

gloss. A brief explanation inserted into a manuscript to explain a point or something unusual in the text.

gnosis, Gnosticism, gnostic (Gk. = "knowledge"). A dualistic system of thought of some early Christians who claimed to have a special higher knowledge of the divine activity and spiritual mysteries. Widespread in the second century, it had early "incipient" forms in the NT era. Generally the gnostics rejected the God of the OT and Jewish forms of religion, and many were ascetic. They saw matter as evil and rejected the notion that the God of Jesus created the world. Docetism is a form of gnostic belief.

Greco-Roman. Descriptive of the period, from the first century B.C. to the fifth century A.D., when Greek culture combined with Roman political dominance.

haggadah/haggadic (Heb. = "narrative," "telling," as in "telling a story"). Postbiblical narrative writing among the rabbis that does not comprise legal prescriptions; stories that illustrate the Torah. (The tradition that focused on the legal implications of the law is called halakah or halakhah.) Anything not included as halakah.

hagiographa (Gk. = "holy writings"). The collection of sacred Scriptures that makes up the third part of the Hebrew Bible. Also called in Hebrew the Ketuvim ("Writings").

halakah/halakic (Heb. = "the way"). Legal regulations of the law, both oral and written, that emerged out of postbiblical Judaism. They were viewed by the rabbis as far more important than the haggadah, or narrative, traditions.

hapax legomenon (Gk. = "said once"). A word found only once in antiquity or in the Bible, or only once in one person's writing in either the OT or NT.

Haustafel (Ger. = "household list"). A list of responsibilities of household members. See Eph 5:22–6:9.

Heilsgeschichte (Ger. = "salvation history"). The sacred activity of God in human history, described or foretold in the Scriptures.

Hellenistic. The period, from the third century B.C. to the fourth century A.D., in which the influence of classical Greek spread throughout the Mediterranean world.

henotheism. The belief in and worship of one god, but without excluding the possibility of there being other gods. See "monotheism."

hermeneutics (Gk. = *hermeneuō*, lit. "I interpret"). The theory and process of interpretation. In biblical studies, the term refers to all that is involved in interpreting the biblical text. See "exegesis."

heterodox. Not "orthodox," or in keeping with what is the generally accepted teaching of the church; heretical.

higher criticism. Interpretation of the text with regard to its literary and historical dimensions, as opposed to lower criticism. A term first widely used in the nineteenth century.

Historie (Ger. = "history"). In theology, an event as it actually happened, or as you can verify that it actually happened. See *"Geschichte."*

hortatory. Referring to language and/or literature that urges a particular course of action or behavior.

hypotaxis. Language that makes use of subordinate grammatical structures, such as participles, phrases, and subordinate clauses, often linked with words such as "because," "while," etc.

inscription. A text written on stone or a similar surface.

interpolation. The insertion of new words into a text.

ipsissima verba (Lat. = "the very words themselves"). Words that can be attributed to the historical Jesus in the biblical tradition and in the agrapha.

ipsissima vox (Lat. = "the very voice"). A thought or notion attributable to the historical Jesus even when the exact words are not discoverable.

Judaizers. Jewish Christians who accepted the law and its traditions and sought to impose circumcision upon the Gentiles. See Gal 2:11–14; Acts 15:1–5.

kerygma (Gk. = "preaching"). Early Christian proclamation and evangelistic activity, as distinct from the teaching (*didachē*) ministry.

Koine (Gk. = "common"). The common language that was used in the composition of the NT writings, as contrasted with the more formal classical Greek. Some writings in the NT are of a more formal literary quality (Luke–Acts, Hebrews, James, 1 Peter), while others are more informal and common (Paul's letters, Mark). All of the NT, however, can be classified as Koine Greek.

koinōnia (Gk. = "fellowship," with the idea of sharing). In the NT, the gatherings of the early Christian community that often involved the breaking of bread together in a common meal.

L The material in Luke's Gospel that is unique to Luke, that is, not found elsewhere. It may stem from the author of the Gospel or from a written or oral source that he used in producing his Gospel.

lacuna. A gap, that which is missing. Often, something absent from a manuscript.

langue. A language system, such as English, Greek, etc. The term is from the early-twentieth-century linguist Ferdinand de Saussure. See *"parole."*

lectionary. A collection of readings from the Scriptures used in liturgical services and fixed according to church calendars. Their use dates back almost to the beginning of the church.

lingua franca. The common language of a large number of people, such as Koine Greek in the Greco-Roman world of the first century A.D.

logion (Gk. = "saying"; pl. logia). A saying of Jesus.

lower criticism. The foundational criticism of establishing the text that one intends to study, as opposed to higher criticism. See also "textual criticism."

LXX (Roman numeral 70). See "Septuagint."

M   The material in Matthew's Gospel that is unique to Matthew. It may stem from the author of the Gospel or from a written or oral source that he used in producing his Gospel.

magi (Gk. = "wise men"). In Matt 2:1–2, the "wise men" who came to honor the newborn king of the Jews. The term was used of masters of the astrological arts (astrologers) but could also have referred to persons who were known as wise sages from the east.

Majority Text. The collection of Byzantine texts that were used in establishing the first modern texts and translations of the Bible. The Byzantine texts constitute the majority of manuscripts. The Majority Text is similar to the Received Text.

majuscule. Script that is written in capital letters, or a manuscript in such script; as opposed to minuscule (lowercase), or cursive, letters; uncial.

Maranatha (Aram. = "Our Lord come!" or "Our Lord has come"). An early Christian affirmation expressing the desired return of Christ. Paul uses this term in its transliterated Greek form in 1 Cor 16:22.

messianism. Belief that messiah will come (Judaism) or that the messiah has come in the person of Jesus (Christianity). How widespread messianism was among Jews in the first century is a matter of debate.

midrash (Heb. = "investigate," "inquire," "search," "interpret"). An interpretation of, or a commentary on, Scripture. The oldest Hebrew commentaries on Scripture are the *Mekilta* on Exodus, the *Sifra* on Leviticus, and the *Sifre* on Numbers and Deuteronomy.

minuscule. Script that is written in lowercase letters, or a manuscript in such script. Most of these manuscripts date from the tenth to the twelfth centuries.

Mishnah (Heb. = "what is repeated," "repetition"). A codified oral tradition that dates from before the time of Jesus to the time of R. Judah ha-Nasi (A.D. 200–219). Indicated by the siglum *m*.

monotheism. The belief that there is only one God; as opposed to polytheism, the belief that there are many gods. See also "henotheism."

mystērion (Gk. = "mystery"). Used of the mystery of God or of the Christian gospel itself (Eph 3:3–6; Col 1:27).

myth. In a specialized sense, the transcendent activity of God spoken of in "this-worldly" categories. Myth is to be interpreted in terms of the reality that produced it. Some scholars speak of this reality in terms of human self-understanding. In other words, myth is a way of speaking about the "other-worldly" activity of God in terms of concrete, "this-worldly" activity.

nomina sacra (Lat. = "sacred names"). Shortened forms of names, such as of God and Jesus, in papyrus and parchment manuscripts.

Old Latin. The Latin versions of the Bible that predate or are independent of Jerome's Vulgate.

ossuary. A box or container in which the bones of a dead person were placed.

ostracon (pl. ostraca). An inscribed potsherd or piece of pottery. A number of ostraca have been found dating to the Hellenistic period, since this was a common writing material for receipts, etc.

paleography (Gk. = "old writing"). The study of ancient handwriting, especially as found on papyri, inscriptions, ostraca, and other sources.

palimpsest (Gk. = "rubbed again"). A manuscript that has been reused, with the first text removed to be replaced by a second text.

papyrus. A plant used in ancient times, especially in Egypt, to make writing material. Many documents written on papyrus have been found in Egypt, and they have helped to illustrate the language and customs of the Hellenistic world. The term "papyrus" is also used for these texts.

parablepsis (Gk. = "look over"). The jumping of one's eyes to a similar expression, resulting in either omission (haplography) or repetition (dittography) of the intervening section.

paraclete (Gk. = "called alongside"). A comforter or advocate; often used of the Holy Spirit in the NT.

parataxis. Language typified by clauses and phrases joined by the simple connective "and."

parenesis, parenetic. Admonitory or exhortative teaching.

parole. A term from the early-twentieth-century linguist Ferdinand de Saussure, indicating an individual's particular use of a language. See "langue."

Parousia (Gk. = "presence"). The returning presence of Christ at the end of this age.

Pastoral Epistles. A term, used since the eighteenth century, referring to 1, 2 Timothy and Titus.

patristics. The study of the church fathers, or their writings, through the sixth or seventh century.

Peloponnese. A mountainous peninsula forming southern Greece, connected to the mainland by the Isthmus of Corinth.

pericope (Gk. = "cut around"). A defined section of biblical material, such as a parable.

pesher (Heb. = "interpretation," "realization"; pl. pesharim). A form of biblical interpretation, similar to midrash, that sees the fulfillment of the passage in the context of the current interpreters. Pesher interpretation was popular at Qumran.

Peshitta. The translation of the Bible of the Syrian church, dating to probably the fifth century.

pleonasm. The use of more words than are necessary to express an idea. Redundancy is implied by a pleonastic construction.

pneumatic (Gk. = "spirit, wind"). Concerned with or related to a spirit, often with reference to the Holy Spirit in the NT.

pre-Tannaim. Rabbinic teachers from 200 B.C. to A.D. 10.

preterist. One who is concerned with the past or with linking the interpretation of a document to past events.

prolegomenon (Gk. = "what is said first"; pl. prolegomena). An introductory section, or introduction.

propitiation. The ancient belief that the wrath or anger of God or the gods must be appeased through sacrifice, and the means of accomplishing this. Romans 3:25 is an important passage for understanding whether the concept is to be found in the NT.

proselyte. A person converted from one belief system to another. In the NT, especially used of Gentiles who convert to Judaism.

protreptic (Gk. = "urge forward"). A form of literature that is exhortatory, that is, that attempts to persuade to a course of action.

provenance. The place of origin of a document.

pseudepigrapha, pseudepigraphical. Documents written under another person's name. Ancient pseudepigrapha were typically done under the name of a famous person, such as Enoch or Plato.

Q (Ger. = Quelle, "source"). A collection of sayings of Jesus; essentially, Gospel material in Matthew and Luke not found in Mark. In much Gospel criticism, Q and Mark are the two primary sources supposedly used by Matthew and Luke.

Qumran. Remains of a settlement, near the Dead Sea, where numerous biblical and extrabiblical texts, commonly known as the Dead Sea Scrolls, were discovered in eleven nearby caves.

Received Text. The Received Text, or Textus Receptus, designates the Greek edition by Erasmus that came to be the text received by the church. The 1633 Elzevir edition was the specific edition to which this name was given.

recension. A revision of a text, and the product of that revision.

redaction. The editing of written material.

Second Sophistic. A Greco-Roman philosophical and rhetorical movement that drew much of its inspiration from the thought of Plato. It especially flourished in the eastern portion of the Roman Empire in the second and third centuries A.D.

seder (Heb. = "order"; pl. sedarim). Division of the Mishnah.

sēmeion (pl. *sēmeia*). Greek word for sign.

Semitic. Concerning or of the Semitic peoples, especially the Jews.

Semitism. An expression, in the Greek of the NT, that betrays an intervention or influence from Hebrew or Aramaic, either directly or indirectly through the LXX (Septuagintalism).

Septuagint. The various translations of the Hebrew Scriptures into Greek that began around 250 B.C. and were completed sometime around 100 B.C. The contents in the time of Jesus are not completely known, but it is used more than 80 percent of the time by the NT writers when quoting or citing the OT. It was the Bible of the early Christian communities as well as the Jews of the Diaspora. According to legend, the translation was made by seventy or seventy-two Jewish scholars brought to Alexandria, Egypt. LXX is the common siglum for the Septuagint.

Shemoneh-Esreh. See "Eighteen Benedictions."

Sitz im Leben (Ger. = "life setting," "life situation"). The social context of a given text, event, or person.

soteriology. The teaching about, and doctrine of, salvation.

stichometry. In textual criticism, the calculation of the letters or syllables on a line and the num-

ber of lines on a page. There are some indications in ancient manuscripts of authors' concerns for these factors. They can be used in trying to reconstruct the parameters of a text.

synchronic (lit. "same time"). Denoting language or events altogether as a complete system. When the whole is viewed together, the term "synchronic" is used. The opposite is "diachronic."

syncretism (Gk. = "mixed together"). The mixing together of various ideas from various sources.

synopsis. A presentation in parallel fashion; especially, so displaying the Gospels to show their relationships.

synoptic problem. Discussion of the issues surrounding the origins and relationships of Matthew, Mark, and Luke, the Synoptic Gospels.

syzygy. Speculation about the divine world as consisting of matched parts, for example, male and female.

Talmud (Heb. = "learning"). The combination of the Mishnah and its Gemara make up the Talmud. The siglum *b.* is used for the Babylonian Talmud and *y.* for the Jerusalem or Palestinian Talmud. See "Gemara."

Tanak. An acronym for the Hebrew Bible, based on the first letters of the three sections, Torah (Law), Neviim (Prophets), and Ketuvim (Writings).

Tannaim (Heb. = "teacher"; more specifically, "reciter," "repeater"). The rabbinic teachers from A.D. 10 to 220.

Targum (Aramic = "translation"). An ancient paraphrase or interpretive translation of the Hebrew Bible into Aramaic.

teleology. The belief in final and ultimate causes. A teleological perspective holds that natural and historical processes are not only causally connected but are directed toward some ultimate and final purpose, such as the kingdom of God.

Tendenz criticism. Examination of the tendencies and development of a tradition. Tendenz criticism has been developed especially in Gospel criticism and criticism of the Book of Acts.

textual criticism. Examination of the principles and standards employed in the establishment and subsequent editing of any text. In biblical studies its goal is to find the earliest and most authentic text of the biblical books.

theism (Gk. theos = "god"). Belief in god or gods, especially the God of the Judaeo-Christian tradition.

Torah. The Law, or the first five books of the OT. The Pentateuch.

Tosefta (Heb. = "supplement"). Material not found in the Mishnah and dating from approximately the same period. Its siglum is *t*.

uncial. A term often used for biblical manuscripts written in capital letters. The majority of uncial manuscripts date from the third to the tenth centuries. See the preferred term "majuscule."

vaticinium ex eventu or vaticinium post eventum (Lat.). A prophecy or prediction made after the event.

Vorlage (Ger. = "lies before"). A document that lies behind another source or tradition, or material that explains the context of another document, person, or activity.

Vulgate. Latin version of the Bible by Jerome, officially adopted by the Catholic Church in the sixteenth century.

INDEX OF MODERN AUTHORS

INDEX OF ANCIENT SOURCES

INDEX OF SUBJECTS

Page references in bold type indicate major discussions. For ancient writings and writers, see also the Index of Ancient Sources.